--- TEAR ALONG PERFORATION ---

WRITER'S MARKET 2019

SYMBOLS KEY

Ⓐ market accepts agented submissions only

⊘ market does not accept unsolicited submissions

◖ Canadian market

◓ market located outside of the U.S. and Canada

$ market pays 0–9¢/word or $0–$150/article

$ $ market pays 10–49¢/word or $151–$750/article

$ $ $ market pays 50–99¢/word or $751–$1,500/article

$ $ $ $ market pays $1/word or more than $1,500/article

◯ comment from the editor of *Writer's Market*

⊶ tips to break into a specific market

ms, mss manuscript(s)

b&w black & white (photo)

SASE self-addressed, stamped envelope

SAE self-addressed envelope

IRC International Reply Coupon, for use when mailing to countries other than your own

P9-DIW-879

For words and expressions relating specifically to writing and publishing, see the glossary in the back of this book.

WRITER'S MARKET 2019

SYMBOLS KEY

- **Ⓐ** market accepts agented submissions only

- **⊘** market does not accept unsolicited submissions

- **Ⓒ** Canadian market

- **☛** market located outside of the U.S. and Canada

- **$** market pays 0–9¢/word or $0–$150/article

- **$$** market pays 10–49¢/word or $151–$750/article

- **$$$** market pays 50–99¢/word or $751–$1,500/article

- **$$$$** market pays $1/word or more than $1,500/article

- **🗩** comment from the editor of *Writer's Market*

- **⚷** tips to break into a specific market

ms, mss manuscript(s)

b&w black & white (photo)

SASE self-addressed, stamped envelope

SAE self-addressed envelope

IRC International Reply Coupon, for use when mailing to countries other than your own

For words and expressions relating specifically to writing and publishing, see the glossary in the back of this book.

TEAR ALONG PERFORATION

WritersMarket.com
Where & How to Sell What You Write

- **MORE UPDATED LISTINGS:** At WritersMarket.com, you'll find thousands of listings, including the listings we couldn't fit in the book, as well as listings from our other best-selling titles, including *Novel & Short Story Writer's Market*, *Children's Writer's & Illustrator's Market*, and *Guide to Literary Agents*. WritersMarket.com provides the most comprehensive database of verified markets available anywhere.

- **EASY-TO-USE, SEARCHABLE DATABASE:** Looking for a specific magazine or book publisher? Just type in its name. Or widen your prospects with the Advanced Search. You can also search for listings that have been recently updated!

- **PERSONALIZED TOOLS:** Store your best-bet markets, and use our popular record-keeping tools to track your submissions. Plus, get new and updated market listings, query reminders, and more—every time you log in!

- **PROFESSIONAL TIPS & ADVICE:** From pay-rate charts to sample query letters, how-to articles to Q&As with literary agents, we have all the resources writers need.

With subscriptions starting at just **$3.33 a month****, WritersMarket.com is the tool you need to take your writing to the next level.

SIGN UP TODAY!

WM19

← **TEAR OUT YOUR HANDY BOOKMARK**
for fast reference to symbols and abbreviations used in this book

** $3.33 a month subscription fee based on average monthly cost for annual subscription, billed in one installment of $39.99. Six-month subscription rate: $24.99. Monthly subscription rate: $5.99. Prices subject to change.

◀ 98TH ANNUAL EDITION ▶

WRITER'S MARKET

2019

Robert Lee Brewer, Editor

WRITER'S DIGEST
BOOKS

WritersDigest.com
Cincinnati, Ohio

Writer's Market website: www.writersmarket.com
Writer's Digest website: www.writersdigest.com

Distributed in the U.K. and Europe by F&W Media International
Pynes Hill Court, Pynes Hill, Rydon Lane
Exeter, EX2 5AZ, United Kingdom
Tel: (+44) 1392 797680, Fax: (+44) 1626-323319
E-mail: postmaster@davidandcharles.co.uk

Library of Congress Catalog Number 31-20772
ISSN: 0084-2729
ISBN-13: 978-1-44035-435-9
ISBN-13: 978-1-44035-436-6 (Writer's Market Deluxe Edition)
ISBN-10: 1-44035-435-9
ISBN-10: 1-44035-436-7 (Writer's Market Deluxe Edition)

Attention Booksellers: This is an annual directory of F + W Media, Inc. Return deadline for this edition is December 31, 2019.

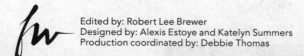

Edited by: Robert Lee Brewer
Designed by: Alexis Estoye and Katelyn Summers
Production coordinated by: Debbie Thomas

CONTENTS

MARKETS

RESOURCES

INDEXES

FROM
THE EDITOR

With each edition of *Writer's Market*, I have two goals: Help writers get published and get paid for their writing. In this edition, a few new articles focus specifically on the latter.

In "Ten-Minute Marketing for Writers," Tania Casselle shares how to work marketing into your schedule without stifling your actual writing time. Michelle Rafter reveals her secrets to "Make Money Covering Live Events," focusing on her own experiences accomplishing just that.

Also new to this edition, Sophia McDonald Bennett explains "Why Every Writer Needs a Business Plan" and how to make it happen. It's easier than you might think. Allen Taylor shares how he dramatically increased his writing income in "Seven Steps to Doubling Your Income in One Year," and Stacy Tornio shows writers "How to Do Video Effectively."

Of course, the listings are still "where it's at" with *Writer's Market*, and this year's book is loaded with them for literary agents, book publishers, consumer magazines, trade journals, and contests. Plus, we've added in two new sections: Playwriting and Screenwriting.

Also, be sure to take advantage of a specially recorded webinar for *Writer's Market* readers. Learn more at www.writersmarket.com/2019-wm-webinar.

Until next we meet, keep writing and marketing what you write.

Robert Lee Brewer
Senior Content Editor
Writer's Market and WritersMarket.com
http://writersdigest.com/editor-blogs/poetic-asides
http://blog.writersmarket.com
http://twitter.com/robertleebrewer

HOW TO USE WRITER'S MARKET

Writer's Market is here to help you decide where and how to submit your writing to appropriate markets. Each listing contains information about the editorial focus of the market, how it prefers material to be submitted, payment information, and other helpful tips.

WHAT'S INSIDE?

Since 1921, *Writer's Market* has been giving you the information you need to knowledgeably approach a market. We've continued to develop improvements to help you access that information more efficiently.

NAVIGATIONAL TOOLS. We've designed the pages of *Writer's Market* with you, the writer, in mind. Within the pages you will find **readable market listings** and **accessible charts and graphs**. One such chart can be found in the ever-popular "How Much Should I Charge?" article.

We've taken all of the updated information in this feature and put it into an easy-to-read-and-navigate chart, making it convenient for you to find the rates that accompany the freelance jobs you're seeking.

ICONS. There are a variety of icons that appear before each listing. A complete Key to Icons & Abbreviations appears on the right. Icons let you know whether a book publisher accepts only agented writers ([A]), comparative pay rates for a magazine ($-$$$$), and more.

CONTACT NAMES, ROYALTY RATES AND ADVANCES. In every section, we identify key contact people with the boldface word **Contact** to help you get your manuscript to the right person.

EDITORS, PAY RATES, ROYALTIES, ADVANCES, AND PERCENTAGE OF MATERIAL WRITTEN BY FREELANCE WRITERS. For Book Publishers, royalty rates and advances are highlighted in boldface, as is other important information on the percentage of first-time writers and unagented writers the company publishes, the number of books published, and the number of manuscripts received each year. In the Consumer Magazines and Trade Journals sections, we identify the amount (percentage) of material accepted from freelance writers, and the pay rates for features, columns and departments, and fillers in boldface to help you quickly identify the information you need to know when considering whether to submit your work.

QUERY FORMATS. We asked editors how they prefer to receive queries and have indicated in the listings whether they prefer them by mail, e-mail, fax or phone. Be sure to check an editor's individual preference before sending your query.

ARTICLES. Writers who want to improve their submission techniques should read the articles in the **Finding Work** section. The **Managing Work** section is geared more toward post-acceptance topics, such as contract negotiation, organization, and self-promotion.

IF THIS BOOK IS NEW TO YOU . . .

Look at the **Contents** pages to familiarize yourself with the arrangement of *Writer's Market*. The three largest sections of the book are the market listings of Book Publishers; Consumer Magazines; and Trade Journals. You will also find other sections of market listings for Literary Agents and Contests & Awards. More opportunities can be found on the WritersMarket.com website.

KEY TO ICONS & ABBREVIATIONS

Ⓐ	market accepts agented submissions only
⊘	market does not accept unsolicited submissions
♻	Canadian market
🌐	market located outside of the U.S. and Canada
$	market pays 0-9¢/word or $0-$150/article
$$	market pays 10-49¢/word or $151-$750/article
$$$	market pays 50-99¢/word or $751-$1,500/article
$$$$	market pays $1/word or over $1,500/article
💬	comment from the editor of Writer's Market
⚷	tips to break into a specific market
MS, MSS	manuscript(s)
B&W	black & white (photo)
SASE	self-addressed, stamped envelope
SAE	self-addressed envelope
IRC	International Reply Coupon, for use when mailing to countries other than your own

---

IMPORTANT LISTING INFORMATION

1. Listings are based on editorial questionnaires and interviews. They are not advertisements; publishers do not pay for their listings. The markets are not endorsed by *Writer's Market* editors. Writer's Digest Books and its employees go to great effort to ascertain the validity of information in this book. However, transactions between users of the information and individuals and/or companies are strictly between those parties.

2. All listings have been verified before publication of this book. If a listing has not changed from last year, then the editor said the market's needs have not changed and the previous listing continues to accurately reflect its policies.

3. *Writer's Market* reserves the right to exclude any listing.

4. When looking for a specific market, check the index. A market may not be listed for one of these reasons:
   - It doesn't solicit freelance material.
   - It doesn't pay for material.
   - It has gone out of business.
   - It has failed to verify or update its listing for this edition.
   - It hasn't answered *Writer's Market* inquiries satisfactorily.

Narrowing your search

After you've identified the market categories that interest you, you can begin researching specific markets within each section.

Consumer Magazines and Trade Journals are categorized by subject within their respective sections to make it easier for you to identify markets for your work.

There is a subject index available for Book Publishers in the back of the book. It is broken into fiction and nonfiction categories and subcategories.

Contests & Awards are categorized by genre of writing. If you want to find journalism contests, you would search the Journalism category; if you have an unpublished novel, check the Fiction category.

Interpreting the markets

Once you've identified companies or publications that cover the subjects in which you're interested, you can begin evaluating specific listings to pinpoint the markets most receptive to your work and most beneficial to you.

In evaluating individual listings, check the location of the company, the types of material it is interested in seeing, submission requirements, and rights and payment policies. Depending on your personal concerns, any of these items could be a deciding factor as you determine which markets you plan to approach. Many listings also include a reporting time.

Whenever possible, obtain submission guidelines before submitting material. You can usually obtain guidelines by sending a SASE to the address in the listing or by checking online. Many of the listings contain instructions on how to obtain sample copies, catalogs or market lists. The more research you do upfront, the better your chances of acceptance, publication and payment.

BEFORE YOUR FIRST SALE

Everything in life has to start somewhere and that somewhere is always at the beginning. Stephen King, Stephenie Meyer, Jeff Kinney, Nora Roberts—they all had to start at the beginning. It would be great to say becoming a writer is as easy as waving a magic wand over your manuscript and "Poof!" you're published, but that's not how it happens. While there's no one true "key" to becoming successful, a long, well-paid writing career *can* happen when you combine four elements:

- Good writing
- Knowledge of writing markets
- Professionalism
- Persistence

Good writing is useless if you don't know which markets will buy your work or how to pitch and sell your writing. If you aren't professional and persistent in your contact with editors, your writing is just that—your writing. But if you are a writer who embraces the above four elements, you have a good chance at becoming a paid, published writer who will reap the benefits of a long and successful career.

As you become more involved with writing, you may read articles or talk to editors and authors with conflicting opinions about the right way to submit your work. The truth is, there are many different routes a writer can follow to get published, but no matter which route you choose, the end is always the same—becoming a published writer.

The following advice on submissions has worked for many writers, but it is by no means the be-all-end-all of proper submission guidelines. It's very easy to get wrapped up in the specifics of submitting (Should I put my last name on every page of my manuscript?) and ignore the more important issues (Will this idea on ice fishing in Alaska be appropriate for a regional magazine in Seattle?). Don't allow yourself to become so blinded by submission procedures that you forget common sense. If you use your common sense and develop professional, courteous relations with editors, you will eventually find your own submission style.

DEVELOP YOUR IDEAS, THEN TARGET THE MARKETS

Writers often think of an interesting story, complete the manuscript, and then begin the search for a suitable publisher or magazine. While this approach is common for fiction, poetry and screenwriting, it reduces your chances of success in many nonfiction writing areas. Instead, choose categories that interest you and study those sections in *Writer's Market*. Select several listings you consider good prospects for your type of writing. Sometimes the individual listings will even help you generate ideas.

Next, make a list of the potential markets for each idea. Make the initial contact with markets using the method stated in the market listings. If you exhaust your list of possibilities, don't give up. Instead, reevaluate the idea or try another angle. Continue developing ideas and approaching markets. Identify and rank potential markets for an idea and continue the process.

As you submit to the various publications listed in *Writer's Market*, it's important to remember that every magazine is published with a particular audience and slant in mind. Probably the number one complaint we receive from editors is the submissions they receive are completely wrong for their magazines or book line. The first mark of professionalism is to know your market well. Gaining that knowledge starts with *Writer's Market*, but you should also do your own detective work. Search out back issues of the magazines you wish to write for, pick up recent issues at your local newsstand, or visit magazines' websites—anything that will help you figure out what subjects specific magazines publish. This research is also helpful in learning what topics have been covered ad nauseum—the topics you should stay away from or approach in a fresh way. Magazines' websites are invaluable as most post the current issue of the magazine, as well as back issues, and most offer writer's guidelines.

The same advice is true for submitting to book publishers. Research publisher websites for their submission guidelines, recently published titles and their backlist. You can use this information to target your book proposal in a way that fits with a publisher's other titles while not directly competing for sales.

Prepare for rejection and the sometimes lengthy wait. When a submission is returned, check your file folder of potential markets for that idea. Cross off the market that rejected the idea. If the editor has given you suggestions or reasons why the manuscript was not accepted, you might want to incorporate these suggestions when revising your manuscript.

After revising your manuscript mail it to the next market on your list.

Take rejection with a grain of salt

Rejection is a way of life in the publishing world. It's inevitable in a business that deals with such an overwhelming number of applicants for such a limited number of positions. Anyone who has published has lived through many rejections, and writers with thin skin are at a distinct disadvantage. A rejection letter is not a personal attack. It simply indicates your submission is not appropriate for that market. Writers who let rejection dissuade them from pursuing their dream or who react to an editor's "No" with indignation or fury do themselves a disservice. Writers who let rejection stop them do not get published. Resign yourself to facing rejection now. You will live through it, and you'll eventually overcome it.

QUERY AND COVER LETTERS

A query letter is a brief, one-page letter used as a tool to hook an editor and get him interested in your idea. When you send a query letter to a magazine, you are trying to get an editor to buy your idea or article. When you query a book publisher, you are attempting to get an editor interested enough in your idea to request your book proposal or your entire manuscript. (Note: Some book editors prefer to receive book proposals on first contact. Check individual listings for which method editors prefer.)

Here are some basic guidelines to help you create a query that's polished and well-organized. For more tips see "Query Letter Clinic" article.

- **LIMIT IT TO ONE PAGE, SINGLE-SPACED,** and address the editor by name (Mr. or Ms. and the surname). *Note*: Do not assume that a person is a Mr. or Ms. unless it is obvious from the name listed. For example, if you are contacting a D.J. Smith, do not assume that D.J. should be preceded by Mr. or Ms. Instead, address the letter to D.J. Smith.
- **GRAB THE EDITOR'S ATTENTION WITH A STRONG OPENING.** Some magazine queries, for example, begin with a paragraph meant to approximate the lead of the intended article.
- **INDICATE HOW YOU INTEND TO DEVELOP THE ARTICLE OR BOOK.** Give the editor some idea of the work's structure and content.
- **LET THE EDITOR KNOW IF YOU HAVE PHOTOS** or illustrations available to accompany your magazine article.
- **MENTION ANY EXPERTISE OR TRAINING THAT QUALIFIES YOU** to write the article or book. If you've been published before, mention it; if not, don't.
- **END WITH A DIRECT REQUEST TO WRITE THE ARTICLE.** Or, if you're pitching a book, ask for the go-ahead to send in a full proposal or the entire manuscript. Give the editor an idea of the expected length and delivery date of your manuscript.

A common question that arises is: If I don't hear from an editor in the reported response time, how do I know when I can safely send the query to another market? Many writers find it helpful to indicate in their queries that if they don't receive a response from the editor (slightly after the listed reporting time), they will assume the editor is not interested. It's best to take this approach, particularly if your topic is timely.

A brief, single-spaced cover letter is helpful when sending a manuscript as it helps personalize the submission. However, if you have previously queried the editor, use the cover letter to politely and briefly remind the editor of that query—when it was sent, what it contained, etc. "Here is the piece on low-fat cooking that I queried you about on December 12. I look forward to hearing from you at your earliest convenience." Do not use the cover letter as a sales pitch.

If you are submitting to a market that accepts unsolicited manuscripts, a cover letter is useful because it personalizes your submission. You can, and should, include information about the manuscript, yourself, your publishing history, and your qualifications.

In addition to tips on writing queries, the "Query Letter Clinic" article offers eight example query letters, some that work and some that don't, as well as comments on why the letters were either successful or failed to garner an assignment or contract.

Querying for fiction

Fiction is sometimes queried, but more often editors prefer receiving material. Many fiction editors won't decide on a submission until they have seen the complete manuscript. When submitting a fiction book idea, most editors prefer to see at least a synopsis and sample chapters (usually the first three). For fiction published in magazines, most editors want to see the complete short story manuscript. If an editor does request a query for fiction, it should include a description of the main theme and story line, including the conflict and resolution. Take a look at individual listings to see what editors prefer to receive.

THE SYNOPSIS

Most fiction books are sold by a complete manuscript, but most editors and agents don't have the time to read a complete manuscript of every wannabe writer. As a result, publishing decision-makers use the synopsis and sample chapters to help the screening process of fiction. The synopsis, on its most basic level, communicates what the book is about.

The length and depth of a synopsis can change from agent to agent or publisher to publisher. Some will want a synopsis that is one to two single-spaced pages; others will want a synopsis that can run up to 25 double-spaced pages. Checking your listings in *Writer's Market*, as well as double-checking with the listing's website, will help guide you in this respect.

The content should cover all the essential points of the novel from beginning to end and in the correct order. The essential points include main characters, main plot points, and, yes, the ending. Of course, your essential points will vary from the editor who wants a one-page synopsis to the editor who wants a 25-page synopsis.

NONFICTION PROPOSALS

Most nonfiction books are sold by a book proposal—a package of materials that details what your book is about, who its intended audience is, and how you intend to write the book. It includes some combination of a cover or query letter, an overview, an outline, author's information sheet, and sample chapters. Editors also want to see information about the audience for your book and about titles that compete with your proposed book.

Submitting nonfiction proposals

A proposal package should include the following items:

- **A COVER OR QUERY LETTER.** This letter should be a short introduction to the material you include in the proposal.
- **AN OVERVIEW.** This is a brief summary of your book. It should detail your book's subject and give an idea of how that subject will be developed.
- **AN OUTLINE.** The outline covers your book chapter by chapter and should include all major points covered in each chapter. Some outlines are done in traditional outline form, but most are written in paragraph form.
- **AN AUTHOR'S INFORMATION SHEET.** This information should acquaint the editor with your writing background and convince her of your qualifications regarding the subject of your book.
- **SAMPLE CHAPTERS.** Many editors like to see sample chapters, especially for a first book. Sample chapters show the editor how you write and develop ideas from your outline.
- **MARKETING INFORMATION.** Facts about how and to whom your book can be successfully marketed are now expected to accompany every book proposal. If you can provide information about the audience for your book and suggest ways the book publisher can reach those people, you will increase your chances of acceptance.
- **COMPETITIVE TITLE ANALYSIS.** Check the *Subject Guide to Books in Print* for other titles on your topic. Write a one- or two-sentence synopsis of each. Point out how your book differs and improves upon existing topics.

For more information on nonfiction book proposals, read Michael Larsen's *How to Write a Book Proposal* (Writer's Digest Books).

A WORD ABOUT AGENTS

An agent represents a writer's work to publishers, negotiates contracts, follows up to see that contracts are fulfilled, and generally handles a writer's business affairs, leaving the writer free to write. Effective agents are valued for their contacts in the publishing industry, their knowledge about who to approach with certain ideas, their ability to guide an author's career, and their business sense.

While most book publishers listed in *Writer's Market* publish books by unagented writers, some of the larger houses are reluctant to consider submissions that have not reached them through a literary agent. Companies with such a policy are noted by an (Ⓐ) icon at the beginning of the listing, as well as in the submission information within the listing.

Writer's Market includes a list of literary agents who are all members of the Association of Authors' Representatives and who are also actively seeking new and established writers.

MANUSCRIPT FORMAT

You can increase your chances of publication by following a few standard guidelines regarding the physical format of your manuscript. It should be your goal to make your manuscript readable. Follow these suggestions as you would any other suggestions: Use what works for you and discard what doesn't.

In general, when submitting a manuscript, you should use white, 8½×11, 20 lb. paper, and you should also choose a legible, professional looking font (i.e., Times New Roman)—no all-italic or artsy fonts. Your entire manuscript should be double-spaced with a 1½-inch margin on all sides of the page. Once you are ready to print your manuscript, you should print either on a laser printer or an ink-jet printer.

ESTIMATING WORD COUNT

All computers provide you with a word count of your manuscript. Your editor will count again after editing the manuscript. Although your computer is counting characters, an editor or production editor is more concerned about the amount of space the text will occupy on a page. Several small headlines or subheads, for instance, will be counted the same by your computer as any other word of text. However, headlines and subheads usually employ a different font size than the body text, so an editor may count them differently to be sure enough space has been estimated for larger type.

For short manuscripts, it's often quickest to count each word on a representative page and multiply by the number of pages. You can get a very rough count by multiplying the

MANUSCRIPT FORMATTING SAMPLE

(1) Your Name
Your Street Address
City State ZIP Code
Day and Evening Phone Numbers
E-mail Address

Website (if applicable)
(2)

50,000 Words **(3)**

(1) Type your real name (even if you use a pseudonym) and contact information **(2)** Double-space twice **(3)** Estimated word count **(4)** Type your title in capital letters, double-space and type "by," double-space again, and type your name (or pseudonym if you're using one) **(5)** Double-space twice, then indent first paragraph and start text of your manuscript **(6)** On subsequent pages, type your name, a dash, and the page number in the upper left or right corner

TITLE

by

(4) Your Name

(5) You can increase your chances of publication by following a few standard guidelines regarding the physical format of your article or manuscript. It should be your goal to make your manuscript readable. Use these suggestions as you would any other suggestions: Use what works for you and discard what doesn't.

In general, when submitting a manuscript, you should use white, 8½×11, 20-lb. bond paper, and you should also choose a legible, professional-looking font (i.e., Times New Roman)—no all-italic or artsy fonts. Your entire manuscript should be double-spaced with a 1½-inch margin on all sides of the page. Once you are ready to print your article or manuscript, you should print either on a laser printer or an ink-jet printer.

Remember, articles should be written after you send a one-page query letter to an editor, and the editor then asks you to write the article. If, however, you are sending an article "on spec" to an editor, you should send both a query letter and the complete article.

Fiction and poetry is a little different from nonfiction articles, in that it is rarely queried. More often than not, poetry and fiction editors want to review the complete manuscript before making a final decision.

number of pages in your manuscript by 250 (the average number of words on a double-spaced typewritten page).

PHOTOGRAPHS AND SLIDES

In some cases, the availability of photographs and slides can be the deciding factor as to whether an editor will accept your submission. This is especially true when querying a publication that relies heavily on photographs, illustrations or artwork to enhance the article (e.g., craft magazines, hobby magazines, etc.). In some instances, the publication may offer additional payment for photographs or illustrations.

Check the individual listings to find out which magazines review photographs and what their submission guidelines are. Most publications prefer you do not send photographs with your submission. However, if photographs or illustrations are available, you should indicate that in your query. As with manuscripts, never send the originals of your photographs or illustrations. Instead, send digital images, which is what most magazine and book publishers prefer to use.

SEND PHOTOCOPIES

If there is one hard-and-fast rule in publishing, it's this: *Never* send the original (or only) copy of your manuscript. Most editors cringe when they find out a writer has sent the only copy of their manuscript. You should always send copies of your manuscript.

Some writers choose to send a self-addressed, stamped postcard with a photocopied submission. In their cover letter they suggest if the editor is not interested in their manuscript, it may be tossed out and a reply sent on the postcard. This method is particularly helpful when sending your submissions to international markets.

MAILING SUBMISSIONS

No matter what size manuscript you're mailing, always include a self-addressed, stamped envelope (SASE) with sufficient return postage. The website for the U.S. Postal Service (www.usps.com) and the website for the Canadian Post (www.canadapost.ca) both have postage calculators if you are unsure how much postage to affix.

A book manuscript should be mailed in a sturdy, well-wrapped box. Enclose a self-addressed mailing label and paper clip your return postage to the label. However, be aware that some book publishers do not return unsolicited manuscripts, so make sure you know the practice of the publisher before sending any unsolicited material.

Types of mail service

There are many different mailing service options available to you whether you are sending a query letter or a complete manuscript. You can work with the U.S. Postal Service, United

Parcel Service, Federal Express, or any number of private mailing companies. The following are the five most common types of mailing services offered by the U.S. Postal Service.

- **FIRST CLASS** is a fairly expensive way to mail a manuscript, but many writers prefer it. First-Class mail generally receives better handling and is delivered more quickly than Standard mail.
- **PRIORITY MAIL** reaches its destination within two or three days.
- **STANDARD MAIL** rates are available for packages, but be sure to pack your materials carefully because they will be handled roughly. To make sure your package will be returned to you if it is undeliverable, print "Return Postage Guaranteed" under your address.
- **CERTIFIED MAIL** must be signed for when it reaches its destination.
- **REGISTERED MAIL** is a high-security method of mailing where the contents are insured. The package is signed in and out of every office it passes through, and a receipt is returned to the sender when the package reaches its destination.

MAILING MANUSCRIPTS

- Fold manuscripts under five pages into thirds, and send in a #10 SASE.
- Mail manuscripts five pages or more unfolded in a 9×12 or 10×13 SASE.
- For return envelope, fold the envelope in half, address it to yourself, and add a stamp, or, if going to Canada or another international destination, International Reply Coupons (available at most post office branches).
- Don't send by Certified Mail—this is a sign of an amateur.

QUERY LETTER CLINIC

//

Many great writers ask year after year, "Why is it so hard to get published?" In many cases, these writers have spent years developing their craft. They submit to the appropriate markets, yet rejection is always the end result. The culprit? A weak query letter.

The query letter is often the most important piece of the publishing puzzle. In many cases, it determines whether editors or agents will even read your manuscript. A good query makes a good first impression; a bad query earns a swift rejection.

ELEMENTS OF A QUERY

A query letter should sell editors or agents on your idea or convince them to request your finished manuscript. The most effective query letters get into the specifics from the very first line. It's important to remember that the query is a call to action, not a listing of features and benefits.

In addition to selling your idea or manuscript, a query can include information on the availability of photographs or artwork. You can include a working title and projected word count. Depending on the piece, you might also mention whether a sidebar might be appropriate and the type of research you plan to conduct. If appropriate, include a tentative deadline and indicate whether the query is being simultaneously submitted.

Biographical information should be included as well, but don't overdo it unless your background actually helps sell the article or proves that you're the only person who could write your proposed piece.

THINGS TO AVOID IN QUERY

The query is not a place to discuss pay rates. This step comes after an editor has agreed to take on your article or book. Besides making an unprofessional impression, it can also work to your disadvantage in negotiating your fee. If you ask too much, an editor may not even contact you to see if a lower rate works. If you ask for too little, you may start an editorial relationship where you make less than the normal rate.

You should also avoid rookie mistakes, such as mentioning your work is copyrighted or including the copyright symbol on your work. While you want to make it clear that you've researched the market, avoid using flattery as a technique for selling your work. It often has the opposite effect of what you intend. In addition, don't hint that you can re-write the piece, as this only leads the editor to think there will be a lot of work involved in shaping up your writing.

Also, never admit several other editors or agents have rejected the query. Always treat your new audience as if they are the first place on your list.

HOW TO FORMAT A QUERY

It's OK to break writing rules in a short story or article, but you should follow the rules when it comes to crafting an effective query. Here are guidelines for query writing.

- Use a normal font and typeface, such as Courier and 10- or 12-point type.
- Include your name, address, phone number, e-mail address and website.
- Use one-inch margin on paper queries.
- Address a specific editor or agent. (Note: It's wise to double-check contact names online or by calling.)
- Limit query to one single-spaced page.
- Include self-addressed, stamped envelope or postcard for response with post submissions.

HOW TO FOLLOW UP

Accidents do happen. Queries may not reach your intended reader. Staff changes or interoffice mail snafus may end up with your query letter thrown away. Or the editor may have set your query off to the side for further consideration and forgotten it. Whatever the case may be, there are some basic guidelines you should use for your follow-up communication.

Most importantly, wait until the reported response time, as indicated in *Writer's Market* or their submission guidelines, has elapsed before contacting an editor or agent. Then, you should send a short and polite e-mail describing the original query sent, the date it was sent, and asking if they received it or made a decision regarding its fate.

The importance of remaining polite and businesslike when following up cannot be stressed enough. Making a bad impression on an editor can often have a ripple effect—as that editor may share his or her bad experience with other editors at the magazine or publishing company. Also, don't call.

HOW THE CLINIC WORKS

As mentioned earlier, the query letter is the most important weapon for getting an assignment or a request for your full manuscript. Published writers know how to craft a well-written, hard-hitting query. What follows are eight queries: four are strong; four are not. Detailed comments show what worked and what did not. As you'll see, there is no cut-and-dried "good" query format; every strong query works on its own merit.

GOOD NONFICTION MAGAZINE QUERY

Jimmy Boaz, editor
American Organic Farmer's Digest
8336 Old Dirt Road
Macon GA 00000

Dear Mr. Boaz,

There are 87 varieties of organic crops grown in the United States, but there's only one farm producing 12 of these—Morganic Corporation. **2**

Located in the heart of Arkansas, this company spent the past decade providing great organic crops at a competitive price helping them grow into the ninth leading organic farming operation in the country. Along the way, they developed the most unique organic offering in North America.

As a seasoned writer with access to Richard Banks, the founder and president of Morganic, I propose writing a profile piece on Banks for your Organic Shakers department. After years of reading this riveting column, I believe the time has come to cover Morganic's rise in the organic farming industry. **3**

This piece would run in the normal 800-1,200 word range with photographs available of Banks and Morganic's operation.

I've been published in *Arkansas Farmer's Deluxe, Organic Farming Today* and in several newspapers. **4**

Thank you for your consideration of this article. I hope to hear from you soon.

Sincerely,

Jackie Service
34 Good St.
Little Rock AR 00000
jackie.service9867@email.com

1 My name is only available on our magazine's website and on the masthead. This writer has done her research. **2** Here's a story that hasn't been pitched before. I didn't know Morganic was so unique in the market. I want to know more. **3** The writer has access to her interview subject, and she displays knowledge of the magazine by pointing out the correct section in which her piece would run. **4** While I probably would've assigned this article based on the idea alone, her past credits do help solidify my decision.

BAD NONFICTION MAGAZINE QUERY

Dear Gentlemen, **1**

I'd like to write the next great article you'll ever publish. My writing credits include amazing pieces I've done for local and community newspapers and for my college English classes. I've been writing for years and years. **2**

Your magazine may not be a big one like *Rolling Stone* or *Sports Illustrated*, but I'm willing to write an interview for you anyway. I know you need material, and I need money. (Don't worry. I won't charge you too much.) **3**

Just give me some people to interview, and I'll do the best job you've ever read. It will be amazing, and I can re-write the piece for you if you don't agree. I'm willing to re-write 20 times if needed. **4**

You better hurry up and assign me an article though, because I've sent out letters to lots of other magazines, and I'm sure to be filled up to capacity very soon. **5**

Later gents,

Carl Bighead
76 Bad Query Lane
Big City NY 00000

1 This is sexist, and it doesn't address any contact specifically. **2** An over-the-top claim by a writer who does not impress me with his publishing background. **3** Insults the magazine and then reassures me he won't charge too much? **4** While I do assign material from time to time, I prefer writers pitch me their own ideas after studying the magazine. **5** I'm sure people aren't going to be knocking down his door anytime soon.

GOOD FICTION MAGAZINE QUERY

Marcus West
88 Piano Drive
Lexington KY 00000

August 8, 2011 **1**

Jeanette Curic, editor
Wonder Stories
45 Noodle Street
Portland OR 00000

Dear Ms. Curic,

Please consider the following 1,200-word story, "Turning to the Melon," a quirky coming-of-age story with a little magical realism thrown in the mix. **2**

After reading *Wonder Stories* for years, I think I've finally written something that would fit with your audience. My previous short story credits include *Stunned Fiction Quarterly* and *Faulty Mindbomb*. **3**

Thank you in advance for considering "Turning to Melon."

Sincerely,

Marcus West
(123) 456-7890
marcusw87452@email.com

Encl: Manuscript and SASE **4**

1 Follows the format we established in our guidelines. Being able to follow directions is more important than many writers realize. **2** Story is in our word count, and the description sounds like the type of story we would consider publishing. It's flattering to know he reads our magazine. While it won't guarantee publication, it does make me a little more hopeful that the story I'm reading will be a good fit. Also, good to know he's been published before. **4** I can figure it out, but it's nice to know what other materials were included in the envelope. This letter is not flashy, but it gives me the basics and puts me in the right frame of mind to read the actual story.

BAD FICTION MAGAZINE QUERY

To: curic@wonderstories808.com (1)
Subject: A Towering Epic Fantasy

Hello there. (2)

I've written a great fantasy epic novel short story of about 25,000 words that may be included in your magazine if you so desire. (3)

More than 20 years, I've spent chained to my desk in a basement writing out the greatest story of our modern time. And it can be yours if you so desire to have it. (4)

Just say the word, and I'll ship it over to you. We can talk money and movie rights after your acceptance. I have big plans for this story, and you can be part of that success. (5)

Yours forever (if you so desire), (6)

Harold
(or Harry for friends)

(1) We do not consider e-mail queries or submissions. (2) This is a little too informal. (3) First off, what did he write? An epic novel or short story? Second, 25,000 words is way over our 1,500-word max. (4) I'm lost for words. (5) Money and movie rights? We pay moderate rates and definitely don't get involved in movies. (6) I'm sure the writer was just trying to be nice, but this is a little bizarre and kind of creepy. I do not so desire more contact with "Harry."

GOOD NONFICTION BOOK QUERY

To: corey@bigbookspublishing.com
Subject: Query: Become a Better Parent in 30 Days **1**

Dear Mr. Corey,

2 As a parent of six and a high school teacher for more than 20 years, I know first hand that being a parent is difficult work. Even harder is being a good parent. My proposed title, **3** *Taking Care of Yourself and Your Kids: A 30-day Program to Become a Better Parent While Still Living Your Life*, would show how to handle real-life situations and still be a good parent.

This book has been years in the making, as it follows the outline I've used successfully in my summer seminars I give on the topic to thousands of parents every year. It really works, because past participants contact me constantly to let me know what a difference my classes have made in their lives. **4**

In addition to marketing and selling *Taking Care of Yourself and Your Kids* at my summer seminars, I would also be able to sell it through my website and promote it through my weekly e-newsletter with over 25,000 subscribers. Of course, it would also make a very nice trade title that I think would sell well in bookstores and possibly retail outlets, such as Wal-Mart and Target. **5**

Please contact me for a copy of my full book proposal today. **6**

Thank you for your consideration.

Marilyn Parent
8647 Query St.
Norman OK 00000
mparent8647@email.com
www.marilynsbetterparents.com

1 Effective subject line. Lets me know exactly what to expect when I open the e-mail. **2** Good lead. Six kids and teaches high school. I already trust her as an expert. **3** Nice title that would fit well with others we currently offer. **4** Her platform as a speaker definitely gets my attention. **5** 25,000 e-mail subscribers? She must have a very good voice to gather that many readers. **6** I was interested after the first paragraph, but every paragraph after made it impossible to not request her proposal.

BAD NONFICTION BOOK QUERY

To: info@bigbookspublishing.com
Subject: a question for you **1**

I really liked this book by Mega Book Publishers called *Build Better Trains in Your Own Backyard*. It was a great book that covered all the basics of model train building. My father and I would read from it together and assemble all the pieces, and it was magical like Christmas all through the year. Why wouldn't you want to publish such a book? **2**

Well, here it is. I've already copyrighted the material for 2006 and can help you promote it if you want to send me on a worldwide book tour. As you can see from my attached digital photo, I'm not the prettiest person, but I am passionate. **3**

There are at least 1,000 model train builders in the United States alone, and there might be even more than that. I haven't done enough research yet, because I don't know if this is an idea that appeals to you. If you give me maybe $500, I could do that research in a day and get back to you on it. **4**

Anyway, this idea is a good one that brings back lots of memories for me.

Jacob **5**

1 The subject line is so vague I almost deleted this e-mail as spam without even opening it. **2** The reason we don't publish such a book is easy—we don't do hobby titles. **3** I'm not going to open an attachment from an unknown sender via e-mail. Also, copyrighting your work years before pitching is the sign of an amateur. **4** 1,000 possible buyers is a small market, and I'm not going to pay a writer to do research on a proposal. **5** Not even a last name? Or contact information? At least I won't feel guilty for not responding.

GOOD FICTION BOOK QUERY

Jeremy Mansfield, editor
Novels R Us Publishing
8787 Big Time Street
New York NY 00000

Dear Mr. Mansfield,

My 62,000-word novel, *The Cat Walk,* is a psychologically complex thriller in the same mold as James Patterson's Alex Cross novels, but with a touch of the supernatural a la Stephenie Meyer. **1**

Rebecca Frank is at the top of the modeling world, posing for magazines in exotic locales all over the world and living life to its fullest. Despite all her success, she feels something is missing in her life. Then she runs into Marcus Hunt, a wealthy bachelor with cold blue eyes and an ambiguous past.

Within 24 hours of meeting Marcus, Rebecca's understanding of the world turns upside down, and she finds herself fighting for her life and the love of a man who may not have the ability to return her the favor.

Filled with demons, serial killers, trolls, maniacal clowns and more, *The Cat Walk* follows Rebecca through a gauntlet of trouble and turmoil, leading up to a final climactic realization that may lead to her own unraveling. **2**

The Cat Walk should fit in well with your other titles, such as *Bone Dead* and *Carry Me Home*, though it is a unique story. Your website mentioned supernatural suspense as a current interest, so I hope this is a good match. **3**

My short fiction has appeared in many mystery magazines, including a prize-winning story in *The Mysterious Oregon Quarterly*. This novel is the first in a series that I'm working on (already half-way through the second). **4**

As stated in your guidelines, I've included the first 30 pages. Thank you for considering *The Cat Walk*.

Sincerely,

Merry Plentiful
54 Willow Road
East Lansing MI 00000
merry865423@email.com

1 Novel is correct length and has the suspense and supernatural elements we're seeking. **2** The quick summary sounds like something we would write on the back cover of our paperbacks. That's a good thing, because it identifies the triggers that draw a response out of our readers. **3** She mentions similar titles we've done and that she's done research on our website. She's not afraid to put in a little extra effort. **4** At the moment, I'm not terribly concerned that this book could become a series, but it is something good to file away in the back of my mind for future use.

Jeremy Mansfield
Novels R Us Publishing
8787 Big Time Street
New York NY 00000

Dear Editor,

My novel has an amazing twist ending that could make it a worldwide phenomenon overnight while you are sleeping. It has spectacular special effects that will probably lead to a multi-million dollar movie deal that will also spawn action figures, lunch boxes, and several other crazy subsidiary rights. I mean, we're talking big-time money here. **1**

I'm not going to share the twist until I have a signed contract that authorizes me to a big bank account, because I don't want to have my idea stolen and used to promote whatever new initiative "The Man" has in mind for media nowadays. Let it be known that you will be rewarded handsomely for taking a chance on me. **2**

Did you know that George Lucas once took a chance on an actor named Harrison Ford by casting him as Han Solo in Star Wars? Look at how that panned out. Ford went on to become a big actor in the Indiana Jones series, *The Fugitive, Blade Runner*, and more. It's obvious that you taking a risk on me could play out in the same dramatic way. **3**

I realize that you've got to make money, and guess what? I want to make money too. So we're on the same page, you and I. We both want to make money, and we'll stop at nothing to do so.

If you want me to start work on this amazing novel with an incredible twist ending, just send a one-page contract agreeing to pay me a lot of money if we hit it big. No other obligations will apply. If it's a bust, I won't sue you for millions. **4**

Sincerely,

Kenzel Pain
92 Bad Writer Road
Austin TX 00000

1 While I love to hear enthusiasm from a writer about his or her work, this kind of unchecked excitement is worrisome for an editor. **2** I need to know the twist to make a decision on whether to accept the manuscript. Plus, I'm troubled by the paranoia and emphasis on making a lot of money. **3** I'm confused. Does he think he's Harrison Ford? **4** So that's the twist: He hasn't even written the novel yet. There's no way I'm going to offer a contract for a novel that hasn't been written by someone with no experience or idea of how the publishing industry works.

WRITE BETTER QUERIES AND SELL MORE ARTICLES

by Krissy Brady

The steps to scoring a byline in your favorite publication are straightforward enough: Come up with a mind-blowing article idea for your target market. Write an attention-grabbing query letter. Submit it to the appropriate editor. Rinse. Repeat. But there's one aspect of the pitching process new writers tend to ignore that could spell disaster for them down the line.

Once you've got the nuts-and-bolts of query writing on lockdown, your primary goal as a writer needs to shift from learning how to write quality pitches to learning how to write them more efficiently. As assignments start rolling in (and they will), you'll inevitably have less time to dedicate to pitches—and the last thing you want is your income stream slowing to a trickle.

By making the following tiny changes now, you'll not only avoid the whole assignments vs. pitches tug-of-war as your portfolio grows, but churn out top notch query letters in a fraction of the time. (This is not a drill.)

1. ESTABLISH YOUR EXACT MISSION

Make sure the focus of your primary writing goal is laser sharp. Don't just decide the category of magazine you want to write for: Pinpoint your exact target demographic within that category, the exact magazines that cater to that demographic, and the exact section you want to break into. Focus your attention on the bullseye, not the entire dartboard. It will make the process of breaking in much less overwhelming—and once you've built a solid relationship with the editor of one department, you'll have an automatic referral once you're ready to branch out into others.

2. KEEP TABS ON YOUR MARKETS

Know your markets better than you know yourself. Keep files on each market you'd like to write for, and track everything you learn about them along the way. Include submission guidelines (which you score by signing up for a Mediabistro.com premium membership), the name of the section you want to break into, as well as the name and e-mail address of the editor who runs that department. If they also accept pitches for their website, add their web editor's info to your roster as well.

For unlimited access to your target markets (not to mention years worth of back issues!), sign up for a Texture.com account. Keep track of the articles that are being published in your section: List each headline and sub-headline in your file, along with a brief description of how each article was packaged (feature with sidebars, list post, as told to, etc.). As each new issue launches, update your file. Finally, visit their website on a daily or weekly basis and track what they're publishing online.

Sure, it's a little cyber-stalkerish, but studying your markets on a regular basis takes the guesswork out of what to pitch, who to pitch to, and how to package your ideas, putting you miles ahead of the competition. Over time, your files will become a treasure trove of information that other writers would hand over a kidney for.

3. FIND THE DIAMONDS IN THE ROUGH

While it's important to subscribe to sites like ScienceDaily and EurekAlert! for the latest news on studies and scientific breakthroughs, they're not the best places for new writers to find interesting stories—especially if you don't already have a relationship with the editor you're pitching the story to. More often than not, a staff writer or regular contributor will have written the story before you've so much as decided on a lede.

Instead, visit sites like Google Scholar (scholar.google.com), PubMed (www.ncbi.nlm.nih.gov/pubmed), and ScienceDirect (www.sciencedirect.com). Search for interesting studies that haven't hit the mainstream using keywords that best describe the topics you're most interested in writing about. Best of all, all three sites let you create alerts based on your fave keywords, so you can have the latest studies sent directly to your inbox on a daily or weekly basis. Not sure if a study is worth writing about? Grab a copy of *Basics for Evaluating Medical Research Studies: A Simplified Approach*, by Sheri Ann Strite and Michael E. Stuart, M.D. (Delfini Group, 2013) to help you wade through the medical jargon.

4. LET THE INFORMATION COME TO YOU

Set up an e-mail address specifically for subscribing to scholarly journals, press release websites, and newsletters by the top experts in your field. Each time you read a new article in your niche, look into the studies that were mentioned, where they were published, and subscribe to notifications from those journals. Add the experts that were quoted to your contact list for future reference, and follow them on social media. If applicable, introduce yourself to the PR people who represent these experts and let them know you'd like to be kept in the loop on interesting developments. Use digital doo-dads like Flipboard (flipboard.com) and Nuzzel (nuzzel.com) to streamline your news hunting experience. Instead of scouring the Internet for new material (which almost always leads to hours of unnecessary Facebook and IMDB creeping), all you'll have to do is check your e-mail and voila—so many ideas, so little time.

5. PITCH LESS

No, but seriously. Focus on the quality of your pitches, not on how fast you can send them out. Once the process of building a solid query is second nature to you, the speed at which you write them will increase naturally. In the meantime, think each of your ideas through from head(line) to toe, and thoughtfully decide which markets you're going to submit them to. I now send one-quarter of the pitches that I used to, but receive (way) more acceptances than rejections—which is the only statistic that matters.

6. BE A PERSONAL PROFESSIONAL

Ditch the business speak and write your pitches like you're writing an e-mail to a friend. Allow the editor to hear your voice as they read your words. I've built an entire writing career using my emotional baggage as bait, and you can too. Define what makes you quirky, and run with it.

7. HONE YOUR PACKAGING SKILLS

Once you've worked with the same editor a few times, you don't have to be as formal with your query letters since they already know you've got the goods. But your pitches still need to pack a punch, and this is where the art of packaging comes in handy. Each time you come up with a new idea, search articles that have been written on the topic in the past and brainstorm ways to package your idea to make it stand out. Consistently putting this habit into practice means the next time a breaking story hits your radar, you'll be able to send your editor an insta-packaged idea that just might lead to an insta-assignment.

8. DON'T LET ANYTHING SLIP THROUGH THE CRACKS

Eventually, you're not only going to have multiple assignments on the go at various stages of completion, but multiple pitches circulating that will need to be followed up on at specific times. Use a program or app like Story Tracker (andrewnicolle.com) to remind yourself of when to touch base with an editor—and when to send your pitch elsewhere.

9. DEVELOP BACKUP ANGLES AND PITCHES

Like you, I was told the odds are slim-to-none that two editors will show interest in the same pitch. And then it happened. Twice. In a row. Naturally, I wasn't prepared, and didn't know whether to do a happy dance or throw up. Save yourself the panic attack by developing 1-2 backup angles for each pitch that can be offered to the second editor if they work for a non-competing market, and a backup pitch that's of equal or higher value if they work for a direct competitor.

10. CREATE YOUR OWN LEARNING EXPERIENCE

Typically, editors only respond to the ideas they're interested in publishing, which means it's on you to determine why your rejected queries were... well, rejected. We've all sent out pitches that were slightly off or "almost" worthy of a sale, and it's important to take stock of what went wrong to refine your process. Compare them to pitches you've nailed in the past, and you'll find the answers are right in front of you: Maybe your intro wasn't catchy enough or your angle was too vague. Maybe your headline was a snore or you sent the pitch from a place of impatience instead of finality. You don't need an editor to write back and confirm your suspicions, because deep down you already know what you need to improve on.

11. PITCH FOR THE RIGHT REASONS

Pitch stories you're drawn to and have a legit interest in covering; don't just pitch an idea because you think it'll sell. If you come across a study that'd make an excellent front-of-book piece for your target market du jour, but you find the subject matter blasé, your query will reflect that. Editors can tell the difference between your heart calling the shots—and your empty wallet.

KRISSY BRADY is so out of shape, it's like she has the innards of an 80-year-old—so naturally, she became a women's health + wellness writer. Since turning her emotional baggage into a writing career, she's been published in magazines like *Cosmopolitan* and *Women's Health*, as well as on websites like Prevention.com and Shape.com. You can follow her shenanigans at writtenbykrissy.com (you know, if you want).

LANDING THE SIX-FIGURE DEAL

What Makes Your Proposal Hot

....

by SJ Hodges

It's the question every first-time author wants to ask:

"If I sell my book, will the advance even cover my rent?"

Authors, I am happy to tell you that, yes, the six-figure book deal for a newbie still exists—even if you're not a celebrity with your own television show! As a ghostwriter, I work with numerous authors and personalities to develop both nonfiction and fiction proposals, and I've seen unknown first-timers land life-changing deals even in a down economy. Is platform the ultimate key to their success? You better believe it's a huge consideration for publishers, but here's the good news: Having a killer platform is only one element that transforms a "nice deal" into a "major deal."

You still have to ensure the eight additional elements of your proposal qualify as major attractions. Daniela Rapp, editor at St. Martin's Press explains, "In addition to platform, authors need to have a fantastic, original idea. They have to truly be an expert in their field and they must be able to write." So how do you craft a proposal that conveys your brilliance, your credentials, your talent and puts a couple extra zeroes on your check?

ONE: NARRATIVE OVERVIEW

Before you've even written word one of your manuscript, you are expected to, miraculously, summarize the entirety of your book in such a compelling and visceral way that a publisher or agent will feel as if they are reading *The New York Times* review. Sound impossible? That's because it is.

That's why I'm going to offer two unorthodox suggestions. First, consider writing the first draft of your overview after you've created your table of contents and your chapter outlines. You'll know much more about the content and scope of your material even if you're not 100 percent certain about the voice and tone. That's why you'll take another pass after you complete your sample chapters. Because then you'll be better acquainted with the voice of your book which brings me to unorthodox suggestion number two… treat your overview as literature.

I believe every proposal component needs to be written "in voice" especially because your overview is the first page the editor sees after the title page. By establishing your voice on the page immediately, your proposal becomes less of a sales document and more of a page-turner. Remember, not everyone deciding your fate works in marketing and sales. Editors still have some buying power and they are readers, first and foremost.

TWO: TABLE OF CONTENTS AND CHAPTER OUTLINES

Television writers call this "breaking" a script. This is where you break your book or it breaks you. This is where you discover if what you plan to share with the world actually merits 80,000 words and international distribution.

Regardless of whether you're writing fiction or nonfiction, this element of your proposal must take your buyer on a journey (especially if it's nonfiction) and once more, I'm a big fan of approaching this component with creativity particularly if you're exploring a specific historical time period, plan to write using a regional dialect, rely heavily on "slanguage," and especially if the material is highly technical and dry.

This means you'll need to style your chapter summaries and your chapter titles as a form of dramatic writing. Think about the arc of the chapters, illuminating the escalating conflict, the progression towards a resolution, in a cinematic fashion. Each chapter summary should end with an "emotional bumper," a statement that simultaneously summarizes and entices in the same way a television show punches you in the gut before they cut to a commercial.

Is it risky to commit to a more creative approach? Absolutely. Will it be perfect the first time you write it? No. The fifth time you write it? No. The tenth time? Maybe. But the contents and chapter summary portion of your proposal is where you really get a chance to show off your skills as an architect of plot and structure and how you make an editor's job much, much easier. According to Lara Asher, acquisitions editor at Globe Pequot Press, it is the single most important component of your proposal. "If I can't easily understand what a book is trying to achieve then I can't present it to my colleagues," Asher says. "It won't make it through the acquisitions process."

THREE: YOUR AUTHOR BIO

Your author bio page must prove that you are more than just a pro, that you are recognized by the world at large as "the definitive expert" on your topic, that you have first-hand experience tackling the problems and implementing your solutions, and that you've seen positive results not only in your personal life but in the lives of others. You have to have walked the walk and talked the talk. You come equipped with a built-in audience, mass media attention, and a strong social network. Your bio assures your buyer that you are the right writer exploring the right topic at the right time.

FOUR: YOUR PLATFORM

Platform, platform, platform. Sit through any writing conference, query any agent, lunch with any editor and you'll hear the "P" word over and over again. What you won't hear is hard-and-fast numbers about just how large this platform has to be in order to secure a serious offer. Is there an audience-to-dollar-amount ratio that seems to be in play? Are publishers paying per head?

"I haven't found this to be the case," says Julia Pastore, former editor for Random House. "It's easier to compel someone to 'Like' you on Facebook or follow you on Twitter than it is to compel them to plunk down money to buy your book. Audience engagement is more important than the sheer number of social media followers."

With that said, if you're shooting for six-figures, publishers expect you'll have big numbers and big plans. Your platform will need to include:

Cross-promotional partnerships

These are organizations or individuals that already support you, are already promoting your brand, your products or your persona. If you host a show on HGTV or Nike designed a tennis racket in your honor, they definitely qualify. If, however, you're not rolling like an A-lister just yet, you need to brainstorm any and every possible connection you have to organizations with reach in the 20,000+ range. Maybe your home church is only 200 people but the larger association serves 40,000 and you often write for their newsletter. Think big. Then think bigger.

Specific, verifiable numbers proving the loyalty of your audience

"Publishers want to see that you have direct contact with a loyal audience," says Maura Teitelbaum, an agent at Folio Literary Management. This means having a calendar full of face-to-face speaking engagements, a personal mailing list, extensive database and verifiable traffic to your author website.

But how much traffic does there need to be? How many public appearances? How many e-mails in your Constant Contact newsletter? Publishers are loathe to quote concrete numbers for "Likes" and "Followers" so I'll stick my neck out and do it instead. At a minimum, to land a basic book deal, meaning a low five-figure sum, you'll need to prove that you've got 15,000-20,000 fans willing to follow you into hell and through high water.

For a big six-figure deal, you'll need a solid base of 100,000 rabid fans plus access to hundreds of thousands more. If not millions. Depressed yet? Don't be. Because we live in a time when things as trivial as Angry Oranges or as important as scientific TED talks can go viral and propel a writer out of obscurity in a matter of seconds. It is only your job to become part of the conversation. And once your foot is in the door, you'll be able to gather…

Considerable media exposure

Publishers are risk averse. They want to see that you're a media darling achieving pundit status. Organize and present all your clips, put together a DVD demo reel of your on-air appearances and be able to quote subscriber numbers and demographics about the publications running your articles or features about you.

Advance praise from people who matter

Will blurbs really make a difference in the size of your check? "I would include as many in a proposal as possible," says Teitelbaum. "Especially if those people are willing to write letters of commitment saying they will promote the book via their platform. That shows your efforts will grow exponentially."

FIVE: PROMOTIONAL PLANS

So what is the difference between your platform and your promotional plan? Your promotional plan must demonstrate specifically how you will activate your current platform and the expected sales results of that activation. These are projections starting three to six months before your book release date and continuing for one year after its hardcover publication. They want your guarantee to sell 15,000 books within that first year.

In addition, your promotional plan also issues promises about the commitments you are willing to make in order to promote the book to an even wider market. This is your expansion plan. How will you broaden your reach and who will help you do it? Publishers want to see that your goals are ambitious but doable.

Think about it this way. If you own a nail salon and you apply for a loan to shoot a movie, you're likely to be rejected. But ask for a loan to open your second salon and your odds get much better. In other words, keep your promotional plans in your wheelhouse while still managing to include:

- Television and radio appearances
- Access to print media
- A massive social media campaign
- Direct e-mail solicitations
- E-commerce and back-of-room merchandising
- New joint partnerships
- Your upcoming touring and speaking schedule with expected audience

You'll notice that I did not include hiring a book publicist as a requirement. Gone are the days when an advance-sucking, three-month contract with a book publicist makes any difference. For a six-figure author, publishers expect there is a team in place: a powerful agent, a herd of assistants and a more generalized media publicist already managing the day-to-day affairs of building your brand, growing your audience. Hiring a book publicist at the last minute is useless.

SIX: YOUR MARKET ANALYSIS

It would seem the odds against a first-time author hitting the jackpot are slim but that's where market analysis provides a glimmer of hope. There are actually markets considered more desirable to publishers. "Broader is generally better for us," says Rapp. "Niche generally implies small. Not something we [St. Martin's Press] can afford to do these days. Current affairs books, if they are explosive and timely, can work. Neuroscience is hot. Animal books (not so much animal memoirs) still work. Military books sell."

"The health and diet category will always be huge," says Asher. "But in a category like parenting which is so crowded, we look for an author tackling a niche topic that hasn't yet been covered."

Niche or broad, your market analysis must position your book within a larger context, addressing the needs of the publishing industry, the relevant cultural conversations happening in the zeitgeist, your potential audience and their buying power, and the potential for both domestic and international sales.

SEVEN: YOUR C.T.A.

Choose the books for your Competitive Title Analysis not only for their topical similarities but also because the author has a comparable profile and platform to your own. Says Pastore, "It can be editorially helpful to compare your book to *Unbroken* by Hillenbrand, but unless your previous book was also a bestseller, this comparison won't be helpful to our sales force."

Limit your C.T.A. to five or six solid offerings then get on BookScan and make sure none of the books sold fewer than 10,000 copies. "Higher sales are preferable," says Rapp. "And you should leave it to the publisher to decide if the market can hold one more title or not. We always do our own research anyway, so just because the book is not mentioned in your line-up doesn't mean we won't know about it."

EIGHT: SAMPLE CHAPTERS

Finally, you have to/get to prove you can … write. Oh yeah, that!

This is the fun part, the pages of your proposal where you really get to shine. It is of upmost importance that these chapters, in harmony with your overview and chapter summaries, allow the beauty, wisdom and/or quirkiness of your voice to be heard. Loud and clear.

"Writing absolutely matters and strong sample chapters are crucial." Pastore explains, "An author must be able to turn their brilliant idea into engaging prose on the page."

Approach the presentation of these chapters creatively. Consider including excerpts from several different chapters and not just offering the standard Introduction, Chapter One and Two. Consider the inclusion of photographs to support the narrative, helping your editor put faces to names. Consider using sidebars or box quotes from the narrative throughout your proposal to build anticipation for the actual read.

NINE: YOUR ONE-PAGER

Lastly, you'll need a one-pager, which is a relatively new addition to the book proposal format. Publishers now expect an author to squeeze a 50- or 60-page proposal down to a one-page summary they can hand to their marketing and sales teams. In its brevity, the one-pager must provide your buyer with "a clear vision of what the book is, why it's unique, why you are the best person to write it, and how we can reach the audience," says Pastore. And it must do that in fewer than 1,000 words. There is no room to be anything but impressive.

And if you're shooting for that six-figure deal, impressive is what each component of your book proposal must be. Easy? No. But still possible? Yes.

SJ HODGES is an 11-time published playwright, ghostwriter and editor. Her most recent book, a memoir co-authored with Animal Planet's "Pit Boss" Shorty Rossi was purchased by Random House/Crown, hit #36 on the Amazon bestseller list and went into its 3rd printing less than six weeks after its release date. As a developmental editor, SJ has worked on books published by Vanguard Press, Perseus Book Group and St. Martin's Press. SJ is a tireless advocate for artists offering a free listing for jobs, grants and fellowships at her Facebook page: facebook.com/constantcreator. She can be reached through her website: sjhodges.com.

TEN-MINUTE MARKETING FOR WRITERS

by Tania Casselle

It's easy to put off marketing until I've got a free afternoon. That afternoon never comes. I pile up lists of story ideas and contacts but by the time I tackle the list half my ideas are out of date or I've missed the boat. Too often freelance writers are overwhelmed by all the marketing we could do, but it takes such a lot of time and energy, doesn't it?

That's a fallacy. Marketing is often just a matter of keeping in touch with editors and clients, even in quite a casual way, to keep your name at the front of their minds when work comes up. Or it can be a matter of a few minutes here and there to nip away at marketing in bite-sized chunks. Ten minutes a day can be enough to make a difference.

All experienced freelancers know that marketing can't be postponed until the calendar is empty of work so you suddenly have to scramble for business. When you are too busy for a full-on marketing push, grab any free 10 minutes in your day and try these quick hit ways to keep the marketing energy flowing.

QUICK QUERIES & PITHY PITCHES

- **Contact former clients or editors you haven't worked with for a while.** It's better than cold pitching to new people, because old clients already know you and the value of your work. Remind them that you exist with a quick e-mail asking how things are going and can you help with anything?
- **Don't be too perfectionist with your pitches.** Sometimes writers delay querying until they have every detail covered—basically they have completely researched and just about written the story! If that's working for you, great! But if the process is so

slow that the story is out of date before you pitch it, or worse, it never gets get finished at all, remember the phrase: "Perfect is the enemy of done." I've found that a quick-and-dirty query is better than none at all, as long as it is professional and to the point.

- **For bigger pitches, tackle one part at a time.** Chunk it down into 10-minute segments, such as research, query draft, choosing clips, etc.
- **Keep a bank of template e-mails for letters of introduction (LOI)**, one for each of your writing niches or business areas. Use them as an introduction to prospective clients, tweaked accordingly. Keep a list of prospects so whenever you have a few minutes to send an LOI, you know who is next on your list.
- **Follow up on a query that hasn't received a reply after a few weeks.** A follow-up takes a minute or two, resending the original query with a brief, friendly note asking if they've had chance to review it yet. I usually follow up two or three times, and it's amazing how often the editor responds with an assignment on that third follow-up!
- **Recycle!** Find an old query that has been rejected and tweak it slightly for another market.
- **Respin!** Think about previous articles that you've written: Did you have excess research and interview quotes that you didn't use? Can you respin your material with a different angle for another market? Once we've done the research and are familiar with a topic, it's time-efficient to see how many other articles we can wring out of it. Obviously make the new spin different enough to satisfy any previous contractual obligations.
- **Browse a magazine editorial calendar to spark ideas for a quick query.** Trade magazine and B2B (business-to-business) publications are especially likely to have an editorial calendar on their websites.

CREATIVE CONNECTIONS

Send editors you've worked with a link to some research in their field or other news that is of interest to them, even if you're not pitching a story. It proves you're a team player, keeping you front-of-mind when they have an assignment.

Katherine Gustafson, whose work has appeared in publications including *Forbes* and *Slate* (katherinegustafson.com) is a fan of contacting clients in a non-salesy way. For example, she e-mailed a former client about potential new work. "I got radio silence," says Gustafson. "It would have been easy to take that non-response as a brush-off, but I was determined to keep contacting them."

However, she wanted to offer something to them rather than just ask for work. She discovered through online searching that the company had recently won an award, so she wrote a congratulations e-mail, without mentioning the prospect of work at all. She immediately received a thank you message, saying the company might need more help from her soon. "Goes to show that following up works, and that simply popping your head in people's virtual doors can be just as effective as—or perhaps more effective than—selling yourself every time you contact someone."

Check jobs boards and forums like JournalismJobs.com and Craigslist. If you spot a full time job that fits your skills, send a quick LOI offering freelance help until they fill the permanent post.

Sometimes a writer needs a little chutzpah. Freelance writer Laurie Lyons-Makaimoku (www.clippings.me/users/llyons) saw a job post for travel writers in certain cities. Her own city wasn't listed but that didn't stop her sending her resume and portfolio. "I said, 'If you ever need writers in Hawaii, let me know!' I didn't think about it again until two months later when the editor responded offering me a contract job. Seriously, it took me three minutes to send the e-mail."

Add a listing to your local Craigslist to advertise yourself as a writer or editor.

Spend a few minutes on housekeeping, ensuring that everywhere you have an online presence is up-to-date. Update clips on your website, your Contently portfolio or your listings in membership organizations. Don't overlook the importance of keywords related to the subjects you write about. I once landed six meaty $2-a-word assignments purely because I'd recently updated my bio in a professional writer group with keywords reflecting my expertise on a specific subject. When an editor searched the group for that subject, my name came up tops, even though others in that group were also competent in the subject. But they didn't have the keyword in their bios! I made it easy for the editor to find me.

Update your e-mail signature with links to recent articles and projects, and forthcoming events, readings and seminars. Keep it brief (nobody reads long signatures) but every time you send an e-mail you are advertising your business.

Touch base with freelance colleagues, including sending leads for gigs that might be perfect for them. My writing community is a major source of business, mainly from referrals and insider info. Sharing tips and participating in professional writer forums and organizations can pay off big time, as well as being great company and support for the work-at-home writer!

SOMETIMES YOU'VE JUST GOT TO ASK

- **Shoot an e-mail to an editor or client you've worked with recently** to say that some time has opened up in your schedule for the next month, is there anything you can help with? Every time I put out a direct ask, I usually find someone responds with a story or project to discuss.
- **Referrals and recommendations are the best kind of marketing** and it only takes a minute to e-mail a client requesting them to please mention you if anyone asks for writer recommendations. Linsey Knerl, writer, content creator and writing course

coach (linseyknerl.com) has an ingenious way of approaching clients for referrals. Each year when she increases her rates for content marketing clients, she e-mails the limited budget start-ups, noting her rate increase but promising to keep their old rate. As a favor in return, will they kindly refer her to other business people? "I usually get at least a couple of introductions from each client, and it keeps me on good terms with my favorite small start-ups that I enjoy helping but realize don't have extra dollars. They are usually very appreciative."

- **Ask satisfied clients for a testimonial for your website.** Make it easy for them, rather than letting them flail around figuring out what to say. (After all, they hired you to write for them for a reason.) Ask them simply to answer a couple of questions. For example: What did you most enjoy about working with me? What did I bring to the project that contributed to its success?

- **If you are a book author, use social media or your mailing list** to ask people to leave reviews on Amazon, but don't call it a review! Ask them simply to leave a comment. People freeze up when asked for "a review" because it sounds so formal and they think they have to write some literary work of art. Again, ask them a couple of specific questions. For example: I'd so appreciate you leaving a brief comment saying what you most enjoyed about my book. Can you name one thing that stood out for you? What did you learn from my self-help book?

SOCIAL MEDIA SAVVY

Whichever social media platforms you use, the objective is not just to promote yourself in a "me-me-me" way, but to build relationships genuinely and keep yourself on an editor or client's radar.

- Share links to your recent work to showcase your skills and help people associate you as the go-to expert for your particular niche.
- Ten minutes is plenty of time to broaden your network by adding editors, corporate prospects or other professionals to your connections.
- Sharing editor or client posts or making comments on them is the simplest 10-minute marketing way to connect.

Freelance food and restaurant writer Julia Antenucci (followyourfork.com) landed an assignment just by commenting on a publication's Instagram feed. Antenucci had just negotiated a freelance gig that was a financial coup for her. "Asking for the pay you deserve and actually receiving it for the very first time is a rush, to say the least. And I was proud."

So when GirlBoss, the online publication for female entrepreneurs, asked Instagram followers about their "GirlBoss Moment," Antenucci left a comment. "I waxed poetic about how I always wanted to be a writer, and now, I wasn't only going to be able to write about the things I cared about, but I was going to pay my rent doing it. Soon after, I got a message from them asking me to write a full essay about my GirlBoss moment."

LINKEDIN LOVE

Many freelance writers get creative with LinkedIn as a way to reach editors and business clients.

Jennifer Goforth Gregory uses the LinkedIn feature that shows who has viewed your profile to contact any potential clients. "If you have the paid version you can see more views," says Gregory, author of *The Freelance Content Marketing Writer: Find Your Perfect Clients, Make Tons of Money and Build a Business You Love* (jennifergregorywriter.com). "But even the free version shows you the past two. I have landed at least five clients this way. It is usually a quick payoff because they are in the market for a writer."

April Blake, who writes about food, craft beer, agriculture, and tourism (theapril-blake.com) got lucky with LinkedIn when she posted a casual update saying: "Yes, actually, I am taking on more freelance content marketing work! If you need some writing done and want to see what I can do in that realm, e-mail me at [address] and I can regale you with as many or few samples as you'd like." Her quick and cheerful message hit home. "I got a message from the guy who owns the roofing company that did my house five years ago asking me to call him about doing web copy and blog posts for their site."

Other writers have connected with clients and editors by writing a LinkedIn update about an event or conference they are planning to attend, or a brief summary of some takeaway tips from after the event.

Finally, make a list of 10-minute tasks. Then you don't waste time deciding what to do when you find a few minutes in your schedule. You can just pull one item from the list and dig in.

TANIA CASSELLE has been a freelance writer and editor for 20+ years, published in books, magazines, newspapers and online media internationally. Her nonfiction, fiction, poetry and radio work have been recognized in numerous awards and anthologies. As a writing coach, she helps writers through individual coaching, online seminars and in-person workshops. www.TCwriter.com

MAKE MONEY COVERING LIVE EVENTS

by Michelle V. Rafter

I've made thousands in Las Vegas without gambling a penny. I don't have a system for beating the house. My secret is more mundane but also more dependably lucrative—I cover conferences, trade shows and live events.

From my first journalism job as a trade magazine associate editor through years of freelancing for newspapers, magazines and online publications, I've covered dozens of conventions and conferences in Las Vegas, New York, Orlando and other popular event destinations. Depending on the occasion, I can come away making two to three times what I spend on travel, lodging and other expenses. The key is planning, pitching ideas based on what I pick up at a show, and working like a crazy person when I'm there.

Here's an example. Because I write about the technology that companies use to manage their workforce, I planned a trip to a major workplace tech conference taking place in Las Vegas. After getting a press pass, a trade publication owned by the company that runs the event asked if I could write daily blog posts about it for their website. Voila, I had $2,000 in assignments to cover an estimated $1,400 in expenses before even heading to the airport. While I was onsite, I did that work. I also scheduled a dozen other interviews I used for other assignments for a different industry magazine where I'm a contributing writer. Over the months that followed, I pitched multiple stories to other publications based on ideas I picked up at the show.

Here are smart things you can do to get the most out of covering a technology, business, science or other industry-specific convention or conference.

Register early to maximize interview opportunities

Convention exhibitors receive press lists and their public relations teams contact reporters in advance about possible interviews. For the Las Vegas technology conference, I got pitched by close to 100 exhibitors, industry analysts and other sources. I chose who I wanted to interview based on existing assignments and topics I wanted to cover. To deal with the crazy amount of e-mail, I set up inbox folders for pending requests, scheduled interviews, companies I wasn't talking to but might visit on the expo floor, and companies I wasn't interviewing or visiting but might want for future reference. I copied everything to Evernote—an app I use to save notes, bookmark websites and keep other background material—in case I needed to reference something at the conference.

Think twice about accepting freebies

In some industries, it's become common for live-event sponsors to offer to pay writers to attend in exchange for coverage. Industries like travel have a long history of comping writers. The practice has spilled over to paying social media influencers to show up and share what they do or learn with their Instagram or YouTube fans. Getting an all-expense paid trip could sound like a sweet deal, but might not be worth it in the long run. Some publications have strict ethics rules prohibiting staff writers from accepting gifts from sources or potential sources, a policy that often extends to freelance contributors. By taking a free trip, you're essentially ruling out any possibility of writing for those publications. Even if you don't formally agree to a quid pro quo, accepting free stuff could create the perception that you can be bought. Is that really the image you want to project? I don't have a problem asking for a conference press pass that otherwise could cost hundreds or thousands of dollars, but I draw the line at accepting anything else.

Hammer out contracts in advance

If you get an assignment to cover a conference or expo, don't let your enthusiasm blind you to the fact that you need to hash out contract terms before doing the work, even if you're under the gun to get details sorted out for an event that's just around the corner. I negotiated the contract for covering the Las Vegas conference before I did anything else, including booking a flight or hotel room. Terms included content I was responsible for filing, total word count, fee, number of revisions (a max of one per article), what constituted acceptance on their part (an "Okay, this is good" e-mail from the editor), and when I could bill. If you're working for a publication for the first time, you'll also need to fill out a W9, and if direct deposit is an option, related banking paperwork.

Plan your time

Before I hit the road, I create a Google Sheet spreadsheet to map out how I'll spend each day. For the Las Vegas trip, I divided days into 30-minute time slots. I plugged in times, names and locations of panels I'd been assigned to cover and added other panels I wanted to attend. Any open slots was time I could use to write, do interviews, take breaks, and attend after-hours events. When I scheduled an interview, I updated the spreadsheet with the source's name, interview location and a cellphone number I could text in case something came up. The nice thing about creating a spreadsheet in the cloud—I could open it on either my laptop or phone and change it on the fly if someone cancelled or switched where we were meeting.

Set up work files in advance

At conventions and events where the schedule is everything, time is your enemy. Anything you can do to give yourself more of it is good. Before I leave home, I create a Word file or Google Doc for each story I'll be filing from the road. If I'm covering a panel, I paste in names, titles and photos of panel speakers copied from the conference website so when I'm filing my story, I don't have to hunt around for any of the information—and the photos help me remember who's who. Once I'm at the conference, I type notes from sessions or follow-up interviews into the same file. When it's time to write, I use Window's split-screen feature to pull up my notes file alongside a file for the story I created in Word.

Get story instructions in advance

Writing stories on deadline isn't the time to learn whether a publication follows the Associated Press Stylebook, The Chicago Manual of Style, or its own style guide. Find out all you can about a publication's preferences for style, grammar, format or other requirements beforehand to save yourself the stress. At the tech conference, I was writing for a new-to-me publication so I got instructions ahead of time for the elements that articles I was writing needed to include (title, description, links, etc.), plus who to send them to. If I hadn't asked, I wouldn't have known about special requirements, such mentioning the names of the panels I was covering in the blog posts I was writing.

Take pictures

I don't get paid for photos. But I take them anyway and share them on Twitter along with captions and conference hashtags. It's another way to take notes, plus a way to share what I learn with my more than 8,000 Twitter followers, including people who aren't at a conference but want to keep tabs on what's happening.

Find room to write

In Las Vegas, I booked accommodations away from the conference hotel because they were cheaper, an important consideration since I was paying my own way. Also, I knew the walk to and from the venue was the only exercise I'd get for the days I was there. However, it meant I was stuck writing in a pressroom that was crowded, noisy and freezing. In hindsight, having a quiet place to write just an elevator ride away would have been worth paying extra, though my step count would have suffered.

Allot more writing time than you think you need

I thought I could hammer out 500-word articles with multiple sources in an hour before heading to the next session or interview. Turns out I needed about twice that to account for navigating an enormous conference venue. It didn't help that some interviews ran long, and I got sidetracked chatting with people in the pressroom. One day I'd booked myself so completely that I didn't file my last blog post until 10 p.m. The next day, I bought myself time by starting to write before the sessions were over. Overestimating the time it takes to finish assignments is easier to deal with than underestimating.

Don't overdo

Earlier in my career, I'd report on conference sessions, do interviews, walk the concrete floors of an exhibit hall all day—in heels—file my stories and then go out with sources or friends until the wee hours. And by the time the trip was over, I was exhausted or caught some kind of bug. I still hit after-hours events because they're a great way to meet sources and pick up tips. But now I'm all about moderation, and getting enough sleep. And the heels stay home.

Put the trip home to good use

The first days back in the office after any kind of trip can be crazy, so anything I can get done on the journey home gets me ahead of the game. One year, I used a five-hour, cross-country flight home from a conference to write a rough draft of an event recap I'd sold to an industry newsletter. The material was so fresh, the article practically wrote itself. I've also used plane flights to organize expense receipts, make notes on business cards I'd collected from potential sources or sent the same people requests to connect on LinkedIn, which I use as a contact manager. Other times I've used plane or train rides to read materials I picked up at the conference that could be useful for future assignments. Sometimes I just read a book, or sleep!

Pitch ideas while they're hot

Back in the office, I scan notes for ideas for trend pieces, profiles and other stories I could pitch to publications I already write for or for new-to-me outlets. I use conference reporting to flesh out a pitch and mention studies or interviews I already have and other research I would do to write a piece. One year, post-conference pitches from the same workplace tech convention resulted in my first bylines for AARP.org and Computerworld, which paved the way for subsequent articles I've done for both.

Michelle V. Rafter is a Portland, Oregon, journalist, author, and ghostwriter.

FUNDS FOR WRITERS 101

Find Money You Didn't Know Existed

....

by C. Hope Clark

When I completed writing my novel over a decade ago, I imagined the next step was simply to find a publisher and watch the book sell. Like most writers, my goal was to earn a living doing what I loved so I could walk away from the day job. No such luck. Between rejection and newfound knowledge that a novel can take years to sell enough for a single house payment, I opened my mind to other writing avenues. I learned that there's no *one* way to find funds to support your writing; instead there are *many*. So many, in fact, that I felt the need to share the volume of knowledge I collected, and I called it FundsforWriters.com.

Funds are money. But obtaining those funds isn't necessarily a linear process, or a one-dimensional path. As a serious writer, you study all options at your fingertips, entertaining financial resources that initially don't make sense as well as the obvious.

GRANTS

Grants come from government agencies, nonprofits, businesses and even generous individuals. They do not have to be repaid, as long as you use the grant as intended. No two are alike. Therefore, you must do your homework to find the right match between your grant need and the grant provider's mission. Grantors like being successful at their mission just as you like excelling at yours. So they screen applicants, ensuring they fit the rules and show promise to follow through.

Don't fear grants. Sure, you're judged by a panel, and rejection is part of the game, but you already know that as a writer. Gigi Rosenberg, author of *The Artist's Guide to*

Grant Writing, states, "If one funder doesn't want to invest in your project, find another who does. And if nobody does, then begin it any way you can. Once you've started, that momentum will help your project find its audience and its financial support."

TYPES OF GRANTS

Grants can send you to retreats, handle emergencies, provide mentors, pay for conferences, or cover travel. They also can be called awards, fellowships, residencies, or scholarships. But like any aspect of your writing journey, define how any tool, even a grant, fits into your plans. Your mission must parallel a grantor's mission.

The cream-of-the-crop grants have no strings attached. Winning recipients are based upon portfolios and an application that defines a work-in-progress. You don't have to be a Pulitzer winner, but you must prove your establishment as a writer.

You find most of these opportunities in state arts commissions. Find them at www.nasaa-arts.org or as a partner listed at the National Endowment for the Arts website, www.nea.gov. Not only does your state's arts commission provide funding, but the players can direct you to other grant opportunities, as well as to artists who've gone before you. Speaking to grant winners gives you a wealth of information and a leg up in designing the best application.

Foundations and nonprofits fund the majority of grants. Most writers' organizations are nonprofits. Both the Mystery Writers of America (www.mysterywriters.org) and Society of Children's Book Writers and Illustrators (www.scbwi.org) offer scholarships and grants.

Many retreats are nonprofits. Journalist and freelancer Alexis Grant (http://alexisgrant.com/) tries to attend a retreat a year. Some ask her to pay, usually on a sliding scale based upon income, and others provide scholarships. Each time, she applies with a clear definition of what she hopes to gain from the two to five-week trips. "It's a great way to get away from the noise of everyday responsibilities, focus on writing well and meet other people who prioritize writing. I always return home with a new perspective." One resource to find writing retreats is the Alliance of Artists Communities (www.artistcommunities.org/).

Laura Lee Perkins won four artist-in-residence slots with the National Park Service (www.nps.gov). The federal agency has 43 locations throughout the United States where writers and artists live for two to four weeks. From Acadia National Park in Maine to Sleeping Bear Dunes National Lakeshore in Michigan, Perkins spoke to tourists about her goals to write a book about Native American music. "Memories of the US National Parks' beauty and profound serenity will continue to enrich my work. Writers find unparalleled inspiration, quietude, housing, interesting staff, and a feeling of being in the root of your artistic desires."

Don't forget writers' conferences. While they may not advertise financial aid, many have funds available in times of need. Always ask as to the availability of a scholarship or work-share program that might enable your attendance.

Grants come in all sizes. FundsforWriters posts emergency grants on its grants page (www.fundsforwriters.com) as well as new grant opportunities such as the Sustainable Arts Foundation (www.sustainableartsfoundation.org) that offers grants to writers and artists with children under the age of 18, or the Awesome Foundation (www.awecomefoundation.org), which gives $1,000 grants to creative projects.

Novelist Joan Dempsey won an Elizabeth George Foundation grant (http://www.elizabethgeorgeonline.com/foundation/index.htm) in early 2012. "I applied to the Foundation for a research grant that included three trips to places relevant to my novel-in-progress, trips I otherwise could not have afforded. Not only does the grant provide travel funds, but it also provides validation that I'm a serious writer worthy of investment, which is great for my psyche and my résumé."

FISCAL SPONSORSHIP

Nonprofits have access to an incredibly large number of grants that individuals do not, and have the ability to offer their tax-exempt status to groups and individuals involved in activities related to their mission. By allowing a nonprofit to serve as your grant overseer, you may acquire funds for your project.

Deborah Marshall is President of the Missouri Writers Guild (www.missouriwritersguild.org) and founder of the Missouri Warrior Writers Project, with ample experience with grants in the arts. "Although grant dollars are available for individual writers, writing the grant proposal becomes difficult without significant publication credits. Partnering with a nonprofit organization, whether it is a writing group, service, community organization, or any 501(c)3, can fill in those gaps to make a grant application competitive. Partnering not only helps a writer's name become known, but it also assists in building that all-important platform."

Two excellent groups that offer fiscal sponsorship for writers are The Fractured Atlas (www.fracturedatlas.org) and Artspire (www.artspire.org), sponsored by the New York Foundation for the Arts and open to all US citizens. Visit The Foundation Center (www.foundationcenter.org) for an excellent tutorial guide to fiscal sponsorship.

CROWD SOURCING

Crowd sourcing is a co-op arrangement where people support artists directly, much like the agricultural co-op movement where individuals fund farming operations in exchange for fresh food. Kickstarter (www.kickstarter.com) has made this funding method successful in the arts.

Basically, the writer proposes his project, and for a financial endorsement as low as $1, donors receive some token in return, like an autographed book, artwork, or bookmark. The higher the donation, the bigger the *wow* factor in the gift. Donors do not receive ownership in the project.

Meagan Adele Lopez (www.ladywholunches.net) presented her debut self-published book *Three Questions* to Kickstarter readers, requesting $4,400 to take her book on tour, create a book trailer, pre-order books, and redesign the cover. Eighty-eight backers pledged a total of $5,202. She was able to hire an editor and a company that designed film trailers. For every $750 she received over her plan, she added a new city to her book tour.

Other up-and-coming crowd sourcing companies include Culture 360 (www.culture360.org) that serves Asia and Europe, and Indiegogo (www.indiegogo.com), as well as Rocket Hub (www.rockethub.com). And nothing stops you from simply asking those you know to support your project. The concept is elementary.

CONTESTS

Contests offer financial opportunity, too. Of course you must win, place or show, but many writers overlook the importance that contests have on a career. These days, contests not only open doors to publishing, name recognition, and money, but listing such achievements in a query letter might make an agent or publisher take a second glance. Noting your wins on a magazine pitch might land a feature assignment. Mentioning your accolades to potential clients could clinch a freelance deal.

I used contests as a barometer when fleshing out my first mystery novel, *A Low-country Bribe* (Bell Bridge Books). After I placed in several contests, earned a total of $750, and reached the semi-finals of the Amazon Breakthrough Novel Award (www.createspace.com/abna), my confidence grew strong enough to pitch agents. My current agent admits that the contest wins drew her in.

Contests can assist in sales of existing books, not only aiding sales but also enticing more deals for future books . . . or the rest of your writing profession.

Whether writing short stories, poetry, novels, or nonfiction, contests abound. As with any call for submission, study the rules. Double checking with entities that screen, like FundsforWriters.com and WinningWriters.com, will help alleviate concerns when selecting where to enter.

FREELANCING

A thick collection of freelancing clips can make an editor sit up and take notice. You've been vetted and accepted by others in the business, and possibly established a following. The more well known the publications, the brighter your aura.

Sooner or later in your career, you'll write an article. In the beginning, articles are a great way to gain your footing. As your career develops, you become more of an expert, and are expected to enlighten and educate about your journey and the knowledge you've acquired. Articles are, arguably, one of the best means to income and branding for writers.

Trade magazines, national periodicals, literary journals, newsletters, newspapers and blogs all offer you a chance to present yourself, earn money, and gain readers for a platform. Do not discount them as income earners.

Linda Formichelli, of Renegade Writer fame (www.therenegadewriter.com) leaped into freelance magazine writing because she simply loved to write, and that love turned her into an expert. "I never loved working to line someone else's pockets." A full-time freelancer since 1997, with credits like *Family Circle*, *Redbook*, and *Writer's Digest*, she also writes articles, books, e-courses, and e-books about her profession as a magazine writer.

JOBS

Part-time, full-time, temporary or permanent, writing jobs hone your skills, pad your resume, and present avenues to movers and shakers you wouldn't necessarily meet on your own. Government and corporate managers hire writers under all sorts of guises like Social Media Specialist and Communications Specialist, as well as the expected Reporter and Copywriter.

Alexis Grant considers her prior jobs as catapults. "Working at a newspaper (*Houston Chronicle*) and a news magazine (*US News & World Report*) for six years provided the foundation for what I'm doing now as a freelancer. Producing stories regularly on tight deadlines will always make you a better writer."

Joan Dempsey chose to return to full-time work and write her novel on the side, removing worries about her livelihood. "My creative writing was suffering trying to freelance. So, I have a day job that supports me now." She still maintains her Facebook presence to continue building her platform for her pending novel.

DIVERSIFICATION

Most importantly, however, is learning how to collect all your funding options and incorporate them into your plan. The successful writer doesn't perform in one arena. Instead, he thrives in more of a three-ring circus.

Grant states it well: "For a long while I thought of myself as only a journalist, but there are so many other ways to use my skills. Today my income comes from three streams: helping small companies with social media and blogging (the biggest source), writing and selling e-guides and courses (my favorite), and taking freelance writing or editing assignments."

Formichelli is proud of being flexible. "When I've had it with magazine writing, I put more energy into my e-courses, and vice versa. Heck, I'm even a certified personal trainer, so if I get really sick of writing I can work out. But a definite side benefit to diversifying is that I'm more protected from the feast-or-famine nature of writing."

Sometimes pursuing the more common sense or lucrative income opportunity can open doors for the dream. When my novel didn't sell, I began writing freelance articles. Then I established FundsforWriters, using all the grant, contest, publisher and market research I did for myself. A decade later, once the site thrived with over 45,000 readers, I used the very research I'd gleaned for my readers to find an agent and sign a publishing contract . . . for the original novel started so long ago.

You can fight to fund one project or study all resources and fund a career. Opportunity is there. Just don't get so wrapped up in one angle that you miss the chance to invest more fully in your future.

C. HOPE CLARK manages FundsForWriters.com and is the author of several books, including *Lowcountry Bribe* and *Palmetto Poison*. Learn more at http://chopeclark.com.

WHY EVERY WRITER NEEDS A BUSINESS PLAN

And Why Writing One Is Easy

by Sophia McDonald Bennett

When I transitioned from being a part-time to full-time writer, I was lucky enough to pick up a full roster of clients quickly. But after my first year I was seriously questioning my decision to become a freelancer. In my rush to build a business, I'd taken on every project I could find regardless of how much it paid, whether it was a good fit with my skills, or whether I really had time for it. The result? I was exhausted, uninspired and had no time to tackle the projects I'd dreamed of doing when I quit my day job.

One evening I sat down with a notepad and started making lists. What did I want to accomplish over the next six months? How much income did I want to report at the end of the year? What did I need to do—and stop doing—in order to meet my goals?

Those lists eventually turned into a rudimentary business plan that guided me through the next six months. I let go of a few poorly-paying clients that weren't helping me build my clip file. Instead of pursuing blogging jobs when I had spare time, I refocused on pitching national magazines. And when I considered new projects, I asked myself if they fit within my plan. If they didn't, it was magically easier to say no.

Since then I've engaged in business planning twice a year. It gives me a chance to reflect on what I've learned about myself and my profession over the preceding months, consider what opportunities are and aren't worth pursuing, and determine if I'm on track toward meeting my professional aspirations. I also use this time to consider how I'm doing at finding that tricky work/life balance. One of the best things about this process is that it's helped me grow my income by 25 percent annually over the last two years.

BUSINESS PLANNING VS. A BUSINESS PLAN

There are a few reason I refer to this process as "business planning" rather than "writing a business plan." It's been my experience that people start shaking in their socks as soon as you utter the words "business plan." That seems to be true even of writers, who I would argue are uniquely positioned to succeed at this particular task.

Why? "When you write a business plan, you're telling your story," says Doug Wilson, MBA, a senior instructor of marketing at the University of Oregon's Lundquist College of Business. "What you want to do is tell it in the most compelling way possible for yourself and your potential customers." Since most writers don't need to apply for bank loans or approach investors to support their business, no one else ever needs to see their business plan. And since we're natural storytellers, I find this approach heartening.

In addition, the document that results from my planning process isn't nearly as extensive as a traditional business plan. It's typically a one- to two-page framework that outlines my goals and tasks for the next six months. Sometimes it's a series of lists or charts. One year, when I was eager to dig into the adult coloring book I'd received for Christmas, I turned my business plan into an art project.

Here, again, Wilson has some sage advice. "Don't be intimidated by the structure or the format," he says. "The real value in the business planning process is not in producing a document, but in having to think through all of the elements a business requires before you start making commitments or signing contracts."

While content matters more than form, there is some value in considering the sections typically included in a business plan. The following five subjects can be quite applicable to writers.

MISSION, VISION AND VALUES STATEMENTS

Most businesses have a set of guiding principles that govern the way they work and serve their clients. Your writing practice is no different. Creating a set of simple statements can serve as a powerful framework for everything you do.

A mission statement broadly describes what you do and what you hope to accomplish. My most recent mission statement reads: "To support myself as a writer, editor and communications consultant who specializes in writing for and about food/beverage and other lifestyle topics, sustainability, business and nonprofits."

A vision statement shares where you envision yourself and your practice in the future. In that sense it's the most goal-oriented of these sections. My vision statement includes things such as writing for more national magazines, doing more work as an editor and engaging in more public speaking.

A values statement often reflects why you do the things you do, but can also encompass the morals or standards you hold yourself to as a professional. My values include providing outstanding customer service, meeting deadlines and working with companies whose belief systems are a good match with mine.

If you don't have one already, this may be a good time to develop a professional bio. Summarize your relevant experience with an eye toward what you can offer a company or publisher. Why should they hire you over someone else?

PRODUCTS AND SERVICES

You're in the business of producing writing. But what kind of writing can you do? Especially if you're just starting your career as a freelancer, it's a good idea to write down the types of services you can provide clients. Are you a technical writer or a news writer? Do you have experience penning articles about business and financial trends or covering lifestyle topics?

After that, think about the types of writing you want to do. Do you want to do less corporate copywriting and more long-form nonfiction or personal essays? Do you want to ditch your focus on covering the healthcare industry from a business perspective and focus on writing about the human impacts of disease and medicine?

Clearly identifying your products and services will help you set goals for your business. To stay focused on my yearly plans, I create a list of both the subjects I want to write about and the kinds of clients I want to work with. I've also found it helpful to create a grid with the different types of services I offer and list my clients under each heading. It's a quick way to assess whether my focus is falling more heavily in areas I want to pursue or those I'm trying to move away from.

The best goals are ambitious but realistic, measureable, and time-bound. You don't want to get your first big byline or earn six figures a year by the time you retire. Presumably you want to do it in the next year, two years or five years. You can write down the details of how you'll reach your goals here or in the timeline section.

FINANCIAL PLAN

While most writers don't need a balance sheet or profile/loss statement, doing some financial planning can be quite beneficial. If you're new to freelancing and are trying to set your rates, consider making a spreadsheet that shows all of your expenses. From there you can determine how much you need to earn per hour to cover them. Keep in mind that you will now have to pay self-employment tax on your earnings. Also, remember that all of the time you spend on business development is unpaid and must be accounted for in your hourly rate.

When I was considering the move to full-time freelancing, I set up an income calculator to estimate how much money I could realistically earn every month. I plugged in the amount I was earning from my existing clients (many of whom paid per piece, not by the hour) and then started playing with the numbers. If I could double the volume of blog posts I produced, would that give me a solid income? Or would I be better off picking up more regional magazines that paid about the same as the other publications I wrote for?

My income calculator is often accompanied by a time calculator that helps me estimate how much time it takes to write certain types of content (articles vs. blog posts vs. press releases) and how many more pieces I can realistically create every month. Figuring out how much time is dedicated to certain projects – including new business development – keeps me from getting too overloaded.

A basic budget that tracks spending on necessities such as office supplies, subscriptions, travel, conference fees and marketing expenses can also be quite helpful. Set projections for the time period of your business plan and track actual expenses so you can make adjustments in future budgets.

MARKETING PLAN

If you've gotten this far into the planning process, you already have answers to some of the hard questions you need to address before creating a bare-bones marketing plan. Now it's about getting down to details.

Start by looking back at the types of writing you want to do. That will help you identify who is in your target market. The next thing you need to do is determine where to find those people. If you want to offer copywriting services to businesses, a Chamber of Commerce, professional association or your personal network are good places to start mining contacts. If you want to write for magazines or author a nonfiction book, you're in luck—you're already in the best place to find people who need writers.

Next, determine how you'll reach out to potential clients. For copywriting, it may be a letter of introduction. For magazines, you'll need to write query letters. For books, start learning how to create a book proposal.

A marketing budget may be useful in years when you plan to shell out cash for promotions. Digital advertising (such as a website, LinkedIn Premium subscription, or paid ads on Google or Facebook) can be an affordable and highly targeted way to reach decision-makers depending on what your professional goals are. Before you invest in advertising, make sure you put some real time into honing your message and understanding your audience.

TIMELINE/WORKPLAN

Now that you have a list of goals and some ideas for marketing your services, list the steps you'll take each month to grow or change your business. You can also place them on your calendar if that makes them easier to remember. Having a plan for how you'll accomplish your goals will keep you moving forward. Setting deadlines will also keep you accountable (even if the only person making sure you check off each item is you).

Once you've wrapped up your business planning process, don't put the resulting document away in a drawer. Revisit it on a regular basis to remind yourself of your vision and goals and revel in your progress. That's another reason to make the document brief, well-organized and even attractive. You'll be much more likely to review a short and sweet pathway to your dreams than one that seems like a long and winding road.

Sophia McDonald Bennett is a freelance writer, editor, communications consultant and marketing instructor in Eugene, Oregon.

SEVEN STEPS TO DOUBLING YOUR INCOME IN ONE YEAR

by Allen Taylor

For almost a decade I rocked along making a living as a freelance writer, envious of those who claimed to be making $100 an hour or more and a six-figure income. Then I made a radical vow to myself. I was going to double my income, do or die.

I did it. But it took a lot of changing. I had to change some bad habits, some bad thinking, and trade a few bad clients for some good ones. After a year-long struggle, I entered the club of freelance writers earning an above-average income. At times, I earned as much as $400 an hour for my work. I now have one client who pays me as much for half a day's work as I used to earn with all of my clients combined. Here's how I doubled my income in less than a year, and how you can do it too with a simple formula that you can tweak to make you own.

THE COLD, HARD TRUTH ABOUT FREELANCE WRITING

The beauty of this formula is that it works for any income range. No matter where you fall on the income scale of writers, you can double your income just by following this 7-step process. It might take a little longer for some, or even a few months less for others, but I'm convinced that anyone can double their income with the right mental focus and motivation.

You'll never make as much money as a general writer as you will if you specialize. What you know about specific niches and types of writing is more important than your ability to craft sentences because it sets you apart from every other writer in the marketplace. You must have a marketable distinction or you're just another person with a pen.

Another thing, targeting your services to low-hanging fruit will keep you frustrated and hungry. Don't get stuck in the rut of marketing to bargain hunters.

Thirdly, if you want to earn higher-than-average income as a writer, then you need to learn new skills. Eccolo Media conducted a survey of American business decision makers and found that white papers and case studies were two of the top three content products they consulted when making buying decisions. Knowing that makes you a writer who can charge top-dollar to deliver the content products decision makers are in the market for.

So the cold, hard truth about freelance writing is this—writing is not your most important skill. Specific knowledge in other areas is far more important if you want to be a high-income freelance writer today.

HOW TO DOUBLE YOUR INCOME IN ONE YEAR OR LESS

I must confess. I learned much of this from Carol Tice's 2X Accelerator, a mastermind course through her Freelance Writer's Den. What I'll share below is some basic information I learned from Carol plus my own insights from working through her program. If you take this template, make it your own, and diligently pursue your goal of doubling your income, you should see similar results to what I and many others have seen.

Step 1: Pick a specialization

Whether you specialize in white paper writing, a specific industry, or a type of client (e.g. small businesses, global enterprise executives, or pro athletes) is up to you. Specializing is the key to freelance writing income acceleration because the knowledge you gain in your area of specialization gives you a competitive edge over every general writer competing on price.

Step 2: Raising prices on your current clients

Starting with the lowest-paying client first, raise your prices. The first time I did this, 90 percent of my clients continued with my services and my income went up immediately. The key is to increase prices in small increments. If you raise your rates by 10 percent, or a measly $20 or $25, it will not hurt your clients much and will serve as a huge encouragement to you. This works because clients will see it as more of a hassle to search for and train another writer rather than pay your small increase. As an alternative, if a client refuses to pay more, you can reduce the amount of writing you do for them, which is effectively a pay raise. I had one client who stuck with me for two more years as I gradually reduced the amount of writing I did for them. I eventually had to cut them off completely to make room for more higher paying clients.

Step 3: Identify your ideal customer and acquire a contact list

LinkedIn's search feature allows you to filter your searches by specific business criteria, and the Premium membership includes company size and revenue filters. Crunchbase, Hoover's, your local business journal, and the public library are also excellent sources for finding companies that match your ideal client profile. After you get your list, start sending out letters of introduction (LOIs) to explain how you are the perfect writer for their writing needs.

Step 4: Revamp your website to reflect your specialty

I don't recommend this step earlier because you need to start marketing yourself aggressively as soon as possible to get in the habit. Sending LOIs should become a regular part of your marketing routine. After sending a few, you'll have better clarity on who your ideal client is and how to present your message to that client more effectively. You can then take what you learn from that process to improve your website.

Step 5: Optimize your LinkedIn profile

Using the same principle, write your LinkedIn profile to appeal to your ideal client. Use a keyword-based title that potential clients would use to find a writer like you. For instance, if you write executive memoirs, then your LinkedIn title and summary should include "executive memoir writer" in them. Every element of your LinkedIn profile should be crafted to appeal to your ideal writer. LinkedIn has become one of my primary sources of new client leads.

Step 6: Become a content publisher

You'll have to put some thought into this as there is no shortage of media for content publishing. The key is to figure out where your ideal clients spend time and put your name in front of them. That could be on a blog attached to your website, your LinkedIn Pulse blog, Medium or Huffington Post, industry newsletters and trade publications, third-party websites that cover a specific industry, and more. You should also write specific content types that match what you do for your clients (white papers, e-books, blog posts, special reports, etc.). Push your content out to social media channels your ideal client uses to pull them in. If your audience is on Twitter, publish on Twitter. If your ideal client is on Instagram, then you should be too. Publish the content that is helpful to your ideal client and share it in places where they will see it and be led back to your website.

Step 7: Tweak, repeat, and adapt

As you go through each step, note what works. If something doesn't work for you, toss it. Put more time into those activities that produce positive results. Keep tweaking, repeating these steps, and adapting your processes until you reach your income goal. You should be able to keep this process going indefinitely and adapt your marketing as your writing business grows.

A WORD ABOUT SETTING GOALS

This process will work better if you set goals. Instead of aiming for the sky, set small, achievable goals in three key areas: 1) Production; 2) Income; and 3) Time.

Production Goals

There are two types of production goals: Writing and marketing.

Writing goals center around deadlines. It's easy to get in the habit of jumping through hoops if you don't pace your projects to complete specific benchmarks prior to hard deadlines. This is especially true of larger projects. Break each project into smaller pieces (i.e. research, first draft, final draft, etc) so that you can manage them better.

Marketing goals are easy to track because you can determine how aggressive you want to be out of the gate. Decide how many LOIs you want to send each week, or how many new contacts you want to make, and be diligent in getting it done. Today's marketing production is directly related to tomorrow's income. After a few days of marketing, you'll learn your average response rate to each marketing activity, which will help you figure out how much of each activity to engage in to attract more clients.

Income Goals

The higher your starting income, the more important it is to set realistic goals from the start. If your income today is $80,000, that means you'll have to work harder to double it than your counterpart starting at $40,000. However, it is doable.

One way to set income goals is to determine your hourly rate based on your current projects. Then you can set a goal to increase that within a certain time frame – for instance, if you make $75 an hour today, you might set a goal to increase it to $100 per hour within six months. If you spend 30 hours writing each week, that's an increase of $750, or $3,000 a month.

Make your goals palatable and achievable and they'll be easier to reach.

Time Goals

Setting goals on your time is very important. Otherwise, you could end up working 80 hours a week with no time left for your family. As your income grows, you might spend more time at your desk, but it shouldn't be overwhelmingly so. When I decided to double my income, I was writing an average of 27 hours a week. I now average 33 and 35 hours per week, and I have more than doubled my annual income. My hourly income has tripled.

Tracking the time you spend on each project helps you better understand the value of your time. If it takes you an hour to write a blog post, then you know what you have to do to increase your income. It's important to know that raising client pay is not the only way to earn more. If you can make more efficient use of your writing time, you can raise your hourly rate by spending less time at the keyboard and more time marketing. I doubled my hourly rate on one client from $200 an hour to $400 an hour just by creating a matrix for each blog post that included title, a summary of main points, keywords, and sources. One hour of brainstorming led to a savings of two hours writing time.

A FINAL WORD OF ENCOURAGEMENT

Doubling your income is a worthwhile goal whether you are a beginning writer, a mid-career writer, or a professional on the last leg of her career. With the proper planning, a positive mindset, and a goal-oriented focus, you can do it. Take it slow, be productive, and set realistic expectations for yourself.

Allen Taylor specializes in FinTech writing. He is the editor of Lending Times and Blockchain Times and the author of "E-book Publishing: Create Your Own Brand of Digital Books," available in e-book form at Amazon, Barnes & Noble, Smashwords, Kobo, and the Apple iBook Store. He is also a published poet and fiction writer. His professional home on the Web is at http://tayloredcontent.com.

HOW TO DEVELOP AN EFFECTIVE AUTHOR BRAND

....

by Leslie Lee Sanders

An author's brand isn't just the specific colors of your website, a catchy tagline, or a recognizable face. Branding is delivering on a promise after setting an expectation. Determining how you want to be perceived and what sets you apart is essential when organizing an author's image, but that is only the tip of the iceberg when it comes to branding. Diving deeper when creating an author brand is a must.

Following is an in-depth look at how to build a successful author brand and become a fierce competitor in the publishing business.

ESTABLISH AN IMAGE

When establishing your image, think beyond color scheme and website layout. Humans are unique for their feeling capabilities, and the way we feel about something usually stays with us longer than any color or image. If applied properly, certain phrases, images, and colors trigger emotions, and this is your main goal when establishing your image. However, you must recognize the emotion you want to convey and how it links people to your brand.

For example, you might want to convey love, calm, excitement, wonder, intrigue, nostalgia, or even hilarity, but deep down the feeling should be universal enough to be relatable.

This is how branding works. A brand effectively engages emotion. Remember the Geico commercial where the massive camel awkwardly strolls through a busy office during the middle of the day asking the workers what day it is? Sure, it is a funny ad, but what is that commercial doing on a deeper level? The commercial is selling a service using a situation most people relate to by making you laugh. Actually, Geico's history of running funny ads have become their brand, from the gecko, the cavemen, Maxwell the Pig, and now the "Hump Day" camel.

Most people relate to the situation of working a demanding nine-to-five and counting the days until the weekend. Most people are probably familiar with a co-worker who, much like the camel, points out the middle of the week in the same tedious way, prompting tired sighs and eye rolls. The commercial triggers something most people "get" and therefore it sticks with them. This is what your brand should do too.

What you do for your readers through your website, blogs, videos, and podcasts is your "service." The books and stories you sell is your "product." How you manage it is your "business." Connect to your audience using emotion to form your reputation and establish your image.

What feelings do you want to trigger?

List the emotions you want others to feel when visiting your website or when reading your books. An easy way to accomplish this is by asking yourself what words you want to associate with your image. Take the third party route, step outside of yourself, and look at what you offer through an objective view. If someone were to describe you and your brand, what words or emotion would you like them to use? Trigger those emotions by using specific words in your content, books, blog posts, and author bio. Use images and colors on your website and book covers to convey your overall message.

What emotion or message do you want to resonate?

Triggering feelings and having them resonate are two different things. The former is what sucks you into the brand. The latter is what you take from it, what you're left with, or what stays with you. What would you like readers to take away from your book after reading it? After visiting your website, what message will they remember you by? Make your mission clear in your work.

What promises do you want to communicate?

By communicating a promise, and most importantly, delivering on that promise, you establish trust that produces satisfied readers, which not only translates into repeat service from avid fans, but generates new readers through word-of-mouth marketing. People will seek you out because you've become the go-to person for your particular service and product. Think Starbucks and coffee. When you've become the go-to person, you have successfully built a brand. Your brand's promise is what your audience comes to expect from your business.

To further expand or maintain your brand requires consistency.

CREATE CONSISTENCY

Being consistent falls under the tier of delivering on your promises. There's a cycle when building a brand; make a promise, deliver, build trust, and repeat. By performing this cycle, you are practicing consistency, which is the reason people come to you instead of your competitor. Take away one of the components and you break the cycle. Break the cycle and your brand might suffer.

You might think to get ahead or to produce sales requires you to beat your competitors, and to be on top means to flaunt what makes you unique. Today, in the writing business, this kind of thinking is retroactive because with so many books and authors flooding the market, being unique is a one in a million chance. The truth is, establishing a brand, building an audience, and keeping your audience satisfied is the trick to success in most businesses. Do this and in return your readers will help you expand your audience by advertising your products and services through recommendations (i.e., word of mouth, social media sharing, and book reviews). This is the tried-and-true formula of every successful brand.

How do you satisfy your audience? Consistency.

Consistency with book releases, series, and the production and design of content

Whatever your service, provide it regularly. Readers expect a new book from you once a year? Meet or exceed that expectation and release a new book every year or sooner. If your newsletter subscribers expect a monthly newsletter and your YouTube videos to highlight important writing techniques for novelist, continue giving them what they come for or give them what they want and more.

Establishing your place within your genre

Sure, you write in a specific genre with no plans of crossing genres anytime soon. Still there are other ways to stay consistent. Do your novels end with happily ever after? Don't try experimenting with the latest story now. You may lose some readers if they're convinced their favorite author or series is becoming something other than what they've grown to love.

Cultivating an overall tone and a distinct voice

Your voice and style, the words you use, and the way you piece them together in your writing is unique to you and your personality. Your audience will grow familiar with your writing mechanics and may even recognize your style in your speaking voice. Keep it consistent. You may have read a book by an author whose writing style reminded you of another author. For example, you may believe the book you are currently hooked on reads like a Stephen King or J.K. Rowling novel. If you're consistent, your style can become recognizable and be a distinctive part of your brand too.

BUILD TRUST

Establishing your image, being consistent, and building trust are some of what it takes to build an effective brand. Let's talk coffee. When mentioning coffee, which establishment do you think of first, Starbucks or McDonalds? Most would say Starbucks. Why? Because Starbucks successfully built their coffeehouse brand.

Starbucks is one of the largest and most successful coffeehouses for many reasons, but one reason is they are consistent with their products, using the same ingredients and measurements to make each coffee the same as the one before. You know exactly how your favorite latte should taste, and they meet that expectation each time. Your brand should build a similar kind of trust with your audience.

Image familiarity, logos, and other insignia

When mentioning branding your business, the next thought might be logos. Your logo is not your brand but the visual symbol of your brand. Your logo is a way to identify your brand in its simplest form, a visual representation of your business.

Here are the best ways to use your logo to maximize your brand's exposure:

- **BOOK SERIES COVER.** A perfect way to use a logo is on the cover of your books in a particular series. It's a recognizable insignia that communicates the promise and trust exchange between you and your readers. When they see that logo on the cover they know each book contains your familiar voice and writing style, and they will know what to expect of the books in that series.
- **STATIONARY, BUSINESS CARDS, BOOKMARKS, LETTERHEAD, ETC.** Office supplies are probably the most obvious place to add your logo. Also make sure your logo appears on business forms like invoices, packing slips, and receipts.
- **ONLINE USE.** Use your logo in place of your profile picture on Twitter and Facebook. Add it to your website header and favicon. Use it in your e-mail signature, in your guest posts, or in your Gravitar (Globally Recognized Avatar) in conjunction with guest posting to get your logo in front of new audiences when commenting on other people's blogs.
- **CUSTOM GOODS.** Add your logo to custom-made apparel, mugs, water bottles, chocolates, pens, totes, etc. Make sure the logo is large enough to be discernable at a distance, and use colors and fonts that can be easily read.

REPUTATION

Overall, your brand, brand identity, logo, content, message, storytelling, and reader experience is your reputation. Your reputation is built from the general feelings, opinions, and beliefs of the majority of people who encounter your brand. And to be just as successful in your niche as Starbucks is to coffee, remember these steps to building your author brand:

1. Establish your image by creating a specific emotion to trigger; message to resonate; and promise to communicate.
2. The following should stay consistent in your brand: identity; voice and style; and production.
3. Build trust by staying consistent; delivering on promises; and creating a visual representation of your business.

LESLIE LEE SANDERS is a published author with over ten years of fiction writing and book publishing experience. She teaches the art and craft of blogging, writing, and publishing on her blog at leslieleesanders.com. Her work has been included in the following Writer's Market books: 2016 Writer's Market, 2016 Novel and Short Story Writer's Market, the 2014 and 2015 editions of Guide to Self-Publishing. She's currently writing the fifth installment of her post-apocalyptic and dystopian book series, Refuge Inc.

E-MAIL NEWSLETTERS FOR WRITERS

....

by Rebecca Pitts

Newsletters are the new blogs. There is simply no better or more direct way to reach your audience in 2018 than to be invited into their inbox. Whether you're just starting out by building a list of loyal readers, or you're an established author who's hoping to convert current fans into subscribers, this article outlines everything you should consider when launching an author's newsletter, from the essential technical questions to big picture strategy.

KNOW YOUR 'WHY' AND 'WHO'

Your list (the e-mail addresses of your subscribers, along with any other information they provide) is a powerful asset and tool that will allow you to:

- communicate directly with readers to share news or exclusive content
- increase your impact by reaching a specific and growing number of people who are interested in your work, invested in your success, and engaged
- sell and market your work directly, if you choose to self-publish
- be more attractive to a publisher, who sees your list as a platform where you can build a relationship with readers and promote your books

Always consider your audience as you develop content for your subscribers. A writer who develops nonfiction craft and DIY books has an audience whose interests likely differ from a travel memoirist living in Istanbul. A homeschooling dad and blogger would likely appeal to parents who are considering this educational arrangement. A writer who is just starting out might not know yet who their people are, and that's ok. You'll likely discover who is opting in to your list (as well as what sort of content you love to share) as you go.

DECIDE WHAT YOU'LL SHARE

Your options for structuring and designing your newsletter are almost endless, but you can't go wrong if you stick to this guiding principle: Your newsletter should feel like a must-have treat that your subscribers truly love to get and read. Here's the good news: You probably have a ton of inspiration in your inbox right now. Spend 30 minutes looking through your inbox at the e-mails you enjoy receiving and reading. What is it about them that keeps you coming back? Are there parts of each e-mail that you find valuable, entertaining, or educational?

> Your newsletter should feel like a must-have treat that your subscribers truly love to get and read.

Here are a few examples of types of formats you might want to consider, along with examples from published authors, journalists, and producers of digital media:

- **The personal letter.** Some of my favorite author newsletters look and feel like a personal letter and are as simple as an essay, delivered in the body of an e-mail. Designer and author Paul Jarvis manages to make each e-mail feel like a letter from a friend, complete with jokes that are actually funny. (https://pjrvs.com/)
- **The interview.** Journalist Nishat Kurwa shares an original interview each week "with dynamic women who rule" in her newsletter Talk Story. (http://tinyletter.com/talkstory)
- **A curated list of links to relevant content around your expertise.** Here's where knowing your audience comes in handy—what are they interested in? Could you save them time by delivering hand-picked content? I open freelance journalist Ann Friedman's e-mail every week for a better sense of what's happening in politics, gender, and the media, delivered via a handful of links to news articles and opinion pieces. (http://www.annfriedman.com/weekly/)
- **A behind-the-scenes peek.** Share a slice of your creative life that isn't available anywhere else—readers will appreciate the insider insight on your thought-process. Author Ryan Holiday does this well in his monthly newsletter, which reads as an annotated bibliography of the books on his nightstand. (https://ryanholiday.net/)

It's worth mentioning that most of the content in these newsletters is exclusive—that is, it's not readily available anywhere else. There's a real reward for a subscriber to join a list—to gain access to information they can't get elsewhere.

If you're consistently delivering value to your audience, promoting your own work will be much easier to do and won't feel like such a struggle. Clearly link to where your readers can buy your books, to specific blog posts on your website, or to event listings you're speaking at. It's a balance: Don't be shy about sharing your wins (like a book deal or a new e-book you're offering) but be sure you're not selling 100% of the time.

CHOOSE AN E-MAIL SERVICE PROVIDER

Choosing the right e-mail service provider will keep you sane and organized. Even if you are just starting out, without a single e-mail address on your list, don't be tempted to cut and paste e-mail addresses into the body of a blank e-mail.

An e-mail service provider:

- manages all of your subscribers in a database
- usually allows for some sort of tagging or organization of those contacts along with additional info like a person's name
- allows you to customize automated emails such as a welcome e-mail
- simplifies design decisions and manages your templates so you're not constantly re-inventing the wheel

TinyLetter, Mailchimp, AWeber, Constant Contact, and ConvertKit are just a few examples of popular e-mail service providers. All of them offer technical support and tutorials for novice users. Several online education platforms, like Skillshare, Lynda.com, and Udemy offer a range of newsletter courses aimed at beginner and advanced students.

> When in doubt, choose a free e-mail service provider if you're just starting out.

When determining the best fit for you and your audience, be sure to consider benefits and costs of each. Many providers offer tiered pricing, with free accounts available to members with lists under a certain number of subscribers. Others, like Tiny Letter, are known for their simplicity of use but lack sophisticated tools like segmentation.

When in doubt, choose a free e-mail service provider if you're just starting out. It's more important that you get started—you can always export your list into a spreadsheet and switch providers once you've gained traction and have outgrown the services offered.

DON'T BE A SPAMMER

It's worth noting upfront that I'm not a lawyer, and you should always consult one for legal advice. Laws around e-mail marketing exist to protect the consumer, and we should all be pleased about this. No one likes getting spam or an unsolicited message. Here are a few things to keep in mind when writing your newsletters and growing your list:

- **You must include a valid mailing address.** Many service providers walk you through this process, and won't let you send an e-mail without your address field populated. If you have privacy concerns, consider getting and using a P.O. box.
- **Don't add people to your list without their consent.** This one couldn't be more plain and simple. Just don't do it. You really don't want people on your list who don't want to be there. Most subscribers will join via an opt-in form (more on this below). If you're speaking at an event, keep a clipboard or notebook open for attendees to join your list. This counts as permission, and later, you can manually add these e-mail addresses to your list.

Does what you're doing feel right?

- **Be thoughtful (and law-abiding) about including your affiliate partnerships.** Affiliate marketing is the promotion of someone else's product or service, with you receiving a commission on the sale. It doesn't cost the customer anything, but it may affect the level of trust a customer has in you (for better or worse). Circle back to your 'why'—if your aim is to communicate with subscribers, share your good news, and grow your list, then you may decide it's not worth promoting someone else's product for the small amount of money you receive. Some affiliate links (like Amazon Associates) aren't even allowed to be shared over e-mail at all. And, finally, if you are sharing affiliate links, you must disclose this information to your subscribers upfront.

Check in with yourself. Does what you're doing feel right? You probably have a good sense of what is and isn't appropriate when growing your list, sharing your ideas, and monetizing your projects.

MAKE IT EASY FOR YOUR READERS TO JOIN YOUR LIST (AND TO TALK TO YOU)

So, you've chosen a provider and have figured out what kind of info you're going to share. It's time to welcome your readers!

- **A newsletter should build on what you're already doing.** Ideally, you have a website as your author platform. It's possible to have a list without a website (I've seen writers with Twitter accounts that link to a 'join' page hosted by an e-mail service provider) but a newsletter list and author website truly go hand-in-hand. Think of the opt-in on your website as a door—you'll want to be clear about what's on the other side, and make the space welcoming and inviting. It doesn't hurt to note that you'll be sharing insider, subscriber-only content as an incentive to your readers.

- **Where should your front door go?** Next, you'll want to determine where you'll place your opt-in on your website. Having a unique URL (in my case, it's rebeccaapitts. com/join) is handy if you're sharing the opt-in elsewhere. In addition, you'll want to include opt-ins on your most heavily trafficked pages as well as your home page.

- **What will you say when a reader walks through your door?** Consider the experience your reader has when they join your list. Be sure to customize the welcome e-mail template within your e-mail service provider—this is a terrific opportunity to write in your own voice, let your sense of humor shine (if that's your thing), and consider adding something of value: either content not shared anywhere else or by linking to the most popular posts on your site.

- **Talk to your readers.** Encourage replies, comments, and questions, just as you would welcome and encourage these on your blog or social media accounts.

GROW YOUR LIST

Numbers are important, sure, but they're not everything. List growth takes time, and is built around consistency and trust.

- **Start with who you already are talking to.** An easy way to gain some momentum is to write a welcome e-mail. Comb through your address book to identify friends, family, and peers that might be interested in hearing from you. Send out an e-mail that explains what you're up to, what you'll be sharing, how often you'll be writing, and ask them to join you if they are interested. Again, don't just add people without their permission.

- **Promote your newsletter.** If you have an existing blog or social media account, use this space to encourage your current followers to join your list. As you develop new content such as a blog post or Instagram post, continue to remind new followers in these spaces that they can keep the conversation going over e-mail by joining your list.

- **Offer a content-upgrade or bonus for subscribers.** A content-upgrade is an offering you make on your blog, social media post, on someone else's website or podcast if you're guest posting, or really in any space where you may meet potential new subscribers.

I've even seen them at the beginning of free e-books. The reader, listener, or viewer will hopefully find the offering valuable and subscribe to your list for access. Examples include: a book club study guide, a mini e-book of your list of favorite books of all time, a printable template referenced in a blog post, and access to exclusive audio or video files relating to your expertise.

Your newsletter is a place where you can (and should) be you. Ultimately, your unique voice is what will keep your readers interested beyond any freebie you're offering.

By being upfront about what you'll deliver in your newsletter, how often you'll deliver it, and by following through on your promises, you'll consistently deliver value over time and ultimately build trust. And trust is what will ultimately keep your readers coming back, will fuel your readers' desire to share your news and offerings, and will open the door to real, two-way communication with your subscribers.

Oh yeah, and when it's time to announce a new book, publicize a speaking event, or offer a self-published product to your list, your readers will be right there alongside you, as invested champions of you and your work.

REBECCA PITTS writes and makes stuff for kids and kids at heart. Her work and ideas have been featured in *Country Living, the Etsy Seller Handbook*, the Martha Stewart American Made Market, Craft Industry Alliance, And North, and Dear Handmade Life. She's got a thing for picture books, public libraries, and digging into the archives of female movers & shakers, writers, and artists. Her weekends are usually spent day-tripping in the Hudson Valley, where she lives with her husband, son, and daughter. Learn more at rebeccaapitts.com.

HOW TO DO VIDEO EFFECTIVELY

With Little to No Budget

....

by Stacy Tornio

Long gone are the days when writers are just writing. I remember those days, both as a writer and an assigning editor, and they were wonderful. Rates were strong, as were creative approaches to stories and in-depth interviews.

Yet the way many of us consume media has changed, requiring editors to seek out different skills and assets for the traditional print and online story. And more often than not, this means video.

I continue to sit on both sides of this—both as a writer and as an editor—and it's a tricky situation. As a writer, I still want my written words to be valued and adequately compensated. Plus, creating video is not easy or cheap. Yet as an editor, I know video is where it's at. I challenge every writer and editor I work with to think of the "video version" of every story. And unfortunately, we can't be spending thousands of dollars to create them—it's just not usually in the budget.

So how do we tackle video creation differently? My business card says, "Master Storyteller," and I really embrace this title. A story can (and should) take multiple forms, including print, online, audio, and video. This means that we as writers have to step up our storytelling game. We need to figure out how to turn our masterful words and great stories into an engaging, effective video. With this in mind, here are seven different video formats that writers can do effectively with little to no budget.

THE GIF VIDEO

WHAT?

This video list goes from easy to hard, and this is definitely the easiest. GIF videos aren't really even videos to be honest. This is where you see a clip or a GIF on screen with just a few words. An example of this might be a clip of the scene from Titanic when Jack is at the front of the boat in the iconic "I'm king of the world!" moment. But instead of those words, you might see something like, "How I feel when I get free guac," or "How I feel when my baby finally sleeps through the night." Of course, the messaging would change based on your story or topic area, but we've all seen examples like this.

HOW?

To create your own GIF videos, you can pull a clip off of Giphy.com (or other GIF platforms) and then set it to words or even music through dozens of different programs. You can do this through Adobe Premiere, Apple's Keynote, or several options. Just google "GIF maker," and you'll find free options. But remember it's just a clip and words on screen. Don't forget to add a logo.

WHY?

Now it doesn't seem like this should be a video, but it counts as one on Facebook and other social media sites. Sometimes you see examples like this reaching millions upon millions of views, which can be great for engagement and gaining new followers. This is an easy one to do for yourself or for brands you write for because it can be a great complement to the story you've written. Plus it's quick (and free) to do.

THE SLIDESHOW VIDEO

WHAT?

You've definitely seen this come across your Facebook feed. Love What Matters and The Dodo are two big media brands that do the slideshow video really well. Essentially, these are feel-good videos told through text, photos, and some video.

HOW?

These are put together the same way people make wedding slideshows, so you probably already have the tools to create one. Mac users will even use iMovie to put one together. The trick here is to gather really compelling videos and photos. Then be short and sweet with your words. It's easy to want to write a lot, but with slideshow videos, a little goes a long way. You want your photos and video footage to say more than your words do.

WHY?

This is one of the easiest and best ways to transfer a traditional written story into a video. Often times, you just take pieces of your story and the photos that you've already gathered, and then you boil it down to just the best of the best to create a 1-minute (or less) video. If you're working on a written story already and get the sense that you might want to create a video version of it, be sure to ask the people you interview with any extra videos or photos. It will really help the story come alive.

THE USER VIDEO

WHAT?

The user or reader is the one who generates the video in this type. It usually involves someone talking directly into the camera, giving a first person and heartfelt account of their story or their take on the story.

HOW?

For this one, just ask your user to record them talking about a specific part of the story. Or if this is you, record yourself. You don't need fancy equipment or microphones to do this. Most people are doing user videos just through the power of their phones. A word of caution—it's easy for this type of video to go on and on and get redundant. To avoid this, think of it like a sound byte you might see on TV. Focus in on something specific and powerful, and capture that on video instead. Once you have your footage, be sure to add a little editing to it at the beginning and end to include branding and/or logos. You can do this through iMovie, Premiere, Final Cut, or other simple editing software options.

WHY?

User videos work well when you're tackling a topic where the voice or the angle of the story really matters. By including a video from a user that you interviewed, it can make your story come alive.

THE TUTORIAL VIDEO

WHAT?

Think of this video as a teaching video. The fancy version might have a mix of on-camera talent, animation, and graphics. But the simplest version can just be a person in front of a camera, explaining how or demonstrating how to do something. These can be especially effective on YouTube because people often search the site for how to do certain things.

HOW?

At the most basic level, you just need a simple camera set-up and a compelling topic. Be sure to research what's already out there on the topic of the video you want to create. If there are already amazing options, you might want to pick something else. If not, be sure you script out the idea before filming to make sure you're covering all the important points. If you want to kick it up a notch but you're still on a budget, see if you can partner with a local high school or college multimedia department who can do motion graphics to make it more professional. I've even found people on Craigslist and online for an affordable rate as they were looking to build their portfolios. Just remember that it's really important to be direct and clear in this video type. Don't have a 3-minute video when a 30-second version will do.

WHY?

It's great for SEO. When people are searching for how to do something, you want your video to show up. Just make sure to check the competition first!

THE JOURNALISTIC VIDEO

WHAT?

Think of this as a story you see on TV news, usually told through interviews and video footage. There are so many stories being told this way, and it's a step up from the slideshow video because you're usually capturing video or sound bytes in person. This one takes a little more skills (and resources), but it's such a great example of modern storytelling.

HOW?

In an ideal scenario, you'd have a decent camera and recording equipment, but don't let this stop you if you don't. By finding a really great background or scene for your story, you can still capture really compelling footage. You will want to invest in a good tripod, though. No one likes a shaky video! Once you have all the pieces for your story, you'll want to construct it in a similar way as you do the slideshow videos.

WHY?

This is storytelling at its best. You have full control over the voice of your story by selecting the footage and quotes that you include. It can be extremely powerful, and a great way to complement the written piece.

THE HOW-TO VIDEO

WHAT?

You know the geniusness of Tasty? They really mastered the how-to video by showing how to do something from a top-down angle. The video itself is not hard to shoot. You just need a compelling topic or really creative idea that people want to watch from start to finish.

HOW?

This is one of the easiest video styles to replicate because it's usually done in a single shot and from a single angle. The trick here is to mount your camera in a way that you truly get a top-down point of view. (If it's slightly off, it'll definitely show.) Then you just need a good hand model to show the steps one by one. After you're done, you speed it up and set it to music (using the same video editors mentioned before). You can add some step-by-step instructions throughout, but that's it! Of course, you can get fancier by shooting secondary footage or showing the tutorial in action. But this is completely optional. If you're just trying this style, start simple. You can even shoot this style entirely with the video on your cell phone. Remember to keep that camera secure—shaking or wobbling on this style is the worst!

WHY?

Because if you want to go viral, this might be the way. When you can find a topic that is really interesting, you'll naturally get people who want to share or tag their friends. Plus it's a really fun style to try.

THE LIVE VIDEO

WHAT?

Live video is very in right now, and it doesn't seem to be going away anytime soon. Luckily, it's incredibly easy to put together. You'll want to make sure you have a compelling reason to go live, but it's a great way to build up the excitement around a specific topic area.

HOW?

If you search "inexpensive Facebook Live equipment," you'll find plenty of articles that tell you what you need. Again, this is one where you can use the camera on your phone, so you don't have to get overly fancy. You will want to use microphones for good sound, but this can easily be achieved through lavalier mics that plug into your phone. Here's another one where it makes a big difference to use a tripod—don't skimp on that. Then when you're ready to go live, just hit the go button, and that's it! It sounds intimidating, but it's not. Just don't overthink it. Sure it's live, but mistakes sometimes happen and the audience will understand (within reason).

WHY?

Live gives people an experience because it's happening right now. If you can find the right topic, you can really make someone feel as if they're in the moment. It's a great way to connect with an audience in a whole new way.

If you've never done video before, it can seem a bit intimidating. But don't get discouraged. At the end of the day, you still have to tell a good story, which is probably something you already do really well.

Start small by studying others who are doing video, looking at what does well and what you personally respond to. This will help you get in the right mindset of turning great content into video. Then seek someone out who does this well. Learn their tips and tricks, and try to get a better handle of how they put stories together. Pretty soon, you won't be able to stop thinking of the "video version" for stories, and you'll be well on your way to creating effective videos for yourself and others.

Stacy Tornio is an author of 15 books, a senior editor with WeAreTeachers.com, and a freelancer writer for websites like *Fodors*, *Prevention*, and others. She loves the challenge of pitching and will always be an ideas person at heart.

CONTRACTS 101

....

by Cindy Ferraino

After you do a victory dance about getting the book deal you always dreamed about or your article hitting the top of the content list of a popular magazine, the celebration quickly comes to a halt when you realize you are not at the finish line yet. Your heart begins to beat faster because you know the next possible hurdle is just around the corner—the contract. For many, the idea of reviewing a contract is like being back in first grade. You know you have to listen to the teacher when you could be playing outside. You know you have to read this contract but why because there are terms in there that look like an excerpt from a foreign language syllabus.

Before I changed my status to self-employed writer, I was working as a grants and contracts administrator at a large medical university in Philadelphia. I helped shepherd the M.D. and Ph.D. researchers through the channels of grants and contracts administration. While the researchers provided the technical and scientific pieces that could potentially be the next cure for diabetes, heart disease, or cancer, I was there to make sure they did their magic within the confines of a budget and imposed contractual regulations. The budget process was easy but when it came to contract regulations—oh well, that was a different story. I became familiar with the terms such as indemnifications, property and intellectual rights, and conditions of payments. I was an integral part of reviewing and negotiating a grant or contract that had the best interests for every party involved.

After my son was born, I left the university and my contracts background went on a brief hiatus. Once my son went off to school, I began freelance writing. After a few writing gigs sprinkled with a few too many rejection slips, I landed an assignment for *Dog Fancy* magazine. I was thrilled and eagerly anticipated the arrival of a contract in my inbox. As I opened the document, the hiatus had lifted. I read through the contract and was able to send it back within a few hours.

For many new freelancers or writers who have been around the block, contract administration is not something that they can list as a perk on their resume. Instead of searching through the Yellow Pages for a contract lawyer or trying to call in a special favor to a writer friend, there are some easy ways for a newbie writer or even a seasoned writer to review a contract before putting a smiley face next to the dotted line.

TAKE A DEEP BREATH, THEN READ ON

Remember breaking those seals on test booklets and the voice in the background telling you, "Please read the directions slowly." As you tried to drown out the voice because your stomach was in knots, little did you know that those imparting words of wisdom would come in handy as you perspired profusely over the legal jargon that unfolded before your eyes. The same words go for contracts.

Many writers, including myself, are anxious to get an assignment underway, but the contract carrot continues to loom over our creative minds. "I'm surprised by writers who just skim a contract and then sign it without understanding what it means," says Kelly James-Enger, author of books including *Six Figure Freelancing: The Writer's Guide to Making More* (Random House) and the blog Dollarsanddeadlines.blogspot.com. "Most of the language in magazine contracts isn't that complicated, but it can be confusing when you're new to the business."

When I receive a contract from a new publisher or editor, I make a second copy. My children call it "my sloppy copy." I take out a highlighter and begin to mark up the key points of the contract: beginning and end date, conditions of payment, how my relationship is defined by the publisher, and what the outline of the article should look like.

The beginning and end date of a contract is crucial. After I recently negotiated a contract, the editor changed the due date of the article in an e-mail. I made sure the contract was changed to reflect the new due date. The conditions of the payments are important because it will describe when the writer will be paid and by what method. Most publishers have turned to incremental payment schedules or payments to be made online like PayPal. How the publisher considers your contractor status is important. If you're a freelance contract writer, the contract should reflect that as well as identify you as an independent contractor for IRS tax purposes. Finally, the contract will highlight an outline of what your article or proposal should look like.

As you slowly digest the terms you are about to agree to for your assignment or book project, you gain a better understanding of what an editor or publisher expects from you and when.

PAYMENT TYPES

There are any number of different arrangements for publishers to pay writers. However, here are three of the most common and what they mean.

- Pays on acceptance. This means a publisher pays (or cuts a check) for the writer upon acceptance of the manuscript. This is usually the best deal a writer can hope to receive.
- Pays on publication. In these cases, a publisher pays (or cuts a check) for the writer by the publication date of the manuscript. For magazines, this could mean several months after the manuscript was accepted and approved. For books, this could mean more than a year.
- Pays after publication. Sometimes contracts will specify exactly how long after publication. Be wary of contracts that leave it open-ended.

CUTTING TO THE LEGAL CHASE

Once you have had a chance to review a contract, you may be scratching your head and saying, "Okay, now what does this all mean to me as a writer?" James-Enger describes three key areas where writers should keep sharp on when it comes to contracts—indemnification, pay and exclusivity provisions.

INDEMNIFICATION is a publisher's way of saying if something goes wrong, we are not responsible. If a claim is brought against another writer's work, a publisher does not want to be responsible for the legal aftermath but you could be the one receiving a notice in the mail. James-Enger warns writers to be on the lookout for indemnification clauses. "In the U.S., anyone can sue anyone over just about anything," she says; "I'm okay with agreeing to indemnification clauses that specify breaches of contract because I know I'm not going to plagiarize, libel or misquote anyone. But I can't promise that the publication will never be sued by anyone whether or not I actually breached the contract."

PAY is where you want the publisher "to show you the money." Writers need to be aware of how publishers will discuss the terms of payment in the contract. James-Enger advises to have "payment on acceptance." This means you will be paid when the editor agrees to accept your manuscript or article. If there is "no payment on acceptance," some publishers will pay when the article is published. "Push for payment whenever you can," she says.

EXCLUSIVITY PROVISIONS are where a particular publisher will not allow the writer to publish an article or manuscript that is "about the same or similar subject" during the time the publisher runs the piece. Because of the nature of the writing business, James-Enger feels writers need to negotiate this part of the contract. "I specialize in health, fitness and nutrition, and I'm always writing about a similar subject," she says.

> ### CONTRACT TIPS
>
> Even seasoned freelancers can find themselves intimidated by contracts. Here are a few things to consider with your contract:
>
> - **KEEP COPY ON RECORD.** If the contract is sent via e-mail, keep a digital copy, but also print up a hard copy and keep it in an easy-to-find file folder.
> - **CHECK FOR RIGHTS.** It's almost never a good idea to sell all rights. But you should also pay attention to whether you're selling any subsidiary or reprint rights. The more rights you release the more payment you should expect (and demand).
> - **WHEN PAYMENT.** Make sure you understand when you are to be paid and have it specified in your contract. You may think that payment will come when the article is accepted or published, but different publishers have different policies. Get it in writing.
> - **HOW MUCH PAYMENT.** The contract should specify exactly how much you are going to be paid. If there is no payment listed on the contract, the publisher could use your work for free.
> - **TURN IN CONTRACT BEFORE ASSIGNMENT.** Don't start working until the contract is signed, and everything is official. As a freelancer, time is as important as money. Don't waste any of your time and effort on any project that is not yet contracted.

WHEN TO HEAD TO THE BARGAINING TABLE

Recently, I became an independent contractor for the American Composites Manufacturing Association (ACMA). When I reviewed the terms of the contract, I was concerned how my independent contractor status was identified. Although I am not an ACMA employee, I wanted to know if I could include my ACMA publications on my resume. Before I signed the contract, I questioned this issue with my editor. My editor told me I may use this opportunity to put on my resume. I signed the contract and finished my assignment.

Writers should be able to talk to an editor or a publisher if there is a question about a term or clause in a contract. "Don't be afraid to talk to the editor about the changes you'd like to make to a contract," James-Enger says; "You don't know what you'll get or if an editor is willing to negotiate it, until you ask."

When writers have to approach an editor for changes to a contract, James-Enger advises writers to act professionally when it comes to the negotiations. "I start out with saying—I am really excited to be working with you on this story and I appreciate the assignment, but I have a couple of issues with the contract that I'd like to talk to you about," she says. "Sure I want a better contract but I also want to maintain a good working relationship with my editor. A scorched-earth policy doesn't benefit any freelancer in the long run."

Negotiating payment terms is a tricky subject for some writers. Writers want to get the most bang for their buck but they don't want to lose a great writing assignment. Do your research first before you decide to ask an editor for more money to complete the assignment. Double check the publisher's website or look to see if the pay scale is equivalent to other publishers in the particular industry. Some publishers have a set publishing fee whereas others may have a little more wiggle room depending on the type of the assignment given. In today's economy, writers are a little more reluctant to ask for a higher rate for an article. If the publisher seems to be open to discussion about the pay scale, just make sure you approach the situation in a professional manner so as to not turn the publisher away from giving you another assignment.

WHO OWNS YOUR WRITING?

Besides payment terms, another area that writers may find themselves on the other end of the negotiation table is with ownership rights. We all want to take credit for the work that we have poured our heart and soul into. Unfortunately, the business of publishing has different ways of saying how a writer can classify their work. Ownership rights vary, but the biggest one that writers have a hard time trying to build up a good case against is "all rights." "All rights" is exactly what it means: *hope you are not in love with what you have just written because you will not be able to use it again.*

In recent months, I have written for two publications that I had given "all rights" to the company. My rationale is that I knew I would never need to use those articles again but I did make sure I was able to include those articles for my byline to show that I have publishing experience.

If you feel that you want to reuse or recycle an article that you had written a few years ago, you might want to consider negotiating an "all rights" clause or maybe going to another publisher. "We don't take all rights so there is no reason for authors to request we change the rights clause," says Angela Hoy, author and owner of WritersWeekly.com and Booklocker.com. "Our contracts were rated 'Outstanding' by Mark Levine (author of *The Fine Print of Self-Publishing*) and has also been called the clearest and fairest in the industry."

James-Enger is also an advocate of negotiating against contracts with an "all rights" clause. "I hate 'all rights' contracts, and try to avoid signing them as they preclude me from ever reselling the piece as a reprint to other markets," she says. "I explain that to editors, and I have been able to get editors to agree to let me retain nonexclusive reprint rights even when they buy all rights—which still lets me market the piece as a reprint." James-Enger also advises that "if the publisher demands all rights, then negotiate if the payment is sub-standard."

So if you are just receiving a contract in the mail for the first time or you are working with a new publisher, you should not be afraid of the legal lingo that blankets the message "we want to work with you." Contracts are meant to protect both the interests of the publishers and writers. Publishers want the commitment from writers that he or she will provide their best work and writers want to be recognized for their best work. But between those contracts lines, the legal lingo can cause writers to feel they need a law degree to review the contract. No, just sit back and relax and enjoy the prose that will take your writing to the next level.

RIGHTS AND WHAT THEY MEAN

A creative work can be used in many different ways. As the author of the work, you hold all rights to the work in question. When you agree to have your work published, you are granting a publisher the right to use your work in any number of ways. Whether that right is to publish the manuscript for the first time in a publication, or to publish it as many times and in as many ways as a publisher wishes, is up to you—it all depends on the agreed-upon terms. As a general rule, the more rights you license away, the less control you have over your work and the money you're paid. You should strive to keep as many rights to your work as you can.

Writers and editors sometimes define rights in a number of different ways. Below you will find a classification of terms as they relate to rights.

- **FIRST SERIAL RIGHTS.** Rights that the writer offers a newspaper or magazine to publish the manuscript for the first time in any periodical. All other rights remain with the writer. Sometimes the qualifier "North American" is added to these rights to specify a geographical limitation to the license. When content is excerpted from a book scheduled to be published, and it appears in a magazine or newspaper prior to book publication, this is also called first serial rights.
- **ONE-TIME RIGHTS.** Nonexclusive rights (rights that can be licensed to more than one market) purchased by a periodical to publish the work once (also known as simultaneous rights). That is, there is nothing to stop the author from selling the work to other publications at the same time.
- **SECOND SERIAL (REPRINT) RIGHTS.** Nonexclusive rights given to a newspaper or magazine to publish a manuscript after it has already appeared in another newspaper or magazine.
- **ALL RIGHTS.** This is exactly what it sounds like. "All rights" means an author is selling every right he has to a work. If you license all rights to your work, you forfeit the right to ever use the work again. If you think you may want to use the article again, you should avoid submitting to such markets or refuse payment and withdraw your material.
- **ELECTRONIC RIGHTS.** Rights that cover a broad range of electronic media, including websites, CD/DVDs, video games, smart phone apps, and more. The contract should

specify if—and which—electronic rights are included. The presumption is unspeci-fied rights remain with the writer.

- **SUBSIDIARY RIGHTS.** Rights, other than book publication rights, that should be cov-ered in a book contract. These may include various serial rights; movie, TV, audio, and other electronic rights; translation rights, etc. The book contract should specify who controls the rights (author or publisher) and what percentage of sales from the licensing of these rights goes to the author.
- **DRAMATIC, TV, AND MOTION PICTURE RIGHTS.** Rights for use of material on the stage, on TV, or in the movies. Often a one-year option to buy such rights is offered (generally for 10 percent of the total price). The party interested in the rights then tries to sell the idea to other people—actors, directors, studios, or TV networks. Some properties are optioned numerous times, but most fail to become full productions. In those cases, the writer can sell the rights again and again.

Sometimes editors don't take the time to specify the rights they are buying. If you sense that an editor is interested in getting stories, but doesn't seem to know what his and the writer's responsibilities are, be wary. In such a case, you'll want to explain what rights you're offering (preferably one-time or first serial rights only) and that you expect addi-tional payment for subsequent use of your work.

The Copyright Law that went into effect January 1, 1978, states writers are primarily sell-ing one-time rights to their work unless they—and the publisher—agree otherwise in writ-ing. Book rights are covered fully by contract between the writer and the book publisher.

CINDY FERRAINO has been blessed with a variety of assignments, including newspaper arti-cles, magazine articles, ghost-written articles, stories for books, and most recently authoring a book on accounting and bookkeeping terminology, *The Complete Dictionary of Accounting & Bookkeeping Terms Explained Simply* (Atlantic Publishing Group).

HOW MUCH SHOULD I CHARGE?

....

by Aaron Belz

//

The first question most aspiring freelance writers ask themselves is, "Where do I find paying gigs?" But once a writer finds that first freelance gig, they often ask, "How much should I charge?"

They ask this question, because often their clients ask them. In the beginning, this can be one of the most stressful parts of the freelancing process: Trying to set rates that don't scare away clients, but that also help put dinner on the table.

Maybe that's why the "How Much Should I Charge?" pay rate chart is one of the most popular and useful pieces of the *Writer's Market*. Freelancers use the rates to justify their worth on the market to potential clients, and clients use the chart as an objective third party authority on what the current market is paying.

Use the following chart to help you get started in figuring out your freelance rates. If you're a beginner, it makes sense to price yourself closer to the lower end of the spectrum, but always use your gut in negotiating rates. The rate on that first assignment often helps set the expectations for future rates.

As you find success in securing work, your rates should naturally increase. If not, consider whether you're building relationships with clients that lead to multiple assignments. Also, take into account whether you're negotiating for higher rates on new assignments with familiar and newer clients.

Remember that smarter freelancers work toward the goal of higher rates, because better rates mean one of two things for writers: Either they're able to earn money, or they're able to earn the same money in less time. For some freelancers, having that extra time is worth more than anything money can buy.

Use the listings in *Writer's Market* to find freelance work for magazines, book publishers, and other traditional publishing markets. But don't restrict your search to the traditional markets if you want to make a serious living as a freelance writer.

As the pay rate chart shows, there are an incredible number of opportunities for writers to make a living doing what they love: writing. Maybe that means writing critiques, editing anthologies, blogging, or something else entirely.

While this pay rate chart covers a wide variety of freelance writing gigs, there are some that are just too unique to get a going rate. If you can't find a specific job listed here, try to find something that is similar to use as a guide for figuring out a rate. There are times when you just have to create the going rate yourself.

Thank you, Aaron Belz, for assembling this pay rate chart and sharing your sources in the sidebar below. I know it will help more than one freelance writer negotiate the freelance rates they deserve.

—*Robert Lee Brewer*

PARTICIPATING ORGANIZATIONS

Here are the organizations surveyed to compile the "How Much Should I Charge?" pay rate chart. You can also find Professional Organizations in the Resources.

- American Medical Writers Association (AMWA), www.amwa.org
- American Society of Journalists & Authors (ASJA), www.asja.org
- American Society of Media Photographers (ASMP), www.asmp.org
- American Society of Picture Professionals (ASPP), www.aspp.com
- American Translators Association (ATA), www.atanet.org
- Association of Independents in Radio (AIR), www.airmedia.org
- Educational Freelancers Association (EFA), www.the-efa.org
- Freelance Success (FLX), www.freelancesucess.com
- Investigative Reporters & Editors (IRE), www.ire.org
- Media Communicators Association International (MCA-I), www.mca-i.org
- National Cartoonists Society (NCS), www.reuben.org/main.asp
- National Writers Union (NWU), www.nwu.org
- National Association of Science Writers (NASW), www.nasw.org
- Society of Professional Journalists (SPJ), www.spj.org
- Women in Film (WIF), www.wif.org
- Writer's Guild of America East (WGAE), www.wgaeast.org
- Writer's Guild of America West (WGA), www.wga.org

AARON BELZ is the author of *The Bird Hoverer* (BlazeVOX), *Lovely, Raspberry* (Persea), and *Glitter Bomb* (Persea). A St. Louis native, he now lives and works in Hillsborough, North Carolina. Visit him online at belz.net or follow him on Twitter @aaronbelz.

ADVERTISING & PUBLIC RELATIONS	PER HOUR			PER PROJECT			OTHER		
	HIGH	LOW	AVG	HIGH	LOW	AVG	HIGH	LOW	AVG
Advertising copywriting	$156	$36	$84	$9,000	$160	$2,760	$3/word	30¢/word	$1.57/word
Advertising editing	$125	$20	$65	n/a	n/a	n/a	$1/word	30¢/word	66¢/word
Advertorials	$182	$51	$93	$1,890	$205	$285	$3/word	85¢/word	$1.58/word
Business public relations	$182	$30	$85	n/a	n/a	n/a	$500/day	$200/day	$356/day
Campaign development or product launch	$156	$36	$100	$8,755	$1,550	$4,545	n/a	n/a	n/a
Catalog copywriting	$156	$25	$71	n/a	n/a	n/a	$350/item	$30/item	$116/item
Corporate spokesperson role	$182	$72	$107	n/a	n/a	n/a	$1,200/day	$500/day	$740/day
Direct-mail copywriting	$156	$36	$85	$8,248	$500	$2,839	$4/word	$1/word	$2.17/word
							$400/page	$200/page	$315/page
Event promotions/publicity	$126	$30	$76	n/a	n/a	n/a	n/a	n/a	$500/day
Press kits	$182	$31	$81	n/a	n/a	n/a	$850/60sec	$120/60sec	$458/60sec
Press/news release	$182	$30	$80	$1,500	$125	$700	$2/word	50¢/word	$1.20/word
							$750/page	$150/page	$348/page

	PER HOUR			PER PROJECT			OTHER		
	HIGH	LOW	AVG	HIGH	LOW	AVG	HIGH	LOW	AVG
Radio commercials	$102	$30	$74	n/a	n/a	n/a	$850/60sec	$120/60sec	$456/60sec
Speech writing/editing for individuals or corporations	$168	$36	$92	$10,000	$2,700	$5,036	$355/minute	$105/minute	$208/minute
BOOK PUBLISHING									
Abstracting and abridging	$125	$30	$74	n/a	n/a	n/a	$2/word	$1/word	$1.48/word
Anthology editing	$80	$23	$51	$7,900	$1,200	$4,588	n/a	n/a	n/a
Book chapter	$100	$35	$60	$2,500	$1,200	$1,758	20¢/word	8¢/word	14¢/word
Book production for clients	$100	$40	$67	n/a	n/a	n/a	$17.50/page	$5/page	$10/page
Book proposal consultation	$125	$25	$66	$1,500	$250	$788	n/a	n/a	n/a
Book publicity for clients	n/a	n/a	n/a	$10,000	$500	$2,000	n/a	n/a	n/a
Book query critique	$100	$50	$72	$500	$75	$202	n/a	n/a	n/a
Children's book writing	$75	$35	$50	n/a	n/a	n/a	$5/word / $5,000/adv	$1/word / $450/adv	$2.75/word / $2,286/adv
Content editing (scholarly/textbook)	$125	$20	$51	$15,000	$500	$4,477	$20/page	$3/page	$6.89/page

	PER HOUR			PER PROJECT			OTHER		
	HIGH	LOW	AVG	HIGH	LOW	AVG	HIGH	LOW	AVG
Content editing (trade)	$125	$19	$54	$20,000	$1,000	$6,538	$20/page	$3.75/page	$8/page
Copyediting (trade)	$100	$16	$46	$5,500	$2,000	$2,892	$6/page	$1/page	$4.22/page
Encyclopedia articles	n/a	n/a	n/a	n/a	n/a	n/a	50¢/word	15¢/word	35¢/word
							$3,000/item	$50/item	$933/item
Fiction book writing (own)	n/a	n/a	n/a	n/a	n/a	n/a	$40,000/adv	$525/adv	$14,193/adv
Ghostwriting, as told to	$125	$35	$67	$47,000	$5,500	$22,892	$100/page	$50/page	$87/page
Ghostwriting, no credit	$125	$30	$73	n/a	n/a	n/a	$3/word	50¢/word	$1.79/word
							$500/page	$50/page	$206/page
Guidebook writing/editing	n/a	n/a	n/a	n/a	n/a	n/a	$14,000/adv	$10,000/adv	$12,000/adv
Indexing	$60	$22	$35	n/a	n/a	n/a	$12/page	$2/page	$4.72/page
Manuscript evaluation and critique	$150	$23	$66	$2,000	$150	$663	n/a	n/a	n/a
Manuscript typing	n/a	n/a	$20	n/a	n/a	n/a	$3/page	95¢/page	$1.67/page
Movie novelizations	n/a	n/a	n/a	$15,000	$5,000	$9,159	n/a	n/a	n/a

	PER HOUR			PER PROJECT			OTHER		
	HIGH	LOW	AVG	HIGH	LOW	AVG	HIGH	LOW	AVG
Nonfiction book writing (collaborative)	$125	$40	$80	n/a	n/a	n/a	$110/page $75,000/adv	$50/page $1,300/adv	$80/page $22,684/adv
Nonfiction book writing (own)	$125	$40	$72	n/a	n/a	n/a	$110/page $50,000/adv	$50/page $1,300/adv	$80/page $14,057/adv
Novel synopsis (general)	$60	$30	$45	$450	$150	$292	$100/page	$10/page	$37/page
Personal history writing/editing (for clients)	$125	$30	$60	$40,000	$750	$15,038	n/a	n/a	n/a
Proofreading	$75	$15	$31	n/a	n/a	n/a	$5/page	$2/page	$3.26/page
Research for writers or book publishers	$150	$15	$52	n/a	n/a	n/a	$600/day	$400/day	$525/day
Rewriting/structural editing	$120	$25	$67	$50,000	$2,500	$13,929	14¢/word	5¢/word	10¢/word
Translation—literary	n/a	n/a	n/a	$95,000	$6,500	$8,000	17¢/target word	4¢/target word	8¢/target word
Translation—nonfiction/technical	n/a	n/a	n/a	n/a	n/a	n/a	30¢/target word	5¢/target word	12¢/target word

BUSINESS

	PER HOUR			PER PROJECT			OTHER		
	HIGH	LOW	AVG	HIGH	LOW	AVG	HIGH	LOW	AVG
Annual reports	$185	$60	$102	$15,000	$500	$5,850	$600	$100	$349
Brochures, booklets, flyers	$150	$45	$91	$15,000	$300	$4,230	$2.50/word $800/page	35¢/word $50/page	$1.21/word $341/page
Business editing (general)	$155	$40	$80	n/a	n/a	n/a	n/a	n/a	n/a
Business letters	$155	$40	$79	n/a	n/a	n/a	$2/word	$1/word	$1.47/word
Business plan	$155	$40	$87	$15,000	$200	$4,115	n/a	n/a	n/a
Business writing seminars	$155	$70	$112	$8,600	$550	$2,919	n/a	n/a	n/a
Consultation on communications	$155	$50	$80	n/a	n/a	n/a	$1,300/day	$530/day	$830/day
Copyediting for business	$155	$35	$65	n/a	n/a	n/a	$4/page	$2/page	$3/page
Corporate histories	$155	$45	$91	160,000	$5,000	$54,525	$2/word	$1/word	$1.50/word
Corporate periodicals, editing	$155	$45	$74	n/a	n/a	n/a	$2.50/word	75¢/word	$1.42/word
Corporate periodicals, writing	$155	$45	$83	n/a	n/a	n/a	$3/word	$1/word	$1.71/word
Corporate profiles	$155	$45	$93	n/a	n/a	n/a	$2/word	$1/word	$1.50/word

	PER HOUR			PER PROJECT			OTHER		
	HIGH	LOW	AVG	HIGH	LOW	AVG	HIGH	LOW	AVG
Ghostwriting for business execs	$155	$45	$89	$3,000	$500	$1,400	$2.50/word	50¢/word	$2/word
Ghostwriting for businesses	$155	$45	$114	$3,000	$500	$1,790	n/a	n/a	n/a
Newsletters, desktop publishing/production	$155	$45	$75	$6,600	$1,000	$3,490	$750/page	$150/page	$429/page
Newsletters, editing	$155	$35	$72	n/a	n/a	$3,615	$230/page	$150/page	$185/page
Newsletters, writing	$155	$35	$82	$6,600	$800	$3,581	$5/word $1,250/page	$1/word $150/page	$2.31/word $514/page
Translation services for business use	$80	$45	$57	n/a	n/a	n/a	$35/target word $1.41/target line	7¢/target word $1/target line	$2.31/target word $1.21/target line
Resume writing	$105	$70	$77	$500	$150	$295	n/a	n/a	n/a
COMPUTER, INTERNET & TECHNICAL									
Blogging—paid	$150	$35	$100	$2,000	$500	$1,250	$500/post	$6/post	$49/post
E-mail copywriting	$135	$30	$85	n/a	n/a	$300	$2/word	30¢/word	91¢/word

	PER HOUR			PER PROJECT			OTHER		
	HIGH	LOW	AVG	HIGH	LOW	AVG	HIGH	LOW	AVG
Educational webinars	$500	$0	$195	n/a	n/a	n/a	n/a	n/a	n/a
Hardware/Software help screen writing	$95	$60	$81	$6,000	$1,000	$4,000	n/a	n/a	n/a
Hardware/Software manual writing	$165	$30	$80	$23,500	$5,000	$11,500	n/a	n/a	n/a
Internet research	$95	$25	$55	n/a	n/a	n/a	n/a	n/a	n/a
Keyword descriptions	n/a	n/a	n/a	n/a	n/a	n/a	$200/page	$130/page	$165/page
Online videos for clients	$95	$60	$76	n/a	n/a	n/a	n/a	n/a	n/a
Social media postings for clients	$95	$25	$62	n/a	n/a	$500	n/a	n/a	$10/word
Technical editing	$150	$30	$65	n/a	n/a	n/a	n/a	n/a	n/a
Technical writing	$160	$30	$80	n/a	n/a	n/a	n/a	n/a	n/a
Web editing	$100	$25	$57	n/a	n/a	n/a	$10/page	$4/page	$5.67/page
Webpage design	$150	$25	$80	$4,000	$200	$1,278	n/a	n/a	n/a
Website or blog promotion	n/a	$30	n/a	$650	$195	$335	n/a	n/a	n/a

	PER HOUR			PER PROJECT			OTHER		
	HIGH	LOW	AVG	HIGH	LOW	AVG	HIGH	LOW	AVG
Website reviews	n/a	$30	n/a	$900	$50	$300	n/a	n/a	n/a
Website search engine optimization	$89	$30	$76	$50,000	$8,000	$12,000	n/a	n/a	n/a
White papers	$135	$30	$82	$10,000	$2,500	$4,927	n/a	n/a	n/a
EDITORIAL/DESIGN PACKAGES									
Desktop publishing	$150	$18	$67	n/a	n/a	n/a	$750/page	$30/page	$202/page
Photo brochures	$125	$60	$87	$15,000	$400	$3,869	$65/picture	$30/picture	$48/picture
Photography	$100	$45	$71	$10,500	$50	$2,100	$2,500/day	$500/day	$1,340/day
Photo research	$75	$45	$49	n/a	n/a	n/a	n/a	n/a	n/a
Picture editing	$100	$45	$64	n/a	n/a	n/a	$65/picture	$30/picture	$53/picture
EDUCATIONAL & LITERARY SERVICES									
Author appearances at national events	n/a	n/a	n/a	n/a	n/a	n/a	$500/hour	$100/hour	$285/hour
							$30,000/event	$500/event	$5,000/event

	PER HOUR			PER PROJECT			OTHER		
	HIGH	LOW	AVG	HIGH	LOW	AVG	HIGH	LOW	AVG
Author appearances at regional events	n/a	n/a	n/a	n/a	n/a	n/a	$1,500/event	$50/event	$615/event
Author appearances at local groups	$63	$40	$47	n/a	n/a	n/a	$400/event	$75/event	$219/event
Authors presenting in schools	$125	$25	$78	n/a	n/a	n/a	$350/class	$50/class	$183/class
Educational grant and proposal writing	$100	$35	$67	n/a	n/a	n/a	n/a	n/a	n/a
Manuscript evaluation for theses/dissertations	$100	$15	$53	$1,550	$200	$783	n/a	n/a	n/a
Poetry manuscript critique	$100	$25	$62	n/a	n/a	n/a	n/a	n/a	n/a
Private writing instruction	$60	$50	$57	n/a	n/a	n/a	n/a	n/a	n/a
Readings by poets, fiction writers	n/a	n/a	n/a	n/a	n/a	n/a	$3,000/event	$50/event	$225/event
Short story manuscript critique	$150	$30	$75	$175	$50	$112	n/a	n/a	n/a
Teaching adult writing classes	$125	$30	$82	n/a	n/a	n/a	$800/class $5,000/course	$115/class $500/course	$450/class $2,667/course

	PER HOUR			PER PROJECT			OTHER		
	HIGH	LOW	AVG	HIGH	LOW	AVG	HIGH	LOW	AVG
Writer's workshop panel or class	$220	$30	$92	n/a	n/a	n/a	$5,000/day	$60/day	$1,186/day
Writing for scholarly journals	$100	$40	$63	$450	$100	$285	n/a	n/a	n/a
FILM, VIDEO, TV, RADIO, STAGE									
Book/novel summaries for film producers	n/a	n/a	n/a	n/a	n/a	n/a	$34/page	$15/page	$23/page $120/book
Business film/video scriptwriting	$150	$50	$97	n/a	n/a	$600	$1,000/run min	$50/run min	$334/run min $500/day
Comedy writing for entertainers	n/a	n/a	n/a	n/a	n/a	n/a	$150/joke $500/group	$5/joke $100/group	$50/joke $283/group
Copyediting audiovisuals	$90	$22	$53	n/a	n/a	n/a	n/a	n/a	n/a
Educational or training film/video scriptwriting	$125	$35	$81	n/a	n/a	n/a	$500/run min	$100/run min	$245/run min
Feature film options	First 18 months, 10% WGA minimum; 10% minimum each 18-month period thereafter.								
TV options	First 180 days, 5% WGA minimum; 10% minimum each 180-day period thereafter.								

	PER HOUR			PER PROJECT			OTHER		
	HIGH	LOW	AVG	HIGH	LOW	AVG	HIGH	LOW	AVG
Industrial product film/video scriptwriting	$150	$30	$99				$500/run min	$100/run min	$300/run min
Playwriting for the stage	5-10% box office/Broadway, 6-7% box office/off-Broadway, 10% box office/regional theatre.								
Radio editorials	$70	$50	$60				$200/run min	$45/run min	$124/run min
							$400/day	$250/day	$325/day
Radio interviews	n/a	n/a	n/a	$1,500	$110	$645	n/a	n/a	n/a
Screenwriting (original screenplay-including treatment)	n/a	n/a	n/a	n/a	n/a	n/a	$118,745	$63,526	$92,153
Script synopsis for agent or film	$2,344/30 min, $4,441/60 min, $6,564/90 min								
Script synopsis for business	$75	$45	$62	n/a	n/a	n/a	n/a	n/a	n/a
TV commercials	$99	$60	$81	n/a	n/a	n/a	$2,500/30 sec	$150/30 sec	$1,204/30 sec
TV news story/feature	$1,550/5 min, $3,000/10 min, $4,200/15 min								
TV scripts (non-theatrical)	Prime Time: $33,700/60 min, $47,500/90 min								
	Not Prime Time: $12,900/30 min, $23,500/60 min, $35,300/90 min								

	PER HOUR			PER PROJECT			OTHER		
	HIGH	LOW	AVG	HIGH	LOW	AVG	HIGH	LOW	AVG
TV scripts (teleplay/MOW)	$70,000/120 min								
MAGAZINES & TRADE JOURNALS									
Article manuscript critique	$130	$25	$69	n/a	n/a	n/a	n/a	n/a	n/a
Arts query critique	$105	$50	$80	n/a	n/a	n/a	n/a	n/a	n/a
Arts reviewing	$100	$65	$84	$335	$95	$194	$1.25/word	12¢/word	63¢/word
Book reviews	n/a	n/a	n/a	$900	$12	$348	$1.50/word	20¢/word	73¢/word
City magazine calendar	n/a	n/a	n/a	$250	$45	$135	$1/word	35¢/word	75¢/word
Comic book/strip writing	$225 original story, $525 existing story, $50 short script.								
Consultation on magazine editorial	$155	$35	$86	n/a	n/a	n/a	n/a	n/a	$100/page
Consumer magazine column	n/a	n/a	n/a	$2,500	$70	$898	$2.50/word	37¢/word	$1.13/word
Consumer front-of-book	n/a	n/a	n/a	$850	$320	$550	n/a	n/a	n/a
Content editing	$130	$30	$62	$6,500	$2,000	$3,700	15¢/word	6¢/word	11¢/word
Contributing editor	n/a	n/a	n/a	n/a	n/a	n/a	$160,000/contract	$22,000/contract	$53,000/contract

	PER HOUR			PER PROJECT			OTHER		
	HIGH	LOW	AVG	HIGH	LOW	AVG	HIGH	LOW	AVG
Copyediting magazines	$105	$18	$55	n/a	n/a	n/a	$10/page	$2.90/page	$5.78/page
Fact checking	$130	$15	$46	n/a	n/a	n/a	n/a	n/a	n/a
Gag writing for cartoonists	$35/gag; 25% sale on spec.								
Ghostwriting articles (general)	$225	$30	$107	$3,500	$1,100	$2,200	$10/word	65¢/word	$2.50/word
Magazine research	$125	$20	$53	n/a	n/a	n/a	$500/item	$100/item	$200/item
Proofreading	$80	$20	$40	n/a	n/a	n/a	n/a	n/a	n/a
Reprint fees	n/a	n/a	n/a	$1,500	$20	$439	$1.50/word	10¢/word	76¢/word
Rewriting	$130	$25	$74	n/a	n/a	n/a	n/a	n/a	$50/page
Trade journal feature article	$128	$45	$80	$4,950	$150	$1,412	$3/word	20¢/word	$1.20/word
Transcribing interviews	$185	$95	$55	n/a	n/a	n/a	$3/min	$1/min	$2/min
MEDICAL/SCIENCE									
Medical/scientific conference coverage	$125	$50	$85	n/a	n/a	n/a	$800/day	$300/day	$600/day
Medical/scientific editing	$96	$15	$33	n/a	n/a	n/a	$12.50/page	$3/page	$4.40/page
							$600/day	$500/day	$550/day

	PER HOUR			PER PROJECT			OTHER		
	HIGH	LOW	AVG	HIGH	LOW	AVG	HIGH	LOW	AVG
Medical/scientific writing	$91	$20	$46	$4,000	$500	$2,500	$2/word	25¢/word	$1.12/word
Medical/scientific multimedia presentations	$100	$50	$75	n/a	n/a	n/a	$100/slide	$50/slide	$77/slide
Medical/scientific proofreading	$80	$18	$50	n/a	n/a	$500	$3/page	$2.50/page	$2.75/page
Pharmaceutical writing	$125	$100	$50	n/a	n/a	n/a	n/a	n/a	n/a
NEWSPAPERS									
Arts reviewing	$69	$30	$53	$200	$15	$101	60¢/word	6¢/word	36¢/word
Book reviews	$69	$45	$58	$350	$15	$140	60¢/word	25¢/word	44¢/word
Column, local	n/a	n/a	n/a	$600	$25	$206	$1/word	38¢/word	50¢/word
Column, self-syndicated	n/a	n/a	n/a	n/a	n/a	n/a	$35/insertion	$4/insertion	$16/insert on
Copyediting	$35	$15	$27	n/a	n/a	n/a	n/a	n/a	n/a
Editing/manuscript evaluation	$75	$25	$35	n/a	n/a	n/a	n/a	n/a	n/a
Feature writing	$79	$40	$63	$1,040	$85	$478	$1.60/word	10¢/word	59¢/word
Investigative reporting	n/a	n/a	n/a	n/a	n/a	n/a	$10,000/grant	$250/grant	$2,250/grant

	PER HOUR			PER PROJECT				OTHER		
	HIGH	LOW	AVG	HIGH	LOW	AVG	HIGH	LOW	AVG
Obituary copy	n/a	n/a	n/a	$225	$35	$124	n/a	n/a	n/a
Proofreading	$45	$15	$23	n/a	n/a	n/a	n/a	n/a	n/a
Stringing	n/a	n/a	n/a	$2,400	$40	$525	n/a	n/a	n/a
NONPROFIT									
Grant writing for nonprofits	$150	$12	$75	$3,000	$400	$1,852	n/a	n/a	n/a
Nonprofit annual reports	$100	$28	$60	n/a	n/a	n/a	n/a	n/a	n/a
Nonprofit writing	$150	$17	$65	$17,600	$100	$4,706	n/a	n/a	n/a
Nonprofit editing	$125	$16	$50	n/a	n/a	n/a	n/a	n/a	n/a
Nonprofit fundraising literature	$110	$35	$74	$3,500	$200	$1,597	$1,000/day	$300/day	$767/day
Nonprofit presentations	$100	$40	$73	n/a	n/a	n/a	n/a	n/a	n/a
Nonprofit public relations	$100	$30	$60	n/a	n/a	n/a	n/a	n/a	n/a
POLITICS/GOVERNMENT									
Government agency writing/editing	$110	$25	$64	n/a	n/a	n/a	$1.25/word	25¢/word	75¢/word

	PER HOUR			PER PROJECT			OTHER		
	HIGH	LOW	AVG	HIGH	LOW	AVG	HIGH	LOW	AVG
Government grant writing/editing	$150	$19	$72	n/a	n/a	n/a	n/a	n/a	n/a
Government-sponsored research	$110	$35	$66	n/a	n/a	n/a	n/a	n/a	$630/day
Public relations for political campaigns	$150	$40	$86	n/a	n/a	n/a	n/a	n/a	n/a
Speechwriting for government officials	$200	$40	$96	$4,550	$1,015	$2,755	$200/run min	$110/run min	$155/run min
Speechwriting for political campaigns	$155	$65	$101	n/a	n/a	n/a	$200/run min	$100/run min	$162/run min

MAKING THE MOST OF THE MONEY YOU EARN

....

by Sage Cohen

Writers who manage money well can establish a prosperous writing life that meets their short-term needs and long-term goals. This article will introduce the key financial systems, strategies, attitudes, and practices that will help you cultivate a writing life that makes the most of your resources and sustains you over time.

DIVIDING BUSINESS AND PERSONAL EXPENSES

If you are reporting your writing business to the IRS, it is important that you keep the money that flows from this source entirely separate from your personal finances. Here's what you'll need to accomplish this:

- **BUSINESS CHECKING ACCOUNT:** Only two types of money go into this account: money you have been paid for your writing and/or "capital investments" you make by depositing your own money to invest in the business. And only two types of payments are made from this account: business-related expenses (such as: subscriptions, marketing and advertisement, professional development, fax or phone service, postage, computer software and supplies), and "capital draws" which you make to pay yourself.
- **BUSINESS SAVINGS ACCOUNT OR MONEY MARKET ACCOUNT:** This account is the holding pen where your quarterly tax payments will accumulate and earn interest. Money put aside for your retirement account(s) can also be held here.
- **BUSINESS CREDIT CARD:** It's a good idea to have a credit card for your business as a means of emergency preparedness. Pay off the card responsibly every month and this will help you establish a good business credit record, which can be useful down the line should you need a loan for any reason.

When establishing your business banking and credit, shop around for the best deals, such as highest interest rates, lowest (or no) monthly service fees, and free checking. Mint.com is a good source for researching your options.

EXPENSE TRACKING AND RECONCILING

Once your bank accounts are set up, it's time to start tracking and categorizing what you earn and spend. This will ensure that you can accurately report your income and itemize your deductions when tax time rolls around every quarter. Whether you intend to prepare your taxes yourself or have an accountant help you, immaculate financial records will be the key to speed and success in filing your taxes.

For the most effective and consistent expense tracking, I highly recommend that you use a computer program such as QuickBooks. While it may seem simpler to do accounting by hand, I assure you that it isn't. Even a luddite such as I, who can't comprehend the most basic principles of accounting, can use QuickBooks with great aplomb to plug in the proper categories for income and expenses, easily reconcile bank statements, and with a few clicks prepare all of the requisite reports that make it easy to prepare taxes.

PAYING BILLS ONLINE

While it's certainly not imperative, you might want to check out your bank's online bill pay option if you're not using this already. Once you've set up the payee list, you can make payments in a few seconds every month or set up auto payments for expenses that are recurring. Having a digital history of bills paid can also come in handy with your accounting.

MANAGING TAXES

Self-employed people need to pay quarterly taxes. A quick, online search will reveal a variety of tax calculators and other online tools that can help you estimate what your payments should be. Programs such as TurboTax are popular and useful tools for automating and guiding you step-by-step through tax preparation. An accountant can also be helpful in understanding your unique tax picture, identifying and saving the right amount for taxes each quarter, and even determining SEP IRA contribution amounts (described later in this article). The more complex your finances (or antediluvian your accounting skills), the more likely that you'll benefit from this kind of personalized expertise.

Once you have forecasted your taxes either with the help of a specialized, tax-planning program or an accountant, you can establish a plan toward saving the right amount for quarterly payments. For example, once I figured out what my tax bracket was and the approximate percentage of income that needed to be set aside as taxes, I would immediately transfer a percentage of every deposit to my savings account, where it would sit and grow a little interest until quarterly tax time came around. When I could afford to do so, I would also set aside the appropriate percentage of SEP IRA contribution from each deposit so that I'd be ready at end-of-year to deposit as much as I possibly could for retirement.

THE PRINCIPLE TO COMMIT TO IS THIS: Get that tax-earmarked cash out of your hot little hands (i.e., checking account) as soon as you can, and create whatever deterrents you need to leave the money in savings so you'll have it when you need it.

INTELLIGENT INVESTING FOR YOUR CAREER

Your writing business will require not only the investment of your time but also the investment of money. When deciding what to spend and how, consider your values and your budget in the three, key areas in the chart below: education, marketing and promotion, and keeping the wheels turning.

This is not an absolute formula for spending—just a snapshot of the types of expenses you may be considering and negotiating over time. My general rule would be: start small and modest with the one or two most urgent and/or inexpensive items in each list, and grow slowly over time as your income grows.

The good news is that these legitimate business expenses may all be deducted from your income—making your net income and tax burden less. Please keep in mind that the IRS allows losses as long as you make a profit for at least three of the first five years you are in business. Otherwise, the IRS will consider your writing a non-deductible hobby.

EDUCATION	MARKETING AND PROMOTION	KEEPING THE WHEELS TURNING
Subscriptions to publications in your field	URL registration and hosting for blogs and websites	Technology and application purchase, servicing and back-up
Memberships to organizations in your field	Contact database subscription (such as Constant Contact) for communicating with your audiences	Office supplies and furniture
Books: on topics you want to learn, or in genres you are cultivating	Business cards and stationery	Insurance for you and/or your business

Conferences and seminars	Print promotions (such as direct mail), giveaways and schwag	Travel, gas, parking
Classes and workshops	Online or print ad placement costs	Phone, fax and e-mail

PREPARATION AND PROTECTION FOR THE FUTURE

As a self-employed writer, in many ways your future is in your hands. Following are some of the health and financial investments that I'd recommend you consider as you build and nurture The Enterprise of You. Please understand that these are a layperson's suggestions. I am by no means an accountant, tax advisor, or financial planning guru. I am simply a person who has educated herself on these topics for the sake of her own writing business, made the choices I am recommending, and benefited from them. I'd like you to benefit from them, too.

SEP IRAS

Individual Retirement Accounts (IRAs) are investment accounts designed to help individuals save for retirement. But I do recommend that you educate yourself about the Simplified Employee Pension Individual Retirement Account (SEP IRA) and consider opening one if you don't have one already.

A SEP IRA is a special type of IRA that is particularly beneficial to self-employed people. Whereas a Roth IRA has a contribution cap of $5,000 or $6,000, depending on your age, the contribution limit for self-employed people in 2011 is approximately 20% of adjusted earned income, with a maximum contribution of $49,000. Contributions for a SEP IRA are generally 100% tax deductible and investments grow tax deferred. Let's say your adjusted earned income this year is $50,000. This means you'd be able to contribute $10,000 to your retirement account. I encourage you to do some research online or ask your accountant if a SEP IRA makes sense for you.

CREATING A 9-MONTH SAVINGS BUFFER

When you're living month-to-month, you are extremely vulnerable to fluctuation in the economy, client budget changes, life emergencies and every other wrench that could turn a good working groove into a frightening financial rut. The best way to prepare for the unexpected is to start (or continue) developing a savings buffer. The experts these days are suggesting that we accumulate nine months of living expenses to help us navigate transition in a way that we feel empowered rather than scared and desperate to take the next thing that comes along.

I started creating my savings buffer by opening the highest-interest money market account I could find and setting up a modest, monthly automatic transfer from my checking account. Then, when I paid off my car after five years of monthly payments, I added my car payment amount to the monthly transfer. (I'd been paying that amount for five years, so I was pretty sure I could continue to pay it to myself.) When I paid off one of my credit cards in full, I added that monthly payment to the monthly savings transfer. Within a year, I had a hefty sum going to savings every month before I had time to think about it, all based on expenses I was accustomed to paying, with money that had never been anticipated in the monthly cash flow.

What can you do today—and tomorrow—to put your money to work for your life, and start being as creative with your savings as you are with language?

DISABILITY INSURANCE

If writing is your livelihood, what happens if you become unable to write? I have writing friends who have become incapacitated and unable to work due to injuries to their brains, backs, hands and eyes. Disability insurance is one way to protect against such emergencies and ensure that you have an income in the unlikely event that you're not physically able to earn one yourself.

Depending on your health, age, and budget, monthly disability insurance payments may or may not be within your means or priorities. But you won't know until you learn more about your coverage options. I encourage you to investigate this possibility with several highly rated insurance companies to get the lay of the land for your unique, personal profile and make an informed decision.

HEALTH INSURANCE

Self-employed writers face tough decisions about health insurance. If you're lucky, there's someone in your family with health coverage also available to you. Without the benefit of group health insurance, chances are that self-costs are high and coverage is low. As in disability insurance, age and health status are significant variables in costs and availability.

Ideally, of course, you'll have reasonably-priced health insurance that helps make preventive care and health maintenance more accessible and protects you in case of a major medical emergency. The following are a few possibilities to check out that could reduce costs and improve access to health coverage:

- Join a group that aggregates its members for group coverage, such as a Chamber of Commerce or AARP. Ask an insurance agent in your area if there are any other group coverage options available to you.

- Consider a high-deductible health plan paired with a Health Savings Account (HSA). Because the deductible is so high, these plans are generally thought to be most useful for a major medical emergency. But an HSA paired with such a plan allows you to put aside a chunk of pre-tax change every year that can be spent on medical expenses or remain in the account where it can be invested and grow.

Establishing effective financial systems for your writing business will take some time and energy at the front end. I suggest that you pace yourself by taking an achievable step or two each week until you have a baseline of financial management that works for you. Then, you can start moving toward some of your bigger, longer-term goals. Once it's established, your solid financial foundation will pay you in dividends of greater efficiency, insight, and peace of mind for the rest of your writing career.

SAGE COHEN is the author of *The Productive Writer* and *Writing the Life Poetic*, both from Writer's Digest Books. She's been nominated for a Pushcart Prize, won first prize in the Ghost Road Press Poetry contest and published dozens of poems, essays and articles on the writing life. Sage holds an MFA in creative writing from New York University and a BA from Brown University. Since 1997, she has been a freelance writer serving clients including Intuit, Blue Shield, Adobe, and Kaiser Permanente.

LITERARY AGENTS

The literary agencies listed in this section are open to new clients and are members of the Association of Authors' Representatives (AAR), which means they do not charge for reading, critiquing, or editing. Some agents in this section may charge clients for office expenses such as photocopying, foreign postage, long-distance phone calls, or express mail services. Make sure you have a clear understanding of what these expenses are before signing any agency agreement.

FOR MORE...

The *2019 Guide to Literary Agents* (Writer's Digest Books) offers more than 800 literary agents, as well as information on writers' conferences. It also offers a wealth of information on the author/agent relationship and other related topics.

SUBHEADS

Each listing is broken down into subheads to make locating specific information easier. In the first section, you'll find contact information for each agency. Further information is provided which indicates an agency's size, its willingness to work with a new or previously unpublished writer, and its general areas of interest.

LITERARY AGENTS

ADAMS LITERARY

7845 Colony Rd., C4 #215, Charlotte NC 28226. (704)542-1440. **Fax:** (704)542-1450. **E-mail:** info@adamsliterary.com. **Website:** www.adamsliterary.com. **Contact:** Tracey Adams, Josh Adams. Estab. 2004. Member of AAR. Other memberships include SCBWI and WNBA.

MEMBER AGENTS Tracey Adams, Josh Adams, Lorin Oberweger.

REPRESENTS Considers these fiction areas: middle grade, picture books, young adult.

HOW TO CONTACT Submit through online form on website only. Send e-mail if that is not operating correctly. All submissions and queries should first be made through the online form on website. Will not review—and will promptly recycle—any unsolicited submissions or queries received by mail. Before submitting work for consideration, review complete guidelines online, as the agency sometimes shuts off to new submissions. Accepts simultaneous submissions. Responds in 6 weeks if interested. "While we have an established client list, we do seek new talent—and we accept submissions from both published and aspiring authors and artists."

TERMS Agent receives 15% commission on domestic sales; 20% on foreign sales. Offers written contract.

BRET ADAMS LTD. AGENCY

Bret Adams, Ltd., 448 W. 44th St., New York NY 10036. (212)765-5630. **Fax:** (212)265-2212. **Website:** bretadamsltd.net. Member of AAR.

MEMBER AGENTS Bruce Ostler; Mark Orsini; Alexis Williams.

REPRESENTS Theatrical stage play, stage plays. **Considers these script areas:** stage plays, theatrical stage play.

HOW TO CONTACT Use the online submission form. Because of this agency's submission policy and interests, it's best to approach with a professional recommendation from a client. Accepts simultaneous submissions.

BETSY AMSTER LITERARY ENTERPRISES

607 Foothill Blvd. #1061, La Canada Flintridge CA 91012. **E-mail:** b.amster.assistant@gmail.com (for adult titles); b.amster.kidsbooks@gmail.com (for children's and young adult). **Website:** www.amsterlit.com; www.cummingskidlit.com. **Contact:** Betsy Amster (adult); Mary Cummings (children's and young adult). Estab. 1992. Member of AAR. Represents more than 75 clients.

REPRESENTS Nonfiction, novels, juvenile books. **Considers these nonfiction areas:** autobiography, biography, business, child guidance, cooking, creative nonfiction, cultural interests, decorating, design, foods, gardening, health, history, horticulture, how-to, interior design, investigative, medicine, memoirs, money, multicultural, parenting, popular culture, psychology, science, self-help, sociology, travel, women's issues, young adult. **Considers these fiction areas:** crime, detective, family saga, juvenile, literary, middle grade, multicultural, mystery, picture books, police, suspense, thriller, women's, young adult.

HOW TO CONTACT "For adult fiction or memoirs, please embed the first 3 pages in the body of your e-mail. For nonfiction, please embed the overview of your proposal. For children's picture books, please embed the entire text in the body of your e-mail. For longer middle-grade and YA fiction and nonfiction, please embed the first 3 pages." Accepts simultaneous submissions. Responds in 1 month to queries; 2 months to mss. Obtains most new clients through recommendations from others, solicitations, and conferences.

TERMS Agent receives 15% commission on domestic sales; 20% commission on foreign sales. Offers written contract, binding for 1 year; three-month notice must be given to terminate contract. Charges for photocopying, postage, messengers, galleys/books used in submissions to foreign and film agents and to magazines for first serial rights. (Please note that it is rare to incur much in the way of expenses now that most submissions are made by e-mail.)

APONTE LITERARY AGENCY

E-mail: agents@aponteliterary.com. **Website:** aponteliterary.com. **Contact:** Natalia Aponte. Member of AAR. Signatory of WGA.

MEMBER AGENTS Natalia Aponte (any genre of mainstream fiction and nonfiction, but she is especially seeking women's novels, historical novels, supernatural and paranormal fiction, fantasy novels, political and science thrillers); Victoria Lea (any category, especially interested in women's fiction, science fiction and speculative fiction).

REPRESENTS Novels. **Considers these fiction areas:** fantasy, historical, paranormal, science fiction, supernatural, thriller, women's.

HOW TO CONTACT E-query. Accepts simultaneous submissions. Responds in 6 weeks if interested.

THE AXELROD AGENCY

55 Main St., P.O. Box 357, Chatham NY 12037. (518)392-2100. **E-mail:** steve@axelrodagency.com. **Website:** www.axelrodagency.com. **Contact:** Steven Axelrod. Member of AAR. Represents 15-20 clients.

MEMBER AGENTS Steven Axelrod, representation; Lori Antonson, subsidiary rights.

REPRESENTS Novels. **Considers these fiction areas:** crime, mystery, new adult, romance, women's.

HOW TO CONTACT Query via e-mail. Accepts simultaneous submissions. Obtains most new clients through recommendations from others.

TERMS Agent receives 15% commission on domestic sales; 20% commission on foreign sales. No written contract.

BARONE LITERARY AGENCY

385 North St., Batavia OH 45103. (513)732-6740. **Fax:** (513)297-7208. **E-mail:** baroneliteraryagency@roadrunner.com. **Website:** www.baroneliteraryagency.com. **Contact:** Denise Barone. Estab. 2010. Member of AAR. Signatory of WGA. Member of RWA. Represents 11 clients.

REPRESENTS Nonfiction, fiction, novels. **Considers these nonfiction areas:** memoirs, theater, young adult. **Considers these fiction areas:** action, adventure, cartoon, comic books, commercial, confession, contemporary issues, crime, detective, erotica, ethnic, experimental, family saga, fantasy, feminist, frontier, gay, glitz, hi-lo, historical, horror, humor, inspirational, juvenile, lesbian, literary, mainstream, metaphysical, military, multicultural, multimedia, mystery, new adult, New Age, occult, paranormal, plays, police, psychic, regional, religious, romance, satire, science fiction, spiritual, sports, supernatural, suspense, thriller, translation, urban fantasy, war, westerns, women's, young adult.

HOW TO CONTACT "Please send a query letter via e-mail. If I like your query letter, I will ask for the first 3 chapters and a synopsis as attachments." Accepts simultaneous submissions. "I make every effort to respond within 4 months." Obtains new clients by queries/submissions via e-mail only.

TERMS Agency receives 15% commission on domestic sales; 20% on foreign sales. Offers written contract.

THE BENT AGENCY

19 W. 21st St., #201, New York NY 10010. **E-mail:** info@thebentagency.com. **E-mail:** Please see website.. **Website:** www.thebentagency.com. **Contact:** Jenny Bent. Estab. 2009. Member of AAR.

MEMBER AGENTS Jenny Bent (adult fiction, including women's fiction, romance, and crime/suspense; she particularly likes novels with magical or fantasy elements that fall outside of genre fiction; young adult and middle-grade fiction; memoir; humor); Nicola Barr (literary and commercial fiction for adults and children, and nonfiction in the areas of sports, popular science, popular culture, and social and cultural history); Molly Ker Hawn (young adult and middle-grade books, including contemporary, historical, fantasy, science fiction, thrillers, and mystery); Gemma Cooper (all ages of children's and young adult books, including picture books; likes historical, contemporary, thrillers, mystery, humor, and science fiction); Louise Fury (children's fiction: picture books, literary middle-grade, and all young adult; adult fiction: speculative fiction, suspense/thriller, commercial fiction, and all subgenres of romance including erotic; nonfiction: cookbooks and pop culture); Sarah Manning (commercial and accessible literary adult fiction and nonfiction in the area of memoir, lifestyle, and narrative nonfiction); Beth Phelan (young adult, thrillers, suspense and mystery, romance and women's fiction, literary and general fiction, cookbooks, lifestyle, and pets/animals); Victoria Cappello (commercial and literary adult fiction as well as narrative nonfiction); Heather Flaherty (young adult and middle-grade fiction: all genres; select adult fiction: upmarket fiction, women's fiction, and female-centric thrillers; select nonfiction: pop culture, humorous, and social media–based projects, as well as teen memoir).

REPRESENTS Nonfiction, novels, short story collections, juvenile books. **Considers these nonfiction areas:** animals, cooking, creative nonfiction, foods, juvenile nonfiction, popular culture, women's issues, young adult. **Considers these fiction areas:** adventure, commercial, crime, erotica, fantasy, feminist, historical, horror, humor, juvenile, literary, mainstream, middle grade, multicultural, mystery, new adult, picture books, romance, short story collections, suspense, thriller, women's, young adult.

HOW TO CONTACT "Tell us briefly who you are, what your book is, and why you're the one to write it. Then include the first 10 pages of your material in the body of your e-mail. We respond to all queries; please resend your query if you haven't had a response within 4 weeks." Accepts simultaneous submissions.

VICKY BIJUR LITERARY AGENCY

27 W. 20th St., Suite 1003, New York NY 10011. E-mail: queries@vickybijuragency.com. **Website:** www.vickybijuragency.com. Estab. 1988. Member of AAR.

MEMBER AGENTS Vicky Bijur; Alexandra Franklin.

REPRESENTS Nonfiction, novels. **Considers these nonfiction areas:** memoirs. **Considers these fiction areas:** commercial, literary, mystery, new adult, thriller, women's, young adult, Campus novels, coming-of-age.

HOW TO CONTACT "Please send a query letter of no more than 3 paragraphs on what makes your book special and unique, a very brief synopsis, its length and genre, and your biographical information, along with the first 10 pages of your manuscript. Please let us know in your query letter if it is a multiple submission, and kindly keep us informed of other agents' interest and offers of representation. If sending electronically, paste the pages in an e-mail as we don't open attachments from unfamiliar senders. If sending by hard copy, please include an SASE for our response. If you want your material returned, include an SASE large enough to contain pages and enough postage to send back to you." Accepts simultaneous submissions. "We generally respond to all queries within 8 weeks of receipt."

DAVID BLACK LITERARY AGENCY

335 Adams St., Suite 2707, Brooklyn NY 11201. (718)-852-5500. **Fax:** (718)852-5539. **Website:** www.davidblackagency.com. **Contact:** David Black, owner. Estab. 1989. Member of AAR. Represents 150 clients.

MEMBER AGENTS David Black; Jenny Herrera; Gary Morris; Joy E. Tutela (narrative nonfiction, memoir, history, politics, self-help, investment, business, science, women's issues, GLBT issues, parenting, health and fitness, humor, craft, cooking and wine, lifestyle and entertainment, commercial fiction, literary fiction, MG, YA); Susan Raihofer (commercial fiction and nonfiction, memoir, pop culture, music, inspirational, thrillers, literary fiction); Sarah Smith (memoir, biography, food, music, narrative history, social studies, literary fiction).

REPRESENTS Nonfiction, novels. **Considers these nonfiction areas:** biography, business, cooking, crafts, gay/lesbian, health, history, humor, inspirational, memoirs, music, parenting, popular culture, politics, science, self-help, sociology, sports, women's issues.

Considers these fiction areas: commercial, literary, middle grade, thriller, young adult.

HOW TO CONTACT "To query an individual agent, please follow the specific query guidelines outlined in the agent's profile on our website. Not all agents are currently accepting unsolicited queries. To query the agency, please send a 1-2 page query letter describing your book, and include information about any previously published works, your audience, and your platform." Do not e-mail your query unless an agent specifically asks for an e-mail. Accepts simultaneous submissions. Responds in 2 months to queries.

BOOK CENTS LITERARY AGENCY, LLC
121 Black Rock Turnpike, Suite #499, Redding Ridge CT 06876. **E-mail:** cw@bookcentsliteraryagency.com. **Website:** www.bookcentsliteraryagency.com. **Contact:** Christine Witthohn. Estab. 2005. Member of AAR. RWA, MWA, SinC, KOD.

REPRESENTS Novels. **Considers these nonfiction areas:** cooking, gardening, travel, women's issues. **Considers these fiction areas:** commercial, mainstream, multicultural, mystery, paranormal, romance, suspense, thriller, urban fantasy, women's, young adult.

HOW TO CONTACT Submit via form on website. Does not accept mail or e-mail submissions.

BOOKENDS LITERARY AGENCY
Website: www.bookendsliterary.com. **Contact:** Jessica Faust, Kim Lionetti, Jessica Alvarez, Moe Ferrara, Tracy Marchini, Rachel Brooks, Natascha Morris, Beth Campbell, James McGowan. Estab. 1999. Member of AAR. RWA, MWA, SCBWI, SFWA. Represents 50+ clients.

MEMBER AGENTS Jessica Faust (women's fiction, mysteries, thrillers, suspense); Kim Lionetti (romance, women's fiction, young adult); Jessica Alvarez (romance, women's fiction, mystery, suspense, thrillers, and nonfiction); Beth Campbell (fantasy, science fiction, young adult, suspense, romantic suspense, and mystery); Moe Ferrara (middle-grade, young adult, and adult: romance, science fiction, fantasy, horror); Tracy Marchini (picture book, middle-grade, and young adult: fiction and nonfiction); Rachel Brooks (young adult, romance, women's fiction, cozy mysteries); Natascha Morris (young adult, middle grade, picture book).

REPRESENTS Nonfiction, novels, juvenile books. **Considers these nonfiction areas:** art, business, creative nonfiction, ethnic, how-to, inspirational, juvenile nonfiction, money, self-help, women's issues, young adult, picture book, middle grade. **Considers these fiction areas:** adventure, comic books, crime, detective, erotica, fantasy, gay, historical, horror, juvenile, lesbian, mainstream, middle grade, multicultural, mystery, paranormal, picture books, police, romance, science fiction, supernatural, suspense, thriller, urban fantasy, women's, young adult.

HOW TO CONTACT Visit website for the most up-to-date guidelines and current preferences. BookEnds agents accept all submissions through their personal Query Manager forms. These forms are accessible on the agency website under Submissions. Accepts simultaneous submissions. "Our response time goals are 6 weeks for queries and 12 weeks on requested partials and fulls."

THE BOOK GROUP
20 W. 20th St., Suite 601, New York NY 10011. (212)803-3360. **E-mail:** submissions@thebookgroup.com. **Website:** www.thebookgroup.com. Estab. 2015. Member of AAR. Signatory of WGA.

MEMBER AGENTS Julie Barer; Faye Bender; Brettne Bloom (fiction: literary and commercial fiction, select young adult; nonfiction, including cookbooks, lifestyle, investigative journalism, history, biography, memoir, and psychology); Elisabeth Weed (upmarket fiction, especially plot-driven novels with a sense of place); Rebecca Stead (innovative forms, diverse voices, and open-hearted fiction for children, young adults, and adults); Dana Murphy (story-driven fiction with a strong sense of place, narrative nonfiction/essays with a pop-culture lean, and YA with an honest voice).

REPRESENTS **Considers these nonfiction areas:** biography, cooking, history, investigative, memoirs, psychology. **Considers these fiction areas:** commercial, literary, mainstream, women's, young adult.

HOW TO CONTACT Send a query letter and 10 sample pages to submissions@thebookgroup.com, with the first and last name of the agent you are querying in the subject line. All material must be in the body of the e-mail, as the agents do not open attachments. "If we are interested in reading more, we will get in touch with you as soon as possible." Accepts simultaneous submissions.

BRADFORD LITERARY AGENCY

5694 Mission Center Rd., #347, San Diego CA 92108. (619)521-1201. **E-mail:** queries@bradfordlit.com. **Website:** www.bradfordlit.com. **Contact:** Laura Bradford, Natalie Lakosil, Sarah LaPolla, Monica Odom. Estab. 2001. Member of AAR. RWA, SCBWI, ALA Represents 130 clients.

MEMBER AGENTS Laura Bradford (romance [historical, romantic suspense, paranormal, category, contemporary, erotic], mystery, women's fiction, thrillers/suspense, middle grade & YA); Natalie Lakosil (children's literature [from picture book through teen and New Adult], romance [contemporary and historical], cozy mystery/crime, upmarket women's/general fiction and select children's nonfiction); Sarah LaPolla (YA, middle grade, literary fiction, science fiction, magical realism, dark/psychological mystery, literary horror, and upmarket contemporary fiction); Monica Odom (nonfiction by authors with demonstrable platforms in the areas of: pop culture, illustrated/graphic design, food and cooking, humor, history and social issues; narrative nonfiction, memoir, literary fiction, upmarket commercial fiction, compelling speculative fiction and magic realism, historical fiction, alternative histories, dark and edgy fiction, literary psychological thrillers, and illustrated/picture books).

REPRESENTS Nonfiction, fiction, novels, juvenile books. **Considers these nonfiction areas:** biography, cooking, creative nonfiction, cultural interests, foods, history, humor, juvenile nonfiction, memoirs, parenting, popular culture, politics, self-help, women's issues, women's studies, young adult. **Considers these fiction areas:** commercial, crime, ethnic, gay, historical, juvenile, lesbian, literary, mainstream, middle grade, multicultural, mystery, new adult, paranormal, picture books, romance, science fiction, thriller, women's, young adult.

HOW TO CONTACT Accepts e-mail queries only; For submissions to Laura Bradford or Natalie Lakosil, send to queries@bradfordlit.com. For submissions to Sarah LaPolla, send to sarah@bradfordlit.com. For submissions to Monica Odom, send to Monica@bradfordlit.com. The entire submission must appear in the body of the e-mail and not as an attachment. The subject line should begin as follows: "QUERY: (the title of the ms or any short message that is important should follow)." For fiction: e-mail a query letter along with the first chapter of ms and a synopsis. Include the genre and word count in your query letter. Nonfiction: e-mail full nonfiction proposal including a query letter and a sample chapter. Accepts simultaneous submissions. Responds in 4 weeks to queries; 10 weeks to mss. Obtains most new clients through queries.

TERMS Agent receives 15% commission on domestic sales; 25% commission on foreign sales. Offers written contract. Charges for extra copies of books for foreign submissions.

BRANDT & HOCHMAN LITERARY AGENTS, INC.

1501 Broadway, Suite 2310, New York NY 10036. (212)840-5760. **Fax:** (212)840-5776. **Website:** brandthochman.com. **Contact:** Gail Hochman. Member of AAR. Represents 200 clients.

MEMBER AGENTS Gail Hochman (works of literary fiction, idea-driven nonfiction, literary memoir and children's books); Marianne Merola (fiction, nonfiction and children's books with strong and unique narrative voices); Bill Contardi (voice-driven young adult and middle grade fiction, commercial thrillers, psychological suspense, quirky mysteries, high fantasy, commercial fiction and memoir); Emily Forland (voice-driven literary fiction and nonfiction, memoir, narrative nonfiction, history, biography, food writing, cultural criticism, graphic novels, and young adult fiction); Emma Patterson (fiction from dark, literary novels to upmarket women's and historical fiction; narrative nonfiction that includes memoir, investigative journalism, and popular history; young adult fiction); Jody Kahn (literary and upmarket fiction; narrative nonfiction, particularly books related to sports, food, history, science and pop culture—including cookbooks, and literary memoir and journalism); Henry Thayer (nonfiction on a wide variety of subjects and fiction that inclines toward the literary). The e-mail addresses and specific likes of each of these agents is listed on the agency website.

REPRESENTS Nonfiction, novels. **Considers these nonfiction areas:** biography, cooking, current affairs, foods, health, history, memoirs, music, popular culture, science, sports, narrative nonfiction, journalism. **Considers these fiction areas:** fantasy, historical, literary, middle grade, mystery, suspense, thriller, women's, young adult.

HOW TO CONTACT "We accept queries by e-mail and regular mail; however, we cannot guarantee a response to e-mailed queries. For queries via regular mail, be sure to include a SASE for our reply. Query letters should be no more than 2 pages and should include a convincing overview of the book project and information about the author and his or her writing credits. Address queries to the specific Brandt & Hochman agent whom you would like to consider your work. Agent e-mail addresses and query preferences may be found at the end of each agent profile on the 'Agents' page of our website." Accepts simultaneous submissions. Obtains most new clients through recommendations from others.

TERMS Agent receives 15% commission on domestic sales; 20% commission on foreign sales.

THE BRATTLE AGENCY

P.O. Box 380537, Cambridge MA 02238. (617)721-5375. **E-mail:** christopher.vyce@thebrattleagency.com. **E-mail:** submissions@thebrattleagency.com. **Website:** thebrattleagency.com. **Contact:** Christopher Vyce. Member of AAR. Signatory of WGA.

REPRESENTS Nonfiction, fiction. **Considers these nonfiction areas:** art, biography, cultural interests, history, literature, popular culture, politics, sports, race studies, American studies. **Considers these fiction areas:** literary, graphic novels.

HOW TO CONTACT Query by e-mail. Include cover letter, brief synopsis, brief CV. Accepts simultaneous submissions. Responds to queries in 72 hours. Responds to approved submissions in 6-8 weeks.

BARBARA BRAUN ASSOCIATES, INC.

7 E. 14th St., #19F, New York NY 10003. **Fax:** (212)604-9023. **E-mail:** bbasubmissions@gmail.com. **Website:** www.barbarabraunagency.com. **Contact:** Barbara Braun. Member of AAR.

REPRESENTS Nonfiction, novels. **Considers these nonfiction areas:** architecture, art, biography, design, film, history, photography, politics, psychology, women's issues, social issues, cultural criticism, fashion, narrative nonfiction. **Considers these fiction areas:** commercial, historical, literary, multicultural, mystery, thriller, women's, young adult, Art-related fiction.

HOW TO CONTACT "We no longer accept submissions by regular mail. Please send all queries via e-mail, marked 'Query' in the subject line. Your query should include: a brief summary of your book, word count, genre, any relevant publishing experience, and the first 5 pages of your manuscript pasted into the body of the e-mail. (No attachments—we will not open these.)" Accepts simultaneous submissions.

TERMS Agent receives 15% commission on domestic sales; 20% commission on foreign sales. No reading fees.

CURTIS BROWN, LTD.

10 Astor Place, New York NY 10003. (212)473-5400. **Fax:** (212)598-0917. **Website:** www.curtisbrown.com. Member of AAR. Signatory of WGA.

MEMBER AGENTS Noah Ballard (literary debuts, upmarket thrillers, narrative nonfiction, always looking for honest and provocative new writers); Tess Callero (young adult, upmarket commercial women's fiction, mysteries/ thrillers, romance, nonfiction: pop culture, business, cookbooks, humor, biography, self-help, and food narrative projects); Ginger Clark (science fiction, fantasy, paranormal romance, literary horror, and young adult and middle grade fiction); Kerry D'Agostino (literary and commercial fiction, as well as narrative nonfiction and memoir); Katherine Fausset (literary fiction, upmarket commercial fiction, journalism, memoir, popular science, and narrative nonfiction); Holly Frederick; Peter Ginsberg, president; Elizabeth Harding, vice president (represents authors and illustrators of juvenile, middle-grade and young adult fiction); Ginger Knowlton, executive vice president (authors and illustrators of children's books in all genres—picture book, middle grade, young adult fiction and nonfiction); Timothy Knowlton, CEO; Jonathan Lyons (biographies, history, science, pop culture, sports, general narrative nonfiction, mysteries, thrillers, science fiction and fantasy, and young adult fiction); Sarah Perillo (middle grade fiction and commercial fiction for adults, nonfiction:history, politics, science, pop culture, and humor, and is especially fond of anything involving animals or food); Laura Blake Peterson, vice president (memoir and biography, natural history, literary fiction, mystery, suspense, women's fiction, health and fitness, children's and young adult, faith issues and popular culture); Steven Salpeter (literary fiction, fantasy, graphic novels, historical fiction, mysteries, thrillers, young adult, narrative nonfiction, gift books, history, humor, and popular science); Maureen Walters, senior vice president (working primarily in women's fiction and nonfiction projects on subjects as eclectic as parenting & child care, popular psychology, inspirational/motivational volumes as well as a few medical/nutritional books); Mitchell Waters (literary and commercial fiction and nonfiction, including mystery, history, biography, memoir, young adult, cookbooks, self-help and popular culture); Monika Woods (plot-driven literary novels, non-fiction that is creatively critical, unique perspectives, a great cookbook, and above all, original prose).

REPRESENTS Nonfiction, fiction, novels, short story collections, juvenile books. **Considers these nonfiction areas:** biography, computers, cooking, current affairs, ethnic, health, history, humor, juvenile nonfiction, memoirs, popular culture, psychology, religious, science, self-help, spirituality, sports. **Considers these fiction areas:** fantasy, horror, humor, juvenile, literary, mainstream, middle grade, mystery, paranormal, picture books, religious, romance, spiritual, sports, suspense, thriller, women's, young adult.

HOW TO CONTACT Please refer to the "Agents" page on the website for each agent's submission guidelines. Accepts simultaneous submissions. Responds in 3 weeks to queries; 5 weeks to mss. Obtains most new clients through recommendations from others, solicitations, conferences.

TERMS Agent receives 15% commission on domestic sales; 20% on foreign sales. Offers written contract. 75-day notice must be given to terminate contract. Charges for some postage (overseas, etc.).

BROWNE & MILLER LITERARY ASSOCIATES

52 Village Place, Hinsdale IL 60521. (312) 922-3063. **E-mail:** mail@browneandmiller.com. **Website:** www.browneandmiller.com. **Contact:** Danielle Egan-Miller, president. Estab. 1971. Member of AAR. RWA, MWA, Authors Guild.

REPRESENTS Nonfiction, fiction, novels. **Considers these fiction areas:** commercial, crime, detective, erotica, family saga, historical, inspirational, literary, mainstream, mystery, police, religious, romance, suspense, thriller, women's, Christian/inspirational fiction.

HOW TO CONTACT Query via e-mail only; no attachments. Do not send unsolicited mss. Accepts simultaneous submissions.

ANDREA BROWN LITERARY AGENCY, INC.

E-mail: andrea@andreabrownlit.com; caryn@andreabrownlit.com; lauraqueries@gmail.com; jennifer@andreabrownlit.com; kelly@andreabrownlit.com; jennL@andreabrownlit.com; jamie@andreabrownlit.com; jmatt@andreabrownlit.com; kathleen@andre-abrownlit.com; lara@andreabrownlit.com; soloway@andreabrownlit.com. **Website:** www.andreabrownlit.com. Member of AAR.

MEMBER AGENTS Andrea Brown (president); Laura Rennert (executive agent); Caryn Wiseman (senior agent); Jennifer Laughran (senior agent); Jennifer Rofé (senior agent); Kelly Sonnack (senior agent); Jamie Weiss Chilton (senior agent); Jennifer Mattson (agent); Kathleen Rushall (agent); Lara Perkins (associate agent, digital manager); Jennifer March Soloway (associate agent).

REPRESENTS Juvenile books. **Considers these nonfiction areas:** juvenile nonfiction, young adult, narrative. **Considers these fiction areas:** juvenile, middle grade, picture books, young adult, middle-grade, all juvenile genres..

HOW TO CONTACT For picture books, submit a query letter and complete ms in the body of the e-mail. For fiction, submit a query letter and the first 10 pages in the body of the e-mail. For nonfiction, submit proposal, first 10 pages in the body of the e-mail. Illustrators: submit a query letter and 2-3 illustration samples (in jpeg format), link to online portfolio, and text of picture book, if applicable. "We only accept queries via e-mail. No attachments, with the exception of jpeg illustrations from illustrators." Visit the agents' bios on our website and choose only one agent to whom you will submit your e-query. Send a short e-mail query letter to that agent with "QUERY" in the subject field. Accepts simultaneous submissions. "If we are interested in your work, we will certainly follow up by e-mail or by phone. However, if you haven't heard from us within 6 to 8 weeks, please assume that we are passing on your project." Obtains most new clients through referrals from editors, clients and agents. Check website for guidelines and information.

TERMS Agent receives 15% commission on domestic sales; 25% commission on foreign sales. Offers written contract.

SHEREE BYKOFSKY ASSOCIATES, INC.

P.O. Box 706, Brigantine NJ 08203. **E-mail:** shereebee@aol.com. **Website:** www.shereebee.com. **Contact:** Sheree Bykofsky. Estab. 1991. Member of AAR. Author's Guild, Atlantic City Chamber of Commerce, PRC Council Represents 1,000+ clients.

MEMBER AGENTS Sheree Bykofsky, Janet Rosen.

REPRESENTS Nonfiction, novels, scholarly books. **Considers these nonfiction areas:** Americana, animals, anthropology, architecture, art, autobiography, biography, business, child guidance, cooking, crafts, creative nonfiction, cultural interests, current affairs, dance, decorating, diet/nutrition, design, economics, education, environment, ethnic, film, foods, gardening, gay/lesbian, government, health, history, hobbies, how-to, humor, inspirational, language, law, literature, medicine, memoirs, metaphysics, military, money, multicultural, music, New Age, parenting, philosophy, photography, popular culture, politics, psychology, recreation, regional, religious, science, self-help, sex, sociology, software, spirituality, sports, technology, theater, translation, travel, true crime, war, women's issues, creative nonfiction. **Considers these fiction areas:** commercial, contemporary issues, crime, detective, literary, mainstream, mystery, women's. **Considers these script areas:** , Dramatic rights represented by Joel Gotler..

HOW TO CONTACT Query via e-mail to submitbee@aol.com. "We only accept e-queries. We respond only to those queries in which we are interested. No attachments, snail mail, or phone calls, please. We do not open attachments." Fiction: one-page query, one-page synopsis, and first three pages of ms in body of the e-mail. Nonfiction: one-page query in the body of the e-mail. Currently we are focusing much more on our nonfiction portfolio. Accepts simultaneous submissions. Responds in 1 month to requested mss. Obtains most new clients through referrals but still reads all submissions closely.

TERMS Agent receives 15% commission on domestic sales. Agent receives 15% commission on foreign sales, plus international co-agent receives another 10%. Offers written contract, binding for 1 year. Charges for international postage.

KIMBERLEY CAMERON & ASSOCIATES

1550 Tiburon Blvd., #704, Tiburon CA 94920. (415)789-9191. **Website:** www.kimberleycameron. com. **Contact:** Kimberley Cameron. Member of AAR. Signatory of WGA.

MEMBER AGENTS Kimberley Cameron; Elizabeth Kracht (temporarily closed to submissions); Amy Cloughley (literary and upmarket fiction, women's, historical, narrative nonfiction, travel or adventure memoir); Mary C. Moore (fantasy, science fiction, upmarket "book club," genre romance, thrillers with female protagonists, and stories from marginalized voices); Lisa Abellera (currently closed to unsolicited

submissions); Douglas Lee, douglas@kimberlycameron.com (only accepting submissions via conference and in-person meetings in the Bay Area); Dorian Maffei (only open to submissions requested through Twitter pitch parties, conferences, or #MSWL).

REPRESENTS **Considers these nonfiction areas:** animals, environment, health, memoirs, science, spirituality, travel, true crime, narrative non-fiction. **Considers these fiction areas:** commercial, fantasy, historical, literary, mystery, romance, science fiction, thriller, women's, young adult, LGBTQ.

HOW TO CONTACT Prefers queries via site. Only query one agent at a time. For fiction, fill out the correct submissions form for the individual agent and attach the first 50 pages and a synopsis (if requested) as a Word doc or PDF. For nonfiction, fill out the correct submission form of the individual agent and attach a full book proposal and sample chapters (includes the first chapter and no more than 50 pages) as a Word doc or PDF. Accepts simultaneous submissions. Obtains new clients through recommendations from others, solicitations.

CYNTHIA CANNELL LITERARY AGENCY

54 W. 40th St., New York NY 10018. (212)396-9595. **Website:** www.cannellagency.com. **Contact:** Cynthia Cannell. Estab. 1997. Member of AAR. Women's Media Group and the Authors Guild

REPRESENTS Nonfiction, fiction. **Considers these nonfiction areas:** biography, current affairs, memoirs, self-help, spirituality.

HOW TO CONTACT "Please query us with an e-mail or letter. If querying by e-mail, send a brief description of your project with relevant biographical information including publishing credits (if any) to info@cannellagency.com. Do not send attachments. If querying by conventional mail, enclose an SASE." Responds if interested. Accepts simultaneous submissions.

CAPITAL TALENT AGENCY

1330 Connecticut Ave. NW, Suite 271, Washington DC 20036. (202)429-4785. **Fax:** (202)429-4786. **E-mail:** literary.submissions@capitaltalentagency.com. **Website:** capitaltalentagency.com/html/literary.shtml. **Contact:** Cynthia Kane. Estab. 2014. Member of AAR. Signatory of WGA.

MEMBER AGENTS Cynthia Kane; Roger Yoerges; Michelle Muntifering; J. Fred Shiffman.

REPRESENTS Nonfiction, fiction, movie scripts, stage plays.

HOW TO CONTACT "We accept submissions only by e-mail. We do not accept queries via postal mail or fax. For fiction and nonfiction submissions, send a query letter in the body of your e-mail. Please note that while we consider each query seriously, we are unable to respond to all of them. We endeavor to respond within 6 weeks to projects that interest us." Accepts simultaneous submissions. 6 weeks

MARIA CARVAINIS AGENCY, INC.

Rockefeller Center, 1270 Avenue of the Americas, Suite 2915, New York NY 10020. (212)245-6365. **Fax:** (212)245-7196. **E-mail:** mca@mariacarvainisagency. com. **E-mail:** mca@mariacarvainisagency.com. **Website:** www.mariacarvainisagency.com. Estab. 1977. Member of AAR. Authors Guild, Women's Media Group, ABA, MWA, RWA Represents 75 clients.

MEMBER AGENTS Maria Carvainis, president/literary agent; Elizabeth Copps, associate agent.

REPRESENTS Nonfiction, novels. **Considers these nonfiction areas:** biography, business, history, memoirs, popular culture, psychology, science. **Considers these fiction areas:** action, adventure, commercial, contemporary issues, crime, family saga, historical, horror, humor, juvenile, literary, mainstream, middle grade, multicultural, mystery, romance, suspense, thriller, women's, young adult.

HOW TO CONTACT If you would like to query the agency, please send a query letter, a synopsis of the work, first 5-10 pages, and note of any writing credentials. Please e-mail queries to mca@mariacarvainisagency.com. All attachments must be either Word documents or PDF files. The agency also accepts queries by mail to Maria Carvainis Agency, Inc., Attention: Query Department. If you want the materials returned to you, please enclose a SASE. Otherwise, please be sure to include your e-mail address. There is no reading fee. Accepts simultaneous submissions. Responds to queries within 1 month. Obtains most new clients through recommendations from others, conferences, query letters.

TERMS Agent receives 15% commission on domestic sales. Agent receives 20% commission on foreign sales. Offers written contract. Charges clients for foreign postage.

CHALBERG & SUSSMAN

115 W. 29th St., Third Floor, New York NY 10001. (917)261-7550. **Website:** www.chalbergsussman.com. Member of AAR. Signatory of WGA.

MEMBER AGENTS Terra Chalberg; Rachel Sussman (narrative journalism, memoir, psychology, history, humor, pop culture, literary fiction); Nicole James (plot-driven fiction, psychological suspense, uplifting female-driven memoir, upmarket self-help, and lifestyle books); Lana Popovic (young adult, middle grade, contemporary realism, speculative fiction, fantasy, horror, sophisticated erotica, romance, select nonfiction, international stories).

REPRESENTS Nonfiction, fiction, novels. **Considers these nonfiction areas:** history, humor, memoirs, popular culture, psychology, self-help, narrative journalism. **Considers these fiction areas:** erotica, fantasy, horror, literary, middle grade, romance, science fiction, suspense, young adult, contemporary realism, speculative fiction.

HOW TO CONTACT To query by e-mail, please contact one of the following: terra@chalbergsussman.com, rachel@chalbergsussman.com, nicole@chalbergsussman.com, lana@chalbergsussman.com. To query by regular mail, please address your letter to one agent and include SASE. Accepts simultaneous submissions.

CK WEBBER ASSOCIATES

E-mail: carlie@ckwebber.com. **Website:** ckwebber.com. **Contact:** Carlisle Webber. Member of AAR. Signatory of WGA.

REPRESENTS Novels, juvenile books. **Considers these fiction areas:** action, adventure, commercial, contemporary issues, crime, detective, family saga, fantasy, feminist, horror, literary, mainstream, middle grade, mystery, new adult, romance, science fiction, suspense, thriller, westerns, women's, young adult.

HOW TO CONTACT Accepts queries via e-mail only. To submit your work for consideration, please send a query letter, synopsis, and the first 30 pages or 3 chapters of your work, whichever is more, to carlie@ckwebber.com and put the word "query" in the subject line of your e-mail. Please include your materials in the body of your e-mail. Blank emails that include an attachment will be deleted unread. Accepts simultaneous submissions.

WM CLARK ASSOCIATES

54 W. 21st St., Suite 809, New York NY 10010. (212)675-2784. **E-mail:** general@wmclark.com. **Website:** www.wmclark.com. **Contact:** William Clark. Estab. 1997. Member of AAR.

REPRESENTS Nonfiction, novels. **Considers these nonfiction areas:** architecture, art, autobiography, biography, creative nonfiction, cultural interests, current affairs, dance, design, economics, ethnic, film, foods, history, inspirational, interior design, literature, memoirs, music, popular culture, politics, religious, science, sociology, technology, theater, translation, travel. **Considers these fiction areas:** historical, literary.

HOW TO CONTACT Accepts queries via online query form only. "We will endeavor to respond as soon as possible as to whether or not we'd like to see a proposal or sample chapters from your manuscript." Responds in 1-2 months to queries.

TERMS Agent receives 15% commission on domestic sales; 20% commission on foreign sales. Offers written contract.

FRANCES COLLIN, LITERARY AGENT

P.O. Box 33, Wayne PA 19087-0033. **E-mail:** queries@francescollin.com. **Website:** www.francescollin.com. Estab. 1948. Member of AAR. Represents 50 clients.

MEMBER AGENTS Frances Collin; Sarah Yake.

REPRESENTS Nonfiction, fiction, novels. **Considers these nonfiction areas:** architecture, art, autobiography, biography, creative nonfiction, cultural interests, dance, environment, history, literature, memoirs, popular culture, science, sociology, travel, women's issues, women's studies. **Considers these fiction areas:** adventure, commercial, experimental, feminist, historical, juvenile, literary, middle grade, multicultural, science fiction, women's, young adult.

HOW TO CONTACT "We ask that writers send a traditional query e-mail describing the project and copy and paste the first 5 pages of the manuscript into the body of the e-mail. We look forward to hearing from you at queries@francescollin.com. Please send queries to that e-mail address. Any queries sent to another e-mail address within the agency will be deleted unread." Accepts simultaneous submissions. Responds in 1-4 weeks for initial queries, longer for full mss.

DON CONGDON ASSOCIATES INC.

110 William St., Suite 2202, New York NY 10038. (212)645-1229. **Fax:** (212)727-2688. **E-mail:** dca@doncongdon.com. **Website:** doncongdon.com. Estab. 1983. Member of AAR.

MEMBER AGENTS Cristina Concepcion (crime fiction, narrative nonfiction, political science, journalism, history, books on cities, classical music, biography, science for a popular audience, philosophy, food and wine, iconoclastic books on health and human relationships, essays, and arts criticism); Michael Congdon (commercial and literary fiction, suspense, mystery, thriller, history, military history, biography, memoir, current affairs, and narrative nonfiction [adventure, medicine, science, and nature]); Katie Grimm (literary fiction, historical, women's fiction, short story collections, graphic novels, mysteries, young adult, middle-grade, memoir, science, academic); Katie Kotchman (business [all areas], narrative nonfiction [particularly popular science and social/cultural issues], self-help, success, motivation, psychology, pop culture, women's fiction, realistic young adult, literary fiction, and psychological thrillers); Maura Kye-Casella (narrative nonfiction, cookbooks, women's fiction, young adult, self-help, and parenting); Susan Ramer (literary fiction, upmarket commercial fiction [contemporary and historical], narrative nonfiction, social history, cultural history, smart pop culture [music, film, food, art], women's issues, psychology and mental health, and memoir).

REPRESENTS Nonfiction, novels, short story collections. **Considers these nonfiction areas:** art, biography, business, cooking, creative nonfiction, cultural interests, current affairs, film, foods, history, humor, literature, medicine, memoirs, military, multicultural, music, parenting, philosophy, popular culture, politics, psychology, science, self-help, sociology, sports, women's issues, young adult. **Considers these fiction areas:** crime, hi-lo, historical, literary, middle grade, mystery, short story collections, suspense, thriller, women's, young adult.

HOW TO CONTACT "For queries via e-mail, you must include the word 'query' and the agent's full name in your subject heading. Please also include your query and sample chapter in the body of the e-mail, as we do not open attachments for security reasons. Please query only one agent within the agency at a time. If you are sending your query via regular mail, please enclose a SASE for our reply. If you would like us to return your materials, please make sure your postage will cover their return." Accepts simultaneous submissions.

CREATIVE MEDIA AGENCY, INC.

(212)812-1494. **E-mail:** paige@cmalit.com. **Website:** www.cmalit.com. **Contact:** Paige Wheeler. Estab. 1997. Member of AAR. WMG, RWA, MWA, Authors Guild. Represents about 30 clients.

REPRESENTS Nonfiction, fiction, novels. **Considers these nonfiction areas:** biography, business, creative nonfiction, diet/nutrition, health, inspirational, memoirs, money, parenting, popular culture, self-help, travel, women's issues, prescriptive nonfiction, narrative nonfiction. **Considers these fiction areas:** commercial, crime, detective, historical, inspirational, mainstream, middle grade, mystery, new adult, romance, suspense, thriller, women's, young adult, general fiction.

HOW TO CONTACT E-query. Write "query" in your e-mail subject line. For fiction, paste in the first 5 pages of the ms after the query. For nonfiction, paste in an extended author bio as well as the marketing section of your book proposal after the query. Accepts simultaneous submissions. Responds in 4-6 weeks.

LAURA DAIL LITERARY AGENCY, INC.

121 W. 27th St., Suite 1201, New York NY 10001. (212)239-7477. **E-mail:** literary@ldlainc.com. **E-mail:** queries@ldlainc.com. **Website:** www.ldlainc.com. Member of AAR.

MEMBER AGENTS Laura Dail; Tamar Rydzinski; Elana Roth Parker.

REPRESENTS Nonfiction, fiction, novels, juvenile books. **Considers these nonfiction areas:** biography, cooking, creative nonfiction, current affairs, government, history, investigative, juvenile nonfiction, memoirs, multicultural, popular culture, politics, psychology, sociology, true crime, war, women's studies, young adult. **Considers these fiction areas:** commercial, contemporary issues, crime, detective, ethnic, fantasy, feminist, gay, historical, juvenile, lesbian, mainstream, middle grade, multicultural, mystery, picture books, thriller, women's, young adult.

HOW TO CONTACT "If you would like, you may include a synopsis and no more than 10 pages. If you are mailing your query, please be sure to include a self-addressed, stamped envelope; without it, you may not hear back from us. To save money, time and trees, we prefer queries by e-mail to queries@ldlainc.com. We get a lot of spam and are wary of computer viruses, so please use the word 'Query' in the subject line and include your detailed materials in the body of your message, not as an attachment." Accepts simultaneous submissions. Responds in 2-4 weeks.

DARHANSOFF & VERRILL LITERARY AGENTS

133 W. 72nd St., Room 304, New York NY 10023. (917)305-1300. **E-mail:** submissions@dvagency.com. **Website:** www.dvagency.com. Member of AAR.

MEMBER AGENTS Liz Darhansoff; Chuck Verrill; Michele Mortimer; Eric Amling.

REPRESENTS Nonfiction, novels. **Considers these nonfiction areas:** creative nonfiction, juvenile nonfiction, memoirs, young adult. **Considers these fiction areas:** literary, middle grade, suspense, young adult.

HOW TO CONTACT Send queries via e-mail. Accepts simultaneous submissions.

RECENT SALES A full list of clients is available on their website.

LIZA DAWSON ASSOCIATES

121 W. 27th St., Suite 1201, New York NY 10001. (212)465-9071. **Website:** www.lizadawsonassociates.com. **Contact:** Caitie Flum. Member of AAR. MWA, Women's Media Group. Represents 50+ clients.

MEMBER AGENTS Liza Dawson, queryliza@lizadawsonassociates.com (plot-driven literary and popular fiction, historical, thrillers, suspense, history, psychology [both popular and clinical], politics, narrative nonfiction, and memoirs); Caitlin Blasdell, querycaitlin@lizadawsonassociates.com (science fiction, fantasy [both adult and young adult], parenting, business, thrillers, and women's fiction); Hannah Bowman, queryhannah@lizadawsonassociates.com (commercial fiction [especially science fiction and fantasy, young adult] and nonfiction in the areas of mathematics, science, and spirituality); Monica Odom, querymonica@lizadawsonassociates.com (nonfiction in the areas of Social Studies, including topics of: identity, race, gender, sexual orientation, socioeconomics, civil rights and social justice, advice/relationships, self-help/self-reflection, how-to, crafting/creativity, food and cooking, humor, pop culture, lifestyle, fashion & beauty, biography, memoir, narrative, business, politics and current affairs, history, science and literary fiction and upmarket fiction, Illustrators with demonstrable platforms, preferably author/illustrators, working on nonfiction, graphic memoirs or graphic novels); Caitie Flum, querycaitie@lizadawsonassociates.com (commercial fiction, especially historical, women's fiction, mysteries, crossover fantasy, young adult, and middle-grade; nonfiction in the areas of theater, current affairs, and pop culture).

REPRESENTS Nonfiction, novels. **Considers these nonfiction areas:** agriculture, Americana, animals, anthropology, archeology, architecture, art, autobiography, biography, business, computers, cooking, creative nonfiction, cultural interests, current affairs, environment, ethnic, film, gardening, gay/lesbian, history, humor, investigative, juvenile nonfiction, memoirs, multicultural, parenting, popular culture, politics, psychology, religious, science, sex, sociology, spirituality, theater, travel, true crime, women's issues, women's studies, young adult. **Considers these fiction areas:** action, adventure, commercial, contemporary issues, crime, detective, ethnic, family saga, fantasy, feminist, gay, historical, horror, humor, juvenile, lesbian, mainstream, middle grade, multicultural, mystery, new adult, police, romance, science fiction, supernatural, suspense, thriller, urban fantasy, women's, young adult.

HOW TO CONTACT Query by e-mail only. No phone calls. Each of these agents has their own specific submission requirements, which you can find online at the agency's website. Obtains most new clients through recommendations from others, conferences, and queries.

TERMS Agent receives 15% commission on domestic sales; 20% commission on foreign sales. Offers written contract.

DEFIORE AND COMPANY

47 E. 19th St., 3rd Floor, New York NY 10003. (212) 925-7744. **E-mail:** submissions@defliterary.com. **Website:** www.defliterary.com. Member of AAR. Represents 40 clients.

MEMBER AGENTS Brian DeFiore; Meredith Kafel; Laurie Abkemeier; Adam Schear; Ashley Collom; Matthew Elblonk; Caryn Karmatz Rudy; Rebecca Strauss; Lisa Gallagher; Nicole Tourtelot; Linda Kaplan; Miriam Altshuler; Reiko Davis; Gabrielle Piraino.

REPRESENTS Novels, short story collections. **Considers these nonfiction areas:** creative nonfiction, how-to, literature, memoirs, multicultural, parenting, psychology, self-help, spirituality, women's

issues, young adult. **Considers these fiction areas:** commercial, family saga, historical, literary, middle grade, short story collections, women's, young adult.

HOW TO CONTACT Please send an email to her at querymiriam@defliterary.com. Miriam only accepts email queries. Include the following: A brief description of your book, a brief, relevant bio, the first chapter pasted in the body of your email. Attachments will not be opened. "I also really want to know what you feel the heart of your book is, in one or two sentences." Accepts simultaneous submissions. Obtains most new clients through recommendations from others.

TERMS Agent receives 15% commission on domestic sales; 20% commission on foreign sales. Charges clients for overseas mailing, photocopies, overnight mail when requested by author.

JOELLE DELBOURGO ASSOCIATES, INC.

101 Park St., Montclair NJ 07042. (973)773-0836. **E-mail:** joelle@delbourgo.com. **E-mail:** submissions@delbourgo.com. **Website:** www.delbourgo.com. **Contact:** Joelle Delbourgo. Estab. 1999. Member of AAR. Represents more than 500 clients.

MEMBER AGENTS Joelle Delbourgo; Jacqueline Flynn.

REPRESENTS Nonfiction, fiction, novels. **Considers these nonfiction areas:** Americana, animals, anthropology, archeology, autobiography, biography, business, child guidance, cooking, creative nonfiction, current affairs, dance, decorating, diet/nutrition, design, economics, education, environment, film, gardening, gay/lesbian, government, health, history, how-to, humor, inspirational, interior design, investigative, juvenile nonfiction, literature, medicine, memoirs, military, money, multicultural, music, parenting, philosophy, popular culture, politics, psychology, science, self-help, sex, sociology, spirituality, sports, translation, travel, true crime, war, women's issues, women's studies. **Considers these fiction areas:** adventure, commercial, contemporary issues, crime, detective, fantasy, feminist, juvenile, literary, mainstream, middle grade, military, mystery, new adult, New Age, romance, science fiction, thriller, urban fantasy, women's, young adult.

HOW TO CONTACT It's preferable if you submit via e-mail to a specific agent. Query 1 agent only. No attachments. Put the word "Query" in the subject line. "While we do our best to respond to each query, if you have not received a response in 60 days you may consider that a pass. Please do not send us copies of self-published books unless requested. Let us know if you are sending your query to us exclusively or if this is a multiple submission. For nonfiction, let us know if a proposal and sample chapters are available; if not, you should probably wait to send your query when you have a completed proposal. For fiction and memoir, embed the *first* 10 pages of manuscript into the e-mail after your query letter. Please no attachments. If we like your first pages, we may ask to see your synopsis and more manuscript. Please do not cold call us or make a follow-up call unless we call you." Accepts simultaneous submissions.

TERMS Agent receives 15% commission on domestic sales and 20% commission on foreign sales as well as television/film adaptation when a co-agent is involved. Offers written contract. Charges clients for postage and photocopying.

SANDRA DIJKSTRA LITERARY AGENCY

1155 Camino del Mar, PMB 515, Del Mar CA 92014. **E-mail:** queries@dijkstraagency.com. **Website:** www.dijkstraagency.com. Member of AAR. Authors Guild, Organization of American Historians, RWA. Represents 200+ clients.

MEMBER AGENTS President: Sandra Dijkstra (adult only). Acquiring Associate agents: Elise Capron (adult only); Jill Marr (adult only); Thao Le (adult and YA); Roz Foster (adult and YA); Jessica Watterson (subgenres of adult romance, and women's fiction); Suzy Evans (adult and YA); Jennifer Kim (adult and YA).

REPRESENTS Nonfiction, fiction, novels, short story collections, juvenile books, scholarly books. **Considers these nonfiction areas:** Americana, animals, anthropology, art, biography, business, creative nonfiction, cultural interests, current affairs, design, economics, environment, ethnic, gardening, government, health, history, juvenile nonfiction, literature, memoirs, multicultural, parenting, popular culture, politics, psychology, science, self-help, sports, true crime, women's issues, women's studies, young adult, narrative. **Considers these fiction areas:** commercial, contemporary issues, detective, family saga, fantasy, feminist, historical, horror, juvenile, literary, mainstream, middle grade, multicultural, mystery, new adult, romance, science fiction, short story collections, sports, suspense, thriller, urban fantasy, women's, young adult.

HOW TO CONTACT "Please see guidelines on our website, www.dijkstraagency.com. Please note that we only accept e-mail submissions. Due to the large number of unsolicited submissions we receive, we are only able to respond those submissions in which we are interested." Accepts simultaneous submissions. Responds to queries of interest within 6 weeks.

TERMS Works in conjunction with foreign and film agents. Agent receives 15% commission on domestic sales and 20% commission on foreign sales. Offers written contract. No reading fee.

DUNHAM LITERARY, INC.

110 William St., Suite 2202, New York NY 10038. (212)929-0994. **E-mail:** query@dunhamlit.com. **Website:** www.dunhamlit.com. **Contact:** Jennie Dunham. Estab. 2000. Member of AAR. SCBWI Represents 50 clients.

MEMBER AGENTS Jennie Dunham, Bridget Smith, Leslie Zampetti.

REPRESENTS Nonfiction, fiction, novels, short story collections, juvenile books. **Considers these nonfiction areas:** anthropology, archeology, art, biography, creative nonfiction, cultural interests, environment, gay/lesbian, health, history, language, literature, medicine, memoirs, multicultural, parenting, popular culture, politics, psychology, science, sociology, technology, women's issues, women's studies, young adult. **Considers these fiction areas:** family saga, fantasy, feminist, gay, historical, humor, juvenile, lesbian, literary, mainstream, middle grade, multicultural, mystery, picture books, science fiction, short story collections, sports, urban fantasy, women's, young adult.

HOW TO CONTACT E-mail queries preferred, with all materials pasted in the body of the e-mail. Attachments will not be opened. Paper queries are also accepted. Please include a SASE for response and return of materials. Please include the first 5 pages with the query. Accepts simultaneous submissions. Responds in 4 weeks to queries; 2 months to mss. Obtains most new clients through recommendations from others, solicitations.

TERMS Agent receives 15% commission on domestic sales; 20% commission on foreign sales.

DUNOW, CARLSON, & LERNER AGENCY

27 W. 20th St., Suite 1107, New York NY 10011. (212)645-7606. **E-mail:** mail@dclagency.com. **Website:** www.dclagency.com. Member of AAR.

MEMBER AGENTS Jennifer Carlson (narrative nonfiction writers and journalists covering current events and ideas and cultural history, as well as literary and upmarket commercial novelists); Henry Dunow (quality fiction–literary, historical, strongly written commercial–and with voice-driven nonfiction across a range of areas–narrative history, biography, memoir, current affairs, cultural trends and criticism, science, sports); Erin Hosier (nonfiction: popular culture, music, sociology and memoir); Betsy Lerner (nonfiction writers in the areas of psychology, history, cultural studies, biography, current events, business; fiction: literary, dark, funny, voice driven); Yishai Seidman (broad range of fiction: literary, postmodern, and thrillers; nonfiction: sports, music, and pop culture); Amy Hughes (nonfiction in the areas of history, cultural studies, memoir, current events, wellness, health, food, pop culture, and biography; also literary fiction); Eleanor Jackson (literary, commercial, memoir, art, food, science and history); Julia Kenny (fiction—adult, middle grade and YA—and is especially interested in dark, literary thrillers and suspense); Edward Necarsulmer IV (strong new voices in teen & middle grade as well as picture books); Stacia Decker; Arielle Datz (fiction—adult, YA, or middle-grade—literary and commercial, nonfiction—essays, unconventional memoir, pop culture, and sociology).

REPRESENTS Nonfiction, fiction, novels, short story collections. **Considers these nonfiction areas:** art, biography, creative nonfiction, cultural interests, current affairs, foods, health history, memoirs, music, popular culture, psychology, science, sociology, sports. **Considers these fiction areas:** commercial, literary, mainstream, middle grade, mystery, picture books, thriller, young adult.

HOW TO CONTACT Query via snail mail with SASE, or by e-mail. E-mail preferred, paste 10 sample pages below query letter. No attachments. Will respond only if interested. Accepts simultaneous submissions. Responds in 4-6 weeks if interested.

DYSTEL, GODERICH & BOURRET LLC

1 Union Square W., Suite 904, New York NY 10003. (212)627-9100. **Fax:** (212)627-9313. **Website:** www.dystel.com. Estab. 1994. Member of AAR. Other membership includes SCBWI. Represents 600+ clients.

MEMBER AGENTS Jane Dystel; Miriam Goderich, miriam@dystel.com (literary and commercial fiction as well as some genre fiction, narrative nonfiction, pop culture, psychology, history, science, art, business books, and biography/memoir); Stacey Glick, sglick@dystel.com (adult narrative nonfiction including memoir, parenting, cooking and food, psychology, science, health and wellness, lifestyle, current events, pop culture, YA, middle grade, children's nonfiction, and select adult contemporary fiction); Michael Bourret, mbourret@dystel.com (middle grade and young adult fiction, commercial adult fiction, and all sorts of nonfiction, from practical to narrative; he's especially interested in food and cocktail related books, memoir, popular history, politics, religion (though not spirituality), popular science, and current events); Jim McCarthy, jmccarthy@dystel.com (literary women's fiction, underrepresented voices, mysteries, romance, paranormal fiction, narrative nonfiction, memoir, and paranormal nonfiction); Jessica Papin, jpapin@dystel.com (plot-driven literary and smart commercial fiction, and narrative non-fiction across a range of subjects, including history, medicine, science, economics and women's issues); Lauren Abramo, labramo@dystel.com (humorous middle grade and contemporary YA on the children's side, and upmarket commercial fiction and well-paced literary fiction on the adult side; adult narrative nonfiction, especially pop culture, psychology, pop science, reportage, media, and contemporary culture; in nonfiction, has a strong preference for interdisciplinary approaches, and in all categories she's especially interested in underrepresented voices); John Rudolph, jrudolph@dystel.com (picture book author/illustrators, middle grade, YA, select commercial fiction, and narrative nonfiction—especially in music, sports, history, popular science, "big think", performing arts, health, business, memoir, military history, and humor); Sharon Pelletier, spelletier@dystel.com (smart commercial fiction, from upmarket women's fiction to domestic suspense to literary thrillers, and strong contemporary romance novels; compelling nonfiction projects, especially feminism and religion); Michael Hoogland, mhoogland@dystel.com (thriller, SFF, YA, upmarket women's fiction, and narrative nonfiction); Erin Young, eyoung@dystel.com (YA/MG, literary and intellectual commercial thrillers, memoirs, biographies, sport and science narratives); Amy Bishop, abishop@dystel.com (commercial and literary women's fiction, fiction from diverse authors, historical fiction, YA, personal narratives, and biographies); Kemi

Faderin, kfaderin@dystel.com (smart, plot-driven YA, historical fiction/non-fiction, contemporary women's fiction, and literary fiction).

REPRESENTS Considers these nonfiction areas: animals, art, autobiography, biography, business, cooking, cultural interests, current affairs, ethnic, foods, gay/lesbian, health, history, humor, inspirational, investigative, medicine, memoirs, metaphysics, military, New Age, parenting, popular culture, politics, psychology, religious, science, sports, women's issues, women's studies. **Considers these fiction areas:** commercial, ethnic, gay, lesbian, literary, mainstream, middle grade, mystery, paranormal, romance, suspense, thriller, women's, young adult.

HOW TO CONTACT Query via e-mail and put "Query" in the subject line. "Synopses, outlines or sample chapters (say, one chapter or the first 25 pages of your manuscript) should either be included below the cover letter or attached as a separate document. We won't open attachments if they come with a blank e-mail." Accepts simultaneous submissions. Responds in 6 to 8 weeks to queries; within 8 weeks to mss. Obtains most new clients through recommendations from others, solicitations, conferences.

TERMS Agent receives 15% commission on domestic sales; 19% commission on foreign sales. Offers written contract.

EDEN STREET LITERARY

P.O. Box 30, Billings NY 12510. **E-mail:** info@edenstreetlit.com. **E-mail:** submissions@edenstreetlit.com. **Website:** www.edenstreetlit.com. **Contact:** Liza Voges. Member of AAR. Signatory of WGA. Represents over 40 clients.

REPRESENTS Nonfiction, fiction, novels, juvenile books. **Considers these fiction areas:** juvenile, middle grade, picture books, young adult.

HOW TO CONTACT E-mail a picture book ms or dummy; a synopsis and 3 chapters of a MG or YA novel; a proposal and 3 sample chapters for nonfiction. Accepts simultaneous submissions. Responds only to submissions of interest.

EINSTEIN LITERARY MANAGEMENT

27 W. 20th St., No. 1003, New York NY 10011. (212)221-8797. **E-mail:** info@einsteinliterary.com. **E-mail:** submissions@einsteinliterary.com.. **Website:** http://einsteinliterary.com. **Contact:** Susanna Einstein. Estab. 2015. Member of AAR. Signatory of WGA.

MEMBER AGENTS Susanna Einstein, Susan Graham, Shana Kelly.

REPRESENTS Nonfiction, fiction, novels, short story collections, juvenile books. **Considers these nonfiction areas:** cooking, creative nonfiction, memoirs, blog-to-book projects. **Considers these fiction areas:** comic books, commercial, crime, fantasy, historical, juvenile, literary, middle grade, mystery, picture books, romance, science fiction, suspense, thriller, women's, young adult.

HOW TO CONTACT Please submit a query letter and the first 10 double-spaced pages of your manuscript in the body of the e-mail (no attachments). Does not respond to mail queries or telephone queries or queries that are not specifically addressed to this agency. Accepts simultaneous submissions. Responds in 6 weeks if interested.

THE LISA EKUS GROUP, LLC

57 North St., Hatfield MA 01038. (413)247-9325. **Fax:** (413)247-9873. **E-mail:** info@lisaekus.com. **Website:** www.lisaekus.com. **Contact:** Sally Ekus. Estab. 1982. Member of AAR.

MEMBER AGENTS Lisa Ekus; Sally Ekus.

REPRESENTS Nonfiction. **Considers these nonfiction areas:** cooking, diet/nutrition, foods, health, how-to, humor, women's issues, occasionally health/well-being and women's issues; humor; lifestyle.

HOW TO CONTACT "For more information about our literary services, visit http://lisaekus.com/services/literary-agency. Submit a query via e-mail or through our contact form on the website. You can also submit complete hard copy proposal with title page, proposal contents, concept, bio, marketing, TOC, etc. Include SASE for the return of materials." Accepts simultaneous submissions. Responds in 4-6 weeks.

EMPIRE LITERARY

115 W. 29th St., 3rd Floor, New York NY 10001. (917)213-7082. **E-mail:** abarzvi@empireliterary.com. **E-mail:** queries@empireliterary.com. **Website:** www.empireliterary.com. Estab. 2013. Member of AAR. Signatory of WGA.

MEMBER AGENTS Andrea Barzvi; Carrie Howland; Kathleen Schmidt; Penny Moore.

REPRESENTS Nonfiction, novels. **Considers these nonfiction areas:** diet/nutrition, health, memoirs, popular culture. **Considers these fiction areas:** literary, middle grade, women's, young adult.

HOW TO CONTACT Please only query one agent at a time. "If we are interested in reading more we will get in touch with you as soon as possible." Accepts simultaneous submissions.

FELICIA ETH LITERARY REPRESENTATION

555 Bryant St., Suite 350, Palo Alto CA 94301-1700. **E-mail:** feliciaeth.literary@gmail.com. **Website:** eth-literary.com. **Contact:** Felicia Eth. Member of AAR.
REPRESENTS Nonfiction, fiction, novels. **Considers these nonfiction areas:** animals, creative nonfiction, cultural interests, current affairs, foods, history, investigative, memoirs, parenting, popular culture, psychology, science, sociology, travel, women's issues. **Considers these fiction areas:** contemporary issues, historical, literary, mainstream, suspense.
HOW TO CONTACT For fiction: Please write a query letter introducing yourself, your book, your writing background. Don't forget to include degrees you may have, publishing credits, awards and endorsements. Please wait for a response before including sample pages. "We only consider material where the manuscript for which you are querying is complete, unless you have previously published." For nonfiction: A query letter is best, introducing idea and what you have written already (proposal, manuscript?). "For writerly nonficiton (narratives, bio, memoir) please let us know if you have a finished manuscript. Also it's important you include information about yourself, your background and expertise, your platform and notoriety, if any. We do not ask for exclusivity in most instances but do ask that you inform us if other agents are considering the same material." Accepts simultaneous submissions. Responds in ideally 2 weeks for query, a month if more.
TERMS Agent receives 15% commission on domestic sales; 20% commission on foreign and film sales. Charges clients for photocopying and express mail service

MARY EVANS INC.

242 E. Fifth St., New York NY 10003. (212)979-0880. **Fax:** (212)979-5344. **E-mail:** info@maryevansinc.com. **Website:** maryevansinc.com. Member of AAR.
MEMBER AGENTS Mary Evans (progressive politics, alternative medicine, science and technology, social commentary, American history and culture); Julia Kardon (literary and upmarket fiction, narrative nonfiction, journalism, and history); Tom Mackay (non-

fiction that uses sport as a platform to explore other issues and playful literary fiction).
REPRESENTS Nonfiction, novels. **Considers these nonfiction areas:** creative nonfiction, cultural interests, history, medicine, politics, science, technology, social commentary, journalism. **Considers these fiction areas:** literary, upmarket.
HOW TO CONTACT Query by mail or e-mail. If querying by mail, include a SASE. If querying by e-mail, put "Query" in the subject line. For fiction: Include the first few pages, or opening chapter of your novel as a single Word attachment. For nonfiction: Include your book proposal as a single Word attachment. Accepts simultaneous submissions. Responds within 4-8 weeks.

FAIRBANK LITERARY REPRESENTATION

P.O. Box Six, Hudson NY 12534-0006. (617)576-0030. **E-mail:** queries@fairbankliterary.com. **Website:** www.fairbankliterary.com and www.publishersmarketplace.com/members/SorcheFairbank/. **Contact:** Sorche Elizabeth Fairbank. Estab. 2002. Member of AAR. Author's Guild, the Agents Round Table, and Grub Street's Literary Advisory Council.
MEMBER AGENTS Sorche Fairbank (narrative nonfiction, commercial and literary fiction, memoir, food and wine); Matthew Frederick, matt@fairbankliterary.com (scout for sports nonfiction, architecture, design).
REPRESENTS Nonfiction, novels, short story collections. **Considers these nonfiction areas:** agriculture, animals, architecture, art, autobiography, biography, cooking, crafts, creative nonfiction, cultural interests, current affairs, decorating, diet/nutrition, design, environment, ethnic, foods, gardening, gay/lesbian, government, hobbies, horticulture, how-to, humor, interior design, investigative, juvenile nonfiction, law, memoirs, photography, popular culture, politics, science, sociology, sports, technology, true crime, women's issues, women's studies. **Considers these fiction areas:** commercial, feminist, literary, mainstream, mystery, picture books, short story collections, sports, suspense, thriller, women's, International voices. Southern voices..
HOW TO CONTACT Query by e-mail queries@fairbankliterary.com or by mail with SASE. Accepts simultaneous submissions. Obtains most new clients through recommendations from others, solicitations, conferences, ideas generated in-house.

TERMS Agent receives 15% commission on domestic sales; 20% commission on foreign sales. Offers written contract, binding for 12 months; 45-day notice must be given to terminate contract.

LEIGH FELDMAN LITERARY

E-mail: assistant@lfliterary.com. **E-mail:** query@lfliterary.com. **Website:** http://lfliterary.com. **Contact:** Leigh Feldman. Estab. 2014. Member of AAR. Signatory of WGA.

REPRESENTS Nonfiction, fiction, novels, short story collections. **Considers these nonfiction areas:** creative nonfiction, memoirs. **Considers these fiction areas:** contemporary issues, family saga, feminist, gay, historical, lesbian, literary, multicultural, short story collections, women's, young adult.

HOW TO CONTACT E-query. "Please include 'query' in the subject line. Due to large volume of submissions, we regret that we can not respond to all queries individually. Please include the first chapter or the first 10 pages of your manuscript (or proposal) pasted after your query letter. I'd love to know what led you to query me in particular, and please let me know if you are querying other agents as well." Accepts simultaneous submissions.

DIANA FINCH LITERARY AGENCY

116 W. 23rd St., Suite 500, New York NY 10011. (917)544-4470. **E-mail:** diana.finch@verizon.net. **Website:** dianafinchliteraryagency.blogspot.com. **Contact:** Diana Finch. Estab. 2003. Member of AAR. Represents approximately 40 active clients clients.

REPRESENTS Nonfiction, fiction, novels, scholarly books. **Considers these nonfiction areas:** autobiography, biography, business, child guidance, computers, cultural interests, current affairs, dance, diet/nutrition, economics, environment, ethnic, film, government, health, history, how-to, humor, investigative, juvenile nonfiction, law, medicine, memoirs, military, money, music, parenting, photography, popular culture, politics, psychology, satire, science, self-help, sex, sports, technology, theater, translation, true crime, war, women's issues, women's studies, young adult. **Considers these fiction areas:** action, adventure, contemporary issues, crime, detective, ethnic, fantasy, historical, literary, mainstream, middle grade, multicultural, new adult, police, science fiction, sports, thriller, urban fantasy, young adult.

HOW TO CONTACT This agency prefers submissions via its online form. Accepts simultaneous submissions. Obtains most new clients through recommendations from others.

TERMS Agent receives 15% commission on domestic sales; 20% commission on foreign sales. Offers written contract. "I charge for overseas postage, galleys, and books purchased, and try to recoup these costs from earnings received for a client, rather than charging outright."

FINEPRINT LITERARY MANAGEMENT

207 W. 106th St., Suite 1D, New York NY 10025. (212)279-1282. **Website:** www.fineprintlit.com. Estab. 2007. Member of AAR.

MEMBER AGENTS Peter Rubie, CEO, peter@fineprintlit.com (nonfiction interests include narrative nonfiction, popular science, spirituality, history, biography, pop culture, business, technology, parenting, health, self help, music, and food; fiction interests include literate thrillers, crime fiction, science fiction and fantasy, military fiction and literary fiction, middle grade and boy-oriented YA fiction); Stephany Evans, stephany@fineprintlit.com (nonfiction: health and wellness, spirituality, lifestyle, food and drink, sustainability, running and fitness, memoir, and narrative nonfiction; fiction interests include mystery/crime, women's fiction, from literary to commercial to romance); Laura Wood, laura@fineprintlit.com (serious nonfiction, especially in the areas of science and nature, along with substantial titles in business, history, religion, and other areas by academics, experienced professionals, and journalists; select genre fiction only (no poetry, literary fiction or memoir) in the categories of science fiction & fantasy and mystery); June Clark, june@fineprintlit.com (nonfiction projects in the areas of entertainment, self-help, parenting, reference/how-to books, food and wine, style/beauty, and prescriptive business titles); Jacqueline Murphy, jacqueline@fineprintlit.com.

REPRESENTS Nonfiction, fiction, novels, short story collections. **Considers these nonfiction areas:** biography, business, cooking, cultural interests, current affairs, diet/nutrition, environment, foods, health, history, how-to, humor, investigative, medicine, memoirs, music, parenting, popular culture, psychology, science, self-help, spirituality, technology, travel, women's issues, fitness, lifestyle. **Considers these fiction areas:** commercial, crime, fantasy, historical, literary, mainstream, middle grade, mystery, romance, science fiction, suspense, thriller, women's, young adult.

HOW TO CONTACT E-query. For fiction, send a query, synopsis, bio, and 30 pages pasted into the e-mail. No attachments. For nonfiction, send a query only; proposal requested later if the agent is interested. Accepts simultaneous submissions. Obtains most new clients through recommendations from others, solicitations.

TERMS Agent receives 15% commission on domestic sales; 20% commission on foreign sales.

FLETCHER & COMPANY

78 Fifth Ave., 3rd Floor, New York NY 10011. **E-mail:** info@fletcherandco.com. **Website:** www.fletcherandco.com. **Contact:** Christy Fletcher. Estab. 2003. Member of AAR.

MEMBER AGENTS Christy Fletcher (referrals only); Melissa Chinchillo (select list of her own authors); Rebecca Gradinger (literary fiction, up-market commercial fiction, narrative nonfiction, self-help, memoir, Women's studies, humor, and pop culture); Gráinne Fox (literary fiction and quality commercial authors, award-winning journalists and food writers, American voices, international, literary crime, upmarket fiction, narrative nonfiction); Lisa Grubka (fiction—literary, upmarket women's, and young adult; and nonfiction — narrative, food, science, and more); Sylvie Greenberg (literary fiction, business, sports, science, memoir and history); Donald Lamm (history, biography, investigative journalism, politics, current affairs, and business); Todd Sattersten (business books); Eric Lupfer; Sarah Fuentes; Veronica Goldstein; Mink Choi; Erin McFadden.

REPRESENTS Nonfiction, novels. **Considers these nonfiction areas:** biography, business, creative nonfiction, current affairs, foods, history, humor, investigative, memoirs, popular culture, politics, science, self-help, sports, women's studies. **Considers these fiction areas:** commercial, crime, literary, women's, young adult.

HOW TO CONTACT Send queries to info@fletcherandco.com. Please do not include e-mail attachments with your initial query, as they will be deleted. Address your query to a specific agent. No snail mail queries. Accepts simultaneous submissions.

FOLIO LITERARY MANAGEMENT, LLC

The Film Center Building, 630 Ninth Ave., Suite 1101, New York NY 10036. (212)400-1494. **Fax:** (212)967-0977. **Website:** www.foliolit.com. Member of AAR. Represents 100+ clients.

MEMBER AGENTS Claudia Cross (romance novels, commercial women's fiction, cooking and food writing, serious nonfiction on religious and spiritual topics); Scott Hoffman (literary and commercial fiction, journalistic or academic nonfiction, narrative nonfiction, pop culture books, business, history, politics, spiritual or religious-themed fiction and nonfiction, sci-fi/fantasy literary fiction, heartbreaking memoirs, humorous nonfiction); Jeff Kleinman (book-club fiction (not genre commercial, like mysteries or romances), literary fiction, thrillers and suspense novels, narrative nonfiction, memoir); Dado Derviskadic (nonfiction: cultural history, biography, memoir, pop science, motivational self-help, health/nutrition, pop culture, cookbooks; fiction that's gritty, introspective, or serious); Frank Weimann (biography, business/investing/finance, history, religious, mind/body/spirit, health, lifestyle, cookbooks, sports, African-American, science, memoir, special forces/CIA/FBI/mafia, military, prescriptive nonfiction, humor, celebrity; adult and children's fiction); Michael Harriot (commercial non-fiction (both narrative and prescriptive) and fantasy/science fiction); Erin Harris (book club, historical fiction, literary, narrative nonfiction, psychological suspense, young adult); Katherine Latshaw (blogs-to-books, food/cooking, middle grade, narrative and prescriptive nonfiction); Annie Hwang (literary and upmarket fiction with commercial appeal; select nonfiction: popular science, diet/health/fitness, lifestyle, narrative nonfiction, pop culture, and humor); Erin Niumata (fiction: commercial women's fiction, romance, historical fiction, mysteries, psychological thrillers, suspense, humor; nonfiction: self-help, women's issues, pop culture and humor, pet care/pets, memoirs, and anything blogger); Ruth Pomerance (narrative nonfiction and commercial fiction); Marcy Posner (adult: commercial women's fiction, historical fiction, mystery, biography, history, health, and lifestyle, commercial novels, thrillers, narrative nonfiction; children's: contemporary YA and MG, mystery series for boys, select historical fiction and fantasy); Jeff Silberman (narrative nonfiction, biography, history, politics, current affairs, health, lifestyle, humor, food/cookbook, memoir, pop culture, sports, science, technology; commercial, literary, and book club fiction); Steve Troha; Emily van Beek (YA, MG, picture books), Melissa White (general nonfiction, literary and commercial fiction, MG, YA); John Cusick (middle grade, picture books, YA); Jamie Chambliss. **REPRESENTS** Nonfiction, novels. **Considers these nonfiction areas:** animals, art, biography, business, cooking, creative nonfiction, economics, environment, foods, health, history, how-to, humor, inspirational, memoirs, military, parenting, popular culture, politics, psychology, religious, satire, science, self-help, technology, war, women's issues, women's studies. **Considers these fiction areas:** commercial, fantasy, horror, literary, middle grade, mystery, picture books, religious, romance, thriller, women's, young adult.

HOW TO CONTACT Query via e-mail only (no attachments). Read agent bios online for specific submission guidelines and e-mail addresses, and to check if someone is closed to queries. "All agents respond to queries as soon as possible, whether interested or not. If you haven't heard back from the individual agent within the time period that they specify on their bio page, it's possible that something has gone wrong, and your query has been lost–in that case, please e-mail a follow-up."

JEANNE FREDERICKS
LITERARY AGENCY, INC.

221 Benedict Hill Rd., New Canaan CT 06840. (203)972-3011. **Fax:** (203)972-3011. **E-mail:** jeanne.fredericks@gmail.com. **Website:** www.jeannefredericks.com. **Contact:** Jeanne Fredericks. Estab. 1997. Member of AAR. Other memberships include Authors Guild. Represents 100+ clients.

REPRESENTS Nonfiction. **Considers these nonfiction areas:** Americana, animals, autobiography, biography, child guidance, cooking, decorating, diet/nutrition, environment, foods, gardening, health, history, how-to, interior design, medicine, parenting, photography, psychology, self-help, women's issues.

HOW TO CONTACT Query first by e-mail, then send outline/proposal, 1-2 sample chapters, if requested and after you have consulted the submission guidelines on the agency website. If you do send requested submission materials, include the word "Requested" in the subject line. Accepts simultaneous submissions. Responds in 3-5 weeks to queries; 2-4 months to mss. Obtains most new clients through recommendations from others, solicitations, conferences.

TERMS Agent receives 15% commission on domestic sales; 25% commission on foreign sales with co-

agent. Offers written contract, binding for 9 months; 2-month notice must be given to terminate contract. Charges client for photocopying of whole proposals and mss, overseas postage, expedited mail services. Almost all submissions are made electronically so these charges rarely apply.

GRACE FREEDSON'S
PUBLISHING NETWORK

7600 Jericho Turnpike, Suite 300, Woodbury NY 11797. (516)931-7757. **Fax:** (516)931-7759. **E-mail:** gfreedson@gmail.com. **Contact:** Grace Freedson. . Estab. 2000. Member of AAR. Women's Media Group; Author's Guild Represents 100 clients.

REPRESENTS Nonfiction, scholarly books. **Considers these nonfiction areas:** animals, business, child guidance, computers, cooking, crafts, creative nonfiction, current affairs, diet/nutrition, economics, education, environment, foods, gardening, health, history, hobbies, horticulture, how-to, humor, inspirational, interior design, juvenile nonfiction, language, law, medicine, memoirs, metaphysics, money, multicultural, parenting, philosophy, popular culture, psychology, recreation, regional, satire, science, self-help, sports, technology, true crime, war, women's issues, women's studies. **Considers these script areas:** , Test Preparation.

HOW TO CONTACT Query with SASE. Submit synopsis, SASE. Responds in 2-6 weeks to queries. Obtains most new clients through recommendations from others.

TERMS Agent receives 15% commission on domestic sales. Offers written contract; 30-day notice must be given to terminate contract.

REBECCA FRIEDMAN LITERARY AGENCY

E-mail: brandie@rfliterary.com. **Website:** www.rfliterary.com. Estab. 2013. Member of AAR. Signatory of WGA.

MEMBER AGENTS Rebecca Friedman (commercial and literary fiction with a focus on literary novels of suspense, women's fiction, contemporary romance, and young adult, as well as journalistic nonfiction and memoir); Susan Finesman, susan@rfliterary.com (fiction, cookbooks, and lifestyle); Abby Schulman, abby@rfliterary.com (YA and nonfiction related to health, wellness, and personal development); Brandie Coonis, brandie@rfliterary.com (MG, YA, SFF, and writers that defy genre).

REPRESENTS Nonfiction, fiction, novels. **Considers these nonfiction areas:** cooking, health, memoirs, young adult, journalistic nonfiction. **Considers these fiction areas:** commercial, family saga, fantasy, feminist, frontier, gay, historical, horror, literary, middle grade, mystery, new adult, romance, science fiction, suspense, thriller, women's, young adult.

HOW TO CONTACT Please submit your brief query letter and first chapter (no more than 15 pages, double-spaced). No attachments. Accepts simultaneous submissions. Tries to respond in 6-8 weeks.

THE FRIEDRICH AGENCY

19 W. 21st St., Suite 201, New York NY 10010. (212)317-8810. **E-mail:** mfriedrich@friedrichagency.com; lcarson@friedrichagency.com; kwolf@friedrichagency.com. **Website:** www.friedrichagency.com. **Contact:** Molly Friedrich; Lucy Carson; Kent D. Wolf. Estab. 2006. Member of AAR. Signatory of WGA. Represents 50+ clients.

MEMBER AGENTS Molly Friedrich, founder and agent (open to queries); Lucy Carson, TV/film rights director and agent (open to queries); Kent D. Wolf, foreign rights director and agent (open to queries).

REPRESENTS Nonfiction, fiction, novels, short story collections. **Considers these nonfiction areas:** autobiography, biography, creative nonfiction, memoirs, true crime, young adult. **Considers these fiction areas:** commercial, detective, family saga, feminist, literary, multicultural, short story collections, suspense, women's, young adult.

HOW TO CONTACT Query by e-mail only. Please query only 1 agent at this agency. Accepts simultaneous submissions. Responds in 2-4 weeks.

FULL CIRCLE LITERARY, LLC

San Diego CA **Website:** www.fullcircleliterary.com. **Contact:** Stefanie Von Borstel. Estab. 2005. Member of AAR. Society of Children's Books Writers & Illustrators, Authors Guild. Represents 100+ clients.

MEMBER AGENTS Stefanie Sanchez Von Borstel; Adriana Dominguez; Taylor Martindale Kean; Lilly Ghahremani.

REPRESENTS **Considers these nonfiction areas:** how-to, multicultural, women's issues, young adult. **Considers these fiction areas:** literary, middle grade, multicultural, young adult.

HOW TO CONTACT Online submissions only via submissions form online. Please complete the form

and submit cover letter, author information and sample writing. For sample writing: fiction please include the first 10 ms pages. For nonfiction, include a proposal with 1 sample chapter. Accepts simultaneous submissions. "Due to the high volume of submissions, please keep in mind we are no longer able to personally respond to every submission. However, we read every submission with care and often share for a second read within the office. If we are interested, we will contact you by email to request additional materials (such as a complete manuscript or additional manuscripts). Please keep us updated if there is a change in the status of your project, such as an offer of representation or book contract."

TERMS Agent receives 15% commission on domestic sales; 25% commission on foreign sales. Offers written contract which outlines responsibilities of the author and the agent.

THE G AGENCY, LLC

P.O. Box 374, Bronx NY 10471. **E-mail:** gagencyquery@gmail.com. **Website:** www.publishersmarketplace.com/members/jeffg/. **Contact:** Jeff Gerecke. Estab. 2012. Member of AAR.

MEMBER AGENTS Jeff Gerecke.

REPRESENTS Nonfiction, fiction. **Considers these nonfiction areas:** biography, business, computers, history, military, money, popular culture, technology. **Considers these fiction areas:** historical, mainstream, military, mystery, suspense, thriller, war.

HOW TO CONTACT E-mail submissions required. Please do attach sample chapters or proposal. Enter "QUERY" along with the title in the subject line of e-mails. "I cannot guarantee replies to every submission. If you do not hear from me the first time, you may send me one reminder. I encourage you to make multiple submissions but want to know that is the case if I ask for a manuscript to read." Accepts simultaneous submissions.

GELFMAN SCHNEIDER / ICM PARTNERS

850 7th Ave., Suite 903, New York NY 10019. **E-mail:** mail@gelfmanschneider.com. **Website:** www.gelfmanschneider.com. **Contact:** Jane Gelfman, Deborah Schneider. Member of AAR. Represents 300+ clients.

MEMBER AGENTS Deborah Schneider (all categories of literary and commercial fiction and nonfiction); Jane Gelfman; Heather Mitchell (particularly interested in narrative nonfiction, historical fiction and young debut authors with strong voices); Penelope Burns, penelope.gsliterary@gmail.com (literary and commercial fiction and nonfiction, as well as a variety of young adult and middle grade).

REPRESENTS Nonfiction, fiction, juvenile books. **Considers these nonfiction areas:** creative nonfiction, popular culture. **Considers these fiction areas:** commercial, fantasy, historical, literary, mainstream, middle grade, mystery, science fiction, suspense, women's, young adult.

HOW TO CONTACT Query. Check Submissions page of website to see which agents are open to queries and further instructions. Accepts simultaneous submissions.

TERMS Agent receives 15% commission on domestic sales; 20% commission on foreign sales; 15% commission on film sales. Offers written contract. Charges clients for photocopying and messengers/couriers.

GHOSH LITERARY

E-mail: submissions@ghoshliterary.com. **Website:** www.ghoshliterary.com. **Contact:** Anna Ghosh. Member of AAR. Signatory of WGA.

REPRESENTS Nonfiction, fiction.

HOW TO CONTACT E-query. Please send an e-mail briefly introducing yourself and your work. Although no specific format is required, it is helpful to know the following: your qualifications for writing your book, including any publications and recognition for your work; who you expect to buy and read your book; similar books and authors. Accepts simultaneous submissions.

GLASS LITERARY MANAGEMENT

138 W. 25th St., 10th Floor, New York NY 10001. (646)237-4881. **E-mail:** alex@glassliterary.com; rick@glassliterary.com. **Website:** www.glassliterary.com. **Contact:** Alex Glass or Rick Pascocello. Estab. 2014. Member of AAR. Signatory of WGA.

MEMBER AGENTS Alex Glass; Rick Pascocello.

REPRESENTS Nonfiction, novels.

HOW TO CONTACT "Please send your query letter in the body of an e-mail and if we are interested, we will respond and ask for the complete manuscript or proposal. No attachments." Accepts simultaneous submissions.

GLOBAL LION INTELLECTUAL PROPERTY MANAGEMENT

P.O. Box 669238, Pompano Beach FL 33066. **E-mail:** queriesgloballionmgt@gmail.com. **Website:** www.

globallionmanagement.com. **Contact:** Peter Miller. Estab. 2013. Member of AAR. Signatory of WGA.

HOW TO CONTACT E-query. Global Lion Intellectual Property Management. Inc. accepts exclusive submissions only. "If your work is under consideration by another agency, please do not submit it to us." Below the query, paste a one page synopsis, a sample of your book (20 pages is fine), a short author bio, and any impressive social media links.

BARRY GOLDBLATT LITERARY LLC

320 7th Ave. #266, Brooklyn NY 11215. **E-mail:** query@bgliterary.com. **Website:** www.bgliterary.com. **Contact:** Barry Goldblatt; Jennifer Udden. Estab. 2000. Member of AAR. Signatory of WGA.

MEMBER AGENTS Barry Goldblatt; Jennifer Udden, query.judden@gmail.com (speculative fiction of all stripes, especially innovative science fiction or fantasy; contemporary/erotic/LGBT/paranormal/historical romance; contemporary or speculative YA; select mysteries, thrillers, and urban fantasies).

REPRESENTS Fiction. **Considers these fiction areas:** fantasy, middle grade, mystery, romance, science fiction, thriller, young adult.

HOW TO CONTACT "E-mail queries can be sent to query@bgliterary.com and should include the word 'query' in the subject line. To query Jen Udden specifically, e-mail queries can be sent to query.judden@gmail.com. Please know that we will read and respond to every e-query that we receive, provided it is properly addressed and follows the submission guidelines below. We will not respond to e-queries that are addressed to no one, or to multiple recipients. Your e-mail query should include the following within the body of the e-mail: your query letter, a synopsis of the book, and the first 5 pages of your manuscript. We will not open or respond to any e-mails that have attachments. If we like the sound of your work, we will request more from you. Our response time is 4 weeks on queries, 6-8 weeks on full manuscripts. If you haven't heard from us within that time, feel free to check in via e-mail." Accepts simultaneous submissions. Obtains clients through referrals, queries, and conferences.

TERMS Agent receives 15% commission on domestic sales; 20% on foreign and dramatic sales. Offers written contract. 60 days notice must be given to terminate contract.

FRANCES GOLDIN LITERARY AGENCY, INC.

214 W. 29th St., Suite 410, New York NY 10001. (212)777-0047. **Fax:** (212)228-1660. **Website:** www.goldinlit.com. Estab. 1977. Member of AAR.

MEMBER AGENTS Frances Goldin, founder/president; Ellen Geiger, vice president/principal (nonfiction: history, biography, progressive politics, photography, science and medicine, women, religion and serious investigative journalism; fiction: literary thriller, and novels in general that provoke and challenge the status quo, as well as historical and multicultural works. Please no New Age, romance, how-to or right-wing politics); Matt McGowan, agent/rights director, mm@goldinlit.com, (literary fiction, essays, history, memoir, journalism, biography, music, popular culture & science, sports [particularly soccer], narrative nonfiction, cultural studies, as well as literary travel, crime, food, suspense and sci-fi); Sam Stoloff, vice president/principal, (literary fiction, memoir, history, accessible sociology and philosophy, cultural studies, serious journalism, narrative and topical nonfiction with a progressive orientation); Ria Julien, agent/counsel; Nina Cochran, literary assistant.

REPRESENTS Nonfiction, novels. **Considers these nonfiction areas:** biography, creative nonfiction, cultural interests, foods, history, investigative, medicine, memoirs, music, philosophy, photography, popular culture, politics, science, sociology, sports, travel, women's issues, crime. **Considers these fiction areas:** historical, literary, mainstream, multicultural, suspense, thriller.

HOW TO CONTACT There is an online submission process you can find online. Responds in 4-6 weeks to queries.

IRENE GOODMAN LITERARY AGENCY

27 W. 24th St., Suite 700B, New York NY 10010. **E-mail:** miriam.queries@irenegoodman.com, barbara.queries@irenegoodman.com, rachel.queries@irenegoodman.com, kim.queries@irenegoodman.com, victoria.queries@irenegoodman.com, irene.queries@irenegoodman.com, brita.queries@irenegoodman.com. **E-mail:** submissions@irenegoodman.com. **Website:** www.irenegoodman.com. **Contact:** Brita Lundberg. Estab. 1978. Member of AAR. Represents 150 clients.

MEMBER AGENTS Irene Goodman, Miriam Kriss, Barbara Poelle, Rachel Ekstrom, Kim Perel, Brita Lundberg, Victoria Marini.

REPRESENTS Nonfiction, fiction, novels, juvenile books. **Considers these nonfiction areas:** animals, autobiography, cooking, creative nonfiction, cultural interests, current affairs, decorating, diet/nutrition, design, foods, health, history, how-to, humor, interior design, juvenile nonfiction, memoirs, parenting, politics, science, self-help, women's issues, young adult, parenting, social issues, francophilia, anglophilia, Judaica, lifestyles, cooking, memoir. **Considers these fiction areas:** action, crime, detective, family saga, historical, horror, middle grade, mystery, romance, science fiction, suspense, thriller, urban fantasy, women's, young adult.

HOW TO CONTACT Query. Submit synopsis, first 10 pages pasted into the body of the email. E-mail queries only! See the website submission page. No e-mail attachments. Query 1 agent only. Accepts simultaneous submissions. Responds in 2 months to queries. Consult website for each agent's submission guidelines.

TERMS 15% commission.

DOUG GRAD LITERARY AGENCY, INC.

156 Prospect Park West, #3L, Brooklyn NY 11215. (718)788-6067. **E-mail:** query@dgliterary.com. **Website:** www.dgliterary.com. **Contact:** Doug Grad. Estab. 2008. Member of AAR. Signatory of WGA. Represents 50+ clients.

MEMBER AGENTS Doug Grad (narrative nonfiction, military, sports, celebrity memoir, thrillers, mysteries, cozies, historical fiction, music, style, business, home improvement, cookbooks, science and theater).

REPRESENTS Nonfiction, fiction, novels. **Considers these nonfiction areas:** Americana, autobiography, biography, business, cooking, creative nonfiction, current affairs, diet/nutrition, design, film, government, history, humor, investigative, language, military, music, popular culture, politics, science, sports, technology, theater, travel, true crime, war. **Considers these fiction areas:** action, adventure, commercial, crime, detective, historical, horror, literary, mainstream, military, mystery, police, romance, science fiction, suspense, thriller, war, young adult.

HOW TO CONTACT Query by e-mail first. No sample material unless requested; no printed submissions by mail. Accepts simultaneous submissions. Due to the volume of queries, it's impossible to give a response time.

SANFORD J. GREENBURGER ASSOCIATES, INC.

55 Fifth Ave., New York NY 10003. (212)206-5600. **Fax:** (212)463-8718. **Website:** www.greenburger.com. Member of AAR. Represents 500 clients.

MEMBER AGENTS Matt Bialer, querymb@sjga.com (fantasy, science fiction, thrillers, and mysteries as well as a select group of literary writers, and also loves smart narrative nonfiction including books about current events, popular culture, biography, history, music, race, and sports); Brenda Bowen, querybb@sjga.com (literary fiction, writers and illustrators of picture books, chapter books, and middle-grade and teen fiction); Faith Hamlin, fhamlin@sjga.com (receives submissions by referral); Heide Lange, queryhl@sjga.com (receives submissions by referral); Daniel Mandel, querydm@sjga.com (literary and commercial fiction, as well as memoirs and nonfiction about business, art, history, politics, sports, and popular culture); Rachael Dillon Fried, rfried@sjga.com (both fiction and nonfiction authors, with a keen interest in unique literary voices, women's fiction, narrative nonfiction, memoir, and comedy); Stephanie Delman, sdelman@sjga.com (literary/upmarket contemporary fiction, psychological thrillers/suspense, and atmospheric, near-historical fiction); Ed Maxwell, emaxwell@sjga.com (expert and narrative nonfiction authors, novelists and graphic novelists, as well as children's book authors and illustrators).

REPRESENTS Nonfiction, fiction, novels, juvenile books. **Considers these nonfiction areas:** art, biography, business, creative nonfiction, current affairs, ethnic, history, humor, memoirs, music, popular culture, politics, sports. **Considers these fiction areas:** commercial, crime, family saga, fantasy, feminist, historical, literary, middle grade, multicultural, mystery, picture books, romance, science fiction, thriller, women's, young adult.

HOW TO CONTACT E-query. "Please look at each agent's profile page for current information about what each agent is looking for and for the correct email address to use for queries to that agent. Please be sure to use the correct query e-mail address for each agent." Agents may not respond to all queries; will respond within 6-8 weeks if interested. Obtains most new clients through recommendations from others.

TERMS Agent receives 15% commission on domestic sales; 20% commission on foreign sales. Charges for photocopying and books for foreign and subsidiary rights submissions.

THE GREENHOUSE LITERARY AGENCY

E-mail: submissions@greenhouseliterary.com. **Website:** www.greenhouseliterary.com. **Contact:** Sarah Davies. Estab. 2008. Member of AAR. Other memberships include SCBWI. Represents 50 clients.

MEMBER AGENTS Sarah Davies, vice president (fiction and nonfiction by North American authors, chapter books through to middle grade and young adult); Polly Nolan, agent (fiction by UK, Irish, Commonwealth–including Australia, NZ and India–authors, plus European authors writing in English, author/illustrators (texts under 1,000 words) to young fiction series, through middle grade and young adult).

REPRESENTS Juvenile books. **Considers these nonfiction areas:** juvenile nonfiction, young adult. **Considers these fiction areas:** juvenile, young adult.

HOW TO CONTACT Query 1 agent only. Put the target agent's name in the subject line. Paste the first 5 pages of your story after the query. Accepts simultaneous submissions.

TERMS Agent receives 15% commission on domestic sales; 25% commission on foreign sales. Offers written contract. This agency occasionally charges for submission copies to film agents or foreign publishers.

GREYHAUS LITERARY

3021 20th St., Pl. SW, Puyallup WA 98373. **E-mail:** scott@greyhausagency.com. **E-mail:** submissions@greyhausagency.com. **Website:** www.greyhausagency.com. **Contact:** Scott Eagan, member RWA. Estab. 2003. Member of AAR. Signatory of WGA.

REPRESENTS Novels. **Considers these fiction areas:** new adult, romance, women's.

HOW TO CONTACT Submissions to Greyhaus can be done in one of three ways: 1) A standard query letter via email. If using this method, do not attach documents or send anything else other than a query letter. 2) Use the Submission Form found on the website on the Contact page. Or 3) send a query, the first 3 pages and a synopsis of no more than 3-5 pages (and a SASE), using a snail mail submission. Accepts simultaneous submissions. Responds in up to 3 months.

JILL GRINBERG LITERARY MANAGEMENT

392 Vanderbilt Ave., Brooklyn NY 11238. (212)620-5883. E-mail: info@jillgrinbergliterary.com. Website: www.jillgrinbergliterary.com. Estab. 1999. Member of AAR.

MEMBER AGENTS Jill Grinberg; Cheryl Pientka; Katelyn Detweiler; Sophia Seidner.

REPRESENTS Nonfiction, fiction, novels. **Considers these nonfiction areas:** biography, creative nonfiction, current affairs, ethnic, history, language, literature, memoirs, parenting, popular culture, politics, science, sociology, spirituality, sports, travel, women's issues, young adult. **Considers these fiction areas:** fantasy, historical, juvenile, literary, mainstream, middle grade, multicultural, picture books, romance, science fiction, women's, young adult.

HOW TO CONTACT "Please send queries via e-mail to info@jillgrinbergliterary.com–include your query letter, addressed to the agent of your choice, along with the first 50 pages of your ms pasted into the body of the e-mail or attached as a doc. or docx. file. We also accept queries via mail, though e-mail is preferred. Please send your query letter and the first 50 pages of your ms by mail, along with a SASE, to the attention of your agent of choice. Please note that unless a SASE with sufficient postage is provided, your materials will not be returned. As submissions are shared within the office, please only query one agent with your project." Accepts simultaneous submissions.

THE JOY HARRIS LITERARY AGENCY, INC.

1501 Broadway, Suite 2310, New York NY 10036. (212)924-6269. **Fax:** (212)540-5776. **E-mail:** contact@joyharrisliterary.com. **E-mail:** submissions@joyharrisliterary.com. **Website:** joyharrisliterary.com. **Contact:** Joy Harris. Estab. 1990. Member of AAR. Represents 100+ clients.

MEMBER AGENTS Joy Harris (literary fiction, strongly-written commercial fiction, narrative nonfiction across a broad range of topics, memoir and biography); Adam Reed (literary fiction, science and technology, and pop culture); Elizabeth Trout.

REPRESENTS Nonfiction, fiction. **Considers these nonfiction areas:** art, biography, creative nonfiction, memoirs, popular culture, science, technology. **Considers these fiction areas:** commercial, literary.

HOW TO CONTACT Please e-mail all submissions, comprised of a query letter, outline or sample chapter, to submissions@joyharrisliterary.com. Accepts simultaneous submissions. Obtains most new clients through recommendations from clients and editors.

TERMS Agent receives 15% commission on domestic sales; 20% commission on foreign sales. Charges clients for some office expenses.

JOHN HAWKINS & ASSOCIATES, INC.

80 Maiden Ln., Suite 1503, New York NY 10038. (212)807-7040. **E-mail:** jha@jhalit.com. **Website:** www.jhalit.com. **Contact:** Moses Cardona (rights and translations); Annie Kronenberg (permissions); Warren Frazier, literary agent; Anne Hawkins, literary agent; William Reiss, literary agent. Estab. 1893. Member of AAR. The Author Guild Represents 100+ clients.

MEMBER AGENTS Moses Cardona, moses@jhalit.com (commercial fiction, suspense, business, science, and multicultural fiction); Warren Frazier, frazier@jhalit.com (fiction; nonfiction, specifically technology, history, world affairs and foreign policy); Anne Hawkins, ahawkins@jhalit.com (thrillers to literary fiction to serious nonfiction; interested in science, history, public policy, medicine and women's issues).

REPRESENTS Nonfiction, fiction, novels, short story collections, novellas, juvenile books. **Considers these nonfiction areas:** biography, business, history, medicine, politics, science, technology, women's issues. **Considers these fiction areas:** commercial, historical, literary, multicultural, suspense, thriller.

HOW TO CONTACT Query. Include the word "Query" in the subject line. For fiction, include 1-3 chapters of your book as a single Word attachment. For nonfiction, include your proposal as a single attachment. E-mail a particular agent directly if you are targeting one. Accepts simultaneous submissions. Responds in 1 month to queries. Obtains most new clients through recommendations from others.

TERMS Agent receives 15% commission on domestic sales; 20% commission on foreign sales. Charges clients for photocopying.

RICHARD HENSHAW GROUP

145 W. 28th St., 12th Floor, New York NY 10001. (212)414-1172. **E-mail:** submissions@henshaw.com. **Website:** www.richardhenshawgroup.com. **Contact:** Rich Henshaw. Member of AAR.

REPRESENTS Novels. **Considers these fiction areas:** fantasy, historical, horror, literary, mainstream, mystery, police, romance, science fiction, thriller, young adult.

HOW TO CONTACT "Please feel free to submit a query letter in the form of an e-mail of fewer than 250 words to submissions@henshaw.com address." No snail mail queries. Accepts simultaneous submissions. Obtains most new clients through recommendations from others, solicitations, conferences.

TERMS Agent receives 15% commission on domestic sales; 20% commission on foreign sales. No written contract. Charges clients for photocopying and book orders.

HOLLOWAY LITERARY

P.O. Box 771, Cary NC 27512. **E-mail:** submissions@ hollowayliteraryagency.com. **Website:** hollowayliteraryagency.com. **Contact:** Nikki Terpilowski. Estab. 2011. Member of AAR. Signatory of WGA. International Thriller Writers and Romance Writers of America Represents 26 clients.

MEMBER AGENTS Nikki Terpilowski (romance, women's fiction, Southern fiction, historical fiction, cozy mysteries, lifestyle no-fiction (minimalism, homesteading, southern, etc.) commercial, upmarket/book club fiction, African-American fiction of all types, literary); Rachel Burkot (young adult contemporary, women's fiction, upmarket/book club fiction, contemporary romance, Southern fiction, nonfiction).

REPRESENTS Nonfiction, fiction, movie scripts, feature film. **Considers these nonfiction areas:** Americana, environment, humor, narrative nonfiction, New Journalism, essays. **Considers these fiction areas:** action, adventure, commercial, contemporary issues, crime, detective, ethnic, family saga, fantasy, glitz, historical, inspirational, literary, mainstream, metaphysical, middle grade, military, multicultural, mystery, new adult, New Age, regional, romance, short story collections, spiritual, suspense, thriller, urban fantasy, war, women's, young adult. **Considers these script areas:** action, adventure, biography, contemporary issues, ethnic, romantic comedy, romantic drama, teen, thriller, TV movie of the week.

HOW TO CONTACT Send query and first 15 pages of ms pasted into the body of e-mail to submissions@ hollowayliteraryagency.com. In the subject header write: (Insert Agent's Name)/Title/Genre. Holloway Literary does accept submissions via mail (query letter and first 50 pages). Expect a response time of at least 3 months. Include e-mail address, phone number, social media accounts, and mailing address on your query letter. Accepts simultaneous submissions. Responds in 6-8 weeks. If the agent is interested, he/she'll respond with a request for more material.

HSG AGENCY

37 W. 28th St., 8th Floor, New York NY 10001. **E-mail:** channigan@hsgagency.com; jsalky@hsgagency.com; jgetzler@hsgagency.com; sroberts@hsgagency.com; leigh@hsgagency.com. **Website:** hsgagency.com. **Contact:** Carrie Hannigan; Jesseca Salky; Josh Getzler; Soumeya Roberts; Leigh Eisenman. Estab. 2011. Member of AAR. Signatory of WGA.

MEMBER AGENTS Carrie Hannigan (children's books, illustrators, YA and MG); Jesseca Salky (literary and mainstream fiction); Josh Getzler (foreign and historical fiction; both women's fiction, straight-ahead historical fiction, and thrillers and mysteries); Soumeya Roberts (literary fiction and narrative nonfiction); Leigh Eisenman (literary and upmarket fiction, foodie/cookbooks, health and fitness, lifestyle, and select narrative nonfiction).

REPRESENTS Nonfiction, fiction, novels, short story collections, juvenile books. **Considers these nonfiction areas:** animals, business, cooking, creative nonfiction, cultural interests, current affairs, diet/nutrition, education, environment, foods, gardening, health, history, hobbies, humor, literature, memoirs, money, multicultural, music, parenting, photography, popular culture, politics, psychology, science, self-help, sports, women's issues, women's studies, young adult. **Considers these fiction areas:** adventure, commercial, contemporary issues, crime, detective, ethnic, experimental, family saga, fantasy, feminist, historical, humor, juvenile, literary, mainstream, middle grade, multicultural, mystery, picture books, science fiction, suspense, thriller, translation, women's, young adult.

HOW TO CONTACT Please send a query letter and the first 5 pages of your ms (within the e-mail–no attachments please) to the appropriate agent for your book. If it is a picture book, please include the entire ms. If you were referred to us, please mention it in the first line of your query. Please note that we do not represent screenplays, romance fiction, or religious fiction. If Carrie and Jesseca have not responded to your query within 10 weeks of submission, please consider this a pass. Due to the volume of queries Leigh receives, she will only respond to those in which she's interested. Soumeya will not be accepting new unsolicited queries until May 1, 2018. All queries received during that time will be deleted. All agents are open to new clients.

HARVEY KLINGER, INC.

300 W. 55th St., Suite 11V, New York NY 10019. (212)581-7068. **E-mail:** queries@harveyklinger.com. **Website:** www.harveyklinger.com. **Contact:** Harvey Klinger. Estab. 1977. Member of AAR. PEN Represents 100 clients.

MEMBER AGENTS Harvey Klinger, harvey@harveyklinger.com; David Dunton, david@harveyklinger.com (popular culture, music-related books, literary fiction, young adult, fiction, and memoirs); Andrea Somberg, andrea@harveyklinger.com (literary fiction, commercial fiction, romance, sci-fi/fantasy, mysteries/thrillers, young adult, middle grade, quality narrative nonfiction, popular culture, how-to, self-help, humor, interior design, cookbooks, health/fitness); Wendy Silbert Levinson, wendy@harveyklinger.com (literary and commercial fiction, occasional children's YA or MG, wide variety of nonfiction); Rachel Ridout, rachel@harveyklinger.com (children's MG and YA).

REPRESENTS Nonfiction, fiction, novels, juvenile books. **Considers these nonfiction areas:** autobiography, biography, business, child guidance, cooking, crafts, creative nonfiction, cultural interests, current affairs, diet/nutrition, foods, gay/lesbian, health, history, how-to, investigative, literature, medicine, memoirs, money, music, popular culture, psychology, science, self-help, sociology, spirituality, sports, technology, true crime, women's issues, women's studies, young adult. **Considers these fiction areas:** action, adventure, commercial, contemporary issues, crime, detective, erotica, family saga, fantasy, gay, glitz, historical, horror, juvenile, lesbian, literary, mainstream, middle grade, mystery, new adult, police, romance, suspense, thriller, women's, young adult.

HOW TO CONTACT Use online e-mail submission form on the website, or query with SASE via snail mail. No phone or fax queries. Don't send unsolicited mss or e-mail attachments. Make submission letter to the point and as brief as possible. Accepts simultaneous submissions. Responds in 2-4 weeks to queries, if interested. Obtains most new clients through recommendations from others.

TERMS Agent receives 15% commission on domestic sales; 25% commission on foreign sales. Offers written

contract. Charges for photocopying mss and overseas postage for mss.

THE KNIGHT AGENCY

232 W. Washington St., Madison GA 30650. **E-mail:** deidre.knight@knightagency.net. **E-mail:** submissions@knightagency.net. **Website:** http://knightagency.net/. **Contact:** Deidre Knight. Estab. 1996. Member of AAR. SCWBI, WFA, SFWA, RWA Represents 200+ clients.

MEMBER AGENTS Deidre Knight (romance, women's fiction, erotica, commercial fiction, inspirational, m/m fiction, memoir and nonfiction narrative, personal finance, true crime, business, popular culture, self-help, religion, and health); Pamela Harty (romance, women's fiction, young adult, business, motivational, diet and health, memoir, parenting, pop culture, and true crime); Elaine Spencer (romance (single title and category), women's fiction, commercial "book-club" fiction, cozy mysteries, young adult and middle grade material); Lucienne Diver (fantasy, science fiction, romance, suspense and young adult); Nephele Tempest (literary/commercial fiction, women's fiction, fantasy, science fiction, romantic suspense, paranormal romance, contemporary romance, historical fiction, young adult and middle grade fiction); Melissa Jeglinski (romance [contemporary, category, historical, inspirational], young adult, middle grade, women's fiction and mystery); Kristy Hunter (romance, women's fiction, commercial fiction, young adult and middle grade material), Travis Pennington (young adult, middle grade, mysteries, thrillers, commercial fiction, and romance [nothing paranormal/fantasy in any genre for now]).

REPRESENTS Nonfiction, fiction, novels. **Considers these nonfiction areas:** autobiography, business, creative nonfiction, cultural interests, current affairs, diet/nutrition, design, economics, ethnic, film, foods, gay/lesbian, health, history, how-to, inspirational, interior design, investigative, juvenile nonfiction, literature, memoirs, military, money, multicultural, parenting, popular culture, politics, psychology, self-help, sociology, technology, travel, true crime, women's issues, young adult. **Considers these fiction areas:** commercial, crime, erotica, fantasy, gay, historical, juvenile, lesbian, literary, mainstream, middle grade, multicultural, mystery, new adult, paranormal, psychic, romance, science fiction, thriller, urban fantasy, women's, young adult.

HOW TO CONTACT E-queries only. "Your submission should include a one page query letter and the first five pages of your manuscript. All text must be contained in the body of your e-mail. Attachments will not be opened nor included in the consideration of your work. Queries must be addressed to a specific agent. Please do not query multiple agents." Accepts simultaneous submissions. Responds in 1-2 weeks on queries, 6-8 weeks on submissions.

TERMS 15% Simple agency agreement with openended commitment. 15% commission on all domestic sales, 20% on foreign and film.

LINDA KONNER LITERARY AGENCY

10 W. 15th St., Suite 1918, New York NY 10011. **E-mail:** ldkonner@cs.com. **Website:** www.lindakonnerliteraryagency.com. **Contact:** Linda Konner. Estab. 1996. Member of AAR. Other memberships include ASJA and Authors Guild. Represents 50 clients.

REPRESENTS Nonfiction. **Considers these nonfiction areas:** business, cooking, diet/nutrition, foods, health, how-to, medicine, money, parenting, popular culture, psychology, science, self-help, women's issues, biography (celebrity), African American and Latino issues, relationships, popular science.

HOW TO CONTACT Query by e-mail (or snail mail with SASE) with synopsis and author bio, including size of social media following, size of website following, appearances in traditional media (print/TV/radio) and frequency/size of speaking engagements. Prefers to read materials exclusively for 2 weeks. Accepts simultaneous submissions. Responds within 2 weeks. Obtains most new clients through recommendations from others, occasional solicitation among established authors/journalists.

TERMS Agent receives 15% commission on domestic sales; 25% commission on foreign sales. Offers written contract. Charges one-time fee for domestic expenses; additional expenses may be incurred for foreign sales.

STUART KRICHEVSKY LITERARY AGENCY, INC.

6 E. 39th St., Suite 500, New York NY 10016. (212)725-5288. **Fax:** (212)725-5275. **Website:** www.skagency.com. Member of AAR.

MEMBER AGENTS Stuart Krichevsky, query@skagency.com (emphasis on narrative nonfiction, literary journalism and literary and commercial fiction); Ross Harris, rhquery@skagency.com (voice-driven humor and memoir, books on popular culture and our society, narrative nonfiction and literary fiction); David Patterson, dpquery@skagency.com (writers of upmarket narrative nonfiction and literary fiction, historians, journalists and thought leaders); Mackenzie Brady Watson, mbwquery@skagency.com (narrative nonfiction, science, history, sociology, investigative journalism, food, business, memoir, and select upmarket and literary YA fiction); Hannah Schwartz, hsquery@skagency; Laura Usselman, luquery@skagency.com.

REPRESENTS Nonfiction, novels. **Considers these nonfiction areas:** business, creative nonfiction, foods, history, humor, investigative, memoirs, popular culture, science, sociology, memoir. **Considers these fiction areas:** commercial, contemporary issues, literary, young adult.

HOW TO CONTACT Please send a query letter and the first few (up to 10) pages of your ms or proposal in the body of an e-mail (not an attachment) to one of the e-mail addresses. No attachments. Responds if interested. Accepts simultaneous submissions. Obtains most new clients through recommendations from others, solicitations.

KT LITERARY, LLC

9249 S. Broadway, #200-543, Highlands Ranch CO 80129. **E-mail:** contact@ktliterary.com. **E-mail:** katequery@ktliterary.com, saraquery@ktliterary.com, reneequery@ktliterary.com, hannahquery@ktliterary.com, hilaryquery@ktliterary.com. **Website:** www.ktliterary.com. **Contact:** Kate Schafer Testerman, Sara Megibow, Renee Nyen, Hannah Fergesen, Hilary Harwell. Estab. 2008. Member of AAR. Other agency memberships include SCBWI, YALSA, ALA, SFWA and RWA. Represents 75 clients.

MEMBER AGENTS Kate Testerman (middle grade and young adult); Renee Nyen (middle grade and young adult); Sara Megibow (middle grade, young adult, romance, science fiction and fantasy); Hannah Fergesen (middle grade, young adult and speculative fiction); and Hilary Harwell (middle grade and young adult). Always LGBTQ and diversity friendly!.

REPRESENTS Fiction. **Considers these fiction areas:** fantasy, middle grade, romance, science fiction, young adult.

HOW TO CONTACT "To query us, please select one of the agents at kt literary at a time. If we pass, you can feel free to submit to another. Please e-mail your query letter and the first 3 pages of your manuscript in the body of the e-mail to either Kate at katequery@ktliterary.com, Sara at saraquery@ktliterary.com, Renee at reneequery@ktliterary.com, Hannah at hannahquery@ktliterary.com, or Hilary at hilaryquery@ktliterary.com. The subject line of your e-mail should include the word 'Query' along with the title of your manuscript. Queries should not contain attachments. Attachments will not be read, and queries containing attachments will be deleted unread. We aim to reply to all queries within 4 weeks of receipt. For examples of query letters, please feel free to browse the About My Query archives on the KT Literary website. In addition, if you're an author who is sending a new query, but who previously submitted a novel to us for which we requested chapters but ultimately declined, please do say so in your query letter. If we like your query, we'll ask for the first 5 chapters and a complete synopsis. For our purposes, the synopsis should include the full plot of the book including the conclusion. Don't tease us. Thanks! We are not accepting snail mail queries or queries by phone at this time. We also do not accept pitches on social media." Accepts simultaneous submissions. Responds in 2-4 weeks to queries; 2 months to mss. Obtains most new clients through query slush pile.

TERMS Agent receives 15% commission on domestic sales; 20% commission on foreign sales. Offers written contract; 30-day notice must be given to terminate contract.

THE LESHNE AGENCY

New York NY **E-mail:** info@leshneagency.com. **E-mail:** submissions@leshneagency.com. **Website:** www.leshneagency.com. **Contact:** Lisa Leshne, agent and owner. Estab. 2011. Member of AAR. Women's Media Group

MEMBER AGENTS Lisa Leshne, agent and owner; Sandy Hodgman, director of foreign rights.

REPRESENTS Nonfiction, fiction, novels. **Considers these nonfiction areas:** business, creative nonfiction, cultural interests, health, how-to, humor, inspirational, memoirs, parenting, politics, science, self-help, sports, women's issues. **Considers these fiction areas:** commercial, middle grade, young adult.

HOW TO CONTACT The Leshne Agency is seeking new and existing authors across all genres. "We are especially interested in narrative; memoir; prescriptive nonfiction, with a particular interest in sports, health, wellness, business, political and parenting topics; and truly terrific commercial fiction, young adult and middle-grade books. We are not interested in screenplays; scripts; poetry; and picture books. If your submission is in a genre not specifically listed here, we are still open to considering it, but if your submission is for a genre we've mentioned as not being interested in, please don't bother sending it to us. All submissions should be made through the Authors.me portal by clicking on this link: https://app.authors.me/#submit/the-leshne-agency." Accepts simultaneous submissions.

LEVINE GREENBERG ROSTAN LITERARY AGENCY, INC.

307 Seventh Ave., Suite 2407, New York NY 10001. (212)337-0934. **Fax:** (212)337-0948. **E-mail:** submit@lgrliterary.com. **Website:** www.lgrliterary.com. Member of AAR. Represents 250 clients.

MEMBER AGENTS Jim Levine (nonfiction, including business, science, narrative nonfiction, social and political issues, psychology, health, spirituality, parenting); Stephanie Rostan (adult and YA fiction; nonfiction, including parenting, health & wellness, sports, memoir); Melissa Rowland; Daniel Greenberg (nonfiction: popular culture, narrative nonfiction, memoir, and humor; literary fiction); Victoria Skurnick; Danielle Svetcov (nonfiction); Lindsay Edgecombe (narrative nonfiction, memoir, lifestyle and health, illustrated books, as well as literary fiction); Monika Verma (nonfiction: humor, pop culture, memoir, narrative nonfiction and style and fashion titles; some young adult fiction (paranormal, historical, contemporary)); Kerry Sparks (young adult and middle grade; select adult fiction and occasional nonfiction); Tim Wojcik (nonfiction, including food narratives, humor, pop culture, popular history and science; literary fiction); Arielle Eckstut (no queries); Sarah Bedingfield (literary and upmarket commercial fiction, Epic family dramas, literary novels with notes of magical realism, darkly gothic stories, psychological suspense).

REPRESENTS Nonfiction, novels. **Considers these nonfiction areas:** business, creative nonfiction, health, history, humor, memoirs, parenting, popular culture, science, spirituality, sports. **Considers these fiction areas:** commercial, literary, mainstream, middle grade, suspense, young adult.

HOW TO CONTACT E-query to submit@lgrliterary.com, or online submission form. "If you would like to direct your query to one of our agents specifically, please feel free to name them in the online form or in the email you send." Cannot respond to submissions by mail. Do not attach more than 50 pages. "Due to the volume of submissions we receive, we are unable to respond to each individually. If we would like more information about your project, we'll contact you within 3 weeks (though we do get backed up on occasion!)." Accepts simultaneous submissions. Obtains most new clients through recommendations from others.

TERMS Agent receives 15% commission on domestic sales; 20% commission on foreign sales. Offers written contract. Charges clients for out-of-pocket expenses—telephone, fax, postage, photocopying—directly connected to the project.

LEVY CREATIVE MANAGEMENT

425 E. 58th St., Suite 37F, New York NY 10022. (212)687-6463. **Fax:** (212)661-4839. **E-mail:** info@levycreative.com. **Website:** www.levycreative.com. **Contact:** Sari S. Schorr. Estab. 1996. Member of AAR. Signatory of WGA

HOW TO CONTACT For first contact, see submission guidelines on website. Accepts simultaneous submissions. Responds only if interested. Finds illustrators through recommendations from others, word of mouth, competitions.

TERMS Offers written contract. Advertising costs are split: 75% paid by illustrators; 25% paid by rep.

STERLING LORD LITERISTIC, INC.

115 Broadway, New York NY 10006. (212)780-6050. **Fax:** (212)780-6095. **E-mail:** info@sll.com. **Website:** www.sll.com. Estab. 1987. Member of AAR. Signatory of WGA.

MEMBER AGENTS Philippa Brophy (represents journalists, nonfiction writers and novelists, and is most interested in current events, memoir, science, politics, biography, and women's issues); Laurie Liss (represents authors of commercial and literary fiction and nonfiction whose perspectives are well developed and unique); Sterling Lord; Peter Matson (abiding interest in storytelling, whether in the service of history, fiction, the sciences); Douglas Stewart (primarily fiction for all ages, from the innovatively literary to the unabashedly commercial); Neeti Madan (memoir, journalism, popular culture, lifestyle, women's issues, multicultural books and virtually any intelligent writing on intriguing topics); Robert Guinsler (literary and commercial fiction (including YA), journalism,

narrative nonfiction with an emphasis on pop culture, science and current events, memoirs and biographies); Jim Rutman; Celeste Fine (expert, celebrity, and corporate clients with strong national and international platforms, particularly in the health, science, self-help, food, business, and lifestyle fields); Martha Millard (fiction and nonfiction, including well-written science fiction and young adult); Mary Krienke (literary fiction, memoir, and narrative nonfiction, including psychology, popular science, and cultural commentary); Jenny Stephens (nonfiction: cookbooks, practical lifestyle projects, transportive travel and nature writing, and creative nonfiction; fiction: contemporary literary narratives strongly rooted in place); Alison MacKeen (idea-driven research books: social scientific, scientific, historical, relationships/parenting, learning and education, sexuality, technology, the life-cycle, health, the environment, politics, economics, psychology, geography, and culture; literary fiction, literary nonfiction, memoirs, essays, and travel writing); John Maas (serious nonfiction, specifically business, personal development, science, self-help, health, fitness, and lifestyle); Sarah Passick (commercial nonfiction in the celebrity, food, blogger, lifestyle, health, diet, fitness and fashion categories).

REPRESENTS Nonfiction, fiction. **Considers these nonfiction areas:** biography, business, cooking, creative nonfiction, current affairs, economics, education, foods, gay/lesbian, history, humor, memoirs, multicultural, parenting, popular culture, politics, psychology, science, technology, travel, women's issues, fitness. **Considers these fiction areas:** commercial, juvenile, literary, middle grade, picture books, science fiction, young adult.

HOW TO CONTACT Query via snail mail. "Please submit a query letter, a synopsis of the work, a brief proposal or the first 3 chapters of the manuscript, a brief bio or resume, and SASE for reply. Original artwork is not accepted. Enclose sufficient postage if you wish to have your materials returned to you. We do not respond to unsolicited e-mail inquiries." Accepts simultaneous submissions.

TERMS Agent receives 15% commission on domestic sales; 20% commission on foreign sales. Offers written contract.

LOWENSTEIN ASSOCIATES INC.

115 E. 23rd St., Floor 4, New York NY 10010. (212)206-1630. **E-mail:** assistant@bookhaven.com. **Website:**

www.lowensteinassociates.com. **Contact:** Barbara Lowenstein. Member of AAR.

MEMBER AGENTS Barbara Lowenstein, president (nonfiction interests include narrative nonfiction, health, money, finance, travel, multicultural, popular culture, and memoir; fiction interests include literary fiction and women's fiction); Mary South (literary fiction and nonfiction on subjects such as neuroscience, bioengineering, women's rights, design, and digital humanities, as well as investigative journalism, essays, and memoir).

REPRESENTS Nonfiction, fiction, novels, short story collections. **Considers these nonfiction areas:** autobiography, biography, business, creative nonfiction, cultural interests, health, humor, literature, memoirs, money, multicultural, popular culture, science, technology, travel, women's issues. **Considers these fiction areas:** commercial, literary, middle grade, science fiction, women's, young adult.

HOW TO CONTACT "For fiction, please send us a 1-page query letter, along with the first 10 pages pasted in the body of the message by e-mail to assistant@bookhaven.com. If nonfiction, please send a 1-page query letter, a table of contents, and, if available, a proposal pasted into the body of the e-mail. Please put the word 'QUERY' and the title of your project in the subject field of your e-mail and address it to the agent of your choice. Please do not send an attachment as the message will be deleted without being read and no reply will be sent." Accepts simultaneous submissions. Will respond if interested. Obtains most new clients through recommendations from others, solicitations, conferences.

TERMS Agent receives 15% commission on domestic sales; 20% commission on foreign sales. Offers written contract. Charges for large photocopy batches, messenger service, international postage.

LR CHILDREN'S LITERARY

(312)659-8325. **E-mail:** submissions@lrchildrensliterary.com. **Website:** www.lrchildrensliterary.com. **Contact:** Loretta Caravette. Member of AAR. Signatory of WGA.

REPRESENTS **Considers these fiction areas:** juvenile, middle grade, picture books, young adult.

HOW TO CONTACT E-query only. Alert this agent if you are contacting other agencies at the same time. If submitting young adult or middle grade, submit the first 3 chapters and a synopsis. If submitting a picture book, send no more than 2 mss. Illustrations (no more than 5MB) can be sent as .JPG or .PDF formats. Accepts simultaneous submissions. Responds in up to 6 weeks.

DONALD MAASS LITERARY AGENCY

1000 Dean St., Suite 252, Brooklyn NY 11238. (212)727-8383. **E-mail:** query.dmaass@maassagency.com. **Website:** www.maassagency.com. Estab. 1980. Member of AAR. Other memberships include SFWA, MWA, RWA. Represents more than 200 clients.

MEMBER AGENTS Donald Maass (mainstream, literary, mystery/suspense, science fiction, romance, women's fiction); Jennifer Jackson (science fiction and fantasy for both adult and YA markets, thrillers that mine popular and controversial issues, YA that challenges traditional thinking); Cameron McClure (literary, mystery/suspense, urban, fantasy, narrative nonfiction and projects with multicultural, international, and environmental themes, gay/lesbian); Katie Shea Boutillier (women's fiction/book club, edgy/dark, realistic/contemporary YA, commercial-scale literary fiction, and celebrity memoir); Paul Stevens (science fiction, fantasy, horror, mystery, suspense, and humorous fiction, LBGT a plus); Jennie Goloboy (fun, innovative, diverse, and progressive science fiction and fantasy for adults); Caitlin McDonald (SF/F - YA/MG/Adult, genre-bending/cross-genre fiction, diversity); Michael Curry (science fiction and fantasy, near future thrillers).

REPRESENTS Nonfiction, fiction, novels, juvenile books. **Considers these nonfiction areas:** autobiography, biography, creative nonfiction, memoirs, popular culture, science. **Considers these fiction areas:** commercial, contemporary issues, crime, detective, ethnic, fantasy, feminist, gay, historical, horror, juvenile, lesbian, literary, mainstream, middle grade, military, multicultural, mystery, paranormal, police, regional, romance, science fiction, supernatural, suspense, thriller, urban fantasy, westerns, women's, young adult.

HOW TO CONTACT Query via e-mail only. All the agents have different submission addresses and instructions. See the website and each agent's online profile for exact submission instructions. Accepts simultaneous submissions.

TERMS Agency receives 15% commission on domestic sales; 20% commission on foreign sales.

GINA MACCOBY LITERARY AGENCY

P.O. Box 60, Chappaqua NY 10514. (914)238-5630. E-mail: query@maccobylit.com. **Website:** www.publishersmarketplace.com/members/ginamaccoby/. **Contact:** Gina Maccoby. Estab. 1986. Member of AAR. AAR Board of Directors; Royalties and Ethics and Contracts subcommittees; Authors Guild, SCBWI.

REPRESENTS Nonfiction, fiction, novels, juvenile books. **Considers these nonfiction areas:** autobiography, biography, cultural interests, current affairs, ethnic, history, juvenile nonfiction, literature, popular culture, women's issues, women's studies, young adult. **Considers these fiction areas:** crime, detective, family saga, historical, juvenile, literary, mainstream, middle grade, multicultural, mystery, new adult, thriller, women's, young adult.

HOW TO CONTACT Query by e-mail only. Accepts simultaneous submissions. Owing to volume of submissions, may not respond to queries unless interested. Obtains most new clients through recommendations.

TERMS Agent receives 15% commission on domestic sales; 20-25% commission on foreign sales, which includes subagents commissions. May recover certain costs, such as purchasing books, shipping books overseas by airmail, legal fees for vetting motion picture contracts, bank fees for electronic funds transfers, overnight delivery services.

CAROL MANN AGENCY

55 Fifth Ave., 18th Floor, New York NY 10003. (212)206-5635. **Fax:** (212)675-4809. **E-mail:** submissions@carolmannagency.com. **Website:** www.carolmannagency.com. **Contact:** Agnes Carlowicz. Member of AAR. Represents Roughly 200 clients.

MEMBER AGENTS Carol Mann (health/medical, religion, spirituality, self-help, parenting, narrative nonfiction, current affairs); Laura Yorke; Gareth Esersky; Myrsini Stephanides (nonfiction areas of interest: pop culture and music, humor, narrative nonfiction and memoir, cookbooks; fiction areas of interest: offbeat literary fiction, graphic works, and edgy YA fiction); Joanne Wyckoff (nonfiction areas of interest: memoir, narrative nonfiction, personal narrative, psychology, women's issues, education, health and wellness, parenting, serious self-help, natural history; also accepts fiction); Lydia Shamah (edgy, modern fiction and timely nonfiction in the areas of business, self-improvement, relationship and gift books, particularly interested in female voices and experiences); Tom Miller (narrative nonfiction, self-help/psychology, popular culture, body-mind-spirit, wellness, business, and literary fiction).

REPRESENTS Nonfiction, fiction, novels. **Considers these nonfiction areas:** anthropology, archeology, architecture, art, autobiography, biography, business, child guidance, cultural interests, current affairs, design, ethnic, government, health, history, humor, law, medicine, memoirs, money, music, parenting, popular culture, politics, psychology, self-help, sociology, sports, women's issues, women's studies. **Considers these fiction areas:** commercial, literary, young adult, graphic works. **Considers these script areas:** romantic drama.

HOW TO CONTACT Please see website for submission guidelines. Accepts simultaneous submissions. Responds in 4 weeks to queries.

TERMS Agent receives 15% commission on domestic sales; 20% commission on foreign sales. Offers written contract.

MANSION STREET LITERARY MANAGEMENT

E-mail: querymansionstreet@gmail.com. **E-mail:** querymichelle@mansionstreet.com. **Website:** mansionstreet.com. **Contact:** Jean Sagendorph; Michelle Witte. Member of AAR. Signatory of WGA.

MEMBER AGENTS Jean Sagendorph, querymansionstreet@gmail.com (pop culture, gift books, cookbooks, general nonfiction, lifestyle, design, brand extensions), Michelle Witte, querymichelle@mansionstreet.com (young adult, middle grade, early readers, picture books (especially from author-illustrators), juvenile nonfiction).

REPRESENTS Nonfiction, novels. **Considers these nonfiction areas:** cooking, design, popular culture. **Considers these fiction areas:** juvenile, middle grade, young adult.

HOW TO CONTACT Send a query letter and no more than the first 10 pages of your ms in the body of an e-mail. Query one specific agent at this agency. No attachments. You must list the genre in the subject line. If the genre is not in the subject line, your query will be deleted. Accepts simultaneous submissions. Responds in up to 6 weeks.

MANUS & ASSOCIATES LITERARY AGENCY, INC.

425 Sherman Ave., Suite 200, Palo Alto CA 94306. (650)470-5151. **Fax:** (650)470-5159. **E-mail:** manuslit@manuslit.com. **Website:** www.manuslit.com. **Contact:** Jillian Manus, Jandy Nelson, Penny Nelson. NYC address: 444 Madison Ave., 39th Floor, New York NY 10022. Member of AAR.

MEMBER AGENTS Jandy Nelson (currently not taking on new clients); Jillian Manus, jillian@manuslit.com (political, memoirs, self-help, history, sports, women's issues, thrillers); Penny Nelson, penny@manuslit.com (memoirs, self-help, sports, nonfiction).

REPRESENTS Nonfiction, novels. **Considers these nonfiction areas:** cooking, history, inspirational, memoirs, politics, psychology, religious, self-help, sports, women's issues. **Considers these fiction areas:** thriller.

HOW TO CONTACT Snail mail submissions welcome. E-queries also accepted. For nonfiction, send a full proposal via snail mail. For fiction, send a query letter and 30 pages (unbound) if submitting via snail mail. Send only an e-query if submitting fiction via e-mail. If querying by e-mail, submit directly to one of the agents. Accepts simultaneous submissions. Responds in 3 months. Obtains most new clients through recommendations from others, solicitations, conferences.

TERMS Agent receives 15% commission on domestic sales; 20-25% commission on foreign sales. Offers written contract, binding for 2 years; 60-day notice must be given to terminate contract. Charges for photocopying and postage/UPS.

DENISE MARCIL LITERARY AGENCY, LLC

483 Westover Rd., Stamford CT 06902. (203)327-9970. **E-mail:** dmla@denisemarcilagency.com; annemarie@denisemarcilagency.com. **E-mail:** dmla@denisemacilagency.com. **Website:** www.denisemarcilagency.com. **Contact:** Denise Marcil, Anne Marie O'Farrell. Address for Anne Marie O'Farrell: 86 Dennis St., Manhasset, NY 11030. Estab. 1977. Member of AAR. Women's Media Group

MEMBER AGENTS Denise Marcil (self-help and popular reference books such as wellness, health, women's issues); Anne Marie O'Farrell (books that convey and promote innovative, practical and cutting edge information and ideas which help people in-

crease their self-awareness and fulfillment and maximize their potential in whatever area they choose; she is dying to represent a great basketball book).

REPRESENTS Nonfiction. **Considers these nonfiction areas:** business, cooking, diet/nutrition, education, health, how-to, New Age, psychology, self-help, spirituality, women's issues. **Considers these fiction areas:** commercial, suspense, thriller, women's.

HOW TO CONTACT E-query. Accepts simultaneous submissions.

TERMS Agent receives 15% commission on domestic sales; 20% commission on foreign sales and film sales. Offers written contract, binding for 2 years.

MARLENA AGENCY

278 Hamilton Ave., Princeton NJ 08540. (609)252-9405. **Fax:** (609)252-9408. **E-mail:** marlena@marlenaagency.com. **Website:** www.marlenaagency.com. Estab. 1990. Member of AAR. Signatory of WGA. Member of Society of Illustrators.

MEMBER AGENTS Staff includes Marlena Torzecka, Anna Pluskota, Tara Barry.

REPRESENTS , We represent Illustrators for Picture Books, Books for Children and Book jackets for all genres.

HOW TO CONTACT For first contact, send tearsheets, photocopies, or e-mail low resolution samples only. Submission guidelines available for #10 SASE. Accepts simultaneous submissions. Finds illustrators through queries/solicitations, magazines and graphic design.

TERMS Exclusive representation required. Offers written contract.

THE EVAN MARSHALL AGENCY

1 Pacio Ct., Roseland NJ 07068-1121. (973)287-6216. **E-mail:** evan@evanmarshallagency.com. **Website:** www.evanmarshallagency.com, www.themarshallplan.net. **Contact:** Evan Marshall. Estab. 1987. Member of AAR. Novelists, Inc. Represents 50+ clients.

REPRESENTS Fiction, novels. **Considers these fiction areas:** action, adventure, crime, detective, erotica, ethnic, family saga, fantasy, feminist, frontier, gay, glitz, historical, horror, humor, inspirational, lesbian, literary, mainstream, military, multicultural, multimedia, mystery, new adult, New Age, occult, paranormal, police, psychic, regional, religious, romance, satire, science fiction, spiritual, sports, supernatural, suspense, thriller, translation, urban fantasy, war, westerns, women's, young adult, romance (contemporary, gothic, historical, regency).

HOW TO CONTACT E-mail query letter, synopsis and first 3 chapters of novel within body of e-mail. Will request full manuscript if interested. Accepts simultaneous submissions. Responds in 1 week to queries if interested. Responds in 2 months to mss. Obtains new clients through queries and through recommendations from editors and current clients.

TERMS Agent receives 15% commission on domestic sales; 20% commission on foreign and film/TV sales. Offers written contract.

MARGRET MCBRIDE LITERARY AGENCY

P.O. Box 9128, La Jolla CA 92038. (858)454-1550. **E-mail:** staff@mcbridelit.com. **Website:** www.mcbridel-iterary.com. Estab. 1981. Member of AAR. Other memberships include Authors Guild.

MEMBER AGENTS Margret McBride; Faye Atchison.

REPRESENTS Nonfiction, fiction, novels. **Considers these nonfiction areas:** autobiography, biography, business, cooking, creative nonfiction, cultural interests, current affairs, diet/nutrition, ethnic, foods, gay/lesbian, health, history, hobbies, how-to, inspirational, investigative, juvenile nonfiction, medicine, memoirs, money, multicultural, music, popular culture, psychology, science, self-help, sex, sociology, theater, travel, true crime, women's issues, young adult. **Considers these fiction areas:** action, adventure, comic books, commercial, confession, contemporary issues, crime, detective, family saga, feminist, historical, horror, juvenile, mainstream, multicultural, multimedia, mystery, new adult, paranormal, police, psychic, regional, supernatural, suspense, thriller, young adult.

HOW TO CONTACT Please check our website, as instructions are subject to change. Only e-mail queries are accepted: staff@mcbridelit.com. In your query letter, provide a brief synopsis of your work, as well as any pertinent information about yourself. We recommend that authors look at book jacket copy of professionally published books to get an idea of the style and content that should be included in a query letter. Essentially, you are marketing yourself and your work to us, so that we can determine whether we feel we can market you and your work to publishers. There are detailed nonfiction proposal guidelines on our website, but we recommend author's get a copy of How to Write a Book Proposal by Michael Larsen for fur-

ther instruction. **Please note: The McBride Agency will not respond to queries sent by mail, and will not be responsible for the return of any material submitted by mail.** Accepts simultaneous submissions. Responds within 8 weeks to queries; 6-8 weeks to requested mss. "You are welcome to follow up by phone or e-mail after 6 weeks if you have not yet received a response."

TERMS Agent receives 15% commission on domestic sales; 25% commission on translation rights sales (15% to agency, 10% to sub-agent). Charges for overnight delivery and photocopying.

MCCORMICK LITERARY

37 W. 20th St., New York NY 10011. (212)691-9726. **E-mail:** queries@mccormicklit.com. **Website:** mccormicklit.com. Member of AAR. Signatory of WGA.

MEMBER AGENTS David McCormick; Pilar Queen (narrative nonfiction, practical nonfiction, and commercial women's fiction); Bridget McCarthy (literary and commercial fiction, narrative nonfiction, memoir, and cookbooks); Alia Hanna Habib (literary fiction, narrative nonfiction, memoir and cookbooks); Edward Orloff (literary fiction and narrative nonfiction, especially cultural history, politics, biography, and the arts); Daniel Menaker; Leslie Falk; Emma Borges-Scott.

REPRESENTS Nonfiction, novels. **Considers these nonfiction areas:** biography, cooking, history, memoirs, politics. **Considers these fiction areas:** literary, women's.

HOW TO CONTACT Snail mail queries only. Send an SASE. Accepts simultaneous submissions.

MCINTOSH & OTIS, INC.

353 Lexington Ave., New York NY 10016. (212)687-7400. **Fax:** (212)687-6894. **E-mail:** info@mcintoshandotis.com. **Website:** www.mcintoshandotis.com. **Contact:** Elizabeth Winick Rubinstein. Estab. 1928. Member of AAR. Signatory of WGA. SCBWI

MEMBER AGENTS Elizabeth Winick Rubinstein, ewrquery@mcintoshandotis.com (literary fiction, women's fiction, historical fiction, and mystery/suspense, along with narrative nonfiction, spiritual/self-help, history and current affairs); Christa Heschke, CHquery@mcintoshandotis.com (picture books, middle grade, young adult and new adult projects); Adam Muhlig, AMquery@mcintoshandotis.com (music–from jazz to classical to punk–popular culture, natural history, travel and adventure, and sports).

REPRESENTS Considers these nonfiction areas: creative nonfiction, current affairs, history, popular culture, self-help, spirituality, sports, travel. **Considers these fiction areas:** fantasy, historical, horror, literary, middle grade, mystery, new adult, paranormal, picture books, romance, science fiction, suspense, urban fantasy, women's, young adult.

HOW TO CONTACT E-mail submissions only. Each agent has their own e-mail address for subs. For fiction: Please send a query letter, synopsis, author bio, and the first 3 consecutive chapters (no more than 30 pages) of your novel. For nonfiction: Please send a query letter, proposal, outline, author bio, and 3 sample chapters (no more than 30 pages) of the ms. For children's & young adult: Please send a query letter, synopsis and the first 3 consecutive chapters (not to exceed 25 pages) of the ms. Accepts simultaneous submissions. Obtains clients through recommendations from others, editors, conferences and queries.

TERMS Agent receives 15% commission on domestic sales; 20% on foreign sales.

MENDEL MEDIA GROUP, LLC

115 W. 30th St., Suite 209, New York NY 10001. (646)239-9896. **E-mail:** query@mendelmedia.com. **Website:** www.mendelmedia.com. Estab. 2002. Member of AAR. Represents 60-90 clients.

REPRESENTS Nonfiction, fiction, novels. **Considers these nonfiction areas:** Americana, animals, anthropology, architecture, art, biography, business, child guidance, cooking, current affairs, dance, education, environment, ethnic, foods, gardening, gay/lesbian, government, health, history, how-to, humor, investigative, language, medicine, memoirs, military, money, multicultural, music, parenting, philosophy, popular culture, psychology, recreation, regional, religious, science, self-help, sex, sociology, software, spirituality, sports, travel, true crime, war, women's issues, women's studies, all narrative projects, and creative nonfiction.. **Considers these fiction areas:** action, adventure, contemporary issues, crime, detective, erotica, ethnic, feminist, gay, glitz, historical, humor, inspirational, juvenile, lesbian, literary, mainstream, mystery, picture books, police, religious, romance, satire, sports, thriller, young adult, commercial and literary fiction..

HOW TO CONTACT You should e-mail your work to query@mendelmedia.com. We no longer accept or read submissions sent by mail, so please do not send inquiries by any other method. If we want to read more or discuss your work, we will respond to you by e-mail or phone. Fiction queries: If you have a novel you would like to submit, please paste a synopsis and the first twenty pages into the body of your email, below a detailed letter about your publication history and the history of the project, if it has been submitted previously to publishers or other agents. Please do not use attachments, as we will not open them. Nonfiction queries: If you have a completed nonfiction book proposal and sample chapters, you should paste those into the body of an e-mail, below a detailed letter about your publication history and the history of the project, if it has been submitted previously to any publishers or other agents. Please do not use attachments, as we will not open them. If we want to read more or discuss your work, we will call or e-mail you directly. If you do not receive a personal response within a few weeks, we are not going to offer representation. In any case, however, please do not call or email to inquire about your query. Accepts simultaneous submissions. Responds within a few weeks, if interested. Obtains most new clients through referrals.

TERMS Agent receives 15% commission on domestic sales; 20% commission on foreign sales.

HOWARD MORHAIM LITERARY AGENCY

30 Pierrepont St., Brooklyn NY 11201. (718)222-8400. **Fax:** (718)222-5056. **E-mail:** info@morhaimliterary.com. **Website:** www.morhaimliterary.com. Member of AAR.

MEMBER AGENTS Howard Morhaim, howard@morhaimliterary.com; Kate McKean, kmckean@morhaimliterary.com; DongWon Song, dongwon@morhaimliterary.com; Kim-Mei Kirtland, kimmei@morhaimliterary.com.

REPRESENTS Considers these nonfiction areas: biography, business, cooking, crafts, creative nonfiction, design, economics, foods, health, humor, memoirs, parenting, self-help, sports. **Considers these fiction areas:** fantasy, historical, literary, middle grade, new adult, romance, science fiction, women's, young adult, LGBTQ young adult, magical realism, fantasy should be high fantasy, historical fiction should be no earlier than the 20th century..

HOW TO CONTACT Query via e-mail with cover letter and 3 sample chapters. See each agent's listing for specifics. Accepts simultaneous submissions.

JEAN V. NAGGAR LITERARY AGENCY, INC.

JVNLA, Inc., 216 E. 75th St., Suite 1E, New York NY 10021. (212)794-1082. **Website:** www.jvnla.com. **Contact:** Jennifer Weltz. Estab. 1978. Member of AAR. Other memberships include Women's Media Group, SCBWI, Pace University's Masters in Publishing Board Member. Represents 450 clients.

MEMBER AGENTS Jennifer Weltz (well-researched and original historicals, thrillers with a unique voice, wry dark humor, and magical realism; enthralling narrative nonfiction; voice driven young adult, middle grade); Alice Tasman (literary, commercial, YA, middle grade, and nonfiction in the categories of narrative, biography, music or pop culture); Ariana Philips (nonfiction both prescriptive and narrative).

REPRESENTS Nonfiction, fiction, novels, short story collections, novellas, juvenile books, scholarly books, poetry books.

HOW TO CONTACT "Visit our website to send submissions and see what our individual agents are looking for. No snail mail submissions please!" Accepts simultaneous submissions. Depends on the agent. No responses for queries unless the agent is interested.

TERMS Agent receives 15% commission on domestic sales; 20% commission on foreign sales. Offers written contract. Charges for overseas mailing, messenger services, book purchases, photocopying—all deductible from royalties received.

NELSON LITERARY AGENCY

1732 Wazee St., Suite 207, Denver CO 80202. (303)292-2805. **E-mail:** query@nelsonagency.com. **E-mail:** querykristin@nelsonagency.com; querydanielle@nelsonagency.com; queryjoanna@nelsonagency.com; queryquressa@nelsonagency.com. **Website:** www.nelsonagency.com. **Contact:** Kristin Nelson, President. Estab. 2002. Member of AAR. RWA, SCBWI, SFWA. Represents 79 clients.

MEMBER AGENTS Danielle Burby; Joanna MacKenzie; Quressa Robinson.

REPRESENTS Fiction, novels. , young adult, middle grade, literary commercial, upmarket women's fiction, single-title romance, science fiction, fantasy. **Considers these fiction areas:** commercial, fantasy, historical, horror, literary, mainstream, middle grade, romance, science fiction, suspense, thriller, urban fantasy, women's, young adult.

HOW TO CONTACT "Please visit our website and carefully read our submission guidelines. We do not accept any queries on Facebook or Twitter. Query by e-mail only. Write the word 'Query' in the e-mail subject line along with the title of your novel. Send no attachments, but please paste the first 10 pages of your novel in the body of the e-mail beneath your query letter." Accepts simultaneous submissions. Makes best efforts to respond to all queries within 3 weeks. Response to full mss requested can take up to 3 months.

TERMS Agent charges industry standard commission.

NEW LEAF LITERARY & MEDIA, INC.

110 W. 40th St., Suite 2201, New York NY 10018. (646)248-7989. **Fax:** (646)861-4654. **E-mail:** query@newleafliterary.com. **Website:** www.newleafliterary.com. Estab. 2012. Member of AAR.

MEMBER AGENTS Joanna Volpe (women's fiction, thriller, horror, speculative fiction, literary fiction and historical fiction, young adult, middle grade, art-focused picture books); Kathleen Ortiz, Director of Subsidiary Rights and literary agent (new voices in YA and animator/illustrator talent); Suzie Townsend (new adult, young adult, middle grade, romance [all subgenres], fantasy [urban fantasy, science fiction, steampunk, epic fantasy] and crime fiction [mysteries, thrillers]); Pouya Shahbazian, Director of Film and Television (no unsolicited queries); Janet Reid, janet@newleafliterary.com; Jaida Temperly (all fiction: magical realism, historical fiction; literary fiction; stories that are quirky and fantastical; nonfiction: niche, offbeat, a bit strange; middle grade; JL Stermer (nonfiction, smart pop culture, comedy/satire, fashion, health & wellness, self-help, and memoir).

REPRESENTS Nonfiction, fiction, novels, novellas, juvenile books, poetry books. **Considers these nonfiction areas:** cooking, crafts, creative nonfiction, science, technology, women's issues, young adult. **Considers these fiction areas:** crime, fantasy, historical, horror, literary, mainstream, middle grade, mystery, new adult, paranormal, picture books, romance, thriller, women's, young adult.

HOW TO CONTACT Send query via e-mail. Please do not query via phone. The word "Query" must be in the subject line, plus the agent's name, i.e.–Subject: Query, Suzie Townsend. You may include up to 5 double-spaced sample pages within the body of the e-mail. No attachments, unless specifically requested. Include all necessary contact information. You will receive an auto-response confirming receipt of your query. "We only respond if we are interested in seeing your work." Responds only if interested. All queries read within 1 month.

DANA NEWMAN LITERARY

1800 Avenue of the Stars, 12th Floor, Los Angeles CA 90067. **E-mail:** dananewmanliterary@gmail.com. **Website:** dananewman.com. **Contact:** Dana Newman. Estab. 2009. Member of AAR. California State Bar. Represents 29 clients.

MEMBER AGENTS Dana Newman (narrative nonfiction, business, lifestyle, current affairs, parenting, memoir, pop culture, sports, health, literary, and upmarket fiction).

REPRESENTS Nonfiction, novels, short story collections. **Considers these nonfiction areas:** architecture, art, autobiography, biography, business, child guidance, cooking, creative nonfiction, cultural interests, current affairs, diet/nutrition, design, education, ethnic, film, foods, gay/lesbian, government, health, history, how-to, inspirational, interior design, investigative, language, law, literature, medicine, memoirs, money, multicultural, music, New Age, parenting, popular culture, politics, psychology, science, self-help, sociology, sports, technology, theater, travel, true crime, women's issues, women's studies. **Considers these fiction areas:** commercial, contemporary issues, family saga, feminist, historical, literary, multicultural, sports, women's.

HOW TO CONTACT E-mail queries only. For both nonfiction and fiction, please submit a query letter including a description of your project and a brief biography. "If we are interested in your project, we will contact you and request a full book proposal (nonfiction) or a synopsis and the first 25 pages (fiction)." Accepts simultaneous submissions. "If we have requested your materials after receiving your query, we usually respond within 4 weeks." Obtains new clients through recommendations from others, queries, and submissions.

TERMS Obtains 15% commission on domestic sales; 20% on foreign sales. Offers 1 year written contract. Notice must be given 1 month prior to terminate a contract.

HAROLD OBER ASSOCIATES

425 Madison Ave., New York NY 10017. (212)759-8600. **Fax:** (212)759-9428. **Website:** www.haroldober.com. **Contact:** Appropriate agent. Member of AAR. Represents 250 clients.

MEMBER AGENTS Phyllis Westberg; Craig Tenney (few new clients, mostly Ober backlist and foreign rights).

HOW TO CONTACT Submit concise query letter addressed to a specific agent with the first 5 pages of the ms or proposal and SASE. No fax or e-mail. Does not handle filmscripts or plays. Responds as promptly as possible. Obtains most new clients through recommendations from others.

TERMS Agent receives 15% commission on domestic sales; 20% commission on foreign sales. Charges clients for express mail/package services.

RUBIN PFEFFER CONTENT

648 Hammond St., Chestnut Hill MA 02467. **E-mail:** info@rpcontent.com. **Website:** www.rpcontent.com. **Contact:** Rubin Pfeffer. Estab. 2014. Member of AAR. Signatory of WGA.

MEMBER AGENTS Melissa Nasson is an associate agent at Rubin Pfeffer Content and an attorney. She previously interned at Zachary Shuster Harmsworth, Perseus Books Group, and East-West Literary Agency before joining Rubin Pfeffer Content. Melissa also works as contracts director at Beacon Press.

REPRESENTS **Considers these nonfiction areas:** juvenile nonfiction, young adult. **Considers these fiction areas:** juvenile, middle grade, picture books, young adult.

HOW TO CONTACT Note: Rubin Pfeffer accepts submissions by referral only. Melissa Nasson is open to queries for picture books, middle-grade, and young adult fiction and nonfiction. To query Melissa, email her at melissa@rpcontent.com, include the query letter in the body of the email, and attach the first 50 pages as a Word doc or PDF. If you wish to query Rubin Pfeffer by referral only, specify the contact information of your reference when submitting. Authors/illustrators should send a query and a 1-3 chapter ms via e-mail (no postal submissions). The query, placed in the body of the e-mail, should include a synopsis of the piece, as well as any relevant information regarding previous publications, referrals, websites, and biographies. The ms may be attached as a .doc or a .pdf file. Specifically for illustrators, attach a PDF of the dummy or artwork to the e-mail. Accepts simultaneous submissions. Strives to respond within 6-8 weeks.

AARON M. PRIEST LITERARY AGENCY

200 W. 41st St., 21st Floor, New York NY 10036. (212)818-0344. **Fax:** (212)573-9417. **E-mail:** info@aar-

onpriest.com. **Website:** www.aaronpriest.com. Estab. 1974. Member of AAR.

MEMBER AGENTS Aaron Priest, querypriest@aaronpriest.com (thrillers, commercial fiction, biographies); Lisa Erbach Vance, queryvance@aaronpriest.com (contemporary fiction, thrillers/suspense, international fiction, narrative nonfiction); Lucy Childs, querychilds@aaronpriest.com (literary and commercial fiction, memoir, edgy women's fiction); Mitch Hoffman, queryhoffman@aaronpriest.com (thrillers, suspense, crime fiction, and literary fiction, as well as narrative nonfiction, politics, popular science, history, memoir, current events, and pop culture).

REPRESENTS Considers these nonfiction areas: biography, current affairs, history, memoirs, popular culture, politics, science. **Considers these fiction areas:** commercial, contemporary issues, crime, literary, middle grade, suspense, thriller, women's, young adult.

HOW TO CONTACT Query one of the agents using the appropriate e-mail listed on the website. "Please do not submit to more than 1 agent at this agency. We urge you to check our website and consider each agent's emphasis before submitting. Your query letter should be about one page long and describe your work as well as your background. You may also paste the first chapter of your work in the body of the e-mail. Do not send attachments." Accepts simultaneous submissions. Responds in 4 weeks, only if interested.

TERMS Agent receives 15% commission on domestic sales.

PROSPECT AGENCY

551 Valley Rd., PMB 377, Upper Montclair NJ 07043. (718)788-3217. **Fax:** (718)360-9582. **Website:** www.prospectagency.com. Estab. 2005. Member of AAR. Signatory of WGA. Represents 130+ clients.

MEMBER AGENTS Emily Sylvan Kim, esk@prospectagency.com (romance, women's, commercial, young adult, new adult); Rachel Orr, rko@prospectagency.com (picture books, illustrators, middle grade, young adult); Becca Stumpf, becca@prospectagency.com (young adult and middle grade [all genres, including fantasy/SciFi, literary, mystery, contemporary, historical, horror/suspense], especially MG and YA novels featuring diverse protagonists and life circumstances. Adult SciFi and Fantasy novels with broad appeal, upmarket women's fiction, smart, spicy romance novels); Carrie Pestritto, carrie@prospectagency.com (narrative nonfiction, general nonfiction, biography, and memoir; commercial fiction with a literary twist, women's fiction, romance, upmarket, historical fiction, high-concept YA and upper MG); Kirsten Carleton, kcarleton@prospectagency.com (upmarket speculative, thriller, and literary fiction for adult and YA).

REPRESENTS Nonfiction, fiction, novels, novellas, juvenile books, scholarly books, textbooks. **Considers these nonfiction areas:** biography, memoirs, popular culture, psychology. **Considers these fiction areas:** commercial, contemporary issues, crime, ethnic, family saga, fantasy, feminist, gay, historical, horror, humor, juvenile, lesbian, literary, mainstream, middle grade, multicultural, mystery, new adult, picture books, romance, science fiction, suspense, thriller, urban fantasy, women's, young adult.

HOW TO CONTACT All submissions are electronic and must be submitted through the portal at prospectagency.com/submissions. We do not accept any submissions through snail mail. Accepts simultaneous submissions. Obtains new clients through conferences, recommendations, queries, and some scouting.

TERMS Agent receives 15% on domestic sales, 20% on foreign sales sold directly and 25% on sales using a subagent. Offers written contract.

REES LITERARY AGENCY

14 Beacon St., Suite 710, Boston MA 02108. (617)227-9014. **E-mail:** lorin@reesagency.com. **Website:** reesagency.com. Estab. 1983. Member of AAR. Represents more than 100 clients.

MEMBER AGENTS Ann Collette, agent10702@aol.com (fiction: literary, upscale commercial women's, crime [including mystery, thriller and psychological suspense], upscale western, historical, military and war, and horror; nonfiction: narrative, military and war, books on race and class, works set in Southeast Asia, biography, pop culture, books on film and opera, humor, and memoir); Lorin Rees, lorin@reesagency.com (literary fiction, memoirs, business books, self-help, science, history, psychology, and narrative nonfiction); Rebecca Podos, rebecca@reesagency.com (young adult and middle grade fiction, particularly books about complex female relationships, beautifully written contemporary, genre novels with a strong focus on character, romance with more at stake than "will they/won't they," and LGBTQ books across all genres).

REPRESENTS Novels. **Considers these nonfiction areas:** biography, business, film, history, humor, memoirs, military, popular culture, psychology, science, war. **Considers these fiction areas:** commercial, crime, historical, horror, literary, middle grade, mystery, suspense, thriller, westerns, women's, young adult.

HOW TO CONTACT Consult website for each agent's submission guidelines and e-mail addresses, as they differ. Accepts simultaneous submissions. Obtains most new clients through recommendations from others, conferences, submissions.

TERMS Agent receives 15% commission on domestic sales; 20% commission on foreign sales.

REGAL HOFFMANN & ASSOCIATES LLC

242 W. 38th St., Floor 2, New York NY 10018. (212)684-7900. **Fax:** (212)684-7906. **E-mail:** submissions@rhaliterary.com. **Website:** www.rhaliterary.com. Estab. 2002. Member of AAR. Represents 70 clients.

MEMBER AGENTS Claire Anderson-Wheeler (nonfiction: memoirs and biographies, narrative histories, popular science, popular psychology; adult fiction: primarily character-driven literary fiction, but open to genre fiction, high-concept fiction; all genres of young adult / middle grade fiction); Markus Hoffmann (international and literary fiction, crime, [pop] cultural studies, current affairs, economics, history, music, popular science, and travel literature); Joseph Regal (literary fiction, international thrillers, history, science, photography, music, culture, and whimsy); Stephanie Steiker (serious and narrative nonfiction, literary fiction, graphic novels, history, philosophy, current affairs, cultural studies, biography, music, international writing); Grace Ross (literary fiction, historical fiction, international narratives, narrative nonfiction, popular science, biography, cultural theory, memoir).

REPRESENTS Nonfiction, fiction, novels, short story collections, juvenile books, scholarly books. **Considers these nonfiction areas:** biography, creative nonfiction, current affairs, economics, history, investigative, juvenile nonfiction, literature, memoirs, music, psychology, science, translation, travel, women's issues, women's studies, young adult. **Considers these** fiction areas: literary, mainstream, middle grade, short story collections, thriller, women's, young adult.

HOW TO CONTACT Query with SASE or via e-mail to submissions@rhaliterary.com. No phone calls. Submissions should consist of a 1-page query letter detailing the book in question, as well as the qualifications of the author. For fiction, submissions may also include the first 10 pages of the novel or one short story from a collection. Responds if interested. Accepts simultaneous submissions. Responds in 4-8 weeks.

TERMS Agent receives 15% commission on domestic sales; 20% commission on foreign sales. We charge no reading fees.

ANGELA RINALDI LITERARY AGENCY

P.O. Box 7875, Beverly Hills CA 90212-7875. (310)842-7665. **Fax:** (310)837-8143. **E-mail:** info@rinaldiliterary.com. **Website:** www.rinaldiliterary.com. **Contact:** Angela Rinaldi. Member of AAR.

REPRESENTS Nonfiction, novels. , TV and motion picture rights (for clients only). **Considers these nonfiction areas:** biography, business, cooking, current affairs, health, memoirs, parenting, psychology, self-help, women's issues, women's studies, narrative nonfiction, food narratives, wine, lifestyle, relationships, wellness, personal finance. **Considers these fiction areas:** commercial, historical, literary, mainstream, mystery, suspense, thriller, women's, contemporary, gothic, women's book club fiction.

HOW TO CONTACT E-queries only. Include the word "Query" in the subject line. For fiction, please send a brief synopsis and paste the first 10 pages into an e-mail. Nonfiction queries should include a detailed cover letter, your credentials and platform information as well as any publishing history. Tell us if you have a completed proposal. Accepts simultaneous submissions. Responds in 2-4 weeks.

TERMS Agent receives 15% commission on domestic sales; 25% commission on foreign sales. Offers written contract.

ANN RITTENBERG LITERARY AGENCY, INC.

15 Maiden Lane, Suite 206, New York NY 10038. (212)684-6936. **E-mail:** info@rittlit.com. **Website:** www.rittlit.com. **Contact:** Ann Rittenberg, president. Estab. 1992. Member of AAR. Represents 30 clients.

MEMBER AGENTS Ann Rittenberg, Rosie Jonker.

REPRESENTS Nonfiction, fiction, novels, juvenile books. **Considers these nonfiction areas:** biography, history, literature, memoirs, popular culture, true crime. **Considers these fiction areas:** crime, detective, family saga, literary, mainstream, mystery, suspense, thriller, women's.

HOW TO CONTACT Query via e-mail or postal mail (with SASE). Submit query letter with 3 sample chapters pasted into the body of the e-mail. If you query by e-mail, we will only respond if interested. If you are making a simultaneous submission, you must tell us in your query. Accepts simultaneous submissions. Responds in 6-8 weeks. However, as noted above, if you don't receive a response to an emailed query, that means it was a pass. Obtains most new clients through referrals from established writers and editors.

TERMS Agent receives 15% commission on domestic sales, and 20% commission on foreign and film deals. This 20% is shared with co-agents. Offers written contract. No charges except for PDFs or finished books for foreign and film submissions.

RLR ASSOCIATES, LTD.

420 Lexington Ave., Suite 2532, New York NY 10170. (212)541-8641. **E-mail:** website.info@rlrassociates. net. **Website:** www.rlrassociates.net. **Contact:** Scott Gould. Member of AAR. Represents 50 clients.

REPRESENTS Nonfiction, novels. **Considers these nonfiction areas:** biography, creative nonfiction, foods, history, humor, popular culture, sports. **Considers these fiction areas:** commercial, literary, mainstream, middle grade, picture books, romance, women's, young adult, genre.

HOW TO CONTACT Query by snail mail. For fiction, send a query and 1-3 chapters (pasted). For nonfiction, send query or proposal. Accepts simultaneous submissions. "If you do not hear from us within 3 months, please assume that your work is out of active consideration." Obtains most new clients through recommendations from others.

TERMS Agent receives 15% commission on domestic sales; 20% commission on foreign sales. Offers written contract.

BJ ROBBINS LITERARY AGENCY

5130 Bellaire Ave., North Hollywood CA 91607-2908. **E-mail:** robbinsliterary@gmail.com. **Website:** www. bjrobbinsliterary.com. **Contact:** (Ms.) BJ Robbins. Estab. 1992. Member of AAR.

REPRESENTS Nonfiction, fiction. **Considers these nonfiction areas:** autobiography, biography, creative nonfiction, cultural interests, current affairs, ethnic,

film, health, history, investigative, medicine, memoirs, multicultural, music, popular culture, psychology, science, sociology, sports, theater, travel, true crime, women's issues, women's studies. **Considers these fiction areas:** contemporary issues, crime, detective, ethnic, historical, literary, mainstream, multicultural, mystery, sports, suspense, thriller, women's.

HOW TO CONTACT E-query with no attachments. For fiction, okay to include first 10 pages in body of e-mail. Accepts simultaneous submissions. Only responds to projects if interested. Obtains most new clients through conferences, referrals.

TERMS Agent receives 15% commission on domestic sales; 20% commission on foreign sales. Offers written contract. No fees.

RODEEN LITERARY MANAGEMENT

3501 N. Southport #497, Chicago IL 60657. **E-mail:** info@rodeenliterary.com. **E-mail:** submissions@rodeenliterary.com. **Website:** www.rodeenliterary.com. **Contact:** Paul Rodeen. Estab. 2009. Member of AAR. Signatory of WGA

REPRESENTS Nonfiction, novels, juvenile books. , illustrations, graphic novels. **Considers these fiction areas:** juvenile, middle grade, picture books, young adult, graphic novels, comics.

HOW TO CONTACT Unsolicited submissions are accepted by e-mail only. Cover letters with synopsis and contact information should be included in the body of your e-mail. An initial submission of 50 pages from a novel or a longer work of nonfiction will suffice and should be pasted into the body of your e-mail. Accepts simultaneous submissions.

LINDA ROGHAAR LITERARY AGENCY, LLC

P.O. Box 3561, Amherst MA 01004. **E-mail:** contact@ lindaroghaar.com. **Website:** www.lindaroghaar.com. **Contact:** Linda L. Roghaar. Member of AAR.

REPRESENTS Nonfiction.

HOW TO CONTACT We prefer e-queries. Please mention 'query' in the subject line, and do not include attachments. For queries by mail, please include an SASE. Accepts simultaneous submissions. Responds within 12 weeks if interested.

TERMS Agent receives 15% commission on domestic sales. Agent receives negotiable commission on foreign sales. Offers written contract.

THE ROSENBERG GROUP

23 Lincoln Ave., Marblehead MA 01945. (781)990-1341. **Fax:** (781)990-1344. **Website:** www.rosenberggroup.com. **Contact:** Barbara Collins Rosenberg. Estab. 1998. Member of AAR. Recognized agent of the RWA. Represents 25 clients.

REPRESENTS Nonfiction, novels, textbooks. , college textbooks only. **Considers these nonfiction areas:** biography, current affairs, foods, music, popular culture, psychology, science, self-help, sports, women's issues, women's studies, women's health, wine/beverages. **Considers these fiction areas:** romance, women's, chick lit.

HOW TO CONTACT Query via snail mail. Your query letter should not exceed one page in length. It should include the title of your work, the genre and/or sub-genre; the manuscript's word count; and a brief description of the work. If you are writing category romance, please be certain to let her know the line for which your work is intended. Accepts simultaneous submissions. Obtains most new clients through recommendations from others, solicitations, conferences.

TERMS Agent receives 15% commission on domestic and foreign sales. Offers written contract; 1-month notice must be given to terminate contract. Charges maximum of $350/year for postage and photocopying.

RITA ROSENKRANZ LITERARY AGENCY

440 West End Ave., #15D, New York NY 10024. (212) 873-6333. **E-mail:** rrosenkranz@mindspring.com. **Website:** www.ritarosenkranzliteraryagency.com. **Contact:** Rita Rosenkranz. Member of AAR. Represents 40 clients.

REPRESENTS Nonfiction. **Considers these nonfiction areas:** agriculture, Americana, animals, anthropology, archeology, architecture, art, autobiography, biography, business, child guidance, computers, cooking, crafts, creative nonfiction, cultural interests, current affairs, dance, decorating, diet/nutrition, design, economics, education, environment, ethnic, film, foods, gardening, gay/lesbian, government, health, history, hobbies, horticulture, how-to, humor, inspirational, interior design, investigative, language, law, literature, medicine, memoirs, military, money, multicultural, music, New Age, parenting, philosophy, photography, popular culture, politics, psychology, regional, religious, satire, science, self-help, sex, software, spirituality, sports, technology, theater, true crime, war, women's issues, women's studies.

HOW TO CONTACT Send query letter only (no proposal) via regular mail or e-mail. Submit proposal package with SASE only on request. No fax queries. Accepts simultaneous submissions. Responds in 2 weeks to queries. Obtains most new clients through directory listings, solicitations, conferences, word of mouth.

TERMS Agent receives 15% commission on domestic sales; 20% commission on foreign sales. Offers written contract, binding for 3 years; 3-month written notice must be given to terminate contract. Charges clients for photocopying. Makes referrals to editing services.

ANDY ROSS LITERARY AGENCY

767 Santa Ray Ave., Oakland CA 94610. (510)238-8965. **E-mail:** andyrossagency@hotmail.com. **Website:** www.andyrossagency.com. **Contact:** Andy Ross. Estab. 2008. Member of AAR. Represents See website for client list. clients.

REPRESENTS Nonfiction, fiction, novels, juvenile books, scholarly books. **Considers these nonfiction areas:** anthropology, autobiography, biography, child guidance, cooking, creative nonfiction, cultural interests, current affairs, economics, education, environment, ethnic, gay/lesbian, government, history, investigative, juvenile nonfiction, language, law, literature, memoirs, military, parenting, philosophy, popular culture, politics, psychology, science, sociology, technology, war, women's issues, women's studies, young adult. **Considers these fiction areas:** commercial, contemporary issues, historical, juvenile, literary, middle grade, picture books, young adult.

HOW TO CONTACT Queries should be less than half page. Please put the word "query" in the title header of the e-mail. In the first sentence, state the category of the project. Give a short description of the book and your qualifications for writing. Accepts simultaneous submissions. Responds in 1 week to queries.

TERMS Agent receives 15% commission on domestic sales; 20% commission on foreign sales or other deals made through a sub-agent. Offers written contract.

JANE ROTROSEN AGENCY LLC

85 Broad St., 28th Floor, New York NY 10004. (212)593-4330. **Fax:** (212)935-6985. **Website:** www.janerotrosen.com. Estab. 1974. Member of AAR. Other memberships include Authors Guild. Represents more than 100 clients.

MEMBER AGENTS Jane Rotrosen Berkey (not taking on clients); Andrea Cirillo, acirillo@janerotrosen.com (general fiction, suspense, and women's fiction); Annelise Robey, arobey@janerotrosen.com (women's fiction, suspense, mystery, literary fiction, and select nonfiction); Meg Ruley, mruley@janerotrosen.com (commercial fiction, including suspense, mysteries, romance, and general fiction); Christina Hogrebe, chogrebe@janerotrosen.com (young adult, new adult, book club fiction, romantic comedies, mystery, and suspense); Amy Tannenbaum, atannenbaum@janerotrosen.com (contemporary romance, psychological suspense, thrillers, and new adult, as well as women's fiction that falls into that sweet spot between literary and commercial, memoir, narrative and prescriptive non-fiction in the areas of health, business, pop culture, humor, and popular psychology); Rebecca Scherer rscherer@janerotrosen.com (women's fiction, mystery, suspense, thriller, romance, upmarket/literary-leaning fiction); Jessica Errera (assistant to Christina and Rebecca).

REPRESENTS Nonfiction, novels. **Considers these nonfiction areas:** business, health, humor, memoirs, popular culture, psychology, narrative nonfiction. **Considers these fiction areas:** commercial, literary, mainstream, mystery, new adult, romance, suspense, thriller, women's, young adult.

HOW TO CONTACT Check website for guidelines. Accepts simultaneous submissions. Obtains most new clients through recommendations from others.

TERMS Agent receives 15% commission on domestic sales; 20% commission on foreign sales. Offers written contract, binding for 3 years; 2-month notice must be given to terminate contract. Charges clients for photocopying, express mail, overseas postage, book purchase.

THE RUDY AGENCY

825 Wildlife Ln., Estes Park CO 80517. (970)577-8500. **E-mail:** mak@rudyagency.com; claggett@rudyagency.com. **Website:** www.rudyagency.com. **Contact:** Maryann Karinch. Estab. 2004. Adheres to AAR canon of ethics. Represents 24 clients.

MEMBER AGENTS Maryann Karinch and Hilary Claggett (selected nonfiction).

REPRESENTS Nonfiction, fiction, novels, scholarly books. **Considers these nonfiction areas:** Americana, anthropology, archeology, architecture, autobiography, biography, business, child guidance, comput-

ers, cooking, creative nonfiction, cultural interests, current affairs, diet/nutrition, design, economics, education, environment, gay/lesbian, government, health, history, how-to, inspirational, investigative, law, literature, medicine, memoirs, military, money, parenting, popular culture, politics, psychology, science, self-help, sex, sociology, sports, technology, theater, true crime, war, women's issues, women's studies. **Considers these fiction areas:** action, adventure, commercial, contemporary issues, crime, erotica, feminist, gay, historical, inspirational, lesbian, literary, military, multicultural, sports, thriller, women's.

HOW TO CONTACT "Query us. If we like the query, we will invite a complete proposal (or complete ms if writing fiction). No phone queries, please. We won't hang up on you, but it makes it easier if you send us a note first." Accepts simultaneous submissions. Responds in under 3 weeks to non-fiction proposals and 8 weeks to invited manuscripts. Obtains most new clients through recommendations from others, solicitations.

TERMS Agent receives 15% commission on domestic sales. Offers written contract, binding for 1 year.

REGINA RYAN PUBLISHING ENTERPRISES, INC.

251 Central Park W., 7D, New York NY 10024. **E-mail:** https://app.authors.me/submit/regina-ryan-books. **Website:** www.reginaryanbooks.com. **Contact:** Regina Ryan. Estab. 1976. Member of AAR.

REPRESENTS Nonfiction. **Considers these nonfiction areas:** Americana, animals, anthropology, archeology, architecture, autobiography, biography, business, child guidance, cooking, cultural interests, diet/nutrition, environment, foods, gardening, health, history, horticulture, medicine, parenting, popular culture, politics, psychology, recreation, science, self-help, sex, sports, travel, true crime, women's issues, women's studies, adult and juvenile nonfiction: narrative nonfiction; natural history (especially birds and birding); popular science, lifestyle, sustainability, mind-body-spirit;.

HOW TO CONTACT All queries must come through the following site https://app.authors.me/submit/regina-ryan-books. Accepts simultaneous submissions. "We try to respond in 4-6 weeks but only if we are interested in pursuing the project. If you don't hear from us in that time frame, it means that we are not interested." Obtains most new clients through internet submissions.

TERMS Agent receives 15% commission on domestic and foreign sales. Offers written contract. Charges clients for all out-of-pocket expenses (e.g., long distance calls, messengers, freight, copying) if it's more than just a nominal amount.

SADLER CHILDREN'S LITERARY

(815)209-6252. **E-mail:** submissions.sadlerliterary@gmail.com. **Website:** www.sadlerchildrensliterary.com. **Contact:** Jodell Sadler. Member of AAR. Signatory of WGA.

REPRESENTS Nonfiction, fiction, novels, juvenile books. **Considers these nonfiction areas:** creative nonfiction, juvenile nonfiction, young adult. **Considers these fiction areas:** juvenile, middle grade, picture books, young adult.

HOW TO CONTACT "E-mail submissions only from conferences and events, including participation in webinars and webinar series courses at KidLitCollege. Your subject line should read 'Code provided—(Genre) Title_by_Author' and specifically addressed to me. I prefer a short letter: Hook (why my agency), pitch for you project, and bio (brief background and other categories you work in). All submissions in body of the e-mail, no attachments. Query and complete picture book text; first 10 pages for longer genre category. If you are an illustrator or author-illustrator, I encourage you to contact me, and please send a link to your online portfolio." Accepts simultaneous submissions. "I only obtain clients through writing conferences and SCBWI, Writer's Digest, and KidLitCollege.com webinars and events."

TERMS Standard rate. Provided on contract.

THE SAGALYN AGENCY / ICM PARTNERS

Chevy Chase MD **E-mail:** info@sagalyn.com. **E-mail:** query@sagalyn.com. **Website:** www.sagalyn.com. Estab. 1980. Member of AAR.

MEMBER AGENTS Raphael Sagalyn; Brandon Coward; Abby Serino.

REPRESENTS Nonfiction. **Considers these nonfiction areas:** biography, business, creative nonfiction, economics, popular culture, science, technology.

HOW TO CONTACT Please send e-mail queries only. Accepts simultaneous submissions.

VICTORIA SANDERS & ASSOCIATES

440 Buck Rd., Stone Ridge NY 12484. (212)633-8811. **E-mail:** queriesvsa@gmail.com. **Website:** www.victoriasanders.com. **Contact:** Victoria Sanders. Estab. 1992. Member of AAR. Signatory of WGA. Represents 135 clients.

MEMBER AGENTS Victoria Sanders; Bernadette Baker-Baughman; Jessica Spivey.

REPRESENTS Nonfiction, fiction, novels, short story collections, juvenile books. **Considers these nonfiction areas:** autobiography, biography, cooking, cultural interests, current affairs, ethnic, film, foods, gay/lesbian, government, history, humor, law, literature, memoirs, music, parenting, popular culture, politics, psychology, satire, theater, translation, women's issues, women's studies. **Considers these fiction areas:** action, adventure, cartoon, comic books, contemporary issues, crime, detective, ethnic, family saga, feminist, gay, historical, humor, inspirational, juvenile, lesbian, literary, mainstream, middle grade, multicultural, multimedia, mystery, new adult, picture books, suspense, thriller, women's, young adult.

HOW TO CONTACT Authors who wish to contact us regarding potential representation should send a query letter with the first 3 chapters (or about 25 pages) pasted into the body of the message to queriesvsa@gmail.com. We will only accept queries via e-mail. Query letters should describe the project and the author in the body of a single, 1-page e-mail that does not contain any attached files. Important note: Please paste the first 3 chapters of your manuscript (or about 25 pages, and feel free to round up to a chapter break) into the body of your e-mail." Accepts simultaneous submissions. Responds in 1-4 weeks, although occasionally it will take longer. "We will not respond to e-mails with attachments or attached files."

TERMS Agent receives 15% commission on domestic sales; 20% commission on foreign/film sales. Offers written contract.

WENDY SCHMALZ AGENCY

402 Union St., #831, Hudson NY 12534. (518)672-7697. **E-mail:** wendy@schmalzagency.com. **Website:** www.schmalzagency.com. **Contact:** Wendy Schmalz. Estab. 2002. Member of AAR.

REPRESENTS Juvenile books. **Considers these nonfiction areas:** young adult, Many nonfiction subjects are of interest to this agency.. **Considers these fiction areas:** middle grade, young adult.

HOW TO CONTACT Accepts only e-mail queries. Paste synopsis into the e-mail. Do not attach the ms or sample chapters or synopsis. Replies to queries only if they want to read the ms. If you do not hear from this agency within 2 weeks, consider that a no. Accepts simultaneous submissions. Obtains clients through recommendations from others.

TERMS Agent receives 15% commission on domestic sales; 20% on foreign sales; 25% for Asia.

SUSAN SCHULMAN LITERARY AGENCY LLC

454 W. 44th St., New York NY 10036. (212)713-1633. **E-mail:** susan@schulmanagency.com. **E-mail:** queries@schulmanagency.com. **Website:** www.publishersmarketplace.com/members/schulman/. **Contact:** Susan Schulman. Estab. 1980. Member of AAR. Signatory of WGA. Other memberships include Dramatists Guild, Writers Guild of America, East, New York Women in Film, Women's Media Group, Agents' Roundtable, League of New York Theater Women.

REPRESENTS Nonfiction, fiction, novels, juvenile books, feature film, TV scripts, theatrical stage play. **Considers these nonfiction areas:** anthropology, archeology, architecture, art, biography, business, child guidance, cooking, creative nonfiction, current affairs, economics, ethnic, government, health, history, juvenile nonfiction, law, money, popular culture, politics, psychology, religious, science, spirituality, women's issues, women's studies, young adult. **Considers these fiction areas:** commercial, contemporary issues, juvenile, literary, mainstream, new adult, religious, women's, young adult. **Considers these script areas:** theatrical stage play.

HOW TO CONTACT "For fiction: query letter with outline and three sample chapters, resume and SASE. For nonfiction: query letter with complete description of subject, at least one chapter, resume and SASE. Queries may be sent via regular mail or e-mail. Please do not submit queries via UPS or Federal Express. Please do not send attachments with e-mail queries Please incorporate the chapters into the body of the e-mail." Accepts simultaneous submissions. Responds in less than 1 week generally to a full query and 6 weeks to a full ms. Obtains most new clients through recommendations from others, solicitations, conferences.

TERMS Agent receives 15% commission on domestic sales; 20% commission on foreign sales. Offers written contract; 30-day notice must be given to terminate contract.

SCOVIL GALEN GHOSH LITERARY AGENCY, INC.

276 Fifth Ave., Suite 708, New York NY 10001. (212)679-8686. **Fax:** (212)679-6710. **E-mail:** info@sgglit.com. **Website:** www.sgglit.com. **Contact:** Russell Galen. Estab. 1992. Member of AAR. Represents 300 clients.

MEMBER AGENTS Russell Galen, russellgalen@sgglit.com (novels that stretch the bounds of reality; strong, serious nonfiction books on almost any subject that teach something new; no books that are merely entertaining, such as diet or pop psych books; serious interests include science, history, journalism, biography, business, memoir, nature, politics, sports, contemporary culture, literary nonfiction, etc.); Jack Scovil, jackscovil@sgglit.com; Anna Ghosh, annaghosh@sgglit.com (nonfiction proposals on all subjects, including literary nonfiction, history, science, social and cultural issues, memoir, food, art, adventure, and travel; adult commercial and literary fiction); Ann Behar, annbehar@sgglit.com (juvenile books for all ages).

HOW TO CONTACT E-mail queries only. Note how each agent at this agency has their own submission e-mail. Accepts simultaneous submissions.

SERENDIPITY LITERARY AGENCY, LLC

305 Gates Ave., Brooklyn NY 11216. **E-mail:** rbrooks@serendipitylit.com; info@serendipitylit.com. **Website:** www.serendipitylit.com; facebook.com/serendipitylit. **Contact:** Regina Brooks. Estab. 2000. Member of AAR. Signatory of WGA. Represents 150 clients.

MEMBER AGENTS Regina Brooks; Dawn Michelle Hardy (nonfiction, including sports, pop culture, blog and trend, music, lifestyle and social science); Folade Bell (literary and commercial women's fiction, YA, literary mysteries & thrillers, historical fiction, African-American issues, gay/lesbian, Christian fiction, humor and books that deeply explore other cultures; nonfiction that reads like fiction, including blog-to-book or pop culture); Nadeen Gayle (romance, memoir, pop culture, inspirational/ religious, women's fiction, parenting, young adult, mystery and political thrillers, and all forms of nonfiction); Rebecca Bugger (narrative nonfiction, investigative journalism, memoir, inspirational self-help, religion/spirituality, international, popular culture, and current affairs; literary and commercial fiction); Christina Morgan (literary fiction, crime fiction, and narrative nonfiction in the categories of pop culture, sports, current events and memoir); Jocquelle Caiby (literary fiction, horror, middle grade fiction, and children's books by authors who have been published in the adult market, athletes, actors, journalists, politicians, and musicians).

REPRESENTS Nonfiction, fiction, novels. **Considers these nonfiction areas:** Americana, anthropology, architecture, art, autobiography, biography, business, cooking, creative nonfiction, cultural interests, current affairs, inspirational, interior design, memoirs, metaphysics, music, parenting, popular culture, religious, self-help, spirituality, sports, travel, true crime, women's issues, women's studies, young adult. **Considers these fiction areas:** commercial, gay, historical, lesbian, literary, middle grade, mystery, romance, thriller, women's, young adult, Christian.

HOW TO CONTACT Check the website, as there are online submission forms for fiction, nonfiction and juvenile. Website will also state if we're temporarily closed to submissions to any areas. Accepts simultaneous submissions. Obtains most new clients through conferences, referrals.

TERMS Agent receives 15% commission on domestic sales; 20% commission on foreign sales. Offers written contract; 2-month notice must be given to terminate contract. Charges clients for office fees, which are taken from any advance.

THE SEYMOUR AGENCY

475 Miner St., Canton NY 13617. (239) 398-8209. **E-mail:** nicole@theseymouragency.com; julie@theseymouragency.com. **Website:** www.theseymouragency.com. Member of AAR. Signatory of WGA. Other memberships include RWA, Authors Guild, RWA, ACFW, HWA, MWA, SCBWI.

MEMBER AGENTS Nicole Rescinti, nicole@theseymouragency.com; Julie Gwinn, julie@theseymouragency.com; Tina Wainscott, tina@theseymouragency.com; Jennifer Wills, jennifer@theseymouragency.com; Lesley Sabga, lesley@theseymourageency.com.

REPRESENTS Nonfiction, fiction, novels, juvenile books. **Considers these nonfiction areas:** business, child guidance, cooking, crafts, cultural interests, decorating, diet/nutrition, design, foods, gardening, gay/lesbian, health, history, hobbies, how-to, humor, inspirational, juvenile nonfiction, literature, memoirs, metaphysics, military, music, New Age, parent-ing, philosophy, photography, popular culture, politics, psychology, religious, self-help, sex, spirituality, sports, theater, travel, true crime, war, women's issues, women's studies, young adult, ; cookbooks; any well-written nonfiction that includes a proposal in standard format and 1 sample chapter.. **Considers these fiction areas:** action, adventure, commercial, contemporary issues, erotica, ethnic, experimental, family saga, fantasy, feminist, frontier, gay, horror, humor, inspirational, lesbian, literary, mainstream, metaphysical, middle grade, military, multicultural, multimedia, mystery, new adult, New Age, occult, paranormal, picture books, police, religious, romance, science fiction, spiritual, sports, supernatural, suspense, thriller, translation, urban fantasy, war, westerns, women's, young adult.

HOW TO CONTACT Accepts e-mail queries. Check online for guidelines. Accepts simultaneous submissions. Responds in 1 month to queries; 3 months to mss.

TERMS Agent receives 12-15% commission on domestic sales.

DENISE SHANNON LITERARY AGENCY, INC.

20 W. 22nd St., Suite 1603, New York NY 10010. **E-mail:** info@deniseshannonagency.com. **E-mail:** submissions@deniseshannonagency.com. **Website:** www.deniseshannonagency.com. **Contact:** Denise Shannon. Estab. 2002. Member of AAR.

REPRESENTS Nonfiction, novels. **Considers these nonfiction areas:** biography, business, health, narrative nonfiction, politics, journalism, social history. **Considers these fiction areas:** literary.

HOW TO CONTACT "Queries may be submitted by post, accompanied by a SASE, or by e-mail to submissions@deniseshannonagency.com. Please include a description of the available book project and a brief bio including details of any prior publications. We will reply and request more material if we are interested. We request that you inform us if you are submitting material simultaneously to other agencies." Accepts simultaneous submissions.

WENDY SHERMAN ASSOCIATES, INC.

138 W. 25th St., Suite 1018, New York NY 10001. (212)279-9027. **E-mail:** submissions@wsherman.com. **Website:** www.wsherman.com. **Contact:** Wendy Sherman. Estab. 1999. Member of AAR.

MEMBER AGENTS Wendy Sherman (women's fiction that hits that sweet spot between literary and mainstream, Southern voices, suspense with a well-developed protagonist, anything related to food, dogs, mothers and daughters).

REPRESENTS Nonfiction, fiction, novels, juvenile books. **Considers these nonfiction areas:** creative nonfiction, foods, humor, memoirs, parenting, popular culture, psychology, self-help, narrative nonfiction. **Considers these fiction areas:** mainstream, Mainstream fiction that hits the sweet spot between literary and commercial.

HOW TO CONTACT Query via e-mail only. "We ask that you include your last name, title, and the name of the agent you are submitting to in the subject line. For fiction, please include a query letter and your first 10 pages copied and pasted in the body of the e-mail. We will not open attachments unless they have been requested. For nonfiction, please include your query letter and author bio. Due to the large number of e-mail submissions that we receive, we only reply to e-mail queries in the affirmative. We respectfully ask that you do not send queries to our individual e-mail addresses." Accepts simultaneous submissions. Obtains most new clients through recommendations from other writers.

TERMS Agent receives standard 15% commission. Offers written contract.

SPENCERHILL ASSOCIATES

8131 Lakewood Main St., Building M, Suite 205, Lakewood Ranch FL 34202. (941)907-3700. **E-mail:** submission@spencerhillassociates.com. **Website:** www.spencerhillassociates.com. **Contact:** Karen Solem, Nalini Akolekar, Amanda Leuck, Sandy Harding, and Ali Herring. Member of AAR.

MEMBER AGENTS Karen Solem; Nalini Akolekar; Amanda Leuck; Sandy Harding; Ali Herring.

REPRESENTS Fiction, novels, juvenile books. **Considers these fiction areas:** commercial, contemporary issues, crime, detective, erotica, family saga, feminist, gay, historical, inspirational, lesbian, literary, mainstream, middle grade, multicultural, mystery, new adult, paranormal, police, religious, romance, suspense, thriller, women's, young adult.

HOW TO CONTACT "We accept electronic submissions only. Please send us a query letter in the body of an e-mail, pitch us your project and tell us about yourself: Do you have prior publishing credits? At-tach the first three chapters and synopsis preferably in .doc, rtf or txt format to your email. Send all queries to submission@spencerhillassociates.com. Or submit through the QueryManager link on our website. We do not have a preference for exclusive submissions, but do appreciate knowing if the submission is simultaneous. We receive thousands of submissions a year and each query receives our attention. Unfortunately, we are unable to respond to each query individually. If we are interested in your work, we will contact you within 12 weeks." Accepts simultaneous submissions. Responds in approximately 12 weeks.

TERMS Agent receives 15% commission on domestic sales; 20% commission on foreign sales. Offers written contract; 3-month notice must be given to terminate contract.

PHILIP G. SPITZER LITERARY AGENCY, INC

50 Talmage Farm Ln., East Hampton NY 11937. (631)329-3650. **Fax:** (631)329-3651. **E-mail:** lukas.ortiz@spitzeragency.com; annelise.spitzer@spitzeragency.com. **E-mail:** kim.lombardini@spitzeragency.com. **Website:** www.spitzeragency.com. **Contact:** Lukas Ortiz. Estab. 1969. Member of AAR.

MEMBER AGENTS Philip G. Spitzer; Anne-Lise Spitzer; Lukas Ortiz.

REPRESENTS Novels. **Considers these nonfiction areas:** biography, current affairs, history, politics, sports, travel. **Considers these fiction areas:** literary, mainstream, suspense, thriller.

HOW TO CONTACT E-mail query containing synopsis of work, brief biography, and a sample chapter (pasted into the e-mail). Be aware that this agency openly says their client list is quite full. Obtains most new clients through recommendations from others.

TERMS Agent receives 15% commission on domestic sales; 20% commission on foreign sales.

STIMOLA LITERARY STUDIO

308 Livingston Ct., Edgewater NJ 07020. **E-mail:** info@stimolaliterarystudio.com. **E-mail:** see submission page on website. **Website:** www.stimolaliterarystudio.com. **Contact:** Rosemary B. Stimola. Estab. 1997. Member of AAR. PEN, Authors Guild, ALA Represents 75 clients.

MEMBER AGENTS Rosemary B. Stimola; Erica Rand Silverman; Allison Remcheck; Adriana Stimola.

REPRESENTS Juvenile books. **Considers these nonfiction areas:** cooking, foods, juvenile nonfiction, young adult. **Considers these fiction areas:** middle grade, picture books, young adult.

HOW TO CONTACT Query via e-mail as per submission guidelines on website. Author/illustrators of picture books may attach text and sample art. A PDF dummy is preferred. Accepts simultaneous submissions. Responds in 3 weeks to queries "we wish to pursue further;" 2 months to requested mss. While unsolicited queries are welcome, most clients come through editor, agent, client referrals.

TERMS Agent receives 15% commission on domestic sales; 20% (if subagents are employed) commission on foreign sales. Offers written contract, binding for all children's projects. 60 days notice must be given to terminate contract.

STONESONG

270 W. 39th St. #201, New York NY 10018. (212)929-4600. **E-mail:** editors@stonesong.com. **E-mail:** submissions@stonesong.com. **Website:** stonesong.com. Member of AAR. Signatory of WGA.

MEMBER AGENTS Alison Fargis; Ellen Scordato; Judy Linden; Emmanuelle Morgen; Leila Campoli (business, science, technology, and self improvement); Maria Ribas (cookbooks, self-help, health, diet, home, parenting, and humor, all from authors with demonstrable platforms; she's also interested in narrative nonfiction and select memoir); Melissa Edwards (children's fiction and adult commercial fiction, as well as select pop-culture nonfiction); Alyssa Jennette (children's and adult fiction and picture books, and has dabbled in humor and pop culture nonfiction); Madelyn Burt (adult and children's fiction, as well as select historical nonfiction).

REPRESENTS Nonfiction, fiction, novels, juvenile books. **Considers these nonfiction areas:** architecture, art, biography, business, cooking, crafts, creative nonfiction, cultural interests, current affairs, dance, decorating, diet/nutrition, design, economics, foods, gay/lesbian, health, history, hobbies, how-to, humor, interior design, investigative, literature, memoirs, money, music, New Age, parenting, photography, popular culture, politics, psychology, science, self-help, sociology, spirituality, sports, technology, women's issues, young adult. **Considers these fiction areas:** action, adventure, commercial, confession, contemporary issues, ethnic, experimental, family saga, fantasy, feminist, gay, historical, horror, humor, juvenile, lesbian, literary, mainstream, middle grade, mili-

tary, multicultural, mystery, new adult, New Age, occult, paranormal, regional, romance, satire, science fiction, supernatural, suspense, thriller, urban fantasy, women's, young adult.

HOW TO CONTACT Accepts electronic queries for fiction and nonfiction. Submit query addressed to a specific agent. Include first chapter or first 10 pages of ms. Accepts simultaneous submissions.

ROBIN STRAUS AGENCY, INC.

The Wallace Literary Agency, 229 E. 79th St., Suite 5A, New York NY 10075. (212)472-3282. **Fax:** (212)472-3833. **E-mail:** info@robinstrausagency.com. **Website:** www.robinstrausagency.com. **Contact:** Ms. Robin Straus. Estab. 1983. Member of AAR.

REPRESENTS Considers these nonfiction areas: biography, cooking, creative nonfiction, current affairs, environment, foods, gay/lesbian, health, history, memoirs, multicultural, music, parenting, popular culture, politics, psychology, science, travel, women's issues, mainstream science. **Considers these fiction areas:** commercial, contemporary issues, fantasy, feminist, literary, mainstream, science fiction, translation, women's.

HOW TO CONTACT E-query only. No physical mail accepted. See our website for full submission instructions. Email us a query letter with contact information, an autobiographical summary, a brief synopsis or description of your book project, submission history, and information on competition. If you wish, you may also include the opening chapter of your manuscript (pasted). While we do our best to reply to all queries, you can assume that if you haven't heard from us after six weeks, we are not interested. Accepts simultaneous submissions.

TERMS Agent receives 15% commission on domestic sales; 20% commission on foreign sales. Offers written contract.

THE STRINGER LITERARY AGENCY LLC

P.O. Box 111255, Naples FL 34108. **E-mail:** mstringer@stringerlit.com. **Website:** www.stringerlit.com. **Contact:** Marlene Stringer. Estab. 2008. Member of AAR. Signatory of WGA. RWA, MWA, ITW, SBCWI Represents 50 clients.

REPRESENTS Fiction, novels. **Considers these fiction areas:** commercial, crime, detective, fantasy, historical, horror, mainstream, multicultural, mystery, new adult, paranormal, police, romance, science fiction, suspense, thriller, urban fantasy, women's, young adult, No space opera SF..

HOW TO CONTACT Electronic submissions through website submission form only. Please make sure your ms is as good as it can be before you submit. Agents are not first readers. For specific information on what we like to see in query letters, refer to the information at www.stringerlit.com under the heading "Learn." Accepts simultaneous submissions. "We strive to respond quickly, but current clients' work always comes first." Obtains new clients through referrals, submissions, conferences.

TERMS Standard commission. "We do not charge fees."

THE STROTHMAN AGENCY, LLC

63 E. 9th St., 10X, New York NY 10003. **E-mail:** info@strothmanagency.com. **E-mail:** strothmanagency@gmail.com. **Website:** www.strothmanagency.com. **Contact:** Wendy Strothman, Lauren MacLeod. Estab. 2003. Member of AAR. Represents 100+ clients.

MEMBER AGENTS Wendy Strothman (history, narrative nonfiction, narrative journalism, science and nature, and current affairs); Lauren MacLeod (young adult fiction and nonfiction, middle grade novels, as well as adult narrative nonfiction, particularly food writing, science, pop culture and history).

REPRESENTS Nonfiction, juvenile books. **Considers these nonfiction areas:** anthropology, archeology, business, cooking, cultural interests, current affairs, economics, environment, foods, government, history, investigative, juvenile nonfiction, language, law, literature, popular culture, politics, science, sociology, true crime, war, women's issues, women's studies, young adult. **Considers these fiction areas:** middle grade, young adult.

HOW TO CONTACT Accepts queries only via e-mail. See submission guidelines online. Accepts simultaneous submissions. "All e-mails received will be responded to with an auto-reply. If we have not replied to your query within 6 weeks, we do not feel that it is right for us." Accepts simultaneous submissions. Obtains most new clients through recommendations from others.

TERMS Agent receives 15% commission on domestic sales; 20% commission on foreign sales. Offers written contract; 30-day notice must be given to terminate contract.

EMMA SWEENEY AGENCY, LLC

245 E 80th St., Suite 7E, New York NY 10075. **E-mail:** info@emmasweeneyagency.com. **E-mail:** queries@emmasweeneyagency.com. **Website:** www.emmasweeneyagency.com. Estab. 2006. Member of AAR. Other memberships include Women's Media Group. Represents 80 clients.

MEMBER AGENTS Emma Sweeney, president; Margaret Sutherland Brown (commercial and literary fiction, mysteries and thrillers, narrative nonfiction, lifestyle, and cookbook); Kira Watson (children's literature).

REPRESENTS Nonfiction, fiction, novels, juvenile books. **Considers these nonfiction areas:** biography, cooking, creative nonfiction, cultural interests, decorating, diet/nutrition, design, foods, gardening, history, how-to, interior design, juvenile nonfiction, literature, memoirs, popular culture, psychology, religious, science, sex, sociology, young adult. **Considers these fiction areas:** commercial, contemporary issues, crime, historical, horror, juvenile, literary, mainstream, middle grade, mystery, new adult, suspense, thriller, women's, young adult.

HOW TO CONTACT "We accept only electronic queries, and ask that all queries be sent to queries@emmasweeneyagency.com rather than to any agent directly. Please begin your query with a succinct (and hopefully catchy) description of your plot or proposal. Always include a brief cover letter telling us how you heard about ESA, your previous writing credits, and a few lines about yourself. We cannot open any attachments unless specifically requested, and ask that you paste the first 10 pages of your proposal or novel into the text of your e-mail." Accepts simultaneous submissions.

TESSLER LITERARY AGENCY, LLC

27 W. 20th St., Suite 1003, New York NY 10011. (212)242-0466. **Website:** www.tessleragency.com. **Contact:** Michelle Tessler. Estab. 2004. Member of AAR. Women's Media Group.

REPRESENTS Nonfiction, fiction, novels. **Considers these nonfiction areas:** animals, autobiography, biography, business, cooking, creative nonfiction, cultural interests, current affairs, diet/nutrition, economics, education, environment, ethnic, foods, gardening, health, history, how-to, humor, investigative, literature, medicine, memoirs, military, money, multicultural, parenting, philosophy, photography, popular culture, psychology, religious, science, self-help, spirituality, technology, travel, women's issues, women's studies. **Considers these fiction areas:** commercial, ethnic, family saga, historical, literary, multicultural, women's.

HOW TO CONTACT Submit query through online query form only. Accepts simultaneous submissions. New clients by queries/submissions through the website and recommendations from others.

TERMS Receives 15% commission on domestic sales; 20% on foreign sales. Offers written contract.

THOMPSON LITERARY AGENCY

115 W. 29th St., Third Floor, New York NY 10001. (347)281-7685. **E-mail:** submissions@thompsonliterary.com. **Website:** thompsonliterary.com. **Contact:** Meg Thompson, founder. Estab. 2014. Member of AAR. Signatory of WGA.

MEMBER AGENTS Cindy Uh, senior agent; Kiele Raymond, senior agent; John Thorn, affiliate agent; Sandy Hodgman, director of foreign rights.

REPRESENTS Nonfiction, fiction, novels, juvenile books. **Considers these nonfiction areas:** autobiography, biography, business, cooking, crafts, creative nonfiction, current affairs, diet/nutrition, design, education, foods, health, history, how-to, humor, inspirational, interior design, juvenile nonfiction, memoirs, multicultural, popular culture, politics, science, self-help, sociology, sports, travel, women's issues, women's studies, young adult. **Considers these fiction areas:** commercial, contemporary issues, experimental, fantasy, feminist, historical, juvenile, literary, middle grade, multicultural, picture books, women's, young adult.

HOW TO CONTACT "For fiction: Please send a query letter, including any salient biographical information or previous publications, and attach the first 25 pages of your manuscript. For nonfiction: Please send a query letter and a full proposal, including biographical information, previous publications, credentials that qualify you to write your book, marketing information, and sample material. You should address your query to whichever agent you think is best suited for your project." Accepts simultaneous submissions. Responds in 6 weeks if interested.

THREE SEAS LITERARY AGENCY

P.O. Box 444, Sun Prairie WI 53590. (608)834-9317. **E-mail:** queries@threeseaslit.com. **Website:** threeseasagency.com. **Contact:** Michelle Grajkowski, Cori Deyoe. Estab. 2000. Member of AAR. Other memberships include RWA (Romance Writers of America), SCBWI Represents 55 clients.

MEMBER AGENTS Michelle Grajkowski (romance, women's fiction, young adult and middle grade fiction, select nonfiction projects); Cori Deyoe (all sub-genres of romance, women's fiction, young adult, middle grade, picture books, thrillers, mysteries and select nonfiction); Linda Scalissi (women's fiction, thrillers, young adult, mysteries and romance).

REPRESENTS Nonfiction, novels. **Considers these fiction areas:** middle grade, mystery, picture books, romance, thriller, women's, young adult.

HOW TO CONTACT E-mail queries only; no attachments, unless requested by agents. For fiction, please e-mail the first chapter and synopsis along with a cover letter. Also, be sure to include the genre and the number of words in your manuscript, as well as pertinent writing experience in your query letter. For nonfiction, e-mail a complete proposal, including a query letter and your first chapter. For picture books, query with complete text. Accepts simultaneous submissions. Obtains most new clients through recommendations from others, conferences.

TERMS Agent receives 15% commission on domestic sales; 20% commission on foreign sales. Offers written contract.

TRIADA US

P.O. Box 561, Sewickley PA 15143. (412)401-3376. **E-mail:** uwe@triadaus.com; brent@triadaus.com; laura@triadaus.com; lauren@triadaus.com; amelia@triadaus.com. **Website:** www.triadaus.com. **Contact:** Dr. Uwe Stender, President. Estab. 2004. Member of AAR.

MEMBER AGENTS Uwe Stender; Brent Taylor; Laura Crockett; Lauren Spieller; Amelia Appel.

REPRESENTS Nonfiction, fiction, novels, juvenile books. **Considers these nonfiction areas:** biography, business, cooking, crafts, creative nonfiction, cultural interests, current affairs, diet/nutrition, economics, education, environment, ethnic, foods, gardening, health, history, how-to, juvenile nonfiction, literature, memoirs, music, parenting, popular culture, politics, science, self-help, sports, true crime, women's issues, young adult. **Considers these fiction areas:** action, adventure, comic books, commercial, contemporary issues, crime, detective, ethnic, family saga, fantasy, gay, historical, horror, juvenile, lesbian, literary, mainstream, middle grade, multicultural, mystery, new adult, occult, picture books, police, suspense, thriller, urban fantasy, women's, young adult.

HOW TO CONTACT E-mail queries preferred. Please paste your query letter and the first 10 pages of your ms into the body of a message e-mailed to the agent of your choice. Please note: a rejection from 1 Triada US agent is a rejection from all. Triada US agents personally respond to all queries and requested material and pride themselves on having some of the fastest response times in the industry. Obtains most new clients through submission inbox (query letters and requested mss), client referrals, and conferences.

TERMS Triada US retains 15% commission on domestic sales and 20% commission on foreign and translation sales. Offers written contract; 30-day notice must be given prior to termination.

TRIDENT MEDIA GROUP

41 Madison Ave., 36th Floor, New York NY 10010. (212)333-1511. **Website:** www.tridentmediagroup. com. **Contact:** Ellen Levine. Member of AAR.

MEMBER AGENTS Kimberly Whalen, ws.assistant@tridentmediagroup (commercial fiction and nonfiction, including women's fiction, romance, suspense, paranormal, and pop culture); Alyssa Eisner Henkin (picture books through young adult fiction, including mysteries, period pieces, contemporary school-settings, issues of social justice, family sagas, eerie magical realism, and retellings of classics; children's/YA nonfiction: history, STEM/STEAM themes, memoir) Scott Miller, smiller@tridentmediagroup.com (commercial fiction, including thrillers, crime fiction, women's, book club fiction, middle grade, young adult; nonfiction, including military, celebrity and pop culture, narrative, sports, prescriptive, and current events); Melissa Flashman, mflashman@tridentmediagroup.com (nonfiction: pop culture, memoir, wellness, popular science, business and economics, technology; fiction: adult and YA, literary and commercial); Don Fehr, dfehr@tridentmediagroup.com (literary and commercial fiction, young adult fiction, narrative nonfiction, memoirs, travel, science, and health); John Silbersack, silbersack.assistant@tridentmediagroup.com (fiction: literary fiction, crime fiction, science fiction and fantasy, children's, thrillers/suspense; nonfiction: narrative nonfiction, science, history, biography, current events, memoirs, finance, pop culture); Erica Spellman-Silverman; Ellen Levine, levine.assistant@tridentmediagroup.com (popular commercial fiction and compelling nonfiction, including memoir, popular culture, narrative nonfiction, history, politics, biography, science, and the odd quirky book); Mark Gottlieb (fiction: science fiction, fantasy, young adult, graphic novels, historical, middle grade, mystery, romance, suspense, thrillers; nonfiction: business, finance, history, religious, health, cookbooks, sports, African-American, biography, memoir, travel, mind/body/spirit, narrative nonfiction, science, technology); Alexander Slater, aslater@tridentmdiagroup.com (children's, middle grade, and young adult fiction); Amanda O'Connor, aoconnor@tridentmediagroup.com; Tara Carberry, tcarberry@tridentmediagroup.com (women's commercial fiction, romance, new adult, young adult, and select nonfiction); Alexa Stark, astark@tridentmediagroup.com (literary fiction, upmarket commercial fiction, young adult, memoir, narrative nonfiction, popular science, cultural criticism and women's issues).

REPRESENTS Considers these nonfiction areas: biography, business, cooking, creative nonfiction, current affairs, economics, health, history, memoirs, military, popular culture, politics, religious, science, sports, technology, travel, women's issues, young adult, middle grade. **Considers these fiction areas:** commercial, crime, fantasy, historical, juvenile, literary, middle grade, mystery, new adult, paranormal, picture books, romance, science fiction, suspense, thriller, women's, young adult.

HOW TO CONTACT Submit through the agency's online submission form on the agency website. Query only one agent at a time. If you e-query, include no attachments. Accepts simultaneous submissions.

THE UNTER AGENCY

23 W. 73rd St., Suite 100, New York NY 10023. (212)401-4068. **E-mail:** jennifer@theunteragency. com. **Website:** www.theunteragency.com. **Contact:** Jennifer Unter. Estab. 2008. Member of AAR. Women Media Group

REPRESENTS Nonfiction, fiction, novels, short story collections, juvenile books. **Considers these nonfiction areas:** animals, art, autobiography, biography, cooking, creative nonfiction, current affairs, diet/nutrition, environment, foods, health, history, how-to, humor, juvenile nonfiction, law, memoirs, popular culture, politics, spirituality, sports, travel, true crime, women's issues, young adult, nature subjects. **Considers these fiction areas:** action, adventure, cartoon, commercial, family saga, inspirational, juvenile, mainstream, middle grade, mystery, paranormal, picture books, thriller, women's, young adult.

HOW TO CONTACT Send an e-query. There is also an online submission form. If you do not hear back from this agency within 3 months, consider that a no. Accepts simultaneous submissions. Responds in 3 months.

UPSTART CROW LITERARY

244 Fifth Avenue, 11th Floor, New York NY 10001. **E-mail:** danielle.submission@gmail.com. **Website:** www.upstartcrowliterary.com. **Contact:** Danielle Chiotti, Alexandra Penfold. Estab. 2009. Member of AAR. Signatory of WGA.

MEMBER AGENTS Michael Stearns (not accepting submissions); Danielle Chiotti (all genres of young adult and middle grade fiction; adult upmarket commercial fiction [not considering romance, mystery/suspense/thriller, science fiction, horror, or erotica]; nonfiction in the areas of narrative/memoir, lifestyle, relationships, humor, current events, food, wine, and cooking); Ted Malawer (not accepting submissions); Alexandra Penfold (not accepting submissions); Susan Hawk (books for children and teens only).

REPRESENTS Considers these nonfiction areas: cooking, current affairs, foods, humor, memoirs. **Considers these fiction areas:** commercial, mainstream, middle grade, picture books, young adult.

HOW TO CONTACT Submit a query and 20 pages pasted into an e-mail. Accepts simultaneous submissions.

VERITAS LITERARY AGENCY

601 Van Ness Ave., Opera Plaza, Suite E, San Francisco CA 94102. (415)647-6964. **Fax:** (415)647-6965. **E-mail:** submissions@veritasliterary.com. **Website:** www.veritasliterary.com. **Contact:** Katherine Boyle. Member of AAR. Other memberships include Author's Guild and SCBWI.

MEMBER AGENTS Katherine Boyle, kboyle@veritasliterary.com (literary fiction, middle grade, young adult, narrative nonfiction/memoir, historical fiction, crime/suspense, history, pop culture, popular science, business/career); Michael Carr, michael@veritasliterary.com (historical fiction, women's fiction, science fiction and fantasy, nonfiction).

REPRESENTS Nonfiction, novels. **Considers these nonfiction areas:** business, history, memoirs, popular culture, women's issues. **Considers these fiction**

areas: commercial, crime, fantasy, historical, literary, middle grade, new adult, science fiction, suspense, women's, young adult.

HOW TO CONTACT This agency accepts short queries or proposals via e-mail only. "Fiction: Please include a cover letter listing previously published work, a one-page summary and the first 5 pages in the body of the e-mail (not as an attachment). Nonfiction: If you are sending a proposal, please include an author biography, an overview, a chapter-by-chapter summary, and an analysis of competitive titles. We do our best to review all queries within 4-6 weeks; however, if you have not heard from us in 12 weeks, consider that a no." Accepts simultaneous submissions. If you have not heard from this agency in 12 weeks, consider that a no.

WALES LITERARY AGENCY, INC.

1508 10th Ave. E. #401, Seattle WA 98102. (206)284-7114. **E-mail:** waleslit@waleslit.com. **Website:** www.waleslit.com. **Contact:** Elizabeth Wales; Neal Swain. Estab. 1990. Member of AAR. Other memberships include Authors Guild.

MEMBER AGENTS Elizabeth Wales; Neal Swain.

REPRESENTS Nonfiction, fiction, novels.

HOW TO CONTACT E-query with no attachments. Submission guidelines can be found at the agency website along with a list of current clients and titles. Accepts simultaneous submissions. Responds in 2 weeks to queries, 2 months to mss.

TERMS Agent receives 15% commission on domestic sales; 20% commission on foreign sales.

WELLS ARMS LITERARY

New York NY **E-mail:** info@wellsarms.com. **Website:** www.wellsarms.com. Estab. 2013. Member of AAR. SCBWI, Society of Illustrators. Represents 25 clients.

REPRESENTS Nonfiction, fiction, novels, juvenile books. , children's book illustrators. **Considers these nonfiction areas:** juvenile nonfiction, young adult. **Considers these fiction areas:** juvenile, middle grade, new adult, picture books, young adult.

HOW TO CONTACT E-query. Put "query" and your title in your e-mail subject line addressed to info@wellsarms.com. Accepts simultaneous submissions. We try to respond in a month's time. If no response, assume it's a no.

WERNICK & PRATT AGENCY

E-mail: submissions@wernickpratt.com. **Website:** www.wernickpratt.com. **Contact:** Marcia Wernick; Linda Pratt; Emily Mitchell. Member of AAR. Signatory of WGA. SCBWI

MEMBER AGENTS Marcia Wernick, Linda Pratt, Emily Mitchell.

REPRESENTS Juvenile books. **Considers these fiction areas:** middle grade, young adult.

HOW TO CONTACT Submit via e-mail only to submissions@wernickpratt.com. "Please indicate to which agent you are submitting." Detailed submission guidelines available on website. "Submissions will only be responded to further if we are interested in them. If you do not hear from us within 6 weeks of your submission, it should be considered declined." Accepts simultaneous submissions. Responds in 6 weeks.

WOLF LITERARY SERVICES, LLC

E-mail: queries@wolflit.com. **Website:** wolflit.com. Estab. 2008. Member of AAR. Signatory of WGA.

MEMBER AGENTS Kirsten Wolf (no queries); Kate Johnson (literary and upmarket fiction, memoir, cultural history, pop science, narrative nonfiction); Allison Devereux (literary and upmarket fiction, narrative nonfiction, cultural history and criticism, memoir, and biography); Rachel Crawford (literary fiction; high concept YA; and narrative nonfiction, particularly environmental and science journalism, ecological memoir, and queer and feminist pop culture).

REPRESENTS Nonfiction, fiction, novels. **Considers these nonfiction areas:** animals, anthropology, art, biography, creative nonfiction, economics, environment, film, foods, gay/lesbian, history, humor, investigative, literature, memoirs, parenting, science, travel, women's issues, women's studies. **Considers these fiction areas:** commercial, contemporary issues, family saga, fantasy, feminist, gay, historical, horror, lesbian, literary, science fiction, suspense, thriller, young adult, LGBTI+.

HOW TO CONTACT To submit a project, please send a query letter along with a 50-page writing sample (for fiction) or a detailed proposal (for nonfiction) to queries@wolflit.com. Samples may be submitted as an attachment or embedded in the body of the e-mail. Accepts simultaneous submissions.

WRITERS HOUSE

21 W. 26th St., New York NY 10010. (212)685-2400. **Fax:** (212)685-1781. **Website:** www.writershouse.com. Estab. 1973. Member of AAR.

MEMBER AGENTS Amy Berkower; Stephen Barr; Susan Cohen; Dan Conaway; Lisa DiMona; Susan Ginsburg; Susan Golomb; Merrilee Heifetz; Brianne Johnson; Daniel Lazar; Simon Lipskar; Steven Malk; Jodi Reamer, Esq.; Robin Rue; Rebecca Sherman; Geri Thoma; Albert Zuckerman; Alec Shane; Stacy Testa; Victoria Doherty-Munro; Beth Miller; Andrea Morrison; Soumeya Roberts.

REPRESENTS Nonfiction, novels. **Considers these nonfiction areas:** biography, business, cooking, economics, history, how-to, juvenile nonfiction, memoirs, parenting, psychology, science, self-help. **Considers these fiction areas:** commercial, fantasy, juvenile, literary, mainstream, middle grade, picture books, science fiction, women's, young adult.

HOW TO CONTACT Individual agent email addresses are available on the website. "Please e-mail us a query letter, which includes your credentials, an explanation of what makes your book unique and special, and a synopsis. Some agents within our agency have different requirements. Please consult their individual Publisher's Marketplace (PM) profile for details. We respond to all queries, generally within six to eight weeks." If you prefer to submit my mail, address it to an individual agent, and please include SASE for our reply. (If submitting to Steven Malk: Writers House, 7660 Fay Ave., #338H, La Jolla, CA 92037.) Accepts simultaneous submissions. "We respond to all queries, generally within 6-8 weeks." Obtains most new clients through recommendations from authors and editors.

TERMS Agent receives 15% commission on domestic sales. Agent receives 20% commission on foreign sales. Offers written contract, binding for 1 year. Agency charges fees for copying mss/proposals and overseas airmail of books.

JASON YARN LITERARY AGENCY

3544 Broadway, No. 68, New York NY 10031. **E-mail:** jason@jasonyarnliteraryagency.com. **Website:** www.jasonyarnliteraryagency.com. Member of AAR. Signatory of WGA.

REPRESENTS Nonfiction, fiction. **Considers these nonfiction areas:** creative nonfiction, current affairs, foods, history, science. **Considers these fiction ar-

eas: commercial, fantasy, literary, middle grade, science fiction, suspense, thriller, young adult, graphic novels, comics.

HOW TO CONTACT Please e-mail your query to jason@jasonyarnliteraryagency.com with the word "Query" in the subject line, and please paste the first 10 pages of your manuscript or proposal into the text of your e-mail. Do not send any attachments. "Visit the About page for information on what we are interested in, and please note that JYLA does not accept queries for film, TV, or stage scripts." Accepts simultaneous submissions.

BOOK PUBLISHERS

///

The markets in this year's Book Publishers section offer opportunities in nearly every area of publishing. There are large, commercial houses and medium-sized presses. Smaller publishers can be found on WritersMarket.com.

The Book Publishers Subject Index is the best place to start your search. You'll find it in the back of the book, before the General Index. Subject areas for both fiction and nonfiction are broken out for all of the book publisher listings.

When you have compiled a list of publishers interested in books in your subject area, read the detailed listings. Pare down your list by cross-referencing two or three subject areas and eliminating the listings only marginally suited to your book. When you have a good list, send for those publishers' catalogs and manuscript guidelines, or check publishers' websites, which often contain catalog listings, manuscript preparation guidelines, current contact names, and other information helpful to prospective authors. You want to use this information to make sure your book idea is in line with a publisher's list but is not a duplicate of something already published.

You should also visit bookstores and libraries to see if the publisher's books are well represented. When you find a couple of books the house has published that are similar to yours, write or call the company to find out who edited those books. This extra bit of research could be the key to getting your proposal to precisely the right editor.

Publishers prefer different methods of submission on first contact. Most like to see a one-page query, especially for nonfiction. Others will accept a brief proposal package that might include an outline and/or a sample chapter. Some publishers will accept submissions from agents only. Each listing in the Book Publishers section includes specific submission methods, if provided by the publisher. Make sure you read each listing carefully to find out exactly what the publisher wants to receive.

When you write your one-page query, give an overview of your book, mention the intended audience, the competition for your book (check local bookstore shelves), and what sets your book apart from the competition. You should also include any previous publishing experience or special training relevant to the subject of your book. For more on queries, read "Query Letter Clinic."

Personalize your query by addressing the editor individually and mentioning what you know about the company from its catalog or books. Under the heading **Contact**, we list the names of editors who acquire new books for each company, along with the editors' specific areas of expertise. Try your best to send your query to the appropriate editor. Editors move around all the time, so it's in your best interest to look online or call the publishing house to make sure the editor you are addressing your query to is still employed by that publisher.

Author-subsidy publishers' not included

Writer's Market is a reference tool to help you sell your writing, and we encourage you to work with publishers that pay a royalty. Subsidy publishing involves paying money to a publishing house to publish a book. The source of the money could be a government, foundation or university grant, or it could be the author of the book. If one of the publishers listed in this book offers you an author-subsidy arrangement (sometimes called "cooperative publishing," "co-publishing," or "joint venture"); or asks you to pay for part or all of the cost of any aspect of publishing (editing services, manuscript critiques, printing, advertising, etc.); or asks you to guarantee the purchase of any number of the books yourself, we would like you to inform us of that company's practices immediately.

BOOK PUBLISHERS

///

ABC-CLIO/GREENWOOD

Acquisitions Department, P.O. Box 1911, Santa Barbara CA 93116. (805)968-1911. **E-mail:** acquisition inquiries@ abc-clio.com. **Website:** www.abc-clio.com. Estab. 1955. ABC-CLIO is an award-winning publisher of reference titles, academic and general interest books, electronic resources, and books for librarians and other professionals. **Publishes 600 titles/year. 20% of books from first-time authors. 90% from unagented writers. Pays variable royalty on net price.** Accepts simultaneous submissions. Catalog and guidelines online.

IMPRINTS ABC-CLIO; Greenwood Press; Praeger; Linworth and Libraries Unlimited.

NONFICTION Subjects include business, child guidance, education, government, history, humanities, language, music, psychology, religion, social sciences, sociology, sports. No memoirs, drama. Query with proposal package, including scope, organization, length of project, whether a complete ms is available or when it will be, CV, and SASE. Check guidelines online for each imprint.

ABDO PUBLISHING CO.

8000 W. 78th St., Suite 310, Edina MN 55439. (800)800-1312. **Fax:** (952)831-1632. **E-mail:** nonfiction@abdopublishing.com. **E-mail:** fiction@abdopublishing.com; illustrations@abdopublishing.com. **Website:** www.abdopublishing.com. Estab. 1985. Publishes hardcover originals. ABDO publishes nonfiction children's books (prekindergarten to 8th grade) for school and public libraries—mainly history, sports, biography, geography, science, and social studies. "Please specify each submission as either nonfiction, fiction, or illustration. **Publishes 300 titles/year.** Accepts simultaneous submissions. Guidelines online.

NONFICTION Subjects include animals, history, science, sports, geography, social studies.

ABINGDON PRESS

Imprint of The United Methodist Publishing House, 201 Eighth Ave. S., P.O. Box 801, Nashville TN 37202. (615)749-6000. **Fax:** (615)749-6512. **E-mail:** submissions@umpublishing.org. **Website:** www.abingdonpress. com. Estab. 1789. Publishes hardcover and paperback originals. Abingdon Press, America's oldest theological publisher, provides an ecumenical publishing program dedicated to serving the Christian community—clergy, scholars, church leaders, musicians, and general readers—with quality resources in the areas of Bible study, the practice of ministry, theology, devotion, spirituality, inspiration, prayer, music and worship, reference, Christian education, and church supplies. **Publishes 120 titles/year. 3,000 queries; 250 mss received/year. 85% from** unagented writers. Pays 7½% royalty on retail price. Publishes ms 2 years after acceptance. Responds in 2 months to queries. Book catalog available free. Guidelines online.

NONFICTION Subjects include education, religion, theology. Query with outline and samples only. The author should retain a copy of any unsolicited material submitted.

FICTION Publishes stories of faith, hope, and love that encourage readers to explore life. Agented submissions only for fiction.

⊘ ABRAMS

115 W. 18th St., 6th Floor, New York NY 10011. (212)206-7715. **Fax:** (212)519-1210. **E-mail:** abrams@ abramsbooks.com. **Website:** www.abramsbooks.com. **Contact:** Managing Editor. Estab. 1951. Publishes hardcover and a few paperback originals. **Publishes 250 titles/year.** Accepts simultaneous submissions.

IMPRINTS Stewart, Tabori & Chang: Abrams Appleseed; Abrams Books for Young Readers; Abrams Image; STC Craft; Amulet Books.

NONFICTION Subjects include recreation.

FICTION Subjects include young adult. Publishes hardcover and "a few" paperback originals. Averages 150 total titles/year.

ACADEMY CHICAGO PUBLISHERS

814 N. Franklin St., Chicago IL 60610. (312)337-0747. **Fax:** (312)337-5985. **Website:** www.chicagoreviewpress.com. **Contact:** Yuval Taylor, senior editor. Estab. 1975. Publishes hardcover and some paperback originals and trade paperback reprints. "We publish quality fiction and nonfiction. Our audience is literate and discriminating. No novelized biography, history, or science fiction. No electronic submissions." **Publishes 10 titles/year. Pays 7-10% royalty on wholesale price.** Publishes ms 18 months after acceptance. Accepts simultaneous submissions. Responds in 3 months. Book catalog online. Guidelines online.

NONFICTION Subjects include history, travel. No religion, cookbooks, or self-help. Submit proposal package, outline, bio, 3 sample chapters.

FICTION Subjects include historical, mystery. "We look for quality work, but we do not publish experimental, avant garde, horror, science fiction, thrillers novels." Submit proposal package, synopsis, 3 sample chapters, and short bio.

Ⓐ⊘ ACE SCIENCE FICTION AND FANTASY

Imprint of the Berkley Publishing Group, Penguin Group (USA), Inc., 375 Hudson St., New York NY 10014. (212)366-2000. **Website:** www. us.penguingroup.com. Estab. 1953. Publishes hardcover, paperback, and trade paperback originals and reprints. Ace publishes science fiction and fantasy exclusively. **Publishes 75 titles/year. Pays royalty. Pays advance.**

FICTION Subjects include fantasy, science fiction. No other genre accepted. No short stories. Due to the high volume of manuscripts received, most Penguin Group (USA) Inc. imprints do not normally accept unsolicited mss.

ACTA PUBLICATIONS

4848 N. Clark St., Chicago IL 60640. **Website:** www. actapublications.com. **Contact:** Acquisitions Editor. Estab. 1958. Publishes trade paperback originals. ACTA publishes nonacademic, practical books aimed at the mainline religious market. **Publishes 12 titles/year. 100 queries received/year. 25 mss received/year. 50% of books from first-time authors. 90% from unagented writers. Pays 10-12% royalty on wholesale price.** Publishes book 1 year after acceptance of ms. Responds in 2-3 months to proposals. Book catalog and guidelines online.

NONFICTION Subjects include religion, spirituality. True Submit outline, 1 sample chapter. No e-mail submissions. Reviews artwork/photos. Send photocopies.

ADDICUS BOOKS, INC.

P.O. Box 45327, Omaha NE 68145. (402)330-7493. **Fax:** (402)330-1707. **E-mail:** info@addicusbooks.com. **Website:** www.addicusbooks.com. **Contact:** Acquisitions Editor. Estab. 1994. Addicus Books, Inc. publishes nonfiction books. "Our focus is on consumer health topics and legal topics for consumers, but we will consider other topics. We publish every book in trade paperback and in 3 e-book formats. We partner with a master book distributor that sells books into the trade—bookstores and libraries; we continually seek other sales channels outside the trade. We need at least 1 solid sales channel outside the bookstore market. To submit your book idea, first e-mail a short description of your book; tell us who the audience is and how they could be reached. If we need more info, we'll ask for it." **Publishes 15 titles/year. 90% of** books from first-time authors. 95% from unagented writers. Standard contract—royalties, paid every 6 months, are based on a percentage of revenue. Publishes ms 9 months after acceptance. Accepts simultaneous submissions. Responds in 1 month or less to inquiries. Catalog and guidelines online.

NONFICTION Subjects include business, economics, health, law, consumer health, consumer legal topics, economics, investment advice. "We are continuously expanding our line of consumer health and consumer legal titles." Submit inquiry in a brief e-mail. "If we are interested, we may ask for a proposal. See proposal guidelines on our Website. Do not send entire ms unless requested. Please do not mail submissions by certified mail."

AHSAHTA PRESS

MFA Program in Creative Writing, Boise State University, 1910 University Dr., MS 1525, Boise ID 83725. (208) 426-3414. **E-mail:** ahsahta@boisestate.edu. **Website:** ahsahtapress.org. **Contact:** Janet Holmes, director. Estab. 1974. Publishes trade paperback originals. A not-for-profit literary publisher, Ahsahta was founded in 1974 at Boise State University to preserve the best works by early poets of the American West. Its name, *ahsahta,* is the Mandan word meaning "Rocky Mountain bighorn sheep," and was first recorded by members of the Lewis and Clark expedition; the founding editors chose the word to honor the press's original mission to publish Western poetry. Peggy Pond Church, H.L. Davis, Hazel Hall, Gwendolen Haste, Haniel Long, and Norman Macleod are among the early Western writers Ahsahta Press restored to print. Soon after its inception, the press began publishing contemporary poetry by Western poets along with its reprint titles. Ahsahta editors discovered and initially published a number of widely popular poets from the West—among them David Baker, Katharine Coles, Wyn Cooper, Gretel Ehrlich, Cynthia Hogue, Leo Romero, and Carolyne Wright. With the inception of the M.F.A. Program in Creative Writing at Boise State University, Ahsahta Press expanded its scope, presenting the work of poets from across the nation whose work is selected through our national competitions or by general submission. These include Julie Carr, Anne Boyer, Kate Greenstreet, Brian Teare, James Meetze, and TC Tolbert. "Ahsahta Press champions and promotes surprising, relevant, and accessible experimental poetry that more commercially minded small presses avoid; in making it widely available, we aim to increase its readership." Publishes 7-10 titles/year. 1,000 mss received/year. 40% of books from first-time authors. 100% from unagented writers. Pays 8% royalty on retail price for first 1,000 sold; 10% thereafter. Does not usually pay advance. Publishes ms 2 years after acceptance. Accepts simultaneous submissions. Responds in 3 months to mss. Book catalog online. Guidelines online; submit through submissions manager.

POETRY "We usually hold an open submissions period in May as well as the Sawtooth Poetry Prize competition in January and February, from which we publish 2-3 mss per year. We no longer publish chapbooks." Submit complete ms. The press publishes runners-up as well as winners of the Sawtooth Poetry Prize. Forthcoming, new, and backlist titles available on website. Most backlist titles: $9.95; most current titles: $18.

⊘ ALADDIN

Simon & Schuster, 1230 Avenue of the Americas, 4th Floor, New York NY 10020. (212)698-7000. **Website:** www.simonandschuster.com. **Contact:** Acquisitions Editor. Publishes hardcover/paperback originals and imprints of Simon & Schuster Children's Publishing Children's Division. Aladdin publishes picture books, beginning readers, chapter books, middle grade and tween fiction and nonfiction, and graphic novels and nonfiction in hardcover and paperback, with an emphasis on commercial, kid-friendly titles. Accepts simultaneous submissions.

FICTION Simon & Schuster does not review, retain or return unsolicited materials or artwork. "We suggest prospective authors and illustrators submit their mss through a professional literary agent."

⊘ ALGONQUIN BOOKS OF CHAPEL HILL

Workman Publishing, P.O. Box 2225, Chapel Hill NC 27515-2225. (919)967-0108. **Website:** www.algonquin.com. **Contact:** Editorial Department. Publishes hardcover originals. Algonquin Books publishes quality literary fiction and literary nonfiction. **Publishes 24 titles/year.** Guidelines online.

IMPRINTS Algonquin Young Readers.

NONFICTION Does not accept unsolicited submissions at this time. "Visit our website for full submission policy to queries."

FICTION Subjects include literary. Does not accept unsolicited submissions at this time.

ALGORA PUBLISHING

222 Riverside Dr., 16th Floor, New York NY 10025-6809. (212)678-0232. **Fax:** (212)666-3682. **Website:** www.algora.com. Estab. 1992. Publishes hardcover and trade paperback originals and reprints. Algora Publishing is an academic-type press, focusing on works by North and South American, European, Asian, and African authors for the educated general reader. **Publishes 25 titles/year. 1,500 queries; 800 mss received/year. 20% of books from first-time authors. 85% from unagented writers. Pays $0-1,000 advance.** Publishes book 10-18 months after acceptance of ms. Accepts simultaneous submissions. Responds in 1 month to queries/proposals; 3 months to mss. Book catalog and guidelines online.

NONFICTION Subjects include anthropology, archeology, creative nonfiction, dance, education, environment, finance, government, history, language, literature, military, money, music, nature, philosophy, politics, psychology, religion, science, sociology, translation, war, womens issues, womens studies, economics. Algora Publishing welcomes proposals for original mss, but "we do not handle self-help, recovery, or children's books." Submit a query or ms by uploading file to our website.

ALLWORTH PRESS

An imprint of Skyhorse Publishing, 307 West 36th St., 11th Floor, New York NY 10018. (212)643-6816. **Fax:** (212)643-6819. **E-mail:** allworthsubmissions@skyhorsepublishing.com. **Website:** www.allworth.com. Estab. 1989. Publishes hardcover and trade paperback originals. Allworth Press publishes business and self-help information for artists, designers, photographers, authors and film and performing artists, as well as books about business, money and the law for the general public. The press also publishes the best of classic and contemporary writing in art and graphic design. Currently emphasizing photography, graphic and industrial design, performing arts, fine arts and crafts, et al. **Publishes 12-18 titles/year. Pays advance.** Responds in 4-6 weeks. Book catalog and ms guidelines free.

NONFICTION Subjects include photography, film, television, graphic design, performing arts, as well as business and legal guides for the public. "We are currently accepting query letters for practical, legal, and technique books targeted to professionals in the arts, including designers, graphic and fine artists, craftspeople, photographers, and those involved in film and the performing arts." Query with 1-2 page synopsis, chapter outline, market analysis, sample chapter, bio, SASE.

AMERICAN CHEMICAL SOCIETY

Publications/Books Division, 1155 16th St. NW, Washington DC 20036. (202)452-2120. **Fax:** (202)513-8819. **Website:** pubs.acs.org/books/. Estab. 1876. Publishes hardcover originals. American Chemical Society publishes symposium-based books for chemistry. **Publishes 35 titles/year. Pays royalty.** Accepts simultaneous submissions. Responds in 2 months to proposals. Book catalog available free. Guidelines online.

NONFICTION Subjects include science. Emphasis is on meeting-based books. Log in to submission site online.

AMERICAN CORRECTIONAL ASSOCIATION

206 N. Washington St., Suite 200, Alexandria VA 22314. (703)224-0000. **Fax:** (703)224-0179. **Website:** www.aca.org. Estab. 1870. Publishes trade paperback originals. American Correctional Association provides practical information on jails, prisons, boot camps, probation, parole, community corrections, juvenile facilities and rehabilitation programs, substance abuse programs, and other areas of corrections. **Publishes 18 titles/year. 90% of books from first-time authors. 100% from unagented writers.** Publishes ms 1 year after acceptance. Accepts simultaneous submissions. Responds in 4 months to queries. Book catalog available free. Guidelines online.

NONFICTION "We are looking for practical, how-to texts or training materials written for the corrections profession. We are especially interested in books on management, development of first-line supervisors, and security-threat group/management in prisons." No autobiographies or true-life accounts by current or former inmates or correctional officers, theses, or dissertations. No fiction or poetry. Query with SASE. Reviews artwork/photos.

AMERICAN FEDERATION OF ASTROLOGERS

6535 S. Rural Rd., Tempe AZ 85283. (480)838-1751. **Fax:** (480)838-8293. **Website:** www.astrologers.com. Estab. 1938. Publishes trade paperback originals and reprints. American Federation of Astrologers publishes astrology books, calendars, charts, and related aids. **Publishes 10-15 titles/year. 10 queries; 20 mss received/year. 50% of books from first-time authors. 100% from unagented writers. Pays 10% royalty.** Publishes book 10 months after acceptance of ms. Accepts simultaneous submissions. Responds in 6 months to mss. Book catalog available free. Guidelines online.

NONFICTION "Our market for beginner books, Sun-sign guides, and similar material is limited and we thus publish very few of these. The ideal word count for a book-length manuscript published by AFA is about 40,000 words, although we will consider manuscripts from 20,000 to 60,000 words." Submit complete ms.

AMERICAN QUILTER'S SOCIETY

5801 Kentucky Dam Rd., Paducah KY 42003. (270)898-7903. **Fax:** (270)898-1173. **Website:** www.americanquilter.com. Estab. 1984. Publishes trade paperbacks. American Quilter's Society publishes how-to and pattern books for quilters (beginners through intermediate skill level). We are not the publisher for non-quilters writing about quilts. We now publish quilt-related craft cozy romance and mystery titles, series only. Humor is good. Graphic depictions and curse words are bad. **Publishes 20-24 titles/year. 100 queries received/year. 60% of books from first-time authors. Pays 5% royalty on retail price for both nonfiction and fiction.** Publishes nonfiction ms 9-18 months after acceptance. Fiction published on a different schedule TBD. Responds in 2 months to proposals. Guidelines online.

NONFICTION No queries; proposals only. Note: 1 or 2 completed quilt projects must accompany proposal.

FICTION Submit a synopsis and 2 sample chapters, plus an outline of the next 2 books in the series.

AMERICAN WATER WORKS ASSOCIATION

6666 W. Quincy Ave., Denver CO 80235. (303)347-6260. **Fax:** (303)794-7310. **E-mail:** submissions@awwa.org. **Website:** www.awwa.org. **Contact:** Senior Manager, Acquisitions and Content. Estab. 1881. Publishes hardcover and trade paperback originals. AWWA strives to advance and promote the safety and knowledge of drinking water and related issues to all audiences—from kindergarten through post-doctorate. **Publishes 25 titles/year.** Responds in 4 months to queries. Book catalog and ms guidelines free.

NONFICTION Subjects include science, software, drinking water and wastewater related topics, operations, treatment, sustainability. Query with SASE. Submit outline, bio, 3 sample chapters. Reviews artwork/photos. Send photocopies.

AMHERST MEDIA, INC.

P.O. Box 538, Buffalo NY 14213. (716)874-4450. **E-mail:** submissions@amherstmedia.com. **Website:** www.amherstmedia.com. **Contact:** Craig Alesse, publisher. Associate Publisher: Kate Neaverth. Estab. 1974. Publishes trade paperback originals and reprints. Amherst Media publishes illustrated books on all subjects including photographic instruction. **Publishes 50 titles/year. 60% of books from first-time authors. 90% from unagented writers. Pays 12-18% royalty. Pays advance.** Publishes book 1 year after acceptance. Accepts simultaneous submissions. Responds in 2 weeks to queries. Book catalog online. Guidelines upon request.

NONFICTION Subjects include agriculture, animals, architecture, art, automotive, communications, contemporary culture, crafts, creative nonfiction, environment, gardening, hobbies, horticulture, house and home, marine subjects, medicine, nature, New Age, photography, pop culture, recreation, transportation, womens issues. Looking for author/photographers for illustrated books. 100-200 high quality photographs around a theme. Reviews artwork/photos.

⊘⊘ AMULET BOOKS

Imprint of Abrams, 115 W. 18th St., 6th Floor, New York NY 10001. **Website:** www.amuletbooks.com. Estab. 2004. *Does not accept unsolicited mss or queries.* **10% of books from first-time authors.** Accepts simultaneous submissions.

FICTION Middle readers: adventure, contemporary, fantasy, history, science fiction, sports. Young adults/teens: adventure, contemporary, fantasy, history, science fiction, sports, suspense.

ANDREWS MCMEEL UNIVERSAL

1130 Walnut St., Kansas City MO 64106. (816)581-7500. **Website:** www.andrewsmcmeel.com. **Contact:** Book Submissions. Estab. 1973. Publishes hardcover and paperback originals. Andrews McMeel publishes general trade books, humor books, miniature gift books, calendars, and stationery products. **Publishes 300 titles/year. Pays royalty on retail price or net** receipts. **Pays advance.** Accepts simultaneous submissions. Guidelines online.

NONFICTION Subjects include cooking, games, comics, puzzles. Submit proposal.

ANKERWYCKE

American Bar Association, 321 N. Clark St., Chicago IL 60654. **Website:** www.ababooks.org. Estab. 1878. Publishes hardcover and trade paperback originals. In 1215, the Magna Carta was signed underneath the ancient Ankerwycke Yew tree, starting the process which led to rule by constitutional law—in effect, giving rights and the law to the people. And today, the ABA's Ankerwycke line of books continues to bring the law to the people. With legal fiction, true crime books, popular legal histories, public policy handbooks, and prescriptive guides to current legal and business issues, Ankerwycke is a contemporary and innovative line of books for everyone from a trusted and vested authority. **Publishes 30-40 titles/year. 1,000's of queries received/year. 25% of books from first-time authors. 50% from unagented writers.** Publishes ms 12-18 months after acceptance. Accepts simultaneous submissions. Responds in 1 month to queries and proposals; 3 months to mss. Book catalog and ms guidelines online.

NONFICTION Subjects include business, consumer legal. "Extremely high quality nonfiction with a legal aspect; business books specifically for service professionals; consumer legal on a wide range of topics—we're actively acquiring in all these areas." Query with cover letter; outline or TOC; and CV/bio including other credits. Include e-mail address for response.

FICTION "We're actively acquiring legal fiction with extreme verisimilitude." Query with cover letter; outline or TOC; and CV/bio including other credits. Include e-mail address for response.

⊙⊘ ANNICK PRESS, LTD.

15 Patricia Ave., Toronto ON M2M 1H9, Canada. (416)221-4802. **Fax:** (416)221-8400. **Website:** www.annickpress.com. **Contact:** The Editors. Publishes picture books, juvenile and YA fiction and nonfiction; specializes in trade books. Annick Press maintains a commitment to high quality books that entertain and challenge. Our publications share fantasy and stimulate imagination, while encouraging children to trust their judgment and abilities. *Does not accept unsolicited mss.* **Publishes 25 titles/year. 5,000 queries received/year. 3,000 mss received/year. 20% of books**

from first-time authors. 80-85% from unagented writers. Pays authors royalty of 5-12% based on retail price. Offers advances (average amount: $3,000). Pays illustrators royalty of 5% minimum.** Publishes a book 2 years after acceptance. Accepts simultaneous submissions. Book catalog and guidelines online.

NONFICTION Works with 20 illustrators/year. Illustrations only: Query with samples.

FICTION Publisher of children's books. Not accepting picture books at this time.

APA BOOKS

American Psychological Association, 750 First St. NE, Washington DC 20002. (202)336-5500. **Website:** www.apa.org/pubs/books/index.aspx. Publishes hardcover and trade paperback originals. Accepts simultaneous submissions. Book catalog online. Guidelines online.

IMPRINTS Magination Press (children's books).

NONFICTION Subjects include education, multicultural, psychology, science, social sciences, sociology. Submit cv and prospectus with TOC, intended audience, selling points, and outside competition.

ARBORDALE PUBLISHING

612 Johnnie Dodds, Suite A2, Mt. Pleasant SC 29464. (843)971-6722. **Fax:** (843)216-3804. **E-mail:** submissions@arbordalepublishing.com. **Website:** www.arbordalepublishing.com. **Contact:** Acquisitions Editor. Estab. 2004. Publishes hardcover, trade paperback, and electronic originals. "The picture books we publish are usually, but not always, fictional stories with nonfiction woven into the story that relate to science or math. All books should subtly convey an educational theme through a warm story that is fun to read and that will grab a child's attention. Each book has a 4-page *'For Creative Minds'* section to reinforce the educational component. This section will have a craft and/or game as well as 'fun facts' to be shared by the parent, teacher, or other adult. Authors do not need to supply this information with their submission, but if their ms is accepted, they may be asked to provide additional information for this section. Mss should be less than 1,000 words and meet all of the following 4 criteria: fun to read—mostly fiction with nonfiction facts woven into the story; national or regional in scope; must tie into early elementary school curriculum; must be marketable through a niche market such as a zoo, aquarium, or museum gift shop." **Publishes 12 titles/year. 1,000 mss received/year. 50% of**

books from first-time authors. 99% from unagented writers. Pays 6 8% royalty on wholesale price. Pays small advance. Publishes book 18 months after acceptance. May hold onto mss of interest for 1 year until acceptance. Accepts simultaneous submissions. Accepts electronic submissions only. Snail mail submissions are discarded without being opened. Acknowledges receipt of ms submission within 1 month. Book catalog and guidelines online.

NONFICTION Subjects include animals, creative nonfiction, environment, ethnic, marine subjects, multicultural, science. Prefer fiction, but will consider nonfiction as well. All mss should be submitted via e-mail. Mss should be less than 1,000 words. Reviews artwork/photos. Send 1-2 JPEGS and link to online portfolio

FICTION Subjects include picture books. Picture books: animal, folktales, nature/environment, science- or math-related. No more than 1,000 words. All mss should be submitted via e-mail to Katie Hall. Mss should be less than 1,000 words.

POETRY "We do not accept books of poetry. Will consider mss written in rhyming verse, but prefer prose."

ARCADE PUBLISHING

Skyhorse Publishing, 307 W. 36th St., 11th Floor, New York NY 10018. (212)643-6816. **Fax:** (212)643-6819. **E-mail:** arcadesubmissions@skyhorsepublishing.com. **Website:** www.arcadepub.com. **Contact:** Acquisitions Editor. Estab. 1988. Publishes hardcover originals, trade paperback reprints. Arcade prides itself on publishing top-notch literary nonfiction and fiction, with a significant proportion of foreign writers. **Publishes 35 titles/year. 5% of books from first-time authors. Pays royalty on retail price and 10 author's copies. Pays advance.** Publishes book 18 months after acceptance. Accepts simultaneous submissions. Responds in 2 months if interested. Book catalog and ms guidelines for #10 SASE.

NONFICTION Subjects include history, memoirs, travel, popular science, current events. Submit proposal with brief query, 1-2 page synopsis, chapter outline, market analysis, sample chapter, bio.

FICTION Subjects include literary, short story collections, translation. No romance, historical, science fiction. Submit proposal with brief query, 1-2 page synopsis, chapter outline, market analysis, sample chapter, bio.

ARCADIA PUBLISHING

420 Wando Park Blvd., Mt. Pleasant SC 29464. (843)853-2070. **Fax:** (843)853-0044. **Website:** www.arcadiapublishing.com. Estab. 1993. Publishes trade paperback originals. Arcadia publishes photographic vintage regional histories. "We have more than 3,000 Images of America series in print. We have expanded our California program." **Publishes 600 titles/year. Pays 8% royalty on retail price.** Publishes book 9 months after acceptance. Accepts simultaneous submissions. Book catalog online. Guidelines available free.

NONFICTION Subjects include history. "Arcadia accepts submissions year-round. Our editors seek proposals on local history topics and are able to provide authors with detailed information about our publishing program as well as book proposal submission guidelines. Due to the great demand for titles on local and regional history, we are currently searching for authors to work with us on new photographic history projects. Please contact one of our regional publishing teams if you are interested in submitting a proposal." Specific proposal form to be completed.

ARCHAIA

Imprint of Boom! Studios, 5670 Wilshire Blvd., Suite 450, Los Angeles CA 90036. **Website:** www.archaia.com. Use online submission form. Accepts simultaneous submissions.

FICTION Subjects include adventure, fantasy, horror, mystery, science fiction. Looking for graphic novel submissions that include finished art. "Archaia is a multi-award-winning graphic novel publisher with more than 75 renowned publishing brands, including such domestic and international hits as *Artesia*, *Mouse Guard*, and a line of Jim Henson graphic novels including *Fraggle Rock* and *The Dark Crystal*. Publishes creator-shared comic books and graphic novels in the adventure, fantasy, horror, pulp noir, and science fiction genres that contain idiosyncratic and atypical writing and art. *Archaia does not generally hire freelancers or arrange for freelance work, so submissions should only be for completed book and series proposals.*"

A-R EDITIONS, INC.

1600 Aspen Commons, Suite 100, Middleton WI 53562. (608)836-9000. **E-mail:** info@areditions.com. **Website:** www.areditions.com. Estab. 1962. A-R Editions publishes modern critical editions of music based on current musicological research. Each edition is devoted to works by a single composer or to a single genre of composition. The contents are chosen for their potential interest to scholars and performers, then prepared for publication according to the standards that govern the making of all reliable, historical editions. **Publishes 30 titles/year. 40 queries; 30 mss received/year. 75% of books from first-time authors. 100% from unagented writers. Pays royalty or honoraria.** Book catalog online. Guidelines online.

NONFICTION Subjects include , historical music editions; computer music and digital audio topics. Computer Music and Digital Audio Series titles deal with issues tied to digital and electronic media, and include both textbooks and handbooks in this area.

ARROW PUBLICATIONS, LLC

7716 Bells Mill Rd., Bethesda MD 20817. (301)299-9422. **Fax:** (240)632-8477. **E-mail:** arrow_info@arrowpub.com. **Website:** www.arrowpub.com. **Contact:** Tom King, managing editor. Estab. 1987. No graphic novels until further notice. **Publishes Publishes 50 e-book titles/year. Paperback version launched in 2009 with 12 English and 12 Spanish titles/year. titles/year. 150 queries; 100 mss received/year. 80% of books from first-time authors. 100% from unagented writers. Makes outright purchase of accepted completed scripts.** Publishes book 4-6 months after acceptance of ms. Accepts simultaneous submissions. Responds in 2 month to queries; 1 month to mss sent upon request. Guidelines online.

NONFICTION Subjects include business, womens issues.

FICTION Subjects include comic books, erotica, ethnic, historical, mainstream, romance. "We are looking for outlines of stories heavy on romance with elements of adventure/intrigue/mystery. We will consider other romance genres such as fantasy, western, inspirational, and historical as long as the romance element is strong." Query with outline first with SASE. Consult submission guidelines online before submitting.

ARSENAL PULP PRESS

#202-211 East Georgia St., Vancouver BC V6A 1Z6, Canada. (604)687-4233. **Fax:** (604)687-4283. **E-mail:** info@arsenalpulp.com. **Website:** www.arsenalpulp.com. **Contact:** Editorial Board. Estab. 1980. Publishes trade paperback originals, and trade paperback reprints. "We are interested in literature that traverses uncharted territories, publishing books that chal-

lenge and stimulate and ask probing questions about the world around us." **Publishes 14-20 titles/year. 500 queries; 300 mss received/year. 30% of books from first-time authors. 100% from unagented writers.** Publishes ms 1 year after acceptance. Accepts simultaneous submissions. Responds in 2-4 months. Book catalog for 9×12 SAE with IRCs or online. Guidelines online.

NONFICTION Subjects include creative nonfiction, ethnic, history, multicultural, sex, sociology, travel, film, visual art. Rarely publishes non-Canadian authors. No poetry at this time. "We do not publish children's books." Each submission must include: "a synopsis of the work, a chapter by chapter outline for nonfiction, writing credentials, a 50-page excerpt from the ms (*do not send more, it will be a waste of postage; if we like what we see, we'll ask for the rest of the manuscript*), and a marketing analysis. If our editorial board is interested, you will be asked to send the entire ms. We do not accept discs or submissions by fax or e-mail, and we do not discuss concepts over the phone." Reviews artwork/photos.

FICTION Subjects include ethnic, feminist, literary, multicultural, short story collections. No children's books or genre fiction, i.e., westerns, romance, horror, mystery, etc. Submit proposal package, outline, clips, 2-3 sample chapters.

ARTE PUBLICO PRESS

University of Houston, 4902 Gulf Fwy, Bldg 19, Rm 100, Houston TX 77204-2004. **Fax:** (713)743-2847. **E-mail:** submapp@uh.edu. **Website:** artepublicopress.com. Estab. 1979. Publishes hardcover originals, trade paperback originals and reprints. Arte Publico Press is the oldest and largest publisher of Hispanic literature for children and adults in the United States. "We are a showcase for Hispanic literary creativity, arts and culture. Our endeavor is to provide a national forum for U.S.-Hispanic literature." **Publishes 25-30 titles/year. 1,000 queries; 2,000 mss received/year. 50% of books from first-time authors. 80% from unagented writers. Pays 10% royalty on wholesale price. Provides 20 author's copies; 40% discount on subsequent copies. Pays $1,000-3,000 advance.** Publishes book 2 years after acceptance of ms. Accepts simultaneous submissions. Responds in 1 month to queries and proposals; 4 months to mss. Book catalog available free. Guidelines online.

NONFICTION Subjects include ethnic, regional, translation. Hispanic civil rights issues for new series: The Hispanic Civil Rights Series. Submissions made through online submission form.

FICTION Subjects include contemporary, ethnic, literary, mainstream. "Written by U.S.-Hispanics." Submissions made through online submission form.

POETRY Submissions made through online submission form.

ASA, AVIATION SUPPLIES & ACADEMICS

7005 132 Place SE, Newcastle WA 98059. (425)235-1500. **E-mail:** feedback@asa2fly.com. **Website:** www.asa2fly.com. ASA is an industry leader in the development and sales of aviation supplies, publications, and software for pilots, flight instructors, flight engineers and aviation technicians. All ASA products are developed by a team of researchers, authors and editors. Book catalog available free.

NONFICTION Subjects include education. "We are primarily an aviation publisher. Educational books in this area are our specialty; other aviation books will be considered." All subjects must be related to aviation education and training. Query with outline. Send photocopies or MS Word files.

ASCEND BOOKS

7221 W. 79th St., Suite 206, Overland Park KS 66204. (913)948-5500. **Fax:** (913)948-7770. **E-mail:** bsnodgrass@ascendbooks.com. **Website:** ascendbooks.com. **Contact:** Robert Snodgrass. Estab. 2008. Ascend Books is positioned to acquire and execute publishing projects in a tightly defined market–that of sports celebrities, including athletes, coaches, and teams, and of significant anniversary celebrations of sports institutions, such as football bowl games, franchises, and halls of fame. Ascend Books also works with clients in the fields of entertainment and business. Ascend Books is a highly specialized publishing company with a burgeoning presence in the sports and commemoration business. Ascend Books is positioned to acquire and execute publishing projects in a tightly defined market–that of sports celebrities, including athletes, coaches, and teams, and of significant anniversary celebrations of sports institutions, such as football bowl games, franchises, and halls of fame. Ascend Books also works with clients in the fields of entertainment and business. Ascend Books differentiates itself from traditional publishers by extending the intellectual property of a book and its author into professional speaking and consulting businesses. Ascend Books specializes in turning media-related ideas into popular books for events, associations, celebrities and organizations across the country. Currently Ascend Books publishes a variety of formats each year—in a variety of subject areas. Our Publishing Initiative can provide a multi-dimensional approach for a select number of titles. Each year groups, associations, charities and teams celebrate significant anniversaries, events or accomplishments with a Custom Book Project. Each year Ascend Books works with the nations leading industry professionals and associations. The Ascend Books distribution team shepherds thousands of books from press to audience each month. Ascend employs professionals in editorial, sales, production, and distribution roles. Our stringent publishing criteria however, limits the number of books we publish each year. When we accept and initiate a book publishing project we put our full resources of talented editors, collaborators, photographers, artists and sales professionals behind each project. Unlike many other publishers, the Ascend Books Team works with setting goals, then establishing defined objectives to maximize the sales opportunities for each project. When the decision is made to proceed on a book, we put the full strength of our sales, editorial, production and distribution resources to work. **Publishes 12-15 titles/year. 50% of books from first-time authors. 75% from unagented writers. Pays advance.** Accepts simultaneous submissions. Responds in 4-6 weeks. Catalog online.

NONFICTION Subjects include entertainment, memoirs, sports.

ASM PRESS

Book division for the American Society for Microbiology, 1752 N St., NW, Washington DC 20036. (202)737-3600. **Fax:** (202)942-9342. **E-mail:** books@asmusa.org. **Website:** www.asmscience.org. Estab. 1899. Publishes hardcover, trade paperback and electronic originals. **Publishes 30 titles/year. 40% of books from first-time authors. 95% from unagented writers. Pays 5-15% royalty on wholesale price. Pays $1,000-10,000 advance.** Publishes book 6-9 months after acceptance. Accepts simultaneous submissions. Responds in 2 months. Book catalog online. Guidelines online.

NONFICTION Subjects include agriculture, animals, education, history, horticulture, science, microbiology and related sciences. "Must have bona fide academic credentials in which they are writing." Query with SASE or by e-mail. Submit proposal package, outline, prospectus. Reviews artwork/photos. Send photocopies.

ASSOCIATION FOR SUPERVISION AND CURRICULUM DEVELOPMENT

ASCD, 1703 N. Beauregard St., Alexandria VA 22311-1714. (703)578-9600. **Fax:** (703)575-5400. **E-mail:** acquisitions@ascd.org. **Website:** www.ascd.org. **Contact:** Genny Ostertag, director, content acquisitions. Estab. 1943. Publishes trade paperback originals. ASCD publishes high-quality professional books for educators. **Publishes 30 titles/year. Receives approximately 200 proposals/year. 30% of books from first-time authors. 95% from unagented writers. Pays negotiable royalty on actual monies received.** Publishes ms 1 year after acceptance. Accepts simultaneous submissions. Responds in 2-3 months to proposals. Book catalog and guidelines online.

NONFICTION Subjects include education. Submit full proposal, 2 sample chapters. Reviews artwork/photos. Send photocopies.

ASTRAGAL PRESS

Finney Company, 5995 149th St. W., Suite 105, Apple Valley MN 55124. (866)543-3045. **E-mail:** info@finneyco.com. **Website:** www.astragalpress.com. Estab. 1983. Publishes trade paperback originals and reprints. Our primary audience includes those interested in antique tool collecting, metalworking, carriage building, early sciences and early trades, and railroading. Accepts simultaneous submissions. Responds in 3 months. Book catalog and ms guidelines free.

NONFICTION Wants books on early tools, trades and technology, and railroads. Query with sample chapters, TOC, book overview, illustration descriptions.

ⒶⓄ ATHENEUM BOOKS FOR YOUNG READERS

Simon & Schuster, 1230 Avenue of the Americas, New York NY 10020. **Website:** kids.simonandschuster.com. Estab. 1961. Publishes hardcover originals. Accepts simultaneous submissions. Guidelines for #10 SASE.

NONFICTION Subjects include Americana, animals, history, photography, psychology, recreation, religion, science, sociology, sports, travel. Publishes hardcover originals, picture books for young kids,

nonfiction for ages 8-12 and novels for middle-grade and young adults. 100% require freelance illustration. Agented submissions only.

FICTION Subjects include adventure, ethnic, experimental, fantasy, gothic, historical, horror, humor, mystery, science fiction, sports, suspense, western, Animal. All in juvenile versions. "We have few specific needs except for books that are fresh, interesting and well written. Fad topics are dangerous, as are works you haven't polished to the best of your ability. We also don't need safety pamphlets, ABC books, coloring books and board books. In writing picture book texts, avoid the coy and 'cutesy,' such as stories about characters with alliterative names." Agented submissions only. No paperback romance-type fiction.

AVALON TRAVEL PUBLISHING

Avalon Publishing Group, 1700 4th St., Berkeley CA 94710. (510)595-3664. **Fax:** (510)595-4228. **E-mail:** avalon.acquisitions@perseusbooks.com. **Website:** www.avalontravelbooks.com. Estab. 1973. Publishes trade paperback originals. Avalon travel guides feature practicality and spirit, offering a traveler-to-traveler perspective perfect for planning an afternoon hike, around-the-world journey, or anything in between. ATP publishes 7 major series. Each one has a different emphasis and a different geographic coverage. "We have expanded our coverage, with a focus on European and Asian destinations. Our main areas of interest are North America, Central America, South America, the Caribbean, and the Pacific. We are seeking only a few titles in each of our major series. Check online guidelines for our current needs. Follow guidelines closely." **Publishes 100 titles/year. 5,000 queries received/year. 25% of books from first-time authors. 95% from unagented writers. Pays up to $17,000 advance.** Publishes ms an average of 9 months after acceptance. Accepts simultaneous submissions. Responds in 4 months. Guidelines online.

NONFICTION Subjects include regional, travel. "We are not interested in fiction, children's books, and travelogues/travel diaries." Submit cover letter, resume, and up to 5 relevant clips.

AVON ROMANCE

Harper Collins Publishers, 10 E. 53 St., New York NY 10022. **E-mail:** info@avonromance.com. **Website:** www.avonromance.com. Estab. 1941. Publishes paperback and digital originals and reprints. Avon has been publishing award-winning books since 1941.

It is recognized for having pioneered the historical romance category and continues to bring the best of commercial literature to the broadest possible audience. **Publishes 400 titles/year.** Accepts simultaneous submissions.

FICTION Subjects include historical, literary, mystery, romance, science fiction, young adult. Submit a query and ms via the online submission form.

BACKBEAT BOOKS

Hal Leonard Publishing Group, 33 Plymouth St., Suite 302, Montclair NJ 07042. (973)337-5034. **E-mail:** bmalavarca@halleonard.com. **Website:** www. backbeatbooks.com. **Contact:** Bernadette Malavarca, senior editor. Publishes hardcover and trade paperback originals; trade paperback reprints. **Publishes 30 titles/year. 30% of books from first-time authors. 60% from unagented writers. Pays modest advance.** Publishes ms 18-24 months after acceptance. Accepts simultaneous submissions. Guidelines online.

NONFICTION Subjects include music, pop culture. Query with TOC, sample chapter, sample illustrations.

BAEN BOOKS

P.O. Box 1188, Wake Forest NC 27588. (919)570-1640. **E-mail:** info@baen.com. **Website:** www.baen.com. Estab. 1983. "We publish only science fiction and fantasy. Writers familiar with what we have published in the past will know what sort of material we are most likely to publish in the future: powerful plots with solid scientific and philosophical underpinnings are the sine qua non for consideration for science fiction submissions. As for fantasy, any magical system must be both rigorously coherent and integral to the plot, and overall the work must at least strive for originality." Accepts simultaneous submissions. Responds to mss within 12-18 months.

FICTION "Style: Simple is generally better; in our opinion good style, like good breeding, never calls attention to itself. Length: 100,000-130,000 words Generally we are uncomfortable with manuscripts under 100,000 words, but if your novel is really wonderful send it along regardless of length." "Query letters are not necessary. We prefer to see complete manuscripts accompanied by a synopsis. We prefer not to see simultaneous submissions. Electronic submissions are strongly preferred. *We no longer accept submissions by e-mail.* Send ms by using the submission form at: http://ftp.baen.com/Slush/submit.aspx. No disks unless requested. Attach ms as a Rich Text Format (.rtf) file. Any other format will not be considered."

ⒶⓄ BAKER BOOKS

Division of Baker Publishing Group, 6030 E. Fulton Rd., Ada MI 49301. (616)676-9185. **Website:** baker-publishinggroup.com/bakerbooks. Estab. 1939. Publishes in hardcover and trade paperback originals, and trade paperback reprints. "We will consider unsolicited work only through one of the following avenues. Materials sent through a literary agent will be considered. In addition, our staff attends various writers' conferences at which prospective authors can develop relationships with those in the publishing industry." Accepts simultaneous submissions. Book catalog for 9½×12½ envelope and 3 first-class stamps. Guidelines online.

NONFICTION Subjects include , Christian doctrines.

Ⓐ BALLANTINE BOOKS

Imprint of Penguin Random House, Inc., 1745 Broadway, 18th Floor, New York NY 10019. (212)782-9000. **Website:** www.penguinrandomhouse.com. Estab. 1952. Publishes hardcover, trade paperback, mass market paperback originals. Ballantine Bantam Dell publishes a wide variety of nonfiction and fiction. Accepts simultaneous submissions. Guidelines online.

NONFICTION Subjects include animals, child guidance, community, creative nonfiction, education, history, memoirs, recreation, religion, sex, spirituality, travel, true crime. Agented submissions only. Reviews artwork/photos. Send photocopies.

FICTION Subjects include confession, ethnic, fantasy, feminist, historical, humor, literary, multicultural, mystery, romance, short story collections, spiritual, suspense, translation, general fiction. Agented submissions only.

Ⓐ BALZER & BRAY

HarperCollins Children's Books, 10 E. 53rd St., New York NY 10022. **Website:** www.harpercollinschildrens.com. Estab. 2008. "We publish bold, creative, groundbreaking picture books and novels that appeal directly to kids in a fresh way." **Publishes 10 titles/year. Offers advances. Pays illustrators by the project.** Publishes book 18 months after acceptance. Accepts simultaneous submissions.

NONFICTION Subjects include animals, cooking, dance, environment, history, multicultural, music, nature, science, social sciences, sports. "We will publish very few nonfiction titles, maybe 1-2 per year." Agented submissions only.

FICTION Picture Books, Young Readers: adventure, animal, anthology, concept, contemporary, fantasy, history, humor, multicultural, nature/environment, poetry, science fiction, special needs, sports, suspense. Middle readers, young adults/teens: adventure, animal, anthology, contemporary, fantasy, history, humor, multicultural, nature/environment, poetry, science fiction, special needs, sports, suspense. Agented submissions only.

ⓐⓞ BANTAM BOOKS

Imprint of Penguin Random House, Inc., 1745 Broadway, New York NY 10019. (212)782-9000. **Website:** www.randomhousebooks.com. *Not seeking mss at this time.* Accepts simultaneous submissions.

ⓞ BAREFOOT BOOKS

2067 Massachusettes Ave., 5th Floor, Cambridge MA 02140. (617)576-0660. **Fax:** (617)576-0049. **E-mail:** help@barefootbooks.com. **Website:** www.barefootbooks.com. **Contact:** Acquisitions Editor. Publishes hardcover and trade paperback originals. "We are a small, independent publishing company that publishes high-quality picture books for children of all ages and specializes in the work of artists and writers from many cultures. We focus on themes that support independence of spirit, encourage openness to others, and foster a life-long love of learning. Prefers full manuscript." **Publishes 30 titles/year. 2,000 queries received/year. 3,000 mss received/year. 35% of books from first-time authors. 60% from unagented writers. Pays advance.** Accepts simultaneous submissions. Book catalog for 9x12 SAE stamped with $1.80 postage.

FICTION Subjects include juvenile. "Barefoot Books only publishes children's picture books and anthologies of folktales. We do not publish novels." Barefoot Books is not currently accepting ms queries or submissions.

BARRICADE BOOKS, INC.

2037 Lemoine Ave., Suite 362, Fort Lee NJ 07024. (201)944-7600. **Fax:** (201)917-4951. **Website:** www.barricadebooks.com. **Contact:** Carole Stuart, publisher. Estab. 1991. Publishes hardcover and trade paperback originals, trade paperback reprints. "Barricade Books publishes nonfiction, mostly of the con-

troversial type, and books we can promote with authors who can talk about their topics on radio and television and to the press." **Publishes 12 titles/year. 200 queries received/year. 100 mss received/year. 80% of books from first-time authors. 50% from unagented writers. Pays 10-12% royalty on retail price for hardcover. Pays advance.** Publishes book 18 months after acceptance. Accepts simultaneous submissions. Responds in 1 month to queries.

NONFICTION Subjects include ethnic, history, psychology, sociology, true crime. "We look for quality nonfiction mss—preferably with a controversial lean." Query with SASE. Submit outline, 1-2 sample chapters. Material will not be returned or responded to without SASE. "We do not accept proposals on disk or via e-mail." Reviews artwork/photos. Send photocopies.

BARRONS EDUCATIONAL SERIES

250 Wireless Blvd., Hauppauge NY 11788. **Fax:** (631)434-3723. **Website:** www.barronseduc.com. **Contact:** Wayne R. Barr, manuscript acquisitions. Estab. 1945. **Pays authors royalty of 10-12% based on net price or buys ms outright for $2,000 minimum. Pays illustrators by the project based on retail price.** Publishes book 1 year after acceptance. Accepts simultaneous submissions. Due to the large volume of unsolicited submissions received, a complete evaluation of a proposal may take 4-6 weeks. Please do not call about the status of individual submissions. Catalog available for 9x12 SASE. Guidelines available on website.

NONFICTION Picture books: concept, reference. Young readers: biography, how-to, reference, self-help, social issues. Middle readers: hi-lo, how-to, reference, self-help, social issues. Young adults: reference, self-help, social issues, sports. Submit outline/synopsis and sample chapters. "Nonfiction submissions must be accompanied by SASE for response."

FICTION Picture books: animal, concept, multicultural, nature/environment. Young readers: adventure, multicultural, nature/environment, fantasy, suspense/mystery. Middle readers: adventure, fantasy, multicultural, nature/environment, problem novels, suspense/mystery. Young adults: problem novels. "Stories with an educational element are appealing." Query via e-mail with no attached files. Full guidelines are listed on the website.

⚑⊘ BASIC BOOKS

Hachette Book Group, 1290 Avenue of the Americas, Suite 1500, New York NY 10104. **Website:** www.basicbooks.com. **Contact:** Editor. Estab. 1952. Publishes hardcover and trade paperback originals and reprints. Accepts simultaneous submissions. Responds in at least 3 months to queries. Book catalog available free. Guidelines online.

NONFICTION Subjects include history, psychology, sociology, politics, current affairs.

BAYLOR UNIVERSITY PRESS

One Bear Place 97363, Waco TX 76798. (254)710-3164. **Fax:** (254)710-3440. **E-mail:** carey_newman@baylor. edu. **Website:** www.baylorpress.com. **Contact:** Dr. Carey C. Newman, director. Estab. 1897. Publishes hardcover and trade paperback originals. "We publish contemporary and historical scholarly works about culture, religion, politics, science, and the arts." **Publishes 30 titles/year. Pays 10% royalty on wholesale price.** Publishes ms 1 year after acceptance. Accepts simultaneous submissions. Responds in 2 months to proposals. Guidelines online.

NONFICTION Submit outline, 1-3 sample chapters via e-mail.

BEACON PRESS

24 Farnsworth St., Boston MA 02210. **E-mail:** editorial@beacon.org. **Website:** www.beacon.org. Estab. 1854. Publishes hardcover originals and paperback reprints. Beacon Press publishes general interest books that promote the following values: the inherent worth and dignity of every person; justice, equity, and compassion in human relations; acceptance of one another; a free and responsible search for truth and meaning; the goal of world community with peace, liberty, and justice for all; respect for the interdependent web of all existence. Currently emphasizing innovative nonfiction writing by people of all colors. De-emphasizing poetry, children's stories, art books, self-help. **Publishes 60 titles/year. 10% of books from first-time authors. Pays royalty. Pays advance.** Accepts simultaneous submissions. Responds in 3 months to queries.

NONFICTION Subjects include child guidance, education, ethnic, philosophy, religion, world affairs. *Strongly prefers agented submissions. Query by e-mail only. Strongly prefers referred submissions, on exclusive.*

BEARMANOR MEDIA

P.O. Box 71426, Albany GA 31708. **E-mail:** books@benohmart.com. **Website:** www.bearmanormedia.com. **Contact:** Ben Ohmart, publisher. Estab. 2000. Publishes trade paperback originals, hardbacks and e-books. "We specialize in entertainment biographies, and books on radio, TV and stage projects, as well as film scripts." **Publishes 70 titles/year. 90% of books from first-time authors. 90% from unagented writers. Negotiable per project. Pays upon acceptance. Occasionally pays advance.** Accepts simultaneous submissions. Responds within a few days. Book catalog online, or free upon request.

IMPRINTS BearManor Bare, MagicImage, BearManor Media.

NONFICTION Subjects include cinema, dance, entertainment, film, memoirs, stage. Only entertainment-related books please. Query with SASE. E-mail queries preferred. Submit proposal package, outline, list of credits on the subject. No.

BEHRMAN HOUSE INC.

11 Edison Place, Springfield NJ 07081. (973)379-7200. **Fax:** (973)379-7280. **E-mail:** customersupport@behrmanhouse.com. **Website:** www.behrmanhouse.com. **Contact:** Editorial Committee. Estab. 1921. Publishes books on all aspects of Judaism: history, cultural, textbooks, holidays. "Behrman House publishes quality books of Jewish content—history, Bible, philosophy, holidays, ethics—for children and adults." **12% of books from first-time authors. Pays authors royalty of 3-10% based on retail price or buys ms outright for $1,000-5,000. Offers advance. Pays illustrators by the project (range: $500-5,000).** Publishes book 18 months after acceptance. Accepts simultaneous submissions. Responds in 1 month to queries; 2 months to mss. Book catalog free on request. Guidelines online.

NONFICTION All levels: Judaism, Jewish educational textbooks. Average word length: young reader—1,200; middle reader—2,000; young adult—4,000. Submit outline/synopsis and sample chapters.

BELLEBOOKS

P.O. Box 300921, Memphis TN 38130. (901)344-9024. **Fax:** (901)344-9068. **E-mail:** bellebooks@bellebooks.com. **Website:** www.bellebooks.com. Estab. 1999. BelleBooks began by publishing Southern fiction. It has become a "second home" for many established authors, who also continue to publish with major publishing houses. **Publishes 30-40 titles/year.** Accepts simultaneous submissions. Guidelines online.

FICTION Subjects include juvenile, young adult. "Yes, we'd love to find the next Harry Potter, but our primary focus for the moment is publishing for the teen market." Query e-mail with brief synopsis and credentials/credits with full ms attached (RTF format preferred).

BELLEVUE LITERARY PRESS

Dept. of Medicine, NYU School of Medicine, 550 First Ave., OBV 612, New York NY 10016. (212)263-7802. **E-mail:** blpsubmissions@gmail.com. **Website:** blpress. org. **Contact:** Erika Goldman, publisher/editorial director. Estab. 2005. "Bellevue Literary Press is devoted to publishing literary fiction and nonfiction at the intersection of the arts and sciences because we believe that science and the humanities are natural companions for understanding the human experience. With each book we publish, our goal is to foster a rich, interdisciplinary dialogue that will forge new tools for thinking and engaging with the world." Accepts simultaneous submissions. Guidelines available.

FICTION Subjects include literary. Submit complete ms.

BENBELLA BOOKS

10300 N. Central Expressway, Suite 530, Dallas TX 75231. (214)750-3600. **E-mail:** glenn@benbellabooks. com. **Website:** www.benbellabooks.com. **Contact:** Glenn Yeffeth, publisher. Estab. 2001. Publishes hardcover and trade paperback originals. **Publishes 30-40 titles/year. Pays 6-15% royalty on retail price.** Publishes ms 10 months after acceptance. Accepts simultaneous submissions. Guidelines online.

NONFICTION Subjects include literary criticism, science. Submit proposal package, including: outline, 2 sample chapters (via e-mail).

BENTLEY PUBLISHERS

1734 Massachusetts Ave., Cambridge MA 02138. (617)547-4170. **Fax:** (617)876-9235. **Website:** www. bentleypublishers.com. Estab. 1950. Publishes hardcover and trade paperback originals and reprints. "Bentley Publishers publishes books for automotive enthusiasts. We are interested in books that showcase good research, strong illustrations, and valuable technical information." Automotive subjects only. Query with SASE. Submit sample chapters, bio, synopsis,

target market. Reviews artwork/photos. Book catalog and ms guidelines online.

NONFICTION Query with SASE. Submit sample chapters, bio, synopsis, target market. Rreviews artwork/photos.

🅐⊘ BERKLEY

Penguin Group (USA) Inc., 375 Hudson St., New York NY 10014. **Website:** penguin.com. President: Ivan Held. Estab. 1955. Publishes paperback and mass market originals and reprints. The Berkley Publishing Group publishes a variety of general nonfiction and fiction including the traditional categories of romance, mystery and science fiction. **Publishes 700 titles/year.**

IMPRINTS Ace; Jove; Heat; Sensation; Berkley Prime Crime; Berkley Caliber.

NONFICTION Subjects include child guidance, creative nonfiction, history, New Age, psychology, true crime, job-seeking communication. No memoirs or personal stories. Prefers agented submissions.

FICTION Subjects include adventure, historical, literary, mystery, romance, spiritual, suspense, western, young adult. No occult fiction. Prefers agented submissions.

BERRETT-KOEHLER PUBLISHERS, INC.

1333 Broadway, Suite #1000, Oakland CA 94612. **E-mail:** bkpub@bkpub.com. **E-mail:** submissions@bk-pub.com. **Website:** www.bkconnection.com. **Contact:** Anna Leinberger, associate editor. Publishes hardcover and trade paperback originals, mass market paperback originals, hardcover and trade paperback reprints. "Berrett-Koehler Publishers' mission is to publish books that support the movement toward a world that works for all. Our titles promote positive change at personal, organizational and societal levels." Please see proposal guidelines online. **Publishes 40 titles/year. 1,300 queries received/year. 800 mss received/year. 20-30% of books from first-time authors. 70% from unagented writers. Pays 10-20% royalty.** Publishes book 10 months after acceptance. Accepts simultaneous submissions. Responds in 1 month. Book catalog online.

NONFICTION Subjects include community, New Age, spirituality. Submit proposal package, outline, bio, 1-2 sample chapters. Hard-copy proposals only. Do not e-mail, fax, or phone please. Reviews artwork/photos. Send photocopies or originals with SASE.

BESS PRESS

3565 Harding Ave., Honolulu HI 96816. (808)734-7159. **Fax:** (808)732-3627. **Website:** www.besspress.com. Estab. 1979. Bess Press is a family-owned independent book publishing company based in Honolulu. For over 30 years, Bess Press has been producing both educational and popular general interest titles about Hawai'i and the Pacific. Accepts simultaneous submissions. Responds in 4 months. Catalog online. Guidelines online.

NONFICTION "We are constantly seeking to work with authors, artists, photographers, and organizations that are developing works concentrating on Hawai'i and the Pacific. Our goal is to regularly provide customers with new, creative, informative, educational, and entertaining publications that are directly connected to or flowing from Hawai'i and other islands in the Pacific region." Not interested in material that is unassociated with Hawai'i or the greater Pacific in theme. Please do not submit works if it does not fall into this regional category. Submit your name, contact information, working title, genre, target audience, short (4-6 sentences) description of your work, identifies target audience(s), explains how your work differs from other books already publishing on the same subject, includes discussion of any additional material with samples. All submissions via e-mail.

⊘ BETHANY HOUSE PUBLISHERS

Division of Baker Publishing Group, 6030 E. Fulton Rd., Ada MI 49301. (616)676-9185. **Fax:** (616)676-9573. **Website:** bakerpublishinggroup.com/bethanyhouse. Estab. 1956. Publishes hardcover and trade paperback originals, mass market paperback reprints. Bethany House Publishers specializes in books that communicate Biblical truth and assist people in both spiritual and practical areas of life. Considers unsolicited work only through a professional literary agent or through manuscript submission services, Authonomy or Christian Manuscript Submissions. Guidelines online. *All unsolicited mss returned unopened.* **Publishes 90-100 titles/year. 2% of books from first-time authors. 50% from unagented writers. Pays royalty on net price. Pays advance.** Publishes a book 1 year after acceptance. Accepts simultaneous submissions. Responds in 3 months to queries. Book catalog for 9 x 12 envelope and 5 first-class stamps.

NONFICTION Subjects include child guidance, Biblical disciplines, personal and corporate renewal, emerging generations, devotional, marriage and family, applied theology, inspirational.

FICTION Subjects include historical, young adult, contemporary.

🅐⊘ BEYOND WORDS PUBLISHING, INC.

20827 NW Cornell Rd., Suite 500, Hillsboro OR 97124. (503)531-8700. **Fax:** (503)531-8773. **E-mail:** info@beyondword.com. **Website:** www.beyondword.com. **Contact:** Submissions Department (for agents only). Estab. 1984. Publishes hardcover and trade paperback originals and paperback reprints. "At this time, we are not accepting any unsolicited queries or proposals, and recommend that all authors work with a literary agent in submitting their work." **Publishes 10-15 titles/year.** Accepts simultaneous submissions.

NONFICTION Subjects include health, young adult. For adult nonfiction, wants whole body health, the evolving human, and transformation. For children and YA, wants health, titles that inspire kids' power to incite change, and titles that allow young readers to explore and/or question traditional wisdom and spiritual practices. Does not want children's picture books, adult fiction, cookbooks, textbooks, reference books, photography books, or illustrated coffee table books. Agent should submit query letter with proposal, including author bio, 5 sample chapters, complete synopsis of book, market analysis, SASE.

FICTION Subjects include juvenile, young adult. Agent should submit query letter with proposal, including author bio, 5 sample chapters, complete synopsis of book, market analysis, SASE.

BILINGUAL REVIEW PRESS

Hispanic Research Center, Arizona State University, P.O. Box 875303, Tempe AZ 85287-5303. (480)965-3867. **Fax:** (480)965-0315. **E-mail:** brp@asu.edu. **Website:** www.asu.edu/brp. **Contact:** Gary Francisco Keller, publisher. Estab. 1973. "We are always on the lookout for Chicano, Puerto Rican, Cuban American, or other U.S. Hispanic themes with strong and serious literary qualities and distinctive and intellectually important topics." Accepts simultaneous submissions. Responds in 3-4 weeks for queries; 3-4 months on requested mss.

NONFICTION Query with SASE. Query should describe book, TOC, sample chapter, and any other information relevant to the rationale, content, audience, etc., for the book.

FICTION Subjects include ethnic, short story collections, translation. Query with SASE. Query should describe book, plot summary, sample chapter, and any other information relevant to the rationale, content, audience, etc., for the book.

POETRY Query with SASE. Query should describe book, TOC, sample poems, and any other information relevant to the rationale, content, audience, etc., for the book.

BLACK DOME PRESS CORP.

649 Delaware Ave., Delmar NY 12054. (518)439-6512. **Fax:** (518)439-1309. **Website:** www.blackdomepress.com. Estab. 1990. Publishes cloth and trade paperback originals and reprints. Do not send the entire work. Mail a cover letter, TOC, introduction, sample chapter (or 2), and your CV or brief biography to the Editor. Please do not send computer disks or submit your proposal via e-mail. If your book will include illustrations, please send us copies of sample illustrations. Do not send originals. Accepts simultaneous submissions. Book catalog and guidelines online.

NONFICTION Subjects include history, photography, regional, Native Americans, grand hotels, genealogy, colonial life, French & Indian War (NYS), American Revolution (NYS), quilting, architecture, railroads, hiking and kayaking guidebooks. New York state regional material only. Submit proposal package, outline, bio.

BLACK LAWRENCE PRESS

E-mail: editors@blacklawrencepress.com. **Website:** www.blacklawrencepress.com. **Contact:** Diane Goettel, executive editor. Estab. 2003. Black Lawrence press seeks to publish intriguing books of literature—novels, short story collections, poetry collections, chapbooks, anthologies, and creative nonfiction. Will also publish the occasional translation from German. Publishes 22-24 books/year, mostly poetry and fiction. Mss are selected through open submission and competition. Books are 20-400 pages, offset-printed or high-quality POD, perfect-bound, with 4-color cover. **Accepts submissions during the months of June and November. Pays royalties.** Accepts simultaneous submissions. Responds in 6 months to mss.

FICTION Subjects include literary, short story collections, translation. Submit complete ms.

POETRY Submit complete ms.

BLACK LYON PUBLISHING, LLC

P.O. Box 567, Baker City OR 97814. **E-mail:** info@blacklyonpublishing.com. **E-mail:** queries@blacklyonpublishing.com. **Website:** www.blacklyonpublishing.com. **Contact:** The Editors. Estab. 2007. Publishes paperback and e-book originals. "Black Lyon Publishing is a small, independent publisher. We are currently closed to all except existing Black Lyon authors through 2017." **Publishes 15-20 titles/year.** Guidelines online.

FICTION Subjects include gothic, historical, romance.

BLACK ROSE WRITING

P.O. Box 1540, Castroville TX 78009. **E-mail:** creator@blackrosewriting.com. **Website:** www.blackrosewriting.com/home. **Contact:** Reagan Rothe. Estab. 2006. Publishes fiction, nonfiction, and illustrated children's books. Black Rose Writing is an independent publishing house that strongly believes in developing a personal relationship with their authors. The Texas-based publishing company doesn't see authors as clients or just another number on a page, but rather as individual people.. people who deserve an honest review of their material and to be paid traditional royalties without ever paying any fees to be published. **Publishes 150+ titles/year. 3,500 submissions received/year. 75% of books from first-time authors. 80% from unagented writers. Royalties start at 20%, e-book royalties 25%** Publishes ms 4-6 months after acceptance. Accepts simultaneous submissions. Responds in 3-6 weeks on queries; 3-6 months on mss. Book catalog online. Guidelines online.

IMPRINTS DigiTerra Publishing, Bookend Design.

NONFICTION Subjects include animals, anthropology, archeology, art, business, creative nonfiction, economics, education, ethnic, health, history, medicine, memoirs, military, politics, psychology, science, sociology, sports, transportation, travel, true crime, war. "Our preferred submission method is via Authors.me, please click 'Submit Here' on our website." Reviews artwork.

FICTION Subjects include adventure, fantasy, historical, horror, humor, juvenile, literary, mainstream, military, mystery, occult, picture books, regional, romance, science fiction, sports, suspense, war, western, young adult. "Our preferred submission method is via Authors.me, please click 'Submit Here' on our website."

BLACK VELVET SEDUCTIONS PUBLISHING

E-mail: ric@blackvelvetseductions.com. **E-mail:** submissions@blackvelvetseductions.com. **Website:** www.blackvelvetseductions.com. **Contact:** Richard Savage, CEO. Estab. 2005. Publishes trade paperback and electronic originals and reprints. "We publish across a wide range of romance sub-genres, from soft sweet romance to supernatural romance, domestic discipline to highly erotic romance stories containing D/s and BDSM relationships. We are looking for authors who take something ordinary and make it extraordinary. We want stories with well-developed multi-dimensional characters with back-stories, a high degree of emotional impact, with strong sexual tension between the heroine and hero, and stories that contain strong internal conflict. We prefer stories told in the third person viewpoint, but will consider first person narratives. We put the emphasis on romance, rather than just the erotic. Although we will consider a high level of erotic content, it needs to be in the context of a romance story line. The plots may twist and turn and be full of passion, but please remember that our audience likes a happy ending. Do not be afraid to approach us with a non-traditional character or plot." **Publishes 25 titles/year. 500 queries; 1,000 mss received/year. 75% of books from first-time authors. 100% from unagented writers. Pays 10% royalty for paperbacks; 50% royalty for electronic books.** Publishes ms 6-12 months after acceptance. Accepts simultaneous submissions. Responds as swiftly as possible. Catalog free or online. Guidelines online.

FICTION Subjects include contemporary, erotica, fantasy, gay, historical, lesbian, romance, short story collections, erotic romance, historical romance, multicultural romance, romance, short story collections romantic stories, romantic suspense, western romance. All stories must have a strong romance element. "There are very few sexual taboos in our erotic line. We tend to give our authors the widest latitude. If it is safe, sane, and consensual we will allow our authors latitude to show us the eroticism. However, we will not consider manuscripts with any of the following: bestiality (sex with animals), necrophilia (sex with dead people), pedophillia (sex with children)." Only accepts electronic submissions.

JOHN F. BLAIR, PUBLISHER

1406 Plaza Dr., Winston-Salem NC 27103. (336)768-1374. **Fax:** (336)768-9194. **E-mail:** editorial@blairpub.com. **Website:** www.blairpub.com. **Contact:** Carolyn Sakowski, president. Estab. 1954. No poetry, young adult, children's, science fiction. Fiction must be set in southern U.S. or author must have strong Southern connection. **Publishes 10-15 titles/year. 1,000 proposals received/year. Pays royalties. Pays negotiable advance.** Publishes ms 18 months after acceptance. Accepts simultaneous submissions. Responds in 3-6 months. Catalog online. Guidelines online.

NONFICTION Subjects include cooking, creative nonfiction, history, literature, memoirs, regional, travel. Does not want self-help or business.

FICTION "We specialize in regional books, with an emphasis on nonfiction categories such as history, travel, folklore, and biography. We publish only one or two works of fiction each year. Fiction submitted to us should have some connection with the Southeast. We do not publish children's books, poetry, or category fiction such as romances, science fiction, or spy thrillers. We do not publish collections of short stories, essays, or newspaper columns." Does not want fiction set outside southern U.S. Accepts unsolicited mss. Any fiction submitted should have some connection with the Southeast, either through setting or author's background. Send a cover letter, giving a synopsis of the book. Include the first 2 chapters (at least 50 pages) of the ms. "You may send the entire ms if you wish. If you choose to send only samples, please include the projected word length of your book and estimated completion date in your cover letter. Send a biography of the author, including publishing credits and credentials."

BLOOMBERG PRESS

Imprint of John Wiley & Sons, Professional Development, 111 River St., Hoboken NJ 07030. **E-mail:** info@wiley.com. **Website:** www.wiley.com. Estab. 1995. Publishes hardcover and trade paperback originals. Bloomberg Press publishes professional books for practitioners in the financial markets. "We publish commercially successful, very high-quality books that stand out clearly from the competition by their brevity, ease of use, sophistication, and abundance of practical tips and strategies; books readers need, will use, and appreciate." **Publishes 18-22 titles/year. 200 queries; 20 mss received/year. 45% from unagented writers. Pays negotiable, competitive royalty. Pays negotiable advance for trade books.** Publishes book

9 months after acceptance. Accepts simultaneous submissions. Responds in 1 month to queries.

NONFICTION Subjects include , professional books on finance, investment and financial services, and books for financial advisors.. "We are looking for authorities and for experienced service journalists. Do not send us unfocused books containing general information already covered by books in the marketplace. We do not publish business, management, leadership, or career books." Submit outline, sample chapters, SAE with sufficient postage. Submit complete ms.

Ⓐ⊘ BLOOMSBURY CHILDREN'S BOOKS

Imprint of Bloomsbury USA, 1385 Broadway, 5th Floor, New York NY 10018. **Website:** www.bloomsbury.com/us/childrens. No phone calls or e-mails. *Agented submissions only.* **Publishes 60 titles/year. 25% of books from first-time authors. Pays royalty. Pays advance.** Accepts simultaneous submissions. Responds in 6 months. Book catalog online. Guidelines online.

FICTION Subjects include adventure, fantasy, historical, humor, juvenile, multicultural, mystery, picture books, poetry, science fiction, sports, suspense, young adult, animal, anthology, concept, contemporary, folktales, problem novels. *Agented submissions only.*

Ⓐ⊘ BLOOMSBURY CONTINUUM

Imprint of Bloomsbury Group, 1385 Broadway, 5th Floor, New York NY 10018. (212)419-5300. **Website:** www.bloomsbury.com/us/bloomsbury/bloomsbury-continuum. Continuum publishes textbooks, monographs, and reference works in religious studies, the humanities, arts, and social sciences for students, teachers, and professionals worldwide. *Does not accept unsolicited submissions.* Book catalog online.

NONFICTION Subjects include education, history, philosophy, religion, sociology, linguistics.

BLUE MOUNTAIN PRESS

Blue Mountain Arts, Inc., P.O. Box 4219, Boulder CO 80306. (800)525-0642. **E-mail:** bmpbooks@sps.com. **Website:** www.sps.com. **Contact:** Patti Wayant, director. Estab. 1971. Publishes hardcover originals, trade paperback originals, electronic originals. "Please note: We are not accepting works of fiction, rhyming poetry, children's books, chapbooks, or memoirs." **Pays royalty on wholesale price. Pays royalty advance.** Publishes ms 12-16 months after acceptance.

Accepts simultaneous submissions. Responds in 2-4 months. E-mail to request submission guidelines.

NONFICTION Subjects include , personal growth, teens/tweens, family, relationships, motivational, and inspirational but not religious. Query with SASE. Submit proposal package including outline and 3-5 sample chapters.

POETRY "We publish poetry appropriate for gift books, self-help books, and personal growth books. We do not publish chapbooks or literary poetry. We do not accept rhyming poetry." Query. Submit 10+ sample poems.

BLUE RIVER PRESS

Cardinal Publishers Group, 2402 N. Shadeland Ave., Suite A, Indianapolis IN 46219. (317)352-8200. **Fax:** (317)352-8202. **E-mail:** dmccormick@cardinalpub.com; tdoherty@cardinalpub.com. **Website:** www.brpressbooks.com; www.cardinalpub.com. **Contact:** Dani McCormick, editor; Tom Doherty, president (adult nonfiction). Estab. 2000. Publishes hardcover, trade paperback, and electronic originals and reprints. Blue River Press released its first book in the spring of 2004. "Today we have more than 100 books and e-books in print on the subjects of sports, health, fitness, games, popular culture, travel and our All About.. series for early readers. Our books have been recognized with awards and national and regional review attention. We have had many titles reach Nielsen BookScan category top 50 status in retail sales; illustrating that readers have responded by purchasing Blue River Press titles. Our distributor, Cardinal Publishers Group, has placed our books in chain and independent book retailers, libraries of all sorts, mass-merchant retailers, gift shops, and many specialty retail and wholesale channels. Our authors, editors and designers always keep the reader in mind when creating and developing the content and designing attractive books that are competitively priced. At Blue River Press our mission is to produce and market books that present the reader with good educational and entertaining information at a value." **Publishes 8-12 titles/year. 200 queries received/year. 25% of books from first-time authors. 80% from unagented writers. Pays 10-15% on wholesale price. Outright purchase of $500-5,000. Offers advance up to $5,000.** Publishes ms 6-12 months after acceptance. Accepts simultaneous submissions. Responds to queries in 2 months. Book catalog for #10 SASE or online. Guidelines available by e-mail.

NONFICTION Subjects include Americana, business, career guidance, education, entertainment, environment, games, health, history, recreation, regional, sports, travel. "Most non-religious adult nonfiction subjects are of interest. We like concepts that can develop into series products. Most of our books are paperback or hardcover in the categories of sport, business, health, fitness, lifestyle, yoga, and educational books for teachers and students."

BNA BOOKS

P.O. Box 7814, Edison NJ 08818. (800)960-1220. **Fax:** (723)346-1624. **Website:** www.bnabooks.com. Estab. 1929. Publishes hardcover and softcover originals. BNA Books publishes professional reference books written by lawyers, for lawyers. Accepts simultaneous submissions. Book catalog online. Guidelines online.

NONFICTION No fiction, biographies, bibliographies, cookbooks, religion books, humor, or trade books. Submit detailed TOC or outline, CV, intended market, estimated word length.

BOA EDITIONS, LTD.

P.O. Box 30971, Rochester NY 14603. (585)546-3410. **Fax:** (585)546-3913. **E-mail:** contact@boaeditions. org. **Website:** www.boaeditions.org. **Contact:** Ron Martin-Dent, director of publicity and production; Peter Conners, publisher. Director of Development and Operations: Kelly Hatton. Estab. 1976. Publishes hardcover, trade paperback, and digital e-book originals. BOA Editions, Ltd., a not-for-profit publisher of poetry, short fiction, and poetry-in-translation, fosters readership and appreciation of contemporary literature. By identifying, cultivating, and publishing both new and established poets and selecting authors of unique literary talent, BOA brings high quality literature to the public. **Publishes 10-12 titles/year. 1,000-2,000 queries and mss received/year. 15% of books from first-time authors. 90% from unagented writers. Negotiates royalties. Pays variable advance.** Publishes ms 18-24 months after acceptance. Accepts simultaneous submissions. Responds in 1 week to queries; 5 months to mss. Book catalog online. Guidelines online.

FICTION Subjects include literary, poetry, short story collections. BOA publishes literary fiction through its American Reader Series. While aesthetic quality is subjective, our fiction will be by authors more concerned with the artfulness of their writing than the twists and turns of plot. Our strongest current interest is in short story collections (and short-short story collections). We strongly advise you to read our published fiction collections. *BOA does not accept novel submissions.*

POETRY Readers who, like Whitman, expect the poet to 'indicate more than the beauty and dignity which always attach to dumb real objects. They expect him to indicate the path between reality and their souls,' are the audience of BOA's books. BOA Editions, a Pulitzer Prize and National Book Award-winning not-for-profit publishing house, acclaimed for its work, reads poetry manuscripts for the American Poets Continuum Series (new poetry by distinguished poets in mid-to-late career), the New Poets of America Series (publication of a poet's first book, selected through the A. Poulin, Jr. Poetry Prize), and the America Reader Series (short fiction and prose on poetics). Check BOA's website for reading periods for the American Poets Continuum Series and the A. Poulin, Jr. Poetry Prize. Please adhere to the general submission guidelines for each series. Guidelines online.

BOLD STROKES BOOKS, INC.

P.O. Box 249, Valley Falls NY 12094. (518)677-5127. **Fax:** (518)677-5291. **E-mail:** sandy@boldstrokesbooks. com. **E-mail:** submissions@boldstrokesbooks.com. **Website:** www.boldstrokesbooks.com. **Contact:** Sandy Lowe, senior editor. Estab. 2004. Publishes trade paperback originals and reprints; electronic originals and reprints. **Publishes 120+ titles/year. 300 queries/year; 300 mss/year. 10-20% of books from first-time authors. 95% from unagented writers. Sliding scale based on sales volume and format. Pays advance.** Publishes ms 6-16 months after acceptance. Responds in 1 month to queries; 2 months to proposals; 4 months to mss. Guidelines online.

IMPRINTS BSB Fiction; Victory Editions Lesbian Fiction; Liberty Editions Gay Fiction; Soliloquy Young Adult; Heat Stroke Erotica.

NONFICTION Subjects include gay, lesbian, memoirs, young adult. Submit completed ms with bio, cover letter, and synopsis electronically only. Does not review artwork.

FICTION Subjects include adventure, erotica, fantasy, gay, gothic, historical, horror, lesbian, literary, mainstream, mystery, romance, science fiction, suspense, western, young adult. "Submissions should have a gay, lesbian, transgendered, or bisexual focus and should be positive and life-affirming." We do not publish any non-lgbtqi focused works. Submit completed ms with bio, cover letter, and synopsis—electronically only.

BOOKFISH BOOKS

E-mail: bookfishbooks@gmail.com. **Website:** bookfishbooks.com. **Contact:** Tammy Mckee, acquisitions editor. BookFish Books is looking for novel lengthed young adult, new adult, and middle grade works in all subgenres. Both published and unpublished, agented or unagented authors are welcome to submit. "Sorry, but we do not publish novellas, picture books, early reader/chapter books or adult novels." Responds to every query. Accepts simultaneous submissions. Guidelines online.

FICTION Query via e-mail with a brief synopsis and first 3 chapters of ms.

⬤ BOOKOUTURE

StoryFire Ltd., 23 Sussex Rd., Ickenham UB10 8P, United Kingdom. **Website:** www.bookouture.com. **Contact:** Oliver Rhodes, founder and publisher. Estab. 2012. Publishes mass market paperback and electronic originals and reprints. **Publishes 40 titles/year. Receives 200 queries/year; 300 mss/year. Pays 45% royalty on wholesale price.** Publishes ms 4 months after acceptance. Accepts simultaneous submissions. Responds in 1 month. Book catalog online.

IMPRINTS Imprint of StoryFire Ltd.

FICTION Subjects include contemporary, erotica, ethnic, fantasy, gay, historical, lesbian, mainstream, mystery, romance, science fiction, suspense, western, crime, thriller, new adult. "We are looking for entertaining fiction targeted at modern women. That can be anything from Steampunk to Erotica, Historicals to thrillers. A distinctive author voice is more important than a particular genre or ms length." Submit complete ms.

BOYDS MILLS PRESS

Highlights for Children, Inc., 815 Church St., Honesdale PA 18431. (570)253-1164. **Website:** www.boydsmillspress.com. Estab. 1990. Boyds Mills Press publishes picture books, nonfiction, activity books, and paperback reprints. Their titles have been named notable books by the International Reading Association, the American Library Association, and the National Council of Teachers of English. They've earned nu-merous awards, including the National Jewish Book Award, the Christopher Medal, the NCTE Orbis Pictus Honor, and the Golden Kite Honor. Boyds Mills Press welcomes unsolicited submissions from published and unpublished writers and artists. Submit a ms with a cover letter of relevant information, including experience with writing and publishing. Label the package "Manuscript Submission" and include an SASE. For art samples, label the package "Art Sample Submission." All submissions will be evaluated for all imprints. Responds to mss within 3 months. Catalog online. Guidelines online.

POETRY Send a book-length collection of poems. Do not send an initial query. Keep in mind that the strongest collections demonstrate a facility with multiple poetic forms.

GEORGE BRAZILLER, INC.

277 Broadway, Suite 708, New York NY 10007. **Website:** www.georgebraziller.com. Publishes hardcover and trade paperback originals and reprints. Accepts simultaneous submissions.

FICTION Subjects include ethnic, gay, lesbian, literary. "We rarely do fiction but when we have published novels, they have mostly been literary novels." Submit 4-6 sample chapter(s), SASE. Agented fiction 20%. Responds in 3 months to proposals.

NICHOLAS BREALEY PUBLISHING

53 State St., 9th Floor, Boston MA 02109. (617)523-3801. **Fax:** (617)523-3708. **Website:** www.nicholasbrealey.com. **Contact:** Aquisitions Editor. Estab. 1992. "Nicholas Brealey Publishing has a reputation for publishing high-quality and thought-provoking business books with international appeal. Over time our list has grown to focus also on careers, professional and personal development, travel narratives and crossing cultures. We welcome fresh ideas and new insights in all of these subject areas." Submit via e-mail and follow the guidelines on the website. Accepts simultaneous submissions.

⬤ BROADVIEW PRESS, INC.

P.O. Box 1243, Peterborough ON K9J 7H5, Canada. (705)743-8990. **Fax:** (705)743-8353. **E-mail:** mather@broadviewpress.com; slatta@broadviewpress.com; dema@broadviewpress.com; brett@broadviewpress.com. **Website:** www.broadviewpress.com. **Contact:** Marjorie Mather, publisher/editor (English studies); Stephen Latta, editor (philosophy); Leslie Dema, acquisitions editor (Broadview Editions in philosophy), Brett McLenithan, acquisitions editor. Estab. 1985. "We publish in a broad variety of subject areas in the arts and social sciences. We are open to a broad range of political and philosophical viewpoints, from liberal and conservative to libertarian and Marxist, and including a wide range of feminist viewpoints." **Publishes over 40 titles/year. 500 queries; 200 mss received/year. 10% of books from first-time authors. 99% from unagented writers. Pays royalty.** Publishes ms 12 months after acceptance. Accepts simultaneous submissions. Responds in 1 month to queries; 2 months to proposals; 4 months to mss. Book catalog available free. Guidelines online.

NONFICTION Subjects include philosophy, religion, politics. "Our focus is very much on English studies and Philosophy, but within those 2 core subject areas we are open to a broad range of academic approaches and political viewpoints. We welcome feminist perspectives, and we have a particular interest in addressing environmental issues. Our publishing program is internationally-oriented, and we publish for a broad range of geographical markets-but as a Canadian company we also publish a broad range of titles with a Canadian emphasis." Query with SASE. Submit proposal package. Reviews artwork/photos. Send photocopies.

🅰🚫 BROADWAY BOOKS

Penguin Random House, 1745 Broadway, New York NY 10019. (212)782-9000. **Fax:** (212)782-9411. **Website:** crownpublishing.com/imprint/broadway-books. Estab. 1995. Publishes hardcover and trade paperback books. "Broadway publishes high quality general interest nonfiction and fiction for adults." **Receives thousands of mss/year. Pays royalty on retail price. Pays advance.** Accepts simultaneous submissions.

IMPRINTS Broadway Books; Broadway Business; Doubleday; Doubleday Image; Doubleday Religious Publishing; Main Street Books; Nan A. Talese.

NONFICTION Subjects include child guidance, contemporary culture, history, memoirs, multicultural, New Age, psychology, sex, spirituality, sports, travel, current affairs, motivational/inspirational, popular culture, consumer reference. *Agented submissions only.*

FICTION *Agented submissions only.*

⊙ THE BRUCEDALE PRESS

P.O. Box 2259, Port Elgin ON N0H 2C0, Canada. (519)832-6025. **E-mail:** info@brucedalepress.ca. **Website:** brucedalepress.ca. Estab. 1994. Publishes hardcover and trade paperback originals. The Brucedale Press publishes books and other materials of regional interest and merit, as well as literary, historical, and/or pictorial works. Accepts works by Canadian authors only. Book submissions reviewed November to January. Submissions to *The Leaf Journal* accepted in September and March only. Manuscripts must be in English and thoroughly proofread before being sent. Use Canadian spellings and style. **Publishes 3 titles/year. 75% of books from first-time authors. 100% from unagented writers. Pays royalty.** Publishes book 1 year after acceptance. Book catalog online. "Unless responding to an invitation to submit, query first by Canada Post with outline and sample chapter to book-length manuscripts. Send full manuscripts for work intended for children." Guidelines online.

NONFICTION Subjects include history, memoirs, photography. Reviews artwork/photos from Canadians only.

FICTION Subjects include fantasy, feminist, historical, humor, juvenile, literary, mystery, plays, poetry, romance, short story collections, young adult.

BUCKNELL UNIVERSITY PRESS

Bucknell University, 1 Dent Dr., Lewisburg PA 17837. (570)577-3674. **E-mail:** universitypress@bucknell.edu. **Website:** www.bucknell.edu/universitypress. **Contact:** Greg Clingham, director. Estab. 1968. Publishes hardcover, paperback, and e-books on various platforms. "In all fields, our criteria are scholarly excellence, critical originality, and interdisciplinary and theoretical expertise and sensitivity." **Publishes 35-40 titles/year.** Book catalog available free. Guidelines online.

NONFICTION Subjects include environment, ethnic, history, law, literary criticism, multicultural, philosophy, psychology, sociology, Luso-Hispanic studies, Latin American studies, 18-century studies, ecocriticism, African studies, Irish literature, cultural studies, historiography, legal theory. Series: Transits: Literature, Thought & Culture 1650-1850; Bucknell Series in Latin American Literature and Theory; Eighteenth-Century Scotland; New Studies in the Age of Goethe; Contemporary Irish Writers; Griot Project

Book Series; Apercus: Histories Texts Cultures. Submit full proposal and CV by Word attachment.

BULLITT PUBLISHING

P.O. Box, Austin TX 78729. **E-mail:** bullittpublishing@yahoo.com. **E-mail:** submissions@bullittpublishing.com. **Website:** bullittpublishing.com. **Contact:** Pat Williams, editor. Estab. 2012. Publishes trade paperback and electronic originals. "Bullitt Publishing is a royalty-offering publishing house specializing in smart, contemporary romance. We are proud to provide print on demand distribution through the world's most comprehensive distribution channels. Whether this is your first novel or your 101st novel, Bullitt Publishing will treat you with the same amount of professionalism and respect. While we expect well-written entertaining manuscripts from all of our authors, we promise to provide high quality, professional product in return." **Publishes 12 titles/year.** Accepts simultaneous submissions.

IMPRINTS Tempo Romance.

FICTION Subjects include romance.

BURFORD BOOKS

101 E. State St., #301, Ithaca NY 14850. (607)319-4373. **E-mail:** info@burfordbooks.com. **Website:** www.burfordbooks.com. **Contact:** Burford Books Editorial Department. Estab. 1997. Publishes hardcover originals, trade paperback originals and reprints. Burford Books publishes books on all aspects of the outdoors, from backpacking to sports, practical and literary, as well as books on food & wine, military history, and the Finger Lakes region of New York State. **Publishes 12 titles/year. 300 queries; 200 mss received/year. 30% of books from first-time authors. 60% from unagented writers. Pays royalty on wholesale price.** Publishes book 18 months after acceptance. Accepts simultaneous submissions. Responds in 1 week to queries; 1 month to proposals; 2 months to mss. Book catalog and ms guidelines online.

NONFICTION Subjects include Americana, animals, cooking, foods, gardening, history, hobbies, military, recreation, sports, travel, war, fitness. "Burford Books welcomes proposals on new projects, especially in the subject areas in which we specialize: sports, the outdoors, golf, nature, gardening, food and wine, travel, and military history. We are not currently considering fiction or children's books. In general it's sufficient to send a brief proposal letter that outlines your idea, which should be e-mailed to info@burfordbooks.com with the word 'query' in the subject line." Reviews artwork/photos. Send digital images.

C&T PUBLISHING

1651 Challenge Dr., Concord CA 94520-5206. (925)677-0377. **Fax:** (925)677-0373. **E-mail:** roxanec@ctpub.com. **E-mail:** support@ctpub.com. **Website:** www.ctpub.com. **Contact:** Roxane Cerda. Estab. 1983. Publishes hardcover and trade paperback originals. "C&T publishes well-written, beautifully designed books on quilting, sewing, fiber crafts, embroidery, dollmaking, mixed media and crafting for children." **Publishes 50 titles/year. 200 50% of books from first-time authors. 90% from unagented writers. Pays royalty.** Accepts simultaneous submissions. Responds in 2 months to queries. Book catalog free; guidelines online.

IMPRINTS Stash Books, Fun Stitch Studio, and Kansas City Star Quilts.

NONFICTION Subjects include art, crafts, hobbies, quilting books, occasional quilt picture books, quilt-related crafts, wearable art, needlework, fiber and surface embellishments, other books relating to fabric crafting and paper crafting.. Extensive proposal guidelines are available on the company's website.

FICTION Subjects include , novels and cozy mysteries aimed at a quilting audience.

CALKINS CREEK

Boyds Mills Press, 815 Church St., Honesdale PA 18431. **Website:** www.boydsmillspress.com. Estab. 2004. "We aim to publish books that are a well-written blend of creative writing and extensive research, which emphasize important events, people, and places in U.S. history." **Pays authors royalty or work purchased outright.** Accepts simultaneous submissions. Guidelines online.

NONFICTION Subjects include history. Submit outline/synopsis and 3 sample chapters.

FICTION Subjects include historical. Submit outline/synopsis and 3 sample chapters.

⚠ ⊘ CANDLEWICK PRESS

99 Dover St., Somerville MA 02144. (617) 661-3330. **Fax:** (617) 661-0565. **E-mail:** bigbear@candlewick.com. **Website:** www.candlewick.com. Estab. 1991. Publishes hardcover and trade paperback originals, and reprints. "Candlewick Press publishes high-quality, illustrated children's books for ages infant through

young adult. We are a truly child-centered publisher." **Publishes 200 titles/year. 5% of books from first-time authors. Pays authors royalty of 2½-10% based on retail price. Offers advance.** Accepts simultaneous submissions.

IMPRINTS Big Picture Press, Candlewick Entertainment, Candlewick Studio, Nosy Crow, Templar Books.

NONFICTION Picture books: concept, biography, geography, nature/environment. Young readers: biography, geography, nature/environment.

FICTION Subjects include juvenile, picture books, young adult. Picture books: animal, concept, contemporary, fantasy, history, humor, multicultural, nature/environment, poetry. Middle readers, young adults: contemporary, fantasy, history, humor, multicultural, poetry, science fiction, sports, suspense/mystery. "We currently do not accept unsolicited editorial queries or submissions. If you are an author or illustrator and would like us to consider your work, please read our submissions policy (online) to learn more."

CAPALL BANN PUBLISHING

Auton Farm, Milverton, Somerset TA4 1NE, United Kingdom. (44)(182)340-1528. **E-mail:** enquiries@ capallbann.co.uk. **Website:** www.capallbann.co.uk. **Contact:** Julia Day (MBS, healing, animals and religion). Publishes trade and mass market paperback originals and trade paperback and mass market paperback reprints. "Our mission is to publish books of real value to enhance and improve readers' lives." **Publishes 46 titles/year. 800 queries; 450 mss received/year. 50% of books from first-time authors. 100% from unagented writers. Pays 10% royalty on net sales.** Publishes ms 4-8 months after acceptance. Accepts simultaneous submissions. Responds in 2-6 weeks to queries; 2 months to proposals and mss. Book catalog free. Guidelines online.

NONFICTION Subjects include animals, astrology, crafts, creative nonfiction, gardening, New Age, philosophy, psychic, religion, spirituality, witchcraft, paganism, druidry, ritual magic. Submit outline. Reviews artwork/photos. Send photocopies.

CAPSTONE PRESS

Capstone Young Readers, 1710 Roe Crest Dr., North Mankato MN 56003. **E-mail:** author.sub@capstonepub.com; il.sub@capstonepub.com. **Website:** www.capstonepub.com. Estab. 1991. The Capstone Press imprint publishes nonfiction with accessible text on topics kids love to capture interest and build confidence and skill in beginning, struggling, and reluctant readers, grades pre-K-9. Responds only if submissions fit needs. Mss and writing samples will not be returned. "If you receive no reply within 6 months, you should assume the editors are not interested." Catalog available upon request. Guidelines online.

THE CAREER PRESS, INC.

12 Parish Dr., Wayne NJ 07470. **Website:** www.careerpress.com. Estab. 1985. Publishes hardcover and paperback originals. Career Press publishes books for adult readers seeking practical information to improve themselves in careers, business, HR, sales, entrepreneurship, and other related topics, as well as titles on supervision, management and CEOs. New Page Books publishes in the areas of New Age, new science, paranormal, the unexplained, alternative history, spirituality. Accepts simultaneous submissions. Guidelines online.

NONFICTION Subjects include recreation, nutrition. Look through our catalog; become familiar with our publications. "We like to select authors who are specialists on their topic." Submit outline, bio, TOC, 2-3 sample chapters, marketing plan, SASE. Or, send complete ms (preferred).

CAROLINA WREN PRESS

120 Morris St., Durham NC 27701. (919)560-2738. **E-mail:** carolinawrenpress@earthlink.net. **Website:** www.carolinawrenpress.org. **Contact:** Robin Miura, Editor & Director. Estab. 1976. "We publish poetry, fiction, and memoirs by or about people of color, women, gay/lesbian issues, and work by writers from, living in, or writing about the U.S. South." Accepts simultaneous submissions, but "let us know if work has been accepted elsewhere." **We pay our authors an honorarium.** Publishes ms 2 year after acceptance. Accepts simultaneous submissions. Responds in 3 months to queries; 6 months to mss. Guidelines online.

NONFICTION Subjects include ethnic, gay, lesbian, literature, multicultural, womens issues.

FICTION Subjects include ethnic, experimental, feminist, literary, poetry, short story collections. "We are no longer publishing children's literature of any topic." Books: 6×9 paper; typeset; various bindings; illustrations. Distributes titles through John F. Blair, Amazon.com, Barnes & Noble, Baker & Taylor, and on their website. "We very rarely accept any unsolicited manuscripts, but we accept submissions for the

Doris Bakwin Award for Writing by a Woman in Jan-June of even-numbered years and submissions for the Lee Smith Novel Prize in Jan-June of odd-numbered years." "We will accept e-mailed queries—a letter in the body of the e-mail describing your project—but please do not send large attachments." All other submissions are accepted via Submittable as part of our annual contests.

POETRY Publishes 2 poetry books/year, "usually through the Carolina Wren Press Poetry Series Contest. Otherwise we primarily publish women, minorities, and authors from, living in, or writing about the U.S. South." Not accepting unsolicited submissions except through Poetry Series Contest. Accepts e-mail queries, but send only letter and description of work, no large files. Carolina Wren Press Poetry Contest for a First or Second Book takes submissions, electronically, from January to June of odd-numbered years.

⊘ CARSON-DELLOSA PUBLISHING CO., INC.

P.O. Box 35665, Greensboro NC 27425. (336)632-0084. **E-mail:** freelancesamples@carsondellosa.com. **Website:** www.carsondellosa.com. Does not accept unsolicited product ideas or book proposals at this time. **Publishes 80-90 titles/year. 15-20% of books from first-time authors. 95% from unagented writers. Makes outright purchase.** Book catalog online. Guidelines available free.

NONFICTION Subjects include education. "We publish supplementary educational materials, such as teacher resource books, workbooks, and activity books." No textbooks or trade children's books, please.

❹⊘ CARTWHEEL BOOKS

Imprint of Scholastic Trade Division, 557 Broadway, New York NY 10012. (212)343-6100. **Website:** www. scholastic.com. Estab. 1991. Publishes novelty books, easy readers, board books, hardcover and trade paperback originals. Cartwheel Books publishes innovative books for children, up to age 8. "We are looking for 'novelties' that are books first, play objects second. Even without its gimmick, a Cartwheel Book should stand alone as a valid piece of children's literature." Accepts simultaneous submissions. Guidelines available free.

NONFICTION Subjects include animals, history, recreation, science, sports. Cartwheel Books publishes for the very young, therefore nonfiction should be written in a manner that is accessible to preschoolers through 2nd grade. Often writers choose topics that are too narrow or "special" and do not appeal to the mass market. Also, the text and vocabulary are frequently too difficult for our young audience. *Accepts mss from agents only.* Reviews artwork/photos. Send Please do not send original artwork.

FICTION Subjects include humor, juvenile, mystery, picture books. Again, the subject should have mass market appeal for very young children. Humor can be helpful, but not necessary. Mistakes writers make are a reading level that is too difficult, a topic of no interest or too narrow, or mss that are too long. *Accepts mss from agents only.*

CATHOLIC UNIVERSITY OF AMERICA PRESS

620 Michigan Ave. NE, Washington DC 20064. (202)319-5052. **E-mail:** cua-press@cua.edu. **Website:** cuapress.org. Estab. 1939. The Catholic University of America Press publishes in the fields of history (ecclesiastical and secular), literature and languages, philosophy, political theory, social studies, and theology. "We have interdisciplinary emphasis on patristics, and medieval studies. We publish works of original scholarship intended for academic libraries, scholars and other professionals and works that offer a synthesis of knowledge of the subject of interest to a general audience or suitable for use in college and university classrooms." **Publishes 30-35 titles/year. 50% of books from first-time authors. 100% from unagented writers. Pays variable royalty on net receipts.** Publishes book 18 months after acceptance. Accepts simultaneous submissions. Responds in 5 days to queries. Book catalog on request. Guidelines online.

NONFICTION Subjects include history, philosophy, religion, Church-state relations. No unrevised doctoral dissertations. Length: 40,000-120,000 words. Query with outline, sample chapter, CV, and list of previous publications.

CATO INSTITUTE

1000 Massachusetts Ave. NW, Washington DC 20001. (202)842-0200. **Website:** www.cato.org. **Contact:** Submissions Editor. Estab. 1977. Publishes hardcover originals, trade paperback originals and reprints. Cato Institute publishes books on public policy issues from a free-market or libertarian perspective. **Publishes 12 titles/year. 25% of books from first-time authors. 90% from unagented writers. Makes outright purchase of $1,000-10,000. Pays advance.** Publishes ms 9 months after acceptance. Accepts simultaneous submissions. Responds in 3 months to queries. Book catalog online.

NONFICTION Subjects include education, sociology, public policy. Query with SASE.

CEDAR FORT, INC.

2373 W. 700 S, Springville UT 84663. (801)489-4084. **Website:** www.cedarfort.com. Estab. 1986. Publishes hardcover, trade paperback originals and reprints, mass market paperback and electronic reprints. "Each year we publish well over 100 books, and many of those are by first-time authors. At the same time, we love to see books from established authors. As one of the largest book publishers in Utah, we have the capability and enthusiasm to make your book a success, whether you are a new author or a returning one. We want to publish uplifting and edifying books that help people think about what is important in life, books people enjoy reading to relax and feel better about themselves, and books to help improve lives. Although we do put out several children's books each year, we are extremely selective. Our children's books must have strong religious or moral values, and must contain outstanding writing and an excellent storyline." **Publishes 150 titles/year. Receives 200 queries/year; 600 mss/year. 60% of books from first-time authors. 95% from unagented writers. Pays 10-12% royalty on wholesale price. Pays $2,000-50,000 advance.** Publishes book 10-14 months after acceptance. Accepts simultaneous submissions. Responds in 1 month on queries; 2 months on proposals; 4 months on mss. Catalog and guidelines online.

IMPRINTS Council Press, Sweetwater Books, Bonneville Books, Front Table Books, Hobble Creek Press, CFI, Plain Sight Publishing, Horizon Publishers, Pioneer Plus.

NONFICTION Subjects include agriculture, Americana, animals, anthropology, archeology, business, child guidance, communications, cooking, crafts, creative nonfiction, economics, education, foods, gardening, health, history, hobbies, horticulture, house and home, military, nature, recreation, regional, religion, social sciences, spirituality, war, womens issues, young adult. Query with SASE; submit proposal package, including outline, 2 sample chapters; or submit completed ms. Reviews artwork as part of the ms package. Send photocopies.

FICTION Subjects include adventure, contemporary, fantasy, historical, humor, juvenile, literary, mainstream, military, multicultural, mystery, regional, religious, romance, science fiction, spiritual, sports, suspense, war, western, young adult. Submit completed ms.

CENTERSTREAM PUBLISHING

P.O. Box 17878, Anaheim Hills CA 92817. (714)779-9390. **Fax:** (714)779-9390. **E-mail:** centerstrm@aol.com. **Website:** www.centerstream-usa.com. **Contact:** Ron Middlebrook. Estab. 1980. Publishes music hardcover and mass market paperback originals, trade paperback and mass market paperback reprints. Centerstream publishes music history and instructional books, all instruments plus DVDs. **Publishes 12-15 titles/year. 15 queries; 15 mss received/year. 80% of books from first-time authors. 100% from unagented writers. Pays 10-15% royalty on wholesale price. Pays advance.** Publishes ms 8 months after acceptance. Accepts simultaneous submissions. Responds in 3 months to queries. Book catalog and ms guidelines for #10 SASE.

NONFICTION Query with SASE.

CHALICE PRESS

CBP Books, Christian Board of Publication, 483 E. Lockwood Ave., Suite 100, St. Louis MO 63119. (314)231-8500. **E-mail:** submissions@chalicepress.com. **Website:** www.chalicepress.com. **Contact:** Brad Lyons, president and publisher. Estab. 1911. Publishes hardcover and trade paperback originals. The mission of CBP/Chalice Press is to publish resources inviting all people into deeper relationship with God, equipping them as disciples of Jesus Christ, and sending them into ministries as the Holy Spirit calls them. CBP is a 501(c)3 not-for-profit organization. **Publishes 20 titles/year. 300 queries; 50 mss received/year. 10% of books from first-time authors. 95% from unagented writers. Pays negotiable advance.** Publishes ms 12-24 months after manuscript submission. Accepts simultaneous submissions. Responds in 2 months to queries; 3 months to proposals and mss. Book catalog online. Guidelines online.

IMPRINTS Chalice Press, TCP Books, CBP, Inside Out Church Camp Curriculum.

NONFICTION Subjects include community, multicultural, public affairs, religion, social sciences, spirituality, womens issues, Christian spirituality, social justice. Submit query as directed on www.chalice-press.com.

S. CHAND & COMPANY LTD.

7361 Ram Nagar, Qutab Rd., New Delhi 110055, India. (91)(11)2367-2080. **Fax:** (91)(11)2367-7446. **Website:** www.schandpublishing.com. Accepts simultaneous submissions. Guidelines online.

NONFICTION Subjects include history, botany, chemistry, engineering, technical, English, mathematics, physics, political science, zoology. Query through website.

CHANGELING PRESS LLC

315 N. Centre St., Martinsburg WV 25404. **E-mail:** submissions.changelingpress@gmail.com. **Website:** www.changelingpress.com. **Contact:** Margaret Riley, publisher. Estab. 2004. Publishes e-books. Erotic romance, novellas only (10,000-30,000 words). "We're currently looking for contemporary and futuristic short fiction, single title, series, and serials in the following genres and themes: sci-fi/futuristic, dark and urban fantasy, paranormal, BDSM, action adventure, guilty pleasures (adult contemporary kink), new adult, menage, bisexual and more, gay, interracial, BBW, cougar (M/F), silver fox (M/M), men and women in uniform, vampires, werewolves, Elves, dragons and magical creatures, other shapeshifters, magic, dark desires (demons and horror), and hentai (tentacle monsters)." **Publishes 165 titles/year. 400+ 5% of books from first-time authors. 100% from unagented writers. Pays 35% gross royalties on site, 50% gross off site monthly. Does not pay advance.** Publishes ms 60-90 days after acceptance. Responds in 1 week to queries. Catalog online. Guidelines online.

FICTION Subjects include adventure, erotica, experimental, fantasy, gay, horror, humor, military, multicultural, romance, science fiction, suspense. Please read and follow our submissions guidelines available at http://changelingpress.com/submissions.php. All submissions which do not follow the submissions guidelines will be rejected unread. No lesbian fiction submissions without prior approval, please. Absolutely no lesbian fiction written by men. E-mail submissions only. Please read and follow our submissions guidelines online. All submissions which do not follow the submissions guidelines will be rejected unread.

CHARLESBRIDGE PUBLISHING

85 Main St., Watertown MA 02472. (617)926-0329. **Fax:** (617)926-5720. **E-mail:** tradeeditorial@charlesbridge.com. **E-mail:** yasubs@charlesbridge.com. **Website:** www.charlesbridge.com. Estab. 1980. Publishes hardcover and trade paperback nonfiction and fiction, children's books for the trade and library markets. "Charlesbridge publishes high-quality books for children, with a goal of creating lifelong readers and lifelong learners. Our books encourage reading and discovery in the classroom, library, and home. We believe that books for children should offer accurate information, promote a positive worldview, and embrace a child's innate sense of wonder and fun. To this end, we continually strive to seek new voices, new visions, and new directions in children's literature. As of September 2015, we are now accepting young adult novels for consideration." **Publishes 45 titles/year. 2,000 submissions/year. 10-20% of books from first-time authors. 50% from unagented writers. Pays royalty. Pays advance.** Publishes ms 2-4 years after acceptance. Accepts simultaneous submissions. Responds in 3 months. Guidelines online.

IMPRINTS Charlesbridge Teen: Charlesbridge Teen features storytelling that presents new ideas and an evolving world. Our carefully curated stories give voice to unforgettable characters with unique perspectives. We publish books that inspire teens to cheer or sigh, laugh or reflect, reread or share with a friend, and ultimately, pick up another book. Our mission—to make reading irresistible!

NONFICTION Subjects include animals, creative nonfiction, history, multicultural, science, social science. Strong interest in nature, environment, social studies, and other topics for trade and library markets. Please submit only 1 or 2 chapters at a time. For nonfiction books longer than 30 ms pages, send a detailed proposal, a chapter outline, and 1-3 chapters of text.

FICTION Subjects include young adult. Strong stories with enduring themes. Charlesbridge publishes both picture books and transitional bridge books (books ranging from early readers to middle-grade chapter books). Our fiction titles include lively, plot-driven stories with strong, engaging characters. No alphabet books, board books, coloring books, activity books, or books with audiotapes or CD-ROMs. Please submit only 1 ms at a time. For picture books and shorter bridge books, please send a complete ms. For fiction books longer than 30 ms pages, please send a detailed plot synopsis, a chapter outline, and 3 chapters of text. If sending a young adult novel, mark the front of the envelope with "YA novel enclosed." Please note, for YA, e-mail submissions are preferred to the following address; yasubs@charlesbridge.com. Only responds if interested. Full guidelines on site.

CHELSEA GREEN PUBLISHING CO.

85 N. Main St., Suite 120, White River Junction VT 05001. (802)295-6300. **Fax:** (802)295-6444. **E-mail:** web@chelseagreen.com. **E-mail:** submissions@chelseagreen.com. **Website:** www.chelseagreen.com. Estab. 1984. Publishes hardcover and trade paperback originals and reprints. "Since 1984, Chelsea Green has been the publishing leader for books on the politics and practice of sustainable living." **Publishes 18-25 titles/year. 600-800 queries; 200-300 mss received/year. 30% of books from first-time authors. 80% from unagented writers. Pays royalty on publisher's net. Pays advance.** Publishes book 18 months after acceptance. Accepts simultaneous submissions. Responds in 2 weeks to queries; 1 month to proposals/mss. Book catalog online. Guidelines online.

NONFICTION Subjects include agriculture, alternative lifestyles, animals, business, community, cooking, creative nonfiction, economics, environment, foods, gardening, government, health, horticulture, humanities, medicine, nature, nutrition, politics, science, social sciences, simple living, renewable energy, and other sustainability topics. Does not want academic, self-help, spiritual. Prefers electronic queries and proposals via e-mail (as a single attachment). If sending via snail mail, submissions will only be returned with SASE. Please review our guidelines on our website carefully before submitting. Reviews artwork/photos.

CHEMICAL PUBLISHING CO., INC.

P.O. Box 676, Revere MA 02151. **Website:** www.chemical-publishing.com. **Contact:** Heather Carr, editor. Estab. 1934. Publishes hardcover originals. Chemical Publishing Co., Inc., publishes professional chemistry-technical titles aimed at people employed in the chemical industry, libraries and graduate courses. "We invite the submission of manuscripts whether they are technical, scientific or serious popular expositions. All submitted manuscripts and planned works will receive prompt attention. The staff will consider finished and proposed manuscripts by authors whose works have not been previously published as sympa-

thetically as those by experienced authors. Please do not hesitate to consult us about such manuscripts or about your ideas for writing them." **Publishes 10-15 titles/year. 20 queries received/year. 50% of books from first-time authors. 100% from unagented writers. Pays 10% royalty on retail price or makes negotiable outright purchase. Pays negotiable advance.** Publishes ms 8 months after acceptance. Responds in 3 weeks to queries; 5 weeks to proposals; 1 months to mss. Book catalog available free. Guidelines online.

NONFICTION Subjects include science, analytical methods, chemical technology, cosmetics, dictionaries, engineering, environmental science, food technology, formularies, industrial technology, medical, metallurgy, textiles. Submit outline, a few pages of 3 sample chapters, SASE. Download CPC submission form online and include with submission. Reviews, artwork and photos should also be part of the ms package.

CHICAGO REVIEW PRESS

814 N. Franklin St., Chicago IL 60610. (312)337-0747 **Fax:** (312)337-5110. **E-mail:** csherry@chicagoreviewpress.com; jpohlen@chicagoreviewpress.com; lreardon@chicagoreviewpress.com; ytaylor@chicagoreviewpress.com. **Website:** www.chicagoreviewpress.com. **Contact:** Cynthia Sherry, publisher; Yuval Taylor, senior editor; Jerome Pohlen, senior editor; Lisa Reardon, senior editor. Estab. 1973. "Chicago Review Press publishes high-quality, nonfiction, educational activity books that extend the learning process through hands-on projects and accurate and interesting text. We look for activity books that are as much fun as they are constructive and informative." **Pays authors royalty of 7.5-12.5% based on retail price. Offers advances of $3,000-6,000. Pays illustrators and photographers by the project (range varies considerably).** Publishes a book 1-2 years after acceptance. Accepts simultaneous submissions. Responds in 2 months. Book catalog available for $3. Ms guidelines available for $3.

IMPRINTS Academy Chicago; Ball Publishing; Chicago Review Press; Lawrence Hill Books; Zephyr Press.

NONFICTION Young readers, middle readers and young adults: activity books, arts/crafts, multicultural, history, nature/environment, science. "We're interested in hands-on, educational books; anything else probably will be rejected." Average length: young readers and young adults—144-160 pages. Enclose cover letter and a brief synopsis of book in 1-2 paragraphs, table of contents and first 3 sample chapters; prefers not to receive e-mail queries. For children's activity books include a few sample activities with a list of the others. Full guidelines available on site.

FICTION Guidelines now available on website.

⊘ CHILDREN'S BRAINS ARE YUMMY (CBAY) BOOKS

P.O. Box 670296, Dallas TX 75367. **E-mail:** submissions@cbaybooks.com. **Website:** www.cbaybooks. blog. **Contact:** Madeline Smoot, publisher. Estab. 2008. "CBAY Books currently focuses on quality fantasy and science fiction books for the middle grade and teen markets. We are not currently accepting unsolicited submissions. We do not publish picture books." **Publishes 3-6 titles/year. 30% of books from first-time authors. 80% from unagented writers. Pays authors royalty 10%-15% based on wholesale price. Offers advances against royalties. Average amount $500. Pays advance.** Publishes ms 24 months after acceptance. Accepts simultaneous submissions. Responds in 2 months. "We are distributed by IPG. Our books can be found in their catalog at www.ipgbooks.com." Brochure and guidelines online.

FICTION Subjects include adventure, fantasy, juvenile, mystery, science fiction, short story collections, suspense, young adult, folktales.

● CHRISTIAN FOCUS PUBLICATIONS

Geanies House, Fearn, Tain Ross-shire Scotland IV20 1TW, United Kingdom. (44)1862-871-011. **Fax:** (44)1862-871-699. **E-mail:** submissions@christian-focus.com. **Website:** www.christianfocus.com. **Contact:** Director of Publishing. Estab. 1975. Specializes in Christian material, nonfiction, fiction, educational material. **Publishes 22-32 titles/year. 2% of books from first-time authors.** Publishes book 1 year after acceptance. Accepts simultaneous submissions. Responds to queries in 2 weeks; mss in 3-6 months.

NONFICTION All levels: activity books, biography, history, religion, science. Average word length: picture books—5,000; young readers—5,000; middle readers—5,000-10,000; young adult/teens—10,000-20,000. Query or submit outline/synopsis and 3 sample chapters. Include Author Information Form from site with submission. Will consider electronic submissions and previously published work.

FICTION Picture books, young readers, adventure, history, religion. Middle readers: adventure, problem novels, religion. Young adult/teens: adventure, history, problem novels, religion. Average word length: young readers—5,000; middle readers—max 10,000; young adult/teen—max 20,000.

CHRONICLE BOOKS

680 Second St., San Francisco CA 94107. **E-mail:** submissions@chroniclebooks.com. **Website:** www.chroniclebooks.com. "We publish an exciting range of books, stationery, kits, calendars, and novelty formats. Our list includes children's books and interactive formats; young adult books; cookbooks; fine art, design, and photography; pop culture; craft, fashion, beauty, and home decor; relationships, mind-body-spirit; innovative formats such as interactive journals, kits, decks, and stationery; and much, much more." **Publishes 90 titles/year. Generally pays authors in royalties based on retail price, "though we do occasionally work on a flat fee basis." Advance varies. Illustrators paid royalty based on retail price or flat fee.** Publishes a book 1-3 years after acceptance. Accepts simultaneous submissions. Responds to queries in 1 month. Book catalog for 9x12 SAE and 8 first-class stamps. Ms guidelines for #10 SASE.

NONFICTION Subjects include art, beauty, cooking, crafts, house and home, New Age, pop culture. "We're always looking for the new and unusual. We do accept unsolicited manuscripts and we review all proposals. However, given the volume of proposals we receive, we are not able to personally respond to unsolicited proposals unless we are interested in pursuing the project." Submit via mail or e-mail (prefers e-mail for adult submissions; only by mail for children's submissions). Submit proposal (guidelines online) and allow 3 months for editors to review and for children's submissions, allow 6 months. If submitting by mail, do not include SASE since our staff will not return materials.

FICTION Only interested in fiction for children and young adults. No adult fiction. Submit complete ms (picture books); submit outline/synopsis and 3 sample chapters (for older readers). Will not respond to submissions unless interested. Will not consider submissions by fax, e-mail or disk. Do not include SASE; do not send original materials. No submissions will be returned.

POETRY Submit via mail only. Children's submissions only. Submit proposal (guidelines online) and allow up to 3 months for editors to review. If submitting by mail, do not include SASE since our staff will not return materials.

CHRONICLE BOOKS FOR CHILDREN

680 Second St., San Francisco CA 94107. (415)537-4200. **Fax:** (415)537-4460. **Website:** www.chroniclekids.com. Publishes hardcover and trade paperback originals. "Chronicle Books for Children publishes an eclectic mixture of traditional and innovative children's books. Our aim is to publish books that inspire young readers to learn and grow creatively while helping them discover the joy of reading. We're looking for quirky, bold artwork and subject matter." **Publishes 100-110 titles/year. 30,000 queries received/year. 6% of books from first-time authors. 25% from unagented writers. Pays variable advance.** Publishes a book 18-24 months after acceptance. Accepts simultaneous submissions. Responds in 2-4 weeks to queries; 6 months to mss. Book catalog for 9x12 envelope and 3 first-class stamps. Guidelines online.

NONFICTION Subjects include animals, multicultural, science. Query with synopsis. Reviews artwork/photos.

FICTION Subjects include multicultural, young adult, picture books. Does not accept proposals by fax, via e-mail, or on disk. When submitting artwork, either as a part of a project or as samples for review, do not send original art.

CHURCH PUBLISHING INC.

19 E. 34th St., New York NY 10016. (800)223-6602. **Fax:** (212)779-3392. **E-mail:** nabryan@cpg.org. **Website:** www.churchpublishing.org. **Contact:** Nancy Bryan, VP editorial. Estab. 1884. "With a religious publishing heritage dating back to 1918 and headquartered today in New York City, CPI is an official publisher of worship materials and resources for The Episcopal Church, plus a multi-faceted publisher and supplier to the broader ecumenical marketplace. In the nearly 100 years since its first publication, Church Publishing has emerged as a principal provider of liturgical and musical resources for The Episcopal Church, along with works on church leadership, pastoral care and Christian formation. With its growing portfolio of professional books and resources, Church Publishing was recognized in 1997 as the official publisher for the General Convention of the Episcopal Church in the United States. Simultaneously through the years, Church Publishing has consciously broadened its program, reach, and service to the church by publishing books for and about the worldwide Anglican Communion." Accepts simultaneous submissions.

IMPRINTS Church Publishing, Morehouse Publishing, Seabury Books.

CITY LIGHTS BOOKS

261 Columbus Ave., San Francisco CA 94133. (415)362-8193. **Fax:** (415)362-4921. **Website:** www.citylights.com. Estab. 1953. Accepts simultaneous submissions.

CLARION BOOKS

Houghton Mifflin Co., 215 Park Ave. S., New York NY 10003. **Website:** www.hmhco.com. Estab. 1965. Publishes hardcover originals for children. "Clarion Books publishes picture books, nonfiction, and fiction for infants through grade 12. Avoid telling your stories in verse unless you are a professional poet. *We are no longer responding to your unsolicited submission unless we are interested in publishing it. Please do not include a SASE. Submissions will be recycled, and you will not hear from us regarding the status of your submission unless we are interested. We regret that we cannot respond personally to each submission, but we do consider each and every submission we receive."* **Publishes 50 titles/year. Pays 5-10% royalty on retail price. Pays minimum of $4,000 advance.** Publishes a book 2 years after acceptance. Accepts simultaneous submissions. Responds in 2 months to queries. Guidelines online.

NONFICTION Subjects include Americana, history, photography, holiday. No unsolicited mss. Query with SASE. Submit proposal package, sample chapters, SASE. Reviews artwork/photos. Send photocopies.

FICTION Subjects include adventure, historical, humor, mystery, suspense, strong character studies, contemporary. "Clarion is highly selective in the areas of historical fiction, fantasy, and science fiction. A novel must be superlatively written in order to find a place on the list. Mss that arrive without an SASE of adequate size will *not* be responded to or returned. Accepts fiction translations." Submit complete ms. No queries, please. Send to only *one* Clarion editor.

Ⓐ CLARKSON POTTER

Penguin Random House, 1745 Broadway, New York NY 10019. (212)782-9000. **Website:** www.clarkson-potter.com. Estab. 1959. Publishes hardcover and trade paperback originals. Accepts agented submissions only. Clarkson Potter specializes in publishing cooking books, decorating and other around-the-house how-to subjects.

NONFICTION Subjects include child guidance, memoirs, photography, psychology, translation. Agented submissions only.

CLEIS PRESS

101 Hudson St., 37th Floor, Suite 3705, Jersey City NJ 07302. **Fax:** (510)845-8001. **Website:** www.cleispress. com. Estab. 1980. Publishes books that inform, enlighten, and entertain. Areas of interest include gift, inspiration, health, family and childcare, self-help, women's issues, reference, cooking. "We do our best to bring readers quality books that celebrate life, inspire the mind, revive the spirit, and enhance lives all around. Our authors are practical visionaries; people who offer deep wisdom in a hopeful and helpful manner." Cleis Press publishes provocative, intelligent books in the areas of sexuality, gay and lesbian studies, erotica, fiction, gender studies, and human rights. **Publishes 45 titles/year. 10% of books from first-time authors. 40% from unagented writers.** Publishes ms 2 years after acceptance. Accepts simultaneous submissions. Responds in 2 month to queries.

NONFICTION Subjects include , sexual politics. "Cleis Press is interested in books on topics of sexuality, human rights and women's and gay and lesbian literature. Please consult our website first to be certain that your book fits our list." Query or submit outline and sample chapters.

FICTION Subjects include feminist, literary. "We are looking for high quality fiction and nonfiction." Submit complete ms. Include brief bio, list of publishing credits. Send SASE for return of ms or send a disposable ms and SASE for reply only.

☼ COACH HOUSE BOOKS

80 bpNichol Ln., Toronto ON M5S 3J4, Canada. (416)979-2217. **Fax:** (416)977-1158. **E-mail:** mail@ch-books.com. **E-mail:** editor@chbooks.com. **Website:** www.chbooks.com. **Contact:** Alana Wilcox, editorial director. Publishes trade paperback originals by Canadian authors. Independent Canadian publisher of innovative poetry, literary fiction, nonfiction, and drama. **Publishes 18 titles/year. 80% of books from first-time authors. Pays 10% royalty on retail price.**

Publishes ms 1 year after acceptance. Responds in 6-8 months to queries. Guidelines online.

NONFICTION Query.

FICTION Subjects include experimental, literary, poetry. We much prefer to receive electronic submissions. Please put your cover letter and CV into one Word or PDF file along with the manuscript and e-mail it to editor@chbooks.com. We'd appreciate it if you would name your file following this convention: Last Name, First Name - MS Title. For fiction and poetry submissions, please send your complete manuscript, along with an introductory letter that describes your work and compares it to at least two current Coach House titles, explaining how your book would fit our list, and a literary CV listing your previous publications and relevant experience.

POETRY We much prefer to receive electronic submissions. Please put your cover letter and CV into one Word or PDF file along with the manuscript and e-mail it to editor@chbooks.com. We'd appreciate it if you would name your file following this convention: Last Name, First Name - MS Title. For fiction and poetry submissions, please send your complete manuscript, along with an introductory letter that describes your work and compares it to at least two current Coach House titles, explaining how your book would fit our list, and a literary CV listing your previous publications and relevant experience.

COFFEE HOUSE PRESS

79 13th Ave. NE, Suite 110, Minneapolis MN 55413. (612)338-0125. **Fax:** (612)338-4004. **Website:** www. coffeehousepress.org. Estab. 1984. Publishes hardcover and trade paperback originals. This successful nonprofit small press has received numerous grants from various organizations including the NEA, the McKnight Foundation and Target. Books published by Coffee House Press have won numerous honors and awards. Example: *The Book of Medicines*, by Linda Hogan won the Colorado Book Award for Poetry and the Lannan Foundation Literary Fellowship. **Publishes 16-18 titles/year.** Accepts simultaneous submissions. Responds in 4-6 weeks to queries; up to 6 months to mss. Book catalog and ms guidelines online.

NONFICTION Subjects include creative nonfiction, memoirs, book-length essays, collections of essays. Query with outline and sample pages during annual reading periods (March 1-31 and September 1-30).

FICTION Seeks literary novels, short story collections and poetry. Query first with outline and samples (20-30 pages) during annual reading periods (March 1-31 and September 1-30).

POETRY Coffee House Press will not accept unsolicited poetry submissions. Please check our web page periodically for future updates to this policy.

COLLEGE PRESS PUBLISHING CO.

P.O. Box 1132, 2111 N. Main St., Suite C, Joplin MO 64801. (800)289-3300. **Fax:** (417)623-1929. **E-mail:** collpressbooks@gmail.com. **Website:** www.college-press.com. **Contact:** Acquisitions Editor. Estab. 1959. Publishes hardcover and trade paperback originals and reprints. College Press is a traditional Christian publishing house. Seeks proposals for Bible studies, topical studies (biblically based), apologetic studies. Accepts simultaneous submissions. Responds in 3 months to proposals; 2 months to mss. Guidelines online.

NONFICTION Seeks Bible studies, topical studies, apologetic studies. No poetry, games/puzzles, books on prophecy from a premillennial or dispensational viewpoint, or any book without a Christian message. Query with SASE.

● COLOURPOINT BOOKS

Jubilee Business Park, 21 Jubilee Rd., Newtownards, Northern Ireland BT23 4YH, United Kingdom. (44)(289)182-0505. **Fax:** (44)(289)182-1900. **E-mail:** info@colourpoint.co.uk. **Website:** www.colourpoint.co.uk. Estab. 1993. **Publishes 25 titles/year. Pays royalty.** Accepts simultaneous submissions. Responds in 2-3 months. Guidelines online.

NONFICTION Subjects include education. "Our specialisms are educational textbooks and transport subjects—mainly trains and buses. When e-mailing queries, please put 'submission query' in the subject line." Does not want fiction, poetry or plays. Query with SASE. Submit outline, outline/proposal, resume, publishing history, bio, 2 sample pages, SASE.

CONARI PRESS

Red Wheel/Weiser, LLC., 665 Third Street Suite 400, San Fransisco CA 94107. **E-mail:** submissions@rwwbooks.com: info@rwwbooks.com. **Website:** www.redwheelweiser.com. Estab. 1987. "Conari Press, an imprint of Red Wheel/Weiser, publishes books on topics ranging from spirituality, personal growth, and relationships to women's issues, parenting, and social

issues. Our mission is to publish quality books that will make a difference in people's lives—how we feel about ourselves and how we relate to one another. We value integrity, compassion, and receptivity, both in the books we publish and in the way we do business." Accepts simultaneous submissions.

NONFICTION Subjects include foods, health, parenting, spirituality, womens issues, womens studies. "Inspire, literally to breathe life into. That's what Conari Press books aim to do—inspire all walks of life, mind, body, and spirit; inspire creativity, laughter, gratitude, good food, good health, and all good things in life." Guidelines online.

CONCORDIA PUBLISHING HOUSE

3558 S. Jefferson Ave., St. Louis MO 63118. (314)268-1187. **Fax:** (314)268-1329. **E-mail:** editorial.concordia@cph.org. **Website:** www.cph.org. Estab. 1869. Publishes hardcover and trade paperback originals. Concordia Publishing House is the publishing arm of The Lutheran Church—Missouri Synod. "We develop, produce, and distribute (1) resources that support pastoral and congregational ministry, and (2) scholary and professional books in exegetical, historical, dogmatic, and practical theology." Accepts simultaneous submissions.

COPPER CANYON PRESS

P.O. Box 271, Port Townsend WA 98368. (360)385-4925. **Fax:** (360)385-4985. **E-mail:** poetry@copper-canyonpress.org. **Website:** www.coppercanyonpress.org. **Contact:** Joseph Bednarik and George Knotek, co-publishers. Managing Editor: Tonaya Craft. Estab. 1972. Copper Canyon Press is a nonprofit publisher that believes poetry is vital to language and living. Since 1972, the press has published poetry exclusively and has established an international reputation for its commitment to authors, editorial acumen, and dedication to the poetry audience. Accepts simultaneous submissions. Catalog online. Guidelines online.

POETRY Has open submission periods throughout the year; see website for details. Charges $35 fee for each submission, which entitles poets to select 2 Copper Canyon Press titles from a list. Submit complete ms via Submittable.

CORNELL UNIVERSITY PRESS

Sage House, 512 E. State St., Ithaca NY 14850. (607)277-2338. **Fax:** (607)277-2374. **Website:** www.cornellpress.cornell.edu. **Contact:** Mahinder Kingra, editor-in-chief; Roger Haydon, executive editor; Emily Andrew, senior editor; James Lance, senior editor; Michael J. McGandy, senior editor. Estab. 1869. Publishes hardcover and paperback originals. "Cornell Press is an academic publisher of nonfiction with particular strengths in anthropology, Asian studies, biological sciences, classics, history, labor and business, literary criticism, politics and international relations, women's studies, Slavic studies, philosophy, urban studies, health care work, regional titles, and security studies. Currently emphasizing sound scholarship that appeals beyond the academic community." **Publishes 150 titles/year. Pays royalty. Pays $0-5,000 advance.** Publishes ms 1 year after acceptance. Accepts simultaneous submissions. Book catalog and guidelines online.

NONFICTION Subjects include agriculture, ethnic, history, philosophy, regional, sociology, translation, classics, life sciences. Submit résumé, cover letter, and prospectus.

CORWIN PRESS, INC.

2455 Teller Rd., Thousand Oaks CA 91320. (800)818-7243. **Fax:** (805)499-2692. **E-mail:** ariel.bartlett@corwin.com; erin.null@corwin.com; jessica.allan@corwin.com. **Website:** www.corwinpress.com. **Contact:** Ariel Bartlett, acquisitions editor; Erin Null, acquisitions editor; Jessica Allan, senior acquisitions editor. Estab. 1990. Publishes paperback originals. **Publishes 150 titles/year.** Publishes ms 7 months after acceptance. Accepts simultaneous submissions. Responds in 1-2 months to queries. Guidelines online.

NONFICTION Subjects include education. Seeking fresh insights, conclusions, and recommendations for action. Prefers theory or research-based books that provide real-world examples and practical, hands-on strategies to help busy educators be successful. Professional-level publications for administrators, teachers, school specialists, policymakers, researchers and others involved with Pre K-12 education. No textbooks that simply summarize existing knowledge or mass-market books. Query with SASE.

☯ COTEAU BOOKS

Thunder Creek Publishing Co-operative Ltd., 2517 Victoria Ave., Regina SK S4P 0T2, Canada. (306)777-0170. **Fax:** (306)522-5152. **E-mail:** coteau@coteaubooks.com. **Website:** www.coteaubooks.com. **Contact:** Geoffrey Ursell, publisher. Estab. 1975. Publishes trade paperback originals and reprints. "Our mission is to publish the finest in Canadian fiction, nonfiction, poetry, drama, and children's literature, with an emphasis on Saskatchewan and prairie writers. De-emphasizing science fiction, picture books." Publishes chapter books for young readers aged 9-12 and novels for older kids ages 13-15 and for ages 15 and up. **Publishes 12 titles/year. 200 queries; 40 mss received/year. 25% of books from first-time authors. 90% from unagented writers. Pays 10% royalty on retail price.** Publishes book 1 year after acceptance. Responds in 3 months. Book catalog available free. Guidelines online.

NONFICTION Subjects include creative nonfiction, ethnic, history, memoirs, regional, sports, travel. *Canadian authors only.* Submit hard copy query, bio, 3-4 sample chapters, SASE.

FICTION Subjects include ethnic, fantasy, feminist, historical, humor, juvenile, literary, multicultural, multimedia, mystery, plays, poetry, regional, short story collections, spiritual, sports, novels/short fiction, adult/middle years. No science fiction. No children's picture books. Query.

POETRY Submit 20-25 sample poems.

COVENANT COMMUNICATIONS, INC.

Deseret Book Company, P.O. Box 416, American Fork UT 84003. (801)756-1041. **Fax:** (801)756-1049. **E-mail:** submissionsdesk@covenant-lds.com. **Website:** www.covenant-lds.com. **Contact:** Kathryn Gordon, managing editor. Estab. 1958. "Currently emphasizing inspirational, doctrinal, historical, biography, and fiction." **Publishes 80-100 titles/year. Receives 1,200 mss/year. 30% of books from first-time authors. 99% from unagented writers. Pays 6-15% royalty on retail price.** Publishes book 6-12 months after acceptance. Responds in 1 month on queries; 4-6 months on mss. Guidelines online.

NONFICTION Subjects include history, religion, spirituality. "We target an audience of members of The Church of Jesus Christ of Latter-day Saints, LDS, or Mormon. All mss must be acceptable to that audience." We do not accept anything dealing with the occult or alternative lifestyles. Submit complete ms. Reviews artwork. Send photocopies.

FICTION Subjects include adventure, historical, mystery, regional, religious, romance, spiritual, suspense. "Manuscripts do not necessarily have to include LDS/Mormon characters or themes, but cannot contain profanity, sexual content, gratuitous violence, witchcraft, vampires, and other such material." We do not accept nor publish young adult, middle grade, science fiction, fantasy, occult, steampunk, or gay/lesbian/bisexual/transgender themes. Submit complete ms. **POETRY** We do not publish poetry.

CQ PRESS
2455 Teller Rd., Thousand Oaks CA 91320. (805)410-7582. **Website:** www.cqpress.com. Estab. 1945. Publishes hardcover and online paperback titles. CQ Press seeks to educate the public by publishing authoritative works on American and international politics, policy, and people. Accepts simultaneous submissions. Book catalog available free.

NONFICTION Subjects include history. "We are interested in American government, public administration, comparative government, and international relations." Submit proposal package, including prospectus, TOC, 1-2 sample chapters.

⊘ CRABTREE PUBLISHING COMPANY
350 Fifth Ave., 59th Floor, New York NY 10118. (212)496-5040; (800)387-7650. **Fax:** (800)355-7166. **Website:** www.crabtreebooks.com. Estab. 1978. Crabtree Publishing Company is dedicated to producing high-quality books and educational products for K-8+. Each resource blends accuracy, immediacy, and eye-catching illustration with the goal of inspiring nothing less than a life-long interest in reading and learning in children. The company began building its reputation in 1978 as a quality children's nonfiction book publisher with acclaimed author Bobbie Kalman's first series about the early pioneers. The Early Settler Life Series became a mainstay in schools as well as historic sites and museums across North America. Accepts simultaneous submissions.

CRAFTSMAN BOOK CO.
6058 Corte Del Cedro, Carlsbad CA 92011. (760)438-7828 or (800)829-8123. **Fax:** (760)438-0398. **E-mail:** jacobs@costbook.com. **Website:** www.craftsman-book.com. **Contact:** Laurence D. Jacobs, editorial manager. Estab. 1957. Publishes paperback originals. Publishes how-to manuals for professional builders. Currently emphasizing construction software for cost estimating, insurance replacement costs, contract and lien writing software and construction forms. **Publishes 10 titles/year. 4 85% of books from first-time authors. 99% from unagented writers. Pays 7-12% royalty on wholesale price and 12-1/2% on retail price. Does not pay advance.** Publishes ms 2 years after acceptance. Accepts simultaneous submissions. Responds in 2 months to queries. Book catalog and ms guidelines free.

NONFICTION Subjects include business, software. All titles are related to construction for professional builders. Reviews artwork/photos.

CRAIGMORE CREATIONS
PMB 114, 4110 SE Hawthorne Blvd., Portland OR 97124. (503)477-9562. **E-mail:** info@craigmorecreations.com. **Website:** www.craigmorecreations.com. Estab. 2009. Accepts simultaneous submissions.

NONFICTION Subjects include animals, anthropology, archeology, creative nonfiction, environment, multicultural, nature, regional, science, young adult, Earth sciences, natural history. "We publish books that make time travel seem possible: nonfiction that explores pre-history and Earth sciences for children." Submit proposal package. See website for detailed submission guidelines. Send photocopies.

FICTION Subjects include juvenile, picture books, young adult. Submit proposal package. See website for detailed submission guidelines.

THE CREATIVE COMPANY
P.O. Box 227, Mankato MN 56002. (800)445-6209. **Fax:** (507)388-2746. **E-mail:** info@thecreativecompany.us. **Website:** www.thecreativecompany.us. Estab. 1932. "We are currently not accepting fiction submissions." **Publishes 140 titles/year.** Publishes a book 2 years after acceptance. Accepts simultaneous submissions. Responds in 3-6 months. Guidelines available for SAE.

IMPRINTS Creative Editions (picture books); Creative Education (nonfiction).

NONFICTION Picture books, young readers, young adults: animal, arts/crafts, biography, careers, geography, health, history, hobbies, multicultural, music/dance, nature/environment, religion, science, social issues, special needs, sports. Average word length: young readers—500; young adults—6,000. Submit outline/synopsis and 2 sample chapters, along with division of titles within the series.

◑ CRESCENT MOON PUBLISHING
P.O. Box 1312, Maidstone Kent ME14 5XU, United Kingdom. (44)(162)272-9593. **E-mail:** cresmopub@yahoo.co.uk. **Website:** www.crmoon.com. **Contact:** Jeremy Robinson, director (arts, media, cinema, literature); Cassidy Hughes (visual arts). Estab. 1988. Pub-

lishes hardcover and trade paperback originals. "Our mission is to publish the best in contemporary work, in poetry, fiction, and critical studies, and selections from the great writers. Currently emphasizing nonfiction (media, film, music, painting). De-emphasizing children's books." **Publishes 25 titles/year. 300 queries; 400 mss received/year. 1% of books from first-time authors. 1% from unagented writers. Pays royalty. Pays negotiable advance.** Publishes ms 18 months after acceptance. Accepts simultaneous submissions. Responds in 2 months to queries; 4 months to proposals and mss. Book catalog and ms guidelines free.

IMPRINTS Joe's Press; Pagan America Magazine; Passion Magazine.

NONFICTION Subjects include Americana, anthropology, cinema, contemporary culture, film, gardening, literary criticism, literature, philosophy, pop culture, religion, social sciences, spirituality, travel, womens issues, womens studies, cinema, the media, cultural studies. Query with SASE. Submit outline, 2 sample chapters, bio. Reviews artwork/photos. Send photocopies.

FICTION Subjects include erotica, experimental, feminist, literary, short story collections, translation. "We do not publish much fiction at present but will consider high quality new work." Query with SASE. Submit outline, clips, 2 sample chapters, bio.

POETRY "We prefer a small selection of the poet's very best work at first. We prefer free verse or nonrhyming poetry. Do not send too much material." Query and submit 6 sample poems.

CROSS-CULTURAL COMMUNICATIONS

Cross-Cultural Literary Editions, CROSS-CULTURAL COMMUNICATIONS, 239 Wynsum Ave., Merrick NY 11566-4725. (516)869-5635. **Fax:** (516) 379-1901. **E-mail:** info@cross-culturalcommunications.com; cccpoetry@aol.com. **Website:** www.cross-culturalcommunications.com. **Contact:** Stanley H. Barkan; Bebe Barkan. Estab. 1971. Publishes hardcover and trade paperback originals. **Publishes 10 titles/year. 200 queries; 50 mss received/year. 10-25% of books from first-time authors. 100% from unagented writers.** Publishes book 1 year after acceptance. Responds in 1 month to proposals; 2 months to mss. Book catalog (sample flyers) for #10 SASE.

NONFICTION Subjects include art, language, literature, memoirs, multicultural. "Query first; we basically do not want the focus on nonfiction." Query with SASE. Reviews artwork/photos. Send photocopies.

FICTION Subjects include historical, literary, multicultural, poetry, poetry in translation, translation, bilingual poetry. Query with SASE.

POETRY For bilingual poetry submit 3-6 short poems in original language with English translation, a brief (3-5 lines) bio of the author and translator(s).

THE CROSSROAD PUBLISHING COMPANY

83 Chestnut Ridge Rd., Chestnut Ridge NY 10977. **Fax:** (845)517-0181. **E-mail:** submissions@crossroadpublishing.com. **Website:** www.crossroadpublishing.com. Estab. 1980. Publishes hardcover and trade paperback originals and reprints. **Publishes 45 titles/year. 1,000 queries received/year. 200 mss received/year. 10% of books from first-time authors. 75% from unagented writers. Pays 6-14% royalty on wholesale price.** Publishes ms 14 months after acceptance. Accepts simultaneous submissions. Responds in 6 weeks to queries and proposals; 12 weeks to mss. Book catalog available free. Guidelines online.

IMPRINTS Crossroad (trade); Herder (classroom/academic).

NONFICTION Subjects include creative nonfiction, ethnic, religion, spirituality, leadership, Catholicism. "We want hopeful, well-written books on religion and spirituality." Query with SASE.

CROSSWAY

A publishing ministry of Good News Publishing, 1300 Crescent St., Wheaton IL 60174. (630)682-4300. **Fax:** (630)682-4785. **E-mail:** info@crossway.org. **E-mail:** submissions@crossway.org. **Website:** www.crossway.org. **Contact:** Jill Carter, editorial administrator. Estab. 1938. "'Making a difference in people's lives for Christ' as its maxim, Crossway Books lists titles written from an evangelical Christian perspective." Member ECPA. Distributes titles through Christian bookstores and catalogs. Promotes titles through magazine ads, catalogs. *Does not accept unsolicited mss.* Please check our website for the types of books we publish. Submission guidelines are posted. **Publishes 85 titles/year. Pays negotiable royalty.** Publishes ms 18 months after acceptance. Accepts simultaneous submissions.

NONFICTION "Send us an e-mail query and, if your idea fits within our acquisitions guidelines, we'll invite a proposal."

ⒶⓄ CROWN PUBLISHING GROUP

Penguin Random House, 1745 Broadway, New York NY 10019. (212)782-9000. **Website:** crownpublishing.com. Estab. 1933. Publishes popular fiction and nonfiction hardcover originals. Accepts simultaneous submissions. *Agented submissions only.* See website for more details.

IMPRINTS Amphoto Books; Back Stage Books; Billboard Books; Broadway Books; Clarkson Potter; Crown; Crown Archetype; Crown Business; Crown Forum; Harmony Books; Image Books; Potter Craft; Potter Style; Ten Speed Press; Three Rivers Press; Waterbrook Multnomah; Watson-Guptill.

CSLI PUBLICATIONS

Condura Hall, Stanford University, 210 Panama St., Stanford CA 94305. (650)723-1839. **Fax:** (650)725-2166. **E-mail:** pubs@csli.stanford.edu. **Website:** csli-publications.stanford.edu. Publishes hardcover and scholarly paperback originals. CSLI Publications, part of the Center for the Study of Language and Information, specializes in books in the study of language, information, logic, and computation. Book catalog available free. Guidelines online.

NONFICTION Subjects include science, logic, cognitive science. "We do not accept unsolicited mss."

CURIOSITY QUILLS

Whampa, LLC, P.O. Box 2160, Reston VA 20195. (800)998-2509. **Fax:** (800)998-2509. **E-mail:** editor@curiosityquills.com. **E-mail:** acquisitions@curiosityquills.com. **Website:** curiosityquills.com. **Contact:** Alisa Gus. Additional Contacts: Eugene Teplitsky, Nikki Tetreault. Estab. 2011. Firm publishes sci-fi, speculative fiction, steampunk, paranormal and urban fantasy, and corresponding romance titles under its new Rebel Romance imprint. Curiosity Quills is a publisher of hard-hitting dark sci-fi, speculative fiction, and paranormal works aimed at adults, young adults, and new adults. **Publishes 75 titles/year. 1,000 submissions/year. 60% of books from first-time authors. 65% from unagented writers. Pays variable royalty. Does not pay advance.** Publishes ms 9-12 months after acceptance. Accepts simultaneous submissions. Responds in 1-6 weeks. Catalog available. Guidelines online.

IMPRINTS Curiosity Quills Press, Rebel Romance.

NONFICTION Writer's guides, on a strictly limited basis.

FICTION Subjects include adventure, contemporary, erotica, fantasy, gay, gothic, hi-lo, historical, horror, humor, juvenile, lesbian, literary, mainstream, multicultural, multimedia, mystery, romance, science fiction, suspense, young adult, steampunk, dieselpunk, space opera. Looking for "thought-provoking, mind-twisting rollercoasters—challenge our mind, turn our world upside down, and make us question. Those are the makings of a true literary marauder." Submit ms using online submission form or e-mail to acquisitions@curiosityquills.com.

ⒶⓄ DA CAPO PRESS

Perseus Books Group, 44 Farnsworth St., 3rd Floor, Boston MA 02210. (617)252-5200. **Website:** www.dacapopress.com. Estab. 1975. Publishes hardcover originals and trade paperback originals and reprints. **Publishes 115 titles/year. 500 queries; 300 mss received/year. 25% of books from first-time authors. 1% from unagented writers. Pays 7-15% royalty. Pays $1,000-225,000 advance.** Publishes book 1 year after acceptance. Accepts simultaneous submissions. Book catalog and guidelines online.

NONFICTION Subjects include contemporary culture, creative nonfiction, history, memoirs, social sciences, sports, translation, travel, world affairs. No unsolicited mss or proposals. Agented submissions only.

Ⓞ DARBY CREEK PUBLISHING

Lerner Publishing Group, 1251 Washington Ave. N., Minneapolis MN 55401. (612)332-3344. **Fax:** (612)332-7615. **Website:** www.lernerbooks.com. "Darby Creek publishes series fiction titles for emerging, striving and reluctant readers ages 7 to 18 (grades 2-12). From beginning chapter books to intermediate fiction and page-turning YA titles, Darby Creek books engage readers with strong characters and formats they'll want to pursue." Darby Creek does not publish picture books. Publishes children's chapter books, middle readers, young adult. Mostly series. **Publishes 25 titles/year. Offers advance-against-royalty contracts.** Accepts simultaneous submissions.

NONFICTION Middle readers: biography, history, science, sports.

FICTION Middle readers, young adult.

DARK HORSE COMICS, INC.

10956 SE Main St., Milwaukie OR 97222. (503)652-8815. **Fax:** (503)654-9440. **E-mail:** dhcomics@darkhorse.com. **E-mail:** dhsubsproposals@darkhouse.com.

com. **Website:** www.darkhorse.com. "In addition to publishing comics from top talent like Frank Miller, Mike Mignola, Stan Sakai and internationally-renowned humorist Sergio Aragonés, Dark Horse is recognized as the world's leading publisher of licensed comics." Accepts simultaneous submissions.

FICTION Subjects include comic books. Comic books, graphic novels. Published *Astro Boy Volume 10 TPB*, by Osamu Tezuka and Reid Fleming; *Flaming Carrot Crossover #1* by Bob Burden and David Boswell. Submit synopsis to dhcomics@darkhorse.com. See website (www.darkhorse.com) for detailed submission guidelines and submission agreement, which must be signed. Include a full script for any short story or single-issue submission, or the first eight pages of the first issue of any series. Submissions can no longer be mailed back to the sender.

🐟 DARTON, LONGMAN AND TODD

1 Spencer Ct., 140-142 Wandsworth High St., London SW18 4JJ, United Kingdom. (44)(208)875-0155. **Fax:** (44)(208)875-0133. **E-mail:** editorial@darton-longman-todd.co.uk. **Website:** www.dltbooks.com. **Contact:** Editorial Department. Estab. 1959. Darton, Longman and Todd is an internationally-respected publisher of brave, ground-breaking, independent books and e-books on matters of heart, mind, and soul that meet the needs and interests of ordinary people. **Publishes 30 titles/year. Pays royalty.** Accepts simultaneous submissions. Guidelines online.

NONFICTION Subjects include counseling, politics, religion, spirituality, womens issues, womens studies. Simultaenous submissions accepted, but inform publisher if submitting elsewhere. Does not want poetry, scholarly monographs or children's books. Query by e-mail only.

⊘ JONATHAN DAVID PUBLISHERS, INC.

68-22 Eliot Ave., Middle Village NY 11379. (718)456-8611. **Fax:** (718)894-2818. **Website:** www.jdbooks.com. **Contact:** David Kolatch, editorial director. Estab. 1948. Publishes hardcover and trade paperback originals and reprints. Jonathan David publishes popular Judaica. **Publishes 20-25 titles/year. 50% of books from first-time authors. 90% from unagented writers. Pays royalty, or makes outright purchase.** Publishes ms 18 months after acceptance. Accepts simultaneous submissions. Responds in 1-2 months. Book catalog and guidelines online.

NONFICTION Subjects include creative nonfiction, ethnic, multicultural, religion, sports. Unsolicited mss are not being accepted at this time.

DAW BOOKS, INC.

Penguin Random House, 375 Hudson St., New York NY 10014. (212)366-2096. **Fax:** (212)366-2090. **E-mail:** daw@penguinrandomhouse.com. **Website:** www.dawbooks.com. **Contact:** Peter Stampfel, submissions editor. Estab. 1971. Publishes hardcover and paperback originals and reprints. DAW Books publishes science fiction and fantasy. **Publishes 50-60 titles/year. Pays in royalties with an advance negotiable on a book-by-book basis.** Responds in 3 months. Guidelines online.

FICTION Subjects include fantasy, science fiction. "Currently seeking modern urban fantasy and paranormals. We like character-driven books with appealing protagonists, engaging plots, and well-constructed worlds. We accept both agented and unagented manuscripts." Submit entire ms, cover letter, SASE. "Do not submit your only copy of anything. The average length of the novels we publish varies but is almost never less than 80,000 words."

KATHY DAWSON BOOKS

Penguin Random House, 375 Hudson St., New York NY 10014. (212)366-2000. **Website:** kathydawsonbooks.tumblr.com. **Contact:** Kathy Dawson, vice-president and publisher. Estab. 2014. Mission statement: Publish stellar novels with unforgettable characters for children and teens that expand their vision of the world, sneakily explore the meaning of life, celebrate the written word, and last for generations. The imprint strives to publish tomorrow's award contenders: quality books with strong hooks in a variety of genres with universal themes and compelling voices—books that break the mold and the heart. Responds only if interested. Guidelines online.

FICTION Accepts fiction queries via snail mail only. Include cover sheet with one-sentence elevator pitch, main themes, author version of catalog copy for book, first 10 pages of ms (double-spaced, Times Roman, 12 point type), and publishing history. No SASE needed. Responds only if interested.

⊘ DC UNIVERSE

1700 Broadway, New York NY 10019. **Website:** www.dccomics.com. Accepts simultaneous submissions.

Ⓐⓩ DELACORTE PRESS

an imprint of Random House Children's Books, a division of Penguin Random House LLC, New York, 1745 Broadway, New York NY 10019. (212)782-9000. **Website:** randomhousekids.com; randomhouseteens. com. Publishes middle grade and young adult fiction in hard cover, trade paperback, mass market and digest formats. Accepts simultaneous submissions.

Ⓐⓩ DEL REY BOOKS

Penguin Random House, 1745 Broadway, 18th Floor, New York NY 10019. (212)782-9000. **Website:** www. penguinrandomhouse.com. Estab. 1977. Publishes hardcover, trade paperback, and mass market originals and mass market paperback reprints. Del Rey publishes top level fantasy, alternate history, and science fiction. **Pays royalty on retail price. Pays competitive advance.**

IMPRINTS Del Rey/Manga, Del Rey/Lucas Books.

FICTION Subjects include fantasy, science fiction, alternate history. *Agented submissions only.*

DIAL BOOKS FOR YOUNG READERS

Imprint of Penguin Group (USA), 345 Hudson St., New York NY 10014. (212)366-2000. **Website:** www. penguin.com/children. Estab. 1961. Publishes hardcover originals. "Dial Books for Young Readers publishes quality picture books for ages 18 months-6 years; lively, believable novels for middle readers and young adults; and occasional nonfiction for middle readers and young adults." **Publishes 50 titles/year. 5,000 queries received/year. 20% of books from first-time authors. Pays royalty. Pays varies advance.** Responds in 4-6 months to queries. Book catalog and guidelines online.

NONFICTION Only responds if interested. "We accept entire picture book manuscripts and a maximum of 10 pages for longer works (novels, easy-to-reads). When submitting a portion of a longer work, please provide an accompanying cover letter that briefly describes your manuscript's plot, genre (i.e. easy-to-read, middle grade or YA novel), the intended age group, and your publishing credits, if any."

FICTION Subjects include adventure, fantasy, juvenile, picture books, young adult. Especially looking for lively and well-written novels for middle grade and young adult children involving a convincing plot and believable characters. The subject matter or theme should not already be overworked in pre-viously published books. The approach must not be demeaning to any minority group, nor should the roles of female characters (or others) be stereotyped, though we don't think books should be didactic, or in any way message-y. No topics inappropriate for the juvenile, young adult, and middle grade audiences. No plays. Accepts unsolicited queries and up to 10 pages for longer works and unsolicited mss for picture books. Will only respond if interested.

Ⓐⓩ DIAL PRESS

1745 Broadway, New York NY 10019. **Website:** www. randomhouse.com/bantamdell/. Estab. 1924. Accepts simultaneous submissions.

FICTION Subjects include literary. *Agented submissions only.*

Ⓐ◑ⓩ DK PUBLISHING

Penguin Random House, 80 Strand, London WC2R 0RL, United Kingdom. **Website:** www.dk.com. "DK publishes photographically illustrated nonfiction for children of all ages." *DK Publishing does not accept unagented mss or proposals.* Accepts simultaneous submissions.

DOVER PUBLICATIONS, INC.

31 E. Second St., Mineola NY 11501. (516)294-7000. **Fax:** (516)873-1401. **Website:** www.doverpublications. com. Estab. 1941. Publishes trade paperback originals and reprints. **Publishes 660 titles/year. Makes outright purchase.** Accepts simultaneous submissions. Book catalog online.

NONFICTION Subjects include agriculture, Americana, animals, history, hobbies, philosophy, photography, religion, science, sports, translation, travel. Publishes mostly reprints. Accepts original paper doll collections, game books, coloring books (juvenile). Query with SASE. Reviews artwork/photos.

⊙ DUNDURN PRESS, LTD.

3 Church St., Suite 500, Toronto ON M5E 1M2, Canada. (416)214-5544. **E-mail:** info@dundurn.com. **E-mail:** submissions@dundurn.com. **Website:** www. dundurn.com. **Contact:** Acquisitions Editor. Estab. 1972. Publishes hardcover, trade paperback, and e-book originals and reprints. Dundurn publishes books by Canadian authors. **600 queries received/ year. 25% of books from first-time authors. 50% from unagented writers.** Publishes ms 1-2 year after acceptance. Accepts simultaneous submissions. Responds in 6 months to queries. Guidelines online.

NONFICTION Subjects include history, regional, art history, theater, serious and popular nonfiction. Submit cover letter, synopsis, CV, TOC, writing sample, e-mail contact. Do not submit original materials. Submissions will not be returned.

FICTION Subjects include literary, mystery, young adult. No romance, science fiction, or experimental."Important note: Dundurn is not currently accepting fiction submissions, including mysteries or YA, nor is it accepting children's non-fiction submissions."

DUNEDIN ACADEMIC PRESS LTD

Hudson House, 8 Albany St., Edinburgh EH1 3QB, United Kingdom. (44)(131)473-2397. **E-mail:** mail@dunedinacademicpress.co.uk. **Website:** www.dunedinacademicpress.co.uk. **Contact:** Anthony Kinahan, director. Estab. 2001. Dunedin Academic Press Ltd is a lively small independent academic publishing house. **Publishes 15-20 titles/year. 5% of books from first-time authors. 100% from unagented writers. Pays royalty.** Book catalog and proposal guidelines online.

NONFICTION Subjects include , earth science, health and social care, child protection. Reviews artwork/photos.

THOMAS DUNNE BOOKS

Imprint of St. Martin's Press, 175 Fifth Ave., New York NY 10010. (212)674-5151. **E-mail:** thomasdunnebooks@stmartins.com. **Website:** www.thomasdunnebooks.com. Estab. 1986. Publishes hardcover and trade paperback originals, and reprints. "Thomas Dunne Books publishes popular trade fiction and nonfiction. With an output of approximately 175 titles each year, his group covers a range of genres including commercial and literary fiction, thrillers, biography, politics, sports, popular science, and more. The list is intentionally eclectic and includes a wide range of fiction and nonfiction, from first books to international bestsellers." Accepts simultaneous submissions. Book catalog and ms guidelines free.

NONFICTION Subjects include history, science, true crime, political commentary. *Accepts agented submissions only.*

FICTION Subjects include mystery, suspense, thrillers, women's. *Accepts agented submissions only.*

DUTTON ADULT TRADE

Penguin Random House, 375 Hudson St., New York NY 10014. (212)366-2000. **Website:** penguin.com. Es-

tab. 1852. Publishes hardcover originals. "Dutton currently publishes 45 hardcovers a year, roughly half fiction and half nonfiction." **Pays royalty. Pays negotiable advance.** Book catalog online.

NONFICTION Agented submissions only. *No unsolicited mss.*

FICTION Subjects include adventure, historical, literary, mystery, short story collections, suspense. Agented submissions only. *No unsolicited mss.*

DUTTON CHILDREN'S BOOKS

Penguin Random House, 375 Hudson St., New York NY 10014. **Website:** www.penguin.com. Estab. 1852. Publishes hardcover originals as well as novelty formats. Dutton Children's Books publishes high-quality fiction and nonfiction for readers ranging from preschoolers to young adults on a variety of subjects. Currently emphasizing middle grade and young adult novels that offer a fresh perspective. De-emphasizing photographic nonfiction and picture books that teach a lesson. **Publishes 100 titles/year. 15% of books from first-time authors. Pays royalty on retail price. Pays advance.** Accepts simultaneous submissions.

NONFICTION Subjects include animals, history, science. Query. Only responds if interested.

FICTION Subjects include juvenile, young adult. Dutton Children's Books has a diverse, general interest list that includes picture books; easy-to-read books; and fiction for all ages, from first chapter books to young adult readers. Query. Responds only if interested.

DZANC BOOKS

Dzanc Books, Inc., 2702 Lillian, Ann Arbor MI 48104. **Website:** www.dzancbooks.org. Accepts simultaneous submissions.

FICTION Subjects include literary. "We're an independent non-profit publishing literary fiction. We also set up writer-in-residence programs and help literary journals develop their subscription bases." Publishes paperback originals. Query with outline/synopsis and 35 sample pages. Accepts queries by e-mail. Include brief bio. Agented fiction: 3%. Accepts unsolicited mss. Considers simultaneous submissions, submissions on CD or disk. Rarely critiques/comments on rejected mss. Responds to mss in 5 months.

THE ECCO PRESS

195 Broadway, New York NY 10007. (212)207-7000. **Fax:** (212)702-2460. **Website:** www.harpercollins.

com. Estab. 1970. Publishes hardcover and trade paperback originals and reprints. **Publishes 60 titles/ year. Pays royalty. Pays negotiable advance.** Publishes ms 1 year after acceptance. Accepts simultaneous submissions.

FICTION Literary, short story collections. "We can publish possibly 1 or 2 original novels a year." *Does not accept unsolicited mss.*

✪ EDGE SCIENCE FICTION AND FANTASY PUBLISHING

Hades Publications, Box 1414, Calgary AB T2P 2L7, Canada. (403)254-0160. **E-mail:** publisher@hadespublications.com. **Website:** www.edgewebsite. com. **Contact:** Editorial Manager. Estab. 1996. Publishes trade paperback and e-book originals. EDGE publishes thought-provoking full length novels and anthologies of Science Fiction, Fantasy and Horror. Featuring works by established authors and emerging new voices, EDGE is pleased to provide quality literary entertainment in both print and pixels. **Publishes 20+ titles/year. 300-400 50% of books from first-time authors. 90% from unagented writers. Pays 10% royalty on net price for distributed printed editions, 30% royalty on net price for eBook editions. Negotiable advance.** Publishes ms 18-20 months after acceptance. Responds in 4-5 months to mss. Catalog online. Guidelines online.

IMPRINTS EDGE, EDGE-Lite, Tesseracts Books, Absolute XPress.

NONFICTION Does not want erotica, juvenile.

FICTION Subjects include contemporary, fantasy, horror, mystery, occult, science fiction. "We are looking for all types of fantasy, science fiction, and horror - except juvenile, erotica, and religious fiction. Short stories and poetry are only required for announced anthologies." Length: 75,000-100,000/words. Does not want juvenile, erotica, and religious fiction. Submit first 3 chapters and synopsis. Check website for guidelines. Include estimated word count.

✪ ÉDITIONS DU NOROÎT

4609 D'Iberville, Bureau 202, Montreal QC H2H 2L9, Canada. (514)727-0005. **Fax:** (514)723-6660. **E-mail:** lenoroit@lenoroit.com. **Website:** www.lenoroit.com. Publishes trade paperback originals and reprints. "Editions du Noiroît publishes poetry and essays on poetry." **Publishes 20 titles/year. 500 queries; 500 mss received/year. Pays 10% royalty on retail price.**

Publishes ms 1 year after acceptance. Accepts simultaneous submissions. Responds in 4 months to mss.

POETRY Submit 40 sample poems.

EDUPRESS, INC.

Teacher Created Resources, 12621 Western Ave., Garden Grove CA 92841. (800)662-4321. **Fax:** (800)525-1254. **Website:** www.edupress.com. **Contact:** Editor-in-Chief. Estab. 1979. Edupress, Inc., publishes supplemental curriculum resources for PK-6th grade. Currently emphasizing Common Core reading and math games and materials. **Work purchased outright from authors.** Publishes ms 1-2 years after acceptance. Accepts simultaneous submissions. Responds in 2-4 months. Catalog online.

NONFICTION Submit complete ms via mail or e-mail with "Manuscript Submission" as the subject line.

WILLIAM B. EERDMANS PUBLISHING CO.

2140 Oak Industrial Dr. NE, Grand Rapids MI 49505. (616)459-4591. **Fax:** (616)459-6540. **E-mail:** info@eerdmans.com. **E-mail:** submissions@eerdmans.com. **Website:** www.eerdmans.com. Estab. 1911. Publishes hardcover and paperback originals and reprints. "The majority of our adult publications are religious and most of these are academic or semi-academic in character (as opposed to inspirational or celebrity books), though we also publish general trade books on the Christian life. Our nonreligious titles, most of them in regional history or on social issues, aim, similarly, at an educated audience." Accepts simultaneous submissions. Responds in 4 weeks. Book catalog and ms guidelines free.

NONFICTION Subjects include history, philosophy, psychology, regional, religion, sociology, translation, Biblical studies. "We prefer that writers take the time to notice if we have published anything at all in the same category as their manuscript before sending it to us." Query with TOC, 2-3 sample chapters, and SASE for return of ms. Reviews artwork/photos.

FICTION Subjects include religious. Query with SASE.

EDWARD ELGAR PUBLISHING, INC.

The William Pratt House, 9 Dewey Ct., Northampton MA 01060. (413)584-5551. **Fax:** (413)584-9933. **E-mail:** info@e-elgar.com. **Website:** www.e-elgar.com. Estab. 1986. "Specializing in research monographs, reference books and upper-level textbooks in highly focused areas, we are able to offer a unique service in terms of editorial, production and worldwide marketing. We have three offices, Cheltenham and Camberley in the UK and Northampton, MA, US. We are actively commissioning new titles and are happy to consider and advise on ideas for monograph books, textbooks, professional law books and academic journals at any stage. Please complete a proposal form in as much detail as possible. We review all prososals with our academic advisors." Accepts simultaneous submissions.

ELM BOOKS

1175 Hwy. 130, Laramie WY 82070. (610)529-0460. **E-mail:** leila.monaghan@gmail.com. **Website:** www.elm-books.com. **Contact:** Leila Monaghan, publisher. "We are eager to publish stories by new writers that have real stories to tell. We are looking for short stories (5,000-10,000 words) with real characters and true-to-life stories. Whether your story is fictionalized autobiography, or other stories of real-life mayhem and debauchery, we are interested in reading them!" **Pays royalties.** Accepts simultaneous submissions.

FICTION "We are looking for short stories (1,000-5,000 words) about kids of color that will grab readers' attentions—mysteries, adventures, humor, suspense, set in the present, near past or near future that reflect the realities and hopes of life in diverse communities." Also looking for middle grade novels (20,000-50,000 words). Send complete ms for short stories; synopsis and 3 sample chapters for novels.

⊗⊘ ENCOUNTER BOOKS

900 Broadway, Suite 601, New York NY 10003. (212)871-6310. **Fax:** (212)871-6311. **Website:** www.encounterbooks.com. **Contact:** Acquisitions. Publisher/President: Roger Kimball. Publishes hardcover, trade paperback, and e-book originals and trade paperback reprints. Encounter Books publishes serious nonfiction—books that can alter our society, challenge our morality, stimulate our imaginations—in the areas of history, politics, religion, biography, education, public policy, current affairs, and social sciences. Encounter Books is an activity of Encounter for Culture and Education, a tax-exempt, non profit corporation dedicated to strengthening the marketplace of ideas and engaging in educational activities to help preserve democratic culture. Accepts simultaneous submissions. Book catalog online. Guidelines online.

NONFICTION Subjects include child guidance, education, ethnic, history, memoirs, multicultural, philosophy, psychology, religion, science, sociology, gender studies. Only considers agented submissions.

ENSLOW PUBLISHERS, INC.

101 W. 23rd St., Suite 240, New York NY 10011. (973)771-9400. **Fax:** (877)980-4454. **E-mail:** customerservice@enslow.com. **Website:** www.enslow.com. Estab. 1977. Publishes hardcover originals. 10% require freelance illustration. Enslow publishes nonfiction and fiction series books for young adults and school-age children. **Publishes 250 titles/year. Pays royalty on net price with advance or flat fee. Pays advance.** Publishes ms 1 year after acceptance. Accepts simultaneous submissions. Responds in 1 month to queries. Guidelines via e-mail.

NONFICTION Subjects include history, recreation, science, sociology, sports. "Interested in new ideas for series of books for young people." No fiction, fictionalized history, or dialogue.

ENTREPRENEUR PRESS

Entrepreneur Media Inc., 18061 Fitch, Irvine CA 92614. (949)261-2325. **Fax:** (949)622-7106. **E-mail:** books@entrepreneur.com. **E-mail:** submissions@entrepreneur.com. **Website:** http://entrepreneurmedia.com/books/. **Contact:** Vanessa Campos, sales & marketing director. Acquisitions Director: Jen Dorsey. Entrepreneur Press specializes in quality paperbacks and e-books that focus on the entrepreneur in us all. Addressing the diverse challenges at all stages of business, each Entrepreneur Press book aims to provide actionable solutions to help entrepreneurs excel in all ventures they take on. **Publishes 18+ titles/year. Pays competitive net royalty.** Accepts simultaneous submissions. Catalog online. Guidelines online.

NONFICTION Subjects include business, career guidance, business start-up, small business management, business planning, marketing, finance, careers, personal finance, accounting, motivation, leadership, legal advise, management. When submitting work to us, please send as much of the proposed book as possible. Proposal should include: cover letter, preface, marketing plan, analysis of competition and comparative titles, author bio, TOC, 2 sample chapters. Go to website for more details. Reviews artwork/photos. Send transparencies and all other applicable information.

EYEWEAR PUBLISHING

E-mail: info@eyewearpublishing.com. **Website:** store.eyewearpublishing.com. **Contact:** Dr. Todd Swift, managing director and editor. Senior Editor: Rosanna Hildyard. Managing Editor: Alexandra Payne. Estab. 2012. Firm publishes fiction, nonfiction, and poetry. Eyewear Publishing Ltd. is a small press founded in 2012 by Todd Swift, based in London, UK, with distribution in the USA. Our books have been recommended by such literary figures as Kaveh Akbar, Stephen Fry, Louis Theroux, Salman Rushdie, Clare Pollard, Vicki Feaver, Thomas Lux, Suhayl Saadi and The Rev. Jesse Jackson. We search for emerging talent, and neglected out-of-work authors, as well as well-established figures. We are welcoming, with a commitment to diversity. **Publishes 60 titles/year. Royalties vary from 10% to 20% Pays variable advance.** Accepts simultaneous submissions. Response time varies. Guidelines online.

IMPRINTS Maida Vale Publishing.

NONFICTION Subjects include Americana, art, business, community, contemporary culture, creative nonfiction, education, electronics, ethnic, games, gay, government, history, humanities, lesbian, literary criticism, literature, memoirs, multicultural, music, philosophy, politics, pop culture, public affairs, regional, religion, social sciences, sociology, software, sports, translation, womens issues, womens studies, world affairs.

FICTION Subjects include contemporary, erotica, ethnic, feminist, lesbian, literary, poetry, poetry in translation, regional, short story collections, translation, young adult.

FACTS ON FILE, INC.

Infobase Learning, 132 W. 31st St., 16th Floor, New York NY 10001. (800)322-8755. **Fax:** (800)678-3633. **E-mail:** llikoff@infobaselearning.com; custserv@infobaselearning.com. **Website:** www.infobaselearning.com. **Contact:** Laurie Likoff. Estab. 1941. Publishes hardcover originals and reprints and e-books as well as reference databases. Facts On File produces high-quality reference materials in print and digital format on a broad range of subjects for the school and public library market and the general nonfiction trade. **Publishes 150-200 titles/year. 10% of books from first-time authors. 45% from unagented writers. Pays 10% royalty on retail price. Pays $3-5,000 advance.** Responds in 6 months to 1 year. Accepts simultaneous submissions. Responds in 2 months to queries. Reference catalog available free. Guidelines online.

IMPRINTS Bloom's Literature; Ferguson's; Chelsea House; World Almanac.

NONFICTION Subjects include career guidance, contemporary culture, education, environment, government, history, literary criticism, multicultural, nutrition, politics, religion, sports, womens studies, young adult, careers, entertainment, natural history, popular culture. "We publish serious, informational books and e-books for a targeted audience. All our books must have strong library interest, but we also distribute books effectively to the trade. Our library books fit the junior and senior high school curriculum." No computer books, technical books, cookbooks, biographies (except YA), pop psychology, humor, fiction or poetry. Query or submit outline and sample chapter with SASE. No submissions returned without SASE.

FAMILIUS

1254 Commerce Way, Sanger CA 93657 (559)876-2170. **Fax:** (559)876-2180. **E-mail:** bookideas@familius.com. **Website:** familius.com. **Contact:** Acquisitions. Design & Digital: David Miles. Managing Editor: Brooke Jorden. Marketing & Publicity: Erika Riggs. Estab. 2011. Publishes hardcover, trade paperback, and electronic originals and reprints. Familius is all about strengthening families. Collective, the authors and staff have experienced a wide slice of the family-life spectrum. Some come from broken homes. Some are married and in the throes of managing a bursting household. Some are preparing to start families of their own. Together, they publish books and articles that help families be happy. **Publishes 40 titles/year. 200 queries; 100 mss received/year. 30% of books from first-time authors. 70% from unagented writers. Authors are paid 10-30% royalty on wholesale price.** Publishes book 12 months after acceptance. Accepts simultaneous submissions. Responds in 1 month to queries and proposals; 2 months to mss. Catalog online and print. Guidelines online.

NONFICTION Subjects include Americana, beauty, child guidance, cooking, counseling, crafts, finance, foods, games, gardening, health, hobbies, medicine, memoirs, military, nutrition, parenting. All mss must align with Familius mission statement to help families succeed. Submit a proposal package, including an outline, 1 sample chapter, competition evaluation, and your author platform. Reviews JPEGS if sent as part of the submission package.

FICTION Subjects include juvenile, picture books. All picture books must align with Familius values statement listed on the website footer. Submit a proposal package, including a synopsis, 3 sample chapters, and your author platform.

FANTAGRAPHICS BOOKS, INC.

7563 Lake City Way NE, Seattle WA 98115. (206)524-1967. **Fax:** (206)524-2104. **Website:** www.fantagraphics.com. **Contact:** Submissions Editor. Estab. 1976. Publishes original trade paperbacks. Publishes comics for thinking readers. Does not want mainstream genres of superhero, vigilante, horror, fantasy, or science fiction. Accepts simultaneous submissions. Responds in 2-3 months to queries. Book catalog online. Guidelines online.

FICTION Subjects include comic books. "Fantagraphics is an independent company with a modus operandi different from larger, factory-like corporate comics publishers. If your talents are limited to a specific area of expertise (i.e. inking, writing, etc.), then you will need to develop your own team before submitting a project to us. We want to see an idea that is fully fleshed-out in your mind, at least, if not on paper. Submit a minimum of 5 fully-inked pages of art, a synopsis, SASE, and a brief note stating approximately how many issues you have in mind."

FARCOUNTRY PRESS

P.O. Box 5630, Helena MT 59604. (800)821-3874. **Fax:** (406)443-5480. **E-mail:** will@farcountrypress.com. **Website:** www.farcountrypress.com. **Contact:** Will Harmon, Sr. Editor. Estab. 1980. Award-winning publisher Farcountry Press specializes in softcover and hardcover color photography books showcasing the nation's cities, states, national parks, and wildlife. Farcountry also publishes several children's series, as well as guidebooks, cookbooks, and regional history titles nationwide. **Publishes The staff produces about 30 books annually; the backlist has grown to more than 400 titles. titles/year.** Accepts simultaneous submissions. Guidelines online.

NONFICTION Subjects include agriculture, Americana, animals, community, cooking, environment, foods, history, memoirs, nature, photography, regional, travel.

FARRAR, STRAUS & GIROUX

18 W. 18th St., New York NY 10011. (646)307-5151. **Website:** us.macmillan.com/fsg. **Contact:** Editorial Department. Estab. 1946. Publishes hardcover originals and trade paperback reprints. "We publish original and well-written material for all ages." **Publishes 75 titles/year. 6,000 queries and mss received/year. 5% of books from first-time authors. 50% from unagented writers. Pays 2-6% royalty on retail price for paperbacks, 3-10% for hardcovers. Pays $3,000-25,000 advance.** Publishes ms 18 months after acceptance. Accepts simultaneous submissions. Responds in 2-3 months. Catalog available by request. Guidelines online.

NONFICTION All levels. Send cover letter describing submission with first 50 pages.

FICTION Subjects include juvenile, picture books, young adult. Do not query picture books; just send ms. Do not fax or e-mail queries or mss. Send cover letter describing submission with first 50 pages.

POETRY Send cover letter describing submission with 3-4 poems. By mail only.

FARRAR, STRAUS & GIROUX FOR YOUNG READERS

Macmillan Children's Publishing Group, 175 Fifth Ave., New York NY 10010. (212)741-6900. **Fax:** (212)633-2427. **E-mail:** childrens.editorial@fsgbooks.com. **Website:** www.fsgkidsbooks.com. Estab. 1946. Accepts simultaneous submissions. Book catalog available by request. Ms guidelines online.

NONFICTION All levels: all categories. "We publish only literary nonfiction." Submit cover letter, first 50 pages by mail only.

FICTION All levels: all categories. "Original and well-written material for all ages." Submit cover letter, first 50 pages by mail only.

POETRY Submit cover letter, 3-4 poems by mail only.

❾ FAT FOX BOOKS

The Den, P.O. Box 579, Tonbridge TN9 9NG, United Kingdom. (44)(0)1580-857249. **E-mail:** hello@fatfoxbooks.com. **Website:** fatfoxbooks.com. "Can you write engaging, funny, original and brilliant stories? We are looking for fresh new talent as well as exciting new ideas from established writers and illustrators. We publish books for children from 3-14, and if we think the story is brilliant and fits our list, then as one of the few publishers who accepts unsolicited material, we will take it seriously. We will consider books of all genres." Accepts simultaneous submissions. Guidelines online. Currently closed to submissions.

FICTION For picture books, send complete ms; for longer works, send first 3 chapters and estimate of final word count.

F+W, A CONTENT + ECOMMERCE COMPANY (BOOK DIVISION)

10151 Carver Rd., Suite 200, Blue Ash OH 45242. (513)531-2690. **Website:** www.fwcommunity.com. Estab. 1913. Publishes trade paperback originals and reprints. F+W connects passionate, like-minded groups of people to share an ongoing exchange of information, ideas, and inspiration. "We are committed to providing the very best experience for our consumers across our niche categories–craft, art, writing, design, outdoors, and lifestyle. We offer exclusive programs and products, best-in-industry customer service, curated kit flash sales, rewards and VIP programs, personalized 1-to-1 marketing, and more." **Publishes 400+ titles/year.** Accepts simultaneous submissions. Guidelines online.

IMPRINTS HOW Books (graphic design, illustrated, humor, pop culture); IMPACT Books (fantasy art, manga, creative comics and popular culture); Interweave (knitting, beading, crochet, jewelry, sewing); Krause Books (antiques and collectibles, automotive, coins and paper money, comics, crafts, games, firearms, militaria, outdoors and hunting, records and CDs, sports, toys); North Light Books (crafts, decorative painting, fine art); Popular Woodworking Books (shop skills, woodworking); Tyrus Books (mystery and literary fiction); Warman's (antiques and collectibles, field guides); Writer's Digest Books (writing and reference).

Ⓐ⊘ FEIWEL AND FRIENDS

Macmillan Children's Publishing Group, 175 Fifth Ave., New York NY 10010. (646)307-5151. **Website:** us.macmillan.com. Feiwel and Friends is a publisher of innovative children's fiction and nonfiction literature, including hardcover, paperback series, and individual titles. The list is eclectic and combines quality and commercial appeal for readers ages 0-16. The imprint is dedicated to "book by book" publishing, bringing the work of distinctive and oustanding authors, illustrators, and ideas to the marketplace. This market does not accept unsolicited mss due to the volume of submissions; they also do not accept unso-

licited queries for interior art. The best way to submit a ms is through an agent. Catalog online.

FENCE BOOKS

Science Library 320, Univ. of Albany, 1400 Washington Ave., Albany NY 12222. (518)591-8162. **E-mail:** jessp.fence@gmail.com. **Website:** www.fenceportal.org. **Contact:** Submissions Manager. Publishes hardcover originals. "Fence Books publishes poetry, fiction, and critical texts and anthologies, and prioritizes sustained support for its authors, many of whom come to us through our book contests and then go on to publish second, third, fourth books." Accepts simultaneous submissions. Guidelines online.

FICTION Subjects include literary, poetry. Submit via contests and occasional open reading periods.

POETRY Submit via contests and occasional open reading periods.

FERGUSON PUBLISHING CO.

Infobase Publishing, 132 W. 31st St., 17th Floor, New York NY 10001. (800)322-8755. **E-mail:** editorial@factsonfile.com. **Website:** www.infobasepublishing.com. Estab. 1940. Publishes hardcover and trade paperback originals. "We are primarily a career education publisher that publishes for schools and libraries. We need writers who have expertise in a particular career or career field (for possible full-length books on a specific career or field)." **Publishes 50 titles/year. Pays by project.** Accepts simultaneous submissions. Responds in 6 months to queries. Guidelines online.

NONFICTION "We publish work specifically for the elementary/junior high/high school/college library reference market. Works are generally encyclopedic in nature. Our current focus is career encyclopedias and young adult career sets and series. We consider manuscripts that cross over into the trade market." No mass market, poetry, scholarly, or juvenile books, please. Query or submit an outline and 1 sample chapter.

Ⓒ FERNWOOD PUBLISHING, LTD.

32 Ocenavista Ln., Black Point NS B0J 1B0, Canada. (902)857-1388. **Fax:** (902) 857-1328. **E-mail:** info@fernpub.ca. **E-mail:** editorial@fernpub.ca. **Website:** www.fernwoodpublishing.ca. **Contact:** Errol Sharpe, publisher. Estab. 1993. Publishes trade paperback originals. "Fernwood's objective is to publish critical works which challenge existing scholarship. We are a political and academic publisher. We publish critical

books in the social sciences and humanities and for the trade market." **Publishes 35-40 titles/year. 120 queries received/year. 50 mss received/year. 40% of books from first-time authors. 100% from unagented writers. Pays 7-10% royalty on wholesale price. Pays advance.** Publishes ms 12-18 months after acceptance. Accepts simultaneous submissions. Responds in 6 weeks to proposals. Guidelines online.

IMPRINTS Roseway Publishing.

NONFICTION Subjects include agriculture, anthropology, communications, community, contemporary culture, creative nonfiction, economics, education, environment, ethnic, gay, government, health, history, humanities, labor, law, lesbian, multicultural, philosophy, politics, regional, sex, social sciences, sociology, translation, womens issues, womens studies, world affairs, young adult, contemporary culture, world affairs. "Our main focus is in the social sciences and humanities, emphasizing Indigenous resistance and resurgence, politics, capitalism, political economy, women, gender, sexuality, crime and law, international development and social work-for use in college and university courses." Submit proposal package, outline, sample chapters. Reviews artwork/photos. Send photocopies.

FICTION Subjects include ethnic, feminist, gay, historical, lesbian, literary, multicultural, regional, young adult, environment. Roseway Publishing is our social justice literary imprint. Roseway publishes fiction, young adult fiction, children's fiction and autobiography that deals with social justice issues. Guidelines online.

DAVID FICKLING BOOKS

31 Beamont St., Oxford OX1 2NP, United Kingdom. (018)65-339000. **Fax:** (018)65-339009. **Website:** www.davidficklingbooks.co.uk. **Contact:** Simon Mason, managing director. David Fickling Books is a story house."For nearly twelve years DFB has been run as an imprint—first as part of Scholastic, then of Random House. Now we've set up as an independent business." **Publishes 12-20 titles/year.** Accepts simultaneous submissions. Responds to mss in 3 months, if interested. Guidelines online. Closed to submissions. Check website for when they open to submissions and for details on the Inkpot competition.

FICTION Considers all categories. Submit cover letter and 3 sample chapters as PDF attachment saved in format "Author Name_Full Title."

FINDHORN PRESS

Inner Traditions Inc., One Park St., Rochester VT 05767. **E-mail:** submissions@findhornpress.com. **Website:** www.findhornpress.com. **Contact:** Sabine Weeke, editorial director. Estab. 1971. Publishes trade paperback originals, CDs, card sets and e-books. **Publishes 18-20 titles/year. 1,000 queries received/year. 50% of books from first-time authors. 70% from unagented writers. Pays 10% royalty on net receipts.** Publishes ms 12-18 months after acceptance. Accepts simultaneous submissions. Responds in 3-4 months to proposals. Book catalog and ms guidelines online.

NONFICTION Subjects include alternative lifestyles, animals, community, health, nature, New Age, psychology, spirituality, alternative health. No autobiographies.

FINISHING LINE PRESS

P.O. Box 1626, Georgetown KY 40324. (502)603-0670. **E-mail:** finishingbooks@aol.com. **Website:** www.finishinglinepress.com. **Contact:** Christen Kincaid, director. Estab. 1998. Finishing Line Press seeks to "discover new talent" and hopes to publish chapbooks by both men and women poets who have not previously published a book or chapbook of poetry. Has published *Parables and Revelations* by T. Crunk, *Family Business* by Paula Sergi, *Putting in a Window* by John Brantingham, and *Dusting the Piano* by Abigail Gramig. Publishes 100+ poetry chapbooks/year. Chapbooks are usually 16-35 pages,and perfect bound. Publishes 50+ full-length books per year. Submit poetry with cover letter, bio, acknowledgments, and **no reading fee in November**. Responds to queries and mss in up to 3 months. Pay varies; pays in author's copies. "Sales profits, if any, go to publish the next new poet." Sample chapbooks available by sending $6 to Finishing Line Press or through website. See The Finishing Line Press Open Chapbook Competition and the New Women's Voices Chapbook Competition. Member of CLMP. **2,500 98% from unagented writers. Pays in copies, or standard royalties contract. Pays advance against royalties for fiction and nonfiction.** Accepts simultaneous submissions.

NONFICTION Subjects include alternative lifestyles, Americana, animals, art, creative nonfiction, entertainment, history, humanities, language, lesbian, literary criticism, literature, memoirs, spirituality, womens issues, womens studies, art history, craft of writing, biography.

FICTION Subjects include comic books, contemporary, ethnic, experimental, feminist, gay, historical, literary, mainstream, multicultural, plays, poetry, poetry in translation, religious, short story collections, spiritual, translation.

ⒶⓄ⊘ FIRST SECOND

Macmillan Children's Publishing Group, 175 5th Ave., New York NY 10010. **E-mail:** mail@firstsecondbooks. com. **Website:** www.firstsecondbooks.com. First Second is a publisher of graphic novels and an imprint of Macmillan Children's Publishing Group. First Second does not accept unsolicited submissions. Responds in about 6 weeks. Catalog online.

⦿⊘ FITZHENRY & WHITESIDE LTD.

195 Allstate Pkwy., Markham ON L3R 4T8, Canada. (905)477-9700. **Fax:** (905)477-2834. **E-mail:** godwit@ fitzhenry.ca. **Website:** www.fitzhenry.ca/. Emphasis on Canadian authors and illustrators, subject or perspective. "Until further notice, we will not be accepting unsolicited submissions." **Publishes 15 titles/ year. 10% of books from first-time authors. Pays authors 8-10% royalty with escalations. Offers "respectable" advances for picture books, split 50/50 between author and illustrator. Pays illustrators by project and royalty. Pays photographers per photo.** Publishes book 1-2 years after acceptance.

FOCAL PRESS

Imprint of Elsevier (USA), Inc., 711 3rd Ave., 8th Floor, New York NY 10017. **Website:** routledge.com/focalpress. Estab. US, 1981; UK, 1938. Publishes hardcover and paperback originals and reprints. "Focal Press provides excellent books for students, advanced amateurs, and working professionals involved in all areas of media technology. Topics of interest include photography (digital and traditional techniques), film/video, audio, broadcasting, and cinematography, through to journalism, radio, television, video, and writing. Currently emphasizing graphics, gaming, animation, and multimedia." **Publishes 80-120 UK-US titles/year; entire firm publishes over 1,000 titles/year. 25% of books from first-time authors. 90% from unagented writers.** Publishes ms 6 months after acceptance. Accepts simultaneous submissions. Responds in 2 months to queries. Guidelines online.

NONFICTION Subjects include photography, film, cinematography, broadcasting, theater and performing arts, audio, sound and media technology. Does not publish collections of photographs or books composed primarily of photographs. To submit a proposal for consideration by Elsevier, complete the proposal form online. "Once we have had a chance to review your proposal in line with our publishing plan and budget, we will contact you to discuss the next steps." Reviews artwork/photos.

FODOR'S TRAVEL PUBLICATIONS, INC.

Imprint of Random House, Inc., 1745 Broadway, 15th Floor, New York NY 10019. **E-mail:** editors@fodors. com. **Website:** www.fodors.com. Estab. 1936. Publishes trade paperback originals. Fodor's publishes travel books on many regions and countries. "Remember that most Fodor's writers live in the areas they cover. Note that we do not accept unsolicited mss." **Most titles are collective works, with contributions as works for hire. Most contributions are updates of previously published volumes.** Accepts simultaneous submissions. Responds in 2 months to queries. Book catalog available free.

NONFICTION Subjects include travel. "We are interested in unique approaches to favorite destinations. Writers seldom review our catalog or our list and often query about books on topics that we're already covering. Beyond that, it's important to review competition and to say what the proposed book will add. Do not send originals without first querying as to our interest in the project. We're not interested in travel literature or in proposals for general travel guidebooks." Submit writing clips and résumé via mail or e-mail. In cover letter, explain qualifications and areas of expertise.

FORDHAM UNIVERSITY PRESS

2546 Belmont Ave., University Box L, Bronx NY 10458. (718)817-4795. **Fax:** (718)817-4785. **Website:** www.fordhampress.com. **Contact:** Tom Lay, acquisitions editor. Editorial Director: Richard W. Morrison. Publishes hardcover and trade paperback originals and reprints. "We are a publisher in humanities, accepting scholarly monographs, collections, occasional reprints and general interest titles for consideration. No fiction." Accepts simultaneous submissions. Book catalog and ms guidelines free.

NONFICTION Subjects include education, history, philosophy, regional, religion, science, sociology, translation, business, Jewish studies, media, music. Submit query letter, CV, SASE.

FOREIGN POLICY ASSOCIATION

470 Park Ave. S., New York NY 10016. (212)481-8100. **Fax:** (212)481-9275. **Website:** www.fpa.org. Publishes 2 periodicals, an annual eight episode PBS Television series with DVD and an occasional hardcover and trade paperback original. The Foreign Policy Association, a nonpartisan, not-for-profit educational organization founded in 1918, is a catalyst for developing awareness, understanding of and informed opinion on US foreign policy and global issues. Through its balanced, nonpartisan publications, FPA seeks to encourage individuals in schools, communities and the workplace to participate in the foreign policy process. Accepts simultaneous submissions. Book catalog available free.

IMPRINTS Headline Series (quarterly); Great Decisions (annual).

NONFICTION Subjects include history, foreign policy.

⊕ FORMAC PUBLISHING CO. LTD.

5502 Atlantic St., Halifax NS B3H 1G4, Canada. (902)421-7022. **Fax:** (902)425-0166. **Website:** www. formac.ca. **Contact:** Acquisitions Editor. Estab. 1977. Publishes hardcover and trade paperback originals. **Publishes 15-20 titles/year. 200 queries received/ year. 150 mss received/year. 20% of books from first-time authors. 75% from unagented writers. Pays 5-10% royalty on wholesale price.** Publishes book 1 year after acceptance of ms. Accepts simultaneous submissions. Responds in 2 months to queries and to proposals; 4 months to mss. Book catalog available free. Guidelines online.

NONFICTION Subjects include animals, creative nonfiction, history, multicultural, regional, travel, marine subjects, transportation. Submit proposal package, outline, 2 sample chapters, CV or résumé of author(s).

FORTRESS PRESS

P.O. Box 1209, Minneapolis MN 55440. (612)330-3300. **Website:** www.fortresspress.com. Publishes hardcover and trade paperback originals. "Fortress Press publishes academic books in Biblical studies, theology, Christian ethics, church history, and professional books in pastoral care and counseling." **Pays royalty**

on retail price. Accepts simultaneous submissions. Book catalog free. Guidelines online.

NONFICTION Subjects include religion, church history, African-American studies. Use online form. Please study guidelines before submitting.

FORWARD MOVEMENT

412 Sycamore St., Cincinnati OH 45202. (513)721-6659; (800)543-1813. **Fax:** (513)721-0729. **E-mail:** editorial@forwardmovement.org. **Website:** www.forwardmovement.org. Estab. 1934. "Forward Movement was established to help reinvigorate the life of the church. Many titles focus on the life of prayer, where our relationship with God is centered, death, marriage, baptism, recovery, joy, the Episcopal Church and more. Currently emphasizing prayer/spirituality." **Publishes 30 titles/year.** Accepts simultaneous submissions. Responds in 1 month. Book catalog free. Guidelines online.

NONFICTION Subjects include religion. "We are an agency of the Episcopal Church. There is a special need for tracts of under 8 pages. (A page usually runs about 200 words.) On rare occasions, we publish a full-length book." Query with SASE or by e-mail with complete ms attached.

FICTION Subjects include juvenile.

WALTER FOSTER PUBLISHING

Quarto Publishing Group, 6 Orchard, Suite 100, Lake Forest CA 92630. (949)380-7510. **Fax:** (949)380-7575. **E-mail:** walterfoster@quarto.com. **Website:** www. quartoknows.com. **Contact:** Publisher. Estab. 1922. Publishes trade paperback originals. Walter Foster publishes instructional/how-to books in the fine art, craft, and hobby categories. 12 months between acceptance and publication. Accepts simultaneous submissions. Guidelines online.

NONFICTION Subjects include art, crafts, hobbies. Art, craft, activity books. Submit proposal package.

THE FOUNDRY PUBLISHING

P.O. Box 419527, Kansas City MO 64141. (816)931-1900. **Fax:** (816)412-8306. **E-mail:** rmcfarland@thefoundrypublishing.com. **Website:** thefoundrypublishing.com. Publishes hardcover and paperback originals. "Beacon Hill Press is a Christ-centered publisher that provides authentically Christian resources faithful to God's word and relevant to life." **Publishes 15 titles/year. Pays royalty.** Publishes ms 2 years after acceptance. Accepts simultaneous submissions. Responds in 3 months to queries.

NONFICTION "Accent on holy living; encouragement in daily Christian life." No felt needs, fiction, autobiography, poetry, short stories, or children's picture books. Query or submit proposal electronically.

FOUR WAY BOOKS

Box 535, Village Station, New York NY 10014. **E-mail:** editors@fourwaybooks.com. **Website:** www.fourwaybooks.com. Estab. 1993. "Four Way Books is a not-for-profit literary press dedicated to publishing poetry and short fiction by emerging and established writers. Each year, Four Way Books publishes the winners of its national poetry competitions, as well as collections accepted through general submission, panel selection, and solicitation by the editors." Accepts simultaneous submissions.

FICTION Open reading period: June 1-30. Book-length story collections and novellas. Submission guidelines will be posted online at end of May. Does not want novels or translations.

POETRY Four Way Books publishes poetry and short fiction. Considers full-length poetry mss only. Books are about 70 pages, offset-printed digitally, perfect-bound, with paperback binding, art/graphics on covers. Does not want individual poems or poetry intended for children/young readers. See website for complete submission guidelines and open reading period in June. Book mss may include previously published poems. Responds to submissions in 4 months. Payment varies. Order sample books from Four Way Books online or through bookstores.

FOX CHAPEL PUBLISHING

1970 Broad St., East Petersburg PA 17520. (800)457-9112. **Fax:** (717)560-4702. **Website:** www.foxchapelpublishing.com. Publishes hardcover and trade paperback originals and trade paperback reprints. Fox Chapel publishes craft, lifestyle, and woodworking titles for professionals and hobbyists. **Publishes 90-150 titles/year. 30% of books from first-time authors. 100% from unagented writers. Pays royalty or makes outright purchase. Pays variable advance.** Accepts simultaneous submissions. Submission guidelines online.

NONFICTION Subjects include cooking, crafts, creative nonfiction.

FRANCES LINCOLN BOOKS

74-77 White Lion St., London N1 9PF, United Kingdom. (44)(20)7284-4009. **Website:** www.franceslincoln.com. Estab. 1977. **Publishes 100 titles/year. 6% of books from first-time authors.** Publishes book 18 months after acceptance. Accepts simultaneous submissions. Responds in 6 weeks to mss.

NONFICTION Subjects include animals, career guidance, cooking, environment, history, multicultural, nature, religion, social issues, special needs. Query by e-mail.

FRANCES LINCOLN CHILDREN'S BOOKS

Frances Lincoln, 74-77 White Lion St., London N1 9PF, United Kingdom. (44)(20)7284-4009. **Website:** www.franceslincoln.com. Estab. 1977. "Our company was founded by Frances Lincoln in 1977. We published our first books two years later, and we have been creating illustrated books of the highest quality ever since, with special emphasis on gardening, walking and the outdoors, art, architecture, design and landscape. In 1983, we started to publish illustrated books for children. Since then we have won many awards and prizes with both fiction and nonfiction children's books." **Publishes 100 titles/year. 6% of books from first-time authors.** Publishes book 18 months after acceptance. Accepts simultaneous submissions. Responds in 6 weeks to mss.

NONFICTION Subjects include animals, career guidance, cooking, environment, history, multicultural, nature, religion, young adult, social issues, special needs. Average word length: picture books—1,000; middle readers—29,768. Query by e-mail.

FICTION Subjects include adventure, fantasy, historical, humor, juvenile, multicultural, picture books, sports, young adult, anthololgy, folktales, nature. Average word length: picture books—1,000; young readers— 9,788; middle readers— 20,653; young adults—35,407. Query by e-mail.

FRANCISCAN MEDIA PRESS

28 W. Liberty St., Cincinnati OH 45202-6498. (513)241-5615. **Fax:** (513)241-0399. **E-mail:** info@franciscanmedia.org. **Website:** www.americancatholic.org. Estab. 1970. Publishes trade paperback originals. "St. Anthony Messenger Press/Franciscan Communications seeks to communicate the word that is Jesus Christ in the styles of Saints Francis and Antho-

ny. Through print and electronic media marketed in North America and worldwide, we endeavor to evangelize, inspire, and inform those who search for God and seek a richer Catholic, Christian, human life. Our efforts help support the life, ministry, and charities of the Franciscan Friars of St. John the Baptist Province, who sponsor our work. Currently emphasizing prayer/spirituality." **Publishes 20-25 titles/year. 300 queries received/year. 50 mss received/year. 5% of books from first-time authors. 99% from unagented writers. Pays $1,000 average advance.** Publishes ms 18 months after acceptance. Accepts simultaneous submissions. Responds in 2 months. Guidelines online.

IMPRINTS Servant Books.

NONFICTION Query with SASE. Submit outline. Reviews artwork/photos.

🅐🅢🅞🚫 FRANKLIN WATTS

Hachette Children's Books, Carmelite House, 50 Victoria Embankment, London EC4Y 0DZ, United Kingdom. (44)(20)7873-6000. **Fax:** (44)(20)7873-6024. **Website:** www.franklinwatts.co.uk. Estab. 1942. Franklin Watts is well known for its high quality and attractive information books, which support the National Curriculum and stimulate children's enquiring minds. *Generally does not accept unsolicited mss.* Accepts simultaneous submissions.

FREE SPIRIT PUBLISHING, INC.

6325 Sandburg Rd., Suite 100, Minneapolis MN 55427-3674. (612)338-2068. **Fax:** (612)337-5050. **E-mail:** acquisitions@freespirit.com. **Website:** www. freespirit.com. Estab. 1983. Publishes trade paperback originals and reprints. "Free Spirit is the leading publisher of learning tools that support young people's social-emotional health and educational needs. We help children and teens think for themselves, overcome challenges, and make a difference in the world." Free Spirit does not accept general fiction, poetry or storybook submissions. **Publishes 25-30 titles/year.** Accepts simultaneous submissions. Responds to proposals in 2-6 months. Book catalog and guidelines online.

NONFICTION Subjects include child guidance, counseling, education, educator resources; early childhood education. "Many of our authors are educators, mental health professionals, and youth workers involved in helping kids and teens." No general fiction or picture storybooks, poetry, single biographies or autobiographies, books with mythical or animal characters, or books with religious or New Age content. "We are not looking for academic or religious materials, or books that analyze problems with the nation's school systems." Query with cover letter stating qualifications, intent, and intended audience and market analysis (comprehensive list of similar titles and detailed explanation of how your book stands out from the field), along with your promotional plan, outline, 2 sample chapters (note: for early childhood submissions, the entire text is required for evaluation), resume, SASE. Do not send original copies of work.

FICTION "Please review catalog and author guidelines (both available online) for details before submitting proposal. If you'd like material returned, enclose a SASE with sufficient postage."

FULCRUM PUBLISHING

4690 Table Mountain Dr., Suite 100, Golden CO 80403. **E-mail:** acquisitions@fulcrumbooks.com. **Website:** www.fulcrum-books.com. **Contact:** T. Baker, acquisitions editor. Estab. 1984. In physics, the word fulcrum denotes the point at which motion begins. We strive to create books that will inspire you to move forward in your life or to take action. Whether it's exploring the world around you or discussing the ideas and issues that shape that world, our books provide the tools to create forward motion in your life. Our mission is simple, yet profound: Publish books that inspire readers to live life to the fullest and to learn something new every day. More than thirty years ago, when Bob Baron started Fulcrum Publishing, his goal was to publish high-quality books from extraordinary authors. Fulcrum recognizes that good books can't exist without the best authors. To that end, we have published books from prominent politicians (Governors Richard Lamm and Bill Ritter, Jr., Senators Gary Hart and Eugene McCarthy), influential Native Americans (Wilma Mankiller, Vine Deloria Jr., and Joseph Bruchac), master gardeners (Lauren Springer, Tom Peace, and Richard Hartlage), and important organizations in the environmental community (Campaign for America's Wilderness, World Wilderness Congress, Defenders of Wildlife). Our books have received accolades from the likes of Tom Brokaw, Elizabeth Dole, Nelson Mandela, Paul Newman, William Sears, MD, Gloria Steinem, Dr. Henry Louis Gates, Jr., and Kurt Vonnegut. In addition, Fulcrum authors have received awards from prestigious organizations such as the American Booksellers Association, American Library Association, Colorado Center for the Book, ForeWord magazine, National Book Foundation, National Parenting Publications, New York Public Library, PEN USA Literary Awards, Smithsonian National Museum of the American Indian, Teacher's Choice, Harvey Awards, and more. **200 40% of books from first-time authors. 90% from unagented writers. Pays authors royalty based on wholesale price. Offers advances.** Ms published 18-24 months after acceptance. Accepts simultaneous submissions. Because of the volume of submissions we receive, we can only reply to submissions we are interested in pursuing, and it may take up to three months for a reply. No editorial remarks will be supplied. We do not provide consulting services for authors on the suitability of their mss. Catalog for SASE. Your submission must include: A proposal of your work, including a brief synopsis; 2-3 sample chapters; a brief biography of yourself; a description of your audience; your assessment of the market for the book; a list of competing titles; what you can do to help market your book.

NONFICTION Subjects include Americana, anthropology, contemporary culture, history, literature, nature, parenting, politics, recreation, regional, science, travel, true crime, young adult. Looking for nonfiction-based graphic novels and comics, U.S. history and culture, Native American history or culture studies, conservation-oriented materials. "We do not accept memoir or fiction manuscripts." "Your submission must include: a proposal of your work, including a brief synopsis, 2-3 sample chapters, brief biography of yourself, description of your audience, your assessment of the market for the book, list of competing titles, and what you can do to help market your book. We are a green company and therefore only accept e-mailed submissions. Paper queries submitted via US Mail or any other means (including fax, FedEx/UPS, and even door-to-door delivery) will not be reviewed or returned. Please help us support the preservation of the environment by e-mailing your query to acquisitions@fulcrumbooks.com."

FUTURE HORIZONS

721 W. Abram St., Arlington TX 76013. (817)277-0727. **Fax:** (817)277-2270. **Website:** www.fhautism.com. **Contact:** Jennifer Gilpin-Yacio, editorial director. Publishes hardcover originals, trade paperback originals and reprints. **Publishes 10 titles/year. 250**

queries received/year. 125 mss received/year. 75% of books from first-time authors. 95% from unagented writers. Pays 10% royalty. Makes outright purchase.** Publishes book 2 months after acceptance of ms. Accepts simultaneous submissions. Responds in 1 month to queries; 2 months to proposals. Book catalog available free. Guidelines online.

NONFICTION Subjects include education, autism. Submit proposal package, outline by mail (no e-mail). Reviews artwork/photos. Send photocopies.

GENEALOGICAL PUBLISHING CO., INC

Genealogical.com, 3600 Clipper Mill Rd., Suite 260, Baltimore MD 21211. (410)837-8271. **Fax:** (410)752-8492. **E-mail:** info@genealogical.com. **E-mail:** jgaronzi@genealogical.com. **Website:** www.genealogical.com. **Contact:** Joe Garonzik, marketing director. Production Manager: Eileen Perkins. Estab. 1959. Publishes hardcover and trade paperback originals and reprints. **Publishes 50 titles/year. Receives 100 queries/year; 20 mss/year. 10% of books from first-time authors. 99% from unagented writers. Pays 10% royalty on selling price. Does not pay advance.** Publishes book 6 months after acceptance. Accepts simultaneous submissions. Responds in 1 month. Catalog free on request.

IMPRINTS Clearfield Company.

NONFICTION Subjects include Americana, ethnic, history, hobbies. Submit outline, 1 sample chapter. Reviews artwork/photos as part of the mss package.

Ⓐ⊘ DAVID R. GODINE, PUBLISHER

15 Court Square, Suite 320, Boston MA 02108. (617)451-9600. **Fax:** (617)350-0250. **E-mail:** info@godine.com. **Website:** www.godine.com. Estab. 1970. "We publish books that matter for people who care." This publisher is no longer considering unsolicited mss of any type. Only interested in agented material. Accepts simultaneous submissions.

IMPRINTS Black Sparrow Books, Verba Mundi, Nonpareil.

NONFICTION Subjects include Americana, art, creative nonfiction, gardening, history, language, law, literary criticism, literature, photography, young adult, typography.

FICTION Subjects include literary, multicultural, poetry, poetry in translation, translation, young adult.

Ⓐ⊘ GOLDEN BOOKS FOR YOUNG

READERS GROUP

1745 Broadway, New York NY 10019. **Website:** www. penguinrandomhouse.com. Estab. 1935. "Random House Books aims to create books that nurture the hearts and minds of children, providing and promoting quality books and a rich variety of media that entertain and educate readers from 6 months to 12 years." *Random House-Golden Books does not accept unsolicited mss, only agented material.* They reserve the right not to return unsolicited material. **2% of books from first-time authors. Pays authors in royalties; sometimes buys mss outright.** Accepts simultaneous submissions. Book catalog free on request.

⊙ GOOSE LANE EDITIONS

500 Beaverbrook Ct., Suite 330, Fredericton NB E3B 5X4, Canada. (506)450-4251. **Fax:** (506)459-4991. **E-mail:** info@gooselane.com. **Website:** www.gooselane. com. Estab. 1954. Publishes hardcover and paperback originals and occasional reprints. "Goose Lane publishes literary fiction and nonfiction from well-read and highly skilled Canadian authors." **Publishes 16-20 titles/year. 20% of books from first-time authors. 60% from unagented writers. Pays 8-10% royalty on retail price. Pays $500-3,000, negotiable advance.** Responds in 6 months to queries.

NONFICTION Subjects include history, regional. Query with SASE.

FICTION Subjects include literary, short story collections, contemporary. Our needs in fiction never change: Substantial, character-centered literary fiction. No children's, YA, mainstream, mass market, genre, mystery, thriller, confessional or science fiction. Query with SAE with Canadian stamps or IRCs. No U.S. stamps.

POETRY Considers mss by Canadian poets only. Submit cover letter, list of publications, synopsis, entire ms, SASE.

⊙⊘ GRAYWOLF PRESS

250 Third Ave. N., Suite 600, Minneapolis MN 55401. (651)641-0077. **Fax:** (651)641-0036. **Website:** www. graywolfpress.org. Estab. 1974. Publishes trade cloth and paperback originals. "Graywolf Press is an independent, nonprofit publisher dedicated to the creation and promotion of thoughtful and imaginative contemporary literature essential to a vital and diverse culture." **Publishes 30 titles/year. Pays royalty on retail price. Pays $1,000-25,000 advance.** Publishes 18 months after acceptance. Accepts simultaneous

submissions. Responds in 3 months to queries. Book catalog free. Guidelines online.

NONFICTION Subjects include contemporary culture, culture. Agented submissions only.

FICTION Subjects include short story collections, literary novels. "Familiarize yourself with our list first." No genre books (romance, western, science fiction, suspense) Agented submissions only.

POETRY "We are interested in linguistically challenging work." Agented submissions only.

GREENHAVEN PRESS

27500 Drake Rd., Farmington Hills MI 48331. (800)877-4523. **Website:** www.gale.com/greenhaven. Estab. 1970. Publishes 220 young adult academic reference titles/year. 50% of books by first-time authors. Greenhaven continues to print quality nonfiction anthologies for libraries and classrooms. "Our well-known Opposing Viewpoints series is highly respected by students and librarians in need of material on controversial social issues." Greenhaven accepts no unsolicited mss. Send query, resume, and list of published works by e-mail. Work purchased outright from authors; write-for-hire, flat fee. Accepts simultaneous submissions.

NONFICTION Young adults (high school): controversial issues, social issues, history, literature, science, environment, health.

⊙⊘ GREENWILLOW BOOKS

HarperCollins Publishers, 10 E. 53rd St., New York NY 10022. (212)207-7000. **Website:** www.greenwillowblog.com. Estab. 1974. Publishes hardcover originals, paperbacks, e-books, and reprints. *Does not accept unsolicited mss.* "Unsolicited mail will not be opened and will not be returned." **Publishes 40-50 titles/year. Pays 10% royalty on wholesale price for first-time authors. Offers variable advance.** Publishes ms 2 years after acceptance. Accepts simultaneous submissions.

FICTION Subjects include fantasy, humor, literary, mystery, picture books. *Agented submissions only.*

⊙⊘ GROSSET & DUNLAP PUBLISHERS

Penguin Random House, 345 Hudson St., New York NY 10014. **Website:** www.penguin.com. Estab. 1898. Publishes hardcover (few) and mass market paperback originals. Grosset & Dunlap publishes children's books that show children that reading is fun, with books that speak to their interests, and that are affordable so that children can build a home library of their own. Focus on licensed properties, series and readers. "Grosset & Dunlap publishes high-interest, affordable books for children ages 0-10 years. We focus on original series, licensed properties, readers and novelty books." **Publishes 140 titles/year. Pays royalty. Pays advance.**

NONFICTION Subjects include science. *Agented submissions only.*

FICTION Subjects include juvenile. *Agented submissions only.*

☯ GROUNDWOOD BOOKS

128 Sterling Rd., Lower Level, Attention: Submissions, Toronto ON M6R 2B7, Canada. (416)363-4343. **Fax:** (416)363-1017. **E-mail:** submissions@groundwoodbooks.com. **Website:** groundwoodbooks.com. "We are always looking for new authors of novel-length fiction for children of all ages. Our mandate is to publish high-quality, character-driven literary fiction. We do not generally publish stories with an obvious moral or message, or genre fiction such as thrillers or fantasy." Publishes 19 picture books/year; 2 young readers/year; 3 middle readers/year; 3 young adult titles/year, approximately 2 nonfiction titles/year. **Offers advances.** Accepts simultaneous submissions. Responds to mss in 6-8 months. Visit website for guidelines.

FICTION Submit a cover letter, synopsis and sample chapters via e-mail. "Due to the large number of submissions we receive, Groundwood regrets that we cannot accept unsolicited manuscripts for picture books."

GROUP PUBLISHING, INC.

1515 Cascade Ave., Loveland CO 80539. **E-mail:** info@group.com. **Website:** www.group.com. Estab. 1974. Publishes trade paperback originals. "Our mission is to equip churches to help children, youth, and adults grow in their relationship with Jesus." **Publishes 65 titles/year. 500 queries; 500 mss received/year. 40% of books from first-time authors. 95% from unagented writers. Pays up to 10% royalty on wholesale price or makes outright purchase or work for hire. Pays up to $1,000 advance.** Publishes ms 18 months after acceptance. Accepts simultaneous submissions. Responds in 1 month to queries; 6 months to proposals and mss. Book catalog for 9x12 envelope and 2 first-class stamps.

NONFICTION Subjects include education, religion. "We're an interdenominational publisher of resource materials for people who work with adults, youth or

children in a Christian church setting. We also publish materials for use directly by youth or children (such as devotional books, workbooks or Bibles stories). Everything we do is based on concepts of active and interactive learning as described in *Why Nobody Learns Much of Anything at Church: And How to Fix It*, by Thom and Joani Schultz. We need new, practical, hands-on, innovative, out-of-the-box ideas—things that no one's doing.. yet." Query with SASE. Submit proposal package, outline, 3 sample chapters, cover letter, introduction to book, and sample activities if appropriate.

ⒶⓄ GROVE/ATLANTIC, INC.

154 W. 14th St., 12th Floor, New York NY 10011. **E-mail:** info@groveatlantic.com. **Website:** www.groveatlantic.com. Estab. 1917. Publishes hardcover and trade paperback originals, and reprints. "Due to limited resources of time and staffing, Grove/Atlantic cannot accept manuscripts that do not come through a literary agent. In today's publishing world, agents are more important than ever, helping writers shape their work and navigate the main publishing houses to find the most appropriate outlet for a project." **Publishes 100 titles/year. 1,000+ queries; 1,000+ mss received/year. 10% of books from first-time authors. Pays 7 ½-12 ½% royalty. Makes outright purchase of $5-500,000.** Book published 9 months after acceptance of ms. Accepts simultaneous submissions. Responds in 1 month to queries; 2 months to proposals; 4 months to mss. Book catalog available online.

IMPRINTS Black Cat, Atlantic Monthly Press, Grove Press.

NONFICTION Subjects include creative nonfiction, education, memoirs, philosophy, psychology, science, social sciences, sports, translation. Agented submissions only.

FICTION Subjects include erotica, horror, literary, science fiction, short story collections, suspense, western. Agented submissions only.

POETRY Agented submissions only.

GRYPHON HOUSE, INC.

P.O. Box 10, 6848 Leon's Way, Lewisville NC 27023. (800)638-0928. **E-mail:** info@ghbooks.com. **Website:** www.gryphonhouse.com. Estab. 1981. Publishes trade paperback originals. "At Gryphon House, our goal is to publish books that help teachers and parents enrich the lives of children from birth through age 8. We strive to make our books useful for teachers at all levels of experience, as well as for parents, care-givers, and anyone interested in working with children." Query. Submit outline/synopsis and 2 sample chapters. Responds to queries/mss in 6 months. Publishes a book 18 months after acceptance. Will consider simultaneous submissions, e-mail submissions. Book catalog and ms guidelines available via website or with SASE. **Publishes 12-15 titles/year. Pays royalty on wholesale price.** Responds in 3-6 months to queries. Guidelines available online.

NONFICTION Subjects include child guidance, education. Currently emphasizing social-emotional intelligence and classroom management; de-emphasizing literacy after-school activities. "We prefer to receive a letter of inquiry and/or a proposal, rather than the entire manuscript. Please include: the proposed title, the purpose of the book, table of contents, introductory material, 20-40 sample pages of the actual book. In addition, please describe the book, including the intended audience, why teachers will want to buy it, how it is different from other similar books already published, and what qualifications you possess that make you the appropriate person to write the book. If you have a writing sample that demonstrates that you write clear, compelling prose, please include it with your letter."

⊙⊘ GUERNICA EDITIONS

1569 Heritage Way, Oakville ON L6M 2Z7, Canada. (905)599-5304. **Fax:** (416)981-7606. **E-mail:** michaelmirolla@guernicaeditions.com. **Website:** www.guernicaeditions.com. **Contact:** Michael Mirolla, editor/publisher (poetry, nonfiction, short stories, novels). Publicist: Anna Geisler (annageisler@guernicaeditions.com). Estab. 1978. Publishes trade paperback originals and reprints. Guernica Editions is a literary press that produces works of poetry, fiction and nonfiction often by writers who are ignored by the mainstream. "We feature an imprint (MiroLand) which accepts memoirs, how-to books, graphic novels, genre fiction with the possibility of children's and cook books." A new imprint, Guernica World Editions, features writers who are non-Canadian. **Publishes 25-30 titles/year. Several hundred mss received/year. 20% of books from first-time authors. 99% from unagented writers. Pays 10% royalty on either cover or retail price. Pays $450-750 advance.** Publishes 24-36 months after acceptance. Accepts simultaneous submissions. Responds in 1 month to queries; 6 months to proposals; 1 year to mss. Book catalog online. Queries and submissions accepted via e-mail January 1-April 30.

IMPRINTS MiroLand, Guernica World Editions.

NONFICTION Subjects include contemporary culture, creative nonfiction, ethnic, gay, history, lesbian, literary criticism, literature, memoirs, multicultural, philosophy, politics, pop culture, psychology, regional, social sciences, translation, womens issues, womens studies. Query by e-mail only. Reviews artwork/photos. Send photocopies.

FICTION Subjects include comic books, contemporary, ethnic, experimental, feminist, gay, historical, lesbian, literary, multicultural, mystery, plays, poetry, poetry in translation, science fiction, short story collections, translation. "We wish to open up into the literary fiction world and focus less on poetry." Does not want fantasy, YA. E-mail queries only.

POETRY Feminist, gay/lesbian, literary, multicultural, poetry in translation. Full books only. Query.

GULF PUBLISHING COMPANY

P.O. Box 2608, Houston TX 77252. (713)529-4301. **Fax:** (713)520-4433. **Website:** www.gulfpub.com. Estab. 1916. Publishes hardcover originals and reprints; electronic originals and reprints. "Gulf Publishing Company is the leading publisher to the oil and gas industry. Our specialized publications reach over 100,000 people involved in energy industries worldwide. Our magazines and catalogs help readers keep current with information important to their field and allow advertisers to reach their customers in all segments of petroleum operations. More than half our editorial staff have engineering degrees. The others are thoroughly trained and experienced business journalists and editors." **Publishes 12-15 titles/year. 3-5 queries and mss received in a year. 30% of books from first-time authors. 80% from unagented writers. Royalties on retail price. Pays $1,000-$1,500 advance.** Publishes ms 8-9 months after acceptance. Accepts simultaneous submissions. Responds in 2 months to queries; 1 month to proposals and mss. Catalog free on request. Guidelines available by e-mail.

NONFICTION Subjects include , Engineering. "We don't publish a lot in the year, therefore we are able to focus more on marketing and sales—we are hoping to grow in the future." Submit outline, 1-2 sample chapters, completed ms. Reviews artwork. Send high res file formats with high dpi in b&w.

HAMPTON ROADS PUBLISHING CO., INC.

65 Parker St, Suite 7, Newburyport MA 01950. E-mail: submissions@rwwbooks.com. **Website:** www.redwheelweiser.com. Estab. 1989. Publishes and distributes hardcover and trade paperback originals on subjects including metaphysics, health, complementary medicine, and other related topics. "Our reason for being is to impact, uplift, and contribute to positive change in the world. We publish books that will enrich and empower the evolving consciousness of mankind. Though we are not necessarily limited in scope, we are most interested in manuscripts on the following subjects: Body/Mind/Spirit, Health and Healing, Self-Help. Please be advised that at the moment we are not accepting fiction or novelized material that does not pertain to body/mind/spirit, channeled writing." **Publishes 35-40 titles/year. 1,000 queries; 1,500 mss received/year. 50% of books from first-time authors. 70% from unagented writers. Pays royalty. Pays $1,000-50,000 advance.** Publishes ms 1 year after acceptance. Accepts simultaneous submissions. Responds in 2-4 months to queries; 1 month to proposals; 6-12 months to mss. Guidelines online.

NONFICTION Subjects include New Age, spirituality. Submit by e-mail.

HANCOCK HOUSE PUBLISHERS

Unit 104, 4550 Birch Bay-Lynden Rd., Blaine WA 98230. (800)938-1114. **Fax:** (604)538-2262. **E-mail:** submissions@hancockhouse.com. **Website:** www.hancockhouse.com. Estab. 1971. Publishes hardcover, trade paperback, and e-book originals and reprints. "Hancock House Publishers is the largest North American publisher of wildlife and Native Indian titles. We also cover Pacific Northwest, fishing, history, Canadiana, biographies. We are seeking agriculture, natural history, and popular science titles with a regional (Pacific Northwest), national, or international focus. Currently emphasizing nonfiction wildlife, cryptozoology, guide books, native history, biography, fishing." **Publishes 12-20 titles/year. 50% of books from first-time authors. 90% from unagented writers. Pays 10% royalty.** Publishes book 1 year after acceptance. Accepts simultaneous submissions. Responds to proposals in 3-6 months. Book catalog available free. Guidelines online.

NONFICTION Subjects include agriculture, animals, ethnic, history, horticulture, regional. Centered around Pacific Northwest, local history, nature guide books, international ornithology, and Native Americans. Query via e-mail, including outline with word count, a short author bio, table of contents, 3 sample chapters. Accepts double-spaced word .docs or PDFs. Reviews artwork/photos. Send photocopies.

HANSER PUBLICATIONS

6915 Valley Ave., Cincinnati OH 45244. (800)950-8977. **Fax:** (513)527-8801. **E-mail:** info@hanserpublications.com. **Website:** www.hanserpublications.com. **Contact:** Development Editor. Estab. 1993. Publishes hardcover and paperback originals, and digital educational and training programs. "Hanser Publications publishes books and electronic media for the manufacturing (both metalworking and plastics) industries. Publications range from basic training materials to advanced reference books." **Publishes 10-15 titles/year. 100 queries received/year. 10-20 mss received/year. 50% of books from first-time authors. 100% from unagented writers.** Publishes ms 10 months after acceptance. Accepts simultaneous submissions. Responds in 2 weeks to queries; 1 month to proposals/mss. Book catalog available free. Guidelines available online.

NONFICTION "We publish how-to texts, references, technical books, and computer-based learning materials for the manufacturing industries. Titles include award-winning management books, encyclopedic references, and leading references." Submit outline, sample chapters, resume, preface, and comparison to competing or similar titles.

⚙ HARLEQUIN BLAZE

225 Duncan Mill Rd., Don Mills ON M3B 3K9, Canada. (416)445-5860. **Website:** www.harlequin.com. **Contact:** Kathleen Scheibling, senior editor. Publishes paperback originals. "Harlequin Blaze is a red-hot series. It is a vehicle to build and promote new authors who have a strong sexual edge to their stories. It is also the place to be for seasoned authors who want to create a sexy, sizzling, longer contemporary story." Accepts simultaneous submissions. Guidelines online.

FICTION Subjects include romance. "Sensuous, highly romantic, innovative plots that are sexy in premise and execution. The tone of the books can run from fun and flirtatious to dark and sensual. Submissions should have a very contemporary feel—what it's like to be young and single today. We are looking for heroes and heroines in their early 20s and up. There should be a a strong emphasis on the physical relationship between the couples. Fully described love scenes along with a high level of fantasy and playfulness." Length: 55,000-60,000 words.

HARLEQUIN DESIRE

233 Broadway, Suite 1001, New York NY 10279. (212)553-4200. **Website:** www.harlequin.com. **Contact:** Stacy Boyd, senior editor. Publishes paperback originals and reprints. Always powerful, passionate, and provocative. "Desire novels are sensual reads and a love scene or scenes are still needed. But there is no set number of pages that needs to be fulfilled. Rather, the level of sensuality must be appropriate to the storyline. Above all, every Silhouette Desire novel must fulfill the promise of a powerful, passionate and provocative read." **Pays royalty. Offers advance.** Accepts simultaneous submissions. Guidelines online.

FICTION Subjects include romance. Looking for novels in which "the conflict is an emotional one, springing naturally from the unique characters you've chosen. The focus is on the developing relationship, set in a believable plot. Sensuality is key, but lovemaking is never taken lightly. Secondary characters and subplots need to blend with the core story. Innovative new directions in storytelling and fresh approaches to classic romantic plots are welcome." Manuscripts must be 50,000-55,000 words.

⊙ HARLEQUIN INTRIGUE

225 Duncan Mill Rd., Don Mills ON M3B 3K9, Canada. **Website:** www.harlequin.com. **Contact:** Denise Zaza, senior editor. Wants crime stories tailored to the series romance market packed with a variety of thrilling suspense and whodunit mystery. Word count: 55,000-60,000. Accepts simultaneous submissions. Guidelines online.

FICTION Subjects include mystery, romance, suspense. Submit online.

⊙ HARLEQUIN SUPERROMANCE

225 Duncan Mill Rd., Don Mills ON M3B 3K9, Canada. **Website:** www.harlequin.com. **Contact:** Victoria Curran, senior editor. Publishes paperback originals. "The Harlequin Superromance line focuses on believable characters triumphing over true-to-life drama and conflict. At the heart of these contemporary stories should be a compelling romance that brings the reader along with the hero and heroine on their journey of overcoming the obstacles in their way and falling in love. Because of the longer length relevant subplots and secondary characters are welcome but not required. This series publishes a variety of story types—family sagas, romantic suspense, Westerns, to name a few—and tones from light to dramatic, emotional to suspenseful. Settings also vary from vibrant urban neighborhoods to charming small towns. The unifying element of Harlequin Superromance stories is the realistic treatment of character and plot. The characters should seem familiar to readers—similar to people they know in their own lives—and the circumstances within the realm of possibility. The stories should be layered and complex in that the conflicts should not be easily resolved. The best way to get an idea of we're looking for is to read what we're currently publishing. The aim of Superromance novels is to produce a contemporary, involving read with a mainstream tone in its situations and characters, using romance as the major theme. To achieve this, emphasis should be placed on individual writing styles and unique and topical ideas." **Pays royalties. Pays advance.** Accepts simultaneous submissions. Guidelines online.

FICTION Subjects include romance. "The criteria for Superromance books are flexible. Aside from length (80,000 words), the determining factor for publication will always be quality. Authors should strive to break free of stereotypes, clichés and worn-out plot devices to create strong, believable stories with depth and emotional intensity. Superromance novels are intended to appeal to a wide range of romance readers." Submit online.

HARMONY INK PRESS

Dreamspinner Press, 5032 Capital Circle SW, Suite 2 PMB 279, Tallahassee FL 32305. (850)632-4648. **Fax:** (888)308-3739. **E-mail:** submissions@harmonyink-press.com. **Website:** harmonyinkpress.com. **Contact:** Anne Regan. Estab. 2010. Teen and new adult fiction featuring at least 1 strong LGBTQ+ main character who shows significant personal growth through the course of the story. **Publishes 26 titles/year. Pays royalty. Pays $500-1,000 advance.** Accepts simultaneous submissions.

FICTION "We are looking for stories in all subgenres, featuring primary characters across the whole LGBTQ+ spectrum between the ages of 14 and 21 that explore all the facets of young adult, teen, and new adult life. Sexual content should be appropriate for the characters and the story." Submit complete ms.

ⒶⓄ HARPERBUSINESS

Imprint of HarperCollins General Books Group, 195 Broadway, New York NY 10007. (212)207-7000. **Website:** www.harpercollins.com. Estab. 1991. Publishes hardcover, trade paperback originals and reprints. HarperBusiness publishes the inside story on ideas that will shape business practices with cutting-edge information and visionary concepts. **Pays royalty on retail price. Pays advance.** Accepts simultaneous submissions.

NONFICTION Subjects include , marketing subjects. "We don't publish how-to, textbooks or things for academic market; no reference (tax or mortgage guides), our reference department does that. Proposals need to be top notch. We tend not to publish people who have no business standing. Must have business credentials." Agented submissions only.

ⒶⓄ HARPERCOLLINS

195 Broadway, New York NY 10007. (212)207-7000. **Website:** www.harpercollins.com. Publishes hardcover and paperback originals and paperback reprints. HarperCollins, one of the largest English language publishers in the world, is a broad-based publisher with strengths in academic, business and professional, children's, educational, general interest, and religious and spiritual books, as well as multimedia titles. **Pays royalty. Pays negotiable advance.** Accepts simultaneous submissions.

NONFICTION Agented submissions only. Unsolicited mss returned unopened.

FICTION Subjects include adventure, fantasy, gothic, historical, literary, mystery, science fiction, suspense, western. "We look for a strong story line and exceptional literary talent." Agented submissions only. *All unsolicited mss returned.*

Ⓐ HARPER PERENNIAL

10 E. 53rd St., New York NY 10022. **E-mail:** harperperennial@harpercollins.com. **Website:** harperperennial.tumblr.com. Harper Perennial is one of the paperback imprints of HarperCollins. "We publish paperback originals and reprints of authors like Ann Patchett, Justin Taylor, Barbara Kingsolver, and Blake Butler. Accepts simultaneous submissions.

ⒶⓄ HARPER VOYAGER

Imprint of HarperCollins General Books Group, 195 Broadway, New York NY 10007. (212)207-7000. **Website:** www.harpercollins.com. Estab. 1998. Publishes hardcover originals, trade and mass market paperback originals, and reprints. Eos publishes quality science fiction/fantasy with broad appeal. **Pays royalty on retail price. Pays variable advance.** Accepts simultaneous submissions. Guidelines online.

FICTION Subjects include fantasy, science fiction. No horror or juvenile. Agented submissions only. *All unsolicited mss returned.*

THE HARVARD COMMON PRESS

100 Cummings Center, Suite 406-L, Beverly MA 01915. (978)282-9590. **Fax:** (978)282-7765. **E-mail:** info@harvardcommonpress.com. **E-mail:** editorial@harvardcommonpress.com. **Website:** https://www.quartoknows.com/Harvard-Common-Press. **Contact:** Submissions. Estab. 1976. Publishes hardcover and trade paperback originals and reprints. "We want strong, practical books that help people gain control over a particular area of their lives. Currently emphasizing cooking, child care/parenting, health. De-emphasizing general instructional books, travel." **Publishes 16 titles/year. 20% of books from first-time authors. 40% from unagented writers. Pays royalty. Pays average $2,500-10,000 advance.** Publishes ms 1 year after acceptance. Accepts simultaneous submissions. Responds in 2 months to queries. Guidelines online.

NONFICTION Subjects include child guidance. "A large percentage of our list is made up of books about cooking, child care, and parenting; in these areas we are looking for authors who are knowledgeable, if not experts, and who can offer a different approach to the subject. We are open to good nonfiction proposals that show evidence of strong organization and writing, and clearly demonstrate a need in the marketplace. First-time authors are welcome." Submit outline. Potential authors may also submit a query letter or e-mail of no more than 300 words, rather than a full proposal; if interested, will ask to see a proposal. Queries and questions may be sent via e-mail. "We will not consider e-mail attachments containing proposals. No phone calls, please."

ⒶⓄ HARVEST HOUSE PUBLISHERS

990 Owen Loop, Eugene OR 97402. (541)343-0123. **Fax:** (541)302-0731. **Website:** www.harvesthouse-

publishers.com. Estab. 1974. Publishes hardcover, trade paperback, and mass market paperback originals and reprints. **Publishes 160 titles/year. 1,500 queries; 1,000 mss received/year. 1% of books from first-time authors. Pays royalty.** Accepts simultaneous submissions.

NONFICTION Subjects include child guidance, religion, Bible studies. *No unsolicited mss.*

FICTION *No unsolicited mss, proposals, or artwork.* Agented submissions only.

Ⓐ HAY HOUSE, INC.

P.O. Box 5100, Carlsbad CA 92018. (760)431-7695. **Fax:** (760)431-6948. **E-mail:** editorial@hayhouse.com. **Website:** www.hayhouse.com. Estab. 1985. Publishes hardcover, trade paperback and e-book/POD originals. "We publish books, audios, and videos that help heal the planet." **Publishes 50 titles/year. Pays standard royalty.** Accepts simultaneous submissions. Guidelines online.

IMPRINTS Hay House Lifestyles; Hay House Insights; Hay House Visions; SmileyBooks.

NONFICTION Subjects include alternative lifestyles, astrology, cooking, education, foods, health, New Age, nutrition, philosophy, psychic, psychology, sociology, spirituality, womens issues, mind/body/spirit. "Hay House is interested in a variety of subjects as long as they have a positive self-help slant to them. No poetry, children's books, or negative concepts that are not conducive to helping/healing ourselves or our planet." Accepts e-mail submissions from agents.

HEALTH COMMUNICATIONS, INC.

3201 SW 15th St., Deerfield Beach FL 33442. (954)360-0909, ext. 232. **Fax:** (954)360-0034. **E-mail:** editorial@hcibooks.com. **Website:** www.hcibooks.com. **Contact:** Editorial Committee. Estab. 1976. Publishes hardcover and trade paperback nonfiction only. "While HCI is a best known for recovery publishing, today recovery is only one part of a publishing program that includes titles in self-help and psychology, health and wellness, spirituality, inspiration, women's and men's issues, relationships, family, teens and children, memoirs, mind/body/spirit integration, and gift books." **Publishes 60 titles/year.** Accepts simultaneous submissions. Responds in 3-6 months. Guidelines online.

NONFICTION Subjects include child guidance, health, parenting, psychology, young adult, self-help.

WILLIAM S. HEIN & CO., INC.

2350 N. Forest Rd., Getzville NY 14068. (716)882-2600. **Fax:** (716)883-8100. **E-mail:** mail@wshein.com. **Website:** www.wshein.com. Estab. 1961. "William S. Hein & Co. publishes reference books for law librarians, legal researchers, and those interested in legal writing. Currently emphasizing legal research, legal writing, and legal education." **Publishes 18 titles/year. 30 queries received/year. 15 mss received/year. 30% of books from first-time authors. 99% from unagented writers. Pays 10-20% royalty on net price for print; higher royalties if published as an e-book.** Publishes book 9 months after acceptance. Accepts simultaneous submissions. Responds in 6 weeks to queries. Book catalog online. Guidelines by e-mail.

NONFICTION Subjects include education, law, world affairs, legislative histories.

HELLGATE PRESS

L&R Publishing, LLC, P.O. Box 3531, Ashland OR 97520. (541)973-5154. **E-mail:** sales@hellgatepress.com. **Website:** www.hellgatepress.com. **Contact:** Harley B. Patrick. Estab. 1996. "Hellgate Press specializes in military history, veteran memoirs, other military topics, travel adventure, and historical/adventure fiction." **Publishes 15-25 titles/year. 85% of books from first-time authors. 95% from unagented writers. Pays royalty.** Publishes ms 6-9 months after acceptance. Accepts simultaneous submissions. Responds in 2 months to queries.

NONFICTION Subjects include history, memoirs, military, war, womens issues, world affairs, young adult. Query/proposal by e-mail only. No phone queries, please. *Do not send mss.*

FICTION Subjects include historical, military, war, young adult.

Ⓞ HENDRICKSON PUBLISHERS, INC.

P.O. Box 3473, Peabody MA 01961. **Fax:** (978)573-8276. **E-mail:** editorial@hendrickson.com. **Website:** www.hendrickson.com. Estab. 1981. Publishes trade reprints, bibles, and scholarly material in the areas of New Testament; Hebrew Bible; religion and culture; patristics; Judaism; and practical, historical, and Biblical theology. "Hendrickson is an academic publisher of Biblical scholarship and trade books that encourage spiritual growth. Currently emphasizing Biblical language and reference, pastoral resources, and Biblical studies." **Publishes 35 titles/year. 800 queries received/year. 10% of books from first-time authors.**

90% from unagented writers. Publishes ms 1 year after acceptance. Guidelines online.

NONFICTION Subjects include contemporary culture, creative nonfiction, education, entertainment, film, history, humanities, language, literature, religion, social sciences, spirituality. "We cannot accept unsolicited mss or book proposals except through one of the 2 following avenues: Materials sent to our editorial staff through a professional literary agent will be considered; Our staff would be happy to discuss book ideas at the various conferences we attend throughout the year (most notably, the AAR/SBL annual meeting)."

HERITAGE BOOKS, INC.

5810 Ruatan St., Berwyn Heights MD 20740. (800)876-6103. **Fax:** (800)876-6103. **E-mail:** info@heritagebooks.com. **E-mail:** submissions@heritagebooks.com. **Website:** www.heritagebooks.com. Estab. 1978. Publishes hardcover and paperback originals and reprints. "Our goal is to celebrate life by exploring all aspects of American life: settlement, development, wars, and other significant events, including family histories, memoirs, etc. Currently emphasizing early American life, early wars and conflicts, ethnic studies." **Publishes 200 titles/year. 25% of books from first-time authors. Pays 10% royalty on list price. Does not pay advance.** Ms published 1-3 months after acceptance. Responds in 3 months to queries. Book catalog and ms guidelines free.

NONFICTION Subjects include Americana, ethnic, history, memoirs, military, regional, war. Military memoirs. Query with SASE. Submit outline via e-mail. Reviews artwork/photos.

☼ HERITAGE HOUSE PUBLISHING CO., LTD.

103-1075 Pendergast St., Victoria BC V8V 0A1, Canada. (250)360-0829. **E-mail:** heritage@heritagehouse.ca. **Website:** www.heritagehouse.ca. **Contact:** Lara Kordic, senior editor. Publishes mostly trade paperback and some hardcovers. "Heritage House publishes books that celebrate the historical and cultural heritage of Canada, particularly Western Canada and the Pacific Northwest. We also publish some children's titles, titles of national interest and a series of books aimed at young and casual readers, called *Amazing Stories*. We accept simultaneous submissions, but indicate on your query that it is a simultaneous submission." **Publishes 25-30 titles/year. 200 queries;**

100 mss received/year. 50% of books from first-time authors. 90% from unagented writers. Pays 12-15% royalty on net proceeds. Advances are rarely paid. Publishes book within 1-2 years of acceptance. Accepts simultaneous submissions. Responds in 6 months to queries. Catalog and guidelines online.

NONFICTION Subjects include animals, anthropology, art, business, community, contemporary culture, creative nonfiction, environment, ethnic, history, humanities, marine subjects, multicultural, politics, pop culture, public affairs, regional, war, womens issues, adventure, contemporary Canadian culture. Query by e-mail. Include synopsis, outline, 2-3 sample chapters with indication of illustrative material available, and marketing strategy.

HEYDAY BOOKS

c/o Acquisitions Editor, Box 9145, Berkeley CA 94709. **Fax:** (510)549-1889. **E-mail:** heyday@heydaybooks.com. **Website:** www.heydaybooks.com. **Contact:** Gayle Wattawa, acquisitions and editorial director. Estab. 1974. Publishes hardcover originals, trade paperback originals and reprints. "Heyday Books publishes nonfiction books and literary anthologies with a strong California focus. We publish books about Native Americans, natural history, history, literature, and recreation, with a strong California focus." **Publishes 12-15 titles/year. 50% of books from first-time authors. 90% from unagented writers. Pays 8% royalty on net price.** Publishes book 18 months after acceptance. Responds in 3 months. Book catalog online. Guidelines online.

NONFICTION Subjects include Americana, ethnic, history, recreation, regional, travel. Books about California only. Query with outline and synopsis. "Query or proposal by traditional post. Include a cover letter introducing yourself and your qualifications, a brief description of your project, a table of contents and list of illustrations, notes on the market you are trying to reach and why your book will appeal to them, a sample chapter, and a SASE if you would like us to return these materials to you." Reviews artwork/photos.

FICTION Publishes picture books, beginning readers, and young adult literature. Submit complete ms for picture books; proposal with sample chapters for longer works. include a chapter by chapter summary. Mark attention: Children's Submission. Reviews manuscript/illustration packages; but may consider art and text separately. Tries to respond to query within 12 weeks.

Ⓐ⊘ HILL AND WANG

Farrar Straus & Giroux, Inc., 18 W. 18th St., New York NY 10011. (212)741-6900. **Fax:** (212)633-9385. **Website:** www.fsgbooks.com. Estab. 1956. Publishes hardcover and trade paperbacks. "Hill and Wang publishes serious nonfiction books, primarily in history, science, mathematics and the social sciences. We are not considering new fiction, drama, or poetry." **Publishes 12 titles/year. 1,500 queries received/year. 50% of books from first-time authors. 50% from unagented writers.** Publishes ms 1 year after acceptance. Accepts simultaneous submissions. Book catalog available free.

NONFICTION Subjects include history. *Agented submissions only.*

LAWRENCE HILL BOOKS

Chicago Review Press, 814 N. Franklin St., 2nd Floor, Chicago IL 60610. (312)337-0747. **Fax:** (312)337-5110. **Website:** www.chicagoreviewpress.com. **Contact:** Yuval Taylor, senior editor. Publishes hardcover originals and trade paperback originals and reprints. **Publishes 3-10 titles/year. 20 queries; 10 mss received/year. 40% of books from first-time authors. 50% from unagented writers. Pays 7-12% royalty on retail price. Pays $3,000-10,000 advance.** Publishes ms 1 year after acceptance. Accepts simultaneous submissions. Responds in 1 month to queries; 2 months to proposals and mss. Book catalog available free.

NONFICTION Subjects include ethnic, history, multicultural. Submit proposal package, outline, 2 sample chapters.

HOLIDAY HOUSE, INC.

425 Madison Ave., New York NY 10017. (212)688-0085. **Fax:** (212)421-6134. **E-mail:** info@holidayhouse.com. **Website:** holidayhouse.com. Estab. 1935. Publishes hardcover originals and paperback reprints. "Holiday House publishes children's and young adult books for the school and library markets. We have a commitment to publishing first-time authors and illustrators. We specialize in quality hardcovers from picture books to young adult, both fiction and nonfiction, primarily for the school and library market." **Publishes 50 titles/year. 5% of books from first-time authors. 50% from unagented writers. Pays royalty on list price, range varies.** Publishes 1-2 years after acceptance. Responds in 4 months. Guidelines for #10 SASE.

NONFICTION Subjects include Americana, history, science, Judaica. Please send the entire ms, whether submitting a picture book or novel. "All submissions should be directed to the Editorial Department, Holiday House. We do not accept certified or registered mail. There is no need to include a SASE. We do not consider submissions by e-mail or fax. Please note that you do not have to supply illustrations. However, if you have illustrations you would like to include with your submission, you may send detailed sketches or photocopies of the original art. Do not send original art." Reviews artwork/photos. Send photocopies-no originals.

FICTION Subjects include adventure, historical, humor, literary, Judaica and holiday, animal stories for young readers.. Children's books only. Query with SASE. No phone calls, please.

TIPS "We need manuscripts with strong stories and writing."

Ⓐ⊘ HENRY HOLT

175 Fifth Ave., New York NY 10011. (646)307-5095. **Fax:** (212)633-0748. **Website:** www.henryholt.com. *Agented submissions only.* Accepts simultaneous submissions.

HOPEWELL PUBLICATIONS

P.O. Box 11, Titusville NJ 08560. **Website:** www.hopepubs.com. **Contact:** E. Martin, publisher. Estab. 2002. Format publishes in hardcover, trade paperback, and electronic originals; trade paperback and electronic reprints. "Hopewell Publications specializes in classic reprints—books with proven sales records that have gone out of print—and new titles of interest. Our catalog spans from 1 to 60 years of publication history. We print fiction and nonfiction, and we accept agented and unagented materials. Submissions are accepted online only." **Publishes 20-30 titles/year. Receives 2,000 queries/year; 500 mss/year. 25% of books from first-time authors. 75% from unagented writers. Pays royalty on retail price.** Publishes ms 6-12 months after acceptance. Accepts simultaneous submissions. Responds in 3 months to queries; 6 months to proposals; 9 months to mss. Catalog online. Guidelines online.

IMPRINTS Hopewell Publications, Egress Books, Legacy Classics.

NONFICTION Subjects include , All nonfiction subjects acceptable. Query online using online guidelines.

FICTION Subjects include adventure, confession, contemporary, experimental, fantasy, feminist, gay, historical, humor, juvenile, literary, mainstream, mystery, plays, science fiction, short story collections, spiritual, suspense, young adult, All fiction subjects acceptable. Query online using our online guidelines.

HOUGHTON MIFFLIN HARCOURT BOOKS FOR CHILDREN

Imprint of Houghton Mifflin Trade & Reference Division, 222 Berkeley St., Boston MA 02116. (617)351-5000. **Fax:** (617)351-1111. **Website:** www.houghton-mifflinbooks.com. Publishes hardcover originals and trade paperback originals and reprints. Houghton Mifflin Harcourt gives shape to ideas that educate, inform, and above all, delight. *Does not respond to or return mss unless interested.* **Publishes 100 titles/year. 5,000 queries received/year. 14,000 mss received/year. 10% of books from first-time authors. 60% from unagented writers. Pays 5-10% royalty on retail price. Pays variable advance.** Publishes ms 2 years after acceptance. Accepts simultaneous submissions. Responds in 4-6 months to queries. Guidelines online.

NONFICTION Subjects include animals, ethnic, history, science, sports. Interested in innovative books and subjects about which the author is passionate. Query with SASE. Submit sample chapters, synopsis. Reviews artwork/photos. Send photocopies.

FICTION Subjects include adventure, ethnic, historical, humor, juvenile, literary, mystery, picture books, suspense, young adult, board books. Submit complete ms.

Ⓐ⊘ HOUGHTON MIFFLIN HARCOURT CO.

222 Berkeley St., Boston MA 02116. (617)351-5000. **Website:** www.hmhco.com. Estab. 1832. Publishes hardcover originals and trade paperback originals and reprints. "Houghton Mifflin Harcourt gives shape to ideas that educate, inform and delight. In a new era of publishing, our legacy of quality thrives as we combine imagination with technology, bringing you new ways to know." Accepts simultaneous submissions.

NONFICTION "We are not a mass market publisher. Our main focus is serious nonfiction. We do practical self-help but not pop psychology self-help." *Agented submissions only. Unsolicited mss returned unopened.*

☺⊘ HOUSE OF ANANSI PRESS

128 Sterling Rd., Lower Level, Toronto ON M6R 2B7, Canada. (416)363-4343. **Fax:** (416)363-1017. **Website:** www.anansi.ca. Estab. 1967. House of Anansi publishes literary fiction and poetry by Canadian and international writers. **Pays 8-10% royalties. Pays $750 advance and 10 author's copies.** Responds to queries within 1 year; to mss (if invited) within 4 months. Accepts simultaneous submissions.

NONFICTION Avoids dry, jargon-filled academic prose and has a literary twist that will interest general readers and experts alike. Query with SASE.

FICTION Publishes literary fiction that has a unique flair, memorable characters, and a strong narrative voice. Query with SASE.

POETRY "We seek to balance the list between well-known and emerging writers, with an interest in writing by Canadians of all backgrounds. We publish Canadian poetry only, and poets must have a substantial publication record—if not in books, then definitely in journals and magazines of repute." Does not want "children's poetry or poetry by previously unpublished poets." Canadian poets should query first with 10 sample poems (typed double-spaced) and a cover letter with brief bio and publication credits. Considers simultaneous submissions. Poems are circulated to an editorial board. Often comments on rejected poems.

HOW BOOKS

F+W, a Content + eCommerce Company, 10151 Carver Rd., Suite 200, Blue Ash OH 45242. (513)531-2690. **Website:** www.howdesign.com. Estab. 1985. Publishes hardcover and trade paperback originals. **Publishes 15 titles/year. 50 queries; 5 mss received/year. 50% of books from first-time authors. 50% from unagented writers. Pays 10% royalty on wholesale price. Pays $2,000-6,000 advance.** Publishes ms 18-24 months after acceptance. Accepts simultaneous submissions. Responds in 1 month to queries and proposals; 3 months to mss. Book catalog available online. Guidelines available online.

NONFICTION Subjects include graphic design, web design, creativity, pop culture. "We look for material that reflects the cutting edge of trends, graphic design, and culture. Nearly all HOW Books are intensely visual, and authors must be able to create or supply art/illustration for their books." Query via e-mail. Submit proposal package, outline, 1 sample chapter, sample art or sample design. Reviews artwork/photos. Send as PDF's.

HUMAN KINETICS PUBLISHERS, INC.

P.O. Box 5076, Champaign IL 61825-5076. (800)747-4457. **Fax:** (217)351-1549. **E-mail:** acquisitions@hkusa.com. **Website:** www.humankinetics.com. Estab. 1974. Publishes hardcover, ebooks, and paperback text and reference books, trade paperback originals, course software and audiovisual. "*Human Kinetics* publishes books which provide expert knowledge in sport and fitness training and techniques, physical education, sports sciences and sports medicine for coaches, athletes and fitness enthusiasts and professionals in the physical action field." **Publishes 160 titles/year. Pays 10-15% royalty on net income.** Publishes ms up to 18 months after acceptance. Accepts simultaneous submissions. Responds in 2 months to queries. Book catalog available free. Guidelines online.

NONFICTION Subjects include education, psychology, recreation, sports. "Here is a current listing of our divisions: Amer. Sport Education; Aquatics Edu.; Professional Edu.; HPERD Div., Journal Div.; STM Div., Trade Div." Submit outline, sample chapters. Reviews artwork/photos.

IBEX PUBLISHERS

P.O. Box 30087, Bethesda MD 20824. (301)718-8188. **Fax:** (301)907-8707. **E-mail:** info@ibexpub.com. **Website:** www.ibexpublishers.com. Estab. 1979. Publishes hardcover and trade paperback originals and reprints. "Ibex publishes books about Iran and the Middle East and about Persian culture and literature." **Publishes 10-12 titles/year. Payment varies.** Accepts simultaneous submissions. Book catalog available free.

IMPRINTS Iranbooks Press.

NONFICTION Subjects include cooking, history, humanities, language, literary criticism, literature, spirituality, translation. Query with SASE, or submit proposal package, including outline and 2 sample chapters.

POETRY "Translations of Persian poets will be considered."

ILR PRESS

Cornell University Press, Sage House, 512 E. State St., Ithaca NY 14850. (607)277-2338. **Fax:** (607)277-2374. **E-mail:** fgb2@cornell.edu. **Website:** www.cornellpress.cornell.edu. **Contact:** Frances Benson, editorial director. Estab. 1945. Publishes hardcover and trade paperback originals and reprints. "We are interested in manuscripts with innovative perspectives on current workplace issues that concern both academics and the general public." **Publishes 10-15 titles/year. Pays royalty.** Responds in 2 months to queries. Book catalog available online. Guidelines online.

NONFICTION Subjects include history, sociology. All titles relate to labor relations and/or workplace issues including relevant work in the fields of history, sociology, political science, economics, human resources, and organizational behavior. Special series: culture and politics of health care work. Query with SASE. Submit outline, sample chapters, CV.

IMAGE COMICS

2701 NW Vaughn St., Suite 780, Portland OR 97210. **E-mail:** submissions@imagecomics.com. **Website:** www.imagecomics.com. Estab. 1992. Publishes creator-owned comic books, graphic novels. See this company's website for detailed guidelines. Does not accept writing samples without art. Accepts simultaneous submissions.

FICTION Query with 1-page synopsis and 5 pages or more of samples. "We do not accept writing (that is plots, scripts, whatever) samples! If you're an established pro, we might be able to find somebody willing to work with you but it would be nearly impossible for us to read through every script that might find its way our direction. Do not send your script or your plot unaccompanied by art—it will be discarded, unread."

IMPACT BOOKS

F+W Media, Inc., 10151 Carver Rd., Suite 300, Blue Ash OH 45242. **Website:** www.northlightshop.com; www.impact-books.com. Estab. 2004. Publishes trade paperback originals. IMPACT Books publishes titles that emphasize illustrated how-to-draw-manga, science-fiction, fantasy and comics art instruction. Currently emphasizing manga and anime art, science fiction, traditional American comics styles, including humor, and pop art. Looking for good science fiction art instruction. This market is for experienced artists who are willing to work with an IMPACT editor to produce a step-by-step how-to book about how to create the art and the artist's creative process. **Publishes 9 titles/year. 50 queries; 10-12 mss received/year. 70% of books from first-time authors. 80% from unagented writers. Pays advance.** Publishes ms 11 months after acceptance. Accepts simultaneous submissions. Responds in 4 months. Visit website for booklist. Guidelines available online.

NONFICTION Subjects include art, contemporary culture, creative nonfiction, hobbies. Submit via e-mail only. Submit proposal package, outline, 1 sample chapter, at least 20 examples of sample art. Reviews artwork/photos. Send digital art.

INCENTIVE PUBLICATIONS, INC.

233 N. Michigan Ave., Suite 2000, Chicago IL 60601. **E-mail:** incentive@worldbook.com. **Website:** www.incentivepublications.com. Estab. 1970. Publishes paperback originals. "Incentive publishes developmentally appropriate teacher/school administrator/parent resource materials and supplementary instructional materials for children in grades K-12. Actively seeking proposals for student workbooks, all grades/all subjects, and professional development resources for pre K-12 classroom teachers and school administrators." **Publishes 10-15 titles/year. 25% of books from first-time authors. 100, but agent proposals welcome% from unagented writers. Pays royalty, or makes outright purchase.** an average of 1 year Accepts simultaneous submissions. Responds in 1 month to queries.

NONFICTION Subjects include education. Instructional, teacher/administrator professional development books in pre-K through 12th grade. Query with synopsis and detailed outline.

INDIANA HISTORICAL SOCIETY PRESS

450 W. Ohio St., Indianapolis IN 46202. (317)233-6073. **Fax:** (317)233-0857. **E-mail:** ihspress@indianahistory.org. **Website:** www.indianahistory.org. **Contact:** Submissions Editor. Estab. 1830. Publishes hardcover and paperback originals. **Publishes 10 titles/year.** Accepts simultaneous submissions. Responds in 1 month to queries.

NONFICTION Subjects include agriculture, ethnic, history, sports, family history, children's books. All topics must relate to Indiana. "We seek book-length manuscripts that are solidly researched and engagingly written on topics related to Indiana: biography, history, literature, music, politics, transportation, sports, agriculture, architecture, and children's books." Query with SASE.

INFORMATION TODAY, INC.

143 Old Marlton Pike, Medford NJ 08055. (609)654-6266. **Fax:** (609)654-4309. **E-mail:** rcolding@infotoday.com. **Website:** www.infotoday.com. **Contact:** Rob Colding, Book Marketing Manager. Publishes hardcover and trade paperback originals. "We look for highly-focused coverage of cutting-edge technology topics. Written by established experts and targeted to a tech-savvy readership. Virtually all our titles focus on how information is accessed, used, shared, and transformed into knowledge that can benefit people, business, and society. Currently emphasizing Web 2.0, internet/online technologies, including their social significance: biography, how-to, technical, reference, scholarly. De-emphasizing fiction." **Publishes 15-20 titles/year. 200 queries; 30 mss received/year. 30% of books from first-time authors. 90% from unagented writers. Pays 10-15% royalty on wholesale price. Pays $500-2,500 advance.** Publishes book 9 months after acceptance. Accepts simultaneous submissions. Responds in 1 month to queries; 2 months to proposals; 3 months to mss. Book catalog free or on website. Proposal guidelines free or via e-mail as attachment.

IMPRINTS ITI (academic, scholarly, library science); CyberAge Books (high-end consumer and business technology books-emphasis on Internet/WWW topics including online research).

NONFICTION Subjects include business, computers, education, science, Internet and cyberculture. Query with SASE. Reviews artwork/photos. Send photocopies.

☺ INSOMNIAC PRESS

520 Princess Ave., London ON N6B 2B8, Canada. (416)504-6270. **Website:** www.insomniacpress.com. Estab. 1992. Publishes trade paperback originals and reprints, mass market paperback originals, and electronic originals and reprints. **Publishes 20 titles/year. 250 queries received/year. 1,000 mss received/year. 50% of books from first-time authors. 80% from unagented writers. Pays 10-15% royalty on retail price. Pays $500-1,000 advance.** Publishes ms 6 months after acceptance. Accepts simultaneous submissions. Guidelines online.

NONFICTION Subjects include multicultural, religion, true crime. Very interested in areas such as true crime and well-written and well-researched nonfiction on topics of wide interest. Query via e-mail, submit proposal package including outline, 2 sample chapters, or submit complete ms. Reviews artwork/photos. Send photocopies.

FICTION Subjects include comic books, ethnic, experimental, humor, literary, mystery, poetry, suspense. "We publish a mix of commercial (mysteries) and literary fiction." Query via e-mail, submit proposal.

POETRY "Our poetry publishing is limited to 2-4 books per year and we are often booked up a year or two in advance." Submit complete ms.

INTERLINK PUBLISHING GROUP, INC.

46 Crosby St., Northampton MA 01060. (413)582-7054. **E-mail:** info@interlinkbooks.com. **E-mail:** submissions@interlinkbooks.com. **Website:** www.interlinkbooks.com. Estab. 1987. Publishes hardcover and trade paperback originals. Interlink is an independent publisher of general trade adult fiction and nonfiction with an emphasis on books that have a wide appeal while also meeting high intellectual and literary standards. "Our list is devoted to works of literature, history, contemporary politics, travel, art, and cuisine from around the world, often from areas underrepresented in Western media." **Publishes 50 titles/year. 30% of books from first-time authors. 50% from unagented writers. Pays 6-8% royalty on retail price. Pays small advance.** Publishes ms 18 months after acceptance. Accepts simultaneous submissions. Responds in 3-6 months to queries. Book catalog and guidelines online.

IMPRINTS Olive Branch Press; Crocodile Books; Interlink Books.

NONFICTION Subjects include contemporary culture, creative nonfiction, ethnic, foods, history, humanities, literary criticism, literature, multicultural, politics, regional, translation, war, womens issues, world affairs. Submit outline and sample chapters via e-mail.

FICTION Subjects include ethnic, feminist, literary, multicultural, translation, international. "We are looking for translated works relating to the Middle East, Africa or Latin America. The only fiction we publish falls into our 'Interlink World Fiction' series. Most of these books, as you can see in our catalog, are translated fiction from around the world. The series aims to bring fiction from other countries to a North American audience. In short, unless you were born outside the United States, your novel will not fit into the series." No science fiction, romance, plays, erotica, fantasy, horror. Query by e-mail. Submit outline, sample chapters.

INTERNATIONAL MARINE

The McGraw-Hill Companies, 90 Mechanic St., Camden ME 04843. (207)236-4838. **Fax:** (207)236-6314. **E-mail:** christopher.brown@mheducation.com. **Website:** www.internationalmarine.com. **Contact:** Acquisitions Editor. Estab. 1969. Publishes hardcover and paperback originals. International Marine publishes the best books about boats. **Publishes 50 titles/year. 500-700 mss received/year. 30% of books from first-time authors. 60% from unagented writers. Pays standard royalties based on net price. Pays advance.** Publishes ms 1 year after acceptance. Accepts simultaneous submissions. Responds in 2 months to queries. Guidelines online.

IMPRINTS Ragged Mountain Press (sports and outdoor books that take you off the beaten path).

NONFICTION All books are illustrated. Material in all stages welcome. Publishes a wide range of subjects include: sea stories, seamanship, boat maintenance, etc. Query first with outline and 2-3 sample chapters. Reviews artwork/photos.

INTERNATIONAL PRESS

P.O. Box 502, Somerville MA 02143. (617)623-3855. **Fax:** (617)623-3101. **E-mail:** ipb-mgmt@intlpress.com. **Website:** www.intlpress.com. **Contact:** Brian Bianchini. Estab. 1992. Publishes hardcover originals and reprints. International Press of Boston, Inc. is an academic publishing company that welcomes book publication inquiries from prospective authors on all topics in Mathematics and Physics. International Press also publishes high-level mathematics and mathematical physics book titles and textbooks. **Publishes 12 titles/year. 200 queries received/year. 500 mss received/year. 10% of books from first-time authors. 100% from unagented writers. Pays 3-10% royalty.** Publishes ms 6 months after acceptance. Responds in 5 months to queries and proposals; 1 year to mss. Book catalog available free. Guidelines online.

NONFICTION Subjects include science. All our books will be in research mathematics. Authors need to provide ready to print latex files. Submit complete ms. Reviews artwork/photos. Send EPS files.

INTERNATIONAL SOCIETY FOR TECHNOLOGY IN EDUCATION (ISTE)

1530 Wilson Blvd., Suite 730, Arlington VA 22209. (703)348-4784. **E-mail:** iste@iste.org. **Website:** www.iste.org. Publishes trade paperback originals. "Currently emphasizing books on educational technology standards, curriculum integration, professional development, and assessment. De-emphasizing software how-to books." **Publishes 10 titles/year. 100 queries received/year. 40 mss received/year. 75% of books from first-time authors. 95% from unagented writers. Pays 10% royalty on retail price.** Publishes ms 6-9 months after acceptance. Accepts simultaneous submissions. Responds in 2 weeks to queries; 1 month to proposals and mss. Book catalog and guidelines online.

NONFICTION Submit proposal package, outline, sample chapters, TOC, vita. Reviews artwork/photos. Send photocopies.

INTERNATIONAL WEALTH SUCCESS INC.

IWS Inc., P.O. Box 186, Merrick NY 11570. (516)766-5850. **Fax:** (516)766-5919. **E-mail:** admin@iwsmoney.com. **Website:** www.iwsmoney.com. **Contact:** Tyler G. Hicks, president. Estab. 1966. International Wealth Success Inc. (IWS) is a full-service newsletter, book and self-study course publisher of print and digital media on small business and income real estate. The company's mission is to help beginning and experienced business people choose, start, finance, and succeed in their own small businesses. Topics include real estate investment, import-export, mail order, home-based business, marketing, fundraising, and financing. **Publishes 10 titles/year. Pays 10% royalty on wholesale or retail price.** Publishes ms 4 months after acceptance. Accepts simultaneous submissions. Responds within 1 month to queries. Catalog online.

NONFICTION Subjects include business, career guidance, finance, real estate, private money, financial institutions, homebased business, marketing, export-import, grants and fundraising. Techniques, methods, sources for building wealth. Personal, how-to-do-it with case histories and examples. Publications are aimed at aspiring wealth builders and are sympathetic to their problems and challenges. Publications present a wide range of business opportunities while providing practical, hands-on, step-by-step instructions aimed at helping readers achieve their personal goals in as short a time as possible while adhering to ethical and professional business standards. Length: 60,000-70,000 words. Does not want anything that doesn't pertain to small business, entrepreneurism, business opportunities, or real estate. Query. Reviews artwork/photos.

INTERVARSITY PRESS

P.O. Box 1400, Downers Grove IL 60515. **E-mail:** email@ivpress.com. **Website:** www.ivpress.com/submissions. Estab. 1947. Publishes hardcover originals, trade paperback and mass market paperback originals. "InterVarsity Press publishes a full line of books from an explicitly Christian perspective targeted to an open-minded audience. We serve those in the university, the academy, the church, and the world." **Publishes 115 titles/year. 1,000 queries; 900 mss received/year. 13% of books from first-time authors. 80% from unagented writers. Pays 14-16% royalty on retail price. Outright purchase is $75-1,500. Pays negotiable advance.** Publishes book 18 months after acceptance. Accepts simultaneous submissions. "We are unable to provide updates on the review process or personalized responses to unsolicited proposals. We regret that submissions will not be returned." Book catalog online. Guidelines online.

IMPRINTS IVP Academic; IVP Connect; IVP Books.

NONFICTION Subjects include business, child guidance, contemporary culture, economics, ethnic, history, multicultural, philosophy, psychology, religion, science, social sciences, sociology, spirituality. "InterVarsity Press publishes a full line of books from an explicitly Christian perspective targeted to an open-minded audience. We serve those in the university, the academy, the church, and the world." "We review The Writer's Edge at writersedgeservice.com." Does not review artwork.

IRISH ACADEMIC PRESS

Tuckmill House, 10 George's St., Newbridge Co. Kildare W12 PX39, Ireland. (353)(45)432497. **E-mail:** info@iap.ie. **E-mail:** conor.graham@iap.ie. **Website:** www.iap.ie. **Contact:** Conor Graham. Estab. 1974. Publishes nonfiction. **Publishes 10 titles/year. Pays royalty.** Accepts simultaneous submissions. Responds in 8 weeks. Guidelines online.

IMPRINTS Merrion Press.

NONFICTION Subjects include art, history, humanities, literary criticism, military, politics, social sciences, womens studies, genealogy, Irish history. Does not want fiction or poetry.

IRON GATE PUBLISHING

P.O. Box 999, Niwot CO 80544. **E-mail:** editor@irongate.com. **Website:** www.irongate.com. **Contact:** Dina C. Carson, publisher (how-to, genealogy, local history). Publishes hardcover and trade paperback originals. "Our readers are people who are looking for solid, how-to advice on self-publishing a family or local history, or who are conducting genealogical or local history research in Colorado." **Publishes 20-30 titles/year. 100 queries; 20 mss received/year. 30% of books from first-time authors. 10% from unagented writers. Pays royalty on a case-by-case basis.** Publishes book 6 months after acceptance. Accepts simultaneous submissions. Responds in 2 months to proposals. Book catalog and writer's guidelines free or online.

NONFICTION Subjects include history, genealogy, local history. Query with SASE, or submit proposal package, including outline, 2 sample chapters, and marketing summary. Reviews artwork/photos. Send photocopies.

JEWISH LIGHTS PUBLISHING

LongHill Partners, Inc., Sunset Farm Offices, Rt. 4, P.O. Box 237, Woodstock VT 05091. (802)457-4000. **Fax:** (802)457-4004. **E-mail:** submissions@turner-publishing.com. **Website:** www.jewishlights.com. Estab. 1990. Publishes hardcover and trade paperback originals, trade paperback reprints. "Jewish Lights publishes books for people of all faiths and all backgrounds who yearn for books that attract, engage, educate and spiritually inspire. Our authors are at the forefront of spiritual thought and deal with the quest for the self and for meaning in life by drawing on the Jewish wisdom tradition. Our books cover topics including history, spirituality, life cycle, children, self-help, recovery, theology and philosophy. We do not publish autobiography, biography, fiction, haggadot, poetry or cookbooks. At this point we plan to do only two books for children annually, and one will be for younger children (ages 4-10)." **Publishes 30 titles/year. 50% of books from first-time authors. 75% from unagented writers. Pays authors royalty of 10% of revenue received; 15% royalty for subsequent printings.** Publishes ms 1 year after acceptance. Accepts simultaneous submissions. Responds in 6 months to queries. Book catalog and guidelines online.

NONFICTION Subjects include history, philosophy, religion, spirituality. Picture book, young readers, middle readers: activity books, spirituality. "We do *not* publish haggadot, biography, poetry, memoirs, or cookbooks." Query. Reviews artwork/photos. Send photocopies.

FICTION Picture books, young readers, middle readers: spirituality. "We are not interested in anything other than spirituality." Query with outline/synopsis and 2 sample chapters; submit complete ms for picture books.

THE JOHNS HOPKINS UNIVERSITY PRESS

2715 N. Charles St., Baltimore MD 21218. (410)516-6900. **Fax:** (410)516-6968. **Website:** www.press.jhu.edu. Estab. 1878. Publishes hardcover originals and reprints, and trade paperback reprints. **Publishes 140 titles/year. Pays royalty.** Publishes ms 1 year after acceptance. Accepts simultaneous submissions.

NONFICTION Subjects include history, humanities, literary criticism, regional, religion, science. Submit proposal package, outline, 1 sample chapter, CV. Reviews artwork/photos. Send photocopies.

POETRY "One of the largest American university presses, Johns Hopkins publishes primarily scholarly books and journals. We do, however, publish short fiction and poetry in the series Johns Hopkins: Poetry and Fiction, edited by John Irwin."

JOHNSON BOOKS

Imprint of Big Earth Publishing, 3005 Center Green Dr., Suite 225, Boulder CO 80301. (303)443-9766. **Fax:** (303)443-9687. **E-mail:** books@bigearthpublishing.com. **Website:** bigearthpublishing.com/johnson-books. Estab. 1979. Publishes hardcover and paperback originals and reprints. Johnson Books specializes in books on the American West, primarily outdoor, useful titles that will have strong national appeal. **Publishes 20-25 titles/year. 30% of books from first-time authors. 90% from unagented writers. Royalties vary.** Publishes ms 1 year after acceptance. Accepts simultaneous submissions. Responds in 4 months to queries. Book catalog for 9 x 12 SAE with 5 first-class stamps. Guidelines available.

NONFICTION Subjects include history, recreation, regional, science, travel, general nonfiction. "We are primarily interested in books for the informed popular market, though we will consider vividly written scholarly works. Looks for good writing, thorough research, professional presentation, and appropriate style. Marketing suggestions from writers are helpful." Submit outline/synopsis, 3 sample chapters and a author bio.

JOSSEY-BASS

John Wiley & Sons, Inc., One Montgomery St., Suite 1000, San Francisco CA 94104. **Website:** www.wiley. com. Jossey-Bass is an imprint of Wiley, specializing in books and periodicals for thoughtful professionals and researchers in the areas of business and management, leadership, human resource development, education, health, psychology, religion, and the public and nonprofit sectors. **Publishes 250 titles/year. Pays variable royalties. Pays occasional advance.** Publishes ms 1 year after acceptance. Accepts simultaneous submissions. Responds in 2-3 months to queries. Guidelines online.

NONFICTION Subjects include education, psychology, religion. Jossey-Bass publishes first-time and unagented authors. Publishes books on topics of interest to a wide range of readers: business and management, conflict resolution, mediation and negotiation, K-12 education, higher and adult education, healthcare management, psychology/behavioral healthcare, nonprofit and public management, religion, human resources and training. Also publishes 25 periodicals. See guidelines online.

JUDAICA PRESS

123 Ditmas Ave., Brooklyn NY 11218. (718)972-6200. **Fax:** (718)972-6204. **E-mail:** submissions@judaicapress.com. **Website:** www.judaicapress.com. Estab. 1963. Publishes hardcover and trade paperback originals and reprints. "We cater to the Orthodox Jewish market." **Publishes 12 titles/year.** Accepts simultaneous submissions. Responds in 3 months to queries. Book catalog in print and online.

NONFICTION Subjects include religion, prayer, holidays, life cycle. Looking for Orthodox Judaica in all genres. Submit ms with SASE.

JUDSON PRESS

P.O. Box 851, Valley Forge PA 19482. (610)768-2127. **Fax:** (610)768-2441. **E-mail:** acquisitions@judsonpress.com. **Website:** www.judsonpress.com. **Contact:** Acquisitions Editor. Estab. 1824. Publishes hardcover and paperback originals. "Our audience is comprised primarily of pastors, leaders, and Christians who seek a more fulfilling personal spiritual life and want to serve God in their churches, communities, and relationships. We have a large African American and multicultural readership. Currently emphasizing Baptist identity and small group resources. Not accepting biography, memoir, children's books, poetry." **Pub-**lishes 10-12 titles/year. 500 queries received/year. 50% of books from first-time authors. 85% from unagented writers. Pays royalty or makes outright purchase.** Publishes ms 12-18 months after acceptance. Accepts simultaneous submissions. Responds in 3-6 months to queries. Catalog online. Guidelines online.

NONFICTION Subjects include community, multicultural, parenting, religion, spirituality, womens issues. Adult religious nonfiction of 30,000-80,000 words. Does not want biography, autobiography, memoir. Query by e-mail or mail. Submit annotated outline, sample chapters, CV, competing titles, marketing plan.

KAEDEN BOOKS

P.O. Box 16190, Rocky River OH 44116. **Website:** www.kaeden.com. Estab. 1986. Publishes paperback originals. "Children's book publisher for education K-3 market: reading stories, fiction/nonfiction, chapter books, science, and social studies materials." **Publishes 12-20 titles/year. 1,000 mss received/year. 30% of books from first-time authors. 95% from unagented writers. Work purchased outright from authors. Pays royalties to previous authors.** Publishes ms 6-9 months after acceptance. Accepts simultaneous submissions. Responds only if interested. Book catalog and guidelines online.

NONFICTION Subjects include animals, creative nonfiction, science, social sciences. Mss should have interesting topics and information presented in language comprehensible to young students. Content should be supported with details and accurate facts. Submit complete ms. "Can be as minimal as 25 words for the earliest reader or as much as 2,000 words for the fluent reader. Beginning chapter books are welcome. Our readers are in kindergarten to third grade, so vocabulary and sentence structure must be appropriate for young readers. Make sure that all language used in the story is of an appropriate level for the students to read independently. Sentences should be complete and grammatically correct." Reviews artwork/photos. Send photocopies.

FICTION Subjects include adventure, fantasy, historical, humor, mystery, short story collections, sports, suspense. "We are looking for stories with humor, surprise endings, and interesting characters that will appeal to children in kindergarten through third grade." No sentence fragments. Please do not submit: queries, ms summaries, or résumés, mss that stereotype or demean individuals or groups, mss that present violence as acceptable behavior. Submit complete ms. "Can be as minimal as 25 words for the earliest reader or as much as 2,000 words for the fluent reader. Beginning chapter books are welcome. Our readers are in kindergarten to third grade, so vocabulary and sentence structure must be appropriate for young readers. Make sure that all language used in the story is of an appropriate level for the students to read independently. Sentences should be complete and grammatically correct."

KALMBACH PUBLISHING CO.

21027 Crossroads Circle, P.O. Box 1612, Waukesha WI 53186. (262)796-8776. **Fax:** (262)798-6468. **Website:** www.kalmbach.com. Estab. 1934. Publishes paperback originals and reprints. **Publishes 40-50 titles/ year. 50% of books from first-time authors. 99% from unagented writers. Pays 7% royalty on net receipts. Pays $1,500 advance.** Publishes ms 18 months after acceptance. Accepts simultaneous submissions. Responds in 2 months to queries.

NONFICTION "Focus on beading, wirework, and one-of-a-kind artisan creations for jewelry-making and crafts and in the railfan, model railroading, plastic modeling and toy train collecting/operating hobbies. Kalmbach publishes reference materials and how-to publications for hobbyists, jewelry-makers, and crafters." Query with 2-3 page detailed outline, sample chapter with photos, drawings, and how-to text. Reviews artwork/photos.

Ⓐ KANE/MILLER BOOK PUBLISHERS

4901 Morena Blvd., Suite 213, San Diego CA 92117. (858)456-0540. **Fax:** (858)456-9641. **E-mail:** submissions@kanemiller.com. **Website:** www.kane-miller.com. **Contact:** Editorial Department. Estab. 1985. "Kane/Miller Book Publishers is a division of EDC Publishing, specializing in award-winning children's books from around the world. Our books bring the children of the world closer to each other, sharing stories and ideas, while exploring cultural differences and similarities. Although we continue to look for books from other countries, we are now actively seeking works that convey cultures and communities within the US. We are committed to expanding our picture book list and are interested in great stories with engaging characters, especially those with particularly American subjects. When writing about the experiences of a particular community, we will ex-

press a preference for stories written from a firsthand experience." Submission guidelines on site. Accepts simultaneous submissions. If interested, responds in 90 days to queries.

NONFICTION Subjects include Americana, history, sports, young adult.

FICTION Subjects include adventure, fantasy, historical, juvenile, multicultural, mystery, picture books. Picture Books: concept, contemporary, health, humor, multicultural. Young Readers: contemporary, multicultural, suspense. Middle Readers: contemporary, humor, multicultural, suspense. "At this time, we are not considering holiday stories (in any age range) or self-published works."

KAR-BEN PUBLISHING

Lerner Publishing Group, 1241 Washington Ave. N., Minneapolis MN 55401. **E-mail:** editorial@karben. com. **Website:** www.karben.com. Estab. 1974. Publishes hardcover, trade paperback and e-books. Kar-Ben publishes exclusively children's books on Jewish themes. **Publishes 20 titles/year. 800 mss received/ year. 20% of books from first-time authors. 70% from unagented writers. Pays 5% royalty on NET sale. Pays $500-2,500 advance.** Most mss published within 2 years. Accepts simultaneous submissions. Responds in 12 weeks. Book catalog online; free upon request. Guidelines online.

NONFICTION Subjects include religion. "In addition to traditional Jewish-themed stories about Jewish holidays, history, folktales and other subjects, we especially seek stories that reflect the rich diversity of the contemporary Jewish community." Picture books, young readers; Jewish history, Israel, Holocaust, folktales, religion, social issues, special needs; must be of Jewish interest. No textbooks, games, or educational materials. Submit completed ms. Reviews artwork separately. Works with 10-12 illustrators/year. Prefers four-color art in any medium that is scannable. Reviews illustration packages from artists. Submit sample of art or online portfolio (no originals).

FICTION "We seek picture book mss 800-1,000 words on Jewish-themed topics for children." Picture books: Adventure, concept, folktales, history, humor, multicultural, religion, special needs; must be on a Jewish theme. Average word length: picture books–1,000. Recently published titles: *The Count's Hanukkah Countdown, Sammy Spider's First Book of*

Jewish Holidays, *The Cats of Ben Yehuda Street*. Submit full ms. Picture books only.

KENSINGTON PUBLISHING CORP.

119 W. 40th St., New York NY 10018. (212)407-1500. **Fax:** (212)935-0699. **E-mail:** jscognamiglio@kensingtonbooks.com. **Website:** www.kensingtonbooks.com. **Contact:** John Scognamiglio, editorial director, fiction (historical romance, Regency romance, women's contemporary fiction, gay and lesbian fiction and nonfiction, mysteries, suspense, mainstream fiction); Michaela Hamilton, editor-in-chief, Citadel Press (thrillers, mysteries, mainstream fiction, true crime, current events); Selena James, executive editor, Dafina Books (African American fiction and nonfiction, inspirational, young adult, romance); Peter Senftleben, assistant editor (mainstream fiction, women's contemporary fiction, gay and lesbian fiction, mysteries, suspense, thrillers, romantic suspense, paranormal romance). Estab. 1975. Publishes hardcover and trade paperback originals, mass market paperback originals and reprints. "Kensington focuses on profitable niches and uses aggressive marketing techniques to support its books." **Publishes over 500 titles/year. 5,000 queries received/year. 2,000 mss received/year. 10% of books from first-time authors. Pays 6-15% royalty on retail price. Makes outright purchase. Pays $2,000 and up advance.** Publishes ms 9-12 months after acceptance. Accepts simultaneous submissions. Responds in 1 month to queries and proposals; 4 months to mss. Book catalog and guidelines online.

NONFICTION Subjects include Americana, animals, child guidance, contemporary culture, history, hobbies, memoirs, multicultural, philosophy, psychology, recreation, regional, sex, sports, travel, true crime, pop culture. Query.

FICTION Subjects include ethnic, historical, horror, mainstream, multicultural, mystery, occult, romance, suspense, western, thrillers, women's. No science fiction/fantasy, experimental fiction, business texts or children's titles. Query.

KENT STATE UNIVERSITY PRESS

P.O. Box 5190, 1118 University Library, Kent OH 44242. **Fax:** (330)672-3104. **E-mail:** ksupress@kent.edu. **Website:** www.kentstateuniversitypress.com. **Contact:** Will Underwood, acquiring editor. Estab. 1965. Publishes hardcover and paperback originals and some reprints. "Kent State publishes primarily scholarly works and titles of regional interest. Currently emphasizing US history, US literary criticism." **Publishes 30-35 titles/year. Non-author subsidy publishes 20% of books. Standard minimum book contract on net sales.** Accepts simultaneous submissions. Responds in 4 months to queries. Book catalog available free.

NONFICTION Subjects include history, literary criticism, regional, true crime, literary criticism, material culture, textile/fashion studies, US foreign relations.. "Especially interested in scholarly works in history (US and world) and US literary studies of high quality, any titles of regional interest for Ohio, scholarly biographies and general nonfiction. Send a letter of inquiry before submitting mss. Decisions based on in-house readings and 2 by outside scholars in the field of study." Please, no faxes, phone calls, or e-mail submissions.

KIDS CAN PRESS

25 Dockside Dr., Toronto ON M5A 0B5, Canada. (416)479-7000. **Fax:** (416)960-5437. **Website:** www.kidscanpress.com. **Contact:** Corus Quay, acquisitions. Estab. 1973. Publishes book 18-24 months after acceptance. Accepts simultaneous submissions. Responds in 6 months only if interested.

NONFICTION Picture books: activity books, animal, arts/crafts, biography, careers, concept, health, history, hobbies, how-to, multicultural, nature/environment, science, social issues, special needs, sports. Young readers: activity books, animal, arts/crafts, biography, careers, concept, history, hobbies, how-to, multicultural. Middle readers: cooking, music/dance. Average word length: picture books 500-1,250; young readers 750-2,000; middle readers 5,000-15,000.

FICTION Picture books, young readers: concepts. "We do not accept young adult fiction or fantasy novels for any age." Adventure, animal, contemporary, folktales, history, humor, multicultural, nature/environment, special needs, sports, suspense/mystery. Average word length: picture books 1,000-2,000; young readers 750-1,500; middle readers 10,000-15,000; young adults over 15,000. Submit outline/synopsis and 2-3 sample chapters. For picture books submit complete ms.

KIRKBRIDE BIBLE CO., INC.

1102 Deloss St., Indianapolis IN 46203. (800)428-4385. **Fax:** (317)633-1444. **E-mail:** info@kirkbride.com. **Website:** www.kirkbride.com. **Contact:** Paula Haggard, David Gage, Bill Cross. Estab. 1915. Publishes Thompson Chain-Reference Bible hardcover originals and quality leather bindings styles and translations of the Bible. Types of books include reference and religious. Specializes in reference and study material. Accepts simultaneous submissions.

KNOPF

Imprint of Random House, 1745 Broadway, New York NY 10019. **Fax:** (212)940-7390. **Website:** knopfdoubleday.com/imprint/knopf. Estab. 1915. Publishes hardcover and paperback originals. **Publishes 200 titles/year. Royalties vary. Offers advance.** Publishes ms 1 year after acceptance. Accepts simultaneous submissions. Responds in 2-6 months to queries.

NONFICTION Usually only accepts mss submitted by agents. However, writers may submit sample 25-50 pages with SASE.

FICTION Publishes book-length fiction of literary merit by known or unknown writers. Length: 40,000-150,000 words. Usually only accepts mss submitted by agents. However, writers may submit sample 25-50 pages with SASE.

KNOX ROBINSON PUBLISHING

Knox Robinson Holdings, LLC, 3104 Briarcliff RD NE #98414, Atlanta GA 30345. (404)478-8696. **E-mail:** info@knoxrobinsonpublishing.com. **Website:** www.knoxrobinsonpublishing.com. Estab. 2010. Publishes fiction and nonfiction. Knox Robinson Publishing began as an international, independent, specialist publisher of historical fiction, historical romance and fantasy. Now open to well-written literature in all genres. **Publishes 20 titles/year. Pays royalty.** Accepts simultaneous submissions. Responds within 6 months to submissions of first 3 chapters. "We do not accept proposals." Catalog available. Guidelines online.

IMPRINTS Under The Maple Tree Books (Children's Literature), Mithras Books (Young Adult Literature).

NONFICTION Subjects include history, humanities, religion, general nonfiction. "Our goal is to publish history books, monographs and historical fiction that satisfies history buffs and encourages general readers to learn more." Submit first 3 chapters and author questionnaire found on website. Reviews artwork/photos. Send photocopies. Does not accept printed submissions; electronic only.

FICTION Subjects include adventure, contemporary, fantasy, historical, horror, literary, mainstream, romance, science fiction. "We are seeking historical fic-

tion featuring obscure historical figures." Submit first 3 chapters and author questionnaire found on website.

KRAUSE PUBLICATIONS

A Division of F+W Media, Inc., 5225 Joerns Dr., Stevens Point WI 54481. (715)445-2214. **Fax:** (715)445-4087. **E-mail:** paul.kennedy@fwcommunity.com. **Website:** www.krausebooks.com. **Contact:** Paul Kennedy (antiques and collectibles, rocks, gems and minerals, music, sports, militaria, numismatics); Chris Berens (outdoors); Brian Earnest (automotive). Estab. 1952. Publishes hardcover and trade paperback originals. "We are the world's largest hobby and collectibles publisher." **Publishes 30 titles/year. 100 queries received/year. 25% of books from first-time authors. 95% from unagented writers. Pays advance. Photo budget.** Publishes ms 18 months after acceptance. Responds in 1 month.

NONFICTION Submit proposal package, including outline, TOC, a sample chapter, and letter explaining your project's unique contributions. Reviews artwork/photos. Accepts only digital photography. Send sample photos.

⊘ KREGEL PUBLICATIONS

2450 Oak Industrial Dr. NE, Grand Rapids MI 49505. (616)451-4775. **Fax:** (616)451-9330. **E-mail:** kregelbooks@kregel.com. **Website:** www.kregelpublications.com. Estab. 1949. Publishes hardcover and trade paperback originals and reprints. "Our mission as an evangelical Christian publisher is to provide—with integrity and excellence—trusted, Biblically based resources that challenge and encourage individuals in their Christian lives. Works in theology and Biblical studies should reflect the historic, orthodox Protestant tradition." **Publishes 90 titles/year. 20% of books from first-time authors. 10% from unagented writers. Pays royalty on wholesale price. Pays negotiable advance.** Publishes ms 12-16 months after acceptance. Accepts simultaneous submissions. Responds in 2-3 months. Guidelines online.

IMPRINTS Kregel Publications, Kregel Academic, Kregel Childrens, Kregel Classics.

NONFICTION Subjects include history, religion. "We serve evangelical Christian readers and those in career Christian service." Finds works through The Writer's Edge and Christian Manuscript Submissions ms screening services.

FICTION Subjects include religious, young adult. Fiction should be geared toward the evangelical

Christian market. Wants books with fast-paced, contemporary storylines presenting a strong Christian message in an engaging, entertaining style. Finds works through The Writer's Edge and Christian Manuscript Submissions ms screening services.

KRIEGER PUBLISHING CO.

1725 Krieger Ln., Malabar FL 32950. (321)724-9542. **Fax:** (321)951-3671. **E-mail:** info@krieger-publishing.com. **Website:** www.krieger-publishing.com. **Contact:** Sharan B. Merriam and Ronald M. Cervero, series editor (adult education); David E. Kyvig, series director (local history); James B. Gardner, series editor (public history). Also publishes in the fields of natural sciences, history and space sciences.. Estab. 1969. Publishes hardcover and paperback originals and reprints. "We are a short-run niche publisher providing accurate and well-documented scientific and technical titles for text and reference use, college level and higher." **Publishes 30 titles/year. 30% of books from first-time authors. 100% from unagented writers. Pays royalty on net price.** Publishes ms 9-18 months after acceptance. Accepts simultaneous submissions. Responds in 3 months to queries. Book catalog online.

IMPRINTS Anvil Series; Orbit Series; Public History; Professional Practices in Adult Education and Lifelong Learning Series.

NONFICTION Subjects include agriculture, animals, education, history, horticulture, science, herpetology. Query with SASE. Reviews artwork/photos.

LANGMARC PUBLISHING

P.O. Box 90488, Austin TX 78709-0488. (512)394-0989. **Fax:** (512)394-0829. **E-mail:** langmarc@booksails.com. **Website:** www.langmarc.com. Publishes trade paperback originals. **Publishes 3 titles/year. 150 queries; 80 mss received/year. 60% of books from first-time authors. 80% from unagented writers. Pays 14% royalty on sales price.** Publishes ms 8-14 months after acceptance. Accepts simultaneous submissions. Responds in 3 months to queries. Book catalog online. Guidelines online.

NONFICTION Subjects include creative nonfiction. Query with SASE.

LEE & LOW BOOKS

95 Madison Ave., #1205, New York NY 10016. (212)779-4400. **E-mail:** general@leeandlow.com. **Website:** www.leeandlow.com. Estab. 1991. Publishes hardcover originals and trade paperback reprints.

"Our goals are to meet a growing need for books that address children of color, and to present literature that all children can identify with. We only consider multicultural children's books. Sponsors a yearly New Voices Award for first-time picture book authors of color. Contest rules online at website or for SASE." **Publishes 12-14 titles/year. Receives 100 queries/year; 1,200 mss/year. 20% of books from first-time authors. 50% from unagented writers. Pays net royalty. Pays authors advances against royalty. Pays illustrators advance against royalty. Photographers paid advance against royalty.** Publishes book 2 years after acceptance. Responds in 6 months to mss if interested. Book catalog available online. Guidelines available online or by written request with SASE.

NONFICTION Picture books: concept. Picture books, middle readers: biography, history, multicultural, science and sports. Average word length: picture books-1,500-3,000. Submit complete ms. Reviews artwork/photos only if writer is also a professional illustrator or photographer. Send photocopies and nonreturnable art samples only.

FICTION Picture books, young readers: anthology, contemporary, history, multicultural, poetry. Picture book, middle reader: contemporary, history, multicultural, nature/environment, poetry, sports. Average word length: picture books—1,000-1,500 words. "We do not publish folklore or animal stories." Submit complete ms.

POETRY Submit complete ms.

LEHIGH UNIVERSITY PRESS

B040 Christmas-Saucon Hall, 14 E. Packer Ave., Bethlehem PA 18015. (610)758-3933. **Fax:** (610)758-6331. **E-mail:** inlup@lehigh.edu. **Website:** https://lupress.cas2.lehigh.edu. **Contact:** Kate Crassons. Estab. 1985. Publishes nonfiction hardcover originals. Currently emphasizing works on 18th-century studies, history of technology, literary criticism, and topics involving Asian Studies. **Publishes 10 titles/year. 90-100 queries; 50-60 mss received/year. 70% of books from first-time authors. 100% from unagented writers. Pays royalty.** Publishes ms 18 months after acceptance. Responds in 3 months to queries. Book catalog available free. Guidelines online.

NONFICTION Subjects include Americana, history, science. Lehigh University Press is a conduit for nonfiction works of scholarly interest to the academic community. Submit proposal package with cover letter, several sample chapters, current CV and SASE.

HAL LEONARD BOOKS

Hal Leonard Publishing Group, 33 Plymouth St., Suite 302, Montclair NJ 07042. (973)337-5034. **Website:** www.halleonardbooks.com. **Contact:** John Cerullo, publisher. **Publishes 30 titles/year.** Accepts simultaneous submissions.

NONFICTION Subjects include music. Query with SASE.

LETHE PRESS

118 Heritage Ave., Maple Shade NJ 8052. (609)410-7391. **Website:** www.lethepressbooks.com. Estab. 2001. "Welcomes submissions from authors of any sexual or gender identity." Accepts simultaneous submissions. Guidelines online.

NONFICTION Query via e-mail.

FICTION Subjects include gay, lesbian, occult, science fiction. "Named after the Greek river of memory and forgetfulness (and pronounced Lee-Thee), Lethe Press is a small press devoted to ideas that are often neglected or forgotten by mainstream, profit-oriented publishers." Distributes/promotes titles. Lethe Books are distributed by Ingram Publications and Bookazine, and are available at all major bookstores, as well as the major online retailers. Query via e-mail.

POETRY "Lethe Press is a small press seeking gay and lesbian themed poetry collections." Lethe Books are distributed by Ingram Publications and Bookazine, and are available at all major bookstores, as well as the major online retailers. Query with 7-10 poems, list of publications.

ARTHUR A. LEVINE BOOKS

Scholastic, Inc., 557 Broadway, New York NY 10012. (212)343-4436. **Fax:** (212)343-6143. **Website:** www.arthuralevinebooks.com. Estab. 1996. Publishes hardcover, paperback, and e-book editions. Publishes a book 18 months after acceptance. Accepts simultaneous submissions. Responds in 1 month to queries; 5 months to mss. Picture Books: Query letter and full text of pb. Novels: Send Query letter, first 2 chapters and synopsis. Other: Query letter, 10-page sample and synopsis/proposal.

NONFICTION Please follow submission guidelines. Works with 8 illustrators/year. Will review ms/illustration packages from artists. Query first. Illus-

trations only: Send postcard sample with tearsheets. Samples not returned.

FICTION Subjects include juvenile, picture books, young adult. "Arthur A. Levine is looking for distinctive literature, for children and young adults, for whatever's extraordinary." Averages 18-20 total titles/year. Query.

◯ LEXISNEXIS CANADA, INC.

111 Gordon Baker Rd., Suite 900, Toronto ON M2H 3R1, Canada. (905)479-2665. **Fax:** (905)479-2826. **Website:** www.lexisnexis.ca. **Contact:** Product Development Director. LexisNexis Canada, Inc., publishes professional reference material for the legal, business, and accounting markets under the Butterworths imprint and operates the Quicklaw and LexisNexis online services. **Publishes 100 titles/year. 50% of books from first-time authors. 100% from unagented writers. Pays 5-15% royalty on wholesale price.** Publishes ms 4 months after acceptance. Accepts simultaneous submissions. Responds in 1 month to queries. Book catalog available free. Guidelines online.

LIGUORI PUBLICATIONS

One Liguori Dr., Liguori MO 63057. (636)464-2500. **Fax:** (636)464-8449. **Website:** www.liguori.org. Estab. 1947. Publishes paperback originals and reprints under the Ligouri and Libros Ligouri imprints. Liguori Publications, faithful to the charism of St. Alphonsus, is an apostolate within the mission of the Denver Province. Its mission, a collaborative effort of Redemptorists and laity, is to spread the gospel of Jesus Christ primarily through the print and electronic media. It shares in the Redemptorist priority of giving special attention to the poor and the most abandoned. Currently emphasizing practical spirituality, prayers and devotions, how-to spirituality. **Publishes 20-25 titles/year. Pays royalty. Makes outright purchase. Pays varied advance.** Publishes ms 2 years after acceptance. Responds in 2-3 months. Guidelines online.

NONFICTION Subjects include religion, spirituality. Mostly adult audience; limited children/juvenile. Mss with Catholic sensibility. Query with SASE. Submit outline, 1 sample chapter.

LILLENAS PUBLISHING CO.

Imprint of Lillenas Drama Resources, P.O. Box 419527, Kansas City MO 64141. (800)877-0700. **Fax:** (816)412-8390. **E-mail:** drama@lillenas.com. **Website:** www.lillenasdrama.com. Publishes mass market paperback and electronic originals. "We purchase only original, previously unpublished materials. Also, we require that all scripts be performed at least once before it is submitted for consideration. We do not accept scripts that are sent via fax or e-mail. Direct all manuscripts to the Drama Resources Editor." **Publishes 50+ titles/year. Pays royalty on net price. Makes outright purchase.** Responds in 4-6 months to material. Guidelines online.

NONFICTION No musicals. Query with SASE. Submit complete ms.

FICTION "Looking for sketch and monologue collections for all ages – adults, children and youth. For these collections, we request 12 - 15 scripts to be submitted at one time. Unique treatments of spiritual themes, relevant issues and biblical messages are of interest. Contemporary full-length and one-act plays that have conflict, characterization, and a spiritual context that is neither a sermon nor an apologetic for youth and adults. We also need wholesome so-called secular full-length scripts for dinner theatres and schools." No musicals.

LINDEN PUBLISHING, INC.

2006 S. Mary, Fresno CA 93721. (559)233-6633. **Fax:** (559)233-6933. **E-mail:** richard@lindenpub.com. **Website:** www.lindenpub.com and www.quilldriverbooks.com. **Contact:** Richard Sorsky, president; Kent Sorsky, vice president. Estab. 1976. Publishes hardcover and trade paperback originals; hardcover and trade paperback reprints. **Publishes 10-12 titles/year. 100+ queries; 25+ mss received/year. 40% of books from first-time authors. 50% from unagented writers. Pays 7½ -12% royalty on wholesale price. Pays $500-6,000 advance.** Publishes ms 18 months after acceptance. Responds in 1 month. Book catalog online. Guidelines available via e-mail.

IMPRINTS Quill Driver Books, Craven Street Books. Pace Press.

NONFICTION Subjects include crafts, health, history, hobbies, regional, true crime, Regional California history. Submit proposal package, outline, 3 sample chapters, bio. Reviews artwork/photos. Send electronic files, if available.

FICTION Subjects include adventure, fantasy, gothic, historical, horror, mystery, occult, science fiction, suspense.

LISTEN & LIVE AUDIO

1700 Manhattan Ave., Union City NJ 07087. (201)558-9000. **Website:** www.listenandlive.com. **Contact:** Alfred C. Martino, president. Independent audiobook publisher. "We also license audiobooks for the download market. We specialize in the following genres: fiction, mystery, nonfiction, self-help, business, children's, and teen." **Publishes 10+ titles/year.** Accepts simultaneous submissions. Catalog online.

Ⓐⱺ LITTLE, BROWN AND CO. ADULT TRADE BOOKS

1290 Avenue of the Americas, New York NY 10104. **Website:** www.littlebrown.com. Estab. 1837. Publishes hardcover originals and paperback originals and reprints. "The general editorial philosophy for all divisions continues to be broad and flexible, with high quality and the promise of commercial success as always the first considerations." **Publishes 100 titles/year. Pays royalty. Offer advance.** Accepts simultaneous submissions. Guidelines online.

NONFICTION *Agented submissions only.*

FICTION Subjects include contemporary, literary, mainstream. *Agented submissions only.*

Ⓐⱺ LITTLE, BROWN BOOKS FOR YOUNG READERS

Hachette Book Group USA, 1290 Avenue of the Americas, New York NY 10104. (212)364-1100. **Fax:** (212)364-0925. **Website:** littlebrown.com. Estab. 1837. "Little, Brown and Co. Children's Publishing publishes all formats including board books, picture books, middle grade fiction, and nonfiction YA titles. We are looking for strong writing and presentation, but no predetermined topics." *Only interested in solicited agented material.* **Publishes 100-150 titles/year. Pays authors royalties based on retail price. Pays illustrators and photographers by the project or royalty based on retail price. Sends galleys to authors; dummies to illustrators. Pays negotiable advance.** Publishes ms 2 years after acceptance. Accepts simultaneous submissions. Responds in 1-2 months.

NONFICTION Subjects include animals, ethnic, history, hobbies, recreation, science, sports. "Writers should avoid looking for the 'issue' they think publishers want to see, choosing instead topics they know best and are most enthusiastic about/inspired by." *Agented submissions only.*

FICTION Subjects include adventure, fantasy, feminist, historical, humor, mystery, science fiction, suspense, chick lit, multicultural. Average word length: picture books—1,000; young readers—6,000; middle readers—15,000- 50,000; young adults—50,000 and up. *Agented submissions only.*

LITTLE PICKLE PRESS

3701 Sacramento St., #494, San Francisco CA 94118. (415)340-3344. **Fax:** (415)366-1520. **E-mail:** info@march4thinc.com. **Website:** www.littlepicklepress.com. Little Pickle Press is a 21st Century publisher dedicated to helping parents and educators cultivate conscious, responsible little people by stimulating explorations of the meaningful topics of their generation through a variety of media, technologies, and techniques. Submit through submission link on site. Includes YA imprint Relish Media. Accepts simultaneous submissions. Uses Author.me for submissions for Little Pickle and YA imprint Relish Media. Guidelines available on site.

Ⓐ⊘ LITTLE SIMON

Imprint of Simon & Schuster, 1230 Avenue of the Americas, New York NY 10020. (212)698-1295. **Fax:** (212)698-2794. **Website:** www.simonandschuster.com/kids. Publishes novelty and branded books only. "Our goal is to provide fresh material in an innovative format for preschool to age 8. Our books are often, if not exclusively, format driven." **Offers advance and royalties.** Accepts simultaneous submissions.

NONFICTION "We publish very few nonfiction titles." No picture books. *Currently not accepting unsolicited mss.*

FICTION Novelty books include many things that do not fit in the traditional hardcover or paperback format, such as pop-up, board book, scratch and sniff, glow in the dark, lift the flap, etc. Children's/juvenile. No picture books. Large part of the list is holiday-themed. *Currently not accepting unsolicited mss.*

LLEWELLYN PUBLICATIONS

Imprint of Llewellyn Worldwide, Ltd., 2143 Wooddale Dr., Woodbury MN 55125. (651)291-1970. **Fax:** (651)291-1908. **E-mail:** submissions@llewellyn.com. **Website:** www.llewellyn.com. Estab. 1901. Publishes trade and mass market paperback originals. "Llewellyn publishes New Age fiction and nonfiction exploring new worlds of mind and spirit. Currently emphasizing astrology, alternative health and healing, tarot. De-emphasizing fiction, channeling." **Publishes 100+ titles/year. 30% of books from first-time authors. 50% from unagented writers. Pays 10% royalty on wholesale or retail price.** Accepts simultaneous submissions. Responds in 3 months to queries. Book catalog online.

NONFICTION Subjects include New Age, psychology. Submit outline, sample chapters. Reviews artwork/photos.

LONELY PLANET PUBLICATIONS

124 Linden St., Oakland CA 94607. (510)250-6400. **Fax:** (510)893-8572. **Website:** www.lonelyplanet.com. Estab. 1973. Publishes trade paperback originals. "Lonely Planet publishes travel guides, atlases, travel literature, phrasebooks, condensed pocket guides, diving and snorkeling guides." **Work-for-hire: 1/3 on contract, 1/3 on submission, 1/3 on approval. Pays advance.** Accepts simultaneous submissions. Responds in 3 months to queries. Book catalog online. Guidelines online.

NONFICTION Subjects include travel. "We only work with contract writers on book ideas that we originate. We do not accept original proposals. Request our writer's guidelines. Send resume and clips of travel writing." Query with SASE.

LOYOLA PRESS

3441 N. Ashland Ave., Chicago IL 60657. (773)281-1818. **Fax:** (773)281-0152. **E-mail:** durepos@loyolapress.com. **Website:** www.loyolapress.org. **Contact:** Joseph Durepos, acquisitions editor.. Estab. 1912. Publishes hardcover and trade paperback. **Publishes 20-30 titles/year. 500 queries received/year. Pays standard royalties. Offers reasonable advance.** Accepts simultaneous submissions. Book catalog online. Guidelines online.

NONFICTION Subjects include memoirs, religion, spirituality, inspirational, prayer, Catholic life, parish and adult faith formation resources with a special focus on Ignatian spirituality and Jesuit history. E-mail query, or snail mail query with SASE.

LRP PUBLICATIONS, INC.

360 Hiatt Dr., Palm Beach Gardens FL 33418. **Website:** www.lrp.com. Estab. 1977. Publishes hardcover and trade paperback originals. "LRP publishes two industry-leading magazines, *Human Resource Executive*® and *Risk & Insurance*®, as well as hundreds of newsletters, books, videos and case reporters in the fields of: human resources, federal employment, workers' compensation, public employment law, dis-

ability, bankruptcy, education administration and law." **Pays royalty.** Book catalog free. Guidelines free.

NONFICTION Subjects include education. Submit proposal package, outline.

LSU PRESS

338 Johnston Hall, Baton Rouge LA 70803. (225)578-6294. **Website:** lsupress.org. Estab. 1935. LSU Press has established itself as one of the nation's outstanding scholarly presses and garners national and international accolades, including 4 Pulitzer Prizes. Accepts simultaneous submissions. Responds in 4-6 months. Catalog online. Guidelines online.

POETRY Poetry proposals should include a cover letter, 4-5 sample pages from the ms, and a current resume.

⊘ THE LYONS PRESS

The Globe Pequot Press, Inc., Box 480, 246 Goose Ln., Guilford CT 6437. (203)458-4500. **Fax:** (203)458-4668. **Website:** www.lyonspress.com. Estab. 1984 (Lyons & Burford), 1997 (The Lyons Press). Publishes hardcover and trade paperback originals and reprints. The Lyons Press publishes practical and literary books, chiefly centered on outdoor subjects—natural history, all sports, gardening, horses, fishing, hunting, survival, self-reliant living, plus cooking, memoir, bio, nonfiction. "At this time, we are not accepting unsolicited mss or proposals." Check back for updates. **Pays $3,000-25,000 advance.** Book catalog online. Guidelines online.

NONFICTION Subjects include agriculture, Americana, animals, history, recreation, sports, adventure, fitness, the sea, woodworking.

✪ MAGENTA FOUNDATION

151 Winchester St., Toronto ON M4X 1B5, Canada. **E-mail:** info@magentafoundation.org. **Website:** www.magentafoundation.org. **Contact:** Submissions. Estab. 2004. "Established in 2004, The Magenta Foundation is Canada's pioneering non-profit, charitable arts publishing house. Magenta was created to organize promotional opportunities for artists, in an international context, through circulated exhibitions and publications. Projects mounted by Magenta are supported by credible international media coverage and critical reviews in all mainstream-media formats (radio, television and print). Magenta works with respected individuals and international organizations to help increase recognition for artists while uniting the global photography community." Accepts simultaneous submissions.

MAGE PUBLISHERS, INC.

1780 Crossroads Dr., Odenton MD 21113. (202)342-1642. **Fax:** (202)342-9269. **E-mail:** as@mage.com. **Website:** www.mage.com. Estab. 1985. Publishes hardcover originals and reprints, trade paperback originals. Mage publishes books relating to Persian/Iranian culture. **Pays royalty.** Accepts simultaneous submissions. Responds in 1 month to queries. Book catalog available free. Guidelines online.

NONFICTION Subjects include ethnic, history, sociology, translation. Submit outline, bio, SASE. Query via mail or e-mail. Reviews artwork/photos. Send photocopies.

FICTION Subjects include ethnic, feminist, historical, literary, short story collections. Must relate to Persian/Iranian culture. Submit outline, SASE. Query via mail or e-mail.

POETRY Must relate to Persian/Iranian culture. Query.

MAGINATION PRESS

750 First St. NE, Washington DC 20002. (202)336-5618. **Fax:** (202)336-5624. **E-mail:** magination@apa.org. **Website:** www.apa.org. Estab. 1988. Magination Press is an imprint of the American Psychological Association. "We publish books dealing with the psycho/therapeutic resolution of children's problems and psychological issues with a strong self-help component." Submit complete ms. Full guidelines available on site. Materials returned only with SASE. **Publishes 12 titles/year. 75% of books from first-time authors.** Publishes a book 18-24 months after acceptance. Accepts simultaneous submissions. Responds to queries in 1-2 months; mss in 2-6 months.

NONFICTION All levels: psychological and social issues, self-help, health, multicultural, special needs.

FICTION All levels: psychological and social issues, self-help, health, parenting concerns and, special needs. Picture books, middle school readers.

MANDALA PUBLISHING

Mandala Publishing and Earth Aware Editions, 800 A St., San Rafael CA 94901. **E-mail:** info@mandalapublishing.com. **Website:** www.mandalaeartheditions.com. Estab. 1989. Publishes hardcover, trade paperback, and electronic originals. "In the traditions of the East, wisdom, truth, and beauty go hand in- hand.

This is reflected in the great arts, music, yoga, and philosophy of India. Mandala Publishing strives to bring to its readers authentic and accessible renderings of thousands of years of wisdom and philosophy from this unique culture-timeless treasures that are our inspirations and guides. At Mandala, we believe that the arts, health, ecology, and spirituality of the great Vedic traditions are as relevant today as they were in sacred India thousands of years ago. As a distinguished publisher in the world of Vedic literature, lifestyle, and interests today, Mandala strives to provide accessible and meaningful works for the modern reader." **Publishes 12 titles/year. 200 queries received/year. 100 mss received/year. 40% of books from first-time authors. 100% from unagented writers. Pays 3-15% royalty on retail price.** Publishes ms 8 months after acceptance. Accepts simultaneous submissions. Responds in 6 months. Book catalog online.

NONFICTION Subjects include education, philosophy, photography, religion, spirituality. Query with SASE. Reviews artwork/photos. Send photocopies and thumbnails.

FICTION Subjects include juvenile, religious, spiritual. Query with SASE.

⊕ MANOR HOUSE PUBLISHING, INC.

452 Cottingham Crescent, Ancaster ON L9G 3V6, Canada. (905)648-2193. **E-mail:** mbdavie@manor-house.biz. **Website:** www.manor-house.biz. **Contact:** Mike Davie, president (novels and nonfiction). Estab. 1998. Publishes hardcover, trade paperback, and mass market paperback originals (and reprints if they meet specific criteria - best to inquire with publisher). Manor House is currently looking for new fully edited, ready-to-run titles to complete our spring-fall 2017 release lineup. This is a rare opportunity for authors, including self-published, to have existing or ready titles picked up by Manor House and made available to retailers throughout the world, while our network of rights agents provide more potential revenue streams via foreign language rights sales. We are currently looking for titles that are ready or nearly ready for publishing to be released this fall. Such titles should be written by Canadian citizens residing in Canada and should be profitable or with strong market sales potential to allow full cost recovery and profit for publisher and author. Of primary interest are business and self-help titles along with other nonfiction, including new age. **Publishes 5-6**

titles/year. 30 queries; 20 mss received/year. 90% of books from first-time authors. 90% from unagented writers. Pays 10% royalty on retail price.** Publishes book 6 mos to 1 year after acceptance. Queries and mss to be sent by e-mail only. "We will respond in 30 days if interested-if not, there is no response. Do not follow up unless asked to do so." Book catalog online. Guidelines available.

NONFICTION Subjects include history, sex, social sciences, sociology, spirituality. We are currently looking for titles that are ready or nearly ready for publishing to be released in 2017 onward. Such titles should be written by Canadian citizens residing in Canada and should be profitable or with strong market sales potential to allow full cost recovery and profit for publisher and author. Of primary interest are Business and self-help titles along with other nonfiction, including new age. We are also open to publishing non-Canadian authors (nonfiction works only) - provided non-Canadian authors can further provide us with a very good indication of demand for their book (Eg: actual or expected advance book orders from speaker venues, corporations, agencies or authors on a non-returnable basis) so we are assured the title will likely be a profitable venture for both author and publisher. Query via e-mail. Submit proposal package, outline, bio, 3 sample chapters. Submit complete ms. Reviews artwork/photos. Send photocopies.

FICTION Subjects include adventure, experimental, gothic, historical, horror, humor, juvenile, literary, mystery, occult, poetry, regional, romance, short story collections, young adult. Stories should mainly be by Canadian authors residing in Canada, have Canadian settings and characters should be Canadian, but content should have universal appeal to wide audience. In some cases, we will consider publishing non-Canadian fiction authors - provided they demonstrate publishing their book will be profitable for author and publisher. Query via e-mail. Submit proposal package, clips, bio, 3 sample chapters. Submit complete ms.

POETRY Poetry should engage, provoke, involve the reader (and be written by Canadian authors residing in Canada).

⊘ MARINER BOOKS

222 Berkeley St., Boston MA 2116. (617)351-5000. **Website:** www.hmco.com. Estab. 1997. Accepts simultaneous submissions.

POETRY Has published poetry by Thomas Lux, Linda Gregerson, and Keith Leonard. Agented submissions only.

MARTIN SISTERS PUBLISHING COMPANY, INC

P.O. Box 1154, Barbourville KY 40906-1499. **Website:** www.martinsisterspublishing.com. Estab. 2011. Firm/imprint publishes trade and mass market paperback originals; electronic originals. **Publishes 12 titles/year. 75% of books from first-time authors. 100% from unagented writers. Pays 7.5% royalty/max on print net; 35% royalty/max on e-book net. No advance offered.** Publishes ms 9 months after acceptance. Accepts simultaneous submissions. Responds in 1 month on queries, 2 months on proposals, 3-6 months on mss. Catalog and guidelines online.

NONFICTION Subjects include Americana, child guidance, contemporary culture, cooking, creative nonfiction, education, gardening, history, house and home, humanities, labor, language, law, literature, memoirs, money, nutrition, parenting, psychology, regional, sociology, spirituality, womens issues, womens studies, western. Does not review artwork.

FICTION Subjects include adventure, confession, fantasy, historical, humor, juvenile, literary, mainstream, military, mystery, poetry in translation, regional, religious, romance, science fiction, short story collections, spiritual, sports, suspense, war, western, young adult. "Please place query letter, marketing plan and the first 5-10 pages of your manuscript (if you are submitting fiction) directly into your e-mail." Guidelines available on site.

MARVEL COMICS

135 W. 50th St., 7th Floor, New York NY 10020. **Website:** www.marvel.com. Publishes hardcover originals and reprints, trade paperback reprints, mass market comic book originals, electronic reprints. **Pays on a per page work for hire basis or creator-owned which is then contracted. Pays negotiable advance.** Responds in 3-5 weeks to queries. Guidelines online.

FICTION Subjects include adventure, comic books, fantasy, horror, humor, science fiction, young adult. Our shared universe needs new heroes and villains; books for younger readers and teens needed. Submit inquiry letter, idea submission form (download from website), SASE.

MASTER BOOKS

P.O. Box 726, Green Forest AR 72638. **E-mail:** submissions@newleafpress.net. **Website:** www.masterbooks.com. **Contact:** Craig Froman, acquisitions editor. Estab. 1975. Publishes 3 middle readers/year; 2 young adult nonfiction titles/year; 10 homeschool curriculum titles; 20 adult trade books/year. **5% of books from first-time authors. 99% from unagented writers. Pays authors royalty of 3-15% based on wholesale price.** Publishes book 1 year after acceptance. Accepts simultaneous submissions. We are no longer able to respond to every query. If you have not heard from us within 90 days, it means we are unable to partner with you on that particular project. Book catalog available upon request. Guidelines online.

NONFICTION Subjects include archeology, religion, science, womens issues, world affairs. Picture books: activity books, animal, nature/environment, creation. Young readers, middle readers, young adults: activity books, animal, biography Christian, nature/environment, science, creation. Submission guidelines on website. http://www.nlpg.com/submissions

☺ MCCLELLAND & STEWART, LTD.

The Canadian Publishers, 320 Front St. W., Suite 1400, Toronto ON M5V 3B6, Canada. (416)364-4449. **Fax:** (416)598-7764. **Website:** www.mcclelland.com. Publishes hardcover, trade paperback, and mass market paperback originals and reprints. **Publishes 80 titles/year. 1,500 queries received/year. 10% of books from first-time authors. 30% from unagented writers. Pays 10-15% royalty on retail price (hardcover rates). Pays advance.** Publishes ms 1 year after acceptance. Accepts simultaneous submissions. Responds in 3 months to proposals.

NONFICTION Subjects include history, philosophy, photography, psychology, recreation, religion, science, sociology, sports, translation, travel, Canadiana. "We publish books primarily by Canadian authors." Submit outline. *All unsolicited mss returned unopened.*

FICTION "We publish work by established authors, as well as the work of new and developing authors." Query. *All unsolicited mss returned unopened.*

POETRY Only Canadian poets should apply. We publish only 4 titles each year. Query. *No unsolicited mss.*

⊘ MARGARET K. MCELDERRY BOOKS

Imprint of Simon & Schuster Children's Publishing Division, 1230 Sixth Ave., New York NY 10020. (212)698-7200. **Website:** imprints.simonandschuster.biz/margaret-k-mcelderry-books. VP/Publisher: Justin Chanda. Estab. 1971. "Margaret K. McElderry Books publishes hardcover and paperback trade books for children from pre-school age through young adult. This list includes picture books, middle grade and teen fiction, poetry, and fantasy. The style and subject matter of the books we publish is almost unlimited. We do not publish textbooks, coloring and activity books, greeting cards, magazines, pamphlets, or religious publications." **Publishes 30 titles/year. 15% of books from first-time authors. 50% from unagented writers. Pays authors royalty based on retail price. Pays illustrator royalty of by the project. Pays photographers by the project. Original artwork returned at job's completion. Offers $5,000-8,000 advance for new authors.** Accepts simultaneous submissions. Guidelines for #10 SASE.

NONFICTION Subjects include history, adventure. *No unsolicited mss. Agented submissions only.*

FICTION Subjects include adventure, fantasy, historical, mystery, picture books, young adult. *No unsolicited mss. Agented submissions only.*

MCFARLAND & CO., INC., PUBLISHERS

Box 611, Jefferson NC 28640. (336)246-4460. **Fax:** (336)246-5018. **E-mail:** info@mcfarlandpub.com. **Website:** www.mcfarlandpub.com. **Contact:** Editorial Department. Estab. 1979. Publishes hardcover and quality paperback originals. "McFarland publishes serious nonfiction in a variety of fields, including general reference, performing arts, popular culture, sports (particularly baseball); women's studies, librarianship, literature, Civil War, history and international studies. Currently emphasizing medieval history, automotive history. De-emphasizing memoirs." **Publishes 350 titles/year. 50% of books from first-time authors. 95% from unagented writers.** Publishes book 10 months after acceptance. Accepts simultaneous submissions. Responds in 1 month to queries. Guidelines online.

NONFICTION Subjects include history, recreation, sociology, African-American studies (very strong). Reference books are particularly wanted—fresh material (i.e., not in head-to-head competition with an established title). "We prefer manuscripts of 250 or more double-spaced pages or at least 75,000 words." No fiction, New Age, exposes, poetry, children's books, devotional/inspirational works, Bible studies, or personal essays. Query with SASE. Submit outline, sample chapters. Reviews artwork/photos.

MCGRAW-HILL PROFESSIONAL BUSINESS

Imprint of The McGraw-Hill Companies, 2 Penn Plaza, New York NY 10121. (212)438-1000. **Website:** www.mcgraw-hill.com. McGraw Hill Professional is a publishing leader in business/investing, management, careers, self-help, consumer health, language reference, test preparation, sports/recreation, and general interest titles. Publisher not responsible for returning mss or proposals. Accepts simultaneous submissions. Guidelines online.

NONFICTION Subjects include child guidance, education, sports, management, consumer reference, English and foreign language reference. Current, up-to-date, original ideas are needed. Good self-promotion is key. Submit proposal package, outline, concept of book, competition and market info, CV.

MC PRESS

3695 W. Quail Heights Ct., Boise ID 83703. (208)629-7275. **Fax:** (208)639-1231. **E-mail:** duptmor@mcpressonline.com. **Website:** www.mc-store.com. **Contact:** David Uptmor, publisher. Editor: Anne Grubb. Estab. 2001. Publishes trade paperback originals. **Publishes 12 titles/year. 50 queries received/year. 15 mss received/year. 50% of books from first-time authors. 100% from unagented writers. Pays 10-16% royalty on wholesale price.** Publishes book 5 months after acceptance. Accepts simultaneous submissions. Responds in 1 month. Book catalog and ms guidelines free.

IMPRINTS MC Press, IBM Press.

NONFICTION "We specialize in computer titles targeted at IBM technologies." Submit proposal package, outline, 2 sample chapters, abstract. Reviews artwork/photos. Send photocopies.

MEDIA LAB BOOKS

Topix Media Lab, 14 Wall St., Suite 4B, New York NY 10005. **E-mail:** phil@topixmedia.com. **Website:** onnewsstandsnow.com. **Contact:** Phil Sexton, vice president and publisher. Estab. 2015. Publishes cooking, children's books, games, puzzles, reference, humor, biography, history. Media Lab Books is a premier imprint that partners with industry leaders to publish branded titles designed to inform, educate and entertain readers around the world. "With brand partners that run the gamut, our books are widely variable in category and topic. From John Wayne to Disney and every brand in between, our partners have loyal followings, strong media presences and amazing stories to tell. While leveraging the platforms of our brand partners, we publish highly visual, illustrated books that surprise and delight readers of all ages. From *Jack Hanna's Big Book of Why* to *The John Wayne Code*, we truly have something for everyone. In the end, our aim is to match great ideas with amazing brands. We're looking for creative nonfiction ideas from authors with a voice (and a platform). Though we specialize in creating visually dynamic books built around big brands, we're also interested in original works focusing on popular or trending topics in most nonfiction categories, but given a unique, one-of-a-kind spin that demands publication. For example, *I'm Just Here for the Drinks* by Sother Teague." **Publishes 25 titles/year. 60 20% of books from first-time authors. 20% from unagented writers.** Publishes ms 12-18 months after acceptance. Accepts simultaneous submissions. Responds in 30 days. Catalog available. Electronic submissions only. On the first page of the document, please include author's name and contact information. Please send full submission packet, including overview, USP (unique selling proposition), comparable titles, proposed TOC, and 1-3 sample chapters (no more than 50 pages).

IMPRINTS Media Lab Books, Media Lab Kids.

MELANGE BOOKS, LLC

White Bear Lake MN 55110-5538. **E-mail:** melange-books@melange-books.com. **E-mail:** submissions@melange-books.com. **Website:** www.melange-books.com. **Contact:** Nancy Schumacher, publisher and acquiring editor for Melange and Satin Romance; Caroline Andrus, acquiring editor for Fire and Ice for Young Adult.. Estab. 2011. Publishes trade paperback originals and electronic originals. Melange is a royalty-paying company publishing e-books and print books. **Publishes 75 titles/year. Receives 1,000 queries/year; 700 mss/year. 65% of books from first-time authors. 75% from unagented writers. Authors receive a minimum of 20% royalty on print sales, 40% on electronic book sales. Does not offer an advance.** Publishes book 12-15 months after acceptance. Accepts simultaneous submissions. Responds

in 1 month on queries; 2 months on proposals; 4-6 months on mss. Send SASE for book catalog. Guidelines online.

IMPRINTS Fire and Ice (young and new adult) www.fireandiceya.com; Satin Romance www.satinromance.com.

FICTION Subjects include adventure, contemporary, erotica, fantasy, gay, gothic, historical, lesbian, mainstream, multicultural, mystery, romance, science fiction, suspense, western, young adult. Submit a clean mss by following guidelines on website. Query electronically by clicking on "submissions" on website. Include a synopsis and 4 chapters.

MELBOURNE UNIVERSITY PUBLISHING, LTD.

Subsidiary of University of Melbourne, Level 1, 11-15 Argyle Pl. S., Carlton VIC 3053, Australia. (61)(3)934-20300. **Fax:** (61)(3)9342-0399. **E-mail:** mup-contact@unimelb.edu.au. **E-mail:** mup-submissions@unimelb.edu.au. **Website:** www.mup.com.au. **Contact:** The Executive Assistant. Estab. 1922. **Publishes 80 titles/year.** Accepts simultaneous submissions. Responds to queries in 4 months if interested. Guidelines online.

IMPRINTS Melbourne University Press; The Miegunyah Press (strong Australian content); Victory Books.

NONFICTION Subjects include philosophy, science, social sciences, Aboriginal studies, cultural studies, gender studies, natural history. Submit using MUP Book Proposal Form available online.

MENASHA RIDGE PRESS

AdventureKEEN, 2204 First Ave. S., Suite 102, Birmingham AL 35233. (205)322-0439. **E-mail:** tim@adventurewithkeen.com. **Website:** www.menasharidge.com. **Contact:** Tim Jackson, acquisitions editor. Publishes hardcover and trade paperback originals. Menasha Ridge Press publishes distinctive books in the areas of outdoor sports, recreation, and travel. We are primarily looking for outdoors guidebooks. "Our authors are among the best in their fields." **Publishes 20 titles/year. 30% of books from first-time authors. 90% from unagented writers. Pays varying royalty. Pays varying advance.** Publishes ms 1 year after acceptance. Accepts simultaneous submissions. Responds in 2 months to queries.

NONFICTION Subjects include nature, recreation, sports, travel, outdoors. Most concepts are generated in-house, but a few come from outside submissions.

Submit proposal package, resume, clips. Reviews art-work/photos.

MERRIAM PRESS

489 South St., Hoosick Falls NY 12090. **E-mail:** ray@merriam-press.com. **Website:** www.merriam-press.com. **Contact:** Ray Merriam, owner. Estab. 1988. Publishes hardcover and softcover trade paperback original works and reprints. Titles are also made available in e-book editions. Merriam Press specializes in military history, particularly World War II history. We are also branching out into other genres, including fiction, historical fiction, poetry, children. Provide brief synopsis of ms. Never send any files in body of e-mail or as an attachment. Publisher will ask for full ms for review. Publisher requires unformatted mss. Mss must be thoroughly edited and error-free. **Publishes 12+ titles/year. 70-90% of books from first-time authors. 100% from unagented writers. Pays 10% royalty for printed editions and 50% royalty for e-book editions. Royalty payment is based on the amount paid to the publisher, not the retail or list prices. Does not pay advance.** Publishes ms 6 months or less after acceptance. Responds quickly (e-mail preferred) to queries. Book catalog available in print and PDF editions. Author guidelines and additional information are available on publisher's website.

NONFICTION Subjects include Americana, creative nonfiction, history, memoirs, military, war. Especially but not limited to military history. Query with SASE or by e-mail first. Do not send ms (in whole or in part) unless requested to do so. When asked to submit ms, include all artwork, photos and other materials.

FICTION Subjects include historical, military, poetry, war. Especially but not limited to military history. Query with SASE or by e-mail first. Do not send ms (in whole or in part) unless requested to do so.

POETRY Especially but not limited to military topics. Query with SASE or by e-mail first. Do not send ms (in whole or in part) unless requested to do so.

MESSIANIC JEWISH PUBLISHERS

6120 Day Long Ln., Clarksville MD 21029. (410)531-6644. **E-mail:** editor@messianicjewish.net. **Website:** www.messianicjewish.net. Publishes hardcover and trade paperback originals and reprints. **Publishes 6-12 titles/year. Pays 7-15% royalty on wholesale price.** Accepts simultaneous submissions. Guidelines via e-mail.

NONFICTION Subjects include religion. Text must demonstrate keen awareness of Jewish culture and thought, and Biblical literacy. Jewish themes only. Query with SASE. Unsolicited mss are not returned.

FICTION Subjects include religious. "We publish very little fiction. Jewish or Biblical themes are a must. Text must demonstrate keen awareness of Jewish culture and thought." Query with SASE. Unsolicited mss are not return.

METAL POWDER INDUSTRIES FEDERATION

105 College Rd. E., Princeton NJ 08540. (609)452-7700. **Fax:** (609)987-8523. **Website:** www.mpif.org. Estab. 1946. Publishes hardcover originals. "Metal Powder Industries publishes monographs, textbooks, handbooks, design guides, conference proceedings, standards, and general titles in the field of powder metallurgy or particulate materials." **Publishes 10 titles/year. Pays 3-12% royalty on wholesale or retail price. Pays $3,000-5,000 advance.** Accepts simultaneous submissions. Responds in 1 month to queries.

NONFICTION Work must relate to powder metallurgy or particulate materials.

MICHIGAN STATE UNIVERSITY PRESS

1405 S. Harrison Rd., Suite 25, East Lansing MI 48823. (517)355-9543. **Fax:** (517)432-2611. **E-mail:** msupress@msu.edu. **Website:** msupress.org. **Contact:** Alex Schwartz and Julie Loehr, acquisitions. Estab. 1947. Publishes hardcover and softcover originals. Michigan State University Press has notably represented both scholarly publishing and the mission of Michigan State University with the publication of numerous award-winning books and scholarly journals. In addition, they publish nonfiction that addresses, in a more contemporary way, social concerns, such as diversity and civil rights. They also publish literary fiction and poetry. **Pays variable royalty.** Book catalog and ms guidelines online.

NONFICTION Distributes books for: University of Calgary Press, University of Alberta Press, and University of Manitoba Press. Submit proposal/outline and sample chapter. Hard copy is preferred but email proposals are also accepted. Initial submissions to MSU Press should be in the form of a short letter of inquiry and a sample chapter(s), as well as our preliminary Marketing Questionnaire, which can be downloaded from their website. We do not accept:

Festschrifts, conference papers, or unrevised dissertations. Reviews artwork/photos.

FICTION Subjects include literary. Publishes literary fiction. Submit proposal.

POETRY Publishes poetry collections. Submit proposal with sample poems.

MICROSOFT PRESS

E-mail: 4bkideas@microsoft.com. **Website:** www.microsoft.com/learning/en/us/microsoft-press-books.aspx. **Publishes 80 titles/year. 25% of books from first-time authors. 90% from unagented writers.** Accepts simultaneous submissions. Book proposal guidelines online.

NONFICTION Subjects include software. A book proposal should consist of the following information: TOC, a resume with author biography, a writing sample, and a questionnaire. "We place a great deal of emphasis on your proposal. A proposal provides us with a basis for evaluating the idea of the book and how fully your book fulfills its purpose."

MILKWEED EDITIONS

1011 Washington Ave. S., Suite 300, Minneapolis MN 55415. (612)332-3192. **Fax:** (612)215-2550. **Website:** www.milkweed.org. Estab. 1979. Publishes hardcover, trade paperback, and electronic originals; trade paperback and electronic reprints. "Milkweed Editions publishes with the intention of making a humane impact on society, in the belief that literature is a transformative art uniquely able to convey the essential experiences of the human heart and spirit. To that end, Milkweed Editions publishes distinctive voices of literary merit in handsomely designed, visually dynamic books, exploring the ethical, cultural, and esthetic issues that free societies need continually to address." **Publishes 15-20 titles/year. 25% of books from first-time authors. 75% from unagented writers. Pays authors variable royalty based on retail price. Offers advance against royalties. Pays varied advance from $500-10,000.** Publishes book in 18 months. Accepts simultaneous submissions. Responds in 6 months. Book catalog online. Only accepts submissions during open submission periods. See website for guidelines.

NONFICTION Subjects include agriculture, animals, art, contemporary culture, creative nonfiction, environment, gardening, gay, government, history, humanities, language, literature, multicultural, na-

ture, politics, translation, world affairs. Does not review artwork.

FICTION Subjects include experimental, short story collections, translation, young adult. Novels for adults and for readers 8-13. High literary quality. For adult readers: literary fiction, nonfiction, poetry, essays. Middle readers: adventure, contemporary, fantasy, multicultural, nature/environment, suspense/mystery. Average length: middle readers—90-200 pages. No romance, mysteries, science fiction. "Please submit a query letter with three opening chapters (of a novel) or three representative stories (of a collection). Publishes YR."

POETRY Milkweed Editions is "looking for poetry manuscripts of high quality that embody humane values and contribute to cultural understanding." Not limited in subject matter. Open to writers with previously published books of poetry or a minimum of 6 poems published in nationally distributed commercial or literary journals. Considers translations and bilingual mss. Query with SASE; submit completed ms.

MINNESOTA HISTORICAL SOCIETY PRESS

Minnesota Historical Society, 345 Kellogg Blvd. W., St. Paul MN 55102. (651)259-3200. **Fax:** (651)297-1345. **E-mail:** ann.regan@mnhs.org. **Website:** www.mnhspress.org. **Contact:** Ann Regan, editor-in-chief. Estab. 1852. Publishes hardcover, trade paperback and electronic originals; trade paperback and electronic reprints. The Minnesota Historical Society Press is a leading publisher of the history and culture of Minnesota and the Upper Midwest. The Minnesota Historical Society Press seeks proposals for book manuscripts relating to the history and culture of Minnesota and the Upper Midwest. We are especially interested in excellent works of history and in well-researched and well-written manuscripts that use the best tools of narrative journalism to tell history for general audiences. Successful manuscripts will address themes or issues that are important to understanding life in this region and will reveal a strong sense of place. Preferred topics include Native American studies, Scandinavian studies, nature and environment, women's history, popular culture, food, adventure and travel, true crime, war and conflict, and the histories of Minnesota's diverse peoples. **Publishes 20 titles/year. 300 queries; 150 mss received/year. 60% of books from first-time authors. 95% from unagented writ-**

ers. **Royalties are negotiated; 5-10% on wholesale price. Pays $1,000 and up.** Publishes ms 16 months after acceptance. Accepts simultaneous submissions. Responds in 1-4 months. Book catalog online. Guidelines online.

NONFICTION Subjects include Americana, community, contemporary culture, cooking, creative nonfiction, ethnic, history, memoirs, multicultural, music, photography, politics, pop culture, regional, Native American studies. Books must have a connection to the Midwest. Regional works only. Submit proposal package, outline, 1 sample chapter and other materials listed in our online website in author guidelines: CV, brief description, intended audience, readership, length of ms, schedule. Reviews artwork/photos. Send photocopies.

MITCHELL LANE PUBLISHERS, INC.

P.O. Box 196, Hockessin DE 33009. (302) 234-9426. **Fax:** (866) 834-4164. **E-mail:** barbaramitchell@mitchelllane.com; customerservice@mitchelllane.com. **Website:** www.mitchelllane.com. **Contact:** Barbara Mitchell. Estab. 1993. Publishes hardcover and library bound originals. **Publishes 80 titles/year. 100 queries received/year. 5 mss received/year. 0% of books from first-time authors. 90% from unagented writers. Work purchased outright from authors (range: $350-2,000). Pays illustrators by the project (range: $40-400).** Publishes ms 1 year after acceptance. Responds only if interested to queries. Book catalog available free.

NONFICTION Subjects include ethnic, multicultural. Young readers, middle readers, young adults: biography, nonfiction, and curriculum-related subjects. Average word length: 4,000-50,000 words. Recently published: *My Guide to US Citizenship*, *Rivers of the World* and *Vote America*. Query with SASE. *All unsolicited mss discarded.*

MONDIAL

203 W. 107th St., Suite 6C, New York NY 10025. 212-864-7095. **Fax:** (208)361-2863. **E-mail:** contact@mondialbooks.com. **Website:** www.mondialbooks.com; www.librejo.com. **Contact:** Andrew Moore, editor. Estab. 1996. Publishes hard cover, trade paperback originals and reprints. Mondial publishes fiction and non-fiction in English, Esperanto, and Hebrew: novels, short stories, poetry, textbooks, dictionaries, books about history, linguistics, and psychology, among others. Since 2007, it has been publishing a literary magazine in Esperanto. **Publishes 20 titles/year. 2,000 queries; 500 mss received/year. 20% of books from first-time authors. 100% from unagented writers. Pays 10% royalty on wholesale price. Does not pay advance.** Publishes ms 4 months after acceptance. Accepts simultaneous submissions. Responds to queries in 3 months, only if interested. Guidelines online.

NONFICTION Subjects include ethnic, history, literary criticism, memoirs, multicultural, philosophy, psychology, sex, sociology, translation. Submit proposal package, outline, 1 sample chapters. Send only electronically by e-mail.

FICTION Subjects include adventure, erotica, ethnic, historical, literary, multicultural, mystery, poetry, romance, short story collections, translation. Query through online submission form.

ⒶⓄ MOODY PUBLISHERS

Moody Bible Institute, 820 N. LaSalle Blvd., Chicago IL 60610. (800)678-8812. **Fax:** (312)329-4157. **Website:** www.moodypublishers.org. **Contact:** Acquisitions Coordinator. Estab. 1894. Publishes hardcover, trade, and mass market paperback originals. "The mission of Moody Publishers is to educate and edify the Christian and to evangelize the non-Christian by ethically publishing conservative, evangelical Christian literature and other media for all ages around the world, and to help provide resources for Moody Bible Institute in its training of future Christian leaders." **Publishes 60 titles/year. 1,500 queries received/year. 2,000 mss received/year. 1% of books from first-time authors. 80% from unagented writers. Royalty varies.** Publishes book 1 year after acceptance. Responds in 2-3 months to queries. Book catalog for 9×12 envelope and 4 first-class stamps. Guidelines online.

NONFICTION Subjects include child guidance, religion, spirituality. "We are no longer reviewing queries or unsolicited manuscripts unless they come to us through an agent, are from an author who has published with us, an associate from a Moody Bible Institute ministry or a personal contact at a writer's conference. Unsolicited proposals will be returned only if proper postage is included. We are not able to acknowledge the receipt of your unsolicited proposal." Does not accept unsolicited nonfiction submissions.

FICTION Subjects include fantasy, historical, mystery, religious, science fiction, young adult. *Agented submissions only.*

MOTORBOOKS

Quarto Publishing Group, 401 2nd Ave. N., Suite 310, Minneapolis MN 55401. (612)344-8100. **Fax:** (612)344-8691. **E-mail:** zack.miller@quarto.com. **Website:** www.quartoknows.com. **Contact:** Zack Miller. Estab. 1973. Publishes hardcover and paperback originals. "Motorbooks is one of the world's leading transportation publishers, covering subjects from classic motorcycles to heavy equipment to today's latest automotive technology. We satisfy our customers' high expectations by hiring top writers and photographers and presenting their work in handsomely designed books that work hard in the shop and look good on the coffee table." **Publishes 200 titles/year. 300 queries; 50 mss received/year. 95% from unagented writers. Pays $5,000 average advance.** Publishes ms 1 year after acceptance. Accepts simultaneous submissions. Responds in 6-8 months to proposals. Book catalog available free. Guidelines online.

NONFICTION Subjects include Americana, history, hobbies, photography, translation. State qualifications for doing book. Transportation-related subjects. Query with SASE. Reviews artwork/photos. Send photocopies.

MOUNTAINEERS BOOKS

The Mountaineers, 1001 SW Klickitat Way, Suite 201, Seattle WA 98134. (206)223-6303. **Fax:** (206)223-6306. **E-mail:** submissions@mountaineersbooks.org. **Website:** www.mountaineersbooks.org. Estab. 1961. Publishes trade hardcover, paperback, and e-book originals and reprints. "Mountaineers Books publishes nonfiction books on outdoor recreation, lifestyle, and conservation topics. The sports in its recreation line are all muscle-powered activities, including climbing, hiking, biking, and others. The lifestyle imprint, Skipstone, focuses on sustainable-living topics, such as cooking and gardening. The conservation titles are published in the Braided River imprint, and are uniquely used in partnership with other conservation organizations to highlight, educate, and advocate for specific environmental concerns. Mountaineers Books is an independent nonprofit publisher." **Publishes 40 titles/year. 25% of books from first-time authors. 98% from unagented writers. Pays advance.**

Publishes ms 1 year after acceptance. Responds in 3 months to queries. Guidelines online.

IMPRINTS Skipstone, Braided River.

NONFICTION Subjects include cooking, environment, gardening, horticulture, memoirs, nature, nutrition, recreation, regional, sports, translation, travel, natural history, conservation. Accepts nonfiction translations. Looks for expert knowledge, good organization. Also interested in nonfiction adventure narratives. Does not want to see anything dealing with hunting, fishing, or motorized travel. Submit outline, 2 sample chapters, bio.

MOUNTAIN PRESS PUBLISHING CO.

P.O. Box 2399, Missoula MT 59806. (406)728-1900 or (800)234-5308. **Fax:** (406)728-1635. **E-mail:** info@mtnpress.com. **Website:** www.mountain-press.com. **Contact:** Jennifer Carey, editor. Estab. 1948. Publishes hardcover and trade paperback originals. "We are expanding our Roadside Geology, Geology Underfoot, and Roadside History series (done on a state-by-state basis). We are interested in well-written regional field guides—plants and flowers—and readable history and natural history." **Publishes 15 titles/year. 50% of books from first-time authors. 90% from unagented writers. Pays 7-12% royalty on wholesale price.** Publishes ms 2 years after acceptance. Accepts simultaneous submissions. Responds in 3 months to queries. Book catalog online.

NONFICTION Subjects include animals, history, regional, science. No personal histories or journals, poetry or fiction. Query with SASE. Submit outline, sample chapters. Reviews artwork/photos.

MSI PRESS

1760-F Airline Hwy, #203, Hollister CA 95023. **Fax:** (831)886-2486. **E-mail:** editor@msipress.com. **Website:** www.msipress.com. **Contact:** Betty Leaver, managing editor (self-help, spirituality, religion, memoir, mind/body/spirit, some humor, popular psychology, foreign tales, parenting). Estab. 2003. Publishes trade paperback originals and corresponding e-books. "We are a small, 'boutique' press that specializes in award-winning quality publications, refined through strong personal interactions and productive working relationships between our editors and our authors. A small advance may be offered to previously published authors with a strong book, strong platform, and solid sales numbers. We will accept first-time authors with credibility in their fields and a strong platform, but we do not offer advances to first-time authors. We may refer authors with a good book but little credibility or lacking a strong platform to San Juan Books, our hybrid publishing venture." **Publishes 15-20 titles/ year. 100-200 10% of books from first-time authors. 100% from unagented writers. Pays 10% royalty on retail price for paperbacks and hard cover books; pays 50% royalty on net for e-books. By exception, pays small advance to previously published authors with good sales history.** Publishes ms 6-10 months after acceptance. Accepts simultaneous submissions. Responds in 2 weeks to queries sent by e-mail and to proposals submitted via the template on our website. If response not received in 2 weeks, okay to query. Catalog online. Guidelines online.

IMPRINTS MSI Press, LLC; San Juan Books.

NONFICTION Subjects include animals, child guidance, counseling, creative nonfiction, education, ethnic, health, humanities, labor, memoirs, multicultural, parenting, philosophy, psychology, regional, religion, spirituality, travel, womens issues, Ask; we are open to new ideas.. "We continue to expand our spirituality, psychology, and self-help lines and are interested in adding to our collection of books in Spanish. We do not do or publish translations." Does not want erotica. Submit proposal package, including: annotated outline, 1 sample chapter, professional resume, platform. Prefers electronic submissions. Note that we are open to foreign writers (non-native speakers of English), but please have an English editor proofread the submission prior to sending; if the query letter or proposal is written in poor English, we will not take a chance on a manuscript. Reviews artwork/photos; send computer disk, or, preferably, e-file.

NAVAL INSTITUTE PRESS

US Naval Institute, 291 Wood Rd., Annapolis MD 21402. (410)268-6110. **Fax:** (410)295-1084. **Website:** www.usni.org. Estab. 1873. "The Naval Institute Press publishes trade and scholarly nonfiction. We are interested in national and international security, naval, military, military jointness, intelligence, and special warfare, both current and historical." **Publishes 80-90 titles/year. 50% of books from first-time authors. 90% from unagented writers.** Accepts simultaneous submissions. Guidelines online.

NONFICTION Submit proposal package with outline, author bio, TOC, description/synopsis, sample chapter(s), page/word count, number of illustrations, ms completion date, intended market; or submit complete ms. Send SASE with sufficient postage for return of ms. Send by postal mail only. No e-mail submissions, please.

⊘ NAVPRESS

3820 N. 30th St., Colorado Springs CO 80904. **Website:** www.navpress.com. Estab. 1975. Publishes hardcover, trade paperback, direct and mass market paperback originals and reprints; electronic books and Bible studies. **Pays royalty. Pays low or no advances.** Accepts simultaneous submissions. Book catalog available free.

NONFICTION Subjects include child guidance.

NBM PUBLISHING

160 Broadway, Suite 700, East Bldg., New York NY 10038. **E-mail:** nbmgn@nbmpub.com. **Website:** nbmpub.com. **Contact:** Terry Nantier, editor. Estab. 1976. Publishes graphic novels for an audience of YA/adults. Types of books include fiction, mystery, biographies and social parodies. **Publishes 16 titles/year. 5% of books from first-time authors. 90% from unagented writers. Advance negotiable.** Publishes ms 1 year after acceptance. Accepts simultaneous submissions. Responds to e-mail 1-2 days; mail 1 week. Catalog online.

NONFICTION Subjects include , biographies.

FICTION Subjects include comic books, contemporary, gay, humor, lesbian, literary, multicultural, mystery, translation, young adult.

❶⊘ THOMAS NELSON, INC.

HarperCollins Christian Publishing, Box 141000, Nashville TN 37214. (615)889-9000. **Website:** www.thomasnelson.com. Publishes hardcover and paperback orginals. Thomas Nelson publishes Christian lifestyle nonfiction and fiction, and general nonfiction. **Publishes 100-150 titles/year. Rates negotiated for each project. Pays advance.** Publishes ms 1-2 years after acceptance. Accepts simultaneous submissions.

NONFICTION Subjects include gardening, religion, spirituality, adult inspirational, motivational, devotional, Christian living, prayer and evangelism, Bible study, personal development, political, biography/autobiography. *Does not accept unsolicited mss.* No phone queries.

FICTION Publishes authors of commercial fiction who write for adults from a Christian perspective. *Does not accept unsolicited mss.* No phone queries.

⊘ TOMMY NELSON

Imprint of Thomas Nelson, Inc., P.O. Box 141000, Nashville TN 37214-1000. (615)889-9000. **Fax:** (615)902-2219. **Website:** www.tommynelson.com. Publishes hardcover and trade paperback originals. "Tommy Nelson publishes children's Christian nonfiction and fiction for boys and girls up to age 14. We honor God and serve people through books, videos, software and Bibles for children that improve the lives of our customers." **Publishes 50-75 titles/year.** Guidelines online.

NONFICTION Subjects include religion. *Does not accept unsolicited mss.*

FICTION Subjects include adventure, juvenile, mystery, picture books, religious. No stereotypical characters. *Does not accept unsolicited mss.*

NEW DIRECTIONS

80 Eighth Ave., New York NY 10011. **Fax:** (212)255-0231. **E-mail:** editorial@ndbooks.com. **Website:** www.ndbooks.com. **Contact:** Editorial Assistant. Estab. 1936. Hardcover and trade paperback originals. "Currently, New Directions focuses primarily on fiction in translation, avant garde American fiction, and experimental poetry by American and foreign authors. If your work does not fall into one of those categories, you would probably do best to submit your work elsewhere." **Publishes 30 titles/year.** Responds in 3-4 months to queries. Book catalog and guidelines online.

FICTION Subjects include ethnic, experimental, historical, humor, literary, poetry, poetry in translation, regional, short story collections, suspense, translation. No juvenile or young adult, occult or paranormal, genre fiction (formula romances, sci-fi or westerns), arts & crafts, and inspirational poetry. Brief query only.

POETRY Query.

♲ NEWEST PUBLISHERS LTD.

201, 8540-109 St., Edmonton AB T6G 1E6, Canada. (780)432-9427. **Fax:** (780)433-3179. **E-mail:** info@ newestpress.com. **E-mail:** submissions@newestpress.com. **Website:** www.newestpress.com. Estab. 1977. Publishes trade paperback originals. NeWest publishes Western Canadian fiction, nonfiction, po-

etry, and drama. **Publishes 13-16 titles/year. 40% of books from first-time authors. 85% from unagented writers. Pays 10% royalty.** Publishes ms 2-3 years after acceptance. Accepts simultaneous submissions. Responds in 6-8 months to queries. Book catalog for 9×12 SASE. Guidelines online.

NONFICTION Subjects include ethnic, history, Canadian. Query.

FICTION Subjects include literary. Submit complete ms.

NEW FORUMS PRESS

New Forums, 1018 S. Lewis St., Stillwater OK 74074. (405)372-6158. **Fax:** (405)377-2237. **E-mail:** contact@ newforums.com. **E-mail:** submissions@newforums. com. **Website:** www.newforums.com. **Contact:** Doug Dollar, president (interests: higher education, Oklahoma-Regional, US military). Estab. 1981. Hardcover and trade paperback originals. "New Forums Press is an independent publisher offering works devoted to various aspects of professional development in higher education, home and office aides, US military, and various titles of a regional interest. We welcome suggestions for thematic series of books and thematic issues of our academic journals—addressing a single issue, problem, or theory." **60% of books from first-time authors. 100% from unagented writers. 10% of Gross Sales paid as royalty. Does not pay advance.** Publishes ms 4 months after acceptance. Accepts simultaneous submissions. Responds in 1-2 weeks. Guidelines online.

NONFICTION Subjects include business, education, history, literature, military, regional, sociology, war. "We are actively seeking new authors—send for review copies and author guidelines, and visit our website." Mss should be submitted as a Microsoft Word document, or a similar standard word processor document (saved in RTF rich text), as an attachment to an e-mail sent to submissions@newforums.com. Otherwise, submit your ms on 8 ½ x 11 inch white bond paper (one original). The name and complete address, telephone, fax number, and e-mail address of each author should appear on a separate cover page, so it can be removed for the blind review process.

NEW HARBINGER PUBLICATIONS

5674 Shattuck Ave., Oakland CA 94609. (510)652-0215. **Fax:** (510)652-5472. **E-mail:** proposals@newharbinger.com. **Website:** www.newharbinger.com. Estab. 1973. "We look for psychology and health self-help books that teach readers how to master essential life skills. Mental health professionals who want simple, clear explanations or important psychological techniques and health issues also read our books. Thus, our books must be simple ane easy to understand but also complete and authoritative. Most of our authors are therapists or other helping professionals." **Publishes 55 titles/year. 1,000 queries received/year. 300 mss received/year. 60% of books from first-time authors. 75% from unagented writers.** Publishes ms 1 year after acceptance. Accepts simultaneous submissions. Responds in 2 weeks to queries; 1 month to proposals; 2 months to mss. Book catalog free. Guidelines online.

NONFICTION Subjects include psychology, psycho spirituality, anger management, anxiety, coping, mindfulness skills. Authors need to be qualified psychotherapists or health practitioners to publish with us. Submit proposal package, outline, 2 sample chapters, TOC, competing titles, and a compelling, supported reason why the book is unique.

⊘ NEW HOPE PUBLISHERS

Iron Stream Media, 5184 Caldwell Mill Rd., Ste. 204-221,, Hoover AL 35244. (888)811-9934. **E-mail:** info@newhopepublishers.com. **E-mail:** proposals@newhopepublishers.com. **Website:** www.newhopepublishers.com. **Contact:** Ramona Richards, associate publisher. Iron Stream Media/New Hope Publishers is a Christian media company providing resources to advance the Gospel of Jesus Christ, making disciples as we go. **Publishes 12-18 titles/year. 50-100 40% of books from first-time authors. 50% from unagented writers. Royalty-based payment. Pays occasional advance.** Publishes ms within 2 years after acceptance. Accepts simultaneous submissions. Catalog online. Guidelines online.

NONFICTION Subjects include religion, church leadership, Christian living. "We publish books dealing with all facets of Christian life for women and families, including health, discipleship, missions, ministry, Bible studies, spiritual development, parenting, and marriage. We currently do not accept children's picture books. We are particularly interested in niche categories and books on lifestyle development and change." We do not accept or review any unsolicited queries, proposals, or mss.

FICTION Subjects include , Romantic Suspense, Cozies, Visionary, Women's Fiction. Does not want romance.

NEW HORIZON PRESS

P.O. Box 669, Far Hills NJ 07931. (908)604-6311. **Fax:** (908)604-6330. **Website:** www.newhorizonpress-books.com. **Contact:** Acquisitions Editor. Estab. 1983. Publishes hardcover and trade paperback originals. "New Horizon publishes adult nonfiction featuring true stories of uncommon heroes, true crime, social issues, and self help." **Publishes 12 titles/year. 90% of books from first-time authors. 50% from unagented writers. Pays standard royalty on net receipts. Pays advance.** Publishes book within 2 years of acceptance. Accepts simultaneous submissions. Book catalog available free. Guidelines online.

IMPRINTS Small Horizons.

NONFICTION Subjects include child guidance, creative nonfiction, psychology, true crime. Submit proposal package, outline, résumé, bio, 3 sample chapters, photo, marketing information.

NEWSAGE PRESS

P.O. Box 607, Troutdale OR 97060. (503)695-2211. **E-mail:** info@newsagepress.com. **Website:** www.newsagepress.com. Estab. 1985. Publishes trade paperback originals. "We focus on nonfiction books. No 'how-to' books or cynical, despairing books. Photo-essay books in large format are no longer published by Newsage Press. No novels or other forms of fiction." Accepts simultaneous submissions. Guidelines online.

NONFICTION Subjects include animals, multicultural, death/dying. Submit 2 sample chapters, proposal (no more than 1 page), SASE.

✪ NEW SOCIETY PUBLISHERS

P.O. Box 189, Gabriola Island BC V0R 1X0, Canada. (250)247-9737. **Fax:** (250)247-7471. **E-mail:** editor@newsociety.com. **Website:** www.newsociety.com. Publishes trade paperback originals and reprints and electronic originals. **Publishes 25 titles/year. 400 queries; 300 mss received/year. 50% of books from first-time authors. 80% from unagented writers. Pays 10-12% royalty on wholesale price. Pays $0-5,000 advance.** Publishes ms about 9 months after acceptance. Accepts simultaneous submissions. Responds in 1-2 months. Book catalog and guidelines online.

NONFICTION Subjects include agriculture, alternative lifestyles, animals, beauty, business, child guidance, communications, community, contemporary culture, cooking, economics, education, environment, fashion, finance, foods, gardening, health, horticulture, house and home, humanities, labor, money, nature, nutrition, parenting, philosophy, politics, regional, science, social sciences, spirituality, sustainability, open building, peak oil, renewable energy, post carbon prep, sustainable living, gardening & cooking, green building, natural building, ecological design & planning, environment & economy. Query with SASE. Submit proposal package, outline, 2 sample chapters. Reviews artwork/photos. Send photocopies.

NEW WORLD LIBRARY

14 Pamaron Way, Novato CA 94949. (415)884-2100. **Fax:** (415)884-2199. **E-mail:** submit@newworldlibrary.com. **Website:** www.newworldlibrary.com. **Contact:** Joel Prins, submissions editor. Estab. 1977. Publishes nonfiction hardcover and trade paperback originals and reprints and e-books. "NWL is dedicated to publishing books that inspire and challenge us to improve the quality of our lives and our world." Prefers e-mail submissions. No longer accepting children's mss. **Publishes 30-35 titles/year. 10% of books from first-time authors. 25% from unagented writers. Pays advance.** Publishes ms 12 months after acceptance. Accepts simultaneous submissions. Responds in 3 months to queries if interested. Reviews all queries. Book catalog free. Guidelines online.

NONFICTION Subjects include alternative lifestyles, animals, business, career guidance, child guidance, contemporary culture, counseling, environment, health, nature, New Age, parenting, philosophy, psychic, religion, spirituality, translation, womens issues. Submit outline, overview, bio, 2-3 sample chapters via e-mail. Does not review artwork.

NEW YORK UNIVERSITY PRESS

838 Broadway, 3rd Floor, New York NY 10003. (212)998-2575. **Fax:** (212)995-3833. **E-mail:** nyupressinfo@nyu.edu. **Website:** www.nyupress.org. **Contact:** Ellen Chodosh, director. Estab. 1916. Hardcover and trade paperback originals. "New York University Press embraces ideological diversity. We often publish books on the same issue from different poles to generate dialogue, engender and resist pat categorizations." **Publishes 100 titles/year. 800-1,000 queries received/year. 30% of books from first-time au-

thors. 90% from unagented writers.** Publishes ms 9-11 months after acceptance. Accepts simultaneous submissions. Responds in 1-4 months (peer reviewed) to proposals. Guidelines online.

NONFICTION Subjects include ethnic, psychology, regional, religion, sociology, American history, anthropology. New York University Press is a publisher primarily of academic books and is a department of the New York University Division of Libraries. NYU Press publishes in the humanities and social sciences, with emphasis on sociology, law, cultural and American studies, religion, American history, anthropology, politics, criminology, media and film, and psychology. The Press also publishes books on New York regional history, politics, and culture. Query with SASE. Submit proposal package, outline, 1 sample chapter. Reviews artwork/photos. Send photocopies.

NOLO

950 Parker St., Berkeley CA 94710. (510)549-1976. **Fax:** (510)859-0025. **Website:** www.nolo.com. **Contact:** Editorial Department. Estab. 1971. Publishes trade paperback originals. "We publish practical, do-it-yourself books, software and various electronic products on financial and legal issues that affect individuals, small business, and nonprofit organizations. We specialize in helping people handle their own legal tasks; i.e., write a will, file a small claims lawsuit, start a small business or nonprofit, or apply for a patent." **Publishes 75 new editions and 15 new titles/year. 20% of books from first-time authors. Pays advance.** Accepts simultaneous submissions. Responds in 3 weeks to queries. Responds in 5 weeks to proposals. Guidelines online.

NONFICTION Subjects include , legal guides in various topics including employment, small business, intellectual property, parenting and education, finance and investment, landlord/tenant, real estate, and estate planning. Query with SASE. Submit outline, 1 sample chapter.

NORTH ATLANTIC BOOKS

2526 Martin Luther King Jr. Way, Berkeley CA 94704. **E-mail:** submissions@northatlanticbooks.com. **Website:** www.northatlanticbooks.com. **Contact:** Acquisitions Board. Estab. 1974. Publishes hardcover, trade paperback, and electronic originals; trade paperback and electronic reprints. **Publishes 60 titles/year. Receives 200 mss/year. 50% of books from first-time authors. 75% from unagented writers. Pays royalty percentage on wholesale price. Publishes ms 14 months after acceptance. Accepts simultaneous submissions. Responds in 3-6 months. Book catalog free on request (if available). Guidelines online.

IMPRINTS Evolver Editions, Blue Snake Books.

NONFICTION Subjects include agriculture, anthropology, archeology, architecture, art, astrology, business, child guidance, community, contemporary culture, cooking, economics, electronics, environment, finance, foods, gardening, gay, health, horticulture, lesbian, medicine, memoirs, money, multicultural, nature, New Age, nutrition, philosophy, politics, psychic, psychology, public affairs, religion, science, social sciences, sociology, spirituality, sports, travel, womens issues, womens studies, world affairs. Submit proposal package including an outline, 3-4 sample chapters, and "a 75-word statement about the book, your qualifications as an author, marketing plan/audience, for the book, and comparable titles." Reviews artwork with ms package.

FICTION Subjects include adventure, literary, multicultural, mystery, regional, science fiction, spiritual. "We only publish fiction on rare occasions." Submit proposal package including an outline, 3-4 sample chapters, and "a 75-word statement about the book, your qualifications as an author, marketing plan/audience, for the book, and comparable titles."

POETRY Submit 15-20 sample poems.
barger.

NORTH LIGHT BOOKS

F+W, a Content + eCommerce Company, 10151 Carver Rd., Suite 300, Blue Ash OH 45242. **E-mail:** mona.clough@fwmedia.com. **Website:** www.fwmedia.com; www.artistsnetwork.com; www.createmixedmedia.com. **Contact:** Noel Rivera, managing content director. Publishes hardcover and trade paperback how-to books. "North Light Books publishes art books, including watercolor, drawing, mixed media, acrylic that emphasize illustrated how-to art instruction. Currently emphasizing drawing including traditional, activity books and creativity and inspiration." **Publishes 50 titles/year. 50% of books from first-time authors. 80% from unagented writers. Pays 8% royalty on net receipts and $3,000 advance. Pays advance.** Publishes ms 10-24 months after acceptance. Accepts simultaneous submissions. Responds in 3 months to queries. Book catalog online. Does not return submissions.

NONFICTION Subjects include art, watercolor, oil painting, acrylic painting realistic drawing, creativity, decorative painting, paper arts, collage and other craft instruction books.. Interested in books on acrylic painting, basic drawing and sketching, journaling, pen and ink, colored pencil, decorative painting, art and how-to. Do not submit coffee table art books without how-to art instruction. Query via e-mail only. Submit outline with JPEG low-resolution images. Submissions via snail mail will not be returned.

✦⊘ W.W. NORTON & COMPANY, INC.

500 Fifth Ave., New York NY 10110. (212)354-5500. **Fax:** (212)869-0856. **Website:** www.wwnorton.com. Estab. 1923. "W. W. Norton & Company, the oldest and largest publishing house owned wholly by its employees, strives to carry out the imperative of its founder to 'publish books not for a single season, but for the years' in fiction, nonfiction, poetry, college textbooks, cookbooks, art books and professional books. Due to the workload of our editorial staff and the large volume of materials we receive, *Norton is no longer able to accept unsolicited submissions.* If you are seeking publication, we suggest working with a literary agent who will represent you to the house." Accepts simultaneous submissions.

NO STARCH PRESS, INC.

245 8th St., San Francisco CA 94103. (415)863-9900. **Fax:** (415)863-9950. **E-mail:** editors@nostarch.com. **Website:** www.nostarch.com. **Contact:** William Pollock, publisher. Estab. 1994. Publishes trade paperback originals. "No Starch Press publishes the finest in geek entertainment—unique books on technology, with a focus on open source, security, hacking, programming, alternative operating systems, LEGO, science, and math. Our titles have personality, our authors are passionate, and our books tackle topics that people care about." **Publishes 25-30 titles/year. 300 queries; 50 mss received/year. 80% of books from first-time authors. 90% from unagented writers. Pays 10-15% royalty on wholesale price. Pays advance.** Publishes ms 4-6 months after acceptance. Accepts simultaneous submissions. Responds in 1-2 weeks. Book catalog online. Guidelines online.

NONFICTION Subjects include computers, electronics, science, software, technology, computing, mathematics, science, STEM, LEGO. Submit outline, bio, 1 sample chapter, market rationale. Reviews artwork/photos. Send digitally please.

NURSESBOOKS.ORG

American Nurses Association, 8515 Georgia Ave., Suite 400, Silver Spring MD 20901. (800)274-4ANA. **Fax:** (301)628-5003. **E-mail:** anp@ana.org. **Website:** www.nursesbooks.org. Publishes professional paperback originals and reprints. "Nursebooks.org publishes books designed to help professional nurses in their work and careers. Through the publishing program, Nursebooks.org provides nurses in all practice settings with publications that address cutting edge issues and form a basis for debate and exploration of this century's most critical health care trends." **Publishes 10 titles/year. 50 queries received/year. 8-10 mss received/year. 75% of books from first-time authors. 100% from unagented writers.** Publishes ms 4 months after acceptance. Responds in 3 months. Book catalog online. Guidelines available free.

NONFICTION Subjects include advanced practice, computers, continuing education, ethics, health care policy, nursing administration, psychiatric and mental health, quality, nursing history, workplace issues, key clinical topics, such as geriatrics, pain management, public health, spirituality and home health. Submit outline, 1 sample chapter, CV, list of 3 reviewers and paragraph on audience and how to reach them. Reviews artwork/photos. Send photocopies.

OAK KNOLL PRESS

310 Delaware St., New Castle DE 19720. (302)328-7232. **Fax:** (302)328-7274. **E-mail:** publishing@oakknoll.com. **Website:** www.oakknoll.com. **Contact:** Robert D. Fleck III, president. Estab. 1976. Publishes hardcover and trade paperback originals and reprints. "Oak Knoll specializes in books about books and manuals on the book arts: preserving the art and lore of the printed word." **Publishes 40 titles/year. 250 queries; 100 mss received/year. 50% of books from first-time authors. 100% from unagented writers.** Publishes ms 1 year after acceptance. Accepts simultaneous submissions. Guidelines online.

NONFICTION Reviews artwork/photos. Send photocopies.

OHIO STATE UNIVERSITY PRESS

1070 Carmack Rd., 180 Pressey Hall, Columbus OH 43210-1002. (614)292-6930. **Fax:** (614)292-2065. **E-mail:** eugene@osupress.org. **E-mail:** lindsay@osupress.org. **Website:** www.ohiostatepress.org. **Contact:** Eugene O'Connor, acquisitions editor (medieval studies and classics); Lindsay Martin, acquisitions editor

(literary studies). Estab. 1957. The Ohio State University Press publishes scholarly nonfiction, and offers short fiction and short poetry prizes. Currently emphasizing history, literary studies, political science, women's health, classics, Victoria studies. **Publishes 30 titles/year. Pays royalty. Pays advance.** Accepts simultaneous submissions. Responds in 3 months to queries. Guidelines online.

NONFICTION Subjects include education, history, literary criticism, multicultural, regional, sociology, criminology, literary criticism, women's health. Query.

POETRY Offers poetry competition through *The Journal.*

OHIO UNIVERSITY PRESS

30 Park Place, Suite 101, Athens OH 45701. (740)593-1159. **Fax:** (740)593-4536. **E-mail:** berchowi@ohio.edu. **Website:** www.ohioswallow.com. **Contact:** Gillian Berchowitz, director. Estab. 1964. Publishes hardcover and trade paperback originals and reprints. "In addition to scholarly works in African studies, Appalachian studies, US history, and other areas, Ohio University Press publishes a wide range of creative works as part of its Hollis Summers Poetry Prize (yearly deadline in December), its Modern African Writing series, and under its trade imprint, Swallow Press." **Publishes 45-50 titles/year. 500 queries; 50 mss received/year. 20% of books from first-time authors. 95% from unagented writers.** Publishes ms 1 year after acceptance. Accepts simultaneous submissions. Responds in 1-3 months. Catalog online. Guidelines online.

NONFICTION Subjects include Americana, anthropology, contemporary culture, creative nonfiction, environment, gardening, government, history, horticulture, humanities, language, literature, memoirs, military, multicultural, nature, politics, pop culture, regional, social sciences, sociology, travel, womens studies, young adult, African studies, Appalachian studies, US history, Midwestern studies, regional interest, guidebooks, military history, sustainability, middle-grade biographies. "We prefer queries or detailed proposals, rather than manuscripts. Editors will request the complete manuscript if it is of interest." Query via e-mail or with SASE. Reviews artwork/photos. Send photocopies.

FICTION Subjects include contemporary, literary, multicultural, poetry, poetry in translation, short story collections, translation.

⬤ ONEWORLD

Oneworld Publications, 10 Bloomsbury St., London WC1B 3SR, United Kingdom. **E-mail:** submissions@oneworld-publications.com. **Website:** www. oneworld-publications.com. Estab. 1986. Publishes hardcover and trade paperback originals and mass market paperback. "We publish general trade nonfiction, which must be accessible but authoritative, mainly by academics or experts for a general readership and where appropriate a cross-over student market. Currently emphasizing current affairs, popular science, history, psychology, politics and business; de-emphasizing self-help. We also publish literary fiction by international authors, both debut and established, throughout the English language world as well as selling translation rights. Our focus is on well-written literary and high-end commercial fiction from a variety of cultures and periods, many exploring interesting themes and issues. In addition we publish fiction in translation, crime fiction and YA fiction." **Publishes 100 titles/year. 20% of books from first-time authors. 20% from unagented writers.** Publishes ms 12-15 months after acceptance. Book catalog online. Guidelines online.

IMPRINTS Point Blank, Rock the Boat.

NONFICTION Submit through online proposal form.

FICTION Submit through online proposal forms.

OPEN COURT PUBLISHING CO.

70 E. Lake St., Suite 800, Chicago IL 60601. **E-mail:** opencourt@cricketmedia.com. **Website:** www.opencourtbooks.com. **Contact:** Acquisitions Editor. Estab. 1887. Publishes hardcover and trade paperback originals. "Regrettably, now, and for the forseeable future, Open Court can consider no new unsolicited manuscripts for publication, with the exception of works suitable for our Popular Culture and Philosophy series." **Publishes 20 titles/year. Pays 5-15% royalty on wholesale price.** Publishes ms 2 years after acceptance. Book catalog online. Guidelines online.

NONFICTION Subjects include philosophy, Asian thought, religious studies and popular culture. Query with SASE. Submit proposal package, outline, 1 sample chapter, TOC, author's cover letter, intended audience.

☁ ORCA BOOK PUBLISHERS

1016 Balmoral Rd., Victoria BC V8T 1A8, Canada. (800)210-5277. **Fax:** (877)408-1551. **E-mail:** orca@orcabook.com. **Website:** www.orcabook.com. **Contact:** Amy Collins, editor (picture books); Sarah Harvey, editor (young readers); Andrew Wooldridge, editor (juvenile and teen fiction); Bob Tyrrell, publisher (YA, teen); Ruth Linka, associate editor (rapid reads).. Estab. 1984. Publishes hardcover and trade paperback originals, and mass market paperback originals and reprints. Only publishes Canadian authors. **Publishes 30-50 titles/year. 2,500 queries; 1,000 mss received/year. 20% of books from first-time authors. 75% from unagented writers. Pays 10% royalty.** Publishes book 12-18 months after acceptance. Responds in 1 month to queries; 2 months to proposals and mss. Book catalog for 8½x11 SASE. Guidelines online.

NONFICTION Subjects include gay, lesbian, marine subjects, multicultural, sports, young adult, picture books. Only publishes Canadian authors. Query with a SASE.

FICTION Subjects include adventure, gay, hi-lo, juvenile, lesbian, literary, multicultural, mystery, picture books, sports, young adult. Picture books: animals, contemporary, history, nature/environment. Middle readers: contemporary, history, fantasy, nature/environment, problem novels, graphic novels. Young adults: adventure, contemporary, hi-lo (Orca Soundings), history, multicultural, nature/environment, problem novels, suspense/mystery, graphic novels. Average word length: picture books—500-1,500; middle readers—20,000-35,000; young adult—25,000-45,000; Orca Soundings—13,000-15,000; Orca Currents—13,000-15,000. No romance, science fiction. Query with SASE. Submit proposal package, outline, clips, 2-5 sample chapters, SASE.

ⓐⓩ ORCHARD BOOKS (US)

557 Broadway, New York NY 10012. **Website:** www.scholastic.com. *Orchard is not accepting unsolicited mss.* **Publishes 20 titles/year. 10% of books from first-time authors. Most commonly offers an advance against list royalties.** Accepts simultaneous submissions.

FICTION Picture books, early readers, and novelty: animal, contemporary, history, humor, multicultural, poetry.

OREGON STATE UNIVERSITY PRESS

121 The Valley Library, Corvallis OR 97331. (541)737-3873. **Fax:** (541)737-3170. **E-mail:** mary.braun@oregonstate.edu. **Website:** osupress.oregonstate.edu. **Contact:** Mary Elizabeth Braun, acquisitions editor. Estab. 1962. Publishes hardcover, paperback, and e-book originals. **Publishes 20-25 titles/year. 40% of books from first-time authors.** Publishes book 1 year after acceptance. Responds in 3 months to queries. Book catalog for 6x9 SAE with 2 first-class stamps. Guidelines online.

NONFICTION Subjects include regional, science. Publishes scholarly books in history, biography, geography, literature, natural resource management, with strong emphasis on Pacific or Northwestern topics and Native American and indigenous studies. Submit outline, sample chapters.

O'REILLY MEDIA

1005 Gravenstein Highway N., Sebastopol CA 95472. (707)827-7000. **Fax:** (707)829-0104. **E-mail:** workwithus@oreilly.com. **Website:** www.oreilly.com. **Contact:** Acquisitions Editor. "We're always looking for new authors and new book ideas. Our ideal author has real technical competence and a passion for explaining things clearly." Accepts simultaneous submissions. Guidelines online.

NONFICTION "At the same time as you might say that our books are written 'by and for smart people,' they also have a down to earth quality. We like straight talk that goes right to the heart of what people need to know." Submit proposal package, outline, publishing history, bio.

OUR SUNDAY VISITOR, INC.

200 Noll Plaza, Huntington IN 46750. **E-mail:** jlindsey@osv.com. **Website:** www.osv.com. Publishes paperback and hardbound originals. "We are a Catholic publishing company seeking to educate and deepen our readers in their faith. Currently emphasizing devotional, inspirational, Catholic identity, apologetics, and catechetics." **Publishes 40-50 titles/year. Pays authors royalty of 10-12% net. Pays illustrators by the project (range: $25-1,500).** Publishes ms 1-2 years after acceptance. Accepts simultaneous submissions. Responds in 2 months. Book catalog for 9×12 envelope and first-class stamps; ms guidelines available online.

NONFICTION Prefers to see well-developed proposals as first submission with annotated outline and definition of intended market; Catholic viewpoints on family, prayer, and devotional books, and Catholic heritage books. Picture books, middle readers, young readers, young adults. Query, submit complete ms, or submit outline/synopsis and 2-3 sample chapters. Reviews artwork/photos.

🌀 PETER OWEN PUBLISHERS

81 Bridge Rd., London N8 9NP, United Kingdom. (44)(208)350-1775. **Fax:** (44)(208)340-9488. **E-mail:** info@peterowen.com. **Website:** www.peterowen.com. Publishes hardcover originals and trade paperback originals and reprints. "We are far more interested in proposals for nonfiction than fiction at the moment. No poetry or short stories." **Publishes 20-30 titles/year. 3,000 queries received/year. 800 mss received/year. 70% from unagented writers. Pays 7½-10% royalty. Pays negotiable advance.** Publishes ms 1 year after acceptance. Responds in 2 months to queries; 3 months to proposals and mss. Book catalog for SASE, SAE with IRC or on website.

NONFICTION Subjects include history, literature, memoirs, translation, travel, art, drama, literary, biography. Query with synopsis, sample chapters.

FICTION "No first novels. Authors should be aware that we publish very little new fiction these days." Query with synopsis, sample chapters.

🌀 OXFORD UNIVERSITY PRESS: SOUTHERN AFRICA

P.O. Box 12119, NI City Cape Town 7463, South Africa. (27)(21)596-2300. **Fax:** (27)(21)596-1234. **E-mail:** oxford.za@oup.com. **Website:** www.oxford.co.za. Academic publisher known for its educational books for southern African schools. Also publishes general and reference titles. **Publishes 150 titles/year.** Accepts simultaneous submissions. Book catalog online. Guidelines online.

NONFICTION Submit cover letter, synopsis, first few chapters, and submission form (available online) via mail.

FICTION Submit cover letter, synopsis.

OZARK MOUNTAIN PUBLISHING, INC.

Cannon Holdings, LLC, P.O. Box 754, Huntsville AR 72740. (479)738-2348. **Fax:** (479)738-2448. **E-mail:** brandy@ozarkmt.com. **Website:** www.ozarkmt.com. **Contact:** Nancy Vernon, general manager. Estab. 1992. Publishes trade paperback originals. "We publish new age/metaphysical, spiritual nonfiction books."

Publishes 8-10 titles/year. 50-75 queries; 150-200 mss received/year. 50% of books from first-time authors. 95% from unagented writers. Pays 10-15% royalty on retail or wholesale price. Pays $250-500 advance. Publishes ms within 18 months after acceptance. Accepts simultaneous submissions. Responds in 6 months to queries; 8 months to mss. Book catalog online. Guidelines online. Postcard included for notification of receipt. No phone call please.

NONFICTION Subjects include astrology, New Age, philosophy, psychic, spirituality, metaphysical. No phone calls please. Query with SASE. Submit TOC and 4-5 sample chapters. Guidelines online. No phone calls please.

P & R PUBLISHING CO.

P.O. Box 817, Phillipsburg NJ 08865. **Fax:** (908)859-2390. **E-mail:** editorial@prpbooks.com. **Website:** www.prpbooks.com. Estab. 1930. Publishes hardcover originals and trade paperback originals and reprints. **Publishes 40 titles/year. Up to 300 queries; 100 mss received/year. 5% of books from first-time authors. 95% from unagented writers. Pays 10-16% royalty on wholesale price.** Accepts simultaneous submissions. Responds in 3 months to proposals. Guidelines online.

NONFICTION Subjects include history, religion, spirituality, translation. Only accepts electronic submission with completion of online Author Guidelines. Hard copy mss will not be returned.

PACIFIC PRESS PUBLISHING ASSOCIATION

Trade Book Division, 1350 N. Kings Rd., Nampa ID 83687. (208)465-2500. **Fax:** (208)465-2531. **Website:** www.pacificpress.com. Estab. 1874. Publishes hardcover and trade paperback originals and reprints. "We publish books that fit Seventh-day Adventist beliefs only. All titles are Christian and religious. For guidance, see www.adventist.org/beliefs/index.html. Our books fit into the categories of this retail site: www.adventistbookcenter.com." **Publishes 35 titles/year. 35% of books from first-time authors. 100% from unagented writers. Pays 8-16% royalty on wholesale price.** Publishes book 2 years after acceptance. Responds in 3 months to queries. Guidelines online.

NONFICTION Subjects include child guidance, philosophy, religion, spirituality, family living, Christian lifestyle, Bible study, Christian doctrine, prophecy. Query with SASE or e-mail, or submit 3 sample chapters, cover letter with overview of book. Electronic submissions accepted. Reviews artwork/photos.

FICTION Subjects include religious. "Pacific Press rarely publishes fiction, but we're interested in developing a line of Seventh-day Adventist fiction in the future. Only proposals accepted; no full manuscripts."

PAJAMA PRESS

181 Carlaw Ave., Suite 207, Toronto ON M4M 2S1, Canada. 4164662222. **E-mail:** annfeatherstone@pajamapress.ca. **Website:** pajamapress.ca. **Contact:** Ann Featherstone, senior editor. Publisher: Gail Winskill (gailwinskill@pajamapress.ca). Estab. 2011. "We publish picture books—both for the very young and for school-aged readers, as well as novels for middle grade readers and contemporary or historical fiction for young adults aged 12+. Our nonfiction titles typically contain a strong narrative element. Pajama Press is also looking for mss from authors of diverse backgrounds. Stories about immigrants are of special interest." **Publishes 15-20 titles/year. 1,000 20% of books from first-time authors. 80% from unagented writers. Pays advance.** Publishes ms 1-3 years after acceptance. Responds in 6 weeks. Guidelines online.

NONFICTION Subjects include animals, contemporary culture, cooking, creative nonfiction, environment, gay, history, literature, nature, science, social sciences, sports, war, young adult. "Our nonfiction titles typically contain a strong narrative element; for example, juvenile biographies and narratives about wildlife rescue." Does not want how-to books, activity books, books for adults, psychology books, educational resources Pajama Press considers digital queries accompanied by picture books texts or the first 3 chapters of novel length projects. Your query should include an overview of your submission and some information about your writing background. Pajama Press prefers not to look at simultaneous submissions. Please notify us if you are submitting your project to another publisher. Please e-mail your queries and submissions to annfeatherstone@pajamapress.ca. In the interest of saving trees, Pajama Press does not accept physical mss. Any mss mailed to our office will be recycled unopened.

FICTION Subjects include contemporary, gay, juvenile, literary, multicultural, mystery, picture books, poetry, sports, young adult, All children's fiction. vampire novels; romance (except as part of a literary novel); fiction with overt political or religious messages

PALADIN PRESS

5540 Central Ave., Suite 200, Boulder CO 80301. (303)443-7250. **Fax:** (303)442-8741. **E-mail:** editorial@paladin-press.com. **Website:** www.paladin-press.com. Estab. 1970. Publishes hardcover originals and paperback originals and reprints, videos. "Paladin Press publishes the action library of nonfiction in military science, police science, weapons, combat, personal freedom, self-defense, survival." **Publishes 50 titles/year. 50% of books from first-time authors. 95% from unagented writers. "We pay royalties in full and on time." Pays advance.** Publishes ms 1 year after acceptance. Accepts simultaneous submissions. Responds in 2 months to proposals. Book catalog available free.

IMPRINTS Sycamore Island Books; Flying Machines Press; Outer Limits Press; Romance Book Classics.

NONFICTION If applicable, send sample photographs and line drawings with complete outline and sample chapters. Paladin Press primarily publishes original manuscripts on military science, weaponry, self-defense, personal privacy, financial freedom, espionage, police science, action careers, guerrilla warfare, and fieldcraft. To submit a book proposal to Paladin Press, send an outline or chapter description along with 1-2 sample chapters (or the entire ms) to the address below. If applicable, samples of illustrations or photographs are also useful. Do not send a computer disk at this point, and be sure keep a copy of everything you send us. We are not accepting mss as electronic submissions at this time. Please allow 2-6 weeks for a reply. If you would like your sample material returned, a SASE with proper postage is required. Editorial Department, Paladin Press Gunbarrel Tech Center, 5540 Central Ave., Boulder, CO 80301, or e-mail us at: editorial@paladin-press.com. Query with SASE. Submitting a proposal for a video project is not much different than a book proposal. See guidelines online and send to: All materials related to video proposals should be addressed directly to: David Dubrow, Video Production Manager.

PALGRAVE MACMILLAN

St. Martin's Press, 175 Fifth Ave., New York NY 10010. (212)982-3900. **Fax:** (212)777-6359. **E-mail:** proposals@palgrave.com. **Website:** www.palgrave.com. Publishes hardcover and trade paperback originals.

"Palgrave wishes to expand on our already successful academic, trade, and reference programs so that we will remain at the forefront of publishing in the global information economy of the 21st century. We publish high-quality academic works and a distinguished range of reference titles, and we expect to see many of our works available in electronic form. We do not accept fiction or poetry." Accepts simultaneous submissions. Book catalog and ms guidelines online.

NONFICTION Subjects include creative nonfiction, education, ethnic, history, multicultural, philosophy, regional, religion, sociology, spirituality, translation, humanities. We are looking for good solid scholarship. Query with proposal package including outline, 3-4 sample chapters, prospectus, cv and SASE. Reviews artwork/photos.

PANTS ON FIRE PRESS

2062 Harbor Cove Way, Winter Garden FL 34787. (863)546-0760. **E-mail:** submission@pantsonfirepress.com. **Website:** www.pantsonfirepress.com. **Contact:** Becca Goldman, senior editor; Emily Gerety, editor. Estab. 2012. Publishes hardcover originals and reprints, trade paperback originals and reprints, and electronic originals and reprints. Pants On Fire Press is an award-winning book publisher of picture, middle-grade, young adult, and adult books. **Publishes 10 titles/year. Receives 36,300 queries and mss per year. 50% of books from first-time authors. 80% from unagented writers. Pays 10-50% royalties on wholesale price.** Publishes ms approximately 7 months after acceptance. Accepts simultaneous submissions. Responds in 3 months. Catalog online. Guidelines online.

FICTION Subjects include adventure, ethnic, fantasy, gothic, historical, horror, humor, juvenile, mainstream, military, multicultural, mystery, picture books, regional, religious, romance, science fiction, spiritual, sports, suspense, war, young adult. Publishes big story ideas with high concepts, new worlds, and meaty characters for children, teens, and discerning adults. Submit a proposal package including a synopsis, 3 sample chapters, and a query letter via e-mail.

PAPERCUTZ

160 Broadway, Suite 700E, New York NY 10038. (646)559-4681. **Fax:** (212)643-1545. **E-mail:** papercutz@papercutz.com. **Website:** www.papercutz.com. Estab. 2004. Publishes major licenses and author created comics. Publisher of graphic novels for kids and

teens. **Publishes 40 titles/year. 5% of books from first-time authors. 90% from unagented writers. Pays advance.** Publishes ms 1 year after acceptance. Accepts simultaneous submissions. Responds in 2-4 weeks.

IMPRINTS SuperGenius, Charmz.

NONFICTION Subjects include literature, pop culture, translation, young adult.

FICTION Subjects include comic books, fantasy, historical, horror, humor, juvenile, literary, mainstream, translation, young adult. "Independent publisher of graphic novels including popular existing properties aimed at the teen and tween market."

PARACLETE PRESS

P.O. Box 1568, Orleans MA 02653. (508)255-4685. **Fax:** (508)255-5705. **E-mail:** phil@paracletepress. com. **Website:** www.paracletepress.com. **Contact:** Phil Fox Rose. Estab. 1981. Publishes hardcover and trade paperback originals. Publisher of books on prayer, Christian living, spirituality, fiction, devotionals, new editions of classics. Also publishes audio and video. **Publishes 40 titles/year. 250 mss received/year.** Publishes ms up to 2 years after acceptance.

NONFICTION Subjects include art, religion, spirituality. E-mail. Submit proposal, with intro plus 2-3 sample chapters, TOC, chapter summaries.

PASSKEY CONSOLIDATED PUBLISHING NEVADA

5438 Vegas Dr., PMB 1670, Las Vegas NV 89108. (702)418-3326. **Fax:** (702)418-3326. **E-mail:** admin@ passkeypublications.com. **Website:** www.passkey-publications.com. Estab. 2007. Publishes trade paperback originals. Publishes hardcover textbooks. Pass-Key Publications is an established textbook publisher that occasionally publishes other genres. **Publishes 15 titles/year. Receives 375 queries/year; 120 mss/year. 15% of books from first-time authors. 90% from unagented writers. Pay varies. Pays advance.** Publishes ms 6 months after acceptance. Accepts simultaneous submissions. Responds in 1 month. Catalog and guidelines online. Submit query and/or partial manuscript in Word or pdf format to the e-mail address listed.

IMPRINTS Passkey Publications, PassKey EA Review, Defiant Press.

NONFICTION Subjects include business, economics, finance, money, real estate, young adult, accounting, taxation, study guides, young adult fiction. Ac-

cepting accounting/taxation nonfiction. No self-help or memoirs. Submit query and partial ms.

PAULINE BOOKS & MEDIA

50 St. Paul's Ave., Boston MA 02130. (617)522-8911. **Fax:** (617)541-9805. **E-mail:** design@paulinemedia. com; editorial@paulinemedia.com. **Website:** www. pauline.org. Estab. 1932. Publishes trade paperback originals and reprints. "Submissions are evaluated on adherence to Gospel values, harmony with the Catholic faith tradition, relevance of topic, and quality of writing." For board books and picture books, the entire manuscript should be submitted. For easy-to-read, young readers, and middle reader books and teen books, please send a cover letter accompanied by a synopsis and two sample chapters. "Electronic submissions are encouraged. We make every effort to respond to unsolicited submissions within 2 months." **Publishes 40 titles/year. 5% from unagented writers. Varies by project, but generally are royalties with advance. Flat fees sometimes considered for smaller works.** Publishes a book approximately 11-18 months after acceptance. Responds in 2 months. Book catalog online. Guidelines online.

NONFICTION Subjects include child guidance, religion, spirituality, young adult. Picture books, young readers, middle readers, teen: religion and fiction. Average word length: picture books—500-1,000; young readers—8,000-10,000; middle readers—15,000-25,000; teen—30,000-50,000. Recently published children's titles: *Bible Stores for Little Ones* by Genny Monchapm; *I Forgive You: Love We Can Hear, Ask For and Give* by Nicole Lataif; *Shepherds To the Rescue* (first place Catholic Book Award Winner) by Maria Grace Dateno; *FSP*; *Jorge from Argentina*; *Prayers for Young Catholics*. Teen Titles: *Teens Share the Mission* by Teens; *Martyred: The Story of Saint Lorenzo Ruiz*; *Ten Commandmenst for Kissing Gloria Jean* by Britt Leigh; *A.K.A. Genius* (2nd Place Catholic Book Award Winner) by Marilee Haynes; *Tackling Tough Topics* with Faith and Fiction by Diana Jenkins. No memoir/autobiography, poetry, or strictly nonreligious works currently considered. Submit proposal package, including outline, 1-2 sample chapters, cover letter, synopsis, intended audience and proposed length.

FICTION Subjects include adventure, comic books, contemporary, juvenile, picture books, religious, romance, spiritual, young adult. Children's and teen fiction only. "We are now accepting submissions for easy-to-read and middle reader chapter, and teen well documented historical fiction. We would also consider well-written fantasy, fairy tales, myths, science fiction, mysteries, or romance if approached from a Catholic perspective and consistent with church teaching. Please see our writer's guidelines." "Submit proposal package, including synopsis, 2 sample chapters, and cover letter; complete ms."

PAULIST PRESS

997 Macarthur Blvd., Mahwah NJ 07430. (201)825-7300. **Fax:** (201)825-8345. **E-mail:** submissions@paulistpress.com. **Website:** www.paulistpress.com. **Contact:** Trace Murphy, Editorial Director. Estab. 1865. Paulist Press publishes ecumenical theology, Roman Catholic studies, and books on scripture, liturgy, spirituality, church history, and philosophy, as well as works on faith and culture. Also publishes 2-3 children's titles a year. **Receives 400 submissions/year. 10% of books from first-time authors. 95% from unagented writers. Royalties and advances are negotiable. Pays negotiable advance.** Publishes a book 12-18 months after receipt of final, edited ms. Responds in 3 months to queries and proposals; 3-4 months on mss. Book catalog online. Guidelines online.

NONFICTION Subjects include religion. Accepts submissions via e-mail.

PEACHTREE PUBLISHERS

Peachtree Publishers, Ltd., 1700 Chattahoochee Ave., Atlanta GA 30318. (404)876-8761. **Fax:** (404)875-2578. **E-mail:** hello@peachtree-online.com. **Website:** www.peachtree-online.com. **Contact:** Helen Harriss, submissions editor. Publishes hardcover and trade paperback originals. "We publish a broad range of subjects and perspectives, with emphasis on innovative plots and strong writing." **Publishes 30 titles/year. 25% of books from first-time authors. 25% from unagented writers. Pays royalty on retail price.** Publishes ms 1 year after acceptance. Accepts simultaneous submissions. Responds in 6 months and mss. Book catalog for 6 first-class stamps. Guidelines online.

NONFICTION Subjects include animals, child guidance, creative nonfiction, education, ethnic, gardening, history, literary criticism, multicultural, recreation, regional, science, social sciences, sports, travel, young adult. No e-mail or fax queries of mss. Submit complete ms with SASE, or summary and 3 sample chapters with SASE.

FICTION Subjects include juvenile, picture books, young adult. Looking for very well-written middle grade and young adult novels. No adult fiction. No collections of poetry or short stories; no romance or science fiction. Submit complete ms with SASE.

ⒶⒸ PENGUIN CANADA, LTD.

The Penguin Group, 320 Front St. W., Suite 1400, Toronto ON M5V 3B6, Canada. (416)364-4449. **Fax:** (416)598-7764. **Website:** www.penguinrandomhouse.ca. Estab. 1974. **Pays advance.**

NONFICTION Any Canadian subject by any Canadian authors. Agented submissions only.

ⒶⓄ PENGUIN GROUP USA

375 Hudson St., New York NY 10014. (212)366-2000. **Website:** www.penguin.com. General interest publisher of both fiction and nonfiction. *No unsolicited mss.* Submit work through a literary agent. DAW Books is the lone exception. Guidelines online.

ⒶⓄ PENGUIN RANDOM HOUSE, LLC

Division of Bertelsmann Book Group, 1745 Broadway, New York NY 10019. (212)782-9000. **Website:** www.penguinrandomhouse.com. Estab. 1925. Penguin Random House LLC is the world's largest English-language general trade book publisher. *Agented submissions only. No unsolicited mss.* Accepts simultaneous submissions.

IMPRINTS Crown Publishing Group; Knopf Doubleday Publishing Group; Random House Publishing Group; Random House Children's Books; RH Digital Publishing Group; RH International.

THE PERMANENT PRESS

Second Chance Press, Attn: Judith Shepard, 4170 Noyac Rd., Sag Harbor NY 11963. (631)725-1101. **E-mail:** judith@thepermanentpress.com; shepard@thepermanentpress.com. **Website:** www.thepermanentpress.com. **Contact:** Judith and Martin Shepard, acquisitions/co-publishers. Estab. 1978. Publishes hardcover originals. Mid-size, independent publisher of literary fiction. "We keep titles in print and are active in selling subsidiary rights." Average print order: 1,000-2,500. Averages 16 total titles. Accepts unsolicited mss. Pays 10-15% royalty on wholesale price. Offers $1,000 advance. *Will not accept simultaneous submissions.* **20% of books from first-time authors. 45% from unagented writers. Pays 10-15% royalty on wholesale price. Offers $1,000 advance.** Publishes ms within 18 months after acceptance. Responds in weeks or months. Catalog available.

NONFICTION Subjects include literature, memoirs, sex, true crime.

FICTION Subjects include adventure, contemporary, erotica, experimental, historical, literary, mainstream, mystery, science fiction, suspense, translation. Promotes titles through reviews. Literary, mainstream/contemporary, mystery. Especially looking for high-line literary fiction, "artful, original and arresting." Accepts any fiction category as long as it is a "well-written, original full-length novel."

PERSEA BOOKS

277 Broadway, Suite 708, New York NY 10007. (212)260-9256. **Fax:** (212)267-3165. **E-mail:** info@perseabooks.com. **Website:** www.perseabooks.com. Estab. 1975. The aim of Persea is to publish works that endure by meeting high standards of literary merit and relevance. "We have often taken on important books other publishers have overlooked, or have made significant discoveries and rediscoveries, whether of a single work or writer's entire oeuvre. Our books cover a wide range of themes, styles, and genres. We have published poetry, fiction, essays, memoir, biography, titles of Jewish and Middle Eastern interest, women's studies, American Indian folklore, and revived classics, as well as a notable selection of works in translation." Accepts simultaneous submissions. Responds in 8 weeks to proposals; 10 weeks to mss. Guidelines online.

NONFICTION Subjects include contemporary culture, literary criticism, literature, memoirs, translation, travel, young adult.

FICTION Subjects include contemporary, literary, short story collections, translation, young adult. Queries should include a cover letter, author background and publication history, a detailed synopsis of the proposed work, and a sample chapter. Please indicate if the work is simultaneously submitted.

POETRY "We have a longstanding commitment to publishing extraordinary contemporary poetry and maintain an active poetry program. At this time, due to our commitment to the poets we already publish, we are limited in our ability to add new collections." Send an e-mail to poetry@perseabooks.com describing current project and publication history, attaching a pdf or Word document with up to 12 sample pages of poetry. "If the timing is right and we are interested in seeing more work, we will contact you."

⊘ PERUGIA PRESS

P.O. Box 60364, Florence MA 01062. **Website:** www.perugiapress.com. **Contact:** Rebecca Olander, director. Estab. 1997. The best new women poets. "Contact us through our website." Accepts simultaneous submissions.

PETER PAUPER PRESS, INC.

202 Mamaroneck Ave., 4th Floor, White Plains NY 10601. **Website:** www.peterpauper.com. Estab. 1928. Publishes hardcover originals. "PPP publishes small and medium format, illustrated gift books for occasions and in celebration of specific relationships such as mom, sister, friend, teacher, grandmother, granddaughter. PPP has expanded into the following areas: books for teens and tweens, activity books for children, organizers, books on popular topics of nonfiction for adults and licensed books by best-selling authors." **Publishes 40-50 titles/year. 100 queries received/year. 150 mss received/year. 5% from unagented writers. Makes outright purchase only. Pays advance.** Publishes ms 1 year after acceptance. Responds in 2 months to queries.

NONFICTION "We do not publish fiction or poetry. We publish brief, original quotes, aphorisms, and wise sayings. Please do not send us other people's quotes." Submit cover letter and hard copy ms.

TIPS "Our readers are primarily female, age 10 and over, who are likely to buy a 'gift' book or gift book set in a stationery, gift, book, or boutique store or national book chain. Writers should become familiar with our previously published work. We publish only small- and medium-format, illustrated, hardcover gift books and sets of between 1,000-4,000 words. We have much less interest in work aimed at men."

PETERSON'S

121 S. 13 St., Lincoln NE 68508. **E-mail:** support@petersons.com. **Website:** www.petersons.com. Estab. 1966. Publishes trade and reference books. Peterson's publishes guides to graduate and professional programs, colleges and universities, financial aid, distance learning, private schools, summer programs, international study, executive education, job hunting and career opportunities, educational and career test prep, as well as online products and services offering educational and career guidance and information

for adult learners and workplace solutions for education professionals. **Pays royalty. Pays advance.** Book catalog available free.

NONFICTION Subjects include education, careers. Looks for appropriateness of contents to our markets, author's credentials, and writing style suitable for audience.

PFEIFFER

John Wiley & Sons, Inc., 989 Market St., San Francisco CA 94103. **Website:** www.wiley.com. Pfeiffer is an imprint of Wiley. **Publishes 250 titles/year. Pays variable royalties. Pays occasional advance.** Publishes ms 1 year after acceptance. Accepts simultaneous submissions. Responds in 2-3 months to queries. Guidelines online.

NONFICTION Subjects include education, psychology, religion. See proposal guidelines online.

PFLAUM PUBLISHING GROUP

3055 Kettering Blvd., Suite 100, Dayton OH 45439. (800)543-4383. **Website:** www.pflaum.com. "Pflaum Publishing Group, a division of Peter Li, Inc., serves the specialized market of religious education, primarily Roman Catholic. We provide high quality, theologically sound, practical, and affordable resources that assist religious educators of and ministers to children from preschool through senior high school." **Publishes 20 titles/year. Payment by outright purchase.** Accepts simultaneous submissions. Book catalog and ms guidelines free.

NONFICTION Query with SASE.

PHAIDON PRESS

65 Bleecker St., 8th Floor, New York NY 10012. (212)652-5400. **Fax:** (212)652-5410. **E-mail:** submissions@phaidon.com. **Website:** www.phaidon.com. Estab. 1923. Publishes hardcover and trade paperback originals and reprints. Phaidon Press is the world's leading publisher of books on the visual arts, with offices in London, Paris, Berlin, Barcelona, Milan, New York and Tokyo. Their books are recognized worldwide for the highest quality of content, design, and production. They cover everything from art, architecture, photography, design, performing arts, decorative arts, contemporary culture, fashion, film, travel, cookery and children's books. **Publishes 100 titles/year. 500 mss received/year. 40% of books from first-time authors. 90% from unagented writers. Pays royalty on wholesale price, if appropriate.** Of-

fers advance, if appropriate. Publishes ms 1 year after acceptance. Accepts simultaneous submissions. Responds in 3 months to proposals. Book catalog available free. Guidelines online.

NONFICTION Subjects include photography, design. Submit proposal package and outline, or submit complete ms. Submissions by e-mail or fax will not be accepted. Reviews artwork/photos. Send photocopies.

PHILOSOPHY DOCUMENTATION CENTER

P.O. Box 7147, Charlottesville VA 22906-7147. (434)220-3300. **Fax:** (434)220-3301. **E-mail:** leaman@pdcnet.org. **Website:** www.pdcnet.org. **Contact:** Dr. George Leaman, director. Estab. 1966. The Philosophy Documentation Center specializes in the publication of scholarly journals, book series, conference proceedings, and reference works. It has a unique commitment to support teaching, research, and professional activities in philosophy and related fields. **Publishes 20 titles/year. 20 queries; 4-6 mss received/year. 20% of books from first-time authors.** Publishes ms 1 year after acceptance. Responds in 1 week to queries.

NONFICTION Subjects include philosophy, social sciences, software. "We want to increase the range of philosophical titles that are available online, and we support online publication of philosophical work in multiple languages." Query with SASE. Submit outline.

🅐⊘ PICADOR USA

MacMillan, 175 Fifth Ave., New York NY 10010. (212)674-5151. **Website:** us.macmillan.com/picador. Estab. 1994. Picador publishes high-quality literary fiction and nonfiction. "We are open to a broad range of subjects, well written by authoritative authors." Publishes hardcover and trade paperback originals and reprints. Does not accept unsolicited mss. *Agented submissions only.* **Publishes 70-80 titles/year. Pays 7-15% on royalty. Advance varies.** Publishes ms 18 months after acceptance. Accepts simultaneous submissions.

⊘ THE PILGRIM PRESS

700 Prospect Ave. E., Cleveland OH 44115-1100. (216)736-3755. **Fax:** (216)736-2207. **Website:** www.thepilgrimpress.com. Publishes hardcover and trade paperback originals. No longer accepting unsolicited ms proposals. **Publishes 25 titles/year. 60% of books from first-time authors. 80% from unagented writers. Pays standard royalties. Pays advance.** Publish-

es ms an average of 18 months after acceptance. Responds in 3 months to queries. Book catalog and ms guidelines online.

NONFICTION Subjects include religion, ethics, social issues with a strong commitment to justice—addressing such topics as public policy, sexuality and gender, human rights and minority liberation—primarily in a Christian context, but not exclusively.

PIÑATA BOOKS

Imprint of Arte Publico Press, University of Houston, 4902 Gulf Fwy., Bldg. 19, Room 100, Houston TX 77204-2004. (713)743-2845. **Fax:** (713)743-3080. **E-mail:** submapp@uh.edu. **Website:** www.artepublicopress.com. Estab. 1994. Publishes hardcover and trade paperback originals. "Piñata Books is dedicated to the publication of children's and young adult literature focusing on U.S. Hispanic culture by U.S. Hispanic authors. Arte Publico's mission is the publication, promotion and dissemination of Latino literature for a variety of national and regional audiences, from early childhood to adult, through the complete gamut of delivery systems, including personal performance as well as print and electronic media." **Publishes 10-15 titles/year. 80% of books from first-time authors. Pays 10% royalty on wholesale price. Pays $1,000-3,000 advance.** Publishes book 2 years after acceptance. Accepts simultaneous submissions. Responds in 2-3 months to queries; 4-6 months to mss. Book catalog and guidelines online.

NONFICTION Subjects include ethnic. Piñata Books specializes in publication of children's and young adult literature that authentically portrays themes, characters and customs unique to U.S. Hispanic culture. Submissions made through online submission form.

FICTION Subjects include adventure, juvenile, picture books, young adult. Submissions made through online submission form.

POETRY Appropriate to Hispanic theme. Submissions made through online submission form.

PINEAPPLE PRESS, INC.

P.O. Box 3889, Sarasota FL 34230. (941)706-2507. **Fax:** (800)746-3275. **Website:** www.pineapplepress.com. **Contact:** June Cussen, executive editor. Estab. 1982. Publishes hardcover and trade paperback originals. "We are seeking quality nonfiction on diverse topics for the library and book trade markets. Our mission is to publish good books about Florida."

Publishes 21 titles/year. 1,000 queries; 500 mss received/year. 50% of books from first-time authors. 95% from unagented writers. Pays authors royalty of 10-15%. Publishes a book 1 year after acceptance. Accepts simultaneous submissions. Responds in 2 months. Book catalog for 9×12 SAE with $1.32 postage. Guidelines online.

NONFICTION Subjects include regional, Florida. Picture books: animal, history, nature/environmental, science. Young readers, middle readers, young adults: animal, biography, geography, history, nature/environment, science. Query or submit outline/synopsis and intro and 3 sample chapters. Reviews artwork/photos. Send photocopies.

FICTION Subjects include regional. Picture books, young readers, middle readers, young adults: animal, folktales, history, nature/environment. Query or submit outline/synopsis and 3 sample chapters.

🄰🚫 POCKET BOOKS

Simon & Schuster, 1230 Avenue of the Americas, New York NY 10020. (212)698-7000. **Website:** www.simonandschuster.com. Estab. 1939. Publishes paperback originals and reprints, mass market and trade paperbacks. Pocket Books publishes commercial fiction and genre fiction (WWE, Downtown Press, Star Trek). Book catalog available free. Guidelines online.

NONFICTION *Agented submissions only.*

FICTION Subjects include mystery, romance, suspense, western. *Agented submissions only.*

POISONED PEN PRESS

4014 N. Goldwater Blvd., Suite 201, Scottsdale AZ 85251. **E-mail:** submissions@poisonedpenpress.com. **Website:** www.poisonedpenpress.com. **Contact:** Diane DiBiase, Assistant Publisher. Estab. 1997. Publishes hardcover and trade paperback originals, and hardcover and trade paperback reprints. "Our publishing goal is to offer well-written mystery novels of crime and/or detection where the puzzle and its resolution are the main forces that move the story forward." *Not currently accepting submissions. Check website.* **Publishes 60 titles/year. 1,000 queries; 300 mss received/year. 35% of books from first-time authors. 65% from unagented writers. Pays 9-15% royalty on retail price.** Publishes book 10-12 months after acceptance. Responds in 2-3 months to queries and proposals; 6 months to mss. Book catalog and guidelines online.

FICTION Subjects include mystery. Mss should generally be longer than 65,000 words and shorter than 100,000 words. Member Publishers Marketing Associations, Arizona Book Publishers Associations, Publishers Association of West. Distributes through Ingram, Baker & Taylor, Brodart. Does not want novels centered on serial killers, spousal or child abuse, drugs, or extremist groups, although we do not entirely rule such works out. Accepts unsolicited mss. Electronic queries only. "Submit clips, first 3 pages. We must receive both the synopsis and ms pages electronically as separate attachments to an e-mail message."

POLIS BOOKS

E-mail: info@polisbooks.com. **E-mail:** submissions@polisbooks.com. **Website:** www.polisbooks.com. Estab. 2013. "Polis Books is an independent publishing company actively seeking new and established authors for our growing list. We are actively acquiring titles in mystery, thriller, suspense, procedural, traditional crime, science fiction, fantasy, horror, supernatural, urban fantasy, romance, erotica, commercial women's fiction, commercial literary fiction, young adult and middle grade books." **Publishes 40 titles/year. 500+ 33% of books from first-time authors. 10% from unagented writers. Offers advance against royalties.** For e-book originals, ms published 6-9 months after acceptance. For front list print titles, 9-15 months. Accepts simultaneous submissions. Only responds to submissions if interested. Guidelines online.

FICTION Query with 3 sample chapters and bio via e-mail.

POPULAR WOODWORKING BOOKS

Imprint of F+W Media, Inc., 10151 Carver Rd., Suite 300, Blue Ash OH 45242. (513) 531-2690. **E-mail:** scott.francis@fwcommunity.com. **Website:** www.popularwoodworking.com. **Contact:** Scott Francis, content editor. Publishes trade paperback and hardcover originals and reprints. "Popular Woodworking Books is one of the largest publishers of woodworking books in the world. From perfecting a furniture design to putting on the final coat of finish, our books provide step-by-step instructions and trusted advice from the pros that make them valuable tools for both beginning and advanced woodworkers. Currently emphasizing woodworking jigs and fixtures, woodworking techniques, furniture and cabinet projects, smaller finely crafted boxes, all styles of furniture. We are also looking for DIY-style maker projects for clever furniture projects or home decor created using wood and woodworking techniques; techniques creating space-saving, modular furniture." **Publishes 8-10 titles/year. 20 queries; 10 mss received/year. 20% of books from first-time authors. 95% from unagented writers.** Accepts simultaneous submissions. Responds in 1 month to queries.

NONFICTION "We publish heavily illustrated how-to woodworking books that show, rather than tell, our readers how to accomplish their woodworking goals." Query with SASE, or electronic query. Proposal package should include an outline and digital photos.

PPI (PROFESSIONAL PUBLICATIONS, INC.)

1250 Fifth Ave., Belmont CA 94002. (650)593-9119. **Fax:** (650)592-4519. **E-mail:** info@ppi2pass.com. **E-mail:** acquisitions@ppi2pass.com. **Website:** www.ppi2pass.com. Estab. 1975. Publishes hardcover, paperback, and electronic products, CD-ROMs and DVDs. "PPI publishes professional, reference, and licensing preparation materials. PPI wants submissions from both professionals practicing in the field and from experienced instructors. Currently emphasizing engineering, interior design, architecture, landscape architecture and LEED exam review." **Publishes 10 titles/year. 5% of books from first-time authors. 100% from unagented writers.** Publishes ms 4-18 months after acceptance. Accepts simultaneous submissions. Responds in 1 month to queries. Book catalog and ms guidelines free.

NONFICTION Subjects include architecture, science, landscape architecture, engineering mathematics, engineering, surveying, interior design, greenbuilding, sustainable development, and other professional licensure subjects.. Especially needs review and reference books for all professional licensing examinations. Please submit ms and proposal outlining market potential, etc. Proposal template available upon request. Reviews artwork/photos.

PRESS 53

560 N. Trade St., Suite 103, Winston-Salem NC 27101. (336)770-5353. **E-mail:** editor@press53.com. **Website:** www.press53.com. **Contact:** Kevin Morgan Watson, publisher.. Estab. 2005. Poetry and short fiction collections only. "Press 53 was founded in October 2005 and quickly earned a reputation for publishing remarkable short fiction and poetry collections." **Publishes 14-15 titles/year. Finds mss through contest,**

referrals, and scouting journals, magazines, and contests. **60% of books from first-time authors. 90% from unagented writers. Pays 10% royalty on gross sales. Pays advance only for contest winners.** Publishes ms 1 year after acceptance. Accepts simultaneous submissions. Catalog online. Guidelines online.

FICTION Subjects include literary, short story collections. "We publish roughly 4-5 short fiction collections each year by writers who are active and earning recognition through publication and awards, plus the winner of our Press 53 Award for Short Fiction." Collections should be between 100 and 250 pages (give or take) with half or more of those stories previously published in journals, magazines, anthologies, etc. Does not want novels. Finds mss through contest, referrals, and scouting magazines, journals, and contests.

POETRY "We love working with poets who have been widely published and are active in the poetry community. We publish roughly 6-8 full-length poetry collections of around 70 pages or more each year, plus the winner of our Press 53 Award for Poetry." Prefers that at least 30-40% of the poems in the collection be previously published in magazines, journals, anthologies, etc. Does not want experimental, overtly political or religious. Finds mss through contest, referrals, and scouting magazines, journals, and contests.

✪ PRESSES DE L'UNIVERSITÉ DE MONTREAL

C.P. 6128, succ. Centre-ville, Montreal QC H3C 3J7, Canada. (514)343-6933. **Fax:** (514)343-2232. **E-mail:** sb@editionspum.ca. **Website:** www.pum.umontreal.ca. **Contact:** Patrick Poirier, director, rights and sales. Estab. 1964. Publishes hardcover and trade paperback originals. **Publishes 40 titles/year.** Publishes ms 6 months after acceptance. Accepts simultaneous submissions. Responds in 1 month. Book catalog and ms guidelines free.

NONFICTION Subjects include anthropology, art, contemporary culture, education, history, philosophy, politics, psychology, sociology, translation, world affairs. Submit outline, 2 sample chapters.

PRESTWICK HOUSE, INC.

P.O. Box 658, Clayton DE 19938. **E-mail:** info@prestwickhouse.com. **Website:** www.prestwickhouse.com. Estab. 1980. Accepts simultaneous submissions.

NONFICTION Submit proposal package, outline, resume, 1 sample chapter, TOC.

🅐⊘ PRICE STERN SLOAN, INC.

Penguin Group, 375 Hudson St., New York NY 10014. (212)366-2000. **Website:** www.penguin.com. Estab. 1963. "Price Stern Sloan publishes quirky mass market novelty series for childrens as well as licensed movie tie-in books." Price Stern Sloan only responds to submissions it's interested in publishing. Accepts simultaneous submissions. Book catalog online.

FICTION Publishes picture books and novelty/board books. *Agented submissions only.*

PRINCETON ARCHITECTURAL PRESS

202 Warren St., Hudson NY 12534. (518)671-6100. **E-mail:** submissions@papress.com. **Website:** www.papress.com. Estab. 1981. Publishes hardcover and trade paperback originals. **Publishes 50 titles/year. 300 queries; 150 mss received/year. 65% of books from first-time authors. 95% from unagented writers. Pays royalty on wholesale price.** Publishes book 1 year after acceptance. Accepts simultaneous submissions. Responds in 2 months. Catalog available in print and online. Princeton Architectural Press accepts proposals concerning architecture, landscape architecture, graphic design, and visual culture. Submissions of illustrated children's books are also welcome. Electronic submissions only. See website for detailed submission guidelines.

NONFICTION Subjects include agriculture, animals, architecture, art, communications, community, contemporary culture, crafts, environment, gardening, history, house and home, humanities, nature, photography, politics, pop culture. Does not publish highly technical or purely academic titles.

PRINCETON UNIVERSITY PRESS

41 William St., Princeton NJ 08540. (609)258-4900. **Fax:** (609)258-6305. **Website:** press.princeton.edu. **Contact:** Susan Stewart, editor. "The Lockert Library of Poetry in Translation embraces a wide geographic and temporal range, from Scandinavia to Latin America to the subcontinent of India, from the Tang Dynasty to Europe of the modern day. It especially emphasizes poets who are established in their native lands and who are being introduced to an English-speaking audience. Manuscripts are judged with several criteria in mind: the ability of the translation to stand on its own as poetry in English; fidelity to the

tone and spirit of the original, rather than literal accuracy; and the importance of the translated poet to the literature of his or her time and country." Accepts simultaneous submissions. Responds in 3-4 months. Guidelines online.

NONFICTION Query with SASE.

POETRY Submit hard copy of proposal with sample poems or full ms. Cover letter is required. Reads submissions year round. Mss will not be returned. Comments on finalists only.

PROMETHEUS BOOKS

59 John Glenn Dr., Amherst NY 14228. (800)421-0351. **Fax:** (716)564-2711. **Website:** www.prometheusbooks. com. Estab. 1969. Publishes hardcover originals, trade paperback originals and reprints. "Prometheus Books is a leading independent publisher in philosophy, social science, popular science, and critical thinking. We publish authoritative and thoughtful books by distinguished authors in many categories. Currently emphasizing popular science, health, psychology, social science, current events, business and economics, atheism and critiques of religion." **Publishes 90-100 titles/year. 30% of books from first-time authors. 40% from unagented writers.** Accepts simultaneous submissions. Responds in 2 months to queries; 3 months to proposals; 4 months to mss. Book catalog and guidelines online.

NONFICTION Subjects include education, history, New Age, philosophy, psychology, religion, contemporary issues. Ask for a catalog, go to the library or our website, look at our books and others like them to get an idea of what our focus is. Submit proposal package including outline, synopsis, potential market, tentative ms length, résumé, and a well-developed query letter with SASE, two or three of author's best chapters. Reviews artwork/photos. Send photocopies.

ⓐⓞ PUFFIN BOOKS

Imprint of Penguin Group (USA), Inc., 375 Hudson St., New York NY 10014. (212)366-2000. **Website:** www.penguin.com. Publishes trade paperback originals and reprints. "Puffin Books publishes high-end trade paperbacks and paperback reprints for preschool children, beginning and middle readers, and young adults." **Publishes 175-200 titles/year.** Publishes book 1 year after acceptance.

NONFICTION Subjects include education, history, womens issues, womens studies. "Women in history

books interest us." *No unsolicited mss. Agented submissions only.*

FICTION Subjects include fantasy, picture books, science fiction, young adult, middle grade, easy-to-read grades 1-3, graphic novels, classics. *No unsolicited mss. Agented submissions only.*

PURDUE UNIVERSITY PRESS

504 West State St., West Lafayette IN 47907-2058. (765)494-2038. **E-mail:** pupress@purdue.edu. **E-mail:** lpennywa@purdue.edu. **Website:** www.thepress.purdue.edu. **Contact:** Leah Pennywark, acquisitions assistant. Estab. 1960. Purdue University Press is administratively a unit of Purdue University Libraries and its Director reports to the Dean of Libraries. There are 3 full-time staff and 2 part-time staff, as well as student assistants. Dedicated to the dissemination of scholarly and professional information, the Press provides quality resources in several key subject areas including business, technology, health, veterinary sciences, and other selected disciplines in the humanities and sciences. As well as publishing 30 books a year, and 5 subscription-based journals, the Press is committed to broadening access to scholarly information using digital technology. As part of this initiative, the Press distributes a number of Open Access electronic-only journals. An editorial board of 9 Purdue faculty members is responsible for the imprint of the Press and meets twice a semester to consider mss and proposals, and guide the editorial program. A management advisory board advises the Director on strategy, and meets twice a year. Purdue University Press is a member of the Association of American University Presses.

ⓐⓞ G.P. PUTNAM'S SONS HARDCOVER

Imprint of Penguin Group (USA), Inc., 375 Hudson, New York NY 10014. (212)366-2000. **Fax:** (212)366-2664. **Website:** www.penguin.com. Publishes hardcover originals. **Pays variable royalties on retail price. Pays varies advance.** Accepts simultaneous submissions. Request book catalog through mail order department.

NONFICTION Subjects include animals, child guidance, contemporary culture, religion, science, sports, travel, celebrity-related topics. *Agented submissions only. No unsolicited mss.*

FICTION Subjects include adventure, literary, suspense, women's. *Agented submissions only.*

QUE

Pearson Education, 800 E. 96th St., Indianapolis IN 46240. (317)581-3500. **E-mail:** greg.wiegand@pearson.com. **Website:** www.quepublishing.com. **Contact:** Greg Wiegand, associate publisher. Estab. 1981. Publishes hardcover, trade paperback and mass market paperback originals and reprints. **Publishes 100 titles/year. 80% from unagented writers. Pays variable royalty on wholesale price or makes work-for-hire arrangements. Pays varying advance.** Accepts simultaneous submissions. Book catalog and guidelines online.

NONFICTION Subjects include , technology, certification. Submit proposal package, resume, TOC, writing sample, competing titles.

QUILL DRIVER BOOKS

Linden Publishing, 2006 S. Mary St., Fresno CA 93721. (559)233-6633. **E-mail:** info@lindenpub.com. **E-mail:** kent@lindenpub.com. **Website:** www.quilldriverbooks.com. **Contact:** Kent Sorsky. Publishes hardcover and trade paperback originals and reprints. Quill Driver Books publishes a mix of nonfiction titles, with an emphasis on how-to books. "Our books, we hope, make a worthwhile contribution to the human community, and we have a little fun along the way." **Publishes 10-12 titles/year. 50% of books from first-time authors. 75% from unagented writers. Pays 4-10% royalty on retail price. Pays $500-5,000 advance.** Publishes ms 12 months after acceptance. Accepts simultaneous submissions. Responds in 1 month to queries and proposals; 3 months to mss. Book catalog and ms guidelines for #10 SASE.

NONFICTION Subjects include regional, writing, aging. Query with SASE. Submit proposal package. Reviews artwork/photos. Send photocopies.

⊘ QUITE SPECIFIC MEDIA GROUP, LTD.

7373 Pyramid Place, Hollywood CA 90046. **E-mail:** info@quitespecificmedia.com; info@silmanjamespress.com. **Website:** www.quitespecificmedia.com. Estab. 1967. Publishes hardcover originals, trade paperback originals and reprints. "Quite Specific Media Group is an umbrella company of 5 imprints specializing in costume and fashion, theater and design." **Publishes 12 titles/year. 75 queries; 30 mss received/year. 75% of books from first-time authors. 85% from unagented writers. Pays royalty on wholesale price. Pays varies advance.** Publishes ms 18 months after acceptance. Accepts simultaneous submissions. Responds to queries. Book catalog online.

NONFICTION Subjects include fashion, history, literary criticism, translation. Query by e-mail please. Reviews artwork/photos.

ⒶⒸ RANDOM HOUSE CHILDREN'S BOOKS

1745 Broadway, New York NY 10019. (212)782-9000. **Website:** www.penguinrandomhouse.com. Estab. 1925. "Producing books for preschool children through young adult readers, in all formats from board to activity books to picture books and novels, Random House Children's Books brings together world-famous franchise characters, multimillion-copy series and top-flight, award-winning authors, and illustrators." Submit mss through a literary agent. Accepts simultaneous submissions.

IMPRINTS Kids@Random; Golden Books; Princeton Review; Sylvan Learning.

FICTION "Random House publishes a select list of first chapter books and novels, with an emphasis on fantasy and historical fiction." Chapter books, middle-grade readers, young adult. *Does not accept unsolicited mss.*

ⒶⒸ RANDOM HOUSE PUBLISHING GROUP

Division of Random House, Inc., 1745 Broadway, New York NY 10019. (212)782-9000. **Website:** www.penguinrandomhouse.com. Estab. 1925. Publishes hardcover and paperback trade books. Random House is the world's largest English-language general trade book publisher. It includes an array of prestigious imprints that publish some of the foremost writers of our time. **Publishes 120 titles/year.** Accepts simultaneous submissions.

IMPRINTS Ballantine Books; Bantam; Delacorte; Dell; Del Rey; Modern Library; One World; Presidio Press; Random House Trade Group; Random House Trade Paperbacks; Spectra; Spiegel & Grau; Triumph Books; Villard.

NONFICTION *Agented submissions only.*

FICTION *Agented submissions only.*

RAZORBILL

Penguin Young Readers Group, 345 Hudson St., New York NY 10014. (212)414-3427. **E-mail:** asanchez@penguinrandomhouse.com; bschrank@penguinrandomhouse.com; jharriton@penguinrandomhouse.

com. **Website:** www.razorbillbooks.com. **Contact:** Jessica Almon, executive editor; Casey McIntyre, associate publisher; Deborah Kaplan, vice president and executive art director, Marissa Grossman; assistant editor, Tiffany Liao; associate editor. Estab. 2003. "This division of Penguin Young Readers is looking for the best and the most original of commercial contemporary fiction titles for middle grade and YA readers. A select quantity of nonfiction titles will also be considered." **Publishes 30 titles/year. Offers advance against royalties.** Publishes book 1-2 after acceptance. Accepts simultaneous submissions. Responds in 1-3 months.

NONFICTION Middle readers and young adults/teens: concept. Submit cover letter with up to 30 sample pages.

FICTION Middle Readers: adventure, contemporary, graphic novels, fantasy, humor, problem novels. Young adults/teens: adventure, contemporary, fantasy, graphic novels, humor, multicultural, suspense, paranormal, science fiction, dystopian, literary, romance. Average word length: middle readers—40,000; young adult—60,000. Submit cover letter with up to 30 sample pages.

RED HEN PRESS

P.O. Box 40820, Pasadena CA 91114. (626)356-4760. **Fax:** (626)356-9974. **Website:** www.redhen.org. **Contact:** Mark E. Cull, publisher/executive director. Managing Editor: Kate Gale. Estab. 1993. Publishes trade paperback originals. "At this time, the best opportunity to be published by Red Hen is by entering one of our contests. Please find more information in our award submission guidelines." **Publishes 22 titles/year. 2,000 queries; 500 mss received/year. 10% of books from first-time authors. 90% from unagented writers.** Publishes ms 1 year after acceptance. Accepts simultaneous submissions. Responds in 1-2 months. Book catalog available free. Guidelines online.

NONFICTION Subjects include ethnic, memoirs, political/social interest. Query with synopsis and either 20-30 sample pages or complete ms using online submission manager.

FICTION Subjects include ethnic, experimental, feminist, historical, literary, poetry, poetry in translation, short story collections. Query with synopsis and either 20-30 sample pages or complete ms using online submission manager.

POETRY Submit to Benjamin Saltman Poetry Award.

○ RED MOON PRESS

P.O. Box 2461, Winchester VA 22604. (540)722-2156. **E-mail:** jim.kacian@redmoonpress.com. **Website:** www.redmoonpress.com. **Contact:** Jim Kacian, editor/publisher. Estab. 1993. English-language haiku, contemporary haiku in other languages in English translation, haiku anthologies, books of haiku theory and criticism, books on related genres (tanka, haibun, haiga, renga, renku, etc.). Red Moon Press "is the largest and most prestigious publisher of English-language haiku and related work in the world." Publishes 10-15 volumes/year, usually 2-3 anthologies, 6-8 individual collections of English-language haiku, and 1-3 books of essays, translations, or criticism of haiku. Under other imprints, the press also publishes chapbooks of various sizes and formats. **Publishes 10-15 titles/year. 100+ 75% of books from first-time authors. 100% from unagented writers. Every book is a separate consideration.** Publishes ms 1 month after acceptance. Accepts simultaneous submissions. Catalog online. Guidelines available.

NONFICTION Subjects include alternative lifestyles, art, contemporary culture, education, environment, ethnic, history, hobbies, humanities, language, literary criticism, literature, memoirs, multicultural, music, nature, New Age, philosophy, photography, pop culture, psychology, recreation, spirituality, translation, travel.

POETRY Query first with book concept (not just "I've written a few haiku ..."); if interested we'll ask for samples. "Each contract separately negotiated."

RED SAGE PUBLISHING, INC.

P.O. Box 4844, Seminole FL 33775. (727)391-3847. **E-mail:** submissions@eredsage.com. **Website:** www.eredsage.com. **Contact:** Alexandria Kendall. Estab. 1995. Publishes books of romance fiction, written for the adventurous woman. **Publishes 12 titles/year. 50% of books from first-time authors. Pays author royalty.** Guidelines online and all submissions via e-mail.

FICTION Subjects include adventure, contemporary, erotica, fantasy, gay, historical, horror, military, multicultural, mystery, occult, regional, romance, science fiction, suspense, war, western, Whatever your imagination can come up with. :). Read guidelines.

RED WHEEL/WEISER

65 Parker St., Suite 7, Newburyport MA 01950. (978)465-0504. **Fax:** (978)465-0504. **E-mail:** sub-

missions@rwwbooks.com. **Website:** www.redwheel-weiser.com. **Contact:** Pat Bryce, acquisitions editor. Estab. 1956. Publishes hardcover and trade paperback originals and reprints. **Publishes 60-75 titles/year. 2,000 queries; 2,000 mss received/year. 20% of books from first-time authors. 50% from unagented writers. Pays royalty.** Publishes ms 1 year after acceptance. Accepts simultaneous submissions. Responds in 3-6 months. Book catalog available free. Guidelines online.

NONFICTION Subjects include New Age, spirituality, parenting. Guidelines online.

REFERENCE SERVICE PRESS

1945 Golden Way, Mountain View CA 94040. **Website:** www.rspfunding.com. Estab. 1977. Publishes hardcover originals. "Reference Service Press focuses on the development and publication of financial aid resources in any format (print, electronic, e-book, etc.). We are interested in financial aid publications aimed at specific groups (e.g., minorities, women, veterans, the disabled, undergraduates majoring in specific subject areas, specific types of financial aid, etc.)." **Publishes 10-20 titles/year. 100% from unagented writers. Pays 10% royalty. Pays advance.** Publishes book 6 months after acceptance. Responds in 2 months to queries. Book catalog for #10 SASE.

NONFICTION Subjects include history, disabled. Submit outline, sample chapters.

RIO NUEVO PUBLISHERS

Imprint of Treasure Chest Books, P.O. Box 5250, Tucson AZ 85703. **Fax:** (520)624-5888. **E-mail:** info@rionuevo.com. **Website:** www.rionuevo.com. Estab. 1975. Publishes hardcover and trade paperback originals and reprints. **Publishes 12-20 titles/year. 30 queries received/year. 10 mss received/year. 30% of books from first-time authors. 100% from unagented writers. Pays $1,000-4,000 advance.** Publishes book 1 year after acceptance. Accepts simultaneous submissions. Responds in 6 months. Book catalog online. Guidelines online.

NONFICTION Subjects include animals, gardening, history, regional, religion, spirituality, travel. "We cover the Southwest but prefer titles that are not too narrow in their focus. We want our books to be of broad enough interest that people from other places will also want to read them." Query with SASE or via e-mail. Submit proposal package, outline, 2 sample chapters. Reviews artwork/photos. Send photocopies.

RIVERHEAD BOOKS

Penguin Putnam, 375 Hudson St., New York NY 10014. **Website:** www.penguin.com. Accepts simultaneous submissions.

FICTION Subjects include contemporary, literary, mainstream. *Submit through agent only. No unsolicited mss.*

ROARING BROOK PRESS

Macmillan Children's Publishing Group, 175 Fifth Ave., New York NY 10010. (646)307-5151. **Website:** us.macmillan.com. Estab. 2000. Roaring Brook Press is an imprint of MacMillan, a group of companies that includes Henry Holt and Farrar, Straus & Giroux. *Roaring Brook is not accepting unsolicited mss.* **Pays authors royalty based on retail price.** Accepts simultaneous submissions.

NONFICTION Picture books, young readers, middle readers, young adults: adventure, animal, contemporary, fantasy, history, humor, multicultural, nature/environment, poetry, religion, science fiction, sports, suspense/mystery. *Not accepting unsolicited mss or queries.*

FICTION Picture books, young readers, middle readers, young adults: adventure, animal, contemporary, fantasy, history, humor, multicultural, nature/environment, poetry, religion, science fiction, sports, suspense/mystery. *Not accepting unsolicited mss or queries.*

RODALE BOOKS

400 S. Tenth St., Emmaus PA 18098. (610)967-5171. **Fax:** (610)967-8961. **Website:** www.rodaleinc.com. Estab. 1932. "Rodale Books publishes adult trade titles in categories such health & fitness, cooking, spirituality, and pet care." Accepts simultaneous submissions.

RONSDALE PRESS

3350 W. 21st Ave., Vancouver BC V6S 1G7, Canada. (604)738-4688. **Fax:** (604)731-4548. **E-mail:** ronsdale@shaw.ca. **Website:** ronsdalepress.com. **Contact:** Ronald B. Hatch (fiction, poetry, nonfiction, social commentary); Veronica Hatch (YA novels and short stories). Estab. 1988. Publishes trade paperback originals. "Ronsdale Press is a Canadian literary publishing house that publishes 12 books each year, four of which are young adult titles. Of particular interest are books involving children exploring and discovering new aspects of Canadian history." **Publishes 12 titles/year. 40 queries; 800 mss received/year. 40% of** books from first-time authors. **95% from unagented writers. Pays 10% royalty on retail price.** Publishes book 1 year after acceptance. Accepts simultaneous submissions. Responds to queries in 2 weeks; mss in 2 months. Book catalog for #10 SASE. Guidelines online.

NONFICTION Subjects include history, literary criticism, literature, regional. Middle readers, young adults: animal, biography, history, multicultural, social issues. Average word length: young readers—90; middle readers—90. "We publish a number of books for children and young adults in the age 10 to 15 range. We are especially interested in YA historical novels. We regret that we can no longer publish picture books." Submit complete ms if you feel it is perfect for Ronsdale Press.

FICTION Subjects include literary, poetry, short story collections, young adult, novels. Young adults: Canadian novels. Average word length: middle readers and young adults—50,000. Submit complete MS if you are certain it is right for Ronsdale Press.

POETRY Poets should have published some poems in magazines/journals and should be well-read in contemporary masters. Submit complete MS if you feel it is right for Ronsdale Press. If you want to save postage, send a sample.

ROWMAN & LITTLEFIELD PUBLISHING GROUP

4501 Forbes Blvd., Suite 200, Lanham MD 20706. (301)459-3366. **Fax:** (301)429-5748. **Website:** www.rowmanlittlefield.com. **Contact:** Linda Ganster. Estab. 1949. Textbooks, nonfiction general interest titles, professional development works, references, and select trade in hardcover and paperback. "We are an independent press devoted to publishing social science and humanities titles that engage, inform and educate: innovative, thought-provoking texts for college courses; research-based titles for professionals eager to remain abreast of developments within their domains; and general interest books intended to convey important trends to an educated readership. Our approach emphasizes thought leadership balanced with a deep understanding of the areas in which we publish. We offer a forum for responsible voices representing the diversity of opinion on college campuses, and take special pride in our commitment to covering critical societal issues." **Pays advance.** Book catalog online. Guidelines online. Please submit to only one R&L editor at a time. Multiple submissions slows down the process, and editors are very good about sharing proposals.

NONFICTION Subjects include alternative lifestyles, Americana, anthropology, archeology, architecture, art, career guidance, child guidance, cinema, communications, community, contemporary culture, counseling, education, environment, ethnic, fashion, film, foods, gay, government, health, history, humanities, lesbian, literary criticism, military, multicultural, music, nutrition, parenting, philosophy, politics, pop culture, psychology, public affairs, religion, sex, sociology, sports, stage, war, womens issues, world affairs, young adult. "Rowman & Littlefield is seeking proposals in the serious nonfiction areas of history, politics, current events, religion, sociology, criminal justice, social work, philosophy, communication and education. All proposal inquiries can be e-mailed or mailed to the respective acquisitions editor listed on the contacts page on our website. "

RUTGERS UNIVERSITY PRESS

106 Somerset St., 3rd Floor, New Brunswick NJ 08901. (732)445-7762. **Fax:** (732)445-7039. **E-mail:** lmitch@rutgers.edu. **Website:** rutgerspress.rutgers.edu. **Contact:** Leslie Mitchner, editor-in-chief/associate director (humanities); Peter Micklaus, editor (social sciences); Kel McGowan, editor (science, health and medicine); Elisabeth Maselli, editor (Jewish studies), Lisa Banning (Asian American Studies, human rights, new media), Kimberly Guinta, editor (higher education, anthropology, women's studies). Estab. 1936. Publishes hardcover and trade paperback originals and reprints. "Our press aims to reach audiences beyond the academic community with accessible scholarly and regional books." **Publishes 100 titles/year. 1,500 queries; 300 mss received/year. 30% of books from first-time authors. 70% from unagented writers. Pays 7 1/2-15% royalty. Pays $1,000-10,000 advance.** Publishes ms 1 year after acceptance. Accepts simultaneous submissions. Responds in 1 month to proposals. Book catalog online. Guidelines online.

NONFICTION Subjects include ethnic, history, multicultural, regional, religion, sociology, African-American studies. Books for use in undergraduate courses. Submit outline, 2-3 sample chapters. Reviews artwork/photos. Send photocopies.

SAE INTERNATIONAL

400 Commonwealth Dr., Warrendale PA 15096-0001. (724)776-4841. **Website:** www.sae.org/writeabook. Estab. 1905. Publishes hardcover and trade paperback originals, e-books. Automotive means anything self-propelled. "We are a professional society serving engineers, scientists, and researchers in the automobile, aerospace, and off-highway industries." **Publishes approximately 10 titles/year. 50 queries received/year. 20 mss received/year. 70% of books from first-time authors. 100% from unagented writers. Pays royalty. Pays possible advance.** Publishes ms 9-10 months after acceptance. Accepts simultaneous submissions. Responds in 4 months to queries. Book catalog free. Guidelines online.

NONFICTION Query with proposal.

SAFER SOCIETY PRESS

P.O. Box 340, Brandon VT 05733. (802)247-3132. **Fax:** (802)247-4233. **E-mail:** maryfalcon@safersociety.org. **Website:** www.safersociety.org. **Contact:** Mary Falcon, editorial director. Estab. 1985. Publishes trade paperback originals. "Our mission is the prevention and treatment of sexual abuse." **Publishes 3-4 titles/year. 15-20 queries received/year. 15-20 mss received/year. 90% of books from first-time authors. 100% from unagented writers. Pays 10% royalty on retail price.** Publishes ms 1 year after acceptance. Accepts simultaneous submissions. Book catalog available free. Guidelines online.

NONFICTION Subjects include psychology. "We are a small, nonprofit, niche press. We want well-researched books dealing with any aspect of sexual abuse: treatment, prevention, understanding; works on subject in Spanish." Memoirs generally not accepted. Query with SASE, submit proposal package, or complete ms Reviews artwork/photos. Send photocopies.

❷⦸ ST. MARTIN'S PRESS, LLC

Holtzbrinck Publishers, 175 Fifth Ave., New York NY 10010. (212)674-5151. **Fax:** (212)420-9314. **Website:** www.stmartins.com. Estab. 1952. Publishes hardcover, trade paperback and mass market originals. General interest publisher of both fiction and nonfiction. **Publishes 1,500 titles/year. Pays royalty. Pays advance.** Accepts simultaneous submissions.

NONFICTION Subjects include sports, general nonfiction. *Agented submissions only. No unsolicited mss.*

FICTION Subjects include contemporary, fantasy, historical, horror, literary, mystery, science fiction, suspense, western, general fiction. *Agented submissions only. No unsolicited mss.*

ST PAULS

Society of St. Paul, 2187 Victory Blvd., Staten Island NY 10314. (718)761-0047. **Fax:** (718)761-0057. **E-mail:** edmund_lane@juno.com. **Website:** www.stpauls.us. **Contact:** Edmund C. Lane, SSP, acquisitions editor. Estab. 1957. Publishes trade paperback and mass market paperback originals and reprints. **Publishes 22 titles/year. 250 queries; 150 mss received/year. 10% of books from first-time authors. 100% from unagented writers. Pays 5-10% royalty.** Publishes ms 10 months after acceptance. Responds in 1 month to queries and proposals; 2 months to mss. Book catalog and ms guidelines free.

NONFICTION Subjects include philosophy, religion, spirituality. Alba House is the North American publishing division of the Society of St. Paul, an International Roman Catholic Missionary Religious Congregation dedicated to spreading the Gospel message via the media of communications. Does not want fiction, children's books, poetry, personal testimonies, or autobiographies. Submit complete ms. Reviews artwork/photos. Send photocopies.

SALEM PRESS, INC.

P.O. Box 56, 4919 Rt. 22, Amenia NY 12501. **E-mail:** lmars@greyhouse.com. **Website:** www.salempress.com. **Contact:** Laura Mars, editorial director. **Publishes 20-22 titles/year. 15 queries received/year. Work-for-hire pays 5-15¢/word.** Accepts simultaneous submissions. Responds in 3 months to queries; 1 month to proposals. Book catalog online.

NONFICTION Subjects include ethnic, history, philosophy, psychology, science, sociology. "We accept vitas for writers interested in supplying articles/entries for encyclopedia-type entries in library reference books. Will also accept multi-volume book ideas from people interested in being a general editor." Query with SASE.

❺ SALMON POETRY

Knockeven, Cliffs of Moher, County Clare , Ireland. 353(0)852318909. **E-mail:** info@salmonpoetry.com. **E-mail:** jessie@salmonpoetry.com. **Website:** www.salmonpoetry.com. **Contact:** Jessie Lendennie, editor. Estab. 1981. Publishes contemporary poetry and literary nonfiction. **Publishes 30 titles/year. 300+ 5% of books from first-time authors. 100% from un-agented writers. Pays advance.** Publishes ms 2 years after acceptance. Responds in 3 months. Guidelines available.

NONFICTION Subjects include literature, marine subjects.

POETRY "Salmon Press is one of the most important publishers in the Irish literary world; specializing in the promotion of new poets, particularly women. Established in 1981 as an alternative voice in Irish literature, Salmon is known for its international list and over the years has developed a cross-cultural literary dialog, broadening Irish Literature and urging new perspectives on established traditions." E-mail query with short biographical note and 5-10 sample poems.

SANTA MONICA PRESS

P.O. Box 850, Solana Beach CA 92075. (858)793-1890; (800)784-9553. **E-mail:** books@santamonicapress.com. **E-mail:** acquisitions@santamonicapress.com. **Website:** www.santamonicapress.com. Estab. 1994. Publishes hardcover and trade paperback originals. Santa Monica Press has been publishing an eclectic line of books since 1994. "Our critically acclaimed titles are sold in chain, independent, online, and university bookstores around the world, as well as in some of the most popular retail outlets in North America. Our authors are recognized experts who are sought after by the media and receive newspaper, magazine, radio, and television coverage both nationally and internationally. At Santa Monica Press, we're not afraid to cast a wide editorial net. Our list of lively and modern non-fiction titles includes books in such categories as popular culture, film history, photography, humor, biography, travel, and reference." **Publishes 12 titles/year. 25% of books from first-time authors. 75% from unagented writers. Pays 6-10% royalty on net price. Pays $500-10,000+ advance.** Publishes book 1 year after acceptance. Accepts simultaneous submissions. Responds in 1-2 months to proposals. Guidelines available.

NONFICTION Subjects include Americana, art, cinema, contemporary culture, creative nonfiction, education, entertainment, film, history, humanities, language, literature, memoirs, music, parenting, photography, pop culture, regional, social sciences, sports, stage, travel. Submit proposal package, including outline, 2-3 sample chapters, biography, marketing and publicity plans, analysis of competitive titles, SASE with appropriate postage. Reviews artwork/photos. Send photocopies.

SARABANDE BOOKS, INC.

822 E. Market St., Louisville KY 40206. (502)458-4028. **Fax:** (502)458-4065. **E-mail:** info@sarabandebooks.org. **Website:** www.sarabandebooks.org. **Contact:** Sarah Gorham, Editor-in-Chief. Estab. 1994. Publishes trade paperback originals. "Sarabande Books was founded to publish poetry, short fiction, and creative nonfiction. We look for works of lasting literary value. Please see our titles to get an idea of our taste. Accepts submissions through contests and open submissions." **Publishes 10 titles/year. 1,500 queries; 3,000 mss received/year. 35% of books from first-time authors. 75% from unagented writers. Pays royalty. 10% on actual income received. Also pays in author's copies. Pays $500-1,000 advance.** Publishes ms 18 months after acceptance. Accepts simultaneous submissions. Book catalog available free. Contest guidelines for #10 SASE or on website.

FICTION Subjects include literary, short story collections, novellas, short novels (300 pages maximum, 150 pages minimum). "We consider novels and nonfiction in a wide variety of genres. We do not consider genre fiction such as science fiction, fantasy, or horror. Our target length is 70,000-90,000 words." Queries can be sent via e-mail, fax, or regular post.

POETRY Poetry of superior artistic quality; otherwise no restraints or specifications. Sarabande Books publishes books of poetry of 48 pages minimum. Wants "poetry that offers originality of voice and subject matter, uniqueness of vision, and a language that startles because of the careful attention paid to it—language that goes beyond the merely competent or functional." Mss selected through literary contests, invitation, and recommendation by a well-established writer.

SAS PUBLISHING

100 SAS Campus Dr., Cary NC 27513. (919)677-8000. **Fax:** (919)677-4444. **E-mail:** saspress@sas.com. **Website:** support.sas.com/saspress. Estab. 1976. Publishes hardcover and trade paperback originals. "SAS publishes books for SAS and JMP software users, both new and experienced." **Publishes 40 titles/year. 50% of books from first-time authors. 100% from un-agented writers. Payment negotiable. Pays negotiable**

advance. Responds in 2 weeks to queries. Book catalog and ms guidelines online.

NONFICTION Subjects include software, statistics. SAS Publishing jointly Wiley and SAS Business Series titles. "Through SAS, we also publish books by SAS users on a variety of topics relating to SAS software. SAS titles enhance users' abilities to use SAS effectively. We're interested in publishing manuscripts that describe or illustrate using any of SAS products, including JMP software. Books must be aimed at SAS or JMP users, either new or experienced." Mss must reflect current or upcoming software releases, and the author's writing should indicate an understanding of SAS and the technical aspects covered in the ms. Query with SASE. Submit outline, sample chapters. Reviews artwork/photos.

SASQUATCH BOOKS

1904 Third Ave., Suite 710, Seattle WA 98101. (206)467-4300. **Fax:** (206)467-4301. **E-mail:** custserv@sasquatchbooks.com. **Website:** www.sasquatchbooks.com. Estab. 1986. Publishes regional hardcover and trade paperback originals. "Sasquatch Books publishes books for and from the Pacific Northwest, Alaska, and California is the nation's premier regional press. Sasquatch Books' publishing program is a veritable celebration of regionally written words. Undeterred by political or geographical borders, Sasquatch defines its region as the magnificent area that stretches from the Brooks Range to the Gulf of California and from the Rocky Mountains to the Pacific Ocean. Our top-selling Best Places® travel guides serve the most popular destinations and locations of the West. We also publish widely in the areas of food and wine, gardening, nature, photography, children's books, and regional history, all facets of the literature of place. With more than 200 books brimming with insider information on the West, we offer an energetic eye on the lifestyle, landscape, and worldview of our region. Considers queries and proposals from authors and agents for new projects that fit into our West Coast regional publishing program. We can evaluate query letters, proposals, and complete mss." **Publishes 30 titles/year. 20% of books from first-time authors. 75% from unagented writers. Pays royalty on cover price. Pays wide range advance.** Publishes book 6-9 months after acceptance. Accepts simultaneous submissions. Responds to queries in 3 months. Guidelines online.

NONFICTION Subjects include animals, gardening, history, recreation, regional, sports, travel, outdoors. "We are seeking quality nonfiction works about the Pacific Northwest and West Coast regions (including Alaska to California). The literature of place includes how-to and where-to as well as history and narrative nonfiction." Picture books: activity books, animal, concept, nature/environment. "We publish a variety of nonfiction books, as well as children's books under our Little Bigfoot imprint." Query first, then submit outline and sample chapters with SASE. Send submissions to The Editors. E-mailed submissions and queries are not recommended. Please include return postage if you want your materials back.

FICTION Young readers: adventure, animal, concept, contemporary, humor, nature/environment.

SCARECROW PRESS, INC.

Imprint of Rowman & Littlefield Publishing Group, 4501 Forbes Blvd., Suite 200, Lanham MD 20706. (301)459-3366. **Fax:** (301)429-5748. **Website:** www.scarecrowpress.com. Estab. 1955. Publishes hardcover originals. Scarecrow Press publishes several series: Historical Dictionaries (includes countries, religions, international organizations, and area studies); Studies and Documentaries on the History of Popular Entertainment (forthcoming); Society, Culture and Libraries. Emphasis is on any title likely to appeal to libraries. Currently emphasizing jazz, Africana, and educational issues of contemporary interest. **Publishes 165 titles/year. 70% of books from first-time authors. 99% from unagented writers. Pays 8% royalty on net of first 1,000 copies; 10% of net price thereafter.** Publishes ms 18 months after acceptance. Responds in 2 months to queries. Catalog and ms guidelines online.

NONFICTION Subjects include religion, sports, annotated bibliographies, handbooks and biographical dictionaries in the areas of women's studies and ethnic studies, parapsychology, fine arts and handicrafts, genealogy, sports history, music, movies, stage, library and information science.. Query with SASE.

SCHIFFER PUBLISHING, LTD.

4880 Lower Valley Rd., Atglen PA 19310. (610)593-1777. **Fax:** (610)593-2002. **E-mail:** info@schifferbooks.com. **Website:** www.schifferbooks.com. Estab. 1975. **Publishes 10-20 titles/year. Pays royalty on wholesale price.** Accepts simultaneous submissions. Responds in 2 weeks to queries. Book catalog available free. Guidelines online.

NONFICTION Art-quality illustrated regional histories. Looking for informed, entertaining writing and lots of subject areas to provide points of entry into the text for non-history buffs who buy a beautiful book because they are from, or love, an area. Full color possible in the case of historic postcards. Fax or e-mail outline, photos, and book proposal.

🅰️⊘ SCHOCKEN BOOKS

Imprint of Knopf Publishing Group, Division of Random House, Inc., 1745 Broadway, New York NY 10019. (212)572-9000. **Fax:** (212)572-6030. **Website:** www. schocken.com. Estab. 1945. Publishes hardcover and trade paperback originals and reprints. "Schocken publishes quality Judaica in all areas-fiction, history, biography, current affairs, spirituality and religious practices, popular culture, and cultural studies." *Does not accept unsolicited mss. Agented submissions only.* **Publishes 9-12 titles/year. Pays varied advance.** Accepts simultaneous submissions.

SCHOLASTIC, INC.

557 Broadway, New York NY 10012. (212)343-6100. **Website:** www.scholastic.com. Accepts simultaneous submissions.

IMPRINTS Arthur A. Levine Books, Cartwheel Books®, Chicken House®, David Fickling Books, Graphix™, Little Shepherd™, Orchard Books®, Point™, PUSH, Scholastic en Español, Scholastic Licensed Publishing, Scholastic Nonfiction, Scholastic Paperbacks, Scholastic Press, Scholastic Reference™, and The Blue Sky Press® are imprints of the Scholastic Trade Books Division. In addition, Scholastic Trade Books included Klutz®, a highly innovative publisher and creator of "books plus" for children.

🅰️ SCHOLASTIC PRESS

Imprint of Scholastic, Inc., 557 Broadway, New York NY 10012. (212)343-6100. **Fax:** (212)343-4713. **Website:** www.scholastic.com. Publishes hardcover originals. Scholastic Press publishes fresh, literary picture book fiction and nonfiction; fresh, literary nonseries or nongenre-oriented middle grade and young adult fiction. Currently emphasizing subtly handled treatments of key relationships in children's lives; unusual approaches to commonly dry subjects, such as biography, math, history, or science. De-emphasizing fairy tales (or retellings), board books, genre, or series fiction (mystery, fantasy, etc.). **Publishes 60 titles/year. 2,500 queries received/year. 1% of books from first-time authors. Pays royalty on retail price. Pays variable advance.** Publishes book 2 years after acceptance. Responds in 3 months to queries; 6-8 months to mss.
NONFICTION Agented submissions and previously published authors only.
FICTION Subjects include juvenile, picture books, novels. Looking for strong picture books, young chapter books, appealing middle grade novels (ages 8-11) and interesting and well-written young adult novels. Wants fresh, exciting picture books and novels—inspiring, new talent. *Agented submissions only.*

🅰️⊘ SCHWARTZ & WADE BOOKS

Random House Children's Books, 1745 Broadway, New York NY 10019. **Website:** www.randomhousekids.com. Estab. 2006. Schwartz & Wade Books is an imprint of Random House Children's Books, co-directed by Anne Schwartz and Lee Wade, who take a unique approach to the creative process and believe that the best books for children grow from a seamless collaboration between editorial and design.

🌑 SCRIBE PUBLICATIONS

18-20 Edward St., Brunswick VIC 3056, Australia. (61)(3)9388-8780. **E-mail:** info@scribepub.com.au. **E-mail:** submissions@scribepub.com.au. **Website:** www.scribepublications.com.au. **Contact:** Anna Thwaites. Estab. 1976. Scribe has been operating as a wholly independent trade-publishing house for almost 40 years. What started off in 1976 as a desire on publisher Henry Rosenbloom's part to publish 'serious non-fiction' as a one-man band has turned into a multi-award-winning company with 20 staff members in two locations — Melbourne, Australia and London, England — and a scout in New York. Scribe publishes over 65 nonfiction and fiction titles annually in Australia and about 40 in the United Kingdom. "We currently have acquiring editors working in both our Melbourne and London offices. We spend each day sifting through submissions and manuscripts from around the world, and commissioning and editing local titles, in an uncompromising pursuit of the best books we can find, help create, and deliver to readers. We love what we do, and we hope you will, too." **Publishes 70 titles/year. 10-20% from unagented writers.** Guidelines online.
IMPRINTS Scribble.
NONFICTION Subjects include environment, history, memoirs, psychology, current affairs, social history. "Please refer first to our website before contacting

us or submitting anything, because we explain there who we will accept proposals from."

FICTION Subjects include contemporary, historical, humor, literary, military, mystery, picture books, poetry, short story collections, suspense, translation, war, young adult. Submit synopsis, sample chapters, CV.

Ⓐ⊘ SCRIBNER

Imprint of Simon & Schuster Adult Publishing Group, 1230 Avenue of the Americas, 12th Floor, New York NY 10020. (212)698-7000. **Website:** www.simonsays. com. Publishes hardcover originals. **Publishes 70-75 titles/year. Thousands queries received/year. 20% of books from first-time authors. Pays 7-15% royalty. Pays variable advance.** Publishes ms 9 months after acceptance. Accepts simultaneous submissions. Responds in 3 months to queries.

NONFICTION Subjects include education, ethnic, history, philosophy, psychology, religion, science, criticism. *Agented submissions only.*

FICTION Subjects include literary, mystery, suspense. *Agented submissions only.*

SEAL PRESS

Perseus Books Group, 1700 4th St., Berkeley CA 94710. (510)595-3664. **E-mail:** seal.press@perseusbooks.com. **E-mail:** emma.rose@perseusbooks.com. **Website:** www.sealpress.com. Estab. 1976. Publishes hardcover and trade paperback originals. "Seal Press is an imprint of the Perseus Book Group, a feminist book publisher interested in original, lively, radical, empowering and culturally diverse nonfiction by women addressing contemporary issues with the goal of informing women's lives. Currently emphasizing women outdoor adventurists, young feminists, political issues, health and fitness, parenting, personal finance, sex and relationships, and LGBT and gender topics. *Not accepting fiction at this time."* **Publishes 30 titles/year. 1,000 queries received/year. 750 mss received/year. 25% of books from first-time authors. 50% from unagented writers. Pays 7-10% royalty on retail price. Pays variable royalty on retail price. Pays wide ranging advance.** Publishes ms 1 year after acceptance. Accepts simultaneous submissions. Responds in 2 months to queries. Book catalog and ms guidelines for SASE or online.

NONFICTION Subjects include alternative lifestyles, Americana, child guidance, contemporary culture, creative nonfiction, ethnic, gay, health, les-

bian, memoirs, multicultural, parenting, politics, pop culture, sex, travel, womens issues, womens studies, popular culture, politics, domestic violence, sexual abuse. Query with SASE. Reviews artwork/photos. Send photocopies. No original art or photos accepted.

SEARCH INSTITUTE PRESS

Search Institute, 615 First Ave. NE, Suite 125, Minneapolis MN 55413. (612)376-8955. **Fax:** (612)692-5553. **E-mail:** si@search-institute.org. **Website:** www. search-institute.org. Estab. 1958. Publishes trade paperback originals. **Publishes 12-15 titles/year. Pays royalty.** Publishes book 1 year after acceptance. Accepts simultaneous submissions. Responds in 6 months. Catalog and guidelines online.

NONFICTION Subjects include career guidance, child guidance, community, counseling, education, entertainment, games, parenting, public affairs, social sciences, youth leadership, prevention, activities. Does not want children's picture books, poetry, New Age and religious-themes, memoirs, biographies, and autobiographies. Query with SASE. Does not review artwork/photos.

SEAWORTHY PUBLICATIONS, INC.

6300 N Wickham Rd, Unit # 130 - 416, Melbourne FL 32940. (321)610-3634. **Fax:** 321-259-6872. **E-mail:** queries@seaworthy.com. **Website:** www.seaworthy. com. **Contact:** Joseph F. Janson, publisher. Estab. 1992. Publishes trade paperback originals, hardcover originals, and reprints. "Seaworthy Publications is a nautical book publisher that primarily publishes books of interest to recreational boaters and bluewater cruisers, including cruising guides, how-to books about boating. We will also consider first-person adventure and nautical fiction. Currently emphasizing cruising guides." **Publishes 10 titles/year. 50 queries; 10 mss received/year. 60% of books from first-time authors. 100% from unagented writers. Pays flat rate per copy sold, based on retail price. No advance.** Publishes ms 6 months after acceptance. Responds in 1 month to queries. Book catalog and guidelines online.

IMPRINTS Tablet Publications, Island Hopping Digital Guides.

NONFICTION Subjects include environment, marine subjects, regional, sports, travel, sailing, boating, regional, boating guide books, boating how-to, Bahamas, Caribbean, travel. Regional guide books, first-person adventure, reference, how-to, technical—all dealing with boating. Query with SASE. Submit TOC and 3 sample chapters. Prefers electronic query via e-mail. Reviews artwork/photos. Send photocopies, color prints, or jpeg files.

⊙ SELF-COUNSEL PRESS

1481 Charlotte Rd., North Vancouver BC V7J 1H1, Canada. **E-mail:** editor@self-counsel.com. **Website:** www.self-counsel.com. **Contact:** Tyler Douglas. Estab. 1971. Publishes trade paperback originals. Self-Counsel Press publishes a range of quality self-help books written in practical, nontechnical style by recognized experts in the fields of business, financial, or legal guidance for people who want to help themselves. **Publishes 20 titles/year. 1,500 queries received/year. 50% of books from first-time authors. 95% from unagented writers. Pays rare advance.** Publishes ms 8-10 months after acceptance. Accepts simultaneous submissions. Responds in 2 months to queries. Book catalog online. Guidelines online.

NONFICTION Subjects include , legal and business issues for lay people. Submit proposal package, outline, resume, 2 sample chapters.

SEVEN STORIES PRESS

140 Watts St., New York NY 10013. (212)226-8760. **Fax:** (212)226-1411. **E-mail:** info@sevenstories.com. **Website:** www.sevenstories.com. **Contact:** Acquisitions. Estab. 1995. Publishes hardcover and trade paperback originals. Founded in 1995 in New York City, and named for the seven authors who committed to a home with a fiercely independent spirit, Seven Stories Press publishes works of the imagination and political titles by voices of conscience. While most widely known for its books on politics, human rights, and social and economic justice, Seven Stories continues to champion literature, with a list encompassing both innovative debut novels and National Book Award–winning poetry collections, as well as prose and poetry translations from the French, Spanish, German, Swedish, Italian, Greek, Polish, Korean, Vietnamese, Russian, and Arabic. **Publishes 40-50 titles/year. 15% of books from first-time authors. 50% from unagented writers. Pays 7-15% royalty on retail price. Pays advance.** Publishes ms 1-3 years after acceptance. Accepts simultaneous submissions. Responds in 1 month. Book catalog and ms guidelines free.

NONFICTION Responds only if interested. Submit cover letter with 2 sample chapters.

FICTION Subjects include literary. Submit cover letter with 2 sample chapters.

Ⓐ❾∅ SEVERN HOUSE PUBLISHERS

Salatin House, 19 Cedar Rd., Sutton, Surrey SM2 5DA, United Kingdom. (44)(208)770-3930. **Fax:** (44)(208)770-3850. **Website:** www.severnhouse.com. Publishes hardcover and trade paperback originals and reprints. Severn House is currently emphasizing suspense, romance, mystery. Large print imprint from existing authors. **Publishes 150 titles/year. 400-500 queries received/year. 50 mss received/year. Pays 7-15% royalty on retail price. Pays $750-5,000 advance.** Accepts simultaneous submissions. Responds in 3 months to proposals. Book catalog available free.

FICTION Subjects include adventure, fantasy, historical, horror, mystery, romance, short story collections, suspense. *Agented submissions only.*

SHAMBHALA PUBLICATIONS, INC.

4720 Walnut St., Boulder CO 80304. **E-mail:** submissions@shambhala.com. **Website:** www.shambhala.com. Estab. 1969. Publishes hardcover and trade paperback originals and reprints. **Publishes 90-100 titles/year. 500 queries; 1,200 mss/proposals received/year. 30% of books from first-time authors. 70% from unagented writers. Pays 8% royalty on retail price.** Publishes ms 1 year after acceptance. Accepts simultaneous submissions. Responds in 4 months. Book catalog free. Guidelines online.

IMPRINTS Roost Books; Snow Lion.

NONFICTION Subjects include cooking, crafts, parenting, Buddhism, martial arts, yoga, natural health, Eastern philosophy, creativity, green living, nature writing. To send a book proposal, include a synopsis of the book, see the submissions guidelines online. "We strongly prefer electronic submissions and do not take phone calls regarding book ideas or proposals."

❾ SHEARSMAN BOOKS, LTD

50 Westons Hills Dr., Emersons Green, Bristol BS16 7DF, United Kingdom. **E-mail:** editor@shearsman.com. **Website:** www.shearsman.com. **Contact:** Tony Frazer, editor. Estab. 1981. Publishes trade paperback originals. **Publishes 45-60 titles/year. Receives 2,000 submissions/year. 10% of books from first-time authors. 95% from unagented writers. Pays 10% royalty on retail price after 150 copies have sold; authors also receive 10 free copies of their books. Does not pay advance.** Publishes ms 9-18

months after acceptance. Accepts simultaneous submissions. Responds in 3 months to mss. Book catalog online. Print copies available on request. Guidelines online.

NONFICTION Subjects include literature, memoirs, translation, essays. All nonfiction has to do with poetry in some way. "We don't publish nonfiction unless it's related to poetry."

POETRY "Shearsman only publishes poetry, poetry collections, and poetry in translation (from any language but with an emphasis on work in Spanish & in German). Some critical work on poetry and also memoirs and essays by poets. Mainly poetry by British, Irish, North American, and Australian poets." No poetry by or for children. No devotional or religious verse.

A ⊘ SIMON & SCHUSTER

1230 Avenue of the Americas, New York NY 10020. (212)698-7000. **Website:** www.simonandschuster. com. *Accepts agented submissions only.* Accepts simultaneous submissions.

IMPRINTS Aladdin; Atheneum Books for Young Readers; Atria; Beach Lane Books; Folger Shakespeare Library; Free Press; Gallery Books; Howard Books; Little Simon; Margaret K. McElderry Books; Pocket; Scribner; Simon & Schuster; Simon & Schuster Books for Young Readers; Simon Pulse; Simon Spotlight; Threshold; Touchstone; Paula Wiseman Books.

A ⊘ SIMON & SCHUSTER BOOKS FOR YOUNG READERS

Imprint of Simon & Schuster Children's Publishing, 1230 Avenue of the Americas, New York NY 10020. (212)698-7000. **Fax:** (212)698-2796. **Website:** www. simonsayskids.com. Publishes hardcover originals. "Simon and Schuster Books For Young Readers is the Flagship imprint of the S&S Children's Division. We are committed to publishing a wide range of contemporary, commercial, award-winning fiction and nonfiction that spans every age of children's publishing. BFYR is constantly looking to the future, supporting our foundation authors and franchises, but always with an eye for breaking new ground with every publication. We publish high-quality fiction and nonfiction for a variety of age groups and a variety of markets. Above all, we strive to publish books that we are passionate about." *No unsolicited mss.* All unsolicited mss returned unopened. **Publishes 75 titles/**

year. **Pays variable royalty on retail price.** Publishes ms 2-4 years after acceptance. Accepts simultaneous submissions. Guidelines online.

NONFICTION Subjects include history, biography. Picture books: concept. All levels: narrative, current events, biography, history. "We're looking for picture books or middle grade nonfiction that have a retail potential. No photo essays." *Agented submissions only.*

FICTION Subjects include fantasy, historical, humor, juvenile, mystery, picture books, science fiction, young adult. *Agented submissions only.*

SKINNER HOUSE BOOKS

The Unitarian Universalist Association, 24 Farnsworth St., Boston MA 02210. (617)742-2100, ext. 603. **Fax:** (617)948-6466. **E-mail:** bookproposals@uua.org. **Website:** www.uua.org/publications/skinnerhouse. **Contact:** Betsy Martin. Estab. 1975. Publishes trade paperback originals and reprints. "We publish titles in Unitarian Universalist faith, liberal religion, history, biography, worship, and issues of social justice. Most of our children's titles are intended for religious education or worship use. They reflect Unitarian Universalist values. We also publish inspirational titles of poetic prose and meditations. Writers should know that Unitarian Universalism is a liberal religious denomination committed to progressive ideals. Currently emphasizing social justice concerns." **Publishes 10-20 titles/year. 30% of books from first-time authors. 100% from unagented writers.** Publishes book 1 year after acceptance. Accepts simultaneous submissions. Responds to queries in 1 month. Book catalog for 6×9 SAE with 3 first-class stamps. Guidelines online.

NONFICTION Subjects include religion, inspirational, church leadership. All levels: activity books, multicultural, music/dance, nature/environment, religion. Query or submit proposal with cover letter, TOC, 2 sample chapters. Reviews artwork/photos. Send photocopies.

FICTION Only publishes fiction for children's titles for religious instruction. Query.

SMITH AND KRAUS PUBLISHERS, INC.

177 Lyme Rd., Hanover NH 03755. (603)643-6431. **E-mail:** editor@smithandkraus.com. **E-mail:** carolb@smithandkraus.com. **Website:** smithandkraus.com. Estab. 1990. Publishes hardcover and trade paperback originals. **Publishes 35-40 titles/year. 10% of books from first-time authors. 10-20% from unagented writers. Pays 7% royalty on retail price. Pays $500-**

2,000 advance. Publishes ms 1 year after acceptance. Responds in 1 month to queries; 2 months to proposals; 4 months to mss. Book catalog available free.

NONFICTION Subjects include , drama. Does not return submissions. Query with SASE.

FICTION Does not return submissions. Query with SASE.

GIBBS SMITH, PUBLISHER

P.O. Box 667, Layton UT 84041. (801)544-9800. **Fax:** (801)546-8853. **Website:** www.gibbs-smith.com. Estab. 1969. Publishes hardcover and trade paperback originals. "We publish books that enrich and inspire humankind. Currently emphasizing interior decorating and design, home reference. De-emphasizing novels and short stories." **Publishes 80 titles/year. 3,000-4,000 queries received/year. 50% of books from first-time authors. 75% from unagented writers. Pays 8-14% royalty on gross receipts. Offers advance based on first year saleability projections.** Publishes ms 1-2 years after acceptance. Accepts simultaneous submissions. Responds in 1 month to queries; 10 weeks to proposals and mss. Guidelines online.

NONFICTION Subjects include regional, interior design, cooking, business, western, outdoor/sports/recreation. Query by e-mail only.

SOFT SKULL PRESS INC.

Counterpoint, 2650 Ninth St., Suite 318, Berkeley CA 94710. (510)704-0230. **Fax:** (510)704-0268. **E-mail:** info@counterpointpress.com. **Website:** www.softskull.com. Publishes hardcover and trade paperback originals. "Here at Soft Skull we love books that are new, fun, smart, revelatory, quirky, groundbreaking, cage-rattling and/or otherwise unusual." **Publishes 40 titles/year. Pays 7-10% royalty. Average advance: $100-15,000.** Publishes ms 6 months after acceptance. Accepts simultaneous submissions. Responds in 2 months to proposals; 3 months to mss. Book catalog and guidelines online.

NONFICTION Subjects include contemporary culture, creative nonfiction, entertainment, literature, pop culture. Send a cover letter describing your project and a full proposal along with 2 sample chapters.

FICTION Subjects include comic books, confession, contemporary, erotica, experimental, gay, lesbian, literary, mainstream, multicultural, short story collections. Does not consider poetry. Soft Skull Press no longer accepts digital submissions. Send a cover let-

ter describing your project in detail and a completed ms. For graphic novels, send a minimum of five fully inked pages of art, along with a synopsis of your storyline. "Please do not send original material, as it will not be returned."

SOHO PRESS, INC.

853 Broadway, New York NY 10003. (212)260-1900. **E-mail:** soho@sohopress.com. **Website:** www.sohopress.com. **Contact:** Bronwen Hruska, publisher; Mark Doten, senior editor. Estab. 1986. Publishes hardcover and trade paperback originals; trade paperback reprints. Soho Press publishes primarily fiction, as well as some narrative literary nonfiction and mysteries set abroad. No electronic submissions, only queries by e-mail. **Publishes 60-70 titles/year. 15-25% of books from first-time authors. 10% from unagented writers. Pays 10-15% royalty on retail price (varies under certain circumstances).** Publishes ms 18 months after acceptance. Accepts simultaneous submissions. Responds in 3 months. Guidelines online.

NONFICTION Subjects include creative nonfiction, ethnic, memoirs. "Independent publisher known for sophisticated fiction, mysteries set abroad, women's interest (no genre) novels and multicultural novels." Publishes hardcover and trade paperback originals and reprint editions. Books: perfect binding; halftone illustrations. First novel print order varies. We do not buy books on proposal. We always need to see a complete ms before we buy a book, though we prefer an initial submission of 3 sample chapters. We do not publish books with color art or photographs or a lot of graphical material." No self-help, how-to, or cookbooks. Submit 3 sample chapters and a cover letter with a synopsis and author bio; SASE. Send photocopies.

FICTION Subjects include ethnic, historical, humor, literary, mystery, In mysteries, we only publish series with foreign or exotic settings, usually procedurals.. Adventure, ethnic, feminist, historical, literary, mainstream/contemporary, mystery (police procedural), suspense, multicultural. Submit 3 sample chapters and cover letter with synopsis, author bio, SASE. *No e-mailed submissions.*

SOURCEBOOKS, INC.

1935 Brookdale Rd., Suite 139, Naperville IL 60563. (630)961-3900. **Fax:** (630)961-2168. **E-mail:** editorialsubmissions@sourcebooks.com. **Website:** www.sourcebooks.com. Estab. 1987. Publishes hardcover and trade paperback originals. "Sourcebooks publishes many forms of fiction and nonfiction titles, including books on parenting, self-help/psychology, business, and health. Focus is on practical, useful information and skills. It also continues to publish in the reference, New Age, history, current affairs, and humor categories. Currently emphasizing gift, women's interest, history, reference, historical fiction, romance genre, and children's." **Publishes 300 titles/year. 30% of books from first-time authors. 25% from unagented writers. Pays royalty on wholesale or list price. Pays advance.** Publishes ms 1 year after acceptance. Accepts simultaneous submissions. Responds in 3 months to queries. Book catalog online. Guidelines online.

NONFICTION Subjects include child guidance, history, psychology, science, sports, contemporary culture. Books for small business owners, entrepreneurs, and students. A key to submitting books to us is to explain how your book helps the reader, why it is different from the books already out there (please do your homework), and the author's credentials for writing this book. Books likely to succeed with us are self-help, parenting and childcare, psychology, women's issues, how-to, history, reference, biography, humor, gift books, or books with strong artwork. "We seek unique books on traditional subjects and authors who are smart and aggressive." Query with SASE, 2-3 sample chapters (not the first). *No complete mss.* Reviews artwork/photos.

SOUTHERN ILLINOIS UNIVERSITY PRESS

1915 University Press Dr., SIUC Mail Code 6806, Carbondale IL 62901. (618)453-2281. **Fax:** (618)453-1221. **E-mail:** angmoore@siu.edu. **Website:** www.siupress. com. **Contact:** Angela Moore-Swafford, business manager. Estab. 1956. Publishes hardcover and trade paperback originals and reprints. Scholarly press specializes in theater studies, rhetoric and composition studies, American history, Civil War, regional and nonfiction trade, poetry. No fiction. Currently emphasizing theater and American history, especially Civil War. **Publishes 30-34 titles/year. 300 queries; 80 mss received/year. 40% of books from first-time authors. 99% from unagented writers. Pays 5-10% royalty on wholesale price. Rarely offers advance.** Publishes ms 1 year after acceptance. Responds in 2 months to queries. Book catalog and ms guidelines free.

NONFICTION Subjects include archeology, history, language, military, regional, stage, transportation, war, womens studies.

POETRY Crab Orchard Series in Poetry. Guidelines online.

SPLASHING COW BOOKS

P.O. Box 867, Manchester VT 05254. **Website:** www. splashingcowbooks.com. **Contact:** Gordon McClellan, publisher. Estab. 2014. Publishes mass market paperback and hardcover books. We do not publish digital books. Splashing Cow Books publishes books under three imprints: Splashing Cow (children), Blue Boot (women) and Yellow Dot (family). **Publishes 10 titles/year. 100% of books from first-time authors. 100% from unagented writers. Pays royalties on retail price. Does not offer an advance.** Accepts simultaneous submissions. We try to reply as soon as possible, but may take up to 3 months. Catalog online. Guidelines online.

IMPRINTS Blue Boot Books imprint publishes books for women. Yellow Dot publishes general interest topics.

NONFICTION Open to any topic that would be of interest to children, women or families.

FICTION Subjects include adventure, comic books, contemporary, ethnic, fantasy, historical, humor, juvenile, literary, mainstream, multicultural, mystery, picture books, romance, science fiction, short story collections, spiritual, sports, suspense, western, young adult. Interested in a wide range of subject matter for children, women and families. Please check our website for submission guidelines.

SQUARE ONE PUBLISHERS, INC.

115 Herricks Rd., Garden City Park NY 11040. (516)535-2010. **Fax:** (516)535-2014. **Website:** www. squareonepublishers.com. **Contact:** Acquisitions Editor. Publishes trade paperback originals. **Publishes 20 titles/year. 500 queries; 100 mss received/year. 95% of books from first-time authors. 95% from unagented writers. Pays 10-15% royalty on wholesale price. Pays variable advance.** Publishes ms 10 months after acceptance. Accepts simultaneous submissions. Responds in 1 month. Book catalog and ms guidelines online.

NONFICTION Subjects include child guidance, cooking, health, hobbies, nutrition, psychology, religion, spirituality, sports, travel, writers' guides, cooking/foods, gaming/gambling. Query with SASE.

Submit proposal package, outline, bio, introduction, synopsis, SASE. Reviews artwork/photos. Send photocopies.

STANFORD UNIVERSITY PRESS

500 Broadway St., Redwood City CA 94063. (650)723-9434. **Fax:** (650)725-3457. **Website:** www.sup.org. Estab. 1925. "Stanford University Press publishes scholarly books in the humanities and social sciences, along with professional books in business, economics and management science; also high-level textbooks and some books for a more general audience." *Submit to specific editor.* **Pays variable royalty (sometimes none). Pays occasional advance.** Guidelines online.

NONFICTION Subjects include ethnic, history, humanities, literary criticism, philosophy, psychology, religion, science, social sciences, sociology, political science, law, education, history and culture of China, Japan and Latin America, European history, linguistics, geology, medieval and classical studies. Query with prospectus and an outline. Reviews artwork/photos.

STAR BRIGHT BOOKS

13 Landsdowne St., Cambridge MA 02139. (617)354-1300. **Fax:** (617)354-1399. **E-mail:** info@starbright-books.com. **Website:** www.starbrightbooks.com. Star Bright Books does accept unsolicited mss and art submissions. "We welcome submissions for picture books and longer works, both fiction and nonfiction." Also beginner readers and chapter books. Query first. **Publishes 18 titles/year. 75% of books from first-time authors. 99% from unagented writers. Pays advance.** Publishes ms 1-2 years after acceptance. Accepts simultaneous submissions. Responds in several months. Catalog available.

NONFICTION Almost anything of interest to children. Very keen on Biographies and any thing of interest to children.

ST. AUGUSTINE'S PRESS

17917 Killington Way, South Bend IN 46614-9773. (574)291-3500. **Fax:** (574)291-3700. **E-mail:** bruce@staugustine.net. **Website:** www.staugustine.net. **Contact:** Bruce Fingerhut, president. Estab. 1996. Publishes hardcover originals and trade paperback originals and reprints. "Our market is scholarly in the humanities. We publish in philosophy, religion, cultural history, and history of ideas only." **Publishes 30+ titles/year. 350 queries; 300 mss received/year. 2% of books from first-time authors. 95% from unagent-**

ed writers. Pays 6-15% royalty. Pays $500-5,000 advance.** Publishes book 8-18 months after acceptance. Accepts simultaneous submissions. Responds in 2-6 months to queries; 3-8 months to proposals; 4-8 months to mss. Book catalog available free.

IMPRINTS Carthage Reprints.

NONFICTION Subjects include humanities, philosophy, religion. Query with SASE. Reviews artwork/photos. Send photocopies.

STENHOUSE PUBLISHERS

P.O. Box 11020, Portland ME 04104. **E-mail:** editors@stenhouse.com. **Website:** www.stenhouse.com. **Contact:** Philippa Stratton, editorial director. Estab. 1993. Publishes paperback originals. Stenhouse publishes exclusively professional books for teachers, K-12. **Publishes 15 titles/year. 300 queries received/year. 30% of books from first-time authors. 99% from unagented writers. Pays royalty on wholesale price.** Accepts simultaneous submissions. Responds in 2 weeks to queries; 1 month to mss. Book catalog free or online. Guidelines online.

NONFICTION Subjects include education, specializing in literary with offerings in elementary and middle level math and science. All of our books are a combination of theory and practice. No children's books or student texts. Query by e-mail (preferred) or SASE. Reviews artwork/photos. Send photocopies.

STERLING PUBLISHING CO., INC.

1166 Avenue of the Americas, 17th Floor, New York NY 10036. (212)532-7160. **Website:** www.sterlingpublishing.com. Publishes hardcover and paperback originals and reprints. "Sterling publishes highly illustrated, accessible, hands-on, practical books for adults and children. Our mission is to publish high-quality books that educate, entertain, and enrich the lives of our readers." **15% of books from first-time authors. Pays royalty or work purchased outright. Offers advances (average amount: $2,000).** Accepts simultaneous submissions. Catalog online. Guidelines online.

NONFICTION Subjects include animals, ethnic, gardening, hobbies, New Age, recreation, science, sports, fiber arts, games and puzzles, children's humor, children's science, nature and activities, pets, wine, home decorating, dolls and puppets, ghosts, UFOs, woodworking, crafts, medieval, Celtic subjects, alternative health and healing, new consciousness. Proposals on subjects such as crafting, decorating, outdoor living, and photography should be sent directly to

Lark Books at their Asheville, North Carolina offices. Complete guidelines can be found on the Lark site: www.larkbooks.com/submissions. Publishes nonfiction only. Submit outline, publishing history, 1 sample chapter (typed and double-spaced), SASE. "Explain your idea. Send sample illustrations where applicable. For children's books, please submit full mss. We do not accept electronic (e-mail) submissions. Be sure to include information about yourself with particular regard to your skills and qualifications in the subject area of your submission. It is helpful for us to know your publishing history—whether or not you've written other books and, if so, the name of the publisher and whether those books are currently in print." Reviews artwork/photocopies.

FICTION Publishes fiction for children. Submit to attention of "Children's Book Editor."

STIPES PUBLISHING LLC

P.O. Box 526, Champaign IL 61824. (217)356-8391. **Fax:** (217)356-5753. **E-mail:** stipes01@sbcglobal.net. **Website:** www.stipes.com. Estab. 1925. Publishes hardcover and paperback originals. "Stipes Publishing is oriented towards the education market and educational books with some emphasis in the trade market." **Publishes 15-30 titles/year. 50% of books from first-time authors. 95% from unagented writers. Pays 15% maximum royalty on retail price.** Publishes ms 4 months after acceptance. Responds in 2 months to queries. Guidelines online.

NONFICTION Subjects include agriculture, recreation, science. "All of our books in the trade area are books that also have a college text market. No books unrelated to educational fields taught at the college level." Submit outline, 1 sample chapter.

STOREY PUBLISHING

210 MASS MoCA Way, North Adams MA 01247. (800)793-9396. **Fax:** (413)346-2199. **E-mail:** feedback@storey.com. **Website:** www.storey.com. Estab. 1983. Publishes hardcover and trade paperback originals and reprints. "The mission of Storey Publishing is to serve our customers by publishing practical information that encourages personal independence in harmony with the environment. We seek to do this in a positive atmosphere that promotes editorial quality, team spirit, and profitability. The books we select to carry out this mission include titles on gardening, small-scale farming, building, cooking, home brewing, crafts, part-time business, home improvement,

woodworking, animals, nature, natural living, personal care, and country living. We are always pleased to review new proposals, which we try to process expeditiously. We offer both work-for-hire and standard royalty contracts." **Publishes 40 titles/year. 600 queries received/year. 150 mss received/year. 25% of books from first-time authors. 60% from unagented writers. We offer both work-for-hire and standard royalty contracts. Pays advance.** Publishes book 2 years after acceptance. Accepts simultaneous submissions. Responds in 1-3 months. Book catalog available free. Guidelines online.

NONFICTION Subjects include animals, gardening, home, mind/body/spirit, birds, beer and wine, crafts, building, cooking. Submit a proposal. Reviews artwork/photos.

STYLUS PUBLISHING, LLC

22883 Quicksilver Dr., Sterling VA 20166. **E-mail:** sylusinfo@styluspub.com. **Website:** styluspub.com. Estab. 1996. Publishes hardcover and trade paperback originals. "We publish in higher education (diversity, professional development, distance education, teaching, administration)." **Publishes 10-15 titles/year. 50 queries received/year. 6 mss received/year. 50% of books from first-time authors. 100% from unagented writers. Pays 5-10% royalty on wholesale price. Pays advance.** Publishes ms 6 months after acceptance. Responds in 1 month to queries. Book catalog available free. Guidelines online.

NONFICTION Query or submit outline, 1 sample chapter with SASE. Reviews artwork/photos. Send photocopies.

SUN BOOKS / SUN PUBLISHING

P.O. Box 5588, Santa Fe NM 87502. (505)471-5177. **E-mail:** info@sunbooks.com. **Website:** www.sunbooks.com. Estab. 1973. Publishes trade paperback originals and reprints. Not accepting new mss at this time. **Publishes 10-15 titles/year. 5% of books from first-time authors. 90% from unagented writers. Pays 5% royalty on retail price. Occasionally makes outright purchase.** Publishes ms 16-18 months after acceptance. Accepts simultaneous submissions. "Will respond within 2 months, via e-mail, to queries if interested." Book catalog online. Queries via e-mail only, please.

NONFICTION Subjects include agriculture, alternative lifestyles, Americana, astrology, career guidance, environment, history, New Age, regional, self-help, leadership, motivational, recovery, inspirational.

SUNBURY PRESS, INC.

PO Box 548, Boiling Springs PA 17007. **E-mail:** info@sunburypress.com. **E-mail:** proposals@sunburypress.com. **Website:** www.sunburypress.com. Estab. 2004. Publishes trade paperback and hardcover originals and reprints; electronic originals and reprints. Sunbury Press, Inc., headquartered in Mechanicsburg, PA is a publisher of trade paperback, hard cover and digital books featuring established and emerging authors in many fiction and non-fiction categories. Sunbury's books are printed in the USA and sold through leading booksellers worldwide. "Please use our online submission form." **Publishes 60 titles/year. Receives 1,000 queries/year; 500 mss/year. 40% of books from first-time authors. 95% from unagented writers. Pays 10% royalty on wholesale price.** Publishes ms 6 months after acceptance. Accepts simultaneous submissions. Responds in 3 months. Catalog and guidelines online. Online submission form.

IMPRINTS Sunbury Press (history and nonfiction); Milford House Press (murder mysteries, historical fiction, young adult fiction); Hellbender Books (horror, thrillers); Brown Posey Press (literary fiction, art); Ars Metaphysica (religion, spiritual, metaphysical, visionary fiction); Speckled Egg Press (juvenile fiction/nonfiction).

NONFICTION Subjects include agriculture, Americana, animals, anthropology, archeology, architecture, art, astrology, business, career guidance, child guidance, cinema, communications, community, computers, contemporary culture, cooking, counseling, crafts, creative nonfiction, economics, education, electronics, entertainment, environment, ethnic, film, finance, government, health, history, hobbies, house and home, humanities, labor, language, law, literature, marine subjects, medicine, memoirs, military, money, multicultural, music, nature, New Age, nutrition, parenting, philosophy, politics, pop culture, psychic, psychology, public affairs, real estate, recreation, regional, religion, science, sex, social sciences, sociology, spirituality, sports, transportation, travel, true crime, war, womens issues, womens studies, world affairs, young adult. "We are currently seeking war memoirs of all kinds and local / regional histories and biographies. We are also looking for American Revolution

manuscripts." Please use our online submission service. Reviews artwork.

FICTION Subjects include adventure, confession, contemporary, ethnic, experimental, fantasy, gothic, historical, horror, humor, juvenile, literary, mainstream, military, multicultural, mystery, occult, regional, religious, romance, science fiction, short story collections, spiritual, sports, suspense, war, western, young adult. "We are seeking manuscripts for our three fiction imprints: Milford House Press, Brown Posey Press, and Hellbender Books." Does not want vampires, zombies, erotica. Please use our online submission service.

POETRY Submit complete ms.

SUNRISE RIVER PRESS

838 Lake St. S., Forest Lake MN 55025. (800)895-4585. **Fax:** (651)277-1203. **E-mail:** info@sunriseriverpress.com. **E-mail:** submissions@sunriseriverpress.com. **Website:** www.sunriseriverpress.com. Estab. 1992. "E-mail is preferred method of contact." Sunrise River Press is currently seeking book proposals from health/medical writers or experts who are interested in authoring consumer-geared trade paperbacks on healthcare, fitness, and nutrition topics. **Publishes 30 titles/year. Pays advance.** Accepts simultaneous submissions. Guidelines online.

NONFICTION Subjects include health, genetics, immune system maintenance, fitness; also some professional healthcare titles. Check website for submission guidelines. No phone calls, please; no originals.

SYRACUSE UNIVERSITY PRESS

621 Skytop Rd., Suite 110, Syracuse NY 13244. (315)443-5534. **Fax:** (315)443-5545. **E-mail:** seguiod@syr.edu; dmmanion@syr.edu. **Website:** syracuseuniversitypress.syr.edu. **Contact:** Suzanne Guiod, editor-in-chief; Deborah Manion, acquisitions editor. Estab. 1943. "Currently emphasizing Middle East studies, Jewish studies, Irish studies, peace studies, disability studies, television and popular culture, sports and entertainment, Native American studies, gender and ethnic studies, New York State." **Publishes 50 titles/year. 25% of books from first-time authors. 95% from unagented writers.** Publishes book 15 months after acceptance. Book catalog online. Guidelines online.

NONFICTION Subjects include anthropology, history, humanities, literature, politics, pop culture, regional, religion, sociology, sports, translation, womens studies. "Special opportunity in our nonfiction program for books on New York state, sports history, Jewish studies, Irish studies, the Middle East, religion and politics, television and popular culture, disability studies, peace studies, Native American studies. Provide precise descriptions of subjects, along with background description of project. The author must make a case for the importance of his or her subject." Submit query via e-mail with the book proposal form found on our website and a copy of your CV. Reviews artwork/photos.

TAFELBERG PUBLISHERS

Imprint of NB Publishers, P.O. Box 879, Cape Town 8000, South Africa. (27)(21)406-3033. **Fax:** (27)(21)406-3812. **E-mail:** engela.reinke@nb.co.za. **Website:** www.tafelberg.com. **Contact:** Engela Reinke. General publisher best known for Afrikaans fiction, authoritative political works, children's/youth literature, and a variety of illustrated and nonillustrated nonfiction. **Publishes 10 titles/year. Pays authors royalty of 15-18% based on wholesale price.** Publishes book 1 year after acceptance. Accepts simultaneous submissions. Responds to queries in 2 weeks; mss in 6 months.

NONFICTION Subjects include memoirs, politics. Submit outline, information on intended market, bio, and 1-2 sample chapters.

FICTION Subjects include juvenile, romance. Picture books, young readers: animal, anthology, contemporary, fantasy, folktales, hi-lo, humor, multicultural, nature/environment, scient fiction, special needs. Middle readers, young adults: animal (middle reader only), contemporary, fantasy, hi-lo, humor, multicultural, nature/environment, problem novels, science fiction, special needs, sports, suspense/mystery. Average word length: picture books—1,500-7,500; young readers—25,000; middle readers—15,000; young adults—40,000. Submit complete ms.

NAN A. TALESE

Imprint of Doubleday, Random House, 1745 Broadway, New York NY 10019. (212)782-8918. **Fax:** (212)782-8448. **Website:** www.nanatalese.com. Publishes hardcover originals. Nan A. Talese publishes nonfiction with a powerful guiding narrative and relevance to larger cultural interests, and literary fiction of the highest quality. **Publishes 15 titles/year. 400 queries received/year. 400 mss received/year. Pays variable royalty on retail price. Pays varying advance.** Accepts simultaneous submissions.

NONFICTION Subjects include contemporary culture, history, philosophy, sociology. *Agented submissions only.*

FICTION Subjects include literary. Well-written narratives with a compelling story line, good characterization and use of language. We like stories with an edge. *Agented submissions only.*

TANTOR MEDIA

Recorded Books, 6 Business Park Rd., Old Saybrook CT 06475. (860)395-1155. **Fax:** (860)395-1154. **E-mail:** rightsemail@tantor.com. **Website:** www.tantor.com. **Contact:** Ron Formica, director of acquisitions. Estab. 2001. Publishes audiobooks only. Tantor Media, a division of Recorded Books, is a leading audiobook publisher, producing more than 100 new titles every month. We do not publish print or e-books. **Publishes 1,500 titles/year.** Accepts simultaneous submissions. Responds in 2 months. Catalog online. Not accepting print or e-book queries. We only publish audiobooks.

NONFICTION Subjects include agriculture, alternative lifestyles, Americana, animals, anthropology, astrology, business, child guidance, communications, contemporary culture, cooking, creative nonfiction, economics, education, entertainment, foods, games, gay, government, health, history, horticulture, law, lesbian, literary criticism, marine subjects, memoirs, military, money, multicultural, music, New Age, philosophy, psychology, religion, science, sex, social sciences, sociology, spirituality, sports, womens issues, womens studies, world affairs, young adult. Not accepting print submissions.

FICTION Subjects include adventure, contemporary, erotica, experimental, fantasy, feminist, gay, gothic, historical, horror, humor, juvenile, lesbian, literary, mainstream, military, multicultural, multimedia, mystery, occult, religious, romance, science fiction, short story collections, spiritual, sports, suspense, western, young adult.

TEACHERS COLLEGE PRESS

1234 Amsterdam Ave., New York NY 10027. (212)678-3929. **Fax:** (212)678-4149. **E-mail:** tcp.cs@aidcvt.com. **Website:** www.teacherscollegepress.com. Estab. 1904. Publishes hardcover and paperback originals and reprints. "Teachers College Press publishes a wide range of educational titles for all levels of students: early childhood to higher education. Publishing books that respond to, examine, and confront issues pertaining to education, teacher training, and school reform." **Publishes 60 titles/year. Pays industry standard royalty. Pays advance.** Publishes ms 1 year after acceptance. Responds in 2 months to queries. Book catalog available free. Guidelines online.

NONFICTION Subjects include education, history, philosophy, sociology. This university press concentrates on books in the field of education in the broadest sense, from early childhood to higher education: good classroom practices, teacher training, special education, innovative trends and issues, administration and supervision, film, continuing and adult education, all areas of the curriculum, computers, guidance and counseling, and the politics, economics, philosophy, sociology, and history of education. We have recently added women's studies to our list. The Press also issues classroom materials for students at all levels, with a strong emphasis on reading and writing and social studies. Submit outline, sample chapters.

TEMPLE UNIVERSITY PRESS

1852 N. 10th St., Philadelphia PA 19122. (215)926-2140. **Fax:** (215)926-2141. **Website:** www.temple.edu/temppress/. Estab. 1969. "Temple University Press has been publishing path-breaking books on Asian-Americans, law, gender issues, film, women's studies and other interesting areas for nearly 40 years." **Publishes 60 titles/year. Pays advance.** Publishes ms 10 months after acceptance. Responds in 2 months to queries. Book catalog available free. Guidelines online.

NONFICTION Subjects include ethnic, history, photography, regional, sociology, labor studies, urban studies, Latin American/Latino, Asian American, African American studies, public policy, women's studies. No memoirs, fiction or poetry. Query with SASE. Reviews artwork/photos.

⊗⊘ TEN SPEED PRESS

Penguin Random House, The Crown Publishing Group, Attn: Acquisitions, 2625 Alcatraz Ave. #505, Berkeley CA 94705. (510)559-1600. **Fax:** (510)524-1052. **Website:** crownpublishing.com/imprint/tenspeed-press. Estab. 1971. Publishes trade paperback originals and reprints. "Ten Speed Press publishes authoritative books for an audience interested in innovative ideas. Currently emphasizing cookbooks, career, business, alternative education, and offbeat general nonfiction gift books." **Publishes 120 titles/**

year. **40% of books from first-time authors. 40% from unagented writers. Pays $2,500 average advance.** Publishes ms 1 year after acceptance. Accepts simultaneous submissions. Responds in 3 months to queries; 6-8 weeks to proposals. Book catalog for 9×12 envelope and 6 first-class stamps. Guidelines online.

NONFICTION Subjects include business, career guidance, cooking, crafts, relationships, how-to, humor, and pop culture. *Agented submissions only.*

TEXAS TECH UNIVERSITY PRESS

1120 Main St., Second Floor, Box 41037, Lubbock TX 79415. (806)742-2982. **Fax:** (806)742-2979. **E-mail:** ttup@ttu.edu. **Website:** www.ttupress.org. Estab. 1971. Texas Tech University Press, the book publishing office of the university since 1971 and an AAUP member since 1986, publishes nonfiction titles in the areas of natural history and the natural sciences; 18th century and Joseph Conrad studies; studies of modern Southeast Asia, particularly the Vietnam War; costume and textile history; Latin American literature and culture; and all aspects of the Great Plains and the American West, especially history, biography, memoir, sports history, and travel. In addition, the Press publishes several scholarly journals, acclaimed series for young readers, an annual invited poetry collection, and literary fiction of Texas and the West. Accepts simultaneous submissions. Guidelines online.

NONFICTION Subjects include environment, ethnic, history, law, literary criticism, literature, regional, sports. Submit proposal that includes introduction, 2 sample chapters, cover letter, working title, anticipated ms length, description of audience, comparison of book to others published on the subject, brief bio or CV.

FICTION Subjects include ethnic, multicultural, religious, western. Fiction rooted in the American West and Southwest, Jewish literature, Latin American and Latino fiction (in translation or English).

POETRY "TTUP publishes an annual invited first-book poetry manuscript (please note that we cannot entertain unsolicited poetry submissions)."

○ THISTLEDOWN PRESS LTD.

410 2nd Ave., Saskatoon SK S7K 2C3, Canada. (306)244-1722. **Fax:** (306)244-1762. **E-mail:** editorial@thistledownpress.com. **Website:** www.thistledownpress.com. **Contact:** Allan Forrie, publisher. Estab. 1975. "Thistledown originates books by Canadian authors only, although we have co-published

titles by authors outside Canada. We do not publish children's picture books." **40% of books from first-time authors. 40% from unagented writers. Pays authors royalty of 10-12% based on net dollar sales. Pays illustrators and photographers by the project (range: $250-750). Rarely pays advance.** Publishes book 1 year after acceptance. Responds to queries in 6 months. Book catalog on website. Guidelines online.

NONFICTION Subjects include environment, literature, young adult.

FICTION Subjects include literary, short story collections. Young adults: adventure, anthology, contemporary, fantasy, humor, poetry, romance, science fiction, suspense/mystery, short stories. Average word length: young adults—40,000. Submit outline/synopsis and sample chapters. *Does not accept mss.* Do not query by e-mail. "Please note: we are not accepting middle years (ages 8-12) nor children's manuscripts at this time." See Submission Guidelines on Website.

POETRY "We do not publish cowboy poetry, inspirational poetry, or poetry for children."

☼ THOMSON REUTERS

One Corporate Plaza, 2075 Kennedy Rd., Toronto ON M1T 3V4, Canada. (416)298-5024. **Fax:** (416)298-5094. **Website:** www.carswell.com. Publishes hardcover originals. "Thomson Carswell is Canada's national resource of information and legal interpretations for law, accounting, tax and business professionals." **Publishes 150-200 titles/year. 30-50% of books from first-time authors. Pays 5-15% royalty on wholesale price.** Publishes ms 6 months after acceptance. Accepts simultaneous submissions. Responds in 3 months to queries. Book catalog and ms guidelines free.

NONFICTION Canadian information of a regulatory nature is our mandate. Submit proposal package, outline, resume.

☼⊘ TIGHTROPE BOOKS

#207-2 College St., Toronto Ontario M5G 1K3, Canada. (416)928-6666. **E-mail:** tightropeasst@gmail.com. **Website:** www.tightropebooks.com. Estab. 2005. Publishes trade paperback originals. **Publishes 12 titles/year. 60% of books from first-time authors. 90% from unagented writers. Pays 5-15% royalty on retail price. Pays advance of $200-300.** Publishes book 1-2 years after acceptance. Accepts simultaneous submissions. Responds if interested. Catalog and guidelines online.

NONFICTION Subjects include alternative lifestyles, art, contemporary culture, creative nonfiction, ethnic, gay, language, lesbian, literary criticism, literature, memoirs, multicultural, womens issues, womens studies. No genres

FICTION Subjects include contemporary, ethnic, experimental, feminist, gay, lesbian, literary, multicultural, poetry, poetry in translation, short story collections, young adult.

TILBURY HOUSE PUBLISHERS

WordSplice Studio, Inc., 12 Starr St., Thomaston ME 04861. (207)582-1899. **Fax:** (207)582-8772. **E-mail:** info@tilburyhouse.com. **Website:** www.tilburyhouse.com. Estab. 1990. **Publishes 24 titles/year. Pays royalty based on wholesale price.** Publishes ms 1 year after acceptance. Accepts simultaneous submissions. Responds to mss in 3-6 months. Guidelines and catalog online.

NONFICTION Regional history/maritime/nature, and children's picture books that deal with issues, such as bullying, multiculturalism, etc. science/nature. Submit complete ms for picture books or outline/synopsis for longer works. Now uses online submission form. Reviews artwork/photos. Send URL.

FICTION Picture books: multicultural, nature/environment. Special needs include books that teach children about and honoring diversity. Send art/photography samples and/or complete ms to info@tilburyhouse.com.

Ⓐ TIN HOUSE BOOKS

2617 NW Thurman St., Portland OR 97210. (503)473-8663. **Fax:** (503)473-8957. **E-mail:** masie@tinhouse.com. **Website:** www.tinhouse.com. **Contact:** Masie Cochran, editor; Tony Perez, editor. Publishes hardcover originals, paperback originals, paperback reprints. "We are a small independent publisher dedicated to nurturing new, promising talent as well as showcasing the work of established writers." Distributes/promotes titles through W. W. Norton. **Publishes 10-12 titles/year.** Publishes ms 1 year after acceptance. Accepts simultaneous submissions. Responds to queries in 2-3 weeks; mss in 2-3 months. Guidelines online.

NONFICTION *Agented mss only.* "We no longer read unsolicited submissions by authors with no representation. We will continue to accept submissions from agents."

FICTION *Agented mss only.* "We no longer read unsolicited submissions by authors with no representation. We will continue to accept submissions from agents."

TITAN PRESS

5805 White Oak Ave. #17897, Encino CA 91316. E-mail: titan91416@yahoo.com. **Website:** https://www.facebook.com/RVClef. **Contact:** Romana Von Clef, editor. Estab. 1981. Publishes hardcover and paperback originals. Little literary publisher. **Publishes 12 titles/year. Receives 100-200 submissions/year. 5% of books from first-time authors. 50% from unagented writers. Pays 20-40% royalty.** Publishes ms 1 year after acceptance. Accepts simultaneous submissions. Responds to queries in 3 months.

NONFICTION Subjects include creative nonfiction, entertainment, literary criticism.

FICTION Subjects include contemporary, literary, mainstream, short story collections. Does not accept unsolicited mss. Query with SASE. Include brief bio, list of publishing credits.

POETRY Literary, not MFA banality.

TOR BOOKS

Tom Doherty Associates, 175 Fifth Ave., New York NY 10010. **Website:** www.tor-forge.com. Tor Books is the "world's largest publisher of science fiction and fantasy, with strong category publishing in historical fiction, mystery, western/Americana, thriller, YA." **Publishes 10-20 titles/year. Pays author royalty. Pays illustrators by the project.** Accepts simultaneous submissions. Book catalog available. Guidelines online.

FICTION Subjects include adventure, fantasy, historical, humor, mystery, picture books, science fiction, suspense, young adult. Submit first 3 chapters, 3-10 page synopsis, dated cover letter, SASE.

◎ TOUCHWOOD EDITIONS

The Heritage Group, 103-1075 Pendergast St., Victoria BC V8V 0A1, Canada. (250)360-0829. **Fax:** (250)386-0829. **E-mail:** edit@touchwoodeditions.com. **Website:** www.touchwoodeditions.com. **Contact:** Renée Layberry, Editor. Publishes trade paperback, originals and reprints. **Publishes 20-25 titles/year. 40% of books from first-time authors. 70% from unagented writers. Pays 15% royalty on net price.** Publishes ms 12-24 months after acceptance. Accepts simultaneous submissions. Responds in 6 months to queries. Book catalog and guidelines online.

NONFICTION Subjects include cooking, creative nonfiction, history, memoirs, recreation, regional, regional travel or guidebooks with a focus on food, wine, art or similar topics, regional history or biography, biography (well-known and western Canadian figures only), cultural studies, aboriginal history and writing, for adult and young readers, historical fiction, relating to western Canada. Submit TOC, outline, word count, 2-3 sample chapters, synopsis. Reviews artwork/photos. Send photocopies.

FICTION Subjects include historical, mainstream, mystery, regional. Submit bio/CV, marketing plan, TOC, outline, word count.

TOWER PUBLISHING

588 Saco Rd., Standish ME 04084. (207)642-5400. **Fax:** (207)642-5463. **E-mail:** info@towerpub.com. **E-mail:** michaell@towerpub.com. **Website:** www.towerpub.com. **Contact:** Michael Lyons, president. Estab. 1772. Publishes hardcover originals and reprints, trade paperback originals. Tower Publishing specializes in legal publications. **Publishes 22 titles/year. 60 queries; 30 mss received/year. 10% of books from first-time authors. 90% from unagented writers.** Publishes ms 6 months after acceptance. Accepts simultaneous submissions. Responds in 1 month to queries; 2 months to proposals and mss. Book catalog and ms guidelines online.

NONFICTION Subjects include law. Looking for legal books of a national stature. Query with SASE. Submit outline.

TRAFALGAR SQUARE BOOKS

388 Howe Hill Rd., P.O. Box 257, North Pomfret VT 05053. (802)457-1911. **Website:** www.horseandriderbooks.com. **Contact:** Rebecca Didier. Estab. 1985. Publishes hardcover and trade paperback originals. "We publish high-quality instructional books for horsemen and horsewomen, always with the horse's welfare in mind." **Publishes 12 titles/year. 50% of books from first-time authors. 80% from unagented writers. Pays royalty. Pays advance.** Publishes ms 18 months after acceptance. Responds in 1 month to queries; 2 months to proposals; 2-3 months to mss. Catalog free on request and by e-mail.

NONFICTION Subjects include animals. "We rarely consider books for complete novices." Query with SASE. Submit proposal package including outline, 1-3 sample chapters, letter of introduction including qualifications for writing on the subject and why the proposed book is an essential addition to existing publications. Reviews artwork/photos as part of the ms package. We prefer color laser thumbnail sheets or duplicate prints (do not send original photos or art!).

TUPELO PRESS

P.O. Box 1767, North Adams MA 01247. (413)664-9611. **Website:** www.tupelopress.org. **Contact:** Sarah Russell, administrative director. Publisher: Jeffrey Levine. Estab. 2001. "We're an independent nonprofit literary press. We publish book-length poetry, poetry collections, translations, short story collections, novellas, literary nonfiction/memoirs and novels." **Publishes 14-18 titles/year. 33% of books from first-time authors. 90% from unagented writers. Standard royalty contract. Pays advance in rare instances.** Publishes ms 2 years after acceptance. Accepts simultaneous submissions. Guidelines online.

NONFICTION Subjects include memoirs, memoir, essays, scholarly. No cookbooks, children's books, inspirational books, graphic novels, or religious books. **Charges $45 reading fee.**

FICTION Subjects include poetry, short story collections, novels. "For Novels—submit no more than 100 pages along with a summary of the entire book. If we're interested we'll ask you to send the rest. We accept very few works of prose (3 or 4 per year)." Submit complete ms. **Charges a $45 reading fee.**

POETRY "Our mission is to publish riveting, smart, visually and "Emotionally and intellectually stimulating books of the highest quality. We want contemporary poetry, etc. by the most diverse list of emerging and established writers in the U.S. Keenly interested in poets of color" Submit complete ms. **Charges $28 reading fee.**

TUTTLE PUBLISHING

364 Innovation Dr., North Clarendon VT 05759. (802)773-8930. **Fax:** (802)773-6993. **E-mail:** submissions@tuttlepublishing.com. **Website:** www.tuttle-publishing.com. Estab. 1832. Publishes hardcover and trade paperback originals and reprints. Tuttle is America's leading publisher of books on Japan and Asia. "Familiarize yourself with our catalog and/or similar books we publish. Send complete book proposal with cover letter, table of contents, 1-2 sample chapters, target audience description, SASE. No e-mail submissions." **Publishes 125 titles/year. 1,000 queries received/year. 20% of books from first-time authors. 40% from unagented writers. Pays 5-10%**

royalty on net or retail price, depending on format and kind of book. **Pays advance.** Publishes book 18 months after acceptance. Accepts simultaneous submissions. Responds in 2-3 months to proposals. Tuttle accepts submissions by mail or e-mail. Please send us duplicate copies only: do not send original copies of any kind, especially artwork.

NONFICTION Publishes Asian cultures, language, martial arts, textbooks, art and design, craft books and kits, cookbooks, religion, philosophy, and more. Query with SASE.

Ⓐ⊘ TYNDALE HOUSE PUBLISHERS, INC.

351 Executive Dr., Carol Stream IL 60188. (800)323-9400. **Fax:** (800)684-0247. **Website:** www.tyndale. com. Estab. 1962. Publishes hardcover and trade paperback originals and mass paperback reprints. "Tyndale House publishes practical, user-friendly Christian books for the home and family." **Publishes 15 titles/year. Pays negotiable royalty. Pays negotiable advance.** Accepts simultaneous submissions. Guidelines online.

NONFICTION Subjects include child guidance, religion, devotional/inspirational. *Agented submissions only. No unsolicited mss.*

FICTION Subjects include juvenile, romance, Christian (children's, general, inspirational, mystery/suspense, thriller, romance). "Christian truths must be woven into the story organically. No short story collections. Youth books: character building stories with Christian perspective. Especially interested in ages 10-14. We primarily publish Christian historical romances, with occasional contemporary, suspense, or standalones." *Agented submissions only. No unsolicited mss.*

THE UNIVERSITY OF AKRON PRESS

120 E. Mill St., Suite 415, Akron OH 44308. **E-mail:** uapress@uakron.edu. **Website:** www.uakron.edu/uapress. **Contact:** Dr. Jon Miller, director and acquisitions. Estab. 1988. Publishes hardcover and paperback originals. "The University of Akron Press is the publishing arm of The University of Akron and is dedicated to the dissemination of scholarly, professional, and regional books and other content." **Publishes 10-12 titles/year. 100 queries; 50-75 mss received/year. 40% of books from first-time authors. 80% from unagented writers. Pays 7-15% royalty.** Publishes book 9-12 months after acceptance. Accepts simultaneous submissions. Responds in 4 weeks to queries/propos-

als; 3-4 months to solicited mss. Query prior to submitting. Guidelines online.

NONFICTION Subjects include Americana, anthropology, archeology, creative nonfiction, environment, foods, history, humanities, labor, law, literary criticism, literature, memoirs, multicultural, politics, pop culture, psychology, regional. "For our readers in and of Northeast Ohio, we are always looking for new books on our history and culture. We've published books on our people and neighborhoods, our institutions, our sports teams, our parks, and through our cookbooks, on our food. For readers all over the world, we publish peer-reviewed books and collections on the history and culture of Akron and Ohio. In our Bliss Institute series, we publish scholarship on applied politics. With the Drs. Nicholas and Dorothy Cummings Center for the History of Psychology, we publish books and textbooks on the history of psychology." Query by e-mail. Mss cannot be returned unless SASE is included.

POETRY "Follow the guidelines and submit mss only for the contest: www.uakron.edu/uapress/poetry. html. The Akron Series in Poetry brings forth at least 2 new books of poetry every year, mainly through our prestigious and long-running Akron Poetry Prize. We also publish scholarship on poetics."

THE UNIVERSITY OF ALABAMA PRESS

200 Hackberry Lane, 2nd Floor, Tuscaloosa AL 35487. (205)348-5180 or (205)348-1571. **Fax:** (205)348-9201. **E-mail:** waterman@uapress.ua.edu. **Website:** www. uapress.ua.edu. **Contact:** Daniel Waterman, editor-in-chief. Publishes nonfiction hardcover and paperbound originals. **Publishes 70-75 titles/year. 70% of books from first-time authors. 95% from unagented writers. Pays advance in very limited number of circumstances.** Accepts simultaneous submissions. Responds in 2-3 weeks to queries. Book catalog available free.

NONFICTION Subjects include history, literary criticism, politics, religion. Considers upon merit almost any subject of scholarly interest, but specializes in communications, military history, public administration, literary criticism and biography, history, Judaic studies, and American archaeology. Accepts nonfiction translations. Query with SASE.

UNIVERSITY OF ALASKA PRESS

P.O. Box 756240, Fairbanks AK 99775-6240. (907)474-5831 or (888)252-6657. **Fax:** (907)474-5502. **Website:** www.uaf.edu/uapress. Estab. 1967. Publishes hardcover originals, trade paperback originals and reprints. "The mission of the University of Alaska Press is to encourage, publish, and disseminate works of scholarship that will enhance the store of knowledge about Alaska and the North Pacific Rim, with a special emphasis on the circumpolar regions." **Publishes 10 titles/year.** Publishes ms within 2 years of acceptance. Accepts simultaneous submissions. Responds in 2 months to queries. Book catalog available free. Guidelines online.

NONFICTION Subjects include Americana, animals, education, ethnic, history, regional, science, translation. Northern or circumpolar only. Query with SASE and proposal. Reviews artwork/photos.

FICTION Subjects include literary. Alaska literary series with Peggy Shumaker as series editor. Publishes 1-3 works of fiction/year. Submit proposal.

THE UNIVERSITY OF ALBERTA PRESS

Ring House 2, Edmonton AB T6G 2E1, Canada. (780)492-3662. **Fax:** (780)492-0719. **E-mail:** pmidgley@ualberta.ca. **Website:** www.uap.ualberta.ca. **Contact:** Peter Midgley. Estab. 1969. Publishes originals and reprints. "We do not accept unsolicited novels, short story collections, or poetry. Please see our website for details." **Publishes 18-25 titles/year. Royalties are negotiated.** Publishes ms within 2 years after acceptance. Responds in 3 months to queries. Guidelines online.

NONFICTION Subjects include history, regional, natural history, social policy. Submit cover letter, word count, CV, 1 sample chapter, TOC.

THE UNIVERSITY OF ARKANSAS PRESS

McIlroy House, 105 N. McIlroy Ave., Fayetteville AR 72701. (479)575-3246. **Fax:** (479)575-6044. **E-mail:** mbieker@uark.edu. **Website:** uapress.com. **Contact:** Mike Bieker, director. Estab. 1980. Publishes hardcover and trade paperback originals and reprints. "The University of Arkansas Press publishes series on Ozark studies, the Civil War in the West, poetry and poetics, food studies, and sport and society." **Publishes 22 titles/year. 30% of books from first-time authors. 95% from unagented writers.** Publishes book 1 year after acceptance. Accepts simultaneous submissions. Responds in 3 months to proposals. Book catalog and ms guidelines online.

BOOK PUBLISHERS

NONFICTION Subjects include architecture, foods, history, humanities, literary criticism, regional, Arkansas. Accepted mss must be submitted electronically. Query with SASE. Submit outline, sample chapters, resume.

FICTION Subjects include historical, regional.

POETRY University of Arkansas Press publishes 4 poetry books per year through the Miller Williams Poetry Prize.

UNIVERSITY OF CALGARY PRESS

2500 University Dr. NW, Calgary AB T2N 1N4, Canada. (403)220-7578. **Fax:** (403)282-0085. **E-mail:** brian.scrivener@ucalgary.ca. **Website:** press.ucalgary.ca. **Contact:** Brian Scrivener, Director. Estab. 1984. Publishes scholarly and trade paperback originals and reprints. **Publishes 10 titles/year. 40% of books from first-time authors. 90% from unagented writers.** Publishes ms 20 months after acceptance. Book catalog available for free. Guidelines online.

NONFICTION Subjects include architecture, art, cinema, communications, environment, film, history, humanities, literary criticism, literature, memoirs, military, politics, public affairs, regional, social sciences, womens studies, Canadian studies, postmodern studies, native studies, history, international relations, arctic studies, Africa, Latin American and Caribbean studies, and heritage of the Canadian and American heartland.

THE UNIVERSITY OF CHICAGO PRESS

1427 E. 60th St., Chicago IL 60637. (773)702-7700. **Fax:** (773)702-9756. **E-mail:** rpetilos@uchicago.edu. **Website:** www.press.uchicago.edu. **Contact:** Randolph Petilos, Poetry and Medieval Studies Editor. Estab. 1891. "The University of Chicago Press has been publishing scholarly books and journals since 1891. Annually, we publish an average of 4 books in our Phoenix Poets series and 2 books of poetry in translation. Occasionally, we may publish a book of poetry outside Phoenix Poets, or as a paperback reprint from another publisher." Has recently published work by Charles Bardes, Charles Bernstein, Stuart Dischell, David Gewanter, Mark Halliday, Haribhatta, Lloyd Schwartz, Virgil, and Katie Willingham. Accepts simultaneous submissions.

UNIVERSITY OF GEORGIA PRESS

Main Library, Third Floor, 320 S. Jackson St., Athens GA 30602. (706)369-6130. **Fax:** (706)369-6131. **Web-**site: www.ugapress.org. **Contact:** Mick Gusinde-Duffy, executive editor; Walter Biggins, executive editor; Pat Allen, acquisitions editor; Beth Snead, assistant acquisitions editor. Estab. 1938. Publishes hardcover originals, trade paperback originals, and reprints. University of Georgia Press is a midsized press that publishes fiction only through the Flannery O'Connor Award for Short Fiction competition. **Publishes 85 titles/year. Pays 7-10% royalty on net receipts. Pays rare, varying advance.** Publishes book 1 year after acceptance. Responds in 2 months to queries. Book catalog and guidelines online.

NONFICTION Subjects include history, regional, environmental studies, literary nonfiction.. Query with SASE. Submit bio, 1 sample chapter. Reviews artwork/photos. Send if essential to book.

FICTION Short story collections published in Flannery O'Connor Award Competition.

TIPS "Please visit our website to view our book catalogs and for all manuscript submission guidelines."

UNIVERSITY OF ILLINOIS PRESS

1325 S. Oak St., Champaign IL 61820-6903. (217)333-0950. **Fax:** (217)244-8082. **E-mail:** uipress@uillinois.edu. **Website:** www.press.uillinois.edu. **Contact:** Laurie Matheson, director; Daniel Nasset, acquisitions editor; Dawn Durante, acquisitions editor; James Engelhardt, acquisitions editor. Estab. 1918. Publishes hardcover and trade paperback originals and reprints. University of Illinois Press publishes scholarly books and serious nonfiction with a wide range of study interests. Currently emphasizing American history, especially immigration, labor, African-American, and military; American religion, music, women's studies, and film. **Publishes 150 titles/year. 35% of books from first-time authors. 95% from unagented writers. Pays $1,000-1,500 (rarely) advance.** Publishes ms 1 year after acceptance. Accepts simultaneous submissions. Responds in 1 month to queries. Guidelines online.

NONFICTION Subjects include Americana, animals, communications, ethnic, history, philosophy, regional, sociology, sports, translation, film/cinema/stage. "Always looking for solid, scholarly books in American history, especially social history; books on American popular music, and books in the broad area of American studies." Query with SASE. Submit outline.

286

UNIVERSITY OF IOWA PRESS

100 Kuhl House, 119 W. Park Rd., Iowa City IA 52242. (319)335-2000. **Fax:** (319)335-2055. **E-mail:** james-mccoy@uiowa.edu. **Website:** www.uiowapress.org. **Contact:** James McCoy, director. Estab. 1969. Publishes hardcover and paperback originals. The University of Iowa Press publishes both trade and academic work in a variety of fields. **Publishes 35 titles/year. 30% of books from first-time authors. 95% from unagented writers.** Accepts simultaneous submissions. Book catalog available free. Guidelines online.

NONFICTION Subjects include agriculture, contemporary culture, creative nonfiction, environment, history, humanities, literary criticism, multicultural, nature, pop culture, regional, travel, true crime, womens studies. "Looks for evidence of original research, reliable sources, clarity of organization, complete development of theme with documentation, supportive footnotes and/or bibliography, and a substantive contribution to knowledge in the field treated. Use *Chicago Manual of Style*." Query with SASE. Submit outline. Reviews artwork/photos.

FICTION Currently publishes the Iowa Short Fiction Award selections. "We do not accept any fiction submissions outside of the Iowa Short Fiction Award. See www.uiowapress.org for contest details."

POETRY Currently publishes winners of the Iowa Poetry Prize Competition and Kuhl House Poets (by invitation only). Competition guidelines available on website.

UNIVERSITY OF MICHIGAN PRESS

839 Greene St., Ann Arbor MI 48106. (734)764-4388. **Fax:** (734)615-1540. **Website:** www.press.umich.edu. **Contact:** Mary Francis, editorial director. "In partnership with our authors and series editors, we publish in a wide range of humanities and social sciences disciplines." Accepts simultaneous submissions. Guidelines online.

NONFICTION Submit proposal.

FICTION Subjects include literary, regional. In addition to the annual Michigan Literary Fiction Awards, this publishes literary fiction linked to the Great Lakes region. Submit cover letter and first 30 pages.

UNIVERSITY OF NEVADA PRESS

Mail Stop 0166, Reno NV 89557. (775)784-6573. **Fax:** (775)784-6200. **Website:** www.unpress.nevada.edu. **Contact:** Justin Race, director. Estab. 1961. Publishes hardcover and paperback originals and reprints. "University Press specializing in regional titles, fiction and memoir, and books in the fields of environmental studies, Basque studies, mining studies, nature, and the American West." **Publishes 25 titles/year.** Publishes ms 18 months after acceptance. Responds in 3-5 weeks. Guidelines online.

NONFICTION Subjects include agriculture, animals, archeology, architecture, creative nonfiction, environment, history, memoirs, nature, regional, western literature, gambling and gaming, Basque studies. No juvenile books. Submit electronically, instructions on website. Reviews artwork/photos. Send electronically.

FICTION Fiction should have some connection to the American West, whether in setting or theme. We do not publish historical fiction.

UNIVERSITY OF NEW MEXICO PRESS

1717 Roma Ave. NE, Albuquerque NM 87106. (505)277-3495 or (800)249-7737. **Fax:** (505)277-3343. **Website:** www.unmpress.com. **Contact:** John W. Byram, Director. Estab. 1929. Publishes hardcover originals and trade paperback originals and reprints. "The Press is well known as a publisher in the fields of anthropology, archeology, Latin American studies, art and photography, architecture and the history and culture of the American West, fiction, some poetry, Chicano/a studies and works by and about American Indians. We focus on American West, Southwest and Latin American regions." **Publishes 75 titles/year. 1,500 submissions received/year. 20% of books from first-time authors. 80% from unagented writers. Pays variable royalty. May pay advance.** Publishes ms 10 months after acceptance. Responds in 6 weeks. Book catalog available free. Guidelines online.

NONFICTION Subjects include Americana, anthropology, archeology, architecture, art, cooking, environment, ethnic, foods, gardening, history, humanities, literary criticism, literature, memoirs, military, multicultural, music, nature, photography, politics, pop culture, public affairs, regional, religion, science, social sciences, sports, translation, travel, true crime, womens issues, womens studies, world affairs, contemporary culture, cinema/stage, true crime, general nonfiction. No how-to, humor, juvenile, self-help, software, technical or textbooks. Query with SASE. Reviews artwork/photos. Send photocopies.

FICTION Subjects include ethnic, literary, multicultural, regional, translation.

THE UNIVERSITY OF NORTH CAROLINA PRESS

116 S. Boundary St., Chapel Hill NC 27514. (919)966-3561. **Fax:** (919)966-3829. **E-mail:** mark_simpson-vos@unc.edu. **Website:** www.uncpress.unc.edu. **Contact:** Mark Simpson-Vos, editorial director. Publishes hardcover originals, trade paperback originals and reprints. "UNC Press publishes nonfiction books for academic and general audiences. We have a special interest in trade and scholarly titles about our region. We do not, however, publish original fiction, drama, or poetry, memoirs of living persons, or festshriften." **Publishes 90 titles/year. 500 queries received/year. 200 mss received/year. 50% of books from first-time authors. 90% from unagented writers. Pays variable royalty on wholesale price. Offers variable advance.** Publishes ms 1 year after acceptance. Accepts simultaneous submissions. Responds in 3-4 weeks. Book catalog and guidelines online.

NONFICTION Subjects include Americana, gardening, history, multicultural, philosophy, photography, regional, religion, translation, African-American studies, American studies, cultural studies, Latin-American studies, American-Indian studies, media studies, gender studies, social medicine, Appalachian studies. Submit proposal package, outline, CV, cover letter, abstract, and TOC. Reviews artwork/photos. Send photocopies.

UNIVERSITY OF NORTH TEXAS PRESS

1155 Union Circle, #311336, Denton TX 76203. (940)565-2142. **Fax:** (940)565-4590. **E-mail:** karen.devinney@unt.edu. **Website:** untpress.unt.edu. **Contact:** Ronald Chrisman, director; Karen De Vinney, assistant director. Estab. 1987. Publishes hardcover and trade paperback originals and reprints. "We are dedicated to producing the highest quality scholarly, academic, and general interest books. We are committed to serving all peoples by publishing stories of their cultures and experiences that have been overlooked. Currently emphasizing military history, Texas history, music, Mexican-American studies." **Publishes 14-16 titles/year. 500 queries received/year. 50% of books from first-time authors. 95% from unagented writers.** Publishes ms 1-2 years after acceptance. Responds in 1 month to queries. Book catalog for 8 ½×11 SASE. Guidelines online.

NONFICTION Subjects include Americana, art, cooking, creative nonfiction, ethnic, government, history, humanities, military, multicultural, music, nature, photography, politics, regional, social sciences, war, womens issues, womens studies. Query by e-mail. Reviews artwork/photos. Send photocopies.

FICTION Subjects include short story collections. "The only fiction we publish is the winner of the Katherine Anne Porter Prize in Short Fiction, an annual, national competition with a $1,000 prize, and publication of the winning ms each Fall."

POETRY "The only poetry we publish is the winner of the Vassar Miller Prize in Poetry, an annual, national competition with a $1,000 prize and publication of the winning ms each Spring." Query.

UNIVERSITY OF OKLAHOMA PRESS

2800 Venture Dr., Norman OK 73069. (405)325-5609. **E-mail:** adam.kane@ou.edu. **Website:** www.oupress.com. **Contact:** Adam C. Kane, editor-in-chief. Estab. 1928. Publishes hardcover and paperback originals and reprints. University of Oklahoma Press publishes books for both scholarly and nonspecialist readers. **Publishes 90 titles/year. Pays standard royalty.** Responds promptly to queries. Book catalog online.

IMPRINTS Plains Reprints.

NONFICTION Subjects include political science (Congressional, area and security studies), history (regional, military, natural), language/literature (American Indian, US West), American Indian studies, classical studies. Query with SASE or by e-mail. Submit outline, resume, 1-2 sample chapters. Use *Chicago Manual of Style* for ms guidelines. Reviews artwork/photos.

☼ UNIVERSITY OF OTTAWA PRESS

542 King Edward Ave., Ottawa ON K1N 6N5, Canada. (613)562-5246. **Fax:** (613)562-5247. **E-mail:** puo-uop@uottawa.ca. **Website:** www.press.uottawa.ca. **Contact:** Lara Mainville, director; Dominike Thomas, acquisitions editor. Estab. 1936. "UOP publishes books and journals, in French and English, and in any and all editions and formats, that touch upon the human condition: anthropology, sociology, political science, psychology, criminology, media studies, economics, education, language and culture, law, history, literature, translation studies, philosophy, public administration, health sciences, and religious studies." Accepts simultaneous submissions. Book catalog and ms guidelines online.

NONFICTION Submit outline, proposal form (please see website), CV, 1-2 sample chapters (for monographs only), ms (for collected works only), TOC, 2-5 page proposal/summary, contributor names, short bios, and citizenships (for collected works only).

UNIVERSITY OF PENNSYLVANIA PRESS

3905 Spruce St., Philadelphia PA 19104. (215)898-6261. **Fax:** (215)898-0404. **E-mail:** agree@upenn.edu. **Website:** www.pennpress.org. **Contact:** Peter Agree, editor-in-chief. Estab. 1890. Publishes hardcover and paperback originals, and reprints. "Manuscript submissions are welcome in fields appropriate for Penn Press's editorial program. The Press's acquiring editors, and their fields of responsibility, are listed in the Contact Us section of our Web site. Although we have no formal policies regarding manuscript proposals and submissions, what we need minimally, in order to gauge our degree of interest, is a brief statement describing the manuscript, a copy of the contents page, and a reasonably current vita. Initial inquiries are best sent by letter, in paper form, to the appropriate acquiring editor." **Publishes 100+ titles/year. 20-30% of books from first-time authors. 95% from unagented writers. Royalty determined on book-by-book basis. Pays advance.** Publishes ms 10 months after acceptance. Responds in 3 months to queries. Book catalog online. Guidelines online.

NONFICTION Subjects include Americana, history, literary criticism, sociology, anthropology, literary criticism, cultural studies, ancient studies, medieval studies, urban studies, human rights. Follow the *Chicago Manual of Style.* "Serious books that serve the scholar and the professional, student and general reader." Query with SASE. Submit outline, resume.

UNIVERSITY OF PITTSBURGH PRESS

7500 Thomas Blvd., Pittsburgh PA 15260. (412)383-2456. **Fax:** (412)383-2466. **E-mail:** info@upress.pitt.edu. **Website:** www.upress.pitt.edu. **Contact:** Sandy Crooms, editorial director. Estab. 1936. The University of Pittsburgh Press is a scholary publisher with distinguished books in several academic areas and in poetry and short fiction, as well as books about Pittsburgh and western Pennsylvania for general readers, scholars, and students. "Our mission is to extend the reach and reputation of the university through the publication of scholarly, artistic, and educational books that advance learning and knowledge and through the publication of regional books that contribute to an understanding of and are of special benefit to western Pennsylvania and the Upper Ohio Val-

ley region. Accepts simultaneous submissions. Book catalog online. Guidelines online.

POETRY Publishes at least 4 books by poets who have previously published full-length collections of poetry. Submit complete ms in September and October only.

UNIVERSITY OF SOUTH CAROLINA PRESS

1600 Hampton St., 5th Floor, Columbia SC 29208. (803)777-5243. **Fax:** (803)777-0160. **E-mail:** batesvc@mailbox.sc.edu. **Website:** www.sc.edu/uscpress. **Contact:** Jonathan Haupt, director. Estab. 1944. Publishes hardcover originals, trade paperback originals and reprints. "We focus on scholarly monographs and regional trade books of lasting merit." **Publishes 50 titles/year. 500 queries received/year. 150 mss received/year. 30% of books from first-time authors. 95% from unagented writers.** Publishes ms 1 year after acceptance. Accepts simultaneous submissions. Responds in 3 months to mss. Book catalog available free. Guidelines online.

NONFICTION Subjects include history, regional, religion, rhetoric, communication. Query with SASE, or submit proposal package and outline, and 1 sample chapter and resume with SASE Reviews artwork/photos. Send photocopies.

POETRY Palmetto Poetry Series, a South Carolina-based original poetry series edited by Nikky Finney. Director: Jonathan Haupt, director (jhaupt@mailbox.sc.edu).

THE UNIVERSITY OF TENNESSEE PRESS

The University of Tennessee, 110 Conference Center, 600 Henley St., Knoxville TN 37996. (865)974-3321. **Fax:** (865)974-3724. **E-mail:** twells@utk.edu. **Website:** www.utpress.org. **Contact:** Thomas Wells, acquisitions editor. Estab. 1940. "Our mission is to stimulate scientific and scholarly research in all fields; to channel such studies, either in scholarly or popular form, to a larger number of people; and to extend the regional leadership of the University of Tennessee by stimulating research projects within the South and by nonuniversity authors." **Publishes 35 titles/year. 35% of books from first-time authors. 99% from unagented writers. Pays negotiable royalty on net receipts. Rarely offers advance.** Publishes ms 18 months after acceptance. Accepts simultaneous submissions. Guidelines online.

NONFICTION Subjects include Americana, archeology, architecture, history, literary criticism, military, music, regional, religion, war, African-American studies, Appalachian studies, folklore/folklife, material culture. Prefers scholarly treatment and a readable style. Authors usually have advanced degrees. Submissions in other fields, fiction or poetry, textbooks, and plays and translations are not invited Submit cover letter, outline, bio or CV, and sample chapters. Reviews artwork/photos.

FICTION The press no longer publishes works of fiction.

UNIVERSITY OF TEXAS PRESS

3001 Lake Austin Blvd., 2.200, Stop E4800, Austin TX 78703. **Fax:** (512)232-7178. **Website:** www.utexaspress.com. Estab. 1952. "In addition to publishing the results of advanced research for scholars worldwide, UT Press has a special obligation to the people of its state to publish authoritative books on Texas. We do not publish fiction or poetry, except as invited by a series editor, and some Latin American and Middle Eastern literature in translation." **Publishes 90 titles/year. 50% of books from first-time authors. 99% from unagented writers. Pays occasional advance.** Publishes ms 18-24 months after acceptance. Responds in 3 months to queries. Guidelines online.

NONFICTION Subjects include ethnic, history, literary criticism, regional, science, translation, natural history, American, Latin American, Native American, Latino, and Middle Eastern studies; classics and the ancient world, film, contemporary regional architecture, geography, ornithology, biology. Also uses specialty titles related to Texas and the Southwest, national trade titles and regional trade titles. Submit cover letter, TOC, CV, sample chapter.

UNIVERSITY OF WASHINGTON PRESS

P.O. Box 359570, Seattle WA 98195. (206)543-4050. **Fax:** (206)543-3932. **E-mail:** uwapress@uw.edu. **E-mail:** lmclaugh@uw.edu. **Website:** www.washington.edu/uwpress/. **Contact:** Laurin McLaughlin, editor-in-chief. Publishes in hardcover originals. **Publishes 70 titles/year.** Accepts simultaneous submissions. Book catalog guidelines online.

NONFICTION Subjects include ethnic, history, multicultural, photography, regional, social sciences. Go to our Book Search page for complete subject listing. We publish academic and general books, especially in anthropology, Asian studies, art, environmental studies, Middle Eastern Studies & regional interests. International Studies with focus on Asia; Jewish Stud-

ies; Art & Culture of the Northwest coast; Indians & Alaskan Eskimos; The Asian-American Experience; Southeast Asian Studies; Korean and Slavic Studies; Studies in Modernity & National Identity; Scandinavian Studies. Query with SASE. Submit proposal package, outline, sample chapters.

UNIVERSITY OF WISCONSIN PRESS

1930 Monroe St., 3rd Floor, Madison WI 53711. **E-mail:** kadushin@wisc.edu; gcwalker@wisc.edu. **Website:** uwpress.wisc.edu. **Contact:** Raphael Kadushin, executive editor; Gwen Walker, editorial director. Estab. 1937. **Publishes 50 titles/year. Pays royalty.** Publishes 10-14 months after acceptance of final ms. Accepts simultaneous submissions. Responds in 1-3 weeks to queries; 3-6 weeks to proposals. Rarely comments on rejected work. See submission guidelines on our website.

NONFICTION Subjects include cinema, contemporary culture, creative nonfiction, entertainment, environment, film, foods, gay, government, history, labor, lesbian, memoirs, politics, public affairs, travel, African Studies, classical studies, human rights, Irish studies, Jewish studies, Latin American studies, Latino/a memoirs, modern Western European history, Slavic studies, Southeast Asian studies.. Does not accept unsolicited mss. See website for submission guidelines.

FICTION Subjects include gay, hi-lo, lesbian, mystery, regional, short story collections. Query with SASE or submit outline, 1-2 sample chapter(s), synopsis.

POETRY The University of Wisconsin Press Awards the Brittingham Prize in Poetry and Felix Pollack Prize in Poetry. More details online.

UNIVERSITY PRESS OF KANSAS

2502 Westbrooke Circle, Lawrence KS 66045. (785)864-4154. **Fax:** (785)864-4586. **E-mail:** upress@ku.edu. **Website:** www.kansaspress.ku.edu. **Contact:** Conrad Roberts, Interim Director & Business Manager; Joyce Harrison, Editor-in-Chief; Kim Hogeland, Acquisitions Editor; David Congdon, Acquisitions Editor. Estab. 1946. Publishes hardcover originals, trade paperback originals and reprints. "The University Press of Kansas publishes scholarly books that advance knowledge and regional books that contribute to the understanding of Kansas, the Great Plains, and the Midwest." **Publishes 55 titles/year. 600 queries received/year. 20% of books from first-time authors. 98% from unagented writers. Pays selective**

advance. Publishes book 10 months after acceptance. Responds in 1 month to proposals. Book catalog and ms guidelines free.

NONFICTION Subjects include Americana, archeology, environment, government, military, nature, politics, regional, war, American history, native studies, American cultural studies. "We are looking for books on topics of wide interest based on solid scholarship and written for both specialists and informed general readers. Do not send unsolicited, complete manuscripts." Submit outline, sample chapters, cover letter, CV, prospectus. Reviews artwork/photos. Send photocopies.

UNIVERSITY PRESS OF KENTUCKY

663 S. Limestone St., Lexington KY 40508. (859)257-8434. **Fax:** (859)323-1873. **E-mail:** adwatk0@email. uky.edu. **Website:** www.kentuckypress.com. **Contact:** Anne Dean Dotson, senior acquisitions editor. Estab. 1943. Publishes hardcover and paperback originals and reprints. "We are a scholarly publisher, publishing chiefly for an academic and professional audience, as well as books about Kentucky, the upper South, Appalachia, and the Ohio Valley." **Publishes 60 titles/ year. Royalty varies.** Publishes ms 1 year after accceptance. Accepts simultaneous submissions. Responds in 2 months to queries. Book catalog available free. Guidelines online.

NONFICTION Subjects include history, regional, political science. No textbooks, genealogical material, lightweight popular treatments, how-to books, or books unrelated to our major areas of interest. The Press does not consider original works of fiction or poetry. Query with SASE.

UNIVERSITY PRESS OF MISSISSIPPI

3825 Ridgewood Rd., Jackson MS 39211. (601)432-6205. **Fax:** (601)432-6217. **E-mail:** press@mississippi.edu. **Website:** www.upress.state.ms.us. **Contact:** Craig W. Gill, Director. Estab. 1970. Publishes hardcover and paperback originals and reprints and e-books. "University Press of Mississippi publishes scholarly and trade titles, as well as special series, including: American Made Music; Conversations with Comics Artists; Conversations with Filmmakers; Faulkner and Yoknapatawpha; Great Comic Artists; Literary Conversations; Hollywood Legends; Caribbean Studies, Willie Morris Books in Memoir and Biography." **Publishes 70 titles/year. 80% of books from first-time authors. 90% from unagented writ-**

ers. **Pays competitive royalties and terms. Pays advance.** Publishes ms 1 year after acceptance. Responds in 3 months to queries.

NONFICTION Subjects include Americana, art, ethnic, history, literary criticism, regional, sports, womens studies, African American studies, comics studies, film studies, folklife, popular culture with scholarly emphasis, literary studies. "We prefer a proposal that describes the significance of the work and a chapter outline." Submit outline, sample chapters, CV.

USBORNE PUBLISHING

83-85 Saffron Hill, London EC1N 8RT, United Kingdom. (44)207430-2800. **Fax:** (44)207430-1562. **E-mail:** mail@usborne.co.uk. **Website:** www.usborne.com. "Usborne Publishing is a multiple-award-winning, worldwide children's publishing company publishing almost every type of children's book for every age from baby to young adult." **Pays authors royalty.** Accepts simultaneous submissions.

FICTION Young readers, middle readers: adventure, contemporary, fantasy, history, humor, multicultural, nature/environment, science fiction, suspense/mystery, strong concept-based or character-led series. Average word length: young readers—5,000-10,000; middle readers—25,000-50,000; young adult—50,000-100,000. *Agented submissions only.*

UTAH STATE UNIVERSITY PRESS

3078 Old Main Hill, Logan UT 84322. **Website:** www. usu.edu/usupress. Estab. 1972. Publishes hardcover and trade paperback originals and reprints. Utah State University Press publishes scholarly works in the academic areas noted below. Currently interested in book-length scholarly mss dealing with folklore studies, composition studies, Native American studies, and history. **Publishes 18 titles/year. 8% of books from first-time authors.** Publishes ms 18 months after acceptance. Responds in 1 month to queries. Book catalog available free. Guidelines online.

NONFICTION Subjects include history, regional, folklore, the West, Native-American studies, studies in composition and rhetoric. Query via online submission form. Reviews artwork/photos. Send photocopies.

VANDERBILT UNIVERSITY PRESS

PMB 351813, 2301 Vanderbilt Place, Nashville TN 37235. (615)322-3585. **Fax:** (615)343-8823. **E-mail:** vupress@vanderbilt.edu. **E-mail:** beth.itkin@vanderbilt.edu. **Website:** www.vanderbiltuniversitypress.com. Publishes hardcover originals and trade paperback originals and reprints. "Vanderbilt University Press publishes books on healthcare, social sciences, education, and regional studies, for both academic and general audiences that are intellectually significant, socially relevant, and of practical importance." **Publishes 20-25 titles/year. 500 queries received/year. 25% of books from first-time authors. 90% from unagented writers. Pays rare advance.** Publishes ms 10 months after acceptance. Accepts simultaneous submissions. Responds in 2 weeks to proposals. Book catalog online. Guidelines online.

NONFICTION Subjects include Americana, education, ethnic, history, multicultural, philosophy. Submit cover letter, TOC, CV, 1-2 sample chapters.

⊘ VÉHICULE PRESS

P.O.B. 42094 BP Roy, Montreal QC H2W 2T3, Canada. (514)844-6073. **Fax:** (514)844-7543. **E-mail:** sd@vehiculepress.com. **E-mail:** admin@vehiculepress.com. **Website:** www.vehiculepress.com. **Contact:** Simon Dardick, nonfiction; Carmine Starnino, poetry; Dimitri Nasrallah, fiction. Estab. 1973. Publishes trade paperback originals by Canadian authors mostly. "Montreal's Véhicule Press has published the best of Canadian and Quebec literature-fiction, poetry, essays, translations, and social history." **Publishes 15 titles/year. 20% of books from first-time authors. 95% from unagented writers. Pays 10-15% royalty on retail price. Pays $200-500 advance.** Publishes ms 1 year after acceptance. Accepts simultaneous submissions. Responds in 4 months to queries. Book catalog for 9 x 12 SAE with IRCs.

IMPRINTS Signal Editions (poetry); Esplanade Editions (fiction).

NONFICTION Subjects include history, memoirs, regional, sociology. Especially looking for Canadian social history. Query with SASE. Reviews artwork/photos.

FICTION Subjects include feminist, literary, regional, translation, literary novels. No romance or formula writing. Query with SASE.

POETRY Vehicle Press is a "literary press with a poetry series, Signal Editions, publishing the work of Canadian poets only." Publishes flat-spined paperbacks. Publishes Canadian poetry that is "first-rate, original, content-conscious."

VERSO

20 Jay St., 10th Floor, Brooklyn NY 11201. (718)246-8160. **Fax:** (718)246-8165. **E-mail:** verso@versobooks.com. **E-mail:** submissions@versobooks.com. **Website:** www.versobooks.com. **Contact:** Editorial Department. Estab. 1970. Publishes hardcover and trade paperback originals. "Our books cover economics, politics, cinema studies, and history (among other topics), but all come from a critical, Leftist viewpoint, on the border between trade and academic." **Publishes 100 titles/year. Pays royalty. Pays advance.** Accepts simultaneous submissions. Book catalog available free. Guidelines online.

NONFICTION Subjects include history, philosophy, sociology. Submit proposal package.

⊘ VERTIGO

DC Universe, Vertigo-DC Comics, 1700 Broadway, New York NY 10019. **Website:** www.vertigocomics.com. At this time, DC Entertainment does not accept unsolicited artwork or writing submissions. Accepts simultaneous submissions.

⊘⊘ VIKING

Imprint of Penguin Group (USA), Inc., 375 Hudson St., New York NY 10014. (212)366-2000. **Website:** www.penguin.com. Estab. 1925. Publishes hardcover and originals. Viking publishes a mix of academic and popular fiction and nonfiction. **Publishes 100 titles/year. Pays 10-15% royalty on retail price.** Publishes ms 18 months after acceptance. Accepts simultaneous submissions.

NONFICTION Subjects include child guidance, history, philosophy. *Agented submissions only.*

FICTION Subjects include literary, mystery, suspense. *Agented submissions only.*

⊘⊘ VIKING CHILDREN'S BOOKS

375 Hudson St., New York NY 10014. **Website:** www.penguin.com. Publishes hardcover originals. "Viking Children's Books is known for humorous, quirky picture books, in addition to more traditional fiction. We publish the highest quality fiction, nonfiction, and picture books for pre-schoolers through young adults." *Does not accept unsolicited submissions.* **Publishes 70 titles/year. Pays 2-10% royalty on retail price or flat fee. Pays negotiable advance.** Publishes book 1-2 years after acceptance. Accepts simultaneous submissions. Responds in 6 months.

NONFICTION All levels: biography, concept, history, multicultural, music/dance, nature/environment, science, and sports. *Agented submissions only.*

FICTION All levels: adventure, animal, contemporary, fantasy, history, humor, multicultural, nature/environment, poetry, problem novels, romance, science fiction, sports, suspense/mystery. *Accepts agented mss only.*

Ⓐ⊘ VILLARD BOOKS

Penguin Random House, 1745 Broadway, New York NY 10019. (212)572-2600. **Website:** www.penguinrandomhouse.com. Estab. 1983. "Villard Books is the publisher of savvy and sometimes quirky, best-selling hardcovers and trade paperbacks." **Pays negotiable royalty. Pays negotiable advance.**

NONFICTION *Agented submissions only.*

FICTION Commercial fiction. *Agented submissions only.*

Ⓐ⊘ VINTAGE ANCHOR PUBLISHING

Penguin Random House, 1745 Broadway, New York NY 10019. **Website:** www.penguinrandomhouse.com. **Pays 4-8% royalty on retail price. Average advance: $2,500 and up.** Publishes ms 1 year after acceptance. Accepts simultaneous submissions.

FICTION Subjects include contemporary, literary, mainstream, short story collections. *Agented submissions only.*

⊘ VIZ MEDIA LLC

P.O. Box 77010, San Francisco CA 94107. (415)546-7073. **Website:** www.viz.com. "VIZ Media, LLC is one of the most comprehensive and innovative companies in the field of manga (graphic novel) publishing, animation and entertainment licensing of Japanese content. Owned by three of Japan's largest creators and licensors of manga and animation, Shueisha Inc., Shogakukan Inc., and Shogakukan-Shueisha Productions, Co., Ltd., VIZ Media is a leader in the publishing and distribution of Japanese manga for English speaking audiences in North America, the United Kingdom, Ireland, and South Africa and is a global ex-Asia licensor of Japanese manga and animation. The company offers an integrated product line including magazines such as *Shonen Jump* and *Shojo Beat*, graphic novels, and DVDs, and develops, markets, licenses, and distributes animated entertainment for audiences and consumers of all ages." Accepts simultaneous submissions.

FICTION "At the present, all of the manga that appears in our magazines come directly from manga that has been serialized and published in Japan."

VOYAGEUR PRESS

401 Second Ave. N., Suite 310, Minneapolis MN 55401. (800)458-0454. **Fax:** (612)344-8691. **Website:** https://www.quartoknows.com/Voyageur-Press. Publisher: Jeff Serena. Estab. 1972. Publishes hardcover and trade paperback originals. "Voyageur Press (and its sports imprint MVP Books) is internationally known as a leading publisher of quality music, sports, country living, crafts, natural history, and regional books. No children's or poetry books." **Publishes 80 titles/year. 1,200 queries received/year. 500 mss received/year. 10% of books from first-time authors. 90% from unagented writers. Pays royalty. Pays advance.** Publishes ms 1 year after acceptance. Accepts simultaneous submissions. Responds in 3 months to queries.

NONFICTION Subjects include Americana, cooking, environment, history, hobbies, music, nature, regional, sports, collectibles, country living, knitting and quilting, outdoor recreation. Query with SASE. Submit outline. Send sample digital images or transparencies (duplicates and tearsheets only).

WALCH PUBLISHING

40 Walch Dr., Portland ME 04103. (207)772-3105. **Fax:** (207)774-7167. **Website:** www.walch.com. Estab. 1927. "We focus on English/language arts, math, social studies and science teaching resources for middle school through adult assessment titles." **Publishes 100 titles/year. 10% of books from first-time authors. 95% from unagented writers. Pays 5-8% royalty on flat rate.** Publishes ms 6 months after acceptance. Accepts simultaneous submissions. Responds in 2 months to queries.

NONFICTION Subjects include education, history, science, technology. "Most titles are assigned by us, though we occasionally accept an author's unsolicited submission. We have a great need for author/artist teams and for authors who can write at third- to seventh-grade levels." Looks for sense of organization, writing ability, knowledge of subject, skill of communicating with intended audience. Formats include teacher resources, reproducibles. "We do *not* want textbooks or anthologies. All authors should have educational writing experience." Query first.

ⓐⓩ WATERBROOK MULTNOMAH PUBLISHING GROUP

10807 New Allegiance Dr., Suite 500, Colorado Springs CO 80921. (719)590-4999. **Fax:** (719)590-8977. **Website:** www.waterbrookmultnomah.com. Estab. 1996. Publishes hardcover and trade paperback originals. **Publishes 70 titles/year. 2,000 queries received/year. 15% of books from first-time authors. Pays royalty.** Publishes book 1 year after acceptance. Accepts simultaneous submissions. Responds in 2-3 months. Book catalog online.

NONFICTION Subjects include child guidance, religion, spirituality, marriage, Christian living. "We publish books on unique topics with a Christian perspective." *Agented submissions only.*

FICTION Subjects include adventure, historical, literary, mystery, religious, romance, science fiction, spiritual, suspense. *Agented submissions only.*

WESTMINSTER JOHN KNOX PRESS

Flyaway Books, Division of Presbyterian Publishing Corp., 100 Witherspoon St., Louisville KY 40202. **Fax:** (502)569-5113. **E-mail:** submissions@wjkbooks.com. **Website:** www.wjkbooks.com. Publishes hardcover and paperback originals. "All WJK books have a religious/spiritual angle, but are written for various markets-scholarly, professional, and the general reader. Flyaway Books is a new children's picture book imprint that is intentionally diverse in content and authorship. **Publishes 60 titles/year. 1,000 submissions received/year. 10% of books from first-time authors. 75% from unagented writers. Pays royalty on net price. Pays advance.** Accepts simultaneous submissions. Responds in 2-3 months. Catalog online. Proposal guidelines online.

IMPRINTS Westminster John Knox Press, Flyaway Books.

NONFICTION Subjects include multicultural, religion, social sciences, spirituality, womens issues. No dissertations. Submit proposal package according to the WJK book proposal guidelines found online. Reviews artwork, but only for children's picture books.

WHITAKER HOUSE

1030 Hunt Valley Circle, New Kensington PA 15068. **E-mail:** publisher@whitakerhouse.com. **Website:** www.whitakerhouse.com. **Contact:** Editorial Department. Estab. 1970. Publishes hardcover, trade paperback, and mass market originals. **Publishes 70 titles/year. 600 queries; 200 mss received/year. 15% of** books from first-time authors. 60% from unagented writers. Pays 5-15% royalty on wholesale price.** Publishes ms 9 months after acceptance. Accepts simultaneous submissions. Responds in 3 months. Book catalog online. Guidelines online.

NONFICTION Subjects include religion. Accepts submissions on topics with a Christian perspective. Query with SASE. Does not review artwork/photos.

FICTION Subjects include religious. All fiction must have a Christian perspective. Query with SASE.

☯ WHITECAP BOOKS, LTD.

210 - 314 W. Cordova St., Vancouver BC V6B 1 E8, Canada. (604)681-6181. **Fax:** (905)477-9179. **Website:** www.whitecap.ca. Publishes hardcover and trade paperback originals. "Whitecap Books is a general trade publisher with a focus on food and wine titles. Although we are interested in reviewing unsolicited ms submissions, please note that we only accept submissions that meet the needs of our current publishing program. Please see some of most recent releases to get an idea of the kinds of titles we are interested in." **Publishes 30 titles/year. 500 queries received/year; 1,000 mss received/year. 20% of books from first-time authors. 90% from unagented writers. Pays royalty. Pays negotiated advance.** Publishes book 1 year after acceptance. Accepts simultaneous submissions. Responds in 2-3 months to proposals. Catalog and guidelines online.

NONFICTION Subjects include animals, gardening, history, recreation, regional, travel. Young children's and middle reader's nonfiction focusing mainly on nature, wildlife and animals. "Writers should take the time to research our list and read the submission guidelines on our website. This is especially important for children's writers and cookbook authors. We will only consider submissions that fall into these categories: cookbooks, wine and spirits, regional travel, home and garden, Canadian history, North American natural history, juvenile series-based fiction. At this time, we are not accepting the following categories: self-help or inspirational books, political, social commentary, or issue books, general how-to books, biographies or memoirs, business and finance, art and architecture, religion and spirituality." Submit cover letter, synopsis, SASE via ground mail. See guidelines online. Reviews artwork/photos. Send photocopies.

FICTION No children's picture books or adult fiction. See guidelines.

ALBERT WHITMAN & COMPANY

250 S. Northwest Hwy., Suite 320, Park Ridge IL 60068. (800)255-7675. **Fax:** (847)581-0039. **E-mail:** submissions@albertwhitman.com. **Website:** www.albertwhitman.com. Estab. 1919. Publishes in original hardcover, paperback, boardbooks. Albert Whitman & Company publishes books for the trade, library, and school library market. Interested in reviewing the following types of projects: Picture book manuscripts for ages 2-8; novels and chapter books for ages 8-12; young adult novels; nonfiction for ages 3-12 and YA; art samples showing pictures of children. Best known for the classic series The Boxcar Children® Mysteries. "We are no longer reading unsolicited queries and manuscripts sent through the US mail. We now require these submissions to be sent by e-mail. You must visit our website for our guidelines, which include instructions for formatting your e-mail. E-mails that do not follow this format may not be read. We read every submission within 4 months of receipt, but we can no longer respond to every one. If you do not receive a response from us after four months, we have declined to publish your submission." **Publishes 60 titles/year. 10% of books from first-time authors. 50% from unagented writers.** Accepts simultaneous submissions. Guidelines online.

NONFICTION Picture books up to 1,000 words. Submit cover letter, brief description.

FICTION Picture books (up to 1,000 words); middle grade (up to 35,000 words); young adult (up to 70,000 words). For picture books, submit cover letter and brief description. For middle grade and young adult, send query, synopsis, and first 3 chapters.

WILDERNESS PRESS

2204 First Ave. S., Suite 102, Birmingham AL 35233. (800)443-7227. **Fax:** (205)326-1012. **Website:** www.wildernesspress.com. Estab. 1967. Publishes paperback originals. "Wilderness Press has a long tradition of publishing the highest quality, most accurate hiking and other outdoor activity guidebooks." **Publishes 12 titles/year.** Publishes ms 8-12 months after acceptance. Accepts simultaneous submissions. Responds in 2 months to queries. Book catalog and ms guidelines online.

NONFICTION Subjects include recreation, trail guides for hikers and backpackers. "We publish books about the outdoors and some general travel guides. Many are trail guides for hikers and backpackers, but

we also publish climbing, kayaking, and other outdoor activity guides, how-to books about the outdoors and urban walking books. The manuscript must be accurate. The author must research an area in person. If writing a trail guide, you must walk all the trails in the area your book is about. Outlook must be strongly conservationist. Style must be appropriate for a highly literate audience." Download proposal guidelines from website.

THE WILD ROSE PRESS

P.O. Box 708, Adams Basin NY 14410-0708. (585)752-8770. **E-mail:** queryus@thewildrosepress.com. **Website:** www.thewildrosepress.com. **Contact:** Rhonda Penders, editor-in-chief. Estab. 2006. Publishes paperback originals, reprints, and e-books in a POD format. **Publishes approx. 60 fiction titles/year. Pays royalty of 7% minimum; 40% maximum. Sends prepublication galleys to author.** Publishes ms 1 year after acceptance. Responds to queries in 4 weeks; mss in 12 weeks. Guidelines online.

FICTION Subjects include adventure, contemporary, erotica, fantasy, gay, gothic, historical, horror, humor, mainstream, multicultural, mystery, romance, science fiction, short story collections, suspense, western, young adult, We accept all genre of fiction and romance including young adult.. *Does not accept unsolicited mss.* Send query letter with outline and synopsis of up to 5 pages. Accepts all queries by e-mail. Include estimated word count, brief bio, and list of publishing credits. Agented fiction less than 1%. Always comments on rejected mss.

JOHN WILEY & SONS, INC.

111 River St., Hoboken NJ 07030. (201)748-6000. **Fax:** (201)748-6088. **Website:** www.wiley.com. Estab. 1807. Publishes hardcover originals, trade paperback originals and reprints. **Pays competitive rates.** Accepts simultaneous submissions. Book catalog online. Guidelines online.

NONFICTION Subjects include business, communications, computers, economics, education, finance, health, psychology, science. Wiley is a global publisher of print and electronic products—including scientific, scholarly, professional, consumer, and educational content. "Please visit our website to review our submissions guidelines for Books and Journals authors."

ⒶⓄ WILLIAM MORROW

HarperCollins, 195 Broadway, New York NY 10007. (212)207-7000. **Fax:** (212)207-7145. **Website:** www. harpercollins.com. Estab. 1926. "William Morrow publishes a wide range of titles that receive much recognition and prestige—a most selective house." **Pays standard royalty on retail price. Pays varying advance.** Accepts simultaneous submissions. Book catalog available free.

NONFICTION Subjects include history. Length 50,000-100,000 words. *No unsolicited mss or proposals. Agented submissions only.*

FICTION Publishes adult fiction. Morrow accepts only the highest quality submissions in adult fiction. *No unsolicited mss or proposals. Agented submissions only.*

WILLOW CREEK PRESS

P.O. Box 147, Minocqua WI 54548. (715)358-7010. **Fax:** (715)358-2807. **Website:** www.willowcreekpress. com. **Contact:** Sara Olson, Designer. Estab. 1986. Publishes hardcover and trade paperback, originals, and reprints. "We specialize in nature, outdoor, and sporting topics, including gardening, wildlife, and animal books. Pets, cookbooks, and a few humor books and essays round out our titles. Currently emphasizing pets (mainly dogs and cats), wildlife, outdoor sports (hunting, fishing). De-emphasizing essays, fiction." **Publishes 25 titles/year. 400 queries; 150 mss received/year. 15% of books from first-time authors. 50% from unagented writers. Pays 6-15% royalty on wholesale price. Pays $2,000-5,000 advance.** Publishes ms 18 months after acceptance. Accepts simultaneous submissions. Responds in 2 months to queries. Guidelines online.

NONFICTION Subjects include animals, gardening, recreation, sports, travel, wildlife, pets. Submit cover letter, chapter outline, 1-2 sample chapters, brief bio, SASE. Reviews artwork/photos.

WISCONSIN HISTORICAL SOCIETY PRESS

816 State St., Madison WI 53706. (608)264-6465. **Fax:** (608)264-6486. **Website:** www.wisconsinhistory.org/whspress/. Estab. 1855. Publishes hardcover and trade paperback originals; trade paperback reprints. **Publishes 12-14 titles/year. 60-75 queries received/year. 20% of books from first-time authors. 90% from unagented writers. Pays royalty on wholesale price.** Publishes ms 2 years after acceptance. Accepts si-multaneous submissions. Book catalog available free. Guidelines online.

NONFICTION Subjects include history. Submit book proposal, form from website. Reviews artwork/photos. Send photocopies.

WISDOM PUBLICATIONS

199 Elm St., Somerville MA 02144. (617)776-7416, ext. 28. **Fax:** (617)776-7841. **E-mail:** editors@wisdompubs. org. **Website:** www.wisdompubs.org. **Contact:** David Kittelstrom, senior editor. Estab. 1976. Publishes hardcover originals and trade paperback originals and reprints. "Wisdom Publications is dedicated to making available authentic Buddhist works for the benefit of all. We publish translations, commentaries, and teachings of past and contemporary Buddhist masters and original works by leading Buddhist scholars. Currently emphasizing popular applied Buddhism, scholarly titles." **Publishes 30-35 titles/year. 300 queries received/year. 50% of books from first-time authors. 95% from unagented writers. Pays 8% royalty on wholesale price. Sometimes pays advance.** Publishes ms within 2 years of acceptance. Book catalog and ms guidelines online.

NONFICTION Subjects include philosophy, psychology, religion, spirituality, Buddhism, Tibet, Mindfulness. Submissions should be made electronically.

ⒶⓄ PAULA WISEMAN BOOKS

1230 Sixth Ave., New York NY 10020. (212)698-7000. **Fax:** (212)698-2796. **Website:** kids.simonandschuster.com. Estab. 2003. Paula Wiseman Books is an imprint of Simon & Schuster Children's Publishing that launched in 2003. It has since gone on to publish over 70 award-winning and bestselling books, including picture books, novelty books, and novels. The imprint focuses on stories and art that are childlike, timeless, innovative, and centered in emotion. "We strive to publish books that entertain while expanding the experience of the children who read them, as well as stories that will endure, including those based in other cultures. We are committed to publishing new talent in both picture books and novels. We are actively seeking submissions from new and published authors and artists through agents and from SCBWI conferences." **Publishes 30 titles/year. 15% of books from first-time authors.** Accepts simultaneous submissions.

NONFICTION Picture books: animal, biography, concept, history, nature/environment. Young readers: animal, biography, history, multicultural, nature/environment, sports. Average word length: picture books—500; others standard length. Does not accept unsolicited or unagented mss. By mail preferably.

FICTION Considers all categories. Average word length: picture books—500; others standard length.

WOODBINE HOUSE

6510 Bells Mill Rd., Bethesda MD 20817. (301)897-3570. **Fax:** (301)897-5838. **E-mail:** info@woodbinehouse.com. **Website:** www.woodbinehouse.com. **Contact:** Acquisitions Editor. Estab. 1985. Publishes trade paperback originals. Woodbine House publishes books for or about individuals with disabilities to help those individuals and their families live fulfilling and satisfying lives in their homes, schools, and communities. **Publishes 10 titles/year. 15% of books from first-time authors. 90% from unagented writers. Pays 10-12% royalty.** Publishes ms 18 months after acceptance. Accepts simultaneous submissions. Responds in 3 months to queries. Guidelines online.

NONFICTION Publishes books for and about children with disabilities. No personal accounts or general parenting guides. Submit outline, and at least 3 sample chapters. Reviews artwork/photos.

FICTION Subjects include picture books. Receptive to stories re: developmental and intellectual disabilities, e.g., autism and cerebral palsy. Submit complete ms with SASE.

WORKMAN PUBLISHING CO.

225 Varick St., New York NY 10014. **E-mail:** info@workman.com. **Website:** www.workman.com. Estab. 1967. Publishes hardcover and trade paperback originals, as well as calendars. "We are a trade paperback house specializing in a wide range of popular nonfiction. We publish no adult fiction and very little children's fiction. We also publish a full range of full-color wall and Page-A-Day calendars." **Publishes 40 titles/year. thousands of queries received/year. Open to first-time authors. Pays variable royalty on retail price. Pays variable advance.** Publishes ms approximately 1 year after acceptance. Accepts simultaneous submissions. Responds in 5 months to queries. Guidelines online.

NONFICTION Subjects include child guidance, gardening, sports, travel. Query.

WRITER'S DIGEST BOOKS

Imprint of F+W, a Content + eCommerce Company, 10151 Carver Rd., Suite 300, Cincinnati OH 45242. **E-mail:** writersdigest@fwmedia.com. **Website:** www.writersdigest.com. **Contact:** Amy Jones. Estab. 1920. Publishes hardcover originals and trade paperbacks. "Writer's Digest Books is the premiere source for instructional books on writing and publishing for an audience of aspirational writers. Typical mss are 80,000 words. E-mail queries strongly preferred; no phone calls please." **Publishes 18-20 titles/year. 300 queries; 50 mss received/year. 30% from unagented writers. Pays average $3,000 advance.** Publishes book 1 year after acceptance. Accepts simultaneous submissions. Responds in 3 months to queries. "Our catalog of titles is available to view online at www.WritersDigestShop.com."

NONFICTION "Our instruction books stress results and how to achieve them. Should be well-researched, yet lively and readable. We do not want to see books telling readers how to crack specific nonfiction markets: *Writing for the Computer Market* or *Writing for Trade Publications*, for instance. We are most in need of fiction-technique books written by published authors. Be prepared to explain how the proposed book differs from existing books on the subject." No fiction or poetry. Query with SASE. Submit outline, sample chapters, SASE.

YALE UNIVERSITY PRESS

P.O. Box 209040, New Haven CT 06520. (203)432-0960. **Fax:** (203)432-0948. **E-mail:** Contact specific editor (see website).. **Website:** yalebooks.com. Estab. 1908. Publishes hardcover and trade paperback originals. "Yale University Press publishes scholarly and general interest books." Accepts simultaneous submissions. Book catalog and ms guidelines online.

NONFICTION Subjects include Americana, education, history, philosophy, psychology, religion, science, sociology. "Our nonfiction has to be at a very high level. Most of our books are written by professors or journalists, with a high level of expertise. *Submit proposals only.* We'll ask if we want to see more. *No unsolicited mss.* We won't return them." Submit sample chapters, cover letter, prospectus, CV, TOC, SASE. Reviews artwork/photos. Send photocopies.

POETRY Submit to Yale Series of Younger Poets Competition. Guidelines online.

ZEBRA BOOKS

Kensington, 119 W. 40th St., New York NY 10018. (212)407-1500. **E-mail:** esogah@kensingtonbooks.com. **Website:** www.kensingtonbooks.com. **Contact:** Esi Sogah, senior editor. Publishes hardcover originals, trade paperback and mass market paperback originals and reprints. Zebra Books is dedicated to women's fiction, which includes, but is not limited to romance. Publishes ms 12-18 months after acceptance. Accepts simultaneous submissions. Book catalog online.

FICTION Query.

ZEST BOOKS

2443 Fillmore St., Suite 340, San Francisco CA 94115. (415)777-8654. **Fax:** (415)777-8653. **E-mail:** info@zestbooks.net. **Website:** zestbooks.net. **Contact:** Dan Harmon, publishing director. Zest Books is a leader in young adult nonfiction, publishing books on entertainment, history, science, health, fashion, and lifestyle advice since 2006. Zest Books is distributed by Houghton Mifflin Harcourt. Accepts simultaneous submissions. Guidelines online.

NONFICTION Submit proposal.

ZUMAYA PUBLICATIONS, LLC

3209 S. Interstate 35, Austin TX 78741. (512)330-4055. **Fax:** (512)276-6745. **E-mail:** business@zumayapublishing.com. **E-mail:** acquisitions@zumayapublications.com. **Website:** www.zumayapublications.com. **Contact:** Elizabeth K. Burton. Estab. 1999. Publishes trade paperback and electronic originals. Zumaya Publications is a digitally-based micro-press publishing mainly in on-demand trade paperback and e-book formats in an effort to reduce environmental impact. "We currently offer approximately 190 fiction titles in the mystery, SF/F, historical, romance, LGBTQ, horror, and occult genres in adult, young adult, and middle reader categories. In 2016, we plan to officially launch our graphic and illustrated novel imprint, Zumaya Fabled Ink. We publish approximately 10-15 new titles annually, at least five of which are from new authors. We do not publish erotica or graphic erotic romance at this time. We accept only electronic queries; all others will be discarded unread. A working knowledge of computers and relevant software is a necessity, as our production process is completely digital." **Publishes 10-15 titles/year. 1,000 queries; 50 mss requested/year. 5% of books from first-time authors. 98% from unagented writers. Pay 20% of net on paperbacks, net defined as cover price less printing and other associated costs; 50% of net on all e-books. Does not pay advance.** Publishes book 2 years after acceptance. Responds in 3 months to queries and proposals; 6 months to mss. Guidelines online. We do *not* accept hard-copy queries or submissions.

IMPRINTS Zumaya Arcane (New Age, inspirational fiction & nonfiction), Zumaya Boundless (GLBTQ); Zumaya Embraces (romance/women's fiction); Zumaya Enigma (mystery/suspense/thriller); Zumaya Thresholds (YA/middle grade); Zumaya Otherworlds (SF/F/H), Zumaya Yesterdays (memoirs, historical fiction, fiction, western fiction); Zumaya Fabled Ink (graphic and illustrated novels).

NONFICTION Subjects include creative nonfiction, memoirs, New Age, psychic, spirituality, true crime, true ghost stories. "The easiest way to figure out what we're looking for is to look at what we've already done. Our main nonfiction interests are in collections of true ghost stories, ones that have been investigated or thoroughly documented, memoirs that address specific regions and eras from a 'normal person' viewpoint and books on the craft of writing. That doesn't mean we won't consider something else." Electronic query only. Reviews artwork/photos. Send digital format.

FICTION Subjects include adventure, contemporary, ethnic, fantasy, feminist, gay, gothic, historical, horror, humor, juvenile, lesbian, literary, military, multicultural, mystery, occult, romance, science fiction, short story collections, spiritual, suspense, war, western, young adult, graphic novels. "We are open to all genres, particularly GLBT and YA/middle grade, historical and western, New Age/inspirational (no overtly Christian materials, please), non-category romance, thrillers. We encourage people to review what we've already published so as to avoid sending us more of the same, at least, insofar as the plot is concerned. While we're always looking for good mysteries, especially cozies, mysteries with historical settings, and police procedurals, we want original concepts rather than slightly altered versions of what we've already published. We do not publish erotica or graphically erotic romance at this time." Does not want erotica, graphically erotic romance, experimental, literary (unless it fits into one of our established imprints). A copy of our rules of submission is posted on our website and can be downloaded. They are rules rather

than guidelines and should be read carefully before
submitting. It will save everyone time and frustration.

THREE THINGS ON WRITING QUERY LETTERS

by Robert Lee Brewer

Whether you're trying to get a book published or earn a magazine byline, query letters are super important to finding success as a writer. Here are three things to consider when tackling your own query letters.

THE HOOK

First up, the hook, or opening element of a query. The best hooks—whether fiction or nonfiction—often present a problem, ask a thought-provoking question, or give an enticing snapshot of what project you're about to pitch. Often, in one juicy sentence.

MORE DETAILS

Then, include important details about the project. Do this in one to three concise paragraphs. But remember: The query covers highlights—not every single detail. In other words, establish a need to share how you plan to answer that need. For fiction, share the most compelling elements of a story to entice the editor or agent to want to read more.

YOUR BIO

Finally, include some form of author bio in a very concise two to three sentences. If you've had a book published or won any relevant awards, include that. If you're an expert in the field on which you plan to write, include that. Do not include your lack of experience, even if it's the truth. Unless your name carries weight, the less you write, the better.

CONSUMER MAGAZINES

///

Selling your writing to consumer magazines is as much an exercise of your marketing skills as it is of your writing abilities. Editors of consumer magazines are looking for good writing which communicates pertinent information to their readers.

Marketing skills will help you successfully discern a magazine's editorial slant, and write queries and articles that prove your knowledge of the magazine's readership. You can gather clues about a magazine's readership—and establish your credibility with the editor—in a number of ways: Read the listing in *Writer's Market*; study a magazine's writer's guidelines; check a magazine's website; and read current issues of the magazine.

Writers who can correctly and consistently discern a publication's audience and deliver stories that speak to that target readership will win out every time over writers who submit haphazardly.

In nonfiction, editors continue to look for short feature articles covering specialized topics. Editors want crisp writing and expertise. If you are not an expert in the area about which you are writing, make yourself one through research. Always query before sending your manuscript.

Fiction editors prefer to receive complete manuscripts. Writers must keep in mind that fiction is competitive, and editors receive far more material than they can publish. For this reason, they often do not respond to submissions unless they are interested in using the story.

Most magazines listed here have indicated pay rates; some give very specific payment-per-word rates, while others state a range. Any agreement you come to with a magazine, whether verbal or written, should specify the payment you are to receive and when you are to receive it.

CONSUMER MAGAZINES

ANIMAL

$$ AKC GAZETTE

American Kennel Club, 260 Madison Ave., New York NY 10016. (212)696-8200. **Website:** www.akc.org/pubs/gazette. **85% freelance written.** Monthly magazine. "Geared to interests of fanciers of purebred dogs as opposed to commercial interests or pet owners. We require solid expertise from our contributors—we are *not* a pet magazine." Estab. 1889. Circ. 60,000. Byline given. Pays on publication. Offers 10% kill fee. Publishes ms an average of 6 months after acceptance. Submit seasonal material 6 months in advance. Accepts queries by mail. Accepts simultaneous submissions. Responds in 2 months to queries. Guidelines for #10 SASE.

NONFICTION Needs general interest, how-to, humor, interview, photo feature, travel, dog art, training and canine performance sports. No poetry, tributes to individual dogs, or fiction. **Buys 30-40 mss/year.** Length: 1,000-3,000 words. **Pays $300-500.** Pays expenses of writers on assignment.

FICTION Annual short fiction contest only. Guidelines for #10 SASE. Send entries to AKC Publications Fiction Contest.

$$$$ THE AMERICAN QUARTER HORSE JOURNAL

AQHA, 1600 Quarter Horse Dr., Amarillo TX 79104. (806)376-4811. **Website:** www.aqha.com. Editor-in-Chief: Becky Newell. **30% freelance written. Prefers to work with published/established writers.** Monthly official publication of the american quarter horse association. covering American Quarter Horses/horse activities/western lifestyle. "Covers the American Wuarter Horse breed and more than 30 disciplines in which Quarter Horses compete. Business stories, lifestyles stories, how-to stories and others related to the breed and horse activities." Estab. 1948. Circ. 60,000. Byline given. Pays on acceptance. Offers 60% kill fee. Publishes ms an average of 3 months after acceptance. Editorial lead time 3 months. Submit seasonal material 3 months in advance. Accepts queries by mail, e-mail. Accepts simultaneous submissions. Responds in 1 week to queries. Responds in 1 month to mss. Sample copy free. Guidelines free.

NONFICTION Needs book excerpts, essays, general interest, historical, how-to, humor, inspirational, interview, "Must be about established horses or people who have made a contribution to the business, new prod, opinion, personal exp, photo, technical, equine updates, new surgery procedures, etc." Special issues: Annual stallion issue dedicated to the breeding of horses. **Buys 10 mss/year.** Query with published clips. Length: 700-3,000 words. **Pays $250-1,500 for assigned articles. Pays $250-1,500 for unsolicited articles.** Pays expenses of writers on assignment.

COLUMNS Quarter's Worth (Industry news); Horse Health (health items), 750 words. **Buys 6 mss/yr. mss/year.** Query with published clips. **Pays $100-$400.**

APPALOOSA JOURNAL

2720 W. Pullman Rd., Moscow ID 83843. (208)882-5578. **Fax:** (208)882-8150. **E-mail:** editor@appaloosajournal.com; designer2@appaloosajournal.com. **Website:** www.appaloosajournal.com. **Contact:** Dana Russell, editor; John Langston, art director. **40% freelance written.** Monthly magazine covering Appaloosa horses. "*Appaloosa Journal* is the authoritative, association-based source for information about the Appaloosa Horse Club, the Appaloosa breed and the Appaloosa industry. Our mission is to cultivate a broader membership base and instill enthusiasm for the breed by recognizing the needs and achievements of the Appaloosa, ApHC members, enthusiasts and our readers. The Appaloosa Horse Club is a not-for-profit organization. Serious inquiries within specified budget only." Estab. 1946. Circ. 25,000. Byline given. Pays on publication. Publishes ms an average of 3 months after acceptance. Accepts simultaneous submissions. Responds in 1 month to queries. Responds in 2 months to mss. Sample copy free. Guidelines available online.

NONFICTION Needs historical, interview. **Buys 15-20 mss/year.** Send complete ms. *Appaloosa Journal* is not responsible for unsolicited materials. All freelance correspondence should be directed to editor Dana Russell via e-mail, with the subject line "'Freelance.' Article-length reports of timely and newsworthy events, such as shows, races, and overseas competition, are welcome but must be pre-approved by the editor. Mss exceeding the preferred word length will be evaluated according to relevance and content matter. Lengthy stories, opinion pieces, or poorly written pieces will be rejected. Mss may be sent on a CD or via e-mail in Microsoft Word or text-only format. If sent via CD, an accompanying hard copy should be printed, double spaced, following the guidelines." Length: 1,500-1,800 words (features); 600-800 words (article-length). **Pays $200-400.** Pays expenses of writers on assignment.

THE CHRONICLE OF THE HORSE

P.O. Box 46, Middleburg VA 20118. (540)687-6341. **Fax:** (540)687-3937. **E-mail:** brasin@coth.com. **Web-**site: www.chronofhorse.com. **Contact:** Beth Rasin, executive editor. **40% freelance written.** Biweekly magazine covering horse sport. "We cover English riding sports, including horse showing, grand prix jumping competitions, steeplechase racing, foxhunting, dressage, endurance riding, para-dressage, and eventing. We feature news, profiles, how-to articles on equitation and horse care and interviews with leaders in the various fields." Estab. 1937. Byline given. Pays for features, news and other items on publication. Publishes an average of 4 months after acceptance. Submit seasonal material 3 months in advance. Accepts queries by mail, e-mail. Accepts simultaneous submissions. Responds in 5-6 weeks to queries. Guidelines online.

NONFICTION Needs essays, expose, general interest, historical, how-to, humor, interview, opinion, profile, technical, travel. No poetry, clinic reports, Western riding articles, personal experience or wild horses. **Buys 300 mss/year.** Send complete ms. Length: 1,500-2,500 words. **Pays $150-400.** Pays expenses of writers on assignment.

COLUMNS Dressage, Eventing, Horse Shows, Horse Care, Racing over Fences, Young Entry (about young riders, geared for youth), Horses and Humanities, Hunting, Vaulting, Para-dressage, Endurance,1,500-2500 words. Query with published clips or send complete ms. **Pays $25-200.**

DOG SPORTS MAGAZINE

Cher Car Kennels, 4215 S. Lowell Rd., St. Johns MI 48879. (989)224-7225. **E-mail:** info@chercarkennels.com. **Website:** www.dogsports.com. **Contact:** Cheryl Carlson, editor. **5% freelance written.** Monthly tabloid covering working dogs. *Dog Sports* online magazine is for all dog trainers. Focuses on the "how" of dog training. You will find articles on police K-9 training, narcotics detection, herding, weight pull, tracking, search and rescue, and how to increase your dog-training business. Brings the latest in techniques from the field, actual dog trainers that are out there, working, titling, and training. French Ring, Mondio, Schutzhund, N.A.P.D. PPDA, K-9 Pro Sports all are featured, as well as spotlight articles on breeds, trainers, judges, or events. Estab. 1979. Circ. 2,000. Byline given. Pays on publication. Publishes ms an average of 1 month after acceptance. Editorial lead time 1 month. Submit seasonal material 1 month in advance. Accepts queries by mail, e-mail. Accepts simultaneous submissions. Sample copy free or online.

NONFICTION Needs essays, general interest, how-to, working dogs, humor, interview, technical. **Buys 5 mss/year.** Send complete ms. **Pays $50.**

💲💲 EQUESTRIAN MAGAZINE

United States Equestrian Federation (USEF), 4047 Iron Works Pkwy., Lexington KY 40511. (859)258-2472. **Fax:** (859)231-6662. **Website:** www.usef.org. **10-30% freelance written.** Magazine published 6 times/year covering the equestrian sport. Estab. 1937. Circ. 77,000. Byline given. Pays on publication. Offers 50% kill fee. Editorial lead time 1-5 months. Accepts queries by mail, e-mail, fax, phone. Accepts simultaneous submissions. Sample copy and writer's guidelines free.

NONFICTION Needs interview, technical, all equestrian-related. **Buys 20-30 mss/year.** Query with published clips. Length: 500-3,500 words. **Pays $200-400.** Pays expenses of writers on assignment.

💲 EQUINE JOURNAL

83 Leicester St., North Oxford MA 01537. (508)987-5886. **Fax:** (508)987-5887. **E-mail:** editorial@morris.com. **Website:** www.equinejournal.com. **Contact:** Kelly Ballou, editor. **90% freelance written.** Monthly tabloid covering horses—all breeds, all disciplines. *Equine Journal* is a monthly, all-breed/discipline regional publication for horse enthusiasts. "The purpose of our editorial is to educate, entertain, and enable amateurs and professionals alike to stay on top of new developments in the field. Every month, the *Equine Journal* presents feature articles and columns spanning the length and breadth of horse-related activities and interests from all corners of the country." Estab. 1988. Circ. 26,000. Byline given. Pays on publication. Editorial lead time 4 months. Accepts queries by e-mail. Accepts simultaneous submissions. Responds in 2 months to queries. Guidelines available online.

NONFICTION Needs general interest, how-to, interview. Does not accept poetry, fiction, or stories told from a first-person perspective. **Buys 100 mss/year.** Query with published clips, or send complete ms. Length: 1,200-1,800 words for features; 300-500 words for event write-ups. Pays expenses of writers on assignment.

COLUMNS Horse Health (health-related topics), 1,200-1,500 words. **Buys 12 mss/year.** Query.

EQUUS

Cruz Bay Publishing, Inc., 656 Quince Orchard Rd., Suite 600, Gaithersburg MD 20878. **Fax:** (301)990-9015. **E-mail:** eqletters@equinetwork.com. **Website:** www.equisearch.com. Monthly magazine covering equine behavior. Provides the latest information from the world's top veternarians, equine researchers, riders, and trainers. Circ. 149,482. No kill fee. Accepts queries by mail. Accepts simultaneous submissions. Guidelines available online.

NONFICTION Send complete ms. Length: 1,600-3,000 words. **Payment depends on quality, length, and complexity of the story.** Pays expenses of writers on assignment.

COLUMNS The Medical Front (research/technology/treatments), 200-400 words; Hands On (everyday horse care), 100-400 words; Roundup (industry news stories), 100-400 words; True Tales (experiences/relationships with horses), 700-2,000 words; Case Report (equine illness/injury), 1,000-2,500 words. Send complete ms. **Payment depends on quality, length, and complexity of the story.**

💲💲 FIDO FRIENDLY MAGAZINE

Fido Friendly, Inc., P.O. Box 160, Marsing ID 83639. **E-mail:** fieldeditor@fidofriendly.com. **Website:** www.fidofriendly.com. **Contact:** Susan Sims, publisher. **95% freelance written.** Quarterly magazine covering travel with your dog. "We want articles about all things travel related with your dog." Estab. 2000. Circ. 50,000. Byline given. Pays on publication. 25% kill fee. Publishes ms an average of 2 months after acceptance. Editorial lead time 1-3 months. Submit seasonal material 3 months in advance. Accepts queries by e-mail. Accepts simultaneous submissions. Responds in 2 weeks to queries; in 1 month to mss. Sample copy: $7. Guidelines free.

NONFICTION Needs essays, general interest, how-to, travel with your dog, humor, inspirational, interview, personal experience, travel. No articles from dog's point of view or in dog's voice. **Buys 24 mss/year.** Query with published clips. Length: 600-1,200 words. **Pays 10-20¢ for assigned articles and unsolicited articles.**

COLUMNS Fido Friendly City (city where dogs have lots of options to enjoy restaurants, dog retail stores, dog parks, sports activity). **Buys 6 mss/yr mss/year.** Query with published clips. **Pays 10-20¢/word.**

FICTION Needs adventure, (dog). Nothing from dog's point of view. Query. Length: 600-1,200 words. **Pays 10-20¢/word.**

$$ FRESHWATER AND MARINE AQUARIUM

Bowtie, Inc., 3 Burroughs, Irvine CA 92618. (949)855-8822. **E-mail:** emizer@bowtieinc.com. **Website:** www.fishchannel.com. Clay Jackson. **Contact:** Ethan Mizer, senior associate editor. **95% freelance written.** The freshwater and marine aquarium hobby. "Our audience tends to be more advanced fish-and coral-keepers as well as planted tank fans. Writers should have aquarium keeping experience themselves. FAMA covers all aspects of fish and coral husbandry." Estab. 1978. Circ. 14,000. Byline given. Pays on publication. Pays $50 kill fee. Publishes ms 6-8 months after acceptance. 3.5 months editorial lead time. Accepts queries by mail, e-mail. Accepts simultaneous submissions. 3 weeks on queries, 2 months on mss. "If we are interested in a query or ms, we'll e-mail an assignment with guidelines included."

NONFICTION Contact: Ethan Mizer, senior associate editor. Needs general interest, how-to, interview, new product, personal experience, technical, aquarium-related articles. Special issues: Three special issues every year. Past issues have included aquarium lighting, invertebrates, planted tanks, food, etc. "No beginner articles, such as keeping guppies and goldfish. If mid-level to advanced aquarists wouldn't get anything new by reading it, don't send it." Writer should query. 1,500-2,000/words. **Pay $300-400; 20¢/word.**

COLUMNS "All of our columns are assigned and written by established columnists." **Pays $250.**

$ THE GREYHOUND REVIEW

P.O. Box 543, Abilene KS 67410. (785)263-4660. **E-mail:** nga@ngagreyhounds.com. **Website:** www.ngagreyhounds.com. **20% freelance written.** Monthly magazine covering greyhound breeding, training, and racing. Estab. 1911. Circ. 3,500. Byline given. Pays on acceptance. No kill fee. Submit seasonal material 2 months in advance. Accepts simultaneous submissions. Responds in 2 weeks to queries. Responds in 1 month to mss. Sample copy for $3. Guidelines free.

NONFICTION Needs how-to, interview, personal experience. Do not submit gambling systems. **Buys 24 mss/year.** Query. Length: 1,000-10,000 words. **Pays $85-150.** Pays expenses of writers on assignment.

REPRINTS Send photocopy. Pays 100% of amount paid for original article.

$$$ HORSE&RIDER

2520 55th St., #210, Boulder CO 80301. **E-mail:** horseandrider@aimmedia.com. **Website:** www.horseandrider.com. **Contact:** Julie Preble, assistant editor. **10% freelance written. "Very little unsolicited freelance accepted."** Monthly magazine covering Western horse industry, competition, recreation. "*Horse&Rider's* mission is to enhance the enjoyment and satisfaction readers derive from horse involvement. We strive to do this by providing the insights, knowledge, and horsemanship skills they need to safely and effectively handle, ride, and appreciate their horses, in and out of the competition arena. We also help them find the time, resources, and energy they need to enjoy their horse to the fullest." Estab. 1961. Circ. 150,000. Byline given. Pays after publication. Publishes ms an average of 1 year after acceptance. Editorial lead time 2 months. Submit seasonal material 6 months in advance. Accepts queries by mail (must be on a CD in a digital format), e-mail (preferred). Responds in 3 months to queries and to mss. Sample copy and writer's guidelines online.

NONFICTION Needs book excerpts, general interest, how-to, horse training, horsemanship, humor, interview, new product, personal experience, photo feature, travel. **Buys 5-10 mss/year.** Send complete ms. Length: 1,000-3,000 words. **Pay depends on length, use, and quality.**

☉ HORSE CANADA

Horse Publications Group, Box 670, Aurora ON L4G 4J9 Canada. (905)727-0107. **Fax:** (905)841-1530. **E-mail:** hceditor@horse-canada.com. **Website:** www.horse-canada.com. **Contact:** Amy Harris, managing editor. **80% freelance written.** National magazine for horse lovers of all ages. Readers are committed horse owners with many different breeds involved in a variety of disciplines—from beginner riders to industry professionals. Circ. 20,000. No kill fee. Editorial lead time 2 months. Accepts queries by e-mail. Accepts simultaneous submissions. Guidelines available online.

NONFICTION Query. Length: 750-1,500 words. **Payment varies.**

COLUMNS Payment varies.

⑨⑨ HORSE ILLUSTRATED

I-5 Publishing, 470 Conway Ct., Suite b-6, Lexington KY 40511. (800)546-7730. **E-mail:** horseillustrated@luminamedia.com. **Website:** www.horseillustrated.com. **Contact:** Elizabeth Moyer, editor. **90% freelance written. Prefers to work with published/established writers, but will work with new/unpublished writers.** Monthly magazine covering all aspects of horse ownership. "Our readers are adults, mostly women, between the ages of 18 and 40; stories should be geared to that age group and reflect responsible horse care." Estab. 1976. Circ. 160,660. Byline given. Pays on publication. Publishes ms an average of 8 months after acceptance. Submit seasonal material 6 months in advance. Accepts queries by mail. Accepts simultaneous submissions. Responds in 3 months to queries. Guidelines available at www.horsechannel.com/horse-magazines/horse-illustrated/submission-guidelines.aspx.

NONFICTION Needs general interest, how-to, inspirational, photo feature. "No little girl horse stories, cowboy and Indian stories, or anything not *directly* relating to horses." **Buys 20 mss/year.** Query or send complete ms. Length: 1,000-2,000 words. **Pays $200-475.** Pays expenses of writers on assignment.

⑨⑨ JUST LABS

Willow Creek Press, 2779 Aero Park Dr., Traverse City MI 49686. (231)946-3712; (800)-447-7367. **E-mail:** jake@villagepress.com; jillian.lacross@villagepress.com. **E-mail:** jillian.lacross@villagepress.com. **Website:** www.justlabsmagazine.com. **Contact:** Jason Smith, editor; Jill LaCross, managing and web editor. **50% freelance written.** Bimonthly magazine covering all aspects of the Labrador Retriever. "*Just Labs* is targeted toward the family Labrador Retriever, and all of our articles help people learn about, live with, train, take care of, and enjoy their dogs. We do not look for articles that pull at the heart strings, but rather we look for articles that teach, inform, and entertain." Estab. 2001. Circ. 15,000. Byline given. Pays on publication. Offers 40% kill fee. Publishes ms an average of 6 months after acceptance. Editorial lead time 6 months. Submit seasonal material 6-8 months in advance. Accepts queries by mail, e-mail. Accepts simultaneous submissions. Responds in 4-6 weeks to queries; in 2 months to mss. Guidelines by e-mail.

NONFICTION Needs essays, how-to, humor, inspirational, interview, photo feature, technical, travel. "We don't want tributes to dogs that have passed on. This is a privilege we reserve for our subscribers." **Buys 30 mss/year.** Query. Length: 1,200-1,800 words. **Pays $250-400.** Pays expenses of writers on assignment.

⑨ MINIATURE DONKEY TALK

Miniature Donkey Talk, Inc., P.O. Box 982, Cripple Creek CO 80813. (719)689-2904. **E-mail:** mike@donkeytalk.com. **Website:** www.web-donkeys.com. **Contact:** Mike Gross. **65% freelance written.** Quarterly magazine covering donkeys, with articles on healthcare, promotion, and management of donkeys for owners, breeders, and donkey lovers. Estab. 1987. Circ. 4,925. Byline given. Pays on acceptance. Publishes ms an average of 4 months after acceptance. Editorial lead time 2 months. Submit seasonal material 3 months in advance. Accepts queries by mail, e-mail. Accepts simultaneous submissions. Responds in 2 weeks to queries; 1 month to mss. Sample copy for $5. Guidelines free.

NONFICTION Needs book excerpts, humor, interview, personal experience. **Buys 6 mss/year.** Query with published clips. Length: 700-5,000 words. **Pays $25-150.**

COLUMNS Columns: Humor: 2,000 words; Healthcare: 2,000-5,000 words; Management: 2,000 words. **Buys 50 mss/year.** Query. **Pays $25-100.**

⑨⑨ MUSHING MAGAZINE

2300 Black Spruce Ct., Fairbanks AK 99709. (907)495-2468. **E-mail:** editor@mushing.com; jake@mushing.com. **Website:** www.mushing.com. **Contact:** Greg Sellentin, publisher and executive editor. Bimonthly magazine covering "all aspects of the growing sports of dogsledding, skijoring, carting, dog packing, and weight pulling. *Mushing* promotes responsible dog care through feature articles and updates on working animal health care, safety, nutrition, and training." Estab. 1987. Circ. 10,000. Byline given. Pays within 3 months of publication. No kill fee. Publishes ms an average of 4 months after acceptance. Submit seasonal material 4 months in advance. Accepts queries by mail, e-mail, fax, phone. Accepts simultaneous submissions. Responds in 8 months to queries. Sample copy: $5 ($6 U.S. to Canada). Guidelines online.

NONFICTION Needs historical, how-to. Special issues: Iditarod (January/February); Skijor/Sprint/Peak of Season (March/April); Health and Nutrition (May/June); Meet the Mushers/Tour Business Directory (July/August); Equipment (September/October);

Races and Places/Sled Dog Events Calendar (November/December). See website for current editorial calendar. Query with or without published clips. "We prefer detailed queries but also consider unsolicited mss. Please make proposals informative yet to the point. Spell out your qualifications for handling the topic. We like to see clips of previously published material but are eager to work with new and unpublished authors, too." Considers complete ms by postal mail (with SASE) or e-mail (as attachment or part of message). Also accepts disk submissions. Length: 1,000-2,500 words. **Pays $50-250.** Pays expenses of writers on assignment.

COLUMNS Query with or without published clips or send complete ms. Length: 150-500 words.

FILLERS Needs anecdotes, facts, newsbreaks, short humor, cartoons, puzzles. Length: 100-250 words. **Pays $20-35.**

💲💲 PAINT HORSE JOURNAL

American Paint Horse Association, P.O. Box 961023, Ft. Worth TX 76161-0023. (817)834-2742. Fax: (817)834-3152. **E-mail:** jhein@apha.com. **Website:** apha.com/phj. **Contact:** Jessica Hein, editor. **10% freelance written. Works with a small number of new/unpublished writers each year.** Monthly magazine for people who raise, breed, and show Paint Horses. Estab. 1966. Circ. 12,000. Byline given. Pays on acceptance. Offers negotiable kill fee. Submit seasonal material 3 months in advance. Accepts queries by mail, e-mail, fax. Accepts simultaneous submissions. Guidelines online.

NONFICTION Needs general interest, historical, how-to. **Buys 4-5 mss/year.** Query. Length: 1,000-2,000 words. **Pays $100-500.** Pays expenses of writers on assignment.

💲💲 REPTILES

i-5 Publishing, 3 Burroughs, Irvine CA 92618. (949)855-8822. **E-mail:** reptiles@i5publishing.com. **Website:** www.reptilesmagazine.com. **20% freelance written.** Monthly magazine covering reptiles and amphibians. *Reptiles* covers "a wide range of topics relating to reptiles and amphibians, including breeding, captive care, field herping, etc." Estab. 1992. Byline given. Pays on publication. Offers 20% kill fee. Publishes ms an average of 6-8 months after acceptance. Accepts queries by mail, e-mail. Accepts simultaneous submissions. Responds in 1 month to queries. Responds in 1-2 months to mss. Sample copy available online. Guidelines available online.

NONFICTION Needs general interest, historical, how-to, interview, personal experience, photo feature, travel. **Buys 10 mss/year.** Query. Length: 1,000-2,000 words. **Pays $350-500.**

💲💲 TROPICAL FISH HOBBYIST MAGAZINE

TFH Publications, Inc., One TFH Plaza, Neptune City NJ 07753. **E-mail:** associateeditor@tfh.com. **Website:** www.tfhmagazine.com. **90% freelance written.** Monthly magazine covering tropical fish. Estab. 1952. Circ. 35,000. Byline given. Pays on acceptance. No kill fee. Editorial lead time 3 months. Submit seasonal material 6 months in advance. Accepts queries by e-mail. Responds immediately on electronic queries. Guidelines available online.

NONFICTION **Buys 100-150 mss/year.** "Manuscripts should be submitted as e-mail attachments. Please break up the text using subheads to categorize topics. We prefer articles that are submitted with photos. Do not insert photos into the text. Photos must be submitted separately." Length: 10,000-20,000 characters with spaces. **Pays $100-250.** Pays expenses of writers on assignment.

💲💲 USDF CONNECTION

United States Dressage Federation, 4051 Iron Works Pkwy., Lexington KY 40511. **E-mail:** connection@usdf.org. **E-mail:** editorial@usdf.org. **Website:** www.usdf.org. **Contact:** Jennifer Bryant. **40% freelance written.** Magazine published 10 times/year covering dressage (an equestrian sport). All material must relate to the sport of dressage in the U.S. Estab. 2000. Circ. 30,000. Byline given. Pays on acceptance. Offers 50% kill fee. Publishes ms an average of 6 months after acceptance. Editorial lead time: 3 months. Submit seasonal material 6 months in advance. Accepts queries by e-mail. Responds in 1 month to queries; 1-2 months to mss. Sample copy: $5. Guidelines online.

NONFICTION Needs book excerpts, essays, how-to, interview, opinion, personal experience, profile. Does not want general-interest equine material or stories that lack a U.S. dressage angle. **Buys 20 mss/year.** Query. Length: 500-2,000 words. **Pays $100-450 for assigned articles. Pays $100-300 for unsolicited articles. Byline only for "The Tail End," a one-page personal or op/ed column pertaining to USDF members' dressage experiences.**

COLUMNS Amateur Hour (profiles of and service pieces of interest to USDF's adult amateur members), 1,200-1,500 words; Under 21 (profiles of and service pieces of interest to USDF's young members), 1,200-1,500 words; Horse-Health Connection (dressage-related horse health), 1,200-1,800 words. **Buys 12 mss/year.** Query with published clips. **Pays $150-300.**

🌓🌓 YOUNG RIDER

2030 Main Street, Irvine CA 92614. (949) 855-8822. **Fax:** (949) 855-3045. **E-mail:** yreditor@i5publishing.com. **Website:** www.youngrider.com. "*Young Rider* magazine teaches young people, in an easy-to-read and entertaining way, how to look after their horses properly, and how to improve their riding skills safely." Byline given. Accepts simultaneous submissions. Guidelines available online.

NONFICTION young adults: animal, careers, famous equestrians, health (horse), horse celebrities, riding. Special issues: Wants "'horsey-interest type stories. Stories or events that will interest kids ALL over the country that the editor is not able to personally attend. We need 4-5 good color photos with stories like this; the pictures must be color and tack sharp." Query with published clips. Length: 800-1,000 words. **Pays $200/story.** Pays expenses of writers on assignment.

FICTION young adults: adventure, animal, horses. "We would prefer funny stories, with a bit of conflict, which will appeal to the 13-year-old age group. They should be written in the third person, and about kids." Query. Length: 800-1,000 words. **Pays $150.**

ART & ARCHITECTURE

🌓🌓 THE ARTIST'S MAGAZINE

F+W Media, 10151 Carver Rd., Suite 300, Blue Ash OH 45242. (513)531-2690, ext. 11731. **Fax:** (513)891-7153. **Website:** www.artistsmagazine.com. **Contact:** Maureen Bloomfield, editor in chief; Brian Roeth, senior art director. **80% freelance written.** Magazine published 10 times/year covering primarily two-dimensional art for working artists. Maureen Bloomfield says, "Ours is a highly visual approach to teaching serious amateur and professional artists techniques that will help them improve their skills and market their work. The style should be crisp and immediately engaging, written in a voice that speaks directly to artists. We do not accept unsolicited mss.

Artists should send digital images of their work; writers should send clips of previously published work, along with a query letter." Circ. 100,000. Bionote given for features and columns. Pays on receiving ms. Offers 8% kill fee. Publishes ms an average of 6 months-1 year after acceptance. Responds in 6 months to queries. Sample copy: $6.99. Guidelines available online.

NONFICTION Needs book excerpts, essays, historical, how-to, interview, new product, profile. No unillustrated articles. **Buys 60 mss/year.** Length: 500-1,200 words. **Pays $300-500 and up.**

🌑🌓🌓 ARTLINK

Artlink Australia, P.O. Box 182, Fullarton SA 5063 Australia. (61)(8)8271-6228. **E-mail:** info@artlink.com.au. **Website:** www.artlink.com.au. **Contact:** Eve Sullivan, executive editor. Quarterly magazine covering contemporary art in Australia. Estab. 1981. Accepts simultaneous submissions. Guidelines available online.

NONFICTION Needs general interest. Special issues: "*Artlink* welcomes proposals for writing and information on associated projects and exhibition programs that relate to forthcoming themed issues." See website for upcoming themes. Write or e-mail the editor with your CV and 2-3 examples of previously published writing. **Pays $300/1,000 words.** Pays expenses of writers on assignment.

🌓🌓🌓🌓 AZURE (ARCHITECTURE, DESIGN, INTERIORS, CURIOSITY)

213 Sterling Rd., Suite 206, Toronto ON M6R 2B2 Canada. 416-203-9674. **E-mail:** editorial@azureonline.com; azure@azureonline.com. **Website:** www.azuremagazine.com. **Contact:** David Dick-Agnew, senior editor. **75% freelance written.** Magazine covering design and architecture. "*AZURE* is an award-winning magazine with a focus on contemporary architecture and design. In 8 visually stunning issues per year, *AZURE* explores inventive projects, emerging trends, and design issues that relate to our changing society. In recent years, *AZURE* has evolved into a media brand offering digital editions, weekly e-newsletters featuring the latest design news, an interactive website updated daily, and an international awards program celebrating excellence in design." Estab. 1985. Byline given. Pays on publication. Offers variable kill fee. Publishes ms an average of 1 month after acceptance. Editorial lead time up to 45 days. Accepts

queries by e-mail. Accepts simultaneous submissions. Responds in 6 weeks to queries.

NONFICTION Needs new product, profile, technical, travel. Special issues: January/February: Houses; March/April: Iconic Buildings; June: Office Spaces; July/August: AZ Awards Annual; October: Trends; December: Interiors and Higher Ed. Does not want "anything other than architecture, design, urbanism and landscape, and tangentially related topics." **Buys 25-30 mss/year.** Length: 300-1,500 words. **Pays $1/word (Canadian).** Pays expenses of writers on assignment.

COLUMNS Groundbreaker (profiles of new, large architectural projects) 350 words; book and documentary reviews, 300 words; Field Trip (profiles of hospitality/travel spaces with design angle), 800 words; Trailer (idiosyncratic design stories) 300 words. **Buys 30 mss/year.** Query. **Pays $1/word (Canadian).**

✿ 💲 💲 C MAGAZINE

C The Visual Arts Foundation, P.O. Box 5, Station B, Toronto ON M5T 2T2 Canada. (416)539-9495. **Fax:** (416)539-9903. **E-mail:** info@cmagazine.com. **E-mail:** amishmorrell@cmagazine.com. **Website:** www.cmagazine.com. **Contact:** Amish Morrell, editor. **80% freelance written.** Quarterly magazine covering international contemporary art. "*C Magazine* is a Toronto-based contemporary art and criticism periodical devoted to providing a forum for significant ideas in visual art and culture. Each quarterly issue explores a new theme through original art writing, criticism, and artists' projects." Estab. 1983. Circ. 7,000. Byline given. Pays on publication. Offers kill fee. Publishes ms an average of 4 months after acceptance. Editorial lead time 3 months. Accepts queries by e-mail. Accepts simultaneous submissions. Responds in 6 weeks to queries; in 4 months to mss. Sample copy: $10 (US). Guidelines online.

NONFICTION Needs essays, general interest, opinion, personal experience, "*C Magazine* welcomes writing on contemporary art and culture that is lively and rigorously engaged with current ideas and debates. C is interested in writing that addresses emergent practices and places them in critical context." **Buys 50 mss/year.** Query with published clips and brief bio by e-mail: amishmorrell@cmagazine.com. Length: 800-1,000 words for book reviews; 2,500-4,000 words for features, cultural analysis, artist profiles, and in-

terviews. **Pays $150-500 (Canadian), $105-350 (US).** Pays expenses of writers on assignment.

✿ 💲 ESPACE

Le Centre de Diffusion 3D, 423-5445 Avenue De Gaspé, Montreal QC H2J 3B2 Canada. (514)907-6147. **E-mail:** info@espaceartactuel.com. **Website:** www.espaceartactuel.com. **Contact:** Serge Fisette, editor. **95% freelance written.** Quarterly magazine covering sculpture events. Estab. 1987. Circ. 1,400. Byline given. Pays on publication. No kill fee. Publishes ms an average of 3 months after acceptance. Editorial lead time 5 months. Submit seasonal material 3 months in advance. Accepts queries by e-mail. Accepts simultaneous submissions. Sample copy free. Guidelines online.

NONFICTION Needs interview, reviews, sculpture events. **Buys 60 mss/year.** Send complete ms. Length: up to 1,000 words for reviews; 1,500-2,000 words for interviews, events. **Pays $65/page.** Pays expenses of writers on assignment.

FORM: PIONEERING DESIGN

Balcony Media, Inc., 812 E. Fremont, Suite 205, South Pasadena CA 91030. (626)460-8339. **E-mail:** edit@formmag.net. **Website:** www.formmag.net. **80% freelance written.** Bimonthly magazine covering architecture, interiors, landscape, and other design disciplines. *Form: Pioneering Design* is interested in architecture, interiors, product, graphics, and landscape design as well as news about the arts. We encourage designers to keep us informed on projects, techniques, and products that are innovative, new, or nationally newsworthy. We are especially interested in new and renovated projects that illustrate a high degree of design integrity and unique answers to typical problems in the urban cultural and physical environment. Estab. 1999. Circ. 20,000. Byline given. Pays on publication. No kill fee. Publishes ms an average of 3 months after acceptance. Editorial lead time 4 months. Submit seasonal material 4 months in advance. Accepts queries by mail, e-mail, fax. Accepts simultaneous submissions. Responds in 1 month.

NONFICTION Needs book excerpts, essays, historical, interview, new product. **Buys 20 mss/year.** Length: 500-2,000 words. **Payment negotiable.**

💲 💲 THE MAGAZINE ANTIQUES

Brant Publications, 110 Greene St., New York NY 10012. (212)941-2800. **Fax:** (212)941-2819. **E-mail:** tmaedit@artnews.com (JavaScript required to view).

Website: www.themagazineantiques.com. **75% freelance written.** Bimonthly. "Articles should present new information in a scholarly format (with footnotes) on the fine and decorative arts, architecture, historic preservation, and landscape architecture." Estab. 1922. Circ. 40,000. Byline given. Pays on publication. No kill fee. Publishes ms an average of 6 months after acceptance. Editorial lead time 6 months. Submit seasonal material 6 months in advance. Accepts simultaneous submissions. Responds in 3 weeks to queries. Responds in 6 months to mss. Sample copy $12 plus shipping costs. Contact tmacustserv@cds-fulfillment.com.

NONFICTION **Buys 50 mss/year.** "For submission guidelines and questions about our articles, please contact the editorial department at tmaedit@artnews.com; you need JavaScript enabled to view it." Length: 2,850-3,500 words. **Pays $250-500.** Pays expenses of writers on assignment.

💲💲💲💲 METROPOLIS

Bellerophon Publications, 205 Lexington Ave., 17th Floor, New York NY 10016. (212)627-9977. **Fax:** (212)627-9988. **E-mail:** edit@metropolismag.com. **Website:** www.metropolismag.com. **Contact:** Claire Barliant, managing editor. **80% freelance written.** Monthly magazine (combined issue July/August) for consumers interested in architecture and design. "*Metropolis* examines contemporary life through design—architecture, interior design, product design, graphic design, crafts, planning, and preservation. Subjects range from the sprawling urban environment to intimate living spaces to small objects of everyday use. In looking for why design happens in a certain way, *Metropolis* explores the economic, environmental, social, cultural, political, and technological context. With its innovative graphic presentation and its provocative voice, *Metropolis* shows how richly designed our world can be." Estab. 1981. Circ. 45,000. Byline given. Pays 60-90 days after acceptance. No kill fee. Publishes ms an average of 3 months after acceptance. Submit seasonal material 3 months in advance. Accepts queries by e-mail. Accepts simultaneous submissions. Responds in 8 months to queries. Sample copy: $7. Guidelines available online.

NONFICTION Needs essays, interview. No profiles on individual architectural practices, information from public relations firms, or fine arts. **Buys 30 mss/year.** Send query via e-mail; no mss. "Describe your idea and why it would be good for our magazine. Be concise, specific, and clear. Also, please include clips or links to a few of your recent stories. The ideal *Metropolis* story is based on strong reporting and includes an examination of current critical issues. A design firm's newest work isn't a story, but the issues that its work brings to light might be." Length: 1,500-4,000 words. **Pays $1,500-4,000.** Pays expenses of writers on assignment.

COLUMNS The Metropolis Observed (architecture, design, and city planning news features), 100-1,200 words, pays $100-1,200; Perspective (opinion or personal observation of architecture and design), 1,200 words, pays $1,200; Enterprise (the business/development of architecture and design), 1,500 words, pays $1,500; In Review (architecture and book review essays), 1,500 words, pays $1,500. **Buys 40 mss/year.** Query with published clips.

💲💲 UNIQUE HOMES

Network Communications, Inc., 327 Wall St., Princeton NJ 08540. (609)688-1110. **Fax:** (609)688-0201. **Website:** www.uniquehomes.com. **30% freelance written.** Bimonthly magazine covering luxury real estate for consumers and the high-end real estate industry. Our focus is the luxury real estate market, i.e., the business of buying and selling luxury homes, as well as regional real estate market trends. Byline given. Pays on publication. No kill fee. Publishes ms an average of 3 months after acceptance. Editorial lead time 4 months. Submit seasonal material 4 months in advance. Accepts queries by mail, e-mail, fax. Accepts simultaneous submissions. Responds in 1 month to queries. Responds in 4 months to mss. Sample copy available online.

NONFICTION Special issues: Golf Course Living; Resort Living; Ski Real Estate; Farms, Ranches and Country Estates; Waterfront Homes; International Homes. **Buys 36 mss/year.** Query with published clips and résumé. Length: 500-1,500 words. **Pays $150-500.** Pays expenses of writers on assignment.

ASSOCIATIONS

💲💲💲 AMERICAN EDUCATOR

American Federation of Teachers, 555 New Jersey Ave. NW, Washington DC 20001. **E-mail:** ae@aft.org. **Website:** www.aft.org/ae. **Contact:** Amy Hightower, editor. **5% freelance written.** Quarterly magazine covering education, condition of children, and labor issues. *American Educator*, the quaterly magazine of the American Federation of Teachers, reaches over 900,000 public school teachers, higher education faculty, and education researchers and policymakers. The magazine concentrates on significant ideas and practices in education, civics, and the condition of children in America and around the world. Estab. 1977. Circ. 900,000. Byline given. Pays on publication. Offers 50% kill fee. Publishes ms an average of 2-6 months after acceptance. Editorial lead time 1 year. Submit seasonal material 6 months in advance. Accepts queries by mail, e-mail. Accepts simultaneous submissions. Responds in 2 months to queries. Responds in 6 months to mss. Sample copy and guidelines online.

NONFICTION Needs book excerpts, essays, historical, interview, discussions of educational research. No pieces that are not supportive of the public schools. **Buys 8 mss/year.** Query with published clips. Length: 1,000-7,000 words. **Pays $750-3,000 for assigned articles. Pays $300-1,000 for unsolicited articles.** Pays expenses of writers on assignment.

$$ BUGLE

Rocky Mountain Elk Foundation, 5705 Grant Creek, Missoula MT 59808. (406)523-4500. **Fax:** (800)225-5355. **E-mail:** bugle@rmef.org. **E-mail:** conservationeditor@rmef.org; huntingeditor@rmef.org; assistanteditor@rmef.org; photos@rmef.org. **Website:** www.rmef.org. **50% freelance.** *Bugle* is the membership publication of the Rocky Mountain Elk Foundation, a nonprofit wildlife conservation group. "Our readers are predominantly hunters, many of them conservationists who care deeply about protecting wildlife habitat." Bimonthly. Magazine: 114-212 pages; 55 lb. Escanaba paper; 80 lb. Steriling cover, b&w, 4-color illustrations; photos. Estab. 1984. Circ. 225,000. Byline given. Pays on acceptance. Kill fee. 3-9 months between acceptance and publication. Accepts queries by mail, e-mail. Accepts simultaneous submissions. Responds in 1 month to queries; 3 months to mss. Sample copy for $5. Guidelines online.

NONFICTION Needs essays, personal experience. Special issues: July/August Bowhunting section. Query or submit complete ms to appropriate e-mail address; see website for guidelines. Length: 750-5,000 words, depending on type of piece. **Pays 30¢/word and 3 contributor's copies.**

FICTION "We accept fiction and nonfiction stories pertaining in some way to elk, other wildlife, hunting, habitat conservation, and related issues. We would like to see more humor." Needs adventure, historical, humorous, novel excerpts, slice-of-life vignettes, western, children's/juvenile, satire, human interest, natural history, conservation—as long as they related to elk. Query or submit complete ms to appropriate e-mail address; see website for guidelines. Length: 1,500-5,000 words; average length: 2,500 words. **Pays 30¢/word and 3 contributor's copies.**

$$ DAC NEWS

Detroit Athletic Club, 241 Madison Ave., Detroit MI 48226. (313)442-1034. **Fax:** (313)442-1047. **E-mail:** kenv@thedac.com. **Website:** www.thedac.com. **20% freelance written.** *DAC News* is the magazine for Detroit Athletic Club members. It covers club news and events, plus general interest features. Published 10 times/year. Estab. 1916. Circ. 5,000. Byline given. Pays on publication. No kill fee. Publishes ms an average of 3 months after acceptance. Editorial lead time 3 months. Submit seasonal material 3 months in advance. Accepts queries by mail, phone. Responds in 1 month to queries. Sample copy free.

NONFICTION Needs general interest, historical, photo feature. "No politics or social issues—this is an entertainment magazine. We do not acccept unsolicited mss or queries for travel articles." **Buys 2-3 mss/year.** Length: 1,000-2,000 words. **Pays $100-500.** Sometimes pays expenses of writers on assignment.

$$$ DATA CENTER MANAGEMENT

AFCOM, 742 E. Chapman Ave., Orange CA 92866. **Fax:** (714)997-9743. **E-mail:** afcom@afcom.com; jmoore@afcom.com. **Website:** www.afcom.com. **Contact:** Karen Riccio, managing editor. **50% freelance written.** Bimonthly magazine covering data center management. *Data Center Management* is the slick, 4-color, bimonthly publication for members of AFCOM, the leading association for data center management. Estab. 1988. Circ. 4,000 worldwide. Byline given. Pays on acceptance for assigned articles and on publication for unsolicited articles. Offers up to 10% kill fee. Publishes ms an average of 3 months after acceptance. Editorial lead time 6-12 months. Submit seasonal material 6 months in advance. Accepts queries by e-mail. Accepts simultaneous submissions. Responds in 1-3 weeks to queries; in 1-3 months to mss. Guidelines available online.

NONFICTION Needs how-to. Special issues: The January/February issue is the annual 'Emerging Technologies' issue. Articles for this issue are visionary and product neutral. No product reviews or general tech articles. **Buys 15+ mss/year.** Query with published clips. Length: up to 2,000 word. **Pays 50¢/word minimum, based on writer's expertise.** Pays expenses of writers on assignment.

🐘🐘 THE ELKS MAGAZINE

425 W. Diversey Pkwy., Chicago IL 60614. (773)755-4900. **E-mail:** magnews@elks.org. **Website:** www.elks.org/elksmag. **Contact:** John P. Sheridan, managing editor. **25% freelance written.** Magazine covers nonfiction only; published 10 times/year with basic mission of being the voice of the elks. All fraternal is written in-house. Estab. 1922. Circ. 800,000. Pays on acceptance. No kill fee. Accepts queries by mail, e-mail. Responds in 1 month with a yes/no on ms purchase. Guidelines available online.

NONFICTION Needs general interest, historical, travel. No fiction, religion, controversial issues, first-person, fillers, or verse. **Buys 20-30 mss/year.** Send complete ms. Length: 1,500-2,000 words. **Pays 25¢/word.** Pays expenses of writers on assignment.

🐘🐘 HUMANITIES

National Endowment for the Humanities, 1100 Pennsylvania Ave. NW, Washington DC 20506. (202)606-8435. **Fax:** (202)606-8451. **E-mail:** dskinner@neh.gov; info@neh.gov. **Website:** www.neh.gov/humanities. **Contact:** David Skinner, editor. **50% freelance written.** Bimonthly magazine covering news in the humanities focused on projects that receive financial support from the agency. Estab. 1980. Circ. 7,500. Byline given. Pays on publication. Publishes ms an average of 2 months after acceptance. Editorial lead time 3 months. Submit seasonal material 4 months in advance. Accepts queries by mail, e-mail, fax, phone. Sample copy available online.

NONFICTION Needs book excerpts, historical, interview, photo feature. **Buys 25 mss/year.** Query with published clips. Length: 400-2,500 words. **Pays $300-600.** Sometimes pays expenses of writers on assignment.

COLUMNS In Focus (directors of state humanities councils), 700 words; Breakout (special activities of state humanities councils), 750 words. **Buys 12 mss/year.** Query with published clips. **Pays $300.**

🐘🐘🐘🐘 LION

Lions Clubs International, 300 W. 22nd St., Oak Brook IL 60523-8842. (630)468-6909. **Fax:** (630)571-1685. **E-mail:** magazine@lionsclubs.org. **Website:** www.lionsclubs.org. **Contact:** Jay Copp, senior editor. **35% freelance written. Works with a small number of new/unpublished writers each year.** Monthly magazine covering service club organization for Lions Club members and their families. Estab. 1918. Circ. 350,000. Byline given. Pays on acceptance. No kill fee. Publishes ms an average of 5 months after acceptance. Accepts queries by mail, e-mail, fax, phone. Accepts simultaneous submissions. Responds in 1 month to queries. Sample copy and writer's guidelines free.

NONFICTION Needs photo feature. No travel, biography, or personal experiences. **Buys 40 mss/year.** "Article length should not exceed 2,000 words, and is subject to editing. No gags, fillers, quizzes or poems are accepted. Photos must be color prints or sent digitally. *LION* magazine pays upon acceptance of material. Advance queries save your time and ours. Address all submissions to Jay Copp, senior editor, by mail or e-mail text and .tif or .jpg (300 dpi) photos." Length: 500-2,000 words. **Pays $100-$1,500.** Pays expenses of writers on assignment.

🐘🐘 NEW MOBILITY

United Spinal Association, 120-34 Queens Blvd., #320, Kew Gardens NY 11415. (718)803-3782. **E-mail:** tgilmer@unitedspinal.org; jbyzek@unitedspinal.org. **Website:** www.spinalcord.org/. **Contact:** Tim Gilmer, editor; Josie Byzek, managing editor. **50% freelance written.** Bimonthly magazine covering living with spinal cord injury/disorder (SCI/D). The bimonthly membership magazine for the National Spinal Cord Injury Association, a program of United Spinal Association. Members include people with spinal cord injury or disorder, as well as caregivers, parents, and some spinal cord injury/disorder professionals. All articles should reflect this common interest of the audience. Assume that your audience is better educated in the subject of spinal cord injury than average, but be careful not to be too technical. Each issue has a theme (available from editor) that unites features in addition to a series of departments focused on building community and providing solutions for the SCI/D community. Articles that feature members, chapters or the organization are preferred, but any article that deals with issue pertinent to SCI/D community will be considered. Estab. 2011. Circ. 35,000. Byline given. Pays on publication. No kill fee. Publishes ms an average of 1-2 months after acceptance. Accepts queries by e-mail. Accepts simultaneous submissions. Sample copy and guidelines available on website.

NONFICTION Needs essays, general interest, how-to, humor, interview, new product, personal experience, photo feature, travel, medical research. Does not want "articles that treat disabilities as an affliction or cause for pity, or that show the writer does not get that people with disabilities are people like anyone else. We aren't interested in 'courageous' or 'inspiring' tales of 'overcoming disability.'" **Buys 36 mss/year.** Query. Length: 800-1,600 words. **Pays 15¢/word for new writers.** Pays expenses of writers on assignment.

COLUMNS Travel (report on access of a single travel destination based on conversations with disabled travelers), Access (hands-on look at how to improve access for a specific type of area), Ask Anything (tap members and experts to answer community question relating to life w/SCI/D), Advocacy (investigation of ongoing advocacy issue related to SCI/D). **Buys 40 mss/year.** Length: 800 words. Query with published clips. **Pays 15¢/word for new writers.**

🟢🟢 PENN LINES

Pennsylvania Rural Electric Association, P.O. Box 1266, Harrisburg PA 17108. **E-mail:** editor@prea.com. **Website:** www.prea.com/content/pennlines.asp. Monthly magazine covering rural life in Pennsylvania. News magazine of Pennsylvania electric cooperatives. Features should be balanced, and they should have a rural focus. Electric cooperative sources (such as consumers) should be used. Estab. 1966. Circ. 165,000. Byline given. Pays on publication. No kill fee. Publishes ms an average of 3 months after acceptance. Editorial lead time 4 months. Submit seasonal material 4 months in advance. Accepts queries by mail, e-mail. Accepts simultaneous submissions. Sample copy available online.

NONFICTION Needs general interest, historical, how-to, interview. Query or send complete ms. Length: 500-2,000 words. **Negotiates payment individually.**

🟢🟢🟢 SCOUTING

Boy Scouts of America, 1325 W. Walnut Hill Lane, P.O. Box 152079, Irving TX 75015-2079. **Website:** www.scoutingmagazine.org. **80% freelance written.** Magazine published 6 times/year covering Scout-ing activities for adult leaders of the Boy Scouts, Cub Scouts, and Venturing. Estab. 1913. Circ. 1 million. Byline given. Pays on acceptance for major features and some shorter features. Publishes ms an average of 18 months after acceptance. Editorial lead time 1 year. Submit seasonal material 1 year in advance. Accepts queries by mail. Accepts simultaneous submissions. Responds in 3 weeks to queries; in 2 months to mss. Sample copy: $2.50 and 9x12 SAE with 4 first-class stamps, or online.

NONFICTION Needs inspirational, interview. **Buys 20-30 mss/year.** Query with SASE. Length: short features, 500-700 words; some longer features, up to 1,200 words, usually the result of a definite assignment to a professional writer. **Pays $650-800 for major articles, $300-500 for shorter features. Rates depend on professional quality of article.** Pays expenses of writers on assignment.

REPRINTS Send photocopy of article and information about when and where the article previously appeared. First-person accounts of meaningful Scouting experiences (previously published in local newspapers, etc.) are a popular subject.

COLUMNS Way It Was (Scouting history), 600-750 words; Family Talk (family, raising kids, etc.), 600-750 words. **Buys 8-12 mss/year.** Query. **Pays $300-500.**

FILLERS Limited to personal accounts of humorous or inspirational Scouting experiences. Needs anecdotes, short humor. **Buys 15-25 mss/year.** Length: 50-150 words. **Pays $25 on publication.**

🟢🟢🟢 TEXAS CO-OP POWER

Texas Electric Cooperatives, Inc., 1122 Colorado St., 24th Floor, Austin TX 78701. (512)486-6243. **E-mail:** clohrmann@texas-ec.org; twidlowski@texas-ec.org. **Website:** www.texascooppower.com. **Contact:** Charles Lohrmann, editor; Tom Widlowski, associate editor. **75% freelance written.** Monthly magazine covering Texas life, travel destinations, people, history and general culture as well as some issue-oriented content both in print and online. *Texas Co-op Power* delivers top-notch writing and photography in features on Texas travel, history, food and culture to more than 1.5 million households and businesses. *Texas Co-op Power* enhances the quality of life of electric co-op member-customers in a well-designed and engaging format, both in print and online. Estab. 1948. Circ. 1.54 million. Byline given. Pays upon final acceptance. Kill fee is negotiated separately. Publishes ms an average of 6 months after acceptance. Editorial lead time 6-12 months. Submit seasonal material 6 months in advance. Accepts queries by e-mail, online submission form. Accepts simultaneous submissions. Responds in 1 month to queries. Responds in 3 months to mss. Magazine content is available online. No sample copies mailed. Guidelines online.

NONFICTION Needs book excerpts, essays, general interest, historical, how-to, humor, inspirational, interview, memoir, personal experience, profile, travel. **Buys 30 mss/year.** Read and review magazine content online at texascooppower.com. Query via e-mail with published clips.Do not query if unfamiliar with magazine content, Texas topics or if seeking general assignments. Length: 800-1,400 words. **Pays $300-1,200.**

💲💲 TOASTMASTER

Toastmasters International, P.O. Box 9052, Mission Viejo CA 92690. 949-858-8255. **E-mail:** submissions@toastmasters.org. **Website:** www.toastmasters.org. **Contact:** submissions@toastmasters.org. **50% freelance written.** Monthly magazine covers public speaking, leadership, communication and club-related topics. The monthly Toastmaster magazine is distributed to members of Toastmasters International, a nonprofit organization and world leader in communication and leadership development. The publications team prizes article originality, depth of research, timeliness, and excellence of expression. Unsolicited article queries and photos are accepted via email. All accepted articles are subject to editing for length and/or clarity. Articles and photos may be published in print and digital versions. Estab. 1924. Circ. 345,000 members in more than 15,800 clubs in 142 countries. Byline given. Pays upon acceptance. No kill fee. Submit seasonal material 3-4 months in advance. Accepts queries by e-mail, online submission form. Accepts simultaneous submissions. Guidelines available at www.toastmasters.org/Submissions. Please refer to the submissions guidelines on the Toastmasters website first, and then submit your query via email to submissions@toastmasters.org. Tip: We highly recommend that you review several issues of the Toastmaster magazine before submitting a query.

NONFICTION Needs how-to, humor, interview, profile, communications, leadership, language use. Articles with political or religious slants or sexist or nationalist language will not be accepted. **Buys 50 mss/year.** Need: Leadership and communication

"How To …" articles, expert advice and tips for public speakers, impromptu speaking, humorous speeches, persuasive speeches, storytelling, and cross-cultural communication. Profiles of prominent international speakers and leaders relative to an international audience. Length: 650-1,800 words. **Compensation for accepted articles (word count: 650–1,800) is $200–$650, and is based on readability, thoroughness of the research performed, compliance with submissions guidelines, and the article's value to the publications team and to members of Toastmasters.**

💲 TRAIL & TIMBERLINE

The Colorado Mountain Club, 710 Tenth St., Suite 200, Golden CO 80401. (303)279-3080. **E-mail:** editor@cmc.org. **Website:** www.cmc.org/about/newsroom/trailandtimberline.aspx. **Contact:** editor. **80% freelance written.** Official quarterly publication for the Colorado Mountain Club. "Articles in *Trail & Timberline* conform to the mission statement of the Colorado Mountain Club to unite the energy, interest, and knowledge of lovers of the Colorado mountains, to collect and disseminate information 'regarding the Colorado mountains in the areas of art, science, literature, and recreation,' to stimulate public interest, and to encourage preservation of the mountains of Colorado and the Rocky Mountain region." Estab. 1918. Circ. 10,500. Byline given. Pays on acceptance. No kill fee. Publishes ms an average of 2 months after acceptance. Editorial lead time 6 months. Submit seasonal material 6 months in advance. Accepts queries by mail, e-mail. Accepts simultaneous submissions. Responds in 1 week to queries.; in 1 month to mss. Sample copy: online, or $3 plus catalog-sized SASE. Make checks payable to CMC. Guidelines online.

NONFICTION Needs essays, humor, opinion, personal experience, photo feature, travel. **Buys 10-15 mss/year.** Send complete ms. Length: 500-2,000 words. **Pays $50.** Pays expenses of writers on assignment.

💲💲💲 VFW MAGAZINE

Veterans of Foreign Wars of the United States, 406 W. 34th St., Kansas City MO 64111. (816)756-3390. **Fax:** (816)968-1169. **E-mail:** kwilliams@vfw.org; magazine@vfw.org. **Website:** www.vfwmagazine.org. **Contact:** Kari Williams, editorial associate. **40% freelance written.** Monthly magazine on veterans' affairs, military history, patriotism, defense, and current events. *VFW Magazine* goes to its members worldwide, all having served honorably in the armed forces overseas from World War II through the Iraq and Afghanistan Wars. Estab. 1904. Circ. 1.3 million. Byline given. Pays on acceptance. Offers 50% kill fee. Publishes ms 3-6 months after acceptance. Editorial lead time is 6 months. Submit seasonal material 6 months in advance. Accepts queries by mail, e-mail, fax. Accepts simultaneous submissions. Responds in 2 months to queries. Sample copy for 9x12 SAE with 5 first-class stamps. Guidelines available online.

NONFICTION Needs general interest, historical, inspirational. **Buys 25-30 mss/year.** Query with two-sentence outline, résumé, and published clips. Do not send unsolicited mss. Length: 1,000 words. **Pays up to $500-1,000 maximum for assigned articles; $500-750 maximum for unsolicited articles.** Pays expenses of writers on assignment.

ASTROLOGY & NEW AGE

🌀 FATE MAGAZINE

Fate Magazine, Inc., P.O. Box 460, Lakeville MN 55044. (952)431-2050. **E-mail:** fate@fatemag.com. **Website:** www.fatemag.com. **Contact:** Phyllis Galde, editor in chief. **75% freelance written.** Covers the paranormal, ghosts, UFOs, strange science. "Reports a wide variety of strange and unknown phenomena. We are open to receiving any well-written, well-documented article. Our readers especially like reports of current investigations, experiments, theories, and experiences." Estab. 1948. Circ. 15,000. Byline given. Pays after publication. Publishes ms 3-6 months after acceptance. Editorial lead time 3-6 months. Accepts queries by mail, e-mail. Accepts simultaneous submissions. Responds in 1-3 months to queries. Sample copy available for free online, by e-mail. Guidelines available online.

NONFICTION Needs general interest, historical, how-to, personal experience, photo feature, technical. "We do not publish poetry, fiction, editorial/opinion pieces, or book-length mss." **Buys 100 mss/year.** Submit complete ms by e-mail or on CD accompanied by hard copy. Length: 1,500-3,000 words. **Pays $50.** Pays expenses of writers on assignment. Pays with merchandise or ad space if requested.

COLUMNS True Mystic Experiences (short reader-submitted stories of strange experiences); My Proof of Survival (short reader-submitted stories of proof of life after death), up to 500 words. Submit complete ms by e-mail or on CD accompanied by hard copy. **Pays $10.**

FILLERS Fillers are especially welcomed and must be fully authenticated. Needs anecdotes and facts. Length: 150-500 words. **Pays $10.**

🌀 WHOLE LIFE TIMES

Whole Life Media, LLC, 23705 Vanowen St., #306, West Hills CA 91307. (877)807-2599. **Fax:** (310)933-1693. **E-mail:** editor@wholelifemagazine.com. **Website:** www.wholelifemagazine.com. Bimonthly regional glossy on holistic living. *Whole Life Times* relies almost entirely on freelance material. Open to stories on natural health, alternative healing, green living, sustainable and local food, social responsibility, conscious business, the environment, spirituality and personal growth—anything relevant to a progressive, healthy lifestyle. Estab. 1978. Circ. 40,000 (print); 5,000 (digital). Byline given. Pays within 30-45 days of publication. 50% kill fee on assigned stories. No kill fee to first-time *WLT* writers or for unsolicited submissions. Publishes ms 2-4 months after acceptance. Accepts simultaneous submissions. Sample copy and writer's guidelines available online.

NONFICTION Special issues: Special issues include: Healing Arts, Food and Nutrition, Spirituality, New Beginnings, Relationships, Longevity, Arts/Cultures Travel, Vitamins and Supplements, Women's Issues, Sexuality, Science and Metaphysics, Eco Lifestyle. **Buys 60 mss/year.** Send complete ms. Submissions are accepted via e-mail. Artwork should also be sent via e-mail as hard copies will not be returned. "Queries should be professionally written and show an awareness of our style and current topics of interest in our subject area. We welcome investigative reporting and are happy to see queries that address topics in a political context. We are especially looking for articles on health and nutrition. No regular columns sought. Submissions should be double-spaced in AP style as an attached unformatted MS Word file (.docx). If you do not have Microsoft Word and must e-mail in another program, please also copy and paste your story in the message section of your e-mail." **Payment varies. "WLT accepts up to 3 longer stories (800-1,100 words) per issue, and pay ranges from $100-175 depending on topic, research required, and writer experience. In addition, we have a number**

of regular departments that pay $35-150 depending on topic, length, research required, and writer experience. We pay by invoice, so please be sure to submit one and to name the file with your name." Pays expenses of writers on assignment.

REPRINTS Rarely publishes reprints.

COLUMNS Local News, Taste of Health (food), Yoga & Spirit, Whole Living, Success Track, Art & Soul (media reviews). Length: 600-750 words. Send complete ms or well-developed query and links to previously published work. Submissions are accepted via e-mail. Artwork should also be sent via e-mail as hard copies will not be returned. **"City of Angels is our FOB section featuring short, newsy blurbs on our coverage topics, generally in the context of Los Angeles. These are generally 350-450 words and pay $25-35 depending on length and topic. This is a great section for writers who are new to us. Back-Words is a 650-word personal essay that often highlights a seminal moment or event in the life of the writer and pays $100. We pay by invoice, so please be sure to submit one, and name the file with your name."**

AUTOMOTIVE & MOTORCYCLE

💲 AMERICAN MOTORCYCLIST

American Motorcyclist Association, 13515 Yarmouth Dr., Pickerington OH 43147. (614)856-1900. **E-mail:** submissions@ama-cycle.org. **Website:** www.americanmotorcyclist.com. **Contact:** Grant Parsons, director of communications; James Holter, managing editor. **25% freelance written.** Monthly magazine for enthusiastic motorcyclists investing considerable time and money in the sport, emphasizing the motorcyclist, not the vehicle. Monthly magazine of the American Motorcyclist Association. Emphasizes people involved in, and events dealing with, all aspects of motorcycling. Readers are "enthusiastic motorcyclists, investing considerable time in road riding or all aspects of the sport." Estab. 1947. Circ. 200,000. Byline given. Pays on publication. No kill fee. Editorial lead time 3 months. Submit seasonal material 4 months in advance. Accepts queries by mail, e-mail. Accepts simultaneous submissions. Responds in 5 weeks to queries. Responds in 6 weeks to mss. Sample copy for $1.50. Guidelines free.

NONFICTION Needs interview, personal experience, travel. **Buys 8 mss/year.** Send complete ms. Length: 1,000-2,500 words. **Pays minimum $8/published column inch.** Pays expenses of writers on assignment.

💲💲💲💲 AUTOWEEK

Crain Communications, Inc., 1155 Gratiot Ave., Detroit MI 48207. (313)446-6000. **Fax:** (313)446-1027. **E-mail:** awletter@autoweek.com. **Website:** www.autoweek.com. Editor: Wes Raynal. **5% freelance written, most by regular contributors.** *AutoWeek* is a biweekly magazine for auto enthusiasts. Estab. 1958. Circ. 300,000. Byline given. Pays on publication. Publishes ms an average of 1 month after acceptance. Accepts queries by e-mail. Accepts simultaneous submissions.

NONFICTION Needs historical, interview. **Buys 5 mss/year.** Query. Length: 100-400 words. **Pays $1/word.** Pays expenses of writers on assignment.

♻💲💲💲 CANADIAN BIKER MAGAZINE

108-2220 Sooke Rd., Victoria BC V9B 0G9 Canada. (250)384-0333. **Website:** www.canadianbiker.com. **Contact:** John Campbell, editor. **65% freelance written.** Magazine covering motorcycling. Estab. 1980. Circ. 20,000. Byline given. Publishes ms an average of 1 year after acceptance. Editorial lead time 3 months. Accepts queries by mail. Accepts simultaneous submissions. Responds in 6 weeks to queries; in 6 months to mss.

NONFICTION Needs general interest, historical, how-to, interview, new product, technical, travel. **Buys 12 mss/year.** Query. Length: 500-1,500 words. **Pays $100-200 for assigned articles. Pays $80-150 for unsolicited articles.** Pays expenses of writers on assignment.

CAR AND DRIVER

Hearst Communications, Inc., 1585 Eisenhower Place, Ann Arbor MI 48108. **E-mail:** editors@caranddriver.com. **Website:** www.caranddriver.com. **Contact:** Eddie Alterman, editor in chief; Mike Fazioli, managing editor. Monthly magazine for auto enthusiasts; readers are college-educated, professional, median 24-35 years of age. Estab. 1956. Circ. 1,212,555. Byline given. Pays on acceptance. Offers 25% kill fee. Accepts queries by mail, e-mail. Accepts simultaneous submissions. Responds in 2 months to queries.

NONFICTION Query with published clips before submitting. Pays expenses of writers on assignment.

⊘ CAR CRAFT

The Enthusiast Network, 831 S. Douglas St., El Segundo CA 90245. (310)531-9900. **E-mail:** inquiries@automotive.com. **Website:** www.hotrod.com/car-craft-magazine. Monthly magazine. Created to appeal to drag racing and high performance auto owners. Circ. 383,334. No kill fee. Editorial lead time 3 months. Accepts simultaneous submissions.

$$ CLASSIC TRUCKS

Primedia/McMullen Argus Publishing, 1733 Alton Parkway, Irvine CA 92606. **E-mail:** inquiries@automotive.com. **Website:** www.classictrucks.com. Monthly magazine covering classic trucks from the 1930s to 1973. Estab. 1994. Circ. 60,000. Byline given. Pays on publication. Editorial lead time 4 months. Submit seasonal material 4 months in advance. Guidelines free.

NONFICTION Needs how-to, interview, new product, technical, travel. Query. Length: 1,500-5,000 words. **Pays $75-200/page. Pays $100/page maximum for unsolicited articles.**

COLUMNS **Buys 24 mss/year.** Query.

$$$ FOUR WHEELER MAGAZINE

831 S. Douglas Street, El Segundo CA 90245. **Website:** www.fourwheeler.com. **20% freelance written. Works with a small number of new/unpublished writers each year.** Monthly magazine covering four-wheel-drive vehicles, back-country driving, competition, and travel adventure. Estab. 1963. Circ. 355,466. Pays on publication. No kill fee. Publishes ms an average of 4 months after acceptance. Submit seasonal material 4 months in advance. Accepts queries by mail.

NONFICTION Query with photos. 1,200-2,000 words; average 4-5 pages when published. **Pays $200-300/feature vehicles; $350-600/travel and adventure; $100-800/technical articles.**

⊘$$ FRICTION ZONE

44489 Town Center Way, Suite D497, Palm Desert CA 92260. (951)751-0442. **E-mail:** amy@friction-zone.com. **Website:** www.friction-zone.com. **60% freelance written.** Monthly magazine covering motorcycles. Estab. 1999. Circ. 26,000. Byline given. Pays on publication. No kill fee. Publishes ms an average of 1 month after acceptance. Editorial lead time 6 weeks. Submit seasonal material 2 months in advance. Responds in to queries. Sample copy for $4.50 or on website.

NONFICTION Needs general interest, historical, how-to, humor, inspirational, interview, new product, opinion, photo feature, technical, travel, medical (relating to motorcyclists), book reviews (relating to motorcyclists). Does not accept first-person writing. **Buys 1 mss/year.** Query. Length: 1,000-3,000 words. **Pays 20¢/word.** Sometimes pays expenses of writers on assignment.

COLUMNS Health Zone (health issues relating to motorcyclists); Motorcycle Engines 101 (basic motorcycle mechanics); Road Trip (California destination review including hotel, road, restaurant), all 2,000 words. **Buys 60 mss/year.** Query. **Pays 20¢/word**

FICTION We want stories concerning motorcycling or motorcyclists. No 'first-person' fiction. Query. Length: 1,000-2,000 words. **Pays 20¢/word.**

FILLERS Needs anecdotes, facts, gags, newsbreaks, short humor. Length: 2,000-3,000 words. **Pays 20¢/word.**

$$ HIGHROADS

AAA Arizona, 2375 E. Camelback Rd., Suite 500, Phoenix AZ 85016. (602)650-2732. **Fax:** (602)241-2917. **E-mail:** highroads@arizona.aaa.com. **Website:** highroads.az.aaa.com. **50% freelance written.** *Highroads*, the AAA Arizona member magazine, offers inspiring travel articles about destinations throughout Arizona and around the world, automotive news and reviews, and educational resources on insurance and finance. The print edition is published bimonthly and has been honored for writing and design with Communicator Awards, Davey Awards, and Maggie Awards. Byline given. Pays on publication. Offers 30% kill fee. Editorial lead time 1 year. Submit seasonal material 6 months in advance. Accepts queries by e-mail. Accepts simultaneous submissions. Sample copy available online. Guidelines available online.

NONFICTION Needs reviews, travel. Does not want fiction, humor, poetry, or pitches for new columns. **Buys 21 mss/year.** Query with published clips. Length: 1,200 words. **Pays 25-40¢/word.** Pays expenses of writers on assignment.

COLUMNS Weekender (a short getaway you can travel to from Arizona), 400 words; Road Trip (driving directions about attractions along a specific stretch of road reachable from Arizona), 800 words; Talk of the Town (an Arizona town with a unique hidden attraction), 400 words. **Buys 10 mss/year. Pays 25-40¢/word.**

❻❺ KEYSTONE MOTORCYCLE PRESS

Blue Moon Publications, P.O. Box 296, Ambridge PA 15003-0296. (724)774-6542. **65% freelance written.** Monthly tabloid covering motorcycling. "Our publication is geared toward all motorcyclists & primarily focuses on people & events in the great PA region; hence it is named after the Keystone State. The KMP features product reviews, motorcycle tests, industry news, motorcycling personalities, book reviews, and coverage of major national events." Estab. 1988. Circ. 15,000, plus 2,000 samples and free copies per month. Byline given. Pays on publication. Offers kill fee. varies Publishes ms an average of 2 months after acceptance. Editorial lead time 1-2 months. Submit seasonal material 3 months in advance. Accepts queries by mail, e-mail. Accepts simultaneous submissions. Responds in 2 weeks to queries. Responds in 1 month to mss. Sample copy free. Guidelines by e-mail.

NONFICTION Needs book excerpts, general interest, historical, how-to, humor, inspirational, interview, new product, opinion, religious, (All must relate to motorcycling.). "We do not want personal diatribes. Witty, okay; pointless is not." **Buys 8 mss/year.** Query with published clips. Length: 250-1,500 words. Pays expenses of writers on assignment.

COLUMNS Contact: Dan Faingnaert. All Things Considered (Various news clips), 70 words; New Products (Short summaries of new products available), 120 words. **Buys 18 mss/yr. mss/year.** Query with published clips. **Pays $20-$200.**

FICTION Buys 2 mss/year. Query with published clips. Length: 500-2,500 words. Payment **varies-negotiable.**

POETRY Needs free verse, haiku, light verse, traditional.

FILLERS Needs anecdotes, facts, gags, newsbreaks, short humor. **Buys 18/yr. mss/year.** Word length variable. **Payment variable.**

❻❺ RIDER MAGAZINE

1227 Flynn Rd., Ste. 304, Camarillo CA 93010. (805)987-5500. **Website:** www.ridermagazine.com. **60% freelance written.** Monthly magazine covering motorcycling. *Rider* serves the all-brand motorcycle lifestyle/enthusiast with a slant toward travel and touring. Estab. 1974. Circ. 135,000. Byline given.

Pays on publication. Publishes ms an average of 6-18 months after acceptance. Editorial lead time 3 months. Submit seasonal material 6 months in advance. Accepts queries by mail, e-mail. Responds in 2 months to queries. Sample copy: $2.95. Guidelines on website.

NONFICTION Needs general interest, historical, how-to, humor, interview, personal experience, travel. Does not want to see fiction or "How I Began Motorcycling" articles. **Buys 40-50 mss/year.** Query. Length: 750-1,800 words. **Pays $150-750.**

COLUMNS Favorite Rides (short trip), 850-1,000 words. **Buys 12 mss/year mss/year.** Query. **Pays $150-750.**

❻❺ ROADBIKE

TAM Communications, 1010 Summer St., Stamford CT 06905. (203)425-8777. **Fax:** (203)425-8775. **E-mail:** info@roadbikemag.com. **Website:** www.roadbikemag.com. **40% freelance written.** Monthly magazine covering motorcycling tours, project and custom bikes, products, news, and tech. Estab. 1993. Circ. 50,000. Byline given. Pays on publication. No kill fee. Publishes ms an average of 6 months after acceptance. Editorial lead time 4 months. Submit seasonal material 6 months in advance. Accepts queries by mail, e-mail, fax, online submission form. Guidelines free.

NONFICTION Needs how-to, motorcycle tech, travel, camping, interview, motorcycle related, new product, photo feature, motorcycle events or gathering places with maximum of 1,000 words text, travel. No fiction. **Buys 100 mss/year.** Send complete ms. Length: 1,000-2,500 words. **Pays $15-400.**

FILLERS Needs facts.

❻❺ ROAD KING

Parthenon Publishing, 102 Woodmount Blvd., Suite 450, Nashville TN 37205. **Website:** www.roadking.com. **25% freelance written.** Bimonthly magazine covering the trucking industry. Byline given. Pays 3 weeks from acceptance. Offers 30% kill fee. Publishes ms an average of 3 months after acceptance. Editorial lead time 3-4 months. Submit seasonal material 4 months in advance. Accepts queries by mail. Accepts simultaneous submissions. Responds in 3-4 weeks to queries. Sample copy for #10 SASE. Guidelines free.

NONFICTION No essays, no humor, no cartoons. **Buys 12 mss/year.** Query with published clips. Length: 100-1,000 words. **Pays $50-500.**

💲 TRUCKIN' MAGAZINE

Source Interlink Media, Inc., 1733 Alton Parkway, Irvine CA 92606. **E-mail:** inquiries@automotive.com. **Website:** www.truckinweb.com. Monthly magazine. Written for pickup drivers and enthusiasts. Circ. 186,606. No kill fee. Editorial lead time 3 months. **NONFICTION** Query first. Submit through mail.

TRUCK TREND

Primedia, 831 S. Douglas Street, El Segundo CA 90245. **Website:** www.trucktrend.com. **60% freelance written.** Bimonthly magazine covering light trucks, SUVs, minivans, vans, and travel. *Truck Trend* readers want to know about what's new in the world of sport-utilities, pickups, and vans. What to buy, how to fix up, and where to go. Estab. 1998. Circ. 125,000. Byline given. Pays on publication. No kill fee. Publishes ms an average of 3 months after acceptance. Editorial lead time 5 months. Submit seasonal material 6 months in advance. Accepts queries by mail. Accepts simultaneous submissions. Sample copy for #10 sase. Guidelines available online.

NONFICTION Needs how-to, travel. **Buys 12 mss/year.** "Contributions are welcomed but editors recommend that contributors query first. Contributions must be accompanied by return postage, and we assume no responsibility for loss or damage thereto. Manuscripts must be typewritten on white paper." Pays expenses of writers on assignment.

AVIATION

AIR & SPACE

Smithsonian Institution, P.O. Box 37012, MRC 513, Washington DC 20013. (202)633-6070. **Fax:** (202)633-6085. **E-mail:** editors@si.edu. **Website:** www.air-spacemag.com. **80% freelance written.** Bimonthly magazine covering aviation and aerospace for a non-technical audience. "*Air & Space* is a general interest magazine about flight. Its goal is to show readers, both the knowledgeable and the novice, facets of the enterprise of flight that they are unlikely to encounter elsewhere. The emphasis is on the human rather than the technological, on the ideas behind events, rather than a simple recounting of details." Estab. 1985. Circ. 225,000. Byline given. Pays on acceptance. Offers kill fee. Accepts queries by mail, e-mail, online submission form. Accepts simultaneous submissions.

Responds in 3 months to queries. Sample copy: $7. Guidelines available online.

NONFICTION Needs book excerpts, essays, general interest, historical, humor, photo feature, technical. **Buys 50 mss/year.** Query with published clips. Length: 1,500-3,000 words. **Pay varies.** Pays expenses of writers on assignment.

COLUMNS Above & Beyond (first-person narrative of an adventure in air or space), 1,500 words; Flights & Fancy (whimsical, brief reflection), 800-1,000 words; Soundings (short, current news items reporting oddball or amusing events, efforts, or situations), 300-1,000 words; Reviews & Previews (a description and critique of a recent or soon-to-be-released book, video, movie, aerospace-related recreational product, or software), 200-450 words. **Buys 25 mss/year.** Query with published clips. **Pay varies.**

💲💲 FLIGHT JOURNAL

Air Age Media, 88 Danbury Rd., Wilton CT 06897. (203)431-9000. **E-mail:** flight@airage.com. **Website:** www.flightjournal.com. Bimonthly magazine covering aviation-oriented material, for the most part with a historical overtone, but also with some modern history in the making reporting. "*Flight Journal* is like no other aviation magazine in the world, covering the world of flight from its simple beginnings to its high-tech, no-holds-barred future. We put readers in the cockpit and let them live the thrill and adventure of the aviation experience, narrated by those who know the technology and made the history. Each issue brings the stories of flight—past, present and future—to life." No kill fee. Accepts queries by mail, e-mail. Accepts simultaneous submissions.

NONFICTION Needs historical, humor, interview, new product, personal experience, photo feature, technical. "We do not want any general aviation articles as in 'My Flight to Baja in my 172,' nor detailed recitations of the technical capabilities of an aircraft. Avoid historically accurate but bland chronologies of events." Send a single page outline of your idea. Provide 1 or more samples of prior articles, if practical. Length: 2,500-3,000 words. Lengthier pieces should be discussed in advance with the editors. **Pays $600.**

💲💲 FLYING ADVENTURES

Aviation Publishing Corporation, El Monte Airport (EMT), P.O. Box 93613, Pasadena CA 91109-3613. (626)618-4000. **E-mail:** editor@flyingadventures.com.

Website: www.flyingadventures.com. **Contact:** Lyn Freeman, Editor in Chief
Li Wu, Editor & Research Chief. **20% freelance written.** Bimonthly magazine covering lifestyle travel for owners and passengers of private aircraft. Articles cover upscale travelers. Estab. 1994. Circ. 135,000. Byline given for features. Pays on acceptance. No kill fee. Editorial lead time 2-8 weeks. Accepts queries by e-mail. Accepts simultaneous submissions. Responds immediately.

NONFICTION "Nothing nonrelevant or not our style. See magazine." Query with published clips. Length: 500-1,500 words. **Pays $150-300 for assigned and unsolicited articles.** Pays expenses of writers on assignment.

COLUMNS Publication has numerous departments; see magazine. **Buys 100+ mss/year.** Query with published clips. **Pays up to $150.**

$$$ KITPLANES

P.O. Box 1295, Dayton NV 89403. **E-mail:** editorial@kitplanes.com. **Website:** www.kitplanes.com. **Contact:** Paul Dye, editor in chief; Mark Schrimmer, managing editor. **50% freelance written. Eager to work with new/unpublished writers.** Monthly magazine covering self-construction of private aircraft for pilots and builders. Estab. 1984. Circ. 72,000. Byline given. Pays on publication. Publishes ms an average of 3 months after acceptance. Submit seasonal material 6 months in advance. Accepts queries by mail, e-mail. Accepts simultaneous submissions. Responds in 1 month to queries; in 6 weeks to mss. Sample copy: $6. Guidelines available online.

NONFICTION Needs general interest, how-to, interview, new product, personal experience, photo feature, technical. No general-interest aviation articles, or "My First Solo" type of articles. **Buys 80 mss/year.** Query. Interested in articles on all phases of aircraft construction, from basic design to flight trials to construction technique in wood, metal, and composite. Length: varies, but feature articles average about 2,000 words. **Pays $250-1,000, including story photos.** Pays expenses of writers on assignment.

$$ PILOT GETAWAYS MAGAZINE

Airventure Publishing, LLC, P.O. Box 550, Glendale CA 91209. (818)241-1890; (877)745-6849. **Fax:** (818)241-1895. **E-mail:** info@pilotgetaways.com; editor@pilotgetaways.com. **Website:** www.pilotgetaways.com. **Contact:** George A. Kounis, editor/publisher. **90% freelance written.** Bimonthly magazine covering aviation travel for private pilots. *Pilot Getaways* is a travel magazine for private pilots. Our articles cover destinations that are easily accessible by private aircraft, including details such as airport transportation, convenient hotels, and attractions. Other regular features include fly-in dining, flying tips, and bush flying. Estab. 1999. Circ. 10,000. Byline given. Pays on publication. No kill fee. Editorial lead time 4 months. Submit seasonal material 9 months in advance. Accepts queries by mail, e-mail, phone. Accepts simultaneous submissions. Responds in 2 weeks to queries; 2 months to mss. Sample copy and writer's guidelines free.

NONFICTION Needs travel. "We rarely publish articles about events that have already occurred, such as travel logs about trips the authors have taken or air show reports." **Buys 24 mss/year.** Query. Length: 1,000-3,500 words. **Pays $100-500.** Pays expenses of writers on assignment.

COLUMNS Weekend Getaways (short fly-in getaways), 2,000 words; Fly-in Dining (reviews of airport restaurants), 1,200 words; Flying Tips (tips and pointers on flying technique), 1,000 words; Bush Flying (getaways to unpaved destinations), 1,500 words. **Buys 20 mss/year.** Query. **Pays $100-500.**

$$ PIPERS MAGAZINE

Jones Publishing, Inc., N7450 Aanstad Rd., Iola WI 54945. (866)697-4737. **Website:** www.piperowner.org. **50% freelance written.** Monthly magazine covering Piper single and twin engine aircraft. *Pipers Magazine* is the official publication of the Piper Owner Society (P.O.S). Therefore, our readers are Piper aircraft owners, renters, pilots, mechanics, and enthusiasts. Articles should deal with buying/selling, flying, maintaining, or modifying Pipers. The purpose of our magazine is to promote safe, fun and affordable flying. Estab. 1988. Circ. 5,000. Pays on publication. Publishes ms an average of 3 months after acceptance. Editorial lead time 1 month. Submit seasonal material 3 months in advance. Accepts queries by mail, e-mail, fax, phone. Responds in 2 weeks to queries. Responds in 1 month to mss. Sample copy free. Guidelines free.

NONFICTION Needs historical, of specific models of Pipers, how-to, aircraft repairs and maintenance, new product, personal experience, photo feature, technical, aircraft engines and airframes. **Buys 48**

mss/year. Query. Length: 1,500-2,000 words. **Pays 12¢/word.**

REPRINTS Send mss by e-mail with rights for sale noted and information about when and where the material previously appeared.

💲💲 PLANE AND PILOT

Werner Publishing Corp., 12121 Wilshire Blvd., 12th Floor, Los Angeles CA 90025-1176. (310)820-1500. **Fax:** (310)826-5008. **E-mail:** editor@planeandpilot-mag.com. **Website:** www.planeandpilotmag.com. **80% freelance written.** Monthly magazine covering general aviation. We think a spirited, conversational writing style is most entertaining for our readers. We are read by private and corporate pilots, instructors, students, mechanics and technicians—everyone involved or interested in general aviation. Estab. 1964. Circ. 150,000. Byline given. Pays on publication. Offers kill fee. Publishes ms an average of 4 months after acceptance. Submit seasonal material 4 months in advance. Responds in 4 months to queries. Sample copy for $5.50. Guidelines available online.

NONFICTION Needs how-to, new product, personal experience, technical, travel, pilot efficiency, pilot reports on aircraft. **Buys 75 mss/year.** Query. Length: 1,200 words. **Pays $200-500.** Pays expenses of writers on assignment.

REPRINTS Send tearsheet, photocopy or typed ms with rights for sale noted and information about when and where the material previously appeared. Pays 50% of amount paid for original article.

COLUMNS Readback (any newsworthy items on aircraft and/or people in aviation), 1,200 words; Jobs & Schools (a feature or an interesting school or program in aviation), 900-1,000 words. **Buys 30 mss/year.** Send complete ms. **Pays $200-500.**

BUSINESS & FINANCE

💲💲 ALASKA BUSINESS MAGAZINE

Alaska Business Publishing Company, Inc., 501 W. Northern Lights Blvd., Ste. 100, Anchorage AK 99503-2577. (907)276-4373; (800)770-4373. **Fax:** (907)279-2900. **E-mail:** editor@akbizmag.com. **Website:** www.akbizmag.com. **Contact:** Kathryn Mackenzie, managing editor. **80% freelance written.** *Alaska Business*, produced in Alaska for Alaskans and other U.S. and international audiences interested in the business affairs of the 49th state, provides thorough and ob-

jective analysis of issues and trends of interest to the Alaska business community. Story queries and pitches should be focused on special sections and topics listed on the editorial calendar, located on the editorial page of the website: www.akbizmag.com/editorial. "We are an Alaska-centric publication and typically feature Alaskan writers. However, we are interested in talented writers from throughout the US with interest in commodities markets, financial writing, and the ability to write about highly-technical subjects." The magazine features stories about individuals, organizations, and companies shaping the Alaska economy. *Alaska Business* emphasizes the importance of enterprise and strives for statewide business coverage. Basic industry sectors are highlighted. Estab. 1985. Circ. 13,000-15,000. Byline given. Pays in month of publication. Offers $50 kill fee. Publishes ms an average of 2 months after acceptance. Assignments are due 2 months before date published. Editorial lead time 2-6 months. Deadlines are 2 months prior to month published. Ideas generally need to be submitted 4-6 months in advance for approval and assignment. Accepts queries by e-mail, online submission form. Responds immediately to queries. Past issues available online. Send to editor@akbizmag.com as inline text of an e-mail.

NONFICTION Needs interview, new product, opinion, photo feature, profile, technical, travel, engineering, architecture, construction, conventions & meetings, oil & gas, transportation, Pacific Northwest, telecom & technology, international trade, environmental services, energy & power, Alaska native corporations, mining, healthcare, resource development, employee relations, small business tips, entrepreneur advice. Special issues: "A different industry is featured each month in a special section. Read our magazine and editorial calendar for an idea of the material we assign." No fiction, poetry, or anything not pertinent to Alaska business. Rarely uses any unsolicited or unassigned articles. **Buys 200 mss/year.** Send query and 3 clips of previously published articles. Do not send complete mss. Does not republish blog posts. Length: 500-2,500 words. **Pays $150-500 for assigned articles.** Does not pay expenses.

REPRINTS Rarely publishes reprints from other publications. Reprint payment varies.

✪$$$$ ALBERTA VENTURE

Venture Publishing Inc., 10339–124 St., #300, Edmonton AB T5N 3W1 Canada. (780)990-0839. **E-mail:** admin@albertaventure.com. **Website:** www.albertaventure.com. **70% freelance written.** Monthly magazine covering business in Alberta. "Our readers are mostly business owners and managers in Alberta who read the magazine to keep up with trends and run their businesses better." Estab. 1997. Circ. 35,000. Byline given. Pays on publication. Offers 30% kill fee. Publishes ms an average of 2 months after acceptance. Editorial lead time 3 months. Submit seasonal material 3 months in advance. Accepts queries by e-mail. Accepts simultaneous submissions. Responds in 2 weeks to queries. Guidelines by e-mail.

NONFICTION Does not want company or product profiles. **Buys 75 mss/year.** Query. Length: 1,000-3,000 words. **Pays $300-2,000 (Canadian).** Pays expenses of writers on assignment.

✪$$ ATLANTIC BUSINESS MAGAZINE

Communications Ten, Ltd., P.O. Box 2356, Station C, St. John's NL A1C 6E7 Canada. (709)726-9300. **Fax:** (709)726-3013. **E-mail:** dchafe@atlanticbusinessmagazine.com. **Website:** www.atlanticbusinessmagazine.net. **Contact:** Dawn Chafe, executive editor. **80% freelance written.** Bimonthly magazine covering business in Atlantic Canada. "We discuss positive business developments, emphasizing that the 4 Atlantic provinces are a great place to do business." Estab. 1989. Circ. 30,000. Byline given. Pays within 30 days of publication. No kill fee. Publishes ms an average of 2 months after acceptance. Editorial lead time 6 months. Accepts queries by e-mail. Accepts simultaneous submissions. Sample copy free. Guidelines online.

NONFICTION Needs general interest, interview, new product. "We don't want religious, technical, or scholarly material. We are not an academic magazine. We are interested only in stories concerning business topics specific to the 4 Canadian provinces of Nova Scotia, New Brunswick, Prince Edward Island, and Newfoundland and Labrador." **Buys 36 mss/year.** Query with published clips. Length: 1,000-1,200 words for features; 3,500-4,000 for cover stories. **Pays 40¢/word.** Pays expenses of writers on assignment.

$$ THE BUSINESS JOURNAL

American City Business Journals, Inc., 125 S. Market, 11th Floor, San Jose CA 95113. (408)295-3800. **Fax:** (408)295-5028. **Website:** http://sanjose.bizjournals.com. **Contact:** Moryt Milo, print editor. **2-5% freelance written.** Weekly tabloid covering a wide cross-section of industries. Estab. 1983. Circ. 13,200. Byline given. Pays on publication. Offers $75 kill fee. Editorial lead time 1 month. Responds in 2 weeks to queries. Sample copy and guidelines free.

NONFICTION **Buys 300 mss/year.** Query. Length: 700-2,500 words. **Pays $175-400.**

$$ CINCY MAGAZINE

Great Lakes Publishing Co., Cincinnati Club Building, 30 Garfield Place, Suite 440, Cincinnati OH 45202. (513)421-2533. **Fax:** (513)421-2542. **E-mail:** dgebhardt-french@cincymagazine.com. **Website:** www.cincymagazine.com. **Contact:** Dianne Gebhardt-French, editor; Tim Curtis, managing editor. **80% freelance written.** Glossy bimonthly color magazine written for business professionals in Greater Cincinnati, published 10 times annually. *Cincy* is written and designed for the interests of business professionals and executives both at work and away from work, with features, trend stories, news and opinions related to business, along with lifestyle articles on home, dining, shopping, travel, health and more. Estab. 2003. Circ. 15,300. Byline given. Pays on publication. Offers 100% kill fee. Publishes ms an average of 3 months after acceptance. Editorial lead time 1-3 months. Submit seasonal material 4 months in advance. Accepts queries by mail, e-mail.

NONFICTION Needs general interest, interview. Does not want stock advice. Length: 200-2,000 words. **Pays $75-600.**

$$$ COLORADOBIZ

6160 S. Syracuse Way, #300, Greenwood Village CO 80111. (303)662-5200. **E-mail:** mtaylor@cobizmag.com. **Website:** www.cobizmag.com. **Contact:** Mike Taylor, managing editor. **70% freelance written.** "*ColoradoBiz* is a monthly magazine that covers people, issues and trends statewide for a sophisticated audience of business owners and executives." Estab. 1973. Circ. 20,000+. Byline given. Pays on publication. Publishes ms 2 months after acceptance. Editorial lead time is 2-3 months. Submit seasonal material 3 months in advance. Accepts queries by e-mail. Accepts simultaneous submissions. Responds in 2 weeks to queries. Sample copy available for $2.95 with SASE. Writer's guidelines free online.

NONFICTION Needs book excerpts, expose, technical, Colorado business. Special issues. Minority business. Does not want humor, first-person, self-promotional. **Buys up to 100 mss/year mss/year.** Query with published clips. Length: 300-3,000 words. Pays expenses of writers on assignment.

COLUMNS State of the State, 150 to 300 word briefs on Colorado business issues. Query.

$ $ $ $ CORPORATE BOARD MEMBER

Board Member Inc., 5110 Maryland Way, Suite 250, Brentwood TN 37027. **Fax:** (615)371-0899. **E-mail:** boardmember@boardmember.com. **Website:** www.boardmember.com. **100% freelance written.** Bimonthly magazine covering corporate governance. "Our readers are the directors and top executives of publicly-held US corporations. We look for detailed and preferably narrative stories about how individual boards have dealt with the challenges that face them on a daily basis: reforms, shareholder suits, CEO pay, firing and hiring CEOs, setting up new boards, firing useless directors. We're happy to light fires under the feet of boards that are asleep at the switch. We also do service-type pieces, written in the second person, advising directors about new wrinkles in disclosure laws, for example." Estab. 1999. Circ. 60,000. Byline given. Pays on acceptance. Offers 25% kill fee. Publishes ms an average of 3 months after acceptance. Editorial lead time 4-5 months. Submit seasonal material 4-5 months in advance. Accepts queries by e-mail. Responds in 1 week to queries. Responds in 1 week to mss. Sample copy available online. Guidelines by e-mail.

NONFICTION Special issues: Best Law Firms in America (July/August); What Directors Think (November/December). Does not want views from 35,000 feet, pontification, opinion, humor, anything devoid of reporting. **Buys 100 mss/year.** Query. Length: 650-2,500 words. **Pays $1,200-5,000.** Pays expenses of writers on assignment.

$ $ CORPORATE CONNECTICUT MAGAZINE

Corporate World LLC, P.O. Box 290724, Wethersfield CT 06129. **E-mail:** editor@corpct.com. **Website:** www.corpct.com. **50% freelance written.** Business magazine. Corporate/business leaders, entrepreneurs, technology, innovation. *Corporate Connecticut* is devoted to people who make business happen in the private sector and who create innovative change across

public arenas. Centered in the Northeast between New York and Boston, Connecticut is positioned in a coastal corridor with a dense affluent population who are highly mobile, accomplished and educated. Estab. 2001. Byline given. Pays on publication. Offers 25% kill fee. Publishes ms an average of 2-3 months after acceptance. Editorial lead time 3-6 months. Submit seasonal material 10-12 months in advance. Accepts queries by mail, e-mail. Responds in 2 weeks to queries. Sample copy for #10 SASE.

NONFICTION Query with published clips. **Varying fees; excellence.** Pays expenses of writers on assignment.

$ CRAIN'S DETROIT BUSINESS

Crain Communications, Inc., 1155 Gratiot, Detroit MI 48207. (313)446-0419. **Fax:** (313)446-1687. **Website:** www.crainsdetroit.com. **10% freelance written.** Weekly tabloid covering business in the Detroit metropolitan area—specifically Wayne, Oakland, Macomb, Washtenaw, and Livingston counties. "*Crain's Detroit Business* has been covering non-automotive business news in Southeast Michigan since 1985. Our focus is Wayne, Oakland, Macomb, Washtenaw, and Livingston counties. Our stories read differently from stories in the metro Detroit dailies or regional weeklies. Our audience is narrower. A lot of general media stories use 1 or 2 sources. We like to include competitors and customers in our company profiles. And we focus on details: Where is the financing coming from? What will this do to the competition? Is this a trend? Who owns the company?" Estab. 1985. Circ. 150,000. Byline given. Pays on publication. No kill fee. Publishes ms an average of 1 month after acceptance. Accepts queries by e-mail, online submission form. Sample copy: $1.50. Guidelines online.

NONFICTION Needs new product, technical, business. **Buys 20 mss/year.** Query the appropriate editor with published clips. E-mail cdbdepartments@crain.com for People and Business Diary items. 30-40 words/column inch **Pays $10-15/column inch.** Pays expenses of writers on assignment.

$ $ DOLLARS & SENSE

Real World Economics, Economic Affairs Bureau, Inc., 89 South St., LL02, Boston MA 02111. (617)447-2177. **Fax:** (617)477-2179. **E-mail:** dollars@dollarsandsense.org. **Website:** www.dollarsandsense.org. **Contact:** Alejandro Reuss and Chris Sturr, co-editors. **10% freelance written.** Bimonthly magazine covering economic, environmental, and social justice. "*Dollars & Sense* publishes economic news and analysis, reports on economic justice activism, primers on economic topics, and critiques of the mainstream media's coverage of the economy. Our readers include professors, students, and activists who value our smart and accessible economic coverage. We explain the workings of the U.S. and international economics and provide left perspectives on current economic affairs." Estab. 1974. Circ. 8,000. Byline given. Pays on publication. No kill fee. Publishes ms an average of 4 months after acceptance. Editorial lead time 3 months. Submit seasonal material 2 months in advance. Accepts queries by mail, e-mail. Accepts simultaneous submissions. Sample copy: $5 or on website. Guidelines online.

NONFICTION Special issues: Wants in-depth articles on a broad range of topics. **Buys 6 mss/year.** Query with published clips. Length: 1,500-3,000 words. **Pays up to $200.** Pays expenses of writers on assignment.

COLUMNS Active Culture (briefs on activism), 250-400 words; Reviews (coverage of recent books, movies, and other media), 700 words. Query with published clips.

❺❺ ELLIOTT WAVE INTERNATIONAL PUBLICATIONS

Elliott Wave International, P.O. Box 1618, Gainesville GA 30503. (770)536-0309. **E-mail:** customercare@elliottwave.com. **Website:** www.elliottwave.com. **10% freelance written.** Our publications are weekly to monthly in print and online formats covering investment markets. An understanding of technical market analysis is indispensible, knowledge of Elliott wave analysis even better. Clear, conversational prose is mandatory. Estab. 1979. Circ. 80,000. Byline sometimes given. Pays on publication. Publishes ms an average of 1 month after acceptance. Editorial lead time 1 month. Accepts queries by e-mail. Accepts simultaneous submissions.

NONFICTION Needs essays, how-to, technical. **Buys 12 mss/year.** Query with published clips. Length: 500-800 words. **Pays $100-200.**

COLUMNS Pop culture and the stock market, 500-800 words. **Buys 12 mss/year.** Query with published clips. **Pays $100-200.**

❺❺❺❺ ENTREPRENEUR MAGAZINE

Entrepreneur Media Inc., 18061 Fitch, Irvine CA 92614. **E-mail:** entmag@entrepreneur.com. **Website:** www.entrepreneur.com. **Contact:** Amy Cosper, editor in chief. **60% freelance written.** "*Entrepreneur* readers already run their own businesses. They have been in business for several years and are seeking innovative methods and strategies to improve their business operations. They are also interested in new business ideas and opportunities, as well as current issues that affect their companies." Circ. 600,000. Byline given. Pays on acceptance. No kill fee. Publishes ms an average of 5 months after acceptance. Submit seasonal material 6 months in advance. Accepts queries by e-mail. Accepts simultaneous submissions. Responds in 3 months to queries. Sample copy: $7.20.

NONFICTION Needs how-to. **Buys 10-20 mss/year.** Query with published clips. Length: 1,800 words. **Payment varies.** Pays expenses of writers on assignment.

COLUMNS Snapshots (profiles of interesting entrepreneurs who exemplify innovation in their marketing/sales technique, financing method or management style, or who have developed an innovative product/service or technology); Money Smarts (financial management); Marketing Smarts; Web Smarts (Internet news); Tech Smarts; Management Smarts; Viewpoint (first-person essay on entrepreneurship), all 300 words. **Pays $1/word.**

❺❺ INGRAM'S

Show-Me Publishing, Inc., 2049 Wyandotte, Kansas City MO 64108. (816)268-6402. **E-mail:** editorial@ingramsonline.com. **Website:** www.ingramsonline.com. **Contact:** Dennis Boone, managing editor. **10% freelance written.** Monthly magazine covering Kansas City business and economic development. "*Ingram's* readers are top-level corporate executives and community leaders, officials, and decision makers. Our editorial content must provide such readers with timely, relevant information and insights." Estab. 1975. Circ. 105,000. Byline given. Pays on publication. No kill fee. Publishes ms an average of 1 month after acceptance. Editorial lead time 1 month. Submit seasonal material 5 months in advance. Accepts queries by e-mail. Accepts simultaneous submissions. Sample copy free.

NONFICTION Needs interview, technical. Does not want humor, inspirational, or anything not related to Kansas City business. **Buys 4-6 mss/year.** Query.

Length: 500-1,500 words. **Pays $75-200 depending on research/feature length.** Pays expenses of writers on assignment.

COLUMNS Say So (opinion), 1,500 words. **Buys 12 mss/year. Pays $75-100 maximum.**

💲💲 THE LANE REPORT

Lane Communications Group, 201 E. Main St., 14th Floor, Lexington KY 40507. (859)244-3500. **E-mail:** markgreen@lanereport.com. **Website:** www.lanereport.com. **Contact:** Mark Green, managing editor. **60% freelance written.** Monthly magazine covering statewide business. *The Lane Report* is an intelligent, enterprising magazine that informs readers and drives a statewide dialogue by highlighting important business stories in Kentucky. Estab. 1985. Circ. 15,000. Byline given. Pays on publication. No kill fee. Editorial lead time 6 weeks. Submit seasonal material 3 months in advance. Accepts queries by mail, e-mail. Accepts simultaneous submissions. Responds in 1 month to queries. Sample copy and writer's guidelines free.

NONFICTION Needs essays, interview, new product, photo feature. **Buys 30-40 mss/year.** Query with published clips. Do not send unsolicited mss. Looking for major trends shaping the state, noteworthy business and practices, and stories with sweeping implications across industry sectors and state regions. Length: 750-3,000 words. **Pays $150-375.** Pays expenses of writers on assignment.

COLUMNS Fast Lane Briefs (recent news and trends and how they might shape the future), 100-400 words; Opinion (opinion on a business or economic issue about which you, the writer, feel passionate and qualified to write), 750 words; Entrepreneurs (profile of a particularly interesting or quirky member of the business community), 750-1,400 words. Query.

💲💲💲 MYBUSINESS MAGAZINE

Imagination Publishing, 600 W. Fulton St., 6th Floor, Chicago IL 60661. (615)872-5800; (800)634-2669. **E-mail:** nfib@imaginepub.com. **Website:** www.nfib.com/business-resources/mybusiness-magazine. **75% freelance written.** Bimonthly magazine for small businesses. "We are a guide to small business success, however that is defined in the new small business economy. We explore the methods and minds behind the trends and celebrate the men and women leading the creation of the new small business economy." Estab. 1999. Circ. 400,000. Byline given. Pays

on publication. Offers 30% kill fee. Publishes ms an average of 4 months after acceptance. Editorial lead time 4-6 months. Submit seasonal material 5 months in advance. Accepts queries by e-mail. Accepts simultaneous submissions. Responds in 3 weeks to queries.

NONFICTION Needs how-to, new product. **Buys 8 mss/year.** "Query with résumé and 2 published clips. We accept pitches for feature stories, which fall under 1 of 3 categories: Own, Operate, and Grow. Story ideas should be small-business focused, with an emphasis on timely problems that small business owners face and real, workable solutions. Trend pieces are also of interest. Copy should be submitted as a Microsoft Word enclosure. Deadlines are 90 days before publication." Length: 200-1,800 words. **Pays $75-1,000.**

💲💲💲💲 NATIONAL BLACK MBA MAGAZINE

400 West Peachtree Street NW, Suite 203, Atlanta GA 30308. (312)236-2622. **Fax:** (312)236-0390. **E-mail:** elaine@naylor.com. **Website:** www.nbmbaa.org. **80% freelance written.** Online magazine covering business career strategy, economic development, and financial management. Estab. 1997. Circ. 45,000. Byline given. Pays after publication. Offers 10-20% or $500 kill fee. Publishes ms an average of 1 month after acceptance. Editorial lead time 2-3 months. Submit seasonal material 3-4 months in advance. Accepts queries by mail, e-mail, fax.

NONFICTION Pays expenses of writers on assignment.

COLUMNS Management Strategies (leadership development), 1,200-1,700 words; Features (business management, entreprenuerial finance); Finance; Technology. Send complete ms. **Pays $500-1,000.**

💲💲 THE NETWORK JOURNAL

The Network Journal Communication, 39 Broadway, Suite 2430, New York NY 10006. (212)962-3791. **Fax:** (212)962-3537. **E-mail:** tnjeditors@tnj.com. **Website:** www.tnj.com. **25% freelance written.** Monthly magazine covering business and career articles. *The Network Journal* caters to black professionals and small-business owners, providing quality coverage on business, financial, technology, and career news germane to the black community. Estab. 1993. Circ. 25,000. Byline given. Pays on publication. Editorial lead time 2 months. Submit seasonal material 3 months in advance. Accepts queries by mail, e-mail, fax, phone.

Accepts simultaneous submissions. Sample copy for $1 or online. Writer's guidelines for SASE.

NONFICTION Needs how-to, interview. Send complete ms. Length: 1,200-1,500 words. **Pays $150-200.** Pays expenses of writers on assignment.

COLUMNS Book reviews, 700-800 words; career management and small business development, 800 words. **Pays $100.**

$$$$ OREGON BUSINESS

MEDIAmerica, Inc., 715 SW Morrison St, Suite 800, Portalnd OR 97205. (503)223-0304. **Fax:** (503)221-6544. **E-mail:** lindab@oregonbusiness.com. **E-mail:** editor@oregonbusiness.com. **Website:** www.oregonbusiness.com. **Contact:** Linda Baker, editor. **15-25% freelance written.** Monthly magazine covering business in Oregon. Subscribers inlcude owners of small and medium-sized businesses, government agencies, professional staffs of banks, insurance companies, ad agencies, attorneys, and other service providers. Accepts *only* stories about Oregon businesses, issues, and trends. Estab. 1981. Circ. 50,000. Byline given. Pays on publication. No kill fee. Editorial lead time 2 months. Accepts queries by mail, e-mail. Sample copy for $4. Guidelines available online.

NONFICTION Query with résumé and 2-3 published clips. Length: 1,200-3,000 words.

COLUMNS First Person (opinion piece on an issue related to business), 750 words; Around the State (recent news and trends, and how they might shape the future), 100-600 words; Business Tools (practical, how-to suggestions for business managers and owners), 400-600 words; In Character (profile of interesting or quirky member of the business community), 850 words. Query with résumé and 2-3 published clips.

$$ PRAIRIE BUSINESS

Grand Forks (ND), Forum Communications Company, 808 Third Ave., #400, Fargo ND 58103. **Fax:** (701)280-9092. **E-mail:** info@prairiebizmag.com; kbevill@prairiebizmag.com. **Website:** www.prairiebizmag.com. **Contact:** Kris Bevill, editor. **30% freelance written.** Monthly magazine covering business on the Northern Plains (North Dakota, South Dakota, Minnesota). "We attempt to be a resource for business owners/managers, policymakers, educators, and nonprofit administrators, acting as a catalyst for growth in the region by reaching out to an audience of decision makers within the region and also venture capitalists, site selectors, and angel visitors from outside the region." Estab. 2000. Circ. 20,000. Byline given. Pays within 2 weeks of mailing date. No kill fee. Publishes ms an average of 1-2 months after acceptance. Editorial lead time 2 months. Submit seasonal material 2 months in advance. Accepts queries by e-mail. Accepts simultaneous submissions. Responds in 2 weeks to queries. Sample copy free. Guidelines free.

NONFICTION Needs interview, technical, basic online research. "Does not want articles that are blatant self-promotion for any interest without providing value for readers." **Buys 36 mss/year.** Query. Length: 800-1,500 words. **Pays 15¢/word.**

🍁$$$$ PROFIT

Rogers Media, 1 Mt. Pleasant Rd., 11th Floor, Toronto ON M4Y 2Y5 Canada. (416)764-1402. **Fax:** (416)764-1404. **E-mail:** profit@profit.rogers.com. **Website:** www.profitguide.com. **80% freelance written.** Magazine published 6 times/year covering small and medium businesses. Profit is Canada's guide to business success. The most-read and best-targeted publication in Canada for entrepreneurs and small business executives. "We specialize in specific, useful information that helps our readers manage their businesses better. We want Canadian stories only." Estab. 1982. Circ. 84,632. Byline given. Pays on acceptance. Offers variable kill fee. Publishes ms an average of 2 months after acceptance. Submit seasonal material 6 months in advance. Accepts queries by e-mail. Accepts simultaneous submissions. Responds in 1 month to queries; in 6 weeks to mss.

NONFICTION Needs how-to. **Buys 50 mss/year.** Query with published clips. Length: 800-2,000 words. **Pays $500-2,000.** Pays expenses of writers on assignment.

COLUMNS Finance (info on raising capital in Canada), 700 words; Marketing (marketing strategies for independent business), 700 words. **Buys 80 mss/year.** Query with published clips. **Pays $150-600.**

$ ROCHESTER BUSINESS JOURNAL

Rochester Business Journal, Inc., 45 E. Ave., Suite 500, Rochester NY 14604. (585)546-8303. **Fax:** (585)546-3398. **E-mail:** rbj@rbj.net. **Website:** www.rbj.net. **10% freelance written.** Weekly tabloid covering local business. The *Rochester Business Journal* is geared toward corporate executives and owners of small businesses, bringing them leading-edge business coverage and analysis first in the market. Estab. 1984. Circ. 10,000.

Byline given. Pays on publication. No kill fee. Publishes ms an average of 1 month after acceptance. Editorial lead time 6 weeks. Accepts queries by mail, fax. Responds in 1 week to queries. Sample copy for free or by e-mail. Guidelines available online.

NONFICTION Needs how-to, business topics, news features, trend stories with local examples. Do not query about any topics that do not include several local examples—local companies, organizations, universities, etc. **Buys 110 mss/year.** Query with published clips. Length: 1,000-2,000 words. **Pays $150.**

💲💲 SMARTCEO MEDIA

SmartCEO, 2700 Lighthouse Point E., Suite 220A, Baltimore MD 21224. (410)342-9510. **Fax:** (410)675-5280. **E-mail:** editorial@smartceo.com. **Website:** www.smartceo.com. **25% freelance written.** Publishes four bi-monthly print magazines covering regional business in the Baltimore, MD, Philadelphia, PA, New York, NY, and Washington, DC areas. Nearly 50,000 offensive-minded, growth-oriented CEOs turn to *SmartCEO* magazine to find ideas and inspiration to help them grow their businesses. Each issue includes behind-the-scenes looks at local success stories, columns written by key opinion leaders and other resources to help the region's middle-market CEOs conquer the daily challenges of running a business. *SmartCEO* magazine is published on a bi-monthly basis with editions in four major markets: *Baltimore SmartCEO*, *New York SmartCEO*, *Philadelphia Smart-CEO* and *Washington SmartCEO*. Estab. 2001. Circ. 45,000. Byline given. Pays on publication. No kill fee. Publishes ms an average of 2 months after acceptance. Editorial lead time 5 months. Submit seasonal material 5 months in advance. Accepts queries by e-mail, phone. Accepts simultaneous submissions. Responds in 4 weeks to queries. Responds in 2 months to mss. Sample copy available online. Guidelines by e-mail.

NONFICTION Needs interview, Business features or tips. "We do not want pitches on CEOs or companies outside the Baltimore, MD, Philadelphia, PA, New York, NY or Washington, DC areas; no product reviews, lifestyle content or book reviews, please." **Buys 20 mss/year. mss/year.** Query. Length: varies. **Pay varies.** Pays expenses of writers on assignment.

COLUMNS Project to Watch (overview of a local development project in progress and why it is of interest to the business community), 600 words; Q&A and tip-focused coverage of business issues and challeng-es (each article includes the opinions of 10-20 CEOs), 500-1,000 words. **Buys 0-5 mss/year mss/year.** Query.

💲💲 TECHNICAL ANALYSIS OF STOCKS & COMMODITIES

4757 California Ave. SW, Seattle WA 98116. (206)938-0570. **E-mail:** editor@traders.com. **Website:** www.traders.com. **90% freelance written.** "Magazine covers methods of investing and trading stocks, bonds and commodities (futures), options, mutual funds, and precious metals using technical analysis." Estab. 1982. Circ. 60,000. Byline given. Pays on publication. No kill fee. Publishes ms an average of 4 months after acceptance. Accepts simultaneous submissions. Responds in 2 months to queries. Sample copy: $5. Guidelines available online.

NONFICTION Needs how-to. No newsletter-type, buy-sell recommendations. The article subject must relate to technical analysis, charting, or a numerical technique used to trade securities or futures. Almost universally requires graphics with every article. **Buys 150 mss/year.** Send complete ms. Length: 1,000-4,000 words. **Pays $3/column inch (two-column format) or $2/column inch (three-column format); $50 minimum.** Pays expenses of writers on assignment.

REPRINTS Send tearsheet with rights for sale noted and information about when and where the material previously appeared.

FILLERS "Must relate to trading stocks, bonds, options, mutual funds, commodities, or precious metals." **Buys 20 mss/year.** Length: 500 words. **Pays $20-50.**

💲💲 VERMONT BUSINESS MAGAZINE

365 Dorset St., South Burlington VT 05403. (802)863-8038. **Fax:** (802)863-8069. **Website:** www.vermontbiz.com. **Contact:** Tim McQuiston, editor. **80% freelance written.** Monthly tabloid covering business in Vermont. Circ. 8,000. Byline given. Pays on publication. No kill fee. Publishes ms an average of 1 month after acceptance. Accepts simultaneous submissions. Responds in 2 months to queries. Sample copy for SAE with 11x14 envelope and 7 first-class stamps.

NONFICTION Buys 200 mss/year. Query with published clips. Length: 800-1,800 words. **Pays $100-200.** Pays expenses of writers on assignment.

REPRINTS Send tearsheet and information about when and where the material previously appeared.

CAREER, COLLEGE & ALUMNI

💲💲 AFRICAN-AMERICAN CAREER WORLD

Equal Opportunity Publications, Inc., 445 Broad Hollow Rd., Suite 425, Melville NY 11747. (631)421-9421. **E-mail:** bloehr@eop.com. **Website:** www.eop.com. **Contact:** Barbara Capella Loehr, editor. **60% freelance written.** Semiannual magazine focused on African-American students and professionals in all disciplines. Estab. 1969. Byline given. Pays on publication. No kill fee. Publishes ms an average of 3 months after acceptance. Editorial lead time 3 months. Accepts queries by mail, e-mail. Accepts simultaneous submissions. Sample copy free. Guidelines free.

NONFICTION Needs how-to, interview, personal experience. "We do not want articles that are too general." Query. Length: 1,500-2,500 words. **Pays $350 for assigned articles.** Pays expenses of writers on assignment.

💲💲 EQUAL OPPORTUNITY

Equal Opportunity Publications, Inc., 445 Broad Hollow Rd., Suite 425, Melville NY 11747. (631)421-9421. **Fax:** (631)421-0359. **E-mail:** jwhitcher@eop.com. **Website:** www.eop.com. **Contact:** Joann Whitcher, director, editorial and production. **70% freelance written. Prefers to work with published/established writers.** Triannual magazine dedicated to advancing the professional interests of African Americans, Hispanics, Asian Americans, and Native Americans. Audience is 90% college juniors and seniors; 10% working graduates. An understanding of educational and career problems of minorities is essential. Estab. 1967. Circ. 11,000. Byline given. Pays on publication. Publishes ms an average of 6 months after acceptance. Editorial lead time 6 months. Submit seasonal material 6 months in advance. Accepts queries by mail, e-mail, fax, phone. Accepts simultaneous submissions. Responds in 2 weeks to queries; in 1 month to mss. Sample copy and writer's guidelines for 9x12 SAE with 5 first-class stamps.

NONFICTION Needs general interest, how-to, interview, opinion, personal experience, technical, coverage of minority interests. **Buys 10 mss/year.** Send complete ms. Length: 1,000-2,000 words. **Pays 10¢/ word.** Pays expenses of writers on assignment.

REPRINTS Send information about when and where the material previously appeared. Pays 10¢/word.

💲💲💲💲 HARVARD MAGAZINE

7 Ware St., Cambridge MA 02138. (617)495-5746. **Fax:** (617)495-0324. **E-mail:** john_rosenberg@harvard.edu. **Website:** www.harvardmagazine.com. **Contact:** John S. Rosenberg, editor. **35-50% freelance written.** Bimonthly magazine for Harvard University faculty, alumni, and students. Estab. 1898. Circ. 245,000. Byline given. Pays on publication. No kill fee. Publishes ms an average of 4 months after acceptance. Editorial lead time 1 year. Accepts queries by mail, e-mail. Accepts simultaneous submissions. Responds in 1 month to queries and mss. Sample copy online.

NONFICTION Needs book excerpts, essays, interview, journalism on Harvard-related intellectual subjects. **Buys 20-30 mss/year.** Query with published clips. Length: 800-10,000 words. **Pays $400-3,000.** Pays expenses of writers on assignment.

💲💲 HISPANIC CAREER WORLD

Equal Opportunity Publications, Inc., 445 Broad Hollow Rd., Suite 425, Melville NY 11747. (631)421-9421, ext. 12. **Fax:** (631)421-1352. **E-mail:** bloehr@eop.com. **Website:** www.eop.com. **Contact:** Barbara Capella Loehr, editor. **60% freelance written.** Semiannual magazine aimed at Hispanic students and professionals in all disciplines. Estab. 1969. Byline given. Pays on publication. No kill fee. Publishes ms an average of 3 months after acceptance. Editorial lead time 3 months. Accepts queries by mail, e-mail, fax, phone. Accepts simultaneous submissions. Responds in 2 weeks to queries; 2 months to mss. Sample copy free. Guidelines free.

NONFICTION Needs how-to, interview, personal experience. Query. Length: 1,500-2,500 words. **Pays $350 for assigned articles.**

💲💲💲💲 NOTRE DAME MAGAZINE

University of Notre Dame, 500 Grace Hall, Notre Dame IN 46556-5612. (574)631-5335. **Fax:** (574)631-6767. **E-mail:** ndmag@nd.edu. **Website:** magazine.nd.edu. **Contact:** Kerry Temple, editor; Kerry Prugh, art director. **50% freelance written.** "We are a university magazine with a scope as broad as that found at a university, but we place our discussion in a moral, ethical and spiritual context reflecting our Catholic heritage." Estab. 1972. Circ. 150,000. Byline given. Pays on acceptance. No kill fee. Publishes ms an average of 1 year after acceptance. Accepts queries by mail, e-mail. Accepts simultaneous submissions. Responds in 2 months to queries. Sample copy available online and by request. Guidelines online.

NONFICTION Needs essays, general interest, personal experience, profile. **Buys 35 mss/year.** Query with published clips. Length: 600-3,000 words. **Pays $250-3,000.** Pays expenses of writers on assignment.

COLUMNS CrossCurrents (essays, deal with a wide array of issues—some topical, some personal, some serious, some light). Query with or without published clips or send complete ms.

💲💲💲💲 OREGON QUARTERLY

5228 University of Oregon, Eugene OR 97403. (541)346-5046; (541) 346-5047. **E-mail:** quarterly@uoregon.edu. **Website:** www.oregonquarterly.com. **85% freelance written.** Quarterly magazine covering people and ideas at the University of Oregon and the Northwest. Estab. 1919. Circ. 100,000. Byline given. Pays on acceptance. Offers 20% kill fee. Publishes ms an average of 3 months after acceptance. Accepts simultaneous submissions. Responds in 2 months to queries Guidelines available online.

NONFICTION **Buys 30 mss/year.** Query with published clips. Length: 300-3,000 words. **Payment varies—75¢-$1/per word** Pays expenses of writers on assignment.

FICTION Rarely publishes novel excerpts by UO professors or grads.

THE PENN STATER

Penn State Alumni Association, 218 Hintz Family Alumni Center, University Park PA 16802 USA. (814)865-2709. **Fax:** (814)863-5690. **E-mail:** pennstater@psu.edu. **E-mail:** pennstater@psu.edu. **Website:** www.pennstatermag.com. **Contact:** Tina Hay, editor. **60% freelance written.** Bimonthly magazine covering Penn State and Penn Staters. Estab. 1910. Circ. 135,000. Byline given. Pays on acceptance. Offers 50% kill fee. Publishes ms an average of 4 months after acceptance. Editorial lead time 3 months. Submit seasonal material 8 months in advance. Accepts queries by mail, e-mail, fax. Responds in 3 months to queries. Sample copy and writer's guidelines free.

NONFICTION Needs book excerpts, general interest, historical, interview, photo feature, profile, book reviews, science/research. No unsolicited mss. **Buys 20 mss/year.** Query with published clips. Length: 200-

3,000 words. **Pays competitive rates.** Pays expenses of writers on assignment.

REPRINTS Send photocopy or PDF, plus information about when and where the material previously appeared. Payment varies.

💲💲 RIPON MAGAZINE

P.O. Box 248, 300 Seward St., Ripon WI 54971-0248. (920)748-8322. **Fax:** (920)748-9262. **Website:** www.ripon.edu/magazine. **15% freelance written.** Quarterly magazine that contains information relating to Ripon College and is mailed to alumni and friends of the college. Estab. 1851. Circ. 14,000. Byline given. Pays on publication. Publishes ms an average of 3 months after acceptance. Accepts queries by mail, e-mail, fax, phone. Accepts simultaneous submissions. Responds in 2 weeks to queries.

NONFICTION Needs historical, interview. **Buys 4 mss/year.** Send complete ms. Length: 250-1,000 words. **Pays $25-350.**

💲💲💲 UAB MAGAZINE

UAB Office of Public Relations and Marketing (University of Alabama at Birmingham), AB 340, 1720 2nd Ave. S., Birmingham AL 35294-0103. (205)975-6577. **E-mail:** charlesb@uab.edu; uabmagazine@uab.edu. **Website:** www.uab.edu/uabmagazine. **Contact:** Charles Buchanan, editor. **70% freelance written.** University magazine published 2 times/year covering University of Alabama at Birmingham. *UAB Magazine* informs readers about the innovation and creative energy that drives UAB's renowned research, educational, and health care programs. The magazine reaches active alumni, faculty, friends and donors, patients, corporate and community leaders, media, and the public. Estab. 1980. Circ. 33,000. Byline given. Pays on acceptance. Offers 50% kill fee. Publishes ms an average of 3-4 months after acceptance. Editorial lead time 3 months. Accepts queries by mail, e-mail. Accepts simultaneous submissions. Sample copy available online.

NONFICTION general interest/interview, science/research. **Buys 40-50 mss/year.** Query with published clips. Length: 500-5,000 words. **Pays $100-1,200.** Pays expenses of writers on assignment.

💲💲 WORKFORCE DIVERSITY FOR ENGINEERING & IT PROFESSIONALS

Equal Opportunity Publications, Inc., 445 Broad Hollow Rd., Suite 425, Melville NY 11747. (631)421-9421.

Fax: (631)421-1352. **E-mail:** info@eop.com; bloehr@eop.com. **Website:** www.eop.com. **Contact:** Barbara Capella Loehr, editor. **60% freelance written.** Quarterly magazine addressing workplace issues affecting technical professional women, members of minority groups, and people with disabilities. Estab. 1969. Byline given. Pays on publication. No kill fee. Publishes ms an average of 3 months after acceptance. Editorial lead time 3 months. Accepts queries by mail, e-mail, fax, phone. Accepts simultaneous submissions. Responds in 2 weeks to queries. Responds in 2 months to mss. Sample copy free. Guidelines free.

NONFICTION Needs how-to, interview, personal experience. We do not want articles that are too general. Query. Length: 1,500-2,500 words. **Pays $350 for assigned articles.** Pays expenses of writers on assignment.

CHILD CARE & PARENTAL GUIDANCE

$$ AMERICAN BABY

Meredith Corp., 125 Park Ave., 6th Floor, New York NY 10017. **Website:** www.americanbaby.com. **Contact:** Dana Points, editor-in-chief. **70% freelance written.** Monthly magazine covering health, medical, and child care concerns for expectant and new parents, particularly those having their first child or those whose child is between the ages of birth and 2 years old. Mothers are the primary readers, but fathers' issues are equally important. Prefers to work with published/established writers; works with a small number of new/unpublished writers each year. Estab. 1938. Circ. 2,000,000. Byline given. Pays on acceptance. Offers 25% kill fee. Publishes ms an average of 6 months after acceptance. Editorial lead time 5 months. Submit seasonal material 6 months in advance. Accepts queries by mail. Accepts simultaneous submissions.

NONFICTION Needs book excerpts, essays, general interest, how-to, humor, new product. No "hearts and flowers" or fantasy pieces. **Buys 60 mss/year.** Length: 1,000-2,000 words. **Pays $800-1,000 for features, depending on article length and whether the author has previously written for** *American Baby*. **First-person experiences pay $500.** Pays expenses of writers on assignment.

REPRINTS Send photocopy and information about when and where the material previously appeared. Pays 50% of original price.

COLUMNS Personal essays (700-1,000 words) and shorter items for Crib Notes (news and features) and Medical Updates (50-350 words) are also accepted. **Pays $200-1,000.**

$ ATLANTA PARENT

2346 Perimeter Park Dr., Atlanta GA 30341. (770)454-7599. **E-mail:** editor@atlantaparent.com; atlantaparent@atlantaparent.com. **Website:** www.atlantaparent.com. **Contact:** Editor. **50% freelance written.** Monthly magazine for parents in the Atlanta metro area with children from birth to 18 years old. "*Atlanta Parent* magazine has been a valuable resource for Atlanta families since 1983. It is the only magazine in the Atlanta area providing pertinent, local, and award-winning family-oriented articles and information. Atlanta parents rely on us for features that are timely, informative, and reader-friendly on important issues such as childcare, family life, education, adolescence, motherhood, health, and teens. Fun, easy, and inexpensive family activities and crafts as well as the humorous side of parenting are also important to our readers." Estab. 1983. Byline given. Pays on publication. Publishes ms an average of 3 months after acceptance. Submit seasonal material 6 months in advance. Accepts queries by mail, e-mail. Accepts simultaneous submissions. Responds in 4 months to queries. Sample copy: $3.

NONFICTION Needs general interest, how-to, humor, interview, travel. No religious or philosophical discussions. **Buys 60 mss/year.** Send complete ms by mail or e-mail. Length: 800-1,200 words. **Pays $5-50.** Pays expenses of writers on assignment.

REPRINTS Send tearsheet or photocopy with rights for sale noted and information about when and where the material previously appeared. Pays $30-50.

$$ BIRMINGHAM PARENT

Evans Publishing LLC, 3590-B Hwy 31S. #289, Pelham AL 35124. (205)987-7700. **Fax:** (205)987-7600. **E-mail:** carol@biringhamparent.com. **Website:** www.birminghamparent.com. **Contact:** Carol Evans, publisher/editor. **75% freelance written.** Monthly magazine covering family issues, parenting, education, babies to teens, health care, anything involving parents raising children. "We are a free, local parenting publication in central Alabama. All of our stories carry some type of local slant. Parenting magazines abound: we are the source for the local market." Estab. 2004. Circ. 30,000. Byline given. Pays within 30 days of publication. Offers 20% kill fee. Publishes ms an average of 3-4 months after acceptance. Editorial lead time 3-4 months. Submit seasonal material 4 months in advance. Accepts queries by e-mail. Accepts simultaneous submissions. Responds in 2-3 weeks to queries. Responds in 2-3 months to mss. Sample copy for $3. Guidelines available online.

NONFICTION Needs book excerpts, general interest, how-to, interview, parenting. Does not want first person pieces. "Our pieces educate and inform; we don't take stories without sources." **Buys 24 mss/ year.** Send complete ms. Length: 350-2,500 words. **Pays $50-350 for assigned articles. Pays $35-200 for unsolicited articles.** Pays expenses of writers on assignment.

COLUMNS Parenting Solo (single parenting), 650 words; Baby & Me (dealing with newborns or pregnancy), 650 words; Teens (raising teenagers), 650-1,500 words. **Buys 36 mss/year.** Query with published clips or send complete ms. **Pays $35-200.**

💲 CHESAPEAKE FAMILY LIFE

Jefferson Communications, 121 Cathedral Street, Third Floor, Annapolis MD 21401. (410) 263-1641. **Fax:** (410) 280-0255. **E-mail:** editor@chesapeakefamily.com; calendar@jecoannapolis.com. **Website:** www.chesapeakefamily.com. **Contact:** Betsy Stein, editor. **80% freelance written.** Monthly magazine, website and e-mail newsletters covering parenting and other topics of interest to parents in Maryland. *Chesapeake Family LIFE* publishes a free, regional parenting publication, annual publications and e-mail newsletters serving readers in the Anne Arundel, Calvert, Prince George's and Queen Anne's counties of Maryland. Our goal is to identify tips, resources, and products that will make our readers' lives easier. "We answer the questions they don't have time to ask, doing the research for them so they have the information they need to make better decisions for their families' health, education, and well-being." Articles must have local angle and resources. Estab. 1990. Circ. 34,000. Byline given. Publishes ms an average of 2 months after acceptance. Editorial lead time 3-6 months. Submit seasonal material 4 months in advance. Accepts queries by mail, e-mail, fax. Accepts simultaneous submissions. Guidelines available online.

NONFICTION Needs how-to, interview, profile, travel. No general personal essays (however, personal anecdotes leading into a story with general applicability is fine). **Buys 25 mss/year.** Send complete ms. Length: 800-1,200 words. **Pays $75-150. Pays $35-50 for unsolicited articles.**

COLUMNS Buys 25 mss/year. Pays $35-50.

💲💲 CHICAGO PARENT

141 S. Oak Park Ave., Oak Park IL 60302. (708)386-5555. **E-mail:** tamara@chicagoparent.com; chiparent@chicagoparent.com. **Website:** www.chicagoparent.com. **Contact:** Tamara O'Shaughnessy, editor. **80% freelance written.** Monthly parenting magazine covering the six-county Chicago metropolitan area. *Chicago Parent* has a distinctly local approach. Offers information, inspiration, perspective, and empathy to Chicago-area parents. Lively editorial mix has a "we're all in this together" spirit, and articles are thoroughly researched and well written. Estab. 1988. Circ. 100,000. Byline given. Pays on publication. Offers 10-50% kill fee. Publishes ms an average of 2 months after acceptance. Editorial lead time 4 months. Submit seasonal material 4 months in advance. Accepts queries by e-mail. Responds in 6 weeks to queries. Sample copy for $4.95 and 11×17 SAE with $1.65 postage direct to circulation. Guidelines available on website.

NONFICTION Needs essays, expose, general interest, how-to, humor, interview, personal experience, profile, travel. No pot-boiler parenting pieces or nonlocal writers (from outside the six-county Chicago metropolitan area and Northwest Indiana). **Buys 40-50 mss/year.** Query with links to published clips. Length: 200-2,500 words. **Pays $50-450 for assigned articles.**

💲 GRAND RAPIDS FAMILY MAGAZINE

Gemini Publications, 549 Ottawa Ave. NW, Suite 201, Grand Rapids MI 49503-1444. (616)459-4545. **Fax:** (616)459-4800. **E-mail:** cvalade@geminipub.com. **Website:** www.grfamilymag.com. **Contact:** Carole Valade, editor. Monthly magazine covering local parenting issues. *Grand Rapids Family* seeks to inform, instruct, amuse, and entertain its readers and their families. Circ. 30,000. Byline given. Pays on publication. Offers $25 kill fee. Editorial lead time 3 months. Submit seasonal material 4 months in advance. Accepts simultaneous submissions. Responds in 2 months to queries. Responds in 6 months to mss. Guidelines with #10 SASE.

NONFICTION Query. **Pays $25-50.** Pays expenses of writers on assignment.

COLUMNS All local: law, finance, humor, opinion, mental health. **Pays $25.**

$ HOMESCHOOLING TODAY

Paradigm Press, LLC, P.O. Box 1092, Somerset KY 42502. (606)485-4105. **E-mail:** editor@homeschoolingtoday.com. **Website:** www.homeschooltoday.com. **Contact:** Alex Wiggers, publisher; Ashley Wiggers and Debbie Strayer, executive editors. **75% freelance written.** Bimonthly magazine covering homeschooling. "We are a practical magazine for homeschoolers with a broadly Christian perspective." Estab. 1992. Circ. 13,000. Byline given. Pays on publication. Offers 25% kill fee. Publishes ms an average of 1 year after acceptance. Editorial lead time 6 months. Submit seasonal material 1 year in advance. Accepts simultaneous submissions. Responds in 4 months to mss. Sample copy free. Guidelines online.

NONFICTION Needs book excerpts, how-to, interview, new product. No fiction. **Buys 30 mss/year.** Send complete ms. Length: 500-2,000 words. **Pays 10¢/word.**

$ HUDSON VALLEY PARENT

The Professional Image, 174 South St., Newburgh NY 12550. (845)562-3606. **E-mail:** editor@excitingread.com. **Website:** www.hvparent.com. **Contact:** Sara Dunn. **95% freelance written.** Monthly magazine covering local parents and families. Estab. 1994. Circ. 80,000. Byline given. Pays on publication. No kill fee. Publishes ms an average of 3 months after acceptance. Editorial lead time 4 months. Submit seasonal material 4 months in advance. Accepts queries by e-mail. Accepts simultaneous submissions. Responds in 2-4 weeks to mss. Sample copy free. Guidelines available online.

NONFICTION Needs expose, general interest, humor, interview, personal experience. **Buys 20 mss/year.** Query. Length: 700-1,200 words. **Pays $80-120 for assigned articles. Pays $25-35 for unsolicited articles.** Pays expenses of writers on assignment.

REPRINTS Pays $25-35 for reprints.

$$ INDY'S CHILD MAGAZINE

Midwest Parenting Publications, 6340 Westfield Blvd., Suite 200, Indianapolis IN 46220. (317)722-8500. **E-mail:** indyschild@indyschild.com. **E-mail:** susan@indyschild.com. **Website:** www.indyschild.com. **Contact:** Susan Bryant, editor. **100% freelance written.** *Indy's Child* Parenting Magazine is a local and nationally award-winning parenting magazine. As an independent publication, we strive to make sure we give our readers exactly what they are looking for. We are a valuable guide for parents, educators, and child care providers, and we are 1 of the only publications to be distributed to a majority of schools, libraries, child care agencies, and other family-oriented facilities." Estab. 1985. Byline given. Pays on publication. No kill fee. Publishes ms an average of 6 months after acceptance. Editorial lead time 3 months. Submit seasonal material 6 months in advance. Accepts queries by e-mail. Accepts simultaneous submissions. Guidelines available online.

NONFICTION Needs expose, general interest, historical, how-to, humor, inspirational, interview, opinion, photo feature, travel. **Buys 50 mss/year.** Query by e-mail. See editorial calendar for upcoming topics. **Pay based on assigned word count.** Pays expenses of writers on assignment.

COLUMNS Query by e-mail. **Pay based on assigned word count.**

🍁$ ISLAND PARENT MAGAZINE

Island Parent Group, 830-A Pembroke St., Victoria BC V8T 1H9 Canada. (250)388-6905. **E-mail:** editor@islandparent.ca. **Website:** www.islandparent.ca. **Contact:** Sue Fast, editor. **98% freelance written.** Monthly magazine covering parenting. Estab. 1988. Circ. 20,000. Byline given. No kill fee. Publishes ms an average of 3 months after acceptance. Editorial lead time 3 months. Submit seasonal material 3 months in advance. Accepts queries by e-mail. Accepts simultaneous submissions. Responds in 6 weeks to queries. Sample copy and guidelines available online.

NONFICTION Needs book excerpts, essays, general interest, how-to, humor, inspirational, interview, opinion, personal experience, travel. **Buys 80 mss/year.** Query. Length: 1,000 words average. **Pays $35.**

FILLERS Needs anecdotes, facts, gags, newsbreaks, short humor. **Buys 10 mss/year.** Length: 400-650 words. **Pays $35.**

$ MEDIA FOR LIVING, VALLEY LIVING MAGAZINE

Shalom Foundation, P.O. Box 1501, Harrisonburg VA 22803. (540)433-5351. **E-mail:** info@valleyliving.org. **E-mail:** melodie@valleyliving.org. **Website:** www.valleyliving.org. Lindsey Shantz. **80% freelance**

written. Quarterly magazine covering family living. Articles focus on giving general encouragement for families of all ages and stages. "Our bias is to use articles *showing* rather than telling readers how to raise families (stories rather than how-to). We aim for articles that are well written, understandable, challenging (not the same old thing you've read elsewhere); they should stimulate readers to dig a little deeper, but not too deep with academic or technical language; that are interesting and fit our theological perspective (Christian) but are not preachy or overly patriotic. No favorable mentions of smoking, drinking, cursing, etc. We want our stories and articles to be very practical and upbeat. We do not assume a Christian audience. Writers need to take this into account. Personal-experience stories are welcome but are not the only approach. Our audience? Children, teenagers, singles, married couples, right on through to retired persons. We cover the wide variety of subjects that people face in the home and workplace. (See theme list in our guidelines online.)" Estab. 1990. Circ. 11,000. Byline given. Pays on publication. No kill fee. Publishes ms an average of 6-12 months after acceptance. Editorial lead time 4-6 months. Submit seasonal material 6 months in advance. Accepts queries by mail, e-mail, online submission form. Accepts simultaneous submissions. Responds in 2 months to queries; 2-4 months to mss. Sample copy for SAE with 9x12 envelope and 4 first-class stamps.

NONFICTION Needs general interest, how-to, humor, inspirational, personal experience. "We do not use devotional materials intended for Christian audiences. We seldom use pet stories and receive way too many grief/death/dealing-with-serious-illness stories. We publish in March, June, September, and December, so holidays that occur in other months are not usually the subject of articles." **Buys 48-52 mss/year.** Query. Length: 500-1,200 words. **Pays $35-60.**

$ METROFAMILY MAGAZINE

Inprint Publishing, 318 NW 13th St., Suite 101, Oklahoma City OK 73103. (405)818-5025. **E-mail:** editor@metrofamilymagazine.com. **Website:** www.metrofamilymagazine.com. **Contact:** Hannah Schmitt, editor. **20% freelance written.** Monthly tabloid covering parenting. Circ. 35,000. Byline given. Pays on publication. No kill fee. Requests ms an average of 2-3 months after acceptance. Editorial lead time 3-6 months. Accepts queries by e-mail. Accepts simultaneous submissions. Responds in 3 weeks to queries (only if interested). Responds in 1 month to mss. Sample copy for SAE with 10x13 envelope and 3 first-class stamps. Guidelines available online.

NONFICTION Family or mom-specific articles; see website for themes. No poetry, fiction (except for humor column), or anything that doesn't support good, solid family values. Submit via e-mail only. "We are interested in well-written, thought-provoking feature stories (800-1,500 words), short features (400-750 words) or shorts (up to 400 words) that focus on timely issues and highlight local experts or conditions." **Pays $40-60, plus 1 contributor's copy.** Pays expenses of writers on assignment.

COLUMNS "Our columns are all written by our regular, staff writers and freelance submissions will not be considered for columns."

$ METROKIDS

Kidstuff Publications, Inc., 1412-1414 Pine St., Philadelphia PA 19102. (215)291-5560, ext. 102. **Fax:** (215)291-5565. **E-mail:** editor@metrokids.com. **Website:** www.metrokids.com. **Contact:** Sara Murphy, managing editor. **25% freelance written.** Monthly magazine providing information for parents and kids in Philadelphia and surrounding counties, South Jersey, and Delaware. "*MetroKids*, a free monthly magazine, is a resource for parents living in the greater Delaware Valley. The Pennsylvania, South Jersey, and Delaware editions of *MetroKids* are available in supermarkets, libraries, daycares, and hundreds of other locations. The magazine and website feature the area's most extensive calendar of day-by-day family events; child-focused camp, day care, and party directories; local family fun suggestions; and articles that offer parenting advice and insights. Other *MetroKids* publications include *The Ultimate Family Guide*, a guide to area attractions, service providers, and community resources; SpecialKids, a resource guide for families of children with special needs; and Educator's Edition, a directory of field trips, assemblies, and school enrichment programs." Estab. 1990. Circ. 90,000. Byline given. Pays on publication. Submit seasonal material 4 months in advance. Accepts queries by e-mail. Accepts simultaneous submissions. Guidelines available by e-mail.

NONFICTION Needs general interest, how-to, new product. Special issues: See editorial calendar online for current needs. **Buys 40 mss/year.** Query with published clips. Length: 575-1,500 words. **Pays $50.** Pays expenses of writers on assignment.

REPRINTS E-mail summary or complete article and information about when and where the material previously appeared. Pays $35, or $50 if localized after discussion.

COLUMNS Tech Talk, Mom Matters, Health, Money, Your Home, Parenting, Toddlers, Tweens/Teens, Education, Food & Nutrition, Play, Toddlers, Camp, Classes, Features, all 650-850 words. **Buys 25 mss/year.** Query. **Pays $25-50.**

$$ METRO PARENT MAGAZINE

Metro Parent Publishing Group, 22041 Woodward Ave., Ferndale MI 48220. (248)398-3400. **Fax:** (248)339-4215. **E-mail:** editor@metroparent.com; jelliott@metroparent.com. **Website:** www.metroparent.com. **Contact:** Julia Elliott, editor. **75% freelance written.** Monthly magazine covering parenting, women's health, education. "MetroParent.com is an online parenting community offering expert advice, stories on parenting trends and issues, and numerous ways for parents to enrich their experience raising the next generation. It is part of Metro Parent Publishing Group, which began in suburban Detroit in 1986. Publications include Metro Parent magazine, Metro Baby, Going Places, Special Edition, Party Book and Big Book of Schools. Metro Parent Publishing Group also brings family-friendly events to southeast Michigan as part of its events department." Circ. 60,000. Byline given. Pays on publication. Publishes ms an average of 3 months after acceptance. Editorial lead time 3 months. Submit seasonal material 3 months in advance. Accepts queries by mail, e-mail. Accepts simultaneous submissions. Responds in 2 weeks to queries. Responds in 3 months to mss. Sample copy for $2.50. Guidelines available online.

NONFICTION Needs essays, humor, inspirational, personal experience. **Buys 100 mss/year.** Send complete ms. Length: 1,500-2,500 words for features, 500-700 words for Getaway pieces, 100-600 words for Parent Pipeline pieces. **Pays $150-300 for feature articles, $35-50 for Parent Pipeline pieces.** Pays expenses of writers on assignment.

COLUMNS Women's Health (latest issues of 20-40 year olds), 750-900 words; Solo Parenting (advice for single parents); Family Finance (making sense of money and legal issues); Tweens 'N Teens (handling teen issues), 750-800 words. **Buys 50 mss/year.** Send complete ms. **Pays $50-75.**

$ PEDIATRICS FOR PARENTS

Pediatrics for Parents, Inc., P.O. Box 219, Gloucester MA 01931. (215)253-4543. **Fax:** (973)302-4543. **E-mail:** editor@pedsforparents.com. **E-mail:** submissions@pedsforparents.com. **Website:** www.pedsforparents.com. **Contact:** Richard J. Sagall, M.D., editor. **50% freelance written.** Monthly newsletter covering children's health. "*Pediatrics For Parents* emphasizes an informed, common-sense approach to childhood health care. We stress preventative action, accident prevention, when to call the doctor, and when and how to handle a situation at home. We are also looking for articles that describe general, medical, and pediatric problems, advances, new treatments, etc. All articles must be medically accurate and useful to parents with children—prenatal to adolescence." Estab. 1981. Circ. 120,000. Byline given. Pays on publication. Publishes ms an average of 4 months after acceptance. Accepts queries by mail, e-mail, fax. Accepts simultaneous submissions. Responds in 1 month to queries. Sample copy available online. Guidelines available online.

NONFICTION No first person or experience. **Buys 25 mss/year.** Send complete ms with cover letter containing contact info. Prefers electronic submissions: Send to submissions@pedsforparents.com. Length: 1,000-1,500 words. **Pays $25 and either a 1-year subscription of print issue or a lifetime subscription to PDF version of the newsletter.** Pays expenses of writers on assignment.

$ PIKES PEAK PARENT

The Gazette/Freedom Communications, 30 S. Prospect St., Colorado Springs CO 80903. **Fax:** (719)476-1625. **Website:** www.pikespeakparent.com. **10% freelance written.** Monthly tabloid covering parenting, family, and grandparenting. We prefer stories with local angle and local stories. We do not accept unsolicited manuscripts. Estab. 1994. Circ. 35,000. Byline given. Pays on publication. No kill fee. Editorial lead time 3 months. Submit seasonal material 4 months in advance. Accepts queries by e-mail. Accepts simultaneous submissions. Responds in 1 month to queries. Sample copy available online.

NONFICTION Needs essays, general interest, how-to, medical related to parenting. **Buys 10 mss/year.**

Query with published clips. Length: 800-1,000 words. **Pays $20-120.**

💲💲 SACRAMENTO PARENT

Family Publishing Inc., 457 Grass Valley Hwy., Suite 5, Auburn CA 95603. (530)888-0573. **Fax:** (530)888-1536. **E-mail:** shelly@sacramentoparent.com. **E-mail:** shannon@sacramentoparent.com. **Website:** www.sacramentoparent.com. **Contact:** Shelly Bokman, editor in chief; Shannon Smith, editor. **50% freelance written.** Monthly magazine covering parenting in the Sacramento region. "We look for articles that promote a developmentally appropriate, healthy, and peaceful environment for children." Estab. 1992. Circ. 50,000. Byline given. Pays on publication. Offers 10% kill fee. Publishes ms an average of 2 months after acceptance. Editorial lead time 3 months. Submit seasonal material 4 months in advance. Accepts queries by e-mail. Accepts simultaneous submissions. Sample copy free. Guidelines available online.

NONFICTION Needs book excerpts, general interest, how-to, humor, interview, opinion, personal experience. **Buys 36 mss/year.** Query. Length: 300-1,000 words. **Pays $50-200 for original articles.** Pays expenses of writers on assignment.

COLUMNS Let's Go! (Sacramento regional family-friendly day trips/excursions/activities), 600 words. **Pays $25-45.**

💲 SAN DIEGO FAMILY MAGAZINE

Special Needs Resource Foundation of San Diego (nonprofit), 1475 6th Ave., 5th Floor, San Diego CA 92101-3200. (619)685-6970. **Fax:** (619)685-6978. **E-mail:** family@sandiegofamily.com. **E-mail:** editor@sandiegofamily.com. **Website:** www.sandiegofamily.com; www.SNRFSD.org. **100% freelance written.** "*San Diego Family Magazine* is a regional monthly family publication. We focus on providing current, informative and interesting editorial about parenting and family life that educates and entertains." Estab. 1982. Circ. 100,000. Byline given. Pays on publication. No kill fee. Publishes an 1-6 months after acceptance. Editorial lead time 4 months. Submit seasonal material 2-6 months in advance. Accepts queries by e-mail. Accepts simultaneous submissions. Responds in 1 week-1 month to queries of interest. Sometimes no response if e-mail is "lost" in inbox. Sample copy for $4.50 to P.O. Box 23960, San Diego CA 92193. Guidelines online.

NONFICTION Needs general interest, how-to, interview, personal experience, technical, informational articles. Special issues: Summer camps: March through June *Flourishing Families*, a guide for families with special needs (annual); *Out and About*, an adventure guide for local and visiting families (annual). Does not want personal essays, opinion pieces. **Buys 350-500 mss/year.** Query. Length: 500-950 words. **Pays $35-120.**

REPRINTS E-mail with rights for sale, ted and information about when and where the material previously appeared.

FILLERS Buys 0-6 mss/year. Send complete ms. Length: 200-600 words.

💲💲 SOUTH FLORIDA PARENTING

6501 Nob Hill Rd., Tamarac FL 33321. (954)698-6397. **Fax:** (954)421-9002. **E-mail:** editor@sfparenting.com. **Website:** www.sfparenting.com. **Contact:** Jennifer Jhon, editor. **90% freelance written.** Monthly magazine covering parenting, family. "*South Florida Parenting* provides news, information, and a calendar of events for readers in Southeast Florida (Palm Beach, Broward and Miami-Dade counties). The focus is on parenting issues, things to do, information about raising children in South Florida." Estab. 1990. Circ. 110,000. Byline given. Pays on publication. No kill fee. Editorial lead time 4 months. Submit seasonal material 4 months in advance. Accepts queries by e-mail, fax. Accepts simultaneous submissions. Responds in 3 months to queries.

NONFICTION family, parenting and children's issues. Special issues: family fitness, education, spring party guide, fall party guide, kids and the environment, toddler/preschool, preteen. **Pays $25-115.** Pays expenses of writers on assignment.

REPRINTS Pays $25-50.

COLUMNS Dad's Perspective, Family Deals, Products for Families, Health/Safety, Nutrition, Baby Basics, Travel, Toddler/Preschool, Preteen, South Florida News.

💲💲 SOUTHWEST FLORIDA PARENT & CHILD

The News-Press, A Gannett Company, 2442 Dr. Martin Luther King, Jr. Blvd., Fort Myers FL 33901. (239)335-0200. **Fax:** (239)344-0708. **E-mail:** editor@swflparentchild.com; phayford@fortmyer.gannett.com. **Website:** http://news-press.com/moms. **Con-**

tact: Pamela Smith Hayford, editor. **75% freelance written.** Monthly magazine covering parenting. "*Southwest Florida Parent & Child* is a regional parenting magazine with an audience of mostly moms but some dads, too. With every article, we strive to give readers information they can use. We aim to be an indispensable resource for our local parents." Estab. 2000. Circ. 25,000. Byline given. Pays on publication. Publishes ms an average of 2-3 months after acceptance. Editorial lead time 2-3 months. Submit seasonal material 3+ months in advance. Accepts queries by mail, e-mail. Accepts simultaneous submissions.

NONFICTION Needs book excerpts, general interest, how-to, humor, interview, new product, personal experience, photo feature, religious, travel. Does not want personal experience or opinion pieces. **Buys 96-120 mss/year.** Send complete ms. Length: 500-700 words. **Pays $25-200.** Sometimes pays expenses of writers on assignment.

✪$$$$ TODAY'S PARENT

Rogers Media, Inc., 1 Mt. Pleasant Rd., 8th Floor, Toronto Ontario M4Y 2Y5 Canada. (416)764-2883. **Fax:** (416)764-2894. **E-mail:** editors@todaysparent.com. **Website:** www.todaysparent.com. **Contact:** Alicia Kowalewski, art director. Monthly magazine for parents with children up to the age of 12. Circ. 2 million. No kill fee. Editorial lead time 5 months. Accepts simultaneous submissions.

NONFICTION Length: 1,800-2,500 words. **Pays $1,500-2,200.** Pays expenses of writers on assignment.

COLUMNS What's New (games/apps/movies/toys); Health (parents and children); Behaviour; Relationships; Steps and Stages; How Does He/She Do It; Bright Idea; Food/In the Kitchen.

✪$$$$ TODAY'S PARENT PREGNANCY & BIRTH

Rogers Media, Inc., One Mt. Pleasant Rd., 8th Floor, Toronto ON M4Y 2Y5 Canada. (416)764-2883. **Fax:** (416) 764-2894. **E-mail:** editors@todaysparent.com. **Website:** www.todaysparent.com. **100% freelance written.** Magazine published 3 times/year. "*P&B* helps, supports and encourages expectant and new parents with news and features related to pregnancy, birth, human sexuality and parenting." Estab. 1973. Circ. 190,000. Pays on acceptance. Publishes ms an average of 8 months after acceptance. Editorial lead time 6 months. Accepts queries by mail. Responds in 6 weeks to queries. Guidelines for SASE.

NONFICTION Buys 12 mss/year. Query with published clips; send detailed proposal. Length: 1,000-2,500 words. **Pays up to $1/word.** Sometimes pays expenses of writers on assignment.

$$ TOLEDO AREA PARENT NEWS

Adams Street Publishing, Co., 1120 Adams St., Toledo OH 43604. (419)244-9859. **E-mail:** cjacobs@adamsstreetpublishing.com; editor@adamsstreetpublishing.com. **Website:** www.toledoparent.com. **Contact:** Collette Jacobs, editor in chief and publisher; Nadine Hariri, assignment editor. Monthly tabloid for Northwest Ohio/Southeast Michigan parents. Estab. 1992. Circ. 40,000. Byline given. Pays on publication. No kill fee. Publishes ms an average of 1 month after acceptance. Editorial lead time 3 months. Accepts queries by mail, e-mail, fax. Responds in 1 month to queries. Sample copy: $1.50.

NONFICTION Needs general interest, interview, opinion. **Buys 10 mss/year.** Length: 1,000-2,500 words. **Pays $75-125.**

$$ TWINS™ MAGAZINE

30799 Pinetree Road, #256, Cleveland OH 44124. (855)758-9567. **Fax:** (855)758-9567. **E-mail:** twinseditor@twinsmagazine.com. **Website:** www.twinsmagazine.com. **Contact:** Christa Reed, editor. **50% freelance written.** "We now publish 8 issues/year—4 print/4 digital covering all aspects of parenting twins/multiples. *Twins* is a national/international publication that provides informational and educational articles regarding the parenting of twins, triplets, and more. All articles must be multiple specific and have an upbeat, hopeful, and/or positive ending." Estab. 1984. Circ. 35,000. Byline given. Pays on publication. Editorial lead time 4 months. Submit seasonal material 6 months in advance. Response time varies. Sample copy for $5 or on website. Guidelines available online.

NONFICTION Needs personal experience, professional experience as it relates to multiples. Nothing on cloning, pregnancy reduction, or fertility issues. **Buys 12 mss/year.** Send complete ms. Length: 650-1,100 words. **Pays $25-250 for assigned articles. Pays $25-125 for unsolicited articles.** Pays expenses of writers on assignment.

COLUMNS A Word From Dad; Double Takes; Mom-2-Mom; LOL: Laugh Out Loud; Family Health; Resource Round Up; Tales From Twins; Twins in the News; Twin Start Spotlight; & Research. Pays $25-75.

Buys 8-10 mss/year. Query with or without published clips or send complete ms. **Pays $40-75.**

COMIC BOOKS

💲 THE COMICS JOURNAL

Fantagraphics Books, 7563 Lake City Way NE, Seattle WA 98115. (206)524-1967. **Fax:** (206)524-2104. **E-mail:** editorial@tcj.com. **Website:** www.tcj.com. Editorial Coordinator: Kristy Valenti. Magazine covering the comics medium from an arts-first perspective on a six-week schedule. *"The Comics Journal* is one of the nation's most respected single-arts magazines, providing its readers with an eclectic mix of industry news, professional interviews, and reviews of current work. Due to its reputation as the American magazine with an interest in comics as an art form, the *Journal* has subscribers worldwide, and in this country serves as an important window into the world of comics for several general arts and news magazines." Byline given. Accepts queries by mail, e-mail. Accepts simultaneous submissions. Guidelines available online.

NONFICTION Needs essays, interview, opinion, reviews. Send complete ms. Length: 2,000-3,000 words. **Pays 4¢/word, and 1 contributor's copy.** Pays expenses of writers on assignment.

COLUMNS On Theory, Art and Craft (2,000-3,000 words); Firing Line (reviews 1,000-5,000 words); Bullets (reviews 400 words or less). Send inquiries, samples **Pays 4¢/word, and 1 contributor's copy.**

CONSUMER SERVICE & BUSINESS OPPORTUNITY

💲💲💲💲 CONSUMERS DIGEST

Consumers Digest Communications LLC, 520 Lake-Cook Rd., Suite 500, Deerfield IL 60015. (847)607-3000. **Fax:** (847)607-3009. **E-mail:** editor@consumersdigest.com. **Website:** www.consumersdigest.com. **95% freelance written.** Bimonthly magazine covering consumer matters, new products/services. *Consumers Digest* is designed to provide opinions and recommendations in regard to consumer issues. Estab. 1959. Byline given. Pays on acceptance. Offers 50% kill fee. Publishes ms an average of 2 months after acceptance. Editorial lead time 3-4 months. Submit seasonal material 8 months in advance. Accepts queries by mail, e-mail. Accepts simultaneous submissions.

NONFICTION Needs expose, general interest, new product. **Buys 70 mss/year.** Query. Length: 1,300-3,500 words. **Pays 75¢-$1/word.** Pays expenses of writers on assignment.

💲💲 HOME BUSINESS MAGAZINE

20664 Jutland Place, Lakeville MN 55044. **E-mail:** editor@homebusinessmag.com. **Website:** www.homebusinessmag.com. **Contact:** Sherilyn Colleen. **75% freelance written.** Covers every angle of the home-based business market including: cutting edge editorial by well-known authorities on sales and marketing, business operations, the home office, franchising, business opportunities, network marketing, mail order, and other subjects to help readers choose, manage, and prosper in a home-based business; display advertising, classified ads and a directory of home-based businesses; technology, the Internet, computers, and the future of home-based business; home-office editorial including management advice, office set-up, and product descriptions; business opportunities, franchising and work-from-home success stories. Estab. 1993. Circ. 105,000. No kill fee. Publishes ms an average of 6 months after acceptance. Editorial lead time 6 months. Submit seasonal material 6 months in advance. Accepts queries by e-mail. Accepts simultaneous submissions. Sample copy for sae with 9x12 envelope and 8 first-class stamps. Guidelines for #10 SASE.

NONFICTION Needs book excerpts, general interest, how-to, inspirational, interview, new product, personal experience, photo feature. No non-home business related topics. **Buys 40 mss/year.** Send complete ms. "Send complete information by e-mail. We encourage writers to submit feature articles (2-3 pages) and departmental articles (1 page). Please submit polished, well-written, organized material. It helps to provide subheadings within the article. Boxes, lists, and bullets are encouraged because they make your article easier to read, use, and reference by the reader. A primary problem in the past is that articles do not stick to the subject of the title. Please pay attention to the focus of your article and to your title. Please don't call to get the status of your submission. We will call if we're interested in publishing the submission." Length: 200-1,000 words. **Pays 20¢/published word for work-for-hire assignments; 50-word byline for**

unsolicited articles. Pays expenses of writers on assignment.

COLUMNS Marketing & Sales; Money Corner; Home Office; Management; Technology; Working Smarter; Franchising; Network Marketing, all 650 words. Send complete ms.

CONTEMPORARY CULTURE

💲💲 A&U

Art & Understanding, Inc., 25 Monroe St., Suite 205, Albany NY 12210-2729. (518)426-9010. **Fax:** (518)436-5354. **E-mail:** chaelneedle@mac.com. **Website:** www.aumag.org. Poetry Editor: Noah Stetzer. **Contact:** Chael Needle, managing editor. **50% freelance written.** Monthly national nonprofit print magazine covering cultural, political, and medical responses to HIV/AIDS, including poetry, fiction and drama. Estab. 1991. Circ. 180,000. Byline given. Pays 1-3 months after publication. Publishes ms an average of 1-3 months after acceptance. Editorial lead time 6 months. Accepts queries by mail, e-mail. Accepts simultaneous submissions. Responds in 1 month to queries; in 2 months to mss. Sample copy: $5. Guidelines online.

NONFICTION Needs book excerpts, essays, general interest, humor, interview, opinion, personal experience, photo feature, profile. **Buys 6 mss/year.** Query with published clips. Length: 800-1,200 words. **Pays $150-300 for assigned articles.**

COLUMNS The Culture of AIDS (reviews of books, music, film), 300 words; Viewpoint (personal opinion), 750 words. **Buys 8 mss/year.** Send complete ms. **Pays $175.**

FICTION Literary electronic submissions, as Word attachments, may be mailed to Brent Calderwood, literary editor, at aumaglit@gmail.com. Pay rate schedule available upon request. Send complete ms. Length: up to 1,500 words. **Pays $50.**

POETRY Contact: Noah Stetzer. Accepts any length/style (shorter works preferred). Buys 8-10 poems/year. **Pays $50.**

♻💲💲 ADBUSTERS

Adbusters Media Foundation, 1243 W. Seventh Ave., Vancouver BC V6H 1B7 Canada. (604)736-9401. **E-mail:** editor@adbusters.org. **Website:** www.adbusters.

org. **50% freelance written.** Bimonthly magazine on consumerism. "Based in Vancouver, British Columbia, Canada, *Adbusters* is a not-for-profit, reader-supported magazine concerned with the erosion of our physical and cultural environments by commercial forces. Since 1989, the magazine has been featured in hundreds of alternative and mainstream newspapers, magazines, television, and radio shows. Known worldwide for sparking Occupy Wall Street, *Adbusters* is also responsible for social media campaigns such as Buy Nothing Day and Digital Detox Week. Included in the magazine are incisive philosophical articles and activist commentary, coupled with impact design that seeks to unbound the traditional magazine format. Issues relevant to our contemporary moment, such as media concentration, climate change, and genetically modified foods, are regularly featured. We seek out a world where economy and ecology exist in harmony. By challenging people to become participants as opposed to spectators, *Adbusters* takes aim at corporate disinformation, global injustice, and the industries and governments who actively pollute and destroy our physical and mental commons." Estab. 1989. Circ. 90,000. Byline given. Pays 1 month after publication. Accepts queries by mail, e-mail, fax. Accepts simultaneous submissions. Guidelines available online.

NONFICTION Needs essays, expose, interview, opinion. **Buys variable mss/year.** Query. Length: 250-3,000 words. **Pays $100/page for unsolicited articles; 50¢/word for solicited articles.** Pays expenses of writers on assignment.

FICTION Inquire about themes.

POETRY Inquire about themes.

💲💲 BOSTON REVIEW

P.O. Box 425786, Cambridge MA 02142. (617)324-1360. **E-mail:** review@bostonreview.net. **Website:** www.bostonreview.net. **Contact:** Deborah Chasman and Joshua Cohen, editors. **90% freelance written.** Online and print magazine of cultural and political analysis, reviews, fiction, and poetry. The editors are committed to a society that fosters human diversity and a democracy in which we seek common grounds of principle amidst our many differences. In the hope of advancing these ideals, *Boston Review* acts as a forum that seeks to enrich the language of public debate. Estab. 1975. Byline given. Time between acceptance and publication is 4 months for nonfiction, 1 year for fiction and poetry. Accepts queries by e-mail, online submission form. Accepts simultaneous submissions. Responds in 4 months to queries. Sample copy for $10 plus shipping; purchase online at bostonreview.net/store. Guidelines online.

NONFICTION Needs book excerpts, essays, expose, general interest, historical, interview, reviews, Philosophy, Political Studies. **Buys 200 mss/year.** Submit query letters and unsolicited nonfiction up to 5,000 words via the online submissions system.

FICTION Currently closed to general fiction submissions but assembling a special issue of fiction on global dystopias, edited by Junot Díaz. See submission page for details. Needs ethnic, experimental, fantasy, horror, science fiction, short stories, Afrofuturist, dystopian, speculative. **Buys 20 mss/year.** Send complete ms. Length: up to 5,000 words, but can be much shorter. **Pays $100-300 and contributor's copies.**

POETRY "We are open to both traditional and experimental forms. What we value most is originality and a strong sense of voice." Send materials for review consideration. Buys 50 poems/year. Submit maximum 6 poems. **Payment varies.**

🍁 $ $ BROKEN PENCIL

P.O. Box 203, Station P, Toronto ON M5S 2S7 Canada. **E-mail:** editor@brokenpencil.com. **Website:** www.brokenpencil.com. Hal Niedzviecki, publisher. **Contact:** Alison Lang, editor. **80% freelance written.** Quarterly magazine covering arts and culture. "*Broken Pencil* is one of the few magazines in the world devoted exclusively to underground culture and the independent arts. We are a great resource and a lively read! *Broken Pencil* reviews the best zines, books, websites, videos, and artworks from the underground and reprints the best articles from the alternative press. From the hilarious to the perverse, *Broken Pencil* challenges conformity and demands attention." Estab. 1995. Circ. 5,000. Byline given. Pays on publication. Publishes ms an average of 2-3 months after acceptance. Accepts queries by mail, e-mail. Accepts simultaneous submissions. Guidelines available online.

NONFICTION Needs essays, general interest, historical, humor, interview, opinion, personal experience, photo feature, reviews, travel. Special issues: Canzine Issue (Fall); Deathmatch Issue (Spring). Does not want anything about mainstream art and culture. **Buys 8 mss/year.** Query with published clips. Length: 400-2,500 words. **Pays $30-300.** Pays expenses of writers on assignment.

COLUMNS Books (book reviews and feature articles); Music (music reviews and feature articles); Film (film reviews and feature articles), all 200-300 words for reviews, and up to 1,000 words for features. **Buys 8 mss/year.** Query with published clips. **Pays $30-300.**

FICTION "We're particularly interested in work from emerging writers." Reads fiction submissions February 1-September 15. Needs adventure, erotica, ethnic, experimental, fantasy, historical, horror, humorous, mystery, romance, science fiction, short stories. Submit via online submissions manager. Length: 50-3,000 words. **Pays $30-300.**

$ $ BUST MAGAZINE

Bust, Inc., 253 36th St., Suite C307, Brooklyn NY 11232. **E-mail:** debbie@bust.com. **E-mail:** submissions@bust.com. **Website:** www.bust.com. **Contact:** Debbie Stoller, editor in chief/publisher. **60% freelance written.** Bimonthly magazine covering pop culture for young women. "*Bust* is the groundbreaking, original women's lifestyle magazine and website that is unique in its ability to connect with bright, cutting-edge, influential young women." Estab. 1993. Circ. 100,000. Byline given. Pays on publication. No kill fee. Publishes ms an average of 4 months after acceptance. Editorial lead time 3-4 months. Submit seasonal material 6 months in advance. Accepts queries by mail, e-mail. Accepts simultaneous submissions. Response time varies. Guidelines online at www.bust.com/info/submit.html.

NONFICTION Needs book excerpts, general interest, historical, how-to, humor, inspirational, interview, new product, personal experience, photo feature, travel. Special issues: "No dates are currently set, but we usually have a fashion issue, a music issue and a *Men We Love* issue periodically." We do not want poetry; no stories not relating to women. **Buys 60+ mss/year.** Query with published clips. Length: 350-3,000 words. **Pays up to $250.** Pays expenses of writers on assignment.

COLUMNS **Contact:** Emily Rems, managing editor. Books (reviews of books by women); Music (reviews of music by/about women); Movies (reviews of movies by/about women), all 300 words; One-Handed-Read (Erotic Fiction for Women), 1,200 words. **Buys 6 mss/year.** Query with published clips. **Pays up to $100.**

FICTION Contact: Jenni Miller, Sex Files editor. Needs erotica. "We only publish erotic fiction. All other content is nonfiction." **Buys 6 mss/year.** Query with published clips. Length: 1,000-1,500 words. **Pays up to $50.**

CANADIAN DIMENSION

2E-91 Albert St., Winnipeg Manitoba R3B 1G5 Canada. (204)957-1519. **E-mail:** editor@canadiandimension.com. **Website:** www.canadiandimension.com. **Contact:** Cy Gonick, publisher and coordinating editor. **80% freelance written.** Bimonthly magazine covering politics and world issues from a socialist perspective. "We bring a socialist perspective to bear on events across Canada and around the world. Our contributors provide in-depth coverage on popular movements, peace, labour, women, aboriginal justice, environment, third world, and eastern Europe." Estab. 1963. Circ. 3,000. Pays on publication. Publishes ms an average of 6 months after acceptance. Submit seasonal materials 2-3 months in advance. Accepts queries by e-mail. Accepts simultaneous submissions. Responds in 6 weeks to queries. Sample copy: $2. Guidelines available online.

NONFICTION Needs interview, opinion, reviews. Special issues: See website for list of upcoming themes. **Buys 8 mss/year.** Query. Length: 500-2,000 words. **Pays $25-100.** Pays expenses of writers on assignment.

REPRINTS Send typed ms with rights for sale noted and information about when and where the material previously appeared.

COMMENTARY

561 7th Ave., 16th Floor, New York NY 10018. (212)891-1400. **E-mail:** submissions@commentarymagazine.com. **Website:** www.commentarymagazine.com. **Contact:** John Podhoretz, editor. Monthly magazine covering Judaism, politics, and culture. "*Commentary* is America's premier monthly magazine of opinion and a pivotal voice in American intellectual life. Since its inception in 1945, and increasingly after it emerged as the flagship of neoconservatism in the 1970s, the magazine has been consistently engaged with several large, interrelated questions: the fate of democracy and of democratic ideas in a world threatened by totalitarian ideologies; the state of American and Western security; the future of the Jews, Judaism, and Jewish culture in Israel, the United States, and around the world; and the preservation of high culture in an age of political correctness and the collapse of critical standards." Estab. 1945. Byline given. Pays on publication. No kill fee. Publishes ms an average of 2 months after acceptance. Accepts queries by mail, e-mail.

NONFICTION Needs essays, opinion. **Buys 4 mss/year.** Query or submit complete ms by e-mail or mail (include SASE). Length: 2,000-8,000 words. **Pays $400-1,200.**

COMMON GROUND

Common Ground Publishing, 3152 W 8th Ave., Vancouver BC V6K 2C3 Canada. (604)733-2215. **Fax:** (604)733-4415. **E-mail:** editor@commonground.ca. **Website:** www.commonground.ca. **90% freelance written.** Monthly tabloid covering health, environment, spirit, creativity, and wellness. "We serve the cultural creative community." Estab. 1982. Circ. 70,000. Byline given. Pays on publication. No kill fee. Publishes ms an average of 1 month after acceptance. Editorial lead time 2 months. Submit seasonal material 3 months in advance. Accepts queries by e-mail. Accepts simultaneous submissions. Responds in 6 weeks to queries. Responds in 3 months to mss. Sample copy for $5. Guidelines available online.

NONFICTION Needs book excerpts, how-to, inspirational, interview, opinion, personal experience, travel, call to action. Send complete ms. Length: 500-2,500 words. **Pays 10¢/word (Canadian).** Pays expenses of writers on assignment.

FLAUNT

1422 N. Highland Ave., Los Angeles CA 90028. (323)836-1000. **E-mail:** info@flauntmagazine.com. **Website:** www.flaunt.com. **Contact:** Luis Barajas, editor in chief. **40% freelance written.** Monthly magazine covering culture, arts, entertainment, music, fashion, and film. "*Flaunt* features the bold work of emerging photographers, writers, artists, and musicians. The quality of the content is mirrored in the sophisticated, interactive format of the magazine, using advanced printing techniques, fold-out articles, beautiful papers, and inserts to create a visually stimulating, surprisingly readable, and intelligent book that pushes the magazine into the realm of art-object. *Flaunt* has, since 1998, made it a point to break new ground, earning itself a reputation as an engine of the avant-garde and an outlet for the culture of the cutting edge. *Flaunt* takes pride in reinventing itself each month, while consistently representing a hybrid of all that is interesting in entertainment, fashion, music, design, film, art, and literature." Estab. 1998. Circ. 100,000. Byline given. No kill fee. Publishes ms an average of 3 months after acceptance. Editorial lead time 3 months. Submit seasonal material 3 months in advance. Accepts queries by mail, e-mail. Accepts simultaneous submissions. Responds in 2 weeks to queries; in 1 month to mss.

NONFICTION Needs book excerpts, essays, general interest, historical, humor, interview, new product, opinion, personal experience, photo feature, travel. Special issues: Special issues: September and March (fashion issues); February (men's issue); May (music issue). **Buys 20 mss/year.** Query with published clips. Length: 500-5,000 words. **Pays up to $500.** Pays expenses of writers on assignment.

●❸ THE LIST

The List, Ltd., 14 High St., Edinburgh EH1 1TE Scotland. (44)(131)550-3050. **Fax:** (44)(131)557-8500. **E-mail:** newwriters@list.co.uk. **Website:** www.list. co.uk. **25% freelance written.** Biweekly general interest magazine covering Glasgow and Edinburgh arts, events, listings, and lifestyle. "*The List* is pitched at educated 18-35 year olds in Scotland. All events listings are published free of charge and are accompanied by informative, independent critical comment offering a guide to readers as to what is worth seeing and why. Articles and features are also included previewing forthcoming events in greater detail." Estab. 1985. Circ. 500,000. Byline given. Pays on publication. Offers 100% kill fee. Publishes ms an average of 2 weeks after acceptance. Editorial lead time 1 month. Submit seasonal material 1 month in advance. Accepts queries by mail, e-mail. Accepts simultaneous submissions.

NONFICTION Needs interview, opinion, travel. Query with published clips. Length: 300 words. **Pays £60-80.** Sometimes pays expenses of writers on assignment.

COLUMNS Reviews, 50-650 words, **pays £16-35**; Book Reviews, 150 words; **pays £14.** Comic Reviews, 100 words; **pays £10.** TV/Video Reviews, 100 words; **pays £10.** Record Reviews, 100 words; **pays £10.** Query with published clips.

❸❸❸❸ MOTHER JONES

Foundation for National Progress, 222 Sutter St., Suite 600, San Francisco CA 94108. (415)321-1700. **E-mail:** query@motherjones.com. **Website:** www.motherjones.com. **Contact:** Mark Murrmann, photo editor;

Ivylise Simones, creative director; Monika Bauerlein and Clara Jeffery, editors. **80% freelance written.** Bimonthly magazine covering politics, investigative reporting, social issues, and pop culture. "*Mother Jones* is a 'progressive' magazine—but the core of its editorial well is reporting (i.e., fact-based). No slant required. Estab. 1976. Circ. 240,000. Byline given. Pays on publication. Offers 33% kill fee. Publishes ms an average of 4 months after acceptance. Editorial lead time 4 months. Submit seasonal material 6 months in advance. Accepts simultaneous submissions. Responds in 2 months to queries. Sample copy for $6 and 9x12 SASE. Guidelines available online.

NONFICTION Needs interview, photo feature, current issues, policy, investigative reporting. **Buys 70-100 mss/year.** Query with published clips. "Please also include your rèsumè and two or three of your most relevant clips. If the clips are online, please provide the complete URLs. Web pieces are generally less than 1,500 words. Because we have staff reporters it is extremely rare that we will pay for a piece whose timeliness or other qualities work for the Web only. Magazine pieces can range up to 5,000 words. There is at least a two-month lead time. No phone calls please." Length: 2,000-5,000 words. **Pays $1/word.** Pays expenses of writers on assignment.

COLUMNS Outfront (short, newsy and/or outrageous and/or humorous items), 200-800 words; Profiles of Hellraisers, 500 words. **Pays $1/word.**

❸❸ SHEPHERD EXPRESS

The Brooklyn Company, Inc., 207 E. Buffalo St., Suite 410, Milwaukee WI 53202. (414)276-2222. **Fax:** (414)276-3312. **E-mail:** info@expressmilwaukee. com. **Website:** http://expressmilwaukee.com. **Contact:** Louis Fortis, editor-in-chief and publisher. **50% freelance written.** Weekly tabloid covering news and arts with a progressive news edge and a hip entertainment perspective. Home of Sheprd Flickr interactive photo feature—Milwaukee-related photography. Estab. 1982. Circ. 58,000. Pays 1 month after publication. No kill fee. Publishes ms an average of 1 month after acceptance. Submit seasonal material 2 months in advance. Accepts simultaneous submissions. Sample copy for $3.

NONFICTION Needs book excerpts, essays, expose, opinion. **Buys 200 mss/year.** Send complete ms. Length: 900-2,500 words. **Pays $35-300 for as-**

signed articles. **Pays $10-200 for unsolicited articles.** Sometimes pays expenses of writers on assignment.

COLUMNS Opinions (social trends, politics, from progressive slant), 800-1,200 words; Books Reviewed (new books only: Social trends, environment, politics), 600-1,200 words. **Buys 10 mss/year.** Send complete ms.

❸❸❸❸ THE SUN

107 N. Roberson St., Chapel Hill NC 27516. (919)942-5282. **Fax:** (919)932-3101. **Website:** www.thesunmagazine.org. **Contact:** Sy Safransky, editor. **90% freelance written.** *The Sun* publishes essays, interviews, fiction, and poetry. "We are open to all kinds of writing, though we favor work of a personal nature." Estab. 1974. Circ. 72,000. Byline given. Pays on publication. Publishes ms an average of 6-12 months after acceptance. Accepts queries by mail. Responds in 3-6 months. Sample copy online. Guidelines online.

NONFICTION Needs essays, interview, memoir, personal experience, Also needs spiritual fields; in-depth philosophical; thoughtful essays on political, cultural, and philosophical themes. **Buys 50 mss/year.** Send complete ms. No fax or e-mail submissions. Length: up to 7,000 words. **Pays $300-2,000 and 1-year subscription.** Pays expenses of writers on assignment.

REPRINTS For reprints, send photocopy and information about when and where the material previously appeared. Pays 50% of standard pay.

FICTION Open to all fiction. Receives 800 unsolicited mss/month. Accepts 20 short stories/year. Recently published work by Sigrid Nunez, Susan Straight, Lydia Peelle, Stephen Elliott, David James Duncan, Linda McCullough Moore, and Brenda Miller. No science fiction, horror, fantasy, or other genre fiction. "Read an issue before submitting." **Buys 20 mss/year.** Send complete ms. Accepts reprint submissions. Length: up to 7,000 words. **Pays $300-1,500 and 1-year subscription.**

POETRY Needs free verse. Submit up to 6 poems at a time. Considers previously published poems but strongly prefers unpublished work. "Poems should be typed and accompanied by a cover letter and SASE." Recently published poems by Tony Hoagland, Ellen Bass, Steve Kowit, Brian Doyle, and Alison Luterman. Rarely publishes poems that rhyme. **Pays $100-200 and 1-year subscription.**

DISABILITIES

❂❸❸ ABILITIES

Canadian Abilities Foundation, 225 Duncan Mill Road, Suite 803, Toronto ON M3B 3H9 Canada. (416)421-7944. **Fax:** (416)421-8418. **E-mail:** abilities@bcsgroup.com. **Website:** www.abilities.ca. **Contact:** Caroline Tapp-McDougall, managing editor. **50% freelance written.** Quarterly magazine covering disability issues. "*Abilities* is Canada's foremost cross-disability lifestyle magazine. The mission of the magazine is to provide **information** about lifestyle topics, including travel, health, careers, education, relationships, parenting, new products, social policy and much more; **inspiration** to participate in organizations, events, and activities and pursue opportunities in sports, education, careers, and more; and **opportunity** to learn about a wealth of Canadian resources that facilitate self empowerment of people with disabilities." Estab. 1987. Circ. 20,000. Byline given. Pays on publication. Offers 50% kill fee. Publishes ms an average of 3 months after acceptance. Editorial lead time 3 months. Submit seasonal material 4 months in advance. Accepts queries by mail, e-mail. Responds in 3 months to queries. Sample copy free. Writer's guidelines for #10 SASE, online, or by e-mail.

NONFICTION Needs general interest, how-to, humor, inspirational, interview, new product, personal experience, photo feature, travel. Does not want articles that 'preach to the converted'—this means info that people with disabilities likely already know, such as what it's like to have a disability. **Buys 30-40 mss/year.** Query or send complete ms. Length: 500-2,000 words. **Pays $50-325 (Canadian) for assigned articles.** Pays expenses of writers on assignment.

REPRINTS Sometimes accepts previously published submissions (if stated as such).

COLUMNS The Lighter Side (humor), 700 words; Profile, 1,200 words.

❸❸❸❸ ARTHRITIS TODAY

Arthritis Foundation, 1355 Peachtree St. NE, 6th Floor, Atlanta GA 30309. **Website:** www.arthritistoday.org. **50% freelance written.** Bimonthly magazine covering living with arthritis and the latest in research/treatment. *Arthritis Today* is a consumer health magazine and is written for the more than 70 million Americans who have arthritis and for the millions of others whose lives are touched by an arthritis-related disease. The editorial content is designed to help the person with arthritis live a more productive, independent, and pain-free life. The articles are upbeat and provide practical advice, information, and inspiration. Estab. 1987. Circ. 650,000. Byline given. Pays on acceptance. Offers kill fee. Offers kill fee. Editorial lead time 6 months. Submit seasonal material 6 months in advance. Accepts queries by mail, online submission form. Accepts simultaneous submissions. Responds in 2 months to queries. Sample copy for 9x11 SAE with 4 first-class stamps.

NONFICTION Needs general interest, how-to, inspirational, new product, opinion, personal experience, photo feature, technical, travel. **Buys 12 unsolicited mss/year.** Query with published clips. Length: 150-2,500 words. **Pays $100-2,500.** Pays expenses of writers on assignment.

COLUMNS Nutrition, 100-600 words; Fitness, 100-600 words; Balance (emotional coping), 100-600 words; MedWatch, 100-800 words; Solutions, 100-600 words; Life Makeover, 400-600 words.

FILLERS Needs facts, gags, short humor. **Buys 2 mss/year.** Length: 40-100 words. **Pays $80-150.**

🟢 CAREERS & THE DISABLED

Equal Opportunity Publications, 445 Broad Hollow Rd., Suite 425, Melville NY 11747. (631)421-9421, ext. 12. **E-mail:** bloehr@eop.com. **Website:** www.eop.com. **Contact:** Barbara Capella Loehr, editor. **60% freelance written.** Magazine published 6 times/year, with Fall, Winter, Spring, Summer, Expo and Veterans' editions, offering role-model profiles and career guidance articles geared toward disabled college students and professionals, and promoting personal and professional growth. Estab. 1968: EOP; 1986: CAREERS & the disABLED magazine. Circ. 10,000. Byline given. Pays on publication. Publishes ms an average of 6 months after acceptance. Editorial lead time 6 months. Submit seasonal material 6 months in advance. Accepts queries by mail, e-mail, phone. Accepts simultaneous submissions. Responds in 3 weeks to queries. Sample copy for 9x12 SAE with 5 first-class stamps. Guidelines free.

NONFICTION Needs essays, general interest, how-to, interview, new product, opinion, personal experience. **Buys 30 mss/year.** Query. Length: 1,000-2,500 words. **Pays 10¢/word.** Pays expenses of writers on assignment.

🟢🟢 DIABETES HEALTH

P.O. Box 1199, Woodacre CA 94973. **E-mail:** editor@diabeteshealth.com. **Website:** www.diabeteshealth.com. **Contact:** Nadia Al-Samarrie, editor in chief. **60% freelance written.** Monthly tabloid covering diabetes care. *Diabetes Health* covers the latest in diabetes care, medications, and patient advocacy. Personal accounts are welcome as well as medical-oriented articles by MDs, RNs, and CDEs (certified diabetes educators). Estab. 1991. Circ. 150,000. Byline given. Pays on publication. No kill fee. Publishes ms an average of 2 months after acceptance. Editorial lead time 2 months. Submit seasonal material 2 months in advance. Accepts queries by e-mail. Accepts simultaneous submissions. Sample copy available online. Guidelines free.

NONFICTION Needs book excerpts, essays, how-to, humor, inspirational, interview, memoir, new product, nostalgic, opinion, personal experience, photo feature, reviews, technical, travel. *Diabetes Health* does not accept mss that promote a product, philosophy, or personal view. **Buys 25 mss/year.** Send complete ms. Length: 400-1,500 words. **Pays 10¢/word.**

POETRY Personal poetry from people living with diabetes.

🟢 DIALOGUE

Blindskills, Inc., P.O. Box 5181, Salem OR 97304. **E-mail:** magazine@blindskills.com. **Website:** www.blindskills.com. **60% freelance written.** Quarterly journal covering visually impaired people. Estab. 1962. Circ. 1,100. Byline given. Pays on publication. Publishes ms an average of 6 months after acceptance. Editorial lead time 3 months. Accepts queries by e-mail. Accepts simultaneous submissions. Sample copy: 1 free copy on request. Available in large print, Braille, digital audio Cartridge, and e-mail. Guidelines online.

NONFICTION Needs essays, general interest, historical, how-to, humor, interview, new product, opinion, personal experience, profile. No controversial, explicit sex, religious, or political topics. **Buys 50-60 mss/year.** Send complete ms. Length: 200-1,200 words. **Pays $15-35 for assigned articles; $15-25 for unsolicited articles.** Pays expenses of writers on assignment.

COLUMNS All material should be relative to blind and visually impaired readers. Living with Low Vision, 1,000 words; Hear's How (dealing with sight loss),

1,000 words; Technology Answer Book, 1,000 words. **Buys 80 mss/year.** Send complete ms. **Pays $25-50.**

💲 KALEIDOSCOPE

United Disability Services, 701 S. Main St., Akron OH 44311-1019. (330)762-9755. **Fax:** (330)762-0912. **E-mail:** kaleidoscope@udsakron.org. **Website:** www.kaleidoscopeonline.org. **Contact:** Gail Willmott, editor in chief. **90% freelance written. Eager to work with new/unpublished writers.** Semiannual free online magazine. Kaleidoscope magazine creatively focuses on the experiences of disability through literature and the fine arts. As a pioneering literary resource for the field of disability studies, this award-winning publication expresses the diversity of the disability experience from a variety of perspectives including: individuals, families, friends, caregivers, educators, and healthcare professionals, among others." Estab. 1979. Byline given. Pays on publication. No kill fee. 1-3 years 3 months prior to publication Accepts queries by mail, e-mail, fax, phone, online submission form. Accepts simultaneous submissions. Responds in 6-9 months. Guidelines available online. Submissions and queries electronically via website and e-mail.

NONFICTION Needs essays, interview, personal experience, reviews, articles relating to both literary and visual arts. For book reviews: "Reviews that are substantive, timely, powerful works about publications in the field of disability and/or the arts. The writer's opinion of the work being reviewed should be clear. The review should be a literary work in its own right." **Buys 40-50 mss/year.** Submit complete ms by website or e-mail. Include cover letter. Length: up to 5,000 words. **Pays $25.**

REPRINTS Send double-spaced, typed ms with complete author's/artist's contact information, rights for sale noted, and information about when and where the material previously appeared. Reprints permitted with credit given to original publication. All rights revert to author upon publication

FICTION Wants short stories with a well-crafted plot and engaging characters. Needs historical, humorous, mainstream, short stories, slice-of-life vignettes. No fiction that is stereotypical, patronizing, sentimental, erotic, or maudlin. No romance, religious or dogmatic fiction; no children's literature. Submit complete ms by website or e-mail. Include cover letter. Length: up to 5,000 words. **Pays $25.**

POETRY Wants poems that have strong imagery, evocative language. Submit up to 5 poems by website or e-mail. Include cover letter. Do not get caught up in rhyme scheme. Reviews any style. **$10 per poem.**

💲💲 PN

PVA Publications, 2111 E. Highland Ave., Suite 180, Phoenix AZ 85016-4702. (602)224-0500. **E-mail:** andy@pvamag.com. **Website:** www.pn-magazine. com. **Contact:** Andy Nemann, editorial coordinator. Monthly magazine covering news and information for wheelchair users. Estab. 1946. Circ. 40,000. Byline given. Pays on publication. Publishes ms an average of 2-4 months after acceptance. Editorial lead time 3 months. Submit seasonal material 3 months in advance. Accepts queries by mail, e-mail, fax. Sample copy and guidelines free.

NONFICTION Needs how-to, interview, new product, opinion. **Buys 10-12 mss/year.** Send complete ms. Length: 1,200-2,500 words. **Pays $25-250.**

💲💲💲💲 POZ

CDM Publishing, LLC, 462 Seventh Ave., 19th Floor, New York NY 10018. (212)242-2163. **Fax:** (212)675-8505. **E-mail:** website@poz.com; editor-in-chief@poz.com. **Website:** www.poz.com. **Contact:** Doriot Kim, art director. **25% freelance written.** Monthly national magazine for people impacted by HIV and AIDS. "*POZ* is a trusted source of conventional and alternative treatment information, investigative features, survivor profiles, essays and cutting-edge news for people living with AIDS and their caregivers. *POZ* is a lifestyle magazine with both health and cultural content." Estab. 1994. Circ. 125,000. Byline given. Pays 30 days after publication. Offers 25% kill fee. Publishes ms an average of 3 months after acceptance. Editorial lead time 4 months. Submit seasonal material 4 months in advance. Accepts simultaneous submissions. Sample copy and writer's guidelines free.

NONFICTION Needs book excerpts, essays, historical, how-to, humor, inspirational, interview, opinion, personal experience, photo feature. Query with published clips. "We take unsolicited mss on speculation only." Length: 200-3,000 words. **Pays $1/word.** Pays expenses of writers on assignment.

💲💲 SPORTS 'N SPOKES

The Magazine for Wheelchair Sports and Recreation, Paralyzed Veterans of America / PVA Publications, 2111 E. Highland Ave., Suite 180, Phoenix AZ 85016-

4702. (602)224-0500. **Fax:** (602)224-0507. **E-mail:** brittany@pvamag.com; john@pvamag.com; andy@pvamag.com; anngarvey@pvamag.com; kerry@pvamag.com. **Website:** www.pvamag.com. **Contact:** Tom Fjerstad, editor; Andy Nemann, assistant editor; John Groth and Brittany Martin, editorial coordinators; Ann Garvey and Kerry Randolph (cartoon and photo submissions). Bimonthly magazine covering wheelchair sports and recreation. Writing must pertain to wheelchair sports and recreation. "*SPORTS 'N SPOKES* is committed to providing a voice for the wheelchair sporting and recreation community." Estab. 1974. Circ. 25,000. Byline given. Pays on publication. Publishes ms an average of 2-3 months after acceptance. Editorial lead time 2-3 months. Submit seasonal material 2-3 months in advance. Accepts queries by mail, e-mail. Accepts simultaneous submissions. Sample copy and guidelines free.

NONFICTION Needs general interest, interview, new product. **Buys 5-6 mss/year.** Query before submitting. Length: 1,200-2,500 words. **Pays $20-250.** Pays expenses of writers on assignment.

ENTERTAINMENT

💲 CINEASTE

Cineaste, Inc., 708 Third Ave., 5th Floor, New York NY 10017-4201. (212)209-3856. **E-mail:** cineaste@cineaste.com. **Website:** www.cineaste.com. **30% freelance written.** Quarterly magazine covering motion pictures with an emphasis on social and political perspective on cinema. Estab. 1967. Circ. 11,000. Byline given. Pays on publication. Offers 50% kill fee. Publishes ms an average of 4 months after acceptance. Editorial lead time 3 months. Submit seasonal material 4 months in advance. Accepts queries by mail, e-mail, fax. Accepts simultaneous submissions. Responds in 1 month to queries. Sample copy: $8. Writer's guidelines on website.

NONFICTION Needs book excerpts, essays, expose, historical, humor, interview, opinion. **Buys 20-30 mss/year.** Query with published clips. Length: 2,000-5,000 words. **Pays $30-100.** Pays expenses of writers on assignment.

COLUMNS Homevideo (topics of general interest or a related group of films); A Second Look (new interpretation of a film classic or a reevaluation of an unjustly neglected release of more recent vintage); Lost

and Found (film that may or may not be released or otherwise seen in the U.S. but which is important enough to be brought to the attention of our readers); all 1,000-1,500 words. Query with published clips. **Pays $50 minimum.**

💲 IN TOUCH WEEKLY

270 Sylvan Ave., Englewood Cliffs NJ 07632. (201)569-6699. **E-mail:** contactus@intouchweekly.com. **Website:** www.intouchweekly.com. **10% freelance written.** Weekly magazine covering celebrity news and entertainment. Estab. 2002. Circ. 1,300,000. No byline given. Pays on publication. Editorial lead time 1 week. Accepts queries by mail, e-mail. Accepts simultaneous submissions.

NONFICTION Needs interview, gossip. **Buys 1,300 mss/year.** Query. Send a tip about a celebrity by e-mail. Length: 100-1,000 words. **Pays $50.** Pays expenses of writers on assignment.

💲💲 MOVIEMAKER MAGAZINE

MovieMaker Media LLC, 2525 Michigan Ave., Building I, Santa Monica CA 90404. (310)828-8388. **E-mail:** tim@moviemaker.com. **Website:** www.moviemaker.com. **Contact:** Timothy Rhys, editor in chief. **75% freelance written.** Bimonthly magazine covering film, independent cinema, and Hollywood. "*MovieMaker's* editorial is a progressive mix of in-depth interviews and criticism, combined with practical techniques and advice on financing, distribution, and production strategies. Behind-the-scenes discussions with Hollywood's top moviemakers, as well as independents from around the globe, are routinely found in *MovieMaker's* pages. E-mail is the preferred submission method, but we will accept queries via mail as well. Please, no telephone pitches. We want to read the idea with clips." Estab. 1993. Circ. 55,000. Byline given. Pays 30 days after newsstand publication. Offers variable kill fee. Publishes ms an average of 2 months after acceptance. Editorial lead time 3 months. Submit seasonal material 4 months in advance. Accepts queries by mail, e-mail. Accepts simultaneous submissions. Responds in 2-4 weeks to queries; in 4-6 weeks to mss. Sample copy available online. Guidelines by email.

NONFICTION Needs expose, general interest, historical, how-to, interview, new product, technical. **Buys 20 mss/year.** Query with published clips. Length: 800-3,000 words. **Pays $75-500 for assigned articles.**

COLUMNS Documentary; Home Cinema (home video/DVD reviews); How They Did It (first-person filmmaking experiences); Festival Beat (film festival reviews); World Cinema (current state of cinema from a particular country). Query with published clips **Pays $75-300.**

$$$ OK! MAGAZINE

American Media, Inc., 4 New York Plaza, New York NY 10004. (212)545-4800. **E-mail:** tips@okmagazine.com. **Website:** www.okmagazine.com. **Contact:** James Heidenry, editor in chief. **10% freelance written.** Weekly magazine covering entertainment news. "We are a celebrity friendly magazine. We strive not to show celebrities in a negative light. We consider ourselves a cross between *People* and *In Style*." Estab. 2005. Circ. 4,800,000. Byline sometimes given. Pays after publication. Publishes ms an average of 1 month after acceptance. Editorial lead time 2 weeks. Accepts queries by mail, e-mail. Accepts simultaneous submissions.

NONFICTION Needs interview, photo feature. **Buys 50 mss/year.** Query with published clips. Length: 500-2,000 words. **Pays $100-1,000.** Pays expenses of writers on assignment.

🍁$$ RUE MORGUE

Marrs Media, Inc., 1411 Dufferin St., Toronto ON M6H 4C7 Canada. **E-mail:** dave@rue-morgue.com. **Website:** www.rue-morgue.com. **Contact:** Dave Alexander, editor in chief. **50% freelance written.** Monthly magazine covering horror entertainment. "A knowledge of horror entertainment (films, books, games, toys, etc.)." Estab. 1997. Byline given. Pays on publication. No kill fee. Publishes ms an average of 2-4 months after acceptance. Editorial lead time 2 months. Submit seasonal material 4 months in advance. Accepts queries by e-mail. Responds in 6 weeks to queries; in 2 months to mss. Guidelines available by e-mail.

NONFICTION Needs essays, exposé, historical, interview, travel, new product. No reviews. Query with published clips or send complete ms. Length: 500-3,500 words.

COLUMNS Classic Cut (historical essays on classic horror films, books, games, comic books, music), 500-700 words. Query with published clips.

$$$$ SOUND & VISION

Source Interlink Media, 2 Park Ave., 10th Floor, New York NY 10016. (212)767-5000. **Fax:** (212)767-5200. **E-mail:** rsabin@enthusiastnetwork.com. **Website:** www.soundandvision.com. **Contact:** Rob Sabin, editor. **40% freelance written.** Magazine published 10 times/year covering home theater consumer products. "Provides readers with authoritative information on the home entertainment technologies and products that will impact their lives." Estab. 1958. Circ. 105,000. Byline given. Pays on acceptance. Publishes ms an average of 4 months after acceptance. Accepts queries by mail, e-mail. Sample copy for SAE with 9x12 envelope and 11 first-class stamps.

NONFICTION Buys 25 mss/year. Query with published clips. Length: 1,500-3,000 words. **Pays $1,000-1,500.**

$ TELEREVISTA

304 Indian Trace #238, Weston FL 33326. (954)689-2428. **Fax:** (954)689-2428. **E-mail:** info@telerevista.com. **Website:** www.telerevista.com. **Contact:** Salvatore Trimarchi, editor. **100% freelance written.** Monthly magazine written in Spanish covering Hispanic entertainment (U.S. and Puerto Rico). "We feature interviews, gossip, breaking stories, behind-the-scenes happenings, etc." Estab. 1986. Byline sometimes given. Pays on publication. Publishes ms an average of 3 months after acceptance. Editorial lead time 2 months. Submit seasonal material 3 months in advance. Accepts queries by mail, e-mail, fax. Sample copy free.

NONFICTION Needs expose, interview, opinion, photo feature. **Buys 200 mss/year.** Query. **Pays $25-75.**

COLUMNS Buys 60 mss/year. Query. **Pays $25-75.**

FILLERS Needs anecdotes, facts, gags, newsbreaks, short humor.

ETHNIC & MINORITY

$$ AMBASSADOR MAGAZINE

National Italian American Foundation, 1860 19th St. NW, Washington DC 20009. (202)939-3108. **E-mail:** don@niaf.org. **Website:** www.niaf.org. **Contact:** Don Oldenburg, director of publications and editor. **65% freelance written.** "We publish original nonfiction articles on the Italian American experience, culture, and traditions. We also publish profiles of Italian Americans (famous and not famous but doing something exceptional) and travel features, especially in Italy, but also relevant U.S. travel pieces. We rarely publish memoir-like pieces." *Ambassador* is a glossy, high-quality consumer magazine for Italian Americans, Italians, and Italophiles. Estab. 1989. Circ. 28,000. Byline given. Pays on publication. $50 kill fee for assigned stories. Time between acceptance and publication varies. Editorial lead time 2-4 months. Accepts queries by e-mail. Responds within 2 months to e-mailed queries. Sample copy online. Writer's guidelines available by e-mail.

NONFICTION Needs essays, general interest, interview, personal experience, photo feature, profile, reviews, travel. Query via e-mail before submitting ms. When submitting ms, send as a Word e-mail attachment. Phone and mailed queries and mss are discouraged. Length: 800-1,500 words. **Pays $300 for full feature or profile; $350 for full feature or profile with photos taken by writer.**

$$$ B'NAI B'RITH MAGAZINE

1120 20th St. NW, Suite 300 N, Washington DC 20036. (202)857-6527. **E-mail:** bbmag@bnaibrith.org. **Website:** www.bnaibrith.org. **90% freelance written.** Quarterly magazine specializing in social, political, historical, religious, cultural, 'lifestyle,' and service articles relating chiefly to the Jewish communities of North America and Israel. Write for the American Jewish audience, i.e., write about topics from a Jewish perspective, highlighting creativity and innovation in Jewish life. Estab. 1886. Circ. 110,000. Byline given. Pays on publication. Publishes ms an average of 6 months after acceptance. Editorial lead time 3 months. Submit seasonal material 5 months in advance. Accepts queries by mail, e-mail. Accepts simultaneous submissions. Responds in 1 month to queries; 6 weeks to mss.

NONFICTION Needs interview, photo feature, religious, travel. No Holocaust memoirs, first-person essays/memoirs, fiction, or poetry. **Buys 14-20 mss/year.** Query with published clips. Length: 1,000-2,500 words. **Pays $300-800 for assigned articles; $300-700 for unsolicited articles.** Pays expenses of writers on assignment.

$$ GERMAN LIFE

Zeitgeist Publishing, Inc., 1068 National Hwy., LaVale MD 21502. **E-mail:** editor@germanlife.com. **Website:** www.germanlife.com. **Contact:** Mark Slider. **80% freelance written.** Bimonthly magazine covering German-speaking Europe (Germany, Austria, Switzerland). "*German Life* is for all interested in the diversity of German-speaking culture—past and present—and in the various ways that the US (and North America in general) has been shaped by its German immigrants. The magazine is dedicated to solid reporting on travel, cultural, historical, social, genealogical, culinary and political topics." Estab. 1994. Circ. 40,000. Byline given. Pays on publication. Editorial lead time 4 months. Submit seasonal material 6-12 months in advance. Accepts queries by mail, e-mail. Responds in 2 months to queries; in 3 months to mss. Sample copy for $4.95 and SASE with 4 first-class stamps. Guidelines available online at www.germanlife.com.

NONFICTION Needs general interest, historical, interview, photo feature, reviews, travel. Special issues: February/March: Food, wine, beer; April/May: travel in Germany and other parts of German-speaking Europe; June/July: German-American travel destinations; August/September: Education; October/November: Oktoberfest;. December/January:Holiday Issue. **Buys 50 mss/year.** Query with published clips. Length: up to 1,200 words. **Pays $100-500.**

COLUMNS German-Americana (regards specific German-American communities, organizations, and/or events past or present), 1,200 words; Profile (portrays prominent Germans, Americans, or German-Americans), 1,000 words; At Home (cuisine, etc. relating to German-speaking Europe), 800 words; Library (reviews of books, videos, CDs, etc.), 300 words. **Buys 30 mss/year.** Query with published clips. **Pays $100-130.**

FILLERS Needs facts, newsbreaks. Length: 100-300 words. **Pays $80.**

$$ HADASSAH MAGAZINE

Hadassah, WZOA, 40 Wall St., Eighth Floor, New York NY 10005. **Fax:** (212)451-6257. **E-mail:** magazine@hadassah.org. **Website:** www.hadassahmagazine.org. **Contact:** Elizabeth Barnea. **90% freelance written.** Bimonthly magazine. Bimonthly publication of the Hadassah Women's Zionist Organization of America. Emphasizes Jewish life, Israel. Readers are 85% females who travel and are interested in Jewish affairs, average age 59. Circ. 255,000. Byline given. Pays on acceptance. Accepts simultaneous submissions. Responds in 4 months to mss. Sample copy and writer's guidelines with 9x12 SASE.

NONFICTION Needs historical. **Buys 10 unsolicited mss/year.** Query. Length: 1,500-2,000 words. Pays expenses of writers on assignment.

COLUMNS "We have a family column and a travel column, but a query for topic or destination should be submitted first to make sure the area is of interest and the story follows our format."

FICTION Wants short stories with strong plots and positive Jewish values. Receives 20-25 unsolicited mss/month. Publishes some new writers/year. Needs ethnic. No personal memoirs, "schmaltzy" or shelter magazine fiction. Length: 1,500-2,000 words. **Pays $500 minimum.**

$ INTERNATIONAL EXAMINER

409 Maynard Ave. S., #203, Seattle WA 98104. (206)624-3925. **Fax:** (206)624-3046. **E-mail:** editor@iexaminer.org. **Website:** www.iexaminer.org. **Contact:** Travis Quezon, editor in chief. **75% freelance written.** Biweekly journal of Asian American news, politics, and arts. "*International Examiner* is about Asian American issues and things of interest to Asian Americans. We do not want stuff about Asian things (stories on your trip to China, Japanese Tea Ceremony, etc. will be rejected). Yes, we are in English." Estab. 1974. Circ. 12,000. Pays on publication. No kill fee. Publishes ms an average of 1 month after acceptance. Editorial lead time 1 month. Submit seasonal material 2 months in advance. Accepts queries by mail, e-mail, fax. Accepts simultaneous submissions. Guidelines for #10 SASE.

NONFICTION Needs essays, general interest, historical, humor, interview, opinion, personal experience, photo feature. **Buys 100 mss/year.** Query with published clips. Length: 750-5,000 words, depending on subject. **Pays $25-100.** Pays expenses of writers on assignment.

REPRINTS Accepts previously published submissions (as long as published in same area). Send typed ms with rights for sale noted and information about when and where the material previously appeared. Payment negotiable.

FICTION Asian American authored fiction by or about Asian Americans only. **Buys 1-2 mss/year.** Query.

$ $ ITALIAN AMERICA

219 E St. NE, Washington DC 20002. (202)547-2900. **Fax:** (202)546-8168. **E-mail:** ddesanctis@osia.org; mfisher@osia.org. **Website:** www.osia.org. **Contact:** Dona De Sanctis, editor; Miles Ryan Fisher, Editor-in-Chief. **20% freelance written.** Quarterly magazine. "*Italian America* provides timely information about OSIA, while reporting on individuals, institutions, issues, and events of current or historical significance in the Italian-American community." Estab. 1996. Circ. 65,000. Byline given. Pays on publication. Offers 50% kill fee. Publishes ms an average of 3 months after acceptance. Editorial lead time 3 months. Accepts queries by mail, e-mail, fax. Accepts simultaneous submissions. Sample copy free. Guidelines available online.

NONFICTION Needs historical, interview, opinion, current events. **Buys 8 mss/year.** Query with published clips. Length: 750-1,000 words. **Pays $50-250.** Pays expenses of writers on assignment.

$ $ JEWISH CURRENTS

P.O. Box 111, Accord NY 12404. (845)626-2427. **E-mail:** editor@jewishcurrents.org. **Website:** jewish-currents.org. **Contact:** Lawrence Bush, editor; Jacob Plitman, associate editor. *Jewish Currents*, published 4 times/year, is a progressive Jewish quarterly magazine that carries on the insurgent tradition of the Jewish left through independent journalism, political commentary, and a 'countercultural' approach to Jewish arts and literature. Our website is an active magazine in its own right, with new material published daily. *Jewish Currents* is 88 pages, magazine-sized, offset-printed, saddle-stapled with a full-color arts section, "JCultcha & Funny Pages." The Winter issue is a 12-month arts calendar. Estab. 1946. Circ. 5,000 print; 45,000 website. Publishes mss 1-4 months after acceptance. Accepts queries by mail, e-mail. Accepts simultaneous submissions. Responds in 1 month or less. Subscription: $30/year. First-year subscription: $18.

NONFICTION Submit complete ms with cover letter. "Writers should include brief biographical information." 2,000 words **$100 for website, $200+ for print** Pays expenses of writers on assignment.

FICTION Jewish, historical, multicultural, feminist, humor, satire, translations, contemporary. Send complete ms with cover letter. "Writers should include brief biographical information." **Pays contributor's copies or small honoraria.**

POETRY Submit 3 poems at a time with a cover letter. "Writers should include brief biographical information." Poems should be typed, double-spaced; include SASE. **Pays contributor's copies.**

$ KHABAR

3635 Savannah Place Dr., Suite 400, Duluth GA 30096. (770)451-3067, ext. 4. **E-mail:** editor@khabar.com. **Website:** www.khabar.com. **50% freelance written.** "*Khabar* is a monthly magazine for the Indian community, free in Georgia, Alabama, Tennessee, and South Carolina. Besides Indian-Americans, *Khabar* also reaches other South Asian immigrants in Georgia—those from countries such as Pakistan, Bangladesh, Nepal, and Sri Lanka who share common needs for good and services. 'Khabar' means 'news' or 'to know' in many Indian languages, but we are a features magazine rather than a news publication." Estab. 1992. Circ. 27,000. Pays on publication. Offers 25% kill fee. Publishes ms an average of 2 months after acceptance. Editorial lead time 2 months. Submit seasonal material 2 months in advance. Accepts queries by e-mail. Accepts simultaneous submissions. Sample copy free. Guidelines by e-mail.

NONFICTION Needs essays, interview, opinion, personal experience, travel. **Buys 5 mss/year.** Send complete ms. Length: 750-4,000 words. **Pays $100-300 for assigned articles. Pays $75 for unsolicited articles.** Pays expenses of writers on assignment.

COLUMNS Book Review, 1,200 words; Music Review, 800 words; Spotlight (profiles), 1,200-3,000 words. **Buys 5 mss/year.** Query with or without published clips or send complete ms. **Pays $75 minimum.**

FICTION Needs ethnic. **Buys 5 mss/year.** Query or send complete ms. **Pays $50-100.**

$$$$ LATINA MAGAZINE

Latina Media Ventures, LLC, 625 Madison Ave., 3rd Floor, New York NY 10022. (212)642-0200. **E-mail:** editor@latina.com. **Website:** www.latina.com. **Contact:** Damarys Ocaña, executive editor. **40-50% freelance written.** Monthly magazine covering Latina lifestyle. *Latina Magazine* is the leading bilingual lifestyle publication for Hispanic women in the US today. Covering the best of Latino fashion, beauty, culture, and food, the magazine also features celebrity profiles and interviews. Estab. 1996. Circ. 250,000. Byline given. Pays on publication. Offers 25% kill fee. Publishes ms an average of 2-3 months after acceptance. Editorial lead time 3 months. Submit seasonal material 4-5 months in advance. Accepts queries by e-mail. Responds in 1 month to queries. Responds in 1-2 months to mss. Sample copy available online.

NONFICTION Needs essays, how-to, humor, inspirational, interview, new product, personal experience. Special issues: The 10 Latinas Who Changed the World (December). We do not feature an extensive amount of celebrity content or entertainment content, and freelancers should be sensitive to this. The magazine does not contain book or album reviews, and we do not write stories covering an artist's new project. We do not attend press junkets and do not cover press conferences. Please note that we are a lifestyle magazine, not an entertainment magazine. **Buys 15-20 mss/year.** Query with published clips. Length: 300-2,200 words. **Pays $1/word.** Pays expenses of writers on assignment.

$$$ MOMENT

4115 Wisconsin Ave. NW, Suite LL10, Washington DC 20016. (202)363-6422. **Fax:** (202)362-2514. **E-mail:** editor@momentmag.com. **Website:** www.momentmag.com. **Contact:** Sarah Breger, deputy editor. **90% freelance written.** Bimonthly magazine on Judaism. *Moment* is committed to portraying intellectual, political, cultural, and religious debates within the community, and to educating readers about Judaism's rich history and contemporary movements, ranging from left to right, fundamentalist to secular. Estab. 1975. Circ. 65,000. Byline given. Pays on publication. Publishes ms an average of 6 months after acceptance. Editorial lead time 3 months. Submit seasonal material 6 months in advance. Accepts queries by mail, e-mail. Accepts simultaneous submissions. Responds in 1 month to queries; in 3 months to mss. Sample copy for $4.50 and SAE. Guidelines available online.

NONFICTION Buys 25-30 mss/year. Query with published clips. Length: 2,500-7,000 words. **Pays $200-1,200.**

COLUMNS 5765 (snappy pieces about quirky events in Jewish communities, news and ideas to improve Jewish living), 250 words maximum; Olam (first-person pieces, humor, and colorful reportage), 600-1,500 words; book eviews (fiction and nonfiction) are accepted but generally assigned, 400-800 words. **Buys 30 mss/year.** Query with published clips. **Pays $50-250.**

$$ NATIVE PEOPLES MAGAZINE

5333 N. Seventh St., Suite C-224, Phoenix AZ 85014. (602)265-4855. **Fax:** (602)265-3113. **E-mail:** sphillips@nativepeoples.com. **Website:** www.nativepeoples.com. **Contact:** Stephen Phillips, Publisher. Bimonthly magazine covering Native Americans. High-quality reproduction with full color throughout. The primary purpose of this magazine is to offer a sensitive portrayal of the arts and lifeways of native peoples of the Americas. Estab. 1987. Circ. 40,000. Byline given. Pays on publication. Accepts queries by mail, e-mail, fax. Accepts simultaneous submissions. Responds in 2 months to queries. Guidelines by request.

NONFICTION Needs personal experience. **Buys 35 mss/year.** Length: 1,000-2,500 words. **Pays 25¢/word.** Pays expenses of writers on assignment.

$$ SCANDINAVIAN REVIEW

The American-Scandinavian Foundation, 58 Park Ave., New York NY 10016. (212)779-3587. **E-mail:** info@amscan.org. **Website:** www.amscan.org. **75% freelance written.** Triannual magazine for contemporary Scandinavia. Audience: Members, embassies, consulates, libraries. Slant: Popular coverage of contemporary affairs in Scandinavia. Estab. 1913. Circ. 4,000. Byline given. Pays on publication. No kill fee. Publishes ms an average of 2 months after acceptance. Editorial lead time 3 months. Submit seasonal material 3 months in advance. Responds in 6 weeks to queries. Sample copy available online. Guidelines free.

NONFICTION Needs general interest, interview, photo feature, travel, must have Scandinavia as topic focus. Special issues: Scandinavian travel. No pornography. **Buys 30 mss/year.** Query with published clips. Length: 1,500-2,000 words. **Pays $300 maximum.**

✪$ WINDSPEAKER

Aboriginal Multi-Media Society, 13245-146 St., Edmonton AB T5L 4S8 Canada. (780)455-2700. **Fax:** (780)455-7639. **E-mail:** market@ammsa.com; dsteel@ammsa.com. **Website:** www.ammsa.com/publications/windspeakerwww.ammsa.com/windspeaker. **Contact:** Paul Macedo, director of publishing operations; Debora Steel, contributing news editor. **25% freelance written.** Monthly tabloid covering native issues. Focus on events and issues that affect and interest native peoples, national or local. Estab. 1983. Circ. 27,000. Byline given. Pays on publication. Offers kill fee. Publishes ms an average of 1 month after acceptance. Editorial lead time 1 month. Submit seasonal material 2 months in advance. Accepts queries by mail, e-mail, phone. Accepts simultaneous submissions. Sample copy free. Guidelines available online.

NONFICTION Needs opinion, photo feature, travel, news interview/profile, reviews: books, music, movies. Special issues: Powwow (June); Travel supplement (May). **Buys 200 mss/year.** Query with published clips and SASE or by e-mail. Length: 500-800 words. **Pays $3-3.60/published inch for a single source story and $4.15/published inch for a multi-source story.** Pays expenses of writers on assignment.

FOOD & DRINK

$ BREW YOUR OWN

Battenkill Communications, 5515 Main St., Manchester Center VT 05255. (802)362-3981. **Fax:** (802)362-2377. **E-mail:** edit@byo.com; byo@byo.com. **Website:** www.byo.com. **Contact:** Betsy Parker, editor. **85% freelance written.** Magazine published 8 times/year covering home brewing. "Our mission is to provide practical information in an entertaining format. We try to capture the spirit and challenge of brewing while helping our readers brew the best beer they can." Estab. 1995. Circ. 50,000. Byline given. Pays on acceptance. Offers 25% kill fee. Publishes ms an average of 4 months after acceptance. Editorial lead time 3 months. Submit seasonal material 3 months in advance. Accepts queries by mail, e-mail, fax. Accepts simultaneous submissions. Responds in 2 months to queries. Guidelines online.

NONFICTION Needs historical, how-to, humor, interview. **Buys 75 mss/year.** Query with published clips or description of brewing expertise, or submit complete ms. Length: 1,500-3,000 words. **Pays $25-200, depending on length, complexity of article, and experience of writer.** Pays expenses of writers on assignment.

COLUMNS Homebrew Nation (short first-person brewing stories and photos of homemade equipment); Last Call (humorous stories about homebrewing), 600-750 words. **Buys 12 mss/year.** Query with or without published clips. **Pays $75 for Last Call; no payment for Homebrew Nation.**

$$$ DRAFT

300 W. Clarendon Ave., Suite 155, Phoenix AZ 85013. **E-mail:** editorial@draftmag.com. **Website:** www.

draftmag.com. **Contact:** Sally Benford. **60% freelance written.** Bimonthly magazine covering beer and lifestyle (including food, travel, sports, and leisure). "*DRAFT* is a national magazine devoted to beer, breweries, and the lifestyle and culture that surrounds it. Read by nearly 300,000, aged 21-45, *DRAFT* offers formal beer reviews, plus coverage of food, travel, sports, and leisure. Writers need not have formal beer knowledge (though that's a plus!), but they should be experienced journalists who can appreciate beer and beer culture." Estab. 2006. Circ. 275,000. Byline given. Pays on publication. Offers 20% kill fee. Publishes ms an average of 2 months after acceptance. Editorial lead time 4 months. Submit seasonal material 6 months in advance. Accepts queries by e-mail. Accepts simultaneous submissions. Responds in 1 month to queries. Sample copy: $3 (magazine can also be found on most newsstands for $4.99). Guidelines available at draft-mag.com/submissions.

NONFICTION Does not want unsolicited mss, beer reviews, brewery profiles. **Buys 80 mss/year.** Query with published clips. Length: 250-2,500 words. **Pays 50-90¢ for assigned articles.** Pays expenses of writers on assignment. Expenses limit agreed upon in advance.

💲💲 KASHRUS MAGAZINE

The Kashrus Institute, P.O. Box 204, Brooklyn NY 11204. (718)336-8544. **Fax:** (718)336-8550. **E-mail:** editorial@kashrusmagazine.com. **Website:** www.kashrusmagazine.com. **Contact:** Rabbi Yosef Wikler, editor. *Kashrus Magazine* is the kosher consumer's most established, authoritative, and independent source of news about kosher foods. Estab. 1981. Circ. 10,000. Byline given. Pays on publication. Offers 50% kill fee. Publishes ms an average of 2 months after acceptance. Submit seasonal material 2 months in advance. Accepts queries by mail, phone. Accepts simultaneous submissions. Responds in 2 weeks. Sample copy by e-mail.

NONFICTION Needs personal experience, photo feature, religious, technical. Special issues: International Kosher Travel (October); Passover Shopping Guide (March); Domestic Kosher Travel Guide (June). **Buys 8-12 mss/year.** Query with published clips. Length: 1,000-1,500 words. **Pays $100-250 for assigned articles. Pays up to $100 for unsolicited articles.** Pays expenses of writers on assignment.

REPRINTS Send tearsheet or photocopy and information about when and where the material previously appeared. Pays 25-50% of amount paid for an original article.

COLUMNS Health/Diet/Nutrition, 1,000-1,500 words; Book Review (cookbooks, food technology, kosher food), 250-500 words; People in the News (interviews with kosher personalities), 1,000-1,500 words; Regional Kosher Supervision (report on kosher supervision in a city or community), 1,000-1,500 words; Food Technology (new technology or current technology with accompanying pictures), 1,000-1,500 words; Kosher Travel (international, national—must include Kosher information and Jewish communities), 1,000-1,500 words; Regional Kosher Cooking, 1,000-1,500 words. **Buys 8-12 mss/year.** Query with published clips. **Pays $50-250.**

💲💲 VEGETARIAN JOURNAL

P.O. Box 1463, Baltimore MD 21203-1463. (410)366-8343. **E-mail:** vrg@vrg.org. **Website:** www.vrg.org. **Contact:** Debra Wasserman, editor. Quarterly nonprofit vegetarian magazine that examines the health, ecological and ethical aspects of veganism. "Highly-educated audience including health professionals." Estab. 1982. Circ. 12,000. Accepts simultaneous submissions. Sample copy: $4.

NONFICTION "The articles we publish are usually written by registered dietitians and individuals with a science background. We are open to non-paid articles by others, and possibly a paid feature for a super idea. If you have a great idea that you would like to be paid for, please send a query letter along with a resume, and indicate that you would like to be paid." **Pays $100-200/article.** Pays expenses of writers on assignment.

POETRY "Please, no submissions of poetry from adults; 18 and under only."

💲💲💲💲 WINE ENTHUSIAST MAGAZINE

Wine Enthusiast Media, 200 Summit Lake Dr., Valhalla NY 10595. **E-mail:** editor@wineenthusiast.net. **E-mail:** jczerwin@wineenthusiast.net; jfink@wineenthusiast.net; lbortolot@wineenthusiast.net. **Website:** www.winemag.com. **Contact:** Lauren Buzzeo, managing editor; Jameson Fink, digital senior editor; Layla Schlack, senior editor. **25% freelance written.** Monthly magazine covering the lifestyle of wine. Demystifying wine without dumbing it down, and tapping into current trends of spirits, travel, entertaining and art through a savvy wine lovers' lens, Wine Enthusiast is the modern tome of popular wine culture—a magazine that provokes and drives global dialogue in one of the world's most vibrant and fast-paced lifestyle categories, educating and entertaining legions of smart and sophisticated consumers. Estab. 1988. Circ. 180,000. Byline given. Pays on acceptance. Offers 25% kill fee. Editorial lead time 4 months. Submit seasonal material 5 months in advance. Accepts queries by e-mail. Responds in 2 weeks to queries; 2 months to mss. **NONFICTION** Needs essays, humor, interview, new product, nostalgic, personal experience, travel. **Buys 5 mss/year.** Submit a proposal (1 or 2 paragraphs) with clips and a resume. Submit short, web items to Jameson Fink; submit feature proposals to Lauren Buzzeo. Submit short, front-of-book items to Layla Schlack. **Pays $1/word.**

💲💲 WINE PRESS NORTHWEST

333 W. Canal Dr., Kennewick WA 99336. (509)582-1564. **Fax:** (509)585-7221. **E-mail:** editor@winepress-nw.com; info@winepressnw.com. **Website:** www.winepressnw.com. **50% freelance written.** Quarterly magazine covering Pacific Northwest wine (Washington, Oregon, British Columbia, Idaho). "Wine Press Northwest is a quarterly magazine for those with an interest in wine, from the novice to the veteran. We publish in March, June, September and December. We focus on Washington, Oregon, Idaho and British Columbia's talented winemakers and the wineries, vintners and restaurants that showcase Northwest wines. We are dedicated to all who savor the fruits of their labor." Estab. 1998. Circ. 12,000. Byline given. Pays on publication. Offers 20% kill fee. Publishes ms an average of 3 months after acceptance. Editorial lead time 3 months. Submit seasonal material 3 months in advance. Accepts queries by mail, e-mail, fax. Accepts simultaneous submissions. Responds in 1 month to queries. Sample copy free or online. Guidelines free.

NONFICTION Needs general interest, historical, interview, new product, photo feature, travel. No beer, spirits, non-NW (California wine, etc.). **Buys 30 mss/year.** Query with published clips. Length: 1,500-2,500 words. **Pays $300.** Pays expenses of writers on assignment.

💲💲💲 WINE SPECTATOR

M. Shanken Communications, Inc., 825 Eighth Ave., 33rd Floor, New York NY 10019. (212)481-8610. **Website:** www.winespectator.com. **20% freelance written. Prefers to work with published/established writers.** Monthly news magazine providing "an exciting, insider's view of the good life, including fine dining, wine travel, and entertainment." Estab. 1976. Circ. 350,000. Byline given. Pays within 30 days of publication. No kill fee. Publishes ms an average of 2 months after acceptance. Submit seasonal material 4 months in advance. Accepts queries by mail. Accepts simultaneous submissions. Responds in 3 months to queries.

NONFICTION Needs general interest, interview, opinion, photo feature, travel, dining and other lifestyle pieces. No winery promotional pieces or articles by writers who lack sufficient knowledge to write below just surface data. Query. Length: 100-2,000 words. **Pays $100-1,000.** Pays expenses of writers on assignment.

GAMES & PUZZLES

💲 THE BRIDGE BULLETIN

American Contract Bridge League, 6575 Windchase Dr., Horn Lake MS 38637-1523. (662)253-3156. **Fax:** (662)253-3187. **E-mail:** editor@acbl.org; brent.manley@acbl.org. **Website:** www.acbl.org. Paul Linxwiler, managing editor. **Contact:** Brent Manley, editor. **20% freelance written.** Monthly magazine covering duplicate (tournament) bridge. Estab. 1938. Circ. 155,000. Byline given. Pays on publication. Publishes ms an average of 3 months after acceptance. Editorial lead time 2 months. Accepts queries by mail, e-mail. Accepts simultaneous submissions.

NONFICTION Needs book excerpts, essays, how-to, humor, interview, new product, personal experience, photo feature, technical, travel. **Buys 6 mss/year.** Query. Length: 500-2,000 words. **Pays $100/page.** Pays expenses of writers on assignment.

💲💲 CHESS LIFE

P.O. Box 3967, Crossville TN 38557. (931)787-1234. **Fax:** (931)787-1200. **E-mail:** dlucas@uschess.org. **Website:** www.uschess.org. **Contact:** Daniel Lucas, editor. **15% freelance written. Works with a small number of new/unpublished writers/year.** Monthly magazine. "Chess Life is the official publication of the United States Chess Federation, covering news of most major chess events, both here and abroad, with special emphasis on the triumphs and exploits of American players." Estab. 1939. Circ. 85,000. Byline given. No kill fee. Publishes ms an average of 6 months after acceptance. Submit seasonal material 6 months in advance. Accepts simultaneous submissions. Responds in 3 months to mss. Sample copy via PDF is available.

NONFICTION Needs general interest, historical, humor, interview, photo feature, technical. No stories about personal experiences with chess. **Buys 30-40 mss/year.** Query with samples if new to publication. 3,000 words maximum. **Pays $100/page (800-1,000 words).** Pays expenses of writers on assignment.

FILLERS Submit with samples and clips. Buys first or negotiable rights to cartoons and puzzles. **Pays $25 upon acceptance.**

💲💲💲 GAMES WORLD OF PUZZLES

Kappa Publishing Group, Inc., 6198 Butler Pike, Suite 200, Blue Bell PA 19422. (215)643-6385. **Fax:** (215)628-3571. **E-mail:** games@kappapublishing.com. **Website:** www.gamesmagazine-online.com. **Contact:** Jennifer Orehowsky, senior editor. **50% freelance written.** *Games World of Puzzles*, published 10 times/year, features visual and verbal puzzles, quizzes, game reviews, contests, and feature articles. Estab. 1977. Circ. 75,000. Byline given. Pays on publication. Offers 25% kill fee. Publishes ms an average of 4 months after acceptance. Editorial lead time 3 months. Submit seasonal material 6 months in advance. Accepts queries by mail, e-mail. Accepts simultaneous submissions. Responds in 6-8 weeks to queries and mss. Sample copy: $5. Guidelines available online.

NONFICTION Needs humor, photo feature, game- and puzzle-related events or people, wordplay. Query or submit complete ms by e-mail. Length: 2,000-2,500 words. **Pays $500-1,000.** Pays expenses of writers on assignment.

COLUMNS Puzzles, tests, quizzes. **Buys 50 mss/year.** Query or send complete ms. **Payment varies.**

💲💲 POKER PRO MAGAZINE

Poker Pro Media, 2101 NE Corporate Blvd., Boca Raton FL 33432. **E-mail:** jwenzel@pokerpromedia.com. **Website:** www.pokerpromagazine.com. **Contact:** John Wenzel, editor. **75% freelance written.** Monthly magazine covering poker, gambling, and nightlife. "We want articles about poker and gambling-related articles only; also nightlife in gaming cities and articles on gaming destinations." Estab. 2005. Circ. 150,000. Byline given. Pays on publication. No kill fee. Publishes ms an average of 1 month after acceptance.

Editorial lead time 1.5 months. Submit seasonal material 2 months in advance. Accepts queries by e-mail. Responds in 1 week to queries; in 1 month to mss. Sample copy and guidelines by e-mail.

NONFICTION Needs book excerpts, essays, expose, general interest, historical, how-to, humor, interview, new product, opinion, personal experience, photo feature, travel. **Buys 125 mss/year.** Query. Length: 800-2,500 words. **Pays $100-$200 for assigned or unsolicited articles.** Sometimes pays expenses of writers on assignment.

GAY & LESBIAN INTEREST

💲💲 THE ADVOCATE

Here Media, Inc., 10990 Wilshire Blvd., Penthouse, Los Angeles CA 90024. (310)806-4288. **Fax:** (310)806-4268. **E-mail:** newsroom@advocate.com. **Website:** www.advocate.com. **Contact:** Matthew Breen, editor in chief; Meg Thomann, managing editor. Biweekly magazine covering national news events with a gay and lesbian perspective on the issues. Estab. 1967. Circ. 120,000. Byline given. Pays on publication. Accepts simultaneous submissions. Responds in 1 month. Sample copy: $3.95. Guidelines on website.

NONFICTION Needs expose. Query. Length: 800 words. **Pays $550.** Pays expenses of writers on assignment.

COLUMNS Arts & Media (news and profiles of well-known gay or lesbians in entertainment); 750 words. Query. **Pays $100-500.**

💲💲 CURVE MAGAZINE

E-mail: editor@curvemag.com; merryn@curvemag.com. **Website:** www.curvemag.com. **Contact:** Merryn Johns, editor-in-chief. **60% freelance written.** Magazine published 4 times/year covering lesbian entertainment, culture, and general interest categories. "We want dynamic and provocative articles that deal with issues, ideas, or cultural moments that are of interest or relevance to gay women." Does not publish fiction or poetry. Estab. 1990. Circ. 250,000. Byline given. Pays on publication. Offers 25% kill fee. Up to 3 months between acceptance and publication. Editorial lead time 6 months. Submit seasonal material 6 months in advance. Accepts queries by mail, e-mail, fax. Accepts simultaneous submissions. Sample copy for $4.95 with $2 postage. Guidelines online.

NONFICTION Needs general interest, interview, new product, photo feature, profile, reviews, travel, celebrity interview/profile. Special issues: See website for calendar. No fiction or poetry. **Buys 100 mss/year.** Query. Length: 200-2,000 words. **Pays 15¢/word.**

☯️💲💲 DAILY XTRA

Pink Triangle Press, 2 Carlton St., Suite 1600, Toronto ON M5B 1J3 Canada. (416)925-6665; (800)268-9872. **Fax:** (416)925-6674. **E-mail:** info@dailyxtra.ca. **Website:** www.dailyxtra.ca. **80% freelance written.** Biweekly tabloid covering gay, lesbian, bisexual, and transgender issues, news, arts, and events of interest in Toronto. "*Daily Xtra* is dedicated to lesbian and gay sexual liberation. We publish material that advocates this end, according to the mission statement of the not-for-profit organization Pink Triangle Press, which operates the paper." Estab. 1984. Circ. 45,000. Byline given. Pays on publication. No kill fee. Editorial lead time 1 month. Accepts queries by e-mail. Accepts simultaneous submissions. Responds in 2 weeks to queries. Sample copy online. Guidelines by e-mail.

NONFICTION Needs book excerpts, essays, interview, opinion, personal experience, travel. Does not want US-based stories or profiles of straight people who do not have a direct connection to the LGBT community. Query with published clips. Length: 200-1,600 words. Pays expenses of writers on assignment. Payment: Limit agreed upon in advance.

COLUMNS *Xtra* rarely publishes unsolicited columns. **Buys 6 columns/year. mss/year.** Query with published clips.

💲 ECHO MAGAZINE

ACE Publishing, Inc., P.O. Box 16630, Phoenix AZ 85011. (602)266-0550, ext. 110. **Fax:** (602)266-0773. **E-mail:** editor@echomag.com. **Website:** www.echomag.com. **Contact:** KJ Philp, managing editor. **30-40% freelance written.** Biweekly magazine covering gay and lesbian issues. *Echo Magazine* is a newsmagazine for gay, lesbian, bisexual, and transgendered persons in the Phoenix metro area and throughout the state of Arizona. Editorial content needs to be pro-gay, that is, supportive of LGBTQ equality in all areas of American life. Estab. 1989. Circ. 15,000-18,000. Byline given. Pays on publication. No kill fee. Publishes ms an average of less than 1 month after acceptance. Editorial lead time 1-2 months. Submit seasonal material 1-2 months in advance. Accepts queries by e-mail. Accepts simultaneous submissions. Responds in 2 weeks

to queries; in 1 month to mss. Sample copy available online. Guidelines by e-mail.

NONFICTION Needs book excerpts, essays, historical, humor, interview, opinion, personal experience, photo feature, travel. Special issues: Pride Festival (April); Arts issue (August); Holiday Gift/Decor (December). No articles on topics unrelated to our LGBTQ readers, or anything that is not pro-gay. **Buys 10-20 mss/year.** Query. Length: 500-2,000 words. **Pays $30-40.** Pays expenses of writers on assignment.

COLUMNS Guest Commentary (opinion on GLBT issues), 500-1,000 words; Arts/Entertainment (profiles of GLBT or relevant celebrities, or arts issues), 800-1,500 words. **Buys 5-10 mss/year.** Query. **Pays $30-40.**

💲 THE GAY & LESBIAN REVIEW

Gay & Lesbian Review, Inc., P.O. Box 16477, Hollywood CA 91615. (844)752-7829. **E-mail:** glreview@hubservice.com. **E-mail:** richard.schneider@glreview.org. **Website:** www.glreview.org. **Contact:** Richard Schneider, Jr., editor. **100% freelance written.** "*The Gay & Lesbian Review* is a bimonthly magazine targeting an educated readership of gay, lesbian, bisexual, and transgendered (GLBT) men and women. Under the tagline 'a bimonthly journal of history, culture, and politics,' the *G&LR* publishes essays in a wide range of disciplines as well as reviews of books, movies, and plays." Estab. 1994. Circ. 12,000. A bimonthly magazine of history, culture, and politics. Pays on publication. No kill fee. Editorial lead time 2 months. Accepts simultaneous submissions. Sample copy free. Guidelines available online at http://www.glreview.org/writers-guidelines-for-submission/.

NONFICTION Needs book excerpts, essays, historical, humor, interview, memoir, opinion, photo feature, reviews, travel, book reviews. Special issues: See website: http://www.glreview.org/writers-guidelines-for-submission/. Query or send complete ms by e-mail. Length: 2,000-4,000 words for features; 600-1,200 words for book reviews. **Pays $50-100.** Pays expenses of writers on assignment.

COLUMNS Guest Opinion (op-ed pieces by GLBT writers and activists), 500-1,000 words; Artist's Profile (focuses on the creative output of a visual artist, musician, or writer), 1,000-1,500 words; Art Memo (reflections on a work or artist of the past who made a difference for gay culture), 1,000-1,500 words; International Spectrum (the state of GLBT rights or culture in city or region outside the U.S.), 1,000-1,500 words. Query or submit complete ms by e-mail.

POETRY Needs avant-garde, free verse, traditional. Submit poems by postal mail (no e-mail submissions) with SASE for reply. Submit maximum 3 poems. Length: "While there is no hard-and-fast limit on length, poems of over 50 lines become hard to accommodate."

💲💲 INSTINCT MAGAZINE

11856 Balboa Blvd., #312, Granada Hills CA 91344. (818)284-4525. **E-mail:** editor@instinctmag.com. **Website:** instinctmagazine.com. **Contact:** Mike Wood, editor-in-chief. **40% freelance written.** Gay men's monthly lifestyle and entertainment magazine. "*Instinct* is a blend of *Cosmo* and *Maxim* for gay men. We're smart, sexy, irreverent, and we always have a sense of humor—a unique style that has made us the #1 gay men's magazine in the US." Estab. 1997. Circ. 115,000. Byline given. Pays on publication. Offers 20% kill fee. Editorial lead time 2-3 months. Accepts queries by mail, e-mail. Accepts simultaneous submissions. Sample copy available online. Guidelines available online. Register online first.

NONFICTION Needs expose, general interest, humor, interview, travel, basically anything of interest to gay men will be considered. Does not want first-person accounts or articles. Send complete ms via online submissions manager. Length: 850-2,000 words. **Pays $50-300.** Pays expenses of writers on assignment.

COLUMNS Health (gay, off-kilter), 800 words; Fitness (irreverent), 500 words; Movies, Books (edgy, sardonic), 800 words; Music, Video Games (indie, underground), 800 words. **Pays $150-250.**

💲💲 METROSOURCE MAGAZINE

137 W. 19th St., 2nd Floor, New York NY 10011. (212)691-5127. **E-mail:** letters@metrosource.com. **Website:** www.metrosource.com. **75% freelance written.** Magazine published 6 times/year. "*MetroSource* is an upscale, glossy, 4-color lifestyle magazine targeted to an urban, professional gay and lesbian readership." Estab. 1990. Circ. 145,000. Byline given. Pays on publication. Publishes ms an average of 2 months after acceptance. Editorial lead time 4 months. Submit seasonal material 4 months in advance. Accepts simultaneous submissions. Sample copy for $5.

NONFICTION Buys 20 mss/year. Query with published clips. Length: 1,000-1,800 words. **Pays $100-400.** Pays expenses of writers on assignment.

COLUMNS Book, film, television, and stage reviews; health columns; and personal diary and opinion pieces. Word lengths vary. Query with published clips. **Pays $200.**

💲 THE WASHINGTON BLADE

P.O. Box 53352, Washington DC 20009. (202)747-2077. **Fax:** (202)747-2070. **E-mail:** knaff@washblade.com. **Website:** www.washblade.com. **Contact:** Kevin Naff, editor. **20% freelance written.** Nation's oldest and largest weekly newspaper covering the lesbian, gay, bisexual and transgender issues. Articles (subjects) should be written from or directed to a gay perspective. Estab. 1969. Circ. 30,000. Byline given. No kill fee. Submit seasonal material 1 month in advance. Accepts queries by mail, e-mail, fax. Accepts simultaneous submissions. Responds in 1 month to queries.

NONFICTION Pays expenses of writers on assignment.

REPRINTS Send typed manuscript with rights for sale noted and information about when and where the material previously appeared.

COLUMNS Send feature submissions to Joey DiGuglielmo, arts editor (joeyd@washblade.com). Send opinion submissions to Kevin Naff, editor (knaff@washblade.com). Pay varies. No sexually explicit material.

GENERAL INTEREST

💲 THE ALMANAC FOR FARMERS & CITY FOLK

Greentree Publishing, Inc., Box 319, 840 S. Rancho Dr., Suite 4, Las Vegas NV 89106. (702)387-6777. **Fax:** (702)385-1370. **Website:** www.thealmanac.com. **30-40% freelance written.** Annual almanac of "down-home, folksy material pertaining to farming, gardening, homemaking, animals, etc." Estab. 1983. Circ. 300,000. Byline given. Pays on publication. No kill fee. Publishes ms an average of 6 months after acceptance. Accepts queries by mail. Accepts simultaneous submissions. Sample copy: $4.99.

NONFICTION Needs essays, general interest, historical, how-to, humor. "No fiction or controversial topics. Please, no first-person pieces!" **Buys 30-40 mss/year.** No queries, please. Editorial decisions made from mss only. Send complete ms by mail. Length: 350-1,400 words. **Pays $45/page.** Pays expenses of writers on assignment.

FILLERS Needs anecdotes, facts, short humor, gardening hints. Length: up to 125 words. **Pays $15 for short fillers or page rate for longer fillers.**

💲💲 THE AMERICAN LEGION MAGAZINE

700 N. Pennsylvania St., P.O. Box 1055, Indianapolis IN 46206-1055. (317)630-1253; (317) 630-1298. **Fax:** (317)630-1280. **E-mail:** magazine@legion.org; mgrills@legion.org; hsoria@legion.org. **Website:** www.legion.org. **Contact:** Matt Grills, cartoon editor; Holly Soria, art director. **70% freelance written. Prefers to work with published/established writers, but works with a small number of new/unpublished writers each year.** Monthly magazine. Working through 15,000 community-level posts, the honorably discharged wartime veterans of The American Legion dedicate themselves to God, country, and traditional American values. They believe in a strong defense; adequate and compassionate care for veterans and their families; community service; and the wholesome development of our nation's youth. Publishes articles that reflect these values. Informs readers and their families of significant trends and issues affecting the nation, the world and their way of life. Major features focus on the American flag, national security, foreign affairs, business trends, social issues, health, education, ethics, and the arts. Also publishes selected general feature articles, articles of special interest to veterans, and question-and-answer interviews with prominent national and world figures. Estab. 1919. Circ. 2,550,000. Byline given. Pays on acceptance. No kill fee. Publishes ms an average of 6 months after acceptance. Accepts queries by mail, e-mail, fax. Accepts simultaneous submissions. Responds in 2 months to queries. Sample copy for $3.50 and 9x12 SAE with 6 first-class stamps. Guidelines for #10 SASE.

NONFICTION Needs general interest, interview. No regional topics or promotion of partisan political agendas. No personal experiences or war stories. **Buys 50-60 mss/year.** Query with SASE should explain the subject or issue, article's angle and organization, writer's qualifications, and experts to be interviewed. Length: 300-2,000 words. **Pays 40¢/word and up.** Pays expenses of writers on assignment.

💲💲 THE AMERICAN SCHOLAR

Phi Beta Kappa, 1606 New Hampshire Ave. NW, Washington DC 20009. (202)265-3808. **Fax:** (202)265-0083. **E-mail:** scholar@pbk.org. **E-mail:** theamericanscholar.submittable.org/submit. **Website:** www.theamericanscholar.org. **Contact:** Robert Wilson, editor. **100% freelance written.** Quarterly magazine dedicated to current events, politics, history, science, culture and the arts. "Our intent is to have articles written by scholars and experts but written in nontechnical language for an intelligent audience. Material covers a wide range in the arts, sciences, current affairs, history, and literature." Estab. 1932. Circ. 30,000. Byline given. Pays on publication. Offers 50% kill fee. Publishes ms an average of 1 year after acceptance. Editorial lead time 6 months. Submit seasonal material 6 months in advance. Accepts queries by online submission form. Accepts simultaneous submissions. Responds in 2 weeks to queries; 2 months to mss. Guidelines online.

NONFICTION Needs essays, general interest, historical, humor, memoir, reviews, travel. **Buys 40 mss/year.** Query. Length: 3,000-5,000 words. **Pays $500 maximum.**

POETRY Contact: Sandra Costich. "We're not considering any unsolicited poetry."

THE ATLANTIC MONTHLY

The Watergate, 600 New Hampshire Ave., NW, Washington DC 20037. (202)266-6000. **Fax:** (202)266-6001. **E-mail:** submissions@theatlantic.com; pitches@theatlantic.com. **Website:** www.theatlantic.com. **Contact:** Scott Stossel, magazine editor; Ann Hulbert, literary editor. Covers poetry, fiction, and articles of the highest quality. General magazine for an educated readership with broad cultural and public-affairs interests. "*The Atlantic* considers unsolicited mss, either fiction or nonfiction. A general familiarity with what we have published in the past is the best guide to our needs and preferences." Estab. 1857. Circ. 500,000. Byline given. Pays on acceptance. No kill fee. Accepts queries by mail, e-mail. Responds in 4-6 weeks to mss. Guidelines online.

NONFICTION Needs book excerpts, essays, general interest, humor, travel. Query with or without published clips to pitches@theatlantic.com, or send complete ms to "Editorial Department" at address above. All unsolicited mss must be accompanied by SASE. "A general familiarity with what we have published in the past is the best guide to our needs and preferences." Length: 1,000-6,000 words **Payment varies.** Pays expenses of writers on assignment. Sometimes pays expenses.

FICTION "Seeks fiction that is clear, tightly written with strong sense of 'story' and well-defined characters." No longer publishes fiction in the regular magazine. Instead, it will appear in a special newsstand-only fiction issue. Receives 1,000 unsolicited mss/month. Accepts 7-8 mss/year. **Publishes 3-4 new writers/year.** literary, contemporary. Submit via e-mail with Word document attachment to submissions@theatlantic.com. Mss submitted via postal mail must be typewritten and double-spaced. Preferred length: 2,000-6,000 words. **Payment varies.**

POETRY *The Atlantic Monthly* publishes some of the most distinguished poetry in American literature. "We read with interest and attention every poem submitted to the magazine and, quite simply, we publish those that seem to us to be the best." Has published poetry by Maxine Kumin, Stanley Plumly, Linda Gregerson, Philip Levine, Ellen Bryant Voigt, and W.S. Merwin. Receives about 60,000 poems/year. Submit 2-6 poems by e-mail or mail. Buys 30-35 poems/year.

💲 THE CHRISTIAN SCIENCE MONITOR

210 Massachussetts Ave., Boston MA 02115. **E-mail:** homeforum@csmonitor.com. **Website:** www.csmonitor.com. **Contact:** Editor, The Home Forum. **95% freelance written.** *The Christian Science Monitor*, a Web-first publication that also publishes a weekly print magazine, regularly features personal nonfiction essays and, occasionally, poetry in its Home Forum section. "We're looking for upbeat essays of 600-800 words and short (20 lines maximum) poems that explore and celebrate daily life." Estab. 1908. Pays on publication. Offers 50% kill fee. Publishes ms 1-8 months after acceptance. Editorial lead time 6-8 weeks. Accepts queries by e-mail, online submission form. Responds in 3 weeks to mss; only responds to accepted mss. Sample copy available online. Guidelines available online or by e-mail (send e-mail with "Submission" in "Subject" field to receive autoreply with link).

NONFICTION Needs essays, humor, personal experience. **Buys 2,000+ mss/year.** Length: 600-800 words. **Pays $150.**

POETRY Accepts submissions via online form. Does not want "work that presents people in helpless or hopeless states; poetry about death, aging, or illness; or dark, violent, sensual poems. No poems that are overtly religious or falsely sweet." Submit maximum 5 poems. Length: up to 20 lines/poem. **Pays $25/haiku; $50/poem.**

💲💲💲💲 FAMILY CIRCLE

Meredith Corp., Articles Department, 805 Third Ave., 24th Floor, New York NY 10022. **Website:** www.familycircle.com. Lisa Kelsey, art director. **80% freelance written.** A national general interest women's magazine that focuses on all subjects relating to the family. Estab. 1932. Circ. 4 million. Byline given. Offers 20% kill fee. Editorial lead time 4 months. Submit seasonal material 4 months in advance. Accepts queries by mail. Accepts simultaneous submissions. Responds in 2 months to queries; in 2 months to mss. Guidelines available online.

NONFICTION Needs essays, opinion, personal experience, women's interest subjects such as family and personal relationships, children, physical and mental health, nutrition, and self-improvement. No fiction or poetry. **Buys 200 mss/year.** Submit detailed outline, 2 clips, cover letter describing your publishing history, SASE or IRCs. Length: 1,000-2,500 words. **Pays $1/word.** Pays expenses of writers on assignment.

💲💲 FORUM

Business Journals, Inc., 1384 Broadway, 11th Floor, New York NY 10018. (212)710-7442. **E-mail:** jillianl@busjour.com. **Website:** www.forum.busjour.com. Lisa Montemorra, project manager. **Contact:** Jillian LaRochelle, managing editor. **80% freelance written.** Semiannual magazine covering luxury fashion (men's 70%, women's 30%), luxury lifestyle. *Forum* directly targets a very upscale reader interested in profiles and service pieces on upscale designers, new fashion trends, and traditional suiting. Lifestyle articles—including wine and spirits, travel, cars, boating, sports, collecting, etc.—are upscale top of the line (i.e., don't write how expensive taxis are). Circ. 150,000. Byline given. Pays on publication. Publishes ms an average of 3-4 months after acceptance. Editorial lead time 6 months. Submit seasonal material 6 months in advance. Accepts queries by mail, e-mail. Responds in 2-3 weeks to queries. Guidelines by e-mail.

NONFICTION Needs general interest, interview, travel, luxury lifestyle trends, fashion service pieces. Does not want personal essays ("we run a few but commission them"). No fiction or single product articles; "in other words, an article should be on what's new in Italian wines, not about 1 superspecial brand." **Buys**

20-25 mss/year. Query. Length: 300-1,500 words. **Pays $300-500.**

COLUMNS Travel, 1,000-1,500 words; Wine + Spirits, 600-1,200 words; Gourmet, 600-1,200 words; Wheels, 600 words. **Buys 10-15 mss/year.** Query. **Pays $300-500.**

$$$$ HARPER'S MAGAZINE

666 Broadway, 11th Floor, New York NY 10012. (212)420-5720. **E-mail:** readings@harpers.org; scg@harpers.org. **Website:** www.harpers.org. **Contact:** Ellen Rosenbush, editor. **90% freelance written.** Monthly magazine for well-educated, socially concerned, widely read men and women who value ideas and good writing. *Harper's Magazine* encourages national discussion on current and significant issues in a format that offers arresting facts and intelligent opinions. By means of its several shorter journalistic forms—Harper's Index, Readings, Forum, and Annotation—as well as with its acclaimed essays, fiction, and reporting, *Harper's* continues the tradition begun with its first issue in 1850: to inform readers across the whole spectrum of political, literary, cultural, and scientific affairs. Estab. 1850. Circ. 230,000. Pays on acceptance. Offers negotiable kill fee. Publishes ms an average of 3 months after acceptance. Accepts queries by mail. Accepts simultaneous submissions. Responds in 6 weeks to queries. Guidelines available online.

NONFICTION Needs humor. No interviews or profiles. **Buys 2 mss/year.** Query. Length: 4,000-6,000 words. **Generally pays 50¢-$1/word.**

REPRINTS Reprints accepted for Readings section. Send typed ms with rights for sale and information about when and where the article previously appeared.

FICTION Will consider unsolicited fiction. Has published work by Rebecca Curtis, George Saunders, Haruki Murakami, Margaret Atwood, Allan Gurganus, Evan Connell, and Dave Bezmosgis. Needs humorous. **Buys 12 mss/year.** Submit complete ms by postal mail. Length: 3,000-5,000 words. **Generally pays 50¢-$1/word.**

$$ THE JOURNAL FOR INNOVATION

MultiTalent Management Incorporated, P.O. Box 2189, Santa Barbara CA 93120. Phone/**Fax:** (888)550-4744. **E-mail:** rick@tjfi.net. **E-mail:** wm@tjfi.net. **Website:** www.tjfi.net. **Contact:** Rick Soto. **50% freelance written.** Covers business, entrepreneurship, venture capital, high technology, entertainment, pageantry, health/fitness, music, fashion, and travel. *The Journal for Innovation* is a digital magazine and online media focused on business, entrepreneurship, venture capital, high technology, entertainment, pageantry, health/fitness, music, fashion, as well as, travel with circulation at 100,000. Estab. 1998. Circ. 100,000. Pays prior to publishing on website and digital magazine. Submit 1 month in advance. Accepts queries by mail, e-mail, fax. Accepts simultaneous submissions. Please submit entire article within e-mail, rather than as an attachment.

NONFICTION Needs interview, reviews, travel. Special issues: Annual digital issue. **Buys 12 mss/year.** Length: 300-3,000. **Pays $0.20/word.**

$$$$ NATIONAL GEOGRAPHIC

P.O. Box 98199, Washington DC 20090-8199. (202)857-7000. **Fax:** (202)828-5460. **Website:** www.nationalgeographic.com. **Contact:** Susan Goldberg, editor in chief; David Brindley, managing editor. **60% freelance written. Prefers to work with published/established writers.** Monthly magazine for members of the National Geographic Society. *National Geographic* magazine is the global leader in empowering people to navigate the world, providing authoritative, unbiased content that addresses today's complex issues, while uncovering the wonders of our time. Each issue captivates millions of curious readers with world-class, award-winning photography and reporting that inspire them to make informed decisions and effect positive change. As part of the world's largest nonprofit scientific, education, and entertainment organizations, *National Geographic* has unmatched reach to a national audience that influences opinions on the Beltway, in the board room, in Silicon Valley, and beyond. Estab. 1888. Circ. 3.1 million. Accepts queries by mail. Accepts simultaneous submissions. Guidelines available online.

NONFICTION Query (500 words with clips of published articles). Do not send mss. Length: 2,000-8,000 words. Pays expenses of writers on assignment.

$$$ NEWSWEEK

The Daily Beast, 251 W. 57th St., New York NY 10019. (212)445-4000. **Website:** www.newsweek.com. **Contact:** Kira Bindrim, managing editor. *Newsweek* is edited to report the week's developments on the newsfront of the world and the nation through news, commentary, and analysis. Estab. 1933. Circ. 3.2 million. No kill fee. Accepts simultaneous submissions.

COLUMNS Contact: myturn@newsweek.com. No longer accepting submissions for the print edition. To submit an essay to website, please e-mail. The My Turn essay should be: A) an original piece, B) 850-900 words, C) generally personal in tone, and D) about any topic, but not framed as a response to a Newsweek story or another My Turn essay. Submissions must not have been published elsewhere. Please include full name, phone number, and address with your entry. The competition is very stiff. Receives 600 entries per month and only prints 1 a week. **Pays $1,000 on publication.**

THE NEW YORKER

1 World Trade Center, New York NY 10007. **E-mail:** themail@newyorker.com. **E-mail:** poetry@newyorker.com. **Website:** www.newyorker.com. **Contact:** David Remnick, editor in chief. A quality weekly magazine of distinct news stories, articles, essays, and poems for a literate audience. Estab. 1925. Circ. 938,600. Pays on acceptance. No kill fee. Accepts queries by mail, e-mail. Responds in 3 months to mss. Subscription: $59.99/year (47 issues), $29.99 for 6 months (23 issues).

NONFICTION Submissions should be sent as PDF attachments. Do not paste them into the message field. Due to volume, cannot consider unsolicited "Talk of the Town" stories or other nonfiction. Pays expenses of writers on assignment.

FICTION Contact: fiction@newyorker.com. Publishes 1 ms/issue. Send complete ms by e-mail (as PDF attachment) or mail (address to Fiction Editor). **Payment varies.**

POETRY Submit up to 6 poems at a time by e-mail (as PDF attachment) or mail (address to Poetry Department). **Pays top rates.**

🟡🟡🟡 THE NEW YORK TIMES MAGAZINE

620 Eighth Ave., New York NY 10018. (212)556-1234. **Fax:** (212)556-3830. **E-mail:** magazine@nytimes.com; nytnews@nytimes.com; executive-editor@nytimes.com. **Website:** www.nytimes.com/pages/magazine. **Contact:** Margaret Editor, public editor. *The New York Times Magazine* appears in the *New York Times* on Sunday. The 'Arts and Leisure' section appears during the week. The 'Op Ed' page appears daily. Circ. 1.8 million. No kill fee. Accepts simultaneous submissions.

🟡🟡🟡 THE OLD FARMER'S ALMANAC

Yankee Publishing, Inc., P.O. Box 520, Dublin NH 03444. (603)563-8111. **Website:** www.almanac.com. **Contact:** Janice Stillman, editor. **95% freelance written.** Annual magazine covering weather, gardening, history, oddities, and lore. *"The Old Farmer's Almanac* is the oldest continuously published periodical in North America. Since 1792, it has provided useful information for people in all walks of life: tide tables for those who live near the ocean; sunrise tables and planting charts for those who live on the farm or simply enjoy gardening; recipes for those who like to cook; and forecasts for those who don't like the question of weather left up in the air. The words of the *Almanac*'s founder, Robert B. Thomas, guide us still: 'Our main endeavor is to be useful, but with a pleasant degree of humour.'" Estab. 1792. Circ. 3,100,000. Byline given. Pays on acceptance. Offers 25% kill fee. Publishes ms an average of 9 months after acceptance. Editorial lead time 6 months. Submit seasonal material 1 year in advance. Accepts queries by mail. Accepts simultaneous submissions. Responds in 3 weeks to queries. Responds in 2 months to mss. Sample copy for $6 at bookstores or online. Guidelines available online.

NONFICTION Needs general interest, historical, how-to. No personal recollections/accounts, personal/family histories. Query with published clips via mail or online contact form. Length: 800-2,500 words. **Pays 65¢/word.** Pays expenses of writers on assignment.

FILLERS Needs anecdotes, short humor. **Buys 1-2 mss/year.** Length: 100-200 words. **Pays $25.**

🟡🟡🟡🟡 OUTSIDE

Mariah Media, Inc., 400 Market St., Santa Fe NM 87501. (505)989-7100. **Fax:** (505)989-4700. **Website:** www.outsidemag.com. **Contact:** Axie Navas, associate managing editor. **60% freelance written.** Monthly magazine covering active lifestyle. *"Outside* is a monthly national magazine dedicated to covering the people, sports and activities, politics, art, literature, and hardware of the outdoors. Although our features are usually assigned to a regular stable of experienced and proven writers, we're always interested in new authors and their ideas. In particular, we look for articles on outdoor events, regions, and activities; informative seasonal service pieces; sports and adventure travel pieces; profiles of engaging outdoor characters; and investigative stories on environmental issues." Estab. 1977. Circ. 665,000. Byline given. Pays on acceptance. Offers 25% kill fee. Publishes ms an average of 3-6 months after acceptance. Accepts queries by mail. Responds is 6-8 weeks. Guidelines on website.

NONFICTION Needs book excerpts, new product, travel. **Buys 300 mss/year.** Query with 2 or 3 relevant clips along with a SASE to: Editorial Department at address above. "Queries should present a clear, original, and provocative thesis, not merely a topic or idea, and should reflect familiarity with the magazine's content and tone. Features are generally 1,500-5,000 words in length. Dispatches articles (100-800 words) cover timely news, events, issues, and short profiles. Destinations pieces (300-1,000 words) include places, news, and advice for adventurous travelers. Review articles (200-1,500 words) examine and evaluate outdoor gear and equipment." Length: 100-5,000 words. **Pays $1.50-2/word for assigned articles. Pays $1-1.50/word for unsolicited articles.** Pays expenses of writers on assignment.

COLUMNS Pays $1.50-$2/word.

💲💲💲💲 PARADE

ParadeNet, Inc., 60 E. 42nd St., New York NY 10165-1910. (212)478-1910. **Website:** parade.com. **95% freelance written.** Weekly magazine for a general interest audience. *Parade* magazine is distributed by more than 600 Sunday newspapers, including the *Atlanta Journal & Constitution, The Baltimore Sun, Boston Globe, Chicago Tribune, Dallas Morning News, Houston Chronicle, The Los Angeles Times, The Miami Herald, The New York Post, The Philadelphia Inquirer, San Francisco Chronicle, Seattle Times & Post Intelligencer,* and *The Washington Post.* Estab. 1941. Circ. 22,000,000. Pays on acceptance. Offers kill fee. Kill fee varies in amount. Publishes ms an average of 5 months after acceptance. Editorial lead time 1 month. Accepts queries by mail, online submission form. Accepts simultaneous submissions. Sample copy and guidelines available online.

NONFICTION Spot news events are not accepted, as *Parade* has a 2-month lead time. No fiction, fashion, travel, poetry, cartoons, nostalgia, regular columns, personal essays, quizzes, or fillers. Unsolicited queries concerning celebrities, politicians or sports figures are rarely assigned. **Buys 150 mss/year.** Query with published clips. Length: 1,200-1,500 words. **Pays**

very competitive amount. Pays expenses of writers on assignment.

💲💲💲💲 PEOPLE

Time, Inc., 1271 Avenue of the Americas, 28th Floor, New York NY 10020. (212)522-1212. **Fax:** (212)522-1359. **E-mail:** editor@people.com. **Website:** www.people.com. Weekly magazine. Designed as a forum for personality journalism through the use of short articles on contemporary news events and people. Circ. 3.4 million. No kill fee. Editorial lead time 3 months. Accepts simultaneous submissions.

💲💲 READER'S DIGEST

The Reader's Digest Association, Inc., Box 100, Pleasantville NY 10572. **E-mail:** letters@rd.com. **E-mail:** articleproposals@rd.com. **Website:** www.rd.com. *Reader's Digest* is an American general interest family magazine, published monthly. "We create content that is real, optimistic, authentic, inspiring, and actionable. *Reader's Digest* is a read of lasting value and importance—an oasis from snark, celebrity hype, and pessimism." Estab. 1922. Circ. 3 million. Accepts queries by e-mail. Accepts simultaneous submissions. Guidelines available online.

NONFICTION Accepts one-page queries that clearly detail the article idea, with special emphasis on the arc of the story, interview access to the main characters, access to documents, etc. Looks for dramatic narratives, articles about everyday heroes, crime dramas, adventure stories. Include a separate page for writing credentials. Pays expenses of writers on assignment.

COLUMNS Life; @Work; Off Base, **pays $300.** Laugh; Quotes, **pays $100.** Address your submission to the appropriate humor category.

♻💲💲💲💲 READER'S DIGEST (CANADA)

1100 Rene Levesque Blvd. W, Montreal QC H3B 5H5 Canada. **E-mail:** editor@rd.com. **Website:** www.readersdigest.ca. **30-50% freelance written.** Monthly magazine of general interest articles and subjects. Estab. 1948. Circ. 1,000,000. Byline given. **Pays on acceptance for original works.** Pays on publication for pickups. Offers $500 (Canadian) kill fee. Submit seasonal material 5 months in advance. Accepts queries by mail, online submission form. Accepts simultaneous submissions. Guidelines available online.

NONFICTION Needs general interest, how-to, humor, inspirational, personal experience, travel, crime, health. Query with published clips. Proposals can be mailed to the above address. We are looking for dramatic narratives, inspirational stories, articles about crime, adventure, travel and health issues. Download our writer's guidelines. If we are interested in pursuing your idea, an editor will contact you. Length: up to 2,500 words. **Pays $1/word (CDN) or more depending on story type.** Pays expenses of writers on assignment.

REPRINTS Query. Payment is negotiable.

$ REUNIONS MAGAZINE

P.O. Box 11727, Milwaukee WI 53211-0727. (414)263-4567. **Fax:** (414)263-6331. **E-mail:** editor@reunionsmag.com. **Website:** www.reunionsmag.com. **Contact:** Edith Wagner, editor. **90% freelance written.** Occasional print magazine covering all aspects of reunion planning. "*Reunions Magazine* is for people planning family, class, military, and other reunions. We want easy, practical ideas about organizing, planning, researching/searching, attending, or promoting reunions. Our only focus is reunion planning; our only audience is reunion planners: the people who make reunion purchasing decisions." Estab. 1990. Circ. 15,000. Byline given. Pays on publication. Publishes ms an average of 1 year after acceptance. Editorial lead time 6 months. Submit seasonal material 1 year in advance. Accepts queries by mail, e-mail. Accepts simultaneous submissions. Acknowledges receipt but may not respond for 1 year. Sample copy, send $3; writer's guidelines send #10 SASE or see issues and guidelines online. Prefer e-mail. See guidelines.

NONFICTION Needs how-to, humor, new product, personal experience, photo feature, travel. Not interested in anything that does not have obvious and automatic interest for reunion planners. **Buys 40 mss/year.** Query with published clips. Length: 500-2,500 (prefers work on the short side). **"Rarely able to pay, but when we can pay $25-50."**

REPRINTS Send tearsheet, photocopy or typed ms with rights for sale noted and information about when and where the material previously appeared. Usually pays $10, if at all.

FILLERS Must be reunion-related. Needs anecdotes, facts, short humor. **Buys 20-40 fillers/year mss/year.** Length: 50-250 words. **Pays $5.**

$$$$ ROBB REPORT

CurtCo Robb Media, LLC, 29160 Heathercliff Rd., Suite #200, Malibu CA 90265. (310)589-7700. **Fax:** (310)589-7701. **E-mail:** editorial@robbreport.com. **Website:** www.robbreport.com. **60% freelance written.** Monthly lifestyle magazine geared toward active, affluent readers. Addresses upscale autos, luxury travel, boating, technology, lifestyles, watches, fashion, sports, investments, collectibles. "For over 30 years, *Robb Report* magazine has served as the definitive authority on connoisseurship for ultra-affluent consumers. *Robb Report* not only showcases the products and services available from the most prestigious luxury brands around the globe, but it also provides its sophisticated readership with detailed insight into a range of these subjects, which include sports and luxury automobiles, yachts, real estate, travel, private aircraft, fashion, fine jewelry and watches, art, wine, state-of-the-art home electronics, and much more. For connoisseurs seeking the very best that life has to offer, *Robb Report* remains the essential luxury resource." Estab. 1976. Circ. 104,000. Byline given. Pays on publication. Offers 25% kill fee. Submit seasonal material 5 months in advance. Accepts queries by mail, fax. Accepts simultaneous submissions. Responds in 2 months to queries; in 1 month to mss. Sample copy: $14, plus s&h.

NONFICTION Needs new product, travel. Special issues: Home (October); Recreation (March). **Buys 60 mss/year.** Query with published clips. Length: 500-2,000 words. **Pays $1/word.** Pays expenses of writers on assignment.

SMITHSONIAN MAGAZINE

Capital Gallery, Suite 6001, MRC 513, P.O. Box 37012, Washington DC 20013. (202)275-2000. **E-mail:** smithsonianmagazine@si.edu. **Website:** www.smithsonianmag.com. **Contact:** Molly Roberts, photo editor; Jeff Campagna, art services coordinator. **90% freelance written.** Monthly magazine for associate members of the Smithsonian Institution; 85% with college education. *Smithsonian Magazine's* mission is to inspire fascination with all the world has to offer by featuring unexpected and entertaining editorial that explores different lifestyles, cultures and peoples, the arts, the wonders of nature and technology, and much more. The highly educated, innovative readers of *Smithsonian* share a unique desire to celebrate life, seeking out the timely as well as timeless, the artistic as well as the academic, and the thought-provoking as well as the humorous. Circ. 2.3 million. Pays on acceptance. Offers 33% kill fee. Publishes ms an average of 6 months after acceptance. Editorial lead time

2 months. Submit seasonal material 3 months in advance. Accepts simultaneous submissions. Sample copy for $5. Guidelines available online.

NONFICTION **Buys 120-130 feature (up to 5,000 words) and 12 short (500-650 words) mss/year.** Use online submission form. *Smithsonian* magazine accepts unsolicited proposals from established freelance writers for features and some departments. Submit a proposal of 250 to 300 words as a preliminary query. Background information and writing credentials are helpful. The proposal text box on the Web submission form holds 10,000 characters (approximately 2,000 words), ample room for a cover letter and proposal. All unsolicited proposals are sent on speculation. Supporting material or clips of previously published work can be provided with links. Article length ranges from a 700-word humor column to a 4,000-word full-length feature. Considers focused subjects that fall within the general range of Smithsonian Institution interests, such as: cultural history, physical science, art and natural history. **Pays various rates per feature, $1,500 per short piece.** Pays expenses of writers on assignment.

COLUMNS Length: 1,000-2,000 words. Last Page humor, 550-700 words. **Buys 12-15 mss/year.** Use online submission form. **Pays $1,000-1,500.**

💲💲💲💲 TOWN & COUNTRY

The Hearst Corp., 300 W. 57th St., New York NY 10019-3794. **E-mail:** tnc@hearst.com. **Website:** www.townandcountrymag.com. **40% freelance written.** Monthly lifestyle magazine. *"Town & Country* is a lifestyle magazine for the affluent market. Features focus on fashion, beauty, travel, interior design, and the arts, as well as individuals' accomplishments and contributions to society.' Estab. 1846. Circ. 488,000. Byline given. Pays on acceptance. Offers 25% kill fee. Accepts queries by mail. Accepts simultaneous submissions. Responds in 2 months to queries.

NONFICTION Needs general interest, interview, travel. "Rarely publishes work not commissioned by the magazine. Does not publish poetry, short stories, or fiction." **Buys 25 mss/year.** Query by mail only with relevant clips before submitting. Column items, 100-300 words; feature stories, 800-2,000 words. **Pays $2/word.**

💲💲💲 YES! MAGAZINE

284 Madrona Way NE, Suite 116, Bainbridge Island WA 98110. **E-mail:** editors@yesmagazine.org. **E-mail:** submissions@yesmagazine.org. **Website:** www.yesmagazine.org. **70% freelance written.** Quarterly magazine covering sustainability, social justice, grassroots activism, contemporary culture; nature, conservation, ecology, politics, and world affairs. *"YES! Magazine* documents how people are creating a more just, sustainable and compassionate world. Each issue includes articles focused on a theme—about solutions to a significant challenge facing our world—and a number of timely, non-theme articles. Our non-theme section provides ongoing coverage of issues like health, climate change, globalization, media reform, faith, democracy, economy and labor, social and racial justice and peace building. To inquire about upcoming themes, send an e-mail to submissions@yesmagazine.org; please be sure to type 'themes' as the subject line." Estab. 1997. Circ. 55,000. Byline given. Pays on publication. Rarely offers kill fee. Publishes ms an average of 1-6 months after acceptance. Editorial lead time 3-6 months. Submit seasonal material 2-6 months in advance. Accepts queries by e-mail. Accepts simultaneous submissions. Responds in 3 months. Sample copy and writer's guidelines online.

NONFICTION Needs book excerpts, opinion. "We don't want stories that are negative or too politically partisan." **Buys 30 mss/year mss/year.** Query with published clips. Length: 100-2,500 words. **Pays $50-1,250 for assigned articles. Pays $50-600 for unsolicited articles.** Pays expenses of writers on assignment.

REPRINTS Send photocopy or typed ms with rights for sale noted and information about when and where the material previously appeared.

COLUMNS Signs of Life (positive news briefs), 100-250 words; Commentary (opinion from thinkers and experts), 500 words; Book and film reviews, 500-800 words. **Pays $20-300.**

HEALTH & FITNESS

💲💲 AMERICAN FITNESS

1750 E. Northrop Blvd., Suite 200, Chandler AZ 85286. (800)446-2322, ext. 200. **E-mail:** americanfitness@afaa.com. **Website:** www.afaa.com. **Contact:** Meg Jordan, editor. **75% freelance written.** Bimonthly magazine covering exercise and fitness, health, and nutrition. "We need timely, in-depth, informative articles on health, fitness, aerobic exercise, sports nutrition, age-specific fitness, and outdoor activity. Absolutely no first-person accounts. Need well-researched articles for professional readers." Estab. 1983. Circ. 42,900. Byline given. Pays 30 days after publication. No kill fee. Publishes ms an average of 6 months after acceptance. Submit seasonal material 4 months in advance. Accepts queries by mail, fax. Accepts simultaneous submissions. Responds in 2 months to queries. Sample copy for $4.50 and SASE with 6 first-class stamps.

NONFICTION Needs historical, inspirational, interview, new product, personal experience, photo feature, travel. No articles on unsound nutritional practices, popular trends, or unsafe exercise gimmicks. **Buys 18-25 mss/year.** Send complete ms. Length: 800-1,200 words. **Pays $200 for features, $80 for news.** Pays expenses of writers on assignment.

COLUMNS Research (latest exercise and fitness findings); Alternative paths (nonmainstream approaches to health, wellness, and fitness); Strength (latest breakthroughs in weight training); Clubscene (profiles and highlights of fitness club industry); Adventure (treks, trails, and global challenges); Food (low-fat/nonfat, high-flavor dishes); Homescene (home-workout alternatives); Clip 'n' Post (concise exercise research to post in health clubs, offices or on refrigerators). Length: 800-1,000 words. Query with published clips or send complete ms. **Pays $100-200.**

$$$ BETTER NUTRITION

Active Interest Media, 512 Main St., Suite 1, El Segundo CA 90245. (310)356-4100. **Fax:** (310)356-4110. **E-mail:** nbrechka@aimmedia.com. **Website:** www.betternutrition.com. **Contact:** Nicole Brechka, editor-in-chief. **57% freelance written.** Monthly magazine covering nutritional news and approaches to optimal health. "The new *Better Nutrition* helps people (men, women, families, old and young) integrate nutritious food, the latest and most effective dietary supplements, and exercise/personal care into healthy lifestyles." Estab. 1938. Circ. 460,000. Byline given. Pays on publication. No kill fee. Publishes ms an average of 2 months after acceptance. Editorial lead time 3 months. Accepts queries by mail, e-mail. Accepts simultaneous submissions. Sample copy free.

NONFICTION **Buys 120-180 mss/year.** Query. Length: 400-1,200 words. **Pays $400-1,000.**

$$ HEALING LIFESTYLES & SPAS

P.O. Box 271207, Louisville CO 80027. (303)917-7124. **E-mail:** editorial@healinglifestyles.com; melissa@healinglifestyles.com. **Website:** www.healinglifestyles.com. **Contact:** Melissa Williams, editor in chief. **90% freelance written.** "*Healing Lifestyles & Spas* is a bimonthly magazine committed to healing, health, and living a well-rounded, more natural life. In each issue we cover retreats, spas, organic living, natural food, herbs, beauty, yoga, alternative medicine, bodywork, spirituality, and features on living a healthy lifestyle." Estab. 1996. Circ. 45,000. Pays on publication. No kill fee. Publishes ms an average of 2-10 months after acceptance. Editorial lead time 6 months. Submit seasonal material 6-9 months in advance. Accepts queries by mail, e-mail. Accepts simultaneous submissions. Responds in 6 weeks to queries.

NONFICTION Needs travel. No fiction or poetry. Query. Length: 1,000-2,000 words. **Pays $150-500, depending on length, research, experience, and availability and quality of images.** Pays expenses of writers on assignment.

COLUMNS All Things New & Natural (short pieces outlining new health trends, alternative medicine updates, and other interesting tidbits of information), 50-200 words; Urban Retreats (focuses on a single city and explores its spas and organic living features), 1,200-1,600 words; Health (features on relevant topics ranging from nutrition to health news and updates), 900-1,200 words; Food (nutrition or spa-focused food articles and recipes), 1,000-1,200 words; Ritual (highlights a specific at-home ritual), 500 words; Seasonal Spa (focuses on a seasonal ingredient on the spa menu), 500-700 words; Spa Origins (focuses on particular modalities and healing beliefs from around the world, 1,000-1,200 words; Yoga, 400-800 words; Retreat (highlights a spa or yoga retreat), 500 words; Spa a la carte (explores a new treatment or modality on the spa menu), 600-1,000 words; Insight (focuses on profiles, theme-related articles, and new therapies, healing practices, and newsworthy items), 1,000-2,000 words. Query.

$$ THE HEALTH JOURNAL

Rian Enterprises, LLC, 4808 Courthouse St., Suite 204, Williamsburg VA 23188. (757)645-4475. **Fax:** (757)645-4473. **Website:** www.thehealthjournals.com. **70% freelance written.** Monthly tabloid covering consumer/family health and wellness in Virginia. "Articles accepted of local and national interest. Health-savvy, college educated audience of all gender, ages, and backgrounds." Estab. 2005. Circ. 81,000. Byline given on most pieces. Pays on publication. Publishes ms an average of 1-2 months after acceptance. Editorial lead time 4-6 months. Submit seasonal material 4-6 months in advance. Accepts queries by online submission form. Accepts simultaneous submissions. Only responds to mss of interest. Guidelines available by request only.

NONFICTION Needs book excerpts, essays, expose, general interest, historical, how-to, humor, inspirational, interview, new product, opinion, personal experience, photo feature, technical, travel. Does not want promotion of products, religious material, or anything over 1,000 words. **Buys 100 mss/year.** Query with published clips. Length: 400-1,000 words. **Pays 15¢/word (starting rate); $50/reprint.** Pays expenses of writers on assignment.

🍁$$ IMPACT MAGAZINE

IMPACT Productions, 2007 Second St. SW, Calgary AB T2S 1S4 Canada. (403)228-0605. **E-mail:** editor@impactmagazine.ca. **E-mail:** info@impactmagazine.ca. **Website:** www.impactmagazine.ca. **Contact:** Chris Welner, editor. **10% freelance written.** Bimonthly magazine covering fitness and sport performance. A leader in the industry, *IMPACT Magazine* is committed to publishing content provided by the best experts in their fields for those who aspire to higher levels of health, fitness, and sport performance. Estab. 1991. Circ. 90,000. Byline given. Pays 30 days after publication. Offers 25% kill fee. Publishes ms an average of 4-6 months after acceptance. Editorial lead time 6 months. Submit seasonal material 6 months in advance. Accepts queries by e-mail. Accepts simultaneous submissions. Responds in 4 weeks to queries. Sample copy and guidelines available online.

NONFICTION Needs general interest, how-to, interview, new product, opinion, technical. **Buys 4 mss/year.** Query before submitting. Length: 600-1,800 words. **Pays 25¢/word maximum for assigned articles. Pays 25¢/word maximum for unsolicited articles.** Pays expenses of writers on assignment.

$$$ MUSCLE & FITNESS

Weider Publications, part of American Media, Inc., 21100 Erwin St., Woodland Hills CA 91367. (818)884-6800. **Fax:** (818)595-0463. **Website:** www.muscleandfitness.com. **50% freelance written.** Monthly magazine covering bodybuilding and fitness for healthy, active men and women. "*Muscle & Fitness* contains a wide range of features and monthly departments devoted to all areas of bodybuilding, health, fitness, sport, injury prevention and treatment, and nutrition. Editorial fulfills 2 functions: information and entertainment. "Special attention is devoted to how-to advice and accuracy. Estab. 1950. Circ. 500,000. Pays on publication. No kill fee. Publishes ms an average of 2 months after acceptance. Editorial lead time 5 months. Submit seasonal material 6 months in advance. Accepts queries by mail. Responds in 1 month to queries.

NONFICTION Needs book excerpts, how-to, training, humor, interview, photo feature. **Buys 120 mss/year.** Query with published clips. Length: 800-1,800 words. **Pays $400-1,000.** Pays expenses of writers on assignment.

REPRINTS Send photocopy with rights for sale noted and information about when and where the material previously appeared. Payment varies.

🍁$$ MUSCLEMAG

Robert Kennedy Publishing, Inc., 400 Matheson Blvd. W., Mississauga ON L5R 3M1. **E-mail:** editorial@musclemag.com. **Website:** www.musclemag.com. **80% freelance written.** Covers hardcore bodybuilding. Monthly magazine on building health, fitness, and physique. Byline given. Pays on acceptance. No kill fee. Publishes ms an average of 6 months after acceptance. Accepts queries by mail, e-mail. Responds in 4 months to queries; in 4 months to mss.

NONFICTION Needs how-to, interview, new product, personal experience, photo feature, bodybuilding, strenth training, health, nutrition, fitness. **Pays $80-400 for assigned, accepted articles submitted on spec.**

FILLERS Needs anecdotes, facts, gags, newsbreaks, fitness, nutrition, health, short humor. **Buys 50-100 mss/year.** Length: 100-200 words.

$$$$ ORGANIC LIFE

Rodale, 400 S. 10th St., Emmaus PA 18098-0099. **E-mail:** rolsubmissions@rodale.com. **Website:** www.organicgardening.com. **75% freelance written.** Bimonthly magazine covering living naturally in the modern world. "Pitches for the front-of-book Gather section, the Food, Home, Garden, or Wellbeing sections, or the back-of-book Almanac section should be succinct yet detailed." Estab. 1942. Circ. 300,000. Byline given. Pays between acceptance and publication.

No kill fee. Accepts queries by mail. Accepts simultaneous submissions. Responds in 3 months to queries.

NONFICTION Query with published clips and outline. **Pays up to $1/word for experienced writers.** Pays expenses of writers on assignment.

❂$$$ OXYGEN

Robert Kennedy Publishing, 400 Matheson Blvd. W., Mississauga Ontario L5R 3M1 Canada. (905)507-3545; (888)254-0767. **Fax:** (905)507-2372. **Website:** www.oxygenmag.com. **70% freelance written.** Monthly magazine covering women's health and fitness. *Oxygen* encourages various exercise, good nutrition to shape, and condition the body. Estab. 1997. Circ. 340,000. Byline given. Pays on acceptance. Offers 25% kill fee. Publishes ms an average of 4 months after acceptance. Editorial lead time 3 months. Submit seasonal material 6 months in advance. Accepts queries by mail, fax. Accepts simultaneous submissions. Responds in 5 weeks to queries. Responds in 2 months to mss. Sample copy for $5.

NONFICTION Needs expose, how-to, humor, inspirational, interview, new product, personal experience, photo feature. No poorly researched articles that do not genuinely help the readers toward physical fitness, health, and physique. **Buys 100 mss/year.** Send complete ms with SASE and $5 for return postage. Length: 1,400-1,800 words. **Pays $250-1,000.** Pays expenses of writers on assignment.

COLUMNS Nutrition (low-fat recipes), 1,700 words; Weight Training (routines and techniques), 1,800 words; Aerobics (how-tos), 1,700 words. **Buys 50 mss/year.** Send complete ms. **Pays $150-500.**

$$$$ SELF

Conde Nast, One World Trade Center, New York NY 10007. (212)286-2860. **Fax:** (212)286-6174. **E-mail:** comments@self.com. **Website:** www.self.com. Monthly magazine for women ages 20-45. Self-confidence, self-assurance, and a healthy, happy lifestyle are pivotal to *Self* readers. This healthy lifestyle magazine delivers by addressing real-life issues from the inside out, with unparalleled energy and authority. From beauty, fitness, health and nutrition to personal style, finance, and happiness, the path to total well-being begins with *Self.* Circ. 1.3 million. Byline given on features and most short items. Pays on acceptance. No kill fee. Accepts queries by online submission form. Accepts simultaneous submissions. Responds in 1 month to queries. Guidelines for #10 SASE.

NONFICTION **Buys 40 mss/year.** Query with published clips. Length: 1,500-5,000 words. **Pays $1-2/word.** Pays expenses of writers on assignment.

COLUMNS Uses short, news-driven items on health, fitness, nutrition, money, jobs, love/sex, psychology and happiness, travel. Length: 300-1,000 words. **Buys 50 mss/year.** Query with published clips. **Pays $1-2/word.**

$$$$ SHAPE

American Media, 4 New York Plaza, 4th Floor, New York NY 10004. (212)545-4800. **Website:** www.shape.com. **70% freelance written. Prefers to work with published/established writers.** Monthly magazine covering health, fitness, nutrition, and beauty for women ages 18-34. *Shape* reaches women who are committed to healthful, active lifestyles. Readers participate in a variety of fitness-related activities in the gym, at home, and outdoors. They are also proactive about their health and are nutrition conscious. Estab. 1981. Circ. 2.5 million. Pays on acceptance. Offers 33% kill fee. Submit seasonal material 8 months in advance. Accepts queries by mail. Accepts simultaneous submissions. Responds in 2 months to queries. Sample copy for SAE with 9x12 envelope and 4 first-class stamps.

NONFICTION Needs book excerpts, expose, how-to. Rarely publishes celebrity question-and-answer stories, celebrity profiles, or menopausal/hormone replacement therapy stories. Query with published clips. Length: 2,500 words for features; 1,000 words for shorter pieces. **Pays $1.50/word (on average).** Pays expenses of writers on assignment.

$$ VIBRANT LIFE

Pacific Press Publishing Association, P.O. Box 5353, Nampa ID 83653-5353. (208)465-2579. **Fax:** (208)465-2531. **E-mail:** vibrantlife@pacificpress.com. **Website:** www.vibrantlife.com. **Contact:** Heather Quintana, Editor. **80% freelance written. Enjoys working with published/established writers; works with a small number of new/unpublished writers each year.** Bimonthly magazine covering health articles (especially from a prevention angle and with a Christian slant). "Whether you are fit and vigorous or have just received a frightening diagnosis, *Vibrant Life* has health information that will help you move closer to the life you were designed to live. It is perfect for sharing with people who may have never heard of this Christian approach to whole-person health. It's a wonderful way to introduce people to God's plan for us to have harmony of mind, body, and spirit. You can give a subscription to neighbors, friends, or coworkers; order a stack to place in a local grocery store, business, or doctor's office; or use it as a part of local church health initiatives, such as blood drives or cooking classes." Estab. 1885. Circ. 30,000. Byline given. Pays on acceptance. Submit seasonal material 9 months in advance. Accepts queries by mail, e-mail, fax. Accepts simultaneous submissions. Sample copy for $1. Guidelines available online.

NONFICTION Needs interview. **Buys 50-60 feature articles/year and 40 short mss/year.** Send complete ms. Length: 1,500-1,800 words for features; 650-750 words for short pieces. **Pays $100-300 for articles.** Pays expenses of writers on assignment.

REPRINTS Send tearsheet and information about when and where the material previously appeared. Pays 50% of amount paid for an original article.

$$$$ VIM & VIGOR

1010 E. Missouri Ave., Phoenix AZ 85014. (602)395-5850; (219) 836-0130. **Fax:** (602)395-5853. **Website:** www.comhs.org/vim_vigor/. **90% freelance written.** Quarterly magazine covering health and healthcare. Estab. 1985. Circ. 800,000. Byline given. Pays on acceptance. Publishes ms an average of 6 months after acceptance. Accepts simultaneous submissions. Sample copy for 9x12 SAE with 8 first-class stamps. Guidelines for #10 SASE.

NONFICTION Send published clips and resume by mail or e-mail. Length: 500-1,200 words. **Pays 90¢-$1/word.** Pays expenses of writers on assignment.

$$$$ YOGA JOURNAL

Active Interest Media, Healthy Living Group, 475 Sansome St., Suite 850, San Francisco CA 94111. (415)591-0555. **Fax:** (415)591-0733. **E-mail:** queries@yjmag.com. **Website:** www.yogajournal.com. **Contact:** Kaitlin Quistgaard, editor in chief. **75% freelance written.** Magazine published 9 times a year covering the practice and philosophy of yoga. Estab. 1975. Circ. 300,000. Byline given. Pays within 90 days of acceptance. Offers kill fee. Offers kill fee on assigned articles. Publishes ms an average of 10 months after acceptance. Submit seasonal material 7 months in advance. Accepts queries by e-mail. Accepts simultaneous submissions. Responds in 6 weeks to queries if interested. Sample copy: $4.99. Guidelines on website.

NONFICTION Needs book excerpts, how-to, interview, opinion, photo feature, travel. Does not want unsolicited poetry or cartoons. "Please avoid New Age jargon and in-house buzz words as much as possible." **Buys 50-60 mss/year.** Query with SASE. Length: 3,000-5,000 words. **Pays $800-2,000.** Pays expenses of writers on assignment.

REPRINTS Send tearsheet or photocopy with rights for sale noted and information about when and where the material previously appeared.

COLUMNS Om: Covers myriad aspects of the yoga lifestyle (150-400 words). This department includes Yoga Diary, a 250-word story about a pivotal moment in your yoga practice. Eating Wisely: A popular, 1,400-word department about relationship to food. Most stories focus on vegetarian and whole-foods cooking, nutritional healing, and contemplative pieces about the relationship between yoga and food. Yoga Scene: Featured on the back page of the magazine, this photo depicts some expression of your yoga practice. Please tell us where the photo is from, what was going on during the moment the photo was taken, and any other information that will help put the photo into context. E-mail a well-written query.

HISTORY

AMERICAN HERITAGE

90 Fifth Ave., New York NY 10011. (212)367-3100. **E-mail:** editor@americanheritage.com. **Website:** www.americanheritage.com. **70% freelance written.** Magazine published 6 times/year. *American Heritage* writes from a historical point of view on politics, business, art, current and international affairs, and our changing lifestyles. The articles are written with the intent to enrich the reader's appreciation of the sometimes nostalgic, sometimes funny, always stirring panorama of the American experience. Circ. 350,000. Byline given. Pays on acceptance. Publishes ms an average of 6-12 months after acceptance. Submit seasonal material 1 year in advance. Accepts simultaneous submissions. Responds in 2 months to queries. Guidelines for #10 sase.

NONFICTION **Buys 10-15 unsolicited mss/year.** Query. Length: 1,500-6,000 words. **Payment varies.** Pays expenses of writers on assignment.

AMERICAN HISTORY

Historynet.com, 1919 Gallows Rd., #400, Vienna VA 22182. **E-mail:** americanhistory@historynet.com. **E-mail:** mdolan@historynet.com. **Website:** www.historynet.com/magazines/american_history. **Contact:** Michael Dolan. **75% freelance written.** Bimonthly magazine of cultural, social, military, and political history published for a general audience. "Presents American history for general-interest readers in an authoritative, informative, thought-provoking, and entertaining style. Lively narratives take readers on an adventure with history, complemented by rare photographs, paintings, illustrations, and maps." Estab. 1966. Circ. 95,000. Byline given. Pays on acceptance. 20% kill fee. Accepts queries by e-mail. Accepts simultaneous submissions. Responds in 10 weeks to queries. Sample copy: $6. Guidelines by e-mail.

NONFICTION *"American History* commissions assignments based on one-page pitches by prospective authors explaining topic, significance, key character(s), setting, and narrative arc. We do not encourage speculative submissions." *Unsolicited mss not considered.* Inappropriate materials include book reviews, travelogues, personal/family narratives not of national significance, articles about collectibles/antiques, living artists, local/individual historic buildings/landmarks, and articles of a current editorial nature. **Buys 30 mss/year.** Query by e-mail with published clips. Length: 1,500-3,000 words. **Payment varies.**

AMERICA'S CIVIL WAR

Weider History Group, 1600 Tysons Blvd., Suite 1140, Tysons VA 22102. **E-mail:** acw@historynet.com. **E-mail:** submissions@historynet.com. **Website:** www.historynet.com/americas-civil-war. **Contact:** editor. **60% freelance written.** Bimonthly magazine covering popular history and straight historical narrative for both the general reader and the American Civil War buff featuring firsthand accounts, remarkable photos, expert commentary, and maps in making the whole story of the most pivotal era in American history accessible and showing why it still matters in the 21st century. Estab. 1988. Circ. 78,000. Byline given. Pays on publication. No kill fee. Accepts queries by e-mail. Accepts simultaneous submissions. Guidelines online.

NONFICTION Buys 18 mss/year. "Query. Submit a page outlining the subject and your approach to it, and why you believe this would be an important article for the magazine. Briefly summarize your prior writing experience in a cover note." Length: 3,500 words; 250-word sidebar. **Pays $300 and up.** Pays expenses of writers on assignment.

THE ARTILLERYMAN

Jack W. Melton Jr. LLC, 520 Folly Road, Suite P-379, Charleston SC 29412. (706)940-2673. **E-mail:** mail@artillerymanmagazine.com. **Website:** www.artillerymanmagazine.com. **Contact:** Jack Melton, Publisher. **60% freelance written.** Quarterly magazine covering antique artillery, fortifications, and crew-served weapons 1750-1900 for competition shooters, collectors, and living history reenactors using artillery. Estab. 1979. Circ. 1,200. Byline given. Pays on publication. Publishes ms an average of 6 months after acceptance. Accepts queries by mail, e-mail, fax. Accepts simultaneous submissions. Responds in 3 weeks to queries. Sample copy online.

NONFICTION Needs historical, how-to, interview, photo feature, technical, travel. **Buys 12 mss/year.** Send complete ms. Length: 300 words minimum. **Pays $40-60.**

AVIATION HISTORY

HistoryNet, LLC, 1919 Gallows Rd., Ste. 400, Vienna VA 22182. **E-mail:** aviationhistory@historynet.com. **Website:** www.historynet.com/aviation-history. **Contact:** Carl von Wodtke, editor. **95% freelance written.** Bimonthly magazine covering military and civilian aviation from first flight to the space age. *"Aviation History* aims to make aeronautical history not only factually accurate and complete but also enjoyable to a varied subscriber and newsstand audience." Estab. 1990. Circ. 50,000. Byline given. Pays on publication. 25% Publishes ms an average of 1-2 years after acceptance. Editorial lead time 6 months. Submit seasonal material 1 year in advance. Accepts queries by mail, e-mail. Accepts simultaneous submissions. Responds in 2 months to queries; 3 months to mss. Sample copy: $6. Guidelines with #10 SASE, or online.

NONFICTION Needs historical, interview, personal experience. **Buys 24 mss/year.** Query. Length: up to 3,000 words, with a 500-word sidebar where appropriate, author bio, and book suggestions for further reading. **Pays minimum $300 for features.** Pays expenses of writers on assignment.

COLUMNS Aviators; Restored; Extremes, all up to 1,100 words. **Pays minimum of $150. Book reviews, 300 words max, pays minimum of $75.**

$$$ CIVIL WAR TIMES

Weider History Group, 19300 Promenade Dr., Leesburg VA 20176-6500. **E-mail:** civilwartimes@weiderhistorygroup.com; cwt@weiderhistorygroup.com. **Website:** www.historynet.com. **Contact:** Dana B. Shoaf, editor. **90% freelance written. Works with a small number of new/unpublished writers each year.** Magazine published 6 times/year covering the history of the American Civil War. "*Civil War Times* is the full-spectrum magazine of the Civil War. Specifically, we look for nonpartisan coverage of battles, prominent military and civilian figures, the home front, politics, military technology, common soldier life, prisoners and escapes, period art and photography, the naval war, blockade-running, specific regiments, and much more." Estab. 1962. Circ. 108,000. Pays on acceptance and on publication. Publishes ms an average of 18 months after acceptance. Submit seasonal material 1 year in advance. Responds in 3-6 months to queries. Sample copy: $6. Guidelines for #10 SASE or by e-mail.

NONFICTION Needs interview, photo feature, Civil War historical material. "Don't send us a comprehensive article on a well-known major battle. Instead, focus on some part or aspect of such a battle, or some group of soldiers in the battle. Similar advice applies to major historical figures like Lincoln and Lee. Positively no fiction or poetry." **Buys 20 freelance mss/year.** Query by mail or e-mail with published clips. **Pays $75-800.**

$ GOOD OLD DAYS

Annie's, 306 E. Parr Rd., Berne IN 46711. **Fax:** (260)589-8093. **E-mail:** editor@goodolddaysmagazine.com. **Website:** www.goodolddaysmagazine.com. **Contact:** Mary Beth Weisenburger, editor. **75% freelance written.** Bimonthly magazine of first-person nostalgia, 1935-1960. "We look for strong narratives showing life as it was in the middle decades of the 20th century. Our readership is composed of nostalgia buffs, history enthusiasts, and the people who actually lived and grew up in this era." Byline given. Pays on contract. No kill fee. Publishes ms an average of 8 months after acceptance. Submit seasonal material 10 months in advance. Accepts queries by mail, e-mail, fax. Responds in 2 months to queries. Sample copy: $2. Guidelines available online.

NONFICTION Needs historical, humor, personal experience, photo feature, favorite food/recipes, year-round seasonal material, biography, memorable events, fads, fashion, sports, music, literature, entertainment. No fiction accepted. **Buys 350 mss/year.** Query or send complete ms. Length: 500-1,500 words. **Pays $15-50, depending on quality and photos.** Pays expenses of writers on assignment.

🍁$ HISTORY MAGAZINE

Moorshead Magazines, 82 Church St. S., Suite 101, Ajax ON L1S 6B3 Canada. **E-mail:** edward@moorshead.com. **Website:** www.history-magazine.com. **Contact:** Edward Zapletal, publisher/editor. **99% freelance written.** Bimonthly magazine covering social history. A general interest history magazine, focusing on social history up to about 1960. Estab. 1999. Byline given. Pays on publication. See author notes. Publishes ms an average of 6 months after acceptance. Editorial lead time 6 months. Submit seasonal material 6 months in advance. Accepts queries by e-mail. Accepts simultaneous submissions. Responds in 1-2 months to queries. Sample PDF copy available on request. Guidelines online.

NONFICTION Needs book excerpts, historical. Does not want first-person narratives or revisionist history. **Buys 50 mss/year.** Query. Do not submit complete ms. "Please note: Submissions must be accompanied by the author's name, telephone number, postal address, and e-mail address. If not present in the ms, we will delay publication until we receive the necessary contact information." Length: 500-2,200 words. **Pays 8¢/word; $7/image submitted and used in the final layout.** Pays expenses of writers on assignment.

$ LEBEN

City Seminary Press, 2150 River Plaza Dr., Suite 150, Sacramento CA 95833. **Website:** www.leben.us. **40% freelance written.** Quarterly magazine presenting the people and events of Christian history from a Reformation perspective. Not a theological journal, per se, but rather a popular history magazine. Estab. 2004. Circ. 5,000. Byline given. Pays on acceptance. Offers 25% kill fee. Publishes ms an average of 6 months after acceptance. Editorial lead time 6 months. Submit seasonal material 6 months in advance. Accepts queries by online submission form. Accepts simultaneous submissions. Responds in 3 weeks to queries; in 2 months to mss. Sample copy: $1.50 (order online or request via e-mail). Guidelines by e-mail.

NONFICTION Historical and biographical material related to Protestant and Reformation subjects. Does not want articles that argue theological issues. "There is a place for that, but not in a popular history/biography magazine aimed at general readership." Query. Length: 500-2,500 words. **Pays 5¢/word for original material.**

💲💲 PERSIMMON HILL

1700 NE 63rd St., Oklahoma City OK 73111. (405)478-2250, ext. 213. **Fax:** (405)478-4714. **E-mail:** editor@nationalcowboymuseum.org. **Website:** www.nationalcowboymuseum.org. **Contact:** Judy Hilovsky. **70% freelance written. Prefers to work with published/established writers; works with a small number of new/unpublished writers each year.** Biannual magazine for an audience interested in Western art, Western history, ranching, and rodeo, including historians, artists, ranchers, art galleries, schools, and libraries. Publication of the National Cowboy and Western Heritage Museum. Estab. 1970. Circ. 7,500. Byline given. Pays on publication. No kill fee. Publishes ms an average of 18 months after acceptance. Accepts simultaneous submissions. Responds in 3 months to queries. Sample copy for $11. Writer's guidelines available on website.

NONFICTION Buys 50-75 mss/year. Query with clips. Length: 1,500 words. **Pays $150-300.** Pays expenses of writers on assignment.

💲 RENAISSANCE MAGAZINE

703 Post Rd., Fairfield CT 06824. (800)232-2224. **Fax:** (800)775-2729. **E-mail:** editortom@renaissancemagazine.com. **Website:** www.renaissancemagazine.com. **Contact:** Tom Hauck, editor. **90% freelance written.** Bimonthly magazine covering the history of the Middle Ages and the Renaissance. "Our readers include historians, reenactors, roleplayers, medievalists, and Renaissance Faire enthusiasts." Estab. 1996. Circ. 33,000. Byline given. Pays 3 weeks after publication. Publishes ms an average of 1 year after acceptance. Editorial lead time 6 months. Submit seasonal material 4 months in advance. Accepts queries by mail, e-mail, fax, phone. Accepts simultaneous submissions. Responds in 3 weeks to queries. Responds in 2 months to mss. Sample copy for $9. Guidelines available online.

NONFICTION Needs essays, expose, historical, how-to, interview, new product, opinion, photo feature, religious, travel. **Buys 25 mss/year.** Query or send ms. Length: 2,000 words. **Pays 10¢/word and 1 contributor's copy.**

💲 TOMBIGBEE COUNTRY MAGAZINE

P.O. Box 621, Gu-Win AL 35563. (205)412-1272. **E-mail:** tombigbeecountrymagazine@yahoo.com. **Website:** www.tombigbeecountry.com. **Contact:** Bo Webster, editor. **50% freelance written.** Monthly magazine covering nostalgia and history. *Tombigbee Country* is a magazine dedicated to the old time tales, history, and humor of northeast Mississippi and northwest Alabama. *Tombigbee Country* is a regional, nostalgia, monthly magazine which features human-interest articles concerning the area surrounding the Upper Tombigbee River (Tenn-Tom Waterway). "We take pride in being a country magazine that uses a mixture of irony, wit, and humor with good folk history." Estab. 2,000. Circ. 10,000. Byline given. No kill fee. Publishes ms an average of 1 month after acceptance. Editorial lead time 2 months. Submit seasonal material 2 months in advance. Accepts queries by mail, e-mail. Accepts simultaneous submissions. Responds in 1 week to queries; 1 month to mss. Sample copy $2. Guidelines free.

NONFICTION Needs book excerpts, essays, general interest, historical, humor, inspirational, personal experience, religious. **Buys 24+ mss/year.** Query. "We are eager for stories on personal experience with celebrities—country musicians, famous southerners." Length: 800-2,000 words.

FILLERS Needs short humor. Length: 25-800 words.

💲 THE TOMBSTONE EPITAPH

Tombstone Epitaph, Inc., P.O. BOX, 1880, Tombstone AZ 85638. (520)457-2211. **E-mail:** info@tombstoneepitaph.com. **Website:** www.tombstoneepitaph.com. **Contact:** Frederick Schoemehl, editor. **60% freelance written.** Monthly tabloid covering American west to 1900 (-1935, if there's an Old West connection). "We seek lively, well-written, sourced articles that examine the history and culture of the Old West." Estab. 1880. Byline given. Pays at end of calendar year. No kill fee. Publishes ms an average of 3 months after acceptance. Editorial lead time 3 months. Submit seasonal material 6 months in advance. Accepts queries by e-mail. Responds in 2 weeks to queries. Responds in 1 month to mss. Sample copy for $3. Guidelines by e-mail.

NONFICTION Needs essays, historical, humor, personal experience, (if historically grounded), travel, Past events as interpreted in film, books, magazines, etc. "We do not want poorly sourced stories, contemporary West pieces, fiction, poetry, big 'tell-all' stories." **Buys 25-40 mss/year.** Query. Length: 1,000-5,000 words. **Pays $30-50 for assigned articles. Pays up to $30 for unsolicited articles.**

💲💲 TRACES OF INDIANA AND MIDWESTERN HISTORY

Indiana Historical Society, 450 W. Ohio St., Indianapolis IN 46202-3269. (317)232-1877. **Fax:** (317)233-0857. **E-mail:** rboomhower@indianahistory.org. **Website:** www.indianahistory.org. **Contact:** Ray E. Boomhower, senior editor. **80% freelance written.** Quarterly popular history magazine on Indiana history. "Conceived as a vehicle to bring to the public good narrative and analytical history about Indiana in its broader contexts of region and nation, *Traces* explores the lives of artists, writers, performers, soldiers, politicians, entrepreneurs, homemakers, reformers, and naturalists. It has traced the impact of Hoosiers on the nation and the world. In this vein, the editors seek nonfiction articles that are solidly researched, attractively written, and amenable to illustration, and they encourage scholars, journalists, and freelance writers to contribute to the magazine." Estab. 1989. Circ. 6,000. Byline given. No kill fee. Publishes ms an average of 6-10 months after acceptance. Submit seasonal material 1 year in advance. Accepts queries by mail, e-mail. Accepts simultaneous submissions. Responds in 3 months to mss. Guidelines online.

NONFICTION Needs historical. **Buys 20 mss/year.** Send complete ms. Length: 2,000-4,000 words. **Pays $100-500.**

💲 TRAINS

Kalmbach Publishing Co., P.O. Box 1612, Waukesha WI 53187-1612. (262)796-8776. **Fax:** (262)796-1142. **E-mail:** editor@trainsmag.com; photoeditor@trainsmag.com. **Website:** www.trn.trains.com. **Contact:** Jim Wrinn, editor; Tom Danneman, art director. Monthly magazine covering railroading. "Appeals to consumers interested in learning about the function and history of the railroad industry." Estab. 1940. Circ. 92,419. No kill fee. Editorial lead time 2 months. Accepts simultaneous submissions.

NONFICTION *Trains* buys news stories and feature articles covering railroading's past and present, including first-person recollections. Before submitting a feature-length article, send a written query via e-mail. Send a brief paragraph explaining the story, its theme, and highlights. Queries should include a possible headline. **Payment: 10¢/word.** Pays expenses of writers on assignment.

💲💲💲 TRUE WEST

True West Publishing, Inc., 6702 E. Cave Creek Rd., Suite 5, P.O. Box 8008, Cave Creek AZ 85327. (888)687-1881. **Fax:** (480)575-1903. **E-mail:** editor@twmag.com. **Website:** www.truewestmagazine.com. **Contact:** Meghan Saar, editor; Bob Boze Bell, executive editor. **45% freelance written. Works with a small number of new/unpublished writers each year.** Magazine published 10 times/year covering Western American history from prehistory 1800 to 1930. "We want reliable research on significant historical topics written in lively prose for an informed general audience. More recent topics may be used if they have a historical angle or retain the Old West flavor of trail dust and saddle leather. True West magazine's features and departments tie the history of the American West (between 1800-1930) to the modern western lifestyle through enticing narrative and intelligent analyses." Estab. 1953. Byline given. Pays on publication. Kill fee applicable only to material assigned by the editor, not for stories submitted on spec based on query written to the editor. 50% of original fee should the story have run in the publication. Editorial lead time 6 months. Accepts queries by mail, e-mail. Accepts simultaneous submissions. Sample copy for $3. Guidelines available online.

NONFICTION No fiction, poetry, or unsupported, undocumented tales. **Buys 30 mss/year.** No unsolicited mss. *True West* seeks to establish long-term relationships with writers who conduct excellent research, provide a fresh look at an old subject, write well, hit deadlines and provide manuscripts at the assigned word length. Such writers tend to get repeat assignments. Send your query and accompanying MSS and photos to: **Meghan Saar**, editor-in-chief, via mail (SASE). Length: 1,500 words for features; 450 words for short features; 200 words for snapshot coverage. **Pays 25¢/word with a $20 payment for each photo the author provides that is published with the article and not already part of True West archives."** Pays expenses of writers on assignment.

FILLERS Needs anecdotes, facts, gags, newsbreaks, short humor. **Buys 30 mss/year.** Length: 50-300 words.

VIETNAM

HistoryNet LLC, Editor, Vietnam Magazine, 1919 Gallows Road, Suite 400, Vienna VA 22182-4038. **E-mail:** vietnam@historynet.com. **Website:** www.historynet.com/vietnam. **Contact:** Chuck Springston, editor. **90% freelance written.** Bimonthly magazine providing in-depth and authoritative accounts of the many complexities that made the war in Vietnam unique, including the people, battles, strategies, perspectives, analysis, and weaponry. Estab. 1988. Circ. 46,000. Byline given. Pays on publication. 20% kill fee. Accepts queries by e-mail. Accepts simultaneous submissions. Send mss in Microsoft Word or plain text documents as e-mail attachments.

NONFICTION Needs historical. **Buys 18 mss/year.** Length: up to 3,000 words, including sidebars. **Payment varies.**

COLUMNS Query.

🜊🜊 WILD WEST

World History Group, Wild West Story Idea, 1919 Gallows Road, Suite 400, Vienna VA 22182-4038. **E-mail:** wildwest@historynet.com. **Website:** www.historynet.com. **Contact:** Gregory J. Lalire, editor. **95% freelance written.** Bimonthly magazine covering the history of the American frontier, from its eastern beginnings to its western terminus. *Wild West* covers the popular (narrative) history of the American West—events, trends, personalities, anything of general interest. Estab. 1988. Circ. 83,500. Byline given. Pays on publication. No kill fee. Publishes ms an average of 2 years after acceptance. Editorial lead time 10 months. Submit seasonal material 1 year in advance. Accepts queries by mail, e-mail. Accepts simultaneous submissions. Responds in 3 months to queries; in 6 months to mss. Single issue: $9.95. Writer's guidelines for #10 SASE or online.

NONFICTION Needs historical. No excerpts, travel, etc. Articles can be adapted from book. No fiction or poetry. Nothing current. **Buys 36 mss/year.** Query. Length: 3,500 words with a 500-word sidebar. **Pays $300.** Pays expenses of writers on assignment.

COLUMNS Gunfighters & Lawmen, 2,000 words; Westerners, 2,000 words; Warriors & Chiefs, 2,000 words; Western Lore, 2,000 words; Guns of the West, 1,500 words; Artists West, 1,500 words; Books Reviews, 250 words. **Buys 36 mss/year.** Query. **Pays $150 for departments; book reviews paid by the word, minimum $40.**

🜊🜊 WORLD WAR II

World History Group, World War II, 1600 Tysons Blvd., Suite 1140, Tysons VA 22102. **E-mail:** worldwar2@weiderhistorygroup.com; worldwar2@historynet.com. **Website:** www.historynet.com/magazines/world-war-ii-magazine. **Contact:** Karen Jensen, editor. **25% freelance written. "Most of our stories are assigned by our staff to professional writers. However, we do accept written proposals for features and for our Time Travel department."** Bimonthly magazine covering military operations in World War II—events, personalities, strategy, the home front, etc. Estab. 1986. Circ. 146,000. Byline given. Pays on acceptance. Offers kill fee. Accepts queries by mail, e-mail. Accepts simultaneous submissions. Writer's guidelines available on website or for SASE.

NONFICTION No fiction. **Buys 24 mss/year.** Query by mail or e-mail with published clips. "Your proposal should convince the editors to cover the subject, describe how you would treat the subject, and give the editors an opportunity to judge your writing ability. Please include your writing credentials and background with your proposal. A familiarity with recent issues of the magazine is the best guide to our editorial needs." Length: 2,500-4,000 words. Pays expenses of writers on assignment.

HOBBY & CRAFT

🜊🜊🜊🜊 AMERICAN CRAFT

American Craft Council, 1224 Marshall St. NE, Suite 200, Minneapolis MN 55413. (612)206-3115. **E-mail:** mmoses@craftcouncil.org. **E-mail:** query@craftcouncil.org. **Website:** www.americancraftmag.org. **Contact:** Monica Moses, editor in chief. **75% freelance written.** Bimonthly magazine covering art, craft, design. "American Craft Council is a national nonprofit aimed at supporting artists and craft enthusiasts. We want to inspire people to live a creative life. *American Craft* magazine celebrates the age-old human impulse to make things by hand." Estab. 1941. Circ. 40,000. Byline given. Pays on acceptance. Offers 25% kill fee. Publishes ms an average of 2 months after acceptance. Editorial lead time 4-6 months. Submit seasonal material 4-6 months in advance. Accepts queries by mail, e-mail. Accepts simultaneous submissions. Responds in 1 month to queries; in 2 months to mss. See writer's guidelines online.

NONFICTION Needs essays, interview, profile, travel, craft artist profiles, art travel pieces, interviews with creative luminaries, essays on creativity. Query with images. Include medium (glass, clay, fiber, metal, wood, paper, etc.) and department in subject line. Length: 500-2,000 words. **Pays $1/word, according to assigned length.** Pays expenses of writers on assignment.

COLUMNS On Our Radar (profiles of emerging artists doing remarkable work); Product Placement (stylish, inventive, practical, and generally affordable goods in production and the people who design them); Shop Talk (Q&As with owners of galleries); Material Matters (an artist using unusual materials to make fine craft); Personal Paths (an artist doing very individual—even idiosyncratic—work from a personal motivation); Spirit of Craft (art forms that might not typically be considered fine craft but may entail the sort of devotion generally associated with craft); Craft in Action (artists or organizations using craft to make the world better); Crafted Lives (photo-driven Q&A with a person or people living in a particularly creative space); Ideas (Q&A with a thinker or practitioner whose views represent a challenge to the status quo); Wide World of Craft (foreign or U.S. travel destination for craft lovers). **Buys 10-12 mss/year.** Query with published clips.

$ ANTIQUE TRADER

F+W, a Content + eCommerce Company, 5225 Joerns Dr., Stevens Point WI 54481. (715)445-2214. **Fax:** (715)445-4087. **E-mail:** karen.knapstein@fwmedia.com. **Website:** www.antiquetrader.com. **Contact:** Karen Knapstein, print editor. **60% freelance written.** Published 24 times per year. "We publish quote-heavy informational articles of timely interest in the antiques field. We also cover antiques shows, auctions, and news events." Estab. 1957. Circ. 50,000. Byline given. Pays on acceptance. No kill fee. Publishes ms an average of 1-3 months after acceptance. Editorial lead time 2 months. Accepts queries by mail, e-mail, fax. Accepts simultaneous submissions. Responds in 1 week to queries; 2 months to mss. Sample copy for cover price, plus postage. No cost for digital (PDF) sample copy. Guidelines online.

NONFICTION Needs book excerpts, essays, general interest, historical, interview, personal experience, show and auction coverage. Does not want the same, dry textbook, historical stories on antiques that appear elsewhere. Our readers want personality and timeliness. **Buys 1,000+ mss/year.** Send complete ms. Length: 900-1,200 words. **Pays $50-150, plus contributor copy.**

COLUMNS Dealer Profile (interviews with interesting antiques dealers), 750-1,200 words; Collector Profile (interviews with interesting collectors), 750-1,000 words. **Buys 30-60 mss/year.** Query with or without published clips or send complete ms.

$ AUTOGRAPH MAGAZINE

P.O. Box 25559, Santa Ana CA 92799. (951)734-9636. **Fax:** (951)371-7139. **E-mail:** steve.cyrkin@autographmagazine.com. **Website:** autographmagazine.com. **Contact:** Steve Cyrkin, publisher. **80% freelance written.** Monthly magazine covering the autograph collecting hobby. The focus of *Autograph* is on documents, photographs, or any collectible item that has been signed by a famous person, whether a current celebrity or historical figure. Articles stress how and where to locate celebrities and autograph material, authenticity of signatures and what they are worth. Byline given. Offers negotiable kill fee. Editorial lead time 2 months. Submit seasonal material 3 months in advance. Accepts queries by mail, e-mail. Accepts simultaneous submissions. Responds in 2 weeks to queries.

NONFICTION Needs historical, how-to, interview, personal experience. **Buys 25-35 mss/year.** Query. Length: 1,600-2,000 words. **Pays 5¢/word.** Pays expenses of writers on assignment.

COLUMNS *Autograph Collector* buys 8-10 columns per month written by regular contributors. **Buys 90-100 mss/year.** Query. **Pays $50 or as determined on a per case basis.**

FILLERS Needs anecdotes, facts. **Buys 20-25 mss/year.** Length: 200-300 words. **$15.**

$$ BLADE MAGAZINE

F+W, A Content and Ecommerce Company, 5225 Joerns Dr., Stevens Point WI 54481. (715)445-2214. **Fax:** (715)445-4087. **E-mail:** steve.shackleford@fwmedia.com. **Website:** www.blademag.com. **Contact:** Steve Shackleford, editor. **5% freelance written.** Monthly magazine covering working and using collectible, popular knives. *Blade* prefers in-depth articles focusing on groups of knives, whether military, collectible, high-tech, pocket knives, or hunting knives, and how they perform. Estab. 1973. Circ. 39,000. Byline given. Pays on publication. No kill fee. Publishes ms an average of 9 months after acceptance. Editorial lead time 9 months. Submit seasonal material 9 months in advance. Accepts queries by e-mail. Accepts simultaneous submissions. Responds in 3 months to queries; in 6 months to mss. Guidelines online.

NONFICTION Needs general interest, historical, how-to, interview, new product, photo feature, technical. "We assign profiles, show stories, hammer-in stories, etc. We don't need those. If you've seen the story on the Internet or in another knife or knife/gun magazine, we don't need it. We don't do stories on knives used for self-defense." Send complete ms. Length: 700-1,400 words. **Pays $150-300.** Pays expenses of writers on assignment.

FILLERS Needs anecdotes, facts, newsbreaks. **Buys 1-2 mss/year.** Length: 50-200 words. **Pays $25-50.**

❂❸❸ CANADIAN WOODWORKING AND HOME IMPROVEMENT

Sawdust Media, Inc., 51 Maple Ave. N., RR #3, Burford ON N0E 1A0 Canada. (519)449-2444. **Fax:** (519)449-2445. **E-mail:** pfulcher@canadianwoodworking.com. **E-mail:** rbrown@canadianwoodworking.com. **Website:** www.canadianwoodworking.com. **20% freelance written.** Bi-monthly magazine covering woodworking and home improvement; only accepts work from Canadian writers. Estab. 1999. Byline given. Pays on publication. Offers 50% kill fee. Accepts queries by e-mail. Accepts simultaneous submissions. Sample copy available online. Guidelines available by e-mail.

NONFICTION Needs how-to, humor, inspirational, new product, personal experience, photo feature, technical. Does not want profile on a woodworker. Query. Length: 500-4,000 words. **Pays $250-600 for assigned articles. Pays $250-400 for unsolicited articles.** Pays expenses of writers on assignment.

❸❸ CERAMICS MONTHLY

600 N. Cleveland Ave., Suite 210, Westerville OH 43082. (614)794-5867. **Fax:** (614)891-8960. **E-mail:** editorial@ceramicsmonthly.org. **Website:** www.ceramicsmonthly.org. **70% freelance written.** Monthly magazine (except July and August) covering the ceramic art and craft field. "Each issue of *Ceramics Monthly* includes articles on potters and ceramics artists from throughout the world, exhibitions, and production processes, as well as critical commentary, book and video reviews, clay and glaze recipes, kiln designs and firing techniques, advice from experts in the field, and ads for available materials and equipment. While principally covering contemporary work, the magazine also looks back at influential artists and events from the past." Estab. 1953. Circ. 39,000. Byline given. Pays on publication. Editorial lead time 3 months. Submit seasonal material 6 months in advance. Accepts queries by mail, e-mail, fax, phone. Responds in 2 months to mss. Guidelines available online.

NONFICTION Needs essays, how-to, interview, opinion, personal experience, technical. **Buys 100 mss/year.** Send complete ms. Length: 500-1,500 words. **Pays 10¢/word.**

COLUMNS Upfront (workshop/exhibition review), 500-1,000 words. **Buys 20 mss/year.** Send complete ms.

❸❸ CLASSIC TOY TRAINS

Kalmbach Publishing Co., P.O. Box 1612, 21027 Crossroads Circle, Waukesha WI 53187. (262)796-8776, ext. 524. **Fax:** (262)796-1142. **E-mail:** editor@classictoytrains.com. **Website:** www.classictoytrains.com. **Contact:** Carl Swanson, editor. **80% freelance written.** Magazine published 9 times/year covering collectible toy trains (O, S, Standard) like Lionel and American Flyer, etc. For the collector and operator of toy trains, *CTT* offers full-color photos of layouts and collections of toy trains, restoration tips, operating information, new product reviews and information, and insights into the history of toy trains. Estab. 1987. Circ. 40,000. Byline given. Pays on acceptance. Publishes ms an average of 1 year after acceptance. Editorial lead time 3 months. Submit seasonal material 6 months in advance. Accepts queries by mail, e-mail. Accepts simultaneous submissions. Responds in 3 weeks to queries; in 1 month to mss. Sample copy for $6.95, plus postage. Guidelines available online.

NONFICTION Needs general interest, historical, how-to, interview, personal experience, photo feature, technical. **Buys 90 mss/year.** Query. Length: 500-3,000 words. **Pays $75-500.** Pays expenses of writers on assignment.

❸ CQ AMATEUR RADIO

CQ Communications, Inc., 17 W. John St., Hicksville NY 11801. (516)681-2922. **Fax:** (516)681-2926. **E-mail:** cq@cq-amateur-radio.com. **E-mail:** w2vu@cq-amateur-radio.com. **Website:** www.cq-amateur-radio.com. **Contact:** Richard Moseson, editor. **40% freelance written.** Monthly magazine covering amateur (ham) radio. "*CQ* is published for active ham radio operators and radio hobbyists. It is read by radio enthusiasts in over 100 countries. All articles must deal with amateur radio, shortwave listening or other types of personal two-way radio. Our focus is on operating and on practical projects. A thorough knowledge of amateur radio is required." Estab. 1945. Circ. 60,000. Byline given. Pays after publication. No kill fee. Publishes ms an average of 6 months after acceptance. Editorial lead time 4 months. Submit seasonal material 4 months in advance. Accepts queries by mail, e-mail, fax. Accepts simultaneous submissions. Responds in 3 weeks to queries; 3 months to mss. Sample copy free. Guidelines online.

NONFICTION Needs historical, how-to, interview, personal experience, technical, all related to amateur radio. Special issues: February: QRP (Low-Power operating); June: Take it to the Field (portable operating); October: Emergency Communications; December: Technology. **Buys 50-60 mss/year.** Query. Length: 2,000-4,000 words. **Pays $.05/published word, $5/published photo.**

💲💲 CREATING KEEPSAKES

Creative Crafts Group, LLC, 14850 Pony Express Rd., Bluffdale UT 84065. (801)984-2070. **E-mail:** editorial@CreatingKeepsakes.com. **Website:** www.creatingkeepsakes.com. Monthly magazine covering scrapbooks. Written for scrapbook lovers and those with a box of photos high in the closet. Circ. 100,000. No kill fee. Editorial lead time 6 weeks. Accepts queries by mail, e-mail. Guidelines available online.

NONFICTION Query with 2 visuals to illustrate your suggested topic. Length: 800-1,200 words.

💲💲 DESIGNS IN MACHINE EMBROIDERY

Great Notions News Corp., 2517 Manana Dr., Dallas TX 75220. (888)739-0555. **Fax:** (413)723-2027. **E-mail:** eroche@dzgns.com. **Website:** www.dzgns.com. **75% freelance written.** Bimonthly magazine covering machine embroidery. Projects in *Designs in Machine Embroidery* must feature machine embroidery and teach readers new techniques. Estab. 1998. Circ. 50,000. Byline given. Pays on publication. Publishes ms an average of 2 months after acceptance. Editorial lead time 4 months. Submit seasonal material 4 months in advance. Accepts queries by mail, e-mail. Responds in 2-3 weeks to queries. Guidelines available online.

NONFICTION Needs how-to, interview, new product, technical. Does not want previously published items. **Buys 60 mss/year.** Query. Length: 250-1,000 words. **Pays $250-500.**

💲💲 DOLLHOUSE MINIATURES

P.O. Box 219, Kasson MN 55944. (507)634-3143. **E-mail:** usoffice@ashdown.co.uk. **Website:** www.dhminiatures.com. **70% freelance written.** Monthly magazine covering dollhouse scale miniatures. *Dollhouse Miniatures* is America's best-selling miniatures magazine and the definitive resource for artisans, collectors, and hobbyists. It promotes and supports the large national and international community of miniaturists through club columns, short reports, and by featuring reader projects and ideas. Estab. 1971. Circ. 25,000. Byline given. Pays on acceptance. Editorial lead time 6 months. Submit seasonal material 6 months in advance. Accepts queries by mail, e-mail. Accepts simultaneous submissions. Responds in 1 month to queries; 2 months to mss. Sample copy: $6.95, plus shipping. Guidelines by e-mail.

NONFICTION Needs how-to, interview, photo feature. No essays or articles on miniature shops. **Buys 50-60 mss/year.** Send complete ms. Length: 500-1,500 words. **Pays $30-250 for assigned articles and up to $150 for unsolicited articles.** Pays expenses of writers on assignment.

💲💲 DOLLS

Jones Publishing, Inc., P.O. Box 5000, N7528 Aanstad Rd., Iola WI 54945. (715)445-5000. **Fax:** (715)445-4053. **E-mail:** joyceg@jonespublishing.com; jonespub@jonespublishing.com. **Website:** www.dollsmagazine.com. **Contact:** Joyce Greenholdt, editor. **75% freelance written.** Magazine published 10 times/year covering dolls, doll artists, and related topics of interest to doll collectors and enthusiasts. "*Dolls* enhances the joy of collecting by introducing readers to the best new dolls from around the world, along with the artists and designers who create them. It keeps readers up to date on shows, sales, and special events in the doll world. With beautiful color photography, *Dolls* offers an array of easy-to-read, informative articles that help our collectors select the best buys." Estab. 1982. Circ. 100,000. Byline given. Pays on publication. No kill fee. Accepts queries by mail, e-mail. Accepts simultaneous submissions. Responds in 1 month to queries.

NONFICTION Needs historical, how-to, interview, new product, photo feature. **Buys 55 mss/year.** Send complete ms. Length: 750-1,200 words. **Pays $75-300.** Pays expenses of writers on assignment.

$$$ FAMILY TREE MAGAZINE

F+W Media, Inc., 10151 Carver Rd., Suite 300, Blue Ash OH 45242. (513)531-2690. **Fax:** (513)891-7153. **Website:** www.familytreemagazine.com. **75% freelance written.** Magazine covering family history, heritage, and genealogy research. "*Family Tree Magazine* is a special-interest consumer magazine that helps readers discover, preserve, and celebrate their family's history. We cover genealogy, ethnic heritage, genealogy websites, and software, photography, and photo preservation, and other ways that families connect with their past." Please note that *Family Tree Magazine* does not cover general family or parenting topics. Estab. 1999. Circ. 75,000. Byline given. Pays on acceptance. Offers 25% kill fee. Publishes ms an average of 6 months after acceptance. Editorial lead time 8 months. Submit seasonal material 8 months in advance. Accepts queries by mail, e-mail. Responds in 6-8 weeks to queries. Sample copy: $8 from website. Guidelines online.

NONFICTION Needs book excerpts, historical, how-to, new product, technical. Does not publish personal experience stories (except brief stories in the Tree Talk column, which does not pay) or histories of specific families. Does not cover general family or parenting topics. **Buys 40 mss/year.** Query with a specific story idea and published clips. Length: 250-4,500 words. **Pays up to $800.**

⭘$ FIBRE FOCUS

The Ontario Handweavers & Spinners, 1188 Walker Lake Dr., RR4, Huntsville ON P1H 2J6 Canada. **E-mail:** ffeditor@ohs.on.ca. **Website:** www.ohs.on.ca. **Contact:** Flannery Surette, editor. **75% freelance written.** Quarterly magazine covering handweaving, spinning, basketry, beading, and other fiber arts. "Our readers are weavers and spinners who also do dyeing, knitting, basketry, feltmaking, papermaking, sheep raising, and craft supply. All articles deal with some aspect of these crafts." Estab. 1957. Circ. 700. Byline given. Pays within 30 days after publication. Publishes ms 2-5 months after acceptance. Editorial lead time 3 months. Submit seasonal material 6 months in advance. Accepts simultaneous submissions. Responds in 1 month to queries. Sample copy: $8 (Canadian). Guidelines available online.

NONFICTION Needs historical, how-to, interview, new product, opinion, personal experience, photo feature, profile, reviews, technical, travel. **Buys 40-60 mss/year.** Contact the *Fibre Focus* editor before undertaking a project or an article. Mss may be submitted c/o Flannery Surette by e-mail for anything you have to contribute for upcoming issues. Feature article deadlines: December 31, March 31, June 30, and September 15. Length: varies, but generally 600-1,800 words. **Pays $30 (Canadian)/published page.**

REPRINTS Pays $20 (Canadian) per published page.

$$ FINE BOOKS & COLLECTIONS

OP Media, LLC, 101 Europa Dr., Suite 150, Chapel Hill NC 27517. (800)662-4834. **Fax:** (919)945-0700. **E-mail:** rebecca@finebooksmagazine.com. **Website:** www.finebooksmagazine.com. **90% freelance written.** Bimonthly magazine covering used and antiquarian bookselling and book collecting. Covers all aspects of selling and collecting out-of-print books. Emphasizes good writing, interesting people, and unexpected view points. Estab. 2002. Circ. 5,000. Byline given. Pays on publication. Offers negotiable kill fee. Publishes ms an average of 4 months after acceptance. Editorial lead time 6+ months. Submit seasonal material 4 months in advance. Accepts queries by mail, e-mail. Accepts simultaneous submissions. Responds in 2 months to queries and mss. Sample copy for $6.50 plus shipping. Guidelines available online.

NONFICTION Needs book excerpts, essays, expose, general interest, historical, how-to, travel. Does not want tales of the "gold in my attic" vein. **Buys 25 mss/year.** Query with published clips. Length: 500-2,000 words. **Pays $125-400.** Sometimes pays expenses of writers on assignment.

COLUMNS Digest (news about collectors, booksellers, and bookselling), 500 words.

$ FINESCALE MODELER

Kalmbach Publishing Co., 21027 Crossroads Circle, P.O. Box 1612, Waukesha WI 53187-1612. (414)796-8776. **Website:** www.finescale.com. **80% freelance written. Eager to work with new/unpublished writers.** Magazine published 10 times/year devoted to how-to-do-it modeling information for scale model builders who build non-operating aircraft, tanks, boats, automobiles, figures, dioramas, and science fiction and fantasy models. Circ. 60,000. Byline given. Pays on acceptance. No kill fee. Publishes ms an average of 14 months after acceptance. Accepts simultaneous submissions. Responds in 6 weeks to queries. Responds in 3 months to mss. Sample copy with 9x12 SASE and 3 first-class stamps. Guidelines available on website.

NONFICTION Needs how-to, technical. Query or send complete ms via www.contribute.kalmbach.com. Length: 750-3,000 words. **Pays $60/published page minimum.** Pays expenses of writers on assignment.

COLUMNS *FSM* Showcase (photos plus description of model); *FSM* Tips and Techniques (model building hints and tips). **Buys 25-50 mss/year.** Send complete ms. **Pays $25-50.**

💲💲 THE FINE TOOL JOURNAL LLC

P.O. Box 737, 9325 Dwight Boyer Rd., Watervliet MI 49098. (269)463-8255. **Fax:** (269)463-3767. **E-mail:** finetoolj@gmail.com; jim@finetooljournal.net. **Website:** www.finetooljournal.net. **Contact:** Jim Gehring. **90% freelance written.** "Quarterly magazine specializing in older or antique hand tools from all traditional trades. Readers are primarily interested in woodworking tools, but some subscribers have interests in such areas as leatherworking, wrenches, kitchen, and machinist tools. Readers range from beginners just getting into the hobby to advanced collectors and organizations." Estab. 1970. Circ. 2,500. Byline given. Pays on publication. Offers $50 kill fee. Publishes ms an average of 6 months after acceptance. Editorial lead time 9 months. Submit seasonal material 6 months in advance. Accepts queries by mail, online submission form. Accepts simultaneous submissions. Responds in 2 months to queries; 3 months to mss. Sample copy for $6. Guidelines for #10 SASE.

NONFICTION Needs general interest, historical, how-to, interview, personal experience, photo feature, technical. **Buys 24 mss/year.** Send complete ms. Length: 1,000-3,000 words. **Pays $50-200.** Pays expenses of writers on assignment.

COLUMNS Stanley Tools (new finds and odd types), 300-400 words; Tips of the Trade (how to use tools), 100-200 words. **Buys 12 mss/year.** Send complete ms. **Pays $30-60.**

💲💲 FINE WOODWORKING

The Taunton Press, Inc., 63 South Main St., P.O. Box 5506, Newtown CT 06470-5506. (203)426-8171. **Fax:** (203)426-3434. **E-mail:** fw@taunton.com. **Website:** www.finewoodworking.com. **Contact:** Tom McKenna, senior editor. Bimonthly magazine on woodworking in the small shop. Estab. 1975. Circ. 270,000.

Byline given. Pays on acceptance. Offers variable kill fee. Submit seasonal material 6 months in advance. Accepts simultaneous submissions. Responds in 1 month to queries. Guidelines online at www.finewoodworking.com/pages/fw_authorguideline.asp.

NONFICTION Needs how-to. **Buys 120 mss/year.** Send article outline, helpful drawings or photos, and proposal letter. **Pays $150/magazine page.** Pays expenses of writers on assignment.

COLUMNS Fundamentals (basic how-to and concepts for beginning woodworkers); Master Class (advanced techniques); Finish Line (finishing techniques); Question & Answer (woodworking Q&A); Methods of Work (shop tips); Tools & Materials (short reviews of new tools). **Buys 400 mss/year. Pays $50-150/published page.**

💲💲 THE HOME SHOP MACHINIST

P.O. Box 629, Traverse City MI 49685. (231)946-3712. **Fax:** (231)946-6180. **E-mail:** gbulliss@villagepress.com; kellywagner@villagepress.com. **Website:** www.homeshopmachinist.net. **Contact:** George Bulliss, editor; Kelly Wagner, managing editor. **95% freelance written.** Bimonthly magazine covering machining and metalworking for the hobbyist. Circ. 34,000. Byline given. Pays on publication. Publishes ms an average of 2 years after acceptance. Accepts simultaneous submissions. Responds in 2 months to queries. Sample copy free. Guidelines for 9x12 SASE.

NONFICTION Needs how-to, technical. No fiction or people features. **Buys 40 mss/year.** Send complete ms. Length: open—"whatever it takes to do a thorough job." **Pays $40/published page, plus $9/published photo.**

COLUMNS "Become familiar with our magazine before submitting." Book Reviews; New Product Reviews; Micro-Machining; Foundry. Length: 600-1,500 words. **Buys 25-30 mss/year.** Query. **Pays $40-70.**

FILLERS **Buys 12-15 mss/year.** Length: 100-300 words. **Pays $30-48.**

💲💲 KNIVES ILLUSTRATED

Engaged Media, Inc., 4635 McEwen Rd., Dallas TX 75244. (800)764-6278. **Website:** www.knivesillustrated.com. **40-50% freelance written.** Bimonthly magazine covering high-quality factory and custom knives. "We publish articles on different types of factory and custom knives, how-to make knives, technical articles, shop tours, articles on knife makers and artists.

Must have knowledge about knives and the people who use and make them. We feature the full range of custom and high tech production knives, from miniatures to swords, leaving nothing untouched. We're also known for our outstanding how-to articles and technical features on equipment, materials and knife making supplies. We do not feature knife maker profiles as such, although we do spotlight some makers by featuring a variety of their knives and insight into their background and philosophy." Estab. 1987. Circ. 35,000. Byline given. Pays on publication. No kill fee. Editorial lead time 3 months. Accepts queries by mail, e-mail, fax. Accepts simultaneous submissions. Responds in 2 weeks to queries. Sample copy available. Guidelines for #10 SASE.

NONFICTION Needs general interest, historical, how-to, interview, new product, photo feature, technical. **Buys 35-40 mss/year.** Query. Length: 400-2,000 words. **Pays $100-500.**

⬛⬛ THE LEATHER CRAFTERS & SADDLERS JOURNAL

315 S Oneida Ave., Suite 104, Rhinelander WI 54501. **E-mail:** charil@leathercraftersjournal.com. **Website:** leathercraftersjournal.com. **Contact:** Charil Reis, editor. **100% freelance written.** Bimonthly magazine covering leatherwork. "A leather-working publication with how-to, step-by-step instructional articles using patterns for leathercraft, leather art, custom saddle, boot, etc. A complete resource for leather, tools, machinery, and allied materials, plus leather industry news." Estab. 1990. Circ. 8,000. Byline given. Pays on publication. Publishes ms an average of 4 months after acceptance. Submit seasonal material 6 months in advance. Accepts queries by mail, e-mail. Accepts simultaneous submissions. Responds in 1 month to mss. Sample copy: $7. Guidelines online.

NONFICTION Needs how-to (step-by-step articles on how to make things with leather). **Buys 75 mss/year.** Send complete ms by e-mail: photos (see online guidelines); text (short introduction, step-by-step instructions, and a list of materials and tools used); patterns (see online guidelines). If patterns are too large to e-mail, send by mail. Length: 500-2,500 words. **Pays $20-250 for assigned articles. Pays $25-150 for unsolicited articles.**

REPRINTS Send tearsheet or photocopy. Pays 50% of amount paid for an original article.

⬛ LINN'S STAMP NEWS

Amos Press, P.O. Box 29, Sidney OH 45365. (937)498-0801. **Fax:** (937)498-0886. **E-mail:** linns@linns.com. **Website:** www.linns.com. **Contact:** Charles Snee, editor. **50% freelance written.** Weekly tabloid on the stamp collecting hobby. "All articles must be about philatelic collectibles. Our goal at *Linn's* is to create the number one website for stamp collectors and a weekly print publication that is indispensable to stamp collectors." Estab. 1928. Circ. 20,000. Byline given. Pays within 1 month of publication. Publishes ms an average of 4 months after acceptance. Submit seasonal material 2 months in advance. Responds in 6 weeks to queries. Sample copy online. Guidelines available online.

NONFICTION Needs general interest, historical, how-to, interview, technical, club and show news, current issues, auction realization, and recent discoveries. No articles merely giving information on background of stamp subject. Must have philatelic information included. **Buys 25 mss/year.** Send complete ms. Length: 1,200 words maximum. **Pays $40-100.** Sometimes pays expenses of writers on assignment.

⬛ LOST TREASURE, INC.

P.O. Box 451589, Grove OK 74345. (866)469-6224. **Fax:** (918)786-2192. **E-mail:** managingeditor@losttreasure.com. **Website:** www.losttreasure.com. **Contact:** Carla Nielsen, Managing Editor. **75% freelance written.** Monthly and annual magazines covering lost treasure. Estab. 1966. Circ. 55,000. Byline given. Pays on publication. Approximately 2 months. Accepts queries by e-mail. Accepts simultaneous submissions. Responds within two weeks to queries via e-mail and website. For a sample copy send #10 SASE. Submission guidelines can be requested by e-mailing managingeditor@losttreasure.com.

NONFICTION Needs historical, how-to, personal experience, technical, All must be related to treasure hunting. **Buys 225 mss/year.** Query on Treasure Cache/Treasure Facts only. "Will buy articles, photographs, and cartoons that meet our editorial approval." Enclose SASE with all editorial submissions. Length: 1,000-2,000 words. **Pays 4¢/word.** Pays expenses of writers on assignment.

⬛⬛ MILITARY TRADER

F+W Media, Inc., 5225 Joerns Dr., Stevens Point WI 54481. **Fax:** (715)445-4087. **E-mail:** john.adams-graf@fwmedia.com. **Website:** www.militarytrader. com. **50% freelance written.** Magazine covering military collectibles. Dedicated to serving people who collect, preserve, and display military relics. Estab. 1994. Circ. 6,500. Byline given. Pays on publication. No kill fee. Publishes ms an average of 1 month after acceptance. Accepts queries by mail, e-mail. Accepts simultaneous submissions. Responds in 1 week to queries; 1 month to mss.

NONFICTION Needs historical, collection comparisons, artifact identification, reproduction alert. **Buys 40 mss/year.** Send complete ms. Length: 1,300-2,600 words. **Pays $0-200.**

COLUMNS Pays $0-50.

💲💲 MILITARY VEHICLES

F+W Media, Inc., 5225 Joerns Dr., Stevens Point WI 54481. (715)445-4612. **Fax:** (715)445-4087. **E-mail:** john.adams-graf@fwmedia.com. **Website:** www.militarytrader.com. **Contact:** John Adams-Graf, editor. **50% freelance written.** Bimonthly magazine covering historic military vehicles. Dedicated to serving people who collect, restore, and drive historic military vehicles. Estab. 1987. Circ. 18,500. Byline given. Pays on publication. No kill fee. Publishes ms an average of 1 month after acceptance. Accepts queries by mail, e-mail. Accepts simultaneous submissions. Responds in 1 week to queries. Responds in 1 month to mss. Sample copy for $5.

NONFICTION Needs historical, how-to, technical. **Buys 20 mss/year.** Send complete ms. Length: 1,300-2,600 words. **Pays $0-200.**

COLUMNS Pays $0-75.

TIPS "Be knowledgeable about military vehicles. This magazine is for a very specialized audience. General automotive journalists will probably not be able to write for this group. The bulk of our content addresses U.S.-manufactured and used vehicles. Plenty of good photos will make it easier to be published in our publication. Write for the collector/restorer: Assume that they already know the basics of historical context. Articles that show how to restore or repair military vehicles are given the highest priority."

💲 MODEL CARS MAGAZINE

Golden Bell Press, 2403 Champa St., Denver CO 80205. (808)754-1378. **E-mail:** gregg@modelcarsmag.com. **Website:** www.modelcarsmag.com. **25% freelance written.** Magazine published 9 times/year covering model cars, trucks, and other automotive models. *Model Cars Magazine* is the how-to authority for the automotive modeling hobbiest. This magazine is on the forefront of the hobby, the editorial staff are model car builders, and every single one of the writers has a passion for the hobby that is evident in the articles and stories that we publish. This is the model car magazine written by and for model car builders. Estab. 1999. Circ. 7,000. Byline given. Pays on publication. Publishes ms an average of 2-3 months after acceptance. Editorial lead time 2-3 months. Accepts queries by mail, e-mail. Accepts simultaneous submissions. Sample copy online. Guidelines available online.

NONFICTION Needs how-to. Send ms or queries via e-mail or to *Model Cars Magazine*, P.O. Box 89530, Honolulu, HI 96830. Length: 600-3,000 words. **Pays $50/page. Pays $25/page for unsolicited articles.** Pays expenses of writers on assignment.

💲 NATIONAL COMMUNICATIONS MAGAZINE

America's Hobby Radio Magazine, SCAN Services Co., P.O. Box 1, Aledo IL 61231-0001. (309)228-8000. **Fax:** (888)287-SCAN. **E-mail:** editor@natcommag.com. **Website:** www.natcommag.com. **Contact:** Chuck Gysi, editor and publisher. **50% freelance written.** Covers scanner radios and listening (VHF/UHF), citizens band (CB) radio, and other hobby two-way radio services such as the General Mobile Radio Service, the Family Radio Service and the Multi-Use Radio Service. *National Communications Magazine* was created for the hobby radio user. "Know our audience. Download a recent sample issue at www.nat-com.org/sample.pdf. We're only interested in scanner radios, citizens band radio, two-way radio, especially the hobby radio services such as GMRS, FRS. and MURS. We do not cover amateur radio, shortwave, broadcasting, etc. We're very focused." Estab. 1988. Circ. 5,000. Byline given. Pays *immediately* on publication. No kill fee. Publishes ms an average of 2 months after acceptance. Editorial lead time 2 months. Submit seasonal material 4 months in advance. Accepts queries by e-mail. Responds in 1 day-1 week. Current-issue sample copy: $6. Free recent PDF sample download at www.nat-com.org/sample.pdf. Contact the editor for any information.

NONFICTION Contact: Chuck Gysi, editor and publisher. Needs how-to, interview, new product, personal experience, photo feature, technical. Does not want articles off-topic of the publication's audience (radio hobbyists). "If you aren't writing about police scanners, CB radios, or two-way radios and don't know our audience, we're not interested in your article. It's essential to know your subject matter." **Buys 18 mss/year.** Query by e-mail only. "Inquire before writing with an outline of your proposed article. We're also interested in working with new authors, but we like to work with them in shaping articles before they are started. Photos and graphics are needed for all articles and must be provided by the author." Length: 2,500-3,000 words. **Pays $75 or more.** No expenses paid.

$$ PAPER CRAFTS MAGAZINE

Primedia Magazines, 14512 S. Center Point Way, Suite 600, Bluffdale UT 84065. (801)816-8300. **Fax:** (801)816-8302. **E-mail:** editor@papercraftsmag.com. **Website:** www.papercraftsmag.com. **Contact:** Jennifer Schaerer, editor-in-chief; Kerri Miller, managing editor. Magazine published 10 times/year designed to help readers make creative and rewarding handmade crafts. The main focus is fresh, craft-related projects our reader can make and display in her home or give as gifts. Estab. 1978. Circ. 300,000. Byline given. Pays on acceptance. Editorial lead time 6 months. Accepts queries by mail, e-mail. Accepts simultaneous submissions. Responds in 1 month to queries. Guidelines for #10 SASE and available online.

NONFICTION Needs how-to. **Buys 300 mss/year.** Query with photo or sketch of how-to project. Do not send the actual project until request. **Pays $100-500.** Pays expenses of writers on assignment.

$ PIECEWORK MAGAZINE

Interweave/F+W Media, 4868 Innovation Dr., Fort Collins CO 80537. (800) 272-2193. **Fax:** (970)669-6117. **E-mail:** piecework@interweave.com. **Website:** www.interweave.com. **90% freelance written.** Bimonthly magazine covering needlework history. *PieceWork* celebrates the rich tradition of needlework and the history of the people behind it. Stories and projects on embroidery, cross-stitch, knitting, crocheting, and quilting, along with other textile arts, are featured in each issue. Estab. 1993. Circ. 30,000. Byline given. Pays on publication. Offers 25% kill fee. Editorial lead time 6 months. Submit seasonal material 6 months in advance. Accepts queries by mail, e-mail. Accepts simultaneous submissions. Responds in 6 months to queries. Writer's guidelines available at pieceworkmagazine.com.

NONFICTION historical articles, book excerpts, new product information. No contemporary needlework articles. **Buys 25-30 mss/year.** Send complete ms. Length: 1,500-4,000 words. Pays expenses of writers on assignment.

$$$ POPULAR MECHANICS

Hearst Corp., 300 W. 57th St., New York NY 10019-5899. (212)649-2000. **E-mail:** popularmechanics@hearst.com; pmwebmaster@hearst.com. **Website:** www.popularmechanics.com. **Contact:** Ryan D'Agostino, editor-in-chief. **Up to 50% freelance written.** Monthly magazine on technology, science, automotive, home, outdoors. A men's service magazine that addresses the diverse interests of today's male, providing him with information to improve the way he lives. Covers stories from do-it-yourself projects to technological advances in aerospace, military, automotive, and so on. Estab. 1902. Circ. 1,200,000. Byline given. Pays on acceptance. **Offers 25% kill fee.** Publishes ms an average of 6 months after acceptance. Submit seasonal material 6 months in advance. Accepts simultaneous submissions. Guidelines available on website.

NONFICTION Query before submitting a ms. Send ms to the appropriate departmental editor. In any article query, be specific as to what makes the development new, better, different, interesting, or less expensive. All articles must be submitted in a word processing app. Editorial interests include automotive, home journal, science/technology/aerospace, boating/outdoors, electronics/photography/telecommunications, and general interest articles. **Pays $300-1,000 for features.** Pays expenses of writers on assignment.

$$ POPULAR WOODWORKING MAGAZINE

F+W, A Content + Ecommerce Company, 8469 Blue Ash Rd., Suite 100, Cincinnati OH 45236. **E-mail:** rodney.wilson@fwmedia.com. **E-mail:** rodney.wilson@fwmedia.com. **Website:** www.popularwoodworking.com. **Contact:** Rodney Wilson, Managing Editor. **75% freelance written.** Magazine published 7 times/year. "*Popular Woodworking Magazine* invites woodworkers of all skill levels into a community of professionals who share their hard-won shop experience through in-depth projects and technique articles, which help readers hone their existing skills and develop new ones for both hand and power tools. Related stories increase the readers' understanding and enjoyment of their craft. Any project submitted must be aesthetically pleasing, of sound construction, and offer a challenge to readers. On the average, we use 5 freelance features per issue. Our primary needs are 'how-to' articles on woodworking. Our secondary need is for articles that will inspire discussion concerning woodworking. Tone of articles should be conversational and informal but knowledgeable, as if the writer is speaking directly to the reader. Our readers are the woodworking hobbyist and small woodshop owner. Writers should have an extensive knowledge of woodworking and excellent woodworking techniques and skills." Estab. 1981. Circ. 150,000. Byline given. Pays on acceptance. No kill fee. Publishes ms an average of 10 months after acceptance. Submit seasonal material 6 months in advance. Accepts queries by mail, e-mail. Responds in 2 months to queries. Sample copy: $6.99 plus 9x12 SAE with 6 first-class stamps, or online. Guidelines available online at http://www.popularwoodworking.com/submission-guidelines.

NONFICTION Needs how-to, profile, technical. No tool reviews. **Buys 35 mss/year.** Query first; see guidelines and sample query on website. Length: 1,200-2,500 words. **Pay starts at $275/published page.**

REPRINTS For previously published material, send photocopy with rights for sale noted and information about when and where the material previously appeared. Pays 25% of amount paid for an original article.

COLUMNS Tricks of the Trade (helpful techniques) 250 words; End Grain (thoughts on woodworking as a profession or hobby, can be humorous or serious) 500-550 words. **Buys 20 mss/year.** Query. **Pays $350 for End Grain and $50-$100 for Tricks of the Trade.**

Ⓢ QST

American Radio Relay League, 225 Main St., Newington CT 06111. (860)594-0200. **Fax:** (860)594-0259. **E-mail:** qst@arrl.org. **Website:** www.arrl.org. **Contact:** Steve Ford, editor. **90% freelance written.** Monthly magazine covering amateur radio. "*QST* is the monthly membership journal of ARRL, the national association for amateur radio, covering subjects of interest to amateur ('ham') radio operators." Estab. 1915. Circ. 150,000. Byline given. Pays on publication. No kill fee. Publishes ms an average of 6 months after acceptance. Editorial lead time 6 months. Submit season-

al material 6 months in advance. Accepts queries by mail, e-mail, fax, phone. Accepts simultaneous submissions. Responds in 1 week to queries; in 1 month to mss. Guidelines available online at: www.arrl.org/qst-author-guide.

NONFICTION Needs general interest, how-to, technical. Send complete ms by mail or e-mail. Length: 900-3,000 words. **Pays $65/published page.** Pays expenses of writers on assignment.

Ⓢ Ⓢ QUILTER'S WORLD

185 Sweet Rd., Lincoln ME 04457. **Website:** www.quiltersworld.com. **100% freelance written. Works with a small number of new/unpublished writers each year.** Bimonthly magazine covering quilting. "*Quilter's World* is a general quilting publication. We accept articles about special quilters, techniques, coverage of unusual quilts at quilt shows, special interest quilts, human interest articles and patterns. We include 2 articles and 12-15 patterns in every issue. Reader is 30-70 years old, midwestern." Circ. 130,000. Byline given. Pays 45 days after acceptance. No kill fee. Submit seasonal material 10 months in advance. Accepts queries by mail, e-mail. Accepts simultaneous submissions. Responds in 3 months to queries. Guidelines available online.

NONFICTION Needs how-to, interview, new product, technical, quilters, quilt products. Query or send complete ms **Pays $100-$200 for articles; $50-550 for quilt designs**

Ⓢ Ⓢ ROCK & GEM

Miller Magazines, Inc., 3585 Maple St., Suite 232, Ventura CA 93003. (805)644-3824. **Fax:** (805)644-3875. **E-mail:** editor@rockngem.com. **Website:** www.rockngem.com. **99% freelance written.** Monthly magazine covering rockhounding field trips, how-to lapidary projects, minerals, fossils, gold prospecting, mining, etc. See guidelines. "This is not a scientific journal. Its articles appeal to amateurs, beginners, and experts, but its tone is conversational and casual, not stuffy. It's for hobbyists." Estab. 1971. Circ. 55,000. Byline given. Pays on publication. No kill fee. Editorial lead time 4 months. Submit seasonal material 6 months in advance. Accepts queries by mail. Guidelines available online.

NONFICTION Needs general interest, how-to, personal experience, photo feature, travel. Does not want to see The 25th Anniversary of the Pet Rock, or anything so scientific that it could be a thesis. **Buys**

156-200 mss/year. Send complete ms. Length: 2,000-4,000 words. **Pays $100-250.**

ⓢ SCALE AUTO

Kalmbach Publishing Co., 21027 Crossroads Circle, P.O. Box 1612, Waukesha WI 53187-1612. (262)796-8776. **Fax:** (262)796-1383. **E-mail:** msavage@kalmbach.com. **Website:** www.scaleautomag.com. Robby DeGraff. **70% freelance written.** Bimonthly magazine covering model car building and die-cast model cars. "We are looking for model builders, collectors, and enthusiasts who feel their models and/or modeling techniques and experiences would be of interest to our readership." Estab. 1979. Circ. 35,000. Byline given. Pays on publication. Publishes ms an average of 6 months after acceptance. Editorial lead time 4 months. Submit seasonal material 4 months in advance. Accepts queries by mail, e-mail, fax, phone. Accepts simultaneous submissions. Responds ASAP to queries. Sample copy online. Guidelines online.

NONFICTION Needs historical, how-to, interview, personal experience, photo feature, reviews, technical. Special issues: Contest Cars annual photo issue. Query or send complete ms Length: 600-2,000 words.

COLUMNS Buys 50 mss/year. Query.

ⓢⓢ SEWNEWS

F+W Media, 741 Corporate Circle, Suite A, Golden CO 80401. **E-mail:** sewnews@sewnews.com. **Website:** www.sewnews.com. **Contact:** Ellen March, editor-in-chief. **70% freelance written. Works with a small number of new/unpublished writers each year.** Monthly magazine covering fashion, gift, and home-dec sewing. "*Sew News* magazine is a monthly publication devoted to the enthusiastic and creative people who wants to sew. We provide them with accurate, helpful, step-by-step information for personalizing ready-to-wear and creating original fashions, accessories, gifts, and home décor that express her personal style." Estab. 1980. Circ. 185,000. Byline given. Pays on publication. No kill fee. Publishes ms an average of 6 months after acceptance. Submit seasonal material 6 months in advance. Accepts queries by mail, e-mail. Accepts simultaneous submissions. Responds in 2 months to mss. Sample copy: $5.99. Guidelines online.

NONFICTION Needs how-to, interview. **Buys 200-240 mss/year.** Query with published clips if available. Length: 500-2,000 words. **Pays $50-500.**

ⓢ SHUTTLE SPINDLE & DYEPOT

Handweavers Guild of America, Inc., 1255 Buford Hwy., Suite 211, Suwanee GA 30024. (678)730-0010. **Fax:** (678)730-0836. **E-mail:** hga@weavespindye.org. **Website:** www.weavespindye.org. **60% freelance written.** Quarterly magazine. Quarterly membership publication of the Handweavers Guild of America, Inc., *Shuttle Spindle & Dyepot* magazine seeks to encourage excellence in contemporary fiber arts and to support the preservation of techniques and traditions in fiber arts. It also provides inspiration for fiber artists of all levels and develops public awareness and appreciation of the fiber arts. *Shuttle Spindle & Dyepot* appeals to a highly educated, creative, and very knowledgeable audience of fiber artists and craftsmen, weavers, spinners, dyers, and basket makers. Estab. 1969. Circ. 30,000. Byline given. Pays on publication. Publishes ms an average of 6 months after acceptance. Editorial lead time 8 months. Submit seasonal material 8 months in advance. Accepts queries by mail, e-mail, fax, phone. Sample copy for $8 plus shipping. Guidelines available online.

NONFICTION Needs inspirational, interview, new product, personal experience, photo feature, technical, travel. No self-promotional and no articles from those without knowledge of area/art/artists. **Buys 40 mss/year.** Query with published clips. Length: 1,000-2,000 words. **Pays $75-150.**

COLUMNS Books and Videos, News and Information, Calendar and Conference, Travel and Workshop (all fiber/art related).

ⓢ SPIN-OFF

Interweave Press, 201 E. 4th St., Loveland CO 80537-5655. **E-mail:** spinoff@interweave.com. **Website:** www.spinningdaily.com. "*Spin-Off* is a quarterly magazine devoted to the interests of handspinners at all skill levels. Informative articles in each issue aim to encourage the novice, challenge the expert, and increase every spinner's working knowledge of this ancient and complex craft." Pays on publication. Editorial lead time is 6-12 months. Responds in 6 months to ms. Guidelines available on website.

NONFICTION Special issues: Wants articles on the following subjects: spinning tips (400 words or less); spinning basics (1,200 words); back page essay (650 words); methods for dyeing with natural and chemical dyes; tools for spinning and preparing fibers; fiber basics (2,000 words); ideas for using handspun yarn in a variety of techniques; profiles of people who spin; a gallery of your work; tips on blending fibers; the history and/or cultural role of spinning. Query or submit full ms by e-mail or mail. Length: 200-2,700 words. **Pays $50/published page.** Pays expenses of writers on assignment.

$ SUNSHINE ARTIST

JP Media LLC, N7528 Aanstad Rd., PO Box 5000, Iola WI 54945. (800)597-2573. **Fax:** (715)445-4053. **E-mail:** editor@sunshineartist.com. **Website:** www.sunshineartist.com. Publisher: Diana Jones. Editor: Stephanie Hintz. Marketing Manager: Justin Van Slooten. Monthly magazine covering art shows in the US. "We are the premiere marketing/reference magazine for artists and crafts professionals who earn their living through art shows nationwide. We list more than 2,000 shows monthly, critique many of them, and publish articles on marketing, selling and other issues of concern to professional show circuit artists." Estab. 1972. Circ. 12,000. Byline given. Pays 60 days from publication date. Pays $50 kill fee. Publishes 1-3 months after acceptance. Accepts queries by e-mail. Accepts simultaneous submissions. Responds in 1 week to queries. Sample copy for $5.

NONFICTION **Buys 5-10 freelance mss/year.** Send complete ms. Length: 1,000-2,000 words. **Pays $30-250.**

REPRINTS Send photocopy and information about when and where the material previously appeared.

$$ TEDDY BEAR & FRIENDS

P.O. Box 5000, Iola WI 54945-5000. (800)331-0038, ext. 150. **Fax:** (715)445-4053. **E-mail:** joyceg@jonespublishing.com. **Website:** www.teddybearandfriends.com. **Contact:** Joyce Greenholdt, editor. **65% freelance written. Works with a small number of new/unpublished writers each year.** Bimonthly magazine on teddy bears for collectors, enthusiasts, and bearmakers. Estab. 1985. Byline given. Payment upon publication on the last day of the month the issue is mailed. Submit seasonal material 6 months in advance. Accepts simultaneous submissions. Sample copy and writer's guidelines for $2 and 9x12 SAE.

NONFICTION Needs historical, how-to, interview. No articles from the bear's point of view. **Buys 30-40 mss/year.** Query with published clips. Length: 900-1,500 words. **Pays $100-350.** Pays expenses of writers on assignment.

$$ THREADS

Taunton Press, 63 S. Main St., P.O. Box 5506, Newtown CT 06470. (203)426-8171. **Fax:** (203)426-3434. **E-mail:** th@taunton.com. **Website:** www.threadsmagazine.com. Bimonthly magazine covering garment sewing, garment design, and embellishments (including quilting and embroidery). Written by sewing experts; magazine is geared primarily to intermediate/advanced sewers. "We're seeking proposals from hands-on authors who first and foremost have a skill. Being an experienced writer is of secondary consideration." Estab. 1985. Circ. 129,000. Byline given. Offers $150 kill fee. Editorial lead time minimum 4 months. Accepts simultaneous submissions. Responds in 1-2 months to queries. Guidelines available online.

NONFICTION Send proposal that includes: "a brief 1- or 2-paragraph summary; an outline of the ideas and points you'll cover; sample photographs of work illustrating the topic (quick snapshots are fine) or supporting fabric swatches if you have them. **Payment varies.** Pays expenses of writers on assignment.

COLUMNS Product reviews; book reviews; Tips; Closures (stories of a humorous nature). Query. **Closures pays $150/page. Each sewing tip printed pays $25.**

$$ TOY FARMER

Toy Farmer Publications, 7496 106 Ave. SE, LaMoure ND 58458-9404. (701)883-5206. **Fax:** (701)883-5209. **E-mail:** info@toyfarmer.com. **Website:** www.toyfarmer.com. **70% freelance written.** Monthly magazine covering farm toys. Estab. 1978. Circ. 27,000. Byline given. Pays on publication. Editorial lead time 2 months. Submit seasonal material 3 months in advance. Accepts queries by mail, e-mail, fax. Responds in 1 month to queries. Responds in 2 months to mss. Guidelines available upon request.

NONFICTION Needs general interest, historical, interview, new product, personal experience, technical, book introductions. **Buys 100 mss/year.** Query with published clips. Length: 800-1,500 words. **Pays 10¢/word.** Sometimes pays expenses of writers on assignment.

$$ TOY TRUCKER & CONTRACTOR

Toy Farmer Publications, 7496 106th Ave. SE, LaMoure ND 58458-9404. (701)883-5206. **Fax:** (701)883-5209. **E-mail:** info@toyfarmer.com. **Website:** www.toytrucker.com. **40% freelance written.**

Monthly magazine covering collectible toys. "We are a magazine on hobby and collectible toy trucks and construction pieces." Estab. 1990. Circ. 6,500. Byline given. Pays on publication. No kill fee. Editorial lead time 2 months. Submit seasonal material 3 months in advance. Accepts queries by mail, e-mail, fax, phone. Responds in 1 month to queries. Responds in 2 months to mss. Writer's guidelines available on request.

NONFICTION Needs historical, interview, new product, personal experience, technical. **Buys 35 mss/year.** Query. Length: 800-1,400 words. **Pays 10¢/word.** Sometimes pays expenses of writers on assignment.

$ TREASURES

Antique to Modern Collectibles, Pioneer Communications, Inc., The Plaza, 300 Walnut, Suite 6, Des Moines IA 50309. (319)415-5839. **Fax:** (319)824-3414. **E-mail:** lkruger@pioneermagazines.com; info@treasuresmagazine.com. **Website:** www.treasuresmagazine.com. **Contact:** Linda Kruger, editor. **20% freelance written. Works with a small number of new/unpublished writers each year.** Magazine-size publication on glossy stock, full cover, covering antiques, collectibles, and nostalgic memorabilia and modern collectibles. Ten issues/year. Estab. 1959. Circ. 11,000. Byline given. Pays on publication. Publishes ms an average of 1 year after acceptance. Submit seasonal material 3 months in advance. Accepts queries by e-mail. Responds in 2 weeks to queries. Responds in 6 weeks to mss. Sample copy for $4 and 9x12 SAE. Guidelines free.

NONFICTION Needs general interest, collectibles, antique to modern, historical, relating to collections or collectors, how-to, display your collection, care for, restore, appraise, locate, add to, etc., interview, covering individual collectors and their hobbies, unique or extensive; celebrity collectors, and limited edition artists, technical, in-depth analysis of a particular antique, collectible, or collecting field, travel, hot antiquing places in the U.S. Special issues: Twelve-month listing of antique and collectible shows, flea markets, and conventions (January includes events January-December; June includes events June-May); Care & Display of Collectibles (September); holidays (October-December). **Buys 36 mss/year.** Query with sample of writing. Length: 800-1,000 words. **Pays $1.10/column inch.**

$ WESTERN & EASTERN TREASURES

People's Publishing Co., Inc., P.O. Box 647, Pacific Grove CA 93950-0647 USA. **E-mail:** editor@wetreasures.com. **Website:** www.wetreasures.com. **100% freelance written.** Monthly magazine on the newsstand, in print and in digital format through subscription, covering hobby/sport of metal detecting/treasure hunting. "*Western & Eastern Treasures* provides concise yet comprehensive coverage of every aspect of the sport/hobby of metal detecting and treasure hunting with a strong emphasis on current, accurate information; innovative, field-proven advice and instruction; and entertaining, effective presentation." Estab. 1966. Circ. 50,000. Byline given. Pays on publication. No kill fee. Publishes ms an average of 3+ months after acceptance. Editorial lead time 4 months. Submit seasonal material 3-4 months in advance. Responds in 2 months to mss. Sample copy for SAE with 9x12 envelope and 5 first-class stamps. Request our current Freelancer's Guidelines by sending an email to: editor@wetreasures.com.

NONFICTION Needs how-to, personal experience. Special issues: *Silver & Gold Annual* (editorial deadline February each year)—looking for articles 1,500+ words, plus photos on the subject of locating silver and/or gold using a metal detector. No fiction, poetry, or puzzles. **Buys 150+ mss/year.** Send complete ms by e-mail or mail (include SASE). Be sure you have read a current copy of our Freelancer's Guidelines before submitting any articles/photos. Simply request a copy via e-mail to: editor@wetreasures.com Thank you. Length: 1,000-2,000 words. **Pays 5¢/word.**

$$ WOOD MAGAZINE

Meredith Corporation, 1716 Locust St., LS221, Des Moines IA 50309. **E-mail:** woodmail@woodmagazine.com. **Website:** www.woodmagazine.com. **3% freelance written.** Magazine published 7 times/year covering woodworking. *Wood* manuscripts are friendly, informative, authoritative in the subject of woodworking, and full of helpful service-related content. Estab. 1984. Circ. 550,000. Byline given. Pays on publication. Editorial lead time 2 months. Submit seasonal material 1 year in advance. Accepts queries by e-mail. Accepts simultaneous submissions. Responds in 3 weeks to queries. Responds in 3 weeks to mss.

NONFICTION Does not want nonwoodworking. **Buys 3-4 mss/year.** Query. Length: 500-2,000 words.

Pays $300/page. Pays expenses of writers on assignment.

HOME & GARDEN

💲💲 THE AMERICAN GARDENER

American Horticultural Society, 7931 E. Boulevard Dr., Alexandria VA 22308-1300. (703)768-5700. E-mail: editor@ahsgardening.org. **Website:** www.ahsgardening.org. **Contact:** David Ellis, Editor. **60% freelance written.** Bimonthly, 64-page, four-color magazine covering gardening and horticulture. "This is the official publication of the American Horticultural Society (AHS), a national, nonprofit, membership organization for gardeners, founded in 1922. The AHS mission is 'to open the eyes of all Americans to the vital connection between people and plants, and to inspire all Americans to become responsible caretakers of the earth, to celebrate America's diversity through the art and science of horticulture, and to lead this effort by sharing the society's unique national resources with all Americans.' All articles are also published in the digital edition." Estab. 1922. Circ. 20,000. Byline given. Pays on publication. Offers 25% kill fee. Publishes ms an average of 6 months after acceptance. Editorial lead time 6 months. Submit seasonal material at least 1 year in advance. Accepts queries by mail, e-mail. Responds in 3-4 months to queries. Sample copy: $8. Writer's guidelines by e-mail and online.

NONFICTION Needs general interest, how-to, photo feature, profile, reviews, travel. No personal essays about your garden. **Buys 20 mss/year.** Query with published clips. Length: 1,500-2,000 words. **Pays $300-600, depending on complexity and author's experience.** Pays expenses of writers on assignment.

REPRINTS Rarely purchases second rights. Send PDF file of article with information about when and where the material previously appeared. Payment varies.

COLUMNS Natural Connections (explains a natural phenomenon—plant and pollinator relationships, plant and fungus relationships, parasites—that may be observed in nature or in the garden), 750-1,000 words; Homegrown Harvest (articles on edible plants delivered in a personal, reassuring voice. Each issue focuses on a single crop, such as carrots, blueberries, or parsley), 800-900 words; Plant in the Spotlight (profiles of a single plant species or cultivar, including a personal perspective on why it's a favored plant), 600 words. **Buys 5 mss/year.** Query with published clips. **Pays $100-250.**

💲💲 ATLANTA HOMES AND LIFESTYLES

Esteem Media, 1117 Perimeter Center W., Suite N118, Atlanta GA 30338. (404)252-6670. **E-mail:** editor@atlantahomesmag.com. **Website:** www.atlantahomesmag.com. **Contact:** Elizabeth Ralls, editor in chief; Elizabeth Anderson, art director. **65% freelance written.** Magazine published 12 times/year. *Atlanta Homes and Lifestyles* is designed for the action-oriented, well-educated reader who enjoys his or her shelter, its design and construction, its environment, and living and entertaining in it. Estab. 1983. Circ. 30,000. Byline given. Pays on publication. Publishes ms an average of 6 months after acceptance. Accepts queries by mail, fax. Accepts simultaneous submissions. Responds in 3 months to queries. Sample copy online.

NONFICTION Needs interview, new product. "We do not want articles outside the respective market area, not written for magazine format, or that are excessively controversial, investigative, or that cannot be appropriately illustrated with attractive photography." **Buys 35 mss/year.** Query with published clips. Length: 500-1,200 words. **Pays $100-500.** Pays expenses of writers on assignment. Sometimes pays expenses of writer on assignment.

COLUMNS Pays $50-200.

💲💲💲💲 BETTER HOMES AND GARDENS

1716 Locust St., Des Moines IA 50309. **Website:** www.bhg.com. **Contact:** Nancy Hopkins, deputy editor, Food and Entertaining; Oma Blaise Ford, senior deputy editor, Home Design; Elvin McDonald, deputy editor, Garden and Outdoor Living; Terry Michael, associate editor, Travel; Laura O'Neil, senior building and environmental editor; Christian Millman, health editor; Stephen George, deputy editor, Features; Brenda Lesch, creative director. **10-15% freelance written.** Magazine providing home service information for people who have a serious interest in their homes. *Better Homes and Gardens* is the vibrant, down-to-earth guide for the woman who is passionate about her home and garden and the life she creates there. Estab. 1922. Circ. 7,605,000. Pays on acceptance. Accepts queries by mail. Accepts simultaneous submissions.

NONFICTION Needs travel, education, gardening, health, cars, home, entertainment. Does not deal with political subjects or with areas not connected with the home, community, and family. No poetry or fiction. **Pay rates vary.**

💲💲 BIRDS & BLOOMS

Reiman Media Group, 1610 N. 2nd St., Suite 102, Milwaukee WI 53212. (414)423-0100. **E-mail:** editors@birdsandblooms.com. **Website:** www.birdsandblooms.com. **15% freelance written.** Bimonthly magazine focusing on "the beauty in your own backyard." *Birds & Blooms* is a sharing magazine that lets backyard enthusiasts chat with each other by exchanging personal experiences. This makes *Birds & Blooms* more like a conversation than a magazine, as readers share tips and tricks on producing beautiful blooms and attracting feathered friends to their backyards. Estab. 1995. Circ. 1,900,000. Byline given. Pays on publication. No kill fee. Publishes ms an average of 7 months after acceptance. Editorial lead time 2 months. Submit seasonal material 4 months in advance. Accepts queries by mail. Accepts simultaneous submissions. Responds in 2 months to queries and mss. Sample copy: $2, plus 9x12 SAE and $1.95 postage. Guidelines online.

NONFICTION Needs essays, how-to, humor, inspirational, personal experience. No bird rescue or captive bird pieces. **Buys 12-20 mss/year.** Query or send complete ms, along with full name, daytime phone number, e-mail address, and mailing address. If submitting for a particular column, note that as well. Each reader contributor whose story, photo, or short item is published receives a *Birds & Blooms* tote bag. See guidelines online. Length: up to 1,000 words. **Pays $100-400.**

COLUMNS Bird Tales (birding experiences); Front Porch (gardening and birding tips and tricks, reader-created gardening, birding DIYs, etc.); From Your Backyard (more casual writing). **Buys 12-20 mss/year.** Send complete ms. **Pays $50-75.**

FILLERS Needs anecdotes, facts, gags. **Buys 25 mss/year.** Length: 10-250 words. **Pays $10-75.**

💲💲 CALIFORNIA HOMES

McFadden-Bray Publishing Corp., P.O. Box 8655, Newport Beach CA 92658. **E-mail:** susan@calhomesmagazine.com. **Website:** www.calhomesmagazine.com. **Contact:** Susan McFadden, editor-in-chief. **80% freelance written.** Bimonthly magazine covering California interiors, architecture, some food, travel, history, and current events in the field. Estab. 1997. Circ. 80,000. Byline given. Pays on publication. Offers 50%

kill fee. Publishes ms an average of 3 months after acceptance. Editorial lead time 3 months. Submit seasonal material 6 months in advance. Accepts queries by mail, e-mail. Accepts simultaneous submissions. Responds in 1 month to queries; in 2 months to mss. Sample copy: $7.50. Guidelines for #10 SASE.

NONFICTION Query. Length: 500-1,000 words. **Pays $250-750.** Pays expenses of writers on assignment.

♻💲💲 CANADIAN HOMES & COTTAGES

The In-Home Show, Ltd., 2650 Meadowvale Blvd., Unit 4, Mississauga Ontario L5N 6M5 Canada. (905)567-1440. **Fax:** (905)567-1442. **E-mail:** jnaisby@homesandcottages.com; editorial@homesandcottages.com. **Website:** www.homesandcottages.com. **Contact:** Janice E. Naisby, editor-in-chief. **75% freelance written.** Magazine published 6 times/year covering home building and renovating in Canada. "*Homes & Cottages* is Canada's largest home improvement magazine. Publishes articles that have a technical slant, as well as those with a more general lifestyle feel." Estab. 1987. Circ. 92,340. Byline given. Pays on acceptance. Offers 10% kill fee. Publishes ms an average of 6 months after acceptance. Editorial lead time 3 months. Submit seasonal material 6 months in advance. Accepts queries by mail. Accepts simultaneous submissions. Sample copy for SAE. Guidelines for #10 SASE.

NONFICTION Needs humor, new product, technical. **Buys 32 mss/year.** Query. Length: 800-1,500 words. **Pays $350-650.** Pays expenses of writers on assignment.

💲💲 CHARLESTON STYLE & DESIGN

P.O. Box 20098, Charleston SC 29413. **E-mail:** editor@charlestonstyleanddesign.com. **Website:** www.charlestonstyleanddesign.com. **Contact:** Mary K. Love, editor. **85% freelance written.** Quarterly magazine covering design (architecture and interior design) and lifestyle (wines, restaurants, fashion, local retailers, and travel). "*Charleston Style & Design* is a full-color magazine for discriminating readers eager to discover new horizons in Charleston and the world beyond. We offer vivid, well-researched articles on trends in home design, fashion, food and wine, health/fitness, antiques/collectibles, the arts, travel, and more. We also profile celebrities and opinion leaders who have a link with Charleston or the area." Need personal essays and local writers for assignments. Estab. 2008. Circ. 45,000. Byline given. Pays on publication. Pays 50% kill fee. Publishes ms 4 months after acceptance. Editorial lead time 3-6 months. Submit seasonal material 3 months in advance. Accepts queries by e-mail. Accepts simultaneous submissions. Responds in 2 weeks to queries; in 2 months to mss. Sample copy available online. Guidelines via e-mail.

NONFICTION Needs essays, general interest. Query with published clips. Length: 300-1,200 words. **Pays $120-500.** Pays expenses of writers on assignment. Sometimes pays expenses of writers on assignment.

COLUMNS Reflections (personal essays), 600 words. "Your essay should present an idea, concept, or experience that you think would be of interest to our readers. We believe that the best personal essays have all the characteristics of a good story, offering compelling descriptions, a narrative line, and, of course, a personal point of view. Beyond that, we look for essays that give readers a 'takeaway,' a thought or insight to which they can relate." Submit personal essay and short two-sentence bio via e-mail with the words "personal essay" in the subject line. **Pays $200.**

🟢🟢🟢🟢 COASTAL LIVING

Southern Progress Corp., 4100 Old Montgomery Hwy., Birmingham AL 35209. (205)445-6007. **E-mail:** letters@coastalliving.com. **E-mail:** ellen.mcgauley@timeinc.com; tracey.minkin@timeinc.com; chris.hughes@timeinc.com; katie_finley@timeinc.com. **Website:** www.coastalliving.com. **Contact:** Ellen McGauley, homes editor; Tracey Minkin, travel editor; Chris Hughes, food and wine editor; Katie Finley, deputy editor. "Bimonthly magazine for those who live or vacation along our nation's coasts. The magazine emphasizes home design and travel, but also covers a wide variety of other lifestyle topics and coastal concerns." Estab. 1997. Circ. 660,000. Pays on acceptance. Offers 25% kill fee. Accepts queries by e-mail. Accepts simultaneous submissions. Responds in 2 months to queries. Guidelines online.

NONFICTION Query with clips and SASE. **Pays $1/word.**

🟢🟢 COLORADO HOMES & LIFESTYLES

Network Communications, Inc., 1780 S. Bellaire St., Suite 505, Denver CO 80222. (303)248-2060. **Fax:** (303)248-2066. **E-mail:** mabel@coloradohomesmag.com. **Website:** www.coloradohomesmag.com. **Contact:** Mary Barthelme Abel, editor-in-chief. **75% freelance written.** Upscale shelter magazine published 9 times/year containing beautiful homes, landscapes,

architecture, calendar, antiques, etc. All of Colorado is included. Geared toward home-related and lifestyle areas, personality profiles, etc. Estab. 1981. Circ. 36,000. Byline given. Pays on acceptance. Offers 15% kill fee. Publishes ms an average of 3 months after acceptance. Editorial lead time 3 months. Submit seasonal material 1 year in advance. Accepts queries by mail, e-mail. Accepts simultaneous submissions. Responds in 2 months to queries. Sample copy for #10 SASE.

NONFICTION No personal essays, religious, humor, or technical submissions. **Buys 50-75 mss/year.** Query with published clips. Provide sources with phone numbers with submissions. Length: 900-1,500 words. **Pays $200-400.** Pays expenses of writers on assignment.

🟢🟢 CONCRETE HOMES

Publications and Communications, Inc. (PCI), 13581 Pond Springs Rd., Suite 450, Austin TX 78729. (512)250-9023. **Fax:** (512)331-3950. **E-mail:** info@concretehomesmagazine.com. **Website:** concretehomesmagazine.com. **85% freelance written.** Bimonthly magazine covering homes built with concrete. *Concrete Homes* is a publication designed to be informative to consumers, builders, contractors, architects, etc., who are interested in concrete homes. The magazine profiles concrete home projects (they must be complete) and offers how-to and industry news articles. Estab. 1999. Circ. 25,000. Byline given. Pays on publication. Offers 100% kill fee. Publishes ms an average of 2 months after acceptance. Editorial lead time 2 months. Submit seasonal material 3-4 months in advance. Accepts queries by mail, e-mail. Accepts simultaneous submissions. Responds in 1 month.

NONFICTION Needs how-to, interview, new product, technical. **Buys 30-40 mss/year.** Query or query with published clips Length: 800-2,000 words. **Pays $200-250.** Pays expenses of writers on assignment.

COUNTRY LIVING

The Hearst Corp., 300 W. 57th St., 22nd Floor, New York NY 10019. (212)649-3501. **E-mail:** countryliving@hearst.com. **Website:** www.countryliving.com. **Contact:** Rachel Hardage Barrett, editor-in-chief; Amy Lower Mitchell, managing editor. Monthly magazine covering home design and interior decorating with an emphasis on country style. A lifestyle magazine for readers who appreciate the warmth and traditions associated with American home and family life. Each monthly issue embraces American country decorating and includes features on furniture, antiques, gardening, home building, real estate, cooking, entertaining and travel. Estab. 1978. Circ. 1,600,000. No kill fee. Accepts simultaneous submissions.

NONFICTION Buys 20-30 mss/year. Query to see if market is currently accepting submissions. Then, send complete ms and SASE. **Payment varies.**

💲💲 EARLY AMERICAN LIFE

Firelands Media Group LLC, 16759 W Park Circle Dr, Chagrin Falls OH 44023. (440)543-8566. **E-mail:** queries@firelandsmedia.com. **Website:** www.earlyamericanlife.com. **Contact:** Jeanmarie Andrews, executive editor. **60% freelance written.** "Our readers are interested in America's founding heritage including antiques, traditional crafts, architecture, restoration, collecting, and re-enacting. We are particularly interested in using antiques and crafts in decorating, restoring old homes and building replicas of period examples, judging and making handcrafts of the period (including how-to's), and experiencing period lifestyles, be it though military re-enacting, playing old games and sports, or cooking on a hearth." *Early American Life* is a bimonthly magazine for people who are interested in experiencing the warmth and beauty of the 1600-1840 period in America, using period style in their homes and lives today, re-enacting past events and how people lived, and visiting historic sites and museums. Estab. 1970. Circ. 90,000. Byline given. Pays on acceptance. 25% kill fee. Publishes ms an average of 1 year after acceptance. For upcoming events, submit material at least four months before the event. We are geared to the seasons, so we prepare a year ahead. Accepts queries by mail, e-mail. Responds within 1 week to queries. Sample copy for 9x12 SAE with $2.50 postage. Guidelines online.

NONFICTION Contact: Jeanmarie Andrews, executive editor. Needs book excerpts, historical, how-to, photo feature, travel, architecture and decorating, antiques, heritage studio crafts, historic destinations. Special issues: Christmas. No material outside our period (1600-1840). **Buys 40 mss/year.** Query. Length: 750-2,500 words. **Pays $250-700; additional payment for photos.** Pays expenses of writers on assignment.

💲 THE FAMILY HANDYMAN

Reader's Digest Association, 2915 Commers Dr., #700, Eagan MN 55121. **E-mail:** editors@thefamilyhandyman.com. **Website:** www.familyhandyman.com. *The Family Handyman* is an American home-Improvement magazine. Estab. 1951. Circ. 1.1 million. Byline given. Pays on acceptance. Accepts queries by online submission form. Accepts simultaneous submissions.

NONFICTION Submit to *Family Handyman* via online submission form. Accepts mss for home projects that writers want to share. **Pays $100/ms.** Pays expenses of writers on assignment.

COLUMNS Accepts mss for Handy Hint, Great Goof, and Shop Tips. Accepts submissions online. **Pays $100/ms.**

💲💲💲 FINE GARDENING

Taunton Press, 63 S. Main St., P.O. Box 5506, Newtown CT 06470-5506. (800)309-9193. **Fax:** (203)426-3434. **E-mail:** fg@taunton.com. **Website:** www.finegardening.com. Bimonthly magazine covering gardening. High-value magazine on landscape and ornamental gardening. Articles written by avid gardeners—first person, handson gardening experiences. Estab. 1988. Circ. 200,000. Byline given. Pays on acceptance. No kill fee. Publishes an average of 6 months after acceptance. Editorial lead time 1 year. Submit seasonal material 1 year in advance. Accepts queries by mail. Accepts simultaneous submissions. Guidelines free.

NONFICTION Needs how-to, personal experience, photo feature. Pays expenses of writers on assignment.

💲💲 FINE HOMEBUILDING

The Taunton Press, Inc., 63 S. Main St., P.O. Box 5506, Newtown CT 06470-5506. (203)426-8171. **Fax:** (203)426-3434. **E-mail:** fh@taunton.com. **Website:** www.finehomebuilding.com. Bimonthly magazine for builders, architects, contractors, owner/builders and others who are seriously involved in building new houses or reviving old ones. Estab. 1981. Circ. 300,000. Byline given. Pays half on acceptance, half on publication. Offers kill fee. Offers on acceptance payment as kill fee. Publishes ms an average of 1 year after acceptance. Accepts simultaneous submissions. Responds in 1 month to queries. Guidelines online.

NONFICTION Query with outline, description, photographs, sketches and SASE. **Pays $150/published page.** Pays expenses of writers on assignment.

COLUMNS Tools & Materials, Reviews, Questions & Answers, Tips & Techniques, Cross Section, What's the Difference?, Finishing Touches, Great Moments,

Breaktime, Drawing Board (design column). Query with outline, description, photographs, sketches and SASE. **Payment varies**

💲💲💲💲 GOOD HOUSEKEEPING

Hearst Corporation, Article Submissions, 300 W. 57th St., 28th Floor, New York NY 10019. **Website:** www. goodhousekeeping.com. Monthly magazine covering women's interests. *Good Housekeeping* is edited for the new traditionalist. Articles which focus on food, fitness, beauty, and childcare draw upon the resources of the Good Housekeeping Institute. Editorial includes human interest stories, articles that focus on social issues, money management, health news, and travel. Circ. 4.3 million. Byline given. Pays on acceptance. Offers 25% kill fee. Submit seasonal material 6 months in advance. Accepts queries by mail. Accepts simultaneous submissions. Responds in 2-3 months to queries and mss. Call for a sample copy. Guidelines online.

NONFICTION Needs personal experience, travel. **Buys 4-6 mss/year.** Query by mail with published clips. Include SASE. Length: 500 words. Pays expenses of writers on assignment.

COLUMNS Blessings (about a person or event that proved to be a blessing), 500 words. Query by mail with published clips. Include SASE. **Pays $1/word.**

💲💲 GREENPRINTS

P.O. Box 1355, Fairview NC 28730. (828)628-1902. **E-mail:** pat@greenprints.com. **Website:** www.green-prints.com. **Contact:** Pat Stone, managing editor. **90% freelance written.** "*GreenPrints* is the 'Weeder's Digest.' We share the human—*not* how-to—side of gardening. We publish true personal gardening stories and essays: humorous, heartfelt, insightful, inspiring. We love good, true, well-told personal *stories*—all must be about gardening!" Estab. 1990. Circ. 11,000. Byline given. No editorial lead time. Accepts queries by mail, e-mail. Accepts simultaneous submissions. Responds in 3 months to mss. Sample: $5. Guidelines available online (look under About Us).

NONFICTION Needs essays, general interest, historical, humor, inspirational, nostalgic, personal experience. Does not want how-to. **Buys 60 mss/year.** Submit complete ms by e-mail or snail. Please include your mailing address and a couple of interesting bio lies—I mean lines!—about yourself. Length: 250-2,500 words. **Pays $50-200 for unsolicited articles.** Pays expenses of writers on assignment.

COLUMNS Broken Trowel (the story of your funniest garden mistake), 300 words. **Buys 12 mss/year.** Submit complete ms. **Pays $50-75.**

FICTION "We run very little fiction." **Buys 2 mss/year.** Submit complete ms. **Pays $75-200.**

POETRY Needs free verse, light verse, traditional. "If it's not hands-on and gardening based, please don't send it." Buys 4 poems/year. Submit maximum 3 poems. **Pays $25.**

FILLERS Wants anecdotes, short humor. Length: 100-300 words. **Pays $50-75.**

💲💲💲 HORTICULTURE

F+W, a Content + eCommerce Company, 10151 Carver Rd., Suite #300, Blue Ash OH 45242. (513)531-2690. **Fax:** (513)891-7153. **E-mail:** edit@hortmag.com. **Website:** www.hortmag.com. Bimonthly magazine. *Horticulture*, the country's oldest gardening magazine, is designed for active home gardeners. Our goal is to offer a blend of text, photographs and illustrations that will both instruct and inspire readers. Circ. 160,000. Byline given. Offers kill fee. Submit seasonal material 10 months in advance. Accepts queries by mail, e-mail, fax. Accepts simultaneous submissions. Responds in 3 months to queries. Guidelines for SASE or by e-mail.

NONFICTION Buys 70 mss/year. Query with published clips, subject background material and SASE. Length: 800-1,000 words. **Pays $500.** Pays expenses of writers on assignment.

COLUMNS Length: 200-600 words. Query with published clips, subject background material and SASE. Include disk where possible. **Pays $250.**

MIDWEST HOME

Greenspring Media, 706 S. Second Ave. S., Suite 1000, Minneapolis MN 55402. (612)371-5800. **Fax:** (612)371-5801. **E-mail:** clee@greenspring.com. **Website:** midwesthomemag.com. **Contact:** Chris Lee, editor. **75% freelance written.** *Midwest Home* is an upscale shelter magazine showcasing innovative architecture, interesting interior design, and beautiful gardens of Minnesota. Estab. 1997. Circ. 50,000. Byline given. Pays on acceptance. Offers 20% kill fee. Accepts queries by e-mail. Accepts simultaneous submissions. Guidelines online.

NONFICTION Needs book excerpts, how-to, interview, new product, photo feature, profile. Query with résumé and writing samples. Length: 300-1,000 words. **Payment negotiable.** Pays expenses of writers on assignment.

💲💲 MOUNTAIN LIVING

Wiesner Media Network Communications, Inc., 1780 S. Bellaire St., Suite 505, Denver CO 80222. (303)248-2060. **Fax:** (303)248-2066. **E-mail:** greatideas@mountainliving.com; hscott@mountainliving.com; cdeorio@mountainliving.com. **Website:** www.mountainliving.com. **Contact:** Holly Scott, publisher; Christine DeOrio, editor-in-chief. **50% freelance written.** Magazine published 7 times/year covering architecture, interior design, and lifestyle issues for people who live in, visit, or hope to live in the mountains. Estab. 1994. Circ. 40,000. Byline given. Pays on acceptance. Offers 15% kill fee. Publishes ms an average of 4 months after acceptance. Editorial lead time 6 months. Submit seasonal material 8-12 months in advance. Responds in 6-8 weeks to queries. Responds in 2 months to mss. Sample copy for $7. Guidelines by e-mail.

NONFICTION Needs photo feature, travel, home features. **Buys 30 mss/year.** Query with published clips. Length: 200-600 words. **Pays $250-600.** Pays expenses of writers on assignment.

COLUMNS ML Recommends; Short Travel Tips; New Product Information; Art; Insider's Guide; Entertaining. Length: 150-400 words.

💲💲 ROMANTIC HOMES

Y-Visionary Publishing, 22840 Savi Ranch Pkwy., Suite 200, Yorba Linda CA 92887. **E-mail:** jdemontravel@beckett.com. **Website:** www.romantichomes.com. **Contact:** Jacqueline DeMontravel, editor. **70% freelance written.** Monthly magazine covering home decor. *Romantic Homes* is the magazine for women who want to create a warm, intimate, and casually elegant home—a haven that is both a gathering place for family and friends and a private refuge from the pressures of the outside world. The *Romantic Homes* reader is personally involved in the decor of her home. Features offer unique ideas and how-to advice on decorating, home furnishings, and gardening. Departments focus on floor and wall coverings, paint, textiles, refinishing, architectural elements, artwork, travel, and entertaining. Every article responds to the reader's need to create a beautiful, attainable environment, providing her with the style ideas and resources to achieve her own romantic home. Estab. 1994. Circ. 200,000. Byline given. Pays 30-60 days upon receipt of invoice. No kill fee. Publishes ms an average of 4

months after acceptance. Editorial lead time 5 months. Submit seasonal material 6 months in advance. Accepts queries by mail, fax. Accepts simultaneous submissions. Responds in 2 weeks to queries. Responds in 2 months to mss. Guidelines for #10 SASE.

NONFICTION Needs essays, how-to, new product, personal experience, travel. **Buys 150 mss/year.** Query with published clips. Length: 1,000-1,200 words. **Pays $500.** Pays expenses of writers on assignment.

COLUMNS Departments cover antiques, collectibles, artwork, shopping, travel, refinishing, architectural elements, flower arranging, entertaining, and decorating. Length: 400-600 words. **Pays $250.**

💲💲 SAN DIEGO HOME/GARDEN LIFESTYLES

McKinnon Enterprises, 4577 Viewridge Avenue, San Diego CA 92123. (858)571-1818. **Fax:** (858)571-1889. **E-mail:** ditler@sdhg.net; nboynton@sdhg.net. **Website:** www.sdhg.net. **Contact:** Eva Ditler, managing editor; Nicole Boynton, associate editor. **30% freelance written.** Monthly magazine covering homes, gardens, food, intriguing people, real estate, art and culture for residents of San Diego city and county. Estab. 1979. Circ. 50,000. Byline given. Pays on publication. No kill fee. Publishes ms an average of 3 months after acceptance. Submit seasonal material 3 months in advance. Accepts queries by mail. Accepts simultaneous submissions. Responds in 3 months to queries. Sample copy: $5.

NONFICTION Query with published clips. Length: 500-1,000 words. **Pays $50-375.** Pays expenses of writers on assignment.

💲💲💲 STYLE AT HOME

Transcontinental Media, G.P., 25 Sheppard Ave. W., Suite 100, Toronto ON M2N 6S7 Canada. (416)733-7600. **Fax:** (416)218-3632. **Website:** www.styleathome.com. **85% freelance written.** Magazine published 12 times/year. "The number one magazine choice of Canadian women aged 25 to 54 who have a serious interest in decorating. Provides an authoritative, stylish collection of inspiring and accessible Canadian interiors, decor projects; reports on style design trends." Estab. 1997. Circ. 235,000. Byline given. Pays on acceptance. Offers 50% kill fee. Editorial lead time 4 months. Submit seasonal material 6 months in advance. Accepts queries by online submission form. Accepts simultaneous submissions. Responds in 1 month to queries; 2 weeks to mss.

NONFICTION Needs interview, new product. No how-to; these are planned in-house. **Buys 80 mss/year.** Query with published clips; include scouting shots with interior story queries. Length: 300-700 words. **Pays $300-1,000.** Pays expenses of writers on assignment.

💲💲💲 SU CASA

Bella Media, 215 W. San Francisco St., Santa Fe NM 87501. (505)344-1783. **Fax:** (505)983-1555. **E-mail:** amygross@sucasamagazine.com. **Website:** www.sucasamagazine.com. **Contact:** Amy Gross, editor. **80% freelance written.** Magazine published 4 times/year covering southwestern homes, building, design, architecture for the reader comtemplating building, remodeling, or decorating a Santa Fe style home. "*Su Casa* is tightly focused on Southwestern home building, architecture and design. In particular, we feature New Mexico homes. We also cover alternative construction, far-out homes and contemporary design. We also cover alternative construction, contemporary design, and some Southwestern trend architecture." Estab. 1995. Circ. 40,000. Byline given. Pays on acceptance. Offers 50% kill fee. Publishes ms an average of 6 months after acceptance. Editorial lead time 6-9 months. Submit seasonal material 9 months in advance. Accepts queries by mail, e-mail, fax, phone. Responds in 1 week to queries. Responds in 1 month to mss. Sample copy free. Guidelines free.

NONFICTION Needs book excerpts, essays, interview, personal experience, photo feature. Special issues: The summer issue covers kitchen and bath topics. Does not want how-to articles, product reviews or features, no trends in southwest homes. **Buys 30 mss/year.** Query with published clips. Length: 1,000-2,500 words. **Pays $250-1,000.** Sometimes pays expenses of writers on assignment. Limit agreed upon in advance.

💲💲 TEXAS GARDENER

Suntex Communications, Inc., P.O. Box 9005, Waco TX 76714. (254)848-9393. **Fax:** (254)848-9779. **E-mail:** info@texasgardener.com. **Website:** www.texasgardener.com. **Contact:** Chris Corby. **80% freelance written. Works with a small number of new/unpublished writers each year.** Bimonthly magazine covering vegetable and fruit production, ornamentals, and home landscape information for home gardeners in Texas. Estab. 1981. Circ. 20,000. Byline given. Pays on publication. No kill fee. Publisher pays at time of publication. Submit seasonal material 6 months in advance. Accepts queries by mail, e-mail, fax. Accepts simultaneous submissions. Responds in 2 months to queries. Sample copy for $6.00 (includes postage). Writers' guidelines available online at website.

NONFICTION Needs how-to, humor, interview, photo feature. **Buys 50-60 mss/year.** Query with published clips. Length: 800-2,400 words. **Pays $50-200.**

COLUMNS Between Neighbors. See sample issue for style and content. **Buys 6 mss/year. Pays $50.**

💲💲💲💲 THIS OLD HOUSE

Time Inc., 262 Harbor Drive, Stamford CT 06902. (475)209-8665. **Fax:** (212)522-9435. **E-mail:** toh_letters@thisoldhouse.com; scott@thisoldhouse.com. **Website:** www.thisoldhouse.com. **Contact:** Scott Omelianuk, editor. **40% freelance written.** Magazine published 10 times/year covering home design, renovation, and maintenance. "*This Old House* is the ultimate resource for readers whose homes are their passions. The magazine's mission is threefold: to inform with lively service journalism and reporting on innovative new products and materials, to inspire with beautiful examples of fine craftsmanship and elegant architectural design, and to instruct with clear step-by-step projects that will enhance a home or help a homeowner maintain one. The voice of the magazine is not that of a rarefied design maven or a linear Mr. Fix It but rather that of an eyes-wide-open, in-the-trenches homeowner who's eager for advice, tools, and techniques that'll help him realize his dream of a home." Estab. 1995. Circ. 960,000. Byline given. Pays on acceptance. Publishes ms an average of 3-6 months after acceptance. Editorial lead time 3-12 months. Submit seasonal material 1 year in advance. Accepts queries by mail, e-mail. Accepts simultaneous submissions.

NONFICTION Needs essays, how-to, new product. **Buys 70 mss/year.** Query with published clips. Length: 250-2,500 words. **Pays $1/word.** Pays expenses of writers on assignment.

COLUMNS Around the House (news, new products), 250 words. **Pays $1/word.**

💲💲💲 VAIL VALLEY HOME

Vail Board of Realtors, 0275 Main St., Suites 003 and 004, Edwards CO 81632. (970)766-1028. **E-mail:** pconnolly@vaildaily.com. **Website:** www.vvhmag.com. **Contact:** Wren Bova, editor. **80% freelance written.** Quarterly magazine covering building, remodeling Colorado homes. "We cater to an affluent population of homeowners (including primary, second and third homeowners) who are planning to build or remodel their Colorado home in the mountains or on the western slope. While we feature luxury homes, we also have a slant toward green building." Estab. 2005. Circ. 35,000. Byline given. Pays on publication. No kill fee. Publishes ms an average of 2-3 months after acceptance. Editorial lead time 1 year. Submit seasonal material 6 months in advance. Accepts queries by e-mail. Accepts simultaneous submissions. Responds in 2-4 weeks to queries; in 1 month to mss. Sample copy available online.

NONFICTION Needs interview, new product, profiles of Colorado homes and features related to them. "We do not want do-it-yourself projects." Query with published clips. **Pays $200-650 for assigned articles. "We do not buy articles; we only assign articles."** Pays expenses of writers on assignment.

COLUMNS Your Green Home (tips for environmentally-conscious building, remodeling and living), 300 words. **Buys 4 mss/year.** Query.

💲💲 VICTORIAN HOMES

Beckett Media, 22840 Savi Ranch Pkwy., Suite 200, Yorba Linda CA 92887. (714)939-9991. **Fax:** (714)939-9909. **E-mail:** ephillips@beckett.com. **Website:** www.victorianhomesmag.com. **Contact:** Elaine K. Phillips, editor; Jacqueline deMontravel, editorial director. **90% freelance written.** Quarterly magazine covering Victorian home restoration and decoration. *Victorian Homes* is read by Victorian home owners, restorers, house museum management, and others interested in the Victorian revival. Feature articles cover home architecture, interior design, furnishings, and the home's history. Photography is very important to the feature. Estab. 1981. Circ. 100,000. Byline given. Pays on acceptance. Offers $50 kill fee. Publishes ms an average of 1 year after acceptance. Editorial lead time 4 months. Submit seasonal material 1 year in advance. Accepts simultaneous submissions. Responds in 6 weeks to queries; in 2 months to mss. Sample copy and writer's guidelines for SAE.

NONFICTION Buys 30-35 mss/year. Query. Length: 500-1,200 words. **Pays $50-150.** Pays expenses of writers on assignment.

HUMOR

💲 FUNNY TIMES

Funny Times, Inc., P.O. Box 18530, Cleveland Heights OH 44118. (216)371-8600. **E-mail:** info@funnytimes.com. **Website:** www.funnytimes.com. **Contact:** Ray Lesser and Susan Wolpert, publishers. **50% freelance written.** Monthly tabloid for humor. "*Funny Times* is a monthly review of America's funniest cartoonists and writers. We are a unique voice in modern American humor with a progressive/peace-oriented/environmental/politically activist slant." Estab. 1985. Circ. 58,000. Byline given. Pays on publication. Publishes ms an average of 6 months after acceptance. Editorial lead time 2 months. Accepts simultaneous submissions. Responds in 3 months to mss. Sample copy for $3 or 9x12 SAE with 3 first-class stamps ($1.61 postage). Guidelines online.

NONFICTION Needs essays, humor, interview, opinion, personal experience. **Buys 60 mss/year.** Send complete ms. Length: 600-800 words. **Pays $60 minimum.** Pays expenses of writers on assignment.

COLUMNS Query with published clips.

FICTION Wants anything funny. Needs humorous. **Buys 6 mss/year.** Query with published clips. Length: 600-800 words. **Pays $50-150.**

💲💲 MAD MAGAZINE

DC Entertainment, 1700 Broadway, New York NY 10019. (212)506-4850. **E-mail:** submissions@madmagazine.com. **Website:** www.madmag.com. **100% freelance written.** Monthly magazine always on the lookout for new ways to spoof and to poke fun at hot trends. Estab. 1952. Byline given. Pays on acceptance. Publishes ms an average of 6 months after acceptance. Submit seasonal material 6 months in advance. Accepts simultaneous submissions. Responds in 10 weeks to queries. Sample copy available online. Guidelines available online.

NONFICTION "We're not interested in formats we're already doing or have done to death like 'what they say and what they really mean.' Don't send previously published submissions, riddles, advice columns, TV or movie satires, book manuscripts, top 10 lists, articles about Alfred E. Neuman, poetry, essays, short stories or other text pieces." **Buys 400 mss/year. Pays minimum of $500/page.** Pays expenses of writers on assignment.

INFLIGHT

💲💲💲 HEMISPHERES

Ink Publishing, 68 Jay St., Brooklyn NY 11201. (347)294-1220. **Fax:** (917)591-6247. **E-mail:** editorial@hemispheresmagazine.com. **Website:** www.hemispheresmagazine.com. **Contact:** Joe Keohane, editor-in-chief. **95% freelance written.** Monthly magazine for the educated, business, and recreational frequent traveler on an airline that spans the globe. *"Hemispheres* is an inflight magazine that interprets 'inflight' to be a mode of delivery rather than an editorial genre. *Hemispheres'* task is to engage, intrigue and entertain its primary readers—an international, culturally diverse group of affluent, educated professionals and executives who frequently travel for business and pleasure on United Airlines. The magazine offers a global perspective and a focus on topics that cross borders as often as the people reading the magazine. Emphasizes ideas, concepts, and culture rather than products, presented in a fresh, artful, and sophisticated graphic environment." Estab. 1992. Circ. 12.3 million. Byline given. Pays on acceptance. Offers 20% kill fee. Publishes ms an average of 4-6 months after acceptance. Editorial lead time 8 months. Submit seasonal material 8 months in advance. Accepts queries by mail. Responds in 2 months to queries. Responds in 4 months to mss. Sample copy for $7.50. Guidelines on website.

NONFICTION Needs general interest, humor, personal experience. No "in this country" phraseology. "Too American" is a frequent complaint for queries. Query with published clips. Length: 500-3,000 words. **Pays 50¢/word and up.**

COLUMNS Making a Difference (Q&A format interview with world leaders, movers, and shakers; a 500-600 word introduction anchors the interview. "We want to profile an international mix of men and women representing a variety of topics or issues, but all must truly be making a difference. No puffy celebrity profiles.); 15 Fascinating Facts (a snappy selection of 1- or 2-sentence obscure, intriguing, or travel-service-oriented items that the reader never knew about a city, state, country, or destination.); Executive Secrets (things that top executives know); Case Study (business strategies of international companies or organizations. No lionizations of CEOs. Strategies should be the emphasis. "We want international candidates.); Weekend Breakaway ("takes us just outside a major city after a week of business for several activities for an action-packed weekend"); Roving Gourmet (insider's guide to interesting eating in major city, resort area, or region. The slant can be anything from ethnic to expensive; not just best. The 4 featured eateries span a spectrum from hole in the wall, to expense account lunch, and on to big deal dining.); Collecting (occasional 800-word story on collections and collecting that can emphasize travel); Eye on Sports (global look at anything of interest in sports); Vintage Traveler (options for mature, experienced travelers); Savvy Shopper (insider's tour of best places in the world to shop. Savvy Shopper (steps beyond all those stories that just mention the great shopping at a particular destination. A shop-by-shop, gallery-by-gallery tour of the best places in the world.); Science and Technology (substantive, insightful stories on how technology is changing our lives and the business world. "Not just another column on audio components or software. No gift guides!"); Aviation Journal (for those fascinated with aviation; topics range widely.); Terminal Bliss ("a great airports guide series"); Grape And Grain (wine and spirits with emphasis on education, "not one-upmanship"); Show Business (films, music, and entertainment); Musings (humor or just curious musings); Quick Quiz (tests to amuse and educate); Travel Trends (brief, practical, invaluable, global, trend-oriented); Book Beat (tackles topics like the Wodehouse Society, the birth of a book, the competition between local bookshops, and national chains. "Please, no review proposals."); What the World's Reading (residents explore how current bestsellers tell us what their country is thinking). Length: 1,400 words. Query with published clips. **Pays 50¢/word and up.**

FICTION Needs adventure, ethnic, historical, humorous, mainstream, mystery, explorations of those issues common to all people but within the context of a particular culture. **Buys 14 mss/year.** Send complete ms. Length: 1,000-4,000 words. **Pays 50¢/word and up.**

💲💲 HORIZON EDITION MAGAZINE

Paradigm Communications Group, 2701 First Ave., Suite 250, Seattle WA 98121. (206)441-5871. **Fax:** (206)448-6939. **E-mail:** info@paradigmcg.com. **Website:** www.alaskaairlinesmagazine.com/horizonedition. **Contact:** Michele Andrus Dill, editor. **90% freelance written.** Monthly inflight magazine covering travel, business, and leisure in the Pacific

Northwest. "*Horizon Edition Magazine* is the monthly in-flight magazine for Horizon Air, reaching more than 574,000 travelers in Washington, Oregon, Idaho, Montana, California, Nevada, Western Canada and Baja, Mexico, each month." Estab. 1990. Byline given. Pays on publication. Offers 33% kill fee. Publishes ms an average of 1 year after acceptance. Editorial lead time 6 months. Submit seasonal material 6 months in advance. Accepts queries by mail, fax. Accepts simultaneous submissions. Sample copy for 9x12 SASE. Guidelines available online.

NONFICTION Needs essays, general interest, historical, how-to, humor, interview, personal experience, photo feature, travel, business. Special issues: Meeting planners' guide, golf, gift guide. No material unrelated to the Pacific Northwest. **Buys approximately 36 mss/year.** Query with published clips. Length: 2,000-2,500 words. **Pays $250 minimum.** Pays expenses of writers on assignment.

COLUMNS Region (Northwest news/profiles), 200-500 words. **Buys 15 mss/year.** Query with published clips. **Pays $100 minimum.**

$$$$ SPIRIT MAGAZINE

Pace Communications, Inc., Suite 360, 2811 McKinney Ave., Dallas TX 75204. (214)580-8070. **Fax:** (214)580-2491. **Website:** www.spiritmag.com. **Contact:** Jay Heinrichs, editorial director. Monthly magazine for passengers on Southwest Airlines. Estab. 1992. Circ. 380,000. Byline given. Pays on acceptance. Responds in 1 month to queries. Guidelines online.

NONFICTION Buys about 40 mss/year. Query by mail only with published clips. 3,000-6,000 words (features). **Pays $1/word.** Pays expenses of writers on assignment.

COLUMNS Length: 800-900 words. **Buys about 21 mss/year.** Query by mail only with published clips.

FILLERS Buys 12 mss/year. 250 words. **variable amount.**

JUVENILE

⊖$ AQUILA

Studio 2 Willowfield Studios, 67a Willowfield Rd., Eastbourne BN22 8AP England. (44)(132)343-1313. **E-mail:** editor@aquila.co.uk. **Website:** www.aquila.co.uk. "*Aquila* is an educational magazine for readers ages 8-13 including factual articles (no pop/celebrity material), arts/crafts, and puzzles." Entire publication aimed at juvenile market. Estab. 1993. Circ. 40,000. Pays on publication. Accepts queries by mail, e-mail. Accepts simultaneous submissions. Sample copy: £5. Guidelines online.

NONFICTION Young Readers: animal, arts/crafts, concept, cooking, games/puzzles, health, history, how-to, interview/profile, math, nature/environment, science, sports. Middle Readers: animal, arts/crafts, concept, cooking, games/puzzles, health, history, interview/profile, math, nature/environment, science, sports. Query. Length: 600-800 words. **Pays £90.** Pays expenses of writers on assignment.

FICTION Young Readers: animal, contemporary, fantasy, folktales, health, history, humorous, multicultural, nature/environment, problem solving, religious, science fiction, sports, suspense/mystery. Middle Readers: animal, contemporary, fantasy, folktales, health, history, humorous, multicultural, nature/environment, problem solving, religious, romance, science fiction, sports, suspense/mystery. Length: 1,000-1,150 words. **Pays £90.**

$$ BABYBUG

Cricket Media, Inc., 7926 Jones Branch Dr., Suite 870, McLean VA 22102. (703)885-3400. **Website:** www.cricketmedia.com. **50% freelance written.** "*Babybug*, a look-and-listen magazine, presents simple poems, stories, nonfiction, and activities that reflect the natural playfulness and curiosity of babies and toddlers." Estab. 1994. Circ. 45,000. Byline given. Pays on publication. Accepts queries by online submission form. Accepts simultaneous submissions. Responds in 3-6 months to mss. Guidelines online.

NONFICTION "First Concepts," a playful take on a simple idea, expressed through very short nonfiction. See recent issues for examples. **Buys 10-20 mss/year.** Submit through online submissions manager: cricketmag.submittable.com/submit. Length: up to 6 sentences. **Pays up to 25¢/word.** Pays expenses of writers on assignment.

FICTION Wants very short, clear fiction. rhythmic, rhyming. **Buys 10-20 mss/year.** Submit complete ms via online submissions manager. Length: up to 6 sentences. **Pays up to 25¢/word.**

POETRY "We are especially interested in rhythmic and rhyming poetry. Poems may explore a baby's day, or they may be more whimsical." Submit via online submissions manager. **Pays up to $3/line; $25 minimum.**

💲💲💲💲 BOYS' LIFE

Boy Scouts of America, P.O. Box 152079, 1325 W. Walnut Hill Ln., Irving TX 75015. **Website:** www.boyslife.org. **Contact:** Paula Murphey, senior editor; Clay Swartz, associate editor. **75% freelance written. Prefers to work with published/established writers; works with small number of new/unpublished writers each year.** *Boys' Life* is a monthly 4-color general interest magazine for boys 7-18, most of whom are Cub Scouts, Boy Scouts, or Venturers. Estab. 1911. Circ. 1.1 million. Byline given. Pays on acceptance. Publishes ms approximately 1 year after acceptance. Accepts queries by mail. Accepts simultaneous submissions. Responds to queries/mss in 2 months. Sample copy: $3.95 plus 9x12 SASE. Guidelines online.

NONFICTION scouting activities and general interests. **Buys 60 mss/year.** Query senior editor with SASE. No phone or e-mail queries. Length: 500-1,500 words. **Pay ranges from $400-1,500.** Pays expenses of writers on assignment.

COLUMNS Science; Nature; Earth; Health; Sports; Space and Aviation; Cars; Computers; Entertainment; Pets; History; Music, all 600 words. Query associate editor. **Pays $100-400.**

💲 BREAD FOR GOD'S CHILDREN

Bread Ministries, INC., P.O. Box 1017, Arcadia FL 34265. (863)494-6214. **E-mail:** bread@breadministries.org. **E-mail:** Do not accept. **Website:** www.breadministries.org. **Contact:** Judith M. Gibbs, editor. **10% freelance written.** An interdenominational Christian teaching publication published 4-6 times/year written to aid children and youth in leading a Christian life. Estab. 1972. Circ. 10,000 (U.S. and Canada). Byline given. Publication No kill fee. Publishes ms an average of 6 months after acceptance. Accepts queries by mail. Accepts simultaneous submissions. Responds in 6 months to mss. Sample copy for 9x12 SAE and 5 first-class stamps. Guidelines for #10 SASE.

NONFICTION Needs inspirational, All levels: how-to. "We do not want anything detrimental to solid family values. Most topics will fit if they are slanted to our basic needs." **Buys 3-4 mss/year.** Send complete ms. Length: 500-800 words. **Pays on publication.**

REPRINTS Send tearsheet and information about when and where the material previously appeared.

COLUMNS Freelance columns: Let's Chat (children's Christian values), 500-700 words; Teen Page (youth Christian values), 600-800 words; Idea Page (games, crafts, Bible drills). **Buys 5-8 mss/year.** Send complete ms. **Pays $30.**

FICTION "We are looking for writers who have a solid knowledge of Biblical principles and are concerned for the youth of today living by those principles. Stories must be well written, with the story itself getting the message across—no preaching, moralizing, or tag endings." Needs historical, religious, Young readers, middle readers, young adult/teen: adventure, religious, problem-solving, sports. Looks for "teaching stories that portray Christian lifestyles without preaching." **Buys 10-15 mss/year.** Send complete ms. Length: 600-800 words for young children; 900-1,500 words for older children. **Pays $40-50.**

💲 CADET QUEST MAGAZINE

Calvinist Cadet Corps, 1333 Alger St. SE, Grand Rapids MI 49507. (616)241-5616. **Fax:** (616)241-5558. **E-mail:** submissions@calvinistcadets.org. **Website:** www.calvinistcadets.org. **Contact:** Steve Bootsma, editor. Magazine published 7 times/year. *Cadet Quest Magazine* shows boys 9-14 how God is at work in their lives and in the world around them. Estab. 1958. Circ. 6,000. Byline given. Pays on acceptance. No kill fee. Publishes ms 4-11 months after acceptance. Accepts queries by mail, e-mail. Accepts simultaneous submissions. Responds in 2 months to mss. Sample copy for 9x12 SASE and $1.45 postage. Guidelines online.

NONFICTION informational. Special issues: New themes list available online in January or for SASE. "Articles about Christian athletes, coaching tips, and developing Christian character through sports are appreciated. Photos of these sports or athletes are also welcomed. Be original in presenting these topics to boys. Articles about camping, nature, and survival should be practical—the 'how-to' approach is best. 'God in nature' articles, if done without being preachy, are appreciated." Send complete ms via postal mail or e-mail (in body of e-mail; no attachments). Length: up to 1,500 words. **Pays 5¢/word and 1 contributor's copy.**

REPRINTS For reprints, send typed ms with rights for sale noted or e-mail (in body of e-mail; no attachments). Payment varies.

COLUMNS Project/Hobby articles (simple projects boys 9-14 can do on their own, made with easily accessible materials; must provide clear, accurate instructions); Cartoons and Puzzles (wholesome and boy-oriented logic puzzles, crosswords, and hidden pictures).

💲💲 CLUBHOUSE MAGAZINE

Focus on the Family, 8605 Explorer Dr., Colorado Springs CO 80920. **Website:** www.clubhousemagazine.com. **Contact:** Stephen O'Rear, editorial assistant. **25% freelance written.** Monthly magazine. *Clubhouse* readers are 8-12 year old boys and girls who desire to know more about God and the Bible. Their parents (who typically pay for the membership) want wholesome, educational material with Scriptural or moral insight. The kids want excitement, adventure, action, humor, or mystery. Your job as a writer is to please both the parent and child with each article. Estab. 1987. Circ. 85,000. Byline given. Pays on acceptance. No kill fee. Publishes ms an average of 12-18 months after acceptance. Editorial lead time 5 months. Submit seasonal material 9 months in advance. Responds in 2 months to mss. Sample copy for $1.50 with 9x12 SASE. Guidelines for #10 SASE.

NONFICTION Contact: Jesse Florea, editor. Needs essays, how-to, humor, inspirational, interview, personal experience, photo feature, religious. Avoid Bible stories. Avoid informational-only, science, or educational articles. Avoid biographies told encyclopedia or textbook style. **Buys 6 mss/year.** Send complete ms. Length: 800-1,200 words. **Pays $25-450 for assigned articles. Pays 15-25¢/word for unsolicited articles.**

FICTION Contact: Jesse Florea, editor. Needs adventure, humorous, mystery, religious, suspense, holiday. Avoid contemporary, middle-class family settings (existing authors meet this need), poems (rarely printed), stories dealing with boy-girl relationships. **Buys 10 mss/year.** Send complete ms. Length: 400-1,500 words. **Pays $200 and up for first time contributor and 5 contributor's copies; additional copies available.**

FILLERS Needs facts, newsbreaks. **Buys 2 mss/year.** Length: 40-100 words.

💲💲 COBBLESTONE

Cricket Media, Inc., **E-mail:** cobblestone@cricketmedia.com. **Website:** www.cricketmedia.com. **50% freelance written.** "*Cobblestone* is interested in articles of historical accuracy and lively, original approaches to the subject at hand." American history magazine for ages 8-14. Circ. 15,000. Byline given. Pays on publication. Offers 50% kill fee. Accepts queries by e-mail. Accepts simultaneous submissions. Sample copy available online. Guidelines available online.

NONFICTION Needs historical, humor, interview, personal experience, photo feature. No material that editorializes rather than reports. **Buys 45-50 mss/year.** Query by e-mail with published clips. Length: 700-800 words for feature articles; 300-600 words for supplemental nonfiction. **Pays 20-25¢/word.** Pays expenses of writers on assignment.

FICTION Needs adventure. **Buys 5 mss/year.** Query by e-mail with published clips. Length: up to 800 words. **Pays 20-25¢/word.**

POETRY Needs free verse, light verse, traditional. Serious and light verse considered. Must have clear, objective imagery. Buys 3 poems/year. Length: up to 100 lines/poem. **Pays on an individual basis.**

FILLERS Crossword and other word puzzles (no word finds), mazes, and picture puzzles that use the vocabulary of the issue's theme or otherwise relate to the theme. Query by e-mail with published clips. **Pays on an individual basis.**

💲💲 CRICKET

Cricket Media, Inc., 7926 Jones Branch Dr., Suite 870, McLean VA 22102. (703)885-3400. **Website:** www.cricketmag.com. *Cricket* is a monthly literary magazine for ages 9-14. Publishes 9 issues/year. Estab. 1973. Circ. 73,000. Byline given. Pays on publication. Accepts queries by online submission form. Accepts simultaneous submissions. Responds in 3-6 months to mss. Sample copy available online. Guidelines available online.

NONFICTION *Cricket* publishes thought-provoking nonfiction articles on a wide range of subjects: history, biography, true adventure, science and technology, sports, inventors and explorers, architecture and engineering, archaeology, dance, music, theater, and art. Articles should be carefully researched and include a solid bibliography that shows that research has gone beyond reviewing websites. Submit via online submissions manager (cricketmag.submittable.com). Length: 1,200-1,800 words. **Pays up to 25¢/word.** Pays expenses of writers on assignment.

FICTION realistic, contemporary, historic, humor, mysteries, fantasy, science fiction, folk/fairy tales, legend, myth. No didactic, sex, religious, or horror stories. **Buys 75-100 mss/year.** Submit via online submissions manager (cricketmag.submittable.com). Length: 1,200-1,800 words. **Pays up to 25¢/word.**

POETRY *Cricket* publishes both serious and humorous poetry. Poems should be well-crafted, with precise and vivid language and images. Poems can explore a variety of themes, from nature, to family and friendships, to whatever you can imagine that will delight our readers and invite their wonder and emotional response. Buys 20-30 poems/year. Submit maximum 6 poems. Length: up to 35 lines/poem. Most poems run 8-15 lines. **Pays up to $3/line.**

FILLERS Crossword puzzles, logic puzzles, math puzzles, crafts, recipes, science experiments, games and activities from other countries, plays, music, art. **Pays $75.**

FACES

Cricket Media, Inc., **E-mail:** faces@cricketmedia.com. **Website:** www.cricketmedia.com. **90-100% freelance written.** "Published 9 times/year, *Faces* covers world culture for ages 9-14. It stands apart from other children's magazines by offering a solid look at 1 subject and stressing strong editorial content, color photographs throughout, and original illustrations. *Faces* offers an equal balance of feature articles and activities, as well as folktales and legends." Estab. 1984. Circ. 15,000. Byline given. Pays on publication. Offers 50% kill fee. Accepts simultaneous submissions. Sample copy available online. Guidelines available online.

NONFICTION Needs historical, interview, personal experience, photo feature, feature articles (in-depth nonfiction highlighting an aspect of the featured culture, interviews, and personal accounts), 700-800 words; supplemental nonfiction (subjects directly and indirectly related to the theme), 300-600 words. Special issues: See website for upcoming themes. **Buys 45-50 mss/year.** Query by e-mail with cover letter, one-page outline, bibliography. **Pays 20-25¢/word.** Pays expenses of writers on assignment.

FICTION Fiction accepted: retold legends, folktales, stories, and original plays from around the world, etc., relating to the theme. Needs ethnic. Query with cover letter, one-page outline, bibliography. **Pays 20-25¢/word.**

FILLERS Needs Puzzles and Games (word puzzles using the vocabulary of the edition's theme, mazes and picture puzzles that relate to the theme); Activities (crafts, games, recipes, projects, etc., which children can do either alone or with adult supervision; should be accompanied by sketches and description of how activity relates to theme), up to 700 words. No crossword puzzles. **Pays on an individual basis.**

THE FRIEND MAGAZINE

The Church of Jesus Christ of Latter-day Saints, 50 E. North Temple St., Salt Lake City UT 84150. (801)240-2210. **Fax:** (801)240-2270. **E-mail:** friend@ldschurch.org. **Website:** www.lds.org/friend. **Contact:** Paul B. Pieper, editor; Mark W. Robison, art director. Monthly magazine for 3-12 year olds. "The *Friend* is published by The Church of Jesus Christ of Latter-day Saints for boys and girls up to 3-12 years of age." Estab. 1971. Available online.

NONFICTION Needs historical, humor, inspirational. Pays expenses of writers on assignment.

FICTION Wants illustrated stories and "For Little Friends" stories. See guidelines online.

POETRY Pays $30 for poems.

GIRLS' LIFE

3 S. Frederick St., Suite 806, Baltimore MD 21202. (410)426-9600. **Fax:** (866)793-1531. **E-mail:** writeforgl@girlslife.com. **Website:** www.girlslife.com. **Contact:** Karen Bokram, founding editor and publisher; Kelsey Haywood, senior editor; Chun Kim, art director. Bimonthly magazine covering girls ages 9-15. Estab. 1994. Circ. 2.16 million. Byline given. Pays on publication. Publishes an average of 3 months after acceptance. Editorial lead time 4 months. Submit seasonal material 5 months in advance. Accepts queries by mail, e-mail. Accepts simultaneous submissions. Responds in 1 month to queries. Sample copy for $5 or online. Guidelines online.

NONFICTION Needs book excerpts, essays, general interest, how-to, humor, inspirational, interview, new product, travel. Special issues: Special issues: Back to School (August/September); Fall, Halloween (October/November); Holidays, Winter (December/January); Valentine's Day, Crushes (February/March); Spring, Mother's Day (April/May); and Summer, Father's Day (June/July). **Buys 40 mss/year.** Query by mail with published clips. Submit complete ms on spec only. "Features and articles should speak to young women ages 10-15 looking for new ideas about relationships, family, friends, school, etc. with fresh, savvy advice. Front-of-the-book columns and quizzes are a good place to start." Length: 700-2,000 words. **Pays $350/regular column; $500/feature.** Pays expenses of writers on assignment.

COLUMNS Buys 20 mss/year. Query with published clips. **Pays $150-450.**

FICTION "We accept short fiction. They should be stand-alone stories and are generally 2,500-3,500 words." Needs short stories.

💲 HIGHLIGHTS FOR CHILDREN

803 Church St., Honesdale PA 18431. (570)253-1080. **Fax:** (570)251-7847. **E-mail:** eds@highlights.com (Do not send submissions to this address.). **E-mail:** Highlights.submittable.com. **Website:** www.highlights.com. **Contact:** Christine French Cully, Editor in Chief. **70% freelance written.** Monthly magazine for children ages 6-12. "This book of wholesome fun is dedicated to helping children grow in basic skills and knowledge, in creativeness, in ability to think and reason, in sensitivity to others, in high ideals, and worthy ways of living—for children are the world's most important people. We publish stories and articles for beginning and advanced readers. Up to 400 words for beginning readers, up to 750 words for advanced readers." Estab. 1946. Circ. Approximately 1 million. Byline given. Pays on acceptance. Accepts queries by online submission form. Accepts simultaneous submissions. Responds in 2 months. Guidelines on Highlights.submittable.com.

NONFICTION See guidelines at Highlights.submittable.com. Up to 400 words for beginning readers. Up to 750 words for advanced readers. **Pays $175 and up for articles; pays $40 and up for crafts, activities, and puzzles.**

FICTION Stories appealing to girls and boys ages 6-12. Vivid, full of action. Engaging plot, strong characterization, lively language. Prefers stories in which a child protagonist solves a dilemma through his or her own resources. No stories glorifying war, crime or violence. See Highlights.submittable.com. Up to 475 words for beginning readers. Up to 750 words for advanced readers. **Pays $175 and up.**

POETRY See Highlights.submittable.com. No previously published poetry. Buys all rights. 16 lines maximum. Pays $50 and up.

FILLERS Buys puzzles, crafts, and activities. See Highlights.submittable.com. Pays $40 and up.

💲 JACK AND JILL

U.S. Kids, P.O. Box 88928, Indianapolis IN 46208. (317)634-1100. **E-mail:** jackandjill@uskidsmags.com. **Website:** www.uskidsmags.com. **50% freelance written.** Bimonthly magazine published for children ages 6-12. *Jack and Jill* is an award-winning magazine for children ages 6-12. It promotes the healthy educational and creative growth of children through interactive activities and articles. The pages are designed to spark a child's curiosity in a wide range of topics through articles, games, and activities. Inside you will find: current real-world topics in articles in stories; challenging puzzles and games; and interactive entertainment through experimental crafts and recipes. Please do not send artwork. "We prefer to work with professional illustrators of our own choosing. Write entertaining and imaginative stories for kids, not just about them. Writers should understand what is funny to kids, what's important to them, what excites them. Don't write from an adult 'kids are so cute' perspective. We're also looking for health and healthful lifestyle stories and articles, but don't be preachy." Estab. 1938. Circ. 40,000. Byline given. Pays on publication. Publishes ms an average of 8 months after acceptance. Submit seasonal material 8 months in advance. Accepts queries by mail. Accepts simultaneous submissions. Responds to mss in 3 months. Guidelines online.

NONFICTION **Buys 8-10 mss/year.** Submit complete ms via postal mail; no e-mail submissions. Queries not accepted. We are especially interested in features or Q&As with regular kids (or groups of kids) in the *Jack and Jill* age group who are engaged in unusual, challenging, or interesting activities. No celebrity pieces, please. Length: up to 700 words. **Pays $25 minimum.** Pays expenses of writers on assignment.

FICTION Submit complete ms via postal mail; no e-mail submissions. The tone of the stories should be fun and engaging. Stories should hook readers right from the get-go and pull them through the story. Humor is very important! Dialogue should be witty instead of just furthering the plot. The story should convey some kind of positive message. Possible themes could include self-reliance, being kind to others, appreciating other cultures, and so on. There are a million positive messages, so get creative! Kids can see preachy coming from a mile away, though, so please focus on telling a good story over teaching a lesson. The message—if there is one—should come organically from the story and not feel tacked on. **Buys 30-35 mss/year.** Length: 600-800 words. **Pays $25 minimum.**

POETRY Submit via postal mail; no e-mail submissions. Wants light-hearted poetry appropriate for the age group. Mss must be typewritten with poet's contact information in upper-right corner of each poem's page. SASE required. Length: up to 30 lines/poem. **Pays $25-50.**

FILLERS Needs puzzles, activities, games. In general, we prefer to use in-house generated material for this category but on occasion we do receive unique and fun puzzles, games, or activities through submissions. Please make sure you are submitting a truly unique activity for our consideration. **Pays $25-40.**

$$$ JUNIOR SCHOLASTIC

Scholastic, Inc., 557 Broadway, New York NY 10012. **Website:** junior.scholastic.com. Magazine published 18 times/year. Edited for students ages 11-14. Circ. 535,000. No kill fee. Editorial lead time 6 weeks. Accepts simultaneous submissions.

$ KEYS FOR KIDS DEVOTIONAL

Keys for Kids Ministries, 2060 43rd St. SE, Grand Rapids MI 49508. **E-mail:** editorial@keysforkids.org. **Website:** www.keysforkids.org. **Contact:** Courtney Lasater, editor. **95% freelance.** Daily devotional featuring stories and Scripture verses for children ages 6-12 that help kids dig into God's Word and apply it to their lives. Please put your name and contact information on the first page of your submission. We strongly prefer receiving submissions via our website. Story length is typically 340-375 words. To see full guidelines or submit a story, please go to www.keysforkids.org/writersguidelines. Estab. 1982. Circ. 50,000 print (not including digital circulation). Byline given. Pays on acceptance. Typically publishes stories 6-9 months after acceptance. Editorial lead time 6-8 months. Accepts queries by e-mail, online submission form. Responds in 2-4 months. Sample copy online. Guidelines online.

FICTION Need short contemporary stories with spiritual applications for kids. Please suggest a key verse and an appropriate Scripture passage, generally 3-10 verses, to reinforce the theme of your story. Length: Up to 375 words. **Pays $30.**

$$ LADYBUG

Cricket Media, Inc., **Website:** www.cricketmag.com. *Ladybug* magazine is an imaginative magazine with art and literature for young children ages 3-6. Publishes 9 issues/year. Estab. 1990. Circ. 125,000. Byline given. Pays on publication. Accepts queries by online submission form. Accepts simultaneous submissions. Responds in 6 months to mss. Guidelines available online.

NONFICTION Seeks "simple explorations of interesting places in a young child's world (such as the library and the post office), different cultures, nature, and science. These articles can be straight nonfiction, or they may include story elements, such as a fictional child narrator." **Buys 35 mss/year.** Submit via online submissions manager: cricketmag.submittable.com. Length: up to 400 words. **Pays up to 25¢/word.** Pays expenses of writers on assignment.

FICTION Wants imaginative contemporary stories, original retellings of fairy and folk tales, multicultural stories. **Buys 30 mss/year.** Submit via online submissions manager: cricket.submittable.com. Length: up to 800 words. **Pays up to 25¢/word.**

POETRY Needs light verse, traditional. Wants poetry that is "rhythmic, rhyming; serious, humorous." Submit via online submissions manager: cricket.submittable.com. Length: up to 20 lines/poem. **Pays up to $3/line ($25 minimum).**

FILLERS Learning activities, games, crafts, songs, finger games. See back issues for types, formats, and length.

$$$⊘ MUSE

Cricket Media, Inc., **E-mail:** muse@cricketmedia.com. **Website:** www.cricketmag.com. "The goal of *Muse* is to give as many children as possible access to the most important ideas and concepts underlying the principal areas of human knowledge. Articles should meet the highest possible standards of clarity and transparency, aided, wherever possible, by a tone of skepticism, humor, and irreverence." Estab. 1996. Circ. 40,000. Accepts queries by e-mail. Accepts simultaneous submissions.

NONFICTION Needs interview, photo feature, profile, entertaining stories from the fields of science, technology, engineering, art, and math. Query by e-mail with published clips. Length: 1,200-1,800 words for features; 500-800 words for profiles and interviews; 100-300 words for photo essays. Pays expenses of writers on assignment.

FICTION Needs science fiction. Query with published clips. Length: 1,000-1,600 words

$$$$ NATIONAL GEOGRAPHIC KIDS

National Geographic Society, 1145 17th St. NW, Washington DC 20036. **E-mail:** ashaw@ngs.org. **E-**

mail: michelle.tyler@natgeo.com. **Website:** www.kids.
nationalgeographic.com. **Contact:** Michelle Tyler,
editorial assistant. **70% freelance written.** Magazine
published 10 times/year. "It's our mission to find fresh
ways to entertain children while educating and exciting them about their world." Estab. 1975. Circ. 1.3
million. Byline given. Pays on acceptance. Offers 10%
kill fee. Publishes ms an average of 6 months after acceptance. Editorial lead time 6+ months. Submit seasonal material 6+ months in advance. Accepts queries
by mail. Accepts simultaneous submissions. Sample
copy for #10 SASE. Guidelines online.

NONFICTION Needs general interest, humor, interview, technical. Query with published clips and
résumé. Length: 100-1,000 words. **Pays $1/word for
assigned articles.** Pays expenses of writers on assignment.

COLUMNS Freelance columns: Amazing Animals
(animal heroes, stories about animal rescues, inter-
esting/funny animal tales), 100 words; Inside Scoop
(fun, kid-friendly news items), 50-70 words. Query
with published clips. **Pays $1/word.**

🝙 NATURE FRIEND MAGAZINE

4253 Woodcock Lane, Dayton VA 22821. (540)867-
0764. **E-mail:** info@naturefriendmagazine.com;
editor@naturefriendmagazine.com; photos@na-
turefriendmagazine.com. **Website:** www.nature-
friendmagazine.com. **Contact:** Kevin Shank, editor.
80% freelance written. Monthly children's magazine covering creation-based nature. *Nature Friend*
includes stories, puzzles, science experiments, and
nature experiments. All submissions need to honor
God as creator. Estab. 1983. Circ. 8,000. Byline given.
Pays on publication. No kill fee. Editorial lead time
4 months. Submit seasonal material 6 months in advance. Accepts simultaneous submissions. Responds
in 6 months to mss. Sample copy: $5, postage paid.
Guidelines available on website.

NONFICTION Needs how-to. No poetry, evolution,
animals depicted in captivity, talking animal stories,
or evolutionary material. **Buys 50 mss/year.** Send
complete ms. Length: 250-900 words. **Pays 5¢/word.**
Pays expenses of writers on assignment.

COLUMNS Learning By Doing, 500-900 words.
Buys 12 mss/year. Send complete ms.

FILLERS Needs Facts, puzzles, and short essays
on something current in nature. **Buys 35 mss/year.**
Length: 150-250 words. **5¢/word.**

🝙🝙 POCKETS

The Upper Room, P.O. Box 340004, Nashville TN
37203. (615)340-7333. **E-mail:** pockets@upperroom.
org. **Website:** pockets.upperroom.org. **Contact:** Lynn
W. Gilliam, editor. **60% freelance written.** Magazine
published 11 times/year. "*Pockets* is a Christian devotional magazine for children ages 6-12. All submissions should address the broad theme of the magazine. Each issue is built around a theme with material
which can be used by children in a variety of ways.
Scripture stories, fiction, poetry, prayers, art, graphics, puzzles and activities are included. Submissions
do not need to be overtly religious. They should help
children experience a Christian lifestyle that is not
always a neatly wrapped moral package but is open
to the continuing revelation of God's will. Seasonal
material, both secular and liturgical, is desired." Estab. 1981. Byline given. Pays on acceptance. No kill
fee. Publishes ms an average of 1 year after acceptance.
Submit seasonal material 1 year in advance. Accepts
simultaneous submissions. Responds in 8 weeks to
mss. Each issue reflects a specific theme. Guidelines
online.

NONFICTION Picture-oriented, young readers,
middle readers: cooking, games/puzzles. Special issues: "*Pockets* seeks biographical sketches of persons,
famous or unknown, whose lives reflect their Christian commitment, written in a way that appeals to
children." Does not accept how-to articles. "Nonfiction should read like a story." Multicultural needs include stories that feature children of various racial/
ethnic groups and do so in a way that is true to those
depicted. **Buys 10 mss/year.** Submit complete ms
by mail. No e-mail submissions. Length: 400-1,000
words. **Pays 14¢/word.** Pays expenses of writers on
assignment.

REPRINTS Accepts one-time previously published
submissions. Send ms with rights for sale noted and
information about when and where the material previously appeared.

PHOTOS Send 4-6 close-up photos of children actively involved in peacemakers at work activities. Send
photos, contact sheets, prints, or digital images. Must
be 300 dpi. Pays $25/photo. Buys one-time rights.

COLUMNS Family Time, 200-300 words; Peacemakers at Work (profiles of children working for
peace, justice, and ecological concerns), 400-600
words. **Pays 14¢/word.** Activities/Games (related to

themes). **Pays $25 and up**. Kids Cook (simple recipes children can make alone or with minimal help from an adult). **Pays $25.**

FICTION "Stories should contain lots of action, use believable dialogue, be simply written, and be relevant to the problems faced by this age group in everyday life." Submit complete ms by mail. No e-mail submissions. Length: 600-1,000 words.

POETRY Both seasonal and theme poems needed. Considers poetry by children. Buys 14 poems/year. Length: up to 20 lines. **Pays $25 minimum.**

TIPS "Theme stories, role models, and retold scripture stories are most open to freelancers. Poetry is also open. It is very helpful if writers read our writers' guidelines and themes on our website."

$ RAINBOW RUMPUS

P.O. Box 6881, Minneapolis MN 55406. **Website:** www.rainbowrumpus.org. **Contact:** Liane Bonin Starr, editor in chief and fiction editor. "*Rainbow Rumpus* is the world's only online literary magazine for children and youth with lesbian, gay, bisexual, and transgender (LGBT) parents. We are creating a new genre of children's and young adult fiction. Please carefully read and observe the guidelines on our website." Estab. 2005. Circ. 300 visits/day. Byline given. Pays on publication. Accepts simultaneous submissions. Guidelines available online.

NONFICTION Pays expenses of writers on assignment.

FICTION "Stories should be written from the point of view of children or teens with lesbian, gay, bisexual, or transgender parents or other family members, or who are connected to the LGBT community. Stories featuring families of color, bisexual parents, transgender parents, family members with disabilities, and mixed-race families are particularly welcome." Query editor through website's Contact page. Be sure to select the Submissions category. Length: 800-2,500 words for stories for 4- to 12-year-olds; up to 5,000 words for stories for 13- to 18-year-olds. **Pays $300/story.**

TIPS "Emerging writers encouraged to submit. You do not need to be a member of the LGBT community to participate."

$ SHINE BRIGHTLY

GEMS Girls' Clubs, 1333 Alger St., SE, Grand Rapids MI 49507. (616)241-5616. **Fax:** (616)241-5558. **E-mail:** shinebrightly@gemsgc.org. **Website:** www.gemsgc.org. **Contact:** Kelli Gilmore, managing editor. **60% freelance written. Works with new and published/established writers.** Monthly magazine from September to May with a double issue for September/October. "Our purpose is to lead girls into a living relationship with Jesus Christ and to help them see how God is at work in their lives and the world around them. Puzzles, crafts, stories, and articles for girls ages 9-14." Estab. 1970. Circ. 13,000. Byline given. Pays on publication. No kill fee. Publishes ms an average of 4 months after acceptance. Submit seasonal material 1 year in advance. Accepts simultaneous submissions. Responds in 2 months to mss. Sample copy with 9x12 SASE with 3 first class stamps and $1. Guidelines online.

NONFICTION Needs humor, inspirational, interview, personal experience, photo feature, religious, travel. Avoid the testimony approach. **Buys 15 unsolicited mss/year.** Submit complete ms in body of e-mail. No attachments. Length: 100-800 words. **Pays up to $35, plus 2 copies.** Pays expenses of writers on assignment.

REPRINTS Send typed manuscript with rights for sale noted and information about when and where the material previously appeared.

PHOTOS Purchased with or without ms. Appreciate multicultural subjects. Reviews 5x7 or 8x10 clear color glossy prints. Pays $25-50 on publication.

COLUMNS How-to (crafts); puzzles and jokes; quizzes. Length: 200-400 words. Send complete ms. **Pay varies.**

FICTION Does not want "unrealistic stories and those with trite, easy endings. We are interested in manuscripts that show how real girls can change the world." Needs ethnic, historical, humorous, mystery, religious, slice-of-life vignettes. Believable only. Nothing too preachy. **Buys 30 mss/year.** Submit complete ms in body of e-mail. No attachments. Length: 700-900 words. **Pays up to $35, plus 2 copies.**

POETRY Needs free verse, haiku, light verse, traditional. **Limited need for poetry. Pays $5-15.**

TIPS Writers: "Please check our website before submitting. We have a specific style and theme that deals with how girls can impact the world. The stories should be current, deal with pre-adolescent problems and joys, and help girls see God at work in their lives through humor as well as problem-solving." Prefers not to see anything on the adult level, secular material, or violence. Writers frequently oversimplify the articles and often write with a Pollyanna attitude. An author should be able to see his/her writing style as exciting and appealing to girls ages 9-14. The style can be fun, but also teach a truth. Subjects should be current and important to *SHINE brightly* readers. Use our theme update as a guide. We would like to receive material with a multicultural slant."

🟢 SPARKLE

GEMS Girls' Clubs, 1333 Alger St. SE, Grand Rapids MI 49507. (616)241-5616. **Fax:** (616)241-5558. **E-mail:** sparkle@gemsgc.org. **Website:** www.gemsgc. org. **Contact:** Kelli Gilmore, managing editor; Lisa Hunter, art director/photo editor. **40% freelance written.** Monthly magazine for girls ages 6-9 from October to March. Mission is to prepare young girls to live out their faith and become world-changers. Strives to help girls make a difference in the world. Looks at the application of scripture to everyday life. Also strives to delight the reader and cause the reader to evalute her own life in light of the truth presented. Finally, attempts to teach practical life skills. Estab. 2002. Circ. 9,000. Byline given. Pays on publication. Editorial lead time 3 months. Submit seasonal material 1 year in advance. Accepts queries by e-mail. Accepts simultaneous submissions. Responds 3 months to mss. Sample copy for 9x13 SAE, 3 first-class stamps, and $1 for coverage/publication cost. Guidelines available for #10 SASE or online.

NONFICTION Contact: Kelli Gilmore. Young readers: animal, arts/crafts, biography, careers, cooking, concept, games/puzzles, geography, health, history, hobbies, how-to, humor, inspirational, interview/profile, math, multicultural, music/drama/art, nature/environment, personal experience, photo feature, problem-solving, quizzes, recipes, religious, science, social issues, sports, travel. Looking for inspirational biographies, stories from Zambia, and ideas on how to live a green lifestyle. Constant mention of God is not necessary if the moral tone of the story is positive. **Buys 10 mss/year.** Send complete ms. Length: 100-400 words. **Pays $35 maximum.** Pays expenses of writers on assignment.

PHOTOS Send photos. Identification of subjects required. Reviews at least 5X7 clear color glossy prints, GIF/JPEG files on CD. Offers $25-50/photo. Buys one-time rights.

COLUMNS Crafts; puzzles and jokes; quizzes, all 200-400 words. Send complete ms. **Payment varies.**

FICTION Young readers: adventure, animal, contemporary, ethnic/multicultural, fantasy, folktale, health, history, humorous, music and musicians, mystery, nature/environment, problem-solving, religious, recipes, service projects, slice-of-life, sports, suspense/mystery, vignettes, interacting with family and friends. **Buys 10 mss/year.** Send complete ms. Length: 100-400 words. **Pays $35 maximum.**

POETRY Prefers rhyming. "We do not wish to see anything that is too difficult for a first grader to read. We wish it to remain light. The style can be fun but should also teach a truth." No violence or secular material. Buys 4 poems/year. Submit maximum 4 poems.

FILLERS Needs facts, short humor. **Buys 6 mss/year.** Length: 50-150 words. **Pays $10-15.**

TIPS "Keep it simple. We are writing to first to third graders. It must be simple yet interesting. Mss should build girls up in Christian character but not be preachy. They are just learning about God and how He wants them to live. Mss should be delightful as well as educational and inspirational. Writers should keep stories simple but not write with a 'Pollyanna' attitude. Authors should see their writing style as exciting and appealing to girls ages 6-9. Subjects should be current and important to *Sparkle* readers. Use our theme as a guide. We would like to receive material with a multicultural slant."

🟢🟢 SPIDER

Cricket Media, Inc., **Website:** www.cricketmag.com. **85% freelance written.** Monthly reading and activity magazine for children ages 6-9. "*Spider* introduces children to the highest-quality stories, poems, illustrations, articles, and activities. It was created to foster in beginning readers a love of reading and discovery that will last a lifetime. We're looking for writers who respect children's intelligence." Estab. 1994. Circ. 70,000. Byline given. Pays on publication. Accepts queries by online submission form. Accepts simultaneous submissions. Responds in 6 months to mss. Sample copy available online. Guidelines available online.

NONFICTION Special issues: Wants "well-researched articles about animals, kids their own age doing amazing things, and cool science discoveries (such as wetsuits for penguins and real-life invisibility cloaks). Nonfiction articles should rise above a simple list of facts; we look for kid-friendly nonfiction shaped into an engaging narrative." Submit complete ms via online submissions manager (cricketmag.submittable. com). Length: 300-800 words. **Pays up to 25¢/word.** Pays expenses of writers on assignment.

REPRINTS Send photocopy with rights for sale noted and information about when and where the material previously appeared.

FICTION Wants "complex and believable" stories. Needs fantasy, humorous. No romance, horror, religious. Submit complete ms via online submissions manager (cricketmag.submittable.com). Length: 300-1,000 words. **Pays up to 25¢/word.**

POETRY Needs free verse, traditional. Submit up to 5 poems via online submissions manager (cricketmag.submittable.com). "Poems should be succinct, imaginative, and accessible; we tend to avoid long narrative poems." Length: up to 20 lines/poem. **Pays up to $3/line.**

FILLERS Needs recipes, crafts, puzzles, games, brainteasers, math and word activities. Submit via online submissions manager (cricketmag.submittable.com). Length: 1-4 pages. **Pays $75.**

TIPS "We'd like to see more of the following: engaging nonfiction, fillers, and 'takeout page' activities; folktales, fairy tales, science fiction, and humorous stories. Most importantly, do not write down to children."

LITERARY & LITTLE

AGNI

Boston University, 236 Bay State Rd., Boston MA 02215. **E-mail:** agni@bu.edu. **Website:** www.agnimagazine.org. **Contact:** Sven Birkerts, editor. **90% freelance written.** Eclectic literary magazine publishing first-rate poems, essays, translations, and stories. Estab. 1972. Circ. 3,000 in print, plus more than 60,000 distinct readers online per year. Byline given. Pays on publication. Publishes ms an average of 6 months after acceptance. Accepts queries by online submission form. Accepts simultaneous submissions. Responds in 4 months to mss. No queries please. Sample copy: $12 or online. Guidelines online.

NONFICTION Contact: Nonfiction Editor. Needs essays, memoir, reviews. Literary only. "We do not publish journalism or academic work." **Buys 20+ mss/year.** Submit online or by regular mail, no more than one essay at a time. E-mailed submissions will not be considered. Include an SASE or your e-mail address if sending by mail. **Pays $20/page up to $300, plus a one-year subscription, and, for print publication, 2 contributor's copies and 4 gift copies.**

FICTION Contact: Fiction Editor. Needs short stories. No genre scifi, horror, mystery, or romance. **Buys 20+ mss/year.** Submit online or by regular mail, no more than 1 story at a time. E-mailed submissions will not be considered. Include a SASE or your e-mail address if sending by mail. **Pays $20/page up to $300, plus a one-year subscription, and, for print publication, 2 contributor's copies and 4 gift copies.**

POETRY Contact: Poetry Editor. Submit online or by regular mail, no more than 5 poems at a time. E-mailed submissions will not be considered. Include a SASE or your e-mail address if sending by mail. Buys 120+ poems/year. Submit maximum 5 poems. **Pays $20/page up to $300, plus a one-year subscription, and, for print publication, 2 contributor's copies and 4 gift copies.**

TIPS "We're also looking for extraordinary translations from little-translated languages. It is important to read work published in *AGNI* before submitting, to see if your own might be compatible."

ALASKA QUARTERLY REVIEW

University of Alaska Anchorage, 3211 Providence Dr., Anchorage AK 99508. **E-mail:** uaa_aqr@uaa.alaska.edu. **Website:** www.uaa.alaska.edu/aqr. **Contact:** Ronald Spatz, editor in chief. **95% freelance written.** "*Alaska Quarterly Review* is a literary journal devoted to contemporary literary art, publishing fiction, short plays, poetry, photo essays, and literary nonfiction in traditional and experimental styles. The editors encourage new and emerging writers, while continuing to publish award-winning and established writers." Estab. 1982. Circ. 2,700. Byline given. Publishes ms an average of 6 months after acceptance. Accepts queries by mail. Accepts simultaneous submissions. Responds in 4 months to queries; in 6 weeks-4 months to mss. Sample copy: $6. Guidelines online.

NONFICTION Needs essays, literary nonfiction in traditional and experimental styles. Submit complete ms by mail. Include cover letter with contact information and SASE for return of ms. Length: up to 50 pages. **Pays contributor's copies and honoraria when funding is available.**

FICTION "Works in *AQR* have certain characteristics: freshness, honesty, and a compelling subject. The voice of the piece must be strong—idiosyncratic enough to create a unique persona. We look for craft, putting it in a form where it becomes emotionally and intellectually complex. Many pieces in *AQR* concern everyday life. We're not asking our writers to go outside themselves and their experiences to the absolute exotic to catch our interest. We look for the experiential and revelatory qualities of the work. We will champion a piece that may be less polished or stylistically sophisticated if it engages me, surprises me, and resonates for me. The joy in reading such a work is in discovering something true. Moreover, in keeping with our mission to publish new writers, we are looking for voices our readers do not know, voices that may not always be reflected in the dominant culture and that, in all instances, have something important to convey." Needs experimental, contemporary, prose poem, novel excerpts, drama: experimental and traditional one-acts. No romance, children's, or inspirational/religious. Submit complete ms by mail. Include cover letter with contact information and SASE for return of ms. Length: up to 50 pages. **Pays contributor's copies and honoraria when funding is available.**

POETRY Needs avant-garde, free verse, traditional. Submit poetry by mail. Include cover letter with contact information and SASE for return of ms. No light verse. Length: up to 20 pages. **Pays contributor's copies and honoraria when funding is available.**

TIPS "Although we respond to e-mail queries, we cannot review electronic submissions."

Ⓢ ALITERATE

Genre, Ltd., P.O. Box 380020, Cambridge MA 02238. **E-mail:** editor@aliterate.org. **E-mail:** submissions@aliterate.org. **Website:** www.aliterate.org. *Aliterate* is a production of Genre, Ltd., a small nonprofit publisher based in Cambridge, Massachusetts. "Much has been said about the gulf between literary and genre literature. *Aliterate* seeks to publish works that span this divide, blending tight prose with the fantastical. *Aliterate* reads during March and April." Estab. 2016. Byline given. Accepts queries by e-mail. Accepts simultaneous submissions. "Our median time to reject is 6 days, while our median acceptance time is about 70 days."

FICTION *Aliterate* is a publisher of literary genre fiction and publishes only science fiction, fantasy, Westerns, pulps, thrillers, horror, romance, etc. "We consider 'comedy' to be a fairly large genre; if you submit a comedy, please ensure it is also falls within another genre." Submissions should be of a 'literary' character, with an emphasis on character and language over clever plotting. Needs adventure, experimental, fantasy, historical, horror, humorous, mystery, romance, science fiction, short stories, suspense, western. Does not want poetry, inspirational, erotica, gore, polemics, fan fiction, or young adult. **Buys 16 mss/year.** Review is conducted by blind jury. Remove all identifying information from your submission. No need to include a cover letter; we'll solicit biographic information on acceptance. The subject line of your e-mail will be used to track your story in our review system. Submit only 1 ms in each reading period. Submission is open to all writers, apart from residents of Crimea, Cuba, Iran, North Korea, Sudan, and Syria. Length: 3,000-12,000 words. **Pays 6¢/word.**

TIPS "We've been asked for examples of authors who would fit the tone of *Aliterate*; they include Samuel Delany, Margaret Atwood, and Walter J. Miller Jr. While we love writers like Asimov, *Aliterate* doesn't aim to be a venue primarily for hard science fiction."

Ⓢ ALLEGORY

P.O. Box 2714, Cherry Hill NJ 08034. **E-mail:** submissions@allegoryezine.com. **Website:** www.allegoryezine.com. **Contact:** Ty Drago, publisher and managing editor. Biannual online magazine specializing in science fiction, fantasy, and horror. "We are an e-zine by writers for writers. Our articles focus on the art, craft, and business of writing. Our links and editorial policy all focus on the needs of fiction authors." *Allegory* (as Peridot Books) won the Page One Award for Literary Contribution. Estab. 1998. Circ. *Allegory* receives upwards of 250,000 hits per year. Pays on acceptance for one-time, electronic rights. Publishes in May and November. Accepts simultaneous submissions. Responds in 2 months to mss. Guidelines online.

NONFICTION Must be related to the craft or business of writing. Length: 1,500 words. **Pays $15/article.**

FICTION Receives 150 unsolicited mss/month. Accepts 12 mss/issue; 24 mss/year. Agented fiction 5%. Publishes 10 new writers/year. Also publishes literary essays, literary criticism. Often comments on rejected mss. "No media tie-ins (*Star Trek*, *Star Wars*, etc., or space opera, vampires)." "All submissions should be sent by e-mail (no letters or telephone calls) in either text or RTF format. Please place 'Submission [Title]-[first and last name]' in the subject line. Include the following in both the body of the e-mail and the attachment: your name, name to use on the story (byline) if different, your preferred e-mail address, your mailing address, the story's title, and the story's word count." Length: 1,500-7,500 words; average length: 2,500 words. **Pays $15/story.**

TIPS "Give us something original, preferably with a twist. Avoid gratuitous sex or violence. Funny always scores points. Be clever and imaginative, but be able to tell a story with proper mood and characterization. Put your name and e-mail address in the body of the story. Read the site and get a feel for it before submitting."

🄢 THE AMERICAN POETRY REVIEW

The University of the Arts, 320 S. Broad St., Hamilton #313, Philadelphia PA 19102. **E-mail:** escanlon@aprweb.org. **Website:** www.aprweb.org. **Contact:** Elizabeth Scanlon, editor. "*The American Poetry Review* is dedicated to reaching a worldwide audience with a diverse array of the best contemporary poetry and literary prose. *APR* also aims to expand the audience interested in poetry and literature, and to provide authors, especially poets, with a far-reaching forum in which to present their work." *APR* has included the work of over 1,500 writers, among whom there are 9 Nobel Prize laureates and 33 Pulitzer Prize winners. Estab. 1972. Circ. 8,000-10,000. Accepts queries by mail, online submission form. Accepts simultaneous submissions. Responds in 6 months. Sample: $5. Guidelines online.

NONFICTION Needs essays, interview, reviews. Submit complete ms via online submissions manager. Pays expenses of writers on assignment.

POETRY Submit up to 5 poems via online submissions manager. Has published poetry by D.A. Powell, James Franco, Dean Faulwell, and Caroline Pittman. **Pays $1 per line.**

🄢🄢 AMERICAN SHORT FICTION

Badgerdog Literary Publishing, P.O. Box 301209, Austin TX 78703. **E-mail:** editors@americanshortfiction.org. **Website:** www.americanshortfiction.org. **Contact:** Rebecca Markovits and Adeena Reitberger, editors. "Issued triannually, *American Short Fiction* publishes work by emerging and established voices: stories that dive into the wreck, that stretch the reader between recognition and surprise, that conjure a particular world with delicate expertise—stories that take a different way home." Estab. 1991. Circ. 2,500. Byline given. Pays on publication. Publishes ms an average of 3 months after acceptance. Accepts queries by online submission form. Accepts simultaneous submissions. Responds in 2 weeks to queries; in 5 months to mss. "Sample copies are available for sale through our publisher's online store." Guidelines online.

FICTION "Open to publishing mystery or speculative fiction if we feel it has literary value." Does not want young adult or genre fiction. **Buys 20-25 mss/year.** *American Short Fiction* seeks "short fiction by some of the finest writers working in contemporary literature, whether they are established, new, or lesser-known authors." Also publishes stories under 2,000 words online. Submit 1 story at a time via online submissions manager ($3 fee). No paper submissions. Length: open. **Writers receive $250-500, 2 contributor's copies, free subscription to the magazine. Additional copies $5.**

TIPS "We publish fiction that speaks to us emotionally, uses evocative and precise language, and takes risks in subject matter and/or form. Try to read a few issues of *American Short Fiction* to get a sense of what we like. Also, to be concise is a great virtue."

🄢 ANCIENT PATHS

E-mail: skylarburris@yahoo.com. **Website:** www.editorskylar.com/magazine/table.html. **Contact:** Skylar H. Burris, editor. **100% freelance written.** *Ancient Paths* provides "a forum for quality spiritual poetry and short fiction. We consider works from writers of all religions, but poets and authors should be comfortable appearing in a predominantly Christian publication. Works published in *Ancient Paths* explore themes such as redemption, sin, forgiveness, doubt, faith, gratitude for the ordinary blessings of life, spiritual struggle, and spiritual growth. Please, no overly didactic works. Subtlety is preferred." Please send seasonally themed works for Lent and Advent at least 1 month prior to the start of each season. Works on other themes may be sent at any time. Estab. 1998. Byline given. Pays on publication. Time between acceptance and publication is 1-4 months. Accepts queries by e-mail. Accepts simultaneous submissions. Responds in 8 weeks, usually sooner. Sample copy of printed back issue: $9. Purchase online. Detailed guidelines are available on the website.

REPRINTS Buys reprints of short fiction and poetry at the regular rate of $1.25/piece.

PHOTOS "We accept submissions of photographs on Christian themes. Send as an attachment." Pays $1.25/published photo. Acquires electronic rights.

FICTION E-mail submissions only. Paste short fiction directly in the e-mail message. Use the subject heading "AP Online Submission (title of your work)." Include name and e-mail address at top of e-mail. Previously published works accepted, provided they are not currently available online. Please indicate if your work has been published elsewhere. Needs humorous, mainstream, novel excerpts, religious, short stories, slice-of-life vignettes, All fiction submissions should be under 2,000 words. Very short submission of under 800 words have a better chance of acceptance. Length: under 800 words preferred; up to 2,000 words. **Pays $1.25/work published. Published authors also receive discount code for $3 off 2 printed back issues.**

POETRY Needs formal verse or free verse on spiritual themes. E-mail all submissions. Paste poems in e-mail message. Use the subject heading "AP Online Submission (title of your work)." Include your name and e-mail address at the top of your e-mail. Poems may be rhymed, unrhymed, free verse, or formal and should have a spiritual theme, which may be explicit or implicit, but which should not be overly didactic. No "preachy" poetry; avoid inconsistent meter and forced rhyme; no stream-of-consciousness or avant-garde work; no esoteric academic poetry; no concrete (shape) poetry; no use of the lowercase *i* for the personal pronoun; do not center poetry. Buys 52 poems/year. Submit maximum 5 poems. Length: 8-60 lines. **Pays $1.25/poem. Published poets also receive discount code for $3 off 2 printed back issues.**

TIPS "Read the great religious poets: John Donne, George Herbert, T.S. Eliot, Lord Tennyson. Remember not to preach. This is a literary magazine, not a pulpit. This does not mean you do not communicate morals or celebrate God. It means you are not overbearing or simplistic when you do so."

♻️💲 THE ANTIGONISH REVIEW

St. Francis Xavier University, P.O. Box 5000, Immaculata Hall, Room 413, Antigonish NS B2G 2W5 Canada. (902)867-3962. **Fax:** (902)867-5563. **E-mail:** tar@stfx.ca. **Website:** www.antigonishreview.com. **Contact:** Gerald Trites, editor. **100% freelance written.** Quarterly literary magazine for thoughtful and creative readers. *The Antigonish Review*, published quarterly, features the writing of new and emerging writers as well as the ideas of established and innovative thinkers through poetry, stories, essays, book reviews and interviews." Estab. 1970. Circ. 650. Byline given. Pays on publication. Offers variable kill fee. Publishes ms an average of 8 months after acceptance. Editorial lead time 4 months. Submit seasonal material 8 months in advance. Accepts queries by mail, e-mail, fax, phone. Accepts simultaneous submissions. Responds in 1 month to queries; 6 months to mss. Guidelines online.

NONFICTION Needs essays, interview, memoir, reviews, book reviews/essays. No academic research. **Buys 15-20 mss/year.** Through website using Submittable. Length: 1,500-3,000 words **Pays $50, 1 print copy and 1 digital copy.**

FICTION Send complete ms only through Submittable on our website. Needs short stories. No erotica. **Buys 35-40 mss/year.** Send complete ms. Length: 500-5,000 words. **Pays $50, 1 print edition and 1 digital edition for stories.**

POETRY Open to poetry on any subject written from any point of view and in any form. However, writers should expect their work to be considered within the full context of old and new poetry in English and other languages. Has published poetry by Andy Wainwright, W.J. Keith, Michael Hulse, Jean McNeil, M. Travis Lane, and Douglas Lochhead. Buys 100-125 poems/year. Submit maximum 8 poems. Submit 6-8 poems at a time. A preferable submission would be 3-4 poems. Lines/poem: not over 80, i.e., 2 pages. **Pays $10/page to a maximum of $50 and 2 contributor's copies.**

TIPS Contact by e-mail (tar@stfx.ca) and submit through the website using Submittable. There is a submission fee.

💲 ANTIOCH REVIEW

P.O. Box 148, Yellow Springs OH 45387-0148. (937)769-1365. **E-mail:** review@antiochcollege.edu. **Website:** www.antiochreview.org. **Contact:** Robert S. Fogarty, editor; Judith Hall, poetry editor. Quarterly magazine for general, literary, and academic audience. Literary and cultural review of contemporary issues and literature for general readership. *The Antioch Review* "is an independent quarterly of critical and creative thought. For well over 75 years, prominent and promising authors, poets, and thinkers have found a friendly reception—regardless of formal reputation. The Antioch Review, founded in 1941, is one of the oldest, continuously publishing literary magazines in America. We publish fiction, essays, and poetry from both emerging as well as established authors. Authors published in our pages are consistently included in Best American anthologies and Pushcart prizes. We continue to serve our readers and our authors and to encourage others to publish the "best words in the best order." We receive thousands of submissions each year from established and emerging authors. The competition is keen. Form and content are so inseparable and reaction is so personal, it is difficult to state requirements or limitations. Studying issues of *The Antioch Review* and reviewing our "Writer's Guidelines should be helpful." Estab. 1941. Circ. 3,000. Byline given. Pays on publication. Publishes ms an average of 10 months after acceptance. Accepts queries by mail, e-mail. Accepts simultaneous submissions. Responds in 3-6 months to mss. Sample copies may be purchased online. Guidelines online.

NONFICTION Nonfiction submissions are not accepted between June 1-August 31. Length: 2,000-8,000 words. **Pays $20/printed page, plus 2 contributor's copies.**

FICTION Quality fiction only, distinctive in style with fresh insights into the human condition. Needs experimental, contemporary. No science fiction, fantasy, or confessions. Send complete ms with SASE, preferably mailed flat. Fiction submissions are not accepted between June 1-August 31. **Pays $20/printed page, plus 2 contributor's copies.**

POETRY Has published poetry by Richard Howard, Jacqueline Osherow, Alice Fulton, Richard Kenney, and others. Receives about thousands of submissions/year. No previously published poems or simultaneous submissions. Include SASE with all submissions. No light or inspirational verse. Poetry submissions are not accepted between between May 1-September 1. Submit maximum 6 poems. **Pays $20/printed page, plus 2 contributor's copies.**

✪ $ ARC POETRY MAGAZINE

Arc Poetry Society, P.O. Box 81060, Ottawa ON K1P 1B1 Canada. **E-mail:** managingeditor@arcpoetry.ca; coordinatingeditor@arcpoetry.ca; arc@arcpoetry.ca. **Website:** www.arcpoetry.ca. **Contact:** Monty Reid, managing editor; Chris Johnson, coordinating editor. Semiannual magazine featuring poetry, poetry-related articles, and criticism. *Arc*'s focus is poetry, and particularly Canadian poetry, although it also publishes writers from elsewhere. Looking for the best poetry from new and established writers. Often publishes special issues. Send a SASE for upcoming special issues and contests. Estab. 1978. Circ. 1,500. Byline given. Pays on publication. Publishes mss an average of 6 months after acceptance. Accepts queries by online submission form. Accepts simultaneous submissions. Responds in 4-6 months. Guidelines available online.

NONFICTION Needs essays, interview, reviews, poetry book reviews. Query first. Length: 500-4,000 words. **Pays $50/printed page (Canadian), and 2 copies.** Pays expenses of writers on assignment.

PHOTOS Contact: Kevin Matthews, the Art Editor; art@arcpoetry.ca. Query first. Pays $50/page upon publication, $100 for art featured on the front cover (CDN). Buys one-time rights.

POETRY Needs contemporary poetry. For over 30 years, *Arc* has been publishing the best in contemporary poetry. *Arc* invites submissions from emerging and established poets. Poets may only submit once each calendar year. Poetry submissions must not exceed 3 poems total. Submissions must be typed and single-spaced (double spaces will be interpreted as blank lines). Include your name, e-mail address, and mailing address on each page. Submit each poem in a separate document with bio. Your submission will be grouped in submission platform. Biographical statements should be 2-3 sentences or approximately 50 words. *Arc* can't promise to respond to inquiries regarding the status of submissions before the completion of an editorial cycle. Buys 60 poems/year. Submit maximum 3 poems. **Pays $50/printed page (Canadian).**

$ ARTS & LETTERS JOURNAL OF CONTEMPORARY CULTURE

Georgia College & State University, Milledgeville GA 31061. (478)445-1289. **Website:** al.gcsu.edu. **Contact:** Laura Newbern, editor; Faith Thompson, managing editor. *Arts & Letters Journal of Contemporary Culture*, published semiannually, is devoted to publishing contemporary work from established and emerging writers. Our editors seek work that doesn't try too hard to grab our attention, but rather guides it toward the human voice and its perpetual struggle into language. We're open to both formal and experimental fiction, nonfiction, and poetry; we're also open to work that defies classification. Above all, we look for work in which we can feel writers surprising themselves. Work published in *Arts & Letters Journal* has received the Pushcart Prize. Estab. 1999. Pays on publication. No kill fee. Accepts simultaneous submissions. Responds in 2-4 months. Guidelines online.

NONFICTION Submit complete ms via online submissions manager. Length: up to 25 pages typed and double-spaced. **Pays $10/printed page (minimum payment: $50) and 1 contributor's copy.** Pays expenses of writers on assignment.

FICTION Needs short stories. No genre fiction. Submit complete ms via online submissions manager. Length: up to 25 pages typed and double-spaced. **Pays $10/printed page (minimum payment: $50) and 1 contributor's copy.**

POETRY Submit via online submissions manager. Include cover letter. "Poems are screened, discussed by group of readers. If approved by group, poems are submitted to poetry editor for final approval." Has published poetry by Margaret Gibson, Marilyn Nelson, Stuart Lishan, R.T. Smith, Laurie Lamon, and Miller Williams. No light verse. Submit maximum 6 poems. **Pays $10/printed page (minimum payment: $50) and 1 contributor's copy.**

🟢 ART TIMES

arttimesjournal, P.O. Box 730, Mount Marion NY 12456. (845)246-6944. **Fax:** (845)246 6944. **E-mail:** info@arttimesjournal.com. **Website:** www.arttimesjournal.com. **Contact:** Raymond J. Steiner, editor. **80% freelance written.** "*Art Times*, now an online-only publication, covers the arts fields with essays about music, dance, theater, film, and art, and includes short fiction and poetry as well as editorials. Our readers are creatives looking for resources and people who appreciate good writing." Estab. 1984. Byline given. Pays on publication for short fiction, poetry and essays. No kill fee. Publishes within 4 months Accepts queries by mail, e-mail. Responds in 3 months Guidelines online.

NONFICTION Needs essays, opinion. **Buys 12+ mss/year.** Send complete ms via mail or e-mail. Length: up to 1,000 words. **Pays $25.**

COLUMNS Open to linking appropriate blogs to art-timesjournal.com **Buys 12 mss/year.** Columns appropriate to Creatives eg: tips for social media, marketing

yourself as a creative, general essays about the arts. **Pays $25.**

FICTION Contact: Raymond J. Steiner. Looking for quality short fiction that aspires to be literary. Publishes up to 4 stories a month. Needs adventure, ethnic, fantasy, historical, humorous, mainstream, science fiction, contemporary. Nothing violent, sexist, erotic, juvenile, racist, romantic, political, off-beat, or related to sports or juvenile fiction. **Buys 25 mss/year.** Send complete ms. Length: up to 1,000 words. **Pays $25.**

POETRY Needs avant-garde, free verse, haiku, light verse, traditional. Send poems by mail or e-mail. Wants "poetry that strives to express genuine observation in unique language. All topics, all forms. We prefer well-crafted 'literary' poems. No excessively sentimental poetry." Publishes 2-3 poems each month. Nothing violent, sexist, erotic, juvenile, racist, romantic, political, off-beat, or related to sports or juvenile fiction. Buys 30-35 poems/year. Submit maximum 6 poems. Length: up to 20 lines. **Pays $5/poem.**

🟢 THE BALTIMORE REVIEW

6514 Maplewood Rd., Baltimore MD 21212. **E-mail:** editor@baltimorereview.org. **Website:** www.baltimorereview.org. **Contact:** Barbara Westwood Diehl, senior editor. **100% freelance written.** *The Baltimore Review* publishes poetry, fiction, and creative nonfiction from Baltimore and beyond. Submission periods are August 1 November 30 and February 1-May 31. Estab. 1996. Byline given. Pays on publication. No kill fee. Publishes ms 2-6 months after acceptance. Accepts simultaneous submissions. Responds in 4 months or less. Guidelines online.

NONFICTION creative nonfiction. Publishes 2-6 mss per online issue. Length: up to 5,000 words. **Pays $40.**

FICTION Needs short stories, literary fiction. Send complete ms using online submission form. Publishes 16-20 mss (combination of poetry, fiction, and creative nonfiction) per online issue. Work published online is also published in annual anthology. Length: 100-5,000 words. **Pays $40.**

POETRY Needs avant-garde, free verse, traditional. Submit 1-3 poems. See editor preferences on submission guidelines on website. **Pays $40.**

TIPS "See editor preferences on staff page of website."

⊕ $ BEATDOM

Beatdom Books, 426 Blowrie St., Dundee Scotland DD3 1AH United Kingdom. **E-mail:** editor@beatdom.com. **Website:** www.beatdom.com. **Contact:** David Wills, editor. **75% freelance written.** Beatdom is a Beat Generation-themed literary journal that publishes essays, short stories, and poems related to the Beats. "We publish studies of Beat texts, figures, and legends; we look at writers and movements related to the Beats; we support writers of the present who take their influence from the Beats." Estab. 2007. Circ. 1,000. Byline given. Pays on publication. No kill fee. Publishes ms 6 months after acceptance. Accepts queries by e-mail. Accepts simultaneous submissions.

NONFICTION Needs essays, interview, profile, reviews. **Buys 10 mss/year.** Query. Length: 1,000-5,000 words. **Pays $50.** Pays expenses of writers on assignment.

FICTION Submit complete ms via e-mail. Length: up to 5,000 words. **Pays $50.**

POETRY "Poems should ideally fit the theme of the issue, or display some sort of connection to the Beat Generation."

$ BIG PULP

Exter Press, P.O. Box 92, Cumberland MD 21501. **E-mail:** editors@bigpulp.com. **Website:** www.bigpulp.com. **Contact:** Bill Olver, editor. Quarterly literary magazine. Submissions accepted by e-mail only. *Big Pulp* defines "pulp fiction" very broadly: It's lively, challenging, thought provoking, thrilling, and fun, regardless of how many or how few genre elements are packed in. It doesn't subscribe to the theory that genre fiction is disposable; a great deal of literary fiction could easily fall under one of their general categories. Places a higher value on character and story than genre elements. Estab. 2008. Byline given. Pays on publication. Offers 100% kill fee. Publishes ms 1 year after acceptance. Accepts queries by e-mail. Accepts simultaneous submissions. Responds in 2 months to mss. Sample copy: $10; excerpts available online at no cost. Guidelines online.

FICTION Needs adventure, fantasy, horror, mystery, romance, science fiction, suspense, western, superhero. Does not want generic slice-of-life, memoirs, inspirational, political, pastoral odes. **Buys 70 mss/year.** Submit complete ms. Length: up to 2,500 words. **Pays $5-25.**

POETRY Needs avant-garde, free verse, haiku, light verse, traditional. All types of poetry are considered, but poems should have a genre connection. Buys 20 poems/year. Submit maximum 3 poems. **Pays $5/poem.**

TIPS "We like to be surprised, and we have few boundaries. Fantasy writers may focus on the mundane aspects of a fantastical creature's life or the magic that can happen in everyday life. Romances do not have to be requited or have happy endings, and the object of one's obsession may not be a person. Mysteries need not focus on 'whodunit?' We're always interested in science or speculative fiction focusing on societal issues, but writers should avoid being partisan or shrill. We also like fiction that crosses genre; for example, a science fiction romance or a fantasy crime story. We have an online archive for fiction and poetry and encourage writers to check it out. That said, *Big Pulp* has a strong editorial bias in favor of stories with monkeys. Especially talking monkeys."

$ BOMB MAGAZINE

80 Hanson Place, Ste. 703, Brooklyn NY 11217. (718)636-9100. **Fax:** (718)636-9200. **E-mail:** saul@bombsite.com. **Website:** www.bombmagazine.com. **Contact:** Saul Anton, senior editor. Quarterly magazine providing interviews between artists, writers, musicians, directors, and actors. "Written, edited, and produced by industry professionals and funded by those interested in the arts, *BOMB Magazine* publishes work which is unconventional and contains an edge, whether it be in style or subject matter." Estab. 1981. Circ. 36,000. Pays on publication. No kill fee. Publishes ms an average of 3-6 months after acceptance. Editorial lead time 3-4 months. Accepts queries by online submission form. Accepts simultaneous submissions. Responds in 3-5 months to mss. Sample copy: $10. Guidelines by e-mail.

FICTION experimental, novel concepts, contemporary. No genre fiction: romance, science fiction, horror, western. *BOMB Magazine* accepts unsolicited poetry and prose submissions for our literary supplement *First Proof* by online submission manager in January and August. Submissions sent outside these months will not be read. Submit complete ms via online submission manager. E-mailed submissions will not be considered. Length: up to 25 pages. **Pays $100 and contributor's copies.**

POETRY *BOMB Magazine* accepts unsolicited poetry and prose submissions for our literary supplement *First Proof* by online submission manager in January and August. Submissions sent outside these months will not be read. Submit 4-6 poems via online submission manager. E-mailed submissions will not be considered. **Pays $100 and contributor's copies.**

TIPS "Mss should be typed, double-spaced, and proofread, and should be final drafts. Purchase a sample issue before submitting work."

$$ BOULEVARD

Opojaz, Inc., 6614 Clayton Rd., Box 325, Richmond Heights MO 63117. **E-mail:** editors@boulevardmagazine.org. **Website:** www.boulevardmagazine.org; boulevard.submittable.com/submit. Managing Editor: Dusty Freund. **Contact:** Jessica Rogen, editor. **100% freelance written.** "*Boulevard* is a diverse literary magazine presenting original creative work by well-known authors as well as by writers of exciting promise." Triannual magazine featuring fiction, poetry, and essays. Sometimes comments on rejected mss. *Boulevard* has been called "one of the half-dozen best literary journals" by Poet Laureate Daniel Hoffman in *The Philadelphia Inquirer.* "We strive to publish the finest in poetry, fiction, and nonfiction. We frequently publish writers with previous credits, and we are very interested in publishing less experienced or unpublished writers with exceptional promise. We've published everything from John Ashbery to Donald Hall to a wide variety of styles from new or lesser known poets. We're eclectic. We are interested in original, moving poetry written from the head as well as the heart. It can be about any topic." *Boulevard* is 175-250 pages, digest-sized, flat-spined, with glossy card cover. Receives over 600 unsolicited mss/month. Accepts about 10 mss/issue. Publishes 10 new writers/year. Recently published work by Joyce Carol Oates, Floyd Skloot, John Barth, Stephen Dixon, David Guterson, Albert Goldbarth, Molly Peacock, Bob Hicok, Alice Friman, Dick Allen, and Tom Disch. Estab. 1985. Circ. 11,000. Byline given. Pays on publication. Offers no kill fee. Publishes ms an average of 9 months after acceptance. Accepts queries by mail, e-mail, online submission form. Accepts simultaneous submissions. Responds in 2 weeks to queries; 4-5 months to mss. Sample copy: $10. Subscription: $16 for 3 issues, $29 for 6 issues, $42 for 9 issues. Foreign subscribers, please add $10. Make checks payable to Opojaz, Inc. Subscriptions are available online at www.boulevardmagazine.org/subscribe.html. Guidelines online.

NONFICTION Needs book excerpts, essays, interview, opinion, photo feature. **Buys 10 mss/year.** Submit by mail or Submittable. Accepts multiple submissions. Does not accept mss May 1-October 1. Include SASE for reply. Length: up to 8,000 words. **Pays $100-300.**

FICTION Submit by mail or Submittable. Accepts multiple submissions. Does not accept mss May 1-October 1. SASE for reply. Needs ethnic, experimental, mainstream, novel excerpts, short stories, slice-of-life vignettes. "We do not want erotica, science fiction, romance, western, horror, or children's stories." **Buys 20 mss/year.** Length: up to 8,000 words. **Pays $50-500 (sometimes higher) for accepted work.**

POETRY Needs avant-garde, free verse, haiku, traditional. Submit by mail or Submittable. Accepts multiple submissions. Does not accept poems May 1-October 1. SASE for reply. Does not consider book reviews. "Do not send us light verse." Does not want "poetry that is uninspired, formulaic, self-conscious, unoriginal, insipid." Buys 80 poems/year. Submit maximum 5 poems. Length: up to 200 lines/poem. **Pays $25-250.**

TIPS "Read the magazine first. The work *Boulevard* publishes is generally recognized as among the finest in the country. We continue to seek more good literary or cultural essays. Send only your best work."

[C] $$ BRICK

Brick, P.O. Box 609, Station P, Toronto ON M5S 2Y4 Canada. **E-mail:** info@brickmag.com. **Website:** www.brickmag.com. **Contact:** Liz Johnston, managing editor. **90% freelance written.** Semiannual magazine covering literature and the arts. "We publish literary nonfiction of a very high quality on a range of arts and culture subjects." Estab. 1977. Circ. 3,000. Byline given. Pays on publication. No kill fee. Publishes ms 3-5 months after acceptance. Editorial lead time 5 months. Accepts simultaneous submissions. Responds in 6 months to mss. Sample copy: $16 plus shipping. Guidelines online.

NONFICTION Needs essays, interview, opinion, travel. No fiction, poetry, personal memoir, or art. **Buys 30-40 mss/year.** Send complete ms. Length: 1,000-5,000 words. **Pays $75-500 (Canadian).** Pays expenses of writers on assignment.

PHOTOS State availability. Reviews transparencies, prints, TIFF/JPEG files. Offers $25-50/photo. Buys one-time rights.

TIPS "*Brick* is interested in polished work by writers who are widely read and in touch with contemporary culture. The magazine is serious but not fusty. We like to feel the writer's personality in the piece, too."

$ BURNSIDE REVIEW

P.O. Box 1782, Portland OR 97207. **Website:** www.burnsidereview.org. **Contact:** Sid Miller, founder and editor; Dan Kaplan, managing editor. *Burnside Review*, published every 9 months, prints "the best poetry and short fiction we can get our hands on. We tend to publish writing that finds beauty in truly unexpected places; that combines urban and natural imagery; that breaks the heart." Estab. 2004. Pays on publication. Publishes ms 9 months after acceptance. Submit seasonal material 3-6 months in advance. Accepts queries by online submission form. Accepts simultaneous submissions. Responds in 1-6 months. Single copy: $8; subscription: $13.

FICTION "We like bright, engaging fiction that works to surprise and captivate us." Needs experimental, short stories. Submit complete ms via online submissions manager. Length: up to 5,000 words. **Pays $25 and 1 contributor's copy.**

POETRY Needs avant-garde, free verse, traditional. Open to all forms. Translations are encouraged. "We like lyric. We like narrative. We like when the two merge. We like whiskey. We like hourglass figures. We like to be surprised. Surprise us." Has published poetry by Linda Bierds, Dorianne Laux, Ed Skoog, Campbell McGrath, Paul Guest, and Larissa Szporluk. Reads submissions year round. "Editors read all work submitted." Seldom comments on rejected work. Submit 3-5 poems via online submissions manager. **Pays $25 and 1 contributor's copy.**

$ THE CAFE IRREAL

E-mail: editors@cafeirreal.com. **Website:** www.cafeirreal.com. **Contact:** G.S. Evans and Alice Whittenburg, co-editors. **90% freelance written.** Quarterly webzine focusing on short stories and short shorts of an irreal nature. Also publishes literary essays, literary criticism. "Our audience is composed of people who read or write literary fiction with fantastic themes, similar to the work of Franz Kafka, Kobo Abe, or Ana María Shua. This is a type of fiction (irreal) that has difficulty finding its way into print in the English-speaking world and defies many of the conventions of American literature especially. As a result, ours is a fairly specialized literary publication, and we would strongly recommend that prospective writers look at our current issue and guidelines carefully." Recently published work by Jiří Kratochvil, Vanessa Gebbie, Paul Blaney, Venita Blackburn, Ian Seed, BE Turner, Hernán Ortiz. Estab. 1998. Circ. 10,000. Byline given. Pays on publication for first electronic rights. Sends galleys to author. No kill fee. Accepts queries by e-mail. Responds in 2-4 months. Sometimes comments on rejected mss. Sample copy online. Guidelines online.

REPRINTS "We sometimes publish fiction that has previously appeared in print but not online."

FICTION Accepts submissions by e-mail. No attachments; include submission in body of e-mail. Include estimated word count. Accepts 6-8 mss/issue; 24-32 mss/year. Needs experimental, fantasy, science fiction. No horror or "slice-of-life" stories; no genre or mainstream science fiction or fantasy. Length: up to 2,000 words. **Pays 1¢/word, $2 minimum.**

TIPS "Forget formulas. Write about what you don't know, take me places I couldn't possibly go, don't try to make me care about the characters. Read short fiction by writers such as Franz Kafka, Jorge Luis Borges, Donald Barthelme, Leonora Carrington, Magnus Mills, and Stanislaw Lem. Also read our website and guidelines."

🍁 $ THE CAPILANO REVIEW

102-281 Industrial Ave., Vancouver BC V6A 2P2 Canada. **E-mail:** contact@thecapilanoreview.ca. **E-mail:** online through submittable. **Website:** www.thecapilanoreview.com. **Contact:** Matea Kulic, managing editor. **100% freelance written.** Triannual visual and literary arts magazine that "publishes only what the editors consider to be the very best fiction, poetry, drama, or visual art being produced. *TCR* editors are interested in fresh, original work that stimulates and challenges readers. Over the years, the magazine has developed a reputation for pushing beyond the boundaries of traditional art and writing. We are interested in work that is new in concept and in execution. We no longer accept submissions by mail. Please review our submission guidelines on our website and submit online through submittable." Estab. 1972. Circ. 800. Byline given. Pays on publication. Publishes work within 1 year after acceptance. Accepts queries by online submission form. Accepts simultaneous submissions. Responds in 4-6 months. Sample copy: $10 (outside of Canada, USD). Guidelines online.

NONFICTION Needs essays, interview, reviews. Pays expenses of writers on assignment.

PHOTOS Pays $50 for cover and $50/page to maximum of $200 Canadian. Additional payment for electronic rights; negotiable. Pays on publication. Credit line given. Buys first North American serial rights only.

FICTION Needs experimental, literary. No traditional, conventional fiction. Wants to see more innovative, genre-blurring work. **Buys 10-15 mss/year.** Length: up to 5,000 words. **Pays $50-150.**

POETRY Needs Experimental poetry. Submit up to 8 pages of poetry. Buys 40 poems/year. Submit maximum 8 poems. **Pays $50-150.**

⊖⊖ CHICKEN SOUP FOR THE SOUL PUBLISHING, LLC

Chicken Soup for the Soul Publishing, LLC, P.O. Box 700, Cos Cob CT 06807. **E-mail:** webmaster@chickensoupforthesoul.com (for all inquires). **Website:** www.chickensoup.com. **95% freelance written.** Paperback with 12 publications/year featuring inspirational, heartwarming, uplifting short stories. Estab. 1993. Circ. Over 200 titles; 100 million books in print. Byline given. Pays on publication. No kill fee. Accepts queries by online submission form. Accepts simultaneous submissions. Responds upon consideration. Guidelines available online.

○ "Stories must be written in the first person."

NONFICTION No sermon, essay, eulogy, term paper, journal entry, political, or controversial issues. **Buys 1,000 mss/year.** Send complete ms. Length: 300-1,200 words. **Pays $200.**

POETRY Needs traditional. No controversial poetry.

TIPS "We no longer accept submissions by mail or fax. Stories and poems can only be submitted on our website. Select the 'Submit Your Story' tab on the left toolbar. The submission form can be found there."

⊖ THE CINCINNATI REVIEW

P.O. Box 210069, Cincinnati OH 45221-0069. (513)556-3954. **Fax:** (513)556-3959. **E-mail:** editors@cincinnatireview.com. **Website:** www.cincinnatireview.com. **Contact:** Michael Griffith, fiction editor; Don Bogen, poetry editor; Kristen Iversen, nonfiction editor. **100% freelance written.** Semiannual magazine containing new literary fiction, creative nonfiction, poetry, book reviews, essays, and interviews. A journal devoted to publishing the best new literary fiction, creative nonfiction, and poetry, as well as book reviews, essays, and interviews. Estab. 2003. Byline given. Pays on publication. No kill fee. Publishes ms an average of 6 months after acceptance. Accepts queries by online submission form. Accepts simultaneous submissions. Responds in 4 months to mss. Always sends prepublication galleys. Sample copy: $7 (back issue). Single copy: $9 (current issue). Subscription: $15. Guidelines available on website.

NONFICTION Submit complete ms via online submissions manager only. Length: up to 40 double-spaced pages. **Pays $25/page.**

FICTION Needs short stories. Does not want genre fiction. **Buys 13 mss/year.** Submit complete ms via online submissions manager only. Length: up to 40 double-spaced pages. **Pays $25/page.**

POETRY Needs avant-garde, free verse, traditional. Submit up to 10 pages of poetry at a time via submission manager only. Buys 120 poems/year. **Pays $30/page.**

TIPS "Each issue includes a translation feature. For more information on translations, please see our website."

⊖⊖ THE CLAREMONT REVIEW

1581-H Hillside Ave., Suite 101, Victoria BC V8T 2C1 Canada. **E-mail:** claremontreview@gmail.com. **Website:** www.theclaremontreview.ca. **Contact:** Ali Blythe, Editor-in-chief. The editors of *The Claremont Review* publish the best poetry, short stories, visual art and photography by youth ages 13-19, from anywhere in the English-speaking world. "We publish work in many styles that range from traditional to modern. We prefer edgy pieces that take chances, show your commitment to craft, explore real characters, and reveal authentic emotion. Read the samples in our resources or in past issues for a clearer understanding of what we accept. We strongly encourage readers to subscribe to our magazine, to read, connect with and support youth writing from all over the world." Estab. 1992. Pays on publication. Accepts queries by online submission form. Accepts simultaneous submissions. Responds in 3-6 months. Guidelines available.

FICTION Needs short stories. Only accepts submissions from writers ages 13-19. Length: up to 2,000 words. **Pays $10.**

POETRY Rarely publishes rhyming poetry. Only accepts submissions from writers ages 13-19. Submit maximum 3 poems. **Pays $10.**

TIPS "We love: Wild minds like yours.don't be afraid to try something new with form or thinking. Images, metaphor, leaps, research, specificity, images, sensory details, images. Writing that reveals YOUR artistic spirit.are you formal? Tricky? Elusive? Allusive? Quiet? Bold? Clean writing: read your piece word by word, then line by line, and fix spelling or grammatical errors. Entries that meet all our guidelines, read them."

$ CLOUDBANK

Journal of Contemporary Writing, P.O. Box 610, Corvallis OR 97339. (541)752-0075 or (877)782-6762. **E-mail:** cloudbank@cloudbankbooks.com. **Website:** www.cloudbankbooks.com. **Contact:** Michael Malan, editor. Journal of contemporary writing open to range of styles; never publishes theme issues. *Cloudbank* publishes poetry, short prose, and book reviews. Estab. 2009. Accepts queries by mail. Accepts simultaneous submissions. Responds in 4 months. Single copy: $8. Subscription: $15. Make checks payable to *Cloudbank*. Guidelines available in magazine, for SASE, by e-mail, or on website.

FICTION flash fiction. Submit flash fiction by mail with SASE. Length: up to 500 words. **Pays $200 prize for 1 poem or flash fiction piece per issue.**

POETRY Submit up to 5 poems by mail with SASE. Cover letter is preferred. Does not accept fax, e-mail, or disk submissions from U.S.; overseas e-mail submissions accepted. Reads year round. Rarely sends pre-publication galleys. Receives 1,600 poems/year; accepts about 8%. Has published poetry by Dennis Schmitz, Christopher Buckley, Stuart Friebert, Dore Kiesselbach, Karen Holmberg, and Vern Rutsala. Length: up to 150 lines/submission. **Pays $200 prize for 1 poem or flash fiction piece per issue.**

TIPS "Please consider reading a copy of *Cloudbank* before submitting."

$ COLORADO REVIEW

Center for Literary Publishing, Colorado State University, 9105 Campus Delivery, Fort Collins CO 80523. (970)491-5449. **E-mail:** creview@colostate.edu. **Website:** coloradoreview.colostate.edu. **Contact:** Stephanie G'Schwind, editor-in-chief and nonfiction editor; Steven Schwartz, fiction editor; Don Revell, Sasha Steensen, and Matthew Cooperman, poetry editors; Harrison Candelaria Fletcher, nonfiction editor; Dan Beachy-Quick, poetry book review editor; Jennifer Wisner Kelly, fiction and nonfiction book review editor. Literary magazine published 3 times/year. Work published in *Colorado Review* has been included in *Best American Essays, Best American Short Stories, Best American Poetry, Best New American Voices, Best Travel Writing, Best Food Writing*, and the *Pushcart Prize Anthology*. Estab. 1956. Circ. 1,000. Byline given. Pays on publication. No kill fee. Publishes ms an average of 6 months after acceptance. Editorial lead time 1 year. Accepts simultaneous submissions. Responds in 2 months to mss. Sample copy: $10. Guidelines online.

NONFICTION Needs essays, memoir, personal experience. **Buys 6-9 mss/year.** Mss for creative nonfiction are read year round. Send no more than 1 submission at a time. Length: up to 10,000 words. **Pays $200.** Pays expenses of writers on assignment.

FICTION Needs experimental, short stories, literary short fiction. No genre fiction. **Buys 12 mss/year.** Send complete ms. Fiction mss are read August 1-April 30. Mss received May 1-July 31 will be returned unread. Send no more than 1 story at a time. Length: up to 10,000 words. **Pays $200.**

POETRY Considers poetry of any style. Poetry mss are read August 1-April 30. Mss received May 1-July 31 will be returned unread. Has published poetry by Sherman Alexie, Laynie Browne, John Gallaher, Mathias Svalina, Craig Morgan Teicher, Pam Rehm, Elizabeth Robinson, Elizabeth Willis, and Rosmarie Waldrop. Buys 60-100 poems/year. Submit maximum 5 poems. **Pays $30 minimum or $10/page for poetry.**

$$ CONFRONTATION

English Department, LIU Post, Brookville NY 11548. **E-mail:** confrontationmag@gmail.com. **Website:** www.confrontationmagazine.org. **Contact:** Jonna G. Semeiks, editor in chief; Belinda Kremer, poetry editor; Terry Kattleman, publicity director/production editor. **75% freelance written.** "*Confrontation* has been in continuous publication since 1968. Our taste and our magazine is eclectic, but we always look for excellence in style, an important theme, a memorable voice. We enjoy discovering and fostering new talent. Each issue contains work by both well-established and new writers. We read August 16-April 15. Do not send mss or e-mail submissions between April 16 and August 15." Estab. 1968. Circ. 2,000. Byline given. Pays on publication. Offers kill fee. Publishes work in the first or second issue after acceptance. Accepts queries by mail, e-mail. Accepts simultaneous submissions. Responds in 10 weeks to mss. "We prefer single submissions. Clear copy. **No e-mail submissions unless writer resides outside the U.S.** Mail submissions with a SASE."

NONFICTION Needs essays, personal experience. Special issues: "We publish personal, cultural, political, and other kinds of essays as well as self-contained sections of memoirs." **Buys 5-10 mss/year.** Send complete ms. Length: 1,500-5,000 words. **Pays $100-150; more for commissioned work.**

FICTION "We judge on quality of writing and thought or imagination, so we will accept genre fiction. However, it must have literary merit or must transcend or challenge genre." experimental as well as more traditional fiction, self-contained novel excerpts, slice-of-life vignettes, lyrical or philosophical fiction. No "proselytizing" literature or conventional genre fiction. **Buys 10-15 mss/year.** Send complete ms. Length: up to 7,200 words. **Pays $175-250; more for commissioned work.**

POETRY Needs avant-garde or experimental as well as traditional poems (and forms), lyric poems, dramatic monologues, satiric or philosophical poems. In short, a wide range of verse. *"Confrontation* is interested in all poetic forms. Our only criterion is high literary merit. We think of our audience as an educated, lay group of intelligent readers." Has published poetry by David Ray, T. Alan Broughton, David Ignatow, Philip Appleman, Jane Mayhall, and Joseph Brodsky. Submit no more than 12 pages at a time (up to 6 poems). *Confrontation* also offers the annual Confrontation Poetry Prize. No sentimental verse. No previously published poems. Buys 20 poems/year. Length: up to 2 pages. **Pays $75-100; more for commissioned work.**

TIPS "We look for literary merit. Keep honing your skills, and keep trying."

⊙⊜ CONTEMPORARY VERSE 2

Contemporary Verse 2, Inc., 207-100 Arthur St., Winnipeg MB R3B 1H3 Canada. (204)949-1365. **Fax:** (204)942-5754. **E-mail:** submissions@contemporaryverse2.ca. **Website:** www.contemporaryverse2.ca. **75% freelance written.** Quarterly magazine covering poetry and critical writing about poetry. *CV2* publishes poetry of demonstrable quality as well as critical writing in the form of interviews, essays, articles, and reviews. With the critical writing we tend to create a discussion of poetry which will interest a broad range of readers, including those who might be skeptical about the value of poetry. Reading period: September 1-May 31. Estab. 1975. Circ. 600. Byline given. Pays on publication. Offers 50% kill fee. Editorial lead time 3-6 months. Submit seasonal material 3-6 months in advance. Accepts queries by online submission form. Accepts simultaneous submissions. Responds in 2-3 weeks to queries; 3-8 months to mss. Guidelines online.

NONFICTION Needs essays, interview, book reviews. No content that is not about poetry. **Buys 10-30 mss/year.** Query. Length: 800-3,000 words. **Pays $40-130 for assigned articles.**

POETRY Needs avant-garde, free verse. No rhyming verse, traditionally inspirational. Buys 110-120 poems/year. Submit maximum 6 poems. **Pays $20/poem.**

⊜ CONTRARY

The Journal of Unpopular Discontent, Chicago IL **E-mail:** chicago@contrarymagazine.com. **Website:** www.contrarymagazine.com. **Contact:** Jeff McMahon, editor; Frances Badgett, fiction editor; Shaindel Beers, poetry editor. **100% freelance written.** *Contrary* publishes fiction, poetry, and literary commentary, and prefers work that combines the virtues of all those categories. Founded at the University of Chicago, it now operates independently and not for profit on the South Side of Chicago. Quarterly. Member CLMP. "We like work that is not only contrary in content but contrary in its evasion of the expectations established by its genre. Our fiction defies traditional story form. For example, a story may bring us to closure without ever delivering an ending. We don't insist on the ending, but we do insist on the closure. And we value fiction as poetic as any poem." Estab. 2003. Circ. 38,000. Byline given. Pays on publication and receipt of invoice. Publishes ms 90 days after acceptance. Editorial lead time 3 months. Accepts queries by online submission form. Accepts simultaneous submissions. Responds in 2 weeks to queries; 3 months to mss. Rarely comments on/critiques rejected mss. Guidelines available online.

NONFICTION Needs book excerpts, essays, general interest, humor, memoir, opinion, personal experience, reviews, lyrical, literary nonfiction. Does not publish expository or argumentative nonfiction. **Buys 4-6 mss/year.** Accepts submissions through website only. Include estimated word count, brief bio, list of publications.

FICTION Receives 650 mss/month. Accepts 6 mss/issue; 24 mss/year. Publishes 14 new writers/year. Has published Sherman Alexie, Andrew Coburn, Amy Reed, Clare Kirwan, Stephanie Johnson, Laurence Davies, and Edward McWhinney. Needs experimental, mainstream, religious, short stories, slice-of-life vignettes, literary. **Buys 8-12 mss/year.** Accepts submissions through website only. Include estimated word count, brief bio, list of publications. Length: up to 2,000 words. Average length: 750 words. Publishes short shorts. Average length of short shorts: 750 words. **Pays $20-60.**

POETRY Accepts submissions through website only. Include estimated word count, brief bio, list of publications. Often comments on rejected poems. Submit maximum 3 poems. **Pays $20 per byline, $60 for featured work.**

TIPS "Beautiful writing catches our eye first. If we realize we're in the presence of unanticipated meaning, that's what clinches the deal. Also, we're not fond of expository fiction. We prefer to be seduced by beauty, profundity, and mystery than to be presented with the obvious. We look for fiction that entrances, that stays the reader's finger above the mouse button. That is, in part, why we favor microfiction, flash fiction, and short shorts. Also, we hope writers will remember that most editors are looking for very particular species of work. We try to describe our particular species in our mission statement and our submission guidelines, but those descriptions don't always convey nuance. That's why many editors urge writers to read the publication itself, in the hope that they will intuit an understanding of its particularities. If you happen to write that particular species of work we favor, your submission may find a happy home with us. If you don't, it does not necessarily reflect on your quality or your ability. It usually just means that your work has a happier home somewhere else."

$ COPPER NICKEL

English Department, Campus Box 175, CU Denver, P.O. Box 173364, Denver CO 80217. **E-mail:** wayne.miller@ucdenver.edu. **Website:** copper-nickel.org. **Contact:** Wayne Miller, editor/managing editor; Brian Barker and Nicky Beer, poetry editors; Joanna Luloff, fiction and nonfiction editor; Teague Bohlen, fiction editor. *Copper Nickel*—the national literary journal housed at the University of Colorado Denver—was founded by poet Jake Adam York in 2002. Work published in *Copper Nickel* has appeared in *Best American Poetry, Best American Short Stories*, and *Pushcart Prize* anthologies. Contributors to *Copper Nickel* have received numerous honors for their work, including the National Book Critics Circle Award; the Kingsley Tufts Poetry Award; the American, California, Colorado, Minnesota, and Washington State Book Awards; the Georg Büchner Prize; the T.S. Eliot and Forward Poetry Prizes; the Anisfield-Wolf Book Award; the Whiting Writers Award; the Alice Fay Di Castagnola Award; the Lambda Literary Award; and fellowships from the National Endowment for the Arts; the Guggenheim, Ingram Merrill, Witter Bynner, Soros, Rona Jaffe, Bush, and Jerome Foundations; the Bunting Institute; Cave Canem; and the American Academy in Rome. Submission period: August 15-April 15. Estab. 2002. Pays on publication. Accepts queries by online submission form. Accepts simultaneous submissions. Tries to respond in 2 months. Guidelines online.

NONFICTION Needs essays. Submit 1 essay at a time through online submissions manager. **Pays $30/printed page, 2 contributor's copies, and a one-year subscription.**

FICTION Submit 1 story or 3 pieces of flash fiction at a time through online submissions manager. **Pays $30/printed page, 2 contributor's copies, and a one-year subscription.**

POETRY Submit 4-6 poems through online submissions manager. **Pays $30/printed page, 2 contributor's copies, and a one-year subscription.**

$ CRAZYHORSE

College of Charleston, Department of English, 66 George St., Charleston SC 29424. (843)953-4470. **E-mail:** crazyhorse@cofc.edu. **Website:** crazyhorse.cofc.edu. **Contact:** Jonathan Bohr Heinen, managing editor; Emily Rosko, poetry editor; Anthony Varallo, fiction editor; Bret Lott, nonfiction editor. "We like to print a mix of writing regardless of its form, genre, school, or politics. We're especially on the lookout for original writing that doesn't fit the categories and that engages in the work of honest communication." Estab. 1960. Circ. 1,500. No kill fee. Publishes ms an average of 6-12 months after acceptance. Accepts queries by online submission form. Accepts simultaneous submissions. Responds in 1 week to queries; 3-4 months to mss. Sample copy: $5. Guidelines online.

NONFICTION "*Crazyhorse* publishes 4-6 stories essays year, so we call for the very best writing, period. We believe literary nonfiction can take any form, from the letter to the list, from the biography to the memoir, from the journal to the obituary. All we call for is precision of word and vision, and that the truth of the matter be the flag of the day." Submit 1 essay through online submissions manager. Length: 2,500-8,500 words. **Pays $20/page ($200 maximum) and 2 contributor's copies.**

FICTION "We are open to all narrative styles and forms, and are always on the lookout for something we haven't seen before. Send a story we won't be able to forget." Submit 1 story through online submissions manager. **Buys 12-15 mss/year.** Length: 2,500-8,500 words. **Pays $20/page ($200 maximum) and 2 contributor's copies.**

POETRY "*Crazyhorse* aims to publish work that reflects the multiple poetries of the 21st century. While our taste represents a wide range of aesthetics, from poets at all stages of their writing careers, we read with a discerning eye for poems that demonstrate a rhetorical and formal intelligence—that is, poems that know why they are written in the manner that they are. We seek poems that exhibit how content works symbiotically with form, evidenced in an intentional art of the poetic line or in poems that employ or stretch lyric modes. Along with this, poems that capture our attention enact the lyric utterance through musical textures, tone of voice, vivid language, reticence, and skillful syntax. For us, overall, the best poems do not idly tell the reader how to feel or think, they engender feeling and thought in the reader. " Submit 3-5 poems at a time through online submissions manager. Buys 80 poems/year. Submit maximum 5 poems. **Pays $20/page ($200 maximum) and 2 contributor's copies.**

TIPS "Write to explore subjects you care about. The subject should be one in which something is at stake. Before sending, ask, 'What's reckoned with that's important for other people to read?'"

🄢 CREATIVE NONFICTION

Creative Nonfiction Foundation, 5119 Coral Street, Pittsburgh PA 15224. (412) 404-2975. **Fax:** (412) 345-3767. **E-mail:** information@creativenonfiction.org. **Website:** www.creativenonfiction.org. **100% free-**

lance written. Magazine published 4 times/year covering nonfiction—personal essay, memoir, literary journalism. *Creative Nonfiction* is the voice of the genre. It publishes personal essays, memoirs, and literary journalism on a broad range of subjects. Interviews with prominent writers, reviews, and commentary about the genre also appear in its pages. Estab. 1993. Circ. 7,000. Byline given. Pays on publication. No kill fee. Publishes ms an average of 1 year after acceptance. Editorial lead time 6 months. Accepts queries by mail, online submission form. Accepts simultaneous submissions. Responds in 6 months to mss. Sample copy: $10. Guidelines online.

NONFICTION Needs essays, interview, memoir, personal experience, narrative journalism. No poetry or fiction. Send complete ms. Length: up to 4,000 words. **Pays $50, plus $10/page—sometimes more for theme issues.**

COLUMNS Contact: Hattie Fletcher. "Have an idea for a literary timeline? An opinion on essential texts for readers and/or writers? An in-depth, working knowledge of a specific type of nonfiction? Pitch us your ideas." Complete guidelines found at www.creativenonfiction.org/submissions/pitch-us-column.

TIPS "Points to remember when submitting to *Creative Nonfiction*: strong reportage; well-written prose, attentive to language, rich with detail and distinctive voice; an informational quality or 'teaching element'; a compelling, focused, sustained narrative that's well-structured and conveys meaning. Mss will not be accepted via fax or e-mail."

🄢 CRUCIBLE

Barton College, P.O. Box 5000, Wilson NC 27893. **E-mail:** crucible@barton.edu. **Website:** www.barton.edu/crucible. *Crucible*, published annually in the fall, publishes poetry and fiction as part of its Poetry and Fiction Contest run each year. Deadline for submissions is May 1. Estab. 1964. Circ. 500. Accepts queries by e-mail. Accepts simultaneous submissions. Notifies winners by October each year. Sample: $8. Guidelines online.

FICTION Needs ethnic. Submit ms by e-mail. Do not include name on ms. Include separate bio. Length: up to 8,000 words. **Pays $150 for first prize, $100 for second prize, contributor's copies.**

POETRY Submit "poetry that demonstrates originality and integrity of craftsmanship as well as thought. Traditional metrical and rhyming poems are difficult to bring off in modern poetry. The best poetry is written out of deeply felt experience which has been crafted into pleasing form." Wants "free verse with attention paid particularly to image, line, stanza, and voice." Does not want "very long narratives, poetry that is forced." Has published poetry by Robert Grey, R.T. Smith, and Anthony S. Abbott. Submit up to 5 poems by e-mail. Do not include name on poems. Include separate bio. **Pays $150 for first prize, $100 for second prize, contributor's copies.**

$ THE DARK

Prime Books, P.O. Box 1152, Germantown MD 20875. **E-mail:** thedarkmagazine@gmail.com. **Website:** www.thedarkmagazine.com. **Contact:** Silvia Moreno-Garcia and Sean Wallace, editors. **100% freelance written.** Monthly electronic magazine publishing horror and dark fantasy. Stories featured in *The Dark* have appeared in *The Best Horror of the Year*, *The Year's Best Dark Fantasy & Horror: 2016*, and *The Year's Best Weird Fiction*. Estab. 2013. Byline given. Pays on acceptance. No kill fee. Publishes ms an average of 2 months after acceptance. Editorial lead time 1 month. Accepts queries by e-mail. Responds in 1-2 days to mss. Always sends prepublication galleys. Sample: $2.99 (back issue). Guidelines online.

REPRINTS See submission guidelines. Pays 1¢/word.

FICTION Needs fantasy, horror, suspense, strange, magic realism, dark fantasy. "Don't be afraid to experiment or to deviate from the ordinary; be different—try us with fiction that may fall out of 'regular' categories. However, it is also important to understand that despite the name, *The Dark* is not a market for graphic, violent horror." **Buys 24 mss/year.** Send complete ms by e-mail attached in Microsoft Word DOC only. No multiple submissions. Length: 2,000-6,000 words. **Pays 3¢/word.**

TIPS "All fiction must have a dark, surreal, fantastical bend to it. It should be out of the ordinary and/or experimental. Can also be contemporary."

$$ DECEMBER

A Literary Legacy Since 1958, December Publishing, P.O. Box 16130, St. Louis MO 63105-0830. (314)301-9980. **E-mail:** editor@decembermag.org. **Website:** decembermag.org. **Contact:** Gianna Jacobson, editor; Jennifer Goldring, managing editor. Committed to distributing the work of emerging writers and artists, and celebrating more seasoned voices through a semiannual nonprofit literary magazine featuring fiction, poetry, creative nonfiction, and visual art. Estab. 1958. Circ. 1,500. Byline given. Pays on publication. Editorial lead time 5 months. Accepts queries by mail, e-mail. Responds in 2 months to mss. Sample copy: $12. Guidelines online.

NONFICTION Needs essays, general interest, humor, memoir, opinion, personal experience, literary journalism. Not interested in straight journalism (news or features). **Buys 4-10 mss/year.** Submit complete ms. Length: 25-6,000 words. **Pays $10/page (minimum $40; maximum $200).**

PHOTOS Photo and art submissions accepted. Send photos with submission. Reviews PNG/JPEG files. Negotiates payment individually. Purchases one-time rights on photos.

FICTION Needs experimental, humorous, novel excerpts, short stories, slice-of-life vignettes, literary fiction, flash fiction. Does not want genre fiction. **Buys 10-20 mss/year.** Send complete ms. Length: up to 10,000 words. **Pays $10/page (minimum $40; maximum $200).**

POETRY Needs avant-garde, free verse, traditional. Buys 100-150 poems/year. Submit maximum 5 poems. No length requirements. **Pays $10/page (minimum $40; maximum $200).**

$ DUCTS

P.O. Box 3203, Grand Central Station, New York NY 10163. **E-mail:** vents@ducts.org. **Website:** www.ducts.org. **Contact:** Mary Cool, editor in chief; Tim Tomlinson, fiction editor; Lisa Kirchner, memoir editor; Amy Lemmon, poetry editor; Jacqueline Bishop, art editor. *Ducts* is a semiannual webzine of personal stories, fiction, essays, memoirs, poetry, humor, profiles, reviews, and art. "*Ducts* was founded in 1999 with the intent of giving emerging writers a venue to regularly publish their compelling, personal stories. The site has been expanded to include art and creative works of all genres. We believe that these genres must and do overlap. *Ducts* publishes the best, most compelling stories, and we hope to attract readers who are drawn to work that rises above." Estab. 1999. Circ. 12,000. Pays on publication. Accepts queries by e-mail. Accepts simultaneous submissions. Responds in 1-6 months. Guidelines available on website.

NONFICTION Needs essays, humor, memoir, profile. For essays: "We welcome new and established writers, fresh voices, and original perspectives on both common and uncommon topics. We do not publish research articles; however, we consider for publication essays that include research, as long as this research is connected to a personal narrative." For humor: "Both satire and humorous fiction pieces will be accepted." For memoir: "Please read through some issues to get an idea of what we like. Generally speaking, we're looking for a fresh take on personal experiences. We like quirky, edgy, witty, and smart. Also the heartfelt and moving. But mostly we like great writing." Submit by e-mail; see online guidelines for appropriate e-mail address. Length: up to 3,000 words for essays; 900-2,000 words for memoirs; 1,000-4,000 words for humor. **Pays $20.**

FICTION Needs experimental, mainstream, short stories. No novel excerpts. Submit by e-mail to julie@ducts.org. **Pays $20.**

POETRY Needs all forms and types. Submit 3-5 poems to poetry@ducts.org. Reads poetry January 1-August 31. **Pays $20.**

TIPS "We prefer writing that tells a compelling story with a strong narrative drive."

$ ELLIPSIS

Westminster College, 1840 S. 1300 E., Salt Lake City UT 84105. (801)832-2321. **E-mail:** ellipsis@westminstercollege.edu. **Website:** ellipsis.westminstercollege.edu. *Ellipsis*, published annually in April, needs good literary poetry, fiction, essays, plays, and visual art. Estab. 1965. Byline given. Pays on publication. No kill fee. Publishes ms an average of 3 months after acceptance. Accepts queries by online submission form. Accepts simultaneous submissions. Responds in 6 months to mss. Sample copy: $7.50. Guidelines available online.

NONFICTION Needs essays, creative nonfiction. Submit complete ms via online submissions manager. Include cover letter. **Pays $50 and 2 contributor's copies.**

FICTION literary fiction, plays. Submit complete ms via online submissions manager. Include cover letter. Length: up to 6,000 words. **Pays $50 and 2 contributor's copies.**

POETRY Submit poems via online submissions manager. Include cover letter. Has published poetry by Allison Joseph, Molly McQuade, Virgil Suaárez, Maurice Kilwein-Guevara, Richard Cecil, and Ron Carlson. Submit maximum 5 poems. **Pays $10/poem and 2 contributor's copies.**

$ EPOCH

251 Goldwin Smith Hall, Cornell University, Ithaca NY 14853-3201. (607)255-3385. **Website:** www.epoch.cornell.edu. **Contact:** Michael Koch, editor; Heidi E. Marschner, managing editor. **100% freelance written.** Literary magazine published 3 times/year. Looking for well-written literary fiction, poetry, personal essays. Newcomers welcome. Open to mainstream and avant-garde writing. Estab. 1947. Circ. 1,000. Byline given. Pays on publication. Offers 100% kill fee. Publishes ms an average of 6 months after acceptance. Editorial lead time 6 months. Submit seasonal material 8 months in advance. Accepts queries by mail. Responds in 2 weeks to queries; in 6 weeks to mss. Sometimes comments on rejected mss. Sample copy: $5. Guidelines online and for #10 SASE.

NONFICTION Needs essays, interview. No inspirational. **Buys 6-8 mss/year.** Send complete ms. **Pay varies; pays up to $150/unsolicited piece.** Pays expenses of writers on assignment.

PHOTOS Send photos. Reviews contact sheets, transparencies, any size prints. Negotiates payment individually. Buys one-time rights.

FICTION Needs ethnic, experimental, mainstream, literary short stories. No genre fiction. Would like to see more Southern fiction (Southern U.S.). **Buys 25-30 mss/year.** Send complete ms. Considers fiction in all forms, short short to novella length. **Pay varies; pays up to $150/unsolicited piece.**

POETRY Needs avant-garde, free verse, haiku, light verse, traditional. Mss not accompanied by SASE will be discarded unread. Occasionally provides criticism on poems. Considers poetry in all forms. Buys 30-75 poems/year. Submit maximum 5 poems. **Pay varies; pays $50 minimum/poem.**

TIPS "Tell your story, speak your poem, straight from the heart. We are attracted to language and to good writing, but we are most interested in what the good writing leads us to, or where."

☺$$ EVENT

Douglas College, P.O. Box 2503, New Westminster British Columbia V3L 5B2 Canada. (604)527-5293. **Fax:** (604)527-5095. **E-mail:** event@douglascollege.ca. **Website:** www.eventmags.com. **100% freelance written.** Magazine published 3 times/year containing fiction, poetry, creative nonfiction, notes on writing, and reviews. "We are eclectic and always open to content that invites involvement. Generally, we like strong narrative." Estab. 1971. Circ. 1,000. Byline given. Pays on publication. Publishes ms an average of 8 months after acceptance. Accepts queries by mail. Accepts simultaneous submissions. Responds in 1 month to queries. Responds in 6 months to mss. Guidelines available online.

NONFICTION Pays expenses of writers on assignment.

FICTION "We look for readability, style, and writing that invites involvement." Submit maximum 2 stories. contemporary. No technically poor or unoriginal pieces. **Buys 12-15 mss/year.** Send complete ms. Length: 5,000 words maximum. **Pays $25/page up to $500.**

POETRY Needs free verse. "We tend to appreciate the narrative and sometimes the confessional modes." No light verse. Buys 30-40 poems/year. Submit maximum 10 poems. **Pays $25-500.**

TIPS "Write well and read some past issues of *EVENT*."

⊙❸ THE FIDDLEHEAD

Campus House, 11 Garland Crt, PO Box 4400, University of New Brunswick, Fredericton NB E3B 5A3 Canada. **E-mail:** fiddlehd@unb.ca. **Website:** www.thefiddlehead.ca. Ross Leckie, editor; Sue Sinclair, associate editor. **Contact:** Kathryn Taglia, managing editor; Ian LeTourneau, secretary/graphic designer. The artwork on the covers of *The Fiddlehead* is drawn from the museums, galleries, and ateliers of Atlantic Canada and solicited from local artists; it is part of our mandate to showcase art from Atlantic Canada, especially New Brunswick art. *The Fiddlehead* is open to good writing in English or translations into English from all over the world and in a variety of styles, including experimental genres. Our editors are always happy to see new unsolicited works in fiction (including novel excerpts), creative nonfiction, and poetry. We also publish reviews, and occasionally other selected creative work such as excerpts from plays. Work is read on an ongoing basis; the acceptance rate is around 1-2% (we are, however, famous for our rejection notes!). We particularly welcome submissions from Indigenous writers, writers of colour, writers with disabilities, LGBTQQIA+ writers, and writers from other intersectional and under-represented communities. If you are comfortable identifying yourself as one or more of the above, please feel free to mention this in your cover letter. *The Fiddlehead*'s mandate is to publish accomplished poetry, short fiction, and Canadian literature reviews; to discover and promote new writing talent; to represent the Atlantic Canada's lively cultural and literary diversity; and to place the best of new and established Canadian writing in an international context. Estab. 1945. Circ. 1,500. Pays on publication. Every attempt is made to publish work with 1-2 issues (3-8 months) of acceptance. If longer wait, editors will usually try to indicate this before final acceptance. Accepts simultaneous submissions. Responds in 3-9 months to mss. Occasionally comments on rejected mss. Sample copy: $15 U.S. Writer's guidelines online.

NONFICTION Creative nonfiction only. No academic articles, general interest journal articles, interviews, political opinion pieces, new product reviews, reference articles, how-to or technical reviews, etc. Works such as these will simply be discarded without a response. Send SASE with **Canadian** postage for response or self-addressed envelope with cheque/money to cover postage (US or CA dollars). May request e-mail response if you do not want ms. returned. No e-mail or faxed submissions. Simultaneous submissions only if stated on cover letter; must contact immediately if accepted elsewhere. *The Fiddlehead* is phasing in a move to an online submission system in 2018, please check website for details. 6,000 words maximum. 1 creative nonfiction work counts as one submission. **Pays up to $60 (Canadian)/published page plus 2 contributor's copies.**

FICTION A short fiction submission should be one story, double spaced. Unless a story is very, very short (under 1,000 words), please send only one story per submission. Please specify at the top of the first page the number of words in the story submitted. Needs experimental, novel excerpts, short stories, Literary short fiction; literary novel and play excerpts. Experimental fiction welcome. No fiction aimed at children. **Buys Receives 100-150 unsolicited mss/month. publishes 3-12 stories/issue; 15-30 stories/year. Publishes high percentage of new and emerging writers/year. mss/year.** Send SASE with **Canadian** postage for response or self-addressed envelope with cheque/money to cover postage (US or CA dollars). May request email response if you do not want ms. returned. No e-mail or faxed submissions. Simultaneous submissions only if stated on cover letter; must contact immediately if accepted elsewhere. *The Fiddlehead* is phasing in a move to an online submission system in 2018, please check website for details. Length: up to

6,000 words. Rarely publishes flash fiction. **Pays up to $60 (Canadian)/published page and 2 contributor's copies.**

POETRY All types of literary poetry considered, including experimental. Poetry series and longer poems are considered. Send SASE with **Canadian** postage for response or self-addressed envelope with cheque/money to cover postage (US or CA dollars). May request email response if you do not want ms. returned. No e-mail or faxed submissions. Simultaneous submissions only if stated on cover letter; must contact immediately if accepted elsewhere. *The Fiddlehead* is phasing in a move to an online submission system in 2018, please check website for details. No poetry aimed at children, limericks, doggerel. Buys Receives 100-150 unsolicited mss/month. publishes 10-70 poems/issue; 30-100 poems/year. Publishes high percentage of new and emerging writers/year. poems/year. Submit maximum 6 poems per submission; *The Fiddlehead* prefers to accept several poems by the same author; please do not limit your submission to a single poem. poems. **Pays up to $60 (Canadian)/published page and 2 contributor's copies.**

TIPS "If you are serious about submitting to *The Fiddlehead*, you should subscribe or read several issues to get a sense of the journal. Contact us if you would like to order sample back issues."

$ FIELD

Contemporary Poetry & Poetics, Oberlin College Press, 50 N. Professor St., Oberlin OH 44074. (440)775-8408. **Fax:** (440)775-8124. **E-mail:** oc.press@oberlin.edu. **Website:** www.oberlin.edu/ocpress. **Contact:** Marco Wilkinson, managing editor. **60% freelance written.** Biannual magazine of poetry, poetry in translation, and essays on contemporary poetry by poets. *FIELD: Contemporary Poetry and Poetics*, published semiannually in April and October, is a literary journal with "emphasis on poetry, translations, and essays by poets. See electronic submission guidelines." Estab. 1969. Circ. 1,500. Byline given. Pays on publication. Editorial lead time 4 months. Accepts queries by online submission form. Responds in 6-8 weeks to mss. Sample copy: $8. Subscription: $16/year, $28 for 2 years. Guidelines available online and for #10 SASE.

POETRY Needs contemporary, prose poems, free verse, traditional. Submissions are read August 1 through May 31. Submit 2-6 of your best poems through online submissions manager. No e-mail submissions. Has published poetry by Michelle Glazer, Tom Lux, Carl Phillips, Betsy Sholl, Charles Simic, Jean Valentine, and translations by Marilyn Hacker and Stuart Friebert. Buys 120 poems/year. **Pays $15/page and 2 contributor's copies.**

TIPS "Keep trying!"

$ THE FIRST LINE

Blue Cubicle Press, LLC, P.O. Box 250382, Plano TX 75025. (214)455-4324. **E-mail:** info@thefirstline.com. **E-mail:** submission@thefirstline.com. **Website:** www.thefirstline.com. Editor: David LaBounty. **Contact:** Robin LaBounty, manuscript coordinator. **100% freelance written.** "*The First Line* is an exercise in creativity for writers and a chance for readers to see how many different directions we can take when we start from the same place. The purpose of *The First Line* is to jump start the imagination—to help writers break through the block that is the blank page. Each issue contains short stories that stem from a common first line; it also provides a forum for discussing favorite first lines in literature." Estab. 1999. Circ. 2,000. Byline given. Pays on acceptance. Publishes ms 1 month after acceptance. Accepts queries by mail, e-mail. Responds 3 weeks after submission time closes. Sample copy and guidelines available online.

NONFICTION Contact: David LaBounty. Needs essays. **Buys 4 mss/year.** Submit complete ms. Length: 300-600 words. **Pays $25.**

FICTION "We only publish stories that start with the first line provided. We are a collection of tales—of different directions writers can take when they start from the same place." Needs adventure, ethnic, experimental, fantasy, historical, horror, humorous, mainstream, mystery, religious, romance, science fiction, short stories, suspense, western. "Stories that do not start with our first line." **Buys 35-50 mss/year.** Submit complete ms. Length: 300-5,000 words. **Pays $25-50.**

POETRY Buys 1-2 poems/year. Submit maximum 1 poems. **Pays $25.**

TIPS "Don't just write the first story that comes to mind after you read the sentence. If it is obvious, chances are other people are writing about the same thing. Don't try so hard. Be willing to accept criticism."

$ FIVE POINTS

Georgia State University, P.O. Box 3999, Atlanta GA 30302-3999. **Website:** www.fivepoints.gsu.edu. **Contact:** David Bottoms, co-editor. *Five Points*, published 3 times/year, is committed to publishing work that compels the imagination through the use of fresh and convincing language. Estab. 1996. Circ. 2,000. No kill fee. Publishes ms an average of 6 months after acceptance. Accepts queries by online submission form. Responds in 2 months. Sample copy: $10. Guidelines available on website.

NONFICTION Needs essays. Submit through online submissions manager. Include cover letter. Reading period: August 15-December 1 and January 11-March 31. Length: up to 7,500 words. **Pays $15/page ($250 maximum), plus free subscription to magazine and 2 contributor's copies; additional copies $4.**

FICTION Receives 250 unsolicited mss/month. Accepts 4 mss/issue; 15-20 mss/year. Reads fiction August 15-December 1 and January 3-March 31. Publishes 1 new writer/year. Sometimes comments on rejected mss. Sponsors awards/contests. Needs short stories. Submit through online submissions manager. Include cover letter. Length: up to 7,500 words. **Pays $15/page ($250 maximum), plus free subscription to magazine and 2 contributor's copies; additional copies $4.**

POETRY Reads poetry August 15-December 1 and January 3-March 31. Submit through online submissions manager. Include cover letter. Submit maximum 2 poems. Length: up to 50 lines/poem.

TIPS "We place no limitations on style or content. Our only criteria is excellence. If your writing has an original voice, substance, and significance, send it to us. We will publish distinctive, intelligent writing that has something to say and says it in a way that captures and maintains our attention."

$ FLYLEAF

Flyleaf, LLC, 6627 Old Oaks Blvd., Pearland TX 77584. **E-mail:** info@flyleafjournal.com. **E-mail:** submissions@flyleafjournal.com. **Website:** www.flyleaf.journal.com. **Contact:** Matthew Jankiewicz, editor; Parker Stockman, managing editor. *Flyleaf Journal* is a literary periodical that publishes one short story every month. Each story is produced as a two-sided, four-panel gatefold that opens up to reveal a literary and graphic landscape. Each story is integrated with the photographs and illustrations of a graphic collaborator, designed exclusively for that story. Estab. 2014. Byline given. Does not offer payment. Publishes 3-4 months after acceptance. Editorial lead time is 3 months. Submit seasonal material 4 months in advance. Accepts queries by e-mail. Accepts simultaneous submissions. Sample copy available for $2.50. Guideliens available online.

NONFICTION Pays expenses of writers on assignment.

FICTION **Contact:** Matthew Jankiewicz, editor. Needs adventure, experimental, historical, horror, humorous, mainstream, mystery, science fiction, suspense. **Buys 14 mss/year.** Send complete ms. Length: 500-2,000 words. **Pays $50 per story.**

TIPS "We love to read unique and memorable voices in fiction. We want to receive stories written out of love, passion, or anger. If it doesn't move the writer, we will most likely not be moved as well. Our fiction celebrates the short memories in life that make the biggest impact on us."

🍁 $ FREEFALL MAGAZINE

FreeFall Literary Society of Calgary, 460, 1720 29th Ave. SW, Calgary AB T2T 6T7 Canada. **E-mail:** editors@freefallmagazine.ca. **Website:** www.freefallmagazine.ca. **Contact:** Ryan Stromquist, managing editor. **100% freelance written.** Magazine published triannually containing fiction, poetry, creative nonfiction, essays on writing, interviews, and reviews. "We are looking for exquisite writing with a strong narrative." Estab. 1990. Circ. 1,000. Pays on publication. Accepts queries by online submission form. Accepts simultaneous submissions. Guidelines and submission forms on website.

NONFICTION Needs essays, interview, creative nonfiction, writing-related and general-audience topics. Submit complete ms online submissions manager. Length: up to 4,000 words. **Pays $10/printed page in the magazine ($100 maximum) and 1 contributor's copy.**

FICTION Needs short stories, slice-of-life vignettes. Submit via online submissions manager. Length: up to 4,000 words. **Pays $10/printed page in the magazine ($100 maximum) and 1 contributor's copy.**

POETRY Submit 2-5 poems via online submissions manager. Accepts any style of poetry. Length: up to 6 pages. **Pays $25/poem and 1 contributor's copy.**

TIPS "Our mission is to encourage the voices of new, emerging, and experienced Canadian writers and provide a platform for their quality work."

THE GEORGIA REVIEW

The University of Georgia, Main Library, Room 706A, 320 S. Jackson St., Athens GA 30602. (706)542-3481. **Fax:** (706)542-0047. **E-mail:** garev@uga.edu. **Website:** thegeorgiareview.com. **Contact:** Stephen Corey, editor. **99% freelance written.** Quarterly journal. "*The Georgia Review* is a literary quarterly committed to the art of editorial practice. We collaborate equally with established and emerging authors of essays, stories, poems, and reviews in the pursuit of extraordinary works that engage with the evolving concerns and interests of intellectually curious readers from around the world. Our aim in curating content is not only to elevate literature, publishing, and the arts, but also to help facilitate socially conscious partnerships in our surrounding communities." $3 online submission fee waived for subscribers. No fees for manuscripts submitted by post. Reading period: August 15-May 15. Estab. 1947. Circ. 3,500. Byline given. Pays on publication. No kill fee. Publishes ms an average of 6 months after acceptance. Accepts queries by mail. Accepts simultaneous submissions. Responds in 2 weeks to queries; in 2-3 months to mss. Sample copy: $15. Guidelines online.

NONFICTION Needs essays. **Buys 12-20 mss/year.** We generally avoid publishing scholarly articles that are narrow in focus and/or overly burdened with footnotes. *The Georgia Review* is interested in provocative, thesis-oriented essays that can engage both the intelligent general reader and the specialist, as well as those that are experimental or lyrical in approach but accessible to a range of readers. **Pays $50/published page.** Pays expenses of writers on assignment.

PHOTOS Send photos. Reviews 5x7 prints or larger. Offers no additional payment for photos accepted with ms. Buys one-time rights.

FICTION "We seek original, excellent short fiction not bound by type. Ordinarily we do not publish novel excerpts or works translated into English, and we discourage authors from submitting these." Needs short stories. **Buys 12-20 mss/year.** Send complete ms via online submissions manager or postal mail. **Pays $50/published page.**

POETRY We seek original, excellent poetry. Submit 3-5 poems at a time. Buys 60-75 poems/year. **Pays $4/line.**

THE GETTYSBURG REVIEW

Gettysburg College, Gettysburg College, 300 N. Washington St., Gettysburg PA 17325. (717)337-6770. **E-mail:** mdrew@gettysburg.edu. **Website:** www.gettysburgreview.com. **Contact:** Mark Drew, editor; Jess L. Bryant, managing editor. Published quarterly, *The Gettysburg Review* considers unsolicited submissions of poetry, fiction, and essays. "Our concern is quality. Mss submitted here should be extremely well written." Reading period September 1-May 31. Estab. 1988. Circ. 2,000. Byline given. Pays on publication. Publishes ms an average of 6 months after acceptance. Editorial lead time 1 year. Submit seasonal material 9 months in advance. Accepts queries by mail. Accepts simultaneous submissions. Responds in 1 month to queries; in 3-6 months to mss. Sample: $15. Guidelines online.

NONFICTION Needs book excerpts, essays, general interest, humor, memoir, personal experience, reviews, travel. **Buys 20 mss/year.** Send complete ms. Length: up to 25 pages. **Pays $25/printed page, a one-year subscription, and 1 contributor's copy.**

FICTION Wants high-quality literary fiction. Needs experimental, historical, humorous, mainstream, novel excerpts, short stories, slice-of-life vignettes, literary, contemporary. "We require that fiction be intelligent and aesthetically written." No genre fiction. **Buys 20 mss/year.** Send complete ms with SASE. Length: 2,000-7,000 words. **Pays $25/printed page, a one-year subscription, and 1 contributor's copy.**

POETRY Considers "well-written poems of all kinds on all subjects." Has published poetry by Rita Dove, Alice Friman, Philip Schultz, Michelle Boisseau, Bob Hicok, Linda Pastan, and G. C. Waldrep. Does not want sentimental, clichéd verse. Buys 50 poems/year. Submit maximum 5 poems. **Pays $2.50/line, a one-year subscription, and 1 contributor's copy.**

GLIMMER TRAIN STORIES

Glimmer Train Press, Inc., P.O. Box 80430, Portland OR 97280. **Fax:** (503)221-0837. **E-mail:** eds@glimmertrain.org. **Website:** www.glimmertrain.org. **Contact:** Susan Burmeister-Brown. **100% freelance written.** Triannual magazine of literary short fiction. "We are interested in literary short stories, particularly by new and emerging writers." Estab. 1991. Circ. 12,000.

Byline given. Pays on acceptance. Publishes ms an average of 15 months after acceptance. Accepts simultaneous submissions. Responds in 2 months to mss. Sometimes comments on rejected mss. Sample: $16 on website. For guidelines and to submit online: www.glimmertrain.org.

NONFICTION Pays expenses of writers on assignment.

FICTION Needs short stories. **Buys 45 mss/year.** Submit via the website at www.glimmertrain.org. In a pinch, send a hard copy and include SASE for response. Receives 36,000 unsolicited mss/year. Accepts 15 mss/issue; 45 mss/year. Agented fiction 1%. Publishes 20 new writers/year. Length: 500-20,000 words. **Pays $700 for standard submissions, up to $3,000 for contest-winning stories.**

TIPS "In the last 2 years, over half of the first-place stories have been their authors' very first publications. See our contest listings in Contests & Awards section."

GRASSLIMB

P.O. Box 420816, San Diego CA 92142. **E-mail:** editor@grasslimb.com. **Website:** www.grasslimb.com. **Contact:** Valerie Polichar, editor. **100.** *Grasslimb* publishes literary prose, poetry, and art. Fiction is best when it is short and avant-garde or otherwise experimental. Estab. 2002. Circ. 200. Acceptance $10 Accepts simultaneous submissions. Responds in 4-6 months to mss. Rarely comments on rejected mss. Sample copy: $3. Guidelines for SASE, e-mail, or on website.

NONFICTION Pays expenses of writers on assignment.

FICTION "Fiction in an experimental, avant-garde, or surreal mode is often more interesting to us than a traditional story." Needs experimental. "Although general topics are welcome, we're less likely to select work regarding romance, sex, aging, and children." Send complete ms via e-mail or postal mail with SASE. Length: up to 2,500 words; average length: 1,500 words. **Pays $10-70 and 2 contributor's copies.**

POETRY Submit poems via e-mail or postal mail with SASE. Submit maximum 5 poems. **Pays $5-20/poem.**

TIPS "We publish brief fiction work that can be read in a single sitting over a cup of coffee. Work is generally 'literary' in nature rather than mainstream. Experimental work welcome. Remember to have your work proofread and to send short work. We cannot

read over 3,000 words and prefer under 2,000 words. Include word count."

GRIST

English Dept., 301 McClung Tower, Univ. of Tennessee, Knoxville TN 37996-0430. **E-mail:** gristeditors@gmail.com. **Website:** www.gristjournal.com. Editor-in-Chief: Jeremy Michael Reed. Annual magazine featuring world class fiction, poetry and creative nonfiction, along with interviews with renowned writers and essays about craft. *Grist* is a nationally distributed journal of fiction, nonfiction, poetry, interviews, and craft essays. We seek work of high literary quality from both emerging and established writers, and we welcome all styles and aesthetic approaches. Each issue is accompanied by Grist Online, which features some of the best work we receive during our reading period. In addition to general submissions, *Grist* holds the ProForma Contest every spring, recognizing unpublished creative work that explores the relationship between content and form, whether in fiction, nonfiction, poetry, or a hybrid genre. Throughout the year, we publish interviews, craft essays, and reviews on our blog, The Writing Life. Estab. 2007. Byline given. Pays on publication. No kill fee. Accepts queries by online submission form. Accepts simultaneous submissions. See website for details.

NONFICTION Needs essays, how-to, interview, memoir. Send complete ms. **One cent per word up to $50.**

FICTION Needs experimental, mainstream. Send complete ms. Length: 7,000 words. **1 cent per word up to $50.**

POETRY Needs avant-garde, free verse, traditional. Submit maximum 3-5 poems. **$10 per page.**

TIPS "*Grist* seeks work from both emerging and established writers, whose work is of high literary quality."

GUD MAGAZINE

Greatest Uncommon Denominator Publishing, P.O. Box 1537, Laconia NH 03247. **E-mail:** spiderbait1@gudmagazine.com. **Website:** www.gudmagazine.com. **99% freelance written.** Semiannual magazine covering literary content and art. *"GUD Magazine* transcends and encompasses the audiences of both genre and literary fiction by featuring fiction, art, poetry, essays and reports, comics, and short drama." Estab. 2006. Byline given. Pays on publication. Publishes ms an average of 6-12 months after acceptance. Editorial lead time 6 months. Submit seasonal material 6 months in advance. Accepts queries by online submission form. Accepts simultaneous submissions. Responds in 6 months to mss. Guidelines available online.

NONFICTION Needs book excerpts, essays, historical, humor, interview, personal experience, photo feature, travel, interesting event. **Buys 2-4 mss/year.** Submit complete ms using online form. Length: up to 15,000 words. **Pays a minimum of $5/piece, or 3¢/word for longer pieces.** Pays expenses of writers on assignment.

PHOTOS Send photos and artwork in electronic format. Model releases required for human images. Reviews GIF/JPEG files. Pays $12. Buys all rights.

FICTION Needs adventure, erotica, ethnic, experimental, fantasy, horror, humorous, science fiction, suspense. **Buys 40 mss/year.** Submit via online submissions manager. Length: up to 15,000 words. **Pays a minimum of $5/piece, or 3¢/word for longer pieces.**

POETRY Needs avant-garde, free verse, haiku, light verse, traditional. Submit only 1 poem per entry form. Buys 12-20 poems/year. **Pays a minimum of $5/piece, or 3¢/word for longer pieces.**

FILLERS Buys comics. Reviews GIF/JPEG files. **Pays $12.**

TIPS "We publish work in any genre, plus artwork, factual articles, and interviews. We'll publish something as short as 20 words or as long as 15,000, as long as it grabs us. Be warned: We read a lot. We've seen it all before. We are not easy to impress. Is your work original? Does it have something to say? Read it again. If you genuinely believe it to be so, send it. We do accept simultaneous submissions, as well as multiple submissions, but read the guidelines first."

$$ GULF COAST

A Journal of Literature and Fine Arts, 4800 Calhoun Rd., Houston TX 77204-3013. (713)743-3223. **E-mail:** editors@gulfcoastmag.org. **Website:** www.gulfcoastmag.org. **Contact:** Luisa Muradyan Tannahill, editor; Michele Nereim, managing editor; Georgia Pearle, digital editor; Henk Rossouw, Dan Chu, and Erika Jo Brown, poetry editors; Alex McElroy, Charlotte Wyatt, and Corey Campbell, fiction editors; Alex Naumann and Nathan Stabenfeldt, nonfiction editors; Jonathan Meyer, online fiction editor; Carolann Madden, online poetry editor; Melanie Brkich, online nonfiction editor. Biannual print magazine covering innovative fiction, nonfiction, poetry, visual art, and critical art writing. GC Online is the companion online journal and publishes unique content. Estab. 1986. Circ. 3,000. No kill fee. Publishes ms 6 months-1 year after acceptance. Accepts queries by mail, e-mail, phone. Accepts simultaneous submissions. Responds in 4-6 months to mss. Sometimes comments on rejected mss. Back issue: $8, plus 7x10 SASE with 4 first-class stamps. Writer's guidelines for #10 SASE or on website.

NONFICTION Needs interview, reviews. *Gulf Coast* reads general submissions, submitted by post or through the online submissions manager, September 1-March 1. Submissions e-mailed directly to the editors or postmarked March 1-September 1 will not be read or responded to. "Please visit our contest page for contest submission guidelines." **Pays $100 per review and $200 per interview.** Pays expenses of writers on assignment.

FICTION "Please do not send multiple submissions; we will read only 1 submission per author at a given time, except in the case of our annual contests." Needs ethnic, multicultural, literary, regional, translations, contemporary. No children's, genre, religious/inspirational. *Gulf Coast* reads general submissions, submitted by post or through the online submissions manager, September 1-March 1. Submissions e-mailed directly to the editors or postmarked March 1-September 1 will not be read or responded to. "Please visit our contest page for contest submission guidelines." Receives 500 unsolicited mss/month. Accepts 6-8 mss/issue; 12-16 mss/year. Agented fiction: 5%. Publishes 2-8 new writers/year. Recently published work by Alan Heathcock, Anne Carson, Bret Anthony Johnston, John D'Agata, Lucie Brock-Broido, Clancy Martin, Steve Almond, Sam Lipsyte, Carl Phillips, Dean Young, and Eula Biss. Publishes short shorts. **Pays $50/page.**

POETRY Submit up to 5 poems at a time. Considers simultaneous submissions with notification; no previously published poems. Cover letter is required. List previous publications and include a brief bio. Reads submissions September-April. **Pays $50/page.**

TIPS "Submit only previously unpublished works. Include a cover letter. Online submissions are strongly preferred. Stories or essays should be typed, double-spaced, and paginated with your name, address, and phone number on the first page and the title on subsequent pages. Poems should have your name, address, and phone number on the first page of each." The Annual Gulf Coast Prizes award publication and $1,500 each in poetry, fiction, and nonfiction; opens in December of each year. Honorable mentions in each category will receive a $250 second prize. Postmark/online entry deadline: March 22 of each year. Winners and honorable mentions will be announced in May. **Entry fee:** $23 (includes one-year subscription). Make checks payable to *Gulf Coast.* Guidelines available on website.

🟢 THE HOLLINS CRITIC

P.O. Box 9538, Hollins University, Roanoke VA 24020-1538. **Website:** www.hollins.edu/who-we-are/news-media/hollins-critic. **100% freelance written.** Magazine published 5 times/year. *The Hollins Critic,* published 5 times/year, presents the first serious surveys of the whole bodies of contemporary writers' work, with complete checklists. In past issues, you'll find essays on such writers as Claudia Emerson (by Allison Seay), Wilma Dykeman (by Casey Clabough), Jerry Mirskin (by Howard Nelson), Sally Mann (by Martha Park), James Alan McPherson (by James Robert Saunders), Elise Partridge (by Nicholas Birns), and Ron Rash (by Jerry Wayne Wells). Estab. 1964. Circ. 400. Byline given. Pays on publication. No kill fee. Publishes ms an average of 1 year after acceptance. Accepts queries by online submission form. Accepts simultaneous submissions. Responds in 2 months to mss. Sample copy: $3. Guidelines for #10 SASE or online.

POETRY Needs avant-garde, free verse, traditional. Submit up to 5 poems at a time using the online submission form at www.hollinscriticsubmissions.com, available September 15-December 1. Submissions received at other times will be returned unread. Publishes 16-20 poems/year. **Pays $25/poem plus 5 contributor's copies.**

TIPS "We accept unsolicited poetry submissions; all other content is by prearrangement."

🟢 HOOT

A Postcard Review of (Mini) Poetry and Prose, 4234 Chestnut St., Apt. 1 R, Philadelphia PA 19104. **E-mail:** info@hootreview.com. **Website:** www.hootreview.com. **Contact:** Jane-Rebecca Cannarella, editor in chief; Amanda Vacharat and Dorian Geisler, editors/co-founders. **100% freelance written.** *HOOT* publishes 1 piece of writing, designed with original art and/or photographs, on the front of a postcard ev-

ery month, as well as 2-3 pieces online. The postcards are intended for sharing, to be hung on the wall, etc. Therefore, *HOOT* looks for very brief, surprising-yet-gimmick-free writing that can stand on its own, that also follows "The Refrigerator Rule"—something that you would hang on your refrigerator and would want to read and look at for a whole month. This rule applies to online content as well. Estab. 2011. Pays on publication. Publishes ms 2 months after acceptance. Accepts queries by mail, online submission form. Accepts simultaneous submissions. Sample copy: $2. Guidelines available online.

NONFICTION Needs personal experience, creative nonfiction. **Buys 6 mss/year.** Submit complete ms. Length: up to 150 words. **Pays $10-100 for assigned and unsolicited pieces.** Pays expenses of writers on assignment.

PHOTOS Send photos (GIF/JPEG files) with submission. Buys one-time rights.

FICTION literary, flash/short short. **Buys 14 mss/year.** Submit complete ms. Length: up to 150 words. **Pays $10-100 for print publication.**

POETRY Needs avant-garde, free verse, haiku, light verse, traditional, prose. Buys 14 poems/year. Submit maximum 2 poems. Length: up to 10 lines. **Pays $10-100 for print publication.**

TIPS "We look for writing with audacity and zest from authors who are not afraid to take risks. We appreciate work that is able to go beyond mere description in its 150 words. We offer free online workshops every other Wednesday for authors who would like feedback on their work from the *HOOT* editors. We also often give feedback with our rejections. We publish roughly 6-10 new writers each year."

🟢 HUBBUB

5344 SE 38th Ave., Portland OR 97202. **Website:** www.reed.edu/hubbub. **Contact:** J. Shugrue and Lisa M. Steinman, co-editors. *Hubbub,* published once/year, is designed "to feature a multitude of voices from interesting, contemporary American poets." Wants "poems that are well crafted, with something to say. We have no single style, subject, or length requirement and in particular will consider long poems." Estab. 1983. Pays on publication. Publishes poems 1-12 months (usually) after acceptance. Accepts queries by mail. Responds in 4 months. Sample: $3.35 (back issues), $7 (current issue). Subscription: $7/year. Guidelines for SASE or online.

POETRY Submit 3-6 typed poems at a time. Include SASE. "We review 2-4 poetry books/year in short (three-page) reviews; all reviews are solicited. We do, however, list books received/recommended." Send materials for review consideration. Has published poetry by Madeline DeFrees, Cecil Giscombe, Carolyn Kizer, Primus St. John, Shara McCallum, and Alice Fulton. Does not want light verse. Buys 40-50 poems/year. Submit maximum 6 poems. No length requirements. **Pays $20/poem.**

🚫 THE HUDSON REVIEW

33 W. 67th St., New York NY 10023. (212)650-0020. **E-mail:** info@hudsonreview.com. **Website:** hudsonreview.com. **Contact:** Paula Deitz, editor. **100% freelance written.** Since its beginning, the magazine has dealt with the area where literature bears on the intellectual life of the time and on diverse aspects of American culture. It has no university affiliation and is not committed to any narrow academic aim or to any particular political perspective. The magazine serves as a major forum for the work of new writers and for the exploration of new developments in literature and the arts. It has a distinguished record of publishing little-known or undiscovered writers, many of whom have become major literary figures. Each issue contains a wide range of material including poetry, fiction, essays on literary and cultural topics, book reviews, reports from abroad, and chronicles covering film, theater, dance, music, and art. *The Hudson Review* is distributed in 25 countries. Unsolicited mss are read according to the following schedule: April 1 through June 30 for poetry, September 1 through November 30 for fiction, and January 1 through March 31 for nonfiction. Estab. 1948. Circ. 2,000. Byline given. Pays on publication. No kill fee. Publishes ms an average of 6 months after acceptance. Editorial lead time 3 months. Accepts queries by mail, online submission form. Responds in 6 months to mss. Sample copy: $11. Guidelines online.

NONFICTION Needs essays, general interest, historical, memoir, reviews. **Buys 4-6 mss/year.** Send complete ms by mail from **January 1 through March 31** only. Length: up to 10,000 words. Pays expenses of writers on assignment.

FICTION If you go through our archives, most of the short stories fall into the nebulous category of "literary fiction." Many stories have elements of mystery, romance, historical fiction, etc. For novel excerpts, we ask that the work be able to stand on its own. For genre stories, we ask that the work go beyond its genre—a religious story would have to be more than a conversion narrative or cautionary tale; a comic story would ideally have a little pathos; a romance or mystery or sci-fi story would have some ambiguities or aesthetic concerns or experimentation. In general, we want stories that a writer has put a lot of thought into, and that readers will think about long after they've finished. Needs short stories. **Buys 3-8 mss/year.** Send complete ms by mail or online submissions manager from **September 1 through November 30** only. Length: up to 10,000 words.

POETRY Needs Anything goes. Formal, free verse, experimental, translations, prose poetry, etc. Submit up to 7 poems by mail from **April 1 through June 30** only. Buys 15-30 poems/year.

TIPS "We do not specialize in publishing any particular 'type' of writing; our sole criterion for accepting unsolicited work is literary quality. The best way for you to get an idea of the range of work we publish is to read a current issue. Unsolicited mss submitted outside of specified reading times will be returned unread. Do not send submissions via e-mail."

🚫 HUNGER MOUNTAIN

Vermont College of Fine Arts, 36 College St., Montpelier VT 05602. (802)828-8517. **E-mail:** hungermtn@vcfa.edu. **Website:** www.hungermtn.org. Editor: Miciah Gault. **Contact:** Cameron Finch, managing editor. Annual perfect-bound journal covering high-quality fiction, poetry, creative nonfiction, craft essays, writing for children, and artwork. Four contests held annually, one in each genre. Accepts high-quality work from unknown, emerging, or successful writers. Publishing fiction, creative nonfiction, poetry, and young adult & children's writing. Four writing contests annually. *Hunger Mountain* is a print and online journal of the arts. The print journal is about 200 pages, 7x9, professionally printed, perfect-bound, with full-bleed color artwork on cover. Press run is 1,000. Over 10,000 visits online monthly. Uses online submissions manager (Submittable). Member: CLMP. Estab. 2002. Circ. 1,000. Byline given. Pays on publication. No kill fee. Publishes ms an average of 1 year after acceptance. General submissions between May 1-October 15. Accepts queries by online submission form. Accepts simultaneous submissions. Responds in 4 months to mss. Single issue: $12; subscription:

$18 for 2 issues/2 years; back issue: $8. Checks payable to Vermont College of Fine Arts, or purchase online. Guidelines online.

NONFICTION "We welcome an array of traditional and experimental work, including, but not limited to, personal, lyrical, and meditative essays, memoirs, collages, rants, and humor. The only requirements are recognition of truth, a unique voice with a firm command of language, and an engaging story with multiple pressure points." No informative or instructive articles, no interviews, and no book reviews please. Payment varies. Submit complete ms using online submissions manager at Submittable. Length: up to 10,000 words. **Pays $50 for general fiction or creative nonfiction, for both children's lit and general adult lit.**

PHOTOS Send photos.

FICTION "We look for work that is beautifully crafted and tells a good story, with characters that are alive and kicking, storylines that stay with us long after we've finished reading, and sentences that slay us with their precision." Needs experimental, humorous, novel excerpts, short stories, slice-of-life vignettes. No genre fiction, meaning science fiction, fantasy, horror, detective, erotic, etc. Submit ms using online submissions manager: https://hungermtn.submittable.com/submit. Length: up to 10,000 words. **Pays $50 for general fiction.**

POETRY Needs avant-garde, free verse, traditional. Submit 1-5 poems at a time. "We are looking for truly original poems that run the aesthetic gamut: lively engagement with language in the act of pursuit. Some poems remind us in a fresh way of our own best thoughts; some poems bring us to a place beyond language for which there aren't quite words; some poems take us on a complicated language ride that is, itself, its own aim. Complex poem-architectures thrill us and still-points in the turning world do, too. Send us the best of what you have." Submit using online submissions manager. No light verse, humor/quirky/catchy verse, greeting card verse. Submit maximum 5 poems. **Pays $25 for poetry up to 2 poems (plus $5/poem for additional poems).**

TIPS "Mss must be typed, prose double-spaced. Poets submit poems as one document. No multiple genre submissions. Fresh viewpoints and human interest are very important, as is originality and diversity. We are committed to publishing an outstanding journal of the arts. Do not send entire novels, mss, or short story collections. Do not send previously published work."

ICONOCLAST

1675 Amazon Rd., Mohegan Lake NY 10547-1804. **Website:** www.iconoclastliterarymagazine.com. **Contact:** Phil Wagner, editor and publisher. *Iconoclast* seeks and chooses the best new writing and poetry available—of all genres and styles and entertainment levels. Its mission is to provide a serious publishing opportunity for unheralded, unknown, but deserving creators, whose work is often overlooked or trampled in the commercial, university, or Internet marketplace. Estab. 1992. Pays on publication. Accepts queries by mail. Responds in 6 weeks to mss. Sample copy: $4. Subscription: $20 for 6 issues.

FICTION "Subjects and styles are completely open (within the standards of generally accepted taste—though exceptions, as always, can be made for unique and visionary works)." Needs adventure, experimental, fantasy, mainstream, short stories. No slice-of-life stories, stories containing alcoholism, incest, and domestic or public violence. Accepts most genres, "with the exception of mysteries." Submit by mail; include SASE. Cover letter not necessary. **Pays 1¢/word and 2 contributor's copies. Contributors get 40% discount on extra copies.**

POETRY "Try for originality; if not in thought than expression. No greeting card verse or noble religious sentiments. Look for the unusual in the usual, parallels in opposites, the capturing of what is unique or often unnoticed in an ordinary or extraordinary moment. What makes us human—and the resultant glories and agonies. The universal usually wins out over the personal. Rhyme isn't as easy as it looks—especially for those unversed in its study." Submit by mail; include SASE. Cover letter not necessary. Length: up to 2 pages. **Pays $2-6/poem and 1 contributor's copy per page or work. Contributors get 40% discount on extra copies.**

TIPS "Please don't send preliminary drafts—rewriting is half the job. If you're not sure about the story, don't truly believe in it, or are unenthusiastic about the subject (we will not recycle your term papers or thesis), then don't send it. This is not a lottery (luck has nothing to do with it)."

💲💲 THE IDAHO REVIEW

Boise State University, 1910 University Dr., Boise ID 83725. **E-mail:** mwieland@boisestate.edu. **Website:** idahoreview.org. **Contact:** Mitch Wieland, editor. *The Idaho Review* is the literary journal of Boise State University. Recent stories appearing in *The Idaho Review* have been reprinted in *The Best American Short Stories, The O. Henry Prize Stories, The Pushcart Prize*, and *New Stories from the South*. Recent contributors include Joyce Carol Oates, Rick Moody, Ann Beattie, T.C. Boyle, and Joy Williams. Reading period: September 15-March 15. Estab. 1998. Pays on publication. Publishes ms 1 year after acceptance. Accepts queries by online submission form. Accepts simultaneous submissions. Responds in 3-5 months. Guidelines online.

NONFICTION Needs book excerpts, essays, interview. Special issues: creative nonfiction. Submit through online submissions manager. Pays expenses of writers on assignment.

FICTION Needs experimental, novel excerpts, short stories, literary. No genre fiction of any type. Submit through online submissions manager. Length: up to 25 double-spaced pages. **Pays $300-$500/story and contributor's copies.**

POETRY Submit up to 5 poems using online submissions manager.

TIPS "We look for strongly crafted work that tells a story that needs to be told. We demand vision and intelligence and mystery in the fiction we publish."

💲 ILLUMEN

Alban Lake Publishing, P.O. Box 141, Colo IA 50056-0141. **E-mail:** illumensdp@yahoo.com. **Website:** albanlake.com. **Contact:** Terrie Leigh Relf, editor. **100% freelance written.** "*Illumen* is a print magazine of speculative poetry. It is published quarterly on the first of January, April, July, and October in perfect-bound digest format. It contains speculative poetry, illustrations, articles, and reviews." Estab. 2004. Byline given. Pays on publication. Offers 100% kill fee. About four months between acceptance and publication. Submit seasonal material 6 months in advance. Accepts queries by e-mail. Accepts simultaneous submissions. Responds in 4 months. Guidelines available online.

NONFICTION Needs essays, how-to, interview, opinion, non-fiction must pertain in some way to poetry. Special issues: Wants articles that address some aspect of speculative poetry. Send complete ms by e-mail. Length: 800-2,000 words. **Pays $12 and 1 contributor's copy.** Pays expenses of writers on assignment.

REPRINTS Pays $3 for reprints.

POETRY Needs avant-garde, free verse, haiku, light verse, traditional. "Speculative poetry is 1 result of the application of imagination to reality. In speculative poetry, one's 'vision' often is taken from a different angle, from another perspective, perhaps even from another time and place. Speculative poetry is usually tinged with 1 or more of the genres. Thus, in speculative poetry you find hints of science fiction, fantasy, folklore, myth, the surreal … and yes, even horror. Good speculative poetry will awaken a sense of adventure in the reader. That's what we're looking for: good, original speculative poetry." Submit poetry by e-mail. "Speculative horror poetry evokes moods, often dark and spooky ones. It should not make you upchuck. Remember: twisted is an attitude, not an action." Buys 40-50 poems/year. Submit maximum 3 poems. Length: up to 100 lines/poem. **Pays 2¢/word, minimum $3.**

TIPS "*Illumen* publishes beginning writers as well as seasoned veterans. Be sure to read and follow the guidelines before submitting your work. The best advice for beginning writers is to send your best effort, not your first draft."

💲 IMAGE

3307 Third Ave. W., Seattle WA 98119. (206)281-2988. **Fax:** (206)281-2979. **E-mail:** image@imagejournal.org. **Website:** www.imagejournal.org. **Contact:** Gregory Wolfe, publisher and editor. **50% freelance written.** Quarterly magazine covering the intersection between art and faith. "*Image* is a unique forum for the best writing and artwork that is informed by—or grapples with—religious faith. We have never been interested in art that merely regurgitates dogma or falls back on easy answers or didacticism. Instead, our focus has been on writing and visual artwork that embody a spiritual struggle, that seek to strike a balance between tradition and a profound openness to the world. Each issue explores this relationship through outstanding fiction, poetry, painting, sculpture, architecture, film, music, interviews, and dance. *Image* also features 4-color reproductions of visual art." Magazine: 7×10; 136 pages; glossy cover stock; illustrations; photos. Estab. 1989. Circ. 4,500. Byline given. Pays on acceptance. No kill fee. Publishes ms an average of 8 months after acceptance. Accepts queries by mail, e-mail. Accepts simultaneous submissions. Responds in 1 month to queries; in 5 months to mss. Sample copy: $16 or available online. Guidelines online.

NONFICTION Needs essays, interview, profile, religious, reviews. No sentimental, preachy, moralistic, or obvious essays. **Buys 10 mss/year.** Send complete ms by postal mail (with SASE for reply or return of ms) or online submissions manager at www.imagejournal.org/journal/submit, or query Mary Mitchell (mkenagy@imagejournal.org). Does not accept e-mail submissions. Length: 3,000-6,000 words. **Pays $20/page and 4 contributor's copies.**

FICTION Needs religious, short stories. No sentimental, preachy, moralistic, obvious stories, or genre stories (unless they manage to transcend their genre). **Buys 8 mss/year.** Send complete ms by postal mail (with SASE for reply or return of ms) or online submissions manager at www.imagejournal.org/journal/submit. Does not accept e-mail submissions. Length: 3,000-6,000 words. **Pays $20/page and 4 contributor's copies.**

POETRY Wants poems that grapple with religious faith, usually Judeo-Christian. Send up to 5 poems by postal mail (with SASE for reply or return of ms) or online submissions manager. Does not accept e-mail submissions. Submit maximum 5 poems. Length: up to 10 pages. **Pays $2/line ($150 maximum) and 4 contributor's copies.**

TIPS "Fiction must grapple with religious faith, though subjects need not be overtly religious."

INDIANA REVIEW

Ballantine Hall 529, 1020 E. Kirkwood Ave., Indiana University, Bloomington IN 47405. **E-mail:** inreview@indiana.edu. **Website:** indianareview.org. **Contact:** See masthead for current editorial staff. **100% freelance written.** Biannual magazine. "*Indiana Review*, a nonprofit organization run by IU graduate students, is a journal of innovative fiction, nonfiction, and poetry. We're interested in energy, originality, and careful attention to craft. While we publish many well-known authors, we also welcome new and emerging poets and fiction writers." See website for open reading periods. Estab. 1976. Circ. 5,000. Byline given. Pays on publication. Publishes ms an average of 6-8 months after acceptance. Accepts queries by online submission form. Accepts simultaneous submissions. We make every effort to respond to work in four months. Back issues available for $10. Guidelines available online. We no longer accept hard-copy submissions. All submissions must be made online.

NONFICTION Needs essays. No coming-of-age/slice-of-life pieces or book reviews. **Buys 5-7 mss/year.** Submit complete ms through online submissions manager. Length: up to 8,000 words. **Pays $5/page ($10 minimum), plus 2 contributor's copies.** Pays expenses of writers on assignment.

FICTION "We look for daring stories which integrate theme, language, character, and form. We like polished writing, humor, and fiction which has consequence beyond the world of its narrator." Needs ethnic, experimental, mainstream, novel excerpts, short stories, literary, short fictions, translations. No genre fiction. **Buys 15-25 mss/year.** Submit via online submissions manager. Length: up to 8,000 words. **Pays $5/page ($10 minimum), plus 2 contributor's copies.**

POETRY "We look for poems that are skillful and bold, exhibiting an inventiveness of language with attention to voice and sonics." Wants experimental, free verse, prose poem, traditional form, lyrical, narrative. Submit poetry via online submissions manager. Buys 40-60 poems/year. Submit maximum 6 poems. **Pays $5/page ($10 minimum), plus 2 contributor's copies.**

TIPS "We're always looking for more nonfiction. We enjoy essays that go beyond merely autobiographical revelation and utilize sophisticated organization and slightly radical narrative strategies. We want essays that are both lyrical and analytical, where confession does not mean nostalgia. Read us before you submit. Back issues are available for $10. Our most recent issues have online previews available for free and accessible through the "Shop" page on our website. Often reading is slower in summer and holiday months. Submit work that 'stacks up' with the work we've published."

THE IOWA REVIEW

308 EPB, The University of Iowa, Iowa City IA 52242. (319)335-0462. **E-mail:** iowa-review@uiowa.edu. **Website:** www.iowareview.org. Lynne Nugent, managing editor. **Contact:** Harilaos Stecopoulos. Triannual magazine covering stories, essays, and poems for a general readership interested in contemporary literature. *The Iowa Review*, published 3 times/year, prints fiction, poetry, essays, reviews, and, occasional-

ly, interviews. Receives about 5,000 submissions/year, accepts up to 100. Press run is 2,900; 1,500 distributed to stores. Estab. 1970. Circ. 3,500. Pays on publication. Publishes ms an average of 12-18 months after acceptance. Accepts queries by mail, online submission form. Accepts simultaneous submissions. Responds to mss in 4 months. Sample: $8.95 and online. Subscription: $20. Guidelines online.

NONFICTION Needs essays, interview. Send complete ms with cover letter. Don't bother with queries. SASE for return of ms. Accepts mss by snail mail (SASE required for response) and online submission form at iowareview.submittable.com/submit; no e-mail submissions. **Pays 8¢/word ($100 minimum), plus 2 contributor's copies.** Pays expenses of writers on assignment.

FICTION "We are open to a range of styles and voices and always hope to be surprised by work we then feel we need." Receives 600 unsolicited mss/month. Accepts 4-6 mss/issue; 12-18 mss/year. Does not read mss January-August. Publishes ms an average of 12-18 months after acceptance. Agented fiction less than 2%. **Publishes some new writers/year.** Recently published work by Johanna Hunting, Bennett Sims, and Pedro Mairal. Needs experimental, mainstream, novel excerpts, short stories. Send complete ms with cover letter. Don't bother with queries. SASE for return of ms. Accepts mss by snail mail (SASE required for response) and online submission form at iowareview.submittable.com/submit; no e-mail submissions. **Pays 8¢/word ($100 minimum), plus 2 contributor's copies.**

POETRY Submit up to 8 pages at a time. Online submissions accepted, but no e-mail submissions. Cover letter (with title of work and genre) is encouraged. SASE required. Reads submissions only during the fall semester, September through November, and then contest entries in the spring. Occasionally comments on rejected poems or offers suggestions on accepted poems. "We simply look for poems that, at the time we read and choose, we find we admire. No specifications as to form, length, style, subject matter, or purpose. Though we print work from established writers, we're always delighted when we discover new talent." **Pays $1.50/line, $40 minimum.**

TIPS "We publish essays, reviews, novel excerpts, stories, poems, and photography. We have no set guidelines regarding content but strongly recommend that writers read a sample issue before submitting."

🄢 THE KENYON REVIEW

Finn House, 102 W. Wiggin, Gambier OH 43022. (740)427-5208. **Fax:** (740)427-5417. **E-mail:** kenyonreview@kenyon.edu. **Website:** www.kenyonreview.org. **Contact:** Alicia Misarti. **100% freelance written.** Bimonthly magazine covering contemporary literature and criticism. "An international journal of literature, culture, and the arts, dedicated to an inclusive representation of the best in new writing (fiction, poetry, essays, interviews, criticism) from established and emerging writers." *The Kenyon Review* receives about 8,000 submissions/year. Also publishes *KR Online*, a separate and complementary online literary magazine. Estab. 1939. Circ. 6,000. Byline given. Pays on publication. No kill fee. Publishes ms an average of 1 year after acceptance. Editorial lead time 1 year. Submit seasonal material 1 year in advance. Accepts queries by online submission form. Accepts simultaneous submissions. Responds in 4 months to mss. Sample: $10; includes s&h. Call or e-mail to order. Guidelines online.

NONFICTION Needs essays, interview, criticism. Only accepts mss via online submissions manager; visit website for instructions. Do not submit via e-mail or mail. Receives 130 unsolicited mss/month. Unsolicited mss accepted September 15-November 1 only. Length: 3-15 typeset pages preferred. **Pays 8¢/published word of prose (minimum payment $80; maximum payment $450); word count does not include title, notes, or citations.**

FICTION Receives 800 unsolicited mss/month. Unsolicited mss accepted September 15-November 1 only. Recently published work by Leslie Blanco, Karl Taro Greenfeld, Charles Johnson, Amit Majmudar, Joyce Carol Oates, and Rion Amilcar Scott. Needs condensed novels, ethnic, experimental, historical, humorous, mainstream, novel excerpts, short stories, contemporary, excerpts from novels, gay/lesbian, literary, translations. Only accepts mss via online submissions manager; visit website for instructions. Do not submit via e-mail or mail. Length: 3-15 typeset pages preferred. **Pays 8¢/published word of prose (minimum payment $80; maximum payment $450); word count does not include title, notes, or citations.**

POETRY Features all styles, forms, lengths, and subject matters. Considers translations. Submit up to 6 poems at a time. No previously published poems. Only accepts mss via online submissions program; visit website for instructions. Do not submit via e-mail or snail mail. Accepts submissions September 15-November 1. Has recently published work by Rae Armantrout, Stephen Burt, Meghan O'Rourke, Carl Phillips, Solmaz Sharif, and Arthur Sze. Submit maximum 6 poems. **Pays 16¢/published word of poetry (minimum payment $40; maximum payment $200); word count does not include title, notes, or citations.**

TIPS "We no longer accept mailed or e-mailed submissions. Work will only be read if it is submitted through our online program on our website. Reading period is September 15 through November 1. We look for strong voice, unusual perspective, and power in the writing."

$ LADY CHURCHILL'S ROSEBUD WRISTLET

Small Beer Press, 150 Pleasant St., #306, Easthampton MA 01027. **E-mail:** info@smallbeerpress.com. **Website:** www.smallbeerpress.com/lcrw. **Contact:** Gavin Grant, editor. *Lady Churchill's Rosebud Wristlet* accepts fiction, nonfiction, poetry, and b&w art. "The fiction we publish tends toward, but is not limited to, the speculative. This does not mean only quietly desperate stories. We will consider items that fall out with regular categories. We do not accept multiple submissions." Semiannual. Estab. 1996. Circ. 1,000. Byline given. Pays on publication. Publishes ms 6-12 months after acceptance. Accepts queries by mail. Responds in 6 months to mss. Sometimes comments on rejected mss. Sample copy: $5. Guidelines online.

NONFICTION Needs essays. Send complete ms with a cover letter. Include estimated word count. Send SASE (or IRC) for return of ms, or send a disposable copy of ms and #10 SASE for reply only. **Pays $0.03 per word, $25 minimum.**

FICTION Receives 100 unsolicited mss/month. Accepts 4-6 mss/issue; 8-12 mss/year. Publishes 2-4 new writers/year. Also publishes literary essays, poetry. Has published work by Ted Chiang, Gwenda Bond, Alissa Nutting, and Charlie Anders. Needs experimental, fantasy, science fiction, short stories. "We do not publish gore, sword and sorcery, or pornography. We can discuss these terms if you like. There are places for them all; this is not one of them." Send complete ms with a cover letter. Include estimated word count. Send SASE (or IRC) for return of ms, or send a disposable copy of ms and #10 SASE for reply only. Length: 200-7,000 words. **Pays $0.03 per word, $25 minimum.**

POETRY Send submission with a cover letter. Include estimated word count. Send SASE (or IRC) for return of submission, or send a disposable copy of submission and #10 SASE for reply only. **Pays $10/poem.**

TIPS "We recommend you read *Lady Churchill's Rosebud Wristlet* before submitting. You can pick up a copy from our website or from assorted book shops."

🍁 $ LINE

6079 Academic Quadrangle, 8888 University Dr., Simon Fraser University, Burnaby BC V5A 1S6 Canada. **E-mail:** wcl@sfu.ca. **Website:** linejournal.tumblr.com/about. "*Line* (formerly *West Coast Line*) is a journal of poetry and critique." Estab. 1990. Circ. 500. Pays on publication. No kill fee. Editorial lead time 4 months. Accepts queries by mail, e-mail. Accepts simultaneous submissions. Responds in 6 months to queries and mss. Sample copy for $15 CAD, $20 U.S. Guidelines for SASE (U.S. must include IRC).

NONFICTION Needs essays, experimental prose. No journalistic articles or articles dealing with nonliterary material. **Buys 8-10 mss/year.** Send complete ms. Length: 1,000-5,000 words. **Pays $8/page, 2 contributor's copies, and a one-year subscription.** Pays expenses of writers on assignment.

FICTION Needs experimental. **Buys 3-6 mss/year.**

POETRY Needs avant-garde. No light verse, traditional. Buys 10-15 poems/year. Submit maximum 5-6 poems. **Pays $8/page.**

TIPS Submissions must be either scholarly or formally innovative. Contributors should be familiar with current literary trends in Canada and the U.S. Scholars should be aware of current schools of theory. All submissions should be accompanied by a brief cover letter; essays should be formatted according to the MLA guide. The publication is not divided into departments. We accept innovative poetry, experimental prose, and scholarly essays.

$ LONG STORY SHORT, AN E-ZINE FOR WRITERS

P.O. Box 475, Lewistown MT 59457. **E-mail:** alongstory_short@aol.com. **Website:** www.alongstoryshort.net. **Contact:** Anisa Claire, Kim Bussey, editors. *Long Story Short, An E-zine for Writers* publishes "the best fiction and poetry from both emerging and established writers. Estab. 2003. Publishes ms up to 6 months after acceptance, depending on theme. Submit seasonal material 6 months in advance. Accepts queries by e-mail. Accepts simultaneous submissions. Guidelines available on website. "Read them!".

NONFICTION Needs essays. Submit by e-mail; no attachments. Length: up to 2,000 words. **Pays $10-15 and 1 contributor's copy.** Pays expenses of writers on assignment.

COLUMNS Only Writers Get It (humorous anecdotes or experiences connected to being a writer), 500 words. Submit by e-mail; no attachments. **Pays 1 contributor's copy.**

FICTION Accepts all genres of flash fiction or prose. Needs short stories, flash fiction. Submit by e-mail; no attachments. Length: up to 2,000 words. **Pays $10-15 and 1 contributor's copy for short stories 1,000-2,000 words. Pays 1 contributor's copy for flash fiction.**

POETRY Submit by e-mail; no attachments. Considers poetry by children (ages 10 and up) and teens. Has published poetry by Michael Lee Johnson, Maria Ercilla, Shonda Buchanan, Patricia Wellingham-Jones, Floriana Hall, and Russell Bittner. Length: up to 32 lines/poem. **Pays 1 contributor's copy.**

✿ⓈⓈ MAISONNEUVE

1051 Boulevard Decarie, P.O. Box 53527, St. Laurent Quebec H4L 5J9 Canada. **E-mail:** submissions@ maisonneuve.org. **Website:** www.maisonneuve.org. **90% freelance written.** Quarterly magazine covering eclectic curiosity. "*Maisonneuve* has been described as a new *New Yorker* for a younger generation, or as *Harper's* meets *Vice*, or as *Vanity Fair* without the vanity—but *Maisonneuve* is its own creature. *Maisonneuve*'s purpose is to keep its readers informed, alert, and entertained, and to dissolve artistic borders between regions, countries, languages, and genres. It does this by providing a diverse range of commentary across the arts, sciences, and daily and social life. The magazine has a balanced perspective and "brings the news" in a wide variety of ways." Estab. 2002. Circ. under 10,000. Byline given. Pays on publication. Offers 25% kill fee. Publishes ms an average of 4-6 months after acceptance. Editorial lead time 4 months. Submit seasonal material 8 months in advance. Accepts simultaneous submissions. Responds in 2 weeks to queries; in 3 months to mss. Sample copy online. Guidelines available online.

NONFICTION Needs essays, general interest, historical, humor, interview, personal experience, photo feature. Submit ms via online submissions manager (maisonneuvemagazine.submittable.com) or by mail. Length: 50-5,000 words. **Pays 10¢/word.** Pays expenses of writers on assignment.

PHOTOS Contact: anna@maisonneuve.org. State availability. Captions, identification of subjects, model releases required. Reviews GIF/JPEG files. Negotiates payment individually. Buys one-time rights.

✿Ⓢ THE MALAHAT REVIEW

The University of Victoria, P.O. Box 1700, STN CSC, Victoria BC V8W 2Y2 Canada. (250)721-8524. **E-mail:** malahat@uvic.ca (for queries only). **Website:** www.malahatreview.ca. **Contact:** John Barton, editor. **100% freelance written. Eager to work with new/ unpublished writers.** Quarterly magazine covering poetry, fiction, creative nonfiction, and reviews. "We try to achieve a balance of views and styles in each issue. We strive for a mix of the best writing by both established and new writers." Estab. 1967. Circ. 2,000. Byline given. Pays on acceptance. No kill fee. Publishes ms an average of 6 months after acceptance. Accepts queries by online submission form. Accepts simultaneous submissions. Responds in 2 weeks to queries; 3-10 months to mss. Sample: $16.95 (U.S.). Guidelines online.

NONFICTION Needs essays, general interest, historical, memoir, personal experience, travel. Submit via online submissions manager. Length: 1,000-3,500 words. **Pays $60/magazine page.** Pays expenses of writers on assignment.

FICTION Buys 12-14 mss/year. Submit via online submissions manager. Length: up to 8,000 words. **Pays $60/magazine page.**

POETRY Needs avant-garde, free verse, traditional. Submit 3-6 poems via online submissions manager. Buys 100 poems/year. Length: up to 6 pages. **Pays $60/ magazine page.**

TIPS "Please do not send more than 1 submission at a time: 3-5 poems, 1 piece of creative nonfiction, or 1 short story (do not mix poetry and prose in the same submission). See *The Malahat Review*'s Open Season Awards for poetry and short fiction, creative nonfiction, long poem, and novella contests in the Awards section of our website."

🌐💲 MĀNOA

A Pacific Journal of International Writing, University of Hawaii at Mānoa, English Department, Honolulu HI 96822. **E-mail:** mjournal-l@lists.hawaii.edu. **Website:** manoajournal.hawaii.edu. **Contact:** Frank Stewart, editor. Semiannual magazine. *Mānoa* is seeking high-quality literary fiction, poetry, essays, and translations for an international audience. In general, each issue is devoted to new work from an area of the Asia-Pacific region. Because we feature different places and have guest editors, please contact us to see if your submission is appropriate for what we're working on. *Mānoa* has received numerous awards, and work published in the magazine has been selected for prize anthologies. See website for recently published issues. Estab. 1989. Circ. 1,000 print, 10,000 digital. Byline given. Pays on publication. Editorial lead time 9 months. Accepts queries by e-mail. Accepts simultaneous submissions. Responds in 3 weeks to queries. Sample: $20. Guidelines online.

NONFICTION No Pacific exotica. Query first. Length: 1,000-5,000 words. **Pays $25/printed page.**

FICTION Query first. Needs mainstream, contemporary, excerpted novel. No Pacific exotica. **Buys 1-2 mss/year.** Send complete ms. Length: 1,000-7,500 words. **Pays $100-500 ($25/printed page).**

POETRY No light verse. Buys 10-20 poems/year. Submit maximum 6 poems. **Pays $25/poem.**

TIPS "Not accepting unsolicited mss at this time because of commitments to special projects. Please query before sending mss as e-mail attachments."

💲 THE MASSACHUSETTS REVIEW

University of Massachusetts, Photo Lab 309, 211 Hicks Way, Amherst MA 01003. (413)545-2689. **E-mail:** massrev@external.umass.edu. **Website:** www.massreview.org. **Contact:** Emily Wojcik, managing editor. Quarterly magazine. Seeks a balance between established writers and promising new ones. Interested in material of variety and vitality relevant to the intellectual and aesthetic questions of our time. Aspire to have a broad appeal. Estab. 1959. Circ. 1,200. Pays on publication. Publishes ms an average of 18 months after acceptance. Accepts queries by mail. Responds in 2-6 months to mss. Sample copy: $8 for back issue, $10 for current issue. Guidelines available online.

NONFICTION No reviews of single books. Articles and essays of breadth and depth are considered, as well as discussions of leading writers; of art, music, and drama; analyses of trends in literature, science, philosophy, and public affairs. Include name and contact information on the first page. Encourages page numbers. Send complete ms or query with SASE. Length: up to 6,500 words. **Pays $50 and 2 contributor's copies.** Pays expenses of writers on assignment.

FICTION Wants short stories. Accepts 1 short story per submission. Include name and contact information on the first page. Encourages page numbers. Has published work by Ahdaf Soueif, Elizabeth Denton, and Nicholas Montemarano. **Buys 30-40 mss/year.** Send complete ms. Length: up to 30 pages or 8,000 words. **Pays $50 and 2 contributor's copies.**

POETRY Has published poetry by Catherine Barnett, Billy Collins, and Dara Wier. Include your name and contact on every page. Submit maximum 6 poems. Length: There are no restrictions for length, but generally poems are less than 100 lines. **Pays $50/publication and 2 contributor's copies.**

TIPS "No manuscripts are considered May-September. Electronic submission process can be found on website. No fax or e-mail submissions. Shorter rather than longer stories preferred (up to 28-30 pages)." Looks for works that "stop us in our tracks." Manuscripts that stand out use "unexpected language, idiosyncrasy of outlook, and are the opposite of ordinary."

💲 MICHIGAN QUARTERLY REVIEW

0576 Rackham Bldg., 915 E. Washington, Ann Arbor MI 48109-1070. (734)764-9265. **E-mail:** mqr@umich.edu. **Website:** www.michiganquarterlyreview.com. **Contact:** Jonathan Freedman, editor; Vicki Lawrence, managing editor. **75% freelance written.** Quarterly journal of literature and the humanities publishing literary essays, fiction, poetry, creative nonfiction, memoir, interviews, and book reviews. *Michigan Quarterly Review* is an eclectic interdisciplinary journal of arts and culture that seeks to combine the best of poetry, fiction, and creative nonfiction with outstanding critical essays on literary, cultural, social, and political matters. The flagship journal of the University of Michigan, *MQR* draws on lively minds here and elsewhere, seeking to present accessible work of all varieties for sophisticated readers from within and without the academy. Estab. 1962. Circ. 1,000. Byline given. Pays on publication. No kill fee. Publishes ms an average of 1 year after acceptance. Accepts queries by mail. Accepts simultaneous submissions. Responds in 2 months to queries and mss. Sample: $4. Guidelines available online.

NONFICTION Needs essays. Special issues: Publishes theme issues. Upcoming themes available in magazine and on website. **Buys 35 mss/year.** Query. Length: 1,500-7,000 words, 5,000 words average. **Payment varies but is usually in the range of $50-$150.** Pays expenses of writers on assignment.

FICTION Contact: Fiction editor. "No restrictions on subject matter or language. We are very selective. We like stories that are unusual in tone and structure, and innovative in language. No genre fiction written for a market. Would like to see more fiction about social, political, and cultural matters, not just centered on a love relationship or dysfunctional family." Receives 300 unsolicited mss/month. Accepts 3-4 mss/issue; 12-16 mss/year. Publishes 1-2 new writers/year. Has published work by Rebecca Makkai, Peter Ho Davies, Laura Kasischke, Gerald Shapiro, and Alan Cheuse. **Buys 10 mss/year.** Send complete ms. Length: 1,500-7,000 words; average length: 5,000 words. **Payment varies but is usually in the range of $50-$150.**

POETRY No previously published poems. No e-mail submissions. Cover letter is preferred. "It puts a human face on the ms. A few sentences of biography is all I want, nothing lengthy or defensive." Prefers typed mss. Reviews books of poetry. "All reviews are commissioned." Length: should not exceed 8-12 pages. **Pays $8-12/published page.**

TIPS "Read the journal and assess the range of contents and the level of writing. We have no guidelines to offer or set expectations; every ms is judged on its unique qualities. On essays, query with a very thorough description of the argument and a copy of the first page. Watch for announcements of special issues, which are usually expanded issues and draw upon a lot of freelance writing. Be aware that this is a university quarterly that publishes a limited amount of fiction and poetry and that it is directed at an educated audience, one that has done a great deal of reading in all types of literature."

THE MISSOURI REVIEW

357 McReynolds Hall, University of Missouri, Columbia MO 65211. (573)882-4474. **E-mail:** question@morreview.com. **Website:** www.missourireview.com. **Contact:** Kate McIntyre. **90% freelance written.** Quarterly magazine. Publishes contemporary fiction, poetry, interviews, personal essays, and special features—

such as History as Literature series, Found Text series, and Curio Cabinet art features—for the literary and the general reader interested in a wide range of subjects. Estab. 1978. Circ. 6,500. Byline given. Pays on publication Editorial lead time 4-6 months. Accepts queries by mail, online submission form. Accepts simultaneous submissions. Responds in 2 weeks to queries; in 10-12 weeks to mss. Sample copy: $10 or online. Guidelines online.

NONFICTION Contact: Evelyn Somers. Needs book excerpts, essays. No literary criticism. **Buys 10 mss/year.** Send complete ms. **Pays $40/printed page.**

FICTION Needs ethnic, humorous, mainstream, short stories, literary. **Buys 25 mss/year.** Send complete ms. Length: No restrictions, but longer mss (9,000-12,000 words) or flash fiction ms (up to 2,000 words) must be truly exceptional to be published. **Pays $40/printed page.**

POETRY *TMR* publishes poetry features only—6-14 pages of poems by each of 3-5 poets per issue. Keep in mind the length of features when submitting poems. Typically, successful submissions include 8-20 pages of unpublished poetry. (Note: Do not send complete mss—published or unpublished—for consideration.) No inspirational verse. **Pays $40/printed page and 3 contributor's copies.**

TIPS "Send your best work."

💲 MODERN HAIKU

P.O. Box 930, Portsmouth RI 02871. **E-mail:** modernhaiku@gmail.com. **Website:** modernhaiku.org. **Contact:** Paul Miller, editor. **85% freelance written.** Magazine published 3 times/year in February, June, and October covering haiku poetry. *Modern Haiku* is the foremost international journal of English-language haiku and criticism and publishes high-quality material only. Haiku and related genres, articles on haiku, haiku book reviews, and translations comprise its contents. It has an international circulation; subscribers include many university, school, and public libraries. *Modern Haiku* is 140 pages (average), digest-sized, printed on heavy-quality stock, with full-color cover illustrations, 4-page full-color art sections. Receives about 15,000 submissions/year, accepts about 1,000. Estab. 1969. Byline given. No kill fee. Publishes ms an average of 6 months after acceptance. Editorial lead time 4 months. Accepts queries by mail, e-mail. Responds in 1 week to queries; in 6-8 weeks to mss. Sample copy: $15 in North America, $16 in Canada,

$20 in Mexico, $22 overseas. Subscription: $35 ppd by regular mail in the U.S. Payment possible by PayPal on the *Modern Haiku* website. Guidelines available for SASE or on website.

NONFICTION Needs essays, general interest. Send complete ms. **Pays $5/page for essays.**

COLUMNS Haiku & Senryu; Haibun; Essays (on haiku and related genres); Reviews (books of haiku or related genres) are assigned. **Buys 40 mss/year.** Send complete ms. **Pays $5/page.**

POETRY Needs haiku, senryu, haibun, haiga. Postal submissions: "Send 5-15 haiku on 1 or 2 letter-sized sheets. Put name and address at the top of each sheet. Include SASE." E-mail submissions: "May be attachments (recommended) or pasted in body of message. Subject line must read: MH Submission. Adhere to guidelines on the website." Publishes 1000 poems/year. Has published haiku by Roberta Beary, Billy Collins, Lawrence Ferlinghetti, Carolyn Hall, Sharon Olds, Gary Snyder, John Stevenson, George Swede, and Cor van den Heuvel. Does not want "general poetry, tanka, renku, linked-verse forms. No special consideration given to work by children and teens." **Offers no payment.**

TIPS "Study the history of haiku, read books about haiku, learn the aesthetics of haiku and methods of composition. Write about your sense perceptions of the suchness of entities; avoid ego-centered interpretations. Be sure the work you send us conforms to the definitions on our website."

❺❺❺❺ NARRATIVE MAGAZINE

2443 Fillmore St., #214, San Francisco CA 94115. **E-mail:** contact@narrativemagazine.com. **Website:** www.narrativemagazine.com. **Contact:** Michael Croft, senior editor; Mimi Kusch, managing editor; Michael Wiegers, poetry editor. **100% freelance written.** Online literary journal that publishes American and international literature 3 times/year. "*Narrative* publishes high-quality contemporary literature in a full range of styles, forms, and lengths. Submit poetry, fiction, and nonfiction, including stories, short shorts, novels, novel excerpts, novellas, personal essays, humor, sketches, memoirs, literary biographies, commentary, reportage, interviews, and short audio recordings of short-short stories and poems. We welcome submissions of previously unpublished mss of all lengths, ranging from short-short stories to complete book-length works for serialization. In addition to submissions for issues of *Narrative* itself, we also encourage submissions for our Story of the Week, Poem of the Week, literary contests, and Readers' Narratives. Please read our Submission Guidelines for all information on mss formatting, word lengths, author payment, and other policies. We accept submissions only through our electronic submission system. We do not accept submissions through postal services or e-mail. You may send us mss for the following submission categories: General Submissions, Narrative Prize, Story of the Week, Poem of the Week, Readers' Narrative, iPoem, iStory, Six-Word Story, or a specific Contest. Your mss must be in one of the following file forms: DOC, RTF, PDF, DOCX, TXT, WPD, ODF, MP3, MP4, MOV, or FLV." Estab. 2003. Circ. 250,000. Byline given. Accepts queries by e-mail. Accepts simultaneous submissions. Responds in 1 month-14 weeks to queries. Guidelines online. **Charges $25 reading fee except for 2 weeks in April.**

NONFICTION Needs book excerpts, essays, general interest, humor, interview, memoir, personal experience, photo feature, travel. Send complete ms.

PHOTOS "We are always on the lookout for photography portfolios and photo essays of exceptional quality."

FICTION Has published work by Alice Munro, Tobias Wolff, Marvin Bell, Jane Smiley, Joyce Carol Oates, E.L. Doctorow, and Min Jin Lee. Publishes new and emerging writers. Fiction, cartoons, graphic art, and multimedia content "to entertain, inspire, and engage." Send complete ms. **Pays on publication between $150-1,000, $1,000-5,000 for book length, plus annual prizes of more than $28,000.**

POETRY Needs poetry of all forms.

TIPS "Log on and study our magazine online. Narrative fiction, graphic art, and multimedia are selected, first and foremost, for quality."

❺ NEW ENGLAND REVIEW

Middlebury College, Middlebury VT 05753. (802)443-5075. **E-mail:** nereview@middlebury.edu. **Website:** www.nereview.com. **Contact:** Marcia Parlow, managing editor. Quarterly literary magazine. *New England Review* is a prestigious, nationally distributed literary journal. Reads September 1-May 31 (postmarked dates). *New England Review* is 200+ pages, 7x10, printed on heavy stock, flat-spined, with glossy cover with art. Receives 3,000-4,000 poetry submissions/year, accepts about 70-80 poems/year. Receives

550 unsolicited mss/month, accepts 6 mss/issue, 24 fiction mss/year. Does not accept mss June-August, December-January. Agented fiction less than 5%. Estab. 1978. Circ. 2,000. Byline given. Pays on publication. No kill fee. Publishes ms an average of 6 months after acceptance. Accepts simultaneous submissions. Responds in 2 weeks to queries; in 3 months to mss. Sometimes comments on rejected mss. Sample copy: $10 (add $5 for overseas). Subscription: $35. Overseas shipping fees add $25 for subscription, $12 for Canada. Guidelines online.

NONFICTION **Buys 20-25 mss/year.** Send complete ms via online submission manager. No e-mail submissions. Length: up to 7,500 words, though exceptions may be made. **Pays $20/page ($40 minimum) and 2 contributor's copies.** Pays expenses of writers on assignment.

FICTION Send 1 story at a time, unless it is very short. Wants only serious literary fiction and novel excerpts. Publishes approximately 10 new writers/year. Has published work by Steve Almond, Christine Sneed, Roy Kesey, Thomas Gough, Norman Lock, Brock Clarke, Carl Phillips, Lucia Perillo, Linda Gregerson, and Natasha Trethewey. **Buys 25 mss/year.** Send complete ms via online submission manager. No e-mail submissions. "Will consider simultaneous submissions, but it must be stated as such and you must notify us immediately if the ms is accepted for publication elsewhere." Length: not strict on word count. **Pays $20/page ($20 minimum), and 2 contributor's copies.**

POETRY Submit up to 6 poems at a time. No previously published or simultaneous submissions for poetry. Accepts submissions by online submission manager only; accepts questions by e-mail. "Cover letters are useful." Address submissions to "Poetry Editor." Buys 75-90 poems/year. Submit maximum 6 poems. **Pays $20/page ($20 minimum), and 2 contributor's copies.**

TIPS "We consider short fiction, including short shorts, novellas, and self-contained extracts from novels in both traditional and experimental forms. In nonfiction, we consider a variety of general and literary but not narrowly scholarly essays; we also publish long and short poems, screenplays, graphics, translations, critical reassessments, statements by artists working in various media, testimonies, and letters from abroad. We are committed to exploration of all forms of contemporary cultural expression in the U.S. and abroad. With few exceptions, we print only work not published previously elsewhere."

$ NEW LETTERS

University of Missouri-Kansas City, 5101 Rockhill Rd., Kansas City MO 64110. (816)235-1168. **Fax:** (816)235-2611. **E-mail:** newletters@umkc.edu. **Website:** www.newletters.org. **Contact:** Robert Stewart, editor-in-chief. **100% freelance written.** "*New Letters*, published quarterly, continues to seek the best new writing, whether from established writers or those ready and waiting to be discovered. In addition, it supports those writers, readers, and listeners who want to experience the joy of writing that can both surprise and inspire us all." Submissions are not read May 1 through October 1. Estab. 1934. Circ. 3,000. Byline given. Pays on publication. No kill fee. Publishes ms an average of 6 months after acceptance. Editorial lead time 6 months. Submit seasonal material 6 months in advance. Accepts queries by mail. Accepts simultaneous submissions. Responds in 1 month to queries; 5 months to mss. Sample copy: $10; sample articles online. Guidelines online.

NONFICTION Needs essays. No self-help, how-to, or nonliterary work. **Buys 8-10 mss/year.** Send complete ms. Length: up to 5,000 words. **Pays $40-100.** Pays expenses of writers on assignment.

PHOTOS Send photos. Reviews contact sheets, 2x4 transparencies, prints. Pays $10-40/photo. Buys one-time rights.

FICTION Needs ethnic, experimental, humorous, mainstream, contemporary. No genre fiction. **Buys 15-20 mss/year.** Send complete ms. Length: up to 5,000 words. **Pays $30-75.**

POETRY Needs avant-garde, free verse, haiku, traditional. No light verse. Buys 40-50 poems/year. Submit maximum 6 poems. Length: open. **Pays $10-25.**

TIPS "We aren't interested in essays that are footnoted or essays usually described as scholarly or critical. Our preference is for creative nonfiction or personal essays. We prefer shorter stories and essays to longer ones (an average length is 3,500-4,000 words). We have no rigid preferences as to subject, style, or genre, although commercial efforts tend to put us off. Even so, our only fixed requirement is good writing."

$ NEW OHIO REVIEW

English Department, 79 S. Court St.; Lindley Hall, Ohio University, Athens OH 45701. (740)707-3191. **E-mail:** noreditors@ohio.edu. **Website:** www.ohiou.edu/nor. **Contact:** David Wanczyk, editor. *New Ohio Review*, published biannually in spring and fall, publishes fiction, nonfiction, and poetry. Member CLMP. Reading period is September 15-December 15 and January 15-April 15. Annual contests, Jan 15th-Apr 15th ($1,000 prizes). Estab. 2007. Byline given. No kill fee. Accepts queries by e-mail, online submission form. Accepts simultaneous submissions. Responds in 2-4 months. Single copy: $9. Subscription: $16. Guidelines online.

NONFICTION Needs essays, general interest, memoir. Submit complete ms. **Pays minimum of $30 in addition to 2 contributor's copies and one-year subscription.** Pays expenses of writers on assignment.

FICTION Considers literary short fiction; no novel excerpts. Send complete ms. **Pays $30 minimum in addition to 2 contributor's copies and one-year subscription.**

POETRY Needs quality free verse, formal, experimental. Please do not submit more than once every 6 months unless requested to do so. Submit maximum 6 poems.

[C] $ $ THE NEW QUARTERLY

St. Jerome's University, 290 Westmount Rd. N., Waterloo ON N2L 3G3 Canada. (519)884-8111, ext. 28290. **E-mail:** editor@tnq.ca; info@tnq.ca. **Website:** www.tnq.ca. Sophie Blom. **95% freelance written.** Quarterly book covering Canadian fiction and poetry. "Emphasis on emerging writers and genres, but we publish more traditional work as well if the language and narrative structure are fresh." Open to Canadian writers only. Reading periods: March 1-August 31; September 1-February 28. Estab. 1981. Circ. 1,000. Byline given. Pays on publication. No kill fee. Editorial lead time 6 months. Accepts queries by mail. Accepts simultaneous submissions. Responds in early January to submissions received March 1-August 31; in early June to submissions received September 1-February 28. Sample copy: $16.95 (cover price, plus mailing). Guidelines online.

NONFICTION Needs essays. Query with a proposal.

FICTION "*Canadian work only.* We are not interested in genre fiction. We are looking for innovative, beautifully crafted, deeply felt literary fiction." literary. **Buys 20-25 mss/year.** Send complete ms with submission cover sheet and bio. Does not accept submissions by e-mail. Accepts simultaneoues submissions if indicated in cover letter. **Pays $250/story.**

POETRY Needs avant-garde, free verse, traditional. *Canadian work only.* Send with submission cover sheet and bio. Does not accept submissions by e-mail. Accepts simultaneoues submissions if indicated in cover letter. Submit maximum 3 poems. **Pays $40/poem.**

TIPS "Reading us is the best way to get our measure. We don't have preconceived ideas about what we're looking for other than that it must be Canadian work (Canadian writers, not necessarily Canadian content). We want something that's fresh, something that will repay a second reading, something in which the language soars and the feeling is complexly rendered."

$ ONE STORY

232 3rd St., #A108, Brooklyn NY 11215. **Website:** www.one-story.com. **Contact:** Maribeth Batcha, publisher. **100% freelance written.** "*One Story* is a literary magazine that contains, simply, 1 story. Approximately every 3-4 weeks, subscribers are sent *One Story* in the mail. *One Story* is artfully designed, lightweight, easy to carry, and ready to entertain on buses, in bed, in subways, in cars, in the park, in the bath, in the waiting rooms of doctor's offices, on the couch, or in line at the supermarket. Subscribers also have access to a website where they can learn more about *One Story* authors and hear about *One Story* readings and events. There is always time to read *One Story*." Estab. 2002. Circ. 3,500. Byline given. Pays on publication. Publishes ms an average of 3-6 months after acceptance. Editorial lead time 3-4 months. Accepts queries by online submission form. Accepts simultaneous submissions. Responds in 2-4 months to mss. Sample copy: $2.50 (back issue). Guidelines available online.

FICTION Needs short stories. *One Story* only accepts short stories. Do not send excerpts. Do not send more than 1 story at a time. **Buys 18 mss/year.** Send complete ms using online submission form. Length: 3,000-8,000 words. **Pays $500 and 25 contributor's copies.**

TIPS "*One Story* is looking for stories that are strong enough to stand alone. Therefore they must be very good. We want the best you can give."

$ OVERTIME

Blue Cubicle Press, LLC, P.O. Box 250382, Plano TX 75025. **E-mail:** overtime@workerswritejournal.com. **Website:** www.workerswritejournal.com/overtime. htm. **Contact:** David LaBounty, editor. **100% freelance written.** Quarterly saddle-stitched chapbook covering working-class literature. Estab. 2006. Circ. 500. Byline given. Pays on acceptance of ms. Publishes ms 6 months after acceptance. Accepts queries by mail, e-mail. Accepts simultaneous submissions. Responds in 1 week to queries; 1 month to mss. Sample copy and writer's guidelines available online.

FICTION Needs adventure, condensed novels, ethnic, experimental, historical, humorous, mainstream, novel excerpts, short stories, slice-of-life vignettes, working-class literature. **Buys 4 mss/year.** Query; send complete ms. Length: 5,000-12,000 words. **Pays $35-50 and one-year print subscription.**

$ PAINTED BRIDE QUARTERLY

Drexel University, Department of English and Philosophy, 3141 Chestnut St., Philadelphia PA 19104. **E-mail:** info@pbqmag.org. **Website:** pbqmag.org. **Contact:** Kathleen Volk Miller and Marion Wrenn, editors. Publishes online each quarter with a print annual each spring. *Painted Bride Quarterly* seeks literary fiction (experimental and traditional), poetry, and artwork and photographs. Estab. 1973. No kill fee. Accepts queries by online submission form. Accepts simultaneous submissions. Responds in 6 months to mss. Guidelines available online and by e-mail.

NONFICTION Needs essays, literary criticism. Submit 1 ms through online submissions manager. Length: up to 3,000 words. **Pays $20.**

FICTION Publishes theme-related work; check website. Holds annual fiction contests. ethnic, experimental, feminist, gay, lesbian, literary, short stories, translations. Send complete ms through online submissions manager. Length: up to 5,000 words. **Pays $20.**

POETRY Submit up to 3 poems through online submissions manager. "We have no specifications or restrictions. We'll look at anything." **Pays $20/poem.**

TIPS "We look for freshness of idea incorporated with high-quality writing. We receive an awful lot of nicely written work with worn-out plots. We want quality in whatever—we hold experimental work to as strict standards as anything else. Many of our readers write fiction; most of them enjoy a good reading. We hope to be an outlet for quality. A good story gives, first, enjoyment to the reader. We've seen a good many of them lately, and we've published the best of them."

$$$$ PAKN TREGER

National Yiddish Book Center, 1021 West St., Amherst MA 01002. (413)256-4900. **E-mail:** aatherley@bikher.org; pt@bikher.org;. **Website:** www.yiddishbookcenter.org. **Contact:** Anne Atherley, editor's assistant. **50% freelance written.** Literary magazine published 3 times/year; focuses on modern and contemporary Jewish and Yiddish culture. Estab. 1980. Circ. 20,000. Byline given. Pays on publication. Publishes ms an average of 3 months after acceptance. Editorial lead time 4 months. Submit seasonal material 3 months in advance. Accepts queries by mail, e-mail, fax. Accepts simultaneous submissions. Responds in 4 weeks to queries. Responds in 3 months to mss. Sample copy available online. Guidelines by e-mail.

NONFICTION Needs essays, humor, interview. Does not want personal memoirs, fiction, or poetry. **Buys 6-10 mss/year.** Query. Length: 1,200-4,000 words. **Pays $800-2,000 for assigned articles. Pays $350-1,000 for unsolicited articles.** Pays expenses of writers on assignment.

PHOTOS State availability. Identification of subjects required. Reviews GIF/JPEG files. Negotiates payment individually. Buys one-time rights.

COLUMNS Let's Learn Yiddish (Yiddish lesson), 1 page Yid/English; Translations (Yiddish-English), 1,200-2,500 words. **Pays $350-1,000.**

TIPS "Read the magazine and visit our website."

$ PANK

PANK, Department of Humanities, 1400 Townsend Dr., Houghton MI 49931-1200. **Website:** www.pank-magazine.com. **100% freelance written.** Annual literary magazine. "*PANK* Magazine fosters access to emerging and experimental poetry and prose, publishing the brightest and most promising writers for the most adventurous readers. To the end of the road, up country, a far shore, the edge of things, to a place of amalgamation and unplumbed depths, where the known is made and unmade, and where unimagined futures are born, a place inhabited by contradictions, a place of quirk and startling anomaly. *PANK*, no soft pink hands allowed." Estab. 2006. Circ. 1,000/print; 18,000/online. Publishes ms an average of 3-12 months after acceptance. Accepts queries by online submission form. Accepts simultaneous submissions. Guidelines available on website.

NONFICTION Needs essays, general interest, historical, humor, nostalgic, opinion. Send complete ms through online submissions manager. **Pays $20, a one-year subscription, and a** *PANK* **t-shirt.** Pays expenses of writers on assignment.

FICTION "Bright, new, energetic, passionate writing, writing that pushes our tender little buttons and gets us excited. Push our tender buttons, excite us, and we'll publish you." Send complete ms through online submissions manager. **Pays $20, a one-year subscription, and a** *PANK* **t-shirt.**

POETRY Submit through online submissions manager. **Pays $20, a one-year subscription, and a** *PANK* **t-shirt.**

TIPS "To read *PANK* is to know *PANK*. Or, read a lot within the literary magazine and small-press universe—there's plenty to choose from. Unfortunately, we see a lot of submissions from writers who have clearly read neither *PANK* nor much else. Serious writers are serious readers. Read. Seriously."

THE PARIS REVIEW

544 West 27th St., New York NY 10001. (212)343-1333. **E-mail:** queries@theparisreview.org. **Website:** www. theparisreview.org. **Contact:** Lorin Stein, editor; Robyn Creswell, poetry editor. Quarterly magazine. *The Paris Review* publishes "fiction and poetry of superlative quality, whatever the genre, style, or mode. Our contributors include prominent, as well as less well-known and previously unpublished writers. The Writers at Work interview series includes important contemporary writers discussing their own work and the craft of writing." Pays on publication. No kill fee. Accepts queries by mail. Accepts simultaneous submissions. Responds in 4 months to mss. Guidelines available online.

NONFICTION Pays expenses of writers on assignment.

FICTION Study the publication. Annual Plimpton Prize award of $10,000 given to a new voice published in the magazine. Recently published work by Ottessa Moshfegh, John Jeremiah Sullivan, and Lydia Davis. Send complete ms. Length: no limit. **Pays $1,000-3,000.**

POETRY **Contact:** Robyn Creswell, poetry editor. Submit no more than 6 poems at a time. Poetry can be sent to the poetry editor (please include a self-addressed, stamped envelope). **Poets receive $100/poem.**

PARNASSUS

Poetry in Review, Poetry in Review Foundation, 205 W. 89th St., #8F, New York NY 10024. (212)787-3569. **E-mail:** info@parnassus.com. **Website:** www. parnassusreview.com. **Contact:** Herbert Leibowitz, editor and publisher. Annual magazine covering poetry and criticism. "We now publish 1 double issue/year." *Parnassus: Poetry in Review* provides "a forum where poets, novelists, and critics of all persuasions can gather to review new books of poetry, including translations—international poetries have occupied center stage from our very first issue—with an amplitude and reflectiveness that Sunday book supplements and even the literary quarterlies could not afford. Our editorial philosophy is based on the assumption that reviewing is a complex art. Like a poem or a short story, a review essay requires imagination; scrupulous attention to rhythm, pacing, and supple syntax; space in which to build a persuasive, detailed argument; analytical precision and intuitive gambits; verbal play, wit, and metaphor. We welcome and vigorously seek out voices that break aesthetic molds and disturb xenophobic habits." Estab. 1972. Circ. 1,800. Byline given. Pays on publication. No kill fee. Publishes ms an average of 12-14 months after acceptance. Accepts queries by mail. Accepts simultaneous submissions. Responds in 2 months to mss. Sample copy: $15.

NONFICTION Needs essays, reviews. **Buys 30 mss/year.** Query with published clips. Length: 1,500-7,500 words. **Pays $200-1,000.** Pays expenses of writers on assignment.

POETRY Needs avant garde, free verse, traditional. Accepts most types of poetry. Buys 3-4 unsolicited poems/year.

TIPS "Be certain you have read the magazine and are aware of the editor's taste. Blind submissions are a waste of everybody's time. We'd like to see more poems that display intellectual acumen and curiosity about history, science, music, etc., and fewer trivial lyrical poems about the self, or critical prose that's academic and dull. Prose should sing."

THE PEDESTAL MAGAZINE

6815 Honors Court, Charlotte NC 28210. **E-mail:** pedmagazine@carolina.rr.com. **Website:** www.the-pedestalmagazine.com. **Contact:** John Amen, editor in chief. Committed to promoting diversity and celebrating the voice of the individual. Estab. 2000. No kill fee. Accepts queries by online submission form.

Accepts simultaneous submissions. Responds in 1-2 months to mss. Guidelines available online.

NONFICTION Needs essays, interview, reviews. **Pays $40.**

PHOTOS Reviews JPEG, GIF files.

FICTION "We are receptive to all sorts of high-quality literary fiction. Genre fiction is encouraged as long as it crosses or comments upon its genre and is both character-driven and psychologically acute. We encourage submissions of short fiction, no more than 3 flash fiction pieces at a time. There is no need to query prior to submitting; please submit via online submissions manager—no e-mail to the editor." Needs adventure, ethnic, experimental, historical, horror, humorous, mainstream, mystery, romance, science fiction, works that don't fit into a specific category. **Buys 10-25 mss/year.** Length: up to 4,000 words for short stories; up to 1,000 words for flash fiction. **Pays 3¢/word.**

POETRY Open to a wide variety of poetry, ranging from the highly experimental to the traditionally formal. Submit all poems in 1 form. No need to query before submitting. Submit maximum 5 poems. No length restriction.

TIPS "If you send us your work, please wait for a response to your first submission before you submit again."

❾❸ PLANET: THE WELSH INTERNATIONALIST

Berw Ltd., P.O. Box 44, Aberystwyth Ceredigion SY23 3ZZ United Kingdom. 01970 622408. **E-mail:** admin@planetmagazine.org.uk. **E-mail:** submissions@planetmagazine.org.uk. **Website:** www.planetmagazine.org.uk. Administrative and Marketing Assistant: Lowri Angharad Pearson. **Contact:** Emily Trahair, editor. Quarterly journal. A literary/cultural/political journal centered on Welsh affairs but with a strong interest in minority cultures in Europe and elsewhere. *Planet: The Welsh Internationalist*, published quarterly, is a cultural magazine centered on Wales, but with broader interests in arts, sociology, politics, history, and science. *Planet* is 96 pages, A5, professionally printed, perfect-bound, with glossy colour card cover. Receives about 500 submissions/year, accepts about 5%. Press run is 1,000 (800 subscribers, about 10% libraries, 200 shelf sales). Estab. 1970. Circ. 900. Publishes ms 4-6 months after acceptance. Accepts queries by mail, e-mail, phone. Responds in 3 months.

Single copy: £6.75; subscription: £22 (£40 overseas). Sample copy: £5. Guidelines online.

NONFICTION Needs essays, general interest, historical, humor, interview, personal experience, reviews, travel. Query. Subscriptions.

FICTION Would like to see more inventive, imaginative fiction that pays attention to language and experiments with form. No magical realism, horror, science fiction. Submit complete ms via mail or e-mail (with attachment). For postal submissions, no submissions returned unless accompanied by an SASE. Writers submitting from abroad should send at least 3 IRCs for return of typescript; 1 IRC for reply only. Length: 1,500-2,750 words. **Pays £50/1,000 words.**

POETRY Wants good poetry in a wide variety of styles. No limitations as to subject matter; length can be a problem. Has published poetry by Nigel Jenkins, Anne Stevenson, and Les Murray. Submit 4-6 poems via mail or e-mail (with attachment). For postal submissions, no submissions returned unless accompanied by an SASE. Writers submitting from abroad should send at least 3 IRCs for return of typescript; 1 IRC for reply only. **Pays £30/poem.**

TIPS "We do not look for fiction that necessarily has a 'Welsh' connection, which some writers assume from our title. We try to publish a broad range of fiction, and our main criterion is quality. Try to read copies of any magazine you submit to. Don't write out of the blue to a magazine which might be completely inappropriate for your work. Recognize that you are likely to have a high rejection rate, as magazines tend to favor writers from their own countries."

❸ PLEIADES

Literature in Context, University of Central Missouri, Department of English, Martin 336, 415 E. Clark St., Warrensburg MO 64093. (660)543-4268. **E-mail:** clintoncrockettp@gmail.com (nonfiction inquiries); pnguyen@ucmo.edu (fiction inquiries); pleiadespoetryeditor@gmail.com (poetry inquiries). **Website:** www.pleiadesmag.com. **Contact:** Clinton Crockett Peters, nonfiction editor; Phong Nguyen, fiction editor; and Jenny Molberg, poetry editor. **100% freelance written.** "We publish contemporary fiction, poetry, interviews, literary essays, special-interest personal essays, and reviews for a general and literary audience from authors from around the world." Reads in the months of July for the summer issue and December for the winter issue. Estab. 1991. Circ. 3,000. Byline given. Pays on publication. No kill fee. Publishes ms an average of 9 months after acceptance. Editorial lead time 9 months. Accepts queries by mail. Accepts simultaneous submissions. Responds in 2 months to queries; in 1-4 months to mss. Sample copy for $5 (back issue); $6 (current issue). Guidelines online.

NONFICTION Needs book excerpts, essays, interview, reviews. "Nothing pedantic, slick, or shallow." **Buys 4-6 mss/year.** Send complete ms via online submission manager. Length: 2,000-4,000 words. **Pays $10 and contributor's copies.**

FICTION Reads fiction year-round. Needs ethnic, experimental, humorous, mainstream, magic realism. No science fiction, fantasy, confession, erotica. **Buys 16-20 mss/year.** Send complete ms via online submission manager. Length: 2,000-6,000 words. **Pays $10 and contributor's copies.**

POETRY Needs Wants avant-garde, free verse, haiku, light verse, traditional. Submit 3-5 poems via online submission manager. "Nothing didactic, pretentious, or overly sentimental." Buys 40-50 poems/year. **Pays $3/poem and contributor copies.**

TIPS "Submit only 1 genre at a time to appropriate editors. Show care for your material and your readers—submit quality work in a professional format. Cover art is solicited directly from artists. We accept queries for book reviews."

$$ PLOUGHSHARES

Emerson College, 120 Boylston St., Boston MA 02116. (617)824-3757. **E-mail:** pshares@pshares.org. **Website:** www.pshares.org. **Contact:** Ladette Randolph, editor-in-chief/executive director; Ellen Duffer, managing editor. *Ploughshares* publishes issues four times a year. 2 of these issues are guest-edited by different, prominent authors. A third issue, a mix of both prose and poetry, is edited by our staff editors. The fourth issue is a collection of longform work edited by our Editor-in-chief, Ladette Randolph; these stories and essays are first published as e-books known as Ploughshares Solos. Translations are welcome if permission has been granted. We accept electronic submissions—there is a $3 fee per submission, which is waived if you are a subscriber. Ploughshares is 200 pages, digest-sized. Receives about 11,000 poetry, fiction, and essay submissions/year. Reads submissions June 1-January 15 (postmark); hosts the Emerging Writer's Contest, for writers who have yet to publish a book-length work, March 1-May 15; mss submitted at all other times will be returned unread. A competitive and highly prestigious market. Rotating and guest editors make cracking the line-up even tougher, since it's difficult to know what is appropriate to send. Estab. 1971. Circ. 6,000. Pays on publication. Publishes ms an average of 6 months after acceptance. Accepts queries by mail, online submission form. Accepts simultaneous submissions. Responds in 3-5 months to mss. Sample copy: $14 for current issue, $7 for back issue; please inquire for shipping rates. Subscription: $30 domestic, $30 plus shipping (see website) foreign. Guidelines online.

NONFICTION Needs essays. Submit complete ms via online submissions form or by mail. Length: up to 6,000 words. **Pays $45/printed page ($90 minimum, $450 maximum); 2 contributor's copies; and one-year subscription.** Pays expenses of writers on assignment.

FICTION Has published work by ZZ Packer, Antonya Nelson, and Stuart Dybek. Submit via online submissions form or by mail. Length: up to 6,000 words **Pays $45/printed page ($90 minimum, $450 maximum); 2 contributor's copies; and one-year subscription.**

POETRY Submit up to 5 poems via online submissions form or by mail. Has published poetry by Donald Hall, Li-Young Lee, Robert Pinsky, Brenda Hillman, and Thylias Moss. **Pays $45/printed page ($90 minimum, $450 maximum); 2 contributor's copies; and one-year subscription.**

$$ POETRY

The Poetry Foundation, 61 W. Superior St., Chicago IL 60654. (312)787-7070. **Fax:** (312)787-6650. **E-mail:** editors@poetrymagazine.org. **Website:** www.poetrymagazine.org. **Contact:** Don Share, editor. **100% freelance written.** Monthly magazine. *Poetry*, published monthly by The Poetry Foundation (see separate listing in Organizations), "has no special ms needs and no special requirements as to form: We examine in turn all work received and accept that which seems best." Has published poetry by the major voices of our time as well as new talent. *Poetry*'s website offers featured poems, letters, reviews, interviews, essays, and web-exclusive features. *Poetry* is elegantly printed, flat-spined. Receives 150,000 submissions/year, accepts about 300-350. Press run is 16,000. Estab. 1912. Circ. 32,500. Byline given. Pays on publication. No kill fee. Publishes ms an average of 9 months after acceptance. Accepts queries by e-mail. Accepts simultaneous submissions. Responds within 6 months to mss and queries. Guidelines online.

NONFICTION Buys 14 mss/year. Query. No length requirements. **Pays $150/page.** Pays expenses of writers on assignment.

POETRY Publishes poetry all styles and subject matter. Submit up to 4 poems via Submittable. Reviews books of poetry, most solicited. Buys 180-250 poems/year. Length: up to 10 pages total. **Pays $10 line (minimum payment of $300).**

🌀💲 POETRY IRELAND REVIEW

Poetry Ireland, 11 Parnell Square E., Dublin 1 Ireland. +353(0)16789815. **E-mail:** publications@poetry-ireland.ie. **Website:** www.poetryireland.ie. 3 times a year covers poetry, reviews, and essays in book form. Estab. 1981. Circ. 2,000. Pays on publication. No kill fee. Accepts queries by mail. Accepts simultaneous submissions. Responds in 1 week to queries; 3 months to mss. Guidelines online.

POETRY Needs contemporary, lyric, avant-garde, free verse, haiku. Buys 120 poems/year. Submit maximum 6 poems. **Pays €40-75/submission.**

🌀💲 THE PRAIRIE JOURNAL

A Magazine of Canadian Literature, P.O. Box 68073, 28 Crowfoot Terrace NW, Calgary AB T3G 3N8 Canada. **E-mail:** editor@prairiejournal.org (queries only); prairiejournal@yahoo.com. **Website:** www.prairie-journal.org. **Contact:** Anne Burke, literary editor. **100% freelance written.** Semiannual magazine publishing quality poetry, short fiction, drama, literary criticism, reviews, bibliography, interviews, profiles, and artwork. "The audience is literary, university, library, scholarly, and creative readers/writers. We welcome newcomers and unsolicited submission of writing and artwork. In addition to the print issues, we publish online long poems, fiction, interviews, drama, and reviews." Estab. 1983. Circ. 650-750. Byline given. Pays on publication. No kill fee. Publishes ms an average of 4-6 months after acceptance. Editorial lead time 2-6 months. Accepts queries by mail. Responds in 2 weeks to queries; 2-6 months to mss. Sample copy: $5. Guidelines online.

NONFICTION Needs essays, humor, interview, profile, reviews, literary. No inspirational, news, religious, or travel. Buys 25-40 mss/year. Query with published clips. Length: 100-3,000 words. **Pays $50-100, plus**

contributor's copy. Pays expenses of writers on assignment.

PHOTOS State availability. Offers additional payment for photos accepted with ms. Rights purchased is negotiable.

COLUMNS Reviews (books from small presses publishing poetry, short fiction, essays, and criticism), 200-1,000 words. Buys 5 mss/year. Query with published clips. **Pays $10-50.**

FICTION Needs mainstream. No genre: romance, horror, western—sagebrush or cowboys—erotic, science fiction, or mystery. Buys 6 mss/year. Send complete ms. No e-mail submissions. Length: 100-3,000 words. **Pays $10-75.**

POETRY Needs avant-garde, free verse, haiku. Seeks poetry "of any length; free verse, contemporary themes (feminist, nature, urban, nonpolitical), aesthetic value, a poet's poetry." Does not want to see "most rhymed verse, sentimentality, egotistical ravings. No cowboys or sage brush." Has published poetry by Liliane Welch, Cornelia Hoogland, Sheila Hyland, Zoe Lendale, and Chad Norman. Receives about 1,000 poems/year, accepts 10%. No heroic couplets or greeting-card verse. Buys 25-35 poems/year. Submit maximum 6-8 poems. Length: 3-50 lines. **Pays $5-50.**

TIPS "We publish many, many new writers and are always open to unsolicited submissions because we are 100% freelance. Do not send U.S. stamps; always use IRCs. We have poems, interviews, stories, and reviews online (query first)."

🌀💲 PRISM INTERNATIONAL

Dept. of Creative Writing, Buch E462, 1866 Main Mall, University of British Columbia, Vancouver BC V6T 1Z1 Canada. (604)822-2514. **Fax:** (604)822-3616. **E-mail:** prismcirculation@gmail.com. **Website:** www.prismmagazine.ca. **100% freelance written. Works with new/unpublished writers.** A quarterly international journal of contemporary writing—fiction, poetry, drama, creative nonfiction and translation. *PRISM international* is digest-sized, elegantly printed, flat-spined, with original colour artwork on a nylon card cover. Readership: public and university libraries, individual subscriptions, bookstores—a world-wide audience concerned with the contemporary in literature. "We have no thematic or stylistic allegiances: Excellence is our main criterion for acceptance of manuscripts." Receives 1,000 submissions/year, accepts about 80. Circulation is for 1,200 subscribers.

Subscription: $35/year for Canadian subscriptions, $40/year for US subscriptions, $45/year for international. Sample: $13. Estab. 1959. Circ. 1,200. Pays on publication. No kill fee. Publishes ms an average of 4 months after acceptance. Accepts queries by mail, e-mail, online submission form. Accepts simultaneous submissions. Responds in 4 months to queries; 3-6 months to mss. Sample copy for $13, more info online. Guidelines online.

NONFICTION No tracts, or scholarly essays. **Prose pays $30/printed page, and 2 copies of issue.** Pays expenses of writers on assignment.

PHOTOS PRISM international buys photography for covers only. Sample copies available for $13 each; art guidelines free for SASE with first-class Canadian postage. Portfolio review not required. Buys first rights. "Image may also be used for promotional purposes related to the magazine." Pays on publication: $300 Canadian and 2 copies of magazine. Portfolio review not required. Buys first rights. "Image may also be used for promotional purposes related to the magazine." Pays on publication: $300 Canadian and 2 copies of magazine.

FICTION For Drama: one-acts/excerpts of no more than 1,500 words preferred. Also interested in seeing dramatic monologues. Needs experimental, traditional. "New writing that is contemporary and literary. Short stories and self-contained novel excerpts. Works of translation are eagerly sought and should be accompanied by a copy of the original. Would like to see more translations. No gothic, confession, religious, romance, pornography, or science fiction." **Buys 12-16 mss/year.** Send complete ms. Length: 25 pages maximum. **Pays $30/printed page, and 2 copies of issue.**

POETRY Needs avant-garde, traditional. Wants "fresh, distinctive poetry that shows an awareness of traditions old and new. We read everything." Considers poetry by children and teens. "Excellence is the only criterion." Has published poetry by Margaret Avison, Elizabeth Bachinsky, John Pass, Warren Heiti, Don McKay, Bill Bissett, and Stephanie Bolster. Submit maximum up to 6 poems. **Pays $40/printed page, and 2 copies of issue.**

TIPS "We are looking for new and exciting fiction. Excellence is still our No. 1 criterion. As well as poetry, imaginative nonfiction and fiction, we are especially open to translations of all kinds, very short fiction pieces and drama which work well on the page. Translations must come with a copy of the original language work."

$ THE RAG

P.O. Box 17463, Portland OR 97217. **E-mail:** submissions@raglitmag.com; seth@raglitmag.com. **Website:** raglitmag.com. **Contact:** Seth Porter, managing editor; Dan Reilly, editor. **90% freelance written.** *The Rag* focuses on the grittier genres that tend to fall by the wayside at more traditional literary magazines. *The Rag*'s ultimate goal is to put the literary magazine back into the entertainment market while rekindling the social and cultural value short fiction once held in North American literature. Estab. 2011. Byline given. Pays prior to publication. Editorial lead time 1-2 months. Accepts queries by e-mail. Accepts simultaneous submissions. Responds in 1 month or less for queries; in 1-2 months for mss. Guidelines available online.

NONFICTION Pays expenses of writers on assignment.

PHOTOS Reviews GIF/JPEG files. Negotiates payment individually. Purchases one-time rights.

FICTION Accepts all styles and themes. Needs humorous, transgressive. **Buys 12 mss/year.** Send complete ms. Length: up to 10,000 words. **Pays 5¢/word, $250 average/story.**

FILLERS Length: 150-1,000 words. **Pays $20-100.**

TIPS "We like gritty material: material that is psychologically believable and that has some humor in it, dark or otherwise. We like subtle themes, original characters, and sharp wit."

$ RALEIGH REVIEW LITERARY & ARTS MAGAZINE

Box 6725, Raleigh NC 27628-6725. **E-mail:** info@raleighreview.org. **Website:** www.raleighreview.org. **Contact:** Rob Greene, editor; Landon Houle, fiction editor; Bryce Emley, poetry editor. **90% freelance written.** Semiannual literary magazine. "*Raleigh Review* is a national nonprofit magazine of poetry, short fiction (including flash), and art. We believe that great literature inspires empathy by allowing us to see the world through the eyes of our neighbors, whether across the street or across the globe. Our mission is to foster the creation and availability of accessible yet provocative contemporary literature. We look for work that is emotionally and intellectually complex." Estab. 2010. Pays on publication. Publishes ms 3-6 months after acceptance. Accepts simultaneous submissions. Responds typically in 1-3 months, though sometimes up to 3-6 months. "Poetry and fiction submissions through Submittable; no prior query required." Sample copy: $15 hardcopy or $4.95 on Kindle. "Sample work also online at website." Guidelines online.

NONFICTION Pays expenses of writers on assignment.

FICTION Needs confessions, ethnic, mainstream, novel excerpts, slice-of-life vignettes. "We prefer work that is physically grounded and accessible, though complex and rich in emotional or intellectual power. We delight in stories from unique voices and perspectives. Any fiction that is born from a relatively unknown place grabs our attention. We are not opposed to genre fiction, so long as it has real, human characters and is executed artfully." **Buys 10-15 mss/year.** Submit complete ms. Length: 250-7,500 words. "While we accept fiction up to 7,500 words, we are more likely to publish work in the 4,500- to 5,000-word range." **Pays $10 maximum.**

POETRY Needs free verse, traditional, lyric, narrative poems of experience. Submit up to 5 poems. "If you think your poems will make a perfect stranger's toes tingle, heart leap, or brain sizzle, then send them our way. We typically do not publish avant garde, experimental, or language poetry. We *do* like a poem that causes—for a wide audience—a visceral reaction to intellectually and emotionally rich material." Buys 30-40 poems/year. Submit maximum 5 poems. Length: open. **Pays $10 maximum.**

TIPS "Please be sure to read the guidelines and look at sample work on our website. Every piece is read for its intrinsic value, so new/emerging voices are often published alongside nationally recognized, award-winning authors."

🌐 $ THE RIALTO

P.O. Box 309, Aylsham, Norwich NR11 6LN England. **E-mail:** info@therialto.co.uk. **Website:** www.therialto.co.uk. **Contact:** Michael Mackmin, editor. *The Rialto*, published 3 times/year, seeks to publish the best new poems by established and beginning poets. Seeks excellence and originality. Has published poetry by Alice Fulton, Jenny Joseph, Les Murray, George Szirtes, Philip Gross, and Ruth Padel. Estab. 1984. Pays on publication. Publishes ms 5 months after acceptance. Accepts queries by mail, online submission form. Accepts simultaneous submissions. Responds in 3-4 months. Guidelines available online.

POETRY Submit up to 6 poems at a time via postal mail (with SASE) or online submissions manager. **Pays £20/poem.**

TIPS *The Rialto* also publishes occasional books and pamphlets. Please do not send book-length mss. Query first. Details available in magazine and on website. Before submitting, "you will probably have read many poems by many poets, both living and dead. You will probably have put aside each poem you write for at least 3 weeks before considering it afresh. You will have asked yourself, 'Does it work technically?'; checked the rhythm, the rhymes (if used), and checked that each word is fresh and meaningful in its context, not jaded and tired. You will hopefully have read *The Rialto*."

🍁 $ ROOM

West Coast Feminist Literary Magazine Society, P.O. Box 46160, Station D, Vancouver BC V6J 5G5 Canada. **E-mail:** contactus@roommagazine.com. **Website:** www.roommagazine.com. "*Room* is Canada's oldest feminist literary journal. Published quarterly by a collective based in Vancouver, *Room* showcases fiction, poetry, reviews, artwork, interviews, and profiles by writers and artists who identify as women or genderqueer. Many of our contributors are at the beginning of their writing careers, looking for an opportunity to get published for the first time. Some later go on to great acclaim. *Room* is a space where women can speak, connect, and showcase their creativity. Each quarter we publish original, thought-provoking works that reflect women's strength, sensuality, vulnerability, and wit." Estab. 1975. Circ. 1,400. Byline given. Pays on publication. Offers kill fee if work is accepted but cannot be published. Accepts queries by online submission form. Accepts simultaneous submissions. Responds in 6 months. Sample copy: $12 or online at website.

NONFICTION **Buys 1-2 mss/year.** Submit complete ms via online submissions manager. Length: up to 3,500 words. **Pays $50-120 CAD, 2 contributor's copies, and a one-year subscription.** Pays expenses of writers on assignment.

FICTION Accepts literature that illustrates the female experience—short stories, creative nonfiction, poetry—by, for, and about women. Submit complete ms via online submissions manager. **Pays $50-120**

CAD, 2 contributor's copies, and a one-year subscription.

POETRY *Room* uses "poetry by women, including trans and genderqueer writers, written from a feminist perspective. Nothing simplistic, clichéd. We prefer to receive up to 5 poems at a time, so we can select a pair or group." Submit via online submissions manager. Pays $50-120 CAD, 2 contributor's copies, and a one-year subscription.

THE SAVAGE KICK LITERARY MAGAZINE

Murder Slim Press, 29 Alpha Rd., Gorleston Norfolk NR31 0LQ United Kingdom. **E-mail:** moonshine@murderslim.com. **Website:** www.murderslim.com. **100% freelance written.** Semiannual magazine. "*Savage Kick* primarily deals with viewpoints outside the mainstream: honest emotions told in a raw, simplistic way. It is recommended that you are very familiar with the *SK* style before submitting. Ensure you have a distinctive voice and story to tell." Estab. 2005. Circ. 500+. Byline given. Pays on acceptance. Publishes ms an average of 2 months after acceptance. Accepts queries by mail, e-mail. Accepts simultaneous submissions. Responds in 7-10 days to queries. Guidelines available online.

NONFICTION Needs interview, personal experience. **Buys 10-20 mss/year.** Send complete ms by postal mail or e-mail. Length: up to 3,000 words. **Pays £15 (U.K.) or $25 (international).** Pays expenses of writers on assignment.

COLUMNS Buys up to 4 mss/year. Query. **Pays $25-35.**

FICTION Needs mystery, slice-of-life vignettes. "Real-life stories are preferred, unless the work is distinctively extreme within the crime genre. No poetry of any kind. No mainstream fiction, Oprah-style fiction, Internet/chat language, teen issues, excessive Shakespearean language, surrealism, overworked irony, or genre fiction (horror, fantasy, science fiction, western, erotica, etc.)." **Buys 10-25 mss/year.** Send complete ms via postal mail or e-mail. Length: up to 8,000 words. **Pays £15 (U.K.) or $25 (international).**

SEQUESTRUM

Sequestrum Publishing, 1023 Garfield Ave., Ames IA 50014. **E-mail:** sequr.info@gmail.com. **Website:** www.sequestrum.org. **Contact:** R.M. Cooper, managing editor. Biweekly literary magazine in tabloid and online formats. All publications are paired with a unique visual component. Regularly holds contests and features well-known authors, as well as promising new and emerging voices. Estab. 2014. Circ. 2,500 monthly. Byline given. Pays on acceptance. 100% kill fee. Publishes ms 2-6 months after acceptance. Editorial lead time: 3 months. Accepts queries by online submission form. Accepts simultaneous submissions. Sample copy available for free online. Guidelines online.

NONFICTION Needs book excerpts, essays, expose, general interest, humor, inspirational, memoir, opinion, personal experience, photo feature, religious, travel, narrative, experimental. Special issues: Two contests yearly: Editor's Reprint Award (for previously published material) and New Writer Awards (for writers yet to publish a book-length manuscript). **Buys 3-5 mss/year.** Submit complete ms via online submissions manager. Length: 500-12,000 words. **Pays $10/article.** Pays expenses of writers on assignment.

PHOTOS Send photos with submission (GIF/JPEG files). Pays $10/photo. Buys one-time rights.

FICTION Needs adventure, confessions, ethnic, experimental, fantasy, horror, humorous, mainstream, mystery, novel excerpts, science fiction, short stories, suspense, western, slipstream. **Buys 20-36 mss/year.** Submit complete ms via online submissions manager. Length: 12,000 words max. **Pays $10-15/story.**

POETRY Needs avant-garde, free verse, light verse, traditional, cross-genre. Buys 20 poems/year. Submit maximum 4 poems. Length: 40 lines. **Pays $10/set of poems.**

TIPS "Reading a past issue goes a long way; there's little excuse not to. Our entire archive is available online to preview, and subscription rates are variable. Send your best, most interesting work. General submissions are always open, and we regularly hold contests and offer awards which are themed."

THE SEWANEE REVIEW

735 University Ave., Sewanee TN 37383. (931)598-1246. **E-mail:** sewaneereview@sewanee.edu. **Website:** thesewaneereview.com. **Contact:** Adam Ross, editor. *The Sewanee Review* is America's oldest continuously published literary quarterly. Publishes original fiction, poetry, essays, and interviews. Does not read mss June 1-July 31. Estab. 1892. Circ. 2,200. Byline given. Pays on publication. Accepts queries by online submission form. Accepts simultaneous submissions. Responds in 1-3 months. Sample copy: $12.00. Guidelines online.

NONFICTION Submit complete ms via online submissions manager. Queries accepted but not preferred. Rarely accepts unsolicited reviews. Length: up to 10,000 words. **Pays $25/page, $300 minimum.**

FICTION literary, contemporary. **Buys 10-15 mss/year.** Submit complete ms via online submissions manager. Length: up to 10,000 words. **Pays $25/page, $300 minimum.**

POETRY Submit up to 6 poems via online submissions manager. Buys 25-30 poems/year. **Pays $3.33/line, $100 minimum.**

$ SHENANDOAH

Washington and Lee University, Lexington VA 24450. (540)458-8908. **E-mail:** shenandoah@wlu.edu. **Website:** shenandoahliterary.org. **Contact:** R.T. Smith, editor; William Wright, assistant editor. Semiannual digital-only literary journal. For more than half a century, *Shenandoah* has been publishing splendid poems, stories, essays, and reviews which display passionate understanding, formal accomplishment, and serious mischief. Estab. 1950. Circ. 2,000. Byline given. Pays on publication. No kill fee. Publishes ms an average of 10 months after acceptance. Accepts queries by online submission form. Accepts simultaneous submissions. Responds in 4-6 weeks to mss. Sample copy: $12. Guidelines online.

NONFICTION Needs essays, interview, reviews. **Buys 6 mss/year.** Send complete ms via online submissions manager. Query for reviews and interviews. Length: up to 20 pages. **Pays $25/page ($250 maximum), one-year subscription, and 1 contributor's copy.**

FICTION Needs mainstream, novel excerpts. No sloppy, hasty, slight fiction. **Buys 15 mss/year.** Send complete ms via online submissions manager. Length: up to 20 pages. **Pays $25/page ($250 maximum), one-year subscription, and 1 contributor's copy.**

POETRY Submit 3-5 poems via online submissions manager. No inspirational, confessional poetry. Buys 70 poems/year. Submit maximum 5 poems. **Pays $2.50/line, one-year subscription, and 1 contributor's copy.**

$ THE SOUTHERN REVIEW

338 Johnston Hall, Louisiana State University, Baton Rouge LA 70803. (225)578-5104. **Fax:** (225)578-6461. **E-mail:** southernreview@lsu.edu. **Website:** thesouthernreview.org. **Contact:** Jessica Faust, co-editor and poetry editor; Emily Nemens, co-editor and prose editor. **100% freelance written. Works with a moderate number of new/unpublished writers each year; reads unsolicited mss.** Quarterly magazine with emphasis on contemporary literature in the U.S. and abroad. "*The Southern Review* is one of the nation's premiere literary journals. Hailed by *Time* as 'superior to any other journal in the English language,' we have made literary history since our founding in 1935. We publish a diverse array of fiction, nonfiction, and poetry by the country's—and the world's—most respected contemporary writers." Reading period: September 1 through December 1 (prose); September 1 through February 1 (poetry). All mss submitted during outside the reading period will be recycled. Estab. 1935. Circ. 2,900. Byline given. Pays on publication. No kill fee. Publishes ms an average of 6 months after acceptance. Accepts queries by mail, online submission form. Accepts simultaneous submissions. Responds in 6 months. Sample copy: $12. Guidelines available online at thesouthernreview.org/submissions.

NONFICTION Needs essays. **Buys 15 mss/year.** Submit ms by mail or through online submission form. Length: up to 8,000 words. **Pays $25/printed page (max $200), 2 contributor's copies, and 1-year subscription.** Pays expenses of writers on assignment.

FICTION Wants short stories of lasting literary merit, with emphasis on style and technique; novel excerpts. "We emphasize style and substantial content. No mystery, fantasy, or religious mss." **Buys 30 mss/year.** Submit 1 ms at a time by mail or through online submission form. "We rarely publish work that is longer than 8,000 words. We consider novel excerpts if they stand alone." Length: up to 8,000 words. **Pays $25/printed page (max $200), 2 contributor's copies, and 1-year subscription.**

POETRY Submit poems by mail. Submit maximum 5 poems. **Pays $25/printed page (max $200); 2 contributor's copies, and 1-year subscription.**

TIPS "Careful attention to craftsmanship and technique combined with a developed sense of the creation of story will always make us pay attention."

$$ THE STRAND MAGAZINE

P.O. Box 1418, Birmingham MI 48012-1418. (800)300-6652. **E-mail:** strandmag@strandmag.com. **Website:** www.strandmag.com. Quarterly magazine covering mysteries, short stories, essays, book reviews. "After an absence of nearly half a century, the magazine known to millions for bringing Sir Arthur Conan Doyle's ingenious detective, Sherlock Holmes, to the world has once again appeared on the literary scene. First launched in 1891, *The Strand* included in its pages the works of some of the greatest writers of the 20th century: Agatha Christie, Dorothy Sayers, Margery Allingham, W. Somerset Maugham, Graham Greene, P.G. Wodehouse, H.G. Wells, Aldous Huxley, and many others. In 1950, economic difficulties in England caused a drop in circulation, which forced the magazine to cease publication." Estab. 1998. Circ. 50,000. Byline given. Pays on acceptance. No kill fee. Publishes ms an average of 4 months after acceptance. Accepts queries by e-mail. Accepts simultaneous submissions. Responds in 1 month to queries; in 4-10 months to mss. Sample copy: $10. Guidelines online.

NONFICTION Query.

FICTION "We are interested in mysteries, detective stories, tales of terror and the supernatural as well as short stories. Stories can be set in any time or place, provided they are well written, the plots interesting and well thought." Occasionally accepts short shorts and short novellas. Needs horror, humorous, mystery, suspense. "We are not interested in submissions with any sexual content." Submit complete ms by postal mail. Include SASE. No e-mail submissions. Length: 2,000-6,000 words. **Pays $25-150.**

TIPS "No gratuitous violence, sexual content, or explicit language, please."

💲💲💲 SUBTROPICS

University of Florida, P.O. Box 112075, 4008 Turlington Hall, Gainesville FL 32611-2075. **E-mail:** subtropics@english.ufl.edu. **Website:** www.english.ufl.edu/subtropics. **Contact:** David Leavitt, editor. **100% freelance written.** Magazine published twice/year through the University of Florida's English department. *Subtropics* seeks to publish the best literary fiction, essays, and poetry being written today, both by established and emerging authors. Will consider works of fiction of any length, from short shorts to novellas and self-contained novel excerpts. Gives the same latitude to essays. Appreciates work in translation and, from time to time, republishes important and compelling stories, essays, and poems that have lapsed out of print by writers no longer living. Member: CLMP. Estab. 2005. Circ. 1,500. Byline given. Pays on acceptance for prose; pays on publication of the issue preceding the issue in which the author's

work will appear for poetry. Publishes ms an average of 6 months after acceptance. Accepts simultaneous submissions. Responds in 1 month to queries and mss. Rarely comments on/critiques rejected mss Sample copy: $12.95. Guidelines online.

NONFICTION No book reviews. **Buys 4-5 mss/year.** Send complete ms via online submissions manager. Length: up to 15,000 words. Average length: 5,000 words. **Pays $1,000.**

FICTION Does not read May 1-August 31. Agented fiction 33%. **Publishes 1-2 new writers/year.** Has published John Barth, Ariel Dorfman, Tony D'Souza, Allan Gurganus, Frances Hwang, Kuzhali Manickavel, Eileen Pollack, Padgett Powell, Nancy Reisman, Jarret Rosenblatt, Joanna Scott, and Olga Slavnikova. No genre fiction. **Buys 10-12 mss/year.** Submit complete ms via online submissions manager. Length: up to 15,000 words. Average length: 5,000 words. Average length of short shorts: 400 words. **Pays $500 for short shorts; $1,000 for full stories; 2 contributor's copies.**

POETRY Submit up to 4 poems via online submissions manager. Buys 50 poems/year. **Pays $100 per poem.**

TIPS "We publish longer works of fiction, including novellas and excerpts from forthcoming novels. Each issue includes a short-short story of about 250 words on the back cover. We are also interested in publishing works in translation for the magazine's English-speaking audience."

💲 TAMPA REVIEW

University of Tampa Press, 401 W. Kennedy Blvd., Tampa FL 33606. (813)253-6266. **Fax:** (813)258-7593. **E-mail:** utpress@ut.edu. **Website:** www.ut.edu/tampareview. **Contact:** Richard Mathews, editor; Daniel Dooghan, nonfiction editor; Shane Hinton and Yuly Restrepo, fiction editors; Geoff Bouvier and Elizabeth Winston, poetry editors. Semiannual magazine published in hardback format. An international literary journal publishing art and literature from Florida and Tampa Bay as well as new work and translations from throughout the world. "We no longer accept paper submissions. Please submit all work via the online submission manager. You will find it on our website under the link titled 'How to Submit.'" Estab. 1988. Circ. 700. Byline given. Pays on publication. No kill fee. Publishes ms an average of 10 months after acceptance. Editorial lead time 18 months. Accepts queries by mail, e-mail. Accepts simultaneous submissions.

Responds in 3-4 months to mss. Sample copy: $12. Guidelines online.

NONFICTION Contact: Daniel Dooghan, nonfiction editor. Needs essays, general interest, personal experience, creative nonfiction. No how-to articles, fads, journalistic reprise, etc. **Buys 6 mss/year.** Send complete ms via online submissions manager. We no longer accept submissions by mail. Length: up to 5,000 words. **Pays $10/printed page, 1 contributor's copy, and offers 40% discount on additional copies.** Pays expenses of writers on assignment.

PHOTOS State availability. Captions, identification of subjects required. Reviews contact sheets, negatives, transparencies, prints, digital files. Offers $10/photo. Buys one-time rights.

FICTION Contact: Yuly Restrepo and Andrew Plattner, fiction editors. Needs ethnic, experimental, fantasy, historical, mainstream, Literary. "We are far more interested in quality than in genre. Nothing sentimental as opposed to genuinely moving, nor self-conscious style at the expense of human truth." **Buys 6 mss/year.** Send complete ms via online submissions manager. We no longer accept submissions by mail. Length: up to 5,000 words. **Pays $10/printed page, 1 contributor's copy, and offers 40% discount on additional copies.**

POETRY Contact: Geoff Bouvier and Elizabeth Winston, poetry editors. Needs avant-garde, free verse, haiku, light verse, traditional. No greeting card verse, hackneyed, sing-song, rhyme-for-the-sake-of-rhyme. Buys 45 poems/year. Submit maximum 6 poems. Length: 2-225 lines. **Pays $10/printed page, 1 contributor's copy, and offers 40% discount on additional copies.**

TIPS "Send a clear cover letter stating previous experience or background. Our editorial staff considers submissions between September and December for publication in the following year."

ⓢ THEMA

Thema Literary Society, P.O. Box 8747, Metairie LA 70011-8747. **E-mail:** thema@cox.net. **E-mail:** For writers living outside the U.S. **Website:** themaliterarysociety.com. **Contact:** Virginia Howard, editor; Gail Howard, poetry editor. **100% freelance written.** "*THEMA* is designed to stimulate creative thinking by challenging writers with unusual 'themes, such as "Is There a Word for That?' and 'The Face in the Photograph.' Appeals to writers, teachers of creative writing, artists, photographers, and general reading audience." *THEMA* is 100 pages, digest-sized professionally printed, with glossy card cover. Receives about 400 poems/year, accepts about 8%. Press run is 400 (230 subscribers, 30 libraries). Subscription: $30 U.S./$40 foreign. Has published poetry by Beverly Boyd, John Grey, James B. Nicola, and Matthew Spireng. Estab. 1988. Byline given. Pays on acceptance. No kill fee. Publishes ms, on average, within 6 months after acceptance. Accepts queries by mail, e-mail. Accepts simultaneous submissions. Responds in 1 week to queries; 5 months to mss (after deadline for submission on given theme). Sample $15 U.S./$25 foreign. Upcoming themes and guidelines available in magazine, for SASE, by e-mail, or on website.

NONFICTION Contact: Virginia Howard, editor. Needs book excerpts, essays, historical, humor, memoir, nostalgic, personal experience. Special issues: Nonfiction must relate to one of the upcoming themes. No salacious subject matter. Length: 300-6,000 words (1-20 double-spaced pages). **Pays $10 for under 1,000 words; $25 for articles over 1,000 words.**

PHOTOS Contact: Virginia Howard, editor. Submitted photograph must relate to one of the upcoming themes. high resolution; portrait orientation. Payment: $10 for interior black-and-white photo; $25 for full-color cover photo. Acquires one-time rights only.

FICTION Contact: Virginia Howard, editor. All stories must relate to one of *THEMA*'s upcoming themes (**indicate the target theme on submission of manuscript**). See website for themes. Needs adventure, ethnic, experimental, fantasy, historical, humorous, mainstream, mystery, religious, science fiction, short stories, slice-of-life vignettes, suspense, Fiction **must** relate to a target theme. No erotica. Send complete ms with SASE, cover letter; include "name and address, brief introduction, **specifying the intended target issue for the mss.**" SASE. Accepts simultaneous, multiple submissions, and reprints. Does not accept e-mailed submissions except from non-USA addresses. Length: 300-6,000 words (1-20 double-spaced pages). **Payment: $10 for under 1,000 words; $25 for stories over 1,000 words, plus one contributor copy.**

POETRY Contact: Gail Howard, poetry editor. Needs All poetry must relate to one of *THEMA*'s upcoming themes (**indicate the target theme on submission of manuscript**). See website for themes. Submit up to 3 poems at a time. Include SASE. All submissions should be typewritten on standard $8\frac{1}{2}$x11 paper. Submissions are accepted all year, but evaluated after specified deadlines. **Specify target theme.** Editor comments on submissions. Each issue is based on an unusual premise. Please send SASE for guidelines before submitting poetry to find out the upcoming themes. Does not want scatologic language or explicit love poetry. Buys 24 published out of 250 submitted poems/year. Submit maximum 3 poems. Length: 1-3 pages. **Payment: $10/poem and 1 contributor's copy.**

💲💲 THE THREEPENNY REVIEW

P.O. Box 9131, Berkeley CA 94709. (510)849-4545. **E-mail:** wlesser@threepennyreview.com. **Website:** www.threepennyreview.com. **Contact:** Wendy Lesser, editor. **100% freelance written. Works with small number of new/unpublished writers each year.** Quarterly tabloid. "We are a general-interest, national literary magazine with coverage of politics, the visual arts, and the performing arts." Reading period: January 1-June 30. Estab. 1980. Circ. 6,000-9,000. Byline given. Pays on acceptance. Publishes ms an average of 1 year after acceptance. Responds in 2 days to 2 months Sample copy: $12, or online. Guidelines online.

NONFICTION Needs essays, historical, memoir, personal experience, reviews, book, film, theater, dance, music, and art reviews. **Buys 40 mss/year.** Send complete ms. Length: 1,500-4,000 words. **Pays $400.**

FICTION No fragmentary, sentimental fiction. **Buys 8 mss/year.** Send complete ms. Length: 800-4,000 words. **Pays $400.**

POETRY Needs free verse, traditional. No poems without capital letters or poems without a discernible subject. Buys 30 poems/year. Submit maximum 5 poems. Length: up to 100 lines/poem. **Pays $200.**

TIPS "Nonfiction (political articles, memoirs, reviews) is most open to freelancers."

💲💲💲 TIN HOUSE

McCormack Communications, P.O. Box 10500, Portland OR 97296. (503)219-0622. **E-mail:** info@tinhouse.com. **Website:** www.tinhouse.com. **Contact:** Cheston Knapp, managing editor; Holly MacArthur, founding editor. **90% freelance written.** "We are a general-interest literary quarterly. Our watchword is quality. Our audience includes people interested in literature in all its aspects, from the mundane to the exalted." Estab. 1999. Circ. 11,000. Byline given. Pays

on publication. No kill fee. Publishes ms an average of 6 months after acceptance. Editorial lead time 6 months. Submit seasonal material 6 months in advance. Accepts queries by mail, online submission form. Accepts simultaneous submissions. Responds in 6 weeks to queries; in 4 months to mss. Sample copy: $15. Guidelines online.

NONFICTION Needs book excerpts, essays, interview, personal experience. Special issues: Check website for upcoming theme issues. Submit via online submissions manager or postal mail. Include cover letter with word count. Length: up to 10,000 words. **Pays $50-800 for assigned articles. Pays $50-500 for unsolicited articles.** Pays expenses of writers on assignment.

FICTION Needs experimental. Submit via online submissions manager or postal mail. Include cover letter with word count. Length up to 10,000 words. **Pays $200-800.**

POETRY Needs avant-garde, free verse, traditional. Submit via online submissions manager or postal mail. Include cover letter. Submit maximum 5 poems. **Pays $50-150.**

💲💲 UPSTREET

Ledgetop Publishing, P.O. Box 105, Richmond MA 01254-0105. (413)441-9702. **E-mail:** editor@upstreet-mag.org. **Website:** www.upstreet-mag.org. **Contact:** Vivian Dorsel, Founding Editor/Publisher. **95% freelance written.** Annual magazine covering literary fiction, nonfiction and poetry; author interview in each issue. Estab. 2005. Circ. 4,000. Byline given. Pays on publication. Publishes ms an average of 6 months after acceptance. Editorial lead time 6 months. Accepts queries by online submission form. Accepts simultaneous submissions. Responds in 2 weeks to queries; 6 months to mss. Sample copy for $12.00, plus shipping. Guidelines online and in each issue.

NONFICTION **Contact:** Richard Farrell, creative nonfiction editor. Needs book excerpts, essays, memoir, personal experience, literary, personal essay/memoir, lyric essay. Does not want journalism, religious, technical, anything but literary nonfiction. **Buys 8 mss/year.** Send complete ms. Length: 5,000 words. **Pays $50-250.**

FICTION **Contact:** Joyce A. Griffin, fiction editor. Needs experimental, mainstream, novel excerpts, short stories, quality literary fiction. Does not want run-of-the-mill genre, children's, anything but literary. **Buys 12 mss/year.** Send complete ms. Length: 5,000 words. **Pays $50-250.**

POETRY Contact: Frances Richey, poetry editor. Needs avant-garde, free verse, traditional. Quality is only criterion. Does not consider unsolicited poetry. Buys 20-25 poems/year. Submit maximum 3 poems. **Pays $50-150.**

TIPS "Get sample copy, submit electronically, and follow guidelines."

⚙️💲 VALLUM: CONTEMPORARY POETRY

5038 Sherbrooke West, P.O. Box 23077, CP Vendome, Montreal QC H4A 1T0 Canada. **E-mail:** info@vallummag.com; editors@vallummag.com. **Website:** www.vallummag.com. **Contact:** Joshua Auerbach and Eleni Zisimatos, editors. Poetry/fine arts magazine published twice/year. Publishes exciting interplay of poets and artists. Content for magazine is selected according to themes listed on website. Material is not filed but is returned upon request by SASE. E-mail response is preferred. Seeking exciting, unpublished, traditional or avant garde poetry that reflects contemporary experience. *Vallum* is 100 pages, digest sized (7x8½), digitally printed, perfect-bound, with color images on coated stock cover. Includes ads. Single copy: $12 CDN; subscription: $20/year CDN; $24 U.S. (shipping included). Make checks payable to *Vallum*. Estab. 2000. Pays on publication. Sample copy online. Guidelines online.

NONFICTION Also publishes reviews, interviews, essays and letters to the editor. Please send queries to editors@vallummag.com before submitting. **Pays $85 for accepted reviews or essays on poetry.** Pays expenses of writers on assignment.

POETRY Pays honorarium for accepted poems.

💲 VERSE

English Department, University of Richmond, Richmond VA 23173. **Website:** versemag.blogspot.com. **Contact:** Brian Henry, co-editor; Andrew Zawacki, co-editor. *Verse*, published 3 times/year, is an international poetry journal which also publishes interviews with poets, essays on poetry, and book reviews. Wants no specific kind; looks for high-quality, innovative poetry. Focus is not only on American poetry, but on all poetry written in English, as well as translations. Has published poetry by James Tate, John Ashbery, Barbara Guest, Gustaf Sobin, and Rae Armantrout. Estab. 1984. Accepts simultaneous submissions. Guidelines available online.

NONFICTION Interested in any nonfiction, plus translations, criticisms, interviews, journals/notebooks, etc. Submissions should be chapbook-length (20-40 pages). **Pays $10/page, $250 minimum.** Pays expenses of writers on assignment.

FICTION Interested in any genre. Submissions should be chapbook-length (20-40 pages). **Pays $10/page, $250 minimum.**

POETRY Submissions should be chapbook-length (20-40 pages). **Pays $10/page, $250 minimum.**

TIPS "Read widely and deeply. Avoid inundating a magazine with submissions; constant exposure will not increase your chances of getting accepted."

💲 VESTAL REVIEW

P.O. Box 35369, Brighton MA 02135. **E-mail:** submissions@vestalreview.net. **Website:** www.vestalreview.org. **Contact:** Mark Budman, editor. **100.** Semi-annual print magazine specializing in flash fiction. The oldest magazine of flash fiction. A paying market. Our reading periods are February-May and August-November. Estab. 2000. Circ. 1,500. Byline given. Pays on publication. No kill fee. Publishes ms an average of 6 months after acceptance. Accepts queries by e-mail. Accepts simultaneous submissions. Responds in 1 week to queries; in 6 months to mss. Guidelines online.

FICTION Only flash fiction under 500 words. Needs ethnic, experimental, fantasy, horror, humorous, mainstream, short stories, flash fiction. No porn, racial slurs, excessive gore, or obscenity. No children's or preachy stories. Nothing over 500 words. Publishes flash fiction. "We accept submissions only through our submission manager." Length: 50-500 words. **Pays $25 and 1 contributor's copy.**

TIPS "We like literary fiction with a plot that doesn't waste words. Don't send jokes masked as stories."

💲💲💲💲 THE VIRGINIA QUARTERLY REVIEW

VQR, P.O. Box 400223, Charlottesville VA 22904. **E-mail:** editors@vqronline.org. **Website:** www.vqronline.org. **Contact:** Allison Wright, executive editor. "*VQR*'s primary mission has been to sustain and strengthen Jefferson's bulwark, long describing itself as 'A National Journal of Literature and Discussion.' And for good reason. From its inception in prohibition, through depression and war, in prosperity and peace, *The Virginia Quarterly Review* has been a haven—and home—for the best essayists, fiction writers, and poets, seeking contributors from every section of the United States and abroad. It has not limited itself to any special field. No topic has been alien: literary, public affairs, the arts, history, the economy. If it could be approached through essay or discussion, poetry or prose, *VQR* has covered it." Press run is 4,000. Estab. 1925. Accepts queries by online submission form. Responds in 3 months to mss. Guidelines available on website.

NONFICTION "We publish literary, art, and cultural criticism; reportage; historical and political analysis; and travel essays. We publish few author interviews or memoirs. In general, we are looking for nonfiction that looks out on the world, rather than within the self." Accepts online submissions only at virginiaquarterlyreview.submittable.com/submit. You can also query via this site. Length: 3,500-10,000 words. **Pays $500 for book reviews; $1,000-3,000 for essays, memoir, criticism, and reportage.** Pays expenses of writers on assignment.

FICTION "We are generally not interested in genre fiction (such as romance, science fiction, or fantasy)." Accepts online submissions only at virginiaquarterlyreview.submittable.com/submit. Length: 2,000-10,000 words. **Pays $1,000-2,500 for short stories; $1,000-4,000 for novellas and novel excerpts.**

POETRY *The Virginia Quarterly Review* prints approximately 12 pages of poetry in each issue. No length or subject restrictions. Issues have largely included lyric and narrative free verse, most of which features a strong message or powerful voice. Accepts online submissions only at virginiaquarterlyreview.submittable.com/submit. Submit maximum 5 poems. **Pays $200/poem.**

❸ WEST BRANCH

Stadler Center for Poetry, Bucknell University, Lewisburg PA 17837-2029. (570)577-1853. **Fax:** (570)577-1885. **E-mail:** westbranch@bucknell.edu. **Website:** www.bucknell.edu/westbranch. **Contact:** G.C. Waldrep, editor. Semiannual literary magazine. *West Branch* publishes poetry, fiction, and nonfiction in both traditional and innovative styles. Byline given. Pays on publication. No kill fee. Accepts queries by online submission form. Accepts simultaneous submissions. Sample copy for $3. Guidelines available online.

NONFICTION Needs essays, general interest, literary. **Buys 4-5 mss/year.** Send complete ms. Length: no more than 30 pages. **Pays 5¢/word, with a maximum of $100.** Pays expenses of writers on assignment.

FICTION Needs novel excerpts, short stories. No genre fiction. **Buys 10-12 mss/year.** Send complete ms. Length: no more than 30 pages. **Pays 5¢/word, with a maximum of $100.**

POETRY Needs free and formal verse. Buys 30-40 poems/year. Submit maximum 6 poems. **Pays $50/submission.**

TIPS "All submissions must be sent via our online submission manager. Please see website for guidelines. We recommend that you acquaint yourself with the magazine before submitting."

❸❸ WESTERLY MAGAZINE

University of Western Australia, The Westerly Centre (M202), Crawley WA 6009 Australia. (61)(8)6488-3403. **Fax:** (61)(8)6488-1030. **E-mail:** westerly@uwa.edu.au. **Website:** westerlymag.com.au. **Contact:** Catherine Noske, editor. *Westerly*, published in July and November, prints quality short fiction, poetry, literary criticism, socio-historical articles, and book reviews with special attention given to Australia, Asia, and the Indian Ocean region. "We assume a reasonably well-read, intelligent audience. Past issues of *Westerly* provide the best guides. Not consciously an academic magazine." Estab. 1956. Time between acceptance and publication may be up to 1 year, depending on when work is submitted. Accepts queries by online submission form. "Please wait for a response before forwarding any additional submissions for consideration."

NONFICTION Submit complete ms by postal mail, e-mail, or online submissions form. Length: up to 5,000 words for essays; up to 3,500 words for creative nonfiction. **Pays $150 and contributor's copies.** Pays expenses of writers on assignment.

FICTION Submit complete ms by mail, e-mail, or online submissions form. Length: up to 3,500 words. **Pays $150 and contributor's copies.**

POETRY "We don't dictate to writers on rhyme, style, experimentation, or anything else. We are willing to publish short or long poems." Submit up to 3 poems by mail, e-mail, or online submissions form. **Pays $75 for 1 page or 1 poem, or $100 for 2 or more pages/poems, and contributor's copies.**

WESTERN HUMANITIES REVIEW

University of Utah, 3528 LNCO / English Department, 255 S. Central Campus Dr., Salt Lake City UT 84112-0494. (801)581-6168. **Fax:** (801)585-5167. **E-mail:** managingeditor.whr@gmail.com. **Website:** www.westernhumanitiesreview.com. **Contact:** Michael Mejia, editor; Emily Dyer Barker, managing editor. A tri-annual magazine for educated readers. *Western Humanities Review* is a journal of contemporary literature and culture housed in the University of Utah English Department. Publishes poetry, fiction, nonfiction essays, artwork, and work that resists categorization. Reading period: September 1 through April 15. All submissions must be sent through online submissions manager. Estab. 1947. Circ. 1,000. Pays in contributor copies. Publishes ms an average of 1 year after acceptance. Accepts simultaneous submissions. Responds in 3-5 months. Sample copy: $10. Guidelines online.

NONFICTION **Buys 6-8 unsolicited mss/year.** Send complete ms. **Pays $5/published page (when funds available).** Pays expenses of writers on assignment.

FICTION Contact: Michael Mejia, fiction editor. Needs experimental, innovative voices. Does not want genre (romance, science fiction, etc.). **Buys 5-8 mss/year.** Send complete ms. Length: 5,000 words. **Pays $5/published page (when funds available).**

POETRY Contact: Poetry editors: Katharine Coles, Tom Stillinger. Considers simultaneous submissions but no more than 5 poems or 25 pages per reading period. No fax or e-mail submissions. Reads submissions September 1 through April 1 only. Wants quality poetry of any form, including translations. Has published poetry by Charles Simic, Olena Kalytiak Davis, Ravi Shankar, Karen Volkman, Dan Beachy-Quick, Lucie Brock-Broido, Christine Hume, and Dan Chiasson. Innovative prose poems may be submitted as fiction or nonfiction to the appropriate editor. **Pays 2 contributor's copies.**

TIPS "Because of changes in our editorial staff, we urge familiarity with recent issues of the magazine. We do not publish writer's guidelines because we think that the magazine itself conveys an accurate picture of our requirements. Please, no e-mail submissions."

WILLOW SPRINGS

668 N. Riverpoint Blvd. #259, Spokane WA 99202. (509)828-1486. **E-mail:** willowspringsewu@gmail.com. **Website:** willowsprings.ewu.edu. **Contact:** Samuel Ligon, editor. **95% freelance written.** *Willow Springs* is a semiannual magazine covering poetry, fiction, literary nonfiction and interviews of notable writers. Published twice a year, in spring and fall. Reading period: September 1 through May 31 for fiction and poetry; year-round for nonfiction. Reading fee: $3/submission. Estab. 1977. Circ. 1,200. Byline given. Publishes ms an average of 3 months after acceptance. Accepts queries by e-mail, online submission form. Accepts simultaneous submissions. Sample copy: $10. Guidelines online.

NONFICTION Needs book excerpts, essays, general interest, humor, personal experience. **Buys 2-6 mss/year.** Submit via online submissions manager. **Pays $100 and 2 contributor's copies.** Pays expenses of writers on assignment.

FICTION "We accept any good piece of literary fiction. Buy a sample copy." Needs adventure, ethnic, experimental, historical, mainstream, mystery, slice-of-life vignettes, suspense, western. Does not want to see genre fiction that does not transcend its subject matter. **Buys 10-15 mss/year.** Submit via online submissions manager. Length: open for short stories; up to 750 words for short shorts. **Pays $100 and 2 contributor's copies for short stories; $40 and 2 contributor's copies for short shorts.**

POETRY Needs avant-garde, free verse, haiku, traditional. "Buy a sample copy to learn our tastes. Our aesthetic is very open." Submit only 3-5 poems at a time. Buys 50-60 poems/year. **Pays $20/poem and 2 contributor's copies.**

TIPS "While we have no specific length restrictions, we generally publish fiction and nonfiction no longer than 10,000 words and poetry no longer than 120 lines, though those are not strict rules. *Willow Springs* values poems and essays that transcend the merely autobiographical and fiction that conveys a concern for language as well as story."

THE YALE REVIEW

The Yale Review, P.O. Box 208243, New Haven CT 06520-8243. (203)432-0499. **Fax:** (203)432-0510. **Website:** www.yale.edu/yalereview. **Contact:** J.D. McClatchy, editor. **20% freelance written.** Quarterly magazine. "Like Yale's schools of music, drama, and architecture, like its libraries and art galleries, *The Yale Review* has helped give the University its leading place in American education. In a land of quick fixes and short view and in a time of increasingly commercial publishing, the journal has an authority that derives from its commitment to bold established writers and promising newcomers, to both challenging literary work and a range of essays and reviews that can explore the connections between academic disciplines and the broader movements in American society, thought, and culture. With independence and boldness, with a concern for issues and ideas, with a respect for the mind's capacity to be surprised by speculation and delighted by elegance, *The Yale Review* proudly continues into its third century." Estab. 1911. Circ. 7,000. Pays prior to publication. No kill fee. Publishes ms an average of 6 months after acceptance. Accepts simultaneous submissions. Responds in 1-3 months to mss. Sample copy online. Guidelines available online.

NONFICTION Send complete ms with cover letter and SASE. **Pays $400-500.** Pays expenses of writers on assignment.

FICTION Submit complete ms with SASE. All submissions should be sent to the editorial office. **Pays $400-500.**

POETRY Submit with SASE. All submissions should be sent to the editorial office. **Pays $100-250.**

🌑🌑🌑 ZOETROPE: ALL-STORY

Zoetrope: All-Story, The Sentinel Bldg., 916 Kearny St., San Francisco CA 94133. **Website:** www.all-story.com. **Contact:** fiction editor. Quarterly magazine specializing in the best of contemporary short fiction. Winner of the National Magazine Award for Fiction as the finest literary publication in the United States. Estab. 1997. Circ. 20,000. Byline given. Publishes ms an average of 5 months after acceptance. Accepts simultaneous submissions. Responds in 8 months (if SASE included). Sample copy: $10 plus shipping. Guidelines online.

FICTION Buys 15-20 (of 10,000+ submissions annually) mss/year. Writers should submit only one story at a time. We do not accept artwork or design submissions. We do not accept unsolicited revisions nor respond to writers who don't include an SASE. Send complete ms by postal mail. Length: up to 7,000 words. Excerpts from larger works, screenplays, treatments, and poetry will be returned unread. **Pays $1,000.**

🌑 ZYZZYVA

57 Post St., Suite 604, San Francisco CA 94104. (415)757-0465. **E-mail:** editor@zyzzyva.org. **Website:** www.zyzzyva.org. **Contact:** Laura Cogan, editor; Oscar Villalon, managing editor. **100% freelance written. Works with a small number of new/unpublished writers each year.** "Every issue is a vibrant mix of established talents and new voices, providing an elegantly curated overview of contemporary arts and letters with a distinctly San Francisco perspective." Estab. 1985. Circ. 2,500. Byline given. Pays on acceptance. No kill fee. Publishes ms an average of 3 months after acceptance. Accepts queries by mail. Accepts simultaneous submissions. Responds in 1 week to queries; in 1 month to mss. Sample copy: $12. Guidelines available online.

NONFICTION Needs book excerpts, general interest, historical, humor, personal experience. **Buys 50 mss/year.** Submit by mail. Include SASE and contact information. Length: no limit. **Pays $50.** Pays expenses of writers on assignment.

PHOTOS Reviews scans only at 300 dpi, 5.5.

FICTION Needs ethnic, experimental, humorous, mainstream. **Buys 60 mss/year.** Send complete ms by mail. Include SASE and contact information. Length: no limit. **Pays $50.**

POETRY Submit by mail. Include SASE and contact information. Buys 20 poems/year. Submit maximum 5 poems. Length: no limit. **Pays $50.**

TIPS "We are not currently seeking work about any particular theme or topic; that said, reading recent issues is perhaps the best way to develop a sense for the length and quality we are looking for in submissions."

MEN'S

🌑🌑🌑🌑 CIGAR AFICIONADO

M. Shanken Communications, Inc., 387 Park Ave. S., 8th Floor, New York NY 10016. (212)684-4224. **Fax:** (212)684-5424. **E-mail:** gmott@mshanken.com. **Website:** www.cigaraficionado.com. **75% freelance written.** Bimonthly magazine for affluent men about the world of cigars. Estab. 1992. Circ. 275,000. Byline given. Pays on acceptance. Offers 25% kill fee. Publishes ms an average of 3-6 months after acceptance. Editorial lead time 6 months. Submit seasonal material 6 months in advance. Accepts queries by e-mail. Responds in 1 month to queries. Responds in 2 months to mss. Sample copy free.

NONFICTION Needs general interest. Query. Length: 1,500-4,000 words. **Pays variable amount.** Pays expenses of writers on assignment.

💲💲💲💲 ESQUIRE

Hearst Media, 300 W. 57th St., New York NY 10019. (212)649-4158. **E-mail:** editor@esquire.com. **Website:** www.esquire.com. Monthly magazine covering the ever-changing trends in American culture. *Esquire* is geared toward smart, well-off men. General readership is college educated and sophisticated, between ages 30 and 45. Written mostly by contributing editors on contract. Rarely accepts unsolicited mss. Estab. 1933. Circ. 720,000. Publishes ms an average of 2-6 months after acceptance. Editorial lead time at least 2 months. Accepts queries by mail, e-mail. Accepts simultaneous submissions. Guidelines on website.

NONFICTION Query. Length: 5,000 words average. **Payment varies.** Pays expenses of writers on assignment.

PHOTOS Uses mostly commissioned photography. Payment depends on size and number of photos.

TIPS "A writer has the best chance of breaking in at *Esquire* by querying with a specific idea that requires special contacts and expertise. Ideas must be timely and national in scope."

💲💲💲💲 KING

1115 Broadway, 8th Floor, New York NY 10010. **Fax:** (212)807-0216. **E-mail:** staff@king-mag.com. **Website:** www.king-mag.com. **75% freelance written.** Men's lifestyle magazine published 80 times/year. *King* is a general interest men's magazine with a strong editorial voice. Topics include lifestyle, entertainment, news, women, cars, music, fashion, investigative reporting. Estab. 2001. Circ. 270,000. Byline given. Pays on publication. Offers 25% kill fee. Editorial lead time 2-3 months. Submit seasonal material 4 months in advance. Accepts queries by e-mail. Accepts simultaneous submissions. Responds in 1 month to queries. Guidelines free.

NONFICTION Needs essays, expose, general interest. Does not want completed articles. Pitches only. Query with published clips. Length: 2,000-5,000 words. **Pays $1-1.50/word.** Pays expenses of writers on assignment.

💲💲💲💲 MEN'S HEALTH

Rodale, 33 E. Minor St., Emmaus PA 18098. (610)967-5171. **Fax:** (610)967-7725. **E-mail:** mhletters@rodale.com. **Website:** www.menshealth.com. **50% freelance written.** Magazine published 10 times/year covering men's health and fitness. *Men's Health* is a lifestyle magazine showing men the practical and positive actions that make their lives better, with articles covering fitness, nutrition, relationships, travel, careers, grooming, and health issues. Estab. 1986. Circ. 1,600,000. Pays on acceptance. Offers 25% kill fee. Accepts queries by mail, e-mail. Accepts simultaneous submissions. Responds in 3 weeks to queries. Guidelines for #10 SASE.

NONFICTION Buys 30 features/year; 360 short mss/year. Query with published clips. Length: 1,200-4,000 words for features; 100-300 words for short pieces. **Pays $1,000-5,000 for features; $100-500 for short pieces.** Pays expenses of writers on assignment.

COLUMNS Length: 750-1,500 words. **Buys 80 mss/year. Pays $750-2,000.**

TIPS "We have a wide definition of health. We believe that being successful in every area of your life is being healthy. The magazine focuses on all aspects of health, from stress issues and nutrition, to exercise and sex. It is 50% staff written, 50% from freelancers. The best way to break in is not by covering a particular subject, but by covering it within the magazine's style. There is a very particular tone and voice to the magazine. A writer has to be a good humor writer as well as a good service writer. Prefers mail queries. No phone calls, please."

MILITARY

💲 AIR FORCE TIMES

Sightline Media Group, 1919 Gallows Road, 4th Floor, Vienna VA 22182. (703)750-8646. **Fax:** (703)750-8601. **Website:** www.airforcetimes.com. **Contact:** Michelle Tan, editor. "Weeklies edited separately for Army, Navy, Marine Corps, and Air Force military personnel and their families. They contain career information such as pay raises, promotions, news of legislation affecting the military, housing, base activities, and features of interest to military people." Estab. 1940. Byline given. Pays on acceptance. Offers kill fee. Accepts queries by mail, e-mail, phone. Accepts simultaneous submissions. Responds in 1 month to queries. Sample copy for #10 SASE. Guidelines for #10 SASE.

NONFICTION No advice pieces. **Buys 150-175 mss/year.** Query. Length: 750-2,000 words. **Pays $100-500.**

COLUMNS Length: 500-900 words. **Buys 75 mss/year. Pays $75-125.**

TIPS "Looking for stories on active duty, reserve and retired military personnel; stories on military matters and localized military issues; stories on successful civilian careers after military service."

$$ ARMY MAGAZINE

Association of the US Army, 2425 Wilson Blvd., Arlington VA 22201. (800)336-4570. **E-mail:** armymag@ausa.org. **Website:** www.ausa.org/publications/armymagazine. Managing Editor: Elizabeth Rathbun. **Contact:** Rick Maze, editor-in-chief. **70% freelance written. Prefers to work with published/established writers.** Monthly magazine emphasizing Army interests. Estab. 1950. Circ. 65,000. Byline given. Pays on publication. Publishes ms an average of 5 months after acceptance. Submit seasonal material 3 months in advance. Accepts queries by mail. Accepts simultaneous submissions. Responds to queries within a week.

NONFICTION Needs essays, historical, interview, photo feature, technical. Special issues: "We would like to see more pieces about little-known episodes involving interesting military personalities. We especially want material lending itself to heavy, contributor-supplied photographic treatment. The first thing a contributor should recognize is that our readership is very savvy militarily. 'Gee-whiz' personal reminiscences get short shrift, unless they hold their own in a company in which long military service, heroism, and unusual experiences are commonplace. At the same time, *ARMY* readers like a well-written story with a fresh slant, whether it is about an experience in a foxhole or the fortunes of a corps in battle." No rehashed history. No unsolicited book reviews. **Buys 40 mss/year.** Submit via e-mail to armymag@ausa.org. Length: 1,000-1,500 words for op-eds and opinion, 1,200-1,800 for features. **Pays 15-20¢/word for articles, more for cover stories.** Pays expenses of writers on assignment. Expenses paid only with prior approval.

PHOTOS **Contact:** armymag@ausa.org. Only high-resolution photos accepted. See our writer's guidelines for details. Send photos. Captions required. Reviews prints and high-resolution digital photos. Payment varies.

$$ ARMY TIMES

Sightline Media Group, 1919 Gallows Rd., 4th Floor, Vienna VA 22182. (703)750-9000. **Fax:** (703)750-8622. **E-mail:** tlombardo@armytimes.com. **Website:** www.armytimes.com. **Contact:** Tony Lombardo, editor. Weekly for Army military personnel and their families containing career information such as pay raises, promotions, news of legislation affecting the military, housing, base activities and features of interest to military people. Estab. 1940. Circ. 230,000. Byline given. Pays on acceptance. Offers kill fee. Accepts queries by mail, e-mail. Accepts simultaneous submissions. Responds in 1 month to queries.

NONFICTION **Buys 150-175 mss/year.** Query. Length: 750-2,000 words. **Pays $100-500.** Pays expenses of writers on assignment.

COLUMNS Length: 500-900 words. **Buys 75 mss/year. Pays $75-125.**

TIPS "Looking for stories on active duty, reserve and retired military personnel; stories on military matters and localized military issues; stories on successful civilian careers after military service."

$$ MARINE CORPS TIMES

Sightline Media Group, 1919 Gallows Rd., 4th Floor, Vienna VA 22182. **Website:** www.marinecorpstimes.com. **Contact:** Andrew Tilghman, editor. Weeklies edited separately for Army, Navy, Marine Corps, and Air Force military personnel and their families. They contain career information such as pay raises, promotions, news of legislation affecting the military, housing, base activities and features of interest to military people. Estab. 1940. Circ. 230,000 (combined). Byline given. Pays on publication. Offers kill fee. Accepts simultaneous submissions. Responds in 1 month.

NONFICTION No advice pieces. **Buys 150-175 mss/year.** Query. Length: 750-2,000 words. **Pays $100-500.**

COLUMNS Length: 500-900 words. **Buys 75 mss/year. Pays $75-125.**

TIPS Looking for stories on active duty, reserve and retired military personnel; stories on military matters and localized military issues; stories on successful civilian careers after military service.

$$$ MILITARY OFFICER

201 N. Washington St., Alexandria VA 22314-2539. **E-mail:** editor@moaa.org; msc@moaa.org. **Website:**

www.moaa.org. **60% freelance written. Prefers to work with published/established writers.** Monthly magazine for officers of the 7 uniformed services and their families. Estab. 1945. Circ. 325,000. Byline given. Pays on acceptance. Publishes ms an average of 1 year after acceptance. Accepts queries by e-mail. Accepts simultaneous submissions. Responds in 3 months to queries. Sample copy and guidelines available online.

NONFICTION "We rarely accept unsolicited mss." **Buys 50 mss/year.** Query with résumé, sample clips. Length: 1,000-2,000 words (features). **Pays 80¢/word (features).**

PHOTOS Query with list of stock photo subjects. Images should be 300 dpi or higher. Pays $75-250 for inside color; $300 for cover.

MUSIC CONSUMER

💲🚫 BLUEGRASS UNLIMITED

Bluegrass Unlimited, Inc., P.O. Box 771, Warrenton VA 20188. (540)349-8181 or (800)BLU-GRAS. **Fax:** (540)341-0011. **E-mail:** editor@bluegrassmusic.com; info@bluegrassmusic.com. **Website:** www.bluegrassmusic.com. **10% freelance written. Prefers to work with published/established writers.** Monthly magazine covering bluegrass, acoustic, and old-time country music. Estab. 1966. Circ. 20,000. Byline given. Pays on publication. Offers negotiated kill fee. Publishes ms an average of 4 months after acceptance. Submit seasonal material 4 months in advance. Accepts queries by mail, e-mail, fax. Responds in 2 weeks to queries. Responds in 2 months to mss. Sample copy free. Guidelines for #10 SASE.

NONFICTION Needs general interest, historical, how-to, interview, personal experience, photo feature, travel. No fan-style articles. **Buys 30-40 mss/year.** Query. Length: Open. **Pays 10-13¢/word.**

REPRINTS Send photocopy with rights for sale noted and information about when and where the material previously appeared. Payment is negotiable.

PHOTOS State availability of or send photos. Identification of subjects required. Reviews 35mm transparencies and 3x5, 5x7, and 8x10 b&w and color prints. Also reviews/prefers digital 300 dpi or better jpg, tif files, index, contact sheet with digital submissions. Pays $50-175 for color; $25-60 for b&w prints; $50-250 for color prints. Buys all rights.

FICTION Needs ethnic, humorous. **Buys 3-5 mss/year.** Query. Length: Negotiable. **Pays 10-13¢/word.**

TIPS "We would prefer that articles be informational, based on personal experience, or an interview with lots of quotes from subject, profile, humor, etc. We print less than 10% freelance at this time."

💲💲 CHAMBER MUSIC

Chamber Music America, 12 W. 32nd St., 7th Floor, New York NY 10001-3813. (212)242-2022. **Fax:** (212)967-9747. **E-mail:** egoldensohn@chamber-music.org. **E-mail:** Ellen Goldensohn, publications director. **Website:** www.chamber-music.org. Bimonthly magazine covering chamber music. Estab. 1977. Circ. 13,000. Byline given. Pays on publication. Offers kill fee. Publishes ms an average of 5 months after acceptance. Editorial lead time 4 months. Accepts queries by mail, e-mail, phone.

NONFICTION Needs book excerpts, essays, humor, opinion, personal experience, issue-oriented stories of relevance to the chamber music fields written by top music journalists and critics, or music practitioners. No artist profiles or stories about opera or symphonic work. **Buys 35 mss/year.** Query with published clips. Length: 2,500-3,500 words. **Pays $500 minimum.** Sometimes pays expenses of writers on assignment.

PHOTOS State availability. Offers no payment for photos accepted with ms.

🌐💲 CHART ATTACK

Chart Communications, Inc., 41 Britain St., Suite 200, Toronto ON M5A 1R7 Canada. (416)363-3101. **Fax:** (416)363-3109. **E-mail:** richard@chartattack.com. **Website:** www.chartattack.com. **Contact:** Richard Trapunski, editor-in-chief. **90% freelance written.** *Chart Attack* is a guide to indie and alternative music. Estab. 1990. Circ. 40,000 (paid). Byline given. Pays on publication. No kill fee. Publishes ms an average of 3-6 months after acceptance. Editorial lead time 2 months. Submit seasonal material 3 months in advance. Accepts queries by e-mail. Responds in 4-6 weeks to queries; 2-3 months to mss. Guidelines free.

NONFICTION Needs book excerpts, essays, expose, humor, interview, personal experience, photo feature. Nothing that isn't related to popular music and pop culture (i.e., film, books, video games, fashion, etc., that would appeal to a hip youth demographic). Query with published clips and send complete ms. Length: varies. **Payment varies.** Pays expenses of writers on assignment.

PHOTOS Contact: Steven Balaban, art director. Send photos. Negotiates payment individually. Buys all rights.

🌐 CHURCH MUSIC QUARTERLY

The Royal School of Church Music, 19 The Close, Salisbury Wiltshire SP1 2EB United Kingdom. (44)(1722)424848. **Fax:** (44)(172)242-4849. **E-mail:** cmq@rscm.com; enquiries@rscm.com. **Website:** www.rscm.com. Quarterly publication that offers advice, information, and inspiration to church music enthusiasts around the world. Each issue offers a variety of articles and interviews by distinguished musicians, theologians, and scholars. Circ. 13,500. Pays upon publication. No kill fee. Accepts queries by e-mail. Guidelines by e-mail.

💬 Does not pay for unsolicited articles.

NONFICTION Submit ms, bio. Length: 1,200-1,400 words **Pays £60/page for commissioned articles.**

PHOTOS Reviews prints, 300 dpi digital images.

$$ GUITAR PLAYER

New Bay Media, LLC, 28 E. 28th St., 12th Floor, New York NY 10016. **E-mail:** etrabb@nbmedia.com. **Website:** www.guitarplayer.com. **50% freelance written.** Monthly magazine for persons interested in guitars, guitarists, manufacturers, guitar builders, equipment, careers, etc. Circ. 150,000. Byline given. Pays on acceptance. No kill fee. Publishes ms an average of 3 months after acceptance. Accepts simultaneous submissions. Responds in 6 weeks to queries.

NONFICTION Buys 30-40 mss/year. Query. Open **Pays $250-450.** Pays expenses of writers on assignment.

PHOTOS Reviews 35 mm color transparencies, b&w glossy prints. Payment varies. Buys one time rights.

$$$ SYMPHONY

League of American Orchestras, 33 W. 60th St., 5th Floor, New York NY 10023. (212)262-5161. **Fax:** (212)262-5198. **E-mail:** clane@americanorchestras.org; jmelick@americanorchestras.org; editor@americanorchestras.org. **Website:** www.symphony.org. **Contact:** Chester Lane, senior editor; Jennifer Melick, managing editor. **50% freelance written.** Quarterly magazine for the orchestra industry and classical music enthusiasts covering classical music, orchestra industry, musicians. *Symphony*, the quarterly magazine of the League of American Orchestras, reports on the critical issues, trends, personalities, and developments of the orchestra world. Every issue includes news, provocative essays, in-depth articles, and cutting-edge research relevant to the entire orchestra field. *Symphony* profiles take readers behind the scenes to meet the people who are making a difference in the orchestra world, while wide-ranging survey articles reveal the strategies and tactics that are helping orchestras meet the challenges of the 21st century. *Symphony* is a matchless source of meaningful information about orchestras and serves as an advocate and connector for the orchestra field. Circ. 18,000. Byline given. Pays on acceptance. No kill fee. Publishes ms an average of 10 weeks after acceptance. Editorial lead time 6 months. Submit seasonal material 8 months in advance. Accepts queries by mail, e-mail. Accepts simultaneous submissions. Guidelines available online.

NONFICTION Needs book excerpts, essays, inspirational, interview, opinion, personal experience, photo feature. Does not want to see reviews, interviews. **Buys 30 mss/year.** Query with published clips. Length: 1,500-3,500 words. **Pays $500-900.** Pays expenses of writers on assignment.

PHOTOS Rarely commissions photos or illustrations. State availability of or send photos. Captions, identification of subjects required. Reviews contact sheets, negatives, prints, electronic photos (preferred). Offers no additional payment for photos accepted with ms. Buys one-time rights.

COLUMNS Repertoire (orchestral music—essays); Comment (personal views and opinions); Currents (electronic media developments); In Print (books); On Record (CD, DVD, video), all 1,000-2,500 words. **Buys 12 mss/year.** Query with published clips.

TIPS "We need writing samples before assigning pieces. We prefer to craft the angle with the writer rather than adapt an existing piece. Pitches and queries should demonstrate a clear relevance to the American orchestra industry and should be timely."

MYSTERY

ALFRED HITCHCOCK'S MYSTERY MAGAZINE

Dell Magazines, 44 Wall St., Suite 904, New York NY 10005. **E-mail:** alfredhitchcockmm@dellmagazines.com. **Website:** www.themysteryplace.com/ahmm. **100% freelance written.** Monthly magazine featuring new mystery short stories. Estab. 1956. Circ. 90,000. Byline given. Pays on publication. No kill fee. Submit seasonal material 7 months in advance. Accepts queries by mail, online submission form. Responds in 3-5 months to mss. Sample copy: $5. Guidelines for SASE or on website.

NONFICTION Pays expenses of writers on assignment.

FICTION Wants "original and well-written mystery and crime fiction. Because this is a mystery magazine, the stories we buy must fall into that genre in some sense or another. We are interested in nearly every kind of mystery: stories of detection of the classic kind, police procedurals, private eye tales, suspense, courtroom dramas, stories of espionage, and so on. We ask only that the story be about crime (or the threat or fear of one). We sometimes accept ghost stories or supernatural tales, but those also should involve a crime." Needs mystery, suspense. No sensationalism. Send complete ms. Length: up to 12,000 words. **Payment varies.**

TIPS "No simultaneous submissions, please. Submissions sent to *Alfred Hitchcock's Mystery Magazine* are not considered for or read by *Ellery Queen's Mystery Magazine*, and vice versa."

$ **ELLERY QUEEN'S MYSTERY MAGAZINE**
44 Wall St., Suite 904, New York NY 10005-2401. E-mail: elleryqueenmm@dellmagazines.com. **Website:** www.themysteryplace.com/eqmm. **100% freelance written.** "*Ellery Queen's Mystery Magazine* welcomes submissions from both new and established writers. We publish every kind of mystery short story: the psychological suspense tale, the deductive puzzle, the private eye case—the gamut of crime and detection from the realistic (including the policeman's lot and stories of police procedure) to the more imaginative (including 'locked rooms' and 'impossible crimes'). We look for strong writing, an original and exciting plot, and professional craftsmanship. We encourage writers whose work meets these general criteria to read an issue of *EQMM* before making a submission." Estab. 1941. Circ. 100,000. Byline given. Pays on acceptance. No kill fee. Publishes ms an average of 6-12 months after acceptance. Accepts queries by online submission form. Accepts simultaneous submissions. Responds in 3 months to mss. Sample copy: $9.50. Make out check to *Ellery Queen Mystery Magazine*, and send to

Ellery Queen Mystery Magazine, Attn: Sandy Marlowe, 6 Prowitt St., Norwalk CT 06855. Guidelines online.

PHOTOS Send photos.

FICTION "We always need detective stories. Special consideration given to anything timely and original." Publishes ms 6-12 months after acceptance. Agented fiction 50%. **Publishes 10 new writers/year.** Recently published work by Jeffery Deaver, Joyce Carol Oates, and Margaret Maron. Sometimes comments on rejected mss. Needs mystery, suspense. No explicit sex or violence, no gore or horror. Seldom publishes parodies or pastiches. "We do not want true detective or crime stories." **Buys up to 120 mss/year.** "*EQMM* uses an online submission system (eqmm.magazine-submissions.com) that has been designed to streamline our process and improve communication with authors. We ask that all submissions be made electronically, using this system, rather than on paper. All stories should be in standard ms format and submitted in .DOC format. We cannot accept .DOCX, .RTF, or .TXT files at this time." Length: 2,500-8,000 words, but occasionally accepts longer and shorter submissions—including minute mysteries of 250 words, stories up to 12,000 words, and novellas of up to 20,000 words from established authors. **Pays 5-8¢/word; occasionally higher for established authors.**

TIPS "*EQMM*'s range in the mystery genre is extensive: Almost any story that involves crime or the threat of crime comes within our purview. However, like all magazines, *EQMM* has a distinctive tone and style, and you can only get a sense of whether your work will suit us by reading an issue."

NATURE, CONSERVATION & ECOLOGY

☼ $ $ **ALTERNATIVES JOURNAL**
Alternatives Inc., 283 Duke St. W., Suite 204A, Kitchener ON N2H 3X7 Canada. (519)578-2327. **E-mail:** david@alternativesjournal.ca. **Website:** www.alternativesjournal.ca. **Contact:** David McConnachie, publisher. **90% freelance written.** Magazine published 4 times/year with special issue(s) covering international environmental issues. "*Alternatives Journal*, Canada's national environmental magazine, delivers thoughtful analysis and intelligent debate on Canadian and world environmental issues, the latest news

and ideas, as well as profiles of environmental leaders who are making a difference. *A/J* is a quarterly+ magazine featuring bright, lively writing by the nation's foremost environmental thinkers and researchers. *A/J* offers a vision of a more sustainable future as well as the tools needed to take us there." Estab. 1971. Circ. 5,000. Byline given. Pays on publication. Offers 50% kill fee. Publishes ms an average of 5 months after acceptance. Editorial lead time 7 months. Submit seasonal material 5 months in advance. Accepts queries by e-mail, online submission form. Accepts simultaneous submissions. Sample copy free for Canadian writers only. Guidelines online.

NONFICTION Needs book excerpts, essays, expose, how-to, humor, interview, opinion, photo feature, profile, reviews, technical. **Buys 50 mss/year.** Query with published clips. Length: 800-3,000 words. **Pays 10¢/word (Canadian).** Pays expenses of writers on assignment.

PHOTOS State availability. Identification of subjects required. Pays $35-75/photo. Buys one-time rights.

FICTION Needs science fiction, short stories.

TIPS "Before responding to this call for submissions, please read several back issues of the magazine so that you understand the nature of our publication. We also suggest you go through our detailed submission procedures to understand the types and lengths of articles we accept. Queries should explain, in less than 300 words, the content and scope of your article, and should convey your intended approach, tone, and style. Please include a list of people you will interview, potential images or sources for images, and the number of words you propose to write. We would also like to receive a very short bio. And if you have not written for *Alternatives* before, please include other examples of your writing. Articles range from about 500-3,000 words in length. Keep in mind that our lead time is several months. Articles should not be so time-bound that they will seem dated once published. *Alternatives* has a limited budget of 10¢ per word for several articles. This stipend is available to professional and amateur writers and students only. Please indicate your interest in this funding in your submission."

💲💲💲 ARIZONA WILDLIFE VIEWS

5000 W. Carefree Hwy., Phoenix AZ 85086. (800)777-0015. **E-mail:** awv@azgfd.gov; hrayment@azgfd.gov. **Website:** www.azgfd.gov/magazine. **Contact:** Heidi Rayment. **50% freelance written.** Bimonthly magazine covering Arizona wildlife, wildlife management, and outdoor recreation (specifically hunting, fishing, wildlife watching, boating and off-highway vehicle recreation). "*Arizona Wildlife Views* is a general interest magazine about Arizona wildlife, wildlife management and outdoor recreation. We publish material that conforms to the mission and policies of the Arizona Game and Fish Department. In addition to Arizona wildlife and wildlife management, topics include habitat issues, outdoor recreation involving wildlife, boating, fishing, hunting, bird-watching, animal observation, off-highway vehicle use, etc., and historical articles about wildlife and wildlife management." Circ. 22,000. Byline given. Pays on publication. No kill fee. Publishes ms an average of 10 months after acceptance. Editorial lead time 1 year. Submit seasonal material 2 months in advance. Accepts queries by mail. Accepts simultaneous submissions. Responds in 1 month to queries. Responds in 2 months to mss. Sample copy free. Guidelines available online.

NONFICTION Needs general interest, historical, how-to, interview, photo feature, technical. Does not want "Me and Joe" articles, anthropomorphism of wildlife, or opinionated pieces not based on confirmable facts. **Buys 20 mss/year.** Query. Length: 1,000-2,500 words. **Pays $450-800.** Pays expenses of writers on assignment.

TIPS "Unsolicited material without proper identification will be returned immediately."

💲💲 THE BEAR DELUXE MAGAZINE

Orlo, 240 N. Broadway, #112, Portland OR 97227. **E-mail:** beardeluxe@orlo.org. **Website:** www.orlo.org. **Contact:** Tom Webb, editor-in-chief; Kristin Rogers Brown, art director. **80% freelance written.** Covers fiction, essay, poetry, other. Do not combine submissions; rather submit poetry, fiction, and essay in separate packages. News essays, on occasion, are assigned if they have a strong element of reporting. Artists contribute to *The Bear Deluxe* in various ways, including: editorial illustration, editorial photography, spot illustration, independent art, cover art, graphic design, and cartoons. "*The Bear Deluxe Magazine* is a national independent environmental arts magazine publishing significant works of reporting, creative nonfiction, literature, visual art, and design. Based in the Pacific Northwest, it reaches across cultural and political divides to engage readers on vital issues effecting the environment. Published twice per year,

The Bear Deluxe includes a wider array and a higher percentage of visual artwork and design than many other publications. Artwork is included both as editorial support and as standalone or independent art. It has included nationally recognized artists as well as emerging artists. As with any publication, artists are encouraged to review a sample copy for a clearer understanding of the magazine's approach. Unsolicited submissions and samples are accepted and encouraged." Estab. 1993. Circ. 19,000. Byline given. Pays on publication. Offers 25% kill fee. Publishes ms an average of 6 months after acceptance. Editorial lead time 6 months. Submit seasonal material 9 months in advance. Accepts queries by mail, e-mail. Accepts simultaneous submissions. Responds in 3-6 months to mail queries. Only responds to e-mail queries if interested. Sample copy: $5. Guidelines online.

NONFICTION Needs essays, general interest, interview, new product, opinion, personal experience, photo feature, travel. Special issues: Publishes 1 theme every 2 years. **Buys 40 mss/year.** Query with published clips. Length: 750-4,000 words. **Pays $25-400, depending on piece.** Pays expenses of writers on assignment. Sometimes pays expenses.

PHOTOS State availability. Identification of subjects, model releases required. Reviews contact sheets, transparencies, 8x10 prints. Offers $30/photo. Buys one-time rights.

COLUMNS Reviews (almost anything), 100-1,000 words; Front of the Book (mix of short news bits, found writing, quirky tidbits), 300-500 words; Portrait of an Artist (artist profiles), 1,200 words; Back of the Book (creative opinion pieces), 650 words. **Buys 16 mss/year.** Query with published clips. **Pays $25-400, depending on piece.**

FICTION "We are most excited by high-quality writing that furthers the magazine's goal of engaging new and divergent readers. We appreciate strong aspects of storytelling and are open to new formats, though we wouldn't call ourselves publishers of 'experimental fiction.'" Needs adventure, condensed novels, historical, horror, humorous, mystery, western. No traditional sci-fi, horror, romance, or crime/action. **Buys 8 mss/year.** Query or send complete ms. Prefers postal mail submissions. Length: up to 4,000 words. **Pays free subscription to the magazine, contributor's copies, and $25-400, depending on piece; additional copies for postage.**

POETRY Needs avant-garde, free verse, haiku, light verse, traditional. Submit 3-5 poems at a time. Poems are reviewed by a committee of 3-5 people. Publishes 1 theme issue per year. Buys 16-20 poems/year. Length: up to 50 lines/poem. **Pays $20, subscription, and contributor's copies.**

FILLERS Needs facts, newsbreaks, short humor. **Buys 10 mss/year.** Length: 100-750 words.

TIPS "Offer to be a stringer for future ideas. Get a copy of the magazine and guidelines, and query us with specific nonfiction ideas and clips. We're looking for original, magazine-style stories, not fluff or PR. Fiction, essay, and poetry writers should know we have an open and blind review policy and they should keep sending their best work even if rejected once. Be as specific as possible in queries."

💲💲 BIRD WATCHER'S DIGEST

P.O. Box 110, Marietta OH 45750. (740)373-5285; (800)879-2473. **E-mail:** submissions@birdwatchersdigest.com. **Website:** www.birdwatchersdigest.com. **Contact:** Bill Thompson III, editor; Dawn Hewitt, managing editor. **30% freelance written.** Bimonthly, digest-sized magazine covering birds, bird watching, travel for birding, and natural history. *Bird Watcher's Digest* is a nontechnical magazine interpreting ornithological material for amateur observers, including the knowledgeable birder, the serious novice, and the backyard bird watcher; strives to provide good reading and good ornithology. Works with a small number of new/unpublished writers each year. Estab. 1978. Circ. 42,000. Byline given. Pays after publication. Publishes ms an average of 2 years after acceptance. Submit seasonal material 6 months in advance. Responds in 4 weeks to queries. Sample copy for $4.99 plus shipping, or access online. Guidelines online.

NONFICTION Needs book excerpts, essays, how-to, humor, new product, personal experience, reviews, travel. Only stories about wild birds, bird watching, bird watchers, birding gear, or birding hot spots are considered. No articles on domestic, pet or caged birds, or raising a baby bird. **Buys 30-40 mss/year.** "We gladly accept e-mail queries and ms submissions. When submitting by e-mail, please use the subject line 'Submission—[your topic].' Attach your submission to your e-mail in either MS Word (DOC) or RichText Format (RTF). Please include full contact information on every page." Length: 600-2,500 words. **Pays up to $200.**

PHOTOS Reviews digital photos only. "Our payment schedule is $75 per image used, regardless of size. Images reused on our table of contents page or on our website will be paid an additional $25. There is no payment or contract for photos used in 'My Way,' or for photos that have been loaned for courtesy use." Buys one-time rights for simultaneous print and digital publication.

POETRY Prints short poems about birds or bird watching only on rare occasion. **Pays $10-25, or complimentary subscription.**

TIPS "Obtain a sample copy of *BWD* from us or at your local newsstand, bird store, or bookstore, and familiarize yourself with the type of material we regularly publish. We rarely repeat coverage of a topic within a period of 2-3 years. We aim at an audience ranging from the backyard bird watcher to the very knowledgeable birder; we include in each issue material that will appeal at various levels. We always strive for a good geographical spread, with material from every section of the country. We leave very technical matters to others, but we want facts and accuracy, depth and quality, directed at the veteran bird watcher and at the enthusiastic novice. We stress the joys and pleasures of bird watching, its environmental contribution, and its value for the individual and society."

💲💲 BIRDWATCHING

Madavor Media, LLC, BirdWatching Editorial Dept., 25 Braintree Hill Office Park, Suite 404, Braintree MA 02184. **E-mail:** mail@birdwatchingdaily.com. **Website:** www.birdwatchingdaily.com. Bimonthly magazine for birdwatchers who actively look for wild birds in the field. "*BirdWatching* concentrates on where to find, how to attract, and how to identify wild birds, and on how to understand what they do." Estab. 1987. Circ. 40,000. Byline given. Pays on publication. Accepts queries by mail, e-mail. Accepts simultaneous submissions. Guidelines online.

NONFICTION Needs book excerpts, essays, how-to, interview, personal experience, photo feature, travel. No poetry, fiction, or puzzles. **Buys 12 mss/year.** Query by mail or e-mail with published clips. Length: 500-2,400 words. **Pays $200-400.**

PHOTOS See photo guidelines online. State availability. Identification of subjects required. Buys one-time rights.

💲💲 EARTH ISLAND JOURNAL

Earth Island Institute, 2150 Allston Way, Suite 460, Berkeley CA 94704. **E-mail:** submissions@earthisland.org. **Website:** www.earthislandjournal.org. **80% freelance written.** Quarterly magazine covering the environment/ecology. *Earth Island Journal*, published quarterly, "combines investigative journalism and thought-provoking essays that make the subtle but profound connections between the environment and other contemporary issues." Does not publish poetry or fiction. Looking for in-depth, vigorously reported stories that reveal the connections between the environment and other contemporary issues. Audience, though modest, includes many of the leaders of the environmental movement. Article pitches should be geared toward this sophisticated audience. Estab. 1985. Circ. 10,000. Byline given. Pays on publication. Publishes ms an average of 4 months after acceptance. Editorial lead time 4 months. Submit seasonal material 4 months in advance. Accepts queries by mail, e-mail. Accepts simultaneous submissions. Responds in 1 month to queries and mss. Sample copy online. Guidelines online.

NONFICTION Needs book excerpts, essays, expose, general interest, interview, opinion, personal experience, photo feature. "We do not want product pitches, services, or company news." **Buys 20 mss/year.** Query with published clips. Length: 750-4,000 words. **Pays 25¢/word.** Pays expenses of writers on assignment.

PHOTOS Send photos. Reviews contact sheets, GIF/JPEG files. Negotiates payment individually.

COLUMNS Voices (first-person reflection about the environment in a person's life), 750 words. **Buys 4 mss/year.** Query. **Pays $50.**

TIPS "Given our audience, we are looking for stories that break new ground when it comes to environmental coverage. We are not going to publish a story 'about recycling.' We may, however, be interested in a story about, say, the waste manager in Kansas City, KS, who developed an innovative technology for sorting trash, and how his/her scheme is being copied around the world. In other words, we are looking for fresh angles on familiar stories, stories that so far have been overlooked by larger publications."

💲💲💲 HIGH COUNTRY NEWS

119 Grand Ave., P.O. Box 1090, Paonia CO 81428. (970)527-4898. **E-mail:** brianc@hcn.org; cindy@hcn.

org. **E-mail:** editor@hcn.org; photos@hcn.org. **Website:** www.hcn.org. **Contact:** Brian Calvert, editor-in-chief; Cindy Wehling, art director. **50% freelance written.** Biweekly nonprofit magazine covering environment, natural resources, and under-represented communities across 11 Western states and Alaska; for journalists, policymakers, environmentalists, conservationists, environmental justice advocates, politicians, companies, college classes, government agencies, grass roots activists, public land managers, and other people with a stake in the modern American West. *High Country News* will consider pitches for well-researched reportage, analysis, opinion, essay or criticism on issues vital to the West—especially under the broad frameworks of science and nature; conservation and preservation; food and agriculture; water; environmental justice and racism; climate change and energy; post-colonialism and the legacy of conquest; the rural-urban divide; environmental law and policy; public lands and resources (including water, mineral, timber, range, wildlife, recreation and preservation); military and nuclear legacies; and economics. We are especially interested in stories and perspectives from under-represented communities where they intersect with these issues. The magazine provides meaningful journalism and writing about the American West, not only as a geography, but also as an idea, part history, part mythology. We are looking for sophisticated storytelling that examines the varied landscapes and people across 11 states west of the 100th meridian—Arizona, California, Colorado, Idaho, Montana, New Mexico, Nevada, Oregon, Utah, Washington, Wyoming—and, because they face similar issues, Alaska and the High Plains. The writing in *High Country News* explores the region through unique stories that only the West can produce and that have broad significance beyond our borders. We emphasize intellectual honesty, clarity and nuance. Estab. 1970. Circ. 30,000. Byline given. Pays on publication. Offers kill fee of 1/4 of agreed rate. Publishes ms an average of 2-6 months after acceptance. Accepts queries by e-mail. Accepts simultaneous submissions. Responds in 2 weeks to queries. Sample copy online. Guidelines online.

NONFICTION Needs book excerpts, essays, expose, humor, personal experience, travel. **Buys 100 mss/year.** Query. Length: up to 4,900 words. **Pays 50¢-$1.50/word.** Pays expenses of writers on assignment.

PHOTOS Send photos. Captions, identification of subjects required. Reviews b&w or color prints.

COLUMNS Back-Page Essay, 700-900 words; Writers on the Range (taut and pithy opinion pieces). Submit back-page essay queries to Brian Calvert (brianc@hcn.org); submit Writers on the Range pieces to Betsy Marston (betsym@hsn.org).

TIPS "Familiarity with the newsmagazine is a must. Start by writing a brief, focused query letter. We are especially looking for stories from writers and communities of color, where they intersect with our core issues."

💲💲💲 MINNESOTA CONSERVATION VOLUNTEER

Minnesota Department of Natural Resources, 500 Lafeyette Rd., St. Paul MN 55155-4046. **Website:** www.dnr.state.mn.us/magazine. **50% freelance written.** Bimonthly magazine covering Minnesota natural resources, wildlife, natural history, outdoor recreation, and land use. *"Minnesota Conservation Volunteer* is a donor-supported magazine advocating conservation and careful use of Minnesota's natural resources. Material must reflect an appreciation of nature and an ethic of care for the environment. We rely on a variety of sources in our reporting. More than 130,000 Minnesota households, businesses, schools, and other groups subscribe to this conservation magazine." Estab. 1940. Circ. 131,000. Byline given. Pays on acceptance. Offers 30% kill fee. Publishes ms an average of 2 months after acceptance. Editorial lead time 9 months. Submit seasonal material 9 months in advance. Accepts queries by mail, e-mail. Accepts simultaneous submissions. Responds in 1 month to queries. Responds in 2 months to mss. Sample copy free or on website. Guidelines available online.

NONFICTION Needs essays, expose, general interest, historical, humor, interview, opinion, personal experience, photo feature, Young Naturalists for children. Rarely publishes poetry or uncritical advocacy. **Buys 12 mss/year.** Query with published clips for features and Field Notes; send full ms for essays. Length: 300-1,800 words. **Pays 50¢/word for features and essays.** Pays expenses of writers on assignment.

PHOTOS Pays $100/photo.

COLUMNS Close Encounters (unusual, exciting, or humorous personal wildlife experience in Minnesota), up to 1,500 words; Sense of Place (first- or third-person essay developing character of a Minnesota place), up to 1,500 words; Viewpoint (well-researched and well-reasoned opinion piece), up to 1,500 words; Minnesota Profile (concise description of emblematic state species or geographic feature), 400 words. **Buys 12 mss/year.** Query with published clips. **Pays 50¢/word.**

TIPS "In submitting queries, look beyond topics to the underlying stories, issues, and personalities. In submitting a query addressing a particular issue, think of its impact on land, wildlife, and people and the sources you might consult. Summarize your idea, the story line, and sources in 2 or 3 short paragraphs. While topics must have relevance to Minnesota and give a Minnesota character to the magazine, feel free to round out your research with out-of-state sources."

⊙⊙⊙⊘ NATIONAL PARKS MAGAZINE

National Parks Conservation Association, 777 Sixth St. NW, Suite 700, Washington DC 20001. (202)223-6722; (800)628-7275. **Fax:** (202)454-3333. **E-mail:** npmag@npca.org. **Website:** www.npca.org/magazine. **Contact:** Scott Kirkwood, editor-in-chief. **60% freelance written. Prefers to work with published/established writers.** Quarterly magazine for a largely unscientific but highly educated audience interested in preservation of National Park System units, natural areas, and protection of wildlife habitat. "*National Parks* magazine publishes articles about areas in the National Park System, proposed new areas, threats to parks or park wildlife, scientific discoveries, legislative issues, and endangered species of plants or animals relevant to national parks. We do not publish articles on general environmental topics, nor do we print articles about land managed by the Fish and Wildlife Service, Bureau of Land Management, or other federal agencies." Estab. 1919. Circ. 340,000. Pays on acceptance. Offers 33% kill fee. Publishes ms an average of 2 months after acceptance. Accepts simultaneous submissions. Responds in 3-4 months to queries. Sample copy for $3 and 9x12 SASE or online. Guidelines available online.

NONFICTION Needs expose, descriptive articles about new or proposed national parks and wilderness parks. No poetry, philosophical essays, or first-person narratives. No unsolicited mss. Length: 1,500 words. **Pays $1,300 for 1,500-word features and travel articles.** Pays expenses of writers on assignment.

PHOTOS Not looking for new photographers. Send photos.

TIPS "Articles should have an original slant or news hook and cover a limited subject, rather than attempt to treat a broad subject superficially. Specific examples, descriptive details, and quotes are always preferable to generalized information. The writer must be able to document factual claims, and statements should be clearly substantiated with evidence within the article. *National Parks* does not publish fiction, poetry, personal essays, or 'My trip to .' stories."

⊙ NEW YORK STATE CONSERVATIONIST

New York State Department of Environmental Conservation, 625 Broadway, Albany NY 12233-4502. (518)402-8047. **Fax:** (518)402-8050. **E-mail:** magazine@dec.ny.gov. **Website:** www.dec.ny.gov/pubs/conservationist.html. **30% freelance written.** Bimonthly magazine covering outdoor education, environmental quality, hunting, fishing, wildlife profiles. Circ. 100,000. Byline given. Pays on publication. No kill fee. Publishes ms an average of 2 months-5 years after acceptance. Editorial lead time 6 months. Submit seasonal material 6-12 months in advance. Accepts queries by mail. Accepts simultaneous submissions. Responds in 2-4 weeks to queries; 2 months to mss. Sample copy online. Guidelines online.

NONFICTION Needs historical, personal experience, photo feature. **Buys 10 mss/year.** Query. **Pays $50-100.**

PHOTOS Send photos. Captions, identification of subjects, model releases required. Reviews transparencies. Offers $15-100/photo. Buys one time rights.

COLUMNS The Backpage (outdoor experiences, feel-good anectdotes), 700 words. **Buys 3 mss/year.** Query with published clips. **Pays $50.**

TIPS "The more organized a writer is, the more likely we are to use the piece. Captions, photos, and solid writing don't hurt, either. People doing things in the outdoors. Well-researched wildlife profiles."

⊙⊙ NORTHERN WOODLANDS MAGAZINE

Center for Woodlands Education, Inc., 1776 Center Rd., P.O. Box 471, Corinth VT 05039-0471. (802)439-6292; (800)290-5232. **Fax:** (802)368-1053. **E-mail:** dave@northernwoodlands.org; mail@northernwoodlands.org. **Website:** www.northernwoodlands.org. **40-60% freelance written.** Quarterly magazine covering natural history, conservation, and forest management in the Northeast. "*Northern Woodlands* strives to inspire landowners' sense of stewardship by increasing their awareness of the natural history and the principles of conservation and forestry that are directly related to their land. We also hope to increase the public's awareness of the social, economic, and environmental benefits of a working forest." Estab. 1994. Circ. 15,000. Byline given. Pays 1 month prior to publication. Publishes ms an average of 6 months after acceptance. Editorial lead time 6 months. Submit seasonal material 6 months in advance. Accepts queries by mail, e-mail. Accepts simultaneous submissions. Responds in 1 month to queries. Responds in 1-2 months to mss. Sample copy and guidelines available online.

NONFICTION No product reviews, first-person travelogues, "cute" animal stories, opinion, or advocacy pieces. **Buys 15-20 mss/year.** Query with published clips. Length: 500-3,000 words. **Pay varies per piece.** Pays expenses of writers on assignment.

PHOTOS State availability. Identification of subjects required. Reviews transparencies, prints, high res digital photos. Offers $35-75/photo. Buys one-time rights.

TIPS "We will work with subject-matter experts to make their work suitable for our audience."

$$$ OUTDOOR AMERICA

Izaak Walton League of America, 707 Conservation Ln., Gaithersburg MD 20878. (301)548-0150. **Fax:** (301)548-9409. **E-mail:** oa@iwla.org. **Website:** www.iwla.org. **Contact:** Dawn Merritt, communications director. Quarterly magazine covering national conservation efforts/issues related to and involving members of the Izaak Walton League. A 4-color publication, *Outdoor America* is received by League members, as well as representatives of Congress and the media. Our audience, located predominantly in the midwestern and mid-Atlantic states, enjoys traditional recreational pursuits, such as fishing, hiking, hunting, as well as conservation activities and educating youth. All have a keen interest in protecting the future of our natural resources and outdoor recreation heritage. Estab. 1922. Circ. 36,500. Pays on acceptance. Offers 1/3 original rate kill fee. Publishes ms an average of 2 months after acceptance. Accepts queries by mail, e-mail. Responds in 2 months to queries. Sample copy for $2.50. Guidelines available online.

NONFICTION No fiction, poetry, or unsubstantiated opinion pieces. Query or send ms for short columns/news pieces (500 words or less). Features are planned 6-12 months in advance. **Pays $1,000-1,500 for features.**

[✪] $ OUTDOORS SPECTACULAR

P.O. Box 52022 NPO, 313 St. Anne's Rd., Winnipeg MB R2M 5P9 Canada. (204)955-0599. **E-mail:** editor@outdoorsspectacular.ca. **Website:** www.outdoorsspectacular.ca. **75% freelance written.** Quarterly magazine covering outdoor tourism industry. Estab. 2005. Circ. 2,000. Byline given. Pays on publication. Offers 50% or $25-50 kill fee. Publishes ms an average of 3-9 months after acceptance. Editorial lead time 3 months. Submit seasonal material 3 months in advance. Accepts queries by mail, e-mail. Accepts simultaneous submissions. Responds in 1 month to queries. Responds in 1 month to mss. Sample copy for $3.95. Guidelines available online.

NONFICTION Needs general interest, how-to, hunting, fishing, camping, traveling, etc., humor, inspirational, interview, new product, personal experience, photo feature, technical, travel, environmental, ecological, science, nature, wildlife. Does not want political, religious, tree-hugger propaganda, etc. **Buys 4-8 mss/year.** Send complete ms. Length: 500-2,000 words. **Pays $50-100.**

PHOTOS Send photos. Reviews 5x4 prints, GIF/JPEG files. Offers no additional payment for photos accepted with ms. Buys one time rights.

FICTION All fiction must have something to do with outdoors! Needs adventure, experimental, horror, humorous, mystery, romance, science fiction, slice-of-life vignettes, suspense, cross genre, inspirational, psychological thrillers. Does not want erotica, splatterpunk, special interest, political, ethnic, confessions, religious. **Buys 4-8 mss/year.** Send complete ms. Length: 1,000-3,000 words. **Pays $50-100.**

POETRY Needs avant-garde, free verse, haiku, light verse, traditional. Does not want erotica, splatterpunk, special interest, political, ethnic, confessionals, religious, or tree-hugger propaganda. We publish one poet per issue exclusively. See guidelines. Buys 20 poems/year. Submit maximum 5 poems. Length: 10-50 lines.

FILLERS Needs facts, newsbreaks, short humor. **Buys 8-16 mss/year.** Length: 250-500 words.

TIPS For nonfiction, follow the three E's of journalism: engage, entertain, educate. For fiction, delight, enchant, scare or thrill us. I like stories with a twist and/or surprise ending.

$$$$ SIERRA

2101 Webster St., Suite 1300, Oakland CA 94612. **E-mail:** submissions.sierra@sierraclub.org. **Website:** www.sierraclub.org. Estab. 1893. Accepts queries by e-mail. Accepts simultaneous submissions. Responds in 6-8 weeks. Sample copy for $5 and SASE, or on. Guidelines available online.

[O] The bimonthly magazine of the Sierra Club.

NONFICTION "*Sierra* is looking for strong, well-researched, literate nonfiction storytelling about significant environmental and conservation issues, adventure travel, nature, self-propelled sports, and trends in green living. Writers should look for ways to cast new light on well-established issues. We look for stories of national or international significance; local issues, while sometimes useful as examples of broader trends, are seldom of interest in themselves. We are always looking for adventure-travel pieces that weave events, discoveries, and environmental insights into the narrative. We are more interested in showcasing environmental solutions than adding to the list of environmental problems. We publish dramatic investigative stories that have the potential to reach a broad audience. Nonfiction essays on the natural world are welcome too. Features often focus on aspects of the Sierra Club's work, but few subjects are taboo. For more information about the Club's current campaigns, visit sierraclub.org." "We do not want descriptive wildlife articles unless larger conservation issues figure strongly in the story. We are not interested in editorials, general essays about environmentalism, or highly technical writing. We do not publish unsolicited cartoons, poetry, or fiction; please do not submit works in these genres." **Buys 30-36 mss/year.** Well-researched, tightly focused queries should be submitted to **Submissions.Sierra@sierraclub.org.** Phone calls are strongly discouraged. "Please do not send slides, prints, or other artwork. If photos or illustrations are required for your submission, we will request them when your work is accepted for publication." Length: 2,000-4,000 words. **Pays $1/word. More for "well-known writers with crackerjack credentials."** Pays expenses of writers on assignment. Expenses may be paid in some cases.

PHOTOS Publishes photographs pertaining to the natural world and the environment. "We use high-quality, mostly color photographs and prefer digital files. Photographers interested in submitting work to Sierra are encouraged to send a link to their website, along with a stock listing of regions and subjects of specialty for us to review. Please do not send unsolicited transparencies and prints. We review photographers' stock lists (subject matter and locations in photographs) and samples and keep the names of potential contributors on file. Photographers are contacted only when subjects they have in stock are needed. We typically do not post our photo-needs list online or elsewhere. Sierra does not accept responsibility for lost or damaged transparencies sent on spec or for portfolio review. Please e-mail Photo.Submissions@sierraclub.org." Send photos.

$ WOODS READER

P.O. Box 46, Warren MN 56762. **E-mail:** editor@woodsreader.com. **Website:** www.woodsreader.com. **Contact:** S Sedgwick. **60%.** A quarterly publication for those who love woodland areas: whether a public preserve, forest, tree farm, backyard woodlot or other patch of trees and wildlife. Will only consider articles based on woodlands. "We are looking for positive, whimsical, interesting articles. Our readers like to hear about others' experiences and insights. Please visit submissions page on website. We encourage stories of personal experience. We also buy forest ecology mss of general interest, DIY (photos must accompany), personal essays, book reviews (query first)." Estab. 2017. Byline given. Pays on acceptance or publication. Does not offer kill fee. Publishes ms 3-12 months after acceptance. Accepts queries by mail, e-mail. Accepts simultaneous submissions. Responds in 3 months or less. Sample copy available online for $8. Guidelines online or query.

NONFICTION Needs general interest, historical, how-to, humor, personal experience, photo feature, reviews, travel. No hunting, logging or political pieces. **Buys 12 mss/year.** Length: 500-700 words, will consider other lengths. **Pays $50-150.**

PHOTOS **Contact:** S Sedgwick. Pays $25 with article, $100 cover. First North American serial and reprint rights, digital and print.

FICTION Short fiction based on woodland setting. Will buy longer fiction for serialization over four issues. Needs short stories, slice-of-life vignettes. Length: 500-2,000 words. **Payment varies.**

POETRY Needs short poetry about woodland topics. Buys 4-8 poems/year. Submit maximum 2 poems. Length: 2-16 lines. **Pays $25.**

PERSONAL COMPUTERS

INFOWORLD

InfoWorld Media Group, 501 2nd St., 6F, San Francisco CA 94107. (415)243-0500. **E-mail:** jason_snyder@infoworld.com; doug_dineley@infoworld.com; eric_knorr@infoworld.com. **Website:** www.infoworld.com. **Contact:** Jason Snyder, features; Doug Dineley, reviews; Eric Knorr, news analysis. *InfoWorld* provides in-depth technical analysis on key products, solutions, and technologies for sound buying decisions and business gain. Contact specific editor. Circ. 220,000. No kill fee. Editorial lead time 2 months. Accepts queries by e-mail. Accepts simultaneous submissions.

NONFICTION Pays expenses of writers on assignment.

PC GAMER

Future Network USA, 1 Lombard St., Suite 200, San Francisco CA 94111. **E-mail:** wesley@pcgamer; tyler@pcgamer. **Website:** www.pcgamer.com. "*PC Gamer* is the global authority on PC games. For more than 20 years we have delivered unrivaled coverage, in print and online, of every aspect of PC gaming." No kill fee. Accepts queries by e-mail. Accepts simultaneous submissions.

NONFICTION Needs general interest, new product. Query. Pays expenses of writers on assignment.

TIPS Audience is serious Windows-based gamers.

⊘ PC WORLD

IDG, One Letterman Dr., Bldg. D, Suite P100, San Francisco CA 94129. **Website:** www.pcworld.com. Monthly magazine covering personal computers. *PC World* was created to give PC-proficient managers advice on which technology products to buy, tips on how to use those products most efficiently, news about the latest technological developments, and alerts regarding current problems with products and manufacturers. Circ. 1,100,000. No kill fee. Editorial lead time 3 months. Accepts queries by mail. Accepts simultaneous submissions. Guidelines by e-mail.

NONFICTION Needs how-to, reviews, news items, features. Query. **Payment varies**

TIPS "Once you're familiar with *PC World*, you can write us a query letter. Your letter should answer the following questions as specifically and consisely as possible. What is the problem, technique, or product you want to discuss? Why will *PC World* readers be interested in it? Which section of the magazine do you think it best fits? What is the specific audience for the piece (e.g., database or LAN users, desktop publishers, and so on)?"

💲💲💲 SMART COMPUTING

Sandhills Publishing, 120 W. Harvest Dr., Lincoln NE 68521. (800)544-1264. **Fax:** (402)479-2104. **E-mail:** editor@smartcomputing.com. **Website:** www.smartcomputing.com. **45% freelance written.** Monthly magazine. "We focus on plain-English computing articles with an emphasis on tutorials that improve productivity without the purchase of new hardware." Estab. 1990. Circ. 200,000. Byline given. Pays on acceptance. Offers 25% kill fee. Publishes ms an average of 2 months after acceptance. Editorial lead time 4 months. Submit seasonal material 4 months in advance. Accepts queries by mail, e-mail. Accepts simultaneous submissions. Responds in 1 month to queries. Sample copy for $7.99. Guidelines for #10 SASE.

NONFICTION Needs how to, new product, technical. No humor, opinion, personal experience. **Buys 250 mss/year.** Query with published clips. Length: 800-3,200 words. **Pays $240-960.** Other Pays expenses of writers on assignment up to $75.

PHOTOS Send photos. Captions required. Offers no additional payment for photos accepted with ms. Buys all rights.

TIPS "Focus on practical, how-to computing articles. Our readers are intensely productivity-driven. Carefully review recent issues. We receive many ideas for stories printed in the last 6 months."

WIRED

Condé Nast Publications, 520 Third St., 3rd Floor, San Francisco CA 94107-1815. **E-mail:** submit@wired.com. **Website:** www.wired.com. **95% freelance written.** Monthly magazine covering technology and digital culture. Covers the digital revolution and related advances in computers, communications, and lifestyles. Estab. 1993. Circ. 500,000. Byline given. Pays on publication. Offers 25% kill fee. Publishes ms an average of 3 months after acceptance. Editorial lead time 3 months. Accepts queries by e-mail. Accepts simultaneous submissions. Responds in 3 weeks to queries. Sample copy: $4.95. Guidelines by e-mail.

NONFICTION Needs essays, interview, opinion. No poetry or trade articles. Query. Pays expenses of writers on assignment.

TIPS "Read the magazine. We get too many inappropriate queries. We need quality writers who understand our audience and who understand how to query."

PHOTOGRAPHY

💲💲 VIDEOMAKER

Videomaker, Inc., York Publishing, 645 Mangrove Ave, Chico CA 95926-3946. (530)891-8410. **Fax:** (530)891-8443. **E-mail:** editor@videomaker.com. **Website:** www.videomaker.com. Monthly magazine covering audio and video production, camcorders, editing, computer video, DVDs. Estab. 1985. Circ. 57,814. Byline given. Pays on publication. No kill fee. Publishes ms an average of 4 months after acceptance. Editorial lead time 5 months. Submit seasonal material 5 months in advance. Accepts queries by mail, e-mail. Accepts simultaneous submissions. Responds in 3 weeks to queries. Sample copy and writer's guidelines available online.

NONFICTION Needs how-to, technical. Special issues: Annual Buyer's Guide in October (13th issue of the year). **Buys 34 mss/year.** Query. Length: 900-2,000 words. **Pays $100-300.** Pays expenses of writers on assignment. Limit agreed upon in advance.

PHOTOS Contact: Melissa Hageman, art director. Model releases required. Negotiates payment individually.

POLITICS & WORLD AFFAIRS

💲💲 ARMS CONTROL TODAY

Arms Control Association, 1313 L St. NW, Suite 130, Washington DC 20005. (202)463-8270. **Fax:** (202)463-8273. **E-mail:** submissions@armscontrol.org; aca@armscontrol.org. **Website:** www.armscontrol.org. **Contact:** Daniel Horner, editor. **50% freelance written.** Published 10 times a year, *Arms Control Today* welcomes submissions on topics in the field of international arms control and disarmament, including nuclear proliferation, strategic weapons reductions, missile defense, chemical and biological weapons, missile proliferation, and conventional arms exports. Proposals for articles on other topics also are welcome. Feature articles should stimulate debate and offer constructive policy suggestions. *ACT* articles are not purely academic discussions or journalistic accounts; also seeks articles that detail and analyze a current policy problem and propose appropriate means for addressing it. Estab. 1971. Circ. 2,000. Byline given. Pays on publication. Time between acceptance and publication is 3 months. Accepts queries by e-mail. Accepts simultaneous submissions. Guidelines available on website.

NONFICTION Needs essays, opinion. **Buys 30-40 mss/year.** Query first. Submit a detailed outline and/or abstract of articles before submission so we have a chance to work with you on the piece and solve problems in the early stages of the process. Length: 2,000-4,000 words. **Pays $150-300 for assigned articles; $150-300 for unsolicited articles.** Pays expenses of writers on assignment.

PHOTOS Generally, the editorial staff chooses images and graphics for articles. If you have any, adhere to these specifications: permission; it must be in high-res (300 dpi) JPG or TIF format. State availability. Provide detailed captions.

COLUMNS Pays $150-300.

TIPS "Our readership includes experts and nonexperts; articles should be written so that they are of value to both groups. Avoid jargon and unnecessary technical detail. If terms of art are used in the article, they should be explained on the first reference. Avoid cluttering the article with abbreviations. Submit articles as a Microsoft Word document. Include in the text your detailed contact information, even if the information is contained in your e-mail cover note."

💲💲 CHURCH & STATE

1301 K Street NW, Suite 850E, Washington DC 20005. (202)466-3234. **Fax:** (202)466-2587. **E-mail:** americansunited@au.org. **Website:** www.au.org. **10% freelance written.** Monthly magazine emphasizing religious liberty and church/state relations matters. "Strongly advocates separation of church and state. Readership is well-educated." Estab. 1947. Circ. 40,000. Pays on acceptance. No kill fee. Publishes ms an average of 2 months after acceptance. Accepts queries by mail. Accepts simultaneous submissions. Responds in 2 months to queries. Sample copy and writer's guidelines for 9x12 SAE with 3 first-class stamps.

NONFICTION Needs expose, general interest, historical, interview. **Buys 11 mss/year.** Query. Length: 800-1,600 words. **Pays $150-300.** Sometimes pays expenses of writers on assignment.

REPRINTS Send tearsheet, photocopy or typed ms with rights for sale noted and information about when and where the material previously appeared.

PHOTOS Send photos. Captions required. Pays negotiable fee for b&w prints. Buys one time rights.

TIPS "We're looking for feature articles on underreported local church-state controversies. We also consider 'viewpoint' essays that offer a unique or personal take on church-state issues. We are not a religious magazine. You need to see our magazine before you try to write for it."

💲💲 COMMONWEAL

Commonweal Foundation, 475 Riverside Dr., Room 405, New York NY 10115. (212)662-4200. **Fax:** (212)662-4183. **E-mail:** editors@commonwealmagazine.org. **Website:** www.commonwealmagazine.org. **Contact:** Paul Baumann, editor; Tiina Aleman, production editor. Biweekly journal of opinion edited by Catholic lay people, dealing with topical issues of the day on public affairs, religion, literature, and the arts. Estab. 1924. Circ. 20,000. Byline given. Pays on publication. No kill fee. Submit seasonal material 4 months in advance. Accepts simultaneous submissions. Responds in 2 months to queries. Sample copy free. Guidelines available online.

NONFICTION Needs essays, general interest, interview, personal experience, religious. **Buys 30 mss/year.** Query with published clips. *Commonweal* welcomes original manuscripts dealing with topical issues of the day on public affairs, religion, literature, and the arts. Looks for articles that are timely, accurate, and well written. Length: 2,000-3,000 words for features. **Pays $200-300 for longer mss; $100-200 for shorter pieces.** Pays expenses of writers on assignment.

COLUMNS Upfronts: (750-1,000 words) brief, newsy reportorials, giving facts, information and some interpretation behind the headlines of the day; Last Word: (750 words) usually of a personal nature, on some aspect of the human condition: spiritual, individual, political, or social.

POETRY Needs free verse, traditional. *Commonweal*, published every 2 weeks, is a Catholic general interest magazine for college-educated readers. Does not publish inspirational poems. Buys 20 poems/year. Length: no more than 75 lines. **Pays 75¢/line plus 2 contributor's copies. Acquires all rights. Returns rights when requested by the author.**

TIPS "Articles should be written for a general but well-educated audience. While religious articles are always topical, we are less interested in devotional and churchy pieces than in articles which examine the links between 'worldly' concerns and religious beliefs."

💲💲 THE FREEMAN: IDEAS ON LIBERTY

1819 Peachtree Road NE, Suite 300, Atlanta GA 30309 United States. (404)554-9980. **Fax:** (404)393-3142. **E-mail:** freeman@fee.org. **E-mail:** editor@fee.org. **Website:** fee.org. James Anderson, deputy publisher. **Contact:** Dan Sanchez, managing editor. **85% freelance written.** Monthly publication for the layman and fairly advanced students of liberty. Estab. 1946. Byline given. Pays on publication. No kill fee. Publishes online within weeks. Some online articles are also published in the quarterly print edition. Accepts queries by e-mail. Guidelines available on website.

NONFICTION **Buys 100 mss/year.** Query with SASE. Length: 3,500 words. **Pays 10¢/word.** Pays expenses of writers on assignment.

TIPS "It's most rewarding to find freelancers with new insights and fresh points of view. Facts, figures, and quotations cited should be fully documented, to their original source, if possible."

💲💲 THE NATION

520 Eighth Avenue, 8th Flo, New York NY 10018. **E-mail:** submissions@thenation.com. **Website:** www.thenation.com. Steven Brower, art director. **Contact:** Roane Carey, managing editor; Ange Mlinko, poetry editor. *The Nation*, published weekly, is a journal of left/liberal opinion, with arts coverage that includes poetry. The only requirement for poetry is excellence. Estab. 1865. Circ. 100,000. Guidelines available online.

NONFICTION civil liberties, civil rights, labor, economics, environmental, feminist issues, politics, the arts. Queries accepted via online form. Length: 750-2,500 words. **Pays $150-500, depending on length.** Pays expenses of writers on assignment.

POETRY **Contact:** Ange Mliko, poetry editor. "Please email poems in a single PDF attachment to PoemNationSubmit@gmail.com. Submissions are not accepted from June 1-September 15." Buys 6 poems/year. Submit maximum 3 poems.

$$$ THE PROGRESSIVE

30 W. Mifflin St., Suite 703, Madison WI 53703. (608)257-4626. **E-mail:** editorial@progressive.org. **Website:** www.progressive.org. **Contact:** Norman Stockwell, publisher. **75% freelance written.** Bimonthly magazine of investigative reporting, political commentary, cultural coverage, activism, interviews, poetry, and humor. It steadfastly stands against militarism, the concentration of power in corporate hands, and the disenfranchisement of the citizenry. It champions peace, social and economic justice, civil rights, civil liberties, human rights, a preserved environment, and a reinvigorated democracy. Its bedrock values are nonviolence and freedom of speech. Estab. 1909. Circ. 35,000. Byline given. Pays on publication. Publishes ms an average of 6 weeks after acceptance. Accepts queries by e-mail. Accepts simultaneous submissions. Responds in 1 month to queries. Sample copy for 9x12 SASE with 4 first-class stamps or sample articles online. Guidelines online.

NONFICTION Needs book excerpts, essays, historical, interview, opinion, photo feature, profile. Query. Length: 500-4,000 words. **Pays $250-1,000.** Pays expenses of writers on assignment. by prior arrangement only

POETRY Publishes 1 original poem a month. "We prefer poems that connect up—in 1 fashion or another, however obliquely—with political concerns." **Pays $150.**

TIPS Sought-after topics include electoral coverage, social movements, foreign policy, activism, and book reviews.

$ PROGRESSIVE POPULIST

Ampersand Publishing Co., P.O. Box 819, Manchaca TX 78652. (512)828-7245. **E-mail:** populist@usa.net. **Website:** www.populist.com. **90% freelance written.** Biweekly tabloid covering politics and economics. "We cover political and economic issues of interest to workers, small businesses, and family farmers and ranchers." Estab. 1994. Circ. 15,000. Byline given. Pays quarterly. No kill fee. Publishes ms an average of 1 month after acceptance. Editorial lead time 3 weeks. Submit seasonal material 1 month in advance. Accepts queries by mail, e-mail, fax, phone. Accepts simultaneous submissions. Sample copy and writer's guidelines free.

NONFICTION Needs essays, general interest, historical, humor, interview, opinion. "We are not much interested in 'sound-off' articles about state or national politics, although we accept letters to the editor. We prefer to see more 'journalistic' pieces in which the writer does enough footwork to advance a story beyond the easy realm of opinion." **Buys 400 mss/year.** Query. Length: 600-1,000 words. **Pays $15-50.** Pays expenses of writers on assignment. Pays writers with contributor copies or other premiums if preferred by writer.

REPRINTS Send photocopy with rights for sale noted and information about when and where the material previously appeared.

PHOTOS State availability. Identification of subjects required. Negotiates payment individually. Buys one-time rights.

TIPS "We do prefer submissions by e-mail. I find it's easier to work with e-mail, and for the writer it probably increases the chances of getting a response."

$$$$ REASON

Reason Foundation, 5737 Mesmer Ave., Los Angeles CA 90230. (310)391-2245. **Fax:** (310)390-8986. **E-mail:** bdoherty@reason.com. **Website:** www.reason.com. **30% freelance written.** Monthly magazine covering politics, current events, culture, ideas. *Reason* covers politics, culture and ideas from a dynamic libertarian perspective. It features reported works, opinion pieces, and book reviews. Estab. 1968. Circ. 55,000. Byline given. Pays on publication. Offers kill fee. Editorial lead time 2 months. Submit seasonal material 3 months in advance. Accepts queries by mail, e-mail. Accepts simultaneous submissions. Responds in 6 weeks to queries. Responds in 2 months to mss. Sample copy for $4. Guidelines available online.

NONFICTION Needs book excerpts, essays, expose, general interest, humor, interview, opinion. No products, personal experience, how-to, travel. **Buys 50-60 mss/year.** Query with published clips. Length: 850-5,000 words. **Payment varies.** Pays expenses of writers on assignment.

TIPS We prefer queries of no more than 1 or 2 pages with specifically developed ideas about a given topic rather than more general areas of interest. Enclosing a few published clips also helps.

💲💲 WASHINGTON MONTHLY

The Washington Monthly Co., 1200 18th St. NW, Suite 330, Washington DC 20036. **E-mail:** editors@ washingtonmonthly.com. **Website:** www.washingtonmonthly.com. **50% freelance written.** Monthly magazine covering politics, policy, media. We are a neo-liberal publication with a long history and specific views—please read our magazine before submitting. Estab. 1969. Circ. 28,000. Byline given. Pays on publication. No kill fee. Publishes ms an average of 2 months after acceptance. Editorial lead time 2 months. Submit seasonal material 4 months in advance. Accepts queries by mail, e-mail, fax, phone. Accepts simultaneous submissions. Responds in 3 weeks to queries. Responds in 2 months to mss. Sample copy for 11×17 SAE with 5 first-class stamps or by e-mail. Guidelines available online.

NONFICTION Needs book excerpts, essays, expose, general interest, historical, interview, opinion, personal experience, technical, first-person political. No humor, how-to, or generalized articles. **Buys 20 mss/ year.** Send complete ms. Length: 1,500-5,000 words. **Pays 10¢/word.** Pays expenses of writers on assignment.

PHOTOS State availability. Reviews contact sheets, prints. Negotiates payment individually. Buys one time rights.

COLUMNS 10 Miles Square (about DC); On Political Books, Booknotes (both reviews of current political books), 1,500-3,000 words. **Buys 10 mss/year.** Query with published clips or send complete ms. **Pays 10¢/ word.**

TIPS Call our editors to talk about ideas. Always pitch articles showing background research. We're particularly looking for first-hand accounts of working in government. We also like original work showing that the government is or is not doing something important. We have writer's guidelines, but do your research first.

PSYCHOLOGY & SELF-IMPROVEMENT

💲💲💲💲 GRADPSYCH

American Psychological Association, 750 First St. NE, Washington DC 20009. **Fax:** (202)336-6103. **Website:** www.apa.org/gradpsych. **50% freelance written.** Quarterly magazine. "We cover issues of interest to psychology graduate students, including career outlook, tips for success in school, profiles of interesting students, and reports on student research. We aim for our articles to be readable, informative, and fun. Grad students have enough dry, technical reading to do at school; we don't want to add to it." Estab. 2003. Circ. 60,000. Byline given. Pays on acceptance. Offers $200 kill fee. Publishes ms an average of 4 months after acceptance. Editorial lead time 3-5 months. Submit seasonal material 4 months in advance. Accepts queries by e-mail. Accepts simultaneous submissions. Responds in 2 weeks to queries. Sample copy online.

NONFICTION Needs general interest, how-to, interview, journalism for grad students. **Buys 25 mss/ year.** Query with published clips. Length: 300-2,000 words. **Pays $300-2,000 for assigned articles.**

PHOTOS State availability. Identification of subjects, model releases required. Reviews GIF/JPEG files. Negotiates payment individually. Buys one-time rights.

TIPS "Check out our website and pitch a story on a topic we haven't written on before or that gives an old topic a new spin. Also, have quality clips."

💲💲💲💲 PSYCHOLOGY TODAY

Sussex Publishers, Inc., 115 E. 23rd St., 9th Floor, New York NY 10010. (212)260-7210. **Fax:** (212)260-7445. **Website:** www.psychologytoday.com. Bimonthly magazine exploring every aspect of human behavior, from the cultural trends that shape the way we think and feel to the intricacies of modern neuroscience. "We're sort of a hybrid of a science magazine, a health magazine and a self-help magazine. While we're read by many psychologists, therapists and social workers, most of our readers are simply intelligent and curious people interested in the psyche and the self." Estab. 1967. Circ. 331,400. Byline given. Pays 30 days after publication. No kill fee. Publishes ms an average of 3 months after acceptance. Editorial lead time 5 months. Accepts queries by online submission form. Accepts simultaneous submissions. Responds in 1 month to queries. Guidelines online.

NONFICTION No fiction, poetry or first-person essays on How I Conquered Mental Disorder X. **Buys 20-25 mss/year.** Query with published clips. Length: 1,500-4,000 words. **Pays $1,000-2,500.**

COLUMNS Contact: News Editor. News & Trends, 150-300 words. Query with published clips. **Pays $150-300.**

TIPS "Send your query to one of the members of our staff."

🟢 ROSICRUCIAN DIGEST

Rosicrucian Order, AMORC, 1342 Naglee Ave., San Jose CA 95191-0001. (408)947-3600. **E-mail:** editorinchief@rosicrucian.org. **Website:** www.rosicrucian.org. **Contact:** Editor-in-Chief. "Quarterly magazine (international) emphasizing mysticism, science, philosophy, and the arts for educated men and women of all ages seeking alternative answers to life's questions." Byline given. Pays on acceptance. No kill fee. Publishes ms an average of 6 months after acceptance. Accepts queries by mail, phone. Responds in 3 months to queries. Guidelines online.

NONFICTION No religious, astrological, or political material, or articles promoting a particular group or system of thought. Most articles are written by members or donated, but we're always open to freelance submissions. No book-length mss. Query. Length: 1,500-2,000 words. **Pays 6¢/word.**

REPRINTS Prefers typed ms with rights for sale noted and information about when and where the article previously appeared, but tearsheet or photcopy acceptable. Pays 50% of amount paid for an original article.

TIPS "We're looking for more pieces on these subjects: our connection with the past—the important contributions of ancient civilizations to today's world and culture and the relevance of this wisdom to now; how to channel teenage energy/angst into positive, creative, constructive results (preferably written by teachers or others who work with young people—written for frustrated parents); and the vital necessity of raising our environmental consciousness if we are going to survive as a species on this planet."

🟢 SPOTLIGHT ON RECOVERY MAGAZINE

R. Graham Publishing Company, 9602 Glenwood Rd., #140, Brooklyn NY 11236. (347)831-9373. **E-mail:** rgraham_100@msn.com. **Website:** www.spotlightonrecovery.com. **Contact:** Robin Graham, publisher and editor-in-chief. **85% freelance written.** Quarterly magazine covering self-help, recovery, and empowerment. "This is the premiere outreach and resource magazine in New York. Its goal is to be the catalyst for which the human spirit could heal. Everybody knows somebody who has mental illness, substance abuse issues, parenting problems, educational issues, or someone who is homeless, unemployed, physically ill, or the victim of a crime. Many people suffer in silence. *Spotlight on Recovery* will provide a voice to those who suffer in silence and begin the dialogue of recovery." Estab. 2001. Circ. 3,000-6,000. Byline sometimes given. Pays on publication. No kill fee. Publishes ms an average of 6 months after acceptance. Editorial lead time 1 month. Submit seasonal material 1 month in advance. Accepts queries by mail, e-mail. Accepts simultaneous submissions. Responds in 2 weeks to queries; 1 month to mss. Sample copy and guidelines free.

NONFICTION Needs book excerpts, inspirational, interview, opinion, personal experience. **Buys 30-50 mss/year.** Query with published clips. Length: 150-1,500 words. **Pays 5¢/word or $75-80/article.**

PHOTOS State availability. Identification of subjects required. Reviews GIF/JPEG files. Pays $5-10/photo. Buys one-time rights.

COLUMNS Buys 4 mss/year. Query with published clips. **Pays 5¢/word or $75-80/column.**

FICTION Needs ethnic, mainstream, slice-of-life vignettes.

POETRY Contact: Robin Graham. Buys 10 poems/year. Submit maximum 2 poems. open **Pays 5 cents/word.**

FILLERS Needs facts, newsbreaks, short humor. **Buys 2 mss/year.**

TIPS "Send a query and give a reason why you would choose the subject posted to write about."

REGIONAL

ALABAMA

🟢🟢 ALABAMA HERITAGE

University of Alabama, Box 870342, Tuscaloosa AL 35487-0342. (205)348-7467. **Fax:** (205)348-7473. **E-mail:** reyno031@bama.ua.edu. **Website:** www.alabamaheritage.com. **Contact:** Susan Reynolds, associate editor. **90% freelance written.** *Alabama Heritage* is a nonprofit historical quarterly published by the University of Alabama and the Alabama Department of Archives and History for the intelligent lay reader. "We are interested in lively, well-written, and thoroughly researched articles on Alabama/Southern history and culture. Readability and accuracy are essential." Estab. 1986. Byline given. Pays on publication. No kill fee. Accepts queries by mail, e-mail. Accepts simultaneous submissions. Guidelines online.

NONFICTION "We do not publish fiction, poetry, articles on current events or living artists, or personal/family reminiscences." Query. Length: 750-4,000 words. **Pays $50-350.**

PHOTOS Identification of subjects required. Reviews contact sheets. Buys one-time rights.

TIPS "Authors need to remember that we regard history as a fascinating subject, not as a dry recounting of dates and facts. Articles that are lively and engaging, in addition to being well researched, will find interested readers among our editors. No term papers, please. All areas are open to freelance writers. Best approach is a written query."

💲 ALABAMA LIVING

Alabama Rural Electric Association, 340 Techna-Center Dr., Montgomery AL 36117. (800)410-2737. **E-mail:** agriffin@areapower.com. **Website:** http://www.areapower.coop. **Contact:** Allison Griffin, editor. **80% freelance written.** Monthly magazine covering topics of interest to rural and suburban Alabamians. "Our magazine is an editorially balanced, informational and educational service to members of rural electric cooperatives. Our mix regularly includes Alabama history, Alabama features, gardening, outdoor, and consumer pieces." Estab. 1948. Circ. 400,000. Byline given. Pays on acceptance. No kill fee. Editorial lead time 4 months. Submit seasonal material 4 months in advance. Accepts queries by mail, e-mail. Accepts simultaneous submissions. Responds in 1 month to queries. Sample copy free.

NONFICTION Needs historical. Special issues: Gardening (March); Travel (April); Home Improvement (May); Holiday Recipes (December). **Buys 20 mss/year.** Send complete ms. Length: 500-750 words. **Pays $250 minimum for assigned articles. Pays $150 minimum for unsolicited articles.**

REPRINTS Send typed manuscript with rights for sale noted. Pays $100.

PHOTOS Buys 1-3 photos from freelancers/issue; 12-36 photos/year. Pays $100 for color cover; $50 for color inside; $60-75 for photo/text package. **Pays on acceptance.** Credit line given. Buys one-time rights for publication and website; negotiable.

TIPS "Preference given to submissions with accompanying art."

ALASKA

💲💲 ALASKA

Morris Communications, 301 Arctic Slope Ave., Suite 300, Anchorage AK 99518-3035. **E-mail:** editor@alaskamagazine.com. **Website:** www.alaskamagazine.com. **Contact:** Michelle Theall, editor; Corrynn Cochran, photo editor. **70% freelance written. Eager to work with new/unpublished writers.** Magazine published 10 times/year covering topics uniquely Alaskan. Estab. 1935. Circ. 180,000. Byline given. Pays on publication. No kill fee. Publishes ms an average of 6 months after acceptance. Submit seasonal material 1 year in advance. Accepts queries by e-mail. Accepts simultaneous submissions. Responds in 2 months to queries and mss. Sample copy: $4.99 plus 9x12 SASE with 7 first-class stamps. Guidelines online.

NONFICTION Needs book excerpts, essays, historical, humor, interview, personal experience, photo feature, travel. No fiction or poetry. **Buys 40 mss/year.** Query. Length: 700-2,000 words **Pays $100-1,250.**

PHOTOS *Alaska* is dedicated to depicting life in Alaska through high-quality images of its people, places, and wildlife. Color photographs from professional freelance photographers are used extensively and selected according to their creative and technical merits. Send photos. Captions, identification of subjects required. Reviews 35mm or larger transparencies, slides labeled with your name. Pays $50 maximum for b&w photos; $75-500 for color photos; $300 maximum/day; $2,000 maximum/complete job; $300 maximum/full page; $500 maximum/cover. Buys limited rights, first North American serial rights, and electronic rights. "Each issue of *Alaska* features a 4-, 6-, and/or 8-page feature. We're looking for themes and photos to show the best of Alaska. We want sharp, artistically composed pictures. Cover photo always relates to stories inside the issue." Photographers on assignment are paid a competitive day rate and reimbursed for approved expenses. All assignments are negotiated in advance.

COLUMNS Escape (gives readers a reason to get out and explore the Last Frontier); Adventure (features a variety of Alaskan outdoor subjects, including fishing, hunting, hiking, camping, birding, adventure sports, and extreme activities); Alaska History; Alaska Native Culture; all 800-1,000 words. Query.

TIPS "We're looking for top-notch writing—original, well researched, lively. Subjects must be distinctly Alaskan. A story on a mall in Alaska, for example, won't work for us; every state has malls. If you've got a story about a Juneau mall run by someone who is also a bush pilot and part-time trapper, maybe we'd be interested. The point is that *Alaska* stories need to be vivid, focused, and unique. Alaska is like nowhere else—we need our stories to be the same way."

ARIZONA

💲💲 ARIZONA FOOTHILLS MAGAZINE

8132 N. 87th Place, Scottsdale AZ 85258. (480)460-5203. **Fax:** (480)443-1517. **Website:** www.azfoothills-mag.com. **10% freelance written.** Monthly magazine covering Arizona lifestyle. Estab. 1996. Circ. 60,000. Byline given. Pays on publication. No kill fee. Publishes ms an average of 6 months after acceptance. Editorial lead time 6 months. Submit seasonal material at least 4 months in advance. Accepts queries by mail, e-mail. Accepts simultaneous submissions. Responds in 1 month to queries. Sample copy for #10 SASE.

NONFICTION Needs general interest, photo feature, travel, fashion, decor, arts, interview. **Buys 10 mss/year.** Query with published clips. Length: 900-2,000 words. **Pays 35-40¢/word for assigned articles.**

PHOTOS Photos may be requested. Captions, identification of subjects, model releases required. Reviews contact sheets, transparencies. Negotiates payment individually. Occasionally buys one-time rights.

COLUMNS Travel, dining, fashion, home decor, design, architecture, wine, shopping, golf, performance & visual arts.

TIPS "We prefer stories that appeal to our affluent audience written with an upbeat, contemporary approach and reader service in mind."

💲💲💲💲 ARIZONA HIGHWAYS

2039 W. Lewis Ave., Phoenix AZ 85009. (602)712-2200. **Fax:** (602)254-4505. **E-mail:** kkramer@azdot. gov. **Website:** www.arizonahighways.com. **Contact:** Kelly Kramer, managing editor. **100% freelance written.** Magazine that is state-owned, designed to help attract tourists into and through Arizona. Estab. 1925. Circ. 425,000. Pays on acceptance. No kill fee. Accepts

queries by mail, e-mail, fax. Accepts simultaneous submissions. Responds in 1 month. Guidelines online.

NONFICTION **Buys 50 mss/year.** Query with a lead paragraph and brief outline of story. Length: 600-1,800 words. **Pays up to $1/word.** Pays expenses of writers on assignment.

PHOTOS Contact: Peter Ensenberger, director of photography. For digital requirements, contact the photography department. Pays $125-600. Buys one-time rights.

COLUMNS Focus on Nature (short feature in first or third person dealing with the unique aspects of a single species of wildlife), 800 words; Along the Way (short essay dealing with life in Arizona, or a personal experience keyed to Arizona), 750 words; Back Road Adventure (personal back-road trips, preferably off the beaten path and outside major metro areas), 1,000 words; Hike of the Month (personal experiences on trails anywhere in Arizona), 500 words. **Pays $50-1,000, depending on department.**

TIPS "Writing must be of professional quality, warm, sincere, in-depth, well peopled, and accurate. Avoid themes that describe first trips to Arizona, the Grand Canyon, the desert, Colorado River running, etc. Emphasis is to be on Arizona adventure and romance as well as flora and fauna, when appropriate, and themes that can be photographed. Double check your manuscript for accuracy. Our typical reader is a 50-something person with the time, the inclination, and the means to travel."

💲💲 TRENDS MAGAZINE

Trends Publishing, 5685 N. Scottsdale Rd., Suite E160, Scottsdale AZ 85250. (480)990-9007. **Fax:** (480)990-0048. **E-mail:** editor@trendspublishing.com. **Website:** www.trendspublishing.com. **Contact:** Bill Dougherty, publisher. **20% freelance written.** Monthly magazine covering society, affluent lifestyle, luxury goods and services. *Trends Magazine* has a focus on the affluent community, especially in Arizona. Estab. 1982. Circ. 45,000. Byline given. Offers 100% kill fee. Editorial lead time 2-3 months. Submit seasonal material 2-3 months in advance. Accepts queries by mail, e-mail, fax, phone. Accepts simultaneous submissions. Responds in 1 month. Sample copy free. Guidelines by e-mail.

NONFICTION Needs general interest, humor, interview, travel. Does not want technical, religious, or political. Query with published clips. Length: 700-1,200 words. **Pays $350-600.**

TIPS "Just think about subjects that would appeal to affluent readers."

💲💲 TUCSON LIFESTYLE

Conley Publishing Group, Ltd., Suite 12, 7000 E. Tanque Verde Rd., Tucson AZ 85715-5318. (520)721-2929. **Fax:** (520)721-8665. **E-mail:** scott@tucsonlifestyle.com. **Website:** www.tucsonlifestyle.com. **Contact:** Scott Barker, executive editor. **90% freelance written. Prefers to work with published/established writers.** Monthly magazine covering Southern Arizona-related events and topics. No fiction, poetry, cartoons, or syndicated columns. Estab. 1982. Circ. 29,000. Byline given. Pays on acceptance. No kill fee. Publishes ms an average of 6 months after acceptance. Submit seasonal material 1 year in advance. Accepts queries by mail, e-mail. Accepts simultaneous submissions. Responds in 2 months to queries; in 3 months to mss. Sample copy: $3.99, plus $3 postage. Guidelines free.

NONFICTION "Avoid obvious tourist attractions and information that most residents of the Southwest are likely to know. No anecdotes masquerading as articles. Not interested in fish-out-of-water, Easterner-visiting-the-Old-West pieces." **Buys 20 mss/year. Pays $50-500.** Pays expenses of writers on assignment.

PHOTOS Query about photos before submitting anything.

TIPS "Read the magazine before submitting anything."

CALIFORNIA

💲💲 CARLSBAD MAGAZINE

Wheelhouse Media, P.O. Box 2089, Carlsbad CA 92018. (760)729-9099. **Fax:** (760)729-9011. **E-mail:** tim@wheelhousemedia.com. **Website:** www.click-oncarlsbad.com. **Contact:** Tim Wrisley. **80% freelance written.** Bimonthly magazine covering people, places, events, arts in Carlsbad, California. "We are a regional magazine highlighting all things pertaining specifically to Carlsbad. We focus on history, events, people, and places that make Carlsbad interesting and unique. Our audience is both Carlsbad residents and visitors or anyone interested in learning more about Carlsbad. We favor a conversational tone that still ad-

heres to standard rules of writing." Estab. 2004. Circ. 35,000. Byline given. Pays on publication. Publishes ms an average of 6 months after acceptance. Editorial lead time 4 months. Submit seasonal material 6-12 months in advance. Accepts queries by mail, e-mail. Accepts simultaneous submissions. Responds in 2 months to queries and mss. Sample copy: $2.31. Guidelines by e-mail.

NONFICTION Needs historical, interview. Does not want self-promoting articles for individuals or businesses, real estate how-tos, advertorials. **Buys 3 mss/year.** Query with published clips. Length: 300-2,700 words. **Pays 20-30¢/word for assigned articles. Pays 20¢/word for unsolicited articles.** Pays expenses of writers on assignment.

PHOTOS State availability. Reviews GIF/JPEG files. Offers $15-400/photo. Buys one-time rights.

COLUMNS Carlsbad Arts (people, places, or things related to cultural arts in Carlsbad); Happenings (events that take place in Carlsbad); Carlsbad Character (unique Carlsbad residents who have contributed to Carlsbad's character); Commerce (Carlsbad business profiles); Surf Scene (subjects pertaining to the beach/surf in Carlsbad), all 500-700 words. Garden (Carlsbad garden feature); Home (Carlsbad home feature), both 700-1,200 words. **Buys 60 mss/year.** Query with published clips. **Pays $50 flat fee or 20¢/word.**

TIPS "The main thing to remember is that any pitches need to be subjects directly related to Carlsbad. If the subjects focus on surrounding towns, they aren't going to make the cut. We are looking for well-written feature magazine-style articles. E-mail is the preferred method for queries; you will get a response."

💲💲 THE EAST BAY MONTHLY

Telegraph Media, 1305 Franklin St., Suite 501, Oakland CA 94612. (510)238-9101. **Fax:** (510)238-9163. **Website:** www.themonthly.com. Andreas Jones, art director. **95% freelance written.** Monthly general interest tabloid covering the San Francisco Bay Area. "We feature distinctive, intelligent articles of interest to *East Bay* readers." Estab. 1970. Circ. 62,000. Byline given. Pays on publication. No kill fee. Editorial lead time 2+ months. Submit seasonal material 3 months in advance. Accepts queries by mail, e-mail. Accepts simultaneous submissions. Responds in 1 month to queries. Responds in 1 month to mss. Sample copy for $3. Writer's guidelines for #10 SASE or by e-mail.

NONFICTION No fiction or poetry. Query with published clips. Length: 1,000-3,000 words. **Pays $100-500.** Pays expenses of writers on assignment.

REPRINTS Send tearsheet and information about when and where the material previously appeared.

PHOTOS State availability. Identification of subjects required. Negotiates payment individually.

COLUMNS First Person, 2,000 words. Query with published clips.

GUESTLIFE

Desert Publications, Inc., 303 N. Indian Canyon Dr., Palm Springs CA 92262. (760)325-2333. **Fax:** (760)325-7008. **Website:** www.guestlife.com. **95% freelance written.** Annual prestige hotel room magazine covering history, highlights, and activities of the area named (i.e., *Monterey Bay GuestLife*). *GuestLife* focuses on its respective area and is placed in hotel rooms in that area for the affluent vacationer. Estab. 1979. Byline given. Pays on publication. Offers negotiable kill fee. Publishes ms an average of 9 months after acceptance. Editorial lead time 6 months. Submit seasonal material 8 months in advance. Accepts queries by e-mail. Accepts simultaneous submissions. Responds in 1 month to queries; in 1 month to mss. Sample copy: $10.

NONFICTION Needs general interest, historical, photo feature, travel. **Buys 3 mss/year.** Query with published clips. Length: 300-1,500 words. **Pays $100-500.** Pays expenses of writers on assignment.

PHOTOS State availability. Identification of subjects required. Reviews contact sheets. Negotiates payment individually. Buys all rights.

FILLERS Needs facts. **Buys 3 mss/year.** Length: 50-100 words. **Pays $50-100.**

JOURNAL PLUS

25 Johe Lane, San Luis Obispo CA 93405. (805) 546-0609. **E-mail:** info@slojournal.com. **Website:** slojournal.com. **Contact:** Tom Meinhold, publisher. **60% freelance written.** Monthly magazine that can be read online covering the 25-year old age group and up, but young-at-heart audience. "The *Journal Plus* is a combination of the *SLO County Journal* and *Plus Magazine*. It is the community magazine written for and by the local people of the Central Coast." Estab. 1981. Circ. 25,000. Byline given. Pays on publication. No kill fee. Publishes ms an average of 2 months after acceptance. Editorial lead time 2 months. Submit

seasonal material 2 months in advance. Accepts queries by e-mail. Accepts simultaneous submissions. Responds in 2 weeks to queries; in 1 month to mss. Sample copy for 9x12 SAE with $2 postage. Guidelines online.

NONFICTION Needs historical, humor, interview, personal experience, profile, travel, book reviews, entertainment, health. Special issues: Christmas (December); Travel (October, April). No finance, heavy humor, poetry, or fiction. **Buys 60-70 mss/year.** Send complete ms. Length: 600-1,400 words. **Pays $50-75.** Pays expenses of writers on assignment.

PHOTOS Send photos. High resolution jpegs.

TIPS "Review an issue on the website before submitting."

PALM SPRINGS LIFE

Desert Publications, Inc., 303 N. Indian Canyon, Palm Springs CA 92262. (760)325-2333. **Fax:** (760)325-7008. **Website:** www.palmspringslife.com. **Contact:** Olga Reyes, managing editor. **80% freelance written.** Monthly magazine covering affluent Palm Springs-area desert resort communities. *Palm Springs Life* celebrates the good life. Estab. 1958. Circ. 20,000. Byline given. Pays on publication. Offers negotiable kill fee. Publishes ms an average of 3 months after acceptance. Submit seasonal material 6 months in advance. Accepts simultaneous submissions. Responds in 4-6 weeks to queries. Guidelines online.

NONFICTION Needs book excerpts, essays, interview, feature stories, celebrity, fashion, spa, epicurean. Query with published clips. Length: 500-2,500 words. **Pays $100-500.**

PHOTOS State availability. Captions, identification of subjects, model releases required. Reviews contact sheets. Pays $75-350/photo. Buys one time rights.

COLUMNS The Good Life (art, fashion, fine dining, philanthropy, entertainment, luxury living, luxury auto, architecture), 250-750 words. **Buys 12 mss/year.** Query with or without published clips. **Pays $200-350.**

SACRAMENTO MAGAZINE

Sacramento Magazines Corp., 231 Lathrop Way, Suite A, Sacramento CA 95815. (916)426-1720. **E-mail:** krista@sacmag.com. **Website:** www.sacmag.com. Publisher: Joe Chiodo. **Contact:** Krista Minard, editorial director. **80% freelance written. Works with a small number of new/unpublished writers each year.**

Monthly magazine with a strictly local angle on local issues, human interest and consumer items for readers in the middle to high income brackets. Prefers to work with writers local to Sacramento area. Estab. 1975. Circ. 50,000. Pays on publication. No kill fee. Publishes ms an average of 3 months after acceptance. Accepts queries by mail. Accepts simultaneous submissions. Responds in 3 months.

NONFICTION Buys 5 unsolicited features mss/ year. Query. 1,500-3,000 words, depending on author, subject matter and treatment. **Pays $400 and up.**

PHOTOS Send photos. Captions, identification of subjects required. Payment varies depending on photographer, subject matter and treatment. Buys one time rights.

COLUMNS Business, home and garden, first person essays, regional travel, gourmet, profile, sports, city arts, health, home and garden, profiles of local people (1,000-1,800 words); UpFront (250-300 words). **Pays $600-800.**

🅢🅢 SACRAMENTO NEWS & REVIEW

Chico Community Publishing, 1124 Del Paso Blvd., Sacramento CA 95815. (916)498-1234. **Fax:** (916)498-7920. **E-mail:** priscillag@newsreview.com. **Website:** www.newsreview.com. **Contact:** Rachel Leibrock, editor; Nick Miller, editor; Priscilla Garcia, creative director. **25% freelance written.** Alternative news and entertainment weekly magazine. "We maintain a high literary standard for submissions; unique or alternative slant. Publication aimed at a young, intellectual audience; submissions should have an edge and strong voice. We have a decided preference for stories with a strong local slant. Our mission: To publish great newspapers that are successful and enduring. To create a quality work environment that encourages employees to grow professionally while respecting personal welfare. To have a positive impact on our communities and make them better places to live." Estab. 1989. Circ. 87,000. Byline given. Pays on publication. Offers 10% kill fee. Publishes ms an average of 2 months after acceptance. Editorial lead time 2 months. Submit seasonal material 2 months in advance. Accepts queries by mail, e-mail. Accepts simultaneous submissions. Responds in 1 month to queries; 2 months to mss. Guidelines online.

NONFICTION Needs essays, expose, general interest, humor, interview, personal experience. Does not want to see travel, product stories, business profile.

Buys 20-30 mss/year. Query with published clips. Length: 750-5,000 words. **Pays $40-500.**

PHOTOS State availability. Identification of subjects required. Reviews 8x10 prints. Negotiates payment individually. Buys one-time rights.

🅢🅢 SAN DIEGO MAGAZINE

San Diego Magazine Publishing Co., 707 Broadway, Suite 1100, San Diego CA 92101-7901. (619)230-9292. **Fax:** (619)230-0490. **E-mail:** erin@sandiegomagazine.com. **Website:** www.sandiegomagazine.com. **Contact:** Erin Chambers Smith, editor. **30% freelance written.** Monthly magazine covering San Diego. "We produce informative and entertaining features and investigative reports about politics; community and neighborhood issues; lifestyle; sports; design; dining; arts; and other facets of life in San Diego." Estab. 1948. Circ. 55,000. Byline given. Pays on publication. Offers 25% kill fee. Publishes ms an average of 2 months after acceptance. Editorial lead time 2 months. Submit seasonal material 4 months in advance. Accepts simultaneous submissions.

NONFICTION Needs expose, general interest, historical, how-to, interview, travel, lifestyle. **Buys 12-24 mss/year.** Send complete ms. Length: 1,000-3,000 words. **Pays $250-750.**

PHOTOS State availability. Offers no additional payment for photos accepted with ms. Buys one time rights.

🅢🅢🅢🅢 SAN FRANCISCO

Modern Luxury, 55 Francisco St., Suite 100, San Francisco CA 94133. (415)398-2800. **E-mail:** preulbach@modernluxury.com. **Website:** modernluxury.com/san-francisco. **Contact:** Paul Reulbach. **50% freelance written. Prefers to work with published/established writers.** Monthly city/regional magazine. Estab. 1968. Circ. 180,000. Byline given. Pays on publication. Offers 25% kill fee. Publishes ms an average of 2 months after acceptance. Submit seasonal material 5 months in advance. Accepts simultaneous submissions. Responds in 2 months.

NONFICTION Needs interview, travel. Query with published clips. Length: 200-4,000 words. **Pays $100-2,000 and some expenses.** Pays expenses of writers on assignment.

CANADIAN & INTERNATIONAL

🍁$$$$ ALBERTA VIEWS

Alberta Views, Ltd., Suite 208, 320 23rd Ave. SW, Calgary AB T2S 0J2 Canada. (403)243-5334; (877)212-5334. **Fax:** (403)243-8599. **E-mail:** queries@albertaviews.ab.ca. **Website:** www.albertaviews.ab.ca. **Contact:** Evan Osenton, editor. **50% freelance written.** Bimonthly magazine covering Alberta culture: politics, economy, social issues, and art. "We are a regional magazine providing thoughtful commentary and background information on issues of concern to Albertans. Most of our writers are Albertans." Estab. 1997. Circ. 30,000. Byline given. Pays on publication. Offers 50% kill fee. Publishes ms an average of 3 months after acceptance. Editorial lead time 4 months. Submit seasonal material 3 months in advance. Accepts queries by e-mail. Accepts simultaneous submissions. Responds in 6 weeks to queries; 2 months to mss. Sample copy free. "If you are a writer, illustrator, or photographer interested in contributing to *Alberta Views*, please see our contributor's guidelines online."

NONFICTION Needs essays. **Buys 18 mss/year.** "Query with written proposal of 300–500 words outlining your intended contribution to *Alberta Views*, why you are qualified to write about your subject, and what sources you intend to use; a résumé outlining your experience and education; recent examples of your published work (tear sheets)." Length: 3,000-5,000 words. **Pays $1,000-1,500 for assigned articles; $350-750 for unsolicited articles.**

PHOTOS State availability. Negotiates payment individually. Buys one-time rights, Web rights.

FICTION Only fiction by Alberta writers via the annual *Alberta Views* fiction contest. **Buys 6 mss/year.** Send complete ms. Length: 2,500-4,000 words. **Pays up to $1,000.**

POETRY Accepts unsolicited poetry. Submit complete ms.

🍁$$$ CANADA'S HISTORY

Bryce Hall, Main Floor, 515 Portage Ave., Winnipeg MB R3B 2E9 Canada. (204)988-9300, ext. 219. **Fax:** (204)988-9309. **E-mail:** editors@canadashistory.ca. **Website:** www.canadashistory.ca. **50% freelance written.** Bimonthly magazine covering Canadian history. Estab. 1920. Circ. 46,000. Byline given. Pays on acceptance. Offers $200 kill fee. Editorial lead time 4 months. Submit seasonal material 8 months in advance. Accepts queries by mail, e-mail. Accepts simultaneous submissions. Responds in 6 weeks to queries; in 2 months to mss. Guidelines online.

NONFICTION Subject matter covers the whole range of Canadian history, with emphasis on social history, politics, exploration, discovery and settlement, aboriginal peoples, business & trade, war, culture, and sport. Does not want anything unrelated to Canadian history. No memoirs. **Buys 30 mss/year.** Query with the word *query* in the subject line if using e-mail; include published clips, SASE if using postal mail. Length: 600-3,500 words. **Pays 50¢/word for major features.**

PHOTOS State availability. Identification of subjects, model releases required. Offers no additional payment for photos accepted with ms. Buys one-time rights.

COLUMNS Currents (news items that alert readers to history-related events, community action, exhibits, trends, websites, historical research and the like), 400 words; Getaway (a history weekend getaway with 3-5 history-linked attractions), 600 words; Moment (features a singular event or incident that can be pinpointed to a day, ideally even the time of day, presented as a snapshot in time), 500 words; Your Story (readers' firsthand experiences with an historic event or personage), 1,000 words. **Buys 15 mss/year.** Query. **Pays $125.**

TIPS "*Canada's History* is directed toward a general audience of educated readers, as well as to historians and scholars. We are in the market for lively, well-written, well-researched, and informative articles about Canadian history that focus on all parts of the country and all areas of human activity. Articles should be written in an expository or interpretive style and present the principal themes of Canadian history in an original, interesting and informative way."

🍁$$ THE CANADIAN CO-OPERATOR

LE COOPÉRATEUR, Atlantic Co-operative Publishers, 500 St. George St., Moncton NB E1C 1Y3 Canada. **E-mail:** editor@theatlanticco-operator.coop. **Website:** www.creativecoop.ca. **Contact:** Rayanne Brennan, editor in chief. **95% freelance written.** Bimonthly, bilingual, and national online and print magazine covering co-operatives. Estab. 1933. Byline given. Pays on publication. No kill fee. Publishes ms an average of 2 months after acceptance. Editorial lead time 2 months. Submit seasonal material 2 months in advance. Accepts queries by mail, e-mail, fax. Accepts simultaneous submissions. Responds in 3 weeks to queries.

NONFICTION Needs expose, general interest, historical, interview. No political stories, economical stories, sports. **Buys 90 mss/year.** Query with published clips. Length: 500-2,000 words. **Pays 22¢/word.** Pays expenses of writers on assignment.

PHOTOS State availability. Identification of subjects required. Reviews prints, GIF/JPEG files. Offers $25/ photo. Buys one-time rights.

COLUMNS Health and Lifestyle (anything from recipes to travel), 800 words; International Page (cooperatives in developing countries, good ideas from around the world). **Buys 10 mss/year.** Query with published clips.

☮︎❾❾❾ CANADIAN GEOGRAPHIC

1155 Lola St., Suite 200, Ottawa ON K1K 4C1 Canada. (613)745-4629. **E-mail:** editor@canadiangeographic. ca. **Website:** www.canadiangeographic.ca. **90% freelance written. Works with a small number of new/ unpublished writers each year.** Bimonthly magazine covering Canada. "*Canadian Geographic's* colorful portraits of our ever-changing population show readers just how important the relationship between the people and the land really is." Estab. 1930. Circ. 240,000. Pays on acceptance. Publishes ms an average of 3 months after acceptance. Submit seasonal materials 1 year in advance. Accepts queries by e-mail. Accepts simultaneous submissions.

NONFICTION Needs photo feature, profile, travel. **Buys 30 mss/year.** Query. Length: 1,500-3,000 words. **Pays 80¢/word minimum.**

PHOTOS Pays $75-400 for color photos, depending on published size.

❾❾ DEVON LIFE

Archant South West, Newberry House, Fair Oak Close, Exeter Airport Business Park, Clyst Honiton Exeter EX5 2UL United Kingdom. (01)(3)9288-8413. **E-mail:** andy.cooper@archant.co.uk. **Website:** www. devonlife.co.uk. **Contact:** Andy Cooper, editor. "*Devon Life* is the county's number one magazine, and celebrates the best of Devon. We cover everything from food and drink and businesses to art and fashion, and everything in between, ensuring everything has a local angle." No kill fee. Accepts queries by mail, e-mail. Accepts simultaneous submissions. Sample copy online. Guidelines by e-mail.

NONFICTION Length: 500-750 words/single-page articles; 1,000-1,200 words/two-page articles. **Pays £60-75/up to 1,200 words; £40-50/up to 750 words.**

PHOTOS Send photos. Captions required. Reviews 300 dpi digital images.

☮︎❾ EDGE YK

Verge Communications Ltd., P.O. Box 2451, 5112 52 St., Yellowknife NT X1A 2P8 Canada. (867)445-8360. **E-mail:** editor@edgeyk.ca. **Website:** www.edgenorth. ca/edge-yk-magazine/. **Contact:** Laurie Sarkadi, editor. Magazine published 6 times/year covering life in Yellowknife, NT, Canada. "*EDGE YK* magazine is a free publication dedicated to showcasing some of the vast creative talent within Yellowknife, Northwest Territories. We're interested in well-told first-person narrative stories, as well as pieces on the issues, ideas, and people affecting the city's past, present, and future." Estab. 2011. Circ. 7,000. Byline given. Pays on publication. Offers 50% kill fee. Publishes ms 1 month after acceptance. Editorial lead time 3 months. Submit seasonal material 3 months in advance. Accepts queries by mail, e-mail. Accepts simultaneous submissions. Responds in 1 month to queries; in 2 months to mss.

NONFICTION Needs book excerpts, essays, general interest, historical, how-to, humor, interview, nostalgic, opinion, personal experience, photo feature, profile, travel. No fiction. Query. Length: 300-2,000 words. **Pays minimum of $100 for assigned and unsolicited articles.** Pays expenses of writers on assignment.

PHOTOS State availability of photos with submission. Reviews GIF/JPEG files. Offers payment for photos accepted with ms; negotiates payment individually.

COLUMNS On EDGE Opinion, any topic/slant, approximately 400-600 words. Query. **Pays $100.**

FICTION "We rarely publish fiction."

POETRY Needs free verse. "We rarely publish poetry submissions." Buys 4 poems/year. Submit maximum 1 poems. No minimum or maximum length.

☮︎❾❾❾❾ HAMILTON MAGAZINE

Town Media, a division of Sun Media, 940 Main St. W., Hamilton ON L8S 1B1 Canada. (905)522-6117. **Fax:**

(905)769-1105. **E-mail:** marc.skulnick@sunmedia.ca; erin.stanley@sunmedia.ca. **Website:** www.hamilton-magazine.com. **Contact:** Marc Skulnick, editor; Erin Stanley, deesign. **50% freelance written.** Quarterly magazine devoted to the Greater Hamilton and Golden Horseshoe area (Ontario, Canada). "Our mandate: to entertain and inform by spotlighting the best of what our city and region has to offer. We invite readers to take part in a vibrant community by supplying them with authoritative and dynamic coverage of local culture, food, fashion, and design. Each story strives to expand your view of the area, every issue an essential resource for exploring, understanding, and unlocking the region. Packed with insight, intrigue, and suspense, *Hamilton Magazine* delivers the city to your doorstep." Estab. 1978. Byline given. Pays on publication. Offers 50% kill fee. Editorial lead time 2-3 months. Submit seasonal material 2-3 months in advance. Accepts queries by e-mail. Responds in 1 week to queries and mss. Sample copy with #10 SASE. Guidelines by e-mail.

NONFICTION Needs book excerpts, essays, expose, historical, how-to, humor, inspirational, interview, personal experience, photo feature, religious, travel. Does not want generic articles that could appear in any mass-market publication. Send complete ms. Length: 800-2,000 words. **Pays $200-1,600 for assigned articles; $100-800 for unsolicited articles.** Pays expenses of writers on assignment.

PHOTOS State availability of or send photos. Identification of subjects required. Reviews 8×10 prints, JPEG files (8×10 at 300dpi). Negotiates payment individually. Buys one-time rights.

COLUMNS A&E Art, 1,200-2,000 words; A&E Music, 1,200-2,000 words; A&E Books, 1,200-1,400 words. **Buys 12 mss/year.** Send complete ms. **Pays $200-400.**

TIPS "Unique local voices are key, and a thorough knowledge of the area's history, politics, and culture is invaluable."

✪$ MONDAY MAGAZINE

Black Press Ltd., 818 Broughton St., Victoria British Columbia V8W 1E4 Canada. (250)382-6188. **E-mail:** editor@mondaymag.com. **Website:** www.mondaymag.com. **Contact:** Sarah Wilson, editor. **10% freelance written.** Weekly tabloid covering local news. "*Monday Magazine* is Victoria's only alternative newsweekly. For more than 35 years, we have published fresh, informative, and alternative perspectives on local events. We prefer lively, concise writing with a sense of humor and insight." Estab. 1975. Circ. 20,000. Byline given. **Currently not accepting freelance articles requiring payment.** Pays 1 month after publication. No kill fee. Publishes ms an average of 1 month after acceptance. Editorial lead time 1-2 months. Submit seasonal material 2 months in advance. Accepts queries by e-mail. Accepts simultaneous submissions. Responds in 6-8 weeks to queries; 3 months to mss. Guidelines online.

NONFICTION Needs expose, general interest, humor, interview, personal experience. Special issues: Body, Mind, Spirit (October); Student Survival Guide (August). Does not want fiction, poetry, or conspiracy theories. Send complete ms. Length: 300-1,000 words. **Pays $25-50. Currently not accepting freelance articles requiring payment.**

PHOTOS Send photos. Captions, identification of subjects required. Reviews GIF/JPEG files (300 dpi at 4x6). Offers no additional payment for photos accepted with ms. Buys one-time rights.

TIPS "Local writers tend to have an advantage, as they are familiar with the issues and concerns of interest to a Victoria audience."

$$ RUSSIAN LIFE

RIS Publications, P.O. Box 567, Montpelier VT 05601. **Website:** russianlife.com. **75% freelance written.** Bimonthly magazine covering Russian culture, history, travel, and business. "Our readers are informed Russophiles with an avid interest in all things Russian. But we do not publish personal travel journals or the like." Estab. 1956. Circ. 15,000. Byline given. Pays on publication. Publishes ms an average of 3-6 months after acceptance. Editorial lead time 2 months. Submit seasonal material 3 months in advance. Accepts queries by mail, e-mail. Responds in 1 month to queries. Guidelines online.

NONFICTION Needs book excerpts, general interest, interview, photo feature, travel. No personal stories, i.e., How I came to love Russia. **Buys 15-20 mss/year.** Query. Length: 1,000-6,000 words. **Pays $100-300.**

REPRINTS Accepts previously published submissions rarely.

PHOTOS Send photos. Captions required. Model/property release preferred. Words with local freelancers only. Reviews contact sheets. Negotiates payment individually. Pays $20-50 (color photo with accompanying story), depending on placement in magazine. Pays on publication. Credit line given. Buys one-time rights.

✪ⓈⓈⓈⓈ TORONTO LIFE

St. Joseph Media Corp., Queen Richmond Centre, Toronto ON M5C 1S2 Canada. (416)364-3333. **Fax:** (416)861-1169. **E-mail:** editorial@torontolife.com; pitch@torontolife.com. **Website:** www.torontolife.com. **Contact:** Sarah Fulford, editor. **95% freelance written. Prefers to work with published/established writers.** Monthly magazine emphasizing local issues and social trends, short humor/satire, and service features for upper income, well-educated and, for the most part, young Torontonians. Circ. 92,039. Byline given. Pays on acceptance. Offers kill fee. Pays 50% kill fee for commissioned articles only. Publishes ms an average of 4 months after acceptance. Responds in 3 weeks to queries.

NONFICTION Query with published clips and SASE. Length: 1,000-6,000 words. **Pays $500-5,000.**

COLUMNS "We run about 5 columns an issue. They are all freelanced, though most are from regular contributors. They are mostly local in concern and cover politics, business, performing arts, media, design, and food." Length: 2,000 words. Query with published clips and SASE. **Pays $2,000.**

TIPS "Submissions should have strong Toronto orientation."

COLORADO

ⓈⓈ STEAMBOAT MAGAZINE

Ski Town Publications, Inc., 1120 S. Lincoln Ave., Suite F, Steamboat Springs CO 80487. (970)871-9413. **Fax:** (970)871-1922. **Website:** www.steamboatmagazine.com. **Contact:** Deborah Olsen, president/publisher; Suzi Mitchell, editor. **80% freelance written.** "Quarterly magazine showcasing the history, people, lifestyles, and interests of Northwest Colorado. Our readers are generally well-educated, well-traveled, upscale, active people visiting our region to ski in winter and recreate in summer. They come from all 50 states and many foreign countries. Writing should be fresh, entertaining, and informative." Estab. 1978. Circ. 20,000. Byline given. Pays 50% on acceptance, 50% on publication. No kill fee. Submit seasonal material 1 year in advance. Accepts queries by mail, e-mail, fax, phone. Responds in 3 months to queries. Guidelines free.

NONFICTION Needs book excerpts, essays, general interest, historical, humor, interview, photo feature, travel. **Buys 10-15 mss/year.** Query with published clips. Length: 150-1,500 words. **Pays $50-300 for assigned articles.**

PHOTOS Prefers to review viewing platforms, JPEGs, and dupes. Will request original transparencies when needed. State availability. Captions, identification of subjects required. Pays $50-250/photo. Buys one-time rights.

TIPS "Stories must be about Steamboat Springs and the Yampa Valley to be considered. We're looking for new angles on ski/snowboard stories in the winter and activity-related stories all year round. Please query first with ideas to make sure subjects are fresh and appropriate. We try to make subjects and treatments 'timeless' in nature because our magazine is a 'keeper' with a multiyear shelf life."

ⓈⓈ TELLURIDE MAGAZINE

Big Earth Publishing, Inc., P.O. Box 888, Telluride CO 81435. (970)728-4245. **Fax:** (866)936-8406. **E-mail:** deb@telluridemagazine.com. **Website:** www.telluridemagazine.com. **Contact:** Deb Dion Kees, editor in chief. **75% freelance written.** Telluride: community, events, recreation, ski resort, surrounding region, San Juan Mountains, history, tourism, mountain living. "*Telluride Magazine* speaks specifically to Telluride and the surrounding mountain environment. Telluride is a resort town supported by the ski industry in winter, festivals in summer, outdoor recreation year round, and the unique lifestyle all of that affords. As a National Historic Landmark District with a colorful mining history, it weaves a tale that readers seek out. The local/visitor interaction is key to Telluride's success in making profiles an important part of the content. Telluriders are an environmentally minded and progressive bunch who appreciate efforts toward sustainability and protecting the natural landscape and wilderness that are the region's number one draw." Estab. 1982. Circ. 70,000. Byline given. Pays 60 days from publication. Editorial lead time and advance on seasonal submissions is 6 months. Accepts queries by e-mail. Accepts simultaneous submissions. Responds in 2 weeks to queries; in 2 months to mss. Sample copy online at website. Guidelines by e-mail.

NONFICTION Needs historical, humor, personal experience, photo feature. No articles about places or adventures other than Telluride. **Buys 10 mss/year.** Query with published clips. Length: 1,000-2,000 words. **Pays $200-700 for assigned articles; $100-700 for unsolicited articles.**

PHOTOS Send no more than 20 jpeg comps (low-res) via e-mail, or send CD/DVD with submission. Reviews JPEG/TIFF files. Offers $35-300 per photo; negotiates payment individually. Buys one-time rights; includes print and web (electronic).

COLUMNS Telluride Turns (news and current topics); Mountain Health (health issues related to mountain sports and living at altitude); Nature Notes (explores the flora, fauna, geology, and climate of San Juan Mountains); Green Bytes (sustainable and environmentally sound ideas and products for home building), all 500 words. **Buys 40 mss/year.** Query. **Pays $50-200.**

FICTION "Please contact us; we are very specific about what we will accept." Needs adventure, historical, humorous, western. **Buys 2 mss/year.** Query with published clips. Length: 800-1,200 words.

POETRY Needs Any poetry must reflect mountains or mountain living. Buys 1 poems/year. Length: 3 lines minimum. **Pays up to to $100.**

FILLERS Wants anecdotes, facts, short humor. Seldom buys fillers. Length: 300-1,000 words. **Pays up to $500.**

🟢🟢 VAIL-BEAVER CREEK MAGAZINE

Rocky Mountain Media, LLC, P.O. Box 1397, Avon CO 81620. (970)476-6600. **Fax:** (970)845-0069. **E-mail:** tkatauskas@vailmag.com. **Website:** www.vail-beavercreekmag.com. Editor: Ted Katauskas. **80% freelance written.** Semiannual magazine showcasing the lifestyles and history of the Vail Valley. "We are particularly interested in personality profiles, home and design features, the arts, winter and summer recreation/adventure stories, and environmental articles." Estab. 1975. Circ. 30,000. Byline given. Pays on acceptance. Offers 100% kill fee. Publishes ms an average of 6 months after acceptance. Editorial lead time 1 year. Submit seasonal material 1 year in advance. Accepts queries by mail, e-mail. Accepts simultaneous submissions. Responds in 1 month to queries; 2 months to mss. Guidelines free.

NONFICTION Needs essays, general interest, historical, humor, interview, personal experience, photo feature. **Buys 20-25 mss/year.** Query with published clips. Length: 500-3,000 words. **Pays 20-30¢/word.**

REPRINTS Send typed ms with rights for sale noted and information about when and where the material previously appeared.

PHOTOS State availability. Captions, identification of subjects, model releases required. Offers $50-250/photo. Buys one-time rights.

TIPS "Be familiar with the Vail Valley and its personality. Approach a story that will be relevant for several years to come. We produce a magazine that is a 'keeper.'"

CONNECTICUT

🟢🟢🟢 CONNECTICUT MAGAZINE

Journal Register Co., 200 Gando Dr., New Haven CT 06513. (203)789-5226. **Fax:** (203)789-5255. **E-mail:** rbendici@connecticutmag.com. **E-mail:** dclement@connecticutmag.com. **Website:** www.connecticutmag.com. **Contact:** Doug Clement, verticals editor; Ray Bendici, content manager. **75% freelance written. "Prefers to work with published/established writers who know the state and live/have lived here.** Monthly magazine for an affluent, sophisticated, suburban audience. "We want only articles that pertain to living in Connecticut." Estab. 1971. Circ. 93,000. Byline given. Pays on publication. Offers 20% kill fee. Publishes ms an average of 4 months after acceptance. Submit seasonal material 4 months in advance. Accepts queries by mail, e-mail, fax. Responds in 6 weeks to queries.

NONFICTION Needs book excerpts, expose, general interest, interview, topics of service to Connecticut readers. Special issues: Dining/entertainment, northeast/travel, home/garden and Connecticut bride twice/year. Also, business (January) and healthcare 4-6/year. No personal essays. **Buys 50 mss/year.** Query with published clips. Length: 3,000 words maximum. **Pays $600-1,200.**

PHOTOS Send photos. Identification of subjects, model releases required. Reviews contact sheets, transparencies. Pays $50 minimum/photo. Buys one time rights.

COLUMNS Business, Health, Politics, Connecticut Calendar, Arts, Dining Out, Gardening, Environment, Education, People, Sports, Media, From the Field (quirky, interesting regional stories with broad appeal). Length: 1,500-2,500 words. **Buys 50 mss/ year.** Query with published clips. **Pays $400-700.**

FILLERS Short pieces about Connecticut trends, curiosities, interesting short subjects, etc. Length: 150 400 words. **Pays $75-150.**

TIPS "Make certain your idea has not been covered to death by the local press and can withstand a time lag of a few months. Again, we don't want something that has already received a lot of press."

DELAWARE

💲💲💲 DELAWARE BEACH LIFE

Endeavours LLC, P.O. Box 417, Rehoboth Beach DE 19971. (302)227-9499. **E-mail:** info@delaware-beachlife.com. **Website:** www.delawarebeachlife. com. **Contact:** Terry Plowman, publisher/editor. Magazine published 8 times/year covering coastal Delaware. "*Delaware Beach Life* focuses on coastal Delaware: Fenwick to Lewes. You can go slightly inland as long as there's water and a natural connection to the coast, e.g., Angola or Long Neck." Estab. 2002. Circ. 15,000. Byline given. Pays on acceptance. 50% kill fee. Publishes ms 4 months after acceptance. Editorial lead time 6 months. Submit seasonal material 1 year in advance. Accepts queries by e-mail. Responds in 2 months to queries; in 6 months to mss. Sample copy available online at website. Guidelines free and by e-mail.

NONFICTION Needs book excerpts, essays, general interest, humor, interview, opinion, photo feature. Does not want anything not focused on coastal Delaware. Query with published clips. Length: 1,200-3,000 words. **Pays $400-1,000 for assigned articles.** Pays expenses of writers on assignment.

PHOTOS Send photos. Photos require captions, identification of subjects. Reviews GIF/JPEG files. Pays $25-100 per photo. Purchases one-time rights.

COLUMNS Profiles, History, Opinion (focused on coastal DE), all 1,200 words. **Buys 32 mss/year.** Query with published clips. **Pays $150-350.**

FICTION Needs adventure, condensed novels, historical, humorous, novel excerpts, Must have coastal theme. Does not want anything not coastal. **Buys 3 mss/year.** Query with published clips. Length: 1,000-2,000 words.

POETRY Needs avant-garde, free verse, haiku, light verse, traditional. Does not want anything not coastal.

No erotic poetry. Buys 6 poems/year. Submit maximum 3 poems. Length: 6-15 lines/poem. **Pays up to $50.**

💲💲 DELAWARE TODAY

Today Media, 3301 Lancaster Pike, Suite 5C, Wilmington DE 19805. (302)656-1809. **Website:** www.delawaretoday.com. **Contact:** Drew Ostroski, managing editor. **50% freelance written.** Monthly magazine geared toward Delaware people, places, and issues. "For more than 50 years, *Delaware Today* has been the lifestyle authority in the First State. The publication boasts various awards for thoughtful commentary and stunning full-color design. As the state's premier magazine, *Delaware Today* helps readers make informed decisions to enhance their lives." Estab. 1962. Circ. 25,000. Byline given. Pays on publication. Offers 50% kill fee. Publishes ms an average of 4 months after acceptance. Editorial lead time 3 months. Submit seasonal material 6 months in advance. Accepts queries by online submission form. Accepts simultaneous submissions. Responds in 2 months to queries.

NONFICTION Needs historical, interview, photo feature, lifestyles, issues. Special issues: Newcomer's Guide to Delaware. **Buys 40 mss/year.** Query with published clips. Length: 100-3,000 words. **Pays $50-750.** Pays expenses of writers on assignment.

PHOTOS State availability. Identification of subjects required. Negotiates payment individually. Buys one-time rights.

COLUMNS Business, Health, History, People, all 1,500 words. **Buys 24 mss/year.** Query with published clips. **Pays $150-250.**

FILLERS Needs anecdotes, newsbreaks, short humor. **Buys 10 mss/year.** Length: 100-200 words. **Pays $50-75.**

TIPS "No story ideas that we would know about, i.e., a profile of the governor. Best bets are profiles of quirky/unique Delawareans whom we'd never know about or think of."

DISTRICT OF COLUMBIA

💲💲 WASHINGTON CITY PAPER

1400 Eye St. NW, Suite 900, Washington DC 20005. (202)332-2100. **Fax:** (202)332-8500. **E-mail:** mail@ washingtoncitypaper.com; listings@washingtoncity-paper.com; contact@washingtoncitypaper.com; ccau-terucci@washingtoncitypaper.com. **E-mail:** editor@

washingtoncitypaper.com. **Website:** www.washingtoncitypaper.com. **50% freelance written.** Relentlessly local alternative weekly in nation's capital covering city and regional politics, media and arts. No national stories. Estab. 1981. Circ. 95,000. Byline given. Pays on publication. Offers kill fee. Offers 10% kill fee for assigned stories. Publishes ms an average of 6 weeks after acceptance. Editorial lead time 7-10 days. Accepts simultaneous submissions. Responds in 1 month to queries. Guidelines available online.

NONFICTION **Buys 100 mss/year.** District Line: 800-1,500 words; Covers: 2,500-10,000 words. **Pays 10-40¢/word.** Pays expenses of writers on assignment.

PHOTOS Make appointment to show portfolio to art director. Pays minimum of $75.

COLUMNS Music Writing (eclectic). **Buys 100 mss/ year.** Query with published clips or send complete ms. **Pays 10-40¢/word.**

TIPS "Think local. Great ideas are a plus. We are willing to work with anyone who has a strong idea, regardless of vita."

💲💲💲 THE WASHINGTONIAN

1828 L St. NW, Suite 200, Washington DC 20036. (202)296-3600. **E-mail:** editorial@washingtonian.com. **Website:** www.washingtonian.com. **20-25% freelance written.** Monthly magazine. "Writers should keep in mind that we are a general interest city-and-regional magazine. Nearly all our articles have a hard Washington connection. And, please, no political satire." Estab. 1965. Circ. 160,000. Byline given. Pays on publication. No kill fee. Publishes ms an average of 3 months after acceptance. Editorial lead time 10 weeks. Accepts queries by mail, fax. Accepts simultaneous submissions. Guidelines available online.

NONFICTION Needs book excerpts, expose, general interest, historical, interview, personal experience, photo feature, travel. **Buys 15-30 mss/year.** Query with published clips. **Pays 50¢/word.**

COLUMNS First Person (personal experience that somehow illuminates life in Washington area), 650-700 words. **Buys 9-12 mss/year.** Query. **Pays $325.**

TIPS "The types of articles we publish include service pieces; profiles of people; investigative articles; rating pieces; institutional profiles; first-person articles; stories that cut across the grain of conventional thinking; articles that tell the reader how Washington got to be the way it is; light or satirical pieces (send the complete ms, not the idea, because in this case execution is everything)."

FLORIDA

💲💲💲💲 BOCA RATON MAGAZINE

JES Publishing, 1000 Clint Moore Rd., Suite 103, Boca Raton FL 33487. (561)997-8683. **Fax:** (561)997-8909. **E-mail:** magazine@bocamag.com. **Website:** www.bocamag.com. Managing Editor: John Thomason. **30% freelance written.** Lifestyle and city/regional magazine devoted to the residents of South Florida, featuring fashion, interior design, food, people, places, and community issues that shape the affluent South Florida market. Estab. 1981. Circ. 25,000. Byline given. Pays 45 days after acceptance. No kill fee. Publishes ms an average of 3 months after acceptance. Submit seasonal material 7 months in advance. Accepts simultaneous submissions. Responds in 1 month to queries. Does not accept unsolicited queries. Guidelines for #10 SASE.

NONFICTION Needs general interest, historical, humor, interview, photo feature, travel. Send complete ms. Length: 800-2,500 words. **Pays $350-1,200.**

REPRINTS Send tearsheet. Payment varies.

PHOTOS Send photos.

COLUMNS Body & Soul (health, fitness and beauty column, general interest); Hitting Home (family and social interactions); History or Arts (relevant to South Florida); all 1,000 words. Query with published clips, or send complete ms. **Pays $350-400.**

TIPS "We prefer shorter ms, highly localized articles, and excellent art/photography."

💲💲 EMERALD COAST MAGAZINE

Rowland Publishing, Inc., 1932 Miccosukee Rd., Tallahassee FL 32308. (850) 878-0554. **Fax:** (850) 656-1871. **E-mail:** zwolfgram@rowlandpublishing.com. **Website:** www.emeraldcoastmagazine.com. **60% freelance written.** Bimonthly lifestyle publication celebrating life on Florida's Emerald Coast. All content has an Emerald Coast (Northwest Florida) connection. This includes communities between Pensacola to Panama City. Estab. 2000. Circ. 22,000. Byline given. Pays on acceptance. No kill fee. Publishes ms an average of 3 months after acceptance. Editorial lead time 4 months. Submit seasonal material 6 months in advance. Accepts queries by mail, e-mail.

Accepts simultaneous submissions. Responds in 3 months. Guidelines by e-mail.

NONFICTION Needs essays, historical, inspirational, interview, new product, personal experience, photo feature. No fiction, poetry, or travel. No general interest—be Northwest Florida specific. **Buys 5 mss/year.** Query with published clips. Length: 500-2,000 words. **Pays $100-350.**

PHOTOS Send photos. Captions, identification of subjects, model releases required. Reviews prints, GIF/JPEG files. Negotiates payment individually. Buys one-time rights.

TIPS "We're looking for fresh ideas and new slants related to Florida's Emerald Coast. Because we work so far in advance, it is difficult to be timely, so be sure to give us ideas that aren't too time specific."

💲💲 FT. MYERS MAGAZINE

And Pat llc, 52 Park Ave. E., Merrick NY 11566. (516)652-6072. **E-mail:** ftmyers@optonline.net. **E-mail:** ftmyers2@optonline.net. **Website:** www.ft-myersmagazine.com. **Contact:** Andrew Elias. **90% freelance written.** Bimonthly magazine covering regional arts and living for educated, active, successful, and creative residents of Lee & Collier counties (FL) and people planning vacations, visits and moves to Southwest Florida. Content: Arts, entertainment, media and culture (fine arts, music, theater, film, literature, television) and living (health/fitness, travel/recreation, sports/recreation, home/garden, nutrition/dining, as well as history/environmental issues). Estab. 2001. Circ. 20,000. Byline given. 30 days after publication. No kill fee. Publishes ms an average of 2-6 months after acceptance. Editorial lead time 2-6 months. Submit seasonal material 2-6 months in advance. Accepts queries by e-mail. Accepts simultaneous submissions. Responds in 3 months to queries and to mss. Guidelines online.

NONFICTION Needs book excerpts, essays, general interest, historical, how-to, humor, interview, personal experience, profile, reviews, travel, reviews, previews, news, informational. **Buys 10-25 mss/year.** Send complete ms. Length: 750-1,750 words. **Pays $75-175 or approximately 10¢/word.**

PHOTOS Contact: Andrew Elias. State availability of or send photos. Captions, identification of subjects required. Negotiates payment individually; generally offers $10-100/photo or art. Buys one-time rights.

💲💲💲 GULFSHORE LIFE

Open Sky Media, 1421 Pine Ridge Rd., Suite 100, Naples FL 34109. (239)449-4111. **Fax:** (239)431-8420. **E-mail:** dsendler@gulfshorelifemag.com. **Website:** www.gulfshorelife.com. **Contact:** David Sendler, editor in chief. **75% freelance written.** Magazine published 10 times/year for southwest Florida. Covers the workings of its natural systems, its history, personalities, culture, and lifestyle. Estab. 1970. Circ. 35,000. Byline given. Pays on publication. Publishes ms an average of 4 months after acceptance. Submit seasonal material 8 months in advance. Accepts queries by mail, e-mail, fax. Accepts simultaneous submissions.

NONFICTION Needs historical, interview. **Buys 100 mss/year.** Query with published clips. Length: 500-3,000 words. **Pays $100-1,000.**

PHOTOS Send photos. Identification of subjects, model releases required. Pays $50-100. Buys one-time rights.

TIPS "We buy superbly written stories that illuminate southwest Florida personalities, places, and issues. Surprise us!"

💲💲 JACKSONVILLE

1261 King St., Jacksonville FL 32204. (904)389-3622. **Fax:** (904)389-3628. **E-mail:** jocelyn@jacksonvillemag.com. **Website:** www.jacksonvillemag.com. **Contact:** Jocelyn Tolbert, assistant editor. **50% freelance written.** Monthly magazine covering life and business in northeast Florida for upwardly mobile residents of Jacksonville and the Beaches, Orange Park, St. Augustine and Amelia Island, Florida. Estab. 1985. Circ. 25,000. Byline given. Pays on publication. Offers kill fee. Offers 25-33% kill fee to writers on assignment. Editorial lead time 3 months. Submit seasonal material 4 months in advance. Accepts queries by e-mail. Accepts simultaneous submissions. Responds in 6 weeks to queries; in 1 month to mss. Sample copy: $5 (includes postage). Guidelines online.

NONFICTION Needs book excerpts, expose, general interest, historical, how-to, humor, interview, personal experience, photo feature, travel, commentary. **Buys 50 mss/year.** Query with published clips. Length: 1,200-3,000 words. **Pays $50-500 for feature length pieces.**

REPRINTS Send photocopy. Payment varies.

PHOTOS State availability. Captions, model releases required. Negotiates payment individually. Buys one-time rights.

COLUMNS Business (trends, success stories, personalities), 1,000-1,200 words; Health (trends, emphasis on people, hopeful outlooks), 1,000-1,200 words; Money (practical personal financial advice using local people, anecdotes, and examples), 1,000-1,200 words; Real Estate/Home (service, trends, home photo features), 1,000-1,200 words; Travel (weekends, daytrips, excursions locally and regionally), 1,000-1,200 words; occasional departments and columns covering local history, sports, family issues, etc. **Buys 40 mss/year. Pays $150-250.**

TIPS "We are a writer's magazine and demand writing that tells a story with flair."

$$ PENSACOLA MAGAZINE

Ballinger Publishing, 314 N. Spring St., Suite A, Pensacola FL 32501. **E-mail:** kelly@ballingerpublishing.com. **Website:** www.ballingerpublishing.com. Executive Editor: Kelly Oden. **75% freelance written.** Monthly magazine. *Pensacola Magazine*'s articles are written in a casual, conversational tone. We cover a broad range of topics that citizens of Pensacola relate to. Most of our freelance work is assigned, so it is best to send a resume, cover letter and 3 clips to the above e-mail address. Estab. 1987. Circ. 10,000. Byline given. Pays at end of shelf life. Offers 20% kill fee. Editorial lead time 1 month. Submit seasonal material 6 months in advance. Accepts queries by e-mail. Accepts simultaneous submissions. Responds in 2 weeks to queries. Sample copy for $1, SASE and 1 First-Class stamp. Guidelines available online.

NONFICTION Special issues: Wedding (February); Home & Garden (May). Query with published clips. Length: 700-2,100 words. **Pays 10-15¢/word.** Pays expenses of writers on assignment.

PHOTOS State availability of or send photos. Captions, identification of subjects, model releases required. Reviews GIF/JPEG files. Offers $7/photo. Buys one time rights.

TIPS We accept submissions for *Pensacola Magazine*, *Northwest Florida's Business Climate*, and *Coming of Age*. Please query by topic via e-mail to shannon@ballingerpublishing.com. If you do not have a specific query topic, please send a resume and three clips via e-mail, and you will be given story assignments if your writing style is appropriate. You do not have to be locally or regionally located to write for us.

$$ TALLAHASSEE MAGAZINE

Rowland Publishing, Inc., 1932 Miccosukee Rd., Tallahassee FL 32308. **Website:** www.tallahasseemagazine.com. **20% freelance written.** Bimonthly magazine covering life in Florida's Capital Region. All content has a Tallahassee, Florida connection. Estab. 1978. Circ. 18,000. Byline given. Pays on acceptance. No kill fee. Publishes ms an average of 2 months after acceptance. Editorial lead time 4 months. Submit seasonal material 6 months in advance. Accepts queries by mail, e-mail. Accepts simultaneous submissions. Responds in 3 months to queries & mss. Sample copy: $4. Guidelines available by e-mail.

NONFICTION Needs book excerpts, essays, historical, inspirational, interview, new product, personal experience, photo feature, travel, sports, business, Calendar items. No fiction, poetry, or travel. No general interest. **Buys 15 mss/year.** Query with published clips. Length: 500-2,500 words. **Pays $100-350.** Pays expenses of writers on assignment.

PHOTOS Send photos. Captions, identification of subjects, model releases required. Reviews prints, GIF/JPEG files. Negotiates payment individually. Buys one time rights.

TIPS "We're looking for fresh ideas and new slants that are related to Florida's Capital Region. Because we work so far in advance, it is difficult to be timely, so be sure to give us ideas that aren't too time specific."

GENERAL

$$ A.T. JOURNEYS

Appalachian Trail Conservancy, P.O. Box 807, 799 Washington St., Harpers Ferry WV 25425-0807. (304)535-6331. **Fax:** (304)535-2667. **E-mail:** editor@appalachiantrail.org. **Website:** www.appalachiantrail.org. Estab. 1925. Accepts queries by mail, e-mail. Accepts simultaneous submissions. Responds in 2 months to queries. Guidelines available online.

NONFICTION Needs general interest, historical, how-to, interview, profile, travel. **Buys 5-10 mss/year.** Query with or without published clips, or send complete ms. Prefers e-mail queries. Length: 250-3,000 words. **Pays $25-300.**

REPRINTS Send photocopy with rights for sale noted and information about when and where the material previously appeared.

PHOTOS State availability. Identification of subjects, model releases required. Reviews contact sheets, 5x7 prints, slides, digital images. Offers $25-150/photo; $200/cover.

TIPS "Contributors should display a knowledge of or interest in the Appalachian Trail. Those who live in the vicinity of the Trail may opt for an assigned story and should present credentials and subject of interest to the editor."

🌀🌀 BLUE RIDGE COUNTRY

Leisure Media360, 3424 Brambleton Ave., Roanoke VA 24018. (540)989-6138. **Fax:** (540)989-7603. **E-mail:** krheinheimer@leisuremedia360.com. **Website:** www.blueridgecountry.com. **Contact:** Kurt Rheinheimer, editor. **90% freelance written.** Bimonthly, full-color magazine covering the Blue Ridge region. "The magazine is designed to celebrate the history, heritage and beauty of the Blue Ridge region. It is aimed at adult, upscale readers who enjoy living or traveling in the mountain regions of Virginia, North Carolina, West Virginia, Maryland, Kentucky, Tennessee, South Carolina, Alabama, and Georgia." Estab. 1988. Circ. 325,000. Byline given. Pays on publication. Offers kill fee. Offers $50 kill fee for commissioned pieces only. Publishes ms an average of 8 months after acceptance. Submit seasonal material 6 months in advance. Accepts queries by mail, e-mail. Accepts simultaneous submissions. Responds in 3-4 months to queries. Responds in 2 months to mss. Sample copy with 9x12 SASE with 6 first-class stamps. Guidelines available online.

NONFICTION Needs historical, personal experience, photo feature, travel. Special issues: "The photo essay will continue to be part of each issue, but for the foreseeable future will be a combination of book and gallery/museum exhibit previews, and also essays of work by talented individual photographers—though we cannot pay, this is a good option for those who are interested in editorial coverage of their work. Those essays will include short profile, web link and contact information, with the idea of getting them, their work and their business directly in front of 425,000 readers' eyes." **Buys 25-30 mss/year.** Send complete ms. Length: 200-1,500 words. **Pays $50-250.** Pays expenses of writers on assignment.

PHOTOS Photos must be shot in region. Outline of region can be found online. Send photos. Identification of subjects required. Reviews transparencies. Pays $40-150 for color inside photo; pays $150 for color cover. Pays on publication. Credit line given. Buys one-time rights.

COLUMNS Inns and Getaways (reviews of inns); Mountain Delicacies (cookbooks and recipes); Country Roads (shorts on regional news, people, destinations, events, history, antiques, books); Inns and Getaways (reviews of inns); On the Mountainside (first-person outdoor recreation pieces excluding hikes). **Buys 30-42 mss/year.** Query. **Pays $25-125.**

TIPS "Would like to see more pieces dealing with contemporary history (1940s-70s). Freelancers needed for regional departmental shorts and macro issues affecting whole region. Need field reporters from all areas of Blue Ridge region, especially more from Kentucky, Maryland and South Carolina. We are also looking for updates on the Blue Ridge Parkway, Appalachian Trail, national forests, ecological issues, preservation movements, affordable travel, and interesting short profiles of regional people."

🌀🌀🌀🌀 COWBOYS & INDIANS MAGAZINE

USFR Media Group, 6688 N. Central Expressway, Suite 650, Dallas TX 75206. (214)750-8222. **E-mail:** queries@cowboysindians.com. **Website:** www.cowboysindians.com. **60% freelance written.** Magazine published 8 times/year covering people and places of the American West. The Premier Magazine of the West, *Cowboys & Indians* captures the romance, drama, and grandeur of the American frontier—both past and present—like no other publication. Undeniably exclusive, the magazine covers a broad range of lifestyle topics: art, home interiors, travel, fashion, Western film, and Southwestern cuisine. Estab. 1993. Circ. 101,000. Byline given. Pays on publication. Offers 20% kill fee. Publishes ms an average of 2 months after acceptance. Editorial lead time 4 months. Submit seasonal material 6 months in advance. Accepts queries by mail, e-mail, fax. Sample copy for $5. Guidelines by email.

NONFICTION Needs book excerpts, expose, general interest, historical, interview, photo feature, travel, art. No essays, humor, poetry, or opinion. **Buys 40-50 mss/year.** Query. Length: 500-3,000 words. **Pays**

$250-5,000 for assigned articles. Pays $250-1,000 for unsolicited articles.

PHOTOS State availability. Captions, identification of subjects required. Reviews contact sheets, 21/4x21/4 transparencies. Negotiates payment individually. Buys one time rights.

COLUMNS Art; Travel; Music; Home Interiors; all 200-1,000 words. **Buys 50 mss/year.** Query. **Pays $200-1,500.**

TIPS "Our readers are educated, intelligent, and well-read Western enthusiasts, many of whom collect Western Americana, read other Western publications, attend shows and have discerning tastes. Therefore, articles should assume a certain level of prior knowledge of Western subjects on the part of the reader. Articles should be readable and interesting to the novice and general interest reader as well. Please keep your style lively, above all things, and fast-moving, with snappy beginnings and endings. Wit and humor are always welcome."

$$ SOUTHERN EDITION

509 Old Wagon Rd., Walhalla SC 29691-5821. **E-mail:** southernedition@live.com. **Website:** southernedition.com. **Contact:** Greg Freeman, editor. **10% freelance written.** Dedicated to celebrating the beauty, character, culture, and heritage of the American South, *Southern Edition* brings to you the sights, sounds, tastes, and hospitality for which the region is known." New content is added consistently throughout the year. Past freelance articles include Dr. Ed Brotak's "Southern Live Oaks: Nature's Great Survivors," Debra Pamplin's travel piece "The Casa Marina Hotel and Jacksonville Beach," Tammy Blue's "The Immigrant Historian: British Expat Enjoys Exploring the South's Past" and Darrell Laurant's "Pierce Street: Lynchburg's Out-of-the-Way Connection with African American History." *Southern Edition* is an online magazine comprised of columns devoted to general interests, travel, food, gardening, history, books, and humor. Estab. 2006. Byline given. Typically pays 10-20 days upon publication. Publishes ms an average of 1 month after acceptance. Editorial lead time is 1-3 months. Submit seasonal material 1-2 months in advance. Accepts queries by mail, e-mail. Responds in 1-3 weeks to queries. Responds in 1 month to ms. Sample copies available online. Guidelines available online or via email. While freelance submissions are not actively solicited, queries from writers, photographers, and visual artists are welcomed and entertained. All ideas must be related to the American South, and must be substantive and of educational value.

NONFICTION Needs essays, general interest, historical, interview, nostalgic, photo feature, profile, travel. Does not want to see any "romanticized" travel stories (think phrases like, "nestled in a quaint little village"), or notions that the Civil War is still ongoing. Query via email. Minimum 350 words for nonfiction articles. Prefer articles in 1200-word range. **Pays between $35-375 for assigned and unsolicited articles.** Pays expenses of writers on assignment.

PHOTOS Freelancers should state availability of photos with submission. Photos require captions and identification of subjects. Reviews GIF/JPEG files. Negotiates payment individually.

COLUMNS *Southern Edition* has 5 different, regular columns: Southern Exposure, which featuresinterviews, history, music reviews, and other features (averages 500 words); Soul Food, which features cooking and Southern cuisine (averages 350 words); Magnolia Eden, which features gardening (averages 500 words); Sunbelt Exursions, which features travel (averages 750 words); and Southern Press, which features author interviews and book reviews (averages 500 words). Writer should query via email. **Columns pay between $35-375.**

TIPS "Demonstrate an ability to write about the American South intelligently and concisely, always recognizing that fact-laden material should be palatable to a general audience."

$$$$ SUNSET MAGAZINE

Sunset Publishing Corp., 55 Harrison St., Ste. 200, Oakland CA 94607. (510)858-3400. **Fax:** (650)327-7537. **E-mail:** readerletters@sunset.com. **Website:** www.sunset.com. Monthly magazine covering the lifestyle of the Western states. *Sunset* is a Western lifestyle publication for educated, active consumers. Editorial provides localized information on gardening and travel, food and entertainment, home building and remodeling. Byline given. Pays on acceptance. No kill fee. Accepts simultaneous submissions. Guidelines available online.

NONFICTION Needs travel. **Buys 50-75 mss/year.** Query before submitting. Freelance articles should be timely and only about the 13 Western states. Garden section accepts queries by mail. Travel section prefers queries by e-mail. Length: 550-750 words. **Pays $1/word.** Pays expenses of writers on assignment.

COLUMNS Building & Crafts, Food, Garden, Travel. Travel Guide length: 300-350 words. Direct queries to specific editorial department.

GEORGIA

💲 ATHENS MAGAZINE

One Press Place, Athens GA 30601. (706)208-2308. **Fax:** (706)208-2339. **Website:** www.athensmagazine. com. **70% freelance written.** Quarterly magazine focused on Athens, GA community and surrounding area (does not include Atlanta metro). Estab. 1989. Circ. 5,000. Byline given. Pays on publication. Offers 20% kill fee. Publishes ms an average of 6 months after acceptance. Editorial lead time 6-9 months. Submit seasonal material 12 months in advance. Accepts queries by mail, e-mail. Accepts simultaneous submissions. Responds in 6-8 weeks to queries. Sample copy free. Guidelines online.

PHOTOS State availability. Captions, identification of subjects required. Reviews GIF/JPEG files. Negotiates payment individually. Buys one time rights.

FILLERS Needs anecdotes, facts, short humor. Length: 25-150 words. **Pays $20-150.**

TIPS "I need freelancers who are well-acquainted with Athens area who can write to its unique audience of students, retirees, etc."

💲💲 ATLANTA TRIBUNE: THE MAGAZINE

875 Old Roswell Rd, Suite C-100, Roswell GA 30076. (770)587-0501. **Fax:** (770)642-6501. **E-mail:** info@ atlantatribune.com. **Website:** www.atlantatribune. com. **30% freelance written.** Monthly magazine covering African-American business, careers, technology, wealth-building, politics, and education. The *Atlanta Tribune* is written for Atlanta's black executives, professionals and entrepreneurs with a primary focus of business, careers, technology, wealth-building, politics, and education. Our publication serves as an advisor that offers helpful information and direction to the black entrepreneur. Estab. 1987. Circ. 30,000. Byline given. Pays on publication. Offers 10% kill fee. Editorial lead time 3 months. Submit seasonal material 4 months in advance. Accepts queries by e-mail. Accepts simultaneous submissions. Responds in 6 weeks to queries. Sample copy online or mail a request. Guidelines available online.

NONFICTION Needs book excerpts, how-to, interview, new product, opinion, technical. **Buys 100 mss/year.** Query with published clips. Length: 1,400-2,500 words. **Pays $250-600.** Pays expenses of writers on assignment.

PHOTOS State availability. Identification of subjects, model releases required. Reviews 21/4x21/4 transparencies. Negotiates payment individually. Buys one time rights.

COLUMNS Business; Careers; Technology; Wealth-Building; Politics and Education; all 400-600 words. **Buys 100 mss/year.** Query with published clips. **Pays $100-200.**

TIPS Send a well-written, convincing query by e-mail that demonstrates that you have thoroughly read previous issues and reviewed our online writer's guidelines.

💲💲 GEORGIA MAGAZINE

Georgia Electric Membership Corp., P.O. Box 1707, 2100 E. Exchange Place, Tucker GA 30085. (770)270-6500. **E-mail:** laurel.george@georgiaemc.com; magazine@georgiamc.com. **Website:** www.georgiamagazine.org. **Contact:** Laurel George, editor. **50% freelance written.** "We are a monthly magazine for and about Georgians, with a friendly, conversational tone and human interest topics." Estab. 1945. Circ. 500,000. Byline given. Pays on acceptance. No kill fee. Publishes ms an average of 6 months after acceptance. Editorial lead time 2 months. Submit seasonal material 6 months in advance. Accepts queries by mail, e-mail. Accepts simultaneous submissions. Responds in 1 month to subjects of interest. Sample copy: $2. Guidelines for #10 SASE, or by e-mail.

NONFICTION Needs general interest, historical, how-to, humor, inspirational, interview, photo feature, travel. Query with published clips. Length: 1,000-1,200 words; 800 words for smaller features and departments. **Pays $350-500.** Pays expenses of writers on assignment.

PHOTOS State availability. Identification of subjects, model releases required. Reviews digital images, websites, and prints. Negotiates payment individually. Buys one-time rights.

💲💲 KNOWATLANTA MAGAZINE

New South Publishing, Inc., 9040 Roswell Rd., Suite 210, Atlanta GA 30350. (770)650-1102. **Fax:** (770)650-2848. **E-mail:** lindsay@knowatlanta.com. **Website:**

www.knowatlanta.com. **Contact:** Lindsay Penticuff, editor. **80% freelance written.** Quarterly magazine covering the Atlanta area. *KNOWAtlanta* is metro Atlanta's premier relocation guide. The magazine provides valuable information to people relocating to the area with articles on homes, healthcare, jobs, finances, temporary housing, apartments, education, county-by-county guides, and so much more. *KNOWAtlanta* puts Atlanta at its readers' fingertips. The magazine is used by executives relocating their companies, realtors working with future Atlantans, and individuals moving to the "capital of the Southeast." Estab. 1986. Circ. 192,000. Byline given. Pays on publication. Offers 100% kill fee. Editorial lead time 2 months. Submit seasonal material 2 months in advance. Accepts queries by e-mail. Accepts simultaneous submissions. Sample copy free.

NONFICTION Needs general interest, how-to, interview, personal experience, photo feature. No fiction. **Buys 20 mss/year.** Query with published clips. Length: 800-1,500 words. **Pays $100-500 for assigned articles. Pays $100-300 for unsolicited articles.** Pays expenses of writers on assignment.

PHOTOS Send photos with submission, if available. Captions, identification of subjects required. Reviews contact sheets. Negotiates payment individually. Buys one-time rights.

💲💲 POINTS NORTH MAGAZINE ATLANTA

All Points Interactive Media Corp., 568 Peachtree Pkwy., Cumming GA 30041-6820. (770)844-0969. **Fax:** (770)844-0968. **E-mail:** editorial@pointsnorthatlanta.com. **Website:** www.pointsnorthatlanta.com. **Contact:** Jennifer Colosimo, managing editor; Heather Brown, senior editor. **15% freelance written.** Monthly magazine covering lifestyle in Atlanta, Georgia. *"Points North* specializes in providing pertinent information for our prestigious audience. In each issue we feature intriguing personalities that have a connection to the Atlanta area, fabulous travel destinations, upcoming local and regional events, topics relating to home improvement, recreation, cultural arts and entertainment, fashion, health, retail shopping and the latest news and information from those north Atlanta communities in our primary coverage area." Estab. 2000. Circ. 70,000. Byline given. Pays on publication. Offers negotiable (for assigned articles only) kill fee. Publishes ms an average of 3 months after acceptance. Editorial lead time 3 months. Submit

seasonal material 6 months in advance. Accepts queries by e-mail only. Responds in 6-8 weeks to queries. Responds in 6-8 months to mss. Sample copy for $3.

NONFICTION Contact: Managing editor. Needs general interest, only topics pertaining to Atlanta area, historical, interview, travel. **Buys 50-60 mss/year.** Query with published clips. Length: 1,200-2,500 words. **Pays $100-250.**

PHOTOS "We do not accept photos until article acceptance. Do not send photos with query." State availability. Captions, identification of subjects, model releases required. Reviews slide transparencies, 4x6 prints, GIF/JPEG files. Offers no additional payment for photos accepted with ms.

TIPS "The best way for a freelancer, who is interested in being published, is to get a sense of the types of articles we're looking for by reading the magazine."

💲💲 SAVANNAH MAGAZINE

Morris Publishing Group, P.O. Box 1088, Savannah GA 31402. **Fax:** (912)525-0611. **E-mail:** editor@savannahmagazine.com. **Website:** www.savannahmagazine.com. **Contact:** Emily Testa, editor-in-chief. **95% freelance written.** Bimonthly magazine focusing on homes and entertaining covering coastal lifestyle of Savannah and South Carolina area. *"Savannah Magazine* publishes articles about people, places, and events of interest to the residents of the greater Savannah areas, as well as coastal Georgia and the South Carolina low country. We strive to provide our readers with information that is both useful and entertaining—written in a lively, readable style." Estab. 1990. Circ. 16,000. Byline given. Pays on publication. Offers 20% kill fee. Publishes ms an average of 2 months after acceptance. Editorial lead time 2 months. Submit seasonal material 4 months in advance. Accepts queries by mail, e-mail, fax. Accepts simultaneous submissions. Responds in 4 weeks to queries; 6 weeks to mss. Sample copy free. Guidelines by e-mail.

NONFICTION Needs general interest, historical, humor, interview, travel. Does not want fiction or poetry. Query with published clips. Length: 500-750 words. **Pays $250-450.** Pays expenses of writers on assignment.

PHOTOS Contact: Contact Michelle Karner, art director. State availability. Reviews GIF/JPEG files. Negotiates payment individually. Offers no additional payment for photos accepted with ms. Buys one-time rights.

HAWAII

$$$ HONOLULU MAGAZINE

PacificBasin Communications, 1000 Bishop Street, Suite 405, Honolulu HI 96813. (808)537-9500. **Fax:** (808)537-6455. **E-mail:** kristinl@honolulumagazine.com. **Website:** www.honolulumagazine.com. Michael Keany, managing editor. **Contact:** Kristin Lipman, creative director. Monthly magazine covering general-interest topics relating to Hawaii residents. Estab. 1888. Circ. 30,000. Byline given. Pays about 30 days after publication. Where appropriate, offers 50% kill fee. Prefers to work with published/established writers. Accepts queries by mail, e-mail. Accepts simultaneous submissions. Guidelines available online.

NONFICTION Needs historical, interview, sports, politics, lifestyle trends, all Hawaii-related. "We write for Hawaii residents, so travel articles about Hawaii are not appropriate." Send complete ms. Length determined when assignments discussed. **Pays $250-1,200.** Pays expenses of writers on assignment.

PHOTOS State availability. Captions, identification of subjects, model releases required. Pays $100 for stock, $200 for assigned shot. Package rates also negotiated.

COLUMNS Length determined when assignments discussed. Query with published clips or send complete ms. **Pays $100-300.**

IDAHO

$$ SUN VALLEY MAGAZINE

Valley Publishing, LLC, 313 N. Main St., Hailey ID 83333. (208)788-0770. **Fax:** (208)788-3881. **E-mail:** adam@sunvalleymag.com; julie@sunvalleymag.com. **Website:** www.sunvalleymag.com. **Contact:** Adam Tanous, managing editor; Julie Molema, art director. **95% freelance written.** Quarterly magazine covering the lifestyle of the Sun Valley area. *Sun Valley Magazine* presents the lifestyle of the Sun Valley area and the Wood River Valley, including recreation, culture, profiles, history and the arts. Estab. 1973. Circ. 17,000. Byline given. Pays on publication. No kill fee. Publishes ms an average of 5 months after acceptance. Editorial lead time 1 year. Submit seasonal material 14 months in advance. Accepts queries by mail. Accepts simultaneous submissions. Responds in 5 weeks to queries. Responds in 2 months to mss. Sample copy for $4.95 and $3 postage. Guidelines for #10 SASE.

NONFICTION Needs historical, interview, photo feature, travel. Special issues: Sun Valley home design and architecture (spring); Sun Valley weddings/wedding planner (summer). Query with published clips. **Pays $40-500.** Pays expenses of writers on assignment.

REPRINTS Only occasionally purchases reprints.

PHOTOS State availability. Identification of subjects, model releases required. Reviews transparencies. Offers $60-275/photo. Buys one-time rights and some electronic rights.

COLUMNS Conservation issues, winter/summer sports, health and wellness, mountain-related activities and subjects, home (interior design), garden. All columns must have a local slant. Query with published clips. **Pays $40-300.**

TIPS "Most of our writers are locally based. Also, we rarely take submissions that are not specifically assigned, with the exception of fiction. However, we always appreciate queries."

ILLINOIS

$$$$ CHICAGO MAGAZINE

435 N. Michigan Ave., Suite 1100, Chicago IL 60611. (312)222-8999. **E-mail:** bfenner@chicagomag.com; tnoland@chicagomag.com. **Website:** www.chicagomag.com. **Contact:** Elizabeth Fenner, editor-in-chief; Terrance Noland, executive editor. **50% freelance written. Prefers to work with published/established writers.** Monthly magazine for an audience which is 95% from Chicago area; 90% college educated; upper income, overriding interests in the arts, politics, dining, good life in the city and suburbs. Most are in 25-50 age bracket, well-read and articulate. "Produced by the city's best magazine editors and writers, Chicago Magazine is the definitive voice on top dining, entertainment, shopping and real estate in the region. It also offers provocative narrative stories and topical features that have won numerous awards. Chicago Magazine reaches 1.5 million readers and is published by Tribune Company." Estab. 1968. Circ. 182,000. Pays on acceptance. No kill fee. Publishes ms an average of 3 months after acceptance. Submit seasonal material 4 months in advance. Accepts queries by mail, e-mail. Responds in 1 month to queries.

For sample copy, send $3 to Circulation Department. Guidelines for #10 SASE.

NONFICTION Needs expose, humor, personal experience, think pieces, profiles, spot news, historical articles. Does not want anything about events outside the city or profiles on people who no longer live in the city. **Buys 100 mss/year.** Query; indicate specifics, knowledge of city and market, and demonstrable access to sources. Length: 200-6,000 words. **Pays $100-3,000 and up.** Pays expenses of writers on assignment.

PHOTOS Usually assigned separately, not acquired from writers. Reviews 35mm transparencies, color and b&w glossy prints.

TIPS "Submit detailed queries, be business-like, and avoid cliche ideas."

$$$$ CHICAGO READER

Sun-Times Media, LLC, 350 N. Orleans St., Chicago IL 60654. (312)321-9613. **E-mail:** mail@chicagoreader.com; letters@chicagoreader.com. **Website:** www.chicagoreader.com. **Contact:** Mara Shalhoup, editor; Jake Malooley, managing editor. **50% freelance written.** Weekly alternative tabloid for Chicago. "The *Chicago Reader* is primarily a staff-written publication, but occasionally we'll run a great feature, insightful criticism, timely blog post, or expertly composed video that comes to us from a freelancer." Estab. 1971. Circ. 120,000. Byline given. Pays on publication. Occasional kill fee. Publishes ms an average of 2 weeks after acceptance. Editorial lead time up to 6 months. Accepts queries by mail, e-mail. Accepts simultaneous submissions. Responds if interested. Sample copy free. Guidelines available online.

NONFICTION **Buys 500 mss/year.** Send complete ms. Length: Features: 1,500 words and longer; Music and culture reviews: 600-1,200 words. **Pays $100-3,000.** Sometimes pays expenses of writers on assignment.

REPRINTS Occasionally accepts previously published submissions.

COLUMNS Local color, 500-2,500 words; arts and entertainment reviews, up to 1,200 words.

TIPS "Our greatest need is for full-length magazine-style feature stories on Chicago topics. We're *not* looking for: hard news (What the Mayor Said About the Schools Yesterday); commentary and opinion (What I Think About What the Mayor Said About the Schools Yesterday); or poetry. We are not particularly interested in stories of national (as opposed to local) scope, or in celebrity for celebrity's sake (a la *Rolling Stone*, *Interview*, etc.). More than half the articles published in the *Reader* each week come from freelancers, and once or twice a month we publish 1 that's come in 'over the transom'—from a writer we've never heard of and may never hear from again. We think that keeping the *Reader* open to the greatest possible number of contributors makes a fresher, less predictable, more interesting paper. We not only publish unsolicited freelance writing, we depend on it. Our last issue in December is dedicated to original fiction."

$ ILLINOIS ENTERTAINER

4223 W. Lake St., Suite 490, Chicago IL 60624. (773)717-5665. **Fax:** (773)717-5666. **E-mail:** service@illinoisentertainer.com. **Website:** www.illinoisentertainer.com. **80% freelance written.** Monthly free magazine covering popular and alternative music, as well as other entertainment (film, media) in Illinois. Estab. 1974. Circ. 55,000. Byline given. Pays on publication. Offers 50% kill fee. Publishes ms an average of 2 months after acceptance. Editorial lead time 2 months. Submit seasonal material 2 months in advance. Accepts queries by mail. Accepts simultaneous submissions. Responds in 2 months to queries. Sample copy: $5.

NONFICTION Needs expose, how-to, humor, interview, new product, reviews. No personal, confessional, or inspirational articles. **Buys 75 mss/year.** Query with published clips. Length: 600-2,600 words. **Pays $15-160.** Pays expenses of writers on assignment.

REPRINTS Send typed ms with rights for sale noted and information about when and where the material previously appeared. Pays 100% of amount paid for an original article.

PHOTOS Send photos. Captions, identification of subjects, model releases required. Reviews contact sheets, transparencies, 5x7 prints. Offers $20-200/photo. Buys one-time rights.

COLUMNS Spins (LP reviews), 100-400 words. **Buys 200-300 mss/year.** Query with published clips. **Pays $8-25.**

TIPS "Send clips, résumé, etc. and be patient. Also, sending queries that show you've seen our magazine and have a feel for it greatly increases your publication chances. Don't send unsolicited material. No e-mail solicitations or queries of any kind."

MIDWESTERN FAMILY MAGAZINE

1100 E. Corrington Ave., Peoria IL 61603. **E-mail:** jrudd@midwesternfamily.com. **Website:** www.midwesternfamily.com. **90% freelance written.** Bimonthly magazine covering family living in Central Illinois. *Midwestern Family* is a comprehensive guide to fun, health, and happiness for Central Illinois families. Estab. 2003. Circ. 23,000. Byline given. Pays on publication. No kill fee. Publishes ms an average of 2 months after acceptance. Editorial lead time 4-6 weeks. Submit seasonal material 4-6 weeks in advance. Accepts queries by e-mail, online submission form. Accepts simultaneous submissions. Responds in 2 weeks to queries; in 4 months to mss. Sample: $1.50. Guidelines by e-mail.

NONFICTION Query. Length: 1,000-1,500 words. **Pays $50.** Pays expenses of writers on assignment.

PHOTOS State availability. Identification of subjects, model releases required. Reviews GIF/JPEG files. Negotiates payment individually. Buys all rights.

COLUMNS Home; Fun; Life; Food; Health; Discovery, all 1,000-1,250 words. **Buys 40 mss/year.** Query. **Pays $100.**

NORTHWEST QUARTERLY MAGAZINE

Hughes Media Corp., 222 Seventh St., Rockford IL 61104. (815)316-2300. **E-mail:** clinden@northwestquarterly.com. **Website:** www.northwestquarterly.com. **Contact:** Chris Linden, editor. **20% freelance written.** Quarterly magazine covering regional lifestyle of Northern Illinois and Southern Wisconsin, and also Kane and McHenry counties (Chicago collar counties), highlighting strengths of living and doing business in the area. Publishes information specifically related to its geographic territory. National stories without a local angle not accepted. Estab. 2004. Circ. 42,000. Byline given. Pays on publication. Publishes ms an average of 4-6 months after acceptance. Editorial lead time 6 months. Submit seasonal material 6 months in advance. Accepts queries by mail, e-mail. Accepts simultaneous submissions. Responds in 2 weeks to queries; in 2 months to mss. Sample copy and guidelines available by e-mail.

NONFICTION Needs historical, interview, photo feature, regional features. Does not want opinion, fiction, or "anything unrelated to our geographic region." **Buys 150 mss/year.** Query. Length: 700-2,500 words. **Pays $25-500.** Pays expenses of writers on assignment.

PHOTOS State availability. Captions required. Reviews GIF/JPEG files. Negotiates payment individually. Buys one-time rights.

COLUMNS Health & Fitness, 1,000-2,000 words; Home & Garden, 1,500 words; Destinations & Recreation, 1,000-2,000 words; Environment & Nature, 2,000-3,000 words. **Buys 120 mss/year.** Query. **Pays $100-500.**

FILLERS Needs short humor. **Buys 24 mss/year.** Length: 100-200 words. **Pays $30-50.**

TIPS "Any interesting, well-documented feature relating to the 16-county area we cover may be considered. Nature, history, geography, culture, and destinations are favorite themes."

WEST SUBURBAN LIVING

C2 Publishing, Inc., P.O. Box 111, Elmhurst IL 60126. (630)834-4995. **Fax:** (630)834-4996. **E-mail:** wsl@westsuburbanliving.net. **Website:** www.westsuburbanliving.net. **80% freelance written.** Bimonthly magazine focusing on the western suburbs of Chicago. Estab. 1996. Circ. 25,000. Byline given. Pays on publication. Publishes ms an average of 2-4 months after acceptance. Accepts queries by mail, e-mail, fax. Sample copy available online.

NONFICTION Needs general interest, how-to, travel. "Does not want anything that does not have an angle or tie-in to the area we cover—Chicago's western suburbs." **Buys 15 mss/year. Pays $100-500.** Pays expenses of writers on assignment.

PHOTOS State availability. Model releases required. Offers $50-700/photo; negotiates payment individually.

INDIANA

EVANSVILLE LIVING

Tucker Publishing Group, 223 NW Second St., Suite 200, Evansville IN 47708. (812)426-2115. **E-mail:** ktucker@evansvilleliving.com. **Website:** www.evansvilleliving.com. **Contact:** Kristen Tucker, publisher and editor. **80-100% freelance written.** Bimonthly magazine covering Evansville, Indiana, and the greater area. *Evansville Living* is the only full-color, glossy, 100+ page city magazine for the Evansville, Indiana, area. Regular departments include: Home

Style, Garden Style, Day Tripping, Sporting Life, and Local Flavor (menus). Estab. 2000. Circ. 50,000. Byline given. Pays on acceptance. No kill fee. Publishes ms an average of 3 months after acceptance. Editorial lead time 6 months. Submit seasonal material 6 months in advance. Accepts queries by mail, e-mail. Accepts simultaneous submissions. Sample copy for $5 or online. Guidelines by e-mail.

NONFICTION Needs essays, general interest, historical, photo feature, travel. **Buys 60-80 mss/year.** Query with published clips. Length: 200-2,000 words. **Pays $100-300.** Pays expenses of writers on assignment.

PHOTOS State availability. Captions, identification of subjects required. Reviews contact sheets, negatives, transparencies, prints. Negotiates payment individually. Buys all rights.

COLUMNS Home Style (home); Garden Style (garden); Sporting Life (sports); Local Flavor (menus), all 1,500 words. Query with published clips. **Pays $100-300.**

$$$ INDIANAPOLIS MONTHLY

Emmis Communications, 1 Emmis Plaza, 40 Monument Circle, Suite 100, Indianapolis IN 46204. (317)237-9288. **Fax:** (317)684-2080. **Website:** www.indianapolismonthly.com. **Contact:** Amanda Heckert, editor in chief. **30% freelance written. Prefers to work with published/established writers.** *Indianapolis Monthly* attracts and enlightens its upscale, well-educated readership with bright, lively editorial on subjects ranging from personalities to social issues, fashion to food. Its diverse content and attention to service make it the ultimate source by which the Indianapolis area lives. Estab. 1977. Circ. 50,000. Byline given. Pays on publication. Offers negotiable kill fee. Publishes ms an average of 2 months after acceptance. Editorial lead time 3 months. Submit seasonal material 3 months in advance. Accepts queries by mail. Accepts simultaneous submissions. Responds in 6 weeks to queries. Sample copy: $6.10.

NONFICTION Needs essays, expose, general interest, interview, photo feature. "No poetry, fiction, or domestic humor; no 'How Indy Has Changed Since I Left Town,' 'An Outsider's View of the 500,' or generic material with no or little tie to Indianapolis/Indiana." **Buys 35 mss/year.** Query by mail with published clips. Length: 200-3,000 words. **Pays $50-1,000.** Pays expenses of writers on assignment.

PHOTOS State availability. Captions, identification of subjects, model releases required. Negotiates payment individually. Buys one-time rights.

TIPS "Our standards are simultaneously broad and narrow: broad in that we're a general interest magazine spanning a wide spectrum of topics, narrow in that we buy only stories with a heavy emphasis on Indianapolis (and, to a lesser extent, Indiana). Simply inserting an Indy-oriented paragraph into a generic national article won't get it: All stories must pertain primarily to things Hoosier. Once you've cleared that hurdle, however, it's a wide-open field. We've done features on national celebrities—Indianapolis native David Letterman and *Mir* astronaut David Wolf of Indianapolis, to name a few—and we've published two-paragraph items on such quirky topics as an Indiana gardening supply house that sells insects by mail. Query with clips showing lively writing and solid reporting. No phone queries, please."

IOWA

$$ THE IOWAN

Pioneer Communications, Inc., 300 Walnut St., Suite 6, Des Moines IA 50309. (515)246-0402. **E-mail:** editor@iowan.com. **Website:** www.iowan.com. **Contact:** Erich Gaukel, editor. **75% freelance written.** Bimonthly magazine covering the state of Iowa. *The Iowan* is a bimonthly magazine exploring everything Iowa has to offer. Each issue travels into diverse pockets of the state to discover the sights, meet the people, learn the history, taste the cuisine, and experience the culture. Estab. 1952. Circ. 20,000. Byline given. Pays 60 days from invoice approval or publication date, whichever comes first. Offers $100 kill fee. Publishes ms an average of 3 months after acceptance. Editorial lead time 9-10 months. Submit seasonal material 6-12 months in advance. Accepts queries by mail, e-mail. Accepts simultaneous submissions. Sample copy for $4.95, plus s&h. Guidelines available online.

NONFICTION Needs essays, general interest, historical, interview, photo feature, travel. Special issues: Each issue offers readers a collection of "shorts" that cover timely issues, current trends, interesting people, noteworthy work, enticing food, historical and historic moments, captivating arts and culture, beckoning recreational opportunities, and more. Features cover every topic imaginable with only 2 primary rules: (1) solid storytelling and (2) great photography potential. **Buys 30 mss/year.** Query with published clips. Length: 500-750 words for "shorts"; 1,000-1,500 words for features. **Pays $150-450.** Pays expenses of writers on assignment.

PHOTOS Send photos. Captions, identification of subjects, model releases required. Reviews contact sheets, GIF/JPEG files (8x10 at 300 dpi minimum). Negotiates payment individually, according to space rates. Buys one-time rights.

COLUMNS Last Word (essay), 800 words. **Buys 6 mss/year.** Query with published clips. **Pays $100.**

TIPS "Must have submissions in writing, either via e-mail or snail mail. Submitting published clips is preferred."

KANSAS

💲💲 KANSAS!

1020 S. Kansas Ave., Suite 200, Topeka KS 66612-1354. (785)296-8478. **Fax:** (785)296-6988. **E-mail:** ksmagazine@sunflowerpub.com. **Website:** www.travelks.com/ks-mag. **Contact:** Andrea Etzel, editor. **90% freelance written.** Quarterly magazine emphasizing Kansas travel attractions and events. Estab. 1945. Circ. 45,000. Byline and courtesy bylines are given to all content. Pays on acceptance. No kill fee. Publishes ms an average of 1 year after acceptance. Submit seasonal material 8 months in advance. Accepts queries by mail, e-mail. Accepts simultaneous submissions. Responds in 2 months to queries. Guidelines available on website.

NONFICTION Needs general interest, photo feature, travel. Query. Length: 750-1,250 words. **Pays $200-350.** Pays expenses of writers on assignment. Mileage reimbursement is available for writers on assignment in the state of Kansas, TBD by assignment editor.

PHOTOS "We are a full-color photograph/ms publication. Send digital photos (original transparencies only or CD with images available in high resolution) with query." Captions and location of the image (county and city) are required. Pays $25-75 for gallery images, $150 for cover. Assignments also available, welcomes queries.

TIPS "History and nostalgia or essay stories do not fit into our format because they can't be illustrated well with color photos. Submit a query letter describing 1

appropriate idea with outline for possible article and suggestions for photos. Do not send unsolicited mss."

KENTUCKY

💲💲💲 KENTUCKY LIVING

Kentucky Association of Electric Co-Ops, P.O. Box 32170, Louisville KY 40232. **Website:** www.kentuckyliving.com. **Contact:** Anita Travis Richter, editor. **Mostly freelance written. Prefers to work with published/established writers.** Monthly feature magazine primarily for Kentucky residents. Estab. 1948. Circ. 500,000. Byline given. Pays on acceptance. No kill fee. Publishes ms an average of 12 months after acceptance. Submit seasonal material at least 6 months in advance. Accepts queries by online submission form. Accepts simultaneous submissions. Responds in 1 month to queries. Sample copy with SASE (9x12 envelope and 4 first-class stamps). Guidelines online.

NONFICTION Special issues: Stories of interest include: Kentucky-related profiles (people, places, or events), business and social trends, history, biography, recreation, travel, leisure or lifestyle articles/book excerpts, articles on contemporary subjects of general public interest, and general consumer-related features. **Buys 18-24 mss/year.** Prefers queries rather than submissions. Length: 500-1,500 words. **Pays $75-935.** Pays expenses of writers on assignment.

PHOTOS State availability of or send photos. Identification of subjects required. Reviews photo e-files at online link or sent CD. Payment for photos included in payment for ms.

COLUMNS Accepts queries for Worth the Trip column. Other columns have established columnists.

TIPS "The quality of writing and reporting (factual, objective, thorough) is considered in setting payment price. We prefer general interest pieces filled with quotes and anecdotes. Avoid boosterism. Well-researched, well-written feature articles are preferred. All articles must have a strong Kentucky connection."

💲💲 KENTUCKY MONTHLY

Vested Interest Publications, P.O. Box 559, 100 Consumer Lane, Frankfort KY 40602-0559. (502)227-0053; (888)329-0053. **Fax:** (502)227-5009. **E-mail:** kymonthly@kentuckymonthly.com; steve@kentuckymonthly.com. **E-mail:** patty@kentuckymonthly.com. **Website:** www.kentuckymonthly.com. **Contact:** Stephen Vest, editor; Patricia Ranft, associate editor. **50%**

freelance written. Monthly magazine. "We publish stories about Kentucky and by Kentuckians, including stories written by those who live elsewhere." Estab. 1998. Circ. 40,000. Byline given. Pays within 3 months of publication. Offers kill fee. Publishes ms an average of 3 months after acceptance. Editorial lead time 4-12 months. Submit seasonal material 4-10 months in advance. Accepts queries by e-mail. Accepts simultaneous submissions. Responds in 1-3 months to queries; in 1 month to mss. Sample copy and writer's guidelines online.

NONFICTION Needs book excerpts, essays, general interest, historical, how-to, humor, interview, photo feature, profile, religious, reviews, travel, All pieces should have a Kentucky angle. Special issues: Kentucky Derby Festival Guide (April); Kentucky Gift Guide (November). **Buys 50 mss/year.** Query. Length: 300-2,000 words. **Pays $45-300 for assigned articles; $50-200 for unsolicited articles.** Pays expenses of writers on assignment.

PHOTOS State availability. Captions required. Reviews negatives. Buys first rights.

FICTION We publish stories about Kentucky and by Kentuckians, including stories written by those who live elsewhere." Needs adventure, historical, mainstream, slice-of-life vignettes, Wants Kentucky-related stories. **Buys 30 mss/year.** Query with published clips. Accepts submissions by e-mail. Length: 1,000-5,000 words. **Pays $50-500.**

TIPS "Please read the magazine to get the flavor of what we're publishing each month. We accept articles via e-mail. Approximately 70% of articles are assigned."

LOUISIANA

⑨⑨ PRESERVATION IN PRINT

Preservation Resource Center of New Orleans, 923 Tchoupitoulos St., New Orleans LA 70130. (504)581-7032. **Fax:** (504)636-3073. **E-mail:** prc@prcno.org. **Website:** www.prcno.org. **Contact:** Danielle Del Sol, editor and director of publications. **30% freelance written.** Monthly magazine covering preservation. Looking for articles about interest in the historic architecture of New Orleans. Estab. 1975. Circ. 10,000. Byline given. Pays on acceptance. No kill fee. Publishes ms an average of 1 month after acceptance. Editorial lead time 1 month. Submit seasonal material 1-2

months in advance. Accepts queries by mail, e-mail, fax, phone. Accepts simultaneous submissions. Sample copy available online. Guidelines free.

NONFICTION Needs essays, historical, interview, photo feature, technical. **Buys 30 mss/year.** Query. Length: 700-1,000 words. **Pays $100-200 for assigned articles.** Sometimes pays expenses of writers on assignment.

MAINE

⑨ DISCOVER MAINE MAGAZINE

10 Exchange St., Suite 208, Portland ME 04101. (207)874-7720. **E-mail:** info@discovermainemagazine.com. **Website:** www.discovermainemagazine.com. **Contact:** Jim Burch, editor and publisher. **100% freelance written.** Monthly magazine covering Maine history and nostalgia. Sports and hunting/fishing topics are also included. "*Discover Maine Magazine* is dedicated to bringing the amazing history of the great state of Maine to readers in every corner of the state and to those from away who love the rich heritage and traditions of Maine. From the history of Maine's mill towns, to the traditions of family farming and coastal fishing, 9 times a year *Discover Maine*'s stories tell of life in the cities and towns across Maine as it was years ago." Estab. 1992. Circ. 12,000. Byline given. Pays on publication. No kill fee. Publishes ms an average of 2-3 months after acceptance. Editorial lead time 3 months. Submit seasonal material 3 months in advance. Accepts queries by mail, e-mail. Accepts simultaneous submissions. Responds in 2 weeks to queries; in 1 month to mss.

NONFICTION Needs historical. Does not want poetry. **Buys 200 mss/year.** Send complete ms. Length: 500-2,000 words. **Pays $20-30.** Pays expenses of writers on assignment.

PHOTOS Send photos. Negotiates payment individually. Buys one-time rights.

TIPS "Call first and talk with the publisher."

MARYLAND

⑨⑨ BALTIMORE

1000 Lancaster St., Suite 400, Baltimore MD 21202. (443)873-3900. **Fax:** (410)625-0280. **E-mail:** wmax@baltimoremagazine.net; mjane@baltimoremagazine.net; blauren@balimoremagazine.net; iken@baltimoremagazine.net; cron@baltimoremagazine.net; wlydia@baltimoremagazine.net. **Website:** www.baltimoremagazine.net. **Contact:** Send correspondence to the appropriate editor: Max Weiss (lifestyle, film, pop culture, general inquiries); Jane Marion (food, travel); Lauren Bell (style, home, beauty, wellness); Ken Iglehart (business, special editions); Ron Cassie (politics, environment, health, sports); Lydia Woolever (calendar, events, party pages). **50-60% freelance written.** Monthly city magazine featuring news, profiles, and service articles. Estab. 1907. Circ. 70,000. Byline given. Pays within 1 month of publication. Offers kill fee in some cases. Submit seasonal material 4 months in advance. Accepts queries by mail, e-mail. Accepts simultaneous submissions. Guidelines online.

NONFICTION Needs book excerpts, essays, general interest, historical, humor, new product, personal experience, photo feature, travel. Does not want anything "that lacks a strong Baltimore focus or angle. Unsolicited personal essays are almost never accepted. We've printed only 2 over the past few years; the last was by a 19-year veteran city judge reminiscing on his time on the bench and the odd stories and situations he encountered there. Unsolicited food and restaurant reviews, whether positive or negative, are likewise never accepted." Query appropriate subject editor by e-mail (preferred), or mail query with published clips. Length: 1,600-2,500 words. **Pays 30-40¢/word.** Pays expenses of writers on assignment. Sometimes pays expenses.

COLUMNS "The shorter pieces are the best places to break into the magazine." Up Front, 300-700 words; Hot Shots and Cameo, 800-2,000 words. Query with published clips.

TIPS "Too many writers send us newspaper-style articles. We are seeking: (1) *Human interest features*—strong, even dramatic profiles of Baltimoreans of interest to our readers; (2) *First-person accounts* of experience in Baltimore or experiences of a Baltimore resident; (3) *Consumer*—according to our editorial needs and with Baltimore sources. Writers should read/familiarize themselves with the style of *Baltimore* before submitting. You're most likely to impress us with writing that demonstrates how well you handle character, dramatic narrative, and factual analysis. We also admire inspired reporting and a clear, surprising style. We strongly prefer receiving queries via e-mail. If you use standard U.S. mail, your query should fit on 1 page."

MASSACHUSETTS

💲💲 CAPE COD LIFE

13 Steeple St., Suite 204, P.O. Box 1439, Mashpee MA 02649. (508)419-7381. **Fax:** (508)477-1225. **Website:** www.capecodlife.com. **Contact:** Jen Dow, Creative Director; Matthew Gill, *Cape Cod LIFE* Editor, Julie Wagner, *Cape Cod HOME* Editor. **80% freelance written.** Cape Cod LIFE Magazine published 7 times/year focusing on area lifestyle, history and culture, people and places, business and industry, and issues and answers for year-round and summer residents of Cape Cod, Nantucket, and Martha's Vineyard as well as nonresidents who spend their leisure time here. Cape Cod Life Magazine has become the premier lifestyle magazine for the Cape & Islands, featuring topics ranging from arts and events, history and heritage, beaches and boating as well as a comprehensive resource for planning the perfect vacation.

Cape Cod ART is published annually.

Cape Cod HOME is published 6 times per year. Estab. 1979. Circ. 45,000. Byline given. Pays 90 days after published. Submit seasonal material 6 months in advance. Accepts queries by mail, e-mail. Accepts simultaneous submissions. Responds in 3 months to queries. Responds in 3 months to mss. Sample copy for $5. Guidelines for #10 SASE.

NONFICTION Needs book excerpts, general interest, historical, interview, photo feature, travel, outdoors, gardening, nautical, nature, arts, antiques, history, housing. **Buys 20 mss/year.** Query. Length: 800-1,500 words. **Pays $200-400.** Pays expenses of writers on assignment.

PHOTOS Photo guidelines for #10 SASE. Captions, identification of subjects required. Pays $25-225. Buys first rights with right to reprint.

TIPS "Freelancers submitting *quality* spec articles with a Cape Cod and Islands angle have a good chance at publication. We like to see a wide selection of writer's clips before giving assignments. We also publish *Cape Cod HOME* covering architecture, landscape design, and interior design with a Cape and Islands focus. Also publish Cape Cod ART annually."

💲💲 CAPE COD MAGAZINE

Lighthouse Media Solutions, 396 Main St., Hyannis MA 02601. (508)534-9291. **E-mail:** editor@capecod-magazine.com. **Website:** www.capecodmagazine.com. **80% freelance written.** Magazine published 9 times/year covering Cape Cod lifestyle. "*Cape Cod Magazine* showcases the people, architecture, history, arts, and entertainment that make living and visiting Cape Cod a rich and rewarding experience. *Cape Cod Magazine* and capecodmagazine.com deliver readers the best dining experiences, most beautiful homes, enriching arts, and cultural experiences daily in a multiplatform experience that brings Cape Cod to life." Estab. 1996. Circ. 16,000. Byline given. Pays 30 days after publication. Offers 25% kill fee. Publishes ms an average of 3 months after acceptance. Editorial lead time 6 months. Submit seasonal material 1 year in advance. Accepts queries by mail, e-mail. Accepts simultaneous submissions. Responds in 3 weeks to queries; in 2 months to mss. Sample copy: $5. Guidelines by e-mail.

NONFICTION Needs book excerpts, essays, general interest, historical, humor, personal experience. Does not want clichéd pieces, interviews, and puff features. **Buys 3 mss/year.** Send complete ms. Length: 800-2,500 words. **Pays $300-500 for assigned articles. Pays $100-300 for unsolicited articles.** Pays expenses of writers on assignment.

PHOTOS State availability of or send photos. Reviews GIF/JPEG files. Negotiates payment individually. Buys one-time rights.

COLUMNS Last Word (personal observations in typical back-page format), 700 words. **Buys 4 mss/year.** Query with or without published clips or send complete ms. **Pays $150-300.**

TIPS "Read good magazines. We strive to offer readers the quality they find in good national magazines, so the more informed they are of what good writing is, the better the chance they'll get published in our magazine. Think of art opportunities. Ideas that do not have good art potential are harder to sell than those that do."

💲💲 WORCESTER MAGAZINE

72 Shrewbury St., Worcester MA 01604. (508)749-3166. **E-mail:** editor@worcestermag.com; wbird@worcestermag.com. **Website:** www.worcestermag.com. **Contact:** Walter Bird, Jr., editor; Kathy Real, publisher. **10% freelance written.** Weekly tabloid emphasizing the central Massachusetts region, especially the city of Worcester. Estab. 1976. Circ. 40,000. Byline given. Pays on publication. No kill fee. Publishes ms an average of 3 weeks after acceptance. Submit seasonal material 2 months in advance. Accepts queries by mail, e-mail, fax. Accepts simultaneous submissions.

NONFICTION Needs essays, expose, general interest, historical, humor, opinion, personal experience, photo feature. **Buys less than 75 mss/year.** Length: 500-1,500 words. **Pays 10¢/word.** Pays expenses of writers on assignment.

MICHIGAN

💲💲💲 ANN ARBOR OBSERVER

Ann Arbor Observer Co., 2390 Winewood, Ann Arbor MI 48103. (734)769-3175. **Fax:** (734)769-3375. **E-mail:** editor@aaobserver.com. **Website:** www.annarborobserver.com. **Contact:** John Hilton, editor. **50% freelance written.** Monthly magazine. "We depend heavily on freelancers, and we're always glad to talk to new ones. We look for the intelligence and judgment to fully explore complex people and situations, and the ability to convey what makes them interesting." Estab. 1976. Circ. 60,000. Byline given in some sections. Pays on publication. No kill fee. Publishes ms an average of 2 months after acceptance. Accepts queries by mail, e-mail, phone. Responds in 3 weeks to queries; several months to mss. Sample copy for 12.5x15 SAE with $3 postage. Guidelines by e-mail or mail for #10 SASE.

NONFICTION **Buys 75 mss/year.** Length: 100-2,500 words. **Pays up to $1,000.** Pays expenses of writers on assignment.

COLUMNS Up Front (short, interesting tidbits), 150 words, pays $150; Inside Ann Arbor (concise stories), 300-500 words, pays $250; Around Town (unusual, compelling anecdotes), 750-1,500 words; pays $250-300.

TIPS "If you have an idea for a story, write a 100- to 200-word description telling us why the story is interesting. We are open most to intelligent, insightful features about interesting aspects of life in Ann Arbor—all stories must have a strong Ann Arbor tie."

💲💲 GRAND RAPIDS MAGAZINE

Gemini Publications, 549 Ottawa Ave. NW, Suite 201, Grand Rapids MI 49503. (616)459-4545. **Fax:** (616)459-4800. **E-mail:** cvalade@geminipub.com;

info@geminipub.com. **Website:** www.grmag.com. *Grand Rapids* is a general interest life and style magazine designed for those who live in the Grand Rapids metropolitan area or desire to maintain contact with the community. Estab. 1964. Circ. 20,000. Byline given. Pays on publication. No kill fee. Editorial lead time 2 months. Submit seasonal material 2 months in advance. Accepts simultaneous submissions. Sample copy for $2 and SASE with $1.50 postage. Guidelines with #10 SASE.

NONFICTION Query. **Pays $25-500.** Pays expenses of writers on assignment.

💲💲 MICHIGAN HISTORY

Michigan History magazine, Historical Society of Michigan, 5815 Executive Dr., Lansing MI 48911. (517)332-1828. **Fax:** (517)324-4370. **E-mail:** hsm@hsmichigan.org. **E-mail:** editor@hsmichigan.org. **Website:** www.hsmichigan.org. Editorial Manager: Christopher N. Blaker. **Contact:** Nancy Feldbush, editor-in-chief. Each full-color, bimonthly issue of *Michigan History* magazine contains seven or more feature stories about Michigan's fascinating past, plus special sections that highlight historical sites to explore; spotlight the histories of communities, institutions, and businesses; feature individuals and groups who have left impressions upon our state; bring readers up to date on Michigan's history-related news; and more. The magazine is offered either as an individual subscription or as an enhancement to a Historical Society of Michigan membership. Bimonthly magazine, 68 colorful pages. "Since 1917, *Michigan History* magazine, published by the nonprofit Historical Society of Michigan, has celebrated the Great Lakes State's diverse history and cultures through intriguing stories and scores of photographs and images." Please query first. In addition to payment, authors receive 5 complimentary copies of issues in which their work appears. Estab. 1917. Circ. 22,000. Byline given. Pays 30 days after publication date. Publishes ms 6-18 months after acceptance. Editorial lead time 1 year. Accepts queries by mail, e-mail. Guidelines online.

NONFICTION "We are not a scholarly journal and do not accept academic papers." **Buys 40-50 mss/year.** "A manuscript submission must be accompanied by a list of sources for fact-checking purposes. Your article should draw upon multiple primary and secondary resources." Length: 1,500-2,500 words. **Pays $100-300.**

PHOTOS Include in your query if high-resolution photos are available to accompany your article. Authors are encouraged to provide illustrations or suggestions for image sources. Please note that the Society is unable to reimburse you for any expenses you incur in obtaining photographs.

TIPS "Articles should revolve around a Michigan history-related subject, and a significant amount of the article's content should take place within Michigan. Articles should approach a subject by finding an interesting angle to explore, rather than just listing its history."

💲💲 TRAVERSE

Prism Publications, Inc., 148 E. Front St., Traverse City MI 49684. (231)941-8174. **Fax:** (231)941-8391. **Website:** www.mynorth.com. **20% freelance written.** Monthly magazine covering northern Michigan life. "Since 1981, our company, Prism Publications, Inc., has been dedicated to sharing stories and photos that embody life in Northern Michigan. For more than 25 years we have accomplished this through our award-winning flagship publication *Traverse, Northern Michigan's Magazine*." Estab. 1981. Circ. 30,000. Byline given. Pays on acceptance. Offers 10% kill fee. Editorial lead time 1 year. Submit seasonal material 1 year in advance. Accepts queries by mail, fax, phone. Accepts simultaneous submissions. Responds in 2 months to queries. Sample copy for $3. Guidelines for #10 SASE.

NONFICTION Needs book excerpts, essays, general interest, historical, humor, interview, personal experience, photo feature, travel. No fiction or poetry. **Buys 24 mss/year.** Send complete ms. Length: 1,000-3,200 words. **Pays $150-500.** Pays expenses of writers on assignment.

PHOTOS State availability. Negotiates payment individually. Buys one-time rights.

COLUMNS Up in Michigan Reflection (essays about northern Michigan); Reflection on Home (essays about northern homes), both 700 words. **Buys 18 mss/year.** Query with published clips or send complete ms. **Pays $100-200.**

TIPS "When shaping an article for us, consider first that it must be strongly rooted in our region. If you send us a piece about peaches, even if it does an admirable job of relaying the history of peaches, their medicinal qualities, their nutritional magnificence, and so on, we are likely to reject if it doesn't include local farms as a reference point. We want sidebars and extended captions designed to bring in a reader not enticed by the main subject. We cover the northern portion of the Lower Peninsula and to a lesser degree the Upper Peninsula. General categories of interest include nature and the environment, regional culture, personalities, the arts (visual, performing, literary), crafts, food & dining, homes, history, and outdoor activities (e.g., fishing, golf, skiing, boating, biking, hiking, birding, gardening). We are keenly interested in environmental and land-use issues but seldom use material dealing with such issues as health care, education, social services, criminal justice, and local politics. We use service pieces and a small number of how-to pieces, mostly focused on small projects for the home or yard. Also, we value research. We need articles built with information. Many of the pieces we reject use writing style to fill in for information voids. Style and voice are strongest when used as vehicles for sound research."

MINNESOTA

💲💲 LAKE COUNTRY JOURNAL

1480 Northern Pacific Road, #2A, Brainerd MN 56401. (218)828-6424, ext. 14. **Fax:** (218)825-7816. **E-mail:** editor@lakecountryjournal.com; info@lakecountry-journal.com. **Website:** www.lakecountryjournal.com. **90% freelance written.** Bimonthly magazine covering central Minnesota's lake country. "Lake Country is one of the fastest-growing areas in the midwest. Each bimonthly issue of *Lake Country Journal* captures the essence of why we work, play, and live in this area. Through a diverse blend of articles from features and fiction, to recreation, recipes, gardening, and nature, this quality lifestyle magazine promotes positive family and business endeavors, showcases our natural and cultural resources, and highlights the best of our people, places, and events." Estab. 1996. Circ. 14,500. Byline given. Pays on publication. Offers 25% kill fee. Publishes ms an average of 6 months after acceptance. Submit seasonal material 1 year in advance. Accepts queries by mail, e-mail. Accepts simultaneous submissions. Responds in 2 months to queries. Responds in 3 months to mss. Sample copy for $6. Guidelines available online.

NONFICTION Needs essays, general interest, how-to, humor, interview, personal experience, photo feature. "No articles that come from writers who are not familiar with our target geographical location." **Buys 30 mss/year.** Query with or without published clips. Length: 1,000-1,500 words. **Pays $100-200.** Pays expenses of writers on assignment.

PHOTOS State availability. Identification of subjects, model releases required. Reviews transparencies. Negotiates payment individually. Buys one-time rights.

COLUMNS Profile-People from Lake Country, 800 words; Essay, 800 words; Health (topics pertinent to central Minnesota living), 500 words. **Buys 40 mss/year.** Query with published clips. **Pays $50-75.**

FICTION Needs adventure, humorous, mainstream. **Buys 6 mss/year.** Length: 1,500 words. **Pays $100-200.**

POETRY Needs free verse. "Never use rhyming verse, avant-garde, experimental, etc." Buys 6 poems/year. Submit maximum 4 poems. Length: 8-32 lines. **Pays $25.**

FILLERS Needs anecdotes, short humor. **Buys 20 mss/year.** Length: 100-300 words. **Pays $25/filler.**

TIPS "Most of the people who will read your articles live in the north central Minnesota lakes area. All have some significant attachment to the area. We have readers of various ages, backgrounds, and lifestyles. After reading your article, we hope to have a deeper understanding of some aspect of our community, our environment, ourselves, or humanity in general."

💲💲 LAKE SUPERIOR MAGAZINE

Lake Superior Port Cities, Inc., P.O. Box 16417, Duluth MN 55816-0417. (218)722-5002. **Fax:** (218)722-4096. **E-mail:** edit@lakesuperior.com. **Website:** www.lake-superior.com. **Contact:** Konnie LeMay, editor. **40% freelance written. Works with a small number of new/unpublished writers each year. Please include phone number and address with e-mail queries.** Bimonthly magazine covering contemporary and historic people, places, and current events around Lake Superior. We are a family-owned business sustained with book and magazine publications as well as a Lake Superior Collection of retail items. Estab. 1979. Circ. 20,000. Byline given. Pays on publication. No kill fee. Publishes ms an average of 10 months after acceptance. Submit seasonal material 1 year in advance. Accepts queries by mail, e-mail. Accepts simultaneous submissions. Responds in 3 months to queries. Sample copy: $4.95 plus 6 first-class stamps. Guidelines online.

NONFICTION Needs book excerpts, essays, general interest, historical, how-to, humor, interview, memoir, nostalgic, personal experience, photo feature, profile, travel, city profiles, regional business, some investigative. **Buys 15 mss/year.** Prefers emailed queries or mss, but accepts mail submissions. Length: 1,600-2,000 words for features. **Pays $200-400.** Pays expenses of writers on assignment. Any expenses must be agreed upon before a story is assigned.

PHOTOS "Quality photography is our hallmark." Send photos. Captions, identification of subjects, model releases required. Reviews electronically only. Offers $50/image; $150 for covers.

COLUMNS Shorter articles on specific topics of interest: Homes, Health & Wellness, Lake Superior Journal, Wild Superior, Heritage, Destinations, Profile, all 800-1,200 words. **Buys 20 mss/year.** Query with published clips. **Pays $75-250.**

FICTION Must be targeted regionally. Needs historical, humorous, mainstream, novel excerpts. Wants stories that are Lake Superior related. Rarely uses fiction stories. **Buys 2-3 mss/year.** Query with published clips. Length: 300-2,500 words. **Pays $50-125.**

TIPS "Well-researched queries are attended to. We actively seek queries from writers in Lake Superior communities. We prefer queries. Provide enough information on why the subject is important to the region and our readers, or why and how something is unique. We want details. The writer must have a thorough knowledge of the subject and how it relates to our region. We prefer a fresh, unused approach to the subject that provides the reader with an emotional involvement. Almost all of our articles feature quality photography in color or b&w. It is a prerequisite of all nonfiction. All submissions should include a *short* biography of author/photographer; mug shot sometimes used. Blanket submissions need not apply."

💲💲💲 MPLS. ST. PAUL MAGAZINE

MSP Communications, 220 S. Sixth St., Suite 500, Minneapolis MN 55402. **E-mail:** edit@mspmag.com. **Website:** www.mspmag.com. **Contact:** Kelly Ryan Kegans, executive editor. Monthly magazine covering the Minneapolis-St. Paul area. *Mpls. St. Paul Magazine* is a city magazine serving upscale readers in the Minneapolis-St. Paul metro area. Circ. 80,000. Pays on publication. Editorial lead time 3 months. Accepts queries by mail, e-mail. Accepts simultaneous submissions. Sample copy: $10.

NONFICTION Needs book excerpts, essays, general interest, historical, interview, personal experience, photo feature, travel. **Buys 150 mss/year.** Query with published clips. Length: 500-4,000 words. **Pays 50-75¢/word for assigned articles.** Pays expenses of writers on assignment.

MISSISSIPPI

💲💲 MISSISSIPPI MAGAZINE

Downhome Publications, 5 Lakeland Circle, Jackson MS 39216. (601)982-8418. **Fax:** (601)982-8447. **E-mail:** editor@mismag.com. **Website:** www.mississippimagazine.com. **Contact:** Melanie M. Ward, editor. **90% freelance written.** Bimonthly magazine covering Mississippi—the state and its lifestyles. "We are interested in positive stories reflecting Mississippi's rich traditions and heritage and focusing on the contributions the state and its natives have made to the arts, literature, and culture. In each issue we showcase homes and gardens, in-state travel, food, design, art, and more." Estab. 1982. Circ. 40,000. Byline given. Pays on publication. Offers 25% kill fee. Publishes ms an average of 6 months after acceptance. Editorial lead time 6 months. Submit seasonal material 1 year in advance. Accepts queries by mail, fax. Responds in 2 months to queries. Guidelines for #10 SASE or online.

NONFICTION Needs general interest, historical, how-to, interview, personal experience, travel. No opinion, political, sports, expose. **Buys 15 mss/year.** Query. Length: 100-1,200 words. **Pays $25-350.**

PHOTOS Send photos with query. Captions, identification of subjects, model releases required. Reviews transparencies, prints, digital images on CD. Negotiates payment individually. Buys one time rights.

COLUMNS Southern Scrapbook (see recent issues for example), 100-600 words; Gardening (short informative article on a specific plant or gardening technique), 800-1,200 words; Culture Center (story about an event or person relating to Mississippi's art, music, theatre, or literature), 800-1,200 words; On Being Southern (personal essay about life in Mississippi; only ms submissions accepted), 750 words. **Buys 6 mss/year.** Query. **Pays $25-250.**

MISSOURI

$$ 417 MAGAZINE

Whitaker Publishing, 2111 S. Eastgate Ave., Springfield MO 65809. (417)883-7417. **Fax:** (417)889-7417. **E-mail:** editor@417mag.com. **Website:** www.417mag.com. **Contact:** Katie Pollock Estes, editor. **50% freelance written.** Monthly magazine. *"417 Magazine* is a regional title serving southwest Missouri. Our editorial mix includes service journalism and lifestyle content on home, fashion and the arts; as well as narrative and issues pieces. The audience is affluent, educated, mostly female." Estab. 1998. Circ. 20,000. Byline given. Pays on acceptance. Publishes ms an average of 2-3 months after acceptance. Editorial lead time 6 months. Accepts queries by e-mail. Accepts simultaneous submissions. Responds in 1-2 months to queries. Sample copy by e-mail. Guidelines online.

NONFICTION Needs essays, expose, general interest, how-to, humor, inspirational, interview, new product, personal experience, photo feature, travel, local book reviews. "We are a local magazine, so anything not reflecting our local focus is something we have to pass on." **Buys 175 mss/year.** Query with published clips. Length: 300-3,500 words. **Pays $30-500, sometimes more.** Pays expenses of writers on assignment.

TIPS "Read the magazine before contacting us. Send specific ideas with your queries. Submit story ideas of local interest. Send published clips. Be a curious reporter, and ask probing questions."

$ RIVER HILLS TRAVELER

Traveler Publishing Co., P.O. Box 245, St. Clair MO 63077-0245. (800)874-8423. **Fax:** (800)874-8423. **E-mail:** stories@rhtrav.com. **Website:** www.riverhilltraveler.com. **Contact:** Emery Styron, editor. **80% freelance written.** Monthly tabloid covering outdoor sports and nature in the southeast quarter of Missouri, the east and central Ozarks. Topics like those in *Field & Stream* and *National Geographic*. Estab. 1973. Circ. 5,000. Byline given. Pays on publication. No kill fee. Publishes ms an average of 2 months after acceptance. Editorial lead time 2 months. Submit seasonal material 1 year in advance. Accepts queries by e-mail. Accepts simultaneous submissions. Responds in 2 months to queries. Sample copy for SAE or online. Guidelines available online.

NONFICTION Needs historical, how-to, humor, opinion, personal experience, photo feature, technical, travel. No stories about other geographic areas. **Buys 80 mss/year.** Query with writing samples. Length: 1,500 word maximum. **Pays $15-50.**

REPRINTS E-mail ms with rights for sale noted and information about when and where the material previously appeared.

PHOTOS Send photos. Reviews JPEG/TIFF files. Negotiates payment individually. Pays $35 for covers. Buys one-time rights.

TIPS "We are a 'poor man's' *Field & Stream* and *National Geographic*—about the eastern Missouri Ozarks. We prefer stories that relate an adventure that causes a reader to relive an adventure of his own or consider embarking on a similar adventure. Think of an adventure in camping or cooking, not just fishing and hunting. How-to is great, but not simple instructions. We encourage good first-person reporting. We like to get stories as part of an e-mail, not an attached document."

MONTANA

$$ MONTANA MAGAZINE

Lee Enterprises, P.O. Box 8689, Missoula MT 59807. **E-mail:** editor@montanamagazine.com. **Website:** www.montanamagazine.com. **90% freelance written.** Strictly Montana-oriented magazine, published bimonthly, that features community profiles, contemporary issues, wildlife and natural history, and travel pieces. Estab. 1970. Circ. 20,000. Byline given. Pays on publication. No kill fee. Publishes ms an average of 1 year after acceptance. Submit seasonal material 1 year in advance. Accepts queries by e-mail. Accepts simultaneous submissions. Responds in 6 months to queries. Sample copy for $5 or online. Guidelines available online.

NONFICTION Needs essays, general interest, interview, photo feature, travel. Special issues: Special features on summer and winter destination points. No "me and Joe" hiking and hunting tales; no blood-and-guts hunting stories; no poetry; no fiction; no sentimental essays. **Buys 30 mss/year.** Query with samples and SASE. Length: 1,000-1,500 words. **Pays negotiable rate.** Pays expenses of writers on assignment.

REPRINTS Send photocopy of article with rights for sale and information about when and where the material previously appeared. Pays 50% of amount paid for an original article.

PHOTOS Send photos. Captions, identification of subjects, model releases required. Photos must be sent digitally in high-res format with cutline information included in file information. Offers additional payment for photos accepted with ms. Buys one-time rights.

COLUMNS Memories (reminisces of early-day Montana life), 800-1,000 words; Outdoor Recreation, 1,500-2,000 words; Community Festivals, 500 words, plus b&w or color photo; Montana-Specific Humor, 800-1,000 words. Query with samples.

TIPS "We avoid commonly known topics so Montanans won't ho-hum through more of what they already know. If it's time to revisit a topic, we look for a unique slant."

NEVADA

💲💲 NEVADA MAGAZINE

401 N. Carson St., Carson City NV 89701. (775)687-0602. **Fax:** (775)687-6159. **E-mail:** editor@nevadamagazine.com. **Website:** www.nevadamagazine.com. **25% freelance written. Works with a small number of new/unpublished writers each year.** Bimonthly magazine published by the state of Nevada to promote tourism. Estab. 1936. Circ. 20,000. Byline given. Pays on publication. No kill fee. Publishes ms an average of 6 months after acceptance. Submit seasonal material 6 months in advance. Accepts simultaneous submissions. Responds in 1 month to queries. Sample copy available by request. Guidelines available online.

NONFICTION Prefers a well-written query or outline with specific story elements before receiving the actual story. Write, e-mail, or call if you have a story that might work. Length: 500-1,500 words. **Pays flat rate of $250 or less. For web stories, pays $100 or $200 depending on the assignment.** Pays expenses of writers on assignment.

PHOTOS Contact: Query art director Sean Nebeker (snebeker@nevadamagazine.com). Reviews digital images. Pays $25-250; cover, $250. Buys one-time rights.

COLUMNS Columns include: Up Front (the latest Nevada news), Visions (emphasizes outstanding photography with extended captions), City Limits (features destination stories for Nevada's larger cities), Wide Open (features destination stories for Ne-

vada's rural towns and regions), Cravings (stories centered on food and drink), Travels (people traveling Nevada, sharing their adventures), History, and Events & Shows.

TIPS "Keep in mind the magazine's purpose is to promote Nevada tourism."

NEW HAMPSHIRE

💲💲 NEW HAMPSHIRE MAGAZINE

McLean Communications, Inc., 150 Dow St., Manchester NH 03101. (603)624-1442. **E-mail:** editor@nhmagazine.com. **Website:** www.nhmagazine.com. **Contact:** Rick Broussard, editor. **50% freelance written.** Monthly magazine devoted to New Hampshire. "We want stories written for, by, and about the people of New Hampshire with emphasis on qualities that set us apart from other states. We feature lifestyle, adventure, and home-related stories with a unique local angle." Estab. 1986. Circ. 32,000. Byline given. Pays on publication. Offers 40% kill fee. Editorial lead time 3 months. Submit seasonal material 1 year in advance. Accepts queries by mail, e-mail, fax. Accepts simultaneous submissions. Responds in 2 months to queries. Responds in 3 months to mss. Guidelines available online.

NONFICTION Needs essays, general interest, historical, photo feature, business. **Buys 30 mss/year.** Send ms or query via e-mail. Length: 300-2,000 words. **Payment varies.** Pays expenses of writers on assignment.

PHOTOS State availability. Captions, identification of subjects, model releases required. Possible additional payment for photos accepted with ms. Rights purchased vary.

FILLERS Length: 200-400 words.

NEW JERSEY

💲💲💲💲 NEW JERSEY MONTHLY

55 Park Place, P.O. Box 920, Morristown NJ 07963-0920. (973)539-8230. **Fax:** (973)538-2953. **E-mail:** kschlager@njmonthly.com. **Website:** www.njmonthly.com. **Contact:** Ken Schlager, editor. **75-80% freelance written.** Monthly magazine covering just about anything to do with New Jersey, from news, politics, and sports to decorating trends and lifestyle issues. Our readership is well-educated, affluent, and on aver-

age our readers have lived in New Jersey 20 years or more. Estab. 1976. Circ. 92,000. Byline given. Pays on completion of fact-checking. Offers 20% kill fee. Publishes ms an average of 3 months after acceptance. Editorial lead time 3 months. Submit seasonal material 6 months in advance. Accepts queries by mail, e-mail, fax, phone. Accepts simultaneous submissions. Responds in 2-3 months to queries. Guidelines available online.

NONFICTION Needs book excerpts, essays, expose, general interest, historical, humor, interview, personal experience, photo feature, travel, arts, sports, politics. No experience pieces from people who used to live in New Jersey or general pieces that have no New Jersey angle. **Buys 90-100 mss/year.** Query with published magazine clips via e-mail. Length: 250-3,000 words. **Payment varies.** Pays expenses of writers on assignment. Pays reasonable expenses of writers on assignment with prior approval.

PHOTOS Contact: Donna Panagakos, art director. State availability. Identification of subjects, model releases required. Reviews transparencies, prints. Payment negotiated. Buys one time rights.

COLUMNS Exit Ramp (back page essay usually originating from personal experience but written in a way that tells a broader story of statewide interest), 500 words; front-of-the-book Garden Variety (brief profiles or articles on local life, 250-350 words; restaurant reviews. **Buys 12 mss/year.** Query with published clips. **Payment varies.**

FILLERS Needs anecdotes, for front-of-book. **Buys 12-15 mss/year.** Length: 200-250 words. **Payment varies.**

TIPS "The best approach: Do your homework! Read the past year's issues to get an understanding of our well-written, well-researched articles that tell a tale from a well-established point of view."

⊛⊛ THE SANDPAPER

The SandPaper, Inc., 1816 Long Beach Blvd., Surf City NJ 08008. (609)494-5900. **Fax:** (609)494-1437. **E-mail:** jaymann@thesandpaper.net; letters@thesandpaper.net; photo@thesandpaper.net. **Website:** www.thesandpaper.net. **Contact:** Jay Mann, managing editor; Gail Travers, executive editor; Ryan Morrill, photography editor. Weekly tabloid covering subjects of interest to Long Island Beach area residents and visitors. Each issue includes a mix of news, human interest features, opinion columns, and entertainment/calendar

listings. Estab. 1976. Circ. 30,000. Byline given. Pays on publication. Offers 100% kill fee. Publishes ms an average of 1 month after acceptance. Submit seasonal material 3 months in advance. Accepts queries by mail, e-mail, fax, phone. Accepts simultaneous submissions. Responds in 1 month to queries.

NONFICTION Pays expenses of writers on assignment.

COLUMNS Speakeasy (opinion and slice-of-life, often humorous); Commentary (forum for social science perspectives); both 1,000-1,500 words, preferably with local or Jersey Shore angle. **Buys 50 mss/year.** Send complete ms. **Pays $40.**

NEW MEXICO

ALBUQUERQUE THE MAGAZINE

1550 Mercantile Ave. NE, Top Floor, Albuquerque NM 87107. (505)842-1110. **Fax:** (505)842-1119. **E-mail:** matt@abqthemag.com. **E-mail:** larryl@abqthemag.com. **Website:** abqthemag.com. **Contact:** Larryl Lynch. **20.** "We love our sorbet-colored sunsets. We love that an inch of snow is reason to stay home for the day. We love seeing roadrunners and wily coyotes on a regular basis. We love that you can even get green chile in your ice cream." *Albuquerque The Magazine* celebrates the quality of life and living in Albuquerque with outstanding words and photographs, all designed to showcase our most interesting people and places. "We love it here." Estab. 2004. Circ. 85,000. Byline given. Pays on publication. Editorial lead time 3 months. Accepts queries by e-mail. Accepts simultaneous submissions. "We welcome ideas from new writers. We prefer that you present your story proposal in a query letter rather than sending us a completed ms or describing your idea over the phone. If you are sending us a query for the first time, please include 3 examples of recent samples of your work (preferably published) and a letter detailing some of your pertinent writing experience. Read our magazine and get a feel for our departments, voice and style; show us why your topic would be the perfect fit for a particular section in the magazine. We're always interested in profiling the people of Albuquerque, and devote half a dozen sections to doing so–but each section is different, so it's important to craft a pitch that shows why your profile subject would fit one section better than another."

NONFICTION Needs interview, personal experience, profile. Anything news-related as we are a 100-percent positive publication about the people, places, businesses, events, and more in the Albuquerque metro area. Length: 600–900 words. **Pays upon publication.** Pays expenses of writers on assignment. Does not pay expenses.

PHOTOS Don James, photo director, don@abqthemag.com. Payment varies based on usage. Buys variable rights based on usage.

💲💲 NEW MEXICO MAGAZINE

Lew Wallace Bldg., 495 Old Santa Fe Trail, Santa Fe NM 87501-2750. (505)827-7447. **E-mail:** artdirector@nmmagazine.com. **Website:** www.nmmagazine.com. **70% freelance written.** Covers areas throughout the state. "We want to publish a lively editorial mix, covering both the down-home (like a diner in Tucumcari) and the upscale (a new bistro in world-class Santa Fe)." Explore the gamut of the Old West and the New Age. "Our magazine is about the power of place—in particular more than 120,000 square miles of mountains, desert, grasslands, and forest inhabited by a culturally rich mix of individuals. It is an enterprise of the New Mexico Tourism Department, which strives to make potential visitors aware of our state's multicultural heritage, climate, environment, and uniqueness." Estab. 1923. Circ. 100,000. Pays on acceptance. 20% kill fee. Publishes ms an average of 3 months after acceptance. Submit seasonal material 1 year in advance. Accepts queries by mail. Accepts simultaneous submissions. Responds to queries if interested. Sample copy for $5. Guidelines available online.

NONFICTION Submit story idea along with a working head and subhead and a paragraph synopsis. Include published clips and a short sum-up about your strengths as a writer. Considers proposal as well as writer's potential to write the conceptualized stories. Pays expenses of writers on assignment.

REPRINTS Rarely publishes reprints, but sometimes publishes excerpts from novels and nonfiction books.

PHOTOS "Purchased as portfolio or on assignment. Photographers interested in photo assignments should reference submission guidelines on the contributors' page of our website."

NEW YORK

💲💲 ADIRONDACK LIFE

P.O. Box 410, Rt. 9N, Jay NY 12941-0410. (518)946-2191. **Fax:** (518)946-7461. **E-mail:** astoltie@adirondacklife.com; khofschneider@adirondacklife.com. **Website:** adirondacklifemag.com. **Contact:** Annie Stoltie, editor; Kelly Hofschneider, photo editor. **70% freelance written. Prefers to work with published/established writers.** Magazine, published bimonthly, that emphasizes the Adirondack region and the North Country of New York State in articles covering outdoor activities, history, and natural history directly related to the Adirondacks. Estab. 1970. Circ. 50,000. Byline given. Pays 30 days after publication. No kill fee. Publishes ms an average of 10 months after acceptance. Submit seasonal material 1 year in advance. Accepts queries by mail, e-mail. Accepts simultaneous submissions. Responds in 1 month to queries. Sample copy for $3 and 9x12 SAE. Guidelines available online.

NONFICTION Special issues: Special issues: Annual Guide to the Great Outdoors (how-to and where-to articles that offer in-depth information about recreational offerings in the park); At Home in the Adirondacks (focuses on the region's signature style). Does not want poetry, fiction, or editorial cartoons. **Buys 20-25 unsolicited mss/year.** Query with published clips. Accepts queries, but not unsolicited mss, via e-mail. Length: 1,500-3,000 words. **Pays 30¢/word.** Pays expenses of writers on assignment.

PHOTOS "All photos must have been taken in the Adirondacks. Each issue contains a photo feature. Purchased with or without ms on assignment. All photos must be individually identified as to the subject or locale and must bear the photographer's name." Send photos. Reviews hi-res (300 dpi) TIFF/JPEG/PSD files via e-mail, or raw files on CD. Pays $150 for full page, b&w, or color; $400 for cover (color only, vertical in format). Credit line given.

COLUMNS Short Carries; Northern Lights; Special Places (unique spots in the Adirondack Park); Skills; Working (careers in the Adirondacks); The Scene; Back Page. Length: 1,000-1,800 words. Query with published clips. **Pays 30¢/word.**

FICTION Considers first-serial novel excerpts in its subject matter and region.

TIPS "Do not send a personal essay about your meaningful moment in the mountains. We need factual pieces about regional history, sports, culture, and business. We are looking for clear, concise, well-organized mss that are strictly Adirondack in subject. Check back issues to be sure we haven't already covered your topic. Check out our guidelines online."

💲💲 BUFFALO SPREE MAGAZINE

Buffalo Spree Publishing, Inc., 100 Corporate Pkwy., Suite 200, Buffalo NY 14226. (716)783-9119. **Fax:** (716)783-9983. **E-mail:** elicata@buffalospree.com. **Website:** www.buffalospree.com. **Contact:** Elizabeth Licata, editor. **90% freelance written.** City regional magazine published 12 times/year. Estab. 1967. Circ. 25,000. Byline given. Pays on publication. No kill fee. Publishes ms an average of 2 months after acceptance. Accepts queries by e-mail. Responds in 6 months to queries. Sample copy for $4.95 and 9x12 SAE with 12 first-class stamps.

NONFICTION Needs interview, travel, issue-oriented features, arts, living, food, regional. Query with resume and published clips. Length: 1,000-2,000 words. **Pays $125-250.**

TIPS "Send a well-written, compelling query or an interesting topic, and *great* clips. We no longer regularly publish fiction or poetry. Prefers material that is Western New York related."

💲💲💲 CITY LIMITS

Community Service Society of New York, 31 E. 32nd St., 3rd Floor, New York NY 10016. (212)481-8484, ext. 313. **E-mail:** editor@citylimits.org. **Website:** www.citylimits.org. **Contact:** Jarrett Murphy, executive editor and publisher. **50% freelance written.** Monthly magazine covering urban politics and policy in New York City. *City Limits* is a nonprofit online magazine focusing on issues facing New York City and its neighborhoods, particularly low-income communities. The magazine is strongly committed to investigative journalism, in-depth policy analysis, hard-hitting profiles, and investigation of pressing civic issues in New York City. Driven by a mission to inform public discourse, the magazine provides the factual reporting, human faces, data, history, and breadth of knowledge necessary to understanding the nuances, complexities, and hard truths of the city, its politics, and its people. Estab. 1976. Byline given. Pays on publication. Offers 50% kill fee. Publishes ms an average of 3 months after acceptance. Editorial lead time 2 months. Accepts queries by mail, e-mail, fax. Accepts simultaneous submissions. Responds in 1 month. Sample copy for $2.95. Guidelines free.

NONFICTION Needs book excerpts, humor, interview, opinion, photo feature. No essays, polemics. **Buys 25 mss/year.** Query with published clips. Length: 400-3,500 words. **Pays $150-2,000 for assigned articles. Pays $100-800 for unsolicited articles.** Pays expenses of writers on assignment.

PHOTOS State availability. Model release required for children. Reviews contact sheets, negatives, transparencies. Buys 20 photos from freelancers/issue; 200 photos/year. Pays $100 for color cover; $50-100 for b&w inside. Pays on publication. Credit line given. Buys rights for use in *City Limits* in print and online; higher rate given for online use.

COLUMNS Making Change (nonprofit business), Big Idea (policy news), Book Review—all 800 words; Urban Legend (profile), First Hand (Q&A)—both 350 words. **Buys 15 mss/year.** Query with published clips.

TIPS "Our specialty is covering low-income communities. We want to report untold stories about news affecting neighborhoods at the grassroots. We're looking for stories about housing, health care, criminal justice, child welfare, education, economic development, welfare reform, politics, and government. We need good photojournalists who can capture the emotion of a scene. We offer huge pay for great photos."

💲💲💲💲 NEW YORK MAGAZINE

New York Media, Editorial Submissions, 75 Varick St., New York NY 10013. **E-mail:** comments@nymag.com. **E-mail:** editorialsubmissions@nymag.com. **Website:** nymag.com. **25% freelance written.** Weekly magazine focusing on current events in the New York metropolitan area. Circ. 405,149. Pays on acceptance. Offers 25% kill fee. Submit seasonal material 2 months in advance. Accepts queries by e-mail. Accepts simultaneous submissions. Responds in 1 month to queries. Guidelines online.

NONFICTION Query by e-mail or mail. **Pays $1/word.** Pays expenses of writers on assignment.

💲💲💲 WESTCHESTER MAGAZINE

Today Media, 2 Clinton Ave., Rye NY 10580. (914)345-0601. **Website:** www.westchestermagazine.com. **35% freelance written.** Monthly magazine covering culture and lifestyle of Westchester County, New York.

Westchester Magazine is an upscale, high-end regional lifestyle publication covering issues specific to Westchester County, New York. All stories must have a local slant. Estab. 2001. Circ. 65,475. Byline given. Pays on publication. Offers 25% kill fee. Publishes ms an average of 3 months after acceptance. Editorial lead time 3 months. Submit seasonal material 3 months in advance. Accepts queries by mail. Sample copy available online.

NONFICTION Needs expose, general interest, interview, local service. Does not want personal essays, reviews, stories not specific to Westchester. **Buys 36 mss/year.** Query with published clips. Length: 150-5,000 words. **Pays $50-1,000.** Pays expenses of writers on assignment.

PHOTOS **Contact:** Contact Aiko Masazumi, creative director. State availability. Captions, identification of subjects required. Reviews GIF/JPEG files. Negotiates payment individually. Negotiates rights individually.

COLUMNS Our Neighbor (profile of a local celebrity), 500 words; Westchester Chronicles (short items of local interest), 300 words; County Golf (articles about the local golf scene), 500 words. **Buys 36 mss/year.** Query with published clips. **Pays $30-200.**

TIPS "Be sure to query ideas applicable *only* to Westchester County that we have not written about before."

NORTH CAROLINA

$$ CARY MAGAZINE

Cherokee Media Group, 301 Cascade Pointe Lane, Cary NC 27513. (919)674-6020. **Fax:** (919)674-6027. **E-mail:** editor@carymagazine.com. **Website:** www.carymagazine.com. **Contact:** Nancy Pardue and Amber Keister, editors. **40% freelance written.** "Lifestyle publication for the affluent communities of Cary, Apex, Morrisville, Holly Springs, and Fuquay-Varina. Our editorial objective is to entertain, enlighten, and inform our readers with unique and engaging editorial and vivid photography." Publishes 8 times/year. Estab. 2004. Circ. 18,000. Byline given. Kill fee negotiated. Editorial lead time 3 months. Submit seasonal material 3 months in advance. Accepts queries by mail, e-mail. Accepts simultaneous submissions. Responds in 2-4 weeks to queries; in 1 month to mss. Sample copy: $4.95. Guidelines free.

NONFICTION Needs historical, inspirational, interview, personal experience. Don't submit articles with no local connection. **Buys 2 mss/year.** Query with published clips.

PHOTOS Freelancers should state the availability of photos with their submission or send the photos with their submission. Identification of subjects required. Reviews GIF/JPEG files. Negotiates payment individually. Buys one-time rights.

TIPS "We prefer experienced feature writers with exceptional interviewing skills who can take a fresh perspective on a topic, write with a unique flare and a good hook to engage the reader and evoke emotion, adhere to AP Style and follows basic journalism conventions, and take deadlines seriously. E-mail inquiries preferred."

$$ CHARLOTTE MAGAZINE

Morris Visitor Publications, 214 W. Tremont Ave., Suite 303, Charlotte NC 28203. (704)335-7181. **Fax:** (704)335-3757. **E-mail:** michael.graff@charlottemagazine.com. **Website:** www.charlottemagazine.com. **Contact:** Michael Graff, publisher. **75% freelance written.** Monthly magazine covering Charlotte life. This magazine tells its readers things they didn't know about Charlotte in an interesting, entertaining, and sometimes provocative style. Circ. 40,000. Byline given. Pays within 30 days of acceptance. Offers 25% kill fee. Publishes ms an average of 3 months after acceptance. Editorial lead time 3 months. Submit seasonal material 6 months in advance. Accepts queries by mail, e-mail. Accepts simultaneous submissions. Responds in 6 months to mss. Sample copy for $6.

NONFICTION Needs book excerpts, expose, general interest, interview, photo feature, travel. **Buys 35-50 mss/year.** Query with published clips. Length: 200-3,000 words. **Pays 20-40¢/word.** Pays expenses of writers on assignment.

PHOTOS State availability. Identification of subjects required. Negotiates payment individually. Buys one-time rights.

COLUMNS **Buys 35-50 mss/year. Pays 20-40¢/word**

TIPS "A story for *Charlotte* magazine could only appear in *Charlotte* magazine. That is, the story and its treatment are particularly germane to this area. Because of this, we rarely work with writers who live outside the Charlotte area."

💲💲 FIFTEEN 501

Weiss and Hughes Publishing, 189 Wind Chime Court, Suite 104, Raleigh NC 27615. (919)870-1722. **Fax:** (919)719-5260. **E-mail:** djackson@whmags.com. **Website:** www.fifteen501.com. **Contact:** Danielle Jackson, editor. **50% freelance written.** Quarterly magazine covering lifestyle issues relevant to residents in the U.S. 15/501 corridor of Durham, Orange, and Chatham counties in North Carolina. "We cover issues important to residents of Durham, Orange and Chatham counties. We're committed to improving our readers' overall quality of life and keeping them informed of the lifestyle amenities there." Estab. 2006. Circ. 30,000. Byline given. Pays within 30 days of publication. Offers 25% kill fee. Publishes ms an average of 2 months after acceptance. Editorial lead time 2-3 months. Submit seasonal material 6 months in advance. Accepts queries by mail, e-mail. Accepts simultaneous submissions. Responds in 2-4 weeks to queries. Sample copy available online. Guidelines by e-mail.

NONFICTION Needs general interest, historical, how-to, inspirational, interview, personal experience, photo feature, technical, travel. Does not want opinion pieces or political or religious topics. Query. Length: 600-1,200 words. **Pays 35¢/word.** Pays expenses of writers on assignment.

PHOTOS State availability. Captions, identification of subjects required. Reviews transparencies, GIF/JPEG files. Offers no additional payment for photos accepted with ms. Rights are negotiable.

COLUMNS Around Town (local lifestyle topics), 1,000 words; Hometown Stories, 600 words; Travel (around North Carolina), 1,000 words; Home Interiors/Landscaping (varies), 1,000 words; Restaurants (local, fine dining), 600-1,000 words. **Buys 20-25 mss/year.** Query. **Pays 35¢/word.**

TIPS "All queries must be focused on the issues that make Durham, Chapel Hill, Carrboro, Hillsborough, and Pittsboro unique and wonderful places to live."

💲💲 WAKE LIVING

Weiss and Hughes Publishing, 189 Wind Chime Ct., Suite 104, Raleigh NC 27615. (919)870-1722. **Fax:** (919)719-5260. **Website:** www.wakeliving.com. **Contact:** Janet Ladenburger, editor. **50% freelance written.** Quarterly magazine covering lifestyle issues in Wake County, North Carolina. "We cover issues important to residents of Wake County. We are com-mitted to improving our readers' overall quality of life and keeping them informed of the lifestyle amenities here." Estab. 2003. Circ. 40,000. Byline given. Pays within 30 days of publication. Offers 25% kill fee. Publishes ms an average of 2 months after acceptance. Editorial lead time 2-3 months. Submit seasonal material 6 months in advance. Accepts queries by mail, e-mail. Accepts simultaneous submissions. Responds in 2-4 weeks to queries.

NONFICTION Needs general interest, historical, how-to, inspirational, interview, personal experience, photo feature, technical, travel. Does not want opinion pieces, political topics, religious articles. Query. Length: 600-1,200 words. **Pays 35¢/word. Pay is per article and varies by complexity of assignment.** Pays expenses of writers on assignment.

PHOTOS State availability. Captions, identification of subjects required. Reviews transparencies, GIF/JPEG files. Offers no additional payment for photos accepted with ms.

COLUMNS Around Town (local lifestyle topics); Hometown Stories, 600 words; Travel (around North Carolina); Home Interiors/Landscaping, all 1,000 words. Restaurants (local restaurants, fine dining), 600-1,000 words. **Buys 20-25 mss/year.** Query. **Pays 35¢/word. Pay is per article and varies by complexity of assignment.**

TIPS "Articles must be specifically focused on Wake County/Raleigh metro issues. We like unusual angles about what makes living here unique from other areas."

NORTH DAKOTA

💲💲 NORTH DAKOTA LIVING MAGAZINE

North Dakota Association of Rural Electric Cooperatives, 3201 Nygren Dr. NW, P.O. Box 727, Mandan ND 58554. (701)663-6501. **Fax:** (701)663-3745. **Website:** www.ndliving.com. **20% freelance written.** Monthly magazine covering information of interest to memberships of electric cooperatives and telephone cooperatives. "We publish a general-interest magazine for North Dakotans. We treat subjects pertaining to living and working in the northern Great Plains. We provide progress reporting on electric cooperatives and telephone cooperatives." Estab. 1954. Circ. 70,000. Byline given. Pays on acceptance. No kill fee. Publishes ms an average of 6 months after acceptance. Editorial lead time 6 months. Submit seasonal material 6 months in advance. Accepts queries by mail, e-mail. Accepts simultaneous submissions.

NONFICTION Needs general interest, historical, how-to, humor, interview, new product, travel. **Buys 20 mss/year.** Query with published clips. Length: 1,500-2,000 words. **Pays $100-500 minimum for assigned articles. Pays $300-600 for unsolicited articles.** Pays expenses of writers on assignment.

PHOTOS State availability. Identification of subjects required. Reviews contact sheets. Negotiates payment individually. Buys one-time rights.

COLUMNS Energy Use and Financial Planning, both 750 words. **Buys 6 mss/year.** Query with published clips. **Pays $100-300.**

FICTION Needs historical, humorous, slice-of-life vignettes, western. **Buys 1 mss/year.** Query with published clips. Length: 1,000-2,500 words. **Pays $100-400.**

TIPS "Deal with what's real: real data, real people, real experiences, real history, etc."

OHIO

💲💲 AKRON LIFE

Baker Media Group, 1653 Merriman Rd., Suite 116, Akron OH 44313. (330)253-0056. **Fax:** (330)253-5868. **E-mail:** editor@bakermediagroup.com. **Website:** www.akronlife.com. **10% freelance written.** Monthly regional magazine covering Summit, Stark, Portage and Medina counties. "*Akron Life* is a monthly lifestyles publication committed to providing information that enhances and enriches the experience of living in or visiting Akron and the surrounding region of Summit, Portage, Medina and Stark counties. Each colorful, thoughtfully designed issue profiles, interesting places, personalities and events in the arts, sports, entertainment, business, politics and social scene. We cover issues important to the Greater Akron area and significant trends affecting the lives of those who live here." Estab. 2002. Circ. 15,000. Byline given. Pays on publication. Offers 50% kill fee. Publishes ms an average of 4-6 months after acceptance. Editorial lead time 2+ months. Submit seasonal material 6 months in advance. Accepts queries by mail, e-mail, fax. Accepts simultaneous submissions. Sample copy free. Guidelines free.

NONFICTION Needs essays, general interest, historical, how-to, humor, interview, photo feature, travel. Query with published clips. Length: 300-2,000 words. **Pays $0.10 max/word.** Pays expenses of writers on assignment.

PHOTOS State availability. Captions, identification of subjects, model releases required. Reviews GIF/JPEG files. Negotiates payment individually. Buys all rights.

TIPS "It's best to submit a detailed query along with samples of previously published works. Include why you think the story is of interest to our readers, and be sure to have a fresh approach."

💲💲💲 CINCINNATI MAGAZINE

Emmis Publishing Corp., 441 Vine St., Suite 200, Cincinnati OH 45202-2039. (513)421-4300. **E-mail:** jwilliams@cincinnatimagazine.com. **Website:** www.cincinnatimagazine.com. **Contact:** Jay Stowe, editor in chief; Amanda Boyd Walters, director of editorial operations. Monthly magazine emphasizing Cincinnati living. Circ. 38,000. Byline given. Pays on publication. Offers kill fee only on assigned pieces. Accepts queries by mail, e-mail. Accepts simultaneous submissions. Send SASE for guidelines; view content on magazine website.

NONFICTION **Buys 12 mss/year.** Query. Length: 2,500-3,500 words. **Pays $500-1,000.** Pays expenses of writers on assignment.

COLUMNS Cincinnati media, arts and entertainment, people, politics, sports, business, regional. Length: 1,500-2,000 words. **Buys 10-15 mss/year.** Query. **Pays $300-400.**

TIPS "It's most helpful on us if you query in writing with clips. All articles have a local focus. No generics, please. Also: No movie, book, theater reviews, poetry, or fiction. For special advertising sections, query special sections editor Sue Goldberg; for *Cincinnati Wedding*, query custom publishing editor Kara Renee Hagerman."

💲💲💲 CLEVELAND MAGAZINE

City Magazines, Inc., 1422 Euclid Ave., Suite 730, Cleveland OH 44115. (216)771-2833. **Fax:** (216)781-6318. **E-mail:** gleydura@clevelandmagazine.com; miller@clevelandmagazine.com. **Website:** www.clevelandmagazine.com. **Contact:** Kristen Miller, design director; Steve Gleydura, editor. **60% freelance written. Mostly by assignment.** Monthly magazine with a strong Cleveland/Northeast Ohio angle. Estab. 1972. Circ. 50,000. Byline given. Pays on publication. No kill fee. Publishes ms an average of 3 months after acceptance. Editorial lead time 6 months. Submit seasonal material 8 months in advance. Accepts queries by mail, e-mail, fax. Accepts simultaneous submissions. Responds in 2 months to queries.

NONFICTION Needs general interest, historical, humor, interview, travel, home and garden. Query with published clips. Length: 800-4,000 words. **Pays $250-1,200.** Pays expenses of writers on assignment.

PHOTOS Buys an average of 50 photos from freelancers/issue; 600 photos/year. Model release required for portraits; property release required for individual homes. Photo captions required; include names, date, location, event, phone. Pays on publication. Credit line given. Buys one-time publication, electronic and promotional rights.

COLUMNS Talking Points (opinion or observation-driven essay), approximately 1,000 words. Query with published clips. **Pays $300.**

⊛⊛⊛ COLUMBUS MONTHLY

Dispatch Magazines, 34 S. Third St., Columbus OH 43215. (614)888-4567. **Fax:** (614)848-3838. **E-mail:** kschmidt@columbusmonthly.com; jross@columbusalive.com. **Website:** www.columbusmonthly.com. **Contact:** Kristen Schmitt, editor; John Ross, assistant editor. **40-60% freelance written. Prefers to work with published/established writers.** Monthly magazine emphasizing subjects specifically related to Columbus and Central Ohio. Circ. 35,000. Byline given. Pays on publication. No kill fee. Publishes ms an average of 2 months after acceptance. Responds in 1 month to queries. Sample copy for $6.50.

NONFICTION Buys 2-3 unsolicited mss/year. Query. Length: 250-4,000 words. **Pays $85-900.** Sometimes pays expenses of writers on assignment.

TIPS "It makes sense to start small—something for our City Journal section, perhaps. Stories for that section run between 250-500 words."

⊛⊛⊛ OHIO MAGAZINE

Great Lakes Publishing Co., 1422 Euclid Ave., Suite 730, Cleveland OH 44115. (216)771-2833. **E-mail:** jvickers@ohiomagazine.com. **Website:** www.ohiomagazine.com. **Contact:** Jim Vickers, editor. **50% freelance written.** "*Ohio Magazine* serves energetic and involved Ohioans by providing award-win-

ning stories and pictures of Ohio's most interesting people, arts, entertainment, history, homes, dining, family life, festivals, and regional travel. We capture the beauty, the adventure, and the fun of life in the Buckeye State." Estab. 1978. Circ. 40,000. Byline given. Pays on publication. 20% kill fee. Publishes ms an average of 6 months after acceptance. Submit seasonal material 6 months in advance. Accepts queries by mail, e-mail. Accepts simultaneous submissions. Responds in 3 months to queries; in 3 months to mss. Guidelines online.

NONFICTION Query with résumé and at least 3 published clips. Length: 1,000-3,000 words. **Pays $300-1,200.** Pays expenses of writers on assignment.

REPRINTS Contact Emily Vanuch, advertising coordinator. Pays 50% of amount paid for an original article.

PHOTOS Contact: Lesley Blake, art director (lblake@ohiomagazine.com). Rate negotiable.

COLUMNS Buys 5 unsolicited mss/year. Pays $100-600.

TIPS "Freelancers should send all queries in writing (either by mail or e-mail), not by telephone. Successful queries demonstrate an intimate knowledge of the publication. We are looking to increase our circle of writers who can write about the state in an informative and upbeat style. Strong reporting skills are highly valued."

OKLAHOMA

⊛⊛ INTERMISSION

Langdon Publishing, 110 E. 2nd St., Tulsa OK 74103. **E-mail:** nbizjack@cityoftulsa.org. **Website:** www.tulsapac.com. **Contact:** Nancy Bizjack, editor. **30% freelance written.** Monthly magazine covering events held at the Tulsa Performing Arts Center. "We feature profiles of entertainers appearing at our center, Q&As, stories on the events, and entertainers slated for the Tulsa PAC." Byline given. Pays on publication. Offers 50% kill fee. Publishes ms an average of 1 month after acceptance. Editorial lead time 2 months. Submit seasonal material 2 months in advance. Accepts queries by mail, e-mail. Accepts simultaneous submissions. Responds in 2 weeks to queries. Sample copy available online. Guidelines by e-mail.

NONFICTION Needs general interest, interview. Does not want personal experience articles. **Buys 35**

mss/year. Query with published clips. Length: 600-1,400 words. **Pays $100-200.**

COLUMNS Q&A (personalities and artists tied in to the events at the Tulsa PAC), 1,100 words. **Buys 12 mss/year.** Query with published clips. **Pays $100-150.**

TIPS "Look ahead at our upcoming events, and find an interesting slant on an event. Interview someone who would be of general interest."

OREGON

💲💲 OREGON COAST

P.O. Box 119, Florence OR 97439. (800)348-8401. **E-mail:** oregoncoasteditor@gmail.com. **Website:** www.oregoncoastmagazine.com. Editor: Rosemary Camozzi (oregoncoasteditor@gmail.com). **Contact:** Alicia Spooner. **65% freelance written.** Quarterly magazine covering the Oregon Coast. Celebrating the beautiful and bold Oregon Coast with stories about history, real estate, food, and happenings on the Coast. Editorial content limited to the Oregon Coast, Southwest Washington Coast, and Northern California Coast. Estab. 1982. Circ. 20000. Byline given. Pays after publication. Offers 25% (on assigned stories only, not on stories accepted on spec) kill fee. Publishes ms an average of up to 1 year after acceptance. Submit seasonal material 6 months in advance. Accepts queries by mail, e-mail. Accepts simultaneous submissions. Responds in 3 months to queries. Sample copy for $5.95. Guidelines available on website.

NONFICTION Needs book excerpts, historical, inspirational, memoir, nostalgic, personal experience, photo feature, profile, travel. **Buys 55 mss/year.** Query with published clips. Length: 500-1,500 words. **Pays $75-350, plus 2 contributor copies.**

REPRINTS Send tearsheet or photocopy and information about when and where the material previously appeared. Pays an average of 60% of the amount paid for an original article.

PHOTOS Photo submissions with no ms or stand alone or cover photos. Send photos. Captions, identification of subjects required. High-resolution digital. $100 full page, $400 cover, payment for smaller usage varies. Buys one time rights.

TIPS "Slant article for readers who do not live at the Oregon Coast. At least 1 historical article is used in each issue. Manuscript/photo packages are preferred over manuscripts with no photos. List photo credits

and captions for each photo. Check all facts, proper names, and numbers carefully in photo/manuscript packages. Must pertain to Oregon Coast somehow."

PENNSYLVANIA

💲💲 BERKS COUNTY LIVING

201 Washington St., Suite 525, GoggleWorks Center for the Arts, Reading PA 19601. (610)763-7500. **Fax:** (610)898-1933. **E-mail:** nmurry@berkscountyliving.com. **Website:** www.berkscountyliving.com. **Contact:** Nikki M. Murry, editor in chief. **90% freelance written.** Bimonthly magazine covering topics of interest to people living in Berks County, Pennsylvania. Estab. 2000. Circ. 36,000. Byline given. Pays on publication. Offers 25% kill fee. Publishes ms an average of 4 months after acceptance. Editorial lead time 3 months. Submit seasonal material 4 months in advance. Accepts queries by mail, e-mail. Accepts simultaneous submissions. Responds in 1 week to queries; 1 month to mss.

NONFICTION Needs general interest, historical, how-to, humor, inspirational, interview, new product, photo feature. **Buys 25 mss/year.** Query. Length: 750-2,000 words. **Pays $150-400.** Pays expenses of writers on assignment.

PHOTOS State availability. Captions, identification of subjects, model releases required. Reviews 35mm or greater transparencies, any size prints. Negotiates payment individually. Buys one-time rights.

💲💲 MAIN LINE TODAY

Today Media, Inc., 4645 West Chester Pike, Newtown Square PA 19073. (610)325-4630. **Fax:** (610)325-4636. **E-mail:** hrowland@mainlinetoday.com; tbehan@mainlinetoday.com; ilynch@mainlinetoday.com. **Website:** www.mainlinetoday.com. **Contact:** Hobart Rowland, editor in chief; Tara Behan, senior editor; Ingrid Lynch, art director. **60% freelance written.** Monthly magazine serving Philadelphia's main line and western suburbs. *Main Line Today*'s high-quality print and electronic media provide authoritative, current and entertaining information on local lifestyle trends, while examining the people, issues and institutions that shape life in Philadelphia's western suburbs. Estab. 1996. Circ. 20,000. Byline given. Pays on publication. Offers 25% kill fee. Publishes ms an average of 3 months after acceptance. Editorial lead time 5 months. Submit seasonal material 5 months in advance. Accepts queries by fax. Accepts simultaneous submissions. Responds in 2 weeks to queries. Responds in 1 month to mss. Sample copy free. Guidelines free.

NONFICTION Needs book excerpts, historical, how-to, humor, interview, opinion, photo feature, travel. Special issues: Health & Wellness Guide (September and March). Query with published clips. Length: 400-3,000 words. **Pays $125-650.** Pays expenses of writers on assignment.

PHOTOS State availability. Identification of subjects, model releases required. Reviews GIF/JPEG files. Negotiates payment individually. Buys one time rights.

COLUMNS Profile (local personality); Neighborhood (local people/issues); End of the Line (essay/humor); Living Well (health/wellness), all 1,600 words. **Buys 50 mss/year.** Query with published clips. **Pays $125-350.**

TIPS "*Main Line Today* values good living, social responsibility and community engagement. We treat all subjects with respect, and always strive to be truthful, fair, accurate and insightful. *Main Line Today* is opinionated, smart, stylish and witty, with an emphasis on superior writing, photography and design."

🌐💲 PENNSYLVANIA

Pennsylvania Magazine Co., P.O. Box 755, Camp Hill PA 17001-0755. (717)697-4660. **E-mail:** editor@pa-mag.com. **Website:** www.pa-mag.com. **Contact:** Matt Holliday, editor. **90% freelance written.** Bimonthly magazine covering people, places, events, and history in Pennsylvania. Estab. 1981. Circ. 30,000. Byline given. Pays on acceptance except for articles (by authors unknown to us) sent on speculation, then we pay on publication. Offers 25% kill fee for assigned articles. Publishes ms an average of 9 months after acceptance. Editorial lead time: a year or more. Submit seasonal material at least 9 months in advance. Accepts queries by mail, e-mail. Responds in 4-6 weeks to queries. Sample copy free. Guidelines online.

NONFICTION Needs essays, general interest, historical, photo feature, profile, travel. Nothing on Amish topics, hunting, or skiing. **Buys 75-120 mss/year.** Query. Length: 750-2,500 words. **Pays 15-20¢/word. Sometimes more for exceptional work.**

REPRINTS For reprints, send photocopy with rights for sale noted and information about when and where the material previously appeared. Pays 10¢/word.

PHOTOS "Contact editor via e-mail for photography instructions. We work primarily with digital images and prefer raw when possible." Photography Essay (highlights annual photo essay contest entries and showcases individual photographers). Captions required. Digital photos (send images and CD or DVD or link to Dropbox folder access). Pays $35-40 for inside photos; $150 to 250 for covers. Buys one-time rights.

COLUMNS Round Up (short items about people, unusual events, museums, historical topics/events, family and individually owned consumer-related businesses), 250-1,300 words; Town and Country (items about people or events illustrated with photos or commissioned art), 500 words. Include SASE. Query. **Pays 15¢/word.**

TIPS "Our publication depends on freelance work—send queries. Remember that a subject isn't an idea. Send the topic and your approach when you query. Answer the question: Would this be interesting to someone across the state? Find things that interest you enough that you'd travel 30-50 miles in a car to see/do/explore it, and send a query on that."

🌐💲 PENNSYLVANIA HERITAGE

Pennsylvania Heritage Foundation/Pennsylvania Historical & Museum Commission, Commonwealth Keystone Bldg., Plaza Level, 400 North St., Harrisburg PA 17120. **E-mail:** kyweaver@pa.gov. **Website:** www.paheritage.org. **Contact:** Kyle Weaver, editor. **65% freelance written. Prefers to work with published/established writers.** History and culture in Pennsylvania. *Pennsylvania Heritage* introduces readers to Pennsylvania's rich culture and historic legacy; educates and sensitizes them to the value of preserving that heritage; and entertains and involves them in such a way as to ensure that Pennsylvania's past has a future. The magazine is intended for intelligent lay readers. Estab. 1974. Byline given. Pays on publication. Publishes ms 1-2 years after acceptance. Accepts queries by mail, e-mail. Accepts simultaneous submissions. Responds in 10 weeks to queries. Responds in 8 months to mss. Send e-mail for guidelines.

NONFICTION **Buys 20-24 mss/year.** Prefers to see mss with suggested illustrations. Considers freelance submissions that are shorter in length; pictorial/photographic essays; biographies of notable Pennsylvanians; and interviews with individuals who have helped shape, make, and preserve the Keystone State's history and heritage. Length: 2,000-3,500 words. **Pays $100-500.**

PHOTOS State availability of or send photos. Captions, identification of subjects required. Buys one-time rights.

TIPS "We are looking for well-written, interesting material that pertains to any aspect of Pennsylvania history or culture. Potential contributors should realize that, although our articles are popularly styled, they are not light, puffy, or breezy; in fact they demand strident documentation and substantiation (sans footnotes). The most frequent mistake made by writers in completing articles for us is making them either too scholarly or too sentimental or nostalgic. We want material which educates, but also entertains. Authors should make history readable and enjoyable. Our goal is to make the Keystone State's history come to life in a meaningful, memorable way."

PHILADELPHIA STYLE

Philadelphia Style Magazine, LLC, 141 League St., Philadelphia PA 19147. (215)468-6670. **Fax:** (215)780-0003. **E-mail:** philadelphiastyle-editorial@greengale.com. **Website:** www.phillystylemag.com. **50% freelance written.** Bimonthly magazine covering upscale living in the Philadelphia region. Topics include: celebrity interviews, fashion (men's and women's), food, home and design, real estate, dining, beauty, travel, arts and entertainment, and more. "Our magazine is a positive look at the best ways to live in the Philadelphia region. Submitted articles should speak to an upscale, educated audience of professionals that live in the Delaware Valley." Estab. 1999. Circ. 60,000. Byline given. Pays on publication. Offers 25% kill fee. Publishes ms an average of 3 months after acceptance. Editorial lead time 2-4 months. Submit seasonal material 6 months in advance. Accepts queries by mail, e-mail. Accepts simultaneous submissions.

NONFICTION Needs general interest, interview, travel, region-specific articles. "We are not looking for articles that do not have a regional spin." **Buys 100+ mss/year.** Send complete ms. Length: 300-2,500 words. **Pays $50-500.**

COLUMNS Declarations (celebrity interviews and celebrity contributors); Currents (fashion news); Manor (home and design news); Liberties (beauty and travel news); Dish (dining news); Life in the City (fresh, quirky, regional reporting on books, real estate, art, retail, dining, events, and little-known sto-ries/facts about the region), 100-500 words; Vanguard (people on the forefront of Philadelphia's arts, media, fashion, business, and social scene), 500-700 words; In the Neighborhood (reader-friendly reporting on up-and-coming areas of the region including dining, shopping, attractions, and recreation), 2,000-2,500 words. Query with published clips or send complete ms. **Pays $50-500.**

TIPS "Mail queries with clips or manuscripts. Articles should speak to a stylish, educated audience."

PITTSBURGH MAGAZINE

WiesnerMedia, Washington's Landing, 600 Waterfront Dr., Suite 100, Pittsburgh PA 15222-4795. (412)304-0900. **Fax:** (412)304-0938. **E-mail:** editors@pittsburghmagazine.com. **Website:** www.pittsburghmagazine.com. **Contact:** Sean Collier, associate editor; Lauren Davidson, associate editor; Betsy Benson, publisher and vice president. **70% freelance written.** Monthly magazine covering the Pittsburgh metropolitan area. *Pittsburgh* presents issues, analyzes problems, and strives to encourage a better understanding of the community. Region is Western Pennsylvania, Eastern Ohio, Northern West Virginia, and Western Maryland. Estab. 1970. Circ. 75,000. Byline given. Pays on publication. Offers kill fee. Publishes ms an average of 2 months after acceptance. Submit seasonal material 6 months in advance. Accepts queries by mail, e-mail. Accepts simultaneous submissions. Responds in 2 months to queries. Guidelines online.

NONFICTION Needs expose, general interest, profile, sports, informational, service, business, medical, food, and lifestyle. "We do not publish fiction, poetry, advocacy, or personal reminiscence pieces." Query in writing with outline and clips. Length: 1,200-4,000 words. **Pays $300-1,500+.** Pays expenses of writers on assignment.

PHOTOS Query. Model releases required. Pays pre-negotiated expenses of writer on assignment.

TIPS "Best bet to break in is through a fresh take on news, sparkling writing, and a pitch with regional import or interest; also seeking fresh ideas for service pieces or profiles with a regional interest. We *never* consider any story without a strong regional focus or demonstrable relevance to our region."

$ SUSQUEHANNA LIFE MAGAZINE

217 Market St., Lewisburg PA 17837. (800)232-1670. **Fax:** (570)524-7796. **E-mail:** susquehannalife@gmail.com. **Website:** www.susquehannalife.com. **80% freelance written.** Quarterly magazine covering Central Pennsylvania lifestyle. Estab. 1993. Circ. 53,000. Byline given. Within two weeks after publication. Offers 50% kill fee. Publishes ms an average of 6-9 months after acceptance. Editorial lead time 3-6 months. Submit seasonal material 4-6 months in advance. Accepts queries by e-mail. Responds in 4-6 weeks to queries; 1-3 months to mss. Sample copy for $4.95, plus 5 first-class stamps. Guidelines available for #10 SASE.

NONFICTION Needs book excerpts, essays, general interest, historical, how-to, humor, inspirational, interview, memoir, nostalgic, personal experience, photo feature, profile, travel. Does not want fiction. **Buys 30-40 mss/year.** Query or send complete ms. Length: 850 words. **Pays $75-125.**

PHOTOS Send photos. High-resolution, high-quality jpgs. Captions, identification of subjects, model releases required. Reviews contact sheets, prints, GIF/JPEG files. Offers $20-25/photo; $100+ for cover photos. Buys one-time rights + use of photos on web site.

POETRY Must have a Central Pennsylvania angle.

TIPS "When you query, do not address letter to 'Dear Sir'; address the letter to the name of the publisher/editor. Demonstrate your ability to write. You need to be familiar with the type of articles we use and the particular flavor of the region. Only accepts submissions with a Central Pennsylvania angle."

SOUTH CAROLINA

$$ HILTON HEAD MONTHLY

Monthly Media LLC, P.O. Box 5926, Hilton Head Island SC 29938. (843)842-6988, ext. 230. **E-mail:** lance@hiltonheadmonthly.com. **Website:** www.hiltonheadmonthly.com. **Contact:** Lance Hanlin, editor in chief. **75% freelance written.** Monthly magazine covering the people, business, community, environment, and lifestyle of Hilton Head, SC, and the surrounding Lowcountry. "Our mission is to offer lively, fresh writing about Hilton Head Island, an upscale, environmentally conscious, and intensely proactive resort community on the coast of South Carolina." Circ. 35,000. Byline given. Pays on publication. Offers 50% kill fee. Publishes ms an average of 6 months after acceptance. Editorial lead time 3 months. Submit seasonal material 4 months in advance. Accepts queries by mail, e-mail. Accepts simultaneous submissions. Responds in 1 week to queries; in 4 months to mss. Sample copy: $3.

NONFICTION Needs general interest, how-to, humor, opinion, personal experience, travel. "Everything is local, local, local, so we're especially interested in profiles of notable residents (or those with Lowcountry ties) and original takes on home design/maintenance, environmental issues, entrepreneurship, health, sports, arts and entertainment, humor, travel, and volunteerism. We like to see how national trends/issues play out on a local level." **Buys 225-250 mss/year.** Query with published clips. Pays expenses of writers on assignment.

PHOTOS State availability. Reviews contact sheets, prints, digital samples. Negotiates payment individually. Buys one-time rights.

COLUMNS News; Business; Lifestyles (hobbies, health, sports, etc.); Home; Around Town (local events, charities, and personalities); People (profiles, weddings, etc.). Query with synopsis. **Pays 20¢/word.**

TIPS "Sure, Hilton Head is known primarily as an affluent resort island, but there's plenty more going on than just golf and tennis; this is a lively community with a strong sense of identity and decades-long tradition of community, volunteerism, and environmental preservation. We don't need any more tales of why you chose to retire here or how you fell in love with the beaches, herons, or salt marshes. Seek out lively, surprising characters—there are plenty—and offer fresh (but not trendy) takes on local personalities, Southern living, and green issues."

TENNESSEE

$$ MEMPHIS

Contemporary Media, 460 Tennessee St., Suite 200, Memphis TN 38103. (901)521-9000. **Fax:** (901)521-0129. **E-mail:** murtaugh@memphismagazine.com. **Website:** www.memphismagazine.com. **Contact:** Frank Murtaugh, managing editor. **30% freelance written. Works with a small number of new/unpublished writers.** Monthly magazine covering Memphis and the local region. Our mission is to provide Memphis with a colorful and informative look at the people, places, lifestyles and businesses that make the Bluff

City unique. Estab. 1976. Circ. 24,000. No byline given. Pays on publication. Submit seasonal material 3 months in advance. Accepts queries by mail, e-mail, fax. Accepts simultaneous submissions.

NONFICTION Needs essays, general interest, historical, interview, photo feature, travel, Interiors/exteriors, local issues and events. Special issues: Restaurant Guide and City Guide. **Buys 20 mss/year.** Query with published clips. Length: 500-3,000 words. **Pays 10-30¢/word.** Pays expenses of writers on assignment.

PHOTOS State availability. Reviews contact sheets, transparencies. Buys one time rights.

FICTION One story published annually as part of contest. Open only to those within 150 miles of Memphis. See website for details.

💲💲 MEMPHIS DOWNTOWNER MAGAZINE

Downtown Productions, Inc., 408 S. Front St., Suite 109, Memphis TN 38103. (901)525-7118. **Fax:** (901)525-7128. **E-mail:** editor@memphisdowntowner. com. **Website:** www.memphisdowntowner.com. **Contact:** Terre Gorham, editor. **50% freelance written.** Bi-monthly magazine covering features on positive aspects with a Memphis tie-in, especially to downtown. "We feature people, companies, nonprofits, and other issues that the general Memphis public would find interesting, entertaining, and informative. All editorial focuses on the positives Memphis has. No negative commentary or personal judgements. Controversial subjects should be treated fairly and balanced without bias." Estab. 1991. Circ. 30,000. Byline given. Pays on 15th of month in which assignment is published. Offers 25% kill fee. Publishes ms an average of 2-6 months after acceptance. Editorial lead time 3-6 months. Submit seasonal material 3-6 months in advance. Accepts queries by mail, e-mail. Responds in 2 weeks to queries. Sample copy free. Guidelines by e-mail.

NONFICTION Needs general interest, historical, how-to, humor, interview, personal experience, photo feature. **Buys 40-50 mss/year.** Query with published clips. Length: 600-2,000 words. **Pays scales vary depending on scope of assignment, but typically runs 15¢/word.** Pays expenses of writers on assignment.

PHOTOS State availability. Identification of subjects required. Reviews GIF/JPEG files (300 DPI). Negotiates payment individually.

COLUMNS So It Goes (G-rated humor), 600-800 words; Discovery 901 (Memphis one-of-a-kinds), 1,000-1,200 words. **Buys 6 mss/year.** Query with published clips. **Pays $100-150.**

FILLERS Unusual, interesting, or how-to or what to look for appealing to a large, general audience.

TIPS "Always pitch an actual story idea. E-mails that simply let us know you're a freelance writer mysteriously disappear from our inboxes. Actually read the magazine before you pitch. Get to know the regular columns and departments. In your pitch, explain where in the magazine you think your story idea would best fit. See website for magazine samples and past issues."

TEXAS

💲 HILL COUNTRY SUN

TD Austin Lane, Inc., 100 Commons Rd., Suite 7, #319, Dripping Springs TX 78620. (512)484-9716. **E-mail:** melissa@hillcountrysun.com. **Website:** www.hillcountrysun.com. **Contact:** Melissa Maxwell Ball, editor. **75% freelance written.** Monthly tabloid covering traveling in the Central Texas Hill Country. Publishes stories of interesting people, places, and events in the Central Texas Hill Country. Estab. 1990. Circ. 34,000. Byline given. Pays on acceptance. Publishes ms an average of 2 months after acceptance. Editorial lead time 1 month. Submit seasonal material 2 months in advance. Accepts queries by e-mail. Accepts simultaneous submissions. Responds in 1 week to queries. Sample copy free. Guidelines available online.

NONFICTION Needs interview, travel. No first-person articles. **Buys 50 mss/year.** Query. Length: 600-800 words. **Pays $60 minimum.**

PHOTOS State availability of or send photos. Identification of subjects required. No additional payment for photos accepted with ms. Buys one-time rights.

TIPS "Writers must be familiar with both the magazine's style and the Texas Hill Country."

💲💲💲 HOUSTON PRESS

1621 Milam, Suite 100, Houston TX 77002. (713)280-2400. **Fax:** (713)280-2444. **Website:** www.houstonpress.com. **Contact:** Margaret Downing, editor. **40% freelance written.** "Weekly tabloid covering news and arts stories of interest to a Houston audience. If the same story could run in Seattle, then it's not for us."

Estab. 1989. Byline given. Pays on publication. No kill fee. Publishes ms an average of 2 weeks after acceptance. Editorial lead time 2 months. Submit seasonal material 3 months in advance. Sample copy for $3.

NONFICTION Needs expose, general interest, interview, arts reviews. Query with published clips. Length: 300-4,500 words. **Pays $10-1,000.** Sometimes pays expenses of writers on assignment.

PHOTOS State availability. Identification of subjects required. Negotiates payment individually. Buys all rights.

💲💲💲 TEXAS HIGHWAYS

P.O. Box 141009, Austin TX 78714-1009. (800)839-4997. **E-mail:** letters05@texashighways.com. **Website:** www.texashighways.com. **70% freelance written.** Monthly magazine encourages travel within the state and tells the Texas story to readers around the world. Estab. 1974. Circ. 250,000. Pays on acceptance. No kill fee. Publishes ms an average of 1 year after acceptance. Accepts queries by mail. Accepts simultaneous submissions. Responds in 2 months to queries. Guidelines available online.

NONFICTION Query with description, published clips, additional background materials (charts, maps, etc.) and SASE. Length: 1,200-1,500 words. **Pays 40-50¢/word.** Pays expenses of writers on assignment.

TIPS "We like strong leads that draw in the reader immediately and clear, concise writing. Be specific and avoid superlatives. Avoid overused words. Don't forget the basics—who, what, where, when, why, and how."

💲💲💲💲 TEXAS MONTHLY

Emmis Publishing LP, P.O. Box 1569, Austin TX 78767. (512)320-6900. **Fax:** (512)476-9007. **Website:** www.texasmonthly.com. **Contact:** Tim Taliaferro, editor-in-chief. **10% freelance written.** Monthly magazine covering Texas. Estab. 1973. Circ. 300,000. Byline given. Pays on acceptance, $1/word and writer's expenses. Publishes ms an average of 1-3 months after acceptance. Editorial lead time 2 months. Submit seasonal material 3 months in advance. Accepts queries by online submission form. Responds in 6-8 weeks to queries and mss. Guidelines available online.

NONFICTION Needs book excerpts, essays, expose, general interest, interview, personal experience, photo feature, travel. Does not want articles without a Texas connection. Query. Length: 2,000-5,000 words. Pays expenses of writers on assignment.

PHOTOS Contact: Leslie Baldwin (lbaldwin@texasmonthly.com).

TIPS "Stories must appeal to an educated Texas audience. *Texas Monthly* covers the state's politics, sports, business, culture and changing lifestyles. We like solidly researched reporting that uncovers issues of public concern, reveals offbeat and previously unreported topics, or uses a novel approach to familiar topics. It contains lengthly features, interviews, essays, book excerpts, and reviews of books and movies. Does not want articles without a Texas connection. Any issue of the magazine would be a helpful guide; sample copy for $7."

VERMONT

💲💲 VERMONT LIFE MAGAZINE

One National Life Dr., 6th Floor, Montpelier VT 05620. (802)828-3241. **Fax:** (802)828-3366. **E-mail:** editors@vtlife.com. **Website:** www.vermontlife.com. **Contact:** Bill Anderson, managing editor. **90% freelance written. Prefers to work with published/established writers.** Quarterly magazine. "We read all story ideas submitted, but we cannot reply individually to each one. If we want to pursue a given manuscript or idea, we will contact you within 30 days of receiving it. Please bear in mind that *Vermont Life* produces pages as much as 6 months in advance of publication and may require photographs to be taken a year ahead of publication. We seek stories that have to do with contemporary Vermont culture and the Vermont way of life. As the state magazine, we are most interested in ideas that present positive aspects of life in Vermont. However, while we are nonpartisan, we have no rules about avoiding controversy when the presentation of the subject can illustrate some aspect of Vermont's unique character. We prefer reporting and journalism built around original ideas and insights, emerging trends, and thought-provoking connections in a Vermont context." Estab. 1946. Circ. 53,000. Byline given. Publishes ms an average of 9 months after acceptance. Submit seasonal material 1 year in advance. Accepts simultaneous submissions. Responds in 1 month to queries. "Read online guidelines before submitting: www.vermontlife.com/guidelines-for-contributors."

NONFICTION Pays expenses of writers on assignment.

PHOTOS Buys seasonal photographs. Gives assignments but only with experienced photographers. Query via e-mail only. Original digital photos from cameras of at least 6 megapixels. Photographs should be current (taken within the last 3 years). Metadata for each image must include captions; photographer's name, the location from which the photo was taken, especially the town; identification of subjects and important landmarks; date; model releases required. Pays $75-200 inside color; $500 for cover. Buys one-time rights.

TIPS "Review online guidelines before submitting queries or photography."

VIRGINIA

💲💲 THE ROANOKER

Leisure Publishing Co., 3424 Brambleton Ave., Roanoke VA 24018. (540)989-6138; (800)548-1672. **Fax:** (540)989-7603. **E-mail:** jwood@leisurepublishing.com; krheinheimer@leisurepublishing.com. **Website:** www.theroanoker.com. **Contact:** Kurt Rheinheimer, editor; Austin Clark, creative director; Patty Jackson, production director. **75% freelance written. Works with a small number of new/unpublished writers each year.** Magazine published 6 times/year. "*The Roanoker* is a general interest city magazine for the people of Roanoke, Virginia and the surrounding area. Our readers are primarily upper-income, well-educated professionals between the ages of 35 and 60. Coverage ranges from hard news and consumer information to restaurant reviews and local history." Estab. 1974. Circ. 10,000. Byline given. Pays on publication. No kill fee. Publishes ms an average of 4 months after acceptance. Submit seasonal material 4 months in advance. Accepts queries by mail, e-mail, fax. Accepts simultaneous submissions. Responds in 2 months to queries. Sample copy for $2 with 9x12 SASE and 5 first-class stamps or online.

NONFICTION Needs historical, how-to, interview, photo feature, travel, periodic special sections on fashion, real estate, media, banking, investing. **Buys 30 mss/year.** Send complete ms. 1,400 words maximum. **Pays $35-200.** Pays expenses of writers on assignment.

PHOTOS Send photos. Captions, model releases required. Reviews color transparencies, digital sub-missions. Pays $25-50/published photograph. Rights purchased vary.

COLUMNS Skinny (shorts on people, Roanoke-related books, local issues, events, arts and culture).

TIPS "We're looking for more pieces on contemporary history (1930s-70s). It helps if freelancer lives in the area. The most frequent mistake made by writers in completing an article for us is not having enough Roanoke-area focus: use of area experts, sources, slants, etc."

💲💲 VIRGINIA LIVING

Cape Fear Publishing, 109 E. Cary St., Richmond VA 23219. **E-mail:** erinparkhurst@capefear.com, taylorpilkington@capefear.com. **Website:** www.virginialiving.com. **Contact:** Erin Parkhurst, editor; Taylor Pilkington, associate editor. **80% freelance written.** Bimonthly magazine covering life and lifestyle in Virginia. "We are a large-format (10x13) glossy magazine covering life in Virginia, from food, architecture, and gardening to issues, profiles, and travel." Estab. 2002. Circ. 70,000. Byline given. Pays on publication. Publishes ms an average of 4-6 months after acceptance. Editorial lead time 2-6 months. Submit seasonal material 1 year in advance. Accepts queries by mail. Accepts simultaneous submissions. Responds in 1-3 month to queries. Sample copy: $5.95.

NONFICTION Needs book excerpts, essays, general interest, historical, interview, new product, personal experience, photo feature. No fiction, poetry, previously published articles, or stories with a firm grasp of the obvious. **Buys 180 mss/year.** Query with published clips or send complete ms. Length: 300-3,000 words. **Pays 50¢/word.** Pays expenses of writers on assignment.

PHOTOS Contact: Sonda Andersson Pappan, art director. Captions, identification of subjects, model releases required. Reviews contact sheets, 6x7 transparencies, 8x10 prints, GIF/JPEG files. Negotiates payment individually. Buys one-time rights.

COLUMNS Beauty; Travel; Books; Events; Sports (all with a unique Virginia slant), all 1,000-1,500 words. **Buys 50 mss/year.** Send complete ms. **Pays $120-200.**

TIPS "Queries should be about fresh subjects in Virginia. Avoid stories about Williamsburg, Chincoteague ponies, Monticello, the Civil War, and other press release-type topics. We prefer to introduce new subjects, faces, and ideas, and get beyond the many clichés of Virginia. Freelancers would also do well to think about what time of the year they are pitching stories for, as well as art possibilities. We are a large-format magazine, so photography is a key component to our stories."

WASHINGTON

💲💲 PUGET SOUND MAGAZINE

2115 Renee Place, Port Townsend WA 98368. (206)414-1589. **Fax:** (206)932-2574. **E-mail:** editorial@pugetsoundmagazine.com. **Website:** www.pugetsoundmagazine.com. **Contact:** David Petrich. **50% freelance written.** Online magazine covering regional focus on adventure, travel, recreation, art, food, wine, culture, wildlife, plants, and healthy living on the shoreline communities of Puget Sound and the Salish Sea. Olympia WA to Campbell River, BC. Writing from a personal experience, human interest perspective. We do profiles, historic pieces, how to—mostly features on water-centric lifestyles. Estab. 2008. Circ. 30,000. Byline given. No kill fee. Publishes ms an average of 2 months after acceptance. Editorial lead time 2 months. Accepts queries by mail, e-mail. Accepts simultaneous submissions. Responds in 4 weeks to queries. Sample copy free. Guidelines available online.

NONFICTION Contact: Kathleen McKelvey. Needs book excerpts, essays, general interest, historical, how-to, humor, inspirational, interview, personal experience, photo feature, travel. Special issues: No special issues at this time. Nothing negative, political, pornographic, religious. Send complete ms. Length: 800-2,000 words. **Pays 10¢ for assigned articles and for unsolicited articles.**

PHOTOS Contact: Dave Petrich, graphics/creative. State availability of or send photos. Photos require captions, identification of subjects. Reviews contact sheets. Negotiates payment individually. Buys all rights.

FICTION Contact: Katherine McKelvey. Needs adventure, historical, humorous, mainstream, mystery, western. **Buys 6 mss/year.** Query with published clips. Word length: 800-1,000 words. **Pays 10¢ word.**

POETRY Contact: Terry Persun, editor. Needs free verse, traditional. Buys 6/yr. poems/year. Submit maximum 3 poems. Length: 25 lines.

TIPS "Pay attention to what we ask for. Read the magazine to get the feel of what we do."

💲💲💲 SEATTLE WEEKLY

307 Third Ave. S., 2nd Floor, Seattle WA 98104. (206)623-0500. **Fax:** (206)467-4338. **E-mail:** editorial@seattleweekly.com; mbaumgarten@seattleweekly.com. **Website:** www.seattleweekly.com. **Contact:** Matt Baumgarten, editor in chief. **20% freelance written.** Weekly tabloid covering arts, politics, food, business and books with local and regional emphasis. The *Seattle Weekly* publishes stories on Northwest politics and art, usually written by regional and local writers, for a mostly upscale, urban audience; writing is high-quality magazine style. Estab. 1976. Circ. 105,000. Byline given. Pays on publication. Offers variable kill fee. Publishes ms an average of 1 month after acceptance. Submit seasonal material 2 months in advance. Accepts simultaneous submissions. Responds in 1 month to queries. Sample copy for $3.

NONFICTION Needs book excerpts, expose, general interest, historical, humor, interview, opinion. **Buys 6-8 mss/year.** Query with cover letter, résumé, published clips, and SASE. Length: 300-4,000 words. **Pays $50-800.** Pays expenses of writers on assignment.

REPRINTS Send tearsheet. Payment varies.

WISCONSIN

💲💲💲💲 MILWAUKEE MAGAZINE

Quad Graphics, Inc., 126 N. Jefferson St., Ste. 100, Milwaukee WI 53202. (414)287-4394. **Fax:** (414)273-0016. **E-mail:** daniel.simmons@milwaukeemag.com; claire.hanan@milwaukeemag.com. **Website:** www.milwaukeemag.com. **Contact:** Daniel Simmons, managing editor; Claire Hanan, senior editor, arts and culture. **40% freelance written.** Monthly magazine covering the people, issues, and places of the Milwaukee, Wisconsin, area. "We publish stories about Milwaukee, of service to Milwaukee-area residents, and exploring the area's changing lifestyle, business, arts, politics, and dining. Our goal has always been to create an informative, literate, and entertaining magazine that will challenge Milwaukeeans with in-depth reporting and analysis of issues of the day, provide useful service features, and enlighten readers with thoughtful stories, essays, and columns. Underlying this mission is the desire to discover what is unique about Wisconsin and its people, to challenge conventional wisdom when necessary, criticize when warranted, heap praise when deserved, and season all with affection and concern for the place we call home." Circ. 35,000. Byline given. Pays on publication. Offers 20% kill fee. Publishes ms an average of 2 months after acceptance. Submit seasonal material 6 months in advance. Accepts queries by e-mail. Accepts simultaneous submissions. Responds in 6 weeks to queries. Sample copy: $6. Guidelines online.

NONFICTION Needs essays, expose, general interest, historical, interview, photo feature, travel, food and dining, other services. Special issues: Health, Weddings (one each per year). No articles without a strong Milwaukee or Wisconsin angle; writers from outside the area are welcome, but please only pitch stories that have a connection to this place. **Buys 30-50 mss/year.** Query with published clips. Length: 2,500-5,000 words for full-length features; 800 words for two-page breaker features (short on copy, long on visuals). **Payment varies.** Pays expenses of writers on assignment.

COLUMNS Insider (inside information on Milwaukee, exposé, slice-of-life, unconventional angles on current scene), up to 500 words; Mini Reviews for Insider, 125 words. Query with published clips.

TIPS "Pitch something for the Insider, or suggest a compelling profile we haven't already done. Submit clips that prove you can do the job. We are actively seeking freelance writers who can deliver lively, readable copy that helps our readers make the most of the Milwaukee area. Because we're only human, we'd like writers who can deliver copy on deadline that fits the specifications of our assignment. If you fit this description, we'd love to work with you."

🟢🟢 WISCONSIN TRAILS

333 W. State St., Milwaukee WI 53201. **Fax:** (414)647-4723. **E-mail:** clewis@jrn.com. **Website:** www.wisconsintrails.com. **Contact:** Chelsey Lewis, assistant editor. **40% freelance written.** Bimonthly magazine for readers interested in Wisconsin and its contemporary issues, personalities, recreation, history, natural beauty, and arts. Estab. 1960. Circ. 55,000. Byline given. Pays 1 month from publication. 20% kill fee, up to $75. Publishes ms an average of 6 months after acceptance. Submit seasonal material 1 year in advance. Accepts queries by mail, e-mail, fax. Accepts simultaneous submissions. Responds in 2-3 months to queries. Sample copy: $4.95. Guidelines for #10 SASE or online.

NONFICTION Does not accept unsolicited mss. Query or send a story idea via e-mail. Length: 250-1,500 words. **Pays 25¢/word.** Pays expenses of writers on assignment.

PHOTOS "Because *Wisconsin Trails* works primarily with professional photographers, we do not pay writers for accompanying images nor do we reimburse for any related expenses. Photos will be credited and the photographer retains all rights." Contact editor. Pays $75-250.

TIPS "When querying, submit well-thought-out ideas about stories specific to people, places, events, arts, outdoor adventures, etc., in Wisconsin. Include published clips with queries. Do some research—many queries we receive are pitching ideas for stories we recently have published. Know the tone, content, and audience of the magazine. Refer to our writer's guidelines, or request them, if necessary."

WYOMING

🟢 WYOMING RURAL ELECTRIC NEWS (WREN)

2710 Thomas Ave., Cheyenne WY 82001. (307)772-1986. **Fax:** (307)634-0728. **E-mail:** wren@wyomingrea.org. **Website:** wyomingrea.org/community/wren-magazine. **40% freelance written.** Monthly magazine (except in January) for audience of rural residents, vacation-home owners, farmers, ranchers and business owners in Wyoming. Estab. 1954. Circ. 39,100. Byline given. Pays on publication. No kill fee. Publishes ms an average of 2 months after acceptance. At least 3 months. Submit seasonal material 2 months in advance. Accepts queries by mail, e-mail. Accepts simultaneous submissions. Responds in 1 month to queries. Sample copy for $2.50 and 9x12 SASE. Guidelines for #10 SASE.

NONFICTION No nostalgia, sarcasm, or tongue-in-cheek. **Buys 4-10 mss/year.** Send complete ms. Length: 600-800 words. **Pays up to $150, plus 3 copies.** Pays expenses of writers on assignment.

REPRINTS Send tearsheet or photocopy and information about when and where the material previously appeared.

PHOTOS Color only.

TIPS "Always looking for fresh, new writers. Submit entire ms. Don't submit a regionally set story from some other part of the country. Photos and illustrations (if appropriate) are always welcomed. We want factual articles that are to the point, accurate."

RELIGIOUS

$ ALIVE NOW

1908 Grand Ave., P.O. Box 340004, Nashville TN 37203. (615)340-7254. **E-mail:** alivenow@upperroom.org. **Website:** www.alivenow.org; alivenow.upperroom.org. **Contact:** Beth A. Richardson, editor. *Alive Now*, published bimonthly, is a devotional magazine that invites readers to enter an ever-deepening relationship with God. "*Alive Now* seeks to nourish people who are hungry for a sacred way of living. Submissions should invite readers to see God in the midst of daily life by exploring how contemporary issues impact their faith lives. Each word must be vivid and dynamic and contribute to the whole. We make selections based on a list of upcoming themes. Mss which do not fit a theme will be returned." Estab. 1971. Circ. 70,000. Pays on acceptance. Accepts queries by mail, e-mail. Accepts simultaneous submissions. Subscription: $17.95/year (6 issues); $26.95 for 2 years (12 issues). Additional subscription information, including foreign rates, available on website. Guidelines available online.

NONFICTION meditations. Prefers electronic submissions attached as Word document. Postal submissions should include SASE. Include name, address, theme on each sheet. Length: 400-500 words. **Pays $35 minimum.** Pays expenses of writers on assignment.

FICTION Needs religious. Prefers electronic submissions attached as Word document. Postal submissions should include SASE. Include name, address, theme on each sheet. Length: 400-500 words. **Pays $35 minimum.**

POETRY Prefers electronic submissions attached as Word document. Postal submissions should include SASE. Include name, address, theme on each sheet. **Pays $35 minimum.**

$ BIBLE ADVOCATE

Church of God (Seventh Day), P.O. Box 33677, Denver CO 80233. (303)452-7973. **E-mail:** bibleadvocate@cog7.org. **Website:** baonline.org. **Contact:** Sherri Langton, associate editor. **25% freelance written.** Religious magazine published 6 times/year. "Our purpose is to advocate the Bible and represent the Church of God (Seventh Day) to a Christian audience." Estab. 1863. Circ. 13,500. Byline given. Pays on publication. No kill fee. Publishes ms an average of 3-9 months after acceptance. Editorial lead time 3 months. Submit seasonal material 6 months in advance. Accepts queries by mail, e-mail. Accepts simultaneous submissions. Responds in 2 months to queries. Sample copy for SAE with 9x12 envelope and 3 first-class stamps. Guidelines online.

NONFICTION Contact: Sherri Langton, associate editor. Needs inspirational, personal experience, religious, Biblical studies. No articles on Christmas or Easter. **Buys 10-20 mss/year.** Send complete ms by e-mail, preferably. Length: 600-1,200 words. **Pays $25-65.**

REPRINTS E-mail ms with rights for sale noted.

POETRY Contact: Sherri Langton, associate editor. Needs Wants free verse, traditional, Christian/Bible themes. Seldom comments on rejected poems. No avant-garde. Buys 10-12 poems/year. Submit maximum 5 poems. Length: 5-20 lines. **Pays $20 and 2 contributor's copies.**

TIPS "Be fresh, not preachy! Articles must be in keeping with the doctrinal understanding of the Church of God (Seventh Day). Therefore, the writer should become familiar with what the Church generally accepts as truth as set forth in its doctrinal beliefs. We reserve the right to edit mss to fit our space requirements, doctrinal stands, and church terminology. Significant changes are referred to writers for approval. No fax or handwritten submissions, please."

$$ CATHOLIC ANSWERS

Catholic Answers, 2020 Gillespie Way, El Cajon CA 92020. (619)387-7200. **Fax:** (619)387-0042. **Website:** www.catholic.com. **60% freelance written.** Monthly magazine covering Catholic apologetics and evangelization. Our content explains, defends and promotes Catholic teaching. Estab. 1990. Circ. 24,000. Byline given. Pays on acceptance. Offers variable kill fee. Publishes ms an average of 4 months after acceptance. Accepts queries by e-mail. Responds in 2-4 weeks to queries. Responds in 1-2 months to mss. Sample copy available online. Guidelines by e-mail.

NONFICTION Needs book excerpts, essays, religious, conversion stories. **Buys 50 mss/year.** Send complete ms. Length: 1,500-3,000 words. **Pays $200-350.**

COLUMNS Damascus Road (stories of conversion to the Catholic Church), 2,000 words. **Buys 10 mss/year.** Send complete ms. **Pays $200.**

☺☺ CATHOLIC DIGEST

2 West Hill Dr via Old English Road, Worcester MA 01609. **E-mail:** queries@catholicdigest.com. **Website:** www.catholicdigest.com. **80% freelance written.** Magazine published 9 times/year on Catholic faith. Publishes features, interviews, and advice on topics ranging from spiritual support and education, family, ethics, and Catholic perspectives on modern-day issues, sacraments, and saints through the ages. "We do not publish fiction or poetry. We review only e-mail queries." Estab. 1936. Circ. 275,000. Byline given. Pays on publication. No kill fee. Editorial lead time 6 months. Submit seasonal material 6 months in advance. Accepts queries by e-mail. Accepts simultaneous submissions. Does not respond to unsolicited ms. Guidelines available on website.

NONFICTION Needs book excerpts, essays, general interest, historical, how-to, humor, inspirational, interview, personal experience, religious, travel. Special issues: Accepts features on the following topics: Marriage, Spirituality, Parish/Work, Parenting, Grandparenting, Art, Relationships. Does not accept unsolicited submissions. Query with 1-2 relevant writing samples. Length: 350-1,500 words. **Pays $100-$500.** Pays expenses of writers on assignment.

REPRINTS Does not publish reprints.

PHOTOS State availability. "If your query is accepted and you have photos that may be used to accompany your submission, please attach them as JPEG files. Photos must be at least 300 dpi to be used in the magazine. Appropriate credit lines and captions should also accompany the photos."

FILLERS Open Door (statements of true incidents through which people are brought into the Catholic faith, or recover the Catholic faith they had lost), 350-600 words, send to opendoor@catholicdigest.com; Last Word (back page, personal, inspirational, reflective essay), 550-700 words, send to queries@catholicdigest.com. Query with 1-2 relevant writing samples.

TIPS "Please read the magazine before querying. Spiritual, self-help, and Q&As are a good bet for us. We would also like to see material with an innovative approach to daily living, articles that show new ways of looking at old ideas and problems. You've got to dig beneath the surface."

☺☺ THE CHRISTIAN CENTURY

104 S. Michigan Ave., Suite 1100, Chicago IL 60603-5901. (312)263-7510. **Fax:** (312)263-7540. **E-mail:** main@christiancentury.org. **E-mail:** submissions@christiancentury.org; poetry@christiancentury.org. **Website:** www.christiancentury.org. **Contact:** Jill Peláez Baumgaertner, poetry editor. **90% freelance written. Works with new/unpublished writers.** Biweekly magazine for ecumenically minded, progressive Protestants, both clergy and lay. "We seek mss that articulate the public meaning of faith, bringing the resources of religious tradition to bear on such topics as poverty, human rights, economic justice, international relations, national priorities, and popular culture. We are also interested in pieces that examine or critique the theology and ethos of individual religious communities. We welcome articles that find fresh meaning in old traditions and that adapt or apply religious traditions to new circumstances. Authors should assume that readers are familiar with main themes in Christian history and theology, are accustomed to the historical-critical study of the Bible and are already engaged in relating faith to social and political issues. Many of our readers are ministers or teachers of religion at the college level. Book reviews are solicited by our books editor. Please note that submissions via e-mail will not be considered. If you are interested in becoming a reviewer for *The Christian Century*, please send your résumé and a list of subjects of interest to "Attn: Book reviews." Authors must have a critical and analytical perspective on the church and be familiar with contemporary theological discussion." Estab. 1884. Circ. 37,000. Byline given. Pays on publication. No kill fee. Editorial lead time 1 month. Submit seasonal material 4 months in advance. Accepts queries by mail, e-mail. Accepts simultaneous submissions. Responds in 4-6 weeks to queries; in 2 months to mss. Sample copy: $3.50. Guidelines available online.

NONFICTION Needs essays, humor, interview, opinion, religious. Does not want inspirational. **Buys 150 mss/year.** Send complete ms; query appreciated but not essential. Length: 1,000-3,000 words. **Pays variable amount for assigned articles. Pays $100-300 for unsolicited articles.** Pays expenses of writers on assignment.

PHOTOS State availability. Reviews any size prints. Buys one-time rights.

COLUMNS "We do not accept unsolicited submissions for our regular columns."

POETRY Contact: Jill Pelàez Baumgaertner, poetry editor. Needs free verse, traditional. Wants "poems that are not statements but experiences, that do not talk about the world but show it. We want to publish poems that are grounded in images and that reveal an awareness of the sounds of language and the forms of poetry even when the poems are written in free verse." Submissions without SASE (or SAE and IRCs) will not be returned. Submit poems typed, double-spaced, 1 poem/page. Include name, address, and phone number on each page. Please submit poetry to poetry@christiancentury.org. Has published poetry by Jeanne Murray Walker, Ida Fasel, Kathleen Norris, Luci Shaw, J. Barrie Shepherd, and Wendell Berry. Prefers shorter poems. Inquire about reprint permission. Does not want "pietistic or sentimental doggerel." Buys 50 poems/year. Length: up to 20 lines/poem. **Usually pays $50/poem plus 1 contributor's copy and discount on additional copies. Acquires all rights.**

TIPS "We suggest reading the poems in the past several issues to gain a clearer idea of the kinds of poetry we are seeking. We publish shorter poems that are grounded in images and that reveal an awareness of the sounds of language and the forms of poetry even when the poems are written in free verse."

$$ CONSCIENCE

Catholics for Choice, 1436 U St. NW, Suite 301, Washington DC 20009. (202)986-6093. **E-mail:** conscience@catholicsforchoice.org. **Website:** www.catholicsforchoice.org. **Contact:** Tamar Abrams. **80% written by nonstaff writers. Publishes 40 freelance submissions yearly; 10% by unpublished writers, 50% by authors who are new to the magazine, 70% by experts.** "Conscience offers in-depth coverage of a range of topics, including contemporary politics, Catholicism, women's rights in society and in religions, U.S. politics, reproductive rights, sexuality and gender, ethics and bioethics, feminist theology, social justice, church and state issues, and the role of religion in formulating public policy." Estab. 1980. Circ. 12,000. Byline given. Pays on publication. No kill fee. Publishes ms an average of 2 months after acceptance. Accepts queries by mail, e-mail. Accepts simultaneous submissions. Responds in 4 months to queries. Sample copy free with 9x12 envelope and $1.85 postage. Guidelines with #10 SASE.

NONFICTION Needs book excerpts, interview, opinion, personal experience, issue analysis. **Buys 4-8 mss/year.** Send complete ms. Length: 1,500-3,500 words. **Pays $200 negotiable.** Pays expenses of writers on assignment.

REPRINTS Send typed manuscript with rights for sale noted and information about when and where the material previously appeared. Pays 20-30% of amount paid for an original article.

PHOTOS Sample copies available. Buys up to 25 photos/year. Model/property release preferred. Photo captions preferred; include title, subject, photographer's name. Reviews photos with or without a manuscript. Pays $300 maximum for color cover; $50 maximum for b&w inside. Pays on publication. Credit line given.

COLUMNS Book Reviews, 600-1,200 words. **Buys 4-8 mss/year. Pays $75.**

TIPS "Our readership includes national and international opinion leaders and policymakers, librarians, members of the clergy and the press, and leaders in the fields of theology, ethics, and women's studies. Articles should be written for a diverse and educated audience."

$$ DECISION

Billy Graham Evangelistic Association, P.O. Box 668886, Charlotte NC 28266. (704)401-2432. **Fax:** (704)401-3009. **E-mail:** submissions@bgea.org. **Website:** www.decisionmag.org. **Contact:** Bob Paulson, editor. **5% freelance written. Works each year with small number of new/unpublished writers.** "Magazine published 11 times/year with a mission to communicate the Good News of Jesus Christ, to inform and challenge readers about key cultural and Biblical issues, and to extend the ministry of the Billy Graham Evangelistic Association." Include telephone number with submission. Estab. 1960. Circ. 400,000. Byline given. Pays on publication. Publishes ms up to 18 months after acceptance. Editorial lead time 6 months. Submit seasonal material 6 months in advance. Accepts queries by mail, e-mail. Sample copy for sae with 9x12 envelope and 4 first-class stamps. Guidelines online.

NONFICTION Needs personal experience, testimony. **Buys approximately 8 mss/year.** Send complete ms. Length: 400-1,000 words. **Pays $200-400.** Pays expenses of writers on assignment.

PHOTOS State availability. Captions, identification of subjects, model releases required. Reviews prints. Buys one time rights.

COLUMNS Finding Jesus (people who have become Christians through Billy Graham Ministries), 500-900 words. **Buys 11 mss/year.** Send complete ms. **Pays $200.**

TIPS "Articles should have some connection to the ministry of Billy Graham or Franklin Graham. For example, you may have volunteered in 1 of these ministries or been touched by them. The article does not need to be entirely about that connection, but it should at least mention the connection. Testimonies and personal experience articles should show how God intervened in your life and how you have been transformed by God. SASE required with submissions."

❸❺ EFCA TODAY

Evangelical Free Church of America, 418 Fourth St., NE, Charlottesville VA 22902. **E-mail:** editor@efca. org. **Website:** efcatoday.org. **Contact:** Diane J. Mc-Dougall, editor. **30% freelance written.** Quarterly digital magazine. "*EFCA Today*'s purpose is to unify church leaders around the overall mission of the EFCA by bringing its stories and vision to life, and to sharpen those leaders by generating conversations over topics pertinent to faith and life in the 21st century." Estab. 1931. Byline given. Pays on acceptance. Offers 50% kill fee. Publishes ms an average of 3 months after acceptance. Editorial lead time 5 months. Submit seasonal material 6 months in advance. Accepts queries by e-mail. Accepts simultaneous submissions. Responds in 6 weeks. Sample available online. Guidelines online.

NONFICTION articles related to *EFCA* themes, book reviews, blog posts. Special issues: "Each *EFCA Today* is devoted to a topic designed to stimulate thoughtful dialogue and leadership growth, and to highlight how EFCA leaders are already involved in living out that theme. Examples of themes are: new paradigms for 'doing church,' church planting, and rural/small-town churches. These articles focus on an issue rather than on an individual, although individuals indeed illustrate each theme." Query with published clips. Length: 500-2,000 words for articles.

Pays 23¢/word. Pays expenses of writers on assignment.

REPRINTS Reprint payment varies.

❸❺ ENRICHMENT

The General Council of the Assemblies of God, 1445 N. Boonville Ave., Springfield MO 65802. (417)862-2781, ext. 4095. **E-mail:** enrichmentjournal@ag.org; rknoth@ag.org. **Website:** www.enrichmentjournal. ag.org. **Contact:** Rick Knoth, managing editor. **15% freelance written.** Quarterly journal covering church leadership and ministry. "*Enrichment* offers enriching and encouraging information to equip and empower spirit-filled leaders." Circ. 33,000. Byline given. Pays on publication. Offers 50% kill fee. Publishes ms an average of 1 year after acceptance. Editorial lead time 18 months. Submit seasonal material 18 months in advance. Accepts queries by mail, e-mail. Accepts simultaneous submissions. Sample copy: $7. Guidelines free.

NONFICTION Needs religious. Send complete ms. Length: 1,000-3,000 words. **Pays up to 15¢/word.** Pays expenses of writers on assignment.

❺ EVANGELICAL MISSIONS QUARTERLY

Billy Graham Center at Wheaton College, 500 College Ave., Wheaton IL 60187. (630)752-7158. **E-mail:** emq@wheaton.edu. **Website:** www.emqonline.com. **Contact:** Laurie Fortunak Nichols, managing editor; A. Scott Moreau, editor. **67% freelance written.** Quarterly magazine covering evangelical missions. *Evangelical Missions Quarterly* is a professional journal serving the worldwide missions community. *EMQ* articles reflect missionary life, thought, and practice. Each issue includes articles, book reviews, editorials, and letters. Subjects are related to worldwide mission and evangelism efforts and include successful ministries, practical ideas, new tactics and strategies, trends in world evangelization, church planting and discipleship, health and medicine, literature and media, education and training, relief and development, missionary family life, and much more. Estab. 1964. Circ. 7,000. Byline given. Pays on publication. Offers negotiable kill fee. Publishes ms an average of 18 months after acceptance. Editorial lead time 1 year. Accepts queries by e-mail. Accepts simultaneous submissions. Responds in 2 weeks to queries. Sample copy free. Guidelines available online.

NONFICTION Needs interview, opinion, personal experience, religious. No sermons, poetry, or straight news. **Buys 24 mss/year.** Query. Length: 3,000 words. **Pays $25-100.** Pays expenses of writers on assignment.

PHOTOS Send photos. Identification of subjects required. Offers no additional payment for photos accepted with ms. Buys first rights.

COLUMNS In the Workshop (practical how tos), 800-2,000 words; Perspectives (opinion), 800 words. **Buys 8 mss/year.** Query. **Pays $50-100.**

TIPS "We prefer articles about deeds done, showing the why and the how, not only claiming success but also admitting failure. Principles drawn from 1 example must be applicable to missions more generally. *EMQ* does not include articles which have been previously published in journals, books, websites, etc."

🍁$ FAITH & FRIENDS

The Salvation Army, 2 Overlea Blvd., Toronto ON M4H 1P4 Canada. (416)422-6226. **Fax:** (416)422-6120. **E-mail:** faithandfriends@can.salvationarmy.org. **Website:** www.faithandfriends.ca. **25% freelance written.** Monthly magazine covering Christian living and religion. "*Faith & Friends*, a contemporary, full-color monthly magazine, is written and designed to show Jesus Christ at work in the lives of real people and to provide spiritual resources for those who are new to the Christian faith. Each issue contains stories about people whose lives have been changed through an encounter with Jesus." Estab. 1996. Circ. 50,000. Byline given. Pays on acceptance. Offers $50 kill fee. Publishes ms an average of 3 months after acceptance. Editorial lead time 3 months. Submit seasonal material 6 months in advance. Accepts queries by mail, e-mail, fax. Accepts simultaneous submissions. Usually responds in 10 days to queries and mss. Sample copy available online. Guidelines by e-mail.

NONFICTION Needs book excerpts, essays, general interest, historical, inspirational, interview, memoir, opinion, personal experience, photo feature, profile, religious, reviews, Testimonial (a first-person conversion testimony, conveying what Christ has done in your life, or the testimony of another, obtained through interview), 1,200 words; Personal Story (a concise narrative relating biblical principles to everyday living, using an anecdote or incident from your own or someone else's life), 750 words. "Articles should avoid references and concepts the unchurched would not understand and should focus on ideas and answers which are compatible with a Christian worldview. Take care not to submit an essay or preach at our readers." **Buys 12-24 mss/year.** Query or send complete ms. Approximately 250 words per page up to 1,000 words for a feature. **Pays approximately $50/page.** Pays expenses of writers on assignment.

PHOTOS Send photos. Captions required. Reviews prints, GIF/JPEG files. Negotiates payment individually. Buys one-time rights.

COLUMNS Faith Builders (reviews that explore the spiritual meaning be-hind popular movies or television shows); God in My Life (personal witness of the power of God in everyday life); Turning Point (how, with God's help, you faced a serious obstacle and got on with your life); Someone Cares (a profile or personal treatment of how you or someone you know was helped by The Salvation Army); Words to Live By (the Bible in action or a Bible message integrated into your life and presented in everyday terms); Big Questions (answers to difficult theological questions in terms that ordinary people can understand); Sacred Space (spiritual tools, exercises, disciplines and social justice issues that encourage new Christians to connect with God and reach out to others); Beyond Borders (inspirational stories of overseas missionaries or Christian workers who engage with the culture in innovative ways); The Bottom Line (Christian businesspeople who live out their be-liefs at work by establishing an ethical workplace with ethical practices); Love & Life (exploring the Christian dimension to spousal and family relationships); all 750 words. **Buys 12-18 mss/year.** Query or send complete ms.

🍁$$ FAITH TODAY

The Evangelical Fellowship of Canada, P.O. Box 5885, West Beaver Creek Post Office, Richmond Hill ON L4B 0B8 Canada. (905)479-5885. **Fax:** (905)479-4742. **E-mail:** editor@faithtoday.ca. **Website:** www.faithtoday.ca. **Over 80% freelance written.** Bimonthly magazine. *Faith Today* is the magazine of an association of more than 40 evangelical denominations in Canada but serves evangelicals in all denominations. In 2016 it added a sister magazine for youth and young adults, called *Love Is Moving*. *Faith Today* focuses on church issues, social issues, and personal faith as they are tied to the Canadian context. Writing should explicitly acknowledge that Canadian evangelical context. Queries should have an explicit content connection to Canadian evangelical Christians.

Estab. 1983. Circ. 20,000. Byline given. Pays on publication. Offers 30-50% kill fee. Publishes ms an average of 4 months after acceptance. Editorial lead time 4 months. Accepts queries by mail, e-mail. Accepts simultaneous submissions. Responds in 6 weeks to queries. Sample copy for SASE in Canadian postage. Guidelines online.

NONFICTION Needs book excerpts, essays, expose, general interest, historical, how-to, humor, interview, opinion, religious, reviews, news feature. Does not want Bible studies, poetry, serialized articles, seasonal material, generic or U.S.-focused Christian-living material. **Buys 75 mss/year.** Query. Length: 400-2,000 words. **Pays $100-500 Canadian.** Pays expenses of writers on assignment.

REPRINTS Pays 50% of amount paid for an original article.

PHOTOS State availability. Buys one-time rights.

TIPS "Query should include brief outline and names of the sources you plan to interview in your research. Use Canadian postage on SASE."

🅢 FORWARD IN CHRIST

WELS Communication Services, 2929 N. Mayfair Rd., Milwaukee WI 53222. (414)256-3210. **Fax:** (414)256-3899. **E-mail:** fic@wels.net. **Website:** www.wels.net. **Contact:** Julie K. Wietzke, managing editor; John A. Braun, executive editor. **5% freelance written.** Official monthly magazine covering Wisconsin Evangelical Lutheran Synod (WELS) news, topics, issues. The material usually must be written by or about WELS members. Estab. 1913. Circ. 42,000. Byline given. Pays on publication. No kill fee. Publishes ms an average of 6 months after acceptance. Editorial lead time 3 months. Submit seasonal material 4 months in advance. Accepts queries by mail, e-mail, fax. Responds in 2 months to queries. Sample copy and writer's guidelines free. Guidelines available on website.

NONFICTION Needs personal experience, religious. Query. Length: 550-1,200 words. **Pays $75/page, $125/2 pages.** Sometimes pays expenses of writers on assignment.

TIPS "Topics should be of interest to the majority of the members of the synod—the people in the pews. Articles should have a Christian viewpoint, but we don't want sermons. We suggest you carefully read at least 5 or 6 issues with close attention to the length, content, and style of the features."

🅢 GUIDE

Pacific Press Publishing Association, P.O. Box 5353, Nampa ID 83653. (208)465-2579. **E-mail:** guide@pacificpress.com. **Website:** www.guidemagazine.org. **Contact:** Randy Fishell, editor; Brandon Reese, designer. *Guide* is a Christian story magazine for young people ages 10-14. The 32-page, 4-color publication is published weekly by the Pacific Press. Their mission is to show readers, through stories that illustrate Bible truth, how to walk with God now and forever. Estab. 1953. Byline given. Pays on acceptance. Accepts queries by mail, e-mail. Accepts simultaneous submissions. Responds in 6 weeks to mss. Sample copy free with 6x9 SAE and 2 first-class stamps. Guidelines available on website.

NONFICTION Needs humor, personal experience, religious. Send complete ms. "Each issue includes 3-4 true stories. *Guide* does not publish fiction, poetry, or articles (devotionals, how-to, profiles, etc.). However, we sometimes accept quizzes and other unique nonstory formats. Each piece should include a clear spiritual element." Looking for pieces on adventure, personal growth, Christian humor, inspiration, biography, story series, and nature. Length: 1,000-1,200 words. **Pays 7-10¢/word.** Pays expenses of writers on assignment.

REPRINTS Send copy with information on when and where the story first appeared. Pays reduced amount for reprints.

FILLERS Needs games and puzzles. Send complete ms. **Pays $25-40.**

TIPS "Children's magazines want mystery, action, discovery, suspense, and humor—no matter what the topic. For us, truth is stronger than fiction."

🅢🅢 GUIDEPOSTS

110 William St., Suite 901, New York NY 10038. **E-mail:** submissions@guidepostsmag.com. **Website:** www.guideposts.com. **Contact:** Edward Grinnan, editor. **40% freelance written. Works with a small number of new/unpublished writers each year.** Monthly magazine featuring personal inspirational stories. *Guideposts* is an inspirational monthly magazine for people of all faiths, in which men and women from all walks of life tell true, first-person narratives of how they overcame obstacles, rose above failures, handled sorrow, gained new spiritual insight, and became more effective people through faith in God.

Estab. 1945. Pays on publication. Offers kill fee. Offers 20% kill fee on assigned stories, but not to first-time freelancers. Publishes ms an average of several months after acceptance. Accepts queries by online submission form. Accepts simultaneous submissions. Guidelines available online.

NONFICTION Needs personal experience. Does not want essays, sermons, or fiction. **Buys 40-60 unsolicited mss/year.** Submit complete ms via online submission form. Length: up to 1,500 words. **Pays $100-500.** Pays expenses of writers on assignment.

TIPS "Study the magazine before you try to write for it. Each story must make a single spiritual point that readers can apply to their own daily lives. And it may be easier to just sit down and write them than to have to go through the process of preparing a query. They should be warm, well written, intelligent, and upbeat. We require personal narratives that are true and have some spiritual aspect, but the religious element can be subtle and should *not* be sermonic. A writer succeeds with us if he or she can write a true article using short-story techniques with scenes, drama, tension, and a resolution of the problem presented."

🄢🄢 HOPE FOR WOMEN

P.O. Box 3241, Muncie IN 47307. **E-mail:** hope@hopeforwomenmag.org. **Website:** www.hopeforwomenmag.com. **90% freelance written.** Bimonthly lifestyle magazine that offers faith, love, and virtue for the modern Christian Woman. *Hope for Women* presents refreshing, inspirational articles in an engaging and authentic tone to women from various walks of life. The magazine encourages readers and deals with real-world issues—all while adhering to Christian values and principles. Estab. 2005. Circ. 10,000. Byline given. Pays on publication. Publishes ms an average of 4-6 months after acceptance. Editorial lead time 4-6 months. Accepts queries by mail, e-mail. Accepts simultaneous submissions. Guidelines by email.

NONFICTION Needs book excerpts, essays, general interest, how-to, humor, inspirational, interview, new product, opinion, personal experience, photo feature, religious, travel. Query. Length: 500 words minimum. **Pays 10-20¢/word.** Pays expenses of writers on assignment.

COLUMNS Relationships (nurturing positive relationships—marriage, dating, divorce, single life), 800-1,200 words; Light (reports on issues such as infidelity, homosexuality, addiction, and domestic violence), 500-800 words; Journey (essays on finding your identity with Christ), 500-800 words; Marketplace (finance/money management), 800-1,200 words); E-Spot (book, music, TV, and film reviews), 500-800 words; Family First (parenting encouragement and instruction), 800-1,500 words; Health/Fitness (nutrition/exercise), 800-1,200 words; The Look (fashion/beauty tips), 500-800 words; Home Essentials (home/garden how-to), 500-800 words. Query. **Pays 10-20¢/word.**

TIPS "Our readers are a diverse group of women, ages 25-54. They want to read articles about real women dealing with real problems. Because our readers are balancing work and family, they want information presented in a no-nonsense fashion that is relevant and readable."

🄢🄢 JEWISH ACTION

Orthodox Union, 11 Broadway, New York NY 10004. (212)563-4000. **E-mail:** ja@ou.org. **Website:** www.ou.org/jewish_action. **Contact:** Nechama Carmel, editor; Rashel Zywica, assistant editor. **80% freelance written.** Quarterly magazine covering a vibrant approach to Jewish issues, Orthodox lifestyle, and values. "*Jewish Action*, the quarterly magazine publication of the Orthodox Union, serves as a forum for a diversity of legitimate opinions within the spectrum of Orthodox Judaism. Our goal is to produce a high-quality, intellectually sophisticated, and relevant publication that conveys Orthodox Jewish values and concerns in a way that will enlighten, educate, and inspire our readers. We aim to attract the best writers and thinkers in the Orthodox Jewish world and to provide lively and thought-provoking articles about issues that affect Orthodox Jewish life today." Estab. 1986. Circ. 40,000. Byline given. Pays 2 months after publication. Submit seasonal material 4 months in advance. Accepts queries by mail, e-mail. Accepts simultaneous submissions. Responds in 3 months to mss. Sample copy available online. Guidelines available online.

NONFICTION Needs essays, historical, humor, reviews, articles related to current ongoing issues of Jewish life and experience, human-interest features. "We are not looking for Holocaust accounts. We welcome essays about responses to personal or societal challenges." **Buys 30-40 mss/year.** Submit complete ms. E-mailed submissions preferred. Length: 1,000-3,000 words. **Pays $100-400 for assigned articles.**

Pays $75-150 for unsolicited articles. Pays expenses of writers on assignment.

PHOTOS Send photos. Identification of subjects required.

COLUMNS Just Between Us (personal opinion on current Jewish life and issues), 1,000 words. **Buys 4 mss/year.**

POETRY Buys limited number of poems/year. **Pays $25-75.**

TIPS "Remember that your reader is well educated and has a strong commitment to Orthodox Judaism. Articles on the holidays, Israel, and other common topics should offer a fresh insight. Because the magazine is a quarterly, we do not generally publish articles which concern specific timely events."

$ LIGHT + LIFE MAGAZINE

Free Methodist Church – USA, 770 N. High School Rd., Indianapolis IN 46214. (317)616-4776. **Fax:** (317)244-1247. **E-mail:** jeff.finley@fmcusa.org. **Website:** lightandlifemagazine.com. **Contact:** Jeff Finley, executive editor. **50% freelance written.** *Light + Life Magazine* is a monthly magazine published by Light + Life Communications, the publishing arm of the Free Methodist Church–USA. Each issue focuses on a specific theme with a cohesive approach in which the articles complement each other. The magazine has a flip format with articles in English and Spanish. Estab. 1868. Circ. 38,000. Byline given. Pays on publication. No kill fee. Accepts queries by e-mail. Accepts simultaneous submissions. Responds in 2 months. Guidelines online.

NONFICTION Needs religious. Query. Length: 2,100 words for feature articles, 800 words for print discipleship articles, 500-1,000 words for online discipleship articles, 500-1,000 words for online articles not published in the magazine. **Pays $50 per article.**

$$ LIGUORIAN

One Liguori Dr., Liguori MO 63057. (636)223-1538. **Fax:** (636)223-1595. **E-mail:** liguorianeditor@liguori. org. **Website:** www.liguorian.org. **Contact:** Elizabeth Herzing, managing editor. **25% freelance written. Prefers to work with published/established writers.** Magazine published 10 times/year for Catholics. "Our purpose is to lead our readers to a fuller Christian life by helping them better understand the teachings of the gospel and the church and by illustrating how these teachings apply to life and the problems confronting them as members of families, the church, and society." Estab. 1913. Circ. 60,000. Pays on acceptance. Submit seasonal material 8 months in advance. Accepts queries by mail, e-mail, fax. Responds in 3 months to mss. Sample copy for 9x12 SAE with 3 first-class stamps or online. Guidelines for #10 SASE and on website.

NONFICTION "No travelogue approach or unresearched ventures into controversial areas. Also, no material found in secular publications—fad subjects that already get enough press, pop psychology, or negative articles. *Liguorian* does not consider *retold* Bible stories." **Buys 30-40 unsolicited mss/year.** Length: 400-2,200 words. **Pays 12-15¢/word and 5 contributor's copies.**

PHOTOS Photographs on assignment only unless submitted with and specific to article.

FICTION Needs religious, inspirational, senior citizen/retirement. Send complete ms. Length: 1,500-2,200 words. **Pays 12-15¢/word and 5 contributor's copies.**

TIPS "First read several issues containing short stories. We look for originality and creative input in each story we read. Consideration requires the author studies the target market and presents a carefully polished manuscript. We publish 1 fiction story per issue. Compare this with the 25 or more we receive over the transom each month. We believe fiction is a highly effective mode for transmitting the Christian message; however, many fiction pieces are written without a specific goal or thrust—an interesting incident that goes nowhere is not a story."

$ LIVE

Gospel Publishing House, 1445 N. Boonville Ave., Springfield MO 65802-1894. (417)862-1447. **E-mail:** rl-live@gph.org. **Website:** www.gospelpublishing. com. **100% freelance written.** Weekly magazine for weekly distribution covering practical Christian living. "*LIVE* is a take-home paper distributed weekly in young adult and adult Sunday school classes. We seek to encourage Christians in living for God through fiction and true stories which apply Biblical principles to everyday problems." Estab. 1928. Circ. 18,000. Byline given. Pays on acceptance. No kill fee. Publishes ms an average of 18 months after acceptance. Editorial lead time 12 months. Submit seasonal material 18 months in advance. Accepts queries by mail, e-mail. Accepts simultaneous submissions. Responds in 6 weeks to queries; in 8 weeks to mss. Sample copy for #10 SASE. Guidelines for #10 SASE or on website: www.gospel-publishing.com/store/startcat.cfm?cat=tWRITGUID.

NONFICTION Needs inspirational, religious. No preachy articles or stories that refer to religious myths (e.g., Santa Claus, Easter Bunny, etc.). **Buys 50-100 mss/year.** Send complete ms. Length: 550-1,100 words. **Pays 7-10¢/word.** Pays expenses of writers on assignment.

REPRINTS Send tearsheet, photocopy, or typed ms with rights for sale noted and information about when and where the material previously appeared. Pays 7¢/word.

PHOTOS Send photos. Identification of subjects required. Reviews 35mm transparencies and 3x4 prints or larger. Higher-resolution digital files also accepted. Offers $35-60/photo. Buys one-time rights.

FICTION Needs religious, inspirational, prose poem. No preachy fiction, fiction about Bible characters, or stories that refer to religious myths (e.g., Santa Claus, Easter Bunny, etc.). No science or Bible fiction. No controversial stories about such subjects as feminism, war, or capital punishment. **Buys 20-50 mss/year.** Send complete ms. Length: 800-1,200 words. **Pays 7-10¢/word.**

POETRY Needs free verse, haiku, light verse, traditional. Buys 15-24 poems/year. Submit maximum 3 poems. Length: 12-25 lines. **Pays $35-60.**

TIPS "Don't moralize or be preachy. Provide human interest articles with Biblical life application. Stories should consist of action, not just thought-life, interaction, or insight. Heroes and heroines should rise above failures, take risks for God, prove that scriptural principles meet their needs. Conflict and suspense should increase to a climax! Avoid pious conclusions. Characters should be interesting, believable, and realistic. Avoid stereotypes. Characters should be active, not just pawns to move the plot along. They should confront conflict and change in believable ways. Describe the character's looks and reveal his personality through his actions to such an extent that the reader feels he has met that person. Readers should care about the character enough to finish the story. Feature racial, ethnic, and regional characters in rural and urban settings."

☼❸❺ LIVE

Canadian Baptist Women of Ontario and Quebec, 5 International Blvd., Etobicoke ON M9W 6H3 Canada. (416)651-8967. **Website:** www.baptistwomen.com. **Contact:** Renee James, editor/director of communications. **15% freelance written.** Magazine published 6 times/year designed to help women grow in their authentic experience of God and in their intimate connection to mission. Vision: evangelical, egalitarian, Canadian. Estab. 1878. Circ. 3,500. Byline given. Pays on publication. No kill fee. Publishes ms an average of 6 months after acceptance. Editorial lead time 2 months. Submit seasonal material 4 months in advance. Accepts simultaneous submissions. Sample copy for 9x12 SAE with 2 first-class Canadian stamps.

NONFICTION Needs inspirational, interview, personal experience, religious. **Buys 15 mss/year.** Query first. Unsolicited mss not accepted. Length: 650-800 words. **Pays 10-12¢/word (Canadian).**

PHOTOS State availability. Captions required. Offers no additional payment for photos accepted with ms. Buys one-time rights.

TIPS "We cannot use unsolicited mss from non-Canadian writers. When submitting by e-mail, please send stories as messages, not as attachments."

❺ THE LIVING CHURCH

Living Church Foundation, P.O. Box 510705, Milwaukee WI 53203-0121. (414)276-5420. **Fax:** (414)276-7483. **E-mail:** jschuessler@livingchurch.org. **E-mail:** tlc@livingchurch.org. **Website:** www.livingchurch.org. **Contact:** John Schuessler, managing editor; Douglas LeBlanc, associate editor. **50% freelance written.** Magazine covering news or articles of interest to members of the Episcopal Church. Weekly magazine that presents news and views of the Episcopal Church and the wider Anglican Communion, along with articles on spirituality, Anglican heritage, and the application of Christianity in daily life. There are commentaries on scripture, book reviews, editorials, letters to the editor, and special thematic issues. Estab. 1878. Circ. 9,500. Byline given. Does not pay unless article is requested. No kill fee. Publishes ms an average of 3 months after acceptance. Editorial lead time 3 weeks. Submit seasonal material 2 months in advance. Accepts queries by mail, e-mail, fax. Responds in 2 weeks to queries. Responds in 1 month to mss. Sample copy free.

NONFICTION Needs opinion, personal experience, photo feature, religious. **Buys 10 mss/year.** Send complete ms. Length: 1,000 words. **Pays $25-100.** Sometimes pays expenses of writers on assignment.

PHOTOS Send photos. Reviews any size prints. Offers $15-50/photo. Buys one-time rights.

COLUMNS Benediction (devotional), 250 words; Viewpoint (opinion), under 1,000 words. Send complete ms. **Pays $50 maximum.**

POETRY Needs light verse, traditional.

💲💲 THE LOOKOUT

Christian Standard Media, 16965 Pine Lane, Ste. 202, Parker CO 80134. (800)543-1353. **E-mail:** lookout@ christianstandardmedia.com. **Website:** www.lookoutmag.com. **Contact:** Shawn McMullen, editor. Monthly magazine for Christian adults, with emphasis on spiritual growth, and discipleship. "Our purpose is to provide Christian adults with practical, Biblical teaching and current information that will help them mature as believers." Send mss only on request. Estab. 1894. Circ. 25,000. Byline given. Pays on acceptance. Offers 33% kill fee. Publishes ms an average of 3-6 months after acceptance. Editorial lead time 6-9 months. Accepts queries by e-mail. Sample on website. Assignment only.

NONFICTION Needs inspirational, interview, opinion, personal experience, religious. No fiction or poetry. **Buys 104-108 mss/year.** Assignments only. Length: 1,200 words. **Pays 11¢/word.**

TIPS "*The Lookout* publishes from a theologically conservative, nondenominational, and noncharismatic perspective. We aim primarily for those aged 30-55. Most readers are married and have elementary to young adult children. Our emphasis is on the needs of ordinary Christians who want to grow in their faith. We value well-informed articles that offer lively and clear writing as well as strong application. We often address tough issues and seek to explore fresh ideas or recent developments affecting today's Christians."

💲💲 THE LUTHERAN

8765 W. Higgins Rd., 5th Floor, Chicago IL 60631-4183. (770)380-2540. **Fax:** (773)380-2409. **E-mail:** lutheran@lutheran.org. **Website:** www.thelutheran.org. **Contact:** Daniel J. Lehmann, editor; Michael D. Watson, art director. **15% freelance written.** Monthly magazine for lay people in church covering news and activities of the Evangelical Lutheran Church in America, news of the world of religion, ethical reflections on issues in society, andpersonal Christian experience. Estab. 1988. Circ. 300,000. Byline given. Pays on acceptance. Offers 50% kill fee. Publishes ms an

average of 6 months after acceptance. Submit seasonal material 4 months in advance. Accepts queries by mail, e-mail. Responds in 6 weeks to queries. Sample copy free. Guidelines available online.

NONFICTION Needs inspirational, interview, personal experience, photo feature, religious. No articles unrelated to the world of religion. **Buys 40 mss/ year.** Query with published clips. Length: 250-1,200 words. **Pays $75-600.** Pays expenses of writers on assignment.

PHOTOS Send photos. Captions, identification of subjects required. Reviews contact sheets, transparencies, prints. Offers $50-175/photo. Buys one-time rights.

COLUMNS Contact editor.

TIPS "Writers have the best chance selling us feature articles."

💲 THE LUTHERAN DIGEST

The Lutheran Digest, Inc., 6160 Carmen Ave., Inver Grove Heights MN 55076. (651)451-9945. **E-mail:** editor@lutherandigest.com. **Website:** www.lutherandigest.com. **Contact:** Nick Skapyak, editor. **95% freelance written.** Quarterly magazine covering Christianity from a Lutheran perspective. Publishes articles, humor, and poetry. Articles frequently reflect a Lutheran Christian perspective but are not intended to be sermonettes. Popular stories show how God has intervened in a person's life to help solve a problem. Estab. 1953. Circ. 20,000. No byline given. Pays on publication. No kill fee. Publishes ms an average of 6 months after acceptance. Editorial lead time 9 months. Submit seasonal material 9 months in advance. "No queries, please." Accepts simultaneous submissions. Responds in 4 months to mss. No response to e-mailed mss unless selected for publication. Sample copy: $3.50. Subscription: $16/year, $22 for 2 years. Guidelines available online.

NONFICTION Needs general interest, historical, how-to, humor, inspirational, personal experience. Does not want to see personal tributes to deceased relatives or friends. These are seldom used unless the subject of the article is well known. Avoids articles about the moment a person finds Christ as his or her personal savior. **Buys 50-60 mss/year.** Send complete ms. Length: up to 1,500 words. **Pays $25-50.** Pays expenses of writers on assignment.

REPRINTS Accepts previously published submissions. "We prefer this as we are a digest and 70-80% of our articles are reprints."

POETRY Submit up to 3 poems at a time. Prefers e-mail submissions but also accepts mailed submissions. Cover letter is preferred. Include SASE only if return is desired. Poems are selected by editor and reviewed by publication panel. Length: up to 25 lines/poem. **Pays 1 contributor's copy.**

TIPS "Reading our writers' guidelines and sample articles online is encouraged and is the best way to get a feel for the type of material we publish."

💲💲 MESSAGE MAGAZINE

North American Division of Seventh-day Adventists, 12501 Old Columbia Pike, Silver Spring MD 20904. (301)680-6598. **E-mail:** editor@messagemagazine.com; associateeditor@messagemagazine.com. **Website:** www.messagemagazine.com. **Contact:** Carmela Monk Crawford, editor. **10-20% freelance written.** Bimonthly magazine. "*Message* is the oldest religious journal addressing ethnic issues in the country. Our audience is predominantly Black and Seventh-day Adventist; however, *Message* is an outreach magazine for the churched and unchurched across cultural lines." Estab. 1898. Circ. 110,000. Byline given. Pays on acceptance. No kill fee. Publishes ms an average of 12 months after acceptance. Editorial lead time 6 months. Submit seasonal material 6 months in advance. Accepts simultaneous submissions. Responds in 9 months to queries. Sample copy by e-mail. Guidelines by e-mail and online.

NONFICTION Send complete ms. Length: 300-900 words. **Pays $75-300 for features.** Pays expenses of writers on assignment.

PHOTOS State availability. Identification of subjects required. Buys one time rights.

COLUMNS Eye on the Times: religious liberty, public affairs, human rights, and news (300 words); Optimal Health: health news, how-tos, and healthy habits (550 words). **Pays $75-150.**

TIPS "Please look at the magazine before submitting mss. *Message* publishes a variety of writing styles as long as the writing style is easy to read and flows. Please avoid highly technical writing styles."

💲💲 ONE

1011 First Ave., New York NY 10022-4195. (212)826-1480. **Fax:** (212)838-1344. **E-mail:** cnewa@cnewa.org; editorial@cnewa.org. **Website:** www.cnewa.org. **Contact:** Deacon Greg Kandra, executive editor. **75% freelance written.** Bimonthly magazine for a Catholic audience with interest in the Near East, particularly its current religious, cultural, and political aspects. Estab. 1974. Circ. 100,000. Byline given. Pays on publication. No kill fee. Publishes ms an average of 6 months after acceptance. Accepts queries by mail, fax. Accepts simultaneous submissions. Responds in 1 month to queries. Sample copy and writer's guidelines for 7½×10½ SAE with 2 first-class stamps.

NONFICTION Query. Length: 1,200-1,800 words. **Pays 20¢/edited word.** Pays expenses of writers on assignment.

PHOTOS "Photographs to accompany ms are welcome; they should illustrate the people, places, ceremonies, etc. which are described in the article. We prefer color transparencies but occasionally use b&w." Pay varies depending on use—scale from $50-300.

TIPS "We are interested in current events in the Near East as they affect the cultural, political, and religious lives of the people."

💲💲 OUTREACH MAGAZINE

5550 Tech Center Dr., Colorado Springs CO 80919. (800)991-6011, ext. 3315. **E-mail:** tellus@outreachmagazine.com. **Website:** www.outreachmagazine.com. **80% freelance written.** Bimonthly magazine covering outreach in Christianity. *Outreach* magazine is the gathering place of ideas, insights and stories for Christian churches focused on reaching out to their community—locally and globally—with the love of Christ. Primary readers are pastors and other church leadership, as well as laity who are passionate about outreach. Practical outreach ideas; church profiles and best practices; essential perspectives for leadership; in-depth interviews with leading pastors; trend-oriented features. Estab. 2003. Circ. 35,000. Byline given. Pays on publication. Offers 10% kill fee. Publishes ms an average of 2-4 months after acceptance. Editorial lead time 6 months. Submit seasonal material 6 months in advance. Accepts queries by mail, e-mail. Accepts simultaneous submissions. Responds in 2 months to queries; 8 months to mss. Sample copy free. Guidelines online.

NONFICTION Needs book excerpts, how-to, inspirational, interview, personal experience, religious. Special issues: Small Church America / Church Planting; The American Megachurch Annual; Leadership;

Outreach Resources of the Year; Evangelism, Discipleship, Service. Does not want fiction, poetry, non-outreach-related articles. **Buys 30 mss/year.** Query with published clips. Length: 1,500-2,500 words. Interview sometimes run as long as 4,000 words (assignment only). **Pays approximately 35 cents/word.** Pays expenses of writers on assignment.

PHOTOS Send photos. Identification of subjects required. Reviews GIF/JPEG files. Negotiates payment individually. Buys all rights.

COLUMNS Ideas—For Any Church, Any Size (short stories about outreach-oriented churches and ministries), 250-350 words; Soulfires—Igniting Ministry (dramatic as-told-to features about average individuals (not paid clergy) who have become passionate about a need and established a ministry to meet it; Leadership—Essential Perspectives for Those Who Lead (assigned). Query with published clips. **Approximately 35 cents/per word.**

FILLERS Needs facts, gag.

TIPS "Study our magazine and writer's guidelines. Send published clips that showcase tight, bright writing as well as your ability to interview; research; and organize numerous sources into an article; and write a 100-word piece as well as a 1,600-word piece."

💲💲 PENTECOSTAL EVANGEL

The General Council of the Assemblies of God, 1445 N. Boonville Ave., Springfield MO 65802. (417)862-2781. **Fax:** (417)862-0416. **E-mail:** pe@ag.org. **Website:** pe.ag.org. **Contact:** Ken Horn, editor. **5-10% freelance written.** Weekly magazine emphasizing news of the Assemblies of God for members of the Assemblies and other Pentecostal and charismatic Christians. "Articles should be inspirational without being preachy. Any devotional writing should take a literal approach to the Bible. A variety of general topics and personal experience accepted with inspirational tie-in." Estab. 1913. Circ. 180,000. Byline given. Pays on acceptance. Offers 100% kill fee. Publishes ms an average of 6 months or more after acceptance. Editorial lead time 3 months. Submit seasonal material 6 months in advance. Accepts queries by e-mail. Accepts simultaneous submissions. Responds in 2 weeks to queries. Responds in 2 months to mss. Sample copy free. Guidelines available online.

NONFICTION Needs book excerpts, general interest, inspirational, personal experience, religious. Does not want poetry, fiction, self-promotional. **Buys 10-**

15 mss/year. Send complete ms. Length: 500-1,200 words. **Pays 6 ¢/word and contributor's copies.**

TIPS "We publish first-person articles concerning spiritual experiences; that is, answers to prayer for help in a particular situation, of unusual conversions or healings through faith in Christ. All articles submitted to us should be related to religious life. We are Protestant, evangelical, Pentecostal, and any doctrines or practices portrayed should be in harmony with the official position of our denomination (Assemblies of God)."

💲 THE PENTECOSTAL MESSENGER

Pentecostal Church of God, P.O. Box 211866, Bedford TX 76095. (817)554-5900; (417)624-7050. **Fax:** (817)391-4101. **E-mail:** info@pcg.org. **Website:** www.pcg.org. Monthly magazine covering Christian, inspirational, religious, leadership news. "Our organization is Pentecostal in nature. Our publication goes out to our ministers and laypeople to educate, inspire and inform them of topics around the world and in our organization that will help them in their daily walk." Estab. 1919. Circ. 5,000. Byline given. Pays on publication. Editorial lead time 6 months. Submit themed material 6 months in advance. Accepts queries by mail. Accepts simultaneous submissions. May contact the *Pentecostal Messenger* for a list of monthly themes.

NONFICTION Needs book excerpts, essays, expose, general interest, inspirational, interview, new product, personal experience, religious. **Buys 12-24 mss/year.** Send complete ms. Length: 750-2,000 words. **Pays $15-40.**

PHOTOS Send photos. Identification of subjects required. Reviews prints. Offers no additional payment for photos accepted with ms. Buys one time rights.

💲💲 THE PLAIN TRUTH

Plain Truth Ministries, 300 W. Green St., Pasadena CA 91129. (800)309-4466. **Fax:** (626)358-4846. **E-mail:** managing.editor@ptm.org. **Website:** www.ptm.org. **90% freelance written.** Bimonthly magazine. "We seek to reignite the flame of shattered lives by illustrating the joy of a new life in Christ." Estab. 1935. Circ. 70,000. Byline given. Pays on publication. Offers $50 kill fee. Publishes ms an average of 8 months after acceptance. Editorial lead time 6 months. Submit seasonal material 6 months in advance. Accepts queries by mail, e-mail. Accepts simultaneous submissions.

Sample copy for sae with 9x12 envelope and 5 first-class stamps. Guidelines available online.

NONFICTION Needs inspirational, interview, personal experience, religious. **Buys 48-50 mss/year.** Query with published clips and SASE. *No unsolicited mss.* Length: 750-2,500 words. **Pays 25¢/word.**

REPRINTS Send tearsheet or photocopy of article or typed ms with rights for sale ted and information about when and where the article previously appeared with SASE for response. Pays 15¢/word.

PHOTOS State availability. Captions required. Reviews transparencies, prints. Negotiates payment individually. Buys one time rights.

TIPS "Material should offer Biblical solutions to real-life problems. Both first-person and third-person illustrations are encouraged. Articles should take a unique twist on a subject. Material must be insightful and practical for the Christain reader. All articles must be well researched and Biblically accurate without becoming overly scholastic. Use convincing arguments to support your Christian platform. Use vivid word pictures, simple and compelling language, and avoid stuffy academic jargon. Captivating anecdotes are vital."

$$ POINT

Converge (Baptist General Conference), 11002 Lake Hart Dr., Mail Code 200, Orlando FL 32832. (407)563-6083. **Fax:** (866)990-8980. **E-mail:** bob.putman@converge.org. **Website:** www.converge.org. **Contact:** Bob Putman, editor. **15% freelance written.** Nonprofit, religious, evangelical Christian magazine published 4 times/year covering Converge. *Point* is the official magazine of Converge (BGC). Almost exclusively uses articles related to Converge, their churches, or by/about Converge people. Circ. 43,000. Byline given. Pays on publication. Offers 50% kill fee. Editorial lead time 6 months. Submit seasonal material 6 months in advance. Accepts queries by e-mail. Accepts simultaneous submissions. Responds in 1 month to queries; in 3 months to mss. Sample upon request. Guidelines available free.

NONFICTION Buys 6-8 mss/year. Query with published clips. Wants "articles about our people, churches, missions. View online at www.converge.org before sending anything." Length: 300-1,500 words. **Pays $60-280.** Pays expenses of writers on assignment.

PHOTOS State availability. Captions, identification of subjects, model releases required. Reviews prints, some high-resolution digital. Offers $15-60/photo. Buys one-time rights.

COLUMNS Converge Connection (blurbs of news happening in Converge Worldwide), 50-150 words. Send complete ms and photos. **Pays $30.**

POETRY Needs We do not publish poetry.

TIPS "Please study the magazine and the denomination. We will send sample copies to interested freelancers and give further information about our publication needs upon request. Freelancers from our churches who are interested in working on assignment are especially welcome."

🍁$ PRAIRIE MESSENGER

Benedictine Monks of St. Peter's Abbey, P.O. Box 190, 100 College Dr., Muenster Saskatchewan S0K 2Y0 Canada. (306)682-1772. **Fax:** (306)682-5285. **E-mail:** pm.canadian@stpeterspress.ca. **Website:** www.prairiemessenger.ca. **Contact:** Maureen Weber, associate editor. **30% freelance written.** Weekly Catholic publication published by the Benedictine Monks of St. Peter's Abbey. Has a strong focus on ecumenism, social justice, interfaith relations, aboriginal issues, arts, and culture. Estab. 1904. Circ. 4,000. Byline given. Pays on publication. No kill fee. Publishes ms an average of 4 months after acceptance. Submit seasonal material 3 months in advance. Accepts queries by mail, e-mail. Accepts simultaneous submissions. Responds only if interested; send nonreturnable samples. Sample copy for 9x12 SASE with $1 Canadian postage or IRCs. Guidelines available online. "Because of government subsidy regulations, we are no longer able to accept non-Canadian freelance material."

NONFICTION Needs book excerpts, essays, interview, opinion, religious. Special issues: Christmas, Easter. **Buys 15 mss/year.** Send complete ms. Length: 500-800 words. **Pays $70/article.**

PHOTOS Send photos. Captions required. Reviews 3x5 prints. Offers $25/photo. Buys all rights.

POETRY Needs Shorter poems preferred. Buys 45 poems/year. Length: up to 35 lines. **Pays $30/published poem.**

$$ PRESBYTERIANS TODAY

Presbyterian Church (U.S.A.), 100 Witherspoon St., Louisville KY 40202-1396. (502)569-5627. **Fax:** (502)569-8887. **E-mail:** editor@pcusa.org. **Website:** www.pcusa.org/today. **Contact:** Patrick David Heery, editor. **25% freelance written. Prefers to work with**

published/established writers. Denominational magazine published 6 times/year covering religion, denominational activities, and public issues for members of the Presbyterian Church (U.S.A.). "The magazine's purpose is to increase understanding and appreciation of what the church and its members are doing to live out their Christian faith." Estab. 1867. Circ. 30,000. Byline given. Pays on acceptance. Publishes ms an average of 6 months after acceptance. Editorial lead time 3 months. Submit seasonal material 3 months in advance. Accepts queries by e-mail. Accepts simultaneous submissions. Responds in 2 weeks to queries. Sample copy free. Guidelines available online.

NONFICTION **Buys 20 mss/year.** Send complete ms. Length: 1,000-1,800 words. **Pays $300 maximum for assigned articles; $75-300 for unsolicited articles.** Pays expenses of writers on assignment.

PHOTOS State availability. Identification of subjects required. Reviews contact sheets, transparencies, color prints, digital images. Negotiates payment individually. Buys one-time rights.

$ PURPOSE

MennoMedia, P.O. Box 866, 100 S. Mason St., Suite B, Harrisonburg VA 22801. **E-mail:** purposeeditor@mennomedia.org. **Website:** www.mennomedia.org/purpose. Publisher: Amy Gingerich. **Contact:** Melodie M. Davis. **80% freelance written.** Magazine focuses on Christian discipleship—how to be a faithful Christian in the midst of everyday life situations. Uses personal story form to present models and examples to encourage Christians in living a life of faithful discipleship. Each issue follows a designated theme. *Purpose* is published monthly by Mennomedia, the publisher for Mennonite Church Canada and Mennonite Church USA. It is a faith-based adult monthly magazine that focuses on discipleship-living, simplicity, and the Christian faith. Check the theme list on the website. Estab. 1968. Circ. 4,400. Byline given. Pays upon publication. No kill fee. Publishes ms 6-9 months after acceptance. Editorial lead time: 9 months. Submit material according to writer guidelines and theme deadlines posted on the website. Accepts queries by e-mail. Responds in 1-3 months. Sample articles can be viewed on the website. Guidelines online.

NONFICTION **Buys 140 mss/year.** E-mail submissions preferred. Length: 500-700 words. **Pays $25-50/story.**

POETRY Needs free verse, light verse, traditional. Poetry must address monthly themes of a spiritual nature. Buys 8-10 poems/year. Length: 12 lines maximum. **Pays $10-20/poem.**

TIPS "We seek true stories that follow monthly themes. Be sure to look at the website for the theme list and deadlines, as we only consider stories that are tied to the themes. Follow the writer guidelines on the website for the latest submission information."

$$ ST. ANTHONY MESSENGER

Franciscan Media, 28 W. Liberty St., Cincinnati OH 45202-6498. (513)241-5615. **Fax:** (513)241-0399. **E-mail:** magazineeditors@franciscanmedia.org. **Website:** www.stanthonymessenger.org. **Contact:** Pat McCloskey, OFM, Franciscan Editor. **55% freelance written.** Monthly general-interest magazine for a national readership of Catholic families, most of which have children or grandchildren in grade school, high school, or college. *St. Anthony Messenger* is a Catholic family magazine which aims to help its readers lead more fully human and Christian lives. "We publish articles that report on a changing church and world, opinion pieces written from the perspective of Christian faith and values, personality profiles, and fiction which entertains and informs. Take our writer's guidelines very seriously. We do!" Estab. 1893. Circ. 70,000. Byline given. Pays on acceptance. No kill fee. Publishes ms within an average of 1 year after acceptance. Submit seasonal material 6 months in advance. Accepts queries by mail, e-mail, fax. Responds in 3 weeks to queries; 2 months to mss. Sample copy for 9x12 SAE with 4 first-class stamps. Please study writer's guidelines at StAnthonyMessenger.org.

NONFICTION Needs how-to, humor, inspirational, interview, opinion, personal experience. **Buys 35-50 mss/year.** Query with published clips. Length: 2,000 words maximum **Pays 20¢/word.** Pays expenses of writers on assignment. Pays expenses as negotiated beforehand.

FICTION Needs mainstream. "We do not want mawkishly sentimental or preachy fiction. Stories are most often rejected for poor plotting and characterization, bad dialogue (listen to how people talk), and inadequate motivation. Many stories say nothing, are 'happenings' rather than stories. No fetal journals, no rewritten Bible stories." **Buys 12 mss/year.** Send complete ms. Length: 2,000 words maximum. **Pays 20¢/word.**

POETRY Submit a few poems at a time. "Please include your phone number and a SASE with your submission. Do not send us your entire collection of poetry. Poems must be original." Submit seasonal poems several months in advance. "Our poetry needs are very limited." Submit maximum 4-5 poems. Length: up to 20-25 lines; "the shorter, the better." **Pays $2/line; $20 minimum.**

TIPS "The freelancer should consider why his or her proposed article would be appropriate for us, rather than for *Redbook* or *Saturday Review*. We treat human problems of all kinds, but from a religious perspective. Articles should reflect Catholic theology, spirituality, and employ a Catholic terminology and vocabulary. We need more articles on prayer, scripture, Catholic worship. Get authoritative information (not merely library research); we want interviews with experts. Write in popular style; use lots of examples, stories, and personal quotes. Word length is an important consideration."

$ SEEK

Standard Publishing, 4050 Lee Vance View Dr., Colorado Springs CO 80918. (800)323-7543. **E-mail:** seek@standardpublishing.com. **Website:** www.standardpub.com. "Inspirational stories of faith-in-action for Christian adults; a Sunday School take-home paper." Quarterly. Estab. 1970. Circ. 27,000. Byline given. Pays on acceptance. No kill fee. Acceptance to publishing time is 1 year. Accepts queries by e-mail. Accepts simultaneous submissions. Guidelines available online.

NONFICTION Send complete ms. Length: 850-1,000 words. **Pays 7¢/word for first rights; 5¢/word for reprint rights.** Pays expenses of writers on assignment.

FICTION List of upcoming themes available online. Accepts 150 mss/year. Send complete ms. Prefers submissions by e-mail. "*SEEK* corresponds to the topics of Standard Publishing's adult curriculum line and is designed to further apply these topics to everyday life." Unsolicited mss must be written to a theme list. Does not want poetry. Send complete ms. Prefers submissions by e-mail. Length: 850-1,000 words. **Pays 7¢/word.**

TIPS "Write a credible story with a Christian slant—no preachments; avoid overworked themes such as joy in suffering, generation gaps, etc. Most mss are rejected by us because of irrelevant topic or message, unrealistic story, or poor character and/or plot development. We use fiction stories that are believable."

$ SOCIAL JUSTICE REVIEW

3835 Westminster Place, St. Louis MO 63108. (314)371-1653. **Fax:** (314)371-0889. **Website:** www.socialjusticereview.org. **25% freelance written. Works with a small number of new/unpublished writers each year.** Bimonthly magazine "to promote a true Christian humanism with respect for the dignity and rights of all human beings." Estab. 1908. No kill fee. Publishes ms an average of 1 year after acceptance. Accepts queries by mail. Sample copy for SAE with 9x12 envelope and 3 first-class stamps.

NONFICTION Query by mail only with SASE. Length: 2,500-3,000 words. **Pays about 2¢/word.**

REPRINTS Send typed ms with rights for sale noted and information about when and where the material previously appeared. Pays about 2¢/word.

TIPS "Write moderate essays completely compatible with papal teaching and readable to the average person."

$ SPIRITUAL LIFE

2131 Lincoln Rd. NE, Washington DC 20002-1199. (888)616-1713; (202)832-5505. **Fax:** (202)832-5711. **E-mail:** edodonnell@aol.com. **Website:** www.spiritual-life.org. **Contact:** Edward O'Donnell, editor. **80% freelance written. Prefers to work with published/established writers.** Quarterly magazine for largely Christian, well-educated, serious readers. Circ. 12,000. Pays on acceptance. No kill fee. Publishes ms an average of 1 year after acceptance. Responds in 2 months to queries. Sample copy and writer's guidelines for 7x10 or larger SAE with 5 first-class stamps.

NONFICTION Sentimental articles or those dealing with specific devotional practices not accepted. No fiction or poetry. **Buys 20 mss/year.** Length: 3,000-5,000 words. **Pays $50 minimum, and 2 contributor's copies.**

$ THE UPPER ROOM

1908 Grand Ave., P.O. Box 340004, Nashville TN 37203. (615)340-7252. **Fax:** (615)340-7267. **E-mail:** theupperroommagazine@upperroom.org. **Website:** submissions.upperroom.org. **95% freelance writ-**

ten. **Eager to work with new/unpublished writers.** Bimonthly magazine offering a daily inspirational message, which includes a Bible reading, text, prayer, "Thought for the Day," and suggestion for further prayer. Each day's meditation is written by a different person and is usually a personal witness about discovering meaning and power for Christian living through scripture study which illuminates daily life. Circ. 2.2 million (US); 385,000 outside US. Byline given. Pays on publication. No kill fee. Publishes ms an average of 1 year after acceptance. Submit seasonal material 14 months in advance. Accepts queries by online submission form. Accepts simultaneous submissions. Sample copy and writer's guidelines with a 4x6 SAE and 2 first-class stamps. Guidelines only for #10 SASE or online, submissions.upperroom.org/guidelines.

NONFICTION Needs inspirational, personal experience, Bible-study insights. Special issues: Lent and Easter; Advent. No poetry or lengthy spiritual journey stories. **Buys 365 unsolicited mss/year.** Send complete ms by mail or use online submission form, submissions.upperroom.org. Length: 300-400 words. **Pays $30/meditation.** Pays expenses of writers on assignment.

TIPS "The best way to break in to our magazine is to send a well-written ms that looks at the Christian faith in a fresh way. Standard stories and sermon illustrations are immediately rejected. We want to find new writers and welcome good material. We are interested in meditations based on Old Testament characters and stories. Good repeat meditations can lead to work on longer assignments for our other publications, which pay more. A writer who can deal concretely with everyday situations, relate them to the Bible and spiritual truths, and write clear, direct prose should be able to write for *The Upper Room*. We want material that provides for interaction on the part of the reader—meditation suggestions, journaling suggestions, space to reflect and link personal experience with the meditation for the day. Meditations that are personal, authentic, exploratory, and full of sensory detail make good devotional writing."

💲💲 U.S. CATHOLIC

Claretian Publications, 205 W. Monroe St., Chicago IL 60606. (312)236-7782. **Fax:** (312)236-8207. **E-mail:** literaryeditor@uscatholic.org. **E-mail:** submissions@claretians.org. **Website:** www.uscatholic.org. **Mostly freelance written.** Monthly magazine covering contemporary issues from a Catholic perspective. "*U.S. Catholic* puts faith in the context of everyday life. With a strong focus on social justice, we offer a fresh and balanced take on the issues that matter most in our world, adding a faith perspective to such challenges as poverty, education, family life, the environment, and even pop culture." Estab. 1935. Circ. 25,000. Byline given. Pays on acceptance. No kill fee. Publishes ms an average of 6 months after acceptance. Editorial lead time 8 months. Submit seasonal material 6 months in advance. Accepts queries by mail, e-mail. Responds in 1 month to queries; in 2 months to mss. Guidelines on website.

NONFICTION Needs essays, inspirational, opinion, personal experience, religious. **Buys 100 mss/year.** Send complete ms. Length: 700-1,400 words. **Pays minimum $200.**

PHOTOS State availability.

FICTION Accepts short stories. "Topics vary, but unpublished fiction should be no longer than 1,500 words and should include strong characters and cause readers to stop for a moment and consider their relationships with others, the world, and/or God. Specifically religious themes are not required; subject matter is not restricted. E-mail submissions@uscatholic.org." Needs ethnic, mainstream, religious, slice-of-life vignettes. **Buys 4-6 mss/year.** Send complete ms. Length: 700-1,500 words. **Pays minimum $200.**

POETRY Needs free verse. Submit 3-5 poems at a time. Accepts e-mail submissions (pasted into body of message or as attachments). Cover letter is preferred. No light verse. Buys 12 poems/year. Length: up to 50 lines/poem. **Pays $75.**

💲💲 THE WAR CRY

The Salvation Army, 615 Slaters Lane, Alexandria VA 22314. (703)684-4128. **Fax:** (703)684-5539. **E-mail:** war_cry@usn.salvationarmy.org. **Website:** publications.salvationarmyusa.org. **10% freelance written.** "Inspirational magazine with evangelical emphasis and portrayals that express the mission of the Salvation Army. Twelve issues published per year, including special Easter and Christmas issues." Estab. 1881. Circ. 200,000 monthly; 1.7 million Christmas; 1.1 million Easter. Byline given. Pays on acceptance. No kill fee. Publishes ms an average of 2 months to 1 year after acceptance. Editorial lead time 2 months before issue date; Christmas and Easter issues 6 months before issue date. Submit Christmas and Easter material 6 months in advance. Accepts simultaneous submissions. Responds in 3-4 weeks to mss. Sample copy, theme list, and writer's guidelines free with #10 SASE or online.

NONFICTION "*The War Cry* represents The Salvation Army's mission through features, news, profiles, commentaries, and stories. It seeks to bring people to Christ, help believers grow in faith and character, and promote redemptive cultural practices from the perspective of The Salvation Army programs, minisitries, and doctrines." No missionary stories, confessions. **Buys 30 mss/year.** Complete mss and reprints accepted through website at publications.salvationarmyusa. org/writers-submissions. Submissions strengthened when photos included where appropriate. **Pays 35¢/ word.** Pays expenses of writers on assignment.

REPRINTS Considers reprints.

PHOTOS Accepts submissions for the "In the Moment" feature appearing in each issue. High-resolution photos (600 dpi) with captions. Identification of subjects required. Pays $50. Buys one-time rights.

FICTION Short stories that do not expound on dogma but depict how faith and life intersect.

POETRY Purchases limited poetry (10 per year maximum).

FILLERS Needs anecdotes, religious news, statistical analysis of trends, and vignettes. **Buys 10-20 mss/ year.** Length: 100-400 words. **Pays 35¢/word.**

🖊️💲 WOMAN ALIVE

Christian Publishing and Outreach, Garcia Estate, Canterbury Rd., Worthing West Sussex BN13 1BW United Kingdom. (44)(1903) 60-4352. **E-mail:** womanalive@cpo.org.uk. **Website:** www.womanalive. co.uk. **Contact:** Jackie Harris, editor; Wendy Longhurst, editorial assistant. *Woman Alive* is a Christian magazine geared specifically toward women. It covers all denominations and seeks to inspire, encourage, and provide resources to women in their faith, helping them to grow in their relationship with God and providing practical help and biblical perspective on the issues impacting their lives. Pays on publication. No kill fee. Accepts queries by mail, e-mail. Accepts simultaneous submissions. Sample copy for £1.50, plus postage. Guidelines available on website.

NONFICTION Needs how-to, personal experience. Submit clips, bio, article summary, ms, SASE. Length: 750-850 words/1-page article; 1,200-1,500 words/2-

page article; 1,600-1,800 words/3-page article. **Pays £75/1-page article; £100/2-page article; £130/3-page article.** Pays expenses of writers on assignment.

PHOTOS Send photos. Reviews 300 dpi digital images.

RETIREMENT

💲💲💲💲 AARP THE MAGAZINE

AARP, c/o Editorial Submissions, 601 E. St. NW, Washington DC 20049. **E-mail:** aarpmagazine@ aarp.org. **Website:** www.aarp.org/magazine. **50% freelance written. Prefers to work with published/ established writers.** Bimonthly magazine covering issues that affect people over the age of 50. *AARP The Magazine* is devoted to the varied needs and active life interests of AARP members, age 50 and over, covering such topics as financial planning, travel, health, careers, retirement, relationships, and social and cultural change. Its editorial content serves the mission of AARP, seeking through education, advocacy, and service to enhance the quality of life for all by promoting independence, dignity, and purpose. Circ. 22,721,661. Byline given. Pays on acceptance. Offers 25% kill fee. Publishes ms an average of 6 months after acceptance. Submit seasonal material 6 months in advance. Accepts queries by mail, e-mail. Accepts simultaneous submissions. Responds in 3 months to queries. Sample copy free. Guidelines available online.

NONFICTION No previously published articles. Query for features, or submit complete ms for personal essays. Submit queries and mss via e-mail or mail. "Story pitches for specific features and departments should be 1 page in length and accompanied by recent writing samples. The pitch should explain the idea for the piece, tell how you would approach it as a writer, give some sense of your writing style, and mention the section of the magazine for which the piece is intended. Your samples should not include the actual story that you are proposing, except in the case of personal essays, which should be submitted in full. Features and departments cover the following categories: Money (investments, savings, retirement, and work issues); Health and Fitness (tips, trends, studies); Food and Nutrition (recipes, emphasis on healthy eating); Travel (tips and trends on how and where to travel); Consumerism (practical information and advice); General Interest (new thinking, research, information on timely topics, trends); Relationships (family matters, caregiving, living arrangements, grandparents); Personal Essay (thoughtful, timely, new takes on matters of importance to people over 50); Personal Best (first-person essays on leisure-time pursuits). Length: up to 2,000 words. **Pays $1/word.** Pays expenses of writers on assignment.

PHOTOS Photos purchased with or without accompanying mss. Pays $250 and up for color; $150 and up for b&w.

TIPS "The most frequent mistake made by writers in completing an article for us is poor follow-through with basic research. The outline is often more interesting than the finished piece. We do not accept unsolicited mss."

💲 CHRISTIAN LIVING IN THE MATURE YEARS

The United Methodist Publishing House, 2222 Rosa L. Parks Blvd., P.O. Box 17890, Nashville TN 37228-7890. **E-mail:** matureyears@umpublishing.org. **Website:** matureyears.submittable.com. **80% freelance written. Prefers to work with published/established writers.** Quarterly magazine designed to help persons in and nearing the retirement years understand and appropriate the resources of the Christian faith in dealing with specific problems and opportunities related to aging. Estab. 1954. Circ. 35,000. Byline given. Pays on acceptance. No kill fee. Publishes ms an average of 1 year after acceptance. Submit seasonal material 14 months in advance. Responds in 2-3 months to mss. Guidelines online.

NONFICTION Needs how-to, humor, inspirational, memoir, personal experience, religious, older adult health, life, faith, finance issues. **Buys 75-80 mss/year.** Send complete ms to matureyears.submittable.com. No longer accepts e-mailed or hard-copy submissions. Length: 500-2,000 words. **Pays 7¢/word.**

PHOTOS Send high-resolution photos. Captions, model releases required. Negotiates pay individually. Typically buys one-time rights.

☯ 💲 INSPIRED SENIOR LIVING

Stratis Publishing Ltd., 3, 3948 Quadra St., Victoria BC V8X 1J6 Canada. (250)479-4705. **E-mail:** editor@ seniorlivingmag.com. **Website:** www.seniorliving-mag.com. **Contact:** Bobbie Jo Reid, managing editor. **100% freelance written.** Magazine published 12 times/year covering active 55+ living. Inspiration

for people over 55. Monthly magazine distributed throughout British Columbia, extensive website, 2 annual 55+ Lifestyle Shows. Estab. 2004. Circ. 50,000. Byline given. Pays quarterly. No kill fee. Publishes an average of 2-3 months after acceptance. Editorial lead time 3 months. Submit seasonal material 6 months in advance. Accepts queries by e-mail. Sample copy available online. Guidelines available.

NONFICTION Needs historical, how-to, humor, inspirational, interview, personal experience, travel, profiles of inspiring people age 55+ who live in British Columbia. Special issues: Special issues: housing, travel, charitable giving, fashion. Does not want politics; religion; promotion of business, service, or products; humor that demeans senior demographic or aging process. Query. Does not accept previously published material. Length: 500-1,200 words. **Pays $35-150 for assigned articles; $35-150 for unsolicited articles.** Pays expenses of writers on assignment. Sometimes pays expenses (limit agreed upon in advance).

PHOTOS Send photos. Identification of subjects, model releases required. Reviews GIF/JPEG files. Offers $10-75 per photo. Buys all rights.

COLUMNS Buys 5-6 mss/year. Query with published clips. **Pays $25-$50.**

TIPS "Editorial must be about or reflect the lifestyles of people age 55+ living in British Columbia."

RURAL

💲💲 BACKWOODS HOME MAGAZINE

P.O. Box 712, Gold Beach OR 97444. (541)247-8900. **Fax:** (541)247-8600. **E-mail:** lisa@backwoodshome. com. **E-mail:** article-submission@backwoodshome. com. **Website:** www.backwoodshome.com. **Contact:** Lisa Nourse, editorial coordinator. **90% freelance written.** Bimonthly magazine covering self-reliance. *Backwoods Home Magazine* is written for people who have a desire to pursue personal independence, self-sufficiency, and their dreams. Offers how-to articles on self-reliance. Estab. 1989. Circ. 38,000. Byline given. Pays on acceptance. Editorial lead time 4-6 months. Submit seasonal material 4-6 months in advance. Accepts queries by mail, e-mail. Sample copy for 9x10 SAE and 6 first-class stamps. Guidelines available online.

NONFICTION Needs general interest, how-to, humor, personal experience, technical. **Buys 120 mss/**

year. Send complete ms via e-mail (no attachments) or postal mail. Looking for straightforward, clear writing similar to what you would find in a good newspaper. Length: 500 words. **Pays $40-200.** Pays expenses of writers on assignment.

PHOTOS Send photos. Captions, identification of subjects, model releases required. Offers no additional payment for photos accepted with ms.

💲💲 COUNTRY

Trusted Media Brands, Inc., 1610 N. 2nd St., Suite 102, Milwaukee WI 53212. **Website:** www.country-magazine.com. *Country* celebrates the breathtaking beauty, engaging people, enduring values, and spirutally rewarding lifestyle of the American countryside. Pays on acceptance. Accepts queries by online submission form. Accepts simultaneous submissions. Guidelines online.

NONFICTION All stories are considered on speculation, do not send a query. Submit via mail or e-mail. Photos and mss submitted through the mail will not be returned. E-mailed stories should be included in the body of an e-mail or in an attached .doc, .docx, .rtf, or .odt file. Word length usually runs 400-500 words for a 1-page story. **Pays $250 for story submissions that run a page or more.** Pays expenses of writers on assignment.

PHOTOS To e-mail photos, attach them as a high-res JPG file (at least 1800 x 1200 pixels or 1 MB file size). Requires caption information.

✪💲💲 THE COUNTRY CONNECTION

Pinecone Publishing, 691 Pinecrest Rd., Boulter ON K0L 1G0 Canada. (866)332-3651; (613)332-3651. **Website:** www.pinecone.on.ca. **Contact:** Gus Zylstra, publisher. **100% freelance written.** Magazine published 4 times/year covering nature, environment, history, heritage, nostalgia, travel and the arts. *The Country Connection* is a magazine for true nature lovers and the rural adventurer. Building on our commitment to heritage, cultural, artistic, and environmental themes, we continually add new topics to illuminate the country experience of people living within nature. Our goal is to chronicle rural life in its many aspects, giving `voice' to the countryside. Estab. 1989. Circ. 4,000. Byline given. Pays on publication. No kill fee. Publishes ms an average of 4 months after acceptance. Editorial lead time 4 months. Accepts queries

by mail, e-mail, phone. Sample copy for $5.64. Guidelines available online.

NONFICTION Needs general interest, historical, humor, opinion, personal experience, travel, lifestyle, leisure, art and culture, vegan recipes. No hunting, fishing, animal husbandry, or pet articles. **Buys 60 mss/year.** Send complete ms. Length: 500-2,000 words. **Pays 10¢/word.**

PHOTOS Send photos. Captions required. Reviews transparencies, prints, digital photos on CD. Offers $10-50/photo. Buys one time rights.

FICTION Needs adventure, fantasy, historical, humorous, slice-of-life vignettes, country living. **Buys 10 mss/year.** Send complete ms. Length: 500-1,500 words. **Pays 10¢/word.**

TIPS Canadian content only with a preference for Ontario subject matter. Send manuscript with appropriate support material such as photos, illustrations, maps, etc.

💲💲 FARM & RANCH LIVING

Trusted Media Brands, Inc., 1610 N. Second St., Suite 102, Milwaukee WI 53212-3906. (414)423-0100. **Fax:** (414)423-8463. **E-mail:** submissions@farmandranchliving.com. **Website:** farmandranchliving.com. **30% freelance written. Eager to work with new/ unpublished writers.** Bimonthly magazine aimed at families that live on, work on, or have ties to a farm or ranch. FRL focuses on people who celebrate the pleasures of living off the land rather than production and profits. Estab. 1978. Byline given. Pays on publication. No kill fee. Publishes ms an average of 6 months after acceptance. Submit seasonal material 6 months in advance. Accepts queries by e-mail. Accepts simultaneous submissions. "We are unable to respond to queries." To purchase a single copy, contact customercare@farmandranchliving.com.

NONFICTION Needs humor, inspirational, interview, personal experience, photo feature, nostalgia, prettiest place in the country (photo/text tour of ranch or farm). No issue-oriented stories (pollution, animal rights, etc.). **Buys 30 mss/year.** Send complete ms. Length: 600-1,200 words. **Pays up to $400 for text/photo package.** Pays expenses of writers on assignment.

REPRINTS Send photocopy with rights for sale noted. Payment negotiable.

PHOTOS "We no longer accept slides. We look for photos of farm animals, people, and rural scenery." State availability. Buys one-time rights.

TIPS "Our readers enjoy stories and features that are upbeat and positive. A freelancer must see *F&RL* to fully appreciate how different it is from other farm publications—ordering a sample is strongly advised. Photo features (about interesting farm or ranch families) and personality profiles are most open to freelancers."

🌐🌐 HOBBY FARMS

I-5 Publishing, 470 Conway Court, Suite B6, Lexington KY 40511. **E-mail:** hobbyfarms@luminamedia. com. **Website:** www.hobbyfarms.com. **85% freelance written.** Bimonthly magazine covering small farms and rural lifestyle. "*Hobby Farms* is the magazine for rural enthusiasts. Whether you have a small garden or 100 acres, there is something in *Hobby Farms* to educate, enlighten, or inspire you." Estab. 2001. Circ. 252,801. Byline given. Pays on publication. Publishes ms an average of 6 months after acceptance. Editorial lead time 4 months. Submit seasonal material 6 months in advance. Accepts queries by mail, e-mail. Accepts simultaneous submissions. Responds in 2 months to queries and mss. Guidelines free.

💬 "Writing tone should be conversational but authoritative."

NONFICTION Needs historical, how-to, interview, personal experience, technical, breed or crop profiles. **Buys 10 mss/year.** Send complete ms. Length: 1,000-1,500 words. Pays expenses of writers on assignment. Limit agreed upon in advance.

PHOTOS State availability of or send photos. Identification of subjects, model releases required. Reviews GIF/JPEG files. Negotiates payment individually. Buys one-time rights.

TIPS "Please state your specific experience with any aspect of farming (livestock, gardening, equipment, marketing, etc)."

🌐 THE LAND

Free Press Co., P.O. Box 3169, Mankato MN 56002-3169. (507)345-4523. **E-mail:** editor@thelandonline. com. **Website:** www.thelandonline.com. **40% freelance written.** Weekly tabloid covering farming and rural life in Minnesota and Northern Iowa. "Although we're not tightly focused on any one type of farming, our articles must be of interest to farmers. In other

words, will your article topic have an impact on people who live and work in rural areas?" Prefers to work with Minnesota or Iowa writers. Estab. 1976. Circ. 33,000. Byline given. Pays on acceptance. No kill fee. Publishes ms an average of 2 months after acceptance. Editorial lead time 2 months. Submit seasonal material 2 months in advance. Accepts queries by mail, e-mail. Accepts simultaneous submissions. Responds in 3 weeks to queries; in 2 months to mss. Sample copy free. Guidelines with #10 SASE.

NONFICTION Needs general interest, how-to. **Buys 80 mss/year.** Query. Length: 750-1000 words. **Pays $50-70 for assigned articles.**

PHOTOS Send photos. Reviews contact sheets. Negotiates payment individually. Buys one-time rights.

COLUMNS Query. **Pays $10-50.**

TIPS "Be enthused about rural Minnesota and Iowa life and agriculture, and be willing to work with our editors. We try to stress relevance. When sending me a query, convince me the story belongs in a Minnesota farm publication."

🌐 MONADNOCK TABLE

The Guide to Our Region's Food, Farms & Community, 60 West St., Keene NH 03431. (603)369-2525. **E-mail:** marcia@monadnocktable.com. **Website:** www. monadnocktable.com. **Contact:** Marcia Passos-Duffy, editor. Quarterly magazine for local food/farms in the Monadnock Region of New Hampshire. Estab. 2010. Circ. 15,000. Byline given. Pays on publication. Offers 25% kill fee. Publishes ms 3 months after acceptance. Editorial lead time 3 months. Submit seasonal material 3 months in advance. Accepts queries by e-mail. Accepts simultaneous submissions. Responds in 1 month. Sample copy online. Guidelines online.

NONFICTION Needs book excerpts, essays, how-to, interview, opinion, personal experience. Query. Length: 500-1,200 words. **Pays $75-125.** Pays expenses of writers on assignment.

PHOTOS Freelancers should state availability of photos with submission. Captions required. Reviews GIF/JPEG files. Offers no additional payment for photos accepted with ms.

COLUMNS Local Farmer (profile of local farmer in Monadnock Region), up to 600 words; Local Eats (profile of local chef and/or restaurant using local food), up to 600 words; Feature (how-to or "think" piece about local foods), up to 1,000 words; Books/

Opinion/Commentary (review of books, book excerpt, commentary, opinion pieces about local food), up to 500 words. **Buys 10 mss/year.** Query.

TIPS "Please query first with your qualifications. Please read magazine first for style (magazines available online). Must have a local (Monadnock Region/ Upper Valley New Hampshire) angle."

$ MOTHER EARTH NEWS

Ogden Publications, 1503 SW 42nd St., Topeka KS 66609-1265. (785)274-4300. **E-mail:** letters@motherearthnews.com. **Website:** www.motherearthnews.com. **Contact:** Oscar "Hank" Will III, editor; Rebecca Martin, managing editor. **Mostly written by staff and team of established freelancers.** Bimonthly magazine emphasizing country living, country skills, natural health, and sustainable technologies for both long-time and would-be ruralists. "*Mother Earth News* promotes self-sufficient, financially independent, and environmentally aware lifestyles. Many of our feature articles are written by our Contributing Editors, but we also assign articles to freelance writers, particularly those who have experience with our subject matter (both firsthand and writing experience)." Circ. 350,000. Byline given. Pays on publication. No kill fee. Submit seasonal material 5 months in advance. Accepts queries by mail, e-mail. Accepts simultaneous submissions. Responds in 6 months to mss. Sample copy: $5. Guidelines available online.

NONFICTION Needs how-to, green building, do-it-yourself, organic gardening, whole foods and cooking, natural health, livestock and sustainable farming, renewable energy, 21st-century homesteading, nature-environment-community, green transportation. No fiction, please. **Buys 35-50 mss/year.** "Query. Please send a short synopsis of the idea, a one-page outline, and any relevant digital photos and samples. If available, please send us copies of 1 or 2 published articles, or tell us where to find them online." **Pays $25-150.**

PHOTOS "We welcome quality photographs for our 2 departments."

COLUMNS Country Lore (helpful how-to tips); 100-300 words; Firsthand Reports (first-person stories about sustainable lifestyles of all sorts), 1,500-2,000 words.

TIPS "Read our magazine, and take a close look at previous issues to learn more abut the various topics we cover. We assign articles about 6-8 months ahead of publication date, so keep in mind timing and the seasonality of some topics. Our articles provide hands-on, useful information for people who want a more fun, conscientious, sustainable, secure, and satisfying lifestyle. Practicality is critical; freelance articles must be informative, well-documented, and tightly written in an engaging and energetic voice. For how-to articles, complete, easy-to-understand instructions are essential."

$$ RANGE

Purple Coyote Corp., 106 E. Adams St., Suite 201, Carson City NV 89706. (775)884-2200. **Fax:** (775)884-2213. **E-mail:** edit@rangemagazine.com. **Website:** www.rangemagazine.com. **Contact:** C.J. Hadley, editor/publisher. **70% freelance written.** *RANGE* covers ranching, farming, and the issues that affect agriculture. *RANGE* magazine is devoted to the issues that threaten the West, its people, lifestyles, lands, and wildlife. No stranger to controversy, *RANGE* is the leading forum for opposing viewpoints in the search for solutions that will halt the depletion of a national resource, the American rancher. Not interested in rodeo or travel stories. Estab. 1991. Pays on publication. Publishes ms an average of 3-6 months after acceptance. Accepts queries by e-mail. Accepts simultaneous submissions. Responds in 1-2 months to queries; in 1-4 months to mss. Sample copy: $2. Guidelines online.

NONFICTION Needs expose, historical, humor, nostalgic, opinion, photo feature, profile. No sports or events. No book reviews. Writer must be familiar with *RANGE*. Query via e-mail. Length: 500-2,000 words. **Pays $50-500.**

PHOTOS State availability of photography. Captions, photo credit, and contact information must be included with all photos. Reviews high-res digitals (JPEGS or TIFFS) via FTP site. Slides (on thumb drive with captions) and prints also reviewed. Pays $25-75, $100 for cover. Buys one-time rights. First North American preferred.

$ RURAL HERITAGE

P.O. Box 2067, Cedar Rapids IA 52406. (319)362-3027. **E-mail:** info@ruralheritage.com. **Website:** www.ruralheritage.com. **Contact:** Joe Mischka, editor. **98% freelance written. Willing to work with a small number of new/unpublished writers.** Bimonthly magazine devoted to the training and care of draft animals. Estab. 1976. Circ. 9,500. Byline given. Pays on publication. No kill fee. Publishes ms an average of 6 months after acceptance. Submit seasonal material 6 months in advance. Accepts queries by mail, e-mail. Accepts simultaneous submissions. Responds in 3 months to queries. Sample copy for $8. Guidelines available online.

NONFICTION Needs how-to, interview, photo feature. No articles on *mechanized* farming. **Buys 200 mss/year.** Query or send complete ms. Length: 1,200-1,500 words. **Pays 5¢/word.** Pays expenses of writers on assignment.

PHOTOS 6 covers/year, animals in harness $200. Photo guidelines with #10 SASE or online. Captions, identification of subjects required. Pays $10. Buys one time rights.

POETRY Needs traditional. **Pays $5-25.**

TIPS "Thoroughly understand our subject: working draft animals in harness. We'd like more pieces on plans and instructions for constructing various horse-drawn implements and vehicles. Always welcome are: 1.) Detailed descriptions and photos of horse-drawn implements, 2.) Prices and other details of draft animal and implement auctions and sales."

💲💲💲 RURALITE

5605 N.E. Elam Young Pkwy., Hillsboro OR 97124. (503)357-2105. **E-mail:** editor@ruralite.org. **E-mail:** curtisc@ruralite.org. **Website:** www.ruralite.org. **Contact:** Curtis Condon, editor. **80% freelance written. Works with new, unpublished writers.** Monthly magazine aimed at members of consumer-owned electric utilities throughout 7 western states. General-interest publication used by 48 rural electric cooperatives and PUDs. Readers are predominantly rural and small-town residents interested in stories about people and issues that affect Northwest lifestyles. Estab. 1954. Circ. 330,000. Byline given. Pays on acceptance. No kill fee. Accepts queries by mail. Accepts simultaneous submissions. Responds within 2 months to queries. Sample copy for 9x12 SAE with $1.61 of postage affixed. Guidelines available online.

NONFICTION Buys 50-60 mss/year. Length: 100-2,000 words. **Pays $50-800.**

REPRINTS Send typed ms with rights for sale noted and information about when and where the material previously appeared.

PHOTOS Illustrated stories are the key to a sale. Stories without art rarely make it. Color prints/negatives, color slides, all formats accepted. No b&w. Inside color is $25-100; cover photo is $250-350.

TIPS "Study recent issues. Follow directions when given an assignment. Be able to deliver a complete package (story and photos). We're looking for regular contributors to whom we can assign topics from our story list after they've proven their ability to deliver quality mss."

SCIENCE

💲💲 AD ASTRA

National Space Society, P.O. Box 98106, Washington DC 20090. (202)429-1600. **Fax:** (703)435-4390. **E-mail:** adastra@nss.org. **Website:** www.nss.org/adastra. **Contact:** Katherine Brick, editor. **90% freelance written.** *Ad Astra* ("to the stars") is the award-winning magazine of the National Space Society, featuring the latest news in space exploration and stunning full-color photography. Published quarterly. "We publish nontechnical, lively articles about all aspects of international space programs, from shuttle missions to planetary probes to plans for the future and commercial space." Estab. 1989. Circ. 25,000. Byline given. Pays on publication. No kill fee. Publishes ms 3-6 months after acceptance. Accepts queries by e-mail. Accepts simultaneous submissions. Responds only when interested. Sample copy for 9x12 SASE.

NONFICTION Needs book excerpts, essays, general interest, interview, opinion, photo feature, technical. No science fiction or UFO stories. Query with published clips. Length: 1,200-2,000 words with 2-8 full-size (8.5x11) color images at 300 dpi; 100-600 words for sidebars; 600-750 words for book reviews. **Pays 25¢/word.** Pays expenses of writers on assignment.

PHOTOS State availability. Identification of subjects required. Reviews color prints, digital, JPEG-IS, GISS. Negotiates pay. Buys one-time rights.

TIPS "We require mss to be in Word or text file formats. Know the field of space technology, programs, and policy. Know the players. Look for fresh angles. And please know how to write!"

💲💲💲💲 AMERICAN ARCHAEOLOGY

The Archaeological Conservancy, 1717 Girard Blvd. NE, Albuquerque NM 87106. (505)266-9668. **Fax:** (505)266-0311. **E-mail:** tacmag@nm.net. **Website:** www.americanarchaeology.org. **Contact:** Michael

Bawaya, editor; Vicki Singer, art director. **60% freelance written.** Quarterly magazine. "We're a popular archaeology magazine. Our readers are very interested in this science. Our features cover important digs, prominent archaeologists, and most any aspect of the science. We only cover North America." Estab. 1997. Circ. 35,000. Byline given. Pays on acceptance. Offers 20% kill fee. Publishes ms an average of 3 months after acceptance. Editorial lead time 3 months. Accepts queries by mail, e-mail, fax. Accepts simultaneous submissions. Responds in 3 weeks to queries; in 1 month to mss.

NONFICTION No fiction, poetry, humor. **Buys 15 mss/year.** Query with published clips. Length: 1,500-3,000 words. **Pays $1,000-2,000.** Pays expenses of writers on assignment.

PHOTOS State availability. Identification of subjects required. Reviews transparencies, prints. Pays $50 and up for occasional stock images; assigns work by project (pay varies); negotiable. **Pays on acceptance.** Credit line given. Buys one-time rights. Offers $400-600/photo shoot. Negotiates payment individually. Buys one-time rights.

TIPS "Read the magazine. Features must have a considerable amount of archaeological detail."

⊜⊜⊜ ASTRONOMY

Kalmbach Publishing, 21027 Crossroads Circle, P.O. Box 1612, Waukesha WI 53187-1612. (800)533-6644. **Fax:** (262)798-6468. **Website:** www.astronomy.com. **Contact:** David J. Eicher, editor; LuAnn Williams Belter, art director (for art and photography). **50% of articles submitted and written by science writers; includes commissioned and unsolicited.** Monthly magazine covering the science and hobby of astronomy. "Half of our magazine is for hobbyists (who are active observers of the sky); the other half is directed toward armchair astronomers who are intrigued by the science." Estab. 1973. Circ. 108,000. Byline given. Pays on acceptance. Does pay a kill fee, although rarely used. Accepts simultaneous submissions. Responds in 1 month to queries. Responds in 3 months to mss. on website.

NONFICTION Needs book excerpts, new product, photo feature, technical, space, astronomy. **Buys 75 mss/year.** Please query on all article ideas Length: 500-3,000 words. **Pays $100-1,000.** Pays expenses of writers on assignment.

TIPS "Submitting to *Astronomy* could be tough—take a look at how technical astronomy is. But if someone is a physics teacher or an amateur astronomer, he or she might want to study the magazine for a year to see the sorts of subjects and approaches we use, and then submit a proposal. Submission guidelines available online."

⊜⊜⊜⊜ BIOSCIENCE

American Institute of Biological Sciences, 1900 Campus Commons Dr., Suite 200, Reston VA 20191. (202)628-1500. **Fax:** (202)628-1509. **Website:** www.aibs.org. **Contact:** Scott L. Collins, editor-in-chief. **5% freelance written.** Monthly peer-reviewed scientific journal covering organisms from molecules to the environment. "We contract professional science writers to write features on assigned topics, including organismal biology and ecology, but excluding biomedical topics." Estab. 1951. Byline given. Publishes ms an average of 3 months after acceptance. Editorial lead time 2 months. Accepts queries by e-mail. Accepts simultaneous submissions. Responds in 2-3 weeks to queries. Sample copy on website. Guidelines free.

NONFICTION Does not want biomedical topics. **Buys 10 mss/year.** Query. Length: 1,500-3,000 words. **Pays $1,500-3,000.** Pays expenses of writers on assignment.

TIPS "Queries can cover any area of biology. The story should appeal to a wide scientific audience, yet be accessible to the interested (and somewhat science-literate) layperson. *BioScience* tends to favor research and policy trend stories and avoids personality profiles."

⊜⊜⊜ CHEMICAL HERITAGE

Chemical Heritage Foundation (CHF), 315 Chestnut St., Philadelphia PA 19106. (215)925-2222. **E-mail:** editor@chemheritage.org. **Website:** www.chemheritage.org. **40% freelance written.** Published 3 times/year. "*Chemical Heritage* reports on the history of the chemical and molecular sciences and industries, on Chemical Heritage Foundation activities, and on other activities of interest to our readers." Estab. 1982. Circ. 17,000. Byline given. Pays on acceptance. Publishes ms an average of 6-12 months after acceptance. Editorial lead time 4 months. Accepts queries by e-mail. Accepts simultaneous submissions. Responds in 1 month to queries and mss. Sample copy free.

NONFICTION Needs book excerpts, essays, historical, interview. "No exposés or excessively technical material. Many of our readers are highly educated professionals, but they may not be familiar with, for example, specific chemical processes." **Buys 3-5 mss/ year.** Query. Length: 1,000-3,500 words. **Pays 50¢-$1/ word.** Pays expenses of writers on assignment.

PHOTOS State availability. Captions required. Offers no additional payment for photos accepted with ms. Buys one-time print and online rights.

COLUMNS Book reviews: 200 or 750 words; CHF collections: 300-500 words; policy: 1,000 words; personal remembrances: 750 words; profiles of CHF awardees and oral history subjects: 600-900 words: buys 3-5 mms/year. **Buys 10 mss/year.** Query.

TIPS "CHF attends exhibits at many scientific trade shows and scholarly conferences. Our representatives are always happy to speak to potential authors genuinely interested in the past, present, and future of chemistry. We are a good venue for scholars who want to reach a broader audience or for science writers who want to bolster their scholarly credentials."

❸❸❸ CHEMMATTERS

American Chemical Society, Education Division, 1155 16th St., NW, Washington DC 20036. (202)872-6164. **Fax:** (202)872-8068. **E-mail:** chemmatters@acs.org. **Website:** www.acs.org/chemmatters. **Contact:** Patrice Pages, editor; Cornithia Harris, art director. **100% freelance written.** Covers topics of interest to teenagers and that can be explained with chemistry. *ChemMatters*, published 4 times/year, is a magazine that helps high school students find connections between chemistry and the world around them. Estab. 1983. Circ. 30,000. Byline given. Pays on acceptance. Publishes ms 6 months after acceptance. Accepts queries by mail, e-mail. Accepts simultaneous submissions. Responds in 4 weeks to queries and mss. Sample copies and writer's guidelines free (available as e-mail attachment upon request).

NONFICTION Query with published clips. **Pays $700-$1,000 for article.** Pays expenses of writers on assignment.

TIPS "Be aware of the content covered in a standard high school chemistry textbook. Choose themes and topics that are timely, interesting, fun, *and* that relate to the content and concepts of the first-year chemistry course. Articles should describe real people involved with real science. Best articles feature young people making a difference or solving a problem."

POPULAR SCIENCE

Bonnier Corporation, 2 Park Ave., 9th Floor, New York NY 10016. **E-mail:** queries@popsci.com; bown@ bonniercorp.com. **Website:** www.popsci.com. **Contact:** Jill C. Shomer, managing editor. **50% freelance written.** Monthly magazine for the well-educated adult, interested in science, technology, new products. *Popular Science* is devoted to exploring (and explaining) to a nontechnical, but knowledgeable, readership the technical world around us. Covers all of the sciences, engineering, and technology, and above all, products. Especially focused on the new, the ingenious, and the useful. Contributors should be as alert to the possibility of selling pictures and short features as they are to major articles. Estab. 1872. Circ. 1,450,000. Byline given. Pays on acceptance. Offers 25% kill fee. Editorial lead time 3 months. Accepts queries by mail, e-mail, fax. Accepts simultaneous submissions. Responds in 1 month to queries. Guidelines available online.

NONFICTION *Popular Science* welcomes pitches from writers who want to tell amazing stories about scientific and technological advances in every realm. Query should include a brief summary of the proposed article and provide some indication of a plan to execute the reporting. Links to past work might also be helpful. Reads every query but will respond only to those that are under serious consideration. Pays expenses of writers on assignment.

TIPS "Probably the easiest way to break in here is by covering a news story in science and technology that we haven't heard about yet. We need people to be acting as scouts for us out there, and we are willing to give the most leeway on these performances. We are interested in good, sharply focused ideas in all areas we cover. We prefer a vivid, journalistic style of writing, with the writer taking the reader along with him, showing the reader what he saw, through words."

❸❸❸❸ SCIENTIFIC AMERICAN

75 Varick St., 9th Floor, New York NY 10013-1917. (212)451-8200. **E-mail:** editors@sciam.com. **Website:** www.sciam.com. **Contact:** Mariette DiChristina, editor-in-chief. Monthly magazine covering developments and topics of interest in the world of science. "*Scientific American* brings its readers directly to the wellspring of exploration and technological innovation. The magazine specializes in first-hand accounts by the people who actually do the work. Their per-

sonal experience provides an authoritative perspective on future growth. Over 100 of our authors have won Nobel Prizes. Complementing those articles are regular departments written by *Scientific American*'s staff of professional journalists, all specialists in their fields. *Scientific American* is the authoritative source of advance information. Authors are the first to report on important breakthroughs, because they're the people who make them. It all goes back to *Scientific American*'s corporate mission: to link those who use knowledge with those who create it." Estab. 1845. Circ. 710,000. Byline given. Pays on publication. No kill fee. Accepts simultaneous submissions. Guidelines available on website.

NONFICTION Query before submitting. **Pays $1/word average.** Pays expenses of writers on assignment.

💲💲💲💲 STARDATE

University of Texas, 2515 Speedway, Stop C1402, Austin TX 78712. (512)475-6763. **E-mail:** rjohnson@stardate.org. **Website:** stardate.org. **Contact:** Rebecca Johnson, editor. **80% freelance written.** Bimonthly magazine covering astronomy and skywatching. *StarDate* is written for people with an interest in astronomy and what they see in the night sky, but no special astronomy training or background. Query with published quips, by email or regular mail. No unsolicited mss. Estab. 1975. Circ. 10,000. Byline given. Pays on acceptance. Offers 25% kill fee. Publishes ms an average of 4 months after acceptance. Editorial lead time 6 months. Submit seasonal material 6 months in advance. Accepts queries by mail, e-mail, fax. Accepts simultaneous submissions. Responds in 6 weeks to queries. Sample copy and writer's guidelines free.

NONFICTION Needs general interest, historical, interview, photo feature, technical, travel. No first-person, first stargazing experiences, or paranormal. **Buys 8 mss/year.** Query with published clips. Length: 1,500-3,000 words. **Pays $800-1,700.** Pays expenses of writers on assignment.

PHOTOS Send photos. Identification of subjects required. Reviews transparencies, prints. Negotiates payment individually. Buys one time rights.

COLUMNS AstroNews (short astronomy news item), 250 words. **Buys 6 mss/year.** Query with published clips. **Pays $150-250.**

TIPS "Keep up to date with current astronomy news and space missions. No technical jargon."

💲💲 WEATHERWISE

Taylor & Francis Group, 530 Walnut Str., Suite 850, Philadelphia PA 19106. (215)625-8900. **E-mail:** margaret.benner@taylorandfrancis.com. **Website:** www.weatherwise.org. **Contact:** Margaret Benner Smidt, editor in chief. **75% freelance written.** Bimonthly magazine covering weather and meteorology. "*Weatherwise* is America's only magazine about the weather. Our readers range from professional weathercasters and scientists to basement-bound hobbyists, but all share a common interest in craving information about weather as it relates to the atmospheric sciences, technology, history, culture, society, art, etc." Estab. 1948. Circ. 11,000. Byline given. Pays on publication. No kill fee. Publishes ms an average of 6 months after acceptance. Editorial lead time 6-9 months. Submit seasonal material 9 months in advance. Accepts queries by mail, e-mail, fax, phone. Accepts simultaneous submissions. Responds in 2 months to queries. Guidelines available online.

NONFICTION Needs book excerpts, essays, general interest, historical, how-to, interview, new product, opinion, personal experience, photo feature, technical, travel. Special issues: Photo Contest (September/October deadline June 2). No blow-by-blow accounts of the biggest storm to ever hit your backyard. **Buys 15-18 mss/year.** Query with published clips. Length: 2,000-3,000 words. **Pays $200-500 for assigned articles. Pays $0-300 for unsolicited articles.** Pays expenses of writers on assignment.

PHOTOS Captions, identification of subjects required. Reviews contact sheets, negatives, prints, electronic files. Negotiates payment individually. Buys one time rights.

COLUMNS Weather Front (news, trends), 300-400 words; Weather Talk (folklore and humor), 650-1,000 words. **Buys 12-15 mss/year.** Query with published clips. **Pays $0-200.**

TIPS "Don't query us wanting to write about broad types like the Greenhouse Effect, the Ozone Hole, El Niño, etc. Although these are valid topics, you can bet you won't be able to cover it all in 2,000 words. With these topics and all others, find the story within the story. And whether you're writing about a historical storm or new technology, be sure to focus on the human element—the struggles, triumphs, and other anecdotes of individuals."

SCIENCE FICTION, FANTASY & HORROR

🖐$ ALBEDO ONE

8 Bachelor's Walk, Dublin 1 Ireland. **E-mail:** bobn@ yellowbrickroad.ie. **Website:** www.albedo1.com. **Contact:** Bob Nielson. "We are always looking for thoughtful, well-written fiction. Our definition of what constitutes science fiction, horror, and fantasy is extremely broad, and we love to see material which pushes at the boundaries or crosses between genres." Estab. 1993. Circ. 900. Pays on publication. Publishes ms 1 year after acceptance. Accepts queries by mail, e-mail. Responds in 3 months to mss. Guidelines on website.

FICTION Needs experimental, fantasy, horror, science fiction, literary. Submit complete ms by mail or e-mail. Length: 2,000-8,000 words. **Pays €6/1,000 words, to a maximum of 8,000 words, and 1 contributor's copy.**

TIPS "We look for good writing, good plot, good characters. Read the magazine, and don't give up."

$ ANALOG SCIENCE FICTION & FACT

Dell Magazines, 44 Wall St., Suite 904, New York NY 10005-2401. **E-mail:** analogsf@dellmagazines.com. **Website:** www.analogsf.com. **Contact:** Trevor Quachri, editor. **100% freelance written. Eager to work with new/unpublished writers.** *Analog* seeks "solidly entertaining stories exploring solidly thought-out speculative ideas. But the ideas, and consequently the stories, are always new. Real science and technology have always been important in *ASF,* not only as the foundation of its fiction but as the subject of articles about real research with big implications for the future." Estab. 1930. Circ. 50,000. Byline given. Pays on acceptance. No kill fee. Publishes ms an average of 10 months after acceptance. Accepts queries by mail, online submission form. Accepts simultaneous submissions. Responds in 2-3 months to mss. Sample copy: $5 and SASE. Guidelines online.

NONFICTION Special issues: Articles should deal with subjects of not only current but future interest, i.e., with topics at the present frontiers of research whose likely future developments have implications of wide interest. **Buys 11 mss/year.** Send complete ms via online submissions manager (preferred) or postal mail. Does not accept e-mail submissions. Length: up to 4,000 words. **Pays 9¢/word.**

FICTION "Basically, we publish science fiction stories. That is, stories in which some aspect of future science or technology is so integral to the plot that, if that aspect were removed, the story would collapse. The science can be physical, sociological, psychological. The technology can be anything from electronic engineering to biogenetic engineering. But the stories must be strong and realistic, with believable people (who needn't be human) doing believable things— no matter how fantastic the background might be." Needs science fiction. No fantasy or stories in which the scientific background is implausible or plays no essential role. Send complete ms via online submissions manager (preferred) or postal mail. Does not accept e-mail submissions. Length: 2,000-7,000 words for short stories, 10,000-20,000 words for novelettes and novellas, and 40,000-80,000 for serials. **Analog pays 8-10¢/word for short stories up to 7,500 words, 8-8.5¢ for longer material, 6¢/word for serials.**

POETRY Send poems via online submissions manager (preferred) or postal mail. Does not accept e-mail submissions. Length: up to 40 lines/poem. **Pays $1/line.**

TIPS "I'm looking for irresistibly entertaining stories that make me think about things in ways I've never done before. Read several issues to get a broad feel for our tastes, but don't try to imitate what you read."

$ APEX MAGAZINE

Apex Publications, LLC, P.O. Box 24323, Lexington KY 40524. **E-mail:** lesley@apex-magazine.com. **Website:** www.apex-magazine.com. **Contact:** Lesley Conner, managing editor. **100% freelance written.** Monthly e-zine publishing dark speculative fiction. "An elite repository for new and seasoned authors with an other-worldly interest in the unquestioned and slightly bizarre parts of the universe. We want science fiction, fantasy, horror, and mash-ups of all three of the dark, weird stuff down at the bottom of your little literary heart." Estab. 2004. Circ. 28,000 unique visits per month. Byline given. Pays 30 days after publication. Publishes mss an average of 6 months after acceptance. Editorial lead time 2 weeks. Submit seasonal material 6 months in advance. Accepts queries by e-mail. Responds in 20-30 days. Sample content online. Guidelines online.

NONFICTION Buys 36 mss/year. Send complete ms. Length: 100-7,500 words. **Pays $50 flat rate.**

REPRINTS Pays 1¢/word.

FICTION Needs fantasy, horror, science fiction, short stories. **Buys 36 mss/year.** Send complete ms. Length: 100-7,500 words. **Pays 6¢/word.**

$ ASIMOV'S SCIENCE FICTION

Dell Magazines, 44 Wall St., Suite 904, New York NY 10005. **E-mail:** asimovs@dellmagazines.com. **Website:** www.asimovs.com. **Contact:** Sheila Williams, editor; Victoria Green, senior art director. **98% freelance written. Works with a small number of new/unpublished writers each year.** *Asimov's*, published 10 times/year, including 2 double issues, is 5.875x8.625 (trim size); 112 pages; 30 lb. newspaper; 70 lb. to 8 pt. C1S cover stock; illustrations; rarely has photos. "Magazine consists of science fiction and fantasy stories for adults and young adults. Publishes the best short science fiction available." Estab. 1977. Circ. 50,000. Pays on acceptance. No kill fee. Publishes ms an average of 6-12 months after acceptance. Accepts queries by mail. Responds in 2 months to queries; in 3 months to mss. Sample copy: $5. Guidelines online or for #10 SASE.

NONFICTION Pays expenses of writers on assignment.

FICTION Wants "science fiction primarily. Some fantasy and humor. It is best to read a great deal of material in the genre to avoid the use of some very old ideas." Submit ms via online submissions manager or postal mail; no e-mail submissions. Needs fantasy, science fiction. No horror or psychic/supernatural, sword and sorcery, explicit sex or violence that isn't integral to the story. Would like to see more hard science fiction. Length: 750-15,000 words. **Pays 8-10¢/word for short stories up to 7,500 words; 8-8.5¢/word for longer material. Works between 7,500-10,000 words by authors who make more than 8¢/word for short stories will receive a flat rate that will be no less than the payment would be for a shorter story.**

TIPS "In general, we're looking for 'character-oriented' stories, those in which the characters, rather than the science, provide the main focus for the reader's interest. Serious, thoughtful, yet accessible fiction will constitute the majority of our purchases, but there's always room for the humorous as well."

$ BEYOND CENTAURI

White Cat Publications, LLC, 33080 Industrial Rd., Suite 101, Livonia MI 48150. (734)237-8522. **Fax:** (313)557-5162. **E-mail:** beyondcentauri@whitecatpublications.com. **Website:** www.whitecatpublications.com/guidelines/beyond-centauri. *Beyond Centauri*, published quarterly, contains fantasy, science fiction, sword and sorcery, very mild horror short stories, poetry, and illustrations for readers ages 10 and up. Estab. 2003. Publishes ms 1-2 months after acceptance. Accepts queries by e-mail. Accepts simultaneous submissions. Responds in 2-3 months. Single copy: $7.

NONFICTION Needs opinion, reviews, short articles about space exploration, science, and technology. Send complete ms in the body of an e-mail, or as an RTF attachment. Length: up to 1,500 words. **Pays $7/piece and 1 contributor's copy.**

FICTION Looks for themes of science fiction or fantasy. "Science fiction and especially stories that take place in outer space will find great favor with us." Needs fantasy, horror, science fiction, short stories. Submit in the body of an e-mail, or as an RTF attachment. Length: up to 2,500 words. **Pays $6/story, $3/reprints, and $2/flash fiction (under 1,000 words), plus 1 contributor's copy.**

POETRY Wants fantasy, science fiction, spooky horror, and speculative poetry for younger readers. Considers poetry by children and teens. Has published poetry by Bruce Boston, Bobbi Sinha-Morey, Debbie Feo, Dorothy Imm, Cythera, and Terrie Leigh Relf. Looks for themes of science fiction and fantasy. Poetry should be submitted in the body of an e-mail, or as an RTF attachment. Does not want horror with excessive blood and gore. Length: up to 50 lines/poem. **Pays $2/original poem, $1/reprints, $1/scifaiku and related form, plus 1 contributor's copy.**

$$ FANGORIA

The Brooklyn Company, 20 Railroad Ave., East Northport NY 11731. **E-mail:** musick@fangoria.com. **Website:** www.fangoria.com. **95% freelance written. Works with a small number of new/unpublished writers each year.** Magazine published 10 times/year covering horror films, TV projects, comics, videos, and literature, and those who create them. "We provide an assignment sheet (deadlines, info) to writers, thus authorizing queried stories that we're buying." Estab. 1979. Byline given. Pays 1-3 months after publication. Publishes ms an average of 3 months after acceptance. Submit seasonal material 4 months in advance. Accepts queries by mail. Accepts simultaneous submissions. Responds in 6 weeks to queries.

NONFICTION Avoids most articles on science-fiction films. **Buys 120 mss/year.** Query with published clips. Length: 1,000-3,500 words. **Pays $100-250.** Pays expenses of writers on assignment.

PHOTOS State availability. Captions, identification of subjects required. Reviews transparencies, prints (b&w, color) electronically.

COLUMNS Monster Invasion (exclusive, early information about new film productions; also mini-interviews with filmmakers and novelists). Query with published clips. **Pays $45-75.**

TIPS "Other than recommending that you study one or several copies of *Fangoria*, we can only describe it as a horror film magazine consisting primarily of interviews with technicians and filmmakers in the field. Be sure to stress the interview subjects' words—not your own opinions as much. We're very interested in small, independent filmmakers working outside of Hollywood. These people are usually more accessible to writers, and more cooperative. *Fangoria* is also sort of a de facto bible for youngsters interested in movie makeup careers and for young filmmakers. We are devoted only to reel horrors—the fakery of films, the imagery of the horror fiction of a Stephen King or a Clive Barker—we do not want nor would we ever publish articles on real-life horrors, murders, etc. A writer must enjoy horror films and horror fiction to work for us. If the photos in *Fangoria* disgust you, if the sight of (stage) blood repels you, if you feel `superior' to horror (and its fans), you aren't a writer for us and we certainly aren't the market for you. We love giving new writers their first chance to break into print in a national magazine. We are currently looking for Louisiana- (New Orleans), New Mexico-, Arizona- and Las Vegas-based correspondents, as well as writers stationed in Spain (especially Barcelona), southern US cities, and Eastern Europe."

HELIOTROPE

E-mail: heliotropeditor@gmail.com. **Website:** www.heliotropemag.com. *Heliotrope* is a quarterly e-zine that publishes fiction, articles, and poetry. Estab. 2006. Pays on publication. No kill fee. Accepts queries by e-mail. Responds in 1 month to mss. Guidelines available online.

NONFICTION Needs opinion. Submit complete ms via e-mail. Length: 2,000 words minimum. **Pays $90.**

FICTION "If your story is something we can't label, we're interested in that, too." Needs fantasy, horror, mystery, science fiction. Submit complete ms via e-mail. Length: up to 5,000 words. **Pays 10¢/word.**

POETRY Submit via e-mail. **Pays $50.**

KASMA MAGAZINE

E-mail: editors@kasmamagazine.com. **Website:** www.kasmamagazine.com. **Contact:** Alex Korovessis, editor. Online magazine. "We publish the best science fiction from promising new and established writers. Our aim is to provide stories that are well written, original, and thought provoking." Estab. 2009. Pays on publication. Publishes mss 2-3 months after acceptance. Editorial lead time 2 months. Submit seasonal material 1 month in advance. Accepts queries by e-mail. Accepts simultaneous submissions. Responds in 1 week to queries, in 3 months to mss. Sample copy online and by e-mail. Guidelines online.

FICTION Needs science fiction. No erotica or excessive violence/language. Submit complete ms via e-mail. Length: 1,000-5,000 words. **Pays $25 CAD.**

TIPS "The type of stories I enjoy the most usually come as a surprise: I think I know what is happening, but the underlying reality is revealed to me as I read on. That said, I've accepted many stories that don't fit this model. Sometimes I'm introduced to a new story structure. Sometimes the story I like reminds me of another story, but it introduces a slightly different spin on it. Other times, the story introduces such interesting and original ideas that structure and style don't seem to matter as much."

LEADING EDGE MAGAZINE

4087 JKB, Provo UT 84602. **E-mail:** editor@leadingedgemagazine.com; fiction@leadingedgemagazine.com; art@leadingedgemagazine.com; poetry@leadingedgemagazine.com; nonfiction@leadingedgemagazine.com. **Website:** www.leadingedgemagazine.com. **Contact:** Heather White, editor-in-chief. **90% freelance written.** Semiannual magazine covering science fiction and fantasy. "*Leading Edge* is a magazine dedicated to new and upcoming talent in the fields of science fiction and fantasy. We strive to encourage developing and established talent and provide high-quality speculative fiction to our readers." Does not accept mss with sex, excessive violence, or profanity. Accepts unsolicited submissions. Estab. 1981. Circ. 200. Byline given. Pays on publication. No kill fee. Publishes ms an average of 2-4 months after acceptance. Accepts queries by mail, e-mail. Responds within 12 months to mss. Single copy: $5.95. "We no longer provide subscriptions, but *Leading Edge* is now available on Amazon Kindle, as well as print-on-demand." Guidelines online.

NONFICTION Needs essays, expose, interview, reviews. Special issues: Because we are a science fiction and fantasy journal, all nonfiction submissions should be related to a specific work or trend within the science fiction and fantasy genres. Send complete ms with cover letter and SASE. Include estimated word count. Length: up to 15,000 words. **Pays 1¢/word; $50 maximum.** Pays expenses of writers on assignment.

FICTION Needs fantasy, science fiction. **Buys 14-16 mss/year.** Send complete ms with cover letter and SASE. Include estimated word count. Length: up to 15,000 words. **Pays 1¢/word; $50 maximum.**

POETRY Needs avant-garde, haiku, light verse, traditional. Publishes 2-4 poems per issue. Poetry should reflect both literary value and popular appeal and should deal with science fiction- or fantasy-related themes. No e-mail submissions. Cover letter is preferred. Include name, address, phone number, length of poem, title, and type of poem at the top of each page. Please include SASE with every submission. Submit maximum 10 poems. Pays $10 for first 4 pages; $1.50/each subsequent page.

TIPS "Buy a sample issue to know what is currently selling in our magazine. Also, make sure to follow the writer's guidelines when submitting."

$ THE MAGAZINE OF FANTASY & SCIENCE FICTION

P.O. Box 3447, Hoboken NJ 07030. (201)876-2551. **E-mail:** fandsf@aol.com. **Website:** www.fandsf.com; submissions.ccfinlay.com/fsf. **Contact:** C.C. Finlay, editor. **100% freelance written.** *The Magazine of Fantasy & Science Fiction* publishes various types of science fiction and fantasy short stories and novellas, making up about 80% of each issue. The balance of each issue is devoted to articles about science fiction, a science column, book and film reviews, cartoons, and competitions. Bimonthly. Estab. 1949. Circ. 40,000. Byline given. Pays on acceptance. No kill fee. Publishes ms an average of 9-12 months after acceptance. Submit seasonal material 8 months in advance. Accepts queries by mail, e-mail. Accepts simultaneous submissions. Responds in 2 months to queries. Sample: $7 ($15 international). Guidelines on website at www.sfsite.com/fsf/glines.htm and on the online submission form at submissions.ccfinly.com/fsf. Send a SASE to receive the guidelines by mail.

NONFICTION Needs memoir. Send complete ms.

REPRINTS Submit potential reprints in the same manner as new work, but be sure to indicate with the submission where it first was published. Pays 5¢/word.

COLUMNS Curiosities (reviews of odd and obscure books), up to 270 words. **Buys 6 mss/year.** Query. **Pays $75.**

FICTION *F&SF* has no formula for fiction. The speculative element may be slight, but it should be present. We prefer character-oriented stories, whether it's fantasy, science fiction, horror, humor, or another genre. *F&SF* is open to diverse voices and perspectives, and has published writers from all over the world. Needs adventure, fantasy, horror, humorous, science fiction, short stories, space fantasy, sword & sorcery, dark fantasy, futuristic, psychological, supernatural, science fiction, hard science/technological, soft/sociological. **Buys 60-70 mss/year.** Send complete ms. Length: up to 25,000 words. **Pays 7-12¢/word.**

POETRY *F&SF* buys only a few poems per year. We want only poetry that deals with the fantastic or the science fictional. In the past, we've published poetry by Rebecca Kavaler, Elizabeth Bear, Sophie M. White, and Robert Frazier. Poetry may be submitted using the same online form for fiction. Buys 4-6 poems/year. Submit maximum 5 poems. Length: up to 40 lines/poem, including blank lines. **Pays $50/poem and 2 contributor's copies.**

TIPS Good storytelling makes a submission stand out. We like to be surprised by stories, either by the character insights, ideas, plots, or prose. Even though we prefer electronic submissions, we need stories in standard mss format (like that described here: www.sfwa.org/writing/vonda/vonda.htm). Read an issue of the magazine before submitting to get a sense of the range of our tastes and interests.

🌐 $ PREMONITIONS

13 Hazely Combe, Arrenton Isle of Wight PO30 3AJ United Kingdom. **E-mail:** mail@pigasuspress.co.uk. **Website:** www.pigasuspress.co.uk. **Contact:** Tony Lee,

editor. "Science fiction and horror stories, plus genre poetry and fantastic artwork." Guidelines available on website.

NONFICTION Pays expenses of writers on assignment.

FICTION Wants "original, high-quality SF/fantasy. Horror must have a science fiction element and be psychological or scary, rather than simply gory. Cutting-edge SF and experimental writing styles (cross-genre scenarios, slipstream, etc.) are always welcome." Needs fantasy, horror, science fiction. "No supernatural fantasy-horror." Submit via mail and include SAE or IRC if you want material returned. "Use a standard manuscript format: double-spaced text, no right-justify, no staples." Do not send submissions via e-mail, unless by special request from editor. Include personalized cover letter with brief bio and publication credits. Length: 500-6,000 words. Send 1 story at a time. **Pays minimum $5 or £5 per 1,000 words, plus copy of magazine.**

POETRY Buys 6 poems/year. Length: up to 50 lines.

TIPS "Potential contributors are advised to study recent issues of the magazine."

$ SCIFAIKUEST

Alban Lake Publishing, P.O. Box 782, Cedar Rapids IA 52406. **E-mail:** gatrix65@yahoo.com. **Website:** albanlake.com/scifaikuest. **Contact:** Tyree Campbell, managing editor; Teri Santitoro, editor. *Scifaikuest*, published quarterly both online and in print, features "science fiction/fantasy/horror minimalist poetry, especially scifaiku, and related forms. We also publish articles about various poetic forms and reviews of poetry collections. The online and print versions of *Scifaikuest* are different." *Scifaikuest* (print edition) is 32 pages, digest-sized, offset-printed, perfect-bound, with color cardstock cover, includes ads. Receives about 500 poems/year, accepts about 160 (32%). Press run is 100/issue; 5 distributed free to reviewers. Member: The Speculative Literature Foundation. Estab. 2003. Time between acceptance and publication is 1-2 months. Submit seasonal poems 6 months in advance. Accepts queries by e-mail. Responds in 6-8 weeks. Single copy: $7; subscription: $20/year, $37 for 2 years. Make checks payable to Tyree Campbell/Alban Lake Publishing. Guidelines online.

NONFICTION "We're looking for articles related in some way to one or more of the poetry forms we publish, or related to similar forms such as sijo." Length: under 1,000 words but considers longer essays. **Pays $6/article and 1 contributor's copy.** Pays expenses of writers on assignment.

POETRY Wants artwork, scifaiku, and speculative minimalist forms such as tanka, haibun, ghazals, senryu. Submit 10 poems at a time. Accepts e-mail submissions (pasted into body of message). No disk submissions; artwork as e-mail attachment or inserted body of e-mail. Submission should include snail-mail address and a short (1-2 lines) bio. Reads submissions year round. Editor Teri Santitoro makes all decisions regarding acceptances. Often comments on rejected poems. Has published poetry by Tom Brinck, Oino Sakai, Deborah P. Kolodji, Aurelio Rico Lopez III, Joanne Morcom, and John Dunphy. No 'traditional' poetry. Length: varies, depending on poem type. **Pays $1/poem, $6/review or article, and 1 contributor's copy.**

$ SPACE AND TIME

458 Elizabeth Ave., Somerset NJ 08873. **Website:** www.spaceandtimemagazine.com. **Contact:** Hildy Silverman, publisher. **100% freelance written.** *Space and Time* is the longest continually published small-press genre fiction magazine still in print. "We pride ourselves in having published the first stories of some of the great writers in science fiction, fantasy, and horror." Estab. 1966. Circ. 2,000. Byline given. Pays on publication. No kill fee. Publishes stories/poems 6-12 months after acceptance. Accepts queries by e-mail. Sample copy: $6. Guidelines online. Only opens periodically—announcements of open reading periods appear on Facebook page and website. No fiction or poetry considered outside of open reading periods.

FICTION "We are looking for creative blends of science fiction, fantasy, and/or horror." Needs fantasy, horror, science fiction, short stories. "Do not send children's stories." Submit electronically as a Word doc or .rtf attachment only during open reading periods. Anything sent outside those period will be rejected out of hand. Length: 1,000-10,000 words. Average length: 6,500 words. Average length of short shorts: 1,000 words. **Pays 1¢/word.**

POETRY **Contact:** Linda Addison. Needs speculative nature—science fiction, fantasy, horror themes and imagery. "Multiple submissions are okay within reason (no more than 3 at a time). Submit embedded in an e-mail, a Word doc, or .rtf attachment. Only submit during open poetry reading periods, which are announced via the Facebook page and on the website. All other poetry submitted outside these reading periods will be rejected out of hand." Poetry without any sort of genre or speculative element. Buys average of 15 per year poems/year. Submit maximum 3 poems. No longer than a single standard page. **Pays $5/poem.**

$ STAR*LINE

Science Fiction and Fantasy Poetry Association, Languages and Literatures, University of Northern Iowa, Cedar Falls IA 50614-0502. **E-mail:** starlineeditor@gmail.com. **Website:** www.sfpoetry.com. **Contact:** Vince Gotera, editor. **All freelance.** *Star*Line*, published quarterly in print and .pdf format by the Science Fiction and Fantasy Poetry Association, is a speculative poetry magazine. "Open to all forms as long as your poetry uses speculative motifs: science fiction, fantasy, or horror." Estab. 1978. Circ. 300. Byline given. After publication. No kill fee. No more than 6 months. Accepts queries by e-mail. Accepts simultaneous submissions. Responds in 1 month. Guidelines online.

NONFICTION Needs reviews.

POETRY Submit 3-5 poems at a time. Accepts e-mail submissions (preferred; pasted into body of message, no attachments). Submit maximum 5 poems. **Pays 3¢/word rounded to the next dollar; minimum $3, maximum $25.**

$ STRANGE HORIZONS

Strange Horizons, Inc., P.O. Box 1693, Dubuque IA 52004-1693. **E-mail:** management@strangehorizons.com; fiction@strangehorizons.com. **Website:** strangehorizons.com. **Contact:** Jane Crowley and Kate Dollarhyde, editors-in-chief. "*Strange Horizons* is a magazine of and about speculative fiction and related nonfiction. Speculative fiction includes science fiction, fantasy, horror, slipstream, and other flavors of fantastica." Work published in *Strange Horizons* has been shortlisted for or won Hugo, Nebula, Rhysling, Theodore Sturgeon, James Tiptree Jr., and World Fantasy Awards. Estab. 2000. Accepts queries by online submission form. Responds in 90 days.

NONFICTION Contact: articles@strangehorizons.com. Needs essays. Special issues: "Nonfiction published in *Strange Horizons* should provide an original contribution to the field's discussion." Query (with the word "query" in subject line) or submit complete ms (with the word "sub" in subject line) by e-mail. Length: 3,000-5,000 words. **Pays $20-80.**

COLUMNS Contact: columns@strangehorizons.com. "We publish 1 column per week. Columns are standalone personal essays of 1,000-2,000 words on topics of interest to *Strange Horizons* readers. In the past we have published columns on SF in a wide range of media, from theatre to video games to comics to literature; debates within the SF community, and about the history of the community; and broader cultural, political, and technological issues of interest to the SF community." Submit complete ms (with the word SUB in subject line) by e-mail. **Pays $40.**

FICTION Contact: fiction@strangehorizons.com (questions only). "We love, or are interested in, fiction from or about diverse perspectives and traditionally under-represented groups, settings, and cultures, written from a nonexoticizing and well-researched position; unusual yet readable styles and inventive structures and narratives; stories that address political issues in complex and nuanced ways, resisting oversimplification; and hypertext fiction." speculative fiction, broadly defined. No excessive gore. Submit via online submissions manager; no e-mail or postal submission accepted. Length: up to 10,000 words (under 5,000 words preferred). **Pays 8¢/word, $50 minimum.**

POETRY Contact: poetry@strangehorizons.com. "We're looking for high-quality SF, fantasy, horror, and slipstream poetry. We're looking for modern, exciting poems that explore the possible and impossible: stories about human and nonhuman experiences, dreams and reality, past and future, the here-and-now and otherwhere-and-elsewhen. We want poems from imaginative and unconventional writers; we want voices from diverse perspectives and backgrounds." Submit up to 6 poems within 2 calendar months via e-mail; 1 poem per e-mail. Include "POETRY SUB: Your Poem Title" in subject line. **Pays $40 per poem.**

$ THREE-LOBED BURNING EYE

Portland OR **Website:** www.3lobedmag.com. *Three-Lobed Burning Eye* is a speculative fiction magazine published online twice per year (usually spring and fall) and as a print anthology every other year. Each issue features six stories. Estab. 1999. Responds in 3 months to mss.

FICTION "We are looking for quality speculative fiction, in the vein of horror and dark fantasy, what you might call magical realism, slipstream, cross genre, or weird fiction. We will consider the occasional science fiction, suspense, or western story, though we prefer that it contain some speculative element. Sword and sorcery, hard SF, space opera, and extreme horror are hard sells. We like voices both literary and pulpy, with unique and flowing but not experimental styles. All labels aside, we want stories that expand genre, that value originality in character, narrative, and plot." Has published work by Gemma Files, DF Lewis, Laird Barron, Brenden Connell, Amy Grech, Neil Ayres, and Tim Waggoner. Needs fantasy, horror, science fiction, flash fiction. Does not want fan or franchise tie-in fiction (*Star Trek, Buffy, D&D,* etc.), serial stories, or novel excerpts. No erotica. Submit via online submissions manager. Length: up to 7,000 for short stories; 500-1,000 words for flash fiction. **Pays 3¢/word, up to $35.**

TIPS "Send only your best fiction, distinct and remarkable tales that the reader cannot forget. We encourage diverse authors, characters and points of view, inclusive of all races, cultures, genders, and orientations."

SPORTS

ARCHERY & BOWHUNTING

💲💲 BOW & ARROW HUNTING

Beckett Media LLC, 22840 Savi Ranch Pkwy., Suite 200, Yorba Linda CA 92887. (714)200-1900. **Fax:** (800)249-7761. **E-mail:** JBell@Beckett.com; editorial@bowandarrowhunting.com. **Website:** www.bowandarrowhunting.com. **Contact:** Joe Bell, editor. **70% freelance written.** Magazine published 9 times/year covering bowhunting. Dedicated to serve the serious bowhunting enthusiast. Writers must be willing to share their secrets so readers can become better bowhunters. Estab. 1962. Circ. 90,000. Byline given. Pays on publication. No kill fee. Publishes ms an average of 2 months after acceptance. Submit seasonal material 6 months in advance. Accepts queries by mail, e-mail. Accepts simultaneous submissions. Responds in 1 month to queries; 6 weeks to mss. Sample copy and writer's guidelines free.

NONFICTION Needs how-to, humor, interview, opinion, personal experience, technical. **Buys 60 mss/year.** Send complete ms. Length: 1,700-3,000 words. **Pays $200-450.**

PHOTOS Send photos. Captions required. Reviews contact sheets, digital images only; no slides or prints accepted. Offers no additional payment for photos accepted with ms. Buys one-time or all rights.

FILLERS Needs facts, newsbreaks. **Buys 12 mss/year.** Length: 500 words. **Pays $20-100.**

TIPS "Inform readers how they can become better at the sport, but don't forget to keep it fun! Sidebars are recommended with every submission."

BASEBALL

BASEBALL AMERICA

Baseball America, Inc., P.O. Box 2089, Durham NC 27702. **Website:** www.baseballamerica.com. **10% freelance written.** Biweekly tabloid covering baseball. *Baseball America* is read by industry insiders and passionate, knowledgeable fans. Writing should go beyond routine baseball stories to include more depth or a unique angle. Estab. 1981. Circ. 80,000. Byline given. Pays on publication. No kill fee. Publishes ms an average of 2 months after acceptance. Editorial lead time 1 month. Submit seasonal material 2 months in advance. Accepts simultaneous submissions. Sample copy for $3.25.

NONFICTION Needs historical, interview, theme or issue-oriented baseball features. No major league player features that don't cover new ground or superficial treatments of baseball subjects. Send complete ms. Length: 100-2,000 words. Pays expenses of writers on assignment.

PHOTOS State availability. Identification of subjects required. Negotiates payment individually. Buys one time rights.

💲 JUNIOR BASEBALL

JSAN Publishing LLC, 14 Woodway Ln., Wilton CT 06897. **E-mail:** publisher@juniorbaseball.com. **Website:** www.juniorbaseball.com. **Contact:** Jim Beecher, editor and publisher. **25% freelance written.** Bimonthly magazine focused on youth baseball players ages 7-17 (including high school) and their parents/coaches. Edited to various reading levels, depending upon age/skill level of feature. Estab. 1996. Circ. 20,000. Byline given. Pays on publication. No kill fee. Publishes ms an average of 4 months after acceptance. Editorial lead time 3 months. Submit seasonal material 4 months in advance. Accepts queries by e-mail. Accepts simultaneous submissions. Responds in 2 weeks to queries; in 1 month to mss. Sample copy: $5 or free online.

NONFICTION "No trite first-person articles about your kid. No fiction or poetry." **Buys 8-12 mss/year.** Query. Length: 500-1,000 words. **Pays $50-100.**

PHOTOS Photos can be e-mailed in 300 dpi JPEGs. State availability. Captions, identification of subjects required. Offers $10-100/photo; negotiates payment individually.

COLUMNS When I Was a Kid (a current Major League Baseball player profile); Parents Feature (topics of interest to parents of youth ball players); all 1,000-1,500 words. In the Spotlight (news, events, new products), 50-100 words; Hot Prospect (written for the 14-and-older competitive player; high school baseball is included, and the focus is on improving the finer points of the game to make the high school team, earn a college scholarship, or attract scouts, written to an adult level), 500-1,000 words. **Buys 8-12 mss/year. Pays $50-100.**

TIPS "Must be well-versed in baseball! Have a child who is very involved in the sport, or have extensive hands-on experience in coaching baseball at the youth, high school, or higher level. We can always use accurate, authoritative skills information, and good photos to accompany is a big advantage! This magazine is read by experts. No fiction, poems, games, puzzles, etc."

BICYCLING

💲💲💲 ADVENTURE CYCLIST

Adventure Cycling Association, P.O. Box 8308, Missoula MT 59807. **Fax:** (406)721-8754. **E-mail:** magazine@adventurecycling.org. **Website:** www.adventurecycling.org/adventure-cyclist. **Contact:** Alex Strickland. **75% freelance written.** Published 9 times/year for Adventure Cycling Association members, emphasizing bicycle tourism and travel. Estab. 1975. Circ. 51,000. Byline given. Pays on publication. Kill fee 25%. Publishes ms 8-12 months after acceptance. Submit seasonal material 12 months in advance. Accepts queries by online submission form. Accepts simultaneous submissions. Sample copy and guidelines for 9x12 SAE with 4 first-class stamps. Guidelines online.

NONFICTION Needs essays, historical, how-to, humor, inspirational, memoir, opinion, personal expe-

rience, photo feature, reviews, travel, U.S. or foreign tour accounts. **Buys 20-25 mss/year.** Length: 1,400-3,000 words. **Inquiries requested prior to complete mss. Pays sliding scale per word.** Expenses must be agreed on before final contract is signed.

PHOTOS State availability. Guidelines online: adventurecycling.org/adventure-cyclist/adventure-cyclist-submissions/photography-guidelines. Photo rates available online.

FICTION We rarely publish fiction but are interested if it's well written and appropriate for our audience. Needs adventure. 1500-3000 **$.30-$.45 per word.**

💲💲 BIKE MAGAZINE

The Enthusiast Network, 2052 Corte Del Nogal, Suite 100, Carlsbad CA 92011. (949)325-6200. **Fax:** (949)325-6196. **E-mail:** nicole@bikemag.com. **Website:** www.bikemag.com. **Contact:** Nicole Formosa, managing editor. **35% freelance written.** Magazine publishes 8 times/year covering mountain biking. Estab. 1993. Circ. 170,000. Byline given. Pays on publication. Offers 25% kill fee. Publishes ms an average of 2 months after acceptance. Editorial lead time 4 months. Submit seasonal material 6 months in advance. Accepts queries by mail, e-mail. Accepts simultaneous submissions. Responds in 2 months to queries. Guidelines online.

NONFICTION Needs humor, interview, personal experience, photo feature, travel. **Buys 20 mss/year.** Query. Length: 1,000-2,500 words. **Pays 50¢/word.** Pays expenses of writers on assignment. Sometimes pays expenses: $500 maximum.

PHOTOS Contact: Anthony Smith, photo editor (anthony@bikemag.com). Send photos. Captions, identification of subjects required. Reviews color transparencies, b&w prints. Negotiates payment individually. Buys one-time rights.

COLUMNS Splatter (news), 300 words; Urb (details a great ride within 1 hour of a major metropolitan area), 600-700 words. **Buys 20 mss/year.** Query. **Pays 50¢/word.**

TIPS "Remember that we focus on hardcore mountain biking, not beginners. We're looking for ideas that deliver the excitement and passion of the sport in ways that aren't common or predictable. Ideas should be vivid, unbiased, irreverent, probing, fun, humorous, funky, quirky, smart, good. Great feature ideas are always welcome, especially features on cultural matters or issues in the sport. However, you're much more likely to get published in *Bike* if you send us great ideas for short articles. In particular we need stories for our Splatter, a front-of-the-book section devoted to news, funny anecdotes, quotes, and odds and ends. We also need personality profiles of 600 words or so for our People Who Ride section. Racers are OK, but we're more interested in grassroots people with interesting personalities—it doesn't matter if they're Mother Theresas or scumbags, so long as they make mountain biking a little more interesting. Short descriptions of great rides are very welcome for our Urb column."

💲💲 CYCLE CALIFORNIA! MAGAZINE

1702 Meridian Ave. Suite L, #289, San Jose CA 95125. (408)924-0270. **E-mail:** cycleca@cyclecalifornia.com. **E-mail:** tcorral@cyclecalifornia.com. **Website:** www.cyclecalifornia.com. **Contact:** Tracy L. Corral, publisher. **75% freelance written.** Magazine published 11 times/year covering Northern California bicycling events, races, people. Issues (topics) covered include bicycle commuting, bicycle politics, touring, racing, nostalgia, history—anything at all to do with riding a bike. Magazine published 11 times/year covering Northern California bicycling events, races, people. Issues (topics) covered include bicycle commuting, bicycle politics, touring, racing, nostalgia, history— anything at all to do with riding a bike. Use e-mail (tcorral@cyclecalifornia.com) or Twitter (@Tlynn48) to query editor. Estab. 1995. Circ. 30,000 print; 3,000 digital subscribers. Byline given. Pays on publication. No kill fee. Publishes ms an average of 3 months after acceptance. Editorial lead time 6 weeks. Submit seasonal material 3-6 months in advance. Accepts queries by e-mail. Accepts simultaneous submissions. Responds in 1 month to queries. Sample copy with 9x12 SASE and $1.75 first-class postage. Guidelines with #10 SASE.

NONFICTION Needs historical, how-to, humor, interview, memoir, opinion, personal experience, profile, technical, travel. Special issues: Bicycle Tour & Travel (January issue). No articles about any sport that doesn't relate to bicycling. No product reviews. **Buys 36 mss/year.** Query. Length: 500-1,000 words. **Pays 10-15¢/word.**

PHOTOS Send photos. Identification of subjects preferred. Identification of location or event required. Negotiates payment individually. Buys one-time rights.

COLUMNS **Buys 2-3 mss/year.** Query with links to published stories. **Pays 10-15¢/word.**

FICTION Needs adventure, humorous.

POETRY Needs Poetry as it relates to bike riding. Buys 1-2 poems/year.

TIPS "E-mail us with good ideas. While we don't exclude writers from other parts of the country, articles really should reflect a West Coast slant or be of general interest to bicyclists. We prefer stories written by people who like and use their bikes."

💲💲 VELONEWS

Inside Communications, Inc., 3002 Sterling Circle, Suite 100, Boulder CO 80301. (303)440-0601. **Fax:** (303)444-6788. **E-mail:** webletters@competitorgroup.com; jbradley@competitorgroup.com. **Website:** www.velonews.com. **Contact:** John Bradley, editor in chief. **40% freelance written.** Monthly tabloid covering bicycle racing. Estab. 1972. Circ. 48,000. Byline given. Pays on publication. No kill fee. Publishes ms an average of 1 month after acceptance. Accepts simultaneous submissions. Responds in 3 weeks to queries. Guidelines available online.

NONFICTION **Buys 80 mss/year.** Query. Length: 300-1,200 words. **Pays $100-400.** Pays expenses of writers on assignment.

REPRINTS Send typed manuscript with rights for sale noted and information about when and where the material previously appeared.

PHOTOS State availability. Captions, identification of subjects required. Buys one time rights.

BOATING

💲💲💲 BOATING

Bonnier Corporation, 460 N. Orlando Ave., Suite 200, Winter Park FL 32789. (407)628-4802. **Fax:** (407)628-7061. **E-mail:** editor@boatingmag.com. **Website:** www.boatingmag.com. **25% freelance written.** Magazine published 11 times/year covering performance boating. Estab. 1973. Circ. 50,000. Byline given. Pays on publication. Offers negotiable kill fee. Publishes ms an average of 3 months after acceptance. Editorial lead time 3 months. Submit seasonal material 4 months in advance. Accepts queries by mail, e-mail. Accepts simultaneous submissions.

NONFICTION Needs how-to, interview, new product, photo feature. No general interest boating stories.

Buys numerous mss/year. Query. Length: 300-2,000 words. **Pays $125-1,200.** Pays expenses of writers on assignment.

PHOTOS State availability. Captions required. Reviews negatives. Buys one-time rights.

🔵🔵 BOATING WORLD MAGAZINE

Duncan McIntosh Co., 18475 Bandilier, Fountain Valley CA 92708. (949)660-6150. **Fax:** (949)660-6172. **Website:** www.boatingworld.com. **60% freelance written.** Magazine published 8 times/year covering recreational trailer boats. "Typical reader owns a power boat between 14 and 32 feet long and has 3-9 years experience. Boat reports are mostly written by staff while features and most departments are provided by freelancers. We are looking for freelancers who can write well and who have at least a working knowledge of recreational power boating and the industry behind it." Estab. 1997. Circ. 100,000. Pays on publication. No kill fee. Publishes ms an average of 4 months after acceptance. Accepts simultaneous submissions. Responds in 3 months to queries. Sample copy free. Guidelines for #10 SASE.

NONFICTION Needs general interest, how-to, humor, new product, personal experience, travel. **Buys 20-25 mss/year.** Query. Length: 1,400-1,600 words. **Pays $150-450.** Pays expenses of writers on assignment.

PHOTOS State availability. Identification of subjects, model releases required. Reviews transparencies, prints, digital images. Offers $50-250/photo. Buys one-time rights.

FILLERS Needs anecdotes, facts, newsbreaks. Length: 250-500 words. **Pays $50-100.**

TIPS "We are looking for solid writers who are familiar with power boating and who can educate, entertain, and enlighten our readers with well-written and researched feature stories."

🔵🔵🔵 CANOE & KAYAK

GrindMedia, LLC, 2052 Corte del Nogal, Suite 100, Carlsbad CA 92011. (425)827-6363. **Website:** www.canoekayak.com. **75% freelance written.** Quarterly magazine covering paddlesports. "*Canoe & Kayak* is North America's No. 1 paddlesports resource. Our readers include flatwater and whitewater canoeists and kayakers of all skill levels. We provide comprehensive information on destinations, technique and equipment. Beyond that, we cover canoe and kayak camping, safety, the environment, and the history of boats and sport." Estab. 1972. Circ. 35,000. Byline given. Pays on or shortly after publication. No kill fee. Publishes ms an average of 6 months after acceptance. Editorial lead time 6 months. Submit seasonal material 8 months in advance. Accepts queries by online submission form. Accepts simultaneous submissions. Responds in 2 months to queries. Guidelines online.

NONFICTION Needs historical, how-to, personal experience, photo feature, technical, travel. Special issues: Kayak Fish. No cartoons, poems, stories in which bad judgement is portrayed or 'Me and Molly' articles. **Buys 25 mss/year.** Send complete ms. Length: 400-2,500 words. **Pays $100-800 for assigned articles; $100-500 for unsolicited articles.** Pays expenses of writers on assignment.

PHOTOS "Some activities we cover are canoeing, kayaking, canoe fishing, camping, canoe sailing or poling, backpacking (when compatible with the main activity) and occasionally inflatable boats. We are not interested in groups of people in rafts, photos showing disregard for the environment or personal safety, gasoline-powered engines unless appropriate to the discussion, or unskilled persons taking extraordinary risks." State availability. Captions, identification of subjects. Reviews 35mm transparencies, 4x6 prints, digital files preferred. Offers $75-500/photo. Buys one-time print and web rights.

COLUMNS Put In (environment, conservation, events), 500 words; Destinations (canoe and kayak destinations in US, Canada), 1,500 words; Essays, 750 words. **Buys 40 mss/year.** Send complete ms. **Pays $100-350.**

FILLERS Needs anecdotes, facts, newsbreaks. **Buys 20 mss/year.** Length: 200-500 words. **Pays $25-50.**

TIPS "Start with Put-In articles (short featurettes) or short, unique equipment reviews. Or give us the best, most exciting article we've ever seen—with great photos. Read the magazine before submitting."

🔵🔵🔵 CHESAPEAKE BAY MAGAZINE

601 Sixth St., Annapolis MD 21403. (410)263-2662. **Fax:** (410)267-6924. **E-mail:** joe@chesapeakebaymagazine.com. **E-mail:** editor@chesapeakebaymagazine.com. **Website:** www.chesapeakebaymagazine.com. **Contact:** Kate Livie, managing editor; Joe Evans, editor. **70% freelance written.** Monthly magazine covering boating and the Chesapeake Bay. "Our readers are boaters—sailors, paddlers, power boaters, anglers,

conservationists, and foodies. Read the magazine before submitting." Estab. 1972. Circ. 25,000. Byline given. Pays on publication. No kill fee. Publishes ms an average of 6 months after acceptance. Editorial lead time 1 year. Submit seasonal material 1 year in advance. Accepts queries by mail, e-mail, fax, phone. Accepts simultaneous submissions. Responds in 2 months to queries; 3 months to mss. Sample copy for $5.19 prepaid and SASE.

NONFICTION Needs book excerpts, essays, historical, how-to, humor, interview, new product, nostalgic, photo feature, profile, technical, travel. **Buys 30 mss/year.** Query with published clips. Length: 300-3,000 words. **Pays $100-1,000.** Pays expenses of writers on assignment.

PHOTOS Captions, identification of subjects required. Offers $75-250/photo, $400/day rate for assignment photography. Pays $275 for color cover; $75-250 for color *stock* inside, depending on size; $200-1,200 for *assigned* photo package. Pays on publication. Credit line given. Buys one-time rights. Buys one-time rights.

TIPS "Send us unedited writing samples (not clips) that show the writer can write, not just string words together. We look for well-organized, lucid, lively, intelligent writing."

☺☻ COAST&KAYAK MAGAZINE

Wild Coast Publishing, P.O. Box 24 Stn. A, Nanaimo British Columbia V9R 5K4 Canada. (360)406-4708; (866)984-6437. **Fax:** (866)654-1937. **E-mail:** editor@coastandkayak.com; kayak@coastandkayak.com. **Website:** www.coastandkayak.com. **Contact:** John Kimantas, editor. **75% freelance written.** Quarterly magazine with a major focus on paddling the Pacific coast. "We promote safe paddling, guide paddlers to useful products and services, and explore coastal environmental issues." Estab. 1991. Circ. 65,000 print and electronic readers. Byline given. Pays on publication. Publishes ms an average of 4 months after acceptance. Editorial lead time 4 months. Submit seasonal material 4 months in advance. Accepts queries by mail, e-mail. Accepts simultaneous submissions. Sample copy and guidelines available online.

NONFICTION Needs how-to, humor, new product, personal experience, technical. **Buys 25 mss/year.** Query. Length: 1,000-1,500 words. **Pays $50-75.** Pays expenses of writers on assignment.

PHOTOS State availability. Captions, identification of subjects required. Reviews low-res JPEGs. Offers $25-50/photo. Buys first and electronic rights.

TIPS "You must know paddling—though novice paddlers are welcome. A strong environmental or wilderness appreciation component is advisable. We are willing to help refine work with flexible people. E-mail queries preferred. Check out our editorial calendar for our upcoming features."

☺☻☻☻ CRUISING WORLD

The Sailing Co., 55 Hammarlund Way, Middletown RI 02842. (401)845-5100. **Fax:** (401)845-5180. **E-mail:** mark.pillsbury@cruisingworld.com. **E-mail:** editor@cruisingworld.com. **Website:** www.cruisingworld.com. **60% freelance written.** Monthly magazine covering sailing, cruising/adventuring, do-it-yourself boat improvements. "*Cruising World* is a publication by and for sailboat owners who spend time in home waters as well as voyaging the world. Its readership is extremely loyal, savvy, and driven by independent thinking." Estab. 1974. Circ. 91,244. Byline given. **Pays on acceptance for articles;** on publication for photography. No kill fee. Publishes ms an average of 18 months after acceptance. Editorial lead time 3 months. Submit seasonal material 1 year in advance. Accepts queries by mail. Accepts simultaneous submissions. Responds in 2 months to queries. Responds in 4 months to mss. Sample copy free. Guidelines available online.

NONFICTION Needs book excerpts, essays, expose, general interest, historical, how-to, humor, interview, new product, opinion, personal experience, photo feature, technical, travel. No travel articles that have nothing to do with cruising aboard sailboats from 20-50 feet in length. **Buys dozens mss/year.** Send complete ms. **Pays $50-1,500 for assigned articles. Pays $50-1,000 for unsolicited articles.** Pays expenses of writers on assignment.

PHOTOS Send high-res (minimum 300 DPI) images on CD. Send photos. Captions required. Payment upon publication. Also buys stand-alone photos. Buys first and one-time rights.

COLUMNS Underway Shoreline (sailing news, people, and short features; contact Elaine Lembo), 300 words maximum; Hands-on Sailor (refit, voyaging, seamanship, how-to), 1,000-1,500 words. **Buys dozens mss/year.** Query with or without published clips or send complete ms.

TIPS *"Cruising World's* readers know exactly what they want to read, so our best advice to freelancers is to carefully read the magazine and envision which exact section or department would be the appropriate place for proposed submissions."

💲💲 HEARTLAND BOATING

The Waterways Journal, Inc., 319 N. Fourth St., Suite 650, St. Louis MO 63102. (314)241-4310. **Fax:** (314)241-4207. **E-mail:** brad@heartlandboating.com. **Website:** www.heartlandboating.com. Zac Metcalf, regional sales manager. **Contact:** Brad Kovach, editor. **75% freelance written.** Magazine published 5 times/year covering recreational boating on the inland waterways of mid-America, from the Great Lakes south to the Gulf of Mexico. "Our writers must have experience with, and a great interest in, boating in mid-America. *HeartLand Boating's* content is both informative and inspirational—describing boating life as the heartland boater knows it. The content reflects the challenge, joy, and excitement of our way of life. We are devoted to both power and sailboating enthusiasts throughout America's inland waterways." Estab. 1989. Circ. 10,000. Byline given. Pays on publication. No kill fee. Editorial lead time two months. Accepts queries by mail. Responds only if interested. Sample copy upon request. Guidelines for #10 SASE.

NONFICTION Needs book excerpts, how-to, humor, inspirational, new product, personal experience, profile, reviews, technical, travel. **Buys 100 mss/year.** Send complete ms. Length: 850-1,500 words. **Pays $150-350.**

REPRINTS Send tearsheet, photocopy or typed ms and information about when and where the material previously appeared.

PHOTOS Magazine published five times/year covering recreational boating on the inland waterways of mid-America, from the Great Lakes south to the Gulf of Mexico and over to the east. Send photos. Model release is required, property release is preferred, photo captions are required. Include names and locations. Reviews prints, digital images. Offers no additional payment for photos accepted with ms. Buys one-time print rights and Web rights of photos.

COLUMNS Query with published clips or send complete ms.

TIPS "We begin planning the next year's schedule starting in August. So submitting material between August 1 and October 15 is the best way to proceed."

💲💲 HOUSEBOAT MAGAZINE

Harris Publishing, Inc., 360 B St., Idaho Falls ID 83402. (208)524-7000. **Fax:** (208)522-5241. **E-mail:** blk@houseboatmagazine.com. **Website:** www.houseboatmagazine.com. **Contact:** Brady L. Kay, executive editor. **15% freelance written.** Bi-monthly magazine for houseboaters who enjoy reading everything that reflects the unique houseboating lifestyle. If it is not a houseboat-specific article, please do not query. Estab. 1990. Circ. 25,000. Byline given. Pays on acceptance. Offers 25% kill fee. Publishes ms an average of 3 months after acceptance. Editorial lead time 2 months. Submit seasonal material 6 months in advance. Accepts simultaneous submissions. Responds in 1 week to queries. Sample copy for $5. Guidelines by e-mail.

NONFICTION Needs how-to, interview, new product, personal experience, travel. **Buys 36 mss/year.** Query before submitting. Length: 1,500-2,200 words. **Pays $200-500.** Pays expenses of writers on assignment.

PHOTOS Often required as part of submission package. Color prints discouraged. Digital prints are unacceptable. Seldom purchases photos without ms, but occasionally buys cover photos. Captions, model releases required. Reviews transparencies, high-resolution electronic images. Offers no additional payment for photos accepted with ms. Buys one-time rights.

COLUMNS Pays $150-300.

TIPS "As a general rule, how-to articles are always in demand. So are stories on unique houseboats or houseboaters. You are less likely to break in with a travel piece that does not revolve around specific people or groups. Personality profile pieces with excellent supporting photography are your best bet."

💲💲 LAKELAND BOATING

O'Meara-Brown Publications, Inc., 630 Davis St., Suite 301, Evanston IL 60201. **E-mail:** info@lakelandboating.com. **Website:** www.lakelandboating.com. **50% freelance written.** Magazine covering Great Lakes boating. Estab. 1946. Circ. 60,000. Byline given. Pays on publication. No kill fee. Accepts queries by e-mail. Accepts simultaneous submissions. Responds in 4 months to queries. Sample copy for $5.50 and 9x12 SAE with 6 first-class stamps. Guidelines free.

NONFICTION Needs book excerpts, historical, how-to, interview, personal experience, photo feature, technical, travel, must relate to boating in Great

Lakes. No inspirational, religious, expose, or poetry. **Buys 20-30 mss/year.** Length: 300-1,500 words. **Pays $100-600.**

PHOTOS State availability. Captions required. Reviews prefers 35mm transparencies, high-res digital shots. Buys one time rights.

COLUMNS Bosun's Locker (technical or how-to pieces on boating), 100-1,000 words. **Buys 40 mss/year.** Query. **Pays $25-200.**

💲 LIVING ABOARD

FTW Publishing, P.O. Box 668, Redondo Beach CA 90277. (888)893-7245. **Fax:** (310)789-3448. **E-mail:** editor@livingaboard.com. **Website:** www.livingaboard.com. **95% freelance written.** Bimonthly magazine covering living on boats/cruising. Estab. 1973. Circ. 10,000. Byline given. Pays on publication. No kill fee. Publishes ms an average of 3-6 months after acceptance. Accepts queries by mail, e-mail, fax. Responds in 1-2 weeks to queries. Responds in 1-2 months to mss. Sample copy available online. Guidelines free.

NONFICTION Needs how-to, buy, furnish, maintain, provision a boat, interview, personal experience, technical, as relates to boats, travel, on the water, Cooking Aboard with Recipes. Send complete ms. **Pays 5¢/word.**

PHOTOS Pays $5/photo; $50/cover photo.

COLUMNS Cooking Aboard (how to prepare healthy and nutritious meals in the confines of a galley; how to entertain aboard a boat), 1,000-1,500 words; Environmental Notebook (articles pertaining to clean water, fish, waterfowl, water environment), 750-1,000 words. **Buys 40 mss/year mss/year.** Send complete ms. **Pays 5¢/word**

TIPS "Articles should have a positive tone and promote the live aboard lifestyle."

♻💲💲 PACIFIC YACHTING

OP Publishing, Ltd., 1166 Alberni St., Suite 802, Vancouver, British Columbia V6E 3Z3 Canada. (604)428-0259. **Fax:** (604)620-0425. **E-mail:** editor@pacificyachting.com; ayates@oppublishing.com. **Website:** www.pacificyachting.com. **Contact:** Dale Miller, editor; Arran Yates, art director. **90% freelance written.** Monthly magazine covering all aspects of recreational boating in the Pacific Northwest. "The bulk of our writers and photographers not only come from the local boating community, many of them were long-

time *PY* readers before coming aboard as a contributor. The *PY* reader buys the magazine to read about new destinations or changes to old haunts on the British Columbia coast and the Pacific Northwest and to learn the latest about boats and gear." Estab. 1968. Circ. 19,000. Byline given. Pays on publication. No kill fee. Publishes ms an average of 6 months after acceptance. Editorial lead time 4 months. Submit seasonal material 6 months in advance. Accepts queries by mail, e-mail, fax. Accepts simultaneous submissions. Sample copy for $6.95, plus postage charged to credit card. Guidelines available online.

NONFICTION Needs historical, how-to, humor, interview, personal experience, technical, travel, cruising, and destination on the British Columbia coast. "No articles from writers who are obviously not boaters!" Query. Length: 800-2,000 words. **Pays $150-500. Pays some expenses of writers on assignment for unsolicited articles.** Pays expenses of writers on assignment.

PHOTOS Send photos. Identification of subjects required. Reviews digital photos transparencies, 4 x 6 prints, and slides. Offers no additional payment for photos accepted with ms. Offers $25-400 for photos accepted alone. Buys one-time rights.

COLUMNS Currents (current events, trade and people news, boat gatherings, and festivities), 50-250 words. Reflections; Cruising, both 800-1,000 words. Query. **Pay varies.**

TIPS "Our reader wants you to balance important navigation details with first-person observations, blending the practical with the romantic. Write tight, write short, write with the reader in mind, write to inform, write to entertain. Be specific, accurate, and historic."

💲💲 PONTOON & DECK BOAT

PDB Magazine, Harris Publishing, Inc., 360 B. St., Idaho Falls ID 83402. (208)524-7000. **Fax:** (208)522-5241. **E-mail:** blk@pdbmagazine.com. **Website:** www.pdbmagazine.com. **Contact:** Brady L. Kay, editor. **15% freelance written.** Magazine published 11 times/year covering boating. A boating niche publication geared toward the pontoon and deck boating lifestyle and consumer market. Audience is comprised of people who utilize these boats for varied family activities and fishing. Magazine is promotional of the PDB industry and its major players. Seeks to give the reader a twofold reason to read publication: to celebrate the lifestyle, and to do it aboard a first-class craft. Estab. 1995. Circ. 84,000. Byline given. Pays on publication. No kill fee. Editorial lead time 2 months. Submit seasonal material 3 months in advance. Accepts queries by mail, e-mail. Accepts simultaneous submissions. Responds in 3 weeks to queries; in 3 months to mss. Sample copy and writer's guidelines available.

NONFICTION Needs how-to, personal experience. "No general boating (must be pontoon or deck boat specific), no humor, fiction, or poetry." **Buys 15 mss/year.** Send complete ms. Length: 600-2,000 words. **Pays $50-300.** Pays expenses of writers on assignment.

PHOTOS State availability. Captions, model releases required. Reviews transparencies. Rights negotiable.

COLUMNS No Wake Zone (short, fun quips); Better Boater (how-to). **Buys 6-12 mss/year.** Query with published clips. **Pays $50-150.**

TIPS "Be specific to pontoon and deck boats. Any general boating material goes to the slush pile. The more you can tie together the lifestyle, attitudes, and the PDB industry, the more interest we'll take in what you send us."

❷❸❸ POWER & MOTORYACHT

10 Bokum Rd., Essex CT 06426. (860)767-3200. **E-mail:** gsass@aimmedia.com. **Website:** www.powerandmotoryacht.com. Erin Kenney, creative director. **Contact:** George Sass, editor-in-chief. **25% freelance written.** Monthly magazine covering powerboats 24 feet and larger with special emphasis on the 35-foot-plus market. "Readers have an average of 33 years experience boating, and we give them accurate advice on how to choose, operate, and maintain their boats as well as what electronics and gear will help them pursue their favorite pastime. In addition, since powerboating is truly a lifestyle and not just a hobby for them, *Power & Motoryacht* reports on a host of other topics that affect their enjoyment of the water: chartering, sportfishing, and the environment, among others. Articles must therefore be clear, concise, and authoritative; knowledge of the marine industry is mandatory. Include personal experience and information for marine industry experts where appropriate." Estab. 1985. Circ. 157,000. Byline given. Pays on acceptance. Offers 33% kill fee. Publishes ms an average of 4-6 months after acceptance. Editorial lead time 4-6 months. Submit seasonal material 4-6 months in advance. Accepts queries by mail, e-mail.

Responds in 1 month to queries. Sample copy with 10x12 SASE. Guidelines with #10 SASE or via e-mail.

NONFICTION Needs how-to, interview, personal experience, photo feature, travel. No unsolicited mss or articles about sailboats and/or sailing yachts (including motorsailers or cruise ships). **Buys 20-25 mss/year.** Query with published clips. Length: 800-1,500 words. **Pays $500-1,000 for assigned articles.** Pays expenses of writers on assignment.

PHOTOS State availability. Captions, identification of subjects required. Reviews 8x10 transparencies, GIF/JPEG files (minimum 300 dpi). Offers no additional payment for photos accepted with ms. Buys one-time print and web rights.

TIPS "Take a clever or even unique approach to a subject, particularly if the topic is dry/technical. Pitch us on yacht cruises you've taken, particularly if they're in off-the-beaten-path locations."

❷❸❸ POWER BOATING CANADA

1121 Invicta Drive Unit 2, Oakville ON L6H 2R2 Canada. (800)354-9145. **Fax:** (905)844-5032. **E-mail:** editor@powerboating.com. **Website:** www.powerboating.com. **70% freelance written.** Bimonthly magazine covering recreational power boating. *Power Boating Canada* offers boating destinations, how-to features, boat tests (usually staff written), lifestyle pieces—with a Canadian slant—and appeal to recreational power boaters across the country. Estab. 1984. Circ. 42,000. Byline given. Pays on publication. No kill fee. Publishes ms an average of 3 months after acceptance. Editorial lead time 2 months. Submit seasonal material 3 months in advance. Responds in 1 month to queries. Responds in 2 months to mss. Sample copy free.

NONFICTION Needs historical, how-to, interview, personal experience, travel, boating destinations. No general boating articles or personal anecdotes. **Buys 40-50 mss/year.** Query. Length: 1,200-2,500 words. **Pays $150-300 (Canadian).** Sometimes pays expenses of writers on assignment.

REPRINTS Send photocopy with rights for sale noted and information about when and where the material previously appeared.

PHOTOS Send photos. Captions, identification of subjects required. Reviews contact sheets, negatives, transparencies, prints. Pay varies; no additional payment for photos accepted with ms. Buys one time rights.

$$$ SAIL

180 Canal St., Suite 301, Boston MA 02114. (860)767-3200. **Fax:** (860)767-1048. **E-mail:** sailmail@sailmagazine.com; pnielsen@sailmagazine.com. **Website:** www.sailmagazine.com. **Contact:** Peter Nielsen, editor-in-chief. **30% freelance written.** Monthly magazine written and edited for everyone who sails—aboard a coastal or bluewater cruiser, trailerable, one-design or offshore racer, or daysailer. How-to and technical articles concentrate on techniques of sailing and aspects of design and construction, boat systems, and gear; the feature section emphasizes the fun and rewards of sailing in a practical and instructive way. Estab. 1970. Circ. 180,000. Byline given. Pays on acceptance. No kill fee. Publishes ms an average of 1 year after acceptance. Accepts queries by mail, e-mail, fax. Accepts simultaneous submissions. Responds in 3 months to queries. Guidelines with SASE or available online.

NONFICTION Needs how-to, personal experience, technical, distance cruising, destinations. Special issues: Cruising, chartering, commissioning, fitting-out, special race (e.g., America's Cup), Top 10 Boats. **Buys 50 mss/year.** Query. Length: 1,500-3,000 words. **Pays $200-800.** Pays expenses of writers on assignment.

PHOTOS Prefers transparencies. High-res digital photos (300 dpi) are also accepted, as are high-quality color prints (preferably with negatives attached). Captions, identification of subjects, True required. Payment varies, up to $1,000 if photo used on cover.

COLUMNS Sailing Memories (short essay); Sailing News (cruising, racing, legal, political, environmental); Under Sail (human interest). Query. **Pays $50-400.**

TIPS "Request an articles' specification sheet. We look for unique ways of viewing sailing. Skim old issues of *Sail* for ideas about the types of articles we publish. Always remember that *Sail* is a sailing magazine. Stay away from gloomy articles detailing all the things that went wrong on your boat. Think constructively and write about how to avoid certain problems. You should focus on a theme or choose some aspect of sailing and discuss a personal attitude or new philosophical approach to the subject. Notice that we have certain issues devoted to special themes—for example, chartering, electronics, commissioning, and the like. Stay away from pieces that chronicle your journey in the day-by-day style of a logbook. These are generally dull and uninteresting. Select specific actions or events (preferably sailing events, not shorebound activities), and build your articles around them. Emphasize the sailing."

$$$ SAILING MAGAZINE

125 E. Main St., P.O. Box 249, Port Washington WI 53074. (262)284-3494. **Fax:** (262)284-7764. **E-mail:** editorial@sailingmagazine.net. **Website:** www.sailingmagazine.net. **Contact:** Greta Schanen, managing editor. Monthly magazine for the experienced sailor. Covers all aspects of sailing, from learning how to sail in a dinghy to crossing the ocean on a large cruiser to racing around the buoys against the best sailors in the world. Typically focuses on sailing in places that are realistic destinations for readers, but will occasionally feature an outstanding and unique sailing destination. Estab. 1966. Circ. 45,000. Pays after publication. No kill fee. Accepts queries by mail, e-mail. Accepts simultaneous submissions. Responds in 3 months to unsolicited submission.

NONFICTION Needs book excerpts, how-to, interview, personal experience. **Buys 15-20 mss/year.** Send complete ms in Word as an attachment, or send via mail. Length: 1,000-3,000 words. **Pays $50-500.** Pays expenses of writers on assignment.

PHOTOS Captions required. Reviews color transparencies. Pays $50-400.

COLUMNS Splashes, short news stories (100-500 words).

$$ SAILING WORLD

Bonnier Corporation, 55 Hammarlund Way, Middletown RI 02842. (401)845-5100. **Fax:** (401)845-5180. **E-mail:** editor@sailingworld.com; dave.reed@sailingworld.com. **Website:** www.sailingworld.com. **Contact:** Dave Reed, editor. **40% freelance written.** Magazine published 8 times/year covering performance sailing. Estab. 1962. Circ. 65,000. Byline given. Pays on publication. No kill fee. Publishes ms an average of 4 months after acceptance. Accepts queries by e-mail. Accepts simultaneous submissions. Responds in 1 month to queries. Sample copy: $7. Guidelines available online.

NONFICTION Needs interview. Special issues: "The emphasis here is on performance sailing: Keep in mind that the *Sailing World* readership is relatively educated about the sport. Unless you are dealing with a totally new aspect of sailing, you can and should discuss ideas on an advanced technical level; however, extensive formulae and graphs don't play well to our audience. When in doubt as to the suitability of an article or idea, submit a written query before time and energy are misdirected." No travelogs. **Buys 5-10 unsolicited mss/year.** Query unsolicited articles to dave.reed@sailingworld.com. No phone queries. Length: up to 2,000 words. **Pays $400 for up to 2,000 words.** Pays expenses of writers on assignment. Does not pay expenses of writers on assignment unless pre-approved.

PHOTOS Reviews color slides, prints, digital.

TIPS "Prospective contributors should study recent issues of the magazine to determine appropriate subject matter."

$$ SEA KAYAKER

Sea Kayaker, Inc., P.O. Box 17029, Seattle WA 98127. (206)789-1326. **Fax:** (206)781-1141. **E-mail:** editorial@seakayakermag.com. **Website:** www.seakayakermag.com. **95% freelance written.** *Sea Kayaker* is a bimonthly publication with a worldwide readership that covers all aspects of kayak touring. It is well known as an important source of continuing education by the most experienced paddlers. Estab. 1984. Circ. 30,000. Byline given. Pays on publication. Offers 10% kill fee. Publishes ms an average of 6 months after acceptance. Editorial lead time 4 months. Submit seasonal material 4 months in advance. Accepts queries by mail, e-mail, fax, phone. Responds in 2 months to queries. Sample copy for $7.30 (US), samples to other countries extra. Guidelines available online.

NONFICTION Needs essays, historical, how-to, on making equipment, humor, new product, personal experience, technical, travel. Unsolicited gear reviews are not accepted. **Buys 50 mss/year.** Send complete ms. Length: 1,500-5,000 words. **Pays 18-20¢/word for assigned articles. Pays 15-17¢/word for unsolicited articles.**

PHOTOS Send photos. Captions, identification of subjects required. Reviews transparencies, prints. Offers $15-400. Buys one time rights.

COLUMNS Technique; Equipment; Do-It-Yourself; Food; Safety; Health; Environment; Book Reviews; all 1,000-2,500 words. **Buys 40-45 mss/year.** Query. **Pays 15-20¢/word.**

TIPS "We consider unsolicited manuscripts that include a SASE, but we give greater priority to brief descriptions (several paragraphs) of proposed articles accompanied by at least 2 samples—published or unpublished—of your writing. Enclose a statement as to why you're qualified to write the piece and indicate whether photographs or illustrations are available to accompany the piece."

$$$$$ SHOWBOATS INTERNATIONAL

Boat International Media, 41-47 Hartfield Rd., London SW19 3RQ United Kingdom. (954)522-2628 (US number). **Fax:** (954)522-2240. **E-mail:** kate.lardy@showboats.com. **Website:** www.boatinternational.com. **Contact:** Marilyn Mower, editorial director. **70% freelance written.** Magazine published 11 times/year covering luxury superyacht industry. Estab. 1995. Circ. 46,000. Byline given. Pays on publication. Offers 30% kill fee. Editorial lead time 2 months. Submit seasonal material 4 months in advance. Accepts queries by e-mail. Accepts simultaneous submissions. Responds in 2 months to mss. Sample copy for $6.00. Guidelines free.

NONFICTION Contact: kate.lardy@showboats.com. Needs profile, travel, Travel/destination pieces that are superyacht related. **Buys 10/year mss/year.** Query. Length: 300-2,000 words. **Pays $300 minimum, $2,000 maximum for assigned articles.** Pays expenses of writers on assignment.

PHOTOS State availability. Captions required. Reviews contact sheets, GIF/JPEG files. negotiates payment individually. Buys all rights.

FICTION NONE

$$ SOUTHERN BOATING

Southern Boating & Yachting, Inc., 330 N. Andrews Ave., Suite 200, Ft. Lauderdale FL 33301. (954)522-5515. **Fax:** (954)522-2260. **E-mail:** liz@southernboating.com. **Website:** www.southernboating.com. **Contact:** Liz Pasch, editorial director; Dan Brooks, art director. **75% freelance written.** Monthly boating magazine. Upscale monthly yachting magazine focusing on the Southeast US, Bahamas, Caribbean, and Gulf of Mexico. Estab. 1972. Circ. 40,000. Byline given Pays 30 days after publication. Publishes ms an average of 3 months after acceptance. Editorial lead time 3 months. Submit seasonal material 6 months in advance. Accepts queries by e-mail. Accepts simultaneous submissions.

NONFICTION Needs how to, new product, profile, reviews, technical, travel. Query. Length: 900-1,200 words. **Pays $400-600 with art.**

PHOTOS State availability of hi-res digital photos. Captions, identification of subjects, model releases required. Reviews digital files. Buys one-time rights.

COLUMNS DIY (how-to/maintenance), 900 words; What's New in Electronics (electronics), 900 words; Engine Room (new developments), 900 words. **Buys 24 mss/year.** Query first; see media kit for special issue focus.

⑨ WATERFRONT TIMES

Storyboard Media Inc., 2787 E. Oakland Park Blvd., Suite 205, Ft. Lauderdale FL 33306. (954)524-9450. **Fax:** (954)524-9464. **E-mail:** editor@waterfronttimes.com. **Website:** www.waterfronttimes.com. **Contact:** Jennifer Heit, editor. **20% freelance written.** Monthly tabloid covering marine and boating topics for the Greater Ft. Lauderdale waterfront community. Estab. 1984. Circ. 20,000. Byline given. Pays on publication. No kill fee. Publishes ms an average of 2 months after acceptance. Submit seasonal material 3 months in advance. Accepts simultaneous submissions. Responds in 1 month to queries. Sample copy for SAE with 9x12 envelope and 4 first-class stamps.

NONFICTION Length: 500-1,000 words. **Pays $100-125 for assigned articles.** Pays expenses of writers on assignment.

PHOTOS Send photos. Reviews JPEG/TIFF files.

TIPS "No fiction. Keep it under 1,000 words. Photos or illustrations help. Send for a sample copy of *Waterfront Times* so you can acquaint yourself with our publication and our unique audience. Although we're not necessarily looking for technical articles, it helps if the writer has sailing or powerboating experience. Writers should be familiar with the region and be specific when dealing with local topics."

⑨⑨ WATERWAY GUIDE

P.O. Box 1125, 16273 General Puller Hwy., Deltaville VA 23043. (804)776-8999. **Fax:** (804)776-6111. **Website:** www.waterwayguide.com. **Contact:** Jani Parker, managing editor. **90% freelance written.** Annual magazine covering intracoastal waterway travel for recreational boats. Six editions cover coastal waters from Maine to Florida, the Bahamas, the Gulf of Mexico, the Great Lakes, and the Great Loop Cruise of America's inland waterways. "Writer must be knowledgeable about navigation and the areas covered by the guide." Estab. 1947. Circ. 30,000. Byline given. Pays on publication. No kill fee. Publishes ms an average of 3 months after acceptance. Editorial lead time 4 months. Submit seasonal material 3 months in advance. Accepts queries by mail, phone. Accepts simultaneous submissions. Responds in 6 weeks to queries. Responds in 2 months to mss. Sample copy: $39.95 with $3 postage and available online.

NONFICTION Needs essays, historical, how-to, photo feature, technical, travel. **Buys 6 mss/year.** Send complete ms. Length: 250-5,000 words. **Pays $50-500.** Pays expenses of writers on assignment.

PHOTOS Send photos. Captions, identification of subjects required. Reviews transparencies, 3 x 5 prints. Offers $25-50/photo. Buys all rights.

TIPS "Must have on-the-water experience and be able to provide new and accurate information on geographic areas covered by *Waterway Guide*."

⑨⑨ WOODENBOAT MAGAZINE

WoodenBoat Publications, Inc., P.O. Box 78, Brookline ME 04616. (207)359-4651. **Website:** www.woodenboat.com. **Contact:** Matthew P. Murphy, editor. **50% freelance written.** Bimonthly magazine for wooden boat owners, builders, and designers. "We are devoted exclusively to the design, building, care, preservation, and use of wooden boats, both commercial and pleasure, old and new, sail and power. We work to convey quality, integrity, and involvement in the creation and care of these craft, to entertain, inform, inspire, and to provide our varied readers with access to individuals who are deeply experienced in the world of wooden boats." Estab. 1974. Circ. 90,000. Byline given. Pays on publication. Offers variable kill fee. Publishes ms an average of 1 year after acceptance. Accepts queries by online submission form. Accepts simultaneous submissions. Responds in 2 months to queries and mss. Sample copy: $5.99. Guidelines available online.

NONFICTION Needs technical. No poetry, fiction. **Buys 50 mss/year.** Query with published clips. Length: 1,500-5,000 words. **Pays $300/1,000 words.** Pays expenses of writers on assignment.

REPRINTS Send tearsheet or typed ms with rights for sale noted and information about when and where the material previously appeared.

PHOTOS Send photos. Identification of subjects required. Reviews negatives. Pays $15-75 b&w, $25-350 color. Buys one time rights.

COLUMNS Currents pays for information on wooden boat-related events, projects, boatshop activities, etc. Uses same columnists for each issue. Length: 250-1,000 words. Send complete information. **Pays $5-50.**

TIPS "We appreciate a detailed, articulate query letter, accompanied by photos, that will give us a clear idea of what the author is proposing. We appreciate samples of previously published work. It is important for a prospective author to become familiar with our magazine. Most work is submitted on speculation. The most common failure is not exploring the subject material in enough depth."

✪✪✪ YACHTING

Bonnier Corporation, 55 Hammarlund Way, Middletown RI 02842. **Website:** www.yachtingmagazine.com. **30% freelance written.** Monthly magazine covering yachts, boats. Monthly magazine written and edited for experienced, knowledgeable yachtsmen. Estab. 1907. Circ. 132,000. Byline given. Pays on acceptance. No kill fee. Editorial lead time 2 months. Submit seasonal material 6 months in advance. Accepts queries by mail, e-mail, fax. Accepts simultaneous submissions. Responds in 1 month to queries. Responds in 3 months to mss. Sample copy free.

NONFICTION Needs personal experience, technical. **Buys 50 mss/year.** Query with published clips. Length: 750-800 words. **Pays $150-1,500.** Pays expenses of writers on assignment.

PHOTOS Send photos. Captions, identification of subjects, model releases required. Reviews transparencies. Negotiates payment individually.

TIPS "We require considerable expertise in our writing because our audience is experienced and knowledgeable. Vivid descriptions of quaint anchorages and quainter natives are fine, but our readers want to know how the yachtsmen got there, too. They also want to know how their boats work. *Yachting* is edited for experienced, affluent boatownerspower and sail—who don't have the time or the inclination to read sub-standard stories. They love carefully crafted stories about places they've never been or a different spin on places they have, meticulously reported pieces on issues that affect their yachting lives, personal accounts of yachting experiences from which they can learn, engaging profiles of people who share their passion for boats, insightful essays that evoke the history and traditions of the sport and compelling photographs of others enjoying the game as much as they do. They love to know what to buy and how things work. They love to be surprised. They don't mind getting their hands dirty or saving a buck here and there, but they're not interested in learning how to make a masthead light out of a mayonnaise jar. If you love what they love and can communicate like a pro (that means meeting deadlines, writing tight, being obsessively accurate and never misspelling a proper name), we'd love to hear from you."

GENERAL INTEREST

✪✪ FCA MAGAZINE

Fellowship of Christian Athletes, 8701 Leeds Rd., Kansas City MO 64129. (816)921-0909; (800)289-0909. **Fax:** (816)921-8755. **E-mail:** mag@fca.org. **Website:** www.fca.org/mag. **Contact:** Clay Meyer, editor; Matheau Casner, creative director. **50% freelance written. Prefers to work with published/established writers, but works with a growing number of new/unpublished writers each year.** Published 6 times/year. *FCA Magazine*'s mission is to serve as a ministry tool of the Fellowship of Christian Athletes by informing, inspiring and involving coaches, athletes and all whom they influence, that they may make an impact for Jesus Christ. Estab. 1959. Circ. 75,000. Byline given. Pays on publication. No kill fee. Publishes ms an average of 4 months after acceptance. Submit seasonal material 6 months in advance. Accepts simultaneous submissions. Responds to queries/mss in 3 months. Sample copy for $2 and 9x12 SASE with 3 first-class stamps. Guidelines available at www.fca.org/mag/media-kit.

NONFICTION Needs inspirational, personal experience, photo feature. **Buys 5-20 mss/year.** Articles should be accompanied by at least 3 quality photos. Query and submit via e-mail. Length: 1,000-2,000 words. **Pays $150-400 for assigned and unsolicited articles.** Pays expenses of writers on assignment.

PHOTOS State availability. Reviews contact sheets. Payment based on size of photo. Buys one-time rights.

TIPS "Profiles and interviews of particular interest to coed athlete, primarily high school and college age. Our graphics and editorial content appeal to youth. The area most open to freelancers is profiles on or interviews with well-known athletes or coaches (male, female, minorities) who have been or are involved in some capacity with FCA."

$ OUTDOORS NW

PMB Box 331, 10002 Aurora Ave. N. #36, Seattle WA 98133. (206)418-0747; (800) 935-1083. **Fax:** (206)418-0746. **E-mail:** info@outdoorsnw.com. **Website:** www.outdoorsnw.com. **80% freelance written.** Monthly magazine covering outdoor recreation in the Pacific Northwest. "Writers must have a solid knowledge of the sport they are writing about. They must be doers." Estab. 1988. Circ. 40,000. Byline given. Pays on publication. No kill fee. Publishes ms an average of 3 months after acceptance. Editorial lead time 2 months. Submit seasonal material 4 months in advance. Accepts queries by mail, e-mail, fax. Accepts simultaneous submissions. Sample copy and writer's guidelines for $3.

NONFICTION Needs interview, new product, travel. Query with published clips. Length: 750-1,500 words. **Pays $25-125.** Sometimes pays expenses of writers on assignment.

PHOTOS Send photos. Captions, identification of subjects, model releases required. Reviews electronic images only. Buys all rights.

COLUMNS Faces, Places, Puruits (750 words). **Buys 4-6 mss/year.** Query with published clips. **Pays $40-75.**

TIPS "*Outdoors NW* is written for the serious Pacific Northwest outdoor recreationalist. The magazine's look, style and editorial content actively engage the reader, delivering insightful perspectives on the sports it has come to be known for—alpine skiing, bicycling, adventure racing, triathlon and multi-sport, hiking, kayaking, marathons, mountain climbing, Nordic skiing, running, and snowboarding. *Outdoors NW* magazine wants vivid writing, telling images, and original perspectives to produce its smart, entertaining monthly."

$ SILENT SPORTS

Journal Community Publishing Group, P.O. Box 620583, Middleton WI 53562. (715)258-4354; (715)369-4859. **E-mail:** info@silentsports.net. **E-mail:** editor@silentsports.net. **Website:** www.silentsports.net. **Contact:** Joel Patenaude, editor. **75% freelance written.** Monthly magazine covering running, cycling, cross-country skiing, canoeing, kayaking, snowshoeing, in-line skating, camping, backpacking, and hiking aimed at people in Wisconsin, Minnesota, northern Illinois, and portions of Michigan and Iowa. "Not a coffee table magazine. Our readers are participants from rank amateur weekend athletes to highly competitive racers." Estab. 1984. Circ. 10,000. Byline given. Pays on publication. Offers 20% kill fee. Publishes ms an average of 3 months after acceptance. Submit seasonal material 4 months in advance. Accepts queries by mail, e-mail, fax. Responds in 3 months to queries. Sample copy and writer's guidelines for 10x13 SAE with 7 first-class stamps.

NONFICTION Needs general interest, how-to, interview, opinion, technical, travel. **Buys 25 mss/year.** Query. Length: 2,500 words maximum. **Pays $15-100.** Sometimes pays expenses of writers on assignment.

REPRINTS Send typed manuscript with rights for sale noted and information about when and where the material previously appeared. Pays 50% of amount paid for an original article.

PHOTOS State availability. Reviews transparencies. Pays $5-15 for b&w story photos; $50-100 for color covers. Buys one time rights.

TIPS "Where-to-go and personality profiles are areas most open to freelancers. Writers should keep in mind that this is a regional, Midwest-based publication. We want only stories/articles with a focus on our region."

GOLF

AFRICAN AMERICAN GOLFER'S DIGEST

80 Wall St., Suite 720, New York NY 10005. (212)571-6559. **E-mail:** debertcook@aol.com. **Website:** www.africanamericangolfersdigest.com. **Contact:** Debert Cook, publisher. **100% freelance written.** Quarterly. Covering golf lifestyle, health, travel destinations and reviews, golf equipment, golfer profiles. "Editorial should focus on interests of our market demographic of African Americans with historical, artistic, musical, educational (higher learning), automotive, sports, fashion, entertainment, and other categories of high interest to them." Estab. 2003. Circ. 20,000. Byline given. No kill fee. Publishes ms an average of 3 months after acceptance. Editorial lead time 3-6 months. Submit seasonal material 3-6 months in advance. Accepts queries by e-mail. Accepts simultaneous submissions. Responds in 3 weeks to queries;

3 months to mss. Sample copy for $8. Guidelines by e-mail.

NONFICTION Needs how-to, interview, new product, opinion, personal experience, photo feature, reviews, technical, travel, golf-related. **Buys 3 mss/year.** Query. Length: 250-1,500 words. **Pays 0.03-0.5¢/word.** Pays expenses of writers on assignment.

PHOTOS State availability. Captions, identification of subjects, model releases required. Reviews GIF/JPEG files (300 dpi or higher at 4x6). Negotiates payment individually. Credit line given. Buys all rights.

COLUMNS Profiles (celebrities, national leaders, entertainers, corporate leaders, etc., who golf); Travel (destination/golf course reviews); Golf Fashion (jewelry, clothing, accessories). **Buys 3 mss/year.** Query. **Pays 10-50¢/word.**

FILLERS Needs anecdotes, facts, gags, newsbreaks, short humor. **Buys 3 mss/year. mss/year.** Length: 20-125 words. **Pays 10-50¢/word.**

TIPS "Emphasize golf and African American appeal."

💲💲 THE GOLFER

59 E. 72nd St., New York NY 10021. (212)867-7070. **Website:** www.thegolferinc.com. **40% freelance written.** Bimonthly magazine covering golf. A sophisticated tone for a lifestyle-oriented magazine. "The Golfer Inc. is an international luxury brand, a new media company that is a driving force in the game. Its website is the source for those who want the best the game has to offer—the classic courses, great destinations, finest accoutrements, most intriguing personalities, and latest trends on and off the course.The magazine has distinguished itself as the highest quality, most innovative in its field. It is written for the top of the market—those who live a lifestyle shaped by their passion for the game. With its stunning photography, elegant design and evocative writing, *The Golfer* speaks to its affluent readers with a sense of style and sophistication—it is a world-class publication with an international flair, celebrating the lifestyle of the game." Estab. 1994. Circ. 253,000. Byline given. Pays on publication. Offers negotiable kill fee. Publishes ms an average of 2 months after acceptance. Editorial lead time 2 months. Submit seasonal material 4 months in advance. Accepts queries by mail. Accepts simultaneous submissions. Sample copy free.

NONFICTION Needs book excerpts, essays, general interest, historical, how-to, humor, inspirational, interview, new product, opinion, personal experience, photo feature, technical, travel. Send complete ms. Length: 300-2,000 words. **Pays $150-600.** Pays expenses of writers on assignment.

PHOTOS Send photos. Reviews any size digital files. Buys one-time rights.

💲💲💲 GOLFING MAGAZINE

Golfer Magazine, Inc., 449 Silas Deane Hwy., Suite 3E, Wethersfield CT 06109. (860)563-1633. **E-mail:** editor@golfingmagazine.net. **Website:** www.golfingmagazineonline.com. **Contact:** John Torsiello, editor. **30% freelance written.** Bimonthly magazine covering golf, including travel, products, player profiles, and company profiles. Estab. 1999. Circ. 175,000. Byline given. Pays on publication. Offers negotiable kill fee. Editorial lead time 2 months. Submit seasonal material 2 months in advance. Accepts queries by mail, e-mail. Accepts simultaneous submissions. Sample copy free.

NONFICTION Needs book excerpts, new product, photo feature, travel. **Buys 4-5 mss/year.** Query. Length: 700-2,500 words. **Pays $250-1,000 for assigned articles. Pays $100-500 for unsolicited articles.** Pays expenses of writers on assignment.

PHOTOS State availability. Captions required. Reviews GIF/JPEG files. Negotiates payment and rights individually.

FILLERS Needs facts, gags. **Buys 2-3 mss/year. Payment individually determined.**

💲💲💲 GOLF TIPS

Madavor Media, 25 Braintree Hill Office Park, Suite 404, Braintree MA 02184. (617)706-9110. **Fax:** (617)536-0102. **E-mail:** editors@golftipsmag.com; vwilliams@madavor.com. **Website:** www.golftipsmag.com. **Contact:** Vic Williams, editor. **95% freelance written.** Magazine published 9 times/year covering golf instruction and equipment. "We provide mostly concise, very clear golf instruction pieces for the serious golfer." Estab. 1986. Circ. 300,000. Byline given. Pays on publication. Offers 33% kill fee. Publishes ms an average of 2 months after acceptance. Editorial lead time 3 months. Submit seasonal material 4 months in advance. Accepts queries by e-mail. Accepts simultaneous submissions. Responds in 1 month to queries. Sample copy free. Guidelines on website.

NONFICTION Needs book excerpts, how-to, interview, new product, photo feature, technical. "Generally, golf essays rarely make it." **Buys 125 mss/year.**

Query. Length: 250-2,000 words. **Pays $300-1,000 for assigned articles. Pays $300-800 for unsolicited articles.** Pays expenses of writers on assignment.

PHOTOS State availability. Captions, identification of subjects required. Reviews 2¼×2¼, 4×5, or 35mm transparencies. Negotiates payment individually. Buys all rights.

COLUMNS Stroke Saver (very clear, concise instruction), 350 words; Lesson Library (book excerpts—usually in a series), 1,000 words; Travel Tips (formatted golf travel), 2,500 words. **Buys 40 mss/year.** Query. **Pays $300-850.**

TIPS "Contact a respected PGA professional and find out if they're interested in being published. A good writer can turn an interview into a decent instruction piece."

❸❸❸ MINNESOTA GOLFER

Minnesota Golf Association, 6550 York Ave. S., Suite 211, Edina MN 55435. (952)927-4643. **Fax:** (952)927-9642. **E-mail:** wp@mngolf.org; editor@mngolf.org; info@mngolf.org. **Website:** www.www.mngolf.org/magazine. **Contact:** W.P. Ryan, editor. **75% freelance written.** Bimonthly magazine covering golf in Minnesota; the official publication of the Minnesota Golf Association. Estab. 1975. Circ. 66,000. Byline given. Pays on acceptance or publication. No kill fee. Editorial lead time 3 months. Accepts queries by mail, e-mail, fax.

NONFICTION Needs historical, interview, new product. Query with published clips. Length: 400-2,000 words. **Pays $50-750.** Pays expenses of writers on assignment.

PHOTOS State availability. Captions, identification of subjects required. Reviews contact sheets, transparencies, digital images. Negotiates payment individually. Image rights by assignment.

COLUMNS Punch shots (golf news and notes); Q School (news and information targeted to beginners, junior golfers and women); Great Drives (featuring noteworthy golf holes in Minnesota); Instruction.

❸❸ TEXAS GOLFER MAGAZINE

Texas Golder Media, 15721 Park Row, Suite 100, Houston TX 77084. (888)863-9899. **E-mail:** zane@texasgolfermagazine.com. **Website:** www.texasgolfermagazine.com. **Contact:** Zane Russell, CEO/publisher. **10% freelance written.** Bi-monthly magazine covering golf in Texas. Estab. 1984. Circ. 50,000. By-

line given. Pays 10 days after publication. No kill fee. Publishes ms an average of 2 months after acceptance. Editorial lead time 2 months. Submit seasonal material 3 months in advance. Accepts simultaneous submissions. Responds in 2 weeks to queries; 1 month to mss. Sample copy free. Prefers direct phone discussion for writer's guidelines.

NONFICTION Needs book excerpts, humor, personal experience, all golf-related. Travel pieces accepted about golf outside of Texas. **Buys 20 mss/year.** Query. **Pays 25-40¢/word.** Pays expenses of writers on assignment.

PHOTOS State availability. Captions, identification of subjects required. Reviews contact sheets, prints. No additional payment for photos accepted with ms, but pays $125 for cover photo. Buys one time rights.

TIPS "Most of our purchases are in the how-to area, so writers must know golf quite well and play the game."

❸❸ VIRGINIA GOLFER

Touchpoint Publishing, Inc., Virginia Golfer, 2400 Dovercourt Dr., Midlothian VA 23113. (804)378-2300, ext. 12. **Fax:** (804)378-2369. **Website:** www.vsga.org. **Contact:** Chris Lang, editor. **65% freelance written.** Bimonthly magazine covering golf in Virginia, the official publication of the Virginia State Golf Association. Estab. 1983. Circ. 45,000. Byline given. Pays on publication. No kill fee. Editorial lead time 6 months. Submit seasonal material 3 months in advance. Accepts queries by mail, e-mail. Accepts simultaneous submissions. Sample copy and writer's guidelines free.

NONFICTION Needs book excerpts, essays, historical, how-to, humor, inspirational, interview, personal experience, photo feature, technical, where to play, golf business. **Buys 30-40 mss/year.** Send complete ms. Length: 500-2,500 words. **Pays $50-200.** Pays expenses of writers on assignment.

PHOTOS State availability. Captions, identification of subjects required. Reviews contact sheets. Negotiates payment individually. Rights purchased varies.

COLUMNS Chip ins & Three Putts (news notes), Rules Corner (golf rules explanations and discussion), Your Game, Golf Travel (where to play), Great Holes, Q&A, Golf Business (what's happening?), Fashion. Query.

GUNS

⊗⊗ GUN DIGEST THE MAGAZINE

F+W, a Content and eCommerce Company, 5225 Joerns Dr., Stevens Point WI 54481. (715)445-2214. **Fax:** (715)445-2164. **E-mail:** gundigestonline@fwmedia. com. **Website:** www.gundigest.com. **90% freelance written.** Bimonthly magazine covering firearms. "*Gun Digest the Magazine* covers all aspects of the firearms community, from collectible guns to tactical gear to reloading and accessories. We also publish gun reviews and tests of new and collectible firearms and news features about firearms legislation. We are 100% pro-gun, fully support the NRA, and make no bones about our support of Constitutional freedoms." Byline given. Pays on publication. Publishes ms 2 months after acceptance. Editorial lead time 3 months. Accepts queries by e-mail. Accepts simultaneous submissions. Responds in 3 weeks to queries; in 1 month to mss. Free sample copy. Guidelines available via e-mail.

NONFICTION Needs historical, how-to, interview, new product, nostalgic, profile, technical. Special issues: All submissions must focus on firearms, accessories, or the firearms industry and legislation. Stories that include hunting reference must have as their focus the firearms or ammunition used. The hunting should be secondary. *Gun Digest* also publishes an annual gear guide. "We do not publish 'Me and Joe' hunting stories." **Buys 50-75 mss/year.** Query. Length: 500-3,500 words. **Pays $175-500 for assigned and for unsolicited articles. Does not pay in contributor copies.** Pays expenses of writers on assignment.

PHOTOS Send photos with submission. Requires captions, identification of subjects. Reviews GIF/JPEG files (and TIF files); 300 dpi submitted on a CD (size). Offers no additional payment for photos accepted with ms. Buys all rights.

TIPS "Be an expert in your field. Submit clear copy using the AP stylebook as your guide."

⊗⊗ MUZZLE BLASTS

P.O. Box 67, Friendship IN 47021. (812)667-5131. **Fax:** (812)667-5136. **E-mail:** llarkin@nmlra.org. **Website:** www.nmlra.org. **Contact:** Lee A. Larkin, editor. **65% freelance written.** Monthly magazine. "Articles must relate to muzzleloading or the muzzleloading era of American history." Estab. 1939. Circ. 17,500. Byline given. Pays on publication. Offers $50 kill fee. Publishes ms an average of 6 months after acceptance. Editorial lead time 4 months. Submit seasonal material 6 months in advance. Accepts queries by mail, e-mail. Responds in 1 month to mss. Sample copy and writer's guidelines free.

NONFICTION Needs general interest, historical, how-to, humor, interview, new product, personal experience, photo feature, technical, travel. No subjects that do not pertain to muzzleloading. **Buys 80 mss/year.** Query. Length: 2,000-2,500 words. **Pays $150 minimum for assigned articles. Pays $50 minimum for unsolicited articles.**

PHOTOS Send photos. Captions, model releases required. Reviews prints and digital images. Negotiates payment individually. Buys one-time rights.

COLUMNS **Buys 96 mss/year.** Query. **Pays $50-200.**

FICTION Must pertain to muzzleloading. Needs adventure, historical, humorous. **Buys 6 mss/year.** Query. Length: 2,500 words. **Pays $50-300.**

FILLERS Needs facts. **Pays $50.**

⊗⊗ SHOTGUN SPORTS MAGAZINE

P.O. Box 6810, Auburn CA 95604. (530)889-2220. **Fax:** (530)889-9106. **E-mail:** shotgun@shotgunsportsmagazine.com. **Website:** www.shotgunsportsmagazine.com. **Contact:** Johnny Cantu, editor-in-chief. **50% freelance written. Welcomes new writers.** Monthly magazine covering all the shotgun sports and shotgun hunting—sporting clays, trap, skeet, hunting, gunsmithing, shotshell patterning, shotsell reloading, mental training for the shotgun sports, shotgun tests, anything shotgun. Pays on publication. No kill fee. Publishes ms an average of 1-6 months after acceptance. Accepts simultaneous submissions. Responds within 3 weeks. Sample copy and writer's guidelines available on the website. Subscription: $32.95 (U.S.); $49.95 (Canada); $79.95 (foreign).

NONFICTION Currently needs anything with a "shotgun" subject. Think pieces, roundups, historical, interviews, etc. No articles promoting a specific club or sponsored hunting trip, etc. Submit complete ms with photos by mail with SASE. Can submit by e-mail. Length: 1,500-3,000 words. **Pays $50-150.** Pays expenses of writers on assignment.

TIPS "Do not fax manuscript. Send good photos. Take a fresh approach. Create a professional yet friendly article. Send diagrams, maps, and photos of unique details, if needed. For interviews, more interested in 'words of wisdom' than a list of accomplishments. Reloading articles must include source information and backup data. Check your facts and data! If you can't think of a fresh approach, don't bother. If it's not about shotguns or shotgunners, don't send it. Never say, 'You don't need to check my data; I never make mistakes.'"

HIKING & BACKPACKING

💲💲💲💲 BACKPACKER MAGAZINE

Cruz Bay Publishing, Inc., Active Interest Media Co., 5720 Flatiron Pkwy., Boulder CO 80301. **E-mail:** dlewon@backpacker.com; mhorjus@aimmedia.com; caseylyons@aimmedia.com; mleister@aimmedia.com. **Website:** www.backpacker.com. **Contact:** Dennis Lewon, editor-in-chief; Casey Lyons, deputy editor; Maren Horjus, destinations editor; Adam Roy, senior digital editor; Eli Bernstein, associate gear editor; Corey Buhay, assistant skills editor; Mike Leister, art director; Giovanni C. Leone, assistant art director; Louisa Albanese, photo assistant; Genny Fullerton, photography director. **50% freelance written.** Magazine published 9 times/year covering wilderness travel for backpackers. "*Backpacker* is the source for backpacking gear reviews, outdoor skills information and advice, and destinations for backpacking, camping, and hiking." E-mail the appropriate editor when querying; list can be found on website. Estab. 1973. Circ. 340,000. Byline given. Pays on acceptance. Offers 25% kill fee. Editorial lead time 6 months. Accepts queries by e-mail. Accepts simultaneous submissions. Responds in 2-4 weeks to queries. Guidelines online.

NONFICTION Needs essays, general interest, how-to, inspirational, interview, new product, opinion, personal experience, reviews, technical, "Features usually fall into a distinct category: destinations, personality, skills, or gear. Gear features are generally staff written. In order to make the grade, a potential feature needs an unusual hook, a compelling story, a passionate sense of place, or unique individuals finding unique ways to improve or enjoy the wilderness." Special issues: See website for upcoming issue themes. "Journal-style articles are generally unacceptable." Query with published clips before sending complete ms. Length: 1,500-5,000 words. **Pays 10¢-$1/word.** Pays expenses of writers on assignment.

PHOTOS Contact: Genny Fullerton, photo director: gfullerton@backpacker.com. Buys 80 photos from freelancers/issue; 720 photos/year. Needs transparen-

cies or hi-res digital of people backpacking, camping, landscapes/scenics. Reviews photos with or without a ms. Model/property release required (if necessary). Accepts images in digital format. Send via ZIP; e-mail as JPEG files at 72 dpi for review (300 dpi needed to print). State availability. Payment varies. Buys one-time rights.

COLUMNS Life List (personal essay telling a story about a premier wilderness destination or experience), 300-400 words; Done in a Day (a hike that can be finished in a day), 500 words; Weekend (a trip of 1-2 nights, 6-10 miles/day, within striking distance of a major city, and seasonally appropriate for the month in which they run); Skills (the advice source for all essential hiking and adventure skills, with information targeted to help both beginners and experts); Gear (short reviews of gear that has been field-tested; unlike other departments, Gear is done by assignment only). **Buys 50-75 mss/year.** Query with published clips. **Pays 10¢-$1/word.**

HOCKEY

💲💲 MINNESOTA HOCKEY JOURNAL

Touchpoint Sports, 505 N. Hwy 169, Ste. 465, Minneapolis MN 55441. (763)595-0808. **Fax:** (763)595-0016. **E-mail:** contactus@minnesotahockeyjournal.com. **E-mail:** aaron@touchpointmedia.com. **Website:** www.minnesotahockeyjournal.com. **Contact:** Aaron Paitich, editor. **50% freelance written.** Journal published 4 times/year covering Minnesota hockey. Estab. 2000. Circ. 40,000. Byline given. Pays on publication. No kill fee. Editorial lead time 6 months. Submit seasonal material 4 months in advance. Accepts simultaneous submissions. Sample copy and writer's guidelines free.

NONFICTION Needs essays, general interest, historical, how-to, humor, inspirational, interview, new product, opinion, personal experience, photo feature. **Buys 3-5 mss/year.** Query. Length: 500-1,500 words. **Pays $100-300.** Pays expenses of writers on assignment.

PHOTOS State availability. Captions, identification of subjects required. Reviews contact sheets. Negotiates payment individually. Rights purchased vary.

💲💲💲 USA HOCKEY MAGAZINE

Touchpoint Sports, 1775 Bob Johnson Dr., Colorado Springs CO 80906. (719)576-8724. **Fax:** (763)538-

1160. **E-mail:** usah@usahockey.org. **Website:** www. usahockeymagazine.com. **Contact:** Harry Thompson, editor-in-chief. **60% freelance written.** Magazine published 10 times/year covering amateur hockey in the U.S. The world's largest hockey magazine, *USA Hockey Magazine* is the official magazine of USA Hockey, Inc., the national governing body of hockey. Estab. 1980. Circ. 444,000. Byline given. Pays on acceptance or publication. No kill fee. Editorial lead time 6 months. Submit seasonal material 4 months in advance. Accepts simultaneous submissions. Sample copy and writer's guidelines free.

NONFICTION Needs essays, general interest, historical, how-to, humor, inspirational, interview, new product, opinion, personal experience, photo feature, hockey camps, pro hockey, juniors, college, NCAA hockey championships, Olympics, youth, etc. **Buys 20-30 mss/year.** Query. Length: 500-5,000 words. **Pays $50-750.** Pays expenses of writers on assignment.

PHOTOS State availability. Captions, identification of subjects required. Reviews contact sheets. Negotiates payment individually. Rights purchased varies.

COLUMNS Short Cuts (news and notes); Coaches' Corner (teaching tips); USA Hockey; Inline Notebook (news and notes). **Pays $150-250.**

FICTION Needs adventure, humorous, slice-of-life vignettes. **Buys 10-20 mss/year. Pays $150-1,000.**

FILLERS Needs anecdotes, facts, gags, newsbreaks, short humor. **Buys 20-30 mss/year.** Length: 10-100 words. **Pays $25-250.**

TIPS "Writers must have a general knowledge and enthusiasm for hockey, including ice, inline, street, and other. The primary audience is youth players in the U.S."

HORSE RACING

AMERICAN TURF MONTHLY

747 Middle Neck Rd., Great Neck NY 11024. (516)773-4075. **Fax:** (516)773-2944. **E-mail:** jcorbett@americanturf.com; editor@americanturf.com. **Website:** www.americanturf.com. **Contact:** Joe Girardi, editor. **90% freelance written.** Monthly magazine squarely focused on Thoroughbred racing, handicapping and wagering. *ATM* is a magazine for horseplayers, not owners, breeders, or 12-year-old girls enthralled with ponies. Estab. 1946. Circ. 30,000. Byline given. Pays on publication. No kill fee. Publishes ms an average

of 4 months after acceptance. Editorial lead time 2 months. Submit seasonal material 2 months in advance. Accepts queries by mail, e-mail. Accepts simultaneous submissions. Responds in 1 month to queries. Sample copy and writer's guidelines free.

NONFICTION No historical essays, bilious 'guest editorials,' saccharine poetry, fiction. Special issues: Triple Crown/Kentucky Derby (May); Saratoga/Del Mar (August); Breeder's Cup (November). **Buys Length: 800-2,000 words. Pays $75-300 for assigned articles. Pays $100-500 for unsolicited articles. mss/year.** Query. Length: 800-2,000 words. **Pays $75-300 for assigned articles. Pays $100-500 for unsolicited articles.** Pays expenses of writers on assignment. No.

PHOTOS Send photos. Identification of subjects required. Reviews 3 x 5 transparencies, prints, 300 dpi TIFF images on CD. Offers $25 for b&w or color interior; $150 min. for color cover. Pays on publication. Credit line given. Buys one-time rights.

FILLERS newsbreaks, short humor Needs newsbreaks, short humor. **Buys 5 mss/year.** Length: 400 words. **Pays $25.**

TIPS "Like horses and horse racing."

💲💲 HOOF BEATS

U.S. Trotting Association, 6130 S. Sunbury Rd., Westerville OH 43081-9309. **E-mail:** hoofbeats@ustrotting.com. **Website:** www.hoofbeatsmagazine.com. **Contact:** T.J. Burkett. **60% freelance written.** Monthly magazine covering harness racing and standardbred horses. "Articles and photos must relate to harness racing or Standardbreds. We do not accept any topics that do not touch on these subjects." Estab. 1933. Circ. 7,000. Byline given. Pays on publication. Offers 25% kill fee. Publishes ms an average of 2-4 months after acceptance. Editorial lead time 6 months. Submit seasonal material 6 months in advance. Accepts queries by mail, e-mail, fax. Accepts simultaneous submissions. Responds in 2 weeks to queries; 1 month to mss. Sample copy online. Guidelines free.

NONFICTION Needs general interest, how-to, interview, personal experience, photo feature, technical. "We do not want any fiction or poetry." **Buys 48-72 mss/year.** Query. Length: 750-2,000 words. **Pays $100-500.** Pays expenses of writers on assignment.

PHOTOS State availability. Identification of subjects required. Reviews contact sheets. We offer $25-100 per photo. Buys one-time rights.

COLUMNS Equine Clinic (Standardbreds who overcame major health issues), 900-1,200 words; Profiles (short profiles on people or horses in harness racing), 600-1,000 words; Industry Trends (issues impacting Standardbreds & harness racing), 1,000-2,000 words. **Buys 60 mss/year mss/year.** Query for column submissions. **Pays $100-500.**

TIPS "We welcome new writers who know about harness racing or are willing to learn about it. Make sure to read *Hoof Beats* before querying to see our slant & style. We look for informative/promotional stories on harness racing—not exposés on the sport."

HUNTING & FISHING

💲💲 AMERICAN ANGLER

Morris Communications Company, LLC, 735 Broad St., Augusta GA 30904. (706)828-3971. **E-mail:** editor@americanangler.com. **Website:** www.americanangler.com. **Contact:** Ben Romans, editor; Wayne Knight, art director. **95% freelance written.** Bimonthly magazine covering fly fishing. "*American Angler* is devoted exclusively to fly fishing. We focus mainly on coldwater fly fishing for trout, steelhead, and salmon, but we also run articles about warmwater and saltwater fly fishing. Our mission is to supply our readers with well-written, accurate articles on every aspect of the sport—angling techniques and methods, reading water, finding fish, selecting flies, tying flies, fish behavior, places to fish, casting, managing line, rigging, tackle, accessories, entomology, history, and any other relevant topics. Each submission should present specific, useful information that will increase our readers' enjoyment of the sport and help them catch more fish." Estab. 1976. Circ. 32,000. Byline given. Pays on publication. No kill fee. Publishes ms an average of 6 months after acceptance. Editorial lead time 3 months. Submit seasonal material 5 months in advance. Accepts queries by e-mail. Accepts simultaneous submissions. Responds in 6 weeks to queries; in 2 months to mss.

NONFICTION Needs general interest, historical, how-to, interview, personal experience, photo feature, profile, technical, travel. "No superficial, broad-brush coverage of subjects. We're interested in queries created with the magazine in mind; not shotgunned ideas. The more specific and unique, the better. Not interested in concepts that don't have a solid structure or

are one-sided opinions. The more journalistic the approach (the inclusion of interviews, data, or other supporting evidence and information), the better. We're interested in someone who's willing to chase a story angle, beat the pavement, and put together a strong package more than we're interested in how well you can write a sentence." **Buys 45-60 mss/year.** Query with published clips. Length: 800-2,200 words. **Pays $200-600.** Pays expenses of writers on assignment.

REPRINTS Send information about when and where the material previously appeared. Pay negotiable.

PHOTOS "How-to pieces—those that deal with tactics, rigging, fly tying, and the like—must be accompanied by appropriate photography or rough sketches for our illustrator. Naturally, where-to stories must be illustrated with shots of scenery, people fishing, anglers holding fish, and other pictures that help flesh out the story and paint the local color. Do not bother sending subpar photographs. We only accept photos that are well lit, tack sharp, and correctly framed. A fly-tying submission should always include samples of flies to send to our staff photographer, even if photos of the flies are included. Send photos. Captions, identification of subjects required. Digital photos only. Offers no additional payment for photos accepted with ms. Pays $600-700 for color cover; $30-350 for color inside. Pays on publication. Credit line given. Buys one-time rights, first rights for covers. "Payment is made just prior to publication. "We don't pay by the word, and length is only one of the variables considered. The quality and completeness of a submission may be more important than its length in determining rates, and articles that include good photography are usually worth more. As a guideline, the following rates generally apply: Feature articles pay $450 (and perhaps a bit more if we're impressed), while short features pay $200-400. Generally, these rates assume that useful photos, drawings, or sketches accompany the words. Buys first rights along with nonexclusive perpetual rights, shared with the author after publication. "Tell us in your query or when you submit your ms that you have no good photo support; if the story is good enough, we'll find photos elsewhere. We buy first North American serial print, electronic, and in-house marketing rights to articles and photos."

COLUMNS One-page shorts (problem solvers), 350-750 words. Query with published clips. **Pays $100-300.**

TIPS "If you are submitting for the first time, please submit complete queries."

$$$$ AMERICAN HUNTER

11250 Waples Mill Rd., Fairfax VA 22030-9400. (800)672-3888. **E-mail:** Publications@nrahq.org; americanhunter@nrahq.org; EmediaHunter@nrahq.org. **Website:** www.americanhunter.org. **Contact:** editor-in-chief. Monthly magazine for hunters who are members of the National Rifle Association (NRA). *American Hunter*, the official journal of the National Rifle Association, contains articles dealing with various sport hunting and related activities both at home and abroad. With the encouragement of the sport as a prime game management tool, emphasis is on technique, sportsmanship, and safety. In each issue, hunting equipment and firearms are evaluated, legislative happenings affecting the sport are reported, lore and legend are retold, and the business of the Association is recorded in the Official Journal section. Circ. 1,000,000. Byline given. Pays on publication. No kill fee. Accepts queries by mail, e-mail. Accepts simultaneous submissions. Responds in 6 months to queries. Guidelines online.

NONFICTION Special issues: Special issues: pheasants, whitetail tactics, black bear feed areas, mule deer, duck hunters' transport by land and sea, tech topics to be decided, rut strategies, muzzleloader moose and elk, fall turkeys, staying warm, goose talk, long-range muzzleloading. Not interested in material on fishing, camping, or firearms knowledge. Query (preferred) or submit complete ms by mail or e-mail. Length: 2,000-3,000 words. **Pays up to $1,500 for full-length features with complete photo packages.** Pays expenses of writers on assignment.

REPRINTS Copies for author will be provided upon publication. No reprints possible.

PHOTOS Captions preferred. Accepts images in digital format only, no slides. Model release required "for every recognizable human face in a photo." Pays $125-600/image; $1,000 for color cover; $400-1,400 for text/photo package. Pays on publication. Credit line given. No additional payment made for photos used with ms. Photos purchased with or without accompanying mss. Buys one-time rights.

COLUMNS Build Your Skills (technical how-to column on hunting-related procedure); Hardware (covers new firearms, ammunition, and optics used for hunting), 800-1,200 words. **Pays $500-1,000.**

TIPS "Although unsolicited mss are accepted, detailed query letters outlining the proposed topic and approach are appreciated and will save both writers and editors a considerable amount of time. If we like your story idea, you will be contacted by mail or phone and given direction on how we'd like the topic covered."

🍁$$$ THE ATLANTIC SALMON JOURNAL

The Atlantic Salmon Federation, P.O. Box 5200, St. Andrews New Brunswick E5B 3S8 Canada. (514)457-8737. **Fax:** (506)529-1070. **E-mail:** savesalmon@asf.ca; martinsilverstone@videotron.ca. **Website:** www.asf.ca. **Contact:** Martin Silverstone, editor. **50-68% freelance written.** Quarterly magazine covering conservation efforts for the Atlantic salmon, catering to the dedicated angler and conservationist. Circ. 11,000. Byline given. Pays on publication. No kill fee. Publishes ms an average of 6 months after acceptance. Submit seasonal material 3 months in advance. Accepts simultaneous submissions. Responds in 2 months to queries. Sample copy for 9x12 SAE with $1 (Canadian), or IRC. Guidelines free.

NONFICTION Needs historical, how-to, humor, interview, new product, opinion, personal experience, photo feature, technical. **Buys 15-20 mss/year.** Query with published clips. Length: 2,000 words. **Pays $400-800 for articles with photos.** Pays expenses of writers on assignment.

PHOTOS State availability. Captions, identification of subjects required. Pays $50 minimum; $350-500 for covers; $300 for 2-page spread; $175 for full page photo; $100 for 1/2-page photo.

COLUMNS Fit To Be Tied (conservation issues and salmon research; the design, construction, and success of specific flies); interesting characters in the sport and opinion pieces by knowledgeable writers, 900 words; Casting Around (short, informative, entertaining reports, book reviews, and quotes from the world of Atlantic salmon angling and conservation). Query. **Pays $50-300.**

TIPS "Articles must reflect informed and up-to-date knowledge of Atlantic salmon. Writers need not be authorities, but research must be impeccable. Clear, concise writing is essential, and submissions must be typed."

✪✪ BASSMASTER MAGAZINE

B.A.S.S. Publications, 1170 Celebration Blvd., Suite 200, Celebration FL 32830. (407)566-2277. **Fax:** (407)566-2072. **Website:** www.bassmaster.com. **80% freelance written.** Magazine published 11 times/year about largemouth, smallmouth, and spotted bass, offering how-to articles for dedicated beginning and advanced bass fishermen, including destinations and new product reviews. Estab. 1968. Circ. 600,000. Byline given. Pays on acceptance. No kill fee. Publishes ms an average of less than 1 year after acceptance. Editorial lead time 2 months. Submit seasonal material 6 months in advance. Accepts queries by mail, e-mail. Accepts simultaneous submissions. Responds in 2 months to queries. Sample copy upon request. Guidelines for #10 SASE.

NONFICTION Needs historical, how-to, interview, new product, travel, conservation related to bass fishing. No first-person, personal experience-type articles. **Buys 100 mss/year.** Query. Length: 500-1,500 words. **Pays $100-300.**

PHOTOS Send photos. Captions, model releases required. Reviews transparencies. Offers no additional payment for photos accepted with ms, but pays $800 for color cover transparencies. Buys all rights.

COLUMNS Short Cast/News/Views/Notes/Briefs (upfront regular feature covering news-related events such as new state bass records, unusual bass fishing happenings, conservation, new products, and editorial viewpoints). Length: 250-400 words. **Pays $100-300.**

TIPS "Editorial direction continues in the short, more direct how-to article. Compact, easy-to-read information is our objective. Shorter articles with good graphics, such as how-to diagrams, step-by-step instruction, etc., will enhance a writer's articles submitted to *Bassmaster Magazine*. The most frequent mistakes made by writers in completing an article for us are poor grammar, poor writing, poor organization, and superficial research. Send in detailed queries outlining specific objectives of article, obtain writer's guidelines. Be as concise as possible."

✪✪✪ BC OUTDOORS HUNTING AND SHOOTING

Outdoor Group Media, 7261 River Place, 201a, Mission BC V4S 0A2 Canada. (604)820-3400; (800)898-8811. **Fax:** (604)820-3477. **E-mail:** mmitchell@outdoorgroupmedia.com. **Website:** www.bcoutdoors-magazine.com. **Contact:** Mike Mitchell, editor. **80% freelance written.** Biannual magazine covering hunting, shooting, camping, and backroads in British Columbia, Canada. *BC Outdoors Magazine* publishes 7 sport fishing issues a year with 2 hunting and shooting supplement issues each summer and fall. "Our magazine is about the best outdoor experiences in BC. Whether you're camping on an ocean shore, hiking into your favorite lake, or learning how to fly-fish on your favourite river, we want to showcase what our province has to offer to sport fishing and outdoor enthusiasts. *BC Outdoors Hunting and Shooting* provides trusted editorial for trapping, deer hunting, big buck, bowhunting, bag limits, baitling, decoys, calling, camouflage, tracking, trophy hunting, pheasant hunting, goose hunting, hunting regulations, duck hunting, whitetail hunting, hunting regulations, hunting trips, and mule deer hunting." Estab. 1945. Circ. 30,000. Byline given. Pays on publication. Offers kill fee. Publishes ms an average of 3 months after acceptance. Accepts queries by e-mail. Accepts simultaneous submissions. Guidelines for 8x10 SASE with 7 Canadian first-class stamps.

NONFICTION Needs how-to, personal experience. **Buys 50 mss/year.** Query the publication before submitting. Do not send unsolicited mss or photos. Submit no more than 100-words outlining exactly what your story will be. "You should be able to encapsulate the essence of your story and show us why our readers would be interested in reading or knowing what you are writing about. Queries need to be clear, succinct and straight to the point. Show us why we should publish your article in 150 words or less." Length: 1,700-2,000 words. **Pays $300-500.** Pays expenses of writers on assignment.

PHOTOS Biannual magazine emphasizing hunting, RV camping, canoeing, wildlife and management issues in British Columbia only. Sample copy available for $4.95 Canadian. Family oriented. "By far, most photos accompany manuscripts. We are always on the lookout for good covers—wildlife, recreational activities, people in the outdoors—of British Columbia, vertical and square format. Photos with manuscripts must, of course, illustrate the story. There should, as far as possible, be something happening. Photos generally dominate lead spread of each story. They are used in everything from double-page bleeds to thumbnails." State availability. Model/property release preferred. Photo captions or at least full identification required. Buys one-time rights.

COLUMNS Column needs basically supplied in-house.

TIPS "Send us material on fishing and hunting. We generally just send back nonrelated work. We want in-depth information and professional writing only. Emphasis on environmental issues. Those pieces with a conservation component have a better chance of being published. Subject must be specific to British Columbia. We receive many mss written by people who obviously do not know the magazine or market. The writer has a better chance of breaking in with short, lesser-paying articles and fillers, because we have a stable of regular writers who produce most main features."

💲 💲 BOWHUNTER

InterMedia Outdoors, 6385 Flank Dr., Suite 800, Harrisburg PA 17112. (717)695-8085. **Fax:** (717)545-2527. **Website:** www.bowhunter.com. **50% freelance written.** Bimonthly magazine covering hunting big and small game with bow and arrow. "We are a special-interest publication, produced by bowhunters for bowhunters, covering all aspects of the sport. Material included in each issue is designed to entertain and inform readers, making them better bowhunters." Estab. 1971. Circ. 126,480. Byline given. Pays on acceptance. No kill fee. Submit seasonal material 8 months in advance. Accepts queries by mail. Accepts simultaneous submissions. Responds in 1 month to queries. Responds in 2 months to mss.

NONFICTION Needs general interest, how-to, interview, opinion, personal experience, photo feature. **Buys 60-plus mss/year.** Query. Length: 250-2,000 words. **Pays $500 maximum for assigned articles; $100-400 for unsolicited articles.** Pays expenses of writers on assignment.

PHOTOS Send photos. Captions required. Reviews high-res digital images. Reviews photos with or without a manuscript. Offers $50-300/photo. Pays $50-125 for b&w inside; $75-300 for color inside; $600 for cover, "occasionally more if photo warrants it." **Pays on acceptance.** Credit line given. Buys one-time publication rights. Buys one-time rights.

TIPS "A writer must know bowhunting and be willing to share that knowledge. Writers should anticipate *all* questions a reader might ask, then answer them in the article itself or in an appropriate sidebar. Articles should be written with the reader foremost in mind;

we won't be impressed by writers seeking to prove how good they are—either as writers or bowhunters. We care about the reader and don't need writers with 'I' trouble. Features are a good bet because most of our material comes from freelancers. The best advice is: Be yourself. Tell your story the same as if sharing the experience around a campfire. Don't try to write like you think a writer writes."

💲 💲 BOWHUNTING WORLD

Grand View Media Group, 200 Croft St., Suite 1, Birmingham AL 35242. (888)431-2877. **E-mail:** bowhunting@omedia.com. **Website:** www.bowhuntingworld.com. **50% freelance written.** Bimonthly magazine with 3 additional issues for bowhunting and archery enthusiasts who participate in the sport year-round. Estab. 1952. Circ. 95,000. Byline given. Pays on acceptance. No kill fee. Publishes ms an average of 5 months after acceptance. Accepts simultaneous submissions. Responds in 1 week to e-mail queries; 6 weeks to mss. Guidelines with #10 SASE.

NONFICTION **Buys 60 mss/year.** Send complete ms. Length: 1,500-2,500 words. **Pays $350-600.** Pays expenses of writers on assignment.

PHOTOS "We are seeking cover photos that depict specific behavioral traits of the more common big game animals (scraping whitetails, bugling elk, etc.) and well-equipped bowhunters in action. Must include return postage."

TIPS "Writers are strongly advised to adhere to guidelines and become familiar with our format, as our needs are very specific. Writers are urged to query by e-mail. We prefer detailed outlines of 6 or so article ideas/query. Assignments are made for the next 18 months."

💲 💲 DEER & DEER HUNTING

F+W, a Content + eCommerce Company, 5225 Joerns Dr., Stevens Point WI 54481. **Website:** www.deeranddeerhunting.com. **Contact:** Daniel E. Schmidt, editor. **95% freelance written.** Magazine published 10 times/year covering white-tailed deer. "Readers include a cross section of the deer hunting population—individuals who hunt with bow, gun, or camera. The editorial content of the magazine focuses on white-tailed deer biology and behavior, management principle and practices, habitat requirements, natural history of deer, hunting techniques, and hunting ethics. We also publish a wide range of how-to articles designed to help hunters locate and get close to deer at all times of the year. The majority of our readership consists of two-season hunters (bow & gun) and approximately one-third camera hunt." Estab. 1977. Circ. 200,000. Byline given. Pays on acceptance. No kill fee. Publishes ms an average of 18 months after acceptance. Editorial lead time 6 months. Submit seasonal material 12 months in advance. Accepts queries by mail, e-mail. Accepts simultaneous submissions. Responds in 1 month to queries; in 2 months to mss. Sample copy for 9x12 SASE. Guidelines available on website.

NONFICTION Needs general interest, historical, how-to, photo feature, technical. No "Joe and me" articles. **Buys 100 mss/year.** Send complete ms. Length: 1,000-2,000 words. **Pays $150-600 for assigned articles.** Pays expenses of writers on assignment.

PHOTOS Send photos. Captions required. Reviews transparencies. Offers $25-200/photo; $500 for cover photos. Buys one-time rights.

COLUMNS Browse (odd occurrences), 200-500 words. **Buys 10 mss/year.** Query. **Pays $25-250.**

TIPS "Feature articles dealing with deer biology or behavior should be documented by scientific research (the author's or that of others) as opposed to a limited number of personal observations."

😊😊 THE DRAKE MAGAZINE

P.O. Box 11546, Denver CO 80211. (720)638-3114. **E-mail:** info@drakemag.com. **Website:** www.drakemag. com. Dawn Wieber. **70% freelance written.** Quarterly magazine for people who love flyfishing. Estab. 1998. Byline given. Pays 1 month after publication. No kill fee. Publishes ms an average of 1 year after acceptance. Editorial lead time 1 year. Submit seasonal material 1 year in advance. Accepts queries by e-mail. Accepts simultaneous submissions. Responds in 6 months to mss. Guidelines available online.

NONFICTION Buys 20-30 mss/year. Query. Length: 650-2,000 words. **Pays 25¢/word, "depending on the amount of work we have to put into the piece."** Pays expenses of writers on assignment.

PHOTOS State availability. Offers $50-200/photo. Buys one-time rights.

😊😊 FLORIDA SPORTSMAN

Wickstrom Communications, Intermedia Outdoors, 2700 S. Kanner Hwy., Stuart FL 34994. (772)219-7400. **Fax:** (772)219-6900. **E-mail:** editor@florida-sportsman.com. **Website:** www.floridasportsman. com. **Contact:** Jeff Weakley, executive editor. **30%**

freelance written. Monthly magazine covering fishing, boating, hunting, and related sports—Florida and Caribbean only. Edited for the boat owner and offshore, coastal, and fresh water fisherman. It provides a how, when, and where approach in its articles, which also includes occasional camping, diving, and hunting stories—plus ecology (in-depth articles and editorials attempting to protect Florida's wilderness, wetlands, and natural beauty). Circ. 115,000. Byline given. Pays on acceptance. No kill fee. Publishes ms an average of 6 months after acceptance. Submit seasonal material 6 months in advance. Accepts queries by mail, e-mail. Accepts simultaneous submissions. Responds in 1 month to queries. Sample copy free. E-mail editor for submission guidelines.

NONFICTION Buys 20-40 mss/year. Query. Length: 1,500-2,500 words. **Pays $475.** Pays expenses of writers on assignment.

PHOTOS High-res digital images on CD preferred. Reviews 35mm transparencies, 4×5 and larger prints. Offers no additional payment for photos accepted with ms. Pays up to $750 for cover photos. Buys all rights.

TIPS "Feature articles are sometimes open to freelancers; however there is little chance of acceptance unless contributor is an accomplished and avid outdoorsman *and* a competent writer-photographer with considerable experience in Florida."

😊😊 FUR-FISH-GAME

2878 E. Main St., Columbus OH 43209-9947. **E-mail:** ffgcox@ameritech.net; subs@furfishgame.com. **Website:** www.furfishgame.com. **Contact:** Mitch Cox, editor. **65% freelance written.** Monthly magazine for outdoorsmen of all ages who are interested in hunting, fishing, trapping, dogs, camping, conservation, and related topics. Estab. 1900. Circ. 118,000. Byline given. Pays on acceptance. No kill fee. Publishes ms an average of 4 months after acceptance. Accepts simultaneous submissions. Responds in 2 months to queries. Sample copy for $1 and 9x12 SASE. Guidelines with #10 SASE.

NONFICTION Query. Length: 500-3,000 words. **Pays $50-250 or more for features depending upon quality, photo support, and importance to magazine.** Pays expenses of writers on assignment.

PHOTOS Send photos. Captions, True required. Reviews transparencies, color 5×7 or 8×10 prints, digital photos on CD only with thumbnail sheet of small images and a numbered caption sheet. Pays $35 for separate freelance photos.

TIPS "We are always looking for quality how-to articles about fish, game animals, or birds that are popular with everyday outdoorsmen but often overlooked in other publications, such as catfish, bluegill, crappie, squirrel, rabbit, crows, etc. We also use articles on standard seasonal subjects such as deer and pheasant, but like to see a fresh approach or new technique. Instructional trapping articles are useful all year. Articles on gun dogs, ginseng, and do-it-yourself projects are also popular with our readers. An assortment of photos and/or sketches greatly enhances any manuscript, and sidebars, where applicable, can also help. No phone queries, please."

$$ GAME & FISH

3330 Chastain Meadows Pkwy. NW, Suite 200, Kennesaw GA 30144. (770)953-9222. **Fax:** (678)279-7512. **E-mail:** ken.dunwoody@imoutdoors.com. **Website:** www.gameandfishmag.com. **Contact:** Ken Dunwoody, editorial director; Ron Sinfelt, photo editor; Allen Hansen, graphic artist. **90% freelance written.** Publishes 28 different monthly outdoor magazines, each covering the fishing and hunting opportunities in a particular state or region (see individual titles to contact editors). Estab. 1975. Circ. 570,000 for 28 state-specific magazines. Byline given. Pays 3 months prior to cover date of issue. Offers negotiable kill fee. Publishes ms an average of 7 months after acceptance. Submit seasonal material 8 months in advance. Accepts queries by mail, e-mail, fax. Accepts simultaneous submissions. Responds in 3 months to queries. Sample copy for $3.50 and 9x12 SASE. Guidelines for #10 SASE.

NONFICTION Length: 1,500-2,400 words. **Pays $150-300; additional payment made for electronic rights.** Pays expenses of writers on assignment.

PHOTOS Captions, identification of subjects required. Reviews transparencies, prints, digital images. Cover photos $250, inside color $75, and b&w $25. Buys one-time rights.

TIPS "Our readers are experienced anglers and hunters, and we try to provide them with useful, specific articles about where, when, and how to enjoy the best hunting and fishing in their state or region. We also cover topics concerning game and fish management. Most articles should be tightly focused and aimed at outdoorsmen in 1 particular state. After familiarizing themselves with our magazine(s), writers should query the appropriate state editor (see individual listings) or send to Ken Dunwoody."

$$$ GRAY'S SPORTING JOURNAL

735 Broad St., Augusta GA 30901. **E-mail:** russ.lumpkin@morris.com; wayne.knight@morris.com. **Website:** www.grayssportingjournal.com. **Contact:** Russ Lumpkin, editor-in-chief; Wayne Knight, art director. **75% freelance written.** "*Gray's Hunting Journal* is published 7 times/year. Because 90% of our readers are bird hunters, 85% are fly fishers, and 67% hunt big game, we're always looking for good upland-bird-hunting, fly-fishing, and big-game mss throughout the year, but don't confine yourself to these themes. Other subjects of interest include waterfowl, turkeys, small game, unusual quarry (feral hogs, etc.), sporting adventures in exciting locales (foreign and domestic) and yarns (tall tales or true)." Estab. 1975. Circ. 32,000. Byline given. Pays on publication. No kill fee. Publishes ms an average of 1 year after acceptance. Editorial lead time 14 months. Submit seasonal material 16 months in advance. Accepts queries by e-mail. Accepts simultaneous submissions. Responds in 3 months to mss. Guidelines online.

NONFICTION Needs essays, historical, humor, personal experience, photo feature, travel. Special issues: Publishes 4 themed issues: the Fly Fishing Edition (March/April), the Upland Bird Hunting Edition (August), the Big Game Edition (September/October), and the Expeditions and Guides Annual (December). Does not want how-to articles. **Buys 20-30 mss/year.** Send complete ms via e-mail with "Gray's Manuscript" in subject line. Length: 1,500-12,000 words. **Pays $600-1,250 (based on quality, not length).** Pays expenses of writers on assignment.

PHOTOS State availability. Reviews GIF/JPEG files. Pays $50-300.

FICTION Accepts quality fiction with some aspect of hunting or fishing at the core. Needs adventure, experimental, historical, humorous, slice-of-life vignettes. If some aspect of hunting or fishing isn't at the core of the story, it has zero chance of interesting *Gray's*. **Buys 20 mss/year.** Send complete ms. Length: 750-1,500 words. **Pays $600.**

POETRY Needs avant-garde, haiku, light verse, traditional. Buys 7 poems/year. Submit maximum 1 poems. Length: up to 1,000 words. **Pays $100.**

TIPS "Write something different, write something well—fiction or nonfiction—write something that goes to the heart of hunting or fishing more elegantly, more inspirationally, than the 1,500 or so other unsolicited mss we review each year."

💲💲 ⊙ THE MAINE SPORTSMAN

183 State St., Suite 101, Augusta ME 04330. (207)622-4242. **Fax:** (207)622-4255. **E-mail:** will.sportster@yahoo.com. **Website:** www.mainesportsman.com. **90% freelance written.** Monthly tabloid-size magazine covering Maine's outdoors, especially hunting, fishing, ATVs and snowmobiles. Willing to work with new/unpublished writers, but because we run over 30 regular columns, it's difficult to get into *The Maine Sportsman* as a beginner. Estab. 1972. Circ. 30,000. Byline given. Pays during month of publication. No kill fee. Publishes an average of 3 months after acceptance. Accepts queries by mail, e-mail. Responds in 2 weeks to queries.

NONFICTION Special issues: Biggest Bucks issue, ATVs, Snowmobiling, Spring trout fishing, moose season, whitetail season, blackpowder season. **Buys 25-40 mss/year.** Send complete ms via e-mail. Length: 200-1,200 words. **Pays $25-250.**

PHOTOS Send JPGs/TIFFs via e-mail. Pays $25-100.

TIPS "We publish numerous special sections each year and are eager to buy Maine-oriented articles on snowmobiling, ice fishing, boating, salt water and deer hunting. Send articles or queries."

💲💲 ⊙ MARLIN

460 N. Orlando Ave., Suite 200, Winter Park FL 32789. (407)628-4802. **Fax:** (407)628-7061. **E-mail:** editor@marlinmag.com. **Website:** www.marlinmag.com. **90% freelance written.** Magazine published 8 times/year covering the sport of big game fishing (billfish, tuna, dorado, and wahoo). "Our readers are sophisticated, affluent, and serious about their sport—they expect a high-class, well-written magazine that provides information and practical advice." Estab. 1982. Circ. 50,000. Byline given. Pays on acceptance. No kill fee. Publishes ms an average of 3 months after acceptance. Submit seasonal material 3 months in advance. Accepts simultaneous submissions. Sample copy free with SASE.

NONFICTION Needs general interest, how-to, new product, personal experience, photo feature, technical, travel. No freshwater fishing stories. No "Me & Joe went fishing'" stories. **Buys 30-50 mss/year.** Query with published clips. Length: 800-3,000 words. **Pays $250-500.** Pays expenses of writers on assignment.

REPRINTS Send photocopy and information about when and where the material previously appeared. Pays 50-75% of amount paid for original article.

PHOTOS State availability. Reviews original slides. Offers $50-300 for inside use, $1,000 for a cover. Buys one time rights.

COLUMNS Tournament Reports (reports on winners of major big game fishing tournaments), 200-400 words; Blue Water Currents (news features), 100-400 words. **Buys 25 mss/year.** Query. **Pays $75-250.**

TIPS "Tournament reports are a good way to break in to *Marlin*. Make them short but accurate, and provide photos of fishing action or winners' award shots (*not* dead fish hanging up at the docks). We always need how-tos and news items. Our destination pieces (travel stories) emphasize where and when to fish, but also include information on where to stay. For features: Crisp, high-action stories with emphasis on exotic nature, adventure, personality, etc.—nothing flowery or academic. Technical/how-to: concise and informational—specific details. News: Again, concise with good details—watch for legislation affecting big game fishing, outstanding catches, new clubs and organizations, new trends, and conservation issues."

💲 ⊙ MICHIGAN OUT-OF-DOORS

P.O. Box 30235, Lansing MI 48912. (517)371-1041. **Fax:** (517)371-1505. **E-mail:** thansen@mucc.org; magazine@mucc.org. **Website:** www.michiganoutofdoors.com. **Contact:** Tony Hansen, editor. **75% freelance written.** Monthly magazine emphasizing Michigan hunting and fishing with associated conservation issues. Estab. 1947. Circ. 40,000. Byline given. Pays on acceptance. No kill fee. Publishes ms an average of 6 months after acceptance. Submit seasonal material 6 months in advance. Accepts simultaneous submissions. Responds in 1 month to queries. Sample copy for $3.50. Guidelines for free.

NONFICTION Needs expose, historical, how-to, interview, opinion, personal experience. Special issues: Archery Deer and Small Game Hunting (October); Firearm Deer Hunting (November); Cross-country Skiing and Early-ice Lake Fishing (December or January); Camping/Hiking (May); Family Fishing (June). No humor or poetry. **Buys 96 mss/year.** Send complete ms. Length: 1,000-2,000 words. **Pays $150 mini-**

mum for feature stories. **Photos must be included with story.** Pays expenses of writers on assignment.

PHOTOS Captions required. Offers no additional payment for photos accepted with ms; others $20-175. Buys one-time rights.

TIPS "Top priority is placed on queries that offer new ideas on hard-core hunting and fishing topics. Submit seasonal material 6 months in advance. Wants to see new approaches to subject matter."

🆂 MIDWEST OUTDOORS

MidWest Outdoors, Ltd., 111 Shore Dr., Burr Ridge IL 60527. (630)887-7722. **Fax:** (630)887-1958. **Website:** www.midwestoutdoors.com. **100% freelance written.** Monthly tabloid emphasizing fishing, hunting, camping, and boating. Estab. 1967. Byline given. Pays on publication. No kill fee. Publishes ms an average of 3 months after acceptance. Submit seasonal material 2 months in advance. Accepts simultaneous submissions. Responds in 3 weeks to queries. Sample copy for $1 or online. Guidelines available online.

NONFICTION Needs how-to. "We do not want to see any articles on 'my first fishing, hunting, or camping experiences,' 'cleaning my tackle box,' 'tackle tune-up,' 'making fishing fun for kids,' or 'catch and release.'" **Buys 1,800 unsolicited mss/year.** Send complete ms. Submissions should be submitted via website's online form as a Microsoft Word doc. Length: 600-1,500 words. **Pays $15-30.**

PHOTOS Captions required. Reviews slides and b&w prints. Offers no additional payment for photos accompanying ms. Buys all rights.

COLUMNS Fishing; Hunting. Send complete ms. **Pays $30.**

TIPS "Break in with a great unknown fishing hole or new technique within 500 miles of Chicago. Where, how, when, and why. Know the type of publication you are sending material to."

🆂🆂 MUSKY HUNTER MAGAZINE

P.O. Box 340, 7978 Hwy. 70 E., St. Germain WI 54558. (715)477-2178. **Fax:** (715)477-8858. **E-mail:** editor@ muskyhunter.com. **Website:** www.muskyhunter.com. **Contact:** Jim Saric, editor. **90% freelance written.** Bimonthly magazine on musky fishing. Serves the vertical market of musky fishing enthusiasts. "We're interested in how-to, where-to articles." Estab. 1988. Circ. 37,000. Byline given. Pays on publication. No kill fee. Publishes ms an average of 4 months after ac-

ceptance. Submit seasonal material 4 months in advance. Accepts simultaneous submissions. Responds in 2 months to queries. Sample copy for 9x12 SASE and $2.79 postage. Guidelines for #10 SASE.

NONFICTION Needs historical, how-to, travel. **Buys 50 mss/year.** Send complete ms. Length: 1,000-2,500 words. **Pays $100-300 for assigned articles. Pays $50-300 for unsolicited articles.** Pays expenses of writers on assignment.

PHOTOS Send photos. Identification of subjects required. Reviews 35mm transparencies, 3x5 prints, high-res digital images preferred. Offers no additional payment for photos accepted with ms. Buys one-time rights.

🆂🆂 NORTH AMERICAN WHITETAIL

Game & Fish, 2250 Newmarket Pkwy., Suite 110, Marietta GA 30067. (770)953-9222. **Fax:** (678)279-7512. **E-mail:** ken.dunwoody@imoutdoors.com. **Website:** www.northamericanwhitetail.com. **Contact:** Ken Dunwoody, editorial director. **70% freelance written.** Magazine published 8 times/year about hunting trophy-class white-tailed deer in North America, primarily the U.S. "We provide the serious hunter with highly sophisticated information about trophy-class whitetails and how, when, and where to hunt them. We are not a general hunting magazine or a magazine for the very occasional deer hunter." Estab. 1982. Circ. 150,000. Byline given. Pays 65 days prior to cover date of issue. Offers negotiable kill fee. Publishes ms an average of 6 months after acceptance. Submit seasonal material 10 months in advance. Accepts queries by mail, e-mail, phone. Responds in 3 months to mss. Sample copy for $3.50 and 9x12 SAE with 7 first-class stamps. Guidelines for #10 SASE.

NONFICTION Needs how-to, interview. **Buys 50 mss/year.** Query. Length: 1,000-3,000 words. **Pays $150-400.**

PHOTOS Send photos. Captions, identification of subjects required. Reviews 35mm transparencies, color prints, high quality digital images. Offers no additional payment for photos accepted with ms. Buys one-time rights.

COLUMNS Trails and Tails (nostalgic, humorous, or other entertaining styles of deer-hunting material, fictional or nonfictional), 1,200 words. **Buys 8 mss/year. mss/year.** Send complete ms. **Pays $150.**

TIPS "Our articles are written by persons who are deer hunters first, writers second. Our hard-core hunting audience can see through material produced by nonhunters or those with only marginal deer-hunting expertise. We have a continual need for expert profiles/interviews. Study the magazine to see what type of hunting expert it takes to qualify for our use, and look at how those articles have been directed by the writers. Good photography of the interviewee and his hunting results must accompany such pieces."

✪❸❸ ONTARIO OUT OF DOORS

Ontario Federation of Anglers and Hunters, P.O. Box 8500, Peterborough ON K9J 0B4 Canada. (705)748-0076. **Fax:** (705)748-9577. **Website:** www.ontariooutofdoors.com. **Contact:** John Kerr, editor-in-chief. **80% freelance written.** Magazine published 10 times/year covering the outdoors (hunting, fishing). Estab. 1968. Circ. 93,865. Byline given. Pays on acceptance. Publishes ms an average of 6 months after acceptance. Editorial lead time 1 year. Submit seasonal material 2 months in advance. Accepts queries by mail, e-mail, fax. Responds in 3 months to queries. Writer's guidelines free.

NONFICTION Needs interview, opinion, technical, travel, wildlife management. No 'Me and Joe' features. **Buys 100 mss/year.** Length: 500-2,500 words. **Pays $950 maximum for assigned articles.**

FICTION Pays $500 maximum.

TIPS "It is suggested that writers query prior to submission."

✪❸❸ OUTDOOR CANADA MAGAZINE

130 Merton St., Suite 200, Toronto ON M4S 1A4 Canada. (416)599-2000. **E-mail:** editorial@outdoorcanada.ca. **Website:** www.outdoorcanada.ca. **60% freelance written. Works with a small number of new/unpublished writers each year.** Estab. 1972. Circ. 110,000. Byline given. Pays on publication. 50% Publishes ms an average of 3 months after acceptance. Submit seasonal ideas 1 year in advance. Accepts queries by mail, e-mail. Accepts simultaneous submissions. Responds in 1 month to queries. Guidelines online.

NONFICTION Needs how-to, fishing, hunting, conservation, outdoor issues, outdoor destinations in Canada. **Buys 35-40 mss/year.** Does not accept unsolicited mss. Length: 1,000-2,500 words **Pays flat rate of $400-600 for a feature.**

PHOTOS Emphasize people in the Canadian outdoors. Captions, model releases required. Fees negotiable.

FILLERS Buys 30-40 mss/year. Length: 100-500 words.

❸❸ RACK MAGAZINE

Buckmasters, Ltd., 10350 U.S. Hwy. 80 E., P.O. Box 244022, Montgomery AL 36117. (800) 240-3337. **Fax:** (334) 215-3535. **E-mail:** mikehandley@mac.com. **Website:** www.buckmasters.com. **Contact:** Mike Handley, editor. **75% freelance written.** Magazine published 10 times/year (February, April/May, June, July, August, September, October, November and Winter). "All features are either first- or third-person narratives detailing the successful hunts for world-class, big game animals—mostly white-tailed deer and other North American species." Ask for writer's guidelines. Estab. 1998. Circ. 75,000. Byline given. Pays on publication. No kill fee. Publishes ms an average of 9 months after acceptance. Editorial lead time 9-12 months. Submit seasonal material 9 months in advance. Accepts queries by mail, e-mail. Accepts simultaneous submissions. Responds in 1 month to queries and mss.

NONFICTION Needs personal experience. "We're interested only in articles chronicling successful hunts." **Buys 150 mss/year.** Query. Length: 1,000 words. **Pays $100-360**

REPRINTS Pays 50 percent of first-time rate.

PHOTOS Send photos. Captions, identification of subjects required. Reviews transparencies, prints, JPEG files. Buys one-time rights.

❸❸ SALT WATER SPORTSMAN

Bonnier Corporation, 460 N. Orlando Ave., Suite 200, Winter Park FL 32789. (407)628-4802. **E-mail:** editor@saltwatersportsman.com. **Website:** www.saltwatersportsman.com. **Contact:** Glenn Law, editor-in-chief. **85% freelance written.** Monthly magazine covering saltwater sport fishing. *Salt Water Sportsman* is edited for serious marine sport fishermen whose lifestyle includes the pursuit of game fish in U.S. waters and around the world. It provides information on fishing trends, techniques, and destinations, both local and international. Each issue reviews offshore and inshore fishing boats, high-tech electronics, innovative tackle, engines, and other new products. Coverage also focuses on sound fisheries management and conservation. Circ. 170,000. Byline given. Pays on acceptance. Offers kill fee. Publishes ms an average of 5 months after acceptance. Submit seasonal material 8 months in advance. Accepts queries by mail, e-mail. Accepts simultaneous submissions. Responds in 1 month to queries. Guidelines available by request.

NONFICTION Needs how-to, personal experience, photo feature, technical, travel. **Buys 100 mss/year.** Query. Length: 900-1,200 words. **Pay for feature/photo package starts at $750.** Pays expenses of writers on assignment.

PHOTOS Captions required. Reviews low-res digital files, requires RAW files for publication. Pays $1,500 minimum for cover.

COLUMNS Sportsman's Tips (short, how-to tips and techniques on salt water fishing; emphasis is on building, repairing, or reconditioning specific items or gear). Send complete ms.

TIPS "There are a lot of knowledgeable fishermen/budding writers out there who could be valuable to us with a little coaching. Many don't think they can write a story for us, but they'd be surprised. We work with writers. Shorter articles that get to the point and are accompanied by good, sharp photos are hard for us to turn down. Having to delete unnecessary wordage—conversation, clichés, etc.—that writers feel is mandatory is annoying. Often they don't devote enough attention to specific, repeatable fishing information."

🌑🌑🌑🌑 SPORT FISHING

Bonnier Corporation, 460 N. Orlando Ave., Suite 200, Winter Park FL 32789. (407)628-4802. **Fax:** (407)628-7061. **E-mail:** Editor@sportfishingmag.com. **Website:** www.sportfishingmag.com. **Contact:** Stephanie Pancratz, senior managing editor. **50% freelance written.** Magazine published 10 times/year covering saltwater angling, saltwater fish and fisheries. "*Sport Fishing*'s readers are middle-aged, affluent, mostly male, who are generally proficient in and very educated to their sport. We are about fishing from boats, not from surf or jetties." Estab. 1985. Circ. 85,0000. Byline given. Pays on acceptance. Offers 25% kill fee. Publishes ms an average of 6-12 months after acceptance. Editorial lead time 2-12 months. Submit seasonal material 1 year in advance. Accepts queries by e-mail. Accepts simultaneous submissions. Responds in 1 week to queries. Responds in 1 month to mss. Sample copy with #10 SASE. Guidelines available online.

NONFICTION Needs general interest, how-to. Query. Length: 2,500-3,000 words. **Pays $500-750 for text** only; **$1,500+ possible for complete package with photos.** Pays expenses of writers on assignment.

PHOTOS State availability. Reviews GIF/JPEG files. Offers $75-400/photo. Buys one time rights.

TIPS "Queries please; no over-the-transom submissions. Meet or beat deadlines. Include quality photos when you can. Quote the experts. Balance information with readability. Include sidebars."

🌑🌑🌑 SPORTS AFIELD

Field Sports Publishing, P.O. Box 271305, Fort Collins CO 80527. **Website:** www.sportsafield.com. **60% freelance written.** Magazine published 6 times/year covering big game hunting. "We cater to the upscale hunting market, especially hunters who travel to exotic destinations like Alaska and Africa. We are not a deer hunting magazine, and we do not cover fishing." Estab. 1887. Circ. 50,000. Byline given. Pays 1 month prior to publication. Publishes ms an average of 6 months after acceptance. Editorial lead time 4 months. Submit seasonal material 5 months in advance. Accepts queries by online submission form. Accepts simultaneous submissions. Responds in 2 months. Guidelines online.

NONFICTION Needs personal experience, travel. **Buys 6-8 mss/year.** Query. Length: 1,500-2,500 words. **Pays $500-800.** Pays expenses of writers on assignment.

PHOTOS State availability. Captions, model releases required. Reviews 35mm slides transparencies, TIFF/JPEG files. Offers no additional payment for photos accepted with ms. Buys first time rights.

FILLERS Needs newsbreaks. **Buys 30 mss/year.** Length: 200-500 words. **Pays $75-150.**

🌑🌑 TRAPPER & PREDATOR CALLER

F+W, A Content + Ecommerce Company, 5225 Joerns Dr., Stevens Point WI 54481. (715)445-2214. **E-mail:** jared.blohm@fwcommunity.com. **Website:** www.trapperpredatorcaller.com. **75% freelance written.** Tabloid published 10 times/year covering trapping and predator calling, fur trade. "Our editorial goal is to inform, educate, and entertain our readers with articles, photographs, and illustrations that promote trapping and predator calling." Must have mid-level to advanced knowledge because *T&PC* is heavily how-to focused. Estab. 1975. Circ. 34,000. Byline given. Pays within 45 days of publication. No kill fee. Publishes ms an average of 6 months after acceptance.

Editorial lead time 1 year. Submit seasonal material 1 year in advance. Accepts queries by e-mail.

NONFICTION Needs how-to, interview, personal experience, travel. **Buys 100 mss/year.** Query or send complete ms via e-mail. Length: 1,500-2,500 words. **Pays $250 for assigned articles.**

PHOTOS Send photos. Reviews high-resolution digital photos, slides, prints. Digital photos should be saved as TIFF or JPEG files. Minimum 300 dpi. Buys one-time rights.

TIPS "Check your facts. An error in fact reduces the credibility of the magazine and hurts your relationship with us. Please double-check spelling, dates, proper names, etc."

🄫🄢 TURKEY COUNTRY

P.O. Box 530, Edgefield SC 29824-0530. (803)637-3106. **E-mail:** turkeycountry@nwtf.net; mjones@nwtf.net. **Website:** www.nwtf.org. **Contact:** Matt Lindler, editor; Michelle Jones, publishing assistant. **50-60% freelance written.** Bimonthly educational magazine for members of the National Wild Turkey Federation. Topics covered include hunting, history, restoration, management, biology, and distribution of wild turkey. Estab. 1973. Circ. 180,000. Byline given. Pays on acceptance. 20% kill fee. Publishes ms an average of 6 months after acceptance. Editorial lead time 1 year. Accepts queries by mail, e-mail. Accepts simultaneous submissions. Responds in 2 months to queries Sample copy: $5 and 9x12 SAE. Guidelines available online.

NONFICTION Query (preferred) or send complete ms. Length: 500-1,200 words. **Pays $350-450.** Pays expenses of writers on assignment.

PHOTOS "We want quality photos submitted with features. Illustrations also acceptable. We are using more and more inside color illustrations. No typical hunter-holding-dead-turkey photos or setups using mounted birds or domestic turkeys. Photos with how-to stories must make the techniques clear (i.e., how to make a turkey call; how to sculpt or carve a bird in wood)." Identification of subjects, model releases required. Reviews transparencies, high-resolution digital images. Pays $150 for half-page, $200 for full page, $300 for two-page spread, $250 for contents pages, and $800 for cover. Buys one-time rights.

COLUMNS Acquires for various departments, all 500-1,000 words. Query. **Pays $350.**

TIPS "The writer should simply keep in mind that the audience is 'expert' on wild turkey management, hunting, life history, and restoration/conservation history. Know the subject."

MARTIAL ARTS

🄫🄢 BLACK BELT

Black Belt Communications, LLC, 24900 Anza Dr., Unit E, Valencia CA 91355. **Fax:** (661)257-3028. **E-mail:** byoung@aimmedia.com. **Website:** www.blackbeltmag.com. **Contact:** Robert W. Young, executive editor. **80% freelance written. Works with a small number of new/unpublished writers each year.** Monthly magazine emphasizing martial arts for both experienced practitioner and layman. Estab. 1961. Circ. 100,000. Pays on publication. No kill fee. Publishes ms an average of 1 year after acceptance. Accepts queries by mail, e-mail. Accepts simultaneous submissions. Responds in 3 weeks to queries. Guidelines online.

NONFICTION Needs expose, how-to, interview, new product, personal experience, technical, travel, Informational. We never use personality profiles. **Buys 40-50 mss/year.** Query with outline 1,200 words minimum. **Pays $150-300 for feature articles with good photos.**

PHOTOS Very seldom buys photographs without accompanying ms. Captions, model releases required. Total purchase price for ms includes payment for photos.

🄢 KUNG FU TAI CHI

TC Media International, 40748 Encyclopedia Circle, Fremont CA 94538. (510)656-5100. **Fax:** (510)656-8844. **E-mail:** gene@kungfumagazine.com. **Website:** www.kungfumagazine.com. **Contact:** Gene Ching. **70% freelance written.** Bimonthly magazine covering Chinese martial arts and culture. *Kung Fu Tai Chi* covers the full range of Kung Fu culture, including healing, philosophy, meditation, Fengshui, Buddhism, Taoism, history, and the latest events in art and culture, plus insightful features on the martial arts. Estab. 1992. Circ. 10,000. Byline given. Pays on publication. No kill fee. Publishes ms 3 or more months after acceptance. Editorial lead time 4 months. Submit seasonal material 4 months in advance. Accepts queries by mail, e-mail, fax, phone. Accepts simultaneous submissions. Responds in 2 months to queries;

in 3 months to mss. Sample copy for $4.99 or online. Guidelines available online.

NONFICTION Needs general interest, historical, interview, personal experience, religious, technical, travel, cultural perspectives. No poetry or fiction. **Buys 70 mss/year.** Query. Length: 500-2,500 words. **Pays $35-125.**

PHOTOS Send photos. Captions, identification of subjects required. Reviews 5x7 prints, GIF/JPEG files. Offers no additional payment for photos accepted with ms. Buys one-time rights.

TIPS "Check out our website and get an idea of past articles."

💲💲 T'AI CHI

Wayfarer Publications, P.O. Box 39938, Los Angeles CA 90039. (323)665-7773. **Fax:** (323)665-1627. **E-mail:** taichi@tai-chi.com. **Website:** www.tai-chi.com. **Contact:** Marvin Smalheiser, editor. **90% freelance written.** Quarterly magazine covering T'ai Chi Ch'uan as a martial art and for health and fitness. "Covers T'ai Chi Ch'uan and other internal martial arts, plus qigong and Chinese health, nutrition, and philosophical disciplines. Readers are practitioners or laymen interested in developing skills and insight for self-defense, health, and self-improvement." Estab. 1977. Circ. 50,000. Byline given. Pays on publication. No kill fee. Publishes ms an average of 3 months after acceptance. Editorial lead time 3 months. Submit seasonal material 6 months in advance. Accepts queries by mail, e-mail, fax. Accepts simultaneous submissions. Responds in 3 weeks to queries. Responds in 3 months to mss. Sample copy: $5.99. Guidelines available online.

NONFICTION Needs essays, how-to, interview, personal experience. "Do not want articles promoting an individual, system, or school." Send complete ms. Length: 1,200-4,500 words. **Pays $75-500.**

PHOTOS Send photos. Captions, identification of subjects, model releases required. Reviews color or b&w 4x6 or 5x7 prints, digital files suitable for print production. "Offers no additional payment for photos accepted with ms, but overall payment takes into consideration the number and quality of photos." Buys one-time and reprint rights.

TIPS "Think and write for practitioners and laymen who want information and insight, and who are trying to work through problems to improve skills and their health through Tai Chi. No promotional material."

MISCELLANEOUS

💲💲 CLIMBING

Cruz Bay Publishing, Inc., 5720 Flatiron Pkwy., Boulder CO 80301. (303)625-1600. **Fax:** (303)440-3618. **E-mail:** queries@climbing.com. **Website:** www.climbing.com. Magazine published 9 times/year covering climbing and mountaineering. Provides features on rock climbing and mountaineering worldwide. Estab. 1970. Circ. 51,000. Pays on publication. No kill fee. Editorial lead time 6 weeks. Accepts queries by e-mail. Accepts simultaneous submissions. Guidelines online.

NONFICTION Needs interview, personal experience. Query. Length: 1,500-3,500 words. **Pays 35¢/word.** Pays expenses of writers on assignment.

PHOTOS State availability. Reviews negatives, 35mm transparencies, prints, digital submissions on CD. Pays $25-800.

COLUMNS Query. **Payment varies.**

💲💲 POINTE MAGAZINE

MacFadden Performing Arts Media, LLC, 333 Seveneth Ave., 11th Floor, New York NY 10001. (212)979-4862. **Fax:** (646)459-4848. **E-mail:** pointe@dancemedia.com. **Website:** www.pointemagazine.com. **Contact:** Amy Cogan, publisher. Bimonthly magazine covering ballet. *Pointe Magazine* is the only magazine dedicated to ballet. It offers practicalities on ballet careers as well as news and features. Estab. 2000. Circ. 38,000. Byline given. Pays on publication. Responds in 1 month to queries. Responds in 1 month to mss. Sample copy for SAE with 9x12 envelope and 6 first-class stamps.

NONFICTION Needs historical, how-to, interview, biography, careers, health, news. **Buys 60 mss/year.** Query with published clips. Length: 400-1,500 words. **Pays $125-400.**

PHOTOS Contact: Colin Fowler, photo editor. State availability. Captions required. Reviews 2 1/4 x 2 1/4 or 35 mm transparencies, 8 x 11 prints. Negotiates payment individually. Buys one time rights.

💲💲 POLO PLAYERS' EDITION

6008 Reynolds Rd., Lake Worth FL 33449. (561)968-5208. **Fax:** (561)968-5209. **E-mail:** gwen@poloplayersedition.com; info@poloplayersedition.com. **Website:** www.poloplayersedition.com. **Contact:** Gwen Rizzo, editor/publisher. Monthly magazine on the sport and lifestyle polo. "Our readers are affluent, well educated, well read, and highly sophisticated." Circ. 6,150. Pays on acceptance. Offers kill fee; varies. Publishes ms an average of 2 months after acceptance. Submit seasonal material 3 months in advance. Accepts queries by mail, e-mail. Accepts simultaneous submissions. Responds in 3 months to queries. Guidelines for #10 SAE with 2 stamps.

NONFICTION Needs historical, interview, personal experience, photo feature, technical, travel. Special issues: Annual Art Issue/Gift Buying Guide; Winter Preview/Florida Supplement. **Buys 20 mss/year.** Send complete ms. Length: 800-3,000 words. **Pays $150-400 for assigned articles. Pays $100-300 for unsolicited articles.** Sometimes pays expenses of writers on assignment.

REPRINTS Send tearsheet or typed ms with rights for sale noted and information about when and where the material previously appeared. Pays 50% of amount paid for an original article.

PHOTOS State availability of or send photos. Captions required. Reviews contact sheets, transparencies, prints. Offers $20-150/photo. Buys one-time rights.

COLUMNS Yesteryears (historical pieces), 500 words; Profiles (clubs and players), 800-1,000 words. **Buys 15 mss/year.** Query with published clips. **Pays $100-300.**

TIPS "Query us on a personality or club profile or historic piece or, if you know the game, state availability to cover a tournament. Keep in mind that ours is a sophisticated, well-educated audience."

🄢 RUGBY MAGAZINE

Rugby Press, Ltd., 459 Columbus Ave., #1200, New York NY 10024. (212)787-1160. **Fax:** (212)787-1161. **E-mail:** alex@rugbymag.com. **Website:** www.rugbymag.com. **Contact:** Alex Goff, editor-in-chief. **75% freelance written.** Monthly magazine. Estab. 1975. Circ. 10,000. Byline given. Pays on publication. No kill fee. Publishes ms an average of 2 months after acceptance. Editorial lead time 1 month. Submit seasonal material 2 months in advance. Accepts queries by mail, e-mail, fax, phone. Accepts simultaneous submissions. Responds in 2 weeks to queries. Responds in 1 month to mss. Sample copy for $4. Guidelines free.

NONFICTION Needs book excerpts, essays, general interest, historical, how-to, humor, interview, new product, opinion, personal experience, photo feature, technical, travel. **Buys 15 mss/year.** Send complete ms.

Length: 600-2,000 words. **Pays $50 minimum.** Pays expenses of writers on assignment.

REPRINTS Send tearsheet or typed ms with rights for sale noted and information about when and where the material previously appeared. Payment varies.

PHOTOS Send photos. Reviews negatives, transparencies, prints. Offers no additional payment for photos accepted with ms. Buys all rights.

COLUMNS Nutrition (athletic nutrition), 900 words; Referees' Corner, 1,200 words. **Buys 2-3 mss/year.** Query with published clips. **Pays $50 maximum.**

FICTION Needs cond novels, humorous, novel concepts, slice-of-life vignettes. **Buys 1-3 mss/year.** Query with published clips. Length: 1,000-2,500 words. **Pays $100.**

TIPS "Give us a call. Send along your stories or photos; we're happy to take a look. Tournament stories are a good way to get yourself published in *Rugby Magazine*."

MOTOR SPORTS

🄢 THE HOOK MAGAZINE

P.O. Box 51324, Bowling Green KY 42104. (270)202-6742. **E-mail:** editor@hookmagazine.com; rblively@hotmail.com. **Website:** www.hookmagazine.com. **Contact:** Bryan Lively, editor-in-chief. **80% freelance written.** Bimonthly magazine covering tractor pulling. Estab. 1992. Circ. 6,000. Byline given. Pays on publication. No kill fee. Editorial lead time 6 months. Submit seasonal material 6 months in advance. Accepts queries by mail, e-mail, fax. Accepts simultaneous submissions. Responds in 3 weeks to queries. Responds in 2 months to mss. Sample copy for 8 1/2x11 SAE with 4 first-class stamps or online. Guidelines for #10 SASE.

NONFICTION Needs how-to, interview, new product, personal experience, photo feature, technical, event coverage. **Buys 25 mss/year.** Send complete ms. Length: 500-1,500 words. **Pays $70 for technical articles; $35 for others.**

PHOTOS Send photos. Captions, identification of subjects, model releases required. Reviews 3x5 prints. Negotiates payment individually. Buys one-time and online rights.

FILLERS Needs anecdotes, short humor. **Buys 6 mss/year.** Length: 100 words.

TIPS "Write 'real'; our readers don't respond well to scholarly tomes. Use your everyday voice in all submissions and your chances will go up radically."

⊙⊙ SAND SPORTS MAGAZINE

Wright Publishing Co., Inc., 3176 Pullman, Suite 107, Costa Mesa CA 92626. (714)979-2560, ext. 107. **E-mail:** info@sandsports.net. **Website:** www.sandsports.net. **Contact:** Michael Sommer, editor. **20% freelance written.** Bimonthly magazine covering vehicles for off-road and sand dunes. Estab. 1995. Circ. 35,000. Byline given. Pays on publication. Editorial lead time 3 months. Submit seasonal material 6 months in advance. Accepts queries by mail. Accepts simultaneous submissions. Sample copy and writer's guidelines free.

NONFICTION Needs how-to, photo feature, technical. **Buys 20 mss/year.** Query. Length: 1,500 words minimum. **Pays $175/page.** Pays expenses of writers on assignment.

PHOTOS Send photos. Captions, identification of subjects, model releases required. Reviews color slides or high-res digital images. Negotiates payment individually. Buys one-time rights.

RUNNING

⊙ INSIDE TEXAS RUNNING

P.O. Box 19909, Houston TX 77224. (713)935-0555. **Fax:** (713)935-0559. **Website:** www.insidetexasrunning.com. **Contact:** Lance Phegley, editor. **70% freelance written.** Monthly (except June and August) tabloid covering running and running-related events. "Our audience is made up of Texas runners who may also be interested in cross training." Estab. 1977. Circ. 10,000. Byline given. Pays on publication. No kill fee. Publishes ms an average of 2 months after acceptance. Submit seasonal material 2 months in advance. Accepts simultaneous submissions. Responds in 1 month to mss. Sample copy: $4.95. Guidelines for #10 SASE.

NONFICTION Special issues: Shoe Review (March); Fall Race Review (September); Marathon Focus (October); Resource Guide (December). **Buys 20 mss/year.** Send complete ms. Length: 500-1,500 words. **Pays $100 maximum for assigned articles. Pays $50 maximum for unsolicited articles.**

REPRINTS Send tearsheet, photocopy, or typed ms with rights for sale noted and information about when and where the material previously appeared.

PHOTOS Send photos. Captions required. Offers $25 maximum/photo. Buys one-time rights.

TIPS "Writers should be familiar with the sport and the publication."

⊙⊙⊙ RUNNER'S WORLD

Rodale, 400 S. Tenth St., Emmaus PA 18098. (610)967-8441. **Fax:** (610)967-8883. **E-mail:** rwedit@rodale.com. **Website:** www.runnersworld.com. **Contact:** David Willey, editor-in-chief; Suzanne Perrault, senior managing editor; Benjamen Purvis, design director. **5% freelance written.** Monthly magazine on running—mainly long-distance running. *Runner's World* is the magazine for and about distance running, training, health and fitness, nutrition, motivation, injury prevention, race coverage, and personalities of the sport. Estab. 1966. Circ. 500,000. Byline given. Pays on publication. No kill fee. Publishes ms an average of 6 months after acceptance. Submit seasonal material 6 months in advance. Accepts queries by mail. Accepts simultaneous submissions. Responds in 2 months to queries. Guidelines online.

NONFICTION Needs how-to, interview, personal experience. No "my first marathon" stories. No poetry. **Buys 5-7 mss/year.** Query. **Pays $1,500-2,000.** Pays expenses of writers on assignment.

PHOTOS State availability. Identification of subjects required. Buys one-time rights.

COLUMNS Finish Line (back-of-the-magazine essay, personal experience, humor). **Buys 24 mss/year.** Send complete ms. **Pays $300.**

TIPS "We are always looking for 'Adventure Runs' from readers—runs in wild, remote, beautiful, and interesting places. These are rarely race stories but more like backtracking/running adventures. Great color slides are crucial; 2,000 words maximum."

⊙⊙ TRAIL RUNNER

Big Stone Publishing, 2567 Dolores Way, Carbondale CO 81623. (970)704-1442. **Fax:** (970)963-4965. **E-mail:** pcunobooth@bigstonepub; mbenge@bigstonepub.com. **Website:** www.trailrunnermag.com. **Contact:** Michael Benge, editor; Paul Cuno-Booth, associate editor. **80% freelance written.** Magazine published 8x year, covering trail runing, ultratanning, fastpacking, adventure racing, and snowshoeing. Covers all aspects of off-road running. "North America's only magazine dedicated to trail running. In-depth editorial and compelling photography informs, entertains and inspires readers of all ages and abilities to enjoy the outdoors and to improve their health and fitness through the sport of trail running." Estab. 1999. Circ. 31,000. Byline given. Pays 30 days post-publication Publishes ms an average of 2 months after acceptance. Editorial lead time is 3 months. Submit seasonal material 5 months in advance. Accepts queries by e-mail. Accepts simultaneous submissions. Responds in 4 weeks to queries. Sample copy for $5. Guidelines online.

NONFICTION Needs expose, historical, how-to, humor, inspirational, interview, personal experience, technical, travel, racing. Does not want "My first trail race." **Buys 30-40 mss/year.** Query with one or two writing samples (preferably previously published articles), including your name, phone number and email address. Identify which department your story would be best suited for. **Pays 25¢/word for assigned and unsolicited articles.** Pays expenses of writers on assignment.

PHOTOS "*Trail Runner* regularly features stunning photography of trail running destinations, races, adventures and faces of the sport." State availability of photos with submission. Captions, identification of subjects. Reviews GIF/JPEG files. Send low-res samples or lightbox to photos@bigstonepub.com. Offers $50-250/photo. Buys one-time rights.

COLUMNS Contact: Michael Benge, editor, or Yitka Winn, associate editor. Making Tracks (news, race reports, athlete Q&A), 300-800 words; Trail Tips, Training Trail Rx (injury prevention/treatment, recovery), Take Your Mark (race previews); Nutrition (sports nutrition, health news), 800-1,000 words; Adventure, Great Escapes (running destinations/trails), Faces (athlete profiles), 1,200 words **Buys 40 mss/year. mss/year.** Query with published clips. **Pays 25 cents/word.**

FILLERS Needs anecdotes, facts, newsbreaks, short humor. **Buys 10 mss/year. mss/year.** Length: 75-400 words. **Pays 30 cents/word.**

TIPS "Demonstrate familiarity with the sport. Best way to break in is with interesting and unique news, stories, insights. Submit thoughtful, detailed queries, not just vague story ideas."

SKIING & SNOW SPORTS

$ AMERICAN SNOWMOBILER

Kalmbach Publishing Co., 21027 Crossroads Circle, P.O. Box 1612, Waukesha WI 53187-1612. **E-mail:** editor@amsnow.com. **Website:** www.amsnow.com. **Contact:** Mark Savage, executive editor. **30% freelance written.** Magazine published 6 times seasonally covering snowmobiling. Estab. 1985. Circ. 54,000. Byline given. Pays on acceptance. No kill fee. Publishes an average of 4 months after acceptance. Editorial lead time 4 months. Submit seasonal material 6 months in advance. Accepts queries by mail, e-mail, fax. Accepts simultaneous submissions. Responds in 1 month to queries. Responds in 2 months to mss. Guidelines available online.

NONFICTION Needs general interest, historical, how-to, interview, personal experience, photo feature, travel. **Buys 10 mss/year.** Query with published clips. Length: 500-1,200 words. **Pay varies for assigned articles. Pays $100 minimum for unsolicited articles.**

PHOTOS State availability. Captions, identification of subjects, model releases required. Offers no additional payment for photos accepted with ms. Buys all rights.

$ SKATING

United States Figure Skating Association, 20 First St., Colorado Springs CO 80906. (719)635-5200. **Fax:** (719)635-9548. **E-mail:** info@usfigureskating.org. **Website:** www.usfsa.org. "*Skating* magazine is the official publication of U.S. Figure Skating, and thus we cover skating at both the championship and grass roots level." Published 10 times/year. Estab. 1923. Circ. 42,000. Byline given. Pays on publication. No kill fee. Publishes ms an average of 3 months after acceptance. Accepts queries by mail, e-mail, fax. Sample copy online.

NONFICTION Needs general interest, historical, how-to, interview, background and interests of skaters, volunteers, or other U.S. Figure Skating members, photo feature, technical and competition reports, figure skating issues and trends, sports medicine. **Buys 10 mss/year.** Query. Length: 500-2,500 words. **Payment varies.**

PHOTOS Photos purchased with or without accompanying ms. Query. Pays $10 for 8x10 or 5x7 b&w

glossy prints, and $25 for color prints or transparencies.

COLUMNS Ice Breaker (news briefs); Foreign Competition Reports; Health and Fitness; In Synch (synchronized skating news); Takeoff (up-and-coming athletes), all 500-2,000 words.

TIPS "We want writing by experienced persons knowledgeable in the technical and artistic aspects of figure skating with a new outlook on the development of the sport. Knowledge and background in technical aspects of figure skating is helpful but not necessary to the quality of writing expected. We would like to see articles and short features on U.S. Figure Skating volunteers, skaters, and other U.S. Figure Skating members who normally wouldn't get recognized, as opposed to features on championship-level athletes, which are usually assigned to regular contributors. Good-quality color photos are a must with submissions. Also would be interested in seeing figure skating 'issues and trends' articles, instead of just profiles. No professional skater material. Synchronized skating and adult skating are the 2 fastest growing aspects of U.S. Figure Skating. We would like to see more stories dealing with these unique athletes."

$$$$ SKIING

Bonnier Corporation, 5720 Flatiron Pkwy., Boulder CO 80301. (303)253-6300. **E-mail:** editor@skiingmag.com. **Website:** www.skinet.com. **Contact:** Sam Bass, editor-in-chief. Magazine published 7 times/year for skiers who "deeply love winter, and who live for travel, adventure, instruction, gear, and news." *Skiing* is the user's guide to winter adventure. It is equal parts jaw-dropping inspiration and practical information, action and utility, attitude, and advice. It relates the lifestyles of dedicated skiers and captures their spirit of daring and exploration. Dramatic photography transports readers to spine-tingling mountains with breathtaking immediacy. Reading *Skiing* is almost as much fun as being there. Estab. 1948. Circ. 400,000. Byline given. Offers 40% kill fee.

NONFICTION **Buys 10-15 (feature) and 12-24 (short) mss/year.** Query. Length: 1,500-2,000 words (feature); 100-500 words (short). **Pays $1,000-2,500/feature; $100-500/short piece.**

COLUMNS Length: 200-1,000 words. **Buys 2-3 mss/year.** Query. **Pays $150-1,000.**

TIPS "Consider less obvious subjects: smaller ski areas, specific local ski cultures, unknown aspects of popular resorts. Be expressive, not merely descriptive. We want readers to feel the adventure in your writing—to tingle with the excitement of skiing steep powder, of meeting intriguing people, of reaching new goals or achieving dramatic new insights. We want readers to have fun, to see the humor in and the lighter side of skiing and their fellow skiers."

$$ SNOWEST MAGAZINE

Harris Publishing, 360 B St., Idaho Falls ID 83402. (208)524-7000. **Fax:** (208)522-5241. **E-mail:** lindstrm@snowest.com. **Website:** http://snowest.com. **10-25% freelance written.** Monthly magazine covering snowmobiling. "*SnoWest* covers the sport of snowmobiling, products, and personalities in the western states. This includes mountain riding, deep powder, and trail riding, as well as destination pieces, tech tips, and new model reviews." Estab. 1972. Circ. 140,000. Byline given. Pays on publication. No kill fee. Publishes ms an average of 2 months after acceptance. Editorial lead time 6 months. Submit seasonal material 3 months in advance. Sample copy and writer's guidelines free.

NONFICTION Needs how-to, fix a snowmobile, make it high performance, new product, technical, travel. **Buys 3-5 mss/year.** Query with published clips. Length: 500-1,500 words. **Pays $150-300.**

PHOTOS Send photos. Captions, identification of subjects required. Negotiates payment individually. Buys one-time rights.

$$ SNOW GOER

3300 Fernbrook Lane N., Suite #200, Plymouth MN 55447. **Fax:** (763)-383-4499. **Website:** www.snowgoer.com. **5% freelance written.** Magazine published 7 times/year covering snowmobiling. "*Snow Goer* is a hard-hitting, tell-it-like-it-is magazine designed for the ultra-active snowmobile enthusiast. It is fun, exciting, innovative, and on the cutting edge of technology and trends." Estab. 1967. Circ. 66,000. Byline given. Pays on publication. No kill fee. Publishes ms an average of 5 months after acceptance. Editorial lead time 5 months. Submit seasonal material 6 months in advance. Accepts queries by mail. Accepts simultaneous submissions. Responds in 3 months to queries. Sample copy for SAE with 8x10 envelope and 4 First-Class stamps.

NONFICTION Needs general interest, how-to, interview, new product, personal experience, photo feature, technical, travel. **Buys 6 mss/year.** Query. Length: 500-4,000 words. **Pays $50-500.** Sometimes pays expenses of writers on assignment.

PHOTOS State availability. Captions, identification of subjects required. Reviews contact sheets, prints. Negotiates payment individually. Buys one-time rights or all rights.

TIPS "*Snow Goer* magazine is written for, and by, mature and discerning snowmobile riders. If you wish to contribute articles and photos to *Snow Goer* please carefully read our editorial guidelines (available by request) before submitting your query. Please query us *by regular mail*; do not e-mail article queries."

WATER SPORTS

◑$ DIVER

216 E. Esplanade St., North Vancouver BC V7L 1A3 Canada. (604)988-0711. **E-mail:** editor@divermag. com. **Website:** www.divermag.com. Magazine published 8 times/year emphasizing sport SCUBA diving, ocean science, and technology for a well-educated, active readership across North America and around the world. Circ. 30,000. No kill fee. Accepts queries by mail, e-mail. Accepts simultaneous submissions.

NONFICTION Query. Length: 500-3,000 words. **Pays 12.5¢/word.** Pays expenses of writers on assignment.

PHOTOS Captions, identification of subjects required. Reviews JPEG/TIFF files (300 dpi), slides, maps, drawings. Pays $100 full page, $50 half page, $25 quarter page or smaller photos inside, $350 for cover photo.

$$ SWIMMING WORLD MAGAZINE

Sports Publications International, 2744 East Glenrosa, Phoenix AZ 85016. (928)284-4005. **Fax:** (928)284-2477. **E-mail:** editorial@swimmingworld.com. **Website:** www.swimmingworldmagazine.com. **Contact:** Jason Marsteller, managing editor. **30% freelance written.** Bimonthly magazine about competitive swimming. Readers are fitness-oriented adults from varied social and professional backgrounds who share swimming as part of their lifestyle. Estab. 1960. Circ. 50,000. Byline given. Pays on publication. Editorial lead time 2 months. Submit seasonal material 3 months in advance. Accepts queries by mail, e-mail,

fax. Accepts simultaneous submissions. Responds in 1 month to queries. Guidelines available online.

NONFICTION Needs book excerpts, essays, expose, general interest, historical, how-to, humor, inspirational, interview, new product, personal experience, photo feature, technical, travel, general health. **Buys 30 mss/year.** Query with a 250-word synopsis of article. Length: 250-2,500 words. **Pays $75-400.** Pays expenses of writers on assignment.

PHOTOS Send photos. Captions, identification of subjects, model releases required. Reviews high-resolution digital images. Negotiates payment individually.

$ THE WATER SKIER

1251 Holy Cow Rd., Polk City FL 33868. (863)324-4341. **Fax:** (863)325-8259. **E-mail:** satkinson@usawaterski.org. **Website:** www.usawaterski.org. **Contact:** Scott Atkinson, editor. **10-20% freelance written.** Magazine published 6 times/year. *The Water Skier* is the membership magazine of USA Water Ski, the national governing body for organized water skiing in the United States. The magazine has a controlled circulation and is available only to USA Water Ski's membership, which is made up of 17,000 active competitive water skiers. The editorial content of the magazine features distinctive and informative writing about the sport of water skiing and wakeboarding. Estab. 1951. Circ. 20,000. Byline given. Editorial lead time 4 months. Submit seasonal material 6 months in advance. Accepts simultaneous submissions. Responds in 2 weeks to queries. Sample copy: $3.50. Guidelines available with #10 SASE.

NONFICTION **Buys 10-15 mss/year.** Query. Length: 1,500-3,000 words. **Pays $100-150.** Pays expenses of writers on assignment.

REPRINTS Send photocopy. Payment negotiable.

PHOTOS State availability. Captions, identification of subjects required. Reviews contact sheets. Negotiates payment individually. Buys all rights.

COLUMNS The Water Skier News (small news items about people and events in the sport), 400-500 words. Other topics include safety, training (3-event, barefoot, disabled, show ski, ski race, kneeboard, and wakeboard); champions on their way; new products. Query. **Pays $50-100.**

TIPS "Contact the editor through a query letter (please, no phone calls) with an idea. Avoid instruction, these articles are written by professionals. Concentrate on articles about the people of the sport. We are always looking for interesting stories about people in the sport."

TEEN & YOUNG ADULT

😊💲 CICADA

Cricket Media, Inc., **E-mail:** cicada@cicadamag.com. **Website:** www.cricketmag.com/cicada. "*Cicada* is a YA lit/comics magazine fascinated with the lyric and strange and committed to work that speaks to teens' truths. We publish poetry, realistic and genre fiction, essay, and comics by adults and teens. (We are also inordinately fond of Viking jokes.) Our readers are smart and curious; submissions are invited but not required to engage young adult themes." Bimonthly literary magazine for ages 14 and up. Publishes 6 issues/year. Estab. 1998. Circ. 6,000. Pays after publication. Accepts queries by online submission form. Accepts simultaneous submissions. Responds in 3-6 months to mss. Sample copy available online. Guidelines available online.

NONFICTION narrative nonfiction (especially teen-written), essays on literature, culture, and the arts. Submit complete ms via online submissions manager (cricketmag.submittable.com). Length: up to 5,000 words. **Pays up to 25¢/word.** Pays expenses of writers on assignment.

FICTION realism, science fiction, fantasy, historical fiction. Wants everything from flash fiction to novellas. Length: up to 9,000 words. **Pays up to 25¢/word.**

POETRY Needs free verse, light verse, traditional. Reviews serious, humorous, free verse, rhyming. Length: no limit. **Pays up to $3/line ($25 minimum).**

TIPS "Favorite writers, YA and otherwise: Bennett Madison, Sarah McCarry, Leopoldine Core, J. Hope Stein, José Olivarez, Sofia Samatar, Erica Lorraine Scheidt, David Levithan, Sherman Alexie, Hilary Smith, Nnedi Okorafor, Teju Cole, Anne Boyer, Malory Ortberg. @cicadamagazine; cicadamagazine.tumblr.com."

💲 DEVOZINE

1908 Grand Ave., P.O. Box 340004, Nashville TN 37203-0004. **E-mail:** devozine@upperroom.org. **Website:** www.devozine.org. **Contact:** Sandy Miller, editor. *devozine,* published bimonthly, is a 64-page devotional magazine for youth (ages 14-19) and adults who care about youth. Offers meditations, scripture, prayers, poems, stories, songs, and feature articles to "aid youth in their prayer life, introduce them to spiritual disciplines, help them shape their concept of God, and encourage them in the life of discipleship." Accepts queries by mail, e-mail, online submission form. Accepts simultaneous submissions.

NONFICTION Special issues: Submit by postal mail with SASE, or by e-mail. Include name, age/birth date (if younger than 25), mailing address, e-mail address, phone number, and fax number (if available). Always publishes theme issues (available for SASE or online). Indicate theme you are writing for. Submit devotionals by mail or e-mail listed above. Submit feature article **queries** by e-mail to smiller@upperroom. org. Length: 150-250 words for devotionals; 500-600 words for feature articles. **Pays $25-100.**

POETRY Needs religious. Considers poetry by teens. Submit by postal mail with SASE, or by e-mail. Include name, age/birth date (if younger than 25), mailing address, e-mail address, phone number, and fax number (if available). Always publishes theme issues (available for SASE or online). Indicate theme you are writing for. Length: 10-20 lines/poem. **Pays $25.**

😊💲 THE NEW ERA

50 E. North Temple St., Room 2414, Salt Lake City UT 84150-0024. (801)240-2951. **Fax:** (801)240-2270. **E-mail:** newera@ldschurch.org. **Website:** www.newera. lds.org. **Contact:** Richard M. Romney, managing editor. **20% freelance written.** Monthly magazine for young people (ages 12-18) of the Church of Jesus Christ of Latter-day Saints (Mormon), their church leaders and teachers. Estab. 1971. Circ. 230,000. Byline given. Pays on acceptance. No kill fee. Publishes ms an average of 1 year after acceptance. Submit seasonal material 1 year in advance. Accepts queries by mail, e-mail, fax. Responds in 2 months to queries. Sample copy for $1.50. Guidelines available online.

NONFICTION Needs how-to, humor, inspirational, interview, personal experience, informational. Query. Length: 150-1,200 words. **Pays $25-350/article.**

PHOTOS Uses b&w photos and transparencies with manuscripts. Individual photos used for *Photo of the Month.* Payment depends on use, $10-125 per photo.

COLUMNS What's Up? (news of young Mormons around the world); How I Know; Scripture Lifeline. **Pays $25-125/article.**

POETRY Needs free verse, light verse, traditional, all other forms. Must relate to editorial viewpoint. **Pays $25 and up.**

TIPS "The writer must be able to write from a Mormon point of view. We're especially looking for stories about successful family relationships and personal growth. Well-written, personal experiences are always in demand."

💲💲 YOUNG SALVATIONIST

The Salvation Army, P.O. Box 269, Alexandria VA 22313-0269. (703)684-5500. **Fax:** (703)684-5539. **E-mail:** ys@usn.salvationarmy.org. **Website:** www.youngsalvationist.org. **Contact:** Captain Pamela Maynor, editor. **10% freelance written.** Monthly magazine for teens and early college youth. "*Young Salvationist* provides young people with biblically based inspiration and resources to develop their spirituality within the context of the Salvation Army." Circ. 40,000. Byline given. Pays on acceptance. No kill fee. Publishes ms an average of 6 months after acceptance. Submit special issues material 6 months in advance. Accepts simultaneous submissions. Responds in 2 months to mss. Sample copy and theme list free with #10 SASE or online.

NONFICTION Needs how-to, humor, inspirational, interview, personal experience, photo feature, religious. **Buys 10 mss/year.** Send complete ms through website at publications.salvationarmyusa.org/writers-submissions. Length: 700-900 words. **Pays 35¢/word.** Pays expenses of writers on assignment.

REPRINTS Considers reprints.

TIPS "Study magazine, familiarize yourself with the unique 'Salvationist' perspective of *Young Salvationist*; learn a little about the Salvation Army; media, sports, sex, and dating are strongest appeal."

TRAVEL, CAMPING & TRAILER

💲💲 AAA MIDWEST TRAVELER

AAA Auto Club of Missouri, 12901 N. 40 Dr., St. Louis MO 63141. (314)523-7350, ext. 6301. **Fax:** (314)523-6982. **E-mail:** dreinhardt@aaamissouri.com. **Website:** services.autoclubmo.aaa.com/traveler/mid. **Contact:** Deborah Reinhardt, managing editor. **80% freelance written.** Bimonthly magazine covering travel and automotive safety and is sent to 560,000 AAA

households in Missouri, southern Illinois, southern Indiana, and eastern Kansas. "We provide members with useful information on travel, auto safety and related topics." Estab. 1901. Circ. 500,000. Byline given. Pays on acceptance. Offers $50 kill fee. Editorial lead time 1 year. Best time to query is January through April. Submit seasonal material 6 months in advance. Accepts queries by mail, e-mail, fax. Accepts simultaneous submissions. Responds in 1 month. Sample copy with 10x13 SASE and 4 First-Class stamps. Guidelines with #10 SASE.

NONFICTION Needs travel. No humor, fiction, poetry or cartoons. **Buys 20-30 mss/year.** Query; query with published clips the first time. Length: 800-1,200 words. **Pays $400.** Pays expenses of writers on assignment.

PHOTOS State availability. Captions required. Reviews transparencies, prints. Offers no additional payment for photos accepted with ms. Buys one-time and electronic rights.

TIPS "Send queries between December and February, as we plan our calendar for the following year. Request a copy. Serious writers ask for media kit to help them target their piece. Travel destinations and tips are most open to freelancers; all departments and auto-related news handled by staff. We see too many 'Here's a recount of our family vacation' manuscripts. Go easy on first-person accounts."

💲 BACKROADS

P.O. Box 620, Augusta NJ 07822. (973)948-4176. **Fax:** (973)948-0823. **E-mail:** editor@backroadsusa.com. **Website:** www.backroadsusa.com. **50% freelance written.** Monthly tabloid covering motorcycle touring. "*Backroads* is a motorcycle tour magazine geared toward getting motorcyclists on the road and traveling. We provide interesting destinations, unique roadside attractions and eateries, plus Rip & Ride Route Sheets. We cater to all brands. Although *Backroads* is geared towards the motorcycling population, it is not by any means limited to just motorcycle riders. Non-motorcyclists enjoy great destinations, too. As time has gone by, *Backroads* has developed more and more into a cutting-edge touring publication. We like to see submissions that give the reader the distinct impression of being part of the ride they're reading. Words describing the feelings and emotions brought on by partaking in this great and exciting lifestyle are encouraged." All submissions must be motorcycle related article and stories with high res images to go with them. Estab. 1995. Circ. 40,000. Byline given. Pays 1-3 months after publication. Editorial lead time 1 month. Submit seasonal material 3 months in advance. Accepts queries by mail, e-mail. Responds in 1 month. Sample copy: $4. Guidelines online.

NONFICTION "What *Backroads* does not want is any 'us vs. them' submissions. We are decidedly non-political and secular. *Backroads* is about getting out and riding, not getting down on any particular group, nor do we feel this paper should be a pulpit for a writer's beliefs . be they religious, political, or personal." Query. Needs travel features: "This type of story offers a good opportunity for prospective contributors. They must feature spectacular photography, color preferably, and may be used as a cover story, if of acceptable quality. All submissions must be accompanied by images, with an SASE of adequate size (10x13) to return all material sent, as well as a copy of the issue in which they were published, and a hard copy printout of the article, including your name, address, and phone number. If none is enclosed, the materials will not be returned. Text submissions are accepted via U.S. mail or e-mail. We can usually convert most file types, although it is easier to submit in plain text format, sometimes called ASCII." **Pays $75 and up; varies.** Pays expenses of writers on assignment.

PHOTOS Digital photos may be sent via U.S. mail on CD or via e-mail if they are in a stuffed file or Drop Box. All images must be no smaller then 300 dpi and at least 4x6. If you are sending images at 72 dpi, they must be no smaller than 20x30 for proper resizing. We do not accept photographs, slides, or negatives. Send photos. Offers no additional payment for photos accepted with ms.

COLUMNS We're Outta Here (weekend destinations), 500-750 words; Great All-American Diner Run (good eateries with great location), 500-750 words; Thoughts from the Road (personal opinion/insights), 400-600 words; Mysterious America (unique and obscure sights), 500-750 words; Big City Getaway (day trips), 500-750 words. **Buys 20-24 mss/year.** Query. **Pays $75/article.**

🟢🟢 ESCAPEES

Sharing the RV Lifestyle, Roving Press, 100 Rainbow Dr., Livingston TX 77351. (888)757-2582. **Fax:** (409)327-4388. **E-mail:** editor@escapees.com. **Website:** escapees.com. **Contact:** Kelly Evans-Hill, editorial assistant. *Escapees* magazine contributors are RVers interested in sharing the RV lifestyle. Our audience includes full- and part-time RVers, RVing snowbirds (those who travel south for the winter), and anyone considering extensive travel. Escapees members have varying levels of RVing experience; therefore, the magazine looks for a wide variety of material typically not found in conventional RV magazines. We welcome submissions on all phases of RV life and for all age demographics. Escapees RV Club members range in age from younger RVers, with or without children, who are working from the road, to retirees. A large majority of members live in their motorhomes, fifth-wheel trailers, or travel trailers, on a full-time basis. Popular topics are mechanical/technical, RV modifications and conversions, lifestyle issues and tips. A bimonthly magazine that provides a total support network to RVers and shares the RV lifestyle. Estab. 1979. Circ. 30,000. Byline given. Pays on publication. Publishes ms an average of 3-6 months after acceptance. Editorial lead time 3 months. Submit seasonal material 6 months in advance. Accepts queries by mail, e-mail. Accepts simultaneous submissions. Responds in 2 weeks to queries; in 3 months to mss. Sample copy available free online. Guidelines available online and by e-mail at departmentseditor@escapees.com. Editor does not accept articles based on queries alone. Decisions for use of material are based on the full article with any accompanying photos, graphics, or diagrams. Only complete articles are considered.

NONFICTION Needs general interest, historical, how-to, humor, inspirational, new product, nostalgic, personal experience, photo feature, profile, technical, travel. Do not send anything religious, political, or unrelated to RVs. Submit complete ms. When submitting an article via e-mail as an attachment, please include the text in the body of the e-mail. Length: 300-1,500 words. Please include word count on first page of article. **Pays $50-200 for unsolicited articles.** Pays expenses of writers on assignment.

PHOTOS Contact: Cole Carter, graphic artist. Freelancers should send photos with submissions. Captions, model releases, and identification of subjects required. Reviews GIF/JPEG files. Negotiates payment individually. Purchases one-time rights.

COLUMNS SKP Stops (short blurbs with photos on unique travel destination stops for RVers), 300-500 words. **Buys 10-15 mss/year.** Submit complete ms. **Pays $25-75.**

TIPS "Use an engaging, conversational tone. Well-placed humor is refreshing. Eliminate any fluff and verbosity. Avoid colloquialisms."

⊖⊖ FAMILY MOTOR COACHING

Family Motor Coach Association, 8291 Clough Pike, Cincinnati OH 45244. (513)474-3622; (800)543-3622. **Fax:** (513)474-2332. **E-mail:** rgould@fmca.com; magazine@fmca.com. **Website:** www.fmca.com. **Contact:** Robbin Gould, editor. **80% freelance written. "We prefer that writers/photographers be experienced RVers or at least knowledgeable of the RV lifestyle."** Monthly magazine covers all aspects of motorhome travel and lifestyle. Includes travel/destination topics; mechanics, maintenance, and other technical information; new RV products; hobbies; personality profiles of motorhome travelers; and more. *Family Motor Coaching* is the official publication of Family Motor Coach Association, an international organization serving motorhome owners and enthusiasts. The magazine is distributed to association members who own motorhomes as a requirement of membership—specifically, self-contained, motorized recreation vehicles—and is also read by prospective members who may or may not own a motorhome. Articles focus on RV travel, recreation, and related lifestyle topics; association news and activities; motorhome maintenance, repair, and DIY projects; new motorhome models; and motorhome components and accessories. Approximately one-third of editorial content is devoted to travel and entertainment, one-third to association news, and one-third to new products, industry news, and motorhome maintenance/technical topics. Estab. 1963. Circ. 75,000. Byline given. Pays on acceptance. Publishes ms an average of 8-12 months after acceptance. Submit seasonal material 4-6 months in advance. Accepts queries by mail, e-mail, fax. Responds in approximately 1-2 months to queries/submissions. Sample copy: $3.99; $5 if paying by credit card. Guidelines with #10 SASE, or request PDF by e-mail.

NONFICTION Needs general interest, how-to, humor, interview, new product, nostalgic, profile, technical, travel, motorhome travel (various areas of North America accessible by motorhome), bus conversions. **Buys approximately 50-75 mss/year.** Query with published clips or description of writing background/credits. Clearly state proposed article subject, length, photo availability, why article would interest motorhomers. Plan to send photos (high-resolution digital images preferred). Submissions are requested on speculation. Length: 1,000-2,000 words. **Pays $100-500, depending on article category.** Pays expenses of writers on assignment. Expenses paid in select cases if discussed in advance.

PHOTOS Hi-res digital images preferred (minimum 300 dpi, 4x6). Typically included in ms payment. In select instances, images are purchased independently. Prefers first North American serial and electronic rights to editorial but will consider one-time rights on photos only.

TIPS "One of our biggest freelance needs are travel articles that focus on North American destinations, routes, regions, attractions, etc. Articles should be oriented toward those traveling via motorhome. Featured sites must be accessible by motorized RV, and road conditions impacting motorhome travel should be noted. No articles focusing on towable RVs (e.g., trailers, fifth-wheels), please. Another need: activities, hobbies, and sports that can be enjoyed during motorhome trips. Queries are preferred over article submissions."

⊖⊖⊖ INNS MAGAZINE

Harworth Publishing Inc., 521 Woolwich St., Guelph ON N1H 3X9 Canada. (519)767-6059. **E-mail:** mary@innsmagazine.com. **Website:** www.innsmagazine.com. **Contact:** Mary Hughes, editor. *Inns* is a national publication for travel, dining, and pastimes. It focuses on inns, beds and breakfasts, resorts, and travel in North America. The magazine is targeted to travelers looking for exquisite getaways. Accepts queries by e-mail. Accepts simultaneous submissions. Guidelines by e-mail.

NONFICTION Needs general interest, interview, new product, opinion, personal experience, travel. Query. Length: 300-600 words. **Pays $175-250 (Canadian).** Pays expenses of writers on assignment.

FILLERS Short quips or nominations, 75 words. All stories submitted must have accompany photos. **Pays $25.**

⊖⊖⊖ INTERNATIONAL LIVING

International Living Publishing, Ltd., Elysium House, Ballytruckle, Waterford Ireland (800)643-2479. **Fax:** 353-51-304-561. **E-mail:** submissions@internationalliving.com; editor@internationalliving.com. **Web-**

site: www.internationalliving.com. **Contact:** Eoin Bassett, editorial director. **50% freelance written.** "*International Living* magazine aims at providing a scope and depth of information about global travel, living, retiring, investing, and real estate that is not available anywhere else at any price." Estab. 1981. Circ. 500,000. Byline given. Pays on publication. Offers 25-50% kill fee. Publishes ms an average of 3 months after acceptance. Editorial lead time 2 months. Submit seasonal material 3 months in advance. Accepts queries by e-mail. Accepts simultaneous submissions. Responds in 2 months to mss. Sample copy available online. Guidelines available online.

NONFICTION Needs how-to, interview, new product, personal experience, travel, health care. No descriptive, run-of-the-mill travel articles. **Buys 100 mss/year.** Query. Length: 840-1,400 words. **Pays $250-400.**

PHOTOS State availability. Identification of subjects required. Reviews contact sheets, negatives, transparencies, prints. Offers $50/photo. Buys all rights.

TIPS "Make recommendations in your articles. We want first-hand accounts. Tell us how to do things: how to catch a cab, order a meal, buy a souvenir, buy property, start a business, etc. *International Living*'s philosophy is that the world is full of opportunities to do whatever you want, whenever you want. We will show you how."

$$$$ ISLANDS

Bonnier Corp., 460 N. Orlando Ave., Suite 200, Winter Park FL 32789. **E-mail:** editor@islands.com. **Website:** www.islands.com. **80% freelance written.** Magazine published 8 times/year. "We cover accessible and once-in-a-lifetime islands from many different perspectives: travel, culture, lifestyle. We ask our authors to give us the essence of the island and do it with literary flair." Estab. 1981. Circ. 250,000. Byline given. Pays on publication. Offers 25% kill fee. Publishes ms an average of 8 months after acceptance. Accepts queries by mail, e-mail. Accepts simultaneous submissions. Responds in 2 months to queries; in 6 weeks to mss. Sample copy: $6. Writer's guidelines by e-mail.

NONFICTION Needs book excerpts, essays, general interest, interview, photo feature, travel, service shorts, island-related material. **Buys 25 feature mss/year.** Send complete ms. Length: 2,000-4,000 words. **Pays $750-2,500.** Pays expenses of writers on assignment.

PHOTOS "Fine color photography is a special attraction of *Islands*, and we look for superb composition, technical quality, and editorial applicability. Will not accept or be responsible for unsolicited images or artwork."

COLUMNS Discovers section (island related news), 100-250 words; Taste (island cuisine), 900-1,000 words; Travel Tales (personal essay), 900-1,100 words; Live the Life (island expat Q&A). Query with published clips. **Pays $25-1,000.**

$$$ MOTORHOME

2750 Park View Court, Suite 240, Oxnard CA 93036. **E-mail:** info@motorhomemagazine.com. **Website:** www.motorhome.com. **Contact:** Eileen Hubbard, editor. **60% freelance written.** Monthly magazine covering topics for RV enthusiasts. "*MotorHome* is a magazine for owners and prospective buyers of motorized recreational vehicles who are active outdoorsmen and wide-ranging travelers. We cover all aspects of the RV lifestyle; editorial material is both technical and nontechnical in nature. Regular features include tests and descriptions of various models of motorhomes, travel adventures, and hobbies pursued in such vehicles, objective analysis of equipment and supplies for such vehicles, and do-it-yourself articles. Guides within the magazine provide listings of manufacturers, rentals, and other sources of equipment and accessories of interest to enthusiasts. Articles must have an RV slant and excellent photography accompanying text." Estab. 1968. Circ. 150,000. Byline given. Pays on acceptance. Offers 30% kill fee. Publishes ms an average of 1 year after acceptance. Editorial lead time 4 months. Submit seasonal material 6 months in advance. Accepts queries by mail. Accepts simultaneous submissions. Responds in 1 month to queries; in 2 months to mss. Guidelines online.

NONFICTION Needs general interest, historical, how-to, humor, interview, new product, personal experience, photo feature, technical. No diaries of RV trips or negative RV experiences. **Buys 120 mss/year.** Query with published clips. Length: 800-2,500 words. **Pays $400-900.** Pays expenses of writers on assignment.

PHOTOS Digital photography accepted. Captions, identification of subjects, model releases required. Reviews hi-res photos at 300 dpi. Offers no additional payment for art accepted with ms. Pays $500 for covers. Buys first North American rights.

COLUMNS Crossroads (offbeat briefs of people, places, and events of interest to travelers), 100-200 words; Keepers (tips, resources). Query with published clips, or send complete ms. **Pays $100.**

TIPS "If a freelancer has an idea for a good article, it's best to send a query and include possible photo locations to illustrate the article. We prefer to assign articles and work with the author in developing a piece suitable to our audience. We are in a specialized field with very enthusiastic readers who appreciate articles by authors who actually enjoy motor homes."

PATHFINDERS

6325 Germantown Ave., Philadelphia PA 19144. (215)438-2140. **Fax:** (215)438-2144. **E-mail:** editors@pathfinderstravel.com; info@pathfinderstravel.com. **Website:** www.pathfinderstravel.com. **75% freelance written.** Bimonthly magazine covering travel for people of color, primarily African-Americans. We look for lively, original, well-written stories that provide a good sense of place, with useful information and fresh ideas about travel and the travel industry. Our main audience is African-Americans, though we do look for articles relating to other persons of color: Native Americans, Hispanics and Asians. Pathfinders Travel Magazine for People of Color is is published quarterly. The magazine, which enjoys a circulation of 100,000 copies, reaches an affluent audience of African American travelers interested in enjoying the good life. Pathfinders tells readers where to go, what to do, where to dine and how to `get there from a cultural perspective. Pathfinders covers domestic and international destinations. The slick, glossy, color magazine is available nationally in Barnes & Nobel, Crown, Borders, Hastings and other independent book stores. Estab. 1997. Circ. 100,000. Byline given. Pays on publication. Accepts queries by mail, e-mail. Accepts simultaneous submissions. Responds in 1 month to queries. Responds in 2 months to mss. Sample copy at bookstores (Barnes & Noble). Guidelines available online.

NONFICTION Needs essays, historical, how-to, personal experience, photo feature, travel. "No more pitches on Jamaica. We get these all the time." **Buys 16-20 mss/year.** Send complete ms. Length: 800-1,000 words for features. **Pays $150.** Pays expenses of writers on assignment.

PHOTOS State availability.

COLUMNS Chef's Table, Post Cards from Home; Looking Back; City of the Month, 500-600 words. Send complete ms. **Pays $150.**

TIPS We prefer seeing finished articles rather than queries. All articles are submitted on spec. Articles should be saved in either WordPerfect or Microsoft Word, double-spaced and saved as a text-only file. Include a hard copy. E-mail articles are accepted only by request of the editor. No historical articles.

PORTHOLE CRUISE MAGAZINE

Panoff Publishing, 4517 NW 31st Ave., Ft. Lauderdale FL 33309-3403. (954)377-7777. **Fax:** (954)377-7000. **E-mail:** editorial@ppigroup.com. **Website:** www.porthole.com. **Contact:** Bill Panoff, publisher/editor-in-chief. **70% freelance written.** Bimonthly magazine covering the cruise industry. *Porthole Cruise Magazine* entices its readers to take a cruise vacation by delivering information that is timely, accurate, colorful, and entertaining. Estab. 1992. Circ. 80,000. Byline given. Pays on publication. Offers 20% kill fee. Publishes ms an average of 6 months after acceptance. Editorial lead time 8 months. Submit seasonal material 5 months in advance. Accepts queries by e-mail. Accepts simultaneous submissions. Guidelines available online.

NONFICTION Needs general interest, cruise related, historical, how-to, pick a cruise, not get seasick, travel tips, humor, interview, crew on board or industry executives, new product, personal experience, photo feature, travel, off-the-beaten-path, adventure, ports, destinations, cruises, onboard fashion, spa articles, duty-free shopping, port shopping, ship reviews. No articles on destinations that can't be reached by ship. **Buys 60 mss/year.** Length: 1,000-1,200 words. **Pays $500-600 for assigned feature articles.**

PHOTOS Contact: Linda Douthat, creative director. State availability. Captions, identification of subjects, model releases required. Reviews digital images and original transparencies. Rates available upon request to ldouthat@ppigroup.com. Buys one-time rights.

RECREATION NEWS

Official Publication of the GovEmployee.com, 2699 Bay Dr., Sparrows Point MD 21219. (410)944-4852. **Fax:** (410)638-6902. **E-mail:** editor@recreationnews.com. **Website:** www.recreationnews.com. **Contact:** Marvin Bond, editor. **75% freelance written.** Monthly guide to leisure-time activities for federal and private industry workers covering Mid-Atlantic travel destinations, outdoor recreation, and cultural activities. Estab. 1982. Circ. 115,000. Byline given. Pays on publication. No kill fee. Publishes ms an average of 3 months after acceptance. Submit seasonal material 10 months in advance. Accepts queries by mail, e-mail, phone. Accepts simultaneous submissions. Responds in 2 months to queries. See sample copy and writer's guidelines online.

NONFICTION Needs travel. No reviews/critiques or material outside of Mid-Atlantic region. Query with published clips or links. Length: 600-1,000 words. **Pays $50-300.**

REPRINTS Send tearsheet or typed ms with rights for sale noted and information about when and where the material previously appeared. Pays $50.

TIPS "Our articles are lively and conversational and deal with specific travel destinations in the Mid-Atlantic. We do not buy international or Caribbean stories. Outdoor recreation of all kinds is good, but avoid first-person narrative. Stories need to include info on nearby places of interest, places to eat, and places to stay. Keep contact information in separate box at end of story."

❾❸❸ TIMES OF THE ISLANDS

Times Publications, Ltd., P.O. Box 234, Lucille Lightbourne Bldg., #1, Providenciales Turks & Caicos Islands British West Indies. (649)946-4788. **Fax:** (649)946-4788. **E-mail:** timespub@tciway.tc. **Website:** www.timespub.tc. **60% freelance written.** Quarterly magazine covering the Turks & Caicos Islands. "*Times of the Islands* is used by the public and private sector to inform visitors and potential investors/developers about the Islands. It goes beyond a superficial overview of tourist attractions with in-depth articles about natural history, island heritage, local personalities, new development, offshore finance, sporting activities, visitors' experiences, and Caribbean fiction." Estab. 1988. Circ. 10,000. Byline given. Pays on publication. No kill fee. Publishes ms an average of 6 months after acceptance. Editorial lead time 4 months. Submit seasonal material at least 4 months in advance. Accepts queries by e-mail. Accepts simultaneous submissions. Responds in 6 weeks to queries. Responds in 2 months to mss. Sample copy for $6. Guidelines available online.

NONFICTION Needs book excerpts, essays, general interest, historical, humor, inspirational, interview, nostalgic, personal experience, photo feature, profile, technical, travel, book reviews, nature, ecology, business (offshore finance), watersports. **Buys 20 mss/year.** Query. Length: 500-3,000 words. **Pays $150-500.**

REPRINTS Send photocopy and information about when and where the material previously appeared. Payment varies

PHOTOS Send photos. Identification of subjects required. Reviews digital photos. Pays $15-150/photo.

COLUMNS On Holiday (unique experiences of visitors to Turks & Caicos), 500-1,500 words. **Buys 4 mss/year. mss/year.** Query. **Pays $150.**

FICTION Needs adventure, ethnic, historical, humorous, novel excerpts, slice-of-life vignettes. **Buys 1 mss/year.** Query. Length: 1,000-3,000 words. **Pays $250-400.**

TIPS "Make sure that the query/article specifically relates to the Turks and Caicos Islands. The theme can be general (ecotourism, for instance), but the manuscript should contain specific and current references to the Islands. We're a high-quality magazine, with a small budget and staff, and are very open-minded to ideas (and manuscripts). Writers who have visited the Islands at least once would probably have a better perspective from which to write."

❸❸ TRAILER LIFE

GS Media & Events, 2750 Park View Ct, Suite 240, Oxnard CA 93036. **Fax:** (805)667-4484. **E-mail:** info@trailerlife.com. **Website:** www.trailerlife.com. Managing Editor: Donya Carlson. **Contact:** Valerie Law, editor. **40% freelance written.** Monthly magazine and website covering the RV-camping lifestyle including recreational vehicles, RV travel, RV upgrades and maintenance, outdoor recreation and activities, and RV campgrounds. "*Trailer Life* is written for active people who enjoy travel and recreation with their RV. Every issue includes recreational vehicle and product tests, travel articles, and other features ranging from lifestyle to vehicle maintenance." Estab. 1941. Circ. 270,000. Byline given. Pays on acceptance. Offers kill fee. Offers 30% kill fee for assigned articles that are not acceptable. Publishes ms an average of 6 months after acceptance. Editorial lead time 4 months. Submit seasonal material 6 months in advance. Accepts queries by mail. Accepts simultaneous submissions. Responds in 2 months. Sample copy free. Guidelines online.

NONFICTION Needs book excerpts, historical, how-to, humor, new product, opinion, personal experience, profile, technical, travel. "Nothing without an RV hook." **Buys 75 mss/year.** Email query. Length: Travel Features: 1,500-2,200 words; Technical Features: 1,000-2,000 words; Do-It-Yourself Features: 1,200 words. **Pays $100-700.** Pays expenses of writers on assignment.

PHOTOS Send photos. Identification of subjects, model releases required for covers. Negotiated upon assignment. Buys one-time print and electronic rights.

COLUMNS Around the Bend (news, trends of interest to RVers), 75-100 words; "10-Minute Tech" (technical RV tips) 50-200 words. **Buys 70 mss/year.** Email query or send complete ms **Pays $75-250.**

TIPS "Prerequisite: Articles must have an RV focus, and digital photos must be magazine quality. These are the two biggest reasons why articles are rejected. Readers are travel and outdoor enthusiasts who own RVs (primarily travel trailers, fifth-wheels, toy haulers, tent campers, teardrop trailers and truck campers) in which they explore North America and embrace the great outdoors in national and state parks and commercial RV campgrounds. They're are an active and adventurous community."

$ TRANSITIONS ABROAD PUBLISHING

P.O. Box 1369, Amherst MA 01004-1369. (413)992-6486. **E-mail:** webeditorial@transitionsabroad.com. **Website:** www.transitionsabroad.com. **Contact:** Gregory Hubbs, editor-in-chief. **70-90% freelance written.** Online resource for educational travel with a strong work-teaching-intern-volunteer component. Long-term, independent, budget, and cultural immersion travel are also covered. The underlying focus is on enriching, informed, affordable, and transformational travel. For over 40 years, Transitions Abroad magazine has been the only travel publication and website dedicated to work, study, volunteering, and living abroad. Its purpose is the dissemination of practical information leading to a greater understanding of other cultures through direct participation in the daily life of the host community. Estab. 1977. Circ. 8,000,000 visitors per year. Byline given. Pays before publication. No kill fee. Accepts queries by e-mail. Accepts simultaneous submissions. Responds in 1-2 weeks to queries and mss if interested. Guidelines online.

NONFICTION Needs book excerpts, travel. **Buys 300-1,000 unsolicited mss/year.** "Submit online. Attach only Microsoft Word documents or Google docs. Send digital photos as attachments or ideally point to them on the Cloud. Include contact info." Length: 800-2,000 words. **Pays $50-150/piece. Average: $100. Regular columnist pay per negotiation. Contests: Hosts 3 different writing contests per year, with winner paid $500; 2nd Place, $150; 3rd Place, $100.**

PHOTOS Send photos with submission. Captions, identification of subjects preferred.

COLUMNS Working Traveler (how to find jobs and what to expect, including short-term jobs, teaching English, volunteering, internships, and international careers); Living Abroad (expatriate advice and participant reports); Worldwide Travel Bargains (destinations, activities, and accommodations for budget travelers); Study Abroad and Educational Travel (for teens to college through seniors); Activity Vacations (travel opportunities that involve action and learning, usually by direct involvement in host culture); Responsible Travel (information on community-organized tours). **Buys 100-200 mss/year mss/year.** Send complete ms. **Pays $50-150; negotiable up for very experienced published freelancers.**

TIPS "We like practical yet inspirational information, especially on how to work, live, study, travel and cut costs abroad in order to facilitate cultural immersion. Our readers want usable information on planning a travel itinerary as well as info on work, study, living, and volunteering abroad. Be specific with links to websites. We are very interested in educational, long-term travel, and study abroad for teens to college students to adults to senior citizens."

$$$$ TRAVEL + LEISURE

American Express Publishing Corp., 1120 Avenue of the Americas, 9th Floor, New York NY 10036. (212)382-5600. **Website:** www.travelandleisure.com. **Contact:** Laura Teusink, managing editor. **95% freelance written.** *Travel + Leisure* is a monthly magazine edited for affluent travelers. It explores the latest resorts, hotels, fashions, foods, and drinks, as well as political, cultural, and economic issues affecting travelers. Circ. 950,000. Byline given. Pays on acceptance. Offers 25% kill fee. Accepts queries by mail, online submission form. Accepts simultaneous submissions. Responds in 6 weeks to queries and mss. Sample copy for $5.50 from (800)888-8728. Guidelines available online.

NONFICTION Needs travel. **Buys 40-50 feature (3,000-5,000 words) and 200 short (125-500 words) mss/year.** Query online or by postal mail. An online query will receive a faster response. Editors are looking for a compelling reason to assign an article: a specific angle, news that makes the subject fresh, a writer's enthusiasm for and familiarity with the topic. **Pays $4,000-6,000/feature; $100-500/short piece.** Pays expenses of writers on assignment.

PHOTOS **Contact:** Photo Dept. Discourages submission of unsolicited transparencies. Captions required. Payment varies. Buys one time rights.

COLUMNS Length: 2,500-3,500 words. **Buys 125-150 mss/year. Pays $2,000-3,500.**

TIPS "Queries should not be generic, but should specify what is new or previously uncovered in a destination or travel-related subject area."

$ TRAVEL SMART

Communications House, Inc., P.O. Box 397, Dobbs Ferry NY 10522. (800)327-3633. **E-mail:** travelsmartnow@aol.com. **Website:** www.travelsmartnewsletter.com. Monthly newsletter covering information on good-value travel. Estab. 1976. Circ. 20,000. Pays on publication. No kill fee. Accepts queries by mail, e-mail. Responds in 6 weeks to queries. Responds in 6 weeks to mss. Sample copy and guidelines for SAE with 9x12 envelope and 3 first-class stamps.

NONFICTION Query. Length: 100-1,500 words. **Pays $150 maximum.**

TIPS When you travel, check out small hotels offering good prices, good restaurants, and send us brief rundown (with prices, phone numbers, addresses). Information must be current. Include your phone number with submission, because we sometimes make immediate assignments.

[C] $ $ VERGE MAGAZINE

Verge Magazine Inc., P.O. Box 147, Peterborough ON K9J 6Y5 Canada. **E-mail:** contributing@vergemagazine.ca. **Website:** www.vergemagazine.com. **Contact:** Jessica Lockhart, contributing editor. **60% freelance written.** Quarterly magazine. "Each issue takes you around the world, with people who are doing something different and making a difference doing it. This is the magazine resource for those wanting to volunteer, work, study or adventure overseas." "*Verge* is the magazine for people who travel with purpose. It explores ways to get out and see the world by volunteering, working, and studying overseas. Our readers are typically young (17-40 years), or young at heart, active, independent travelers. Editorial content is intended to inform and motivate the reader by profiling unique individuals and experiences that are timely and socially relevant. We look for articles that are issue driven and combine an engaging and well-told story with nuts and bolts how-to information. Wherever possible and applicable, efforts should be made to provide sources where readers can find out more about the subject, or ways in which readers can become involved in the issue covered." Estab. 2002. Circ. 10,000. Byline given. Pays on publication. No kill fee. Publishes ms an average of 6 months after acceptance. Submit seasonal material 8-12 months in advance. Accepts queries by mail, e-mail. Accepts simultaneous submissions. Responds in 8 weeks to queries. Responds in 2 months to mss. Sample copy for $6, plus shipping. Guidelines available online.

NONFICTION Needs how-to, humor, interview. "We do not want pure travelogues, predictable tourist experiences, luxury travel, stories highighting a specific company, or organisation." **Buys 30-40 mss/year.** Send complete ms. Length: 800-2,500 words. **Pays $0.10 (CAD) per word to first-time contributors.** Pays expenses of writers on assignment.

PHOTOS Send link to online portfolio to contributing@vergemagazine.com or mail portfolio on CD or DVD to *Verge Magazine*. Captions required. Reviews GIF/JPEG files. Negotiates payment individually.

COLUMNS **Buys 20-30 mss/year.** Query with published clips. **Pays $0.10 (CAD) per word to first-time contributors.**

TIPS "Writers should read the guidelines and tell us which department their query fits best. Refer to travel undertaken in the past year if possible."

WOMEN'S

$ $ $ BRIDAL GUIDE

RFP, LLC, 228 E. 45th St., 11th Floor, New York NY 10017. (212)838-7733; (800)472-7744. **Fax:** (212)308-7165. **E-mail:** editorial@bridalguide.com. **Website:** www.bridalguide.com. **20% freelance written.** Bimonthly magazine covering relationships, sexuality, fitness, wedding planning, psychology, finance, and travel. Only works with experienced/published writers. Pays on acceptance. No kill fee. Accepts queries by mail. Responds in 3 months to queries and mss. Sample copy for $5 and SAE with 4 first-class stamps. Guidelines available.

NONFICTION "Please do not send queries concerning beauty, fashion, or home design stories since we produce them in-house. We do not accept personal wedding essays, fiction, or poetry. Address travel queries to travel editor. All correspondence accompanied by an SASE will be answered." **Buys 100 mss/year.** Query with published clips from national consumer magazines. Length: 1,000-2,000 words. **Pays 50¢/word.**

PHOTOS Photography and illustration submissions should be sent to the art department.

TIPS "We are looking for service-oriented, well-researched pieces that are journalistically written. Writers we work with use at least 3 top expert sources, such as physicians, book authors, and business people in the appropriate field. Our tone is conversational, yet authoritative. Features are also generally filled with real-life anecdotes. We also do features that are completely real-person based—such as roundtables of bridesmaids discussing their experiences, or grooms-to-be talking about their feelings about getting married. In queries, we are looking for a well-thought-out idea, the specific angle of focus the writer intends to take, and the sources he or she intends to use. Queries should be brief and snappy—and titles should be supplied to give the editor an even better idea of the direction the writer is going in."

❂❸❸❸❸ CHATELAINE

1 Mount Pleasant Rd., 8th Floor, Toronto ON M4Y 2Y5 Canada. (416)764-2000. **Fax:** (416)764-1888. **E-mail:** storyideas@chatelaine.rogers.com; brendan. fisher@chatelaine.rogers.com. **Website:** www.chatelaine.com. **Contact:** Laura Brown, managing editor; Brendan Fisher, deputy art director. Monthly magazine covering Canadian women's lifestyles. "*Chatelaine* is edited for Canadian women ages 25-49, their changing attitudes and lifestyles. Key editorial ingredients include health, finance, social issues, and trends, as well as fashion, beauty, food, and home décor. Regular departments include Health pages, Entertainment, Money, Home, Humour, and How-to." Byline given. Pays on acceptance. Offers 25-50% kill fee. Accepts queries by e-mail. Accepts simultane-

ous submissions. Responds in 2 months to queries. Guidelines online.

NONFICTION Query with published clips. **Pays $1/word.** Pays expenses of writers on assignment.

ESSENCE

225 Liberty Street, 9th Flor, New York NY 10048. **Website:** www.essence.com. Monthly magazine. *Essence* is the magazine for today's black women. Edited for career-minded, sophisticated, and independent achievers, *Essence*'s editorial is dedicated to helping its readers attain their maximum potential in various lifestyles and roles. The editorial content includes career and educational opportunities, fashion and beauty, investing and money management, health and fitness, parenting, information on home decorating and food, travel, cultural reviews, and profiles of achievers and celebrities. Estab. 1970. Circ. 1 million. Byline given. Pays on acceptance. Offers 25% kill fee. Editorial lead time 6 months. Submit seasonal material 6 months in advance. Accepts queries by mail, fax. Accepts simultaneous submissions. Responds in 2 months to queries; in 2 months to mss. Sample copy: $3.25. Guidelines available online.

NONFICTION Needs book excerpts. **Buys 200 mss/year.** Query with published clips. Address to specific editor. Departments include Arts and Entertainment; Books and Poetry; Beauty and Style; Health, Relationships, and Food; Personal Essays; News; Money and Power; Feature Articles/Personal Growth. See online guidelines for specific editors. Length is given upon assignment. **Pays competitive rate.** Pays expenses of writers on assignment.

REPRINTS Send tearsheet and information about when and where the material previously appeared. Pays 50% of the amount paid for the original article.

PHOTOS "Would like to see photographs for our travel section that feature Black travelers". State availability. Model releases required. Pays $200 minimum depending on the size of the image.

❂❸❸❸❸ FLARE MAGAZINE

Rogers Communications, One Mt. Pleasant Rd., 8th Floor, Toronto ON M4Y 2Y5 Canada. (416)764-1829. **Fax:** (416)764-2866. **E-mail:** editors@flare.com. **Website:** www.flare.com. **Contact:** Miranda Purves, editor. Monthly magazine for women ages 17-35. Byline given. Offers 50% kill fee. Accepts queries by e-mail. Response time varies. Sample copy for #10 SASE.

Guidelines available online at www.flare.com/about/writers-guidelines.

NONFICTION **Buys 24 mss/year.** Query. Length: 200-1,200 words. **Pays $1/word.** Pays expenses of writers on assignment.

TIPS Study our masthead to determine if your topic is handled by regular contributing staff or a staff member.

$$$$ GLAMOUR

Condé Nast, 4 Times Square, 16th Floor, New York NY 10036. (212)286-2860. **Fax:** (212)286-8336. **Website:** www.glamour.com. **Contact:** Cyndi Leive, editor-in-chief. Monthly magazine covering subjects ranging from fashion, beauty, health, personal relationships, career, travel, food, and entertainment. *Glamour* is edited for the contemporary woman. It informs her of current trends, recommends how she can adapt them to her needs, and motivates her to take action. Estab. 1939. Circ. 2.3 million. No kill fee. Accepts queries by mail. Accepts simultaneous submissions.

NONFICTION Needs personal experience, travel. Pays expenses of writers on assignment.

PHOTOS Only uses professional photographers.

$$$$ LADIES' HOME JOURNAL

Meredith Corp., P.O.Box 37508, Boone IA 50037. 212-499-2087. **E-mail:** lhjcustserv@cdsfulfillment.com. **Website:** www.divinecaroline.com/ladies-home-journal. **50% freelance written.** Monthly magazine focusing on issues of concern to women 30-45. *Ladies' Home Journal* is for active, empowered women who are evolving in new directions. It addresses informational needs with highly focused features and articles on a variety of topics: self, style, family, home, world, health, and food. Estab. 1882. Circ. 4.1 million. Pays on acceptance. Offers 25% kill fee. Publishes ms an average of 4-12 months after acceptance. Editorial lead time 4 months. Accepts queries by mail, e-mail. Accepts simultaneous submissions. Responds in 3 months to queries. Guidelines available online.

NONFICTION Send 1-2 page query, SASE, résumé, and clips via mail or e-mail (preferred). Length: 2,000-3,000 words. **Pays $2,000-4,000.** Pays expenses of writers on assignment.

PHOTOS *LHJ* arranges for its own photography almost all the time. State availability. Captions, identification of subjects, model releases required. Offers variable payment for photos accepted with ms. Rights bought vary with submission.

FICTION Only short stories and novels submitted by an agent or publisher will be considered. No poetry of any kind. **Buys 12 mss/year.** Send complete ms. Length: 2,000-2,500 words.

$$ LONG ISLAND WOMAN

P.O. Box 176, Malverne NY 11565. **E-mail:** editor@liwomanonline.com. **Website:** www.liwomanonline.com. **20% freelance written.** Monthly magazine covering issues of importance to women (age 45-69) in Nassau and Suffolk counties in New York—health, finance, arts, entertainment, fitness, travel, home. Estab. 2001. Circ. 30,000. Byline given. Pays within 1 month of publication. Offers 20% kill fee. Publishes an average of 3 months after acceptance. Editorial lead time 3 months. Submit seasonal material 3 months in advance. Accepts queries by e-mail. Accepts simultaneous submissions. Auto response and response when/if interested. Sample copy for $5. Guidelines online.

NONFICTION Needs essays, humor, interview, memoir, nostalgic, travel. **Buys 12-15 mss/year.** Send complete ms. Length: 600-2,250 words. **Pays $70-200.**

REPRINTS Length: 500-2,250 words. Pays $40-100.

PHOTOS State availability of or send photos. Captions, identification of subjects, model releases required.

COLUMNS Humor; Health Issues; Adult Family Issues; Financial and Business Issues; Book Reviews and Books; Arts and Entertainment; Travel and Leisure; Home and Garden; Fitness.

$$$$ MS. MAGAZINE

433 S. Beverly Dr., Beverly Hills CA 90212. (310)556-2515. **Fax:** (310)556-2514. **E-mail:** shallett@msmagazine.com. **Website:** www.msmagazine.com. **Contact:** Michele Kort, senior editor. **80-90% freelance written.** Quarterly magazine on women's issues and news. Estab. 1972. Circ. 150,000. Byline given. Offers 25% kill fee. Accepts simultaneous submissions. Responds in 3 months to queries. Responds in 3 months to mss. Sample copy for $9. Guidelines available online.

NONFICTION Does not consider articles on fashion, beauty, fitness, travel, food, or of a "self-help" variety. **Buys 4-5 feature (2,000-3,000 words) and 4-5 short (500 words) mss/year.** Query with published clips and a brief bio. *Ms.* is looking for pieces that use a feminist lens: considers articles on politics, social commentary, popular culture, law, education, art, and the environment. Length: 300-3,500 words. **Pays $1/word; 50¢/word for news stories and book reviews.** Pays expenses of writers on assignment.

COLUMNS Buys 6-10 mss/year. **Pays $1/word.**

FICTION "*Ms.* welcomes the highest-quality original fiction and poetry, but is publishing these infrequently as of late."

🛑🛑 NA'AMAT WOMAN

21515 Vanowen Street, Suite 102, Canoga Park CA 91303. (818)431-2200. **E-mail:** naamat@naamat.org; judith@naamat.org. **Website:** www.naamat.org. **Contact:** Judith Sokoloff, editor. **80% freelance written.** Published 3 times per year, covering Jewish issues/subjects. "Magazine covering a wide variety of subjects of interest to the Jewish community— including political and social issues, arts, profiles; many articles about Israel and women's issues. Fiction must have a Jewish theme. Readers are the American Jewish community." Estab. 1926. Circ. 10,000. Byline given. Pays on publication. No kill fee. Publishes ms an average of 6 months after acceptance. Submit seasonal material 6 months in advance. Accepts queries by e-mail. Accepts simultaneous submissions. Responds in 4 weeks to queries. Responds in 3 months to mss. Sample copy for $2. Guidelines by e-mail.

NONFICTION Needs book excerpts, essays, historical, interview, personal experience, photo feature, travel, Jewish topics & issues, political & social issues & women's issues. **Buys 16-20 mss/year.** Send complete ms. **Pays 10-20¢/word for assigned and unsolicited articles.** Pays expenses of writers on assignment.

PHOTOS State availability. Reviews GIF/JPEG files. Negotiates payment individually. Buys one-time rights.

FICTION "We want serious fiction, with insight, reflection and consciousness." Needs novel excerpts, literary with Jewish content. "We do not want fiction that is mostly dialogue. No corny Jewish humor. No Holocaust fiction." **Buys 1-2 mss/year. mss/year.** Query with published clips or send complete ms. Length: 2,000-3,000 words. **Pays 10-20¢/word for assigned articles and for unsolicited articles.**

TIPS "No maudlin nostalgia or romance; no hackneyed Jewish humor."

💲💲 SKIRT!

Morris Communications, 1 Henrietta St., First Floor, Charleston SC 29403. (843)958-0027. **Fax:** (843)958-0029. **E-mail:** submissions@skirt.com. **Website:** www.skirt.com. **Contact:** Shelley Young, editor. **10 percent freelance written.** Monthly magazine covering women's interest. *Skirt!* is all about women—their work, play, families, creativity, style, health, wealth, bodies, and souls. The magazine's attitude is spirited, independent, outspoken, serious, playful, irreverent, sometimes controversial, and always passionate. Estab. 1994. Circ. 285,000. Byline given. Pays on publication. No kill fee. Publishes ms an average of 2 months after acceptance. Editorial lead time 2 months. Submit seasonal material 2 months in advance. Accepts queries by e-mail. Accepts simultaneous submissions. Responds in 1-2 months. Guidelines online.

NONFICTION Needs essays, personal experience. "Do not send feature articles. We only accept submissions of completed personal essays that will work with our monthly themes available online." **Buys 100+ mss/year.** Send complete ms (preferably as a Rich Text Format attachment) via e-mail. Publishes personal essays on topics related to women and women's interests. Length: 800-1,100 words. **Pays $100-200.**

TIPS "Surprise and charm us. We look for fearless essays that take chances with content and subject. *Skirt!* is not your average women's magazine. We push the envelope and select content that makes our readers think. Please review guidelines and themes online before submitting."

♻💲💲 TODAY'S BRIDE

Family Communications, 65 The East Mall, Toronto ON M8Z SW3 Canada. (416)537-2604. **Fax:** (416)538-1794. **E-mail:** erind@canadianbride.com. **Website:** www.todaysbride.ca; www.canadianbride.com. **20% freelance written.** Semiannual magazine on wedding planning. Magazine provides information to engaged couples on all aspects of wedding planning, including tips, fashion advice, etc. Also contains beauty, home, groom, and honeymoon travel sections. Estab. 1979. Circ. 102,000. Byline given. Pays on acceptance. No kill fee. Editorial lead time 6 months. Accepts queries by mail, e-mail. Accepts simultaneous submissions. Responds in 2 weeks-1 month.

NONFICTION Needs humor, opinion, personal experience. No travel pieces. Send complete ms. Length: 800-1,400 words. **Pays $250-300.**

PHOTOS Send photos. Identification of subjects required. Reviews transparencies, prints. Negotiates payment individually. Rights purchased negotiated on individual basis.

TIPS "Send us tight writing about topics relevant to all brides and grooms. Stories for grooms, especially those written by/about grooms, are also encouraged."

$ TRUE CONFESSIONS

105 E. 34th St., Box 141, New York NY 10016. **E-mail:** shazell@truerenditionsllc.com. **E-mail:** trueswriters@yahoo.com. **Website:** www.truerenditionsllc.com. **Contact:** Samantha Hazell, editor. "*True Confessions* is a women's magazine featuring true-to-life stories about working-class women and their families. The stories must be in first-person and generally deal with family problems, relationship issues, romances, single moms, abuse, and any other realistic issue women face in our society. The stories we look for are true or at least believable. We look for stories that evoke some sort of emotion, be it happiness or sadness, but in the end there needs to be some sort of moral or lesson learned." Pays on last week of the month after publication. Editorial lead time 3 months. Submit seasonal material 6 months in advance. Guidelines available online.

NONFICTION E-mail submissions preferred (trueswriters@yahoo.com). Include contact information and brief synopsis of story. To submit by postal mail, include disk saved in Word, a hard copy, and SASE for return of materials. Length: 3,000-7,000 words. **Pays 3¢/word.** Pays expenses of writers on assignment.

COLUMNS My Man! (about a special man in your life); That's Incredible! (about an experience in your life that reaffirms your faith); The Life I Live (about an inspirational time in your life); My Moment with God (thoughts during a meditative moment, quiet reflection, or prayer); Phenomenal Woman (about a special woman in your life). E-mail submissions preferred (trueswriters@yahoo.com). Include contact information and brief synopsis of story. To submit by postal mail, include disk saved in Word, a hard copy, and SASE for return of materials. **Pays $65-100.**

FICTION "Stories should be written in first person and past tense. We generally look for more serious stories. The underlying theme is overcoming adversities in life. These are supposed to be 'true' stories—or at least stories that could be true!" E-mail submissions preferred (trueswriters@yahoo.com). Include contact

information and brief synopsis of story. To submit by postal mail, include disk saved in Word, a hard copy, and SASE for return of materials. Length: 3,000-7,000 words. **Pays 3¢/word.**

$$$$ VOGUE

Condè Nast, One World Trade Center, New York NY 10007. (212)286-2860. **Website:** www.vogue.com. Monthly magazine. *Vogue* mirrors the changing roles and concerns of women, covering not only evolutions in fashion, beauty and style, but the important issues and ideas of the arts, health care, politics, and world affairs. Estab. 1892. Circ. 1.1 million. Byline sometimes given. Pays on acceptance. Offers 25% kill fee. Accepts simultaneous submissions. Responds in 3 months to queries. Guidelines for #10 SASE.

NONFICTION Query with published clips. 2,500 words maximum. **Pays $1-2/word.** Pays expenses of writers on assignment.

TIPS "Sophisticated, surprising and compelling writing a must. Please note: *Vogue* accepts *very* few unsolicited manuscripts. Most stories are generated in-house and are written by staff."

$$ WOMAN'S LIFE

A Publication of Woman's Life Insurance Society, 1338 Military St., P.O. Box 5020, Port Huron MI 48061-5020. (800)521-9292, ext. 181. **Fax:** (810)985-6970. **E-mail:** website@womanslife.org. **Website:** www.womanslife.org. **Contact:** Karen Deschaine, managing editor. **30% freelance written.** Quarterly magazine published for a primarily female membership to help them care for themselves and their families. Estab. 1892. Circ. 32,000. Byline given. Pays on publication. No kill fee. Publishes ms an average of 1 year after acceptance. Submit seasonal material 6 months in advance. Accepts queries by mail, e-mail, fax. Accepts simultaneous submissions. Responds in 1 year to queries and to mss. Sample copy for SAE with 9X12 envelope and 4 first-class Sample copy available online. Guidelines for #10 SASE.

NONFICTION Buys 4-10 mss/year. Send complete ms. Length: 1,000-2,000 words. **Pays $150-500.** Pays expenses of writers on assignment.

REPRINTS Send tearsheet, photocopy or typed ms with rights for sale noted and information about when and where the material previously appeared. Pays 15% of amount paid for an original article

PHOTOS Only interested in photos included with ms. Identification of subjects, model releases required.

$ WOMEN IN BUSINESS

American Business Women's Association (The ABWA Co., Inc.), 9820 Metcalf Ave., Suite 110, Overland Park KS 66212. (913)732-5100. **Fax:** (913)660-0101. **E-mail:** abwa@abwa.org; rstreet@abwa.org. **Website:** www.abwa.org. **Contact:** Rene Street, executive director. **30% freelance written.** Bimonthly magazine covering issues affecting working women. "How-to features for career women on business trends, small-business ownership, self-improvement, and retirement issues. Profiles business women." Estab. 1949. Circ. 45,000. Byline given. Pays on acceptance. No kill fee. Publishes ms an average of 3 months after acceptance. Editorial lead time 3 months. Accepts queries by mail, e-mail, fax. Accepts simultaneous submissions. Responds in 3 weeks to queries. Responds in 2 months to mss. Sample copy for SAE with 9x12 envelope and 4 first-class stamps. Guidelines for #10 SASE.

NONFICTION Needs how-to. No fiction or poetry. **Buys 3% of submitted. mss/year.** Query. Length: 500-1,000 words. **Pays $100/500 words.** Pays expenses of writers on assignment.

PHOTOS State availability. Identification of subjects required. Reviews prints. Offers no additional payment for photos accepted with ms. Buys all rights.

COLUMNS Life After Business (concerns of retired business women); It's Your Business (entrepreneurial advice for business owners); Health Spot (health issues that affect women in the work place). Length: 500-750 words. Query. **Pays $100/500 words.**

TRADE JOURNALS

Many writers who pick up *Writer's Market* for the first time do so with the hope of selling an article to one of the popular, high-profile consumer magazines found on newsstands and in bookstores. Many of those writers are surprised to find an entire world of magazine publishing exists outside the realm of commercial magazines—trade journals. Writers who *have* discovered trade journals have found a market that offers the chance to publish regularly in subject areas they find interesting, editors who are typically more accessible than their commercial counterparts, and pay rates that rival those of the big-name magazines.

Trade journal is the general term for any publication focusing on a particular occupation or industry. Other terms used to describe the different types of trade publications are business, technical, and professional journals. They are read by truck drivers, bricklayers, farmers, fishermen, heart surgeons, and just about everyone else working in a trade or profession. Trade periodicals are sharply angled to the specifics of the professions on which they report. They offer business-related news, features, and service articles that will foster their readers' professional development.

Writers for trade journals have to either possess knowledge about the field in question or be able to report it accurately from interviews with those who do. Writers who have or can develop a good grasp of a specialized body of knowledge will find trade magazine editors who are eager to hear from them.

An ideal way to begin your foray into trade journals is to write for those that report on your present profession. If you don't have experience in a profession but can demonstrate an ability to understand (and write about) the intricacies and issues of a particular trade that interests you, editors will still be willing to hear from you.

TRADE JOURNALS

ADVERTISING, MARKETING & PR

$ DECA DIRECT

1908 Association Dr., Reston VA 20191. (703)860-5000. **E-mail:** info@deca.org. **E-mail:** christopher_young@deca.org. **Website:** www.decadirect.org. **Contact:** Christopher Young, editor in chief. **30% freelance written.** Quarterly magazine covering marketing, professional development, business, and career training during school year (no issues published May-August). *DECA Direct* is the membership magazine for DECA—The Association of Marketing Students, primarily ages 15-19 in all 50 states, the U.S. territories, Germany, and Canada. The magazine is delivered through the classroom. Students are interested in developing professional, leadership, and career skills. Estab. 1947. Circ. 160,000. Byline given. Pays on publication. No kill fee. Editorial lead time 3 months. Submit seasonal material 4 months in advance. Accepts queries by e-mail. Accepts simultaneous submissions. Sample copy free online.

NONFICTION Needs essays, general interest, how-to, interview, personal experience. **Buys 10 mss/year.** Submit a paragraph description of your article by e-mail. Length: 500-1,000 words. **Pays $125 for assigned articles. Pays $100 for unsolicited articles.** Pays expenses of writers on assignment.

REPRINTS Send typed ms and information about when and where the material previously appeared. Pays 85% of amount paid for an original article.

COLUMNS Professional Development; Leadership, 500-1,000 words. **Buys 6 mss/year.** Send complete ms. **Pays $75-100.**

$ FORMAT MAGAZINE

315 5th Ave. NW, St. Paul MN 55112. **Website:** www.formatmag.com. **90% freelance written.** Estab. 1954. Circ. 6,000. Byline given. Pays on publication. No kill fee. Editorial lead time 1 months. Accepts simultaneous submissions.

NONFICTION Needs general interest, historical, humor, interview, photo feature. **Buys 2 mss/year.** Length: 300-800 words. **Pays $25-50.**

COLUMNS Advertising (ad humor), 400 words. **Buys 12 mss/year. Pays $25-50.**

FILLERS Needs anecdotes, facts, gags, newsbreaks, short humor. **Buys 12 mss/year.** Length: 100-300 words. **Pays $10-25.**

💲💲💲 INCENTIVE

Northstar Travel Media LLC, 100 Lighting Way, Secaucus NJ 07094. (646)380-6247; (646)380-6251. E-mail: valonzo@ntmllc.com; apalmer@successful-meetings.com. **Website:** www.incentivemag.com. **Contact:** Vincent Alonzo, editor in chief; Alex Palmer, managing editor. Monthly magazine covering sales promotion and employee motivation: managing and marketing through motivation. Estab. 1905. Circ. 41,000. Byline given. Pays on acceptance. No kill fee. Publishes ms an average of 3 months after acceptance. Accepts queries by mail, e-mail. Accepts simultaneous submissions. Responds in 1 month to queries; in 2 months to mss. Sample copy for SAE with 9x12 envelope.

NONFICTION Needs general interest, how-to, interview, travel, corporate case studies. **Buys 48 mss/year.** Query with published clips. Length: 1,000-2,000 words. **Pays $250-700 for assigned articles. Does not pay for unsolicited articles.** Pays expenses of writers on assignment.

REPRINTS Send tearsheet and information about when and where the material previously appeared. Pays 50% of the amount paid for an original article.

💲💲 MIDWEST MEETINGS®

Hennen Publishing, 302 Sixth St. W., Suite A, Brookings SD 57006. (605)692-9559. **Fax:** (605)692-9031. **E-mail:** info@midwestmeetings.com; editor@midwestmeetings.com. **Website:** www.midwestmeetings.com. **Contact:** Randy Hennen. **20% freelance written.** Quarterly magazine covering meetings/conventions industry. "We provide information and resources to meeting/convention planners with a Midwest focus." Estab. 1996. Circ. 28,500. Byline given. Pays on acceptance. Publishes ms an average of 5 months after acceptance. Editorial lead time 3 months. Submit seasonal material 3 months in advance. Accepts queries by e-mail. Accepts simultaneous submissions. Sample copy free. Guidelines by e-mail.

NONFICTION Needs essays, general interest, historical, how-to, humor, interview, personal experience, travel. Does not want marketing pieces related to specific hotels/meeting facilities. **Buys 15-20 mss/year.** Send complete ms. Length: 500-1,000 words. **Pays 5-50¢/word.** Pays expenses of writers on assignment.

💲💲 PROMO MAGAZINE

Access Intelligence, 761 Main Avenue, Norwalk CT 06851. (203)899-8442. **E-mail:** podell@accessintel.com. **Website:** www.chiefmarketer.com/promotional-marketing. **Contact:** Patricia Odell, senior editor. **5% freelance written.** Monthly magazine covering promotion marketing. *Promo* serves marketers, and stories must be informative, well written, and familiar with the subject matter. Estab. 1987. Circ. 25,000. Byline given. Pays on publication. Offers 25% kill fee. Publishes ms an average of 2 months after acceptance. Editorial lead time 3 months. Submit seasonal material 3 months in advance. Accepts simultaneous submissions. Responds in 1 month to queries. Sample copy for $5.

NONFICTION Needs general interest, how-to, interview, new product. No general marketing stories not heavily involved in promotions. Generally does not accept unsolicited mss; query first. **Buys 6-10 mss/year.** Query with published clips. **Pays $1,000 maximum for assigned articles. Pays $500 maximum for unsolicited articles.** Pays expenses of writers on assignment.

💲💲 SIGN BUILDER ILLUSTRATED

Simmons-Boardman Publishing Corp., 55 Broad St., 26th Floor, New York NY 10004. (212)620-7244. **E-mail:** jwooten@sbpub.com; abray@sbpub.com. **Website:** www.signshop.com. **Contact:** Jeff Wooten, editor; Ashley Bray, managing editor. **40% freelance written.** Monthly magazine covering sign and graphic industry. *Sign Builder Illustrated* targets sign professionals where they work: on the shop floor. Topics cover the broadest spectrum of the sign industry, from design to fabrication, installation, maintenance, and repair. Readers own a similarly wide range of shops, including commercial, vinyl, sign erection and maintenance, electrical and neon, architectural, and awnings. Estab. 1987. Circ. 19,000. Byline given. Pays on acceptance. Offers 10% kill fee. Publishes ms an average of 3 months after acceptance. Editorial lead time 3 months. Submit seasonal material 4 months in advance. Accepts queries by mail, e-mail, phone. Accepts simultaneous submissions. Responds in 1 month to queries. Sample copy and writer's guidelines free.

NONFICTION Needs how-to, interview, photo feature, technical. **Buys 50-60 mss/year.** Query. Length: 1,000-1,500 words. **Pays $250-400 for assigned articles.** Pays expenses of writers on assignment.

💲💲 SOCAL MEETINGS + EVENTS MAGAZINE

Tiger Oak Publications, One Tiger Oak Plaza, 900 S. Third St., Minneapolis MN 55415. **Fax:** (612)338-0532. **E-mail:** bobby.hart@tigeroak.com. **Website:** http://meetingsmags.com. **Contact:** Bobby Hart, managing editor. **80% freelance written.** Meetings + Events Media Group, including Minnesota Meetings + Events, Illinois Meetings + Events, Colorado Meetings & Events, Michigan Meetings + Events, California Meetings + Events, Texas Meetings + Events, Northwest Meetings + Events, Mountain Meetings, Pennsylvania Meetings + Evens and New Jersey Meetings + Events is a group of premier quarterly trade magazines for meetings planners and hospitality service providers throughout the US. Thesemagazines aim to report on and promote businesses involved in the meetings and events industry, covering current and emerging trends, people and venues in the meetings and events industry in their respective regions. Estab. 1993. Circ. approximately 20,000 per title. Byline given. Pays on acceptance. Offers 20% kill fee. Publishes ms an average of 4 months after acceptance. Editorial lead time 4-6 months. Submit seasonal material 6 months in advance. Accepts queries by mail. Accepts simultaneous submissions. Responds in 1-2 weeks to queries.

NONFICTION Needs general interest, historical, interview, new product, opinion, personal experience, photo feature, technical, travel. **Buys 30 mss/year.** "Each query should tell us: What the story will be about; how you will tell the story (what sources you will use, how you will conduct research, etc.); why is the story pertinent to the market audience. Please also attach PDFs of 3 published magazine articles." Length: 600-1,500 words. **The average department length story (4-700 words) pays about $2-300 and the average feature length story (1,000-1,200 words) pays up to $800, depending on the story. These rates are not guaranteed and vary.**

COLUMNS Meet + Eat (restaurant reviews); Facility Focus (venue reviews); Regional Spotlight (city review), 1,000 words. **Buys 30 mss/year.** Query with published clips. **Pays $400-600.**

💲💲💲 TEXAS MEETINGS + EVENTS

Tiger Oak Publications, One Tiger Oak Plaza, 900 S. 3rd St., Minneapolis MN 55401. (612)548-3180. **Fax:** (612)548-3181. **E-mail:** bobby.hart@tigeroak.com. **Website:** http://tx.meetingsmags.com. **Contact:** Bobby Hart, managing editor. **80% freelance written.** Quarterly magazine covering meetings and events industry. *Texas Meetings & Events* magazine is the premier trade publication for meetings planners and hospitality service providers in the state. This magazine aims to report on and promote businesses involved in the meetings and events industry. The magazine covers current and emerging trends, people and venues in the meetings and events industry in the state. Estab. 1993. Circ. 20,000. Byline given. Pays on acceptance. Offers 20% kill fee. Publishes ms an average of 4 months after acceptance. Editorial lead time 4-6 months. Submit seasonal material 6 months in advance. Accepts queries by mail. Accepts simultaneous submissions. Responds in 1-2 weeks to queries. Guidelines online.

NONFICTION Needs general interest, historical, interview, new product, opinion, personal experience, photo feature, technical, travel. **Buys 30 mss/year.** Query with published clips of 3 magazine articles. Length: 600-1,500 words. **Pays $400-800.**

COLUMNS Meet + Eat (restaurant reviews); Facility Focus (venue reviews); Regional Spotlight (city review), 1,000 words. **Buys 30 mss/year.** Query with published clips. **Pays $400-600.**

ART, DESIGN & COLLECTIBLES

💲💲 AIRBRUSH ACTION MAGAZINE

Action, Inc., P.O. Box 438, Allenwood NJ 08720. (732)223-7878; (800)876-2472. **E-mail:** ceo@airbrushaction.com. **Website:** www.airbrushaction.com. **Contact:** Cliff Stieglitz, publisher. **80% freelance written.** Bimonthly magazine covering the spectrum of airbrush applications: automotive and custom paint applications, illustration, T-shirt airbrushing, fine art, automotive and sign painting, hobby/craft applications, wall murals, fingernails, temporary tattoos, artist profiles, reviews, and more. Estab. 1985. Circ. 35,000. Byline given. Pays 1 month after publication.

Publishes ms an average of 6 months after acceptance. Editorial lead time 6 months. Submit seasonal material 6 months in advance. Accepts queries by mail, e-mail. Accepts simultaneous submissions.

NONFICTION Needs how-to, humor, inspirational, interview, new product, personal experience, technical. Doesn't want anything unrelated to airbrush. Query with published clips. **Pays 15¢/word.** Pays expenses of writers on assignment.

COLUMNS Query with published clips.

$$ ANTIQUEWEEK

MidCountry Media, 27 N. Jefferson St., P.O. Box 90, Knightstown IN 46148. (800)876-5133, ext. 131. **Fax:** (800)695-8153. **E-mail:** connie@antiqueweek.com. **Website:** www.antiqueweek.com. **Contact:** Connie Swaim, managing editor. **90% freelance written.** Weekly tabloid covering antiques and collectibles with 3 editions: Eastern, Central, and National, plus the monthly *AntiqueWest*. *AntiqueWeek* has a wide range of readership from dealers and auctioneers to collectors, both advanced and novice. Readers demand accurate information presented in an entertaining style. Estab. 1968. Circ. 50,000. Byline given. Pays the month after publication. Offers 10% kill fee or $25. Submit seasonal material 1 month in advance. Accepts queries by e-mail. Accepts simultaneous submissions. Sample copy free. Guidelines by e-mail.

NONFICTION Needs historical, how-to, interview, opinion, personal experience, antique show and auction reports, feature articles on particular types of antiques and collectibles. **Buys 400-500 mss/year.** Query. Length: 1,000-2,000 words. **Pays $50-250.** Pays expenses of writers on assignment.

REPRINTS Send electronic copy with rights for sale noted and information about when and where the material previously appeared.

$ THE APPRAISERS STANDARD

New England Appraisers Association, 6973 Crestridge Dr., Memphis TN 38119. (901)758-2659. **E-mail:** etuten551@aol.com. **Website:** www.newenglandappraisers.org. **Contact:** Edward Tuten, editor. **50% freelance written. Works with a small number of new/unpublished writers each year.** Quarterly publication covering the appraisals of antiques, art, collectibles, jewelry, coins, stamps, and real estate. Estab. 1980. Circ. 1,000. Short bio and byline given. Pays on publication. No kill fee. Publishes ms an average of 1 year after acceptance. Submit seasonal material 2 months in advance. Accepts queries by mail, e-mail. Accepts simultaneous submissions. Responds in 1 month to queries. Responds in 2 months to mss. Sample copy for 9x12 SAE with $1 postage. Guidelines for #10 SASE.

NONFICTION Needs interview, personal experience, technical, travel. Send complete ms. Length: 700 words. **Pays $60.**

REPRINTS "Send typed manuscript with rights for sale noted and information about when and where the material previously appeared."

$$ ART MATERIALS RETAILER

Fahy-Williams Publishing, Inc., 171 Reed St., P.O. Box 1080, Geneva NY 14456. (315)789-0458. **Fax:** (315)789-4263. **E-mail:** tmanzer@fwpi.com. **Website:** www.artmaterialsretailer.com. Publisher: J. Kevin Fahy (kfahy@fwpi.com). **Contact:** Tina Manzer, editorial director. **10% freelance written.** Quarterly magazine covering retail stores that sell art materials. Offers book reviews, retailer-recommended products, and profiles of stores from around the country. Estab. 1998. Byline given. Pays on publication. No kill fee. Editorial lead time 2 months. Submit seasonal material 3 months in advance. Accepts simultaneous submissions. Responds in 3 weeks to queries. Responds in 3 months to mss. Sample copy and writer's guidelines free.

NONFICTION Needs book excerpts, how-to, interview, personal experience. **Buys 2 mss/year.** Send complete ms. Length: 1,500-3,000 words. **Pays $50-250.** Pays expenses of writers on assignment.

FILLERS Needs anecdotes, facts, newsbreaks. **Buys 5 mss/year.** Length: 500-1,500 words. **Pays $50-125.**

$$$ HOW

F+W, a Content + eCommerce Company, 10151 Carver Rd., Suite 300, Blue Ash OH 45242. (513)531-2690. **Fax:** (513)531-2902. **E-mail:** editorial@howdesign.com. **Website:** www.howdesign.com. **75% freelance written.** Bi-monthly magazine covering graphic design profession. *HOW: Design Ideas at Work* strives to serve the business, technological and creative needs of graphic-design professionals. The magazine provides a practical mix of essential business information, up-to-date technological tips, the creative whys and hows behind noteworthy projects, and profiles of professionals who are impacting design. The ultimate goal of *HOW* is to help designers, whether they work for a design firm or for an inhouse design department, run successful, creative, profitable studios. Estab. 1985. Circ. 40,000. Byline given. Pays on acceptance. No kill fee. Accepts simultaneous submissions. Responds in 6 weeks to queries.

NONFICTION Special issues: Self-Promotion Annual (September/October); Business Annual (November/December); In-House Design Annual (January/February); International Annual of Design (March/April); Creativity/Paper/Stock Photography (May/June); Digital Design Annual (July/August). No how-to articles for beginning artists or fine-art-oriented articles. **Buys 40 mss/year.** Query with published clips and samples of subject's work, artwork, or design. Length: 1,500-2,000 words. **Pays $700-900.** Pays expenses of writers on assignment.

COLUMNS Creativity (focuses on creative exercises and inspiration) 1,200-1,500 words. In-House Issues (focuses on business and creativity issues for corporate design groups), 1,200-1,500 words. Business (focuses on business issue for design firm owners), 1,200-1,500 words. **Buys Number of columns: 35. mss/year.** Query with published clips. **Pays $250-400.**

🟢🟢 THE PASTEL JOURNAL

F+W, 10151 Carver Rd., Suite 300, Cincinnati OH 45242. (513)531-2690. **Fax:** (513)891-7153. **E-mail:** pjedit@fwcommunity.com. **Website:** www.pastel-journal.com. **Contact:** Anne Hevener, editor; Jessica Canterbury, managing editor. Bimonthly magazine covering pastel art. *Pastel Journal* is the only national magazine devoted to the medium of pastel. Addressing the working professional as well as passionate amateurs, *Pastel Journal* offers inspiration, information, and instruction to our readers. Estab. 1999. Circ. 22,000. Byline given. Pays on acceptance. Offers 25% kill fee. Publishes ms an average of 3-6 months after acceptance. Editorial lead time 6 months. Submit seasonal material 6 months in advance. Accepts queries by mail, e-mail. Accepts simultaneous submissions. Responds in 4-6 weeks to queries. Guidelines online.

NONFICTION Needs how-to, interview, new product, profile. Does not want articles that aren't art-related. Review magazine before submitting. Query with or without published clips. Length: 500-2,000 words. **Payment does not exceed $600.**

🟢🟢 PRINT

F+W, a Content + eCommerce Company, 10151 Carver Rd., Suite 300, Blue Ash OH 45242. (513)531-2690. **E-mail:** info@printmag.com. **Website:** www.print-

mag.com. **75% freelance written.** Quarterly magazine covering graphic design and visual culture. *PRINT*'s articles, written by design specialists and cultural critics, focus on the social, political and historical context of graphic design, and on the places where consumer culture and popular culture meet. Aims to produce a general interest magazine for professionals with engagingly written text and lavish illustrations. By covering a broad spectrum of topics, both international and local, *Print* tries to demonstrate the significance of design in the world at large. Estab. 1940. Circ. 45,000. Byline given. Pays on acceptance. Offers 25% kill fee. Publishes ms an average of 2 months after acceptance. Editorial lead time 3 months. Submit seasonal material 3 months in advance. Accepts queries by e-mail. Accepts simultaneous submissions. Responds in 2 weeks to queries. Responds in 1 month to mss.

NONFICTION Needs book excerpts, essays, interview, opinion, photo feature, profile, reviews. **Buys 35-40 mss/year.** Query with published clips. Length: 500-3,500 words. **Pays 50¢/word.**

COLUMNS Query with published clips. **Pays 50¢/word.**

🟢🟢 PROFESSIONAL ARTIST

Turnstile Media Group, 1500 Park Center Dr., Orlando FL 32835. (407)563-7000. **Fax:** (407)563-7099. **E-mail:** nhassanein@professionalartistmag.com. **Website:** www.professionalartistmag.com. **Contact:** Nada Hassanein, associate editor. **75% freelance written.** Monthly magazine. *Professional Artist* is dedicated to providing independent visual artists from all backgrounds with the insights, encouragement and business strategies they need to make a living with their artwork. Estab. 1986. Circ. 20,000. Pays on publication. No kill fee. Accepts simultaneous submissions. Sample print copy for $5. Guidelines online.

NONFICTION Needs essays, how-to, interview, cartoons, art law, including pending legislation that affects artists (copyright law, Internet regulations, etc.). Does not run reviews or art historical pieces, nor writing characterized by "critic-speak," philosophical hyperbole, psychological arrogance, politics, or New Age religion. Also, does not condone a get-rich-quick attitude. Send complete ms. **Pays $150-350.**

REPRINTS Send photocopy or typed ms and information about when and where the material previously appeared. Pays $50.

COLUMNS "If an artist or freelancer sends us good articles regularly, and based on results we feel that he is able to produce a column at least 3 times per year, we will invite him to be a contributing writer. If a gifted artist-writer can commit to producing an article on a monthly basis, we will offer him a regular column and the title contributing editor." Send complete ms.

💲💲 WATERCOLOR ARTIST

F+W, a Content + eCommerce Company, 10151 Carver Rd., Suite 200, Blue Ash OH 45242. (513)531-2690. **Fax:** (513)891-7153. **E-mail:** wcamag@fwmedia.com. **Website:** www.watercolorartistmagazine.com. **Contact:** Jennifer Hoffman, art director; Kelly Kane, editor. Bimonthly magazine covering water media arts. Estab. 1984. Circ. 44,000. Byline given. Pays on acceptance. Publishes ms an average of 3-6 months after acceptance. Editorial lead time 6 months. Submit seasonal material 6 months in advance. Accepts queries by mail. Accepts simultaneous submissions. Writer's guidelines available at www.artistsnetwork.com/contactus.

NONFICTION Needs book excerpts, essays, how-to, inspirational, interview, new product, personal experience. Does not want articles that aren't art-related. Review magazine before submitting. **Buys 36 mss/year.** Send query letter with images. Length: 350-2,500 words. **Pays $150-600.** Pays expenses of writers on assignment.

AUTO & TRUCK

💲💲 AUTO RESTORER

i5 Publishing, Inc., 3 Burroughs, Irvine CA 92618. (213)385-2222. **Fax:** (213)385-8565. **E-mail:** tkade@i5publishing.com. **Website:** www.autorestorermagazine.com. **Contact:** Ted Kade, editor. **85% freelance written.** Monthly magazine covering auto restoration. "Our readers own old cars, and they work on them. We help our readers by providing as much practical, how-to information as we can about restoration and old cars." Estab. 1989. Circ. 60,000. Pays on publication. Publishes mss 3 months after acceptance. Submit seasonal material 4 months in advance. Accepts queries by mail, e-mail, fax. Accepts simultaneous submissions. Responds in 2 months to queries. Sample copy: $7. Guidelines free.

NONFICTION Needs how-to, new product, photo feature. **Buys 60 mss/year.** Query first. Length: 250-2,000 words. **Pays $150/published page, including photos and illustrations.** Pays expenses of writers on assignment.

💲💲 BUSINESS FLEET

Bobit Publishing, 3520 Challenger St., Torrance CA 90503. (310)533-2400. **E-mail:** chris.brown@bobit.com. **Website:** www.businessfleet.com. **Contact:** Chris Brown, executive editor. **10% freelance written.** Bimonthly magazine covering businesses which operate 10-50 company vehicles. Estab. 2000. Circ. 100,000. Byline given. Pays on publication. Offers 25% kill fee. Publishes ms an average of 3 months after acceptance. Editorial lead time 2 months. Submit seasonal material 2 months in advance. Accepts queries by mail, e-mail, fax. Accepts simultaneous submissions. Responds in 3 weeks to queries; 2 months to mss. Sample copy and guidelines free.

NONFICTION Needs how-to, interview, new product, personal experience, photo feature, technical. **Buys 16 mss/year.** Query with published clips. Length: 500-2,000 words. **Pays $100-400.** Pays expenses of writers on assignment.

💲💲 FENDERBENDER

DeWitt Publishing, 571 Snelling Avenue North, St. Paul MN 55104. (651)224-6207. **Fax:** (651)224-6212. **E-mail:** news@fenderbender.com; jweyer@fenderbender.com. **Website:** www.fenderbender.com. **Contact:** Jake Weyer, editor. **50% freelance written.** Monthly magazine covering automotive collision repair. Estab. 1999. Circ. 58,000. Byline given. Pays on publication. Offers 20% kill fee. Publishes ms an average of 2 months after acceptance. Editorial lead time 3 months. Submit seasonal material 6 months in advance. Accepts queries by e-mail. Accepts simultaneous submissions. Responds in 1-2 months to queries; 2-3 months to mss. Sample copy for SAE with 10x13 envelope and 6 first-class stamps. Guidelines online.

NONFICTION Needs expose, how-to, inspirational, interview, technical. Does not want personal narratives or any other first-person stories. No poems or creative writing mss. Query with published clips. Length: 1,800-2,500 words. **Pays 25-60¢/word.** Pays expenses of writers on assignment.

COLUMNS Q&A, 600 words; Shakes, Rattles & Rollovers; Rearview Mirror. Query with published clips. **Pays 25-35¢/word.**

💲💲 FLEETSOLUTIONS

NAFA Fleet Management Association, 125 Village Blvd., Suite 200, Princeton NJ 08540. (609)986-1063; (609)720-0882. **Fax:** (609)452-8004. **E-mail:** publications@nafa.org; ddunphy@nafa.org. **Website:** www.nafa.org. **Contact:** Donald W. Dunphy, communications manager/editor. **10% freelance written.** Magazine published 6 times/year covering automotive fleet management. Generally focuses on car, van, and light-duty truck management in US and Canadian corporations, government agencies, and utilities. Editorial emphasis is on general automotive issues; improving jobs skills, productivity, and professionalism; legislation and regulation; alternative fuels; safety; interviews with prominent industry personalities; technology; association news; public service fleet management; and light-duty truck fleet management. Estab. 1957. Circ. 4,000. Bylines provided. Pays on publication. No kill fee. Publishes ms an average of 4 months after acceptance. Editorial lead time 2 months. Accepts queries by mail. Accepts simultaneous submissions. Responds in 1 month to queries. Sample copy online.

NONFICTION Needs interview, technical. **Buys 24 mss/year.** Query with published clips. Length: 500-3,000 words. **Pays $500 maximum.**

💲💲💲💲 OVERDRIVE

Randall-Reilly Publishing, 3200 Rice Mine Rd. NE, Tuscaloosa AL 35406. (205)349-2990. **Fax:** (205)750-8070. **E-mail:** mheine@rrpub.com. **Website:** www.etrucker.com. **Contact:** Max Heine, editorial director. **5% freelance written.** Monthly magazine for independent truckers. Estab. 1961. Circ. 100,000. Byline given. Pays on publication. Offers 10% kill fee. Publishes ms an average of 2 months after acceptance. Accepts simultaneous submissions. Responds in 2 months to queries. Sample copy for 9x12 SASE. Digital copy online.

NONFICTION Needs essays, expose, how-to, interview, personal experience, photo feature, technical. Send complete ms. Length: 500-2,500 words. **Pays $300-1,500 for assigned articles.**

☉💲💲 TIRE NEWS

Rousseau Automotive Communication, 455, Notre-Dame East, Suite 311, Montreal QC H2Y 1C9 Canada. (514)289-0888; 1-877-989-0888. **Fax:** (514)289-5151. **E-mail:** info@autosphere.ca. **E-mail:** news@auto-sphere.ca. **Website:** www.autosphere.ca. Bimonthly magazine covering the Canadian tire industry. *Tire News* focuses on education/training, industry image, management, new tires, new techniques, marketing, HR, etc. Estab. 2004. Circ. 18,725. Byline given. Pays on publication. Publishes ms an average of 2 months after acceptance. Editorial lead time 2 months. Submit seasonal material 2 months in advance. Accepts simultaneous submissions. Responds in 2 weeks to queries. Responds in 2 months to mss. Sample copy free. Guidelines by e-mail.

NONFICTION Needs general interest, how-to, inspirational, interview, new product, technical. Does not want opinion pieces. **Buys 5 mss/year.** Query with published clips. Length: 550-610 words. **Pays up to $200 (Canadian).**

FILLERS Needs facts. **Buys 2 mss/year.** Length: 550-610 words. **Pays $0-200.**

☉💲💲 WESTERN CANADA HIGHWAY NEWS

Craig Kelman & Associates, 2020 Portage Ave., 3rd Floor, Winnipeg MB R3J 0K4 Canada. (204)985-9785. **Fax:** (204)985-9795. **E-mail:** terry@kelman.ca. **Website:** highwaynews.ca. **Contact:** Terry Ross, editor. **30% freelance written.** Quarterly magazine covering trucking. The official magazine of the Alberta, Saskatchewan, and Manitoba trucking associations. As the official magazine of the trucking associations in Alberta, Saskatchewan and Manitoba, *Western Canada Highway News* is committed to providing leading edge, timely information on business practices, technology, trends, new products/services, legal and legislative issues that affect professionals in Western Canada's trucking industry. Estab. 1995. Circ. 4,500. Byline given. Pays on publication. No kill fee. Publishes ms an average of 2 months after acceptance. Editorial lead time 3 months. Submit seasonal material 3 months in advance. Accepts simultaneous submissions. Responds in 1 month. Sample copy for 10x13 SAE with 1 IRC. Guidelines for #10 SASE.

NONFICTION Needs essays, general interest, how-to, interview, new product, opinion, personal experience, photo feature, technical, profiles in excellence (bios of trucking or associate firms enjoying success). **Buys 8-10 mss/year.** Query. Length: 500-3,000 words. **Pays 18-25¢/word.** Pays expenses of writers on assignment.

AVIATION & SPACE

💲💲💲💲 AEROSAFETY WORLD MAGAZINE

Flight Safety Foundation, 701 N. Fairfax St., Suite 4250, Alexandria VA 22314-2058. (703)739-6700. **Fax:** (703)739-6708. **E-mail:** jackman@flightsafety.org. **Website:** www.flightsafety.org. **Contact:** Frank Jackman, vice president of communications. Monthly newsletter covering safety aspects of airport operations. Full-color monthly magazine offers in-depth analysis of important safety issues facing the industry, with emphasis on timely news coverage in a convenient format and eye-catching contemporary design. Estab. 2006. Pays on publication. Accepts queries by mail, e-mail. Guidelines available online.

NONFICTION Needs technical. Query. **Pays $300-1,500.**

💲💲 AVIATION INTERNATIONAL NEWS

AIN Publications, 214 Franklin Ave., Midland Park NJ 07432. (201)444-5075. **E-mail:** aineditor@ain-online.com. **Website:** www.ainonline.com. **Contact:** Mark Phelps, executive editor. **30% freelance written.** Monthly magazine covering business and commercial aviation with news features, special reports, aircraft evaluations and surveys on business aviation worldwide, written for business pilots and industry professionals. Sister print products include daily onsite issues published at 6 conventions and 4 international air shows. Electronic products include four-times-weekly AINalerts, once-weekly AIN Air Transport Perspective and AIN Defense Perspective, and AINonline website. "While the heartbeat of *AIN* is driven by the news it carries, the human touch is not neglected. We pride ourselves on our people stories about the industry's 'movers and shakers' and others in aviation who make a difference." Estab. 1972. Circ. 40,000. Byline given. Pays on acceptance and upon receipt of writer's invoice. Offers variable kill fee. Publishes ms an average of 2 months after acceptance. Editorial lead time 2 months. Submit seasonal material 3 months in advance. Accepts queries by mail, e-mail. Responds in 6 weeks to queries; 2 months to mss. Sample copy for $10.

NONFICTION Needs how-to, interview, new product, opinion, personal experience, photo feature, technical. No place for puff pieces. "Our readers expect serious, real news. We don't pull any punches. *AIN* is not a 'good news' publication; it tells the story, both good and bad." **Buys 150-200 mss/year.** Query with published clips or links to online material. Length: 200-3,000 words. **Pays 45¢/word to first timers, higher rates to proven** *AIN* **freelancers.** Pays expenses of writers on assignment.

💲💲💲 PROFESSIONAL PILOT

Queensmith Communications Corp., 5290 Shawnee Road, Suite 201, Alexandria VA 22312. (703)370-0606. **Fax:** (703)370-7082. **E-mail:** editor@propilotmag.com; editorial@propilotmag.com. **E-mail:** rafael@propilotmag.com. **Website:** www.propilotmag.com. **Contact:** Murray Smith, editor/publisher; Rafael Henriquez, associate editor. **75% freelance written.** Monthly magazine covering corporate, noncombat government, law enforcement, and various other types of professional aviation. The typical reader of *Professional Pilot* has a sophisticated grasp of piloting/aviation knowledge and is interested in articles that help him/her do the job better or more efficiently. Estab. 1967. Circ. 40,000. Byline given. Pays on publication. Offers kill fee. Kill fee negotiable. Publishes ms an average of 2-3 months after acceptance. Accepts queries by mail, e-mail. Accepts simultaneous submissions.

NONFICTION Buys 40 mss/year. Query. Length: 750-2,500 words. **Pays $200-1,000, depending on length. A fee for the article will be established at the time of assignment.** Pays expenses of writers on assignment.

BEAUTY & SALON

💲💲 ASCP SKIN DEEP

Associated Skin Care Professionals, 25188 Genesee Trail Rd., Suite 200, Golden CO 80401. (800)789-0411. **E-mail:** editor@ascpskincare.com; getconnected@ascpskincare.com. **Website:** www.ascpskincare.com. **Contact:** Mary Abel, editor. **80% freelance written.** Bimonthly member magazine of Associated Skin Care Professionals (ASCP), covering technical, educational, and business information for estheticians with an emphasis on solo practitioners and spa/salon employees or independent contractors. Audience is the U.S. individual skin care practitioner who may work on her own and/or in a spa or salon setting. Magazine keeps her up to date on skin care trends and techniques and ways to earn more income doing waxing, facials, peels, microdermabrasion, body wraps, and other skin treatments. Product-neutral stories may include novel spa treatments within the esthetician scope of practice. Does not cover mass-market retail products, hair care, nail care, physician-only treatments/products, cosmetic surgery, or invasive treatments like colonics or ear candling. Successful stories have included how-tos on paraffin facials, aromatherapy body wraps, waxing tips, how to read ingredient labels, how to improve word-of-mouth advertising, and how to choose an online scheduling software package. Estab. 2003. Circ. 14,000+. Byline given. Pays on acceptance. No kill fee. Publishes ms an average of 4-6 months after acceptance. Editorial lead time 4-5 months. Submit seasonal material 7 months in advance. Accepts queries by e-mail. Accepts simultaneous submissions. Responds in 2-4 weeks to queries. Sample copy online at www.ascp-skindeepdigital.com.

NONFICTION Needs how-to. "We don't run general consumer beauty material or products, and very rarely run a new product that is available through retail outlets. 'New' products means introduced in the last 12 months. We do not run industry personnel announcements or stories on individual spas/salons or getaways. We don't cover hair or nails." **Buys 12 mss/year.** Query. Length: 1,200-1,600 words. **Pays $75-300 for assigned articles.** Pays expenses of writers on assignment.

❷❸ BEAUTY STORE BUSINESS

Creative Age Communications, 7628 Densmore Ave., Van Nuys CA 91406. (818)782-7328 or (800)442-5667. **E-mail:** khenderson@creativeage.com. **Website:** www.beautystorebusiness.com. **Contact:** Kim Henderson, executive editor; Breanna Armstrong, managing editor. **50% freelance written.** Monthly magazine covering beauty store business management, news, and beauty products. The primary readers of the publication are owners, managers, and buyers at open-to-the-public beauty stores, including general-market and multicultural market-oriented ones with or without salon services. Secondary readers are those at beauty stores only open to salon industry professionals. Also goes to beauty distributors. Estab. 1994. Circ. 15,000. Byline given. Pays on acceptance. Offers negotiable kill fee. Publishes ms an average of 3 months after acceptance. Editorial lead time 3 months.

Submit seasonal material 4 months in advance. Accepts queries by mail, e-mail. Accepts simultaneous submissions. Responds in 2 weeks, if interested. Sample copy free.

NONFICTION Needs how-to, interview. **Buys 20-30 mss/year.** Query. Length: 1,800-2,200 words. **Pays $250-525 for assigned articles.** Pays expenses of writers on assignment.

❂❷❸ COSMETICS

Rogers Publishing Limited, 420 Britannia Road East, Suite 102, Mississauga ON L4Z 3L5 Canada. (905)890-5161. **E-mail:** jhicks@cctfa.com. **Website:** www.cosmeticsmag.com. **Contact:** Jim Hicks. **10% freelance written.** Bimonthly magazine covering cosmetics for industry professionals. Estab. 1972. Circ. 13,000. Byline given. Pays on acceptance. Offers 50% kill fee. Publishes ms an average of 3 months after acceptance. Editorial lead time 4 months. Submit seasonal material 4 months in advance. Accepts queries by mail. Accepts simultaneous submissions. Responds in 1 month to queries. Sample copy for $6 (Canadian) and 8% GST.

NONFICTION Needs general interest, interview, photo feature. **Buys 1 mss/year.** Query. Length: 250-1,200 words. **Pays 25¢/word.** Pays expenses of writers on assignment.

COLUMNS "All articles assigned on a regular basis from correspondents and columnists that we know personally from the industry."

❷❸ DAYSPA

Creative Age Publications, 7628 Densmore Ave., Van Nuys CA 91406. (818)782-7328, ext. 301. **Fax:** (818)782-7450. **Website:** www.dayspamagazine.com. **Contact:** Lesley McCave, executive editor. **50% freelance written.** Monthly magazine covering the business of day spas, multiservice/skincare salons, and resort/hotel spas. *Dayspa* includes only well-targeted business and trend articles directed at the owners and managers. It serves to enrich, enlighten, and empower spa/salon professionals. Estab. 1996. Circ. 31,000. Byline given. Pays on acceptance. No kill fee. Publishes ms an average of 4 months after acceptance. Editorial lead time 4 months. Submit seasonal material 4 months in advance. Accepts queries by online submission form. Accepts simultaneous submissions. Responds in 2 months to queries. Sample copy: $5.

NONFICTION **Buys 40 mss/year.** Query. Length: 1,500-1,800 words. **Pays $150-500.**

COLUMNS Legal Pad (legal issues affecting salons/spas); Money Matters (financial issues); Management Workshop (spa management issues); Health Wise (wellness trends), all 1,200-1,500 words. **Buys 20 mss/year.** Query. **Pays $150-400.**

💲 💲 MASSAGE MAGAZINE

820 A1A N. Highway, Suite W18, Ponte Vedra Beach FL 32082. **E-mail:** kmenehan@massagemag.com. **Website:** www.massagemag.com. **Contact:** Karen Menehan, editor-in-chief. **50% freelance written.** Magazine about massage and other touch therapies published 12 times/year. Readers are professional therapists who have been in practice for several years. About 70% are self-employed; 95% live in the U.S. The techniques they practice include Swedish, sports, and geriatric massage and energy work. Readers work in settings ranging from home-based studios to spas to integrated clinics. Readers care deeply that massage is portrayed in a professional manner. "We publish articles on self-care, news on integrative care and massage, business, marketing and techniques. Understand the profession of massage therapy." Estab. 1985. Circ. 50,000. Byline given. Pays the month of publication. Offers kill fee. Publishes ms an average of 1-3 months after submission. Editorial lead time 1 month. Advance time 1 month. Accepts queries by e-mail. Responds in 2 weeks to queries. Do not send ms without querying first. Sample copy: $6.95; however; sample articles available via e-mail. Guidelines available by request.

NONFICTION Needs general interest, how-to, interview, personal experience, profile, News: hard news, features and profiles. "We do not publish humorous travel pieces about unusual massage experiences. We do not publish cartoons." **Buys 200 mss/year.** Length: 700-1,500 words for news; 1,600 words for features. **Pays $80-200.**

COLUMNS Profiles; News and Current Events; Practice Building (business); Technique; Mind/Body/Spirit. Length: 200-2,500 words. See website for details.

FILLERS Needs Facts, newsbreaks.

💲 💲 NAILPRO

Creative Age Publications, 7628 Densmore Ave., Van Nuys CA 91406. (800)442-5667; (818)782-7328. **Fax:** (818)782-7450. **E-mail:** nailpro@creativeage.com. **Website:** www.nailpro.com. **Contact:** Stephanie Lavery, executive editor. **20% freelance written.** Monthly magazine written for manicurists and salon owners working as an independent contractor or in a full-service salon or nails-only salons. Estab. 1989. Circ. 65,000. Byline given. Pays on acceptance. 25% kill fee. Publishes ms an average of 6 months after acceptance. Editorial lead time 3 months. Submit seasonal material 3 months in advance. Accepts queries by e-mail. Accepts simultaneous submissions. Responds in 6 weeks to queries only if interested. Sample copy: $2 and 9x12 SASE.

NONFICTION Needs book excerpts, how-to, humor, inspirational, interview, personal experience, photo feature, profile, technical. No general interest articles or business articles not geared to the nail-care industry. **Buys 50 mss/year.** Query. Length: 1,000-3,000 words. **Pays $150-450.** Pays expenses of writers on assignment.

COLUMNS Business (articles on building salon business, marketing and advertising, dealing with employees), 1,500-2,500 words; Attitudes (aspects of operating a nail salon and trends in the nail industry), 1,200-2,500 words. **Buys 50 mss/year.** Query. **Pays $250-350.**

💲 💲 NAILS

Bobit Business Media, 3520 Challenger St., Torrance CA 90503. (310)533-2457. **E-mail:** judy.lessin@bobit.com. **Website:** www.nailsmag.com. **Contact:** Judy Lessin, senior managing editor. **10% freelance written.** Monthly magazine. *NAILS* seeks to educate its readers on new techniques and products, nail anatomy and health, customer relations, working safely and ergonomically, salon sanitation, and the business aspects of running a salon. Estab. 1983. Circ. 55,000. Byline given. Pays on acceptance. No kill fee. Editorial lead time 3 months. Submit seasonal material 4 months in advance. Accepts queries by e-mail. Responds in 1 month to queries. Visit website to view past issues.

NONFICTION Needs how-to, inspirational, interview, personal experience, photo feature, profile, technical. No articles on one particular product, company profiles, or articles slanted toward a particular company or manufacturer. **Buys 20 mss/year.** Query with published clips. Length: 750-1,600 words. **Pays $100-350.** Pays expenses of writers on assignment.

💲 💲 PULSE MAGAZINE

HOST Communications Inc., 2365 Harrodsburg Rd., Suite A325, Lexington KY 40504. (859)226-4326. **Fax:** (859)226-4445. **E-mail:** mae.manacap-johnson@

ispastaff.com. **Website:** www.experienceispa.com/media/pulse-magazine. **Contact:** Mae Manacap-Johnson, editor. **20% freelance written.** Magazine published 10 times/year covering spa industry. *Pulse* is the magazine for the spa professional. As the official publication of the International SPA Association, its purpose is to advance the business of the spa professionals by informing them of the latest trends and practices and promoting the wellness aspects of spa. *Pulse* connects people, nurtures their personal and professional growth, and enhances their ability to network and succeed in the spa industry. Estab. 1991. Circ. 5,300. Byline given. Pays on publication. Publishes ms an average of 1 month after acceptance. Editorial lead time 3 months. Submit seasonal material 4 months in advance. Accepts queries by e-mail. Accepts simultaneous submissions. Sample copy for #10 SASE. Guidelines by e-mail.

NONFICTION Needs general interest, how-to, interview, new product. Does not want articles focused on spas that are not members of ISPA, consumer-focused articles (market is the spa industry professional), or features on hot tubs ("not *that* spa industry"). **Buys 8-10 mss/year.** Query with published clips. Length: 800-2,000 words. **Pays $250-500.** Pays expenses of writers on assignment.

⑨⑨ SKIN INC. MAGAZINE

Allured Business Media, P.O. Box 3009, Northbrook IL 60065. (1-800)362-2192. **Fax:** (1-847)291-4816. **E-mail:** kanderson@allured.com. **Website:** www.skininc.com. **Contact:** Katie Anderson, managing editor. **30% freelance written.** Magazine published 12 times/year as an educational resource for skin care professionals interested in business solutions, treatment techniques, and skin science. Estab. 1988. Circ. 30,000. Byline given. Pays on publication. No kill fee. Publishes ms an average of 6 months after acceptance. Editorial lead time 6 months. Submit seasonal material 1 year in advance. Accepts queries by mail, e-mail, fax, phone. Accepts simultaneous submissions. Responds in 3 weeks to queries; 1 month to mss. Sample copy and guidelines free.

NONFICTION Needs general interest, how-to, interview, personal experience, technical. **Buys 6 mss/year.** Query with published clips. Length: 2,000 words. **Pays $100-300 for assigned articles. Pays $50-200 for unsolicited articles.**

COLUMNS Finance (tips and solutions for managing money), 2,000-2,500 words; Personnel (managing personnel), 2,000-2,500 words; Marketing (marketing tips for salon owners), 2,000-2,500 words; Retail (retailing products and services in the salon environment), 2,000-2,500 words. Query with published clips. **Pays $50-200.**

FILLERS Needs facts, newsbreaks. **Buys Buys 6 mss/year. mss/year.** Length: 250-500 words. **Pays $50-100.**

BEVERAGES & BOTTLING

♻⑨⑨ BAR & BEVERAGE BUSINESS MAGAZINE

Mercury Publications, 1313 Border St., Unit 16, Winnipeg MB R3H 0X4 Canada. (204)954-2085, ext. 213. **Fax:** (204)954-2057. **E-mail:** edufault@mercurypublications.ca. **Website:** www.barandbeverage.com. **Contact:** Elaine Dufault, associate publisher and national account manager. **33% freelance written.** Bimonthly magazine providing information on the latest trends, happenings, and buying/selling of beverages and product merchandising. Estab. 1998. Circ. 15,000+. Byline given. Pays 30-45 days from receipt of invoice. Offers 33% kill fee. Submit seasonal material 3 months in advance. Accepts simultaneous submissions. Sample copy and writer's guidelines free or by e-mail.

NONFICTION Needs how-to, interview. Does not want industry reports, profiles on companies. Query with published clips. Length: 500-9,000 words. **Pays 25-35¢/word.** Pays expenses of writers on assignment.

COLUMNS Out There (bar and beverage news in various parts of the country), 100-500 words. Query. **Pays up to $100.**

⑨⑨ BARTENDER® MAGAZINE

Foley Publishing, P.O. Box 157, Spring Lake NJ 07762. (732)449-4499. **E-mail:** info@bartender.com. **Website:** bartender.com/mixologist.com. **Contact:** Jackie Foley, editor. **75% freelance written. Prefers to work with published/established writers; eager to work with new/unpublished writers.** Quarterly publication for full-service on-premise establishments able to serve a mixed drink on-premise. Features bartenders, bars, creative cocktails, signature drinks, jokes, cartoons, wine, beer, liquor, new products and those products aligned to the field. Estab. 1979. Circ.

150,000. Byline given. Pays on publication. No kill fee. Publishes ms an average of 3 months after acceptance. Submit seasonal material 3 months in advance. Accepts simultaneous submissions. Responds in 2 months to mss. Sample copy with 9x12 SAE and 4 first-class stamps.

NONFICTION Needs general interest, historical, how-to, humor, new product, opinion, personal experience, photo feature. Special issues: Special issues: Annual Calendar and Daily Cocktail Recipe Guide. Send complete ms and SASE. Length: 100-1,000 words. Pays expenses of writers on assignment.

REPRINTS Send tearsheet and information about when and where the material previously appeared. Pays 25% of amount paid for an original article.

COLUMNS Bar of the Month; Bartender of the Month; Creative Cocktails; Bar Sports; Quiz; Bar Art; Wine Cellar; Tips from the Top (from prominent figures in the liquor industry); One For the Road (travel); Collectors (bar or liquor-related items); Photo Essays. Length: 200-1,000 words. Query by mail only with SASE. **Pays $50-200.**

FILLERS Needs anecdotes, newsbreaks, short humor, clippings, jokes, gags. Length: 25-100 words. **Pays $5-25.**

MICHIGAN HOSPITALITY REVIEW
Michigan Licensed Beverage Association, 101 S. Washington Sq., Suite 800, Lansing MI 48933. (800)292-2896; (517)374-9611. **Fax:** (517)374-1165. **E-mail:** editor@mlba.org; mdoerr@mlba.org. **Website:** www.mlba.org. **Contact:** Mason Doerr, editor. **40-50% freelance written.** Monthly trade magazine devoted to the beer, wine, and spirits industry in Michigan. It is dedicated to serving those who make their living serving the public and the state through the orderly and responsible sale of beverages. Estab. 1983. Circ. 4,200. Pays on publication. No kill fee. Editorial lead time 3 months. Submit seasonal material 3 months in advance. Accepts queries by mail, e-mail. Accepts simultaneous submissions. Responds in 2 weeks to queries. Responds in 1 month to mss. Sample copy for $5 or online.

NONFICTION Needs essays, general interest, historical, how-to, humor, interview, new product, opinion, personal experience, photo feature, technical. **Buys 24 mss/year.** Send complete ms. Length: 1,000 words. **Pays $20-200.**

COLUMNS Open to essay content ideas. Interviews (legislators, others), 750-1,000 words; personal experience (waitstaff, customer, bartenders), 500 words. **Buys 12 mss/year.** Send complete ms. **Pays $25-100.**

VINEYARD & WINERY MANAGEMENT
P.O. Box 14459, Santa Rosa CA 95402-6459. (707)577-7700. **Fax:** (707)577-7705. **E-mail:** jfpowers@vwmmedia.com. **Website:** www.vwmmedia.com. **Contact:** Julie Fadda Powers, editor in chief. **80% freelance written.** Bimonthly magazine of professional importance to grape growers, winemakers, and winery sales and business people. Headquartered in Sonoma County, California, *Vineyard & Winery Management* proudly remains a leading independent wine trade magazine serving all of North America. Estab. 1975. Circ. 6,500. Byline given. Pays on publication. 20% kill fee. Accepts queries by e-mail. Accepts simultaneous submissions. Responds in 3 weeks to queries. Responds in 1 month to mss. Sample copy free. Guidelines available by e-mail.

NONFICTION Needs how-to, interview, new product, technical. **Buys 30 mss/year.** Query. Length: 1,500-2,000 words. **Pays approximately $500/feature.** Pays expenses of writers on assignment.

WINES & VINES
Wine Communications Group, 65 Mitchell Blvd., Suite A, San Rafael CA 94903. (415)453-9700; (866)453-9701. **Fax:** (415)453-2517. **E-mail:** edit@winesandvines.com; info@winesandvines.com. **Website:** www.winesandvines.com. **Contact:** Jim Gordon, editor; Kate Lavin, managing editor. **50% freelance written.** Monthly magazine covering the North American winegrape and winemaking industry. "Since 1919, *Wines & Vines Magazine* has been the authoritative voice of the wine and grape industry—from prohibition to phylloxera, we have covered it all. Our paid circulation reaches all 50 states and many foreign countries. Because we are intended for the trade—including growers, winemakers, winery owners, wholesalers, restauranteurs, and serious amateurs—we accept more technical, informative articles. We do not accept wine reviews, wine country tours, or anything of a wine consumer nature." Estab. 1919. Circ. 5,000. Byline given. Pays 30 days after acceptance. No kill fee. Publishes ms an average of 3 months after acceptance. Editorial lead time 2 months. Submit seasonal material 4 months in advance. Accepts queries by e-mail. Accepts simultaneous sub-

missions. Responds in 2-3 weeks to queries. Sample copy: $5. Guidelines free.

NONFICTION Needs interview, new product, technical. "No wine reviews, wine country travelogues, 'lifestyle' pieces, or anything aimed at wine consumers. Our readers are professionals in the field." **Buys 60 mss/year.** Query with published clips. Length: 1,000-2,000 words. **Pays flat fee of $500 for assigned articles.** Pays expenses of writers on assignment.

BOOK & BOOKSTORE

💲 AMERICAN BOOK REVIEW

The Writer's Review, Inc., School of Arts & Sciences, Univ. of Houston-Victoria, 3007 N. Ben Wilson, Victoria TX 77901. (361)570-4848. **E-mail:** americanbookreview@uhv.edu. **Website:** www.americanbookreview.org. Bimonthly magazine covering book reviews. "We specialize in reviewing books published by independent presses." Estab. 1977. Circ. 15,000. Byline given. Pays on publication. Offers $50 kill fee. Publishes ms an average of 2-4 months after acceptance. Editorial lead time 1 month. Accepts queries by mail, e-mail, fax, phone. Accepts simultaneous submissions. Responds in 2 weeks to queries; 1-2 months to mss. Sample copy for $4. Guidelines online.

NONFICTION Does not want fiction, poetry, or interviews. Query with published clips. Length: 750-1,250 words. **Pays $50.** Pays expenses of writers on assignment.

💲💲 FOREWORD REVIEWS

425 Boardman Ave., Traverse City MI 49684. (231)933-3699. **Fax:** (231)933-3899. **E-mail:** victoria@forewordreviews.com. **E-mail:** mschingler@forewordreviews.com. **Website:** www.forewordreviews.com. **Contact:** Michelle Anne Schingler, managing editor. **75% freelance written.** Quarterly magazine covering reviews of good books independently published. In each issue of the magazine, there are 3 to 4 feature *ForeSight* articles focusing on trends in popular categories. These are in addition to the 100 or more critical reviews of forthcoming titles from independent and university presses in the *Review* section. Look online for review submission guidelines or view editorial calendar. Estab. 1998. Circ. 10,000 (about 80% librarians, 10% bookstores, 10% publishing professionals). Byline given. Pays 1 month after submissions. $20 kill fee. Publishes ms an average

of 2-3 months after acceptance. Editorial lead time 2-3 months. Submit seasonal material 5 months in advance. Accepts queries by mail, e-mail. Accepts simultaneous submissions. Responds in 1 month. Sample copy for $5.99 and 8 ½ x11 SASE with $1.50 postage.

NONFICTION Contact: Matt Sutherland. Needs book excerpts, interview, profile. **Buys 4 mss/year.** Query with published clips. All review submissions should be sent to the book review editor. Submissions should include a fact sheet or press release. Length: 400-1,500 words. **Pays $50-250 for assigned articles.**

💲 VIDEO LIBRARIAN

3435 NE Nine Boulder Dr., Poulsbo WA 98370. (360)626-1259. **Fax:** (360)626-1260. **E-mail:** vidlib@videolibrarian.com. **Website:** www.videolibrarian.com. **75% freelance written.** Bimonthly magazine covering DVD/Blu-ray reviews for librarians. "*Video Librarian* reviews approximately 225 titles in each issue: children's, documentaries, how-to's, movies, TV, music and anime." Estab. 1986. Circ. 2,000. Byline given. Pays on publication. Publishes ms an average of 2 months after acceptance. Editorial lead time 2 months. Accepts queries by e-mail. Accepts simultaneous submissions. Responds in 1 week to queries. Sample copy: $11.

NONFICTION Buys 500+ mss/year. Query with published clips. Length: 200-300 words. **Pays $10-20/review.** Pays expenses of writers on assignment.

BRICK, GLASS & CERAMICS

💲 STAINED GLASS

Stained Glass Association of America, 9313 East 63rd St., Raytown MO 64133. (800)438-9581. **Fax:** (816)737-2801. **E-mail:** webmaster@sgaaonline.com. **Website:** www.stainedglassquarterly.com. **Contact:** Richard Gross, editor and media director. **70% freelance written.** Quarterly magazine. *Stained Glass* is the official voice of the Stained Glass Association of America. As the oldest, most respected stained glass publication in North America, *Stained Glass* preserves the techniques of the past as well as illustrates the trends of the future. This vital information, of significant value to the professional stained glass studio, is also of interest to those for whom stained glass is an avocation or hobby. Estab. 1906. Circ. 8,000. Byline given. Pays on publication. No kill fee. Publishes ms an average of 1 year after acceptance. Editorial lead time 6 months. Submit seasonal material 8 months in advance. Accepts queries by mail, e-mail, fax. Accepts simultaneous submissions. Responds in 3 months to queries. Sample copy free. Guidelines on website.

NONFICTION Needs how-to, humor, interview, new product, opinion, photo feature, technical. **Buys 9 mss/year.** Query or send complete ms, but must include photos or slides—very heavy on photos. Length: 2,500-3,500 words. **Pays $125/illustrated article; $75/nonillustrated.**

REPRINTS Accepts previously published submissions from stained glass publications only. Send tearsheet of article. Payment negotiable.

COLUMNS Columns must be illustrated. Teknixs (technical, how-to, stained and glass art), word length varies by subject. **Buys 4 mss/year.** Query or send complete ms, but must be illustrated.

❸❺ US GLASS, METAL & GLAZING

Key Communications, Inc., 20 PGA Dr., Suite 201, Stafford VA 22554. (540)720-5584, ext.118. **Fax:** (540)720-5687. **E-mail:** info@usglassmag.com. **E-mail:** erogers@glass.com. **Website:** www.usglassmag.com. **Contact:** Ellen Rogers, editor. **25% freelance written.** Monthly magazine for companies involved in the flat glass trades. Estab. 1966. Circ. 27,000. Byline given. Pays on publication. No kill fee. Publishes ms an average of 3 months after acceptance. Editorial lead time 3 months. Submit seasonal material 2 months in advance. Accepts queries by mail, e-mail. Accepts simultaneous submissions. Responds in 1 month to queries. Responds in 2 months to mss. Sample copy online.

NONFICTION Buys 12 mss/year. Query with published clips. **Pays $300-600 for assigned articles.** Pays expenses of writers on assignment.

BUILDING INTERIORS

❸❺ FABRICS + FURNISHINGS INTERNATIONAL

SIPCO Publications + Events, 3 Island Ave., Suite 6i, Miami Beach FL 33139. **E-mail:** eric@sipco.net. **Website:** www.fandfi.com. **Contact:** Eric Schneider, editor/publisher. **10% freelance written.** Bimonthly magazine covering commercial, hospitality interior design, and manufacturing. *F+FI* covers news from vendors who supply the hospitality interiors industry. Estab. 1990. Circ. 11,000+. Byline given. Pays on publication. Offers $100 kill fee. Editorial lead time 3 months. Submit seasonal material 3 months in advance. Accepts queries by e-mail. Accepts simultaneous submissions. Sample copy available online.

NONFICTION Needs interview, technical. Does not want opinion or consumer pieces. Readers must learn something from our stories. Query with published clips. Length: 500-1,000 words. **Pays $250-350.** Pays expenses of writers on assignment.

❸❺ KITCHEN & BATH DESIGN NEWS

SOLA Group Inc., 724 12th St., Suite 1W, Wilmette IL 60091. (631)581-2029 or (516)605-1426. **E-mail:** anita@solabrands.com; janice@solabrands.com. **Website:** www.kitchenbathdesign.com. **15% freelance written.** Monthly tabloid for kitchen and bath dealers and design professionals, offering design, business, and marketing advice to help readers be more successful. It is not a consumer publication about design, a book for do-it-yourselfers, or a magazine created to showcase pretty pictures of kitchens and baths. Rather, the magazine covers the professional kitchen and bath design industry in depth, looking at the specific challenges facing these professionals, and how they address these challenges. Estab. 1983. Circ. 51,000. Byline given. Pays on publication. Publishes ms an average of 2-3 months after acceptance. Editorial lead time 2 months. Accepts queries by mail, e-mail. Accepts simultaneous submissions. Responds in 2-4 weeks to queries. Sample copy available online. Guidelines by e-mail.

NONFICTION Needs how-to, interview. Does not want consumer stories, generic business stories, or "I remodeled my kitchen and it's so beautiful" stories. This is a magazine for trade professionals, so stories need to be both slanted for these professionals, as well as sophisticated enough that people who have been working in the field 30 years can still learn something from them. **Buys 16 mss/year.** Query with published clips. Length: 1,100-3,000 words. **Pays $200-650.** Pays expenses of writers on assignment.

❸❺ QUALIFIED REMODELER

SOLA Group, Inc., 1880 Oak Ave., Suite 350, Evanston IL 60201. (847)920-9513. **Website:** www.forresidentialpros.com. Publisher/Editorial Director: Patrick L. O'Toole. **5% freelance written.** Monthly magazine covering residential remodeling. Estab. 1975. Circ.

83,500. Byline given. Pays on acceptance. No kill fee. Publishes ms an average of 1 month after acceptance. Editorial lead time 3 months. Submit seasonal material 2 months in advance. Accepts queries by mail, e-mail, fax, phone. Accepts simultaneous submissions. Sample copy available online.

NONFICTION Needs how-to, new product. **Buys 12 mss/year.** Query with published clips. Length: 1,200-2,500 words. **Pays $300-600 for assigned articles. Pays $200-400 for unsolicited articles.** Pays expenses of writers on assignment.

COLUMNS Query with published clips. **Pays $400.**

$$$$ REMODELING

HanleyWood, LLC, One Thomas Circle NW, Suite 600, Washington DC 20005. (202)452-0800. **Fax:** (202)785-1974. **E-mail:** cwebb@hanleywood.com. **Website:** www.remodelingmagazine.com. **Contact:** Craig Webb, editor. **10% freelance written.** Monthly magazine covering residential and light commercial remodeling. "We cover the best new ideas in remodeling design, business, construction and products." Estab. 1985. Circ. 80,000. Byline given. Pays on publication. Offers 5¢/word kill fee. Publishes ms an average of 3 months after acceptance. Accepts queries by mail, e-mail, fax. Accepts simultaneous submissions. Sample copy free.

NONFICTION Needs interview, new product, technical, small business trends. **Buys 6 mss/year.** Query with published clips. Length: 250-1,000 words. **Pays $1/word.** Pays expenses of writers on assignment.

$$ WALLS & CEILINGS

2401 W. Big Beaver Rd., Suite 700, Troy MI 48084. **Fax:** (248)362-5103. **E-mail:** wyattj@bnpmedia.com; mark@wwcca.org. **Website:** www.wconline.com. **Contact:** John Wyatt, editor; Mark Fowler, editorial director. **20% freelance written.** Monthly magazine for contractors involved in lathing and plastering, drywall, acoustics, fireproofing, curtain walls, and movable partitions, together with manufacturers, dealers, and architects. Estab. 1938. Circ. 30,000. Byline given. Pays on publication. No kill fee. Publishes ms an average of 6 months after acceptance. Submit seasonal material 4 months in advance. Accepts queries by mail, e-mail. Accepts simultaneous submissions. Responds in 6 months to queries. Sample copy for 9x12 SAE with $2 postage. Guidelines for #10 SASE.

NONFICTION Needs how-to, technical. **Buys 20 mss/year.** Query or send complete ms. Length: 1,000-1,500 words. **Pays $50-500.** Pays expenses of writers on assignment.

REPRINTS Send tearsheet or photocopy with rights for sale noted and information about when and where the material previously appeared. Pays 50% of the amount paid for an original article.

BUSINESS MANAGEMENT

$$$$ BEDTIMES

International Sleep Products Association, 501 Wythe St., Alexandria VA 22314. (336)500-3816. **E-mail:** mbest@sleepproducts.org. **Website:** www.bedtimesmagazine.com. **Contact:** Mary Best, editorial director. **20-40% freelance written.** *BedTimes*, published monthly, focuses on news, trends, and issues of interest to mattress manufacturers and their suppliers, as well as more general business stories. Estab. 1917. Circ. 3,800. Byline given. Pays on acceptance. No kill fee. Publishes ms an average of 3 months after acceptance. Editorial lead time 2 months. Accepts queries by e-mail. Accepts simultaneous submissions. Responds in 1 month to queries. Sample copy: $4. Guidelines by e-mail or online.

NONFICTION Buys 15-25 mss/year. Query with published clips. Length: 500-2,500 words. **Pays 50-$1/word for short features; $2,000 for cover story.**

$$$ BUSINESS TRAVEL EXECUTIVE

5768 Remington Dr., Winston-Salem NC 27104. (336)766-1961. **E-mail:** dbooth@askbtc.com. **Website:** www.askbte.com. **Contact:** Dan Booth, managing editor. **90% freelance written.** Monthly magazine covering corporate procurement of travel services. Byline given. Pays on publication. No kill fee. Publishes ms an average of 2 months after acceptance. Editorial lead time 0-3 months. Accepts queries by e-mail. Accepts simultaneous submissions.

NONFICTION Needs how-to, technical. **Buys 48 mss/year.** Please send unsolicited submissions, at your own risk. Please enclose a SASE for return of material. Submission of letters implies the right to edit and publish all or in part. Length: 800-2,000 words. **Pays $200-800.** Pays expenses of writers on assignment.

COLUMNS Meeting Place (meeting planning and management); Hotel Pulse (hotel negotiations, contracting and compliance); Security Watch (travel safety); all 1,000 words. **Buys 24 mss/year.** Query. **Pays $200-400.**

⊛⊛ CHRISTIAN MARKET

CBA, the Association for Christian Retail, 1365 Garden of the Gods Rd., Suite 105, Colorado Springs CO 80907. **Fax:** (719)272-3510. **E-mail:** cellis@cbaonline.org; info@cbaonline.org. **Website:** www.cbaonline.org. **Contact:** Cathy Ellis. **80% freelance written.** Monthly trade magazine covering the Christian products industry. Writers must have knowledge of and direct experience in the Christian products industry. Subject matter must specifically pertain to the Christian products audience. Estab. 1968. Byline given. Pays on publication. No kill fee. Publishes ms an average of 3 months after acceptance. Editorial lead time 3 months. Submit seasonal material 6 months in advance. Accepts queries by e-mail. Accepts simultaneous submissions. Responds in 2 months to queries. Sample copy for $9.50 or online.

NONFICTION **Buys 24 mss/year.** Query. Length: 650-1,500 words. **Pays 25¢/word.**

⊛⊛ CONTRACTING PROFITS

Trade Press Publishing, 2100 W. Florist Ave., Milwaukee WI 53209. (414)228-7701; (800)727-7995. **Fax:** (414)228-1134. **E-mail:** dan.weltin@tradepress.com. **Website:** www.cleanlink.com/cp. **Contact:** Dan Weltin, editor-in-chief. **40% freelance written.** Magazine published 10 times/year covering building service contracting and business management advice. The pocket MBA for this industry—focusing not only on cleaning-specific topics, but also discussing how to run businesses better and increase profits through a variety of management articles. Estab. 1995. Circ. 32,000. Byline given. Pays within 30 days of acceptance. No kill fee. Editorial lead time 2 months. Submit seasonal material 3 months in advance. Accepts queries by mail, e-mail. Accepts simultaneous submissions. Responds in weeks to queries. Sample copy available online. Guidelines free.

NONFICTION Needs expose, how-to, interview, technical. No product-related reviews or testimonials. **Buys 30 mss/year.** Query with published clips. Length: 1,000-1,500 words. **Pays $100-500.** Pays expenses of writers on assignment.

COLUMNS Query with published clips.

⊛⊛ CONTRACT MANAGEMENT

National Contract Management Association, 21740 Beaumeade Circle, Suite 125, Ashburn VA 20147. (571)382-0082. **Fax:** (703)448-0939. **E-mail:** khansen@ncmahq.org. **Website:** www.ncmahq.org. **Contact:** Kerry McKinnon Hansen, director of publications and editor-in-chief. **10% freelance written.** Monthly magazine covering contract and business management. Most of the articles published in *Contract Management (CM)* are written by NCMA members, although one does not have to be an NCMA member to be published in the magazine. Articles should concern some aspect of the contract management profession, whether at the level of a beginner or that of the advanced practitioner. Estab. 1960. Circ. 23,000. Byline given. Pays on publication. No kill fee. Publishes ms an average of 3 months after acceptance. Editorial lead time 10 weeks. Submit seasonal material 3 months in advance. Accepts queries by mail, e-mail, fax, phone. Accepts simultaneous submissions. Responds in 2 weeks to queries. Responds in 1 month to mss. Sample copy and writer's guidelines available online.

NONFICTION Needs essays, general interest, how-to, humor, inspirational, new product, opinion, technical. No company or CEO profiles. Read a copy of publication before submitting. **Buys 6-10 mss/year.** Query with published clips. Send an inquiry including a brief summary (150 words) of the proposed article to the managing editor before writing the article. Length: 1,800-4,000 words. **Pays $300.**

COLUMNS Professional Development (self-improvement in business), 1,000-1,500 words; Back to Basics (basic how-tos and discussions), 1,500-2,000 words. **Buys 2 mss/year.** Query with published clips. **Pays $300.**

⊛⊛ INTENTS

Industrial Fabrics Association International, 1801 County Rd. B W, Roseville MN 55113. (651)222-2508. **Fax:** (651)631-9334. **E-mail:** generalinfo@ifai.com. **Website:** intentsmag.com. **50% freelance written.** Bimonthly magazine covering tent-rental and special-event industries. *InTents* is the official publication of IFAI's Tent Rental Division, delivering "the total tent experience." *InTents* offers focused, credible information needed to stage and host safe, successful tented events. Issues of the magazine include news, trends and behind-the-scenes coverage of the latest events in tents. Estab. 1995. Circ. 12,000. Byline given. Pays on acceptance. No kill fee. Publishes ms an average of 2 months after acceptance. Editorial lead time 3 months. Accepts queries by mail, e-mail, fax. Accepts simultaneous submissions. Sample copy and writer's guidelines free.

NONFICTION Needs how-to, interview, new product, photo feature, technical. **Buys 12-18 mss/year.** Query. Length: 800-2,000 words. **Pays $300-500.** Pays expenses of writers on assignment.

💲💲 MAINEBIZ

Mainebiz Publications, Inc., 48 Free St., Portland ME 04101. (207)761-8379. **Fax:** (207)761-0732. **E-mail:** pvanallen@mainebiz.biz; editorial@mainebiz.biz. **Website:** www.mainebiz.biz. **Contact:** Peter Van Allen, editor. **25% freelance written.** Biweekly tabloid covering business in Maine. *Mainebiz* is read by business decision makers across the state. Readers look to the publication for business news and analysis. Estab. 1994. Circ. 13,000. Byline given. Pays on publication. Offers 10% kill fee. Publishes ms an average of 1 month after acceptance. Editorial lead time 1 month. Submit seasonal material 2 months in advance. Accepts queries by mail, e-mail. Accepts simultaneous submissions. Responds in 3 weeks to queries. Sample copy online.

NONFICTION Needs essays, expose, interview, business trends. Special issues: See website for editorial calendar. **Buys 50+ mss/year.** Query with published clips. Length: 500-2,500 words. **Pays $75-350.** Pays expenses of writers on assignment.

💲💲💲 RETAIL INFO SYSTEMS NEWS

Edgell Communications, 4 Middlebury Blvd., Randolph NJ 07869. (973)607-1300. **Fax:** (973)607-1395. **E-mail:** ablair@edgellmail.com; jskorupa@edgellmail.com. **Website:** www.risnews.com. **Contact:** Adam Blair, editor; Joe Skorupa, group editor-in-chief. **65% freelance written.** Monthly magazine covering retail technology. Estab. 1988. Circ. 22,000. Byline sometimes given. Pays on publication. No kill fee. Publishes ms an average of 2 months after acceptance. Editorial lead time 3 months. Submit seasonal material 3 months in advance. Accepts queries by mail. Accepts simultaneous submissions. Sample copy available online.

NONFICTION Needs essays, how-to, humor, interview, technical. **Buys 80 mss/year.** Query with published clips. Length: 700-1,900 words. **Pays $600-**

1,200 for assigned articles. Pays expenses of writers on assignment.

COLUMNS News/trends (analysis of current events), 150-300 words. **Buys 4 articles/year mss/year.** Query with published clips. **Pays $100-300.**

💲💲 RTOHQ: THE MAGAZINE

1504 Robin Hood Trail, Austin TX 78703. (800)204-2776. **Fax:** (512)794-0097. **E-mail:** nferguson@rtohq.org; bkeese@rtohq.org. **Website:** www.rtohq.org. **Contact:** Neil Ferguson, art director; Bill Keese, executive editor. **50% freelance written.** Bimonthly magazine covering the rent-to-own industry. *RTOHQ: The Magazine* is the only publication representing the rent-to-own industry and members of APRO. The magazine covers timely news and features affecting the industry, association activities, and member profiles. Awarded best 4-color magazine by the American Society of Association Executives in 1999. Estab. 1980. Circ. 5,500. Byline given. Pays on acceptance. Offers 25% kill fee. Publishes ms an average of 2 months after acceptance. Editorial lead time 2 months. Submit seasonal material 4 months in advance. Accepts queries by mail, e-mail, fax, phone, online submission form. Accepts simultaneous submissions. Responds in 1 month to queries. Responds in 2 months to mss. Sample copy free.

NONFICTION Needs expose, general interest, how-to, inspirational, interview, technical, industry features. **Buys 12 mss/year.** Query with published clips. Length: 1,200-2,500 words. **Pays $150-700.** Pays expenses of writers on assignment.

💲💲 SECURITY DEALER & INTEGRATOR

Southcomm, 12735 Morris Road Bldg. 200 Suite 180, Alpharetta GA 30004. (800)547-7377, ext 2226. **E-mail:** paul.rothman@cygnus.com. **Website:** www.securityinfowatch.com/magazine. **Contact:** Paul Rothman, editor-in-chief. **25% freelance written.** Circ. 25,000. Byline sometimes given. Pays 3 weeks after publication. No kill fee. Publishes ms an average of 3 months after acceptance. Accepts queries by e-mail. Accepts simultaneous submissions.

NONFICTION Needs how-to, interview, technical. No consumer pieces. Query by e-mail. Length: 1,000-3,000 words. **Pays $250.** Pays expenses of writers on assignment.

COLUMNS Query by mail only.

🪙🪙 SMART BUSINESS

Smart Business Network, Inc., 835 Sharon Dr., Suite 200, Cleveland OH 44145. (440)250-7000. **Fax:** (440)250-7001. **E-mail:** mscott@sbnonline.com. **Website:** www.sbnonline.com. **Contact:** Mark Scott, senior associate editor. **5% freelance written.** Monthly business magazine with an audience made up of business owners and top decision makers. *Smart Business* is one of the fastest growing national chains of regional management journals for corporate executives. Every issue delves into the minds of the most innovative executives in each of our regions to report on how market leaders got to the top and what strategies they use to stay there. Estab. 1989. Byline given. Pays on publication. Offers 50% kill fee. Publishes ms an average of 2 months after acceptance. Editorial lead time 3 months. Submit seasonal material 3 months in advance. Accepts queries by mail, e-mail. Accepts simultaneous submissions. Responds in 2 weeks to queries. Responds in 1 month to mss. Sample copy available online. Guidelines by e-mail.

NONFICTION Needs how-to, interview. No breaking news or news features. **Buys 10-12 mss/year.** Query with published clips. Length: 1,150-2,000 words. **Pays $200-500.** Pays expenses of writers on assignment.

🪙🪙 STAMATS MEETINGS MEDIA

615 5th St. SE, Cedar Rapids IA 52401. **Fax:** (319)364-4278. **E-mail:** tyler.davidson@meetingsfocus.com. **Website:** www.meetingsfocus.com. **Contact:** Tyler Davidson, chief content director. **75% freelance written.** Monthly tabloid covering meeting, event, and conference planning. Estab. 1986. Circ. *Meetings East* and *Meetings South* 22,000; *Meetings West* 26,000. Byline given. Pays 1 month after publication. No kill fee. Publishes ms an average of 1 month after acceptance. Editorial lead time 3 months. Submit seasonal material 3 months in advance. Accepts queries by mail, e-mail, fax. Accepts simultaneous submissions. Responds in 3 weeks to queries. Sample copy for DSR with 9x13 envelope and 5 first-class stamps.

NONFICTION Needs how-to, travel. "No first-person fluff—this is a business magazine." **Buys 150 mss/year.** Query with published clips. Length: 1,200-2,000 words. **Pays $500 flat rate/package.**

🪙 THE STATE JOURNAL

WorldNow, P.O. Box 11848, Charleston WV 25339. (304)395-1313. **E-mail:** aali@wowktv.com. **Website:** www.statejournal.com. **Contact:** Ann Ali, managing editor. **30% freelance written.** Weekly journal dedicated to providing stories of interest to the business community in West Virginia. Estab. 1984. Circ. 10,000. Byline given. Pays on publication. No kill fee. Publishes ms an average of 3 weeks after acceptance. Submit seasonal material 4 months in advance. Accepts queries by mail, e-mail, fax. Sample copy and writer's guidelines for #10 SASE.

NONFICTION Needs general interest, interview, new product, (all business related). **Buys 400 mss/year.** Query. Length: 250-1,500 words. **Pays $50.** Sometimes pays expenses of writers on assignment.

🪙 SUPERVISION MAGAZINE

National Research Bureau, 320 Valley St., Burlington IA 52601. (319)752-5415. **E-mail:** articles@supervisionmagazine.com. **Website:** www.supervisionmagazine.com/. **Contact:** Todd Darnall. **80% freelance written.** Monthly magazine covering management and supervision. *Supervision Magazine* explains complex issues in a clear and understandable format. Articles written by both experts and scholars provide practical and concise answers to issues facing today's supervisors and managers. Estab. 1939. Circ. 500. Byline given. Pays on acceptance. Publishes ms an average of 1 month after acceptance. Editorial lead time 1 month. Submit seasonal material 2 months in advance. Accepts queries by e-mail. Accepts simultaneous submissions. Sample copy free. Guidelines available online.

NONFICTION Needs personal experience, "We can use articles dealing with motivation, leadership, human relations and communication." Send complete ms. Length: 1,500-2,000 words. **Pays 4¢/word.** Pays expenses of writers on assignment.

🪙🪙🪙 VENECONOMY/VENECONOMA

VenEconomia, Edificio Gran Sabana, Piso 1, Ave. Abraham Lincoln, No. 174, Blvd. de Sabana Grande, Caracas Venezuela. (58)(212)761-8121. **Fax:** (58)(212)762-8160. **E-mail:** mercadeo@veneconomia.com. **Website:** www.veneconomia.com; www.veneconomy.com. **70% freelance written.** Monthly business magazine covering business, political, and social issues in Venezuela. *VenEconomy*'s subscribers are mostly business people, both Venezuelans and foreigners doing business in Venezuela. Some academics and diplomats also read our magazine. The magazine is published monthly both in English and Spanish. Freelancers may query in either language. Slant is decidedly pro-business, but not dogmatically conservative. Development, human rights, political, and environmental issues are covered from a business-friendly angle. Estab. 1983. Byline given. Pays on publication. Offers 50% kill fee. Publishes ms an average of 1 month after acceptance. Editorial lead time 1-2 months. Submit seasonal material 1 month in advance. Accepts queries by e-mail. Accepts simultaneous submissions. Responds in 2 weeks to queries. Responds in 4 months to mss. Sample copy by e-mail.

NONFICTION Contact: Francisco Toro, political editor. Needs essays, expose, interview, new product, opinion. No first-person stories or travel articles. **Buys 50 mss/year.** Query. Length: 1,100-3,200 words. **Pays 10-15¢/word for assigned articles.** Pays expenses of writers on assignment.

CHURCH ADMINISTRATION & MINISTRY

$ CHRISTIAN COMMUNICATOR

American Christian Writers, 9118 W. Elmwood Dr., Suite 1G, Niles IL 60714-5820. (847)296-3964. **E-mail:** ljohnson@wordprocommunications.com. **Website:** acwriters.com. **Contact:** Lin Johnson, managing editor; Sally Miller, poetry editor (sallymiller@ameritech.net). **50% freelance written.** Bimonthly magazine covering Christian writing and speaking. Estab. 1988. Circ. 1,000. Byline given. Pays on publication. No kill fee. Publishes ms an average of 6-12 months after acceptance. Editorial lead time 3 months. Submit seasonal material 9 months in advance. Accepts queries by e-mail. Responds in 6-8 weeks to queries; in 8-12 weeks to mss. Sample copy for SAE and 4 first-class stamps. Writers guidelines by email or on website.

NONFICTION Needs essays, how-to, interview, reviews. "Articles on writing nonfiction, research, creativity." **Buys 24 mss/year.** Query or send complete ms only by e-mail. Length: 700-1,000 words. **Pays $10. $5 for reviews. ACW CD for anecdotes.**

REPRINTS Same as first rights.

POETRY Needs free verse, light verse, traditional. Buys Publishes 12 poems/year. poems/year. Submit maximum 2 poems. Length: 4-20 lines. **Pays $5.**

FILLERS Needs anecdotes, short humor.

$ $ THE JOURNAL OF ADVENTIST EDUCATION

General Conference of SDA, 12501 Old Columbia Pike, Silver Spring MD 20904. (301)680-5069. **Fax:** (301)622-9627. **E-mail:** mcgarrellf@gc.adventist.org; goffc@gc.adventist.org. **Website:** jae.adventist.org. **Contact:** Faith-Ann McGarrell, editor; Chandra Goff, editorial assistant. A quarterly professional journal for Christian teachers, administrators, and stakeholders, with specific emphasis on educators in Seventh-day Adventist schools. Published 4 times per year in English, French, Spanish, and Portuguese. Emphasizes procedures, philosophy, and subject matter of Christian education. Estab. 1939. Circ. 14,000 in English; 13,000 in other languages. Byline given. Pays on publication. No kill fee. Publishes ms an average of 1 year after acceptance. Editorial lead time 1 year. Accepts queries by mail, e-mail, fax, phone. Accepts simultaneous submissions. Responds in 6 weeks to queries; 4 months to mss. Sample copy for SAE with 10x12 envelope and 5 first-class stamps. Guidelines online.

NONFICTION Needs book excerpts, essays, how-to, personal experience, photo feature, religious. "No brief first-person stories about Sunday Schools." Query. All articles must be submitted in electronic format to http://www.editorialmanager.com/jae/default.aspx. Store in Word or .rtf format. If you submit a CD, include a printed copy of the article with the CD. Articles should be 6-8 pages long, with a max of 10 pages, including references. Two-part articles will be considered. Length: 1,500-2,500 words. **Pays $25-300.**

REPRINTS Send tearsheet or photocopy and information about when and where the material previously appeared.

$ $ LEADERSHIP JOURNAL

Christianity Today International, 465 Gundersen Dr., Carol Stream IL 60188. (630)260-6200. **Fax:** (630)260-0114. **E-mail:** ljeditor@leadershipjournal.net. **Website:** www.christianitytoday.com/le. Skye Jethani, managing editor. **Contact:** Marshall Shelley, editor-in-chief. **75% freelance written. Works with a small number of new/unpublished writers each year.** Quarterly magazine. Writers must have a knowledge of and sympathy for the unique expectations placed on pastors and local church leaders. Each article must support points by illustrating from real life experiences in local churches. Estab. 1980. Circ. 48,000. Byline given. Pays on acceptance. Offers 33% kill fee. Publishes ms an average of 6 months after acceptance. Editorial lead time 6 months. Submit seasonal material 6 months in advance. Accepts queries by mail, e-mail, fax. Accepts simultaneous submissions. Responds in 2 weeks to queries. Responds in 2 months to mss. Sample copy for free or online.

NONFICTION Needs how-to, humor, interview, personal experience, sermon illustrations. No articles from writers who have never read our journal. No unsolicited ms. **Buys 60 mss/year.** Query with proposal. Send a brief query letter describing your idea and how you plan to develop it. Length: 300-3,000 words. **Pays $35-400.** Pays expenses of writers on assignment.

COLUMNS **Contact:** Skye Jethanis, managing editor. Toolkit (book/software reviews), 500 words. **Buys 8 mss/year. mss/year.** Query.

$ MOMENTUM

National Catholic Educational Association, 1005 N. Glebe Rd., Suite 525, Arlington VA 22201. (800)711-6232. **Fax:** (703)243-0025. **E-mail:** momentum@ncea.org. **Website:** www.ncea.org/publications/momentum. **Contact:** Gabrielle Gallagher, editor. **65% freelance written.** Quarterly educational journal covering educational issues in Catholic schools and parishes. *Momentum* is a membership journal of the National Catholic Educational Association. The audience is educators and administrators in Catholic schools K-12, and parish programs. Estab. 1970. Circ. 19,000. Byline given. Pays on publication. No kill fee. Publishes ms an average of 3 months after acceptance. Accepts queries by e-mail. Accepts simultaneous submissions. Sample copy for $5 SASE and 8 first-class stamps. Guidelines online.

NONFICTION No articles unrelated to educational and catechesis issues. **Buys 40-60 mss/year.** Query and send complete ms. Length: 1,500 words for feature articles; 700-1,000 words for columns, "From the Field," and opinion pieces or essays; 500-750 words for book reviews. **Pays $75 maximum.**

$$ THE PRIEST

Our Sunday Visitor, Inc., 200 Noll Plaza, Huntington IN 46750. (800)348-2440. **Fax:** (260)356-8472. **E-mail:** tpriest@osv.com. **Website:** www.osv.com. **Contact:** Editorial Department. **40% freelance written.** Monthly magazine that publishes articles to aid priests in their day-to-day parish ministry. Includes items on spirituality, counseling, administration, theology, personalities, the saints, etc. Byline given. Pays on acceptance. No kill fee. Editorial lead time 3 months. Submit seasonal material 4 months in advance. Accepts queries by mail, e-mail, fax, phone, online submission form. Accepts simultaneous submissions. Responds in 5 weeks to queries; 3 months to mss. Sample copy free. Guidelines available online.

NONFICTION Needs essays, historical, humor, inspirational, opinion, personal experience, photo feature, religious. **Buys 96 mss/year.** Send complete ms. Length: 2,500 words maximum. **Pays $200 minimum for assigned articles; $50 minimum for unsolicited articles.**

$ RTJ'S CREATIVE CATECHIST

Twenty-Third Publications, P.O. Box 6015, New London CT 06320. (800)321-0411, ext. 188. **Fax:** (860)437-6246. **E-mail:** creativesubs@rtjscreativecatechist.com; editor@rtjscreativecatechist.com; pat.gohn@bayard-inc.com. **Website:** www.rtjscreativecatechist.com. **Contact:** Pat Gohn, editor. Monthly magazine for Catholic catechists and religion teachers. The mission of *RTJ's Creative Catechist* is to encourage and assist Catholic DREs and catechists in their vocation to proclaim the gospel message and lead others to the joy of following Jesus Christ. *RTJ* provides professional support, theological content, age appropriate methodology, and teaching tools. Estab. 1966. Circ. 30,000. Byline given. Pays on acceptance. Publishes ms an average of 3-20 months after acceptance. Editorial lead time 4 months. Submit seasonal material 6 months in advance. Accepts queries by mail, e-mail. Accepts simultaneous submissions. Responds in 1-2 weeks to queries. Responds in 1-2 months to mss. Sample copy for SAE with 9x12 envelope and 3 first-class stamps. Guidelines free.

NONFICTION Needs how-to, inspirational, personal experience, religious, articles on celebrating church seasons, sacraments, on morality, on prayer, on saints. Special issues: Sacraments; Prayer; Advent/Christmas; Lent/Easter. All should be written by people who have experience in religious education, or a good background in Catholic faith. Does not want fiction, poems, plays, articles written for Catholic school teachers (i.e., math, English, etc.), or articles that are academic rather than catechetical in nature. **Buys 35-**

40 mss/year. Send complete ms. Length: 600-1,300 words. **Pays $100-125 for assigned articles. Pays $75-125 for unsolicited articles.**

COLUMNS Catechist to Catechist (brief articles on crafts, games, etc., for religion lessons); Faith and Fun (full-page religious word games, puzzles, mazes, etc., for children). **Buys 30 mss/year.** Send complete ms. **Pays $20-125.**

🌐💲 TODAY'S CATHOLIC TEACHER

Peter Li Education Group, 3055 Kettering Blvd., Suite 100, Dayton OH 45439. (937)293-1415; (800)523-4625, x1139. **Fax:** (937)293-1310. **E-mail:** bshepard@peterli.com; danielle.bean@bayard-inc.com. **E-mail:** bshepard@peterli.com. **Website:** www.catholicteacher.com. **Contact:** Dr. Lisa D'Souza, editor; Danielle Bean, publisher. **60% freelance written.** Magazine published 6 times/year during school year covering Catholic education for grades K-12. Looks for topics of interest and practical help to teachers in Catholic elementary schools in all curriculum areas including religion technology, discipline, and motivation. Estab. 1972. Circ. 50,000. Byline given. Pays on publication. No kill fee. Publishes ms an average of 2 months after acceptance. Editorial lead time 3 months. Submit seasonal material 6 months in advance. Accepts queries by mail, e-mail, fax. Accepts simultaneous submissions. Responds in 1 month to queries. Responds in 3 months to mss. Sample copy for $3 or on website. Guidelines available online.

NONFICTION Needs essays, how-to, humor, interview, personal experience. No articles pertaining to public education. **Buys 15 mss/year.** Query or send complete ms. Query letters are encouraged. E-mail, write, call, or fax the editor for editorial calendar. Articles may be submitted as hard copy; submission by e-mail with accompanying hard copy is appreciated. Length: 600-1,500 words. **Pays $100-250.** Pays expenses of writers on assignment.

🌐💲 YOUTHWORKER JOURNAL

Salem Publishing/CCM Communications, 402 BNA Dr., Suite 400, Nashville TN 37217-2509. **E-mail:** ALee@SalemPublishing.com. **Website:** www.youthworker.com. **Contact:** Steve Rabey, editor; Amy L. Lee, managing editor. **100% freelance written.** Website and bimonthly magazine covering professional youth ministry in the church and parachurch. Estab. 1984. Circ. 20,000. Byline given. Pays on publication. No kill fee. Publishes ms an average of 3 months after ac-

ceptance for print; immediately online. Editorial lead time 6 months for print; immediately online. Submit seasonal material 6 months in advance for print. Accepts queries by e-mail, online submission form. Accepts simultaneous submissions. Responds within 6 weeks to queries. Sample copy for $5. Guidelines available online.

NONFICTION Needs essays, new product, personal experience, photo feature, religious. Special issues: See website for themes in upcoming issues. Query. Length: 250-3,000 words. **Pays $15-200.**

CLOTHING

🌐💲💲 FOOTWEAR PLUS

9 Threads, 135 West 20th Street, 4th Floor, New York NY 10011. (646)278-1550. **Fax:** (646)278-1553. **E-mail:** editorialrequests@9threads.com. **Website:** www.footwearplusmagazine.com. **Contact:** Brittany Leitner, assistant editor. **20% freelance written.** Monthly magazine covering footwear fashion and business. A business-to-business publication targeted at footwear retailers. Covers all categories of footwear and age ranges with a focus on new trends, brands and consumer buying habits, as well as retailer advice on operating the store more effectively. Estab. 1990. Circ. 18,000. Byline given. Pays on publication. No kill fee. Publishes ms an average of 1-2 months after acceptance. Editorial lead time 1-2 months. Accepts simultaneous submissions. Sample copy for $5.

NONFICTION Needs interview, new product, technical. Does not want pieces unrelated to footwear/fashion industry. **Buys 10-20 mss/year.** Query. Length: 500-2,500 words. **Pays $1,000 maximum.** Pays expenses of writers on assignment.

🌐💲 IMPRESSIONS

Emerald Expositions, 1145 Sanctuary Pkwy., Suite 355, Alpharetta GA 30009-4772. (800)241-9034; (770)291-5412. **Fax:** (770)777-8733. **E-mail:** mderryberry@impressionsmag.com; jlaster@impressionsmag.com; michelle.havich@emeraldexpo.com. **Website:** www.impressionsmag.com. **Contact:** Marcia Derryberry, editor in chief; Jamar Laster, senior editor; Michelle Havich, managing editor. **30% freelance written.** Magazine, published 13 times/year, covering computerized embroidery and digitizing design. Features authoritative, up-to-date information on screen printing, embroidery, heat-applied graphics, and ink-jet-to-garment printing. Readable, practical business and/or technical articles show readers how to succeed in their profession. Estab. 1994. Circ. 20,000. Byline given. Pays on publication. No kill fee. Publishes ms an average of 3 months after acceptance. Editorial lead time 3 months. Submit seasonal material 6 months in advance. Accepts queries by mail, e-mail. Accepts simultaneous submissions. Sample copy: $10.

NONFICTION Needs how-to, interview, new product, photo feature, technical. **Buys 40 mss/year.** Query. Length: 800-2,000 words. **Pays $200 and up for assigned articles.** Pays expenses of writers on assignment.

💲💲 TEXTILE WORLD

Billian Publishing Co., P.O. Box 683155, Marietta GA 30068. (678)483-6102; (404)518-9599. **Fax:** (770)952-0669. **E-mail:** editor@textileworld.com; rsdavis@textileworld.com. **Website:** www.textileworld.com. **Contact:** editor. **5% freelance written.** Bimonthly magazine covering the business of textile, apparel, and fiber industries with considerable technical focus on products and processes. Estab. 1868. Byline given. Pays on publication. No kill fee. Accepts simultaneous submissions.

NONFICTION No puff pieces pushing a particular product. **Buys 10 mss/year.** Query. Length: 500 words minimum. **Pays $200/published page.**

CONSTRUCTION & CONTRACTING

💲💲 AUTOMATED BUILDER

CMN Associates, Inc., 2401 Grapevine Dr., Oxnard CA 93036. (805)351-5931. **Fax:** (805)351-5755. **E-mail:** cms03@pacbell.net. **Website:** www.automatedbuilder.com. **Contact:** Don O. Carlson, editor/publisher. **5% freelance written.** "*Automated Builder* covers management, production and marketing information on all 7 segments of home, apartment and commercial construction. These include: (1) production (site) builders, (2) panelized home manufacturers, (3) HUD-code (mobile) home manufacturers, (4) modular home manufacturers, (5) component manufacturers, (6) special unit (commercial) manufacturers, and (7) all types of builders and builders/dealers. The in-plant material is technical in content and covers new machine technologies and improved methods for in-plant building and erecting. Home and commercial buyers will see the latest in homes and commercial structures." Estab. 1964. Circ. 75,000 when printed. Byline given if desired. Pays on acceptance. Publishes ms an average of 2 months after acceptance. Editorial lead time 2 months. Accepts queries by mail, e-mail, fax. Accepts simultaneous submissions. Responds in 2 weeks to queries.

NONFICTION "No fiction and no planned 'dreams.' Housing projects must be built or under construction. Same for commercial structures." **Buys 6-8 mss/year.** Phone queries OK. Length: 500-750 words. **Pays $250 for stories including photos.** Pays expenses of writers on assignment.

💲💲 CONCRETE CONSTRUCTION

Hanley Wood, 5600 N. River Rd., Suite 250, Rosemont IL 60018. (773)824-2400. **E-mail:** bpalmer@hanleywood.com. **Website:** www.concreteconstruction.net/magazine. **Contact:** William D. Palmer Jr., editor-in-chief.. **20% freelance written.** Monthly magazine for concrete contractors, engineers, architects, specifiers, and others who design and build residential, commercial, industrial, and public works, cast-in-place concrete structures. It also covers job stories and new equipment in the industry. Estab. 1956. Circ. 80,000. Byline given. Pays on acceptance. No kill fee. Publishes ms an average of 4 months after acceptance. Editorial lead time 4 months. Submit seasonal material 4 months in advance. Accepts queries by mail, e-mail, fax. Accepts simultaneous submissions. Responds in 2 weeks to queries; 1 month to mss. Sample copy and writer's guidelines free.

NONFICTION Needs how-to, new product, personal experience, photo feature, technical, job stories. **Buys 7-10 mss/year.** Query with published clips. 2,000 words maximum **Pays $250 or more for assigned articles; $200 minimum for unsolicited articles.** Pays expenses of writers on assignment.

💲💲💲 THE CONCRETE PRODUCER

Hanley-Wood, LLC, 8725 W. Higgins Rd., Suite 600, Chicago IL 60631. (773)824-2400 or (773)824-2496. **E-mail:** tbagsarian@hanleywood.com; ryelton@hanleywood.com; tcpeditor@hanleywood.com. **Website:** www.theconcreteproducer.com. **Contact:** Tom Bagsarian, group managing editor; Richard Yelton, editor-at-large. **25% freelance written.** Monthly magazine covering concrete production. Audience consists of producers who have succeeded in making concrete the preferred building material through management, operating, quality control, use of the latest technology, or use of superior materials. Estab. 1982. Circ. 18,000. Byline given. Pays on acceptance. No kill fee. Publishes ms an average of 2 months after acceptance. Editorial lead time 4 months. Accepts queries by mail, e-mail, fax, phone. Accepts simultaneous submissions. Responds in 1 week to queries; in 2 months to mss. Sample copy: $4. Guidelines free.

NONFICTION Needs how-to, new product, technical. **Buys 10 mss/year.** Send complete ms. Length: 500-2,000 words. **Pays $200-1,000.** Pays expenses of writers on assignment.

💲 HARD HAT NEWS

Lee Publications, Inc., 6113 State Highway 5, P.O. Box 121, Palatine Bridge NY 13428. (518)673-3763 or (800)218-5586. **Fax:** (518)673-2381. **E-mail:** jcasey@leepub.com. **Website:** www.hardhat.com. **Contact:** Jon Casey, editor. **50% freelance written.** Biweekly tabloid covering heavy construction, equipment, road, and bridge work. "Our readers are contractors and heavy construction workers involved in excavation, highways, bridges, utility construction, and underground construction." Estab. 1980. Circ. 15,000. Byline given. No kill fee. Editorial lead time 2 weeks. Submit seasonal material 2 weeks in advance. Accepts queries by mail, e-mail, fax, phone. Sample copy and writer's guidelines free.

NONFICTION Needs interview, new product, opinion, photo feature, technical. Send complete ms. Length: 800-2,000 words. **Pays $2.50/inch.** Pays expenses of writers on assignment.

COLUMNS Association News; Parts and Repairs; Attachments; Trucks and Trailers; People on the Move.

💲💲 HOME ENERGY MAGAZINE

Energy Auditor & Retrofitter, 1250 Addison St., Suite 211B, Berkeley CA 94702. (510) 524-5405. **Fax:** (510) 981-1406. **E-mail:** contact@homeenergy.org; jpgunshinan@homeenergy.org. **Website:** www.homeenergy.org. **Contact:** Jim Gunshinan, editor. **10% freelance written.** Quarterly print and digital magazine plus online articles and blog covering green home building and renovation. Readers are building contractors, energy auditors, and weatherization professionals. They expect technical detail, accuracy, and brevity. Estab. 1984. Circ. 5,000. Byline given. Pays on publication. Offers 10% kill fee. Publishes ms an average of 4 months after acceptance. Editorial lead time 4 months. Accepts queries by e-mail. Accepts simultaneous submissions. Responds in 2 weeks to queries; 2 months to mss. Guidelines online.

NONFICTION Needs interview, technical. Does not want articles for consumers/general public. **Buys 6 mss/year.** Query with published clips. Submit article via e-mail. Length: 400-2,500 words. **Pays 20¢/word; $400 maximum for both assigned and unsolicited articles.**

COLUMNS "Trends" are short stories explaining a single advance or research result (400-1,500 words). "Features" are longer pieces that provide more indepth information (1,500-2,500 words). "Field Notes" provide readers with first-person testimonials (1,500-2,500 words). "Columns" provide readers with direct answers to their specific questions (400-1,500 words). Submit columns via e-mail. Accepts Word, RTF documents, Text documents, and other common formats.

💲💲 INTERIOR CONSTRUCTION

Ceilings & Interior Systems Construction Association, 1010 Jorie Blvd., Suite 30, Oak Brook IL 60523. (630)584-1919. **Fax:** (866)560-8537. **E-mail:** cisca@cisca.org; csmith@naylor.com. **E-mail:** csmith@naylor.com. **Website:** www.cisca.org. **Contact:** Cody Smith. Quarterly magazine on acoustics and commercial specialty ceiling construction. The resource for the Ceilings & Interior Systems Construction Industry. Features examine leading industry issues and trends like specialty ceilings, LEED, acoustics, and more. Each issue features industry news, new products, columns from industry experts, and CISCA news and initiatives. Estab. 1950. Circ. 3,000. Byline given. Pays on publication. No kill fee. Publishes ms an average of 1 1/2 months after acceptance. Editorial lead time 2-3 months. Accepts queries by e-mail. Accepts simultaneous submissions. Sample copy by e-mail. Guidelines available.

NONFICTION Needs new product, technical. Query with published clips. Publishes 1-2 features per issue. Length: 700-1,700 words. **Pays $400 minimum, $800 maximum for assigned articles.**

💲💲 METAL ROOFING MAGAZINE

a Division of F+W Media, Inc., 700 E. Iola St., Iola WI 54990-0001. 715-203-4523. **Fax:** (715)445-4087. **E-mail:** sharon.glorioso@fwmedia.com. **Website:** www.constructionmagnet.com/metal-roofing. **Contact:** Sharon Glorioso. **10% freelance written.** Bimonthly magazine covering roofing. *Metal Roofing Magazine* offers contractors, designers, suppliers, architects, and others in the construction industry a wealth of information on metal roofing—a growing segment of the roofing trade. Estab. 2000. Circ. 26,000. Byline given. Pays on publication. Publishes ms an average of 3 months after acceptance. Editorial lead time 3 months. Submit seasonal material 3 months in advance. Accepts queries by mail. Accepts simultaneous submissions. Sample copy free.

NONFICTION Needs book excerpts, historical, how-to, interview, new product, opinion, photo feature, technical. No advertorials. **Buys 15 mss/year.** Query with published clips. Length: 750 words minimum. **Pays $100-500 for assigned articles.**

COLUMNS Gutter Opportunities; Stay Cool; Metal Roofing Details; Spec It. **Buys 15 mss/year.** Send complete ms. **Pays $0-500.**

❸❸❸ NETCOMPOSITES

4a Broom Business Park, Bridge Way Chesterfield S41 9QG UK. **E-mail:** info@netcomposites.com. **Website:** www.netcomposites.com. **1% freelance written.** Bimonthly newsletter covering advanced materials and fiber-reinforced polymer composites, plus a weekly electronic version called *Composite eNews. Advanced Materials & Composites News* covers markets, applications, materials, processes, and organizations for all sectors of the global hi-tech materials world. Audience is management, academics, researchers, government, suppliers, and fabricators. Focus on news about growth opportunities. Estab. 1978. Circ. 15,000+. Byline sometimes given. Pays on publication. No kill fee. Publishes ms an average of 1 month after acceptance. Editorial lead time 2 weeks. Submit seasonal material 1 month in advance. Accepts queries by e-mail. Accepts simultaneous submissions. Responds in 1 week to queries. Responds in 1 month to mss. Sample copy for #10 SASE.

NONFICTION Needs new product, technical, industry information. **Buys 4-6 mss/year.** Query. 300 words. **Pays $200/final printed page.**

❸❸ POB MAGAZINE

BNP Media, 2401 W. Big Beaver Rd., Suite 700, Troy MI 48084. (248)362-3700. **E-mail:** trunickp@bnpmedia.com. **Website:** www.pobonline.com. **Contact:** Perry Trunick, editor. **5% freelance written,.** Monthly magazine covering surveying, mapping, and geomatics. Estab. 1975. Circ. 39,000. Byline given. Pays on publication. Publishes ms an average of 3 months af-

ter acceptance. Editorial lead time 3 months. Accepts queries by e-mail, phone. Accepts simultaneous submissions. Sample copy and guidelines available online.

NONFICTION Query. Document should be saved in Microsoft Word or text-only format. Also include an author byline and biography. Length: 1,700-2,200 words, with 2 graphics included. **Pays $400.**

❸❸❸ PRECAST INC.

National Precast Concrete Association, 1320 City Center Dr., Suite 200, Carmel IN 46032. (317)571-9500. **Fax:** (317)571-0041. **E-mail:** npca@precast.org; sgreer@precast.org. **Website:** www.precast.org. **Contact:** Sara Geer, managing editor. **75% freelance written.** Bimonthly magazine covering manufactured concrete products. *Precast Inc.* is a publication for owners and managers of plant-produced concrete products used in construction. Publishes business articles, technical articles, company profiles, safety articles, and project profiles, with the intent of educating our readers in order to increase the quality and use of precast concrete. Estab. 1995. Circ. 4,500. Byline given. Pays on acceptance. No kill fee. Publishes ms an average of 6 months after acceptance. Editorial lead time 3 months. Accepts queries by mail, e-mail, fax. Accepts simultaneous submissions. Responds in 1 month to queries; 2 months to mss. Sample copy online. Guidelines online.

NONFICTION Needs how-to, interview, technical. No humor, essays, fiction, or fillers. **Buys 8-14 mss/year.** Query or send complete ms. Length: 1,500-2,500 words. **Pays $250-750.** Pays expenses of writers on assignment.

❸❸ RURAL BUILDER

F+W Media, Inc., 5225 Joerns Dr., Stevens Point WI 54481. (715)445-4612, ext. 13644. **Fax:** (715)445-4087. **E-mail:** sharon.thatcher@fwmedia.com. **Website:** www.ruralbuilder.com. **5% freelance written.** Magazine published 8 times/year covering rural building. "*Rural Builder* serves diversified town and country builders, offering them help managing their businesses through editorial and advertising material about metal, wood, post-frame, and masonry construction." Estab. 1967. Circ. 29,000. Byline given. Pays on publication. Publishes ms an average of 3 months after acceptance. Editorial lead time 3 months. Submit seasonal material 3 months in advance. Accepts queries by mail, e-mail. Accepts simultaneous submissions. Sample copy free.

NONFICTION Needs how-to, photo feature, technical. No advertorials. **Buys 10 mss/year.** Query with published clips. Length: 750 words minimum. **Pays $100-300.**

COLUMNS Tech Talk (computers for builders); Tool Talk (tools); Management Insights (business management); all 1,000 words. **Buys 10 mss/year.** Send complete ms. **Pays $0-250.**

$ TEXAS ARCHITECT

Texas Society of Architects, 500 Chicon St., Austin TX 78702. (512)478-7386. **Fax:** (512)478-0528. **Website:** www.texasarchitect.org. **Contact:** Aaron Seward, editor. **30% freelance written. Mostly written by unpaid members of the professional society.** Bimonthly journal covering architecture and architects of Texas. *Texas Architect* is a highly visually-oriented look at Texas architecture, design, and urban planning. Articles cover varied subtopics within architecture. Readers are mostly architects and related building professionals. Estab. 1951. Circ. 12,500. Byline given. Pays on publication. No kill fee. Publishes ms an average of 3 months after acceptance. Submit seasonal material 4 months in advance. Accepts queries by mail, e-mail. Accepts simultaneous submissions. Responds in 6 weeks to queries. Guidelines online.

NONFICTION Needs interview, photo feature, technical, book reviews. Query with published clips. Length: 100-2,000 words. **Pays $50-100 for assigned articles.**

COLUMNS News (timely reports on architectural issues, projects, and people), 100-500 words. **Buys 10 articles/year mss/year.** Query with published clips. **Pays $50-100.**

$$$ UNDERGROUND CONSTRUCTION

Gulf Publishing Company, Inc., 2 Greenway Plaza, Suite 1020, Houston TX 77046. (713)520-4420. **Fax:** (281)558-7029. **E-mail:** rcarpenter@oildom.com. **Website:** www.ucononline.com. **Contact:** Robert Carpenter, editor-in-chief; Cathy Schmermund, managing editor; Brian Nessen, publisher; Elizabeth Fitzpatrick, art director. **50% freelance written.** Monthly magazine covering underground utilities and pipeline construction and rehabilitation. Markets include: water and sewer pipelines, underground telecommunications, underground power. Content is for contractors, owners/municipalities, consulting engineers. Estab. 1945. Circ. 40,000. Byline given, if independent writer not affiliated with vendor/manufacturer. Roughly every 2 weeks No kill fee. Publishes ms an average of 6 months after acceptance. Editorial lead time 3 months. Accepts queries by mail, e-mail, phone. Accepts simultaneous submissions. Responds in 1 month to mss. Sample copy for SAE.

NONFICTION Needs how-to, interview, new product, technical, project stories and industry issues. Query with published clips. Length: 1,000-2,000 words. **Pays $300-1,200.** Pays expenses of writers on assignment.

EDUCATION & COUNSELING

$ ARTS & ACTIVITIES

Publishers' Development Corp., 12345 World Trade Dr., San Diego CA 92128. (858)605-0242. **Fax:** (858)605-0247. **E-mail:** ed@artsandactivities.com. **Website:** www.artsandactivities.com. **Contact:** Maryellen Bridge, editor-in-chief. **95% freelance written. Eager to work with new/unpublished writers.** Monthly (except July and August) magazine covering art education at levels from preschool through college for educators and therapists engaged in arts and crafts education and training. Estab. 1932. Circ. 20,000. Byline given. Pays on publication. No kill fee. Publishes ms 6 months to 3 years after acceptance. Submit seasonal material 6 months in advance. Accepts queries by mail, e-mail. Responds in 3 months to queries. Sample copy for SAE with 9x12 envelope and 8 first-class stamps. Guidelines available on website.

NONFICTION Needs historical, how-to. **Buys 80-100 mss/year.** Length: 500-1,500 words. **Pays $35-150.**

🍁$ THE ATA MAGAZINE

11010 142nd St. NW, Edmonton Alberta T5N 2R1 Canada. (780)447-9400. **Fax:** (780)455-6481. **E-mail:** government@teachers.ab.ca. **Website:** www.teachers.ab.ca. Quarterly magazine covering education. Estab. 1920. Circ. 42,100. Byline given. Pays on publication. No kill fee. Publishes ms an average of 4 months after acceptance. Editorial lead time 2 months. Submit seasonal material 2 months in advance. Accepts queries by mail, e-mail, fax, phone. Accepts simultaneous submissions. Responds in 2 months to queries. Previous articles available for viewing online. Guidelines available online.

NONFICTION Query with published clips. Length: 500-1,500 words. **Pays $100 (Canadian).** Pays expenses of writers on assignment.

💲💲 DANCE TEACHER

McFadden Performing Arts Media, 333 Seventh Ave., 11th Floor, New York NY 10001. **E-mail:** khildebrand@dancemedia.com; jsullivan@dancemedia.com. **Website:** www.dance-teacher.com. **Contact:** Karen Hildebrand, editor in chief; Joe Sullivan, managing editor. **60% freelance written.** Monthly magazine. Estab. 1979. Circ. 25,000. Byline given. Pays on publication. No kill fee. Publishes ms an average of 3 months after acceptance. Submit seasonal material 6 months in advance. Accepts queries by e-mail. Accepts simultaneous submissions. Responds in 3 months to mss. Sample copy for SAE with 9x12 envelope and 6 first-class stamps. Guidelines available for free.

NONFICTION Needs how-to. Special issues: Summer Programs (January); Music & More (May); Costumes and Production Preview (November); College/Training Schools (December). No PR or puff pieces. All articles must be well researched. **Buys 50 mss/year.** Query. Length: 700-2,000 words. **Pays $100-300.** Pays expenses of writers on assignment.

💲 THE FORENSIC TEACHER MAGAZINE

Wide Open Minds Educational Services, P.O. Box 5263, Wilmington DE 19808. **E-mail:** admin@theforensicteacher.com. **Website:** www.theforensicteacher.com. **Contact:** Dr. Mark R. Feil, editor. **70% freelance written.** Quarterly magazine covering forensic education. Readers are middle, high and post-secondary teachers who are looking for better, easier and more engaging ways to teach forensics as well as law enforcement and scientific forensic experts. Writers understand this and are writing from a forensic or educational background, or both. Prefers a first-person writing style. Estab. 2006. Circ. 16,000. Byline given. Pays 60 days after publication. No kill fee. Publishes ms an average of 6 months after acceptance. Editorial lead time 6 months. Submit seasonal material 6 months in advance. Accepts queries by e-mail. Accepts simultaneous submissions. Responds in 2 weeks to queries; 2 months to mss. Sample copy online. Guidelines online.

NONFICTION Needs general interest, historical, how-to, memoir, personal experience, photo feature, technical. Does not want poetry, fiction, or anything unrelated to medicine, law, forensics or teaching.

Buys 18 mss/year. Send complete ms. Length: 400-3,000 words. **Pays 2¢/word.**

COLUMNS Needs lesson experiences or ideas, personal or professional experiences with a branch of forensics. "If you've done it in your classroom please share it with us. Also, if you're a professional, please tell our readers how they can duplicate the lesson/demo/experiment in their classrooms. Please share what you know."

FILLERS Needs Needs facts, newsbreaks. **Buys 15 mss/year.** Length: 50-200 words. **Pays 2¢/word.**

💲💲 THE HISPANIC OUTLOOK IN HIGHER EDUCATION

299 Market Street, Suite 145, Saddle Brook NJ 07663. (800)587-8800. **Fax:** (201)587-9105. **Website:** www.hispanicoutlook.com. **Contact:** Mary Ann Cooper, editor in chief. **50% freelance written.** Biweekly magazine (except during the summer) covering higher education of Hispanics. Looking for higher education story articles, with a focus on Hispanics and the advancements made by and for Hispanics in higher education. Circ. 28,000. Byline given. Pays on publication. No kill fee. Publishes ms an average of 2 months after acceptance. Editorial lead time 2 months. Submit seasonal material 3 months in advance. Accepts queries by mail, e-mail, fax. Accepts simultaneous submissions. Sample copy free.

NONFICTION Needs historical. **Buys 20-25 mss/year.** Query with published clips. Length: 1,800-2,200 words. **Pays $400 minimum for print articles, and $300 for online articles when accepted.** Pays expenses of writers on assignment.

💲💲 PTO TODAY

School Family Media Inc., 100 Stonewall Blvd., Suite 3, Wrentham MA 02093. (800)644-3561. **E-mail:** queries@ptotoday.com. **Website:** www.ptotoday.com. **Contact:** Emily Graham, chief content editor. **30% freelance written.** Magazine published 6 times during the school year covering the work of school parent-teacher groups. Celebrates the work of school parent group volunteers and provide resources to help parent group leaders do that work more effectively. Estab. 1999. Circ. 80,000. Byline given. Pays on acceptance, net 30 days. Offers 30% kill fee. Publishes ms an average of 4-6 months after acceptance. Editorial lead time 4-6 months. Submit seasonal material 4-6 months in advance. Accepts queries by e-mail. Accepts simultaneous submissions. Sample copy by request. Guidelines by e-mail or online.

NONFICTION Needs general interest, how-to, interview, personal experience. **Buys 8-10 mss/year.** Query. "We review but do not encourage unsolicited submissions." Features are roughly 800-1,500 words. Average assignment is 1,000-1,200 words. Department pieces are 600-900 words. **Payment depends on the difficulty of the topic and the experience of the writer. "We pay by the assignment, not by the word; our pay scale ranges from $200 to $500 for features and $150 to $400 for departments. We occasionally pay more for high-impact stories and highly experienced writers. We buy all rights, and we pay on acceptance (within 30 days of invoice)."**

💲 SCHOOLARTS MAGAZINE

Davis Art, 50 Portland St., Worcester MA 01608. **E-mail:** lmarkey@schoolartsmagazine.com. **E-mail:** sa-submissions@davisart.com. **Website:** schoolartsmagazine.com. **Contact:** Lorraine Markey. **85% freelance written.** Monthly magazine (September-July), serving arts and craft education profession, K-12, higher education, and museum education programs written by and for art teachers. Estab. 1901. Pays on publication (honorarium and 6 copies). No kill fee. Publishes ms an average of 24 months after acceptance. Accepts queries by mail. Responds in 2-4 months to queries. Guidelines available online.

NONFICTION Query or send complete ms and SASE. E-mail submissions are also accepted. See website for details. Length: 800 words maximum. **Pays $30-150.** Pays expenses of writers on assignment.

💲 TEACHERS & WRITERS MAGAZINE

Teachers & Writers Collaborative, 540 President St., 3rd Floor, Brooklyn NY 11215. (212)691-6590. **Fax:** (212)675-0171. **E-mail:** editors@twc.org. **Website:** http://teachersandwritersmagazine.org/. **Contact:** Amy Swauger. **30% freelance written.** *Teachers & Writers Magazine* covers a cross-section of contemporary issues and innovations in education and writing, and engages writers, educators, critics, and students in a conversation on the nature of creativity and the imagination. Estab. 1967. Circ. 7,000. Byline given. Pays on publication. No kill fee. Publishes ms an average of 2-4 months after acceptance. Editorial lead time 2-4 months. Submit seasonal material 2-4 months in advance. Accepts queries by e-mail. Accepts simulta-

neous submissions. Responds in 1-2 months to queries and submissions. Guidelines online.

NONFICTION Needs book excerpts, essays, how-to, interview, opinion, personal experience, creative writing exercises. Length: 500-2,500 words. **Pays $50-150.**

💲 TEACHERS OF VISION

A Publication of Christian Educators Association, P.O. Box 45610, Westlake OH 44145. (888)798-1124. **E-mail:** TOV@ceai.org. **Website:** www.ceai.org. **70% freelance written.** Magazine published 3 times/year for Christians in public education. *Teachers of Vision*'s articles inspire, inform, and equip teachers and administrators in the educational arena. Readers look for teacher tips, integrating faith and work, and general interest education articles. Topics include subject matter, religious expression and activity in public schools, and legal rights of Christian educators. Audience is primarily public school educators. Other readers include teachers in private schools, university professors, school administrators, parents, and school board members. Estab. 1953. Circ. 10,000. Byline given. Pays on publication. No kill fee. Publishes ms an average of 6 months after acceptance. Editorial lead time 4 months. Submit seasonal material 4 months in advance. Accepts queries by mail, e-mail. Accepts simultaneous submissions. Responds in 1 month to queries; 3-4 months to mss. Sample copy for SAE with 9x12 envelope and 4 first-class stamps. Guidelines available online.

NONFICTION Needs how-to, humor, inspirational, interview, opinion, personal experience, religious. No preaching. **Buys 30-50 mss/year.** Query or send complete ms if 2,000 words or less. Length: 1,500 words. **Pays $25-50.** Pays expenses of writers on assignment.

REPRINTS Buys reprints.

COLUMNS Query. **Pays $25-50.**

POETRY Will accept poetry if it pertains to education.

FILLERS Send with SASE—must relate to public education.

💲💲 TEACHING THEATRE

Educational Theatre Association, 2343 Auburn Ave., Cincinnati OH 45219-2815. (513)421-3900. **E-mail:** gbossler@schooltheatre.org; publicationsdept@schooltheatre.org. **Website:** www.schooltheatre.org. **Contact:** Gregory Bossler, managing editor. **65% free-**

lance written. Quarterly magazine covering education theater K-12; primary emphasis on middle and secondary level education. Estab. 1989. Circ. 5,000. Byline given. Pays on acceptance. No kill fee. Publishes ms an average of 3 months after acceptance. Editorial lead time 2 months. Accepts queries by mail, e-mail. Accepts simultaneous submissions. Responds in 4-6 weeks to queries. Responds in 3 months to mss. Sample copy available online. Guidelines available online.

NONFICTION Needs book excerpts, essays, how-to, interview. **Buys 12-15 mss/year.** Query. A typical issue might include: an article on theatre curriculum development; a profile of an exemplary theatre education program; a how-to teach piece on acting, directing, or playwriting; and a news story or 2 about pertinent educational theatre issues and events. Once articles are accepted, authors are asked to supply their work electronically via e-mail. Length: 750-4,000 words. **Pays $150-500.** Pays expenses of writers on assignment.

$$$$ TEACHING TOLERANCE

A Project of The Southern Poverty Law Center, 400 Washington Ave., Montgomery AL 36104. (334)956-8374. **Fax:** (334)956-8488. **E-mail:** editor@teachingtolerance.org. **Website:** www.teachingtolerance.org. **Contact:** Adrienne van der Valk, managing editor. **30% freelance written.** Semiannual magazine. Estab. 1991. Circ. 400,000. Byline given. Pays on acceptance. No kill fee. Editorial lead time 6 months. Submit seasonal material 6 months in advance. Accepts queries by mail, fax, online submission form. Accepts simultaneous submissions. Sample copy avialble online. Guidelines available online.

NONFICTION Needs essays, how-to, personal experience, photo feature. No jargon, rhetoric or academic analysis. No theoretical discussions on the pros/cons of multicultural education. **Buys 2-4 mss/year.** Submit outlines or complete mss. Length: 400-1,600 words. **Pays $1/word.** Pays expenses of writers on assignment.

COLUMNS Features (stories and issues related to anti-bias education), 800-1,600 words; Why I Teach (personal reflections about life in the classroom), 600 words or less; Story Corner (designed to be read by or to students and must cover topics that are appealing to children), 600 words; Activity Exchange (brief descriptions of classroom lesson plans, special projects or other school activities that can be used by others to promote tolerance), 400 words. **Buys 8-12 mss/year.** Query with published clips. Does not accept unsolicited mss. **Pays $1/ word.**

$ TECH DIRECTIONS

Prakken Publications, Inc., P.O. Box 8623, Ann Arbor MI 48107-8623. (734)975-2800. **Fax:** (734)975-2787. **E-mail:** vanessa@techdirections.com. **Website:** www.techdirections.com. **Contact:** Vanessa Revelli, managing editor. **100% freelance written. Eager to work with new/unpublished writers.** Monthly (except June and July) magazine covering issues, trends, and activities of interest to science, technical, and technology educators at the elementary through post-secondary school levels. Estab. 1934. Circ. 40,000. Byline given. Pays on publication. No kill fee. Publishes ms an average of 1 year after acceptance. Responds in 1 month to queries. Sample copy for $5. Guidelines available online.

NONFICTION Needs general interest, how-to, personal experience, technical, think pieces. **Buys 50 unsolicited mss/year.** Length: 2,000 words. **Pays $50-150.** Pays expenses of writers on assignment.

COLUMNS Direct from Washington (education news from Washington, DC); Technology Today (new products under development); Technologies Past (profiles the inventors of last century); Mastering Computers, Technology Concepts (project orientation).

ELECTRONICS & COMMUNICATION

$ THE ACUTA JOURNAL

Information Communications Technology in Higher Education, 152 W. Zandale Dr., Suite 200, Lexington KY 40503. (859)278-3338. **Fax:** (859)278-3268. **E-mail:** pscott@acuta.org. **Website:** www.acuta.org. **Contact:** Pat Scott, director of communications. **20% freelance written.** Quarterly professional association journal covering information communications technology (ICT) in higher education. Audience includes, primarily, middle to upper management in the IT/telecommunications department on college/university campuses. They are highly skilled, technology-oriented professionals who provide data, voice, and video communications services for residential and academic purposes. Estab. 1997. Circ. 2,200. Byline given. Pays on publication. No kill fee. Publishes ms an average of 6 months after acceptance. Editorial lead time 6 months. Accepts queries by mail, e-mail, fax, phone. Accepts simultaneous submissions. Responds in 2 weeks to queries. Request a sample copy by calling (859)721-1659. Guidelines online.

NONFICTION Needs how-to, technical, case study, college/university application of technology. **Buys 6-8 mss/year.** Query. Length: 1,200-4,000 words. **Pays 8-10¢/word.** Pays expenses of writers on assignment.

💲💲 DIGITAL OUTPUT

Rockport Custom Publishing, LLC, 100 Cummings Center, Suite 321E, Beverly MA 01915. (978)921-7850, ext. 13. **E-mail:** mdonovan@rdigitaloutput.net; edit@rockportpubs.com. **Website:** www.digitaloutput.net. **Contact:** Melissa Donovan, editor. **70% freelance written.** Monthly magazine covering electronic prepress, desktop publishing, and digital imaging, with articles ranging from digital capture and design to electronic prepress and digital printing. *Digital Output* is a national business publication for electronic publishers and digital imagers, providing monthly articles which examine the latest technologies and digital methods and discuss how to profit from them. Readers include service bureaus, prepress and reprographic houses, designers, commercial printers, wide-format printers, ad agencies, corporate communications, sign shops, and others. Estab. 1994. Circ. 25,000. Byline given. Pays on publication. Offers 10-20% kill fee. Publishes ms an average of 2 months after acceptance. Editorial lead time 3 months. Submit seasonal material 3 months in advance. Accepts queries by mail, e-mail. Accepts simultaneous submissions. Responds in 3 weeks to queries. Responds in 1 month to mss. Sample copy for $4.50 or online.

NONFICTION Needs how-to, interview, technical, case studies. **Buys 36 mss/year.** Query with published clips or hyperlinks to posted clips. Length: 1,500-4,000 words. **Pays $250-600.**

💲💲 ELECTRICAL APPARATUS

Barks Publications, Inc., Suite 901, 500 N. Michigan Ave., Chicago IL 60611. (312)321-9440. **Fax:** (312)321-1288. **E-mail:** eamagazine@barks.com. **Website:** www.barks.com. **Contact:** Elizabeth Van Ness, publisher; Kevin N. Jones, senior editor. Monthly magazine for persons working in electrical and electronic maintenance, in industrial plants and service and sales centers, who install and service electric mo-

tors, transformers, generators, controls, and related equipment. Contact staff members by telephone for their preferred e-mail addresses. Estab. 1967. Circ. 16,000. Byline given. Pays on publication. No kill fee. Publishes ms an average of 1 month after acceptance. Accepts queries by mail, e-mail, fax. Accepts simultaneous submissions. Responds in 1 week to queries sent by US mail.

NONFICTION Needs technical. Length: 1,500-2,500 words. **Pays $250-500 for assigned articles.** Pays expenses of writers on assignment.

💲💲 SOUND & VIDEO CONTRACTOR

NewBay Media, LLC, 28 E. 28th St., 12th Floor, New York NY 10016. (818)236-3667. **Fax:** (913)514-3683. **E-mail:** cwisehart@nbmedia.com; jgutierrez@nbmedia.com. **Website:** www.svconline.com. Cynthia Wisehart, editor. **Contact:** Cynthia Wisehart, editor; Jessaca Gutierrez, managing and online editor. **60% freelance written.** Monthly magazine covering professional audio, video, security, acoustical design, sales, and marketing. Estab. 1983. Circ. 24,000. Byline given. Pays on acceptance. No kill fee. Publishes ms an average of 3 months after acceptance. Editorial lead time 3 months. Accepts queries by mail, e-mail, fax, phone. Accepts simultaneous submissions. Responds ASAP to queries. Sample copy and writer's guidelines free.

NONFICTION Needs historical, how-to, photo feature, technical, professional audio/video applications, installations, product reviews. No opinion pieces, advertorial, interview/profile, expose/gossip. **Buys 60 mss/year.** Query. Length: 1,000-2,500 words. **Pays $200-1,200 for assigned articles. Pays $200-650 for unsolicited articles.**

REPRINTS Accepts previously published submissions.

COLUMNS Security Technology Review (technical install information); Sales & Marketing (techniques for installation industry); Video Happenings (Pro video/projection/storage technical info), all 1,500 words. **Buys 30 mss/year.** Query. **Pays $200-350.**

💲💲 SQL SERVER MAGAZINE

Penton Media, 221 E. 29th St., Loveland CO 80538. (970)663-4700. **Fax:** (970)667-2321. **E-mail:** Debra.Donston-Miller@penton.com. **Website:** www.sqlmag.com. **Contact:** Deb Donston-Miller, editor. **35% freelance written.** Monthly magazine covering Microsoft SQL Server. *SQL Server Magazine* is the only magazine completely devoted to helping developers and DBAs master new and emerging SQL Server technologies and issues. It provides practical advice and lots of code examples for SQL Server developers and administrators, and includes how-to articles, tips, tricks, and programming techniques offered by SQL Server experts. Estab. 1999. Circ. 20,000. Byline given. "Penton Media pays for articles upon publication. Payment rates are based on the author's writing experience and the quality of the article submitted. We will discuss the payment rate for your article when we notify you of its acceptance." Offers $100 kill fee. Publishes ms an average of 6 months after acceptance. Editorial lead time 4+ months. Accepts queries by mail, e-mail. Accepts simultaneous submissions. Responds in 6 weeks to queries. Responds in 2-3 months to mss. Sample copy available online. Guidelines available online.

NONFICTION Needs how-to, technical, SQL Server administration and programming. Nothing promoting third-party products or companies. **Buys 25-35 mss/year.** Send complete ms. Length: 1,800-2,500 words. **Pays $200 for feature articles; $500 for Focus articles.**

COLUMNS Contact: R2R Editor. Reader to Reader (helpful SQL Server hints and tips from readers), 200-400 words. **Buys 6-12 mss/year.** Send complete ms. **Pays $50**

ENERGY & UTILITIES

⊘ $ $ ELECTRICAL BUSINESS

CLB Media, Inc., 222 Edward St., Aurora ON L4G 1W6 Canada. (905)727-0077; (905)713-4391. **Fax:** (905)727-0017. **E-mail:** acapkun@annexweb.com. **Website:** www.ebmag.com. **Contact:** Anthony Capkun, editor. **35% freelance written.** Tabloid published 10 times/year covering the Canadian electrical industry. *Electrical Business* targets electrical contractors and electricians. It provides practical information readers can use right away in their work and for running their business and assets. Estab. 1964. Circ. 18,097. Byline given. Pays on acceptance. Offers 50% kill fee. Publishes ms an average of 1-2 months after acceptance. Editorial lead time 3 months. Submit seasonal material 6 months in advance. Accepts queries by e-mail, phone. Accepts simultaneous submissions. Responds in 1 month. Sample copy online. Guidelines online.

NONFICTION Needs how-to, technical. Special issues: Summer Blockbuster issue (June/July); Special Homebuilders' issue (November/December). **Buys 15 mss/year.** Query. Length: 800-1,200 words. **Pays 40¢/word.** Pays expenses of writers on assignment.

COLUMNS Atlantic Focus (stories from Atlantic Canada); Western Focus (stories from Western Canada, including Manitoba); Trucks for the Trade (articles pertaining to the vehicles used by electrical contractors); Tools for the Trade (articles pertaining to tools used by contractors); all 800 words. **Buys 6 mss/year.** Query. **Pays 40¢/word.**

$ $ PUBLIC POWER

2451 Crystal Dr., Suite 1000, Arlington VA 22202-4804. (202)467-2900. **Fax:** (202)467-2910. **E-mail:** news@publicpower.org; ldalessandro@publicpower.org; rthomas@publicpower.org. **Website:** www.publicpower.org. **Contact:** Laura D'Alessandro, editor; Robert Thomas, art director. **60% freelance written. Prefers to work with published/established writers.** Publication of the American Public Power Association, published 6 times a year. Emphasizes electric power provided by cities, towns, and utility districts. Estab. 1942. Circ. 14,000. Byline given. Pays on acceptance. No kill fee. Publishes ms an average of 3 months after acceptance. Accepts queries by mail, e-mail, fax. Accepts simultaneous submissions. Responds in 6 months to queries. Sample copy and writer's guidelines free.

NONFICTION **Pays $500 and up.** Pays expenses of writers on assignment.

ENGINEERING & TECHNOLOGY

⊘ $ $ $ CANADIAN CONSULTING ENGINEER

Business Information Group, 80 Valleybrook Dr., Toronto ON M3B 2S9 Canada. (416)510-5119. **Fax:** (416)510-5134. **E-mail:** dpicklyk@ccemag.com. **Website:** www.canadianconsultingengineer.com. **Contact:** Doug Picklyk, editor. **20% freelance written.** Bimonthly magazine covering consulting engineering in private practice. Estab. 1958. Circ. 8,900. Byline given depending on length of story. Pays on publication. Offers 50% kill fee. Publishes ms an average of 4 months after acceptance. Editorial lead time 6 months.

Accepts simultaneous submissions. Responds in 3 months to mss. Sample copy free.

NONFICTION Needs historical, new product. **Buys 8-10 mss/year.** Query with published clips. Length: 300-1,500 words. **Pays $200-1,000 (Canadian).** Pays expenses of writers on assignment.

COLUMNS Export (selling consulting engineering services abroad); Management (managing consulting engineering businesses); On-Line (trends in CAD systems); Employment; Business; Construction and Environmental Law (Canada); all 800 words. **Buys 4 mss/year.** Query with published clips. **Pays $250-400.**

☺☺ COMPOSITES MANUFACTURING MAGAZINE

American Composites Manufacturers Association, 3033 Wilson Blvd., Suite 420, Arlington VA 22201. (703)525-0511. **E-mail:** communications@acmanet. org; info@acmanet.org. **Website:** www.acmanet.org. Monthly magazine covering any industry that uses reinforced composites: marine, aerospace, infrastructure, automotive, transportation, corrosion, architecture, tub and shower, sports, and recreation. Primarily publishes educational pieces, the how-to of the shop environment. Also publishes marketing, business trends, and economic forecasts relevant to the composites industry. Estab. 1979. Circ. 12,000. Byline given. Pays on acceptance. No kill fee. Publishes ms an average of 2-3 months after acceptance. Editorial lead time 2 months. Accepts queries by e-mail. Accepts simultaneous submissions. Responds in 1 week to queries. Responds in 1 month to mss. Sample copy free. Guidelines by e-mail and online. Specific details on submission types available online.

NONFICTION Needs how-to, new product, technical, marketing, related business trends and forecasts. Special issues: "Each January we publish a World Market Report where we cover all niche markets and all geographic areas relevant to the composites industry. Freelance material will be considered strongly for this issue." No need to query company or personal profiles unless there is an extremely unique or novel angle. **Buys 5-10 mss/year.** Query. *Composites Manufacturing* invites freelance feature submissions, all of which should be sent via e-mail as a Microsoft Word attachment. A query letter is required. Length: 1,500-2,000 words. **Pays 20-40¢/word (negotiable).** Pays expenses of writers on assignment.

COLUMNS "We publish columns on HR, relevant government legislation, industry lessons learned, regulatory affairs, and technology. Average word length for columns is 500 words. We would entertain any new column idea that hits hard on industry matters." Query. **Pays $300-350.**

♻☺☺ CONNECTIONS+

The Magazine for ICT Professionals, Business Information Group, 80 Valleybrook Dr., Toronto ON M3B 2S9 Canada. (416)510-6752. **Fax:** (416)510-5134. **E-mail:** pbarker@connectionsplus.ca. **Website:** www. connectionsplus.ca. **Contact:** Paul Barker, editor. **50% freelance written.** Magazine published 6 times/year covering the structured cabling/telecommunications industry. Estab. 1998. Circ. 15,000 print; 45,000 electronic. Byline given. Pays on publication. No kill fee. Publishes ms an average of 1 month after acceptance. Editorial lead time 3 months. Submit seasonal material 1 month in advance. Accepts queries by mail, e-mail, phone. Accepts simultaneous submissions. Sample copy available online. Guidelines free.

NONFICTION Needs technical. No reprints or previously written articles. All articles are assigned by editor based on query or need of publication. **Buys 12 mss/year.** Query with published clips. Length: 1,500-2,500 words. **Pays 40-50¢/word.** Pays expenses of writers on assignment.

COLUMNS Focus on Engineering/Design; Focus on Installation; Focus on Maintenance/Testing; all 1,500 words. **Buys 7 mss/year.** Query with published clips. **Pays 40-50¢/word.**

☺☺☺ ENTERPRISE MINNESOTA MAGAZINE

Enterprise Minnesota, Inc., 310 Fourth Ave. S., Suite 7050, Minneapolis MN 55415. (612)373-2900. **Fax:** (612)373-2901. **E-mail:** editor@enterpriseminnesota.org. **Website:** www.enterpriseminnesota.org. **90% freelance written.** Magazine published 5 times/year. *Enterprise Minnesota Magazine* is for the owners and top management of Minnesota's technology and manufacturing companies. The magazine covers technology trends and issues, global trade, management techniques, and finance. Profiles new and growing companies, new products, and the innovators and entrepreneurs of Minnesota's technology sector. Estab. 1991. Circ. 16,000. Byline given. Pays on publication. Offers 10% kill fee. Publishes ms an average of 3 months after acceptance. Editorial lead time 1 month.

Submit seasonal material 1 year in advance. Accepts queries by mail, e-mail. Accepts simultaneous submissions. Guidelines free.

NONFICTION Needs general interest, how-to, interview. **Buys 60 mss/year.** Query with published clips. **Pays $150-1,000.** Pays expenses of writers on assignment.

COLUMNS Feature Well (Q&A format, provocative ideas from Minnesota business and industry leaders), 2,000 words; Up Front (mini profiles, anecdotal news items), 250-500 words. Query with published clips.

⊗⊕ MFRTECH EJOURNAL

Manufacturers Group Inc., P.O. Box 4310, Lexington KY 40544. **E-mail:** editor@mfrtech.com. **Website:** www.mfrtech.com. **40% freelance written.** Magazine published daily online covering manufacturing and technology from news throughout the U.S. Editorial includes anufacturing news, expansions, acquisition white papers, case histories, new product announcements, feature submissions, book synopsis. Estab. 1976 (print). Circ. 60,000+ weekly subscribers (e-mail); 750,000 monthly online visitors. Byline given. Pays 30 days following publication. Offers 25% kill fee. Publishes ms 3-4 days after acceptance. Editorial lead time 2 weeks. Submit seasonal material 2 weeks in advance. Accepts simultaneous submissions. Sample copy online. Guidelines by e-mail.

NONFICTION Needs new product, opinion, technical. Does not want general interest, inspirational, personal, travel, book excerpts. Length: 750-1,500 words; byline: 75 words. **Pays $0.20/word published (prior to approval from editor).**

COLUMNS New Plant Announcement, Acquisitions, Expansions, New Technology, Federal, Case Histories, Human Resources, Marketing. Query. **Pays $0.20/word (prior to approval from editor).**

⊗⊕ MINORITY ENGINEER

Equal Opportunity Publications, Inc., 445 Broad Hollow Rd., Suite 425, Melville NY 11747. (631)421-9421. **Fax:** (516)421-0359. **E-mail:** bloehr@eop.com; info@eop.com. **Website:** www.eop.com. **Contact:** Barbara Capella Loehr, editor. **60% freelance written. Prefers to work with published/established writers.** Triannual magazine covering career guidance for minority engineering students and minority professional engineers. Estab. 1969. Circ. 15,000. Byline given. Pays on publication. No kill fee. Publishes ms an average of 3 months after acceptance. Editorial lead time 3 months.

Accepts queries by mail, e-mail, fax, phone. Accepts simultaneous submissions. Responds in 2 weeks to queries. Responds in 2 months to mss. Sample copy and writer's guidelines for 9x12 SAE with 5 first-class stamps. Guidelines free.

NONFICTION Needs book excerpts, general interest, how-to, interview, opinion, personal experience, technical, articles on job search techniques, role models. No general information. Query. Length: 1,500-2,500 words. **Pays $350 for assigned articles.** Pays expenses of writers on assignment.

REPRINTS Send typed ms with rights for sale noted and information about when and where the material previously appeared. Pays 100% of amount paid for an original article.

⊗⊕ WOMAN ENGINEER

Equal Opportunity Publications, Inc., 445 Broad Hollow Rd., Suite 425, Melville NY 11747. (631)421-9421. **Fax:** (631)421-1352. **E-mail:** info@eop.com; bloehr@eop.com. **Website:** www.eop.com. **Contact:** Barbara Capella Loehr, editor. **60% freelance written. Works with a small number of new/unpublished writers each year.** Triannual magazine aimed at advancing the careers of women engineering students and professional women engineers. Estab. 1968. Circ. 16,000. Byline given. Pays on publication. No kill fee. Publishes ms an average of 3 months after acceptance. Editorial lead time 3 months. Accepts queries by mail, e-mail, fax, phone. Accepts simultaneous submissions. Responds in 2 weeks to queries. Responds in 2 months to mss. Sample copy and writer's guidelines free.

NONFICTION Needs how-to, interview, personal experience. Query. Length: 1,500-2,500 words. **Pays $350 for assigned articles.** Pays expenses of writers on assignment.

ENTERTAINMENT & THE ARTS

⊗⊕⊗⊕ AMERICAN CINEMATOGRAPHER

American Society of Cinematographers, 1782 N. Orange Dr., Hollywood CA 90028. (800)448-0145; outside US: (323)969-4333. **Fax:** (323)876-4973. **E-mail:** stephen@ascmag.com. **E-mail:** jon@ascmag.com. **Website:** www.theasc.com. **Contact:** Stephen Pizzello, editor-in-chief and publisher; Jon Witmer, Jon Witmer, managing editor (jon@ascmag.com). **90% freelance written.** Monthly magazine covering cinematography (motion picture, TV, music video, commercial). "*American Cinematographer* is a trade publication devoted to the art and craft of cinematography. Our readers are predominantly film industry professionals." Estab. 1919. Circ. 33,000. Byline given. Pays on publication. Offers 50% kill fee. Publishes ms an average of 2-3 months after acceptance. Editorial lead time 2 months. Submit seasonal material 3 months in advance. Accepts queries by mail, e-mail, phone. Responds in 2 weeks to queries; 2 months to mss. Sample copy and guidelines free.

NONFICTION Needs interview, new product, technical. No reviews or opinion pieces. **Buys 20-25 mss/year.** Query with published clips. Length: 1,000-4,000 words. **Pays $400-1,500.** Pays expenses of writers on assignment.

🌐🌐 AMERICAN THEATRE

Theatre Communications Group, 520 Eighth Ave., 24th Floor, New York NY 10018. (212)609-5900. **Fax:** (212)609-5902. **E-mail:** rwkendt@tcg.org. **Website:** www.tcg.org. **Contact:** Rob Weinert-Kendt, editor-in-chief. **60% freelance written.** Monthly magazine covering theatre. Focus is on American regional non-profit theatre. *American Theatre* typically publishes 2-3 features and 4-6 back-of-the-book articles covering trends and events in all types of theatre, as well as economic and legislative developments affecting the arts. *American Theatre* rarely publishes articles about commercial, amateur, or university theatre, nor about works that would widely be classified as dance or opera, except at the editors' discretion. While significant productions may be highlighted in the Critic's Notebook section, *American Theatre* does not review productions (but does review theatre-related books). Estab. 1982. Circ. 100,000. Byline given. Pays on publication. Editorial lead time 2 months. Submit seasonal material 3 months in advance. Accepts queries by mail, e-mail, online submission form. Accepts simultaneous submissions. Responds in 2 months to queries. Sample copy and guidelines available online.

NONFICTION Needs book excerpts, essays, general interest, historical, how-to, humor, inspirational, interview, opinion, personal experience, photo feature, travel. Special issues: Training (January); International (May/June); Season Preview (October). No unsolicited submissions (rarely accepted). No reviews. Writers wishing to submit articles to *American Theatre* should mail or e-mail a query to editor-in-chief

Rob Weinert-Kendt outlining a particular proposal; unsolicited material is rarely accepted. Include a brief résumé and sample clips. Planning of major articles usually occurs at least 3 months in advance of publication. All mss are subject to editing. Length: 200-2,000 words. **"While fees are negotiated per ms, we pay an average of $350 for full-length (2,500-3,500 words) features, and less for shorter pieces."** Pays expenses of writers on assignment.

🌐🌐 DRAMATICS MAGAZINE

Educational Theatre Association, 2343 Auburn Ave., Cincinnati OH 45219. (513)421-3900. **E-mail:** gbossler@schooltheatre.org. **Website:** schooltheatre.org. **Contact:** Gregory Bossler, editor-in-chief. *Dramatics* is for students (mainly high school age) and teachers of theater. The magazine wants student readers to grow as theater artists and become a more discerning and appreciative audience. Material is directed to both theater students and their teachers, with strong student slant. Tries to portray the theater community in all its diversity. Estab. 1929. Circ. 45,000. Byline given. Pays on acceptance. Publishes ms 3 months after acceptance. Accepts queries by mail, e-mail. Accepts simultaneous submissions. Sample copy available for 9x12 SAE with 4-ounce first-class postage. Guidelines available for SASE.

NONFICTION Needs how-to, profile, practical articles on acting, directing, design, production, and other facets of theater; career-oriented profiles of working theater professionals. Special issues: College Theater Programs (November); Summer Theater Work and Study Opportunities (January). Does not want academic treatises. **Buys 50 mss/year.** Submit complete ms. Length: 750-3,000 words. **Pays $50-500 for articles.** Pays expenses of writers on assignment.

FICTION Young adults: drama (one-act and full-length plays). "We prefer unpublished scripts that have been produced at least once." Does not want to see plays that show no understanding of the conventions of the theater. No plays for children, no Christmas or didactic "message" plays. Submit complete ms. Buys 5-9 plays/year. Emerging playwrights have better chances with résumé of credits. Length: 10 minutes to full length. **Pays $100-500 for plays.**

🌐🌐🌐 EMMY

Television Academy, 5220 Lankershim Blvd., North Hollywood CA 91601. (818)754-2800. **E-mail:** emmymag@emmys.org. **Website:** www.emmys.com/emmy-magazine. **Contact:** Editor. **90% freelance written. Prefers to work with published/established writers.** Bimonthly magazine on television for TV professionals. "From the executive suite to the editing bay, *emmy* magazine goes behind the scenes of television and digital entertainment to cover the people who make the magic happen. *Emmy*'s core readers include the members of the Television Academy and other television industry professionals. Articles must appeal to the television and digital entertainment professional while being understandable to the enthusiast." Circ. 14,000. Byline given. Pays on publication or within 6 months. Offers 25% kill fee. Publishes ms an average of 4 months after acceptance. Accepts queries by mail. Accepts simultaneous submissions. Responds in 1 month to queries. Sample copy for SAE with 9x12 envelope and 6 first-class stamps. Guidelines available online.

NONFICTION "We do not run highly technical articles, nor do we accept academic or fan-magazine approaches." Query with published clips. Length: 1,500-2,000 words. **Pays $1,000-1,200.** Pays expenses of writers on assignment.

COLUMNS Mostly written by regular contributors, but newcomers can break in with filler items with In the Mix or short profiles in Labors of Love. Length: 250-500 words, depending on department. Query with published clips. **Pays $250-500.**

💲💲 MAKE-UP ARTIST MAGAZINE
12808 NE 95th St., Vancouver WA 98682. (360)882-3488. **E-mail:** heatherw@kpgmedia.com. **Website:** www.makeupmag.com; www.makeup411.com; www.imats.net. **Contact:** Heather Wisner, managing editor. **90% freelance written.** Bimonthly magazine covering all types of professional make-up artistry. Audience is a mixture of high-level make-up artists, make-up students, fashion and movie buffs. Writers should be comfortable with technical writing, and should have substantial knowledge of at least one area of make-up, such as effects or fashion. This is an entertainment-industry magazine, so writing should have an element of fun and storytelling. Good interview skills required. Estab. 1996. Circ. 16,000. Byline given. Pays within 30 days of publication. No kill fee. Editorial lead time 6 weeks. Submit seasonal material 2 months in advance. Accepts queries by e-mail. Accepts simultaneous submissions. Sample copy for $7. Guidelines available via e-mail.

NONFICTION "Does not want fluff pieces about consumer beauty products." **Buys 20+ mss/year.** Query with published clips. Length: 500-3,000 words. **Pays 20-50¢/word.** Pays expenses of writers on assignment.

COLUMNS Lab Tech, how-to advice for effects artists, written by a current make-up artist working in a lab (700 words + photos); Backstage (behind the scenes info on a theatrical production's make-up (700 words + photos): Out of the Kit, written by make-up artists working on sets (700 words + photos); Industry Buzz (industry news), length varies. Query with published clips. .

💲 SCREEN MAGAZINE
Screen Enterprises, Inc., 676 N. LaSalle Blvd., #501, Chicago IL 60654. (312)640-0800. **Fax:** (312)640-1928. **E-mail:** editor@screenmag.com. **Website:** www.screenmag.com. **Contact:** Andrew Schneider, editor. **5% freelance written.** Biweekly Chicago-based trade magazine covering advertising and film production in the Midwest and national markets. *Screen* is written for Midwest producers (and other creatives involved) of commercials, AV, features, independent corporate, and multimedia. Estab. 1979. Circ. 15,000. Byline given. Pays on publication. No kill fee. Accepts queries by e-mail. Accepts simultaneous submissions. Responds in 3 weeks to queries. Sample copy available online.

NONFICTION Needs interview, new product, technical. No general AV; nothing specific to other markets; no no-brainers or opinion. **Buys 26 mss/year.** Query with published clips. Length: 750-1,500 words. **Pays $50.** Pays expenses of writers on assignment.

💲 SOUTHERN THEATRE
Southeastern Theatre Conference, 1175 Revolution Mill Drive, Studio 14, Greensboro NC 27405. (336)272-3645. **E-mail:** kim@setc.org. **Website:** www.setc.org/southern-theatre. **Contact:** Kim Doty. **100% freelance written.** Quarterly magazine covering all aspects of theater in the Southeast, from innovative theater companies, to important trends, to people making a difference in the region. All stories must be written in a popular magazine style but with subject matter appropriate for theater professionals (not the general public). The audience includes members of the Southeastern Theatre Conference, founded in 1949 and the nation's largest regional theater organization. These members include individuals involved in professional, community, college/university, chil-

dren's, and secondary school theater. The magazine also is purchased by more than 100 libraries. Estab. 1962. Circ. 4,200. Byline given. Pays on publication. No kill fee. Publishes ms an average of 3 months after acceptance. Editorial lead time 3 months. Submit seasonal material 6 months in advance. Accepts queries by mail, e-mail. Accepts simultaneous submissions. Responds in 3 months to queries. Responds in 6 months to mss. Sample copy for $10. Guidelines available online.

NONFICTION Needs general interest, interview. Special issues: Playwriting (Fall issue, all stories submitted by January 1). No scholarly articles. **Buys 15-20 mss/year.** Send complete ms. Length: 1,000-3,000 words. **Pays $50 for feature stories.** Pays expenses of writers on assignment.

COLUMNS *Outside the Box* (innovative solutions to problems faced by designers and technicians), 800-1,000 words; *400 Words* (column where the theater professionals can sound off on issues), 400 words; 800-1,000 words; *Words, Words, Words* (reviews of books on theater), 400 words. Query or send complete ms **No payment for columns.**

FARM

AGRICULTURAL EQUIPMENT

💲 AG WEEKLY

Lee Agri-Media, P.O. Box 918, Bismarck ND 58501. (701)255-4905. **Fax:** (701)255-2312. **E-mail:** editor@ theprairiestar.com. **Website:** www.agweekly.com. **40% freelance written.** *Ag Weekly* is an agricultural publication covering production, markets, regulation, politics. Writers need to be familiar with Idaho agricultural commodities. No printed component; website with 6,000 monthly unique visitors; weekly email newsletter with 3,000 subscribers. Byline given. Pays on publication. Publishes ms an average of 1 month after acceptance. Editorial lead time 1 month. Submit seasonal material 1 month in advance. Accepts queries by e-mail. Accepts simultaneous submissions. Responds in 2 weeks to queries. Responds in 1 month to mss. Sample copy available online. Guidelines with #10 SASE.

NONFICTION Needs interview, new product, opinion, travel, ag-related. Does not want anything other than local/regional ag-related articles. No cowboy poetry. **Buys 100 mss/year.** Query. Length: 250-700 words. **Pays $40-70.** Pays expenses of writers on assignment.

💲💲 FLORIDA GROWER

Meister Media Worldwide, 37733 Euclid Ave., Willoughby OH 44094. (440)942-2000. **E-mail:** fgiles@ meistermedia.com; pprusnak@meistermedia.com. **Website:** www.growingproduce.com/magazine/florida-grower; www.meistermedia.com/publications/florida-grower. **Contact:** Frank Giles, editor; Paul Rusnak, managing editor. **10% freelance written.** Monthly magazine edited for the Florida farmer with commercial production interest primarily in citrus, vegetables, and other ag endeavors. Goal is to provide articles that update and inform on such areas as production, ag financing, farm labor relations, technology, safety, education, and regulation. Estab. 1907. Circ. 12,200. Byline given. Pays on publication. No kill fee. Editorial lead time 2 months. Submit seasonal material 3 months in advance. Accepts queries by mail, e-mail, fax, phone. Accepts simultaneous submissions. Responds in 1 month to queries. Sample copy for SAE with 9x12 envelope and 5 First-Class stamps. Guidelines free.

NONFICTION Needs interview, photo feature, technical. Query with published clips. Length: 700-1,000 words. **Pays $150-250.**

CROPS & SOIL MANAGEMENT

💲💲 AMERICAN AGRICULTURIST

Farm Progress Company/Informa, 5227 Baltimore Pike, Littlestown PA 17340. (717)359-0150. **Fax:** (717)359-0250. **E-mail:** john.vogel@informa.com. **Website:** www.americanagriculturist.com. **Contact:** John Vogel, editor. **20% freelance written.** Monthly magazine covering cutting-edge technology and news to help farmers improve their operations. Publishes cutting-edge technology with ready on-farm application. Estab. 1842. Circ. 32,000. Pays on publication. No kill fee. Publishes ms an average of 3 months after acceptance. Editorial lead time 3 months. Submit seasonal material 3 months in advance. Accepts queries by e-mail, fax. Responds in 2 weeks to queries; in 1 month to mss. Guidelines for #10 SASE.

NONFICTION Needs how-to, interview, new product, technical. No stories without a strong tie to Northeast and Mid-Atlantic farming. **Buys 20 mss/ year.** Query. Length: 500-1,000 words. **Pays $250-500.** Pays expenses of writers on assignment.

💲💲 AMERICAN FRUIT GROWER AND WESTERN FRUIT GROWER

Meister Media Worldwide, 37733 Euclid Ave., Willoughby OH 44094. (290)573-8740. **E-mail:** deddy@meistermedia.com. **Website:** www.fruitgrower.com. **Contact:** David Eddy, editor. **3% freelance written.** Annual magazines covering commercial fruit growing. "Founded in 1880, *American Fruit Grower* and *Western Fruit Grower* magazines reaches producers, shippers, and other influencers who serve the fresh and processing markets for deciduous fruits, citrus, grapes, berries, and nuts. *Western Fruit Grower* has additional reach to producers and others who work with unique varieties and climate and market conditions in the American West." Estab. 1880. Circ. 44,000. Byline given. Pays on publication. No kill fee. Publishes ms an average of 4 months after acceptance. Editorial lead time 2 months. Submit seasonal material 4 months in advance. Accepts queries by mail, e-mail, fax, phone. Accepts simultaneous submissions. Responds in 2 weeks to queries; in 2 months to mss. Sample copy and writer's guidelines free.

NONFICTION Needs how-to. **Buys 6-10 mss/year.** Send complete ms. Length: 800-1,200 words. **Pays $200-250.** Pays expenses of writers on assignment.

💲💲 COTTON GROWER MAGAZINE

Meister Media Worldwide, Cotton Media Group, 8000 Centerview Pkwy., Suite 114, Cordova TN 38018-4246. (901)756-8822. **E-mail:** mccue@meister-media.com. **Website:** www.cotton247.com. **Contact:** Mike McCue, editor. **5% freelance written.** Monthly magazine covering cotton production, cotton markets, and related subjects. Circ. 43,000. Byline given. Pays on acceptance. No kill fee. Publishes ms an average of 2 months after acceptance. Editorial lead time 2 months. Submit seasonal material 2 months in advance. Accepts queries by mail, e-mail, fax, phone. Accepts simultaneous submissions. Sample copy free.

NONFICTION Needs interview, new product, photo feature, technical. No fiction or humorous pieces. **Buys 5-10 mss/year.** Query with published clips.

Length: 500-800 words. **Pays $200-400.** Pays expenses of writers on assignment.

💲💲 DIGGER

Oregon Association of Nurseries, 29751 SW Town Center Loop W., Wilsonville OR 97070. (503)682-5089. **Fax:** (503)682-5099. **E-mail:** ckipp@oan.org; info@oan.org. **Website:** www.diggermagazine.com. **Contact:** Curt Kipp, editor. **50% freelance written.** Monthly magazine covering the nursery and greenhouse industry. *Digger* is a monthly magazine that focuses on industry trends, regulations, research, marketing, and membership activities. In August the magazine becomes *Digger Farwest Edition*, with all the features of *Digger* plus a complete guide to the annual Farwest Show, one of North America's top-attended nursery industry trade shows. Circ. 8,000. Byline given. Pays on receipt of copy. Offers 100% kill fee. Publishes ms an average of 2 months after acceptance. Editorial lead time 6 weeks. Submit seasonal material 2 months in advance. Accepts queries by mail, e-mail, fax, phone. Accepts simultaneous submissions. Sample copy and writer's guidelines free.

NONFICTION Needs general interest, how-to, interview, personal experience, technical. Special issues: Farwest Edition (August): "This is a triple-size issue that runs in tandem with our annual trade show (14,500 circulation for this issue)." No articles not related or pertinent to nursery and greenhouse industry. **Buys 20-30 mss/year.** Query. Length: 800-2,000 words. **Pays $125-400 for assigned articles. Pays $100-300 for unsolicited articles.** Pays expenses of writers on assignment.

💲💲 FRUIT GROWERS NEWS

Great American Publishing, P.O. Box 128, Sparta MI 49345. (616)887-9008. **Fax:** (616)887-2666. **E-mail:** fgnedit@fruitgrowersnews.com. **Website:** www.fruit-growersnews.com. **Contact:** Matt Milkovich, managing editor; Lee Dean, editorial director. **10% freelance written.** Monthly tabloid covering agriculture. "Our objective is to provide commercial fruit growers of all sizes with information to help them succeed." Estab. 1961. Circ. 16,429. Pays on publication. No kill fee. Publishes ms an average of 2 months after acceptance. Editorial lead time 1-2 months. Submit seasonal material 3 months in advance. Accepts queries by mail, e-mail, fax. Accepts simultaneous submissions. Responds in 2 weeks to queries. Responds in 1 month to mss. Sample copy free.

NONFICTION Needs general interest, interview, new product. No advertorials or other puff pieces. **Buys 25 mss/year.** Query with published clips and résumé. Length: 600-1,000 words. **Pays $150-250.** Pays expenses of writers on assignment.

🅢🅢 GOOD FRUIT GROWER

Washington State Fruit Commission, 105 S. 18th St., Suite 217, Yakima WA 98901. (509)853-3520. **Fax:** (509)853-3521. **E-mail:** casey.corr@goodfruit.com. **Website:** www.goodfruit.com. **Contact:** O. Casey Corr, managing editor. **10% freelance written.** Semimonthly magazine covering tree fruit/grape growing. Estab. 1946. Circ. 11,000. Byline given. Pays on acceptance. Publishes ms an average of 2 months after acceptance. Accepts queries by mail, e-mail. Accepts simultaneous submissions. Responds in 1 week to queries; in 1 month to mss. Sample copy free. Guidelines free.

NONFICTION Buys 20 mss/year. Query. Length: 500-1,500 words. **Pays 40-50¢/word.** Pays expenses of writers on assignment.

🅢 GRAIN JOURNAL

Country Journal Publishing Co., 3065 Pershing Court, Decatur IL 62526. (800)728-7511. **E-mail:** ed@grain-net.com. **Website:** www.grainnet.com. **Contact:** Ed Zdrojewski, editor. **5% freelance written.** Bimonthly magazine covering grain handling and merchandising. *Grain Journal* serves the North American grain industry, from the smallest country grain elevators and feed mills to major export terminals. Estab. 1972. Circ. 12,000. Byline sometimes given. Pays on publication. No kill fee. Publishes ms an average of 2 months after acceptance. Editorial lead time 2 months. Submit seasonal material 2 months in advance. Accepts simultaneous submissions. Sample copy free.

NONFICTION Needs how-to, interview, new product, technical. Query. 750 words maximum. **Pays $100.** Pays expenses of writers on assignment.

🅢🅢 ONION WORLD

Columbia Publishing, P.O. Box 333, Roberts ID 83444. (208)520-6461. **Fax:** (509)248-4056. **E-mail:** dkeller@columbiapublications.com. **Website:** www.onionworld.net. **Contact:** Denise Keller, editor. **25% freelance written.** Monthly magazine covering the world of onion production and marketing for onion growers and shippers. Estab. 1985. Circ. 5,500. Byline given. Pays on publication. No kill fee. Publishes ms

an average of 1 month after acceptance. Submit seasonal material 1 month in advance. Accepts simultaneous submissions. Responds in 1 month to queries. Sample copy for SAE with 9x12 envelope and 5 first-class stamps.

NONFICTION Needs general interest, historical, interview. Special issues: Editorial calendar available online. **Buys 30 mss/year.** Query. Length: 1,200-1,250 words. **Pays $100-250 per article, depending upon length. Mileage paid, but query first.**

REPRINTS Send photocopy and information about when and where the material previously appeared. Pays 50% of amount paid for an original article.

🅢 THE VEGETABLE GROWERS NEWS

Great American Publishing, P.O. Box 128, Sparta MI 49345. (616)887-9008, ext. 102. **Fax:** (616)887-2666. **E-mail:** vgnedit@vegetablegrowersnews.com. **Website:** www.vegetablegrowersnews.com. **Contact:** Matt Milkovich, managing editor. **10% freelance written.** Monthly tabloid covering agriculture. Estab. 1970. Circ. 16,000. Pays on publication. No kill fee. Publishes ms an average of 2 months after acceptance. Editorial lead time 1-2 months. Submit seasonal material 3 months in advance. Accepts queries by mail, e-mail, fax. Accepts simultaneous submissions. Responds in 2 weeks to queries. Responds in 1 month to mss. Sample copy free.

NONFICTION Needs general interest, interview, new product. No advertorials, other puff pieces. **Buys 25 mss/year.** Query with published clips and résumé. Length: 800-1,200 words. **Pays $100-125.** Pays expenses of writers on assignment.

LIVESTOCK

🅢🅢🅢 ANGUS JOURNAL

Angus Productions, Inc., 3201 Frederick Ave., St. Joseph MO 64506-2997. (816)383-5270. **E-mail:** shermel@angusjournal.com. **Website:** www.angusjournal.com. **40% freelance written.** Monthly magazine covering Angus cattle. *Angus Journal* is the official magazine of the American Angus Association. Its primary function as such is to report to the membership association activities and information pertinent to raising Angus cattle. Estab. 1919. Circ. 13,500. Byline given. Pays on publication. No kill fee. Publishes ms an average of 3 months after acceptance. Editorial lead time 2 months. Submit seasonal material 3 months in advance. Accepts queries by mail, e-mail. Accepts simultaneous submissions. Responds in 3 weeks to queries; in 2 months to mss. Sample copy: $5. Guidelines with #10 SASE.

NONFICTION Needs how-to, interview, technical. **Buys 20-30 mss/year.** Query with published clips. Length: 800-3,500 words. **Pays $50-1,000.** Pays expenses of writers on assignment.

$$ BEE CULTURE

623 W Liberty St., Medina OH 44256-0706. (330)725-6677; (800)289-7668. **Fax:** (330)725-5624. **E-mail:** kim@beeculture.com; info@beeculture.com. **Website:** www.beeculture.com. **Contact:** Mr. Kim Flottum, editor. **50% freelance written.** Covers the natural science of honey bees, and honey bee management. "Monthly magazine for beekeepers and those interested in the natural science of honey bees, with environmentally-oriented articles relating to honey bees or pollination." Estab. 1873. Pays on publication. No kill fee. Publishes ms an average of 4 months after acceptance. Accepts queries by mail, e-mail. Accepts simultaneous submissions. Responds in 1 month to mss. Sample copy with 9x12 SASE and 5 first-class stamps. Guidelines and sample copy available online.

NONFICTION Needs interview, personal experience, photo feature. No "How I Began Beekeeping" articles. Length: 2,000 words average. **Pays $200-250.**

REPRINTS Send photocopy and information about when and where the material previously appeared. Pays about the same as for an original article, on negotiation.

$$ THE BRAHMAN JOURNAL

Carl and Victoria Lambert, 915 12th St., Hempstead TX 77445. (979)826-4347. **Fax:** (979)826-2007. **E-mail:** info@brahmanjournal.com; vlambert@brahmanjournal.com. **Website:** www.brahmanjournal.com. **Contact:** Victoria Lambert, editor. **10% freelance written.** Monthly magazine promoting, supporting, and informing the owners and admirers of American Brahman Cattle through honest and forthright journalism. *The Brahman Journal* provides timely and useful information about one of the largest and most dynamic breeds of beef cattle in the world. In each issue, *The Brahman Journal* reports on Brahman shows, events, and sales as well as technical articles and the latest research as it pertains to the Brahman Breed. Estab. 1971. Circ. 4,000. Byline given. Pays on publication. No kill fee. Publishes ms an average of 2 months after acceptance. Submit seasonal material 3 months in advance. Accepts simultaneous submissions. Sample copy for SAE with 9x12 envelope and 5 first-class stamps.

NONFICTION Needs general interest, historical, interview. Special issues: See the Calendar online for special issues. **Buys 3-4 mss/year.** Query with published clips. Length: 1,200-3,000 words. **Pays $100-250.** Pays expenses of writers on assignment.

REPRINTS Send typed ms with rights for sale noted. Pays 50% of amount paid for an original article.

$$ THE CATTLEMAN

Texas and Southwestern Cattle Raisers Association, 1301 W. Seventh St., Suite 201, Fort Worth TX 76102. (817)332-7064. **Fax:** (817)332-6441. **E-mail:** ehbrisendine@tscra.org. **Website:** www.tscra.org. **Contact:** Ellen H. Brisendine, editor. **25% freelance written.** Monthly magazine covering the Texas/Oklahoma beef cattle industry. Specializes in in-depth, management-type articles related to range and pasture, beef cattle production, animal health, nutrition, and marketing. Wants "how-to" articles. Estab. 1914. Circ. 18,000. Byline given. Pays on acceptance. No kill fee. Publishes ms an average of 2 months after acceptance. Editorial lead time 2 months. Submit seasonal material 6 months in advance. Accepts queries by e-mail. Accepts simultaneous submissions. Sample copy free. Guidelines online.

NONFICTION Needs how-to, interview, new product, personal experience, technical. Does not want to see anything not specifically related to beef production in the Southwest. **Buys 20 mss/year.** Query with published clips. Length: 1,500-2,000 words. **Pays $350-500 for assigned articles. Pays $100-350 for unsolicited articles.** Pays expenses of writers on assignment.

$$ FEED LOT

Feed Lot Magazine, Inc., P.O. Box 850, Dighton KS 67839. (800)798-9515. **Fax:** (620)397-2839. **E-mail:** feedlot@st-tel.net. **Website:** www.feedlotmagazine.com. Annita Lorimor. **Contact:** Jill Dunkel, editor. **80% freelance written.** Published 8 times/year. Magazine provides readers with the most up-to-date information on the beef industry in concise, easy-to-read articles designed to increase overall awareness among the feedlot community. "The editorial information content fits a dual role: large feedlots and their related cow/calf operations, and large 500+ cow/calf,

100+ stocker operations. The information covers all phases of production from breeding, genetics, animal health, nutrition, equipment design, research through finishing fat cattle. *Feed Lot* publishes a mix of new information and timely articles which directly affect the cattle industry." Estab. 1992. Circ. 11,000. Byline given. Pays on publication. Offers 50% kill fee. Publishes ms an average of 2 months after acceptance. Editorial lead time 2 months. Submit seasonal material 6 months in advance. Accepts queries by mail, e-mail, fax. Accepts simultaneous submissions. Responds in 1 month to queries. Sample copy and guidelines by e-mail.

NONFICTION Needs interview, new product, photo feature. Send complete ms; original material only. Length: 100-700 words. **Pays 30¢/word.** Pays expenses of writers on assignment.

🟢 SHEEP! MAGAZINE

Countryside Publications, Ltd., 145 Industrial Dr., Medford WI 54451. (715)785-7979; (800)551-5691. **Fax:** (715)785-7414 **E-mail:** sheepmag@tds.net; singersol@countrysidemag.com. **Website:** www.sheepmagazine.com. **Contact:** Nathan Griffith, editor. **35% freelance written. Prefers to work with published/established writers.** Bimonthly magazine published in north-central Wisconsin. Estab. 1980. Circ. 11,000. Byline given. Pays on publication. Offers $30 kill fee. Submit seasonal material 3 months in advance. Accepts simultaneous submissions.

NONFICTION Needs book excerpts, how-to, interview, new product, technical. **Buys 80 mss/year.** Send complete ms. Length: 750-2,500 words. **Pays $45-150.** Pays expenses of writers on assignment.

MANAGEMENT

🟢 AG JOURNAL

Gatehouse Media, Inc., 422 Colorado Ave., (P.O. Box 500), La Junta CO 81050. (719)384-1453. **E-mail:** publisher@ljtdmail.com; bcd@ljtdmail.com. **Website:** www.agjournalonline.com. **Contact:** Candi Hill, publisher/editor; Jennifer Justice, assistant editor. **20% freelance written.** Weekly journal covering agriculture. Estab. 1949. Circ. 11,000. Byline given. Pays on publication. No kill fee. Publishes ms an average of 2 weeks after acceptance. Editorial lead time 1 month. Submit seasonal material 1 month in advance. Accepts queries by e-mail. Accepts simulta-

neous submissions. Responds in 2 weeks to queries. Sample copy and writer's guidelines free.

NONFICTION Needs how-to, interview, new product, opinion, photo feature, technical. Query by e-mail only. **Pays 4¢/word.** Pays expenses of writers on assignment.

🟢🟢🟢 NEW HOLLAND NEWS AND ACRES MAGAZINE

P.O. Box 1895, New Holland PA 17557-0903. (610)621-2253. **E-mail:** contact@newhollandmediakit.com. **Website:** www.newholland.com/na; agriculture.newholland.com. **Contact:** Gary Martin, editor. **75% freelance written. Works with a small number of new/unpublished writers each year.** Each magazine published 4 times/year covering agriculture and non-farm country living; designed to entertain and inform farm families and rural homeowners and provide ideas for small acreage outdoor projects. Estab. 1960. Byline given. Pays on acceptance. Offers negotiable kill fee. Publishes ms an average of 8 months after acceptance. Submit seasonal material 8 months in advance. Accepts queries by mail. Responds in 2 months to queries. Sample copy and writer's guidelines for 9x12 SAE with 2 first-class stamps.

NONFICTION **Buys 40 mss/year.** Query. **Pays $700-900.** Pays expenses of writers on assignment.

🟢🟢🟢 PRODUCE BUSINESS

Phoenix Media Network Inc., P.O. Box 810425, Boca Raton FL 33481. (561)994-1118. **E-mail:** kwhitacre@phoenixmedianet.com; info@producebusiness.com. **Website:** www.producebusiness.com. **Contact:** Ken Whitacre, publisher/editorial director. **90% freelance written.** Monthly magazine covering produce and floral marketing. Addresses the buying end of the produce/floral industry, concentrating on supermarkets, chain restaurants, etc. Estab. 1985. Circ. 16,000. Byline given. Pays 30 days after publication. Offers $50 kill fee. Editorial lead time 2 months. Accepts queries by e-mail. Sample copy and guidelines free.

NONFICTION Does not want unsolicited articles. **Buys 150 mss/year.** Query with published clips. Length: 1,200-10,000 words. **Pays $240-1,200.** Pays expenses of writers on assignment.

🟢🟢 PRODUCE RETAILER

Vance Publishing Corp., 10901 W. 84th Ter., Suite 200, Lenexa KS 66214. (913)438-0603; (512)906-0733. **E-mail:** PamelaR@produceretailer.com; treyes@produceretailer.com. **Website:** produceretailer.com. **Contact:** Pamela Riemenschneider, editor; Tony Reyes, art director. **10% freelance written.** Monthly magazine. "*Produce Merchandising* is the only monthly journal on the market that is dedicated solely to produce merchandising information for retailers. Our purpose is to provide information about promotions, merchandising, and operations in the form of ideas and examples." Estab. 1988. Circ. 12,000. Byline given. Pays on acceptance. No kill fee. Publishes ms an average of 3 months after acceptance. Editorial lead time 3 months. Accepts queries by mail. Accepts simultaneous submissions. Responds in 2 weeks to queries. Sample copy free.

NONFICTION Needs how-to, interview, new product, photo feature, technical. **Buys 48 mss/year.** Query with published clips. Length: 1,000-1,500 words. **Pays $200-600.** Pays expenses of writers on assignment.

COLUMNS **Contact:** Contact editor for a specific assignment.. **Buys 30 mss/year.** Query with published clips. **Pays $200-450.**

$ SMALL FARM TODAY

Missouri Farm Publishing, Inc., Ridge Top Ranch, 3903 W. Ridge Trail Rd., Clark MO 65243-9525. (573)687-3525. **E-mail:** smallfarm@socket.net. **Website:** www.smallfarmtoday.com. Bimonthly magazine for small farmers and small-acreage landowners interested in diversification, direct marketing, alternative crops, horses, draft animals, small livestock, exotic and minor breeds, home-based businesses, gardening, vegetable and small fruit crops. Estab. 1984 as *Missouri Farm Magazine*. Circ. 12,000. Byline given. Pays 60 days after publication. No kill fee. Publishes ms an average of 6 months to 1 year after acceptance. Submit seasonal material 4 months in advance. Accepts queries by mail, e-mail. Accepts simultaneous submissions. Responds in 3 months to queries. Sample copy for $3. Guidelines available online.

NONFICTION Special issues: Poultry (January); Wool & Fiber (March); Aquaculture (July); Equipment (November). Query letters recommended. Length: 1,400-2,600 words. **Pays 3.5¢/word.** Pays expenses of writers on assignment.

REPRINTS Send tearsheet, photocopy or typed ms with rights for sale noted and information about when and where the material previously appeared. Pays 2¢/word of original article.

🌐 $ SMALLHOLDER MAGAZINE

Newsquest Media Group, 3 Falmouth Business Park, Bickland Water Rd., Falmouth Cornwall TR11 4SZ United Kingdom. (01)326-213338. **Fax:** (01)326-212084. **E-mail:** editorial@smallholder.co.uk. **Website:** www.smallholder.co.uk. **Contact:** Paul Armstrong, editor. *Smallholder* magazine is the leading monthly publication for the small producer and self-reliant household and has a publishing history spanning more than 100 years. The magazine has a reputation for quality and informed editorial content, and back issues are highly collectable. It is available nationally, through newsagent sales, specialist retail outlets and by subscription. No kill fee. Accepts queries by e-mail. Accepts simultaneous submissions. Sample copy available online. Guidelines by e-mail.

NONFICTION Length: 700-1,400 words. **Pays 4£/word.** Pays expenses of writers on assignment.

MISCELLANEOUS

$ $ ACRES U.S.A.

P.O. Box 1690, Greeley CO 80632. 800-355-5313. **E-mail:** editor@acresusa.com. **Website:** www.acresusa.com. **Contact:** Tara Maxwell. "Monthly trade journal written by people who have a sincere interest in the principles of organic and sustainable agriculture." Estab. 1971. Circ. 20,000. Byline given. Pays on publication. No kill fee. Editorial lead time 3 months. Submit seasonal material 6 months in advance. Accepts queries by mail, e-mail. Accepts simultaneous submissions. Sample copy and writer's guidelines free.

NONFICTION Needs book excerpts, expose, how-to, interview, new product, personal experience, photo feature, profile, technical. Special issues: Seeds (January), Poultry (March), Permaculture (May), Livestock (June), Homesteading (August), Soil Fertility & Testing (October). Does not want poetry, fillers, product profiles, or anything with an overly promotional tone. **Buys about 50 mss/year.** Send complete ms. Length: 500-3,000 words. **Pays 10¢/word.** Pays expenses of writers on assignment.

REGIONAL

⊜⊜ MAINE ORGANIC FARMER & GARDENER

Maine Organic Farmers & Gardeners Association, P.O. Box 170, Unity ME 04988. (207)568-4142. **Fax:** (207)568-4141. **E-mail:** jenglish@tidewater.ne. **Website:** www.mofga.org. **40% freelance written. Prefers to work with published/established local writers.** Quarterly newspaper. "The *MOF&G* promotes and encourages sustainable agriculture and environmentally sound living. Our primary focus is organic farming, gardening, and forestry, but we also deal with local, national, and international agriculture, food, and environmental issues." Estab. 1976. Circ. 10,000. Byline and bio offered. Pays on publication. No kill fee. Publishes ms an average of 8 months after acceptance. Submit seasonal material 1 year in advance. Accepts queries by mail, e-mail. Accepts simultaneous submissions. Responds in 2 months to queries. Sample copy for $2 and SAE with 7 first-class stamps; from MOFGA, P.O. Box 170, Unity ME 04988. Guidelines available at www.mofga.org.

NONFICTION Buys 30 mss/year. Send complete ms. Length: 250-3,000 words. **Pays $25-300.** Pays expenses of writers on assignment.

REPRINTS E-mail manuscript with rights for sale noted and information about when and where the material previously appeared. Pays 50% of amount paid for an original article.

FINANCE

✪⊜⊜⊜ ADVISOR'S EDGE

Rogers Media, Inc., 333 Bloor St. E., 6th Floor, Toronto ON M4W 1G6 Canada. **E-mail:** melissa.shin@rci.rogers.com. **Website:** www.advisor.ca. **Contact:** Melissa Shin, editor. Monthly magazine covering the financial industry (financial advisors and investment advisors). *Advisor's Edge* focuses on sales and marketing opportunities for the financial advisor (how they can build their business and improve relationships with clients). Estab. 1998. Circ. 36,000. Byline given. Pays on publication. Offers 25% kill fee. Publishes ms an average of 3 months after acceptance. Editorial lead time 3 months. Accepts queries by e-mail. Ac-

cepts simultaneous submissions. Sample copy available online.

NONFICTION Needs how-to, interview. No articles that aren't relevant to how a financial advisor does his/her job. **Buys 12 mss/year.** Query with published clips. Length: 1,500-2,000 words. **Pays $900 (Canadian).** Pays expenses of writers on assignment.

⊜⊜⊜⊜ AFP EXCHANGE

Association for Financial Professionals, 4520 East West Hwy., Suite 750, Bethesda MD 20814. (301)907-2862. **E-mail:** exchange@afponline.org. **Website:** www.afponline.org/exchange. **20% freelance written.** Monthly magazine covering corporate treasury, corporate finance, B2B payments issues, corporate risk management, accounting, and regulatory issues from the perspective of corporations. Welcomes interviews with CFOs and senior-level practitioners. Best practices and practical information for corporate CFOs and treasurers. Tone is professional, intended to appeal to financial professionals on the job. Most accepted articles are written by professional journalists and editors, many featuring high-level AFP members in profile and case studies. Estab. 1979. Circ. 25,000. Byline given. Pays on publication. Offers kill fee. Pays negotiable kill fee in advance. Editorial lead time 2 months. Submit seasonal material 3 months in advance. Accepts queries by e-mail. Accepts simultaneous submissions. Responds in 1 week to queries; in 1 month to mss.

NONFICTION Needs book excerpts, how-to, interview, personal experience, technical. No PR-type articles pointing to any type of product or solution. **Buys 3-4 mss/year.** Query. Length: 1,100-1,800 words. **Pays 75¢-$1/word for assigned articles.** Pays expenses of writers on assignment.

COLUMNS Cash Flow Forecasting (practical tips for treasurers, CFOs); Financial Reporting (insight, practical tips); Risk Management (practical tips for treasurers, CFOs); Corporate Payments (practical tips for treasurers), all 1,000-1,300 words. Professional Development (success stories, career related, about high-level financial professionals), 1,100 words. **Buys 10 mss/year.** Query. **Pays $75¢-$1/word.**

FILLERS Needs anecdotes. Length: 400-700 words. **Pays 75¢/word.**

⊜⊜⊜ CREDIT TODAY

P.O. Box 20091, Roanoke VA 24018. (540)343-7500. **E-mail:** robl@credittoday.net; editor@credittoday.net.

Website: www.credittoday.net. **Contact:** Rob Lawson, publisher. **10% freelance written.** Web-based publication covering business or trade credit. Estab. 1997. No byline given. Pays on acceptance. Publishes ms an average of 1 week after acceptance. Editorial lead time 1-2 months. Accepts queries by e-mail. Sample copy free. Guidelines free.

NONFICTION Needs how-to, interview, technical. Does not want "puff" pieces promoting a particular product or vendor. **Buys 20 mss/year.** Send complete ms. Length: 700-1,800 words. **Pays $200-1,400.** Pays expenses of writers on assignment.

💲💲 CREDIT UNION MANAGEMENT

Credit Union Executives Society, 5710 Mineral Point Road, Madison WI 53705. (800)231-4211. **E-mail:** apeterson@cuna.com. **Website:** www.cuna. org. **Contact:** Ann Hayes Peterson, editor in chief. **44% freelance written.** Monthly magazine covering credit union, banking trends, management, HR, and marketing issues. "Our philosophy mirrors the credit union industry of cooperative financial services." Estab. 1978. Circ. 7,413. Pays on acceptance. No kill fee. Publishes ms an average of 2 months after acceptance. Editorial lead time 3 months. Submit seasonal material 4 months in advance. Accepts queries by mail. Accepts simultaneous submissions. Responds in 2 weeks to queries; 1 month to mss. Sample copy and writer's guidelines free.

NONFICTION Needs book excerpts, how-to, interview, technical. **Buys 74 mss/year.** Query with published clips. Length: 700-2,400 words. **$250-350 for assigned features.** Pays expenses of writers on assignment.

COLUMNS Management Network (book/Web reviews, briefs), 300 words; e-marketing, 700 words; Point of Law, 700 words; Best Practices (new technology/operations trends), 700 words. Query with published clips.

💲💲💲 THE FEDERAL CREDIT UNION

National Association of Federal Credit Unions, 3138 10th St. N., Arlington VA 22201. (703)522-4770; (800)336-4644. **Fax:** (703)524-1082. **E-mail:** msc@nafcu.org; sbroaddus@nafcu.org. **Website:** www. nafcu.org/tfcuonline. **Contact:** Susan Broaddus, managing editor. **30% freelance written.** Published bimonthly, *The Federal Credit Union* is the official publication of the National Association of Federal Credit Unions. The magazine is dedicated to providing credit union management, staff, and volunteers with in-depth information (HR, technology, security, board management, etc.) they can use to fulfill their duties and better serve their members. The editorial focus includes coverage of management issues, operations, and technology as well as volunteer-related issues. Looking for writers with financial, banking, or credit union experience, but will work with inexperienced (unpublished) writers based on writing skill. Estab. 1967. Circ. 8,000. Byline given. Pays on publication. No kill fee. Publishes ms an average of 3 months after acceptance. Submit seasonal material 5 months in advance. Accepts queries by mail, e-mail, fax. Accepts simultaneous submissions. Responds in 2 months to queries. Sample copy for SAE with 10x13 envelope and 5 first-class stamps. Guidelines for #10 SASE.

NONFICTION Needs humor, inspirational, interview. Query with published clips and SASE. Length: 1,200-2,000 words. **Pays $400-1,000.**

FLORISTS, NURSERIES & LANDSCAPERS

💲 GROWERTALKS

Ball Publishing, 622 Town Rd., P.O. Box 1660, West Chicago IL 60186. (630)231-3675; (630)588-3401. **Fax:** (630)231-5254. **E-mail:** info@ballpublishing.com. **E-mail:** cbeytes@ballpublishing.com. **Website:** www. growertalks.com. **Contact:** Chris Beytes, editor. **50% freelance written.** Monthly magazine covering horticulture. *GrowerTalks* serves the commercial greenhouse grower. Editorial emphasis is on floricultural crops: bedding plants, potted floral crops, foliage, and fresh cut flowers. Readers are growers, managers, and owners. Looking for writers who've had experience in the greenhouse industry. Estab. 1937. Circ. 9,500. Byline given. Pays on publication. No kill fee. Publishes ms an average of 3 months after acceptance. Editorial lead time 4 months. Submit seasonal material 3 months in advance. Accepts queries by mail, e-mail, fax. Accepts simultaneous submissions. Responds in 1 month to queries. Sample copy and writer's guidelines free.

NONFICTION Needs how-to, interview, personal experience, technical. No articles that promote only 1 product. **Buys 36 mss/year.** Query. Length: 1,200-

1,600 words. **Pays $125 minimum for assigned articles. Pays $75 minimum for unsolicited articles.**

💲 TREE CARE INDUSTRY MAGAZINE

Tree Care Industry Association, 136 Harvey Rd., Suite 101, Londonderry NH 03053. (800)733-2622 or (603)314-5380. **Fax:** (603)314-5386. **E-mail:** editor@tcia.org; dstaruk@TCIA.org. **Website:** www.tcia.org. **Contact:** Don Staruk, editor. **50% freelance written.** Monthly magazine covering tree care and landscape maintenance. Estab. 1990. Circ. 24,000. Byline given. Pays within 1 month of publication. No kill fee. Publishes ms an average of 3 months after acceptance. Editorial lead time 10 weeks. Submit seasonal material 3 months in advance. Accepts queries by e-mail. Accepts simultaneous submissions. Responds within 2 days to queries; 2 months to mss. Sample copies online. Guidelines free.

NONFICTION Needs book excerpts, historical, interview, new product, technical. **Buys 60 mss/year.** Query with published clips. Length: 900-3,500 words. **Pays negotiable rate.**

COLUMNS Buys 40 mss/year. Send complete ms. **Pays $100 and up.**

GOVERNMENT & PUBLIC SERVICE

💲💲 AMERICAN CITY & COUNTY

Penton Media, 6151 Powers Ferry Rd. NW, Suite 200, Atlanta GA 30339. (770)618-0401. **E-mail:** bill.wolpin@penton.com; derek.prall@penton.com. **Website:** www.americancityandcounty.com. **Contact:** Bill Wolpin, editorial director; Derek Prall, managing editor. **40% freelance written.** Monthly magazine covering local and state government in the U.S. Estab. 1909. Circ. 65,000. Byline given. Pays on publication. Offers 25% kill fee. Publishes ms an average of 2 months after acceptance. Editorial lead time 3 months. Accepts queries by e-mail. Accepts simultaneous submissions. Sample copy available online. Guidelines by e-mail.

NONFICTION Needs new product. **Buys 36 mss/year.** Query. Length: 600-2,000 words. **Pays 30¢/published word.** Pays expenses of writers on assignment.

COLUMNS Issues & Trends (local and state government news analysis), 500-700 words. **Buys 24 mss/year.** Query. **Pays $150-250.**

💲💲 COUNTY

Texas Association of Counties, 1210 San Antonio St., Austin TX 78701. (512)478-8753. **Fax:** (512)481-1240. **E-mail:** marias@county.org. **Website:** www.county.org. **Contact:** Maria Sprow, managing editor. **15% freelance written.** Bimonthly magazine covering county and state government in Texas. Provides elected and appointed county officials with insights and information that help them do their jobs and enhances communications among the independent office-holders in the courthouse. Estab. 1988. Circ. 5,500. Byline given. Pays on acceptance. No kill fee. Publishes ms an average of 2 months after acceptance. Editorial lead time 2 months. Submit seasonal material 4 months in advance. Accepts queries by mail, e-mail, phone. Accepts simultaneous submissions. Responds in 2 weeks to queries. Responds in 1 month to mss. Sample copy and writer's guidelines for 8x10 SAE with 3 first-class stamps.

NONFICTION Needs historical. **Buys 5 mss/year.** Query with published clips. Length: 1,000-3,000 words. **Pays $500-700.** Pays expenses of writers on assignment.

COLUMNS Safety; Human Resources; Risk Management (all directed toward education of Texas county officials), maximum length 1,000 words. **Buys Buys 2 mss/year. mss/year.** Query with published clips. **Pays $500.**

💲💲 FIRE CHIEF

Primedia Business, 330 N. Wabash Ave., Suite 2300, Chicago IL 60611. (312)595-1080. **Fax:** (312)595-0295. **E-mail:** Rick.Markley@praetoriangroup.com. **Website:** www.firechief.com. **Contact:** Rick Markley, editor in chief. **60% freelance written.** Monthly magazine covering the fire chief occupation. "*Fire Chief* is the management magazine of the fire service, addressing the administrative, personnel, training, prevention/education, professional development, and operational issues faced by chiefs and other fire officers, whether in paid, volunteer, or combination departments. We're potentially interested in any article that can help them do their jobs better, whether that's as incident commanders, financial managers, supervisors, leaders, trainers, planners, or ambassadors to municipal officials or the public." Estab. 1956. Circ. 53,000. Byline given. Pays on publication. Offers kill fee. Kill fee negotiable. Publishes ms an average of 6 months after acceptance. Editorial lead time 2 months. Submit seasonal material 4 months in advance. Accepts queries by mail, e-mail, fax. Responds in 1 month to queries. Responds in 2 months to mss. Sample copy and submission guidelines free.

NONFICTION Needs how-to, technical. "We do not publish fiction, poetry, or historical articles. We also aren't interested in straightforward accounts of fires or other incidents, unless there are one or more specific lessons to be drawn from a particular incident, especially lessons that are applicable to a large number of departments." **Buys 50-60 mss/year.** Query first with published clips. Length: 1,000-10,000 words. **Pays $50-400.** Pays expenses of writers on assignment.

COLUMNS Training Perspectives; EMS Viewpoints; Sound Off; Volunteer Voice; all 1,000-1,800 words.

⊗⊗ FIREHOUSE MAGAZINE

Cygnus Business Media, 1233 Janesville Ave., Fort Atkinson WI 53538. (800)547-7377. **E-mail:** janelle@firehouse.com. **Website:** www.firehouse.com. **Contact:** Janelle Foskett, executive editor. **85% freelance written. Works with a small number of new/unpublished writers each year.** Monthly magazine. *Firehouse* covers major fires nationwide, controversial issues and trends in the fire service, the latest firefighting equipment and methods of firefighting, historical fires, firefighting history and memorabilia. Fire-related books, fire safety education, hazardous-materials incidents, and the emergency medical services are also covered. Estab. 1976. Circ. 83,538 (print). Byline given. Pays on publication. No kill fee. Accepts queries by mail, e-mail, fax, online submission form. Sample copy for SAE with 9x12 envelope and 8 first-class stamps.

NONFICTION Needs book excerpts, historical, how-to, trends in the fire service. No profiles of people or departments that are not unusual or innovative, reports of nonmajor fires, articles not slanted toward firefighters' interests. No poetry. **Buys 100 mss/year.** Query. "If you have any story ideas, questions, hints, tips, etc., please do not hesitate to call." Length: 500-3,000 words. The average length of each article is between 2-3 pages, including visuals. **Pays $50-400 for assigned articles.**

COLUMNS Training (effective methods); Book Reviews; Fire Safety (how departments teach fire safety to the public); Communicating (PR, dispatching); Arson (efforts to combat it). Length: 750-1,000 words.

Buys 50 mss/year. Query or send complete ms. **Pays $100-300.**

⊗⊗ FIRERESCUE

PennWell Corporation, 21-00 Route 208 South, Fair Lawn NJ 07410. (973)251-5055. **E-mail:** frm.editor@pennwell.com; dianer@pennwell.com. **Website:** www.firefighternation.com. **Contact:** Diane Rothschild, executive editor. "FireRescue covers the fire and rescue markets. Our 'Read It Today, Use It Tomorrow' mission weaves through every article and image we publish. Our readers consist of fire chiefs, company officers, training officers, firefighters, and technical rescue personnel." Estab. 1997. Circ. 50,000. Pays on publication. Accepts queries by mail, e-mail. Responds in 1 month to mss. Guidelines available online.

NONFICTION Needs general interest, how-to, interview, new product, technical. "All story ideas must be submitted with a cover letter that outlines your qualifications and includes your name, full address, phone, and e-mail address. We accept story submissions in 1 of the following 2 formats: query letters and mss." Length: 800-2,200 words. **Pays $100—$200 for features.** Pays expenses of writers on assignment.

⊗⊗ LAW ENFORCEMENT TECHNOLOGY MAGAZINE

Cygnus Business Media, 1233 Janesville Ave., Fort Atkinson WI 53538. (800)547-7377. **Website:** www.officer.com. **40% freelance written.** Monthly magazine covering police management and technology. Estab. 1974. Circ. 30,000. Byline given. Pays on publication. No kill fee. Publishes ms an average of 4 months after acceptance. Editorial lead time 6 months. Accepts simultaneous submissions. Responds in 1 month to queries; 2 months to mss. Guidelines free.

NONFICTION Needs how-to, interview, photo feature, police management and training. **Buys 30 mss/year.** Query. Length: 1,200-2,000 words. **Pays $75-400 for assigned articles.**

REPRINTS Send typed ms with rights for sale noted and information about when and where the material previously appeared. Payment negotiable.

⊗⊗⊗⊗ PLANNING

American Planning Association, 205 N. Michigan Ave., Suite 1200, Chicago IL 60601. (312)431-9100. **Fax:** (312)786-6700. **E-mail:** mstromberg@planning.org. **Website:** www.planning.org. **Contact:** Meghan Stromberg, executive editor; Sylvia Lewis, editor; Joan

Cairney, art director. **30% freelance written.** Monthly magazine emphasizing urban planning for adult, college-educated readers who are regional and urban planners in city, state, or federal agencies or in private business, or university faculty or students. Estab. 1972. Circ. 44,000. Byline given. Pays on publication. No kill fee. Publishes ms an average of 2 months after acceptance. Accepts queries by mail, e-mail. Accepts simultaneous submissions. Responds in 5 weeks to queries. Guidelines available online.

NONFICTION Special issues: Transportation issue. Also needs news stories up to 500 words. **Buys 44 features and 33 news stories mss/year.** Length: 500-3,000 words. **Pays $150-1,500.** Pays expenses of writers on assignment.

🌑🌑 POLICE AND SECURITY NEWS

Performance Publishing, LLC, 15 S. Main St., PO Box 1185, Quakertown PA 18951-1520. (215)538-1240. **Fax:** (215)538-1208. **E-mail:** jdevery@policeandsecuritynews.com. **E-mail:** amenear@policeandsecuritynews.com. **Website:** www.policeandsecuritynews.com. **Contact:** Al Menear, publisher. **40% freelance written.** A nationally circulated bimonthly magazine serving law enforcement and Homeland Security, reaching all levels: municipal/city; county; state and federal law enforcement personnel. *Police and Security News* edits its content for the expert–in a manner even the non-expert can understand and utilize. Every issue features useful, hard to find information which is, oftentimes, entertaining and always contemporary and relevant. Every edition provides in-depth articles by industry known writers; current news and information; useful tips and guidelines; and the latest innovations. *P&SN* is always looking for quality articles and information pertaining to all levels of law enforcement and Homeland Security. Estab. 1984. Circ. 24,000. Byline given. Pays on publication. No kill fee. Publishes ms an average of 2 months after acceptance. 4-6 weeks 4 weeks Accepts queries by mail, e-mail, fax, phone. Accepts simultaneous submissions. Responds immediately. Sample copy online.

NONFICTION Contact: James Devery, managing editor. Needs book excerpts, historical, how-to, humor, interview, new product, nostalgic, opinion, personal experience, photo feature, reviews, technical. **Buys 12 mss/year.** Query. Length: 200-2,500 words. **Pays 10¢/word. Sometimes pays in trade-out of services.** Pays expenses of writers on assignment.

REPRINTS Send tearsheet, photocopy or emailed manuscript with rights for sale noted and information about when and where the material previously appeared. Pays 10¢/word.

FILLERS Contact: James Devery. Law Enforcement- related topics Needs facts, newsbreaks, short humor. **Buys 6 mss/year.** Length: 200-2,000 words. **10¢/word.**

🌑🌑🌑🌑 YOUTH TODAY

Kennesaw State University, 1000 Chastain Rd., MD 2212, Bldg. 22, Kennesaw GA 30144. (678)797-2899. **E-mail:** jfleming@youthtoday.org. **Website:** www.youthtoday.org. **Contact:** John Fleming, editor. **50% freelance written.** Bi-monthly newspaper covering businesses that provide services to youth. Audience is people who run youth programs—mostly nonprofits and government agencies—who want help in providing services and getting funding. Estab. 1994. Circ. 9,000. Byline given. Pays on publication. Offers $200 kill fee for features. Editorial lead time 2 months. Accepts queries by mail. Accepts simultaneous submissions. Responds in 2 weeks to queries. Responds in 1 month to mss. Sample copy for $5. Guidelines available on website.

NONFICTION Needs general interest, technical. "No feel-good stories about do-gooders. We examine the business of youth work." **Buys 5 mss/year.** Query. Send rèsumè, short cover letter, clips. Length: 600-2,500 words. **Pays $150-2,000 for assigned articles.** Pays expenses of writers on assignment.

COLUMNS "*Youth Today* also publishes 750-word guest columns, called Viewpoints. These pieces can be based on the writer's own experiences or based on research, but they must deal with an issue of interest to our readership and must soundly argue an opinion, or advocate for a change in thinking or action within the youth field."

GROCERIES & FOOD PRODUCTS

🌑🌑 CONVENIENCE DISTRIBUTION

American Wholesale Marketers Association, 11311 Sunset Hills Road, Reston VA 20190. (703)208-3358. **Fax:** (703)573-5738. **E-mail:** info@awmanet.org; joanf@awmanet.org. **Website:** www.cdaweb.net. **Contact:** Joan Fay, associate publisher and editor. **70% freelance written.** Magazine published 10 times/year. See website for editorial calendar. Covers trends in candy, tobacco, groceries, beverages, snacks, and other product categories found in convenience stores, grocery stores, and drugstores, plus distribution topics. Contributors should have prior experience writing about the food, retail, and/or distribution industries. Editorial includes a mix of columns, departments, and features (2-6 pages). Also covers AWMA programs. Estab. 1948. Circ. 11,000. Byline given. Pays on acceptance. No kill fee. Publishes ms an average of 2 months after acceptance. Editorial lead time 3-4 months. Accepts simultaneous submissions. Guidelines available online.

NONFICTION Needs how-to, technical, industry trends, also profiles of distribution firms. No comics, jokes, poems, or other fillers. **Buys 40 mss/year.** Query with published clips. Length: 1,200-3,600 words. **Pays 50¢/word.** Pays expenses of writers on assignment.

⊗⊗ FRESH CUT MAGAZINE

Great American Publishing, P.O. Box 128, 75 Applewood Dr., Suite A, Sparta MI 49345. (616)887-9008. **Fax:** (616)887-2666. **E-mail:** fcedit@freshcut.com. **Website:** www.freshcut.com. **Contact:** Lee Dean, editorial director. **20% freelance written.** Monthly magazine covering the value-added and pre-cut fruit and vegetable industry. Interested in articles that focus on what different fresh-cut processors are doing. Estab. 1993. Circ. 16,000. Byline given. Pays on publication. No kill fee. Publishes ms an average of 2 months after acceptance. Editorial lead time 2 months. Accepts queries by mail, e-mail, fax, phone, online submission form. Accepts simultaneous submissions. Responds in 1 month to queries. Responds in 2 months to mss. Sample copy for SAE with 9x12 envelope. Guidelines for #10 SASE.

NONFICTION Needs historical, new product, opinion, technical. **Buys 2-4 mss/year.** Query with published clips.

REPRINTS Send tearsheet with rights for sale noted and information about when and where the material previously appeared. Pays 50% of amount paid for an original article.

COLUMNS Packaging; Food Safety; Processing/Engineering. **Buys 20 mss/year.** Query. **Pays $125-200.**

⊗ THE PRODUCE NEWS

800 Kinderkamack Rd., Suite 100, Oradell NJ 07649. (201)986-7990. **Fax:** (201)986-7996. **E-mail:** groh@ theproducenews.com. **Website:** www.theproduce-news.com. **Contact:** John Groh, editor/publisher. **10% freelance written. Works with a small number of new/unpublished writers each year.** Weekly magazine for commercial growers and shippers, receivers, and distributors of fresh fruits and vegetables, including chain store produce buyers and merchandisers. Estab. 1897. Pays on publication. No kill fee. Publishes ms an average of 2 weeks after acceptance. Accepts queries by mail, e-mail. Accepts simultaneous submissions. Responds in 1 month to queries. Sample copy and writer's guidelines for 10x13 SAE and 4 first-class stamps.

NONFICTION Query. **Pays $1/column inch minimum.** Pays expenses of writers on assignment.

♻⊗⊗ WESTERN GROCER MAGAZINE

Mercury Publications Ltd., 1313 Border Ave., Unit 16, Winnipeg MB R3H 0X4 Canada. (204)954-2085, ext. 219; (800)337-6372. **Fax:** (204)954-2057. **E-mail:** rbradley@mercurypublications.ca. **Website:** www. westerngrocer.com. **Contact:** Robin Bradley, associate publisher and national account manager. **75% freelance written.** Bimonthly magazine covering the grocery industry. Reports for the Western Canadian grocery, allied non-food and institutional industries. Each issue features a selection of relevant trade news and event coverage from the West and around the world. Feature reports offer market analysis, trend views, and insightful interviews from a wide variety of industry leaders. *The Western Grocer* target audience is independent retail food stores, supermarkets, manufacturers and food brokers, distributors and wholesalers of food, and allied non-food products, as well as bakers, specialty and health food stores, and convenience outlets. Estab. 1916. Circ. 15,500. Byline given. Pays 30-45 days from receipt of invoice. Offers 33% kill fee. Submit seasonal material 3 months in advance. Sample copy and writer's guidelines free.

NONFICTION Needs how-to, interview. Does not want industry reports and profiles on companies. Query with published clips. Length: 500-9,000 words. **Pays 25-35¢/word.** Pays expenses of writers on assignment.

HOME FURNISHINGS & HOUSEHOLD GOODS

$ $ HOME FURNISHINGS RETAILER

National Home Furnishings Association (NHFA), 500 Giuseppe Ct., Suite 6, Roseville CA 95678. (336)801-6156; (800)422-3778. **E-mail:** wynnryan@rcn.com. **Website:** www.nhfa.org. **Contact:** Mary Wynn Ryan, editor-in-chief. **75% freelance written.** Monthly magazine published by NHFA covering the home furnishings industry. "We hope home furnishings retailers view our magazine as a profitability tool. We want each issue to help them make or save money." Estab. 1927. Circ. 15,000. Byline given. Pays on acceptance. No kill fee. Publishes ms an average of 6 weeks after acceptance. Editorial lead time 3 months. Accepts queries by mail, e-mail. Accepts simultaneous submissions. Responds in 1 month to queries. Sample copy available with proper postage. Guidelines available.

NONFICTION Query. "When submitting a query or requesting a writing assignment, include a résumé, writing samples, and credentials. When articles are assigned, *Home Furnishings Retailer* will provide general direction along with suggestions for appropriate artwork. The author is responsible for obtaining photographs or other illustrative material. Assigned articles should be submitted via e-mail or on disc along with a list of sources with telephone numbers, fax numbers, and e-mail addresses." Length: 3,000-5,000 words (features). **Pays $350-500.**

COLUMNS Columns cover business and product trends that shape the home furnishings industry. Advertising and Marketing; Finance; Technology; Training; Creative Leadership; Law; Style and Operations. Length: 1,200-1,500 words. Query with published clips.

HOSPITALS, NURSING & NURSING HOMES

$ $ CURRENT NURSING IN GERIATRIC CARE

Freiberg Press Inc., P.O. Box 612, Cedar Falls IA 50613. (319)553-0642; (800)354-3371. **Fax:** (319)553-0644. **E-mail:** bfreiberg@cfu.net. **Website:** www.care4elders.com. **Contact:** Bill Freiberg. **25% freelance written.** Bimonthly trade journal covering medical information and new developments in research for geriatric nurses and other practitioners. Estab. 2006. Byline sometimes given. Pays on acceptance. No kill fee. Accepts queries by e-mail. Accepts simultaneous submissions. Sample copy free; send e-mail to Kathy Freiderg at kfreiberg@cfu.net.

NONFICTION Query. Length: 500-1,500 words. **Pays 15¢/word for assigned articles.** Pays expenses of writers on assignment.

$ $ $ NURSEWEEK

Gannett Healthcare Group, 1721 Moon Lake Blvd., Suite 540, Hoffman Estates IL 60169. **E-mail:** editor@nurse.com. **Website:** www.nurse.com. **Contact:** Nick Hut, editor. **98% freelance written.** Biweekly magazine covering nursing news. Covers nursing news about people, practice, and the profession. Review several issues for content and style. Also consider e-mailing your idea to the editorial director in your region (see list online). The editorial director can help you with the story's focus or angle, along with the organization and development of ideas. Estab. 1999. Circ. 155,000. Byline given. Pays on publication. Offers $200 kill fee. Publishes ms an average of 2 months after acceptance. Editorial lead time 2-3 months. Submit seasonal material 4 months in advance. Accepts queries by e-mail. Accepts simultaneous submissions. Sample copy free. Guidelines on website.

NONFICTION Needs interview, personal experience, articles on innovative approaches to clinical care and evidence-based nursing practice, health-related legislation and regulation, community health programs, healthcare delivery systems, and professional development and management, advances in nursing specialties such as critical care, geriatrics, perioperative care, women's health, home care, long-term care, emergency care, med/surg, pediatrics, advanced practice, education, and staff development. **Buys 20 mss/year mss/year.** Query with a 50-word summary of story and a list of RN experts you plan to interview. Length: 900 words. **Pays $200-800 for assigned or unsolicited articles.**

HOTELS, MOTELS, CLUBS, RESORTS & RESTAURANTS

💲💲 CRUISE INDUSTRY NEWS

441 Lexington Ave., Suite 809, New York NY 10017. (212)986-1025. **Fax:** (212)986-1033. **E-mail:** oivind@cruiseindustrynews.com. **Website:** www.cruiseindustrynews.com. **Contact:** Oivind Mathisen, editor. **20% freelance written.** Quarterly magazine covering cruise shipping. Magazine about the business of cruise shipping for the industry, including cruise lines, shipyards, financial analysts, etc. Estab. 1991. Circ. 10,000. Byline given. Pays on acceptance or on publication. Offers 25% kill fee. Publishes ms an average of 4 months after acceptance. Editorial lead time 3 months. Accepts queries by mail. Accepts simultaneous submissions. Reponse time varies. Sample copy for $15. Guidelines for #10 SASE.

NONFICTION Needs interview, new product. No travel stories. **Buys more than 20 mss/year.** Query with published clips. Length: 500-1,500 words. **Pays $.50/word published.** Pays expenses of writers on assignment.

💲💲 EL RESTAURANTE

P.O. Box 2249, Oak Park IL 60303-2249. (708)267-0023. **E-mail:** kfurore@comcast.net. **Website:** www.restmex.com. **Contact:** Kathleen Furore, editor. Bimonthly magazine covering Mexican and other Latin cuisines. "*el Restaurante* offers features and business-related articles that are geared specifically to owners and operators of Mexican, Tex-Mex, Southwestern, and Latin cuisine restaurants and other foodservice establishments that want to add that type of cuisine." Estab. 1997. Circ. 25,000. Byline given. Pays on publication. No kill fee. Publishes ms an average of 3 months after acceptance. Accepts simultaneous submissions. Responds in 2 months to queries. Sample copy free.

NONFICTION "No specific knowledge of food or restaurants is needed; the key qualification is to be a good reporter who knows how to slant a story toward the Mexican restaurant operator." **Buys 2-4 mss/year.** Query with published clips. Length: 800-1,200 words. **Pays $250-300.**

💲💲💲💲 HOSPITALITY TECHNOLOGY

EnsembleIQ, 1 Gateway Center, 11-43 Raymond PLZ Fl 16, Newark NJ 07102. (973)607-1300. **E-mail:** dcreamer@ensembleiq.com; mescobar@ensembleiq.com; jbinns@ensembleiq.com. **Website:** www.ht-magazine.com. **Contact:** Dorothy Creamer, editor; Jessica Binns, senior editor; Michal Christine Escobar, managing editor. **40% freelance written.** Magazine published 8 times/year covering restaurant and lodging executives who manage hotels, casinos, cruise lines, quick service restaurants, etc. Covers the technology used in restaurants and lodging. Readers are the operators, who have significant IT responsibilities. This publication will not respond to all inquiries, due to the number of submissions—only those that are of particular interest to the editor. Estab. 1996. Circ. 16,000. Byline given. Pays on acceptance. No kill fee. Publishes ms an average of 1 month after acceptance. Editorial lead time 2 months. Accepts queries by mail, e-mail. Accepts simultaneous submissions. Responds in 2 weeks to queries.

NONFICTION Needs how-to, interview, new product, technical. Special issues: Publishes 3 studies each year: the Restaurant Industry Technology Study; the Lodging Industry Technology Study and the Customer Engagement Technology Study. No unsolicited mss. **Buys 40 mss/year.** Query with published clips. Length: 800-1,200 words. **Pays $1/word.** Pays expenses of writers on assignment.

♻💲💲 HOTELIER

Kostuch Media Ltd., 101-23 Lesmill Rd., Toronto ON M3B 3P6 Canada. (416)447-0888. **Fax:** (416)447-5333. **E-mail:** rcaira@foodservice.ca. **Website:** www.hoteliermagazine.com. **Contact:** Rosanna Caira, editor & publisher. **40% freelance written.** Magazine published 8 times/year covering the Canadian hotel industry. Canada's leading hotel publication. Provides comprehensive and insightful content focusing on business developments, trend analysis, and profiles of the industry's movers and shakers. Estab. 1989. Circ. 9,000. Byline given. Pays on publication. No kill fee. Editorial lead time 3 months. Submit seasonal material 2 months in advance. Accepts queries by mail, fax. Accepts simultaneous submissions. Query for free sample copy. Query for free guidelines.

NONFICTION Needs how-to, new product. No case studies. **Buys 30-50 mss/year.** Query. Length: 700-

1,500 words. **Pays 35¢/word (Canadian) for assigned articles.** Pays expenses of writers on assignment.

😊😊 PIZZA TODAY

Macfadden Protech, LLC, 908 S. 8th St., Suite 200, Louisville KY 40203. (502)736-9500. **Fax:** (502)736-9502. **E-mail:** jwhite@pizzatoday.com. **Website:** www.pizzatoday.com. **Contact:** Jeremy White, editor-in-chief. **30% freelance written. Works with published/established writers; occasionally works with new writers.** Monthly magazine for the pizza industry, covering trends, features of successful pizza operators, business and management advice, etc. Estab. 1984. Circ. 44,000. Byline given. Pays on acceptance. No kill fee. Publishes ms an average of 2 months after acceptance. Submit seasonal material 3 months in advance. Accepts queries by mail, e-mail, fax. Accepts simultaneous submissions. Responds in 2 months to queries. Responds in 3 weeks to mss. Sample copy for sae with 10x13 envelope and 6 first-class stamps. Guidelines for #10 SASE and online.

NONFICTION Needs interview, entrepreneurial slants, pizza production and delivery, employee training, hiring, marketing, and business management. No fillers, humor, or poetry. **Buys 85 mss/year.** Length: 1,000 words. **Pays 50¢/word, occasionally more.** Pays expenses of writers on assignment.

😊😊😊 SANTÉ MAGAZINE

On-Premise Communications, 160 Benmont Ave., Suite 92, Third Floor, West Wing, Bennington VT 05201. (802)442-6771. **Fax:** (802)442-6859. **E-mail:** mvaughan@santemagazine.com. **Website:** www.isantemagazine.com. **Contact:** Mark Vaughan, editor. **75% freelance written.** Four issues/year magazine covering food, wine, spirits, and management topics for restaurant professionals. Information and specific advice for restaurant professionals on operating a profitable food and beverage program. Writers should "speak" to readers on a professional-to-professional basis. Estab. 1996. Circ. 45,000. Byline given. Pays on publication. Offers 50% kill fee. Publishes ms an average of 2 months after acceptance. Editorial lead time 3 months. Submit seasonal material 6 months in advance. Accepts queries by e-mail. Accepts simultaneous submissions. Responds in 2 weeks to queries. Does not accept mss. Sample copy available. Guidelines by e-mail.

NONFICTION Needs interview, restaurant business news. Does not want consumer-focused pieces. **Buys**

20 mss/year. Query with published clips. Length: 650-1,800 words. Pays expenses of writers on assignment.

COLUMNS Due to a Redesign, 650 words; Bar Tab (focuses on 1 bar's unique strategy for success), 1,000 words; Restaurant Profile (a business-related look at what qualities make 1 restaurant successful), 1,000 words; Maximizing Profits (covers 1 great profit-maximizing strategy per issue from several sources), Signature Dish (highlights 1 chef's background and favorite dish with recipe), Sommeliers Choice (6 top wine managers recommend favorite wines; with brief profiles of each manager), Distillations (6 bar professionals offer their favorite drink for a particular type of spirit; with brief profiles of each manager), 1,500 words; Provisions (like The Goods only longer; an in-depth look at a special ingredient), 1,500 words. **Buys 20 mss/year.** Query with published clips. **Pays $300-800.**

😊😊😊 WESTERN HOTELIER MAGAZINE

Mercury Publications, Ltd., 1313 Border St., Unit 16, Winnipeg MB R3H 0X4 Canada. (800)337-6372 ext. 221. **Fax:** (204)954-2057. **E-mail:** dbastable@mercurypublications.ca. **Website:** www.westernhotelier.com. **Contact:** David Bastable, associate publisher and national accounts manager. **33% freelance written.** Quarterly magazine covering the hotel industry. *Western Hotelier* is dedicated to the accommodation industry in Western Canada and U.S. western border states. *WH* offers the West's best mix of news and feature reports geared to hotel management. Feature reports are written on a sector basis and are created to help generate enhanced profitability and better understanding. Circ. 4,342. Byline given. Pays 30-45 days from receipt of invoice. Offers 33% kill fee. Submit seasonal material 3 months in advance. Accepts queries by mail, fax. Accepts simultaneous submissions. Responds in 2 weeks to queries. Sample copy and writer's guidelines free.

NONFICTION Needs how-to, interview. Industry reports and profiles on companies. Query with published clips. Length: 500-9,000 words. **Pays 25-35¢/word.** Pays expenses of writers on assignment.

😊😊😊 WESTERN RESTAURANT NEWS

Mercury Publications, Ltd., 1313 Border St., Unit 16, Winnipeg MB R3H 0X4 Canada. (800)337-6372 ext. 213. **Fax:** (204)954-2057. **E-mail:** editorial@mercury.mb.ca; edufault@mercurypublications.ca. **Website:** www.westernrestaurantnews.com; www.mercury.

mb.ca. **Contact:** Elaine Dufault, associate publisher and national accounts manager. **20% freelance written.** Bimonthly magazine covering the restaurant trade in Western Canada. Reports profiles and industry reports on associations, regional business developments, etc. *Western Restaurant News* is the authoritative voice of the food service industry in Western Canada. Offering a total package to readers, *WRN* delivers concise news articles, new product news, and coverage of the leading trade events in the West, across the country, and around the world. Estab. 1994. Circ. 14,532. Byline given. Pays 30-45 days from receipt of invoice. Offers 33% kill fee. Submit seasonal material 3 months in advance. Accepts queries by mail, fax. Accepts simultaneous submissions. Sample copy and writer's guidelines free.

NONFICTION Needs how-to, interview. Industry reports and profiles on companies. Query with published clips. "E-mail, fax, or mail a query outlining your experience, interests, and pay expectations. Include clippings." Length: 500-9,000 words. **Pays 25-35¢/word.** Pays expenses of writers on assignment.

INDUSTRIAL OPERATIONS

☼$$ COMMERCE & INDUSTRY

Mercury Publications, Ltd., 1313 Border Street, Unit 16, Winnipeg MB R3H 0X4 Canada. (204)954-2085. **Fax:** (204)954-2057. **E-mail:** editorial@mercury.mb.ca. **Website:** www.commerceindustry.ca. **Contact:** Nicole Sherwood, editorial coordinator. **75% freelance written.** Bimonthly magazine covering the business and industrial sectors. Offers new product news, industry event coverage, and breaking trade specific business stories. Industry reports and company profiles provide readers with an in-depth insight into key areas of interest in their profession. Estab. 1948. Circ. 18,876. Byline given. Pays 30-45 days from receipt of invoice. Offers 33% kill fee. Submit seasonal material 3 months in advance. Accepts queries by mail, e-mail, fax. Accepts simultaneous submissions. Responds in 2 weeks to queries. Sample copy and writer's guidelines free or by e-mail.

NONFICTION Needs how-to, interview. Industry reports and profiles on companies. Query with published clips. Length: 500-9,000 words. **Pays 25-35¢/word.** Pays expenses of writers on assignment.

$$ INDUSTRIAL WEIGH & MEASURE

WAM Publishing Company, Inc., P.O. Box 2247, Hendersonville TN 37077. (615)239-8087. **E-mail:** dave.mathieu@comcast.net. **Website:** www.weighproducts.com. **Contact:** David M. Mathieu, publisher and editor. Bimonthly magazine for users of industrial scales; covers material handling and logistics industries. Estab. 1914. Circ. 13,900. Byline given. Pays on acceptance. Offers 20% kill fee. Accepts queries by mail, e-mail, phone. Accepts simultaneous submissions. Responds in 2 weeks to queries. Sample copy available online.

NONFICTION Needs general interest, technical. **Buys 15 mss/year.** Query on technical articles; submit complete ms for general interest material. Length: 1,000-2,500 words. **Pays $175-300.** Pays expenses of writers on assignment.

☾$$$ MACHINERY & EQUIPMENT MRO

Annex Business Media, 111 Gordon Baker Rd., Suite 400, Toronto ON M2H 3R1 Canada. (416)510-6851. **Fax:** (416)510-5134. **E-mail:** rbegg@annexweb.com. **Website:** www.mromagazine.com. **Contact:** Rehana Begg, Editor. **30% freelance written.** Bimonthly magazine looking for informative articles on issues that affect plant floor operations and maintenance. Estab. 1985. Circ. 18,000. Byline given. Pays on publication. No kill fee. Publishes ms an average of 3 months after acceptance. Editorial lead time 4 months. Submit seasonal material 4 months in advance. Accepts simultaneous submissions. Responds in 3 weeks to queries; 1 month to mss. Sample copy free. Guidelines available.

NONFICTION Needs essays, how-to, interview, new product, profile, technical. **Buys 6 mss/year.** Query with published clips. Length: 750-4,000 words. **Pays $200-1,400 (Canadian).** Pays expenses of writers on assignment.

$$ MODERN MATERIALS HANDLING

Peerless Media, 111 Speen St., Suite 200, Framingham MA 01701. (508)663-1500. **E-mail:** mlevans@ehpub.com; robert.trebilcock@myfairpoint.net. **Website:** www.mmh.com. **Contact:** Michael Levans, editorial director. **40% freelance written.** Magazine published 13 times/year covering warehousing, distribution centers, and inventory. *Modern Materials Handling* is a national magazine read by managers of warehouses and distribution centers. Focuses on lively, well-written articles telling readers how they can achieve maximum facility productivity and efficiency. Covers technology, too. Estab. 1945. Circ. 81,000. Byline given. Pays on acceptance (allow 4-6 weeks for invoice processing). No kill fee. Publishes ms an average of 1 month after acceptance. Editorial lead time 3 months. Accepts queries by mail, e-mail, fax. Accepts simultaneous submissions. Sample copy and guidelines free.

NONFICTION Needs how-to, new product, technical. Special issues: State-of-the-Industry Report, Peak Performer, Salary and Wage survey, Warehouse of the Year. Doesn't want anything that doesn't deal with the topic of warehousing. No general-interest profiles or interviews. **Buys 25 mss/year.** Query with published clips. **Pays $300-650.**

INFORMATION SYSTEMS

$ JOURNAL OF INFORMATION ETHICS

McFarland & Co., Inc., Publishers, P.O. Box 611, Jefferson NC 28640. (336)246-4460. **E-mail:** hauptman@stcloudstate.edu. **90% freelance written.** Semiannual scholarly journal covering all of the information sciences. Addresses ethical issues in all of the information sciences with a deliberately interdisciplinary approach. Topics range from electronic mail monitoring to library acquisition of controversial material to archival ethics. The *Journal*'s aim is to present thoughtful considerations of ethical dilemmas that arise in a rapidly evolving system of information exchange and dissemination. Estab. 1992. Byline given. Pays on publication. No kill fee. Publishes ms an average of 2 years after acceptance. Submit seasonal material 8 months in advance. Accepts queries by mail, e-mail, phone. Accepts simultaneous submissions. Sample copy for $30. Guidelines free.

NONFICTION Needs essays, reviews. **Buys 10-12 mss/year.** Send complete ms. Length: 500-3,500 words. **Pays $25-50, depending on length.**

$$ SYSTEM INEWS

Penton Technology Media, 748 Whalers Way, Fort Collins CO 80525. (970)663-4700; (800)621-1544. **E-mail:** editors@iprodeveloper.com. **Website:** www.iprodeveloper.com. **40% freelance written.** Magazine, published 12 times/year, focused on programming, networking, IS management, and technology for users of IBM AS/400, iSERIES, SYSTEM i, AND IBM i platform. Estab. 1982. Circ. 30,000 (international). Byline given. Pays on publication. Offers 50% kill fee. Publishes ms an average of 3 months after acceptance. Editorial lead time 4 months. Submit seasonal material 4 months in advance. Accepts queries by e-mail. Accepts simultaneous submissions. Responds in 3 weeks to queries. Responds in 5 weeks to mss. Guidelines available online.

NONFICTION Needs technical. Query. Length: 1,500-2,500 words. **Pays $300/$500 flat fee for assigned articles, depending on article quality and technical depth.** Pays expenses of writers on assignment.

REPRINTS Send photocopy. Payment negotiable.

COLUMNS Load'n'go (complete utility).

$$$$ TECHNOLOGY REVIEW

MIT, One Main St., 13th Floor, Cambridge MA 02142. (617)475-8000. **Fax:** (617)475-8042. **E-mail:** jason.pontin@technologyreview.com; david.rotman@technologyreview.com. **Website:** www.technologyreview.com. **Contact:** Jason Pontin, editor in chief; David Rotman, editor. Magazine published 10 times/year covering information technology, biotech, material science, and nanotechnology. *Technology Review* promotes the understanding of emerging technologies and their impact. Estab. 1899. Circ. 310,000. Byline given. Pays on acceptance. Accepts queries by mail, e-mail. Accepts simultaneous submissions.

NONFICTION Query with a pitch via online contact form. Length: 2,000-4,000 words. **Pays $1-3/word.** Pays expenses of writers on assignment.

FILLERS Short tidbits that relate laboratory prototypes on their way to market in 1-5 years. Length: 150-250 words. **Pays $1-3/word.**

JEWELRY

$ ADORNMENT

The Magazine of Jewelry & Related Arts, Association for the Study of Jewelry & Related Arts, 5070 Bonnie Branch Rd., Ellicott City MD 21043. **E-mail:** elyse@jewelryandrelatedarts.com. **Website:** www.jewelryandrelatedarts.com; www.asjra.net; www.jewelryconference.com. **50% freelance written.** Quarterly magazine covering jewelry, from antique to modern. "This magazine is a perk of membership in the Association for the Study of Jewelry & Related Arts. It is not sold as a stand-alone publication. It is delivered electronically. Readers are collectors, appraisers, antique jewelry dealers, gemologists, jewelry artists, museum curators—anyone with an interest in jewelry. You need to have a good working knowledge of jewelry subjects or we are not interested." Estab. 2002. Circ. 1,000+. Byline given. Pays on publication. No kill fee. Publishes ms an average of 3 months after acceptance. Editorial lead time 3 months. Accepts queries by mail, e-mail. Responds in 1-2 weeks to queries; 1 month to mss. Sample copy free as an e-mailed PDF. Guidelines free.

NONFICTION Needs book excerpts, historical, interview, exhibition reviews—in-depth articles on jewelry subjects. "We do not want articles about retail jewelry. We write about ancient, antique, period, and unique and studio jewelers." **Buys 12-15 mss/year.** Query with published clips. Length: 1,000-3,000 words. **Pays up to $125 for assigned articles. Does not pay for unsolicited articles.**

🟢🟢 BEAD & BUTTON

Kalmbach Publishing, P.O. Box 1612, 21027 Crossroads Circle, Waukesha WI 53187-1612. **E-mail:** editor@beadandbutton.com. **Website:** www.beadandbutton.com. **Contact:** Julia Gerlach, editor. **50% freelance written.** "*Bead & Button* is a bimonthly magazine devoted to techniques, projects, designs, and materials relating to making beaded jewelry. Our readership includes both professional and amateur bead and button makers, hobbyists, and enthusiasts who find satisfaction in making beautiful things." Estab. 1994. Circ. 100,000. Byline given. Pays on acceptance. Offers $75 kill fee. Publishes ms an average of 4-12 months after acceptance. Editorial lead time 4-5 months. Accepts queries by e-mail. Accepts simultaneous submissions. Responds to queries in 4-6 weeks. Guidelines online.

NONFICTION Needs how-to, interview, profile. **Buys 20-25 mss/year.** Query. Length: 1,000-1,200 words. **Pays $75-400.**

🟢🟢 THE ENGRAVERS JOURNAL

P.O. Box 318, Brighton MI 48116. (810)229-5725. **Fax:** (810)229-8320. **E-mail:** editor@engraversjournal.com. **Website:** www.engraversjournal.com. **Contact:** Senior editor. **70% freelance written.** Monthly magazine covering the recognition and personalization industry (engraving, sublimation, digital printing, sandcarving, personalized products, promotional products, awards and incentives, and signage). "We provide practical information for the education and advancement of our readers, mainly retail business owners." Estab. 1975. Byline given. Pays on accep-

tance. No kill fee. Publishes ms an average of 3-9 months after acceptance. Accepts queries by mail, e-mail, fax. Accepts simultaneous submissions. Responds in 2 weeks to mss. Sample copy free. Guidelines free.

NONFICTION Needs general interest, how-to, technical. No general overviews of the industry. Length: 1,000-5,000 words. **Pays $200 and up.**

REPRINTS Send tearsheet, photocopy, or typed ms with rights for sale noted, and information about when and where the material previously appeared. Pays 50-100% of amount paid for original article.

JOURNALISM & WRITING

🟢🟢🟢🟢 AMERICAN JOURNALISM REVIEW

University of Maryland Foundation, Knight Hall, University of Maryland, College Park MD 20742. (301)405-8805. **E-mail:** editor@ajr.org. **Website:** www.ajr.org. **Contact:** Lucy Dalglish, dean and publisher. **80% freelance written.** Bimonthly magazine covering print, broadcast, and online journalism. *American Journalism Review* covers ethical issues, trends in the industry, and coverage that falls short. Circ. 25,000. Byline given. Pays 1 month after publication. Offers 25% kill fee. Publishes ms an average of 2 months after acceptance. Editorial lead time 1 month. Accepts queries by mail, e-mail. Responds in 1 month to queries and unsolicited mss. Sample copy: $4.95 prepaid or online. Guidelines available online.

NONFICTION Needs expose. Query or send complete ms. Length: 2,000-4,000 words. **Pays $1,500-2,000.** Pays expenses of writers on assignment.

FILLERS Needs anecdotes, facts, short humor, short pieces. Length: 150-1,000 words. **Pays $100-250.**

🟢 BOOK DEALERS WORLD

North American Bookdealers Exchange, P.O. Box 606, Cottage Grove OR 97424. (541)942-7455. **E-mail:** nabe@bookmarketingprofits.com. **Website:** www.bookmarketingprofits.com. **Contact:** Al Galasso. **50% freelance written.** Magazine covering writing, self-publishing, and marketing books by mail. Publishes 3 issues/year online. Estab. 1980. Circ. 20,000. Byline given. Pays on publication. No kill fee. Publishes ms an average of 3 months after acceptance. Accepts queries by mail, e-mail. Accepts simultaneous submissions. Responds in 1 month to queries. Sample copy available online.

NONFICTION Needs book excerpts, how-to, interview. **Buys 10 mss/year.** Send complete ms. Length: 1,000-1,500 words. **Pays $25-50.**

REPRINTS Send typed ms with rights for sale noted and information about when and where the material previously appeared. Pays 80% of amount paid for an original article.

COLUMNS Publisher Profile (on successful self-publishers and their marketing strategy), 250-1,000 words. **Buys 20 mss/year.** Send complete ms. **Pays $5-20.**

FILLERS Needs fillers concerning writing, publishing, or books. **Buys 6 mss/year.** Length: 100-250 words. **Pays $3-10.**

✪$$$$ CANADIAN SCREENWRITER

Writers Guild of Canada, 366 Adelaide St. W., Suite 401, Toronto ON M5V 1R9 Canada. (416)979-7907. **Fax:** (416)979-9273. **E-mail:** info@wgc.ca. **Website:** www.wgc.ca. **Contact:** Li Robbins, director of communications. **80% freelance written.** Magazine published 3 times/year covering Canadian screenwriting for television, film, and digital media. *Canadian Screenwriter* profiles Canadian screenwriters, provides industry news, and offers practical writing tips for screenwriters. Estab. 1998. Circ. 4,000. Byline given. Pays on acceptance. Offers 50% kill fee. Publishes ms an average of 1 month after acceptance. Editorial lead time 2 months. Submit seasonal material 2 months in advance. Accepts queries by e-mail. Accepts simultaneous submissions. Responds in 1 week to queries; in 1 month to mss. Sample copy free. Guidelines by e-mail.

NONFICTION Needs how-to, humor, interview. Does not want writing on foreign screenwriters; the focus is on Canadian-resident screenwriters. **Buys 12 mss/year.** Query with published clips. Length: 750-2,200 words. **Pays $1/word.** Pays expenses of writers on assignment.

✪$ ECONTENT MAGAZINE

Information Today, Inc., 143 Old Marlton Pike, Medford NJ 08055. **E-mail:** theresa.cramer@infotoday.com. **Website:** www.econtentmag.com. **Contact:** Theresa Cramer, editor. **90% freelance written.** Quarterly magazine covering digital content trends, strategies, etc. *EContent* is a leading authority on the businesses of digital publishing, media, and marketing, targeting executives and decision-makers in these fast-changing markets. By covering the latest tools, strategies, and thought-leaders in the digital content ecosystem, *EContent* magazine and EContentmag.com keep professionals ahead of the curve in order to maximize their investment in digital content strategies while building sustainable, profitable business models. Visit our About page for writer's guidelines and more information about what kinds of pitches we look for. Estab. 1979. Circ. 12,000. Byline given. Pays within 1 month of publication. No kill fee. Editorial lead time 3-4 months. Accepts simultaneous submissions. Responds in 3 weeks to queries; in 1 month to mss. Sample copy and writer's guidelines online.

NONFICTION Needs expose, how-to, interview, new product, opinion. No academic or straight Q&A. **Buys 48 mss/year.** Query with published clips. Submit electronically as e-mail attachment. Length: 1,000 words. Pays expenses of writers on assignment.

COLUMNS Profiles (short profile of unique company, person or product), 1,200 words; New Features (breaking news of content-related topics), up to 500 words. **Buys 40 mss/year.** Query with published clips. **Pays 30-40¢/word.**

✪$ FELLOWSCRIPT

InScribe Christian Writers' Fellowship, P.O. Box 99509, Edmonton AB T5B 0E1 Canada. **E-mail:** fellowscripteditor2@gmail.com. **Website:** www.inscribe.org. Vice President: Tracy Krauss. **Contact:** Nina Faye Morey, editor. **100% freelance written.** Quarterly writers' magazine focused on Christian faith and writing. Most open to instructional articles on specific topics of interest to Christian writers. Readers are Christians with a commitment to writing. Among readership are best-selling authors and unpublished beginning writers. Submissions should include practical information, i.e., something the reader can immediately put into practice. Estab. 1983. Circ. 200. Byline given. Pays on publication. No kill fee. Publishes ms an average of 6-12 months after acceptance. Editorial lead time 3 months. Submit seasonal material 4 months in advance. Accepts queries by e-mail. Accepts simultaneous submissions. Responds in 1 month to queries and mss. Sample copy for $9, 9x12 SAE, and 3 first-class stamps (Canadian) or IRCs. Guidelines online.

NONFICTION Needs book excerpts, essays, how-to, humor, inspirational, interview, new product, opinion, personal experience, profile, religious, reviews, technical. Does not want memoir, autobiography, testimony, or scholarly articles. **Buys 30-45 mss/ year.** Send complete ms attached in doc or rtf format. Length: 350-750 words. **Pays 2 1/2¢/word (first rights); 1 1/2¢/word reprints (Canadian funds).**

REPRINTS Pays 1 1/2¢/word reprints (Canadian funds).

COLUMNS Contact: Carol Schafer, Columns Editor, E: schaferc@telus.net. Columnists are contracted for four issues. Send a query about your proposed column to the columns editor. Regular Columns, 501-600 words; Mini-Columns, up to 300 words. **Buys 1-4. mss/year.** Send complete ms attached in doc format. **Pays $18 (Canadian) for regular columns; no payment for mini-columns; 1 contributor's copy.**

FICTION Contact: Nina Faye Morey, Editor, E: fellowscripteditor2@gmail.com. Christian short stories or book excerpts. Needs novel excerpts, short stories. **Buys 1-4 mss/year.** Send complete ms attached in doc format. Length: Maximum 750 words **Pays 2 1/2¢/ word (first rights); 1 1/2¢/word reprints (Canadian funds).**

POETRY Contact: Violet Nesdoly, Poetry Editor, E: fspoetryeditor@gmail.com. Poetry related to faith or writing; traditional or free-verse. Buys 8-12 poems/ year. Submit maximum 3-6 poems. Length: 4-20 lines. **Pays $10 for original, unpublished; $5 for original, previously published (Canadian funds).**

FILLERS Contact: Nina Faye Morey, Editor, E: fellowscripteditor2@gmail.com. Book reviews (writing or faith related), members' profiles, members' books and book launches (150–300 words), writers' tips, anecdotes, market updates (50–300 words), quotes, humour. **Buys 5-10 mss/year.** Send complete ms attached in doc format. Length: 25-300 words. **Pays 1 contributor's copy.**

FREELANCE MARKET NEWS

The Writers Bureau Ltd., 8-10 Dutton St., Manchester M3 1LE England. (44)(161)819-9919. **Fax:** (44)(161)819-2842. **E-mail:** fmn@writersbureau.com. **Website:** www.freelancemarketnews.com. **15% freelance written.** Monthly newsletter covering freelance writing. For all writers, established and new, *Freelance Market News* is an excellent source of the most up-to-date information about the publishing world. It is packed with news, views and the latest advice about new publications, plus the trends and developments in established markets, in the UK and around the world. Informs readers about publications that are looking for new writers and even warn about those writers should avoid. Estab. 1968. Byline given. Pays on acceptance. No kill fee. Publishes ms an average of 3 months after acceptance. Editorial lead time 3 months. Submit seasonal material 3 months in advance. Accepts queries by mail, e-mail. Sample copy and guidelines available online.

NONFICTION Buys 12 mss/year. Length: 1,00 words. **Pays £50/1,000 words.** Pays expenses of writers on assignment.

COLUMNS New Markets (magazines which have recently been published); Fillers & Letters; Overseas Markets (obviously only English-language publications); Market Notes (established publications accepting articles, fiction, reviews, or poetry). All should be between 40 and 200 words. **Pays £40/1,000 words.**

FREELANCE WRITER'S REPORT

CNW Publishing, Inc., 45 Main St., P.O. Box A, North Stratford NH 03590-0167. (603)922-8338. **E-mail:** fwrwm@writers-editors.com. **Website:** www.writers-editors.com. **10% freelance written.** Monthly newsletter covering the business of freelance writing. *FWR* covers the marketing and business/office management aspects of running a freelance writing business. Articles must be of value to the established freelancer; nothing basic. Estab. 1982. Byline given. Pays on publication. No kill fee. Publishes ms an average of 12 months after acceptance. Editorial lead time 2 months. Submit seasonal material 2 months in advance. Accepts simultaneous submissions. Responds in 1 week to queries; 2 weeks to mss. Sample copy for 6x9 SAE with 2 first-class stamps (for back copy); $4 for current copy. Guidelines and sample copy available online.

NONFICTION Needs book excerpts. Does not want articles about the basics of freelancing. **Buys 5 mss/ year.** Send complete ms by e-mail. Length: up to 900 words. **Pays 10¢/word.** Pays expenses of writers on assignment.

MSLEXIA

Mslexia Publications Ltd., P.O. Box 656, Newcastle upon Tyne NE99 1PZ United Kingdom. (44)(191)204-8860. **E-mail:** submissions@mslexia.co.uk; postbag@mslexia.co.uk; debbie@mslexia.co.uk. **Website:** www.mslexia.co.uk. **Contact:** Debbie Taylor, editorial director. **60% freelance written.** Quarterly magazine plus monthly email supplement offering advice and publishing opportunities for women writers, plus publication of poetry, fiction, memoir, reportage, journalism, reviews, etc. from open submissions and commissions. "*Mslexia* tells you all you need to know about exploring your creativity and getting into print. No other magazine provides *Mslexia*'s unique mix of advice and inspiration; news, reviews, interviews; competitions, events, grants; all served up with a challenging selection of new poetry and prose. *Mslexia* is read by authors and absolute beginners. A quarterly master class in the business and psychology of writing, it's the essential magazine for women who write. We accept submissions from any woman from any country writing in English. There are 14 ways of submitting to the magazine, for every kind of writing, and we pay for everything we publish. Submissions guidelines are on our website. We also run a series of women's fiction competitions with top cash prizes and career development opportunities for finalists." Estab. 1997. Circ. 8,000. Byline given. Pays on publication. Offers 50% kill fee. Publishes ms an average of 1 month after acceptance. Editorial lead time 3 months. Submit seasonal material 3 months in advance. Accepts queries by mail, e-mail, phone. Accepts simultaneous submissions. Responds in 3 months to mss. Purchase of single issues via office or website. Writer's guidelines online or by e-mail.

NONFICTION Needs how-to, inspirational, interview, opinion, personal experience, profile. No general items about women or academic features. "We are only interested in features (for tertiary-educated readership) about women's writing and literature." **Buys 40 mss/year.** Query with published clips. Length: 500-3,000 words by commission only. **Pays $70-600 for assigned articles; $70-300 for unsolicited articles.** Pays expenses of writers on assignment.

COLUMNS "We are open to suggestions, but would only commission 1 new column/year, probably from a UK-based writer." **Buys 12 mss/year.** Query with published clips.

FICTION See guidelines on website. "Submissions not on 1 of our current themes will be returned (if submitted with a SASE) or destroyed." **Buys 30 mss/year.** Send complete ms. Length: 50-2,200 words. **Pays £15 per 1,000 words prose plus contributor's copies.**

POETRY Needs avant-garde, free verse, haiku, traditional. Buys 40 poems/year. Submit maximum 4 poems. **Pays £25 per poem plus contributor's copies.**

💲💲 POETS & WRITERS MAGAZINE

90 Broad St., Suite 2100, New York NY 10004. (212)226-3586. **E-mail:** editor@pw.org. **Website:** www.pw.org/magazine. **Contact:** Kevin Larimer, editor. **95% freelance written.** Bimonthly professional trade journal for poets and fiction writers and creative nonfiction writers. Estab. 1987. Circ. 60,000. Byline given. Pays on publication. Offers 25% kill fee. Publishes ms an average of 4 months after acceptance. Submit seasonal material 4 months in advance. Accepts queries by mail, e-mail. Accepts simultaneous submissions. Responds in 2 months to mss. Sample copy: $5.95. Guidelines available online.

NONFICTION Needs how-to. **Buys 35 mss/year.** Send complete ms. Length: 700-3,000 words (depending on topic). Pays expenses of writers on assignment.

COLUMNS Literary and Publishing News, 700-1,000 words; Profiles of Emerging and Established Poets, Fiction Writers and Creative Nonfiction Writers, 2,000-3,000 words; Craft Essays and Publishing Advice, 2,000-2,500 words. Query with published clips or send complete ms. **Pays $225-500.**

💲 QUILL & SCROLL MAGAZINE

Quill and Scroll International Honorary Society for High School Journalists, University of Iowa, School of Journalism and Mass Communication, 100 Adler Journalism Bldg., Iowa City IA 52242. (319)335-3457. **Fax:** (319)335-3989. **E-mail:** quill-scroll@uiowa.edu. **Website:** www.quillandscroll.org. **Contact:** Jeffrey Browne, executive director; Judy Hauge. **20% freelance written.** Fall and spring issues covering scholastic journalism-related topics during school year. Primary audience is high school journalism students working on and studying topics related to newspapers, yearbooks, radio, television, and online media; secondary audience is their teachers and others interested in this topic. Invites journalism students and advisers to submit mss about important lessons learned or obstacles overcome. Estab. 1926. Circ. 8000. Byline given. Pays on acceptance and publication. No kill fee. Publishes ms an average of 4 months after acceptance. Editorial lead time 2 months. Accepts queries by mail, e-mail. Accepts simultaneous submissions. Responds in 2 weeks to queries. Guidelines available.

NONFICTION Needs essays, how-to, humor, interview, new product, opinion, personal experience, photo feature, technical, travel, types on topic. Does not want articles not pertinent to high school student journalists. Query with your submission. Length: 600-1,000 words. **Pays $10-100 for assigned articles.** Pays expenses of writers on assignment.

💲💲💲 QUILL MAGAZINE

Society of Professional Journalists, 3909 N. Meridian St., Indianapolis IN 46208. (317)927-8000, ext. 211. **Fax:** (317)920-4789. **E-mail:** sleadingham@spj.org. **E-mail:** quill@spj.org. **Website:** www.spj.org/quill.asp. **Contact:** Scott Leadingham, editor. **75% freelance written.** Monthly magazine covering journalism and the media industry. *Quill* is a how-to magazine written by journalists. Focuses on the industry's biggest issues while providing tips on how to become better journalists. Estab. 1912. Circ. 10,000. Byline given. Pays on acceptance. Offers 25% kill fee. Publishes ms an average of 2 months after acceptance. Editorial lead time 2-3 months. Submit seasonal material 2-3 months in advance. Accepts queries by e-mail. Accepts simultaneous submissions. Sample copy available online.

NONFICTION Needs general interest, how-to, technical. Does not want personality profiles and straight research pieces. **Buys 12 mss/year.** Query. Length: 800-2,500 words. **Pays $150-800.**

💲 THE WRITER'S CHRONICLE

Association of Writers & Writing Programs (AWP), 4400 University Drive, George Mason University, Fairfax VA 22030-4444. (703)993-4301. **Fax:** (703)993-4302. **E-mail:** chronicle@awpwriter.org. **Website:** www.awpwriter.org. **90% freelance written.** Published 6 times during the academic year; 3 times a semester. Magazine covering the art and craft of writing. "*Writer's Chronicle* strives to: present the best essays on the craft and art of writing poetry, fiction, and nonfiction; help overcome the over-specialization of the literary arts by presenting a public forum for the appreciation, debate, and analysis of contemporary literature; present the diversity of accomplishments and points of view within contemporary literature; provide serious and committed writers and students of writing the best advice on how to manage their professional lives; provide writers who teach with new pedagogical approaches for their classrooms; provide the members and subscribers with a literary commu-

nity as a compensation for a devotion to a difficult and lonely art; provide information on publishing opportunities, grants, and awards; and promote the good works of AWP, its programs, and its individual members." Estab. 1967. Circ. 35,000. Byline given. Pays on publication. No kill fee. Editorial lead time 3 months. Accepts simultaneous submissions. Responds in 2 weeks to queries. Sample copy free. Guidelines online. Reading period: February 1 through September 30.

NONFICTION Needs essays, interview, opinion. No personal essays. **Buys 15-20 mss/year.** Send complete ms. Length: 2,500-7,000 words. **Pays $18/100 words for assigned articles.**

💲💲💲 WRITER'S DIGEST

F+W Media, Inc., 10151 Carver Rd., Suite #200, Blue Ash OH 45242. (513)531-2690. **E-mail:** wdsubmissions@fwmedia.com. **Website:** www.writersdigest.com. **75% freelance written.** Magazine for those who want to write better, get published, and participate in the vibrant culture of writers. Readers look for specific ideas and tips that will help them succeed, whether success means getting into print, finding personal fulfillment through writing, or building and maintaining a thriving writing career and network. *Writer's Digest*, the No. 1 magazine for writers, celebrates the writing life and what it means to be a writer in today's publishing environment. Estab. 1920. Byline given. Pays on acceptance. Offers 25% kill fee. Publishes ms an average of 4 months after acceptance. Accepts simultaneous submissions. Responds in 1-4 months to queries and mss. Guidelines and editorial calendar available online (writersdigest.com/submission-guidelines).

NONFICTION , essays; short front-of-book pieces; how-to (writing craft, business of publishing, etc.); humor; inspirational; interviews/profiles (rarely, as those are typically handled in house). Does not accept phone, snail mail, or fax queries, and queries of this nature will receive no response. Does not buy newspaper clippings or reprints of articles previously published in other mainstream media, whether in print or online. Product reviews are handled in-house. **Buys 80 mss/year.** A query should include a thorough outline that introduces your article proposal and highlights each of the points you intend to make. Your query should discuss how the article will benefit readers, why the topic is timely, and why you're the appropriate writer to discuss the topic. Please include your publishing credential related to your topic with your submission. Do not send attachments. Length: 800-2,400 words. **Pays 30-50¢/word.** Pays expenses of writers on assignment.

😊😊😊😊 WRITTEN BY

7000 W. Third St., Los Angeles CA 90048. (323)782-4574. **Fax:** (323)782-4800. **Website:** www.writtenby.com. **40% freelance written.** Magazine published 9 times/year. *Written By* is the premier magazine written by and for America's screen and TV writers. Focuses on the craft of screenwriting and covers all aspects of the entertainment industry from the perspective of the writer. Audience is screenwriters and most entertainment executives. Estab. 1987. Circ. 12,000. Byline given. Pays on acceptance. Offers 10% kill fee. Publishes ms an average of 2 months after acceptance. Editorial lead time 4 months. Submit seasonal material 4 months in advance. Accepts queries by mail, e-mail, fax, phone, online submission form. Accepts simultaneous submissions. Guidelines for #10 SASE or online contact form.

NONFICTION Needs book excerpts, essays, historical, humor, interview, opinion, personal experience, photo feature, technical. No beginner pieces on how to break into Hollywood or how to write scripts. **Buys 20 mss/year.** Query with published clips. Length: 500-3,500 words. **Pays $500-3,500 for assigned articles.** Pays expenses of writers on assignment.

COLUMNS Pays $1,000 maximum.

LAW

😊😊😊😊 ABA JOURNAL

American Bar Association, 321 N. Clark St., 20th Floor, Chicago IL 60654. (312)988-6018. **Fax:** (312)988-6014. **E-mail:** releases@americanbar.org. **Website:** www.abajournal.com. **Contact:** Molly McDonough. **10% freelance written.** Monthly magazine covering the trends, people, and finances of the legal profession from Wall Street to Main Street to Pennsylvania Avenue. The *ABA Journal* is an independent, thoughtful, and inquiring observer of the law and the legal profession. The magazine is edited for members of the American Bar Association. Circ. 380,000. Byline given. Pays on acceptance. No kill fee. Accepts queries by e-mail, fax. Accepts simultaneous submissions. Sample copy free. Guidelines available online.

NONFICTION "We don't want anything that does not have a legal theme. No poetry or fiction." **Buys 5 mss/year.** "We use freelancers with experience reporting for legal or consumer publications; most have law degrees. If you are interested in freelancing for the *Journal*, we urge you to include your résumé and published clips when you contact us with story ideas." Length: 500-3,500 words. **Pays $300-2,000 for assigned articles.** Pays expenses of writers on assignment.

COLUMNS The National Pulse/Ideas from the Front (reports on legal news and trends), 650 words; eReport (reports on legal news and trends), 500-1,500 words. "The *ABA Journal eReport* is our weekly online newsletter sent out to members." **Buys 25 mss/year.** Query with published clips. **Pays $300, regardless of story length.**

😊😊😊😊 BENCH & BAR OF MINNESOTA

Minnesota State Bar Association, 600 Nicollet Mall #380, Minneapolis MN 55402. (612)333-1183; 800-882-6722. **Fax:** (612)333-4927. **E-mail:** jhaverkamp@mnbar.org. **Website:** www.mnbar.org. **Contact:** Judson Haverkamp, editor. **5% freelance written.** Magazine published 11 times/year. *Bench & Bar* seeks reportage, analysis, and commentary on changes in the law, trends and issues in the law and the legal profession, especially in Minnesota. Preference to items of practical/professional human interest to lawyers and judges. Audience is mostly Minnesota lawyers. Estab. 1931. Circ. 17,000. Byline given. Pays on acceptance. No kill fee. Publishes ms an average of 3 months after acceptance. Accepts simultaneous submissions. Responds in 1 month to queries. Guidelines for free online or by mail.

NONFICTION Does not want one-sided opinion pieces or advertorial. **Buys 2-3 mss/year.** Send query or complete ms. Length: 1,000-3,500 words. **Pays $500-1,500.** Pays expenses of writers on assignment.

😊😊😊😊 CALIFORNIA LAWYER

Daily Journal Corp., 44 Montgomery St., Suite 500, San Francisco CA 94104. (415)296-2400. **Fax:** (415)296-2440. **E-mail:** cl_contributingeditor@dailyjournal.com; bo_links@dailyjournal.com. **Website:** www.callawyer.com. **Contact:** Bo Links, legal editor; Marsha Sessa, art director. **30% freelance written.** Monthly magazine of law-related articles and general-interest subjects of appeal to lawyers and judges. Primary mission is to cover the news of the world as it affects the law and lawyers, helping readers better comprehend the issues of the day and to cover changes and trends in the legal profession. Readers are all California lawyers, plus judges, legislators, and corporate executives. Although the magazine focuses on California and the West, they have subscribers in every state. *California Lawyer* is a general interest magazine for people interested in law. Estab. 1981. Circ. 140,000. Byline given. Pays on acceptance. Offers 25% kill fee. Publishes ms an average of 3 months after acceptance. Editorial lead time 3 months. Accepts queries by e-mail. Accepts simultaneous submissions. Guidelines available online.

NONFICTION Needs essays, general interest, profile, "We will consider well-researched, in-depth stories on the law, including legal trends of statewide and national significance, thought-provoking legal issues, and profiles of lawyers doing groundbreaking work. We will consider local issues if they have statewide or national implications or if you have a new unique angle to the story." **Buys 12 mss/year.** Query contributing editor: cl_contributingeditor@dailyjournal.com. Please do not send unsolicited mss. Length: 500-5,000 words. **Pays $50-2,000.** Pays expenses of writers on assignment.

COLUMNS Expert Advice (specific, practical tips on an area of law or practice management), 650-750 words; Tech (lawyers and technology), up to 1,000 words; First Person (personal experience), 700 words; In House (working as corporate counsel in California), up to 1,000 words. Query appropriate editor (see website submission guidelines). **Pays $50-250.**

$$$$ INSIDECOUNSEL

ALM Media, LLC, 120 Broadway, 5th Floor, New York NY 10271. (212)457-9400. **E-mail:** apaonita@alm.com. **Website:** www.insidecounsel.com. **Contact:** Anthony Paonita, editor-in-chief. **50% freelance written.** Monthly tabloid covering legal information for attorneys. *InsideCounsel* is a monthly national magazine that gives general counsel and inhouse attorneys information on legal and business issues to help them better manage corporate law departments. It routinely addresses changes and trends in law departments, litigation management, legal technology, corporate governance and inhouse careers. Law areas covered monthly include: intellectual property, international, technology, project finance, e-commerce, and litigation. All articles need to be geared toward

the inhouse attorney's perspective. Estab. 1991. Circ. 45,000. Byline given. Pays on publication. No kill fee. Publishes ms an average of 3 months after acceptance. Editorial lead time 3 months. Submit seasonal material 3 months in advance. Accepts queries by mail, e-mail. Accepts simultaneous submissions. Responds in 3 weeks to queries. Sample copy for $17. Guidelines available online.

NONFICTION **Buys 12-25 mss/year.** Query with published clips. Length: 500-3,000 words. **Pays $500-2,000.**

♻$$$$ NATIONAL

The Canadian Bar Association, 865 Carling Ave., Ottawa ON K1S 5S8 Canada. (613)237-2925. **Fax:** (613)237-0185. **E-mail:** beverleys@cba.org; national@cba.org. **Website:** www.nationalmagazine.ca. **Contact:** Beverley Spencer, editor in chief. **90% freelance written.** Magazine published 8 times/year covering practice trends and business developments in the law, with a focus on technology, innovation, practice management, and client relations. Estab. 1993. Circ. 37,000. Byline given. Pays on acceptance. Offers 50% kill fee. Publishes ms an average of 2 months after acceptance. Editorial lead time 2 months. Accepts queries by e-mail. Accepts simultaneous submissions. Sample copy free.

NONFICTION **Buys 25 mss/year.** Query with published clips. Length: 1,000-2,500 words. **Pays $1/word.** Pays expenses of writers on assignment.

$$ THE NATIONAL JURIST AND PRE LAW

Cypress Magazines, 7670 Opportunity Rd #105, San Diego CA 92111. (858)300-3201; (800)296-9656. **Fax:** (858)503-7588. **E-mail:** jack@cypressmagazines.com; callahan@cypressmagazines.com. **Website:** www.nationaljurist.com. **Contact:** Jack Crittenden, editor in chief. **25% freelance written.** Bimonthly magazine covering law students and issues of interest to law students. Estab. 1991. Circ. 145,000. Pays on publication. No kill fee. Accepts queries by mail, e-mail. Accepts simultaneous submissions.

NONFICTION Needs general interest, how-to, humor, interview. **Buys 4 mss/year.** Query. Length: 750-3,000 words. **Pays $100-500.** Pays expenses of writers on assignment.

COLUMNS **Pays $100-500.**

PARALEGAL TODAY

Conexion International Media, Inc., 6030 Marshalee Dr., Suite 455, Elkridge MD 21075-5935. (443)445-3057. **Fax:** (443)445-3257. **E-mail:** pinfanti@connexionmedia.com. **Website:** www.paralegaltoday.com. **Contact:** Patricia E. Infanti, editor in chief; Charles Buckwalter, publisher. Quarterly magazine geared toward all legal assistants/paralegals throughout the U.S. and Canada, regardless of specialty (litigation, corporate, bankruptcy, environmental law, etc.). How-to articles to help paralegals perform their jobs more effectively are most in demand, as are career and salary information, technolgoy tips, and trends pieces. Estab. 1983. Circ. 8,000. Byline given. Pays on publication. Offers kill fee ($25-50 standard rate). Editorial lead time is 10 weeks. Submit seasonal material 3 months in advance. Accepts queries by mail, e-mail, fax, online submission form. Accepts simultaneous submissions. Responds in 2 months to mss. Sample copy available online. Guidelines available online.

NONFICTION Needs interview, news (brief, hard news topics regarding paralegals), features (present information to help paralegals advance their careers). Send query letter first; if electronic, send submission as attachment. **Pays $75-300.** Pays expenses of writers on assignment.

THE PENNSYLVANIA LAWYER

Pennsylvania Bar Association, 100 South St., P.O. Box 186, Harrisburg PA 17108. **E-mail:** editor@pabar.org. **Website:** www.pabar.org. **Contact:** Editor. **25% freelance written. Prefers to work with published/established writers.** Bimonthly magazine published as a service to the legal profession and the members of the Pennsylvania Bar Association. Estab. 1979. Circ. 26,000. Byline given. Pays on acceptance. No kill fee. Publishes ms an average of 6 months after acceptance. Submit seasonal material 6 months in advance. Accepts queries by mail, e-mail. Accepts simultaneous submissions. Responds in 2 months. Sample copy for $2. Writer's guidelines for #10 SASE or by e-mail.

NONFICTION Needs how-to, interview, law-practice management, technology. **Buys 8-10 mss/year.** Query. Length: 1,200-1,500 words. **Pays $50 for book reviews; $75-400 for assigned articles; $150 for unsolicited articles.** Pays expenses of writers on assignment.

SUPER LAWYERS

Thomson Reuters, 610 Opperman Dr., Eagan MN 55123. (877)787-5290. **Website:** www.superlawyers.com. **Contact:** Erik Lundegaard, editor. **100% freelance written.** Monthly magazine covering law and politics. Publishes glossy magazines in every region of the country; all serve a legal audience and have a storytelling sensibility. Writes profiles of interesting attorneys exclusively. Estab. 1990. Byline given. Pays on acceptance. Offers 25% kill fee. Publishes ms an average of 1 month after acceptance. Editorial lead time 6 months. Submit seasonal material 6 months in advance. Accepts queries by phone, online submission form. Accepts simultaneous submissions. Sample copy free. Guidelines free.

NONFICTION Needs general interest, historical. Query. Length: 500-2,000 words. **Pays 50¢-$1.50/word.** Pays expenses of writers on assignment.

LUMBER

PALLET ENTERPRISE

Industrial Reporting, Inc., 10244 Timber Ridge Dr., Ashland VA 23005. (804)550-0323. **Fax:** (804)550-2181. **E-mail:** edb@ireporting.com; mbrindleypallet@gmail.com. **Website:** www.palletenterprise.com. **Contact:** Edward C. Brindley, Jr., Ph.D., publisher; Melissa Brindley, editor. **40% freelance written.** Monthly magazine covering lumber and pallet operations. The *Pallet Enterprise* is a monthly trade magazine for the sawmill, pallet, remanufacturing, and wood processing industries. Articles should offer technical, solution-oriented information. Anti-forest articles are not accepted. Articles should focus on machinery and unique ways to improve profitability/make money. Estab. 1981. Circ. 14,500. Pays on publication. Editorial lead time 2 months. Submit seasonal material 2 months in advance. Accepts queries by mail, e-mail, fax, phone. Accepts simultaneous submissions. Sample copy available online. Guidelines free.

NONFICTION Needs interview, new product, opinion, technical, industry news, environmental, forests operation/plant features. No lifestyle, humor, general news, etc. **Buys 20 mss/year.** Query with published clips. Length: 1,000-3,000 words. **Pays $200-400 for assigned articles. Pays $100-400 for unsolicited articles.** Pays expenses of writers on assignment.

COLUMNS Green Watch (environmental news/opinion affecting US forests), 1,500 words. **Buys 12 mss/year.** Query with published clips. **Pays $200-400.**

$$ TIMBERWEST

TimberWest Publications, LLC, P.O. Box 610, Edmonds WA 98020. (425)778-3388. **Fax:** (425)771-3623. **E-mail:** timberwest@forestnet.com; diane@forestnet.com. **Website:** www.forestnet.com. **Contact:** Diane Mettler, managing editor. **75% freelance written.** Monthly magazine covering logging and lumber segment of the forestry industry in the Northwest. Primarily publishes profiles on loggers and their operations—with an emphasis on the machinery—in Washington, Oregon, Idaho, Montana, Northern California, and Alaska. Some timber issues are highly controversial, and although the magazine will report on the issues, this is a pro-logging publication. Does not publish articles with a negative slant on the timber industry. Estab. 1975. Circ. 10,000. Byline given. Pays on acceptance. No kill fee. Editorial lead time 2 months. Accepts queries by mail, fax. Accepts simultaneous submissions. Responds in 3 weeks to queries. Sample copy: $2. Guidelines for #10 SASE.

NONFICTION Needs historical, interview, new product. No articles that put the timber industry in a bad light, such as environmental articles against logging. **Buys 50 mss/year.** Query with published clips. Length: 1,100-1,500 words. **Pays $400.** Pays expenses of writers on assignment.

FILLERS Needs facts, newsbreaks. **Buys 10 mss/year.** Length: 400-800 words. **Pays $100-250.**

MACHINERY & METAL

$$$ AMERICAN MACHINIST

Penton Media, 1300 E. 9th St., Cleveland OH 44114. (216)696-7000. **Fax:** (913)696-8208. **E-mail:** robert.brooks@penton.com. **Website:** www.americanmachinist.com. **Contact:** Robert Brooks, editor-in-chief. **10% freelance written.** Monthly online website covering all forms of metalworking covering all forms of metalworking. Accepts contributed features and articles. *American Machinist* is an essential online source dedicated to metalworking in the United States. Readers are the owners and managers of metalworking shops. Publishes articles that provide the managers and owners of job shops, contract shops, and captive shops the information they need to make their operations more efficient, more productive, and more profitable. Articles are technical in nature and must be focused on technology that will help these shops to become more competitive on a global basis. Readers are skilled machinists. This is not the place for lightweight items about manufacturing. Not interested in articles on management theories. Estab. 1877. Circ. 80,000. Byline sometimes given. Offers 20% kill fee. Publishes ms an average of 1-2 months after acceptance. Editorial lead time 3-6 months. Submit seasonal material 4-6 months in advance. Accepts queries by mail, e-mail, phone. Accepts simultaneous submissions. Responds in 1-2 weeks to queries; 1 month to mss. Sample copy online.

NONFICTION Needs general interest, how-to, new product, opinion, personal experience, photo feature, technical. Query with published clips. Length: 600-2,400 words. **Pays $300-1,200.** Pays expenses of writers on assignment.

FILLERS Needs anecdotes, facts, gags, newsbreaks, short humor. **Buys 12-18 mss/year. mss/year.** Length: 50-200 words. **Pays $25-100.**

$$$ CUTTING TOOL ENGINEERING

CTE Publications, Inc., 1 Northfield Plaza, Suite 240, Northfield IL 60093 USA. (847)714-0175. **Fax:** (847)559-4444. **E-mail:** alanr@jwr.com. **Website:** www.ctemag.com. **Contact:** Alan Richter, editor. **40% freelance written.** Monthly magazine covering industrial metal cutting tools and metal cutting and grinding operations. *Cutting Tool Engineering* serves owners, managers, and engineers who work in manufacturing, specifically manufacturing that involves cutting or grinding metal or other materials. Writing should be geared toward improving manufacturing processes. Estab. 1948. Circ. 60,000. Byline given. Pays on publication. Offers 50% kill fee. Publishes ms an average of 2 months after acceptance. Editorial lead time 2 months. Accepts queries by mail, e-mail, phone. Responds in 2 months to mss. Sample copy and guidelines free.

NONFICTION Needs how-to, opinion, personal experience, profile, technical. Does not want fiction or articles that don't relate to manufacturing. **Buys 10 mss/year.** Length: 1,500-2,000 words. **Pays $750-1,100.** Pays expenses of writers on assignment.

✪$$ EQUIPMENT JOURNAL

Pace Publishing, 5160 Explorer Dr., Unit 6, Mississauga ON L4W 4T7 Canada. (416)459-5163. **E-mail:**

editor@equipmentjournal.com. **E-mail:** editor@equipmentjournal.com. **Website:** www.equipment-journal.com. **Contact:** Nathan Medcalf. **5% freelance written.** Canada's national heavy equipment newspaper. Focuses on the construction, material handling, mining, forestry, and on-highway transportation industries. Estab. 1966. Circ. 22,000. Byline given. Pays on publication. Kill fee: $50. Publishes ms an average of 1-2 months after acceptance. Editorial lead time 2-3 months. Accepts queries by e-mail, phone. Accepts simultaneous submissions. Sample copy and guidelines free.

NONFICTION Needs how-to, interview, new product, photo feature, technical. Does not want "material that falls outside of *Equipment Journal*'s mandate—the Canadian equipment industry." **Buys 15 mss/year.** Send complete ms. "We prefer electronic submissions." Length: 400-900 words. **Pays 40-50¢/word.** Pays expenses of writers on assignment.

REPRINTS Reprint payment negotiable.

COLUMNS Contact: Nathan Medcalf, editor. **Buys 2 mss/year.**

🟡🟡 ORNAMENTAL & MISCELLANEOUS FABRICATOR

P. O. Box 492167, Lawrenceville GA 30049. (888)516-8585. **Fax:** (888)279-7994. **E-mail:** editor@nomma.org; todd@nomma.org. **Website:** www.nomma.org. **Contact:** Todd Daniel, editor. **20% freelance written.** "Bimonthly magazine to inform, educate, and inspire members of the ornamental and miscellaneous metalworking industry." Estab. 1959. Circ. 9,000. Byline given. Pays on publication. No kill fee. Editorial lead time 1-2 months. Accepts queries by mail, e-mail, fax. Accepts simultaneous submissions. Responds by e-mail in 1 month (include e-mail address in query). Guidelines by email.

NONFICTION Needs book excerpts, essays, general interest, historical, how-to, humor, interview, opinion, personal experience, technical. **Buys 8-12 mss/year.** Query. Length: 1,200-2,000 words. **Pays $250-400.** Pays expenses of writers on assignment.

REPRINTS Send tearsheet, photocopy or typed ms with rights for sale noted and information about when and where the material previously appeared. Pays 100% of amount paid for an original article.

COLUMNS 700-900 words. **Pays $50-100.**

🟡🟡🟡 PRACTICAL WELDING TODAY

FMA Communications, Inc., 2135 Point Blvd., Elgin IL 60123. (815)399-8700. **E-mail:** amandac@thefabricator.com. **Website:** www.thefabricator.com. **Contact:** Amanda Carlson, editor. **15% freelance written.** Bimonthly magazine covering welding. "We generally publish how-to and educational articles that teach people about a process or how to do something better." Estab. 1997. Circ. 40,000. Byline given. Pays on publication. No kill fee. Editorial lead time 6 months. Accepts queries by mail, e-mail. Accepts simultaneous submissions. Responds in 2 weeks to queries; 2 months to mss. Sample copy free. Guidelines online.

NONFICTION Needs how-to, technical, company profiles. Special issues: Forecast issue on trends in welding (January/February). No promotional, one-sided, persuasive articles or unsolicited case studies. **Buys 5 mss/year.** Query with published clips. Length: 800-1,200 words. **Pays 40-80¢/word.** Pays expenses of writers on assignment.

🟡🟡 SNIPS MAGAZINE

BNP Media, 2401 W. Big Beaver Rd., Suite 700, Troy MI 48084. (248)244-6416. **Fax:** (248)362-0317. **E-mail:** mcconnellm@bnpmedia.com. **Website:** www.snipsmag.com. **Contact:** Michael McConnell, editor. **2% freelance written.** Monthly magazine for sheet metal, heating, ventilation, air conditioning, and metal roofing contractors. Estab. 1932. No kill fee. Publishes ms an average of 3 months after acceptance. Accepts queries by mail, e-mail, fax, phone. Accepts simultaneous submissions. Call for writer's guidelines.

NONFICTION Length: under 1,000 words unless on special assignment. **Pays $200-300.** Pays expenses of writers on assignment.

🟡🟡 SPRINGS

Spring Manufacturers Institute, 2001 Midwest Rd., Suite 106, Oak Brook IL 60523-1335. (630)495-8588. **Fax:** (630)495-8595. **E-mail:** lynne@smihq.org. **Website:** www.smihq.org. **Contact:** Lynne Carr, general manager. **10% freelance written.** Quarterly magazine covering precision mechanical spring manufacture. Articles should be aimed at spring manufacturers. Estab. 1962. Circ. 10,800. Byline given. Pays on publication. No kill fee. Publishes ms an average of 3-6 months after acceptance. Editorial lead time 4 months. Accepts simultaneous submissions. Sample copy free. Guidelines available online.

NONFICTION Needs general interest, how-to, interview, opinion, personal experience, technical. **Buys 4-6 mss/year.** Length: 2,000-10,000 words. **Pays $100-600 for assigned articles.**

$ $ $ STAMPING JOURNAL

Fabricators & Manufacturers Association (FMA), 2135 Point Blvd., Elgin IL 60123. (815)399-8700. **Fax:** (815)381-1370. **E-mail:** kateb@thefabricator.com. **Website:** www.thefabricator.com. **Contact:** Dan Davis, editor-in-chief; Kate Bachman, editor. **15% freelance written.** Bimonthly magazine covering metal stamping. Looks for how-to and educational articles—nonpromotional. Estab. 1989. Circ. 35,000. Byline given. Pays on publication. No kill fee. Editorial lead time 6 months. Accepts queries by mail, e-mail, phone. Accepts simultaneous submissions. Responds in 2 weeks to queries. Sample copy and writer's guidelines free.

NONFICTION Pays 40-80¢/word. Pays expenses of writers on assignment.

$ $ $ TPJ—THE TUBE & PIPE JOURNAL

Fabricators & Manufacturers Association (FMA), 2135 Point Blvd., Elgin IL 60123. (815)399-8700. **Fax:** (815)381-1370. **E-mail:** ericl@thefabricator.com. **Website:** www.thefabricator.com. **Contact:** Eric Lundin, editor. **15% freelance written.** Magazine published 8 times/year covering metal tube and pipe. Educational perspective—emphasis is on how-to articles to accomplish a particular task or improve on a process. New trends and technologies are also important topics. Estab. 1990. Circ. 30,000. Byline given. Pays on publication. No kill fee. Editorial lead time 6 months. Accepts queries by mail, e-mail. Accepts simultaneous submissions. Responds in 2 weeks to queries; 2 months to mss. Sample copy free. Guidelines online.

NONFICTION Needs how-to, technical. Special issues: Forecast issue (January). No unsolicited case studies. **Buys 5 mss/year.** Query with published clips. Length: 800-1,200 words. **Pays 40-80¢/word.** Pays expenses of writers on assignment.

$ $ $ WELDING DESIGN & FABRICATION

Penton Media, 1300 E. 9th St., Cleveland OH 44114. (216)696-7000. **Fax:** (216)931-9524. **E-mail:** wdeditor@penton.com; robert.brooks@penton. **Website:** www.weldingdesign.com. **Contact:** Robert E. Brooks, editor. **10% freelance written.** Bimonthly magazine covering all facets of welding and running a welding business. *Welding Design & Fabrication* provides information to the owners and managers of welding shops, including business, technology and trends. We include information on engineering and technological developments that could change the business as it is currently known, and feature stories on how welders are doing business with the goal of helping our readers to be more productive, efficient, and competitive. Welding shops are very local in nature and need to be addressed as small businessmen in a field that is consolidating and becoming more challenging and more global. We do not write about business management theory as much as we write about putting into practice good management techniques that have proved to work at similar businesses. Estab. 1930. Circ. 40,000. Byline given. Pays on publication. Offers 20% kill fee. Publishes ms an average of 1-2 months after acceptance. Editorial lead time 3-6 months. Submit seasonal material 4-6 months in advance. Accepts queries by mail, e-mail, phone. Accepts simultaneous submissions. Responds in 1-2 weeks to queries. Responds in 1 month to mss. Sample copy available online.

NONFICTION Needs general interest, how-to, new product, opinion, personal experience, photo feature, technical. Query. Length: 600-2,400 words. **Pays $300-1,200.** Pays expenses of writers on assignment.

FILLERS Needs anecdotes, facts, gags, newsbreaks, short humor. **Buys 12-18 mss/year.** Length: 50-200 words. **Pays $25-100.**

$ $ WIRE ROPE NEWS & SLING TECHNOLOGY

Wire Rope News LLC, P.O. Box 871, Clark NJ 07066. (908)486-3221. **Fax:** (732)396-4215. **E-mail:** info@wireropenews.com. **Website:** www.wireropenews.com. **Contact:** Edward Bluvias III, publisher and editorial director. **100% freelance written.** Bimonthly magazine published for manufacturers and distributors of wire rope, chain, cordage, related hardware, and sling fabricators. Content includes technical articles, news and reports describing the manufacturing and use of wire rope and related products in marine, construction, mining, aircraft and offshore drilling operations. Estab. 1979. Circ. 4,300. Byline sometimes given. Pays on acceptance. No kill fee. Publishes ms an average of 6 months after acceptance. Editorial lead time 2 months. Submit seasonal material 2 months in advance. Accepts queries by mail, fax. Accepts simultaneous submissions.

NONFICTION Needs general interest, historical, interview, photo feature, technical. **Buys 30 mss/year.** Send complete ms. Length: 2,500-5,000 words. **Pays $300-500.** Pays expenses of writers on assignment.

MAINTENANCE & SAFETY

💲💲 AMERICAN WINDOW CLEANER MAGAZINE

12Twelve Publishing Corp., 750-B NW Broad St., Southern Pines NC 28387. (910)693-2644. **Fax:** (910)246-1681. **E-mail:** info@awcmag.com; karen@awcmag.com. **Website:** www.awcmag.com. **Contact:** Karen Grinter, creative director. **20% freelance written.** Bimonthly magazine on window cleaning. Produces articles to help window cleaners become more profitable, safe, professional, and feel good about what they do. Estab. 1986. Circ. 8,000. Byline given. Pays on acceptance. Offers 33% kill fee. Publishes ms an average of 4-8 months after acceptance. Editorial lead time 2 months. Submit seasonal material 3 months in advance. Accepts simultaneous submissions. Responds in 2 weeks to queries; in 1 month to mss. Sample copy free.

NONFICTION Needs how-to, humor, inspirational, interview, personal experience, photo feature. "We do not want PR-driven pieces. We want to educate—not push a particular product." **Buys 20 mss/year.** Query. Length: 500-5,000 words. **Pays $50-250.** Pays expenses of writers on assignment.

COLUMNS Window Cleaning Tips (tricks of the trade); 1,000-2,000 words; Humor-anecdotes-feel good-abouts (window cleaning industry); Computer High-Tech (tips on new technology), all 1,000 words. **Buys 12 mss/year.** Query. **Pays $50-100.**

💲💲 PEST MANAGEMENT PROFESSIONAL

North Coast Media, 1360 E. 9th St., Suite 1070, Cleveland OH 44114. (216)706-3754. **Fax:** (216)706-3711. **E-mail:** hgooch@northcoastmedia.net. **Website:** www.mypmp.net. **Contact:** Heather Gooch, editor. Monthly magazine for professional pest management professionals and sanitarians. Estab. 1933. Circ. 20,000. Pays on publication. No kill fee. Submit seasonal material 3 months in advance. Accepts queries by mail, e-mail, phone. Accepts simultaneous submissions. Responds in 1 month to mss.

NONFICTION Needs how-to, humor, inspirational, interview, new product, personal experience, case histories, new technological breakthroughs. No general information type of articles desired. **Buys 3 mss/year.** Query. Length: 1,000-1,400 words. **Pays $150-400 minimum.**

COLUMNS Regular columns use material oriented to this profession, 550 words.

MANAGEMENT & SUPERVISION

💲💲💲 HUMAN RESOURCE EXECUTIVE

LRP Publications Magazine Group, P.O. Box 980, Horsham PA 19044-0980. (215)784-0910. **Fax:** (215)784-0275. **E-mail:** kfrasch@lrp.com. **E-mail:** tgarrison@lrp.com. **Website:** www.hronline.com. **Contact:** Kristen B. Frasch, managing editor; Terri Garrison, editorial assistant. **30% freelance written.** Magazine published 16 times/year serving the information needs of chief human resource professionals/executives in companies, government agencies, and nonprofit institutions with 500 or more employees. Estab. 1987. Circ. 75,000. Byline given. Pays on acceptance. Offers kill fee. Pays 50% kill fee on assigned stories. Publishes ms an average of 2 months after acceptance. Accepts queries by mail, e-mail, fax. Accepts simultaneous submissions. Responds in 1 month to mss. Guidelines available online.

NONFICTION Needs book excerpts, interview. **Buys 16 mss/year.** Query with published clips. Length: 1,800 words. **Pays $200-1,000.** Pays expenses of writers on assignment.

💲💲 PLAYGROUND MAGAZINE

Harris Publishing, P.O. Box 595, Ashton ID 83420. (208)652-3683. **Fax:** (208)652-7856. **Website:** www.playgroundmag.com. **25% freelance written.** Magazine published quarterly covering playgrounds, play-related issues, equipment, and industry trends. *Playground Magazine* targets park and recreation management, elementary school teachers and administrators, child care facilities, and parent-group leader readership. Articles should focus on play and the playground market as a whole, including aquatic play and surfacing. Estab. 2000. Circ. 35,000. Byline given. Pays on publication. No kill fee. Publishes ms an average of 6 months after acceptance. Editorial lead time 2 months. Submit seasonal material 1 year in advance. Accepts queries by mail, e-mail. Accepts simultaneous submissions. Responds in 1 month to queries. Responds in 2 months to mss. Sample copy for $5. Guidelines for #10 SASE.

NONFICTION Needs how-to, interview, new product, opinion, personal experience, photo feature, technical, travel. *Playground Magazine* does not publish any articles that do not directly relate to play and the playground industry. **Buys 4-6 mss/year.** Query. Length: 800-1,500 words. **Pays $50-300 for assigned articles.** Pays expenses of writers on assignment.

COLUMNS Dream Spaces (an article that profiles a unique play area and focuses on community involvement, unique design, or human interest), 800-1,200 words. **Buys 2 mss/year.** Query. **Pays $100-300.**

MARINE & MARITIME INDUSTRIES

💲💲 CURRENTS

Marine Technology Society, 1100 H St. NW, Suite LL-100, Washington DC 20005. (202)717-8705. **Fax:** (202)347-4302. **E-mail:** morganteeditorial@verizon.net. **Website:** www.mtsociety.org. **Contact:** Amy Morgante, managing editor. Bimonthly newsletter covering commercial, academic, scientific marine technology. Readers are engineers and technologists who design, develop ,and maintain the equipment and instruments used to understand and explore the oceans. The newsletter covers society news, industry news, science and technology news, and similar news. Estab. 1963. Circ. 3,200. Byline given. Pays on acceptance. No kill fee. Editorial lead time 1-2 months. Accepts queries by e-mail. Accepts simultaneous submissions. Responds in 4 weeks to queries Sample copy free.

NONFICTION Needs interview, technical. **Buys 1-6 mss/year.** Query. Length: 250-500 words. **Pays $100-500 for assigned articles.** Pays expenses of writers on assignment.

💲💲 PROFESSIONAL MARINER

Navigator Publishing, P.O. Box 569, Portland ME 04112. (207)772-2466. **Fax:** (207)772-2879. **E-mail:** rmiller@professionalmariner.com. **Website:** www.professionalmariner.com. **Contact:** Rich Miller, editor. **75% freelance written.** Bimonthly magazine covering professional seamanship and maritime industry news. Estab. 1993. Circ. 29,000. Byline given. Pays on

publication. No kill fee. Editorial lead time 3 months. Accepts queries by mail, e-mail. Accepts simultaneous submissions.

NONFICTION Buys 15 mss/year. Query. Length: varies; short clips to long profiles/features. **Pays 25¢/word.** Pays expenses of writers on assignment.

MEDICAL

💲💲 AHIP COVERAGE

America's Health Insurance Plans, 601 Pennsylvania Ave. NW, South Bldg., Suite 500, Washington DC 20004. (202)778-3200. **Fax:** (202)331-7487. **E-mail:** ahip@ahip.org. **Website:** www.ahip.org. **75% freelance written.** Bimonthly magazine geared toward administrators in America's health insurance companies. Articles should inform and generate interest and discussion about topics on anything from patient care to regulatory issues. Estab. 1990. Circ. 12,000. Byline given. Pays within 30 days of acceptance of article in final form. Offers 30% kill fee. Publishes ms an average of 2 months after acceptance. Editorial lead time 2 months. Submit seasonal material 4 months in advance. Accepts queries by mail, e-mail, fax. Accepts simultaneous submissions. Sample copy free.

NONFICTION Needs book excerpts, how-to, opinion. "We do not accept stories that promote products." Send complete ms. Length: 1,800-2,500 words. **Pays 65¢/word minimum.** Pays expenses of writers on assignment. Pays phone expenses of writers on assignment.

💲💲 JEMS: JOURNAL OF EMERGENCY MEDICAL SERVICES

PennWell Corporation, 1421 S. Sheridan Rd., Tulsa OK 74112. (800)331-4463. **E-mail:** rkelley@pennwell.com. **Website:** www.jems.com. Senior Editor: Sarah Ferguson. **Contact:** Ryan Kelley, Managing Editor. **95% freelance written.** Monthly magazine directed to personnel who serve the pre-hospital emergency medicine industry: paramedics, EMTs, emergency physicians and nurses, administrators, EMS consultants, etc. *JEMS (Journal of Emergency Medical Services)* seeks to improve patient care in the prehospital setting and promote positive change in EMS by delivering information and education from industry leaders, change makers and emerging voices. With a rich tradition of editorial excellence and an unparalleled consortium of subject matter experts and state-of-the-science content, *JEMS* fulfills its commitment to EMS providers, instructors and administrators through all media channels including online and print. Estab. 1980. Circ. 50,000. Byline given. Pays on publication. No kill fee. Publishes ms an average of 6 months after acceptance. Submit seasonal material 6 months in advance. Accepts queries by e-mail. Responds in 2-3 months to queries. Sample copy free by request when available. Guidelines online.

NONFICTION Needs general interest, how-to, interview, new product, personal experience, photo feature, profile, technical, All articles should be focused on emergency medical services and prehospital care. Does not want stories, poems, and personal stories. **Buys 80 mss/year.** Query Ryan Kelley with contact information, suggested title, ms document (can be an outline), a summary, a general ms classification, and photos or figures to be considered with the ms. Please also submit professional CV/resume. Length: 1,800-2,400 words, plus references. **Pays $100-300.**

COLUMNS Length: up to 850 words. Query with or without published clips. **Pays $50-250.**

⑨⑨⑨ MANAGED CARE

780 Township Line Rd., Yardley PA 19067. (267)685-2788. **Fax:** (267)685-2966. **E-mail:** pwehrwein@medimedia.com. **Website:** www.managedcaremag.com. **Contact:** Peter Wehrwein, editor. **75% freelance written.** Monthly magazine that delivers high-interest, full-length articles and shorter features on clinical and business aspects of the health care industry. Emphasizes practical, usable information that helps HMO medical directors and pharmacy directors cope with the options, challenges, and hazards in the rapidly changing health care industry. Estab. 1992. Circ. 60,000. Byline given. Pays on acceptance. Offers 20% kill fee. Publishes ms an average of 6 weeks after acceptance. Editorial lead time 3 months. Submit seasonal material 4 months in advance. Accepts queries by mail, e-mail, fax. Accepts simultaneous submissions. Responds in 3 weeks to queries. Responds in 2 months to mss. Sample copy free. Guidelines available online.

NONFICTION Needs book excerpts, general interest, how-to, original research and review articles that examine the relationship between health care delivery and financing. Also considered occasionally are personal experience, opinion, interview/profile, and humor pieces, but these must have a strong managed care angle and draw upon the insights of (if they are not written by) a knowledgeable managed care professional. **Buys 40 mss/year.** Query with published clips. Length: 1,000-3,000 words. **Pays 75¢/word.** Pays expenses of writers on assignment.

✪⑨⑨ OPTICAL PRISM

250 The East Mall, Suite 1113, Toronto ON M9B 6L3 Canada. (416)233-2487. **Fax:** (416)233-1746. **E-mail:** info@opticalprism.ca. **Website:** www.opticalprism.ca. **30% freelance written.** Magazine published 10 times/year. Covers the health, fashion, and business aspects of the optical industry in Canada. Estab. 1982. Circ. 10,000. Byline given. Pays on publication. Publishes ms an average of 2 months after acceptance. Editorial lead time 3 months. Submit seasonal material 3 months in advance. Accepts queries by mail, e-mail. Accepts simultaneous submissions. Digital copy available online.

NONFICTION Needs interview, related to optical industry. Special issues: Editorial themes and feature topics available online in media kit. Query. Length: 1,000-1,600 words. **Pays 40¢/word (Canadian).** Pays expenses of writers on assignment.

COLUMNS Insight (profiles on people in the eyewear industry—also sometimes schools and businesses), 700-1,000 words. **Buys 5 mss/year.** Query. **Pays 40¢/word.**

⑨⑨ PHYSICIAN MAGAZINE

Physicians News Network, 10755 Scripps Poway Parkway, Suite 615, San Diego CA 92131. (858)226-7647. **E-mail:** sheri@physiciansnetwork.com; editors@physiciansnetwork.com. **Website:** www.physiciansnewsnetwork.com. **Contact:** Sheri Carr, COO/editor. **25% freelance written.** Monthly magazine covering non-technical articles of relevance to physicians. Estab. 1908. Circ. 18,000. Byline given. Pays on acceptance. Offers 10% kill fee. Publishes ms an average of 2-3 months after acceptance. Editorial lead time 2-3 months. Accepts queries by e-mail. Accepts simultaneous submissions. Responds in 4 weeks to queries. Responds in 2 months to mss. Sample copy available online.

NONFICTION Needs general interest. **Buys 12-24 mss/year.** Query with published clips. Length: 600-3,000 words. **Pays $200-600 for assigned articles.**

COLUMNS Medical World (tips/how-to's), 800-900 words. Query with published clips. **Pays $200-600.**

💲💲 PLASTIC SURGERY NEWS

American Society of Plastic Surgeons, 444 E. Algonquin Rd., Arlington Heights IL 60005. **Fax:** (847)981-5458. **E-mail:** mss@plasticsurgery.org. **Website:** www.plasticsurgery.org. **Contact:** Mike Stokes, managing editor. **15% freelance written.** Monthly tabloid covering plastic surgery. *Plastic Surgery News* readership is comprised primarily of plastic surgeons and those involved with the specialty (nurses, techs, industry). The magazine is distributed via subscription and to all members of the American Society of Plastic Surgeons. The magazine covers a variety of specialty-specific news and features, including trends, legislation, and clinical information. Estab. 1960. Circ. 6,000. Byline given. Pays on acceptance. Offers 25% kill fee. Publishes ms an average of 1-2 months after acceptance. Editorial lead time 1-3 months. Accepts queries by e-mail. Accepts simultaneous submissions. Responds in 2 weeks to queries. Responds in 3 months to mss. Sample copy for 10 first-class stamps. Guidelines by e-mail.

NONFICTION Needs expose, how-to, new product, technical. Does not want celebrity or entertainment based pieces. **Buys 20 mss/year.** Query with published clips. Length: 1,000-3,500 words. **Pays 20-40¢/word.** Pays expenses of writers on assignment.

COLUMNS Digital Plastic Surgeon (technology), 1,500-1,700 words.

💲💲 PODIATRY MANAGEMENT

Kane Communications, Inc., Rosemont Plaza, 1062 Lancaster Ave., Rosemont PA 19010. (718)897-9700. **Fax:** (718)896-5747. **E-mail:** bblock@podiatrym.com. **Website:** www.podiatrym.com. Magazine published 9 times/year for practicing podiatrists. Aims to help the doctor of podiatric medicine to build a bigger, more successful practice, to conserve and invest his money, to keep him posted on the economic, legal, and sociological changes that affect him. Estab. 1982. Circ. 16,500. Byline given. Pays on publication. $75 kill fee. Submit seasonal material 4 months in advance. Accepts queries by e-mail. Accepts simultaneous submissions. Responds in 2 weeks to queries. Sample copy for $5 and 9x12 SAE. Guidelines for #10 SASE.

NONFICTION Buys 35 mss/year. Length: 1,500-3,000 words. **Pays $350-600.** Pays expenses of writers on assignment.

REPRINTS Send photocopy. Pays 33% of amount paid for an original article.

💲💲 PRIMARY CARE OPTOMETRY NEWS

SLACK Inc., 6900 Grove Rd., Thorofare NJ 08086-9447. (856)848-1000. **Fax:** (856)848-5991. **E-mail:** editor@healio.com; optometry@healio.com. **Website:** www.healio.com/optometry. **Contact:** Michael D. DePaolis, editor. **5% freelance written.** Monthly tabloid covering optometry. *Primary Care Optometry News* strives to be the optometric professional's definitive information source by delivering timely, accurate, authoritative and balanced reports on clinical issues, socioeconomic and legislative affairs, ophthalmic industry, and research developments, as well as updates on diagnostic and thereaputic regimens and techniques to enhance the quality of patient care. Estab. 1996. Circ. 39,000. Byline given. Pays on publication. Offers 50% kill fee. Publishes ms an average of 2 months after acceptance. Editorial lead time 2 months. Accepts queries by mail, e-mail, fax, phone. Accepts simultaneous submissions. Responds in 2 weeks to queries. Sample copy available online. Guidelines by e-mail.

NONFICTION Needs how-to, interview, new product, opinion, technical. **Buys 20 mss/year.** Query. Length: 800-1,000 words. **Pays $350-500.** Pays expenses of writers on assignment.

COLUMNS What's Your Diagnosis (case presentation), 800 words. **Buys 40 mss/year.** Query. **Pays $100-500.**

💲💲 STRATEGIC HEALTH CARE MARKETING

Health Care Communications, 11 Heritage Ln., P.O. Box 594, Rye NY 10580. (914)967-6741; (866)641-4548. **Fax:** (914)967-3054. **E-mail:** mhumphrey@plainenglishmedia.com. **Website:** www.strategichealthcare.com. **Contact:** Matt Humphrey, publisher. **90% freelance written.** Monthly newsletter covering health care marketing and management in a wide range of settings, including hospitals, medical group practices, home health services, and managed care organizations. Emphasis is on strategies and techniques employed within the health care field and relevant applications from other service industries. Works with published/established writers only. *Strategic Health Care Marketing* is specifically seeking writers with expertise/contacts in managed care, patient satisfaction, and e-health. Estab. 1984. Byline given. Pays on publication. Offers 25% kill fee. Publishes ms an average of 2 months after acceptance. Accepts queries by mail, e-mail. Accepts simultaneous submissions.

Responds in 1 month to queries. Sample copy for SAE with 9x12 envelope and 3 first-class stamps. Guidelines sent with sample copy only.

NONFICTION Needs how-to, interview, new product, technical. **Buys 50 mss/year.** Query. Length: 1,000-1,800 words. **Pays $100-500.** Pays expenses of writers on assignment. Sometimes pays expenses of writers on assignment with prior authorization.

MUSIC

💲 INTERNATIONAL BLUEGRASS

International Bluegrass Music Association, 4206 Gallatin Pk., Nashville TN 37216. (615)256-3222. **Fax:** (615)256-0450. **E-mail:** info@ibma.org. **Website:** www.ibma.org. **10% freelance written.** Bimonthly newsletter of the International Bluegrass Music Association. *International Bluegrass* is the business publication for the bluegrass music industry. Interested in hard news and features concerning how to reach that potential and how to conduct business more effectively. Estab. 1985. Circ. 4,500. Byline given. Pays on publication. No kill fee. Publishes ms an average of 2 months after acceptance. Submit seasonal material 4 months in advance. Accepts queries by mail, e-mail, phone. Accepts simultaneous submissions. Responds in 1 month to queries. Sample copy for SAE with 6x9 envelope and 2 first-class stamps.

NONFICTION Needs book excerpts, essays, how-to, new product, opinion. No interview/profiles/feature stories of performers (rare exceptions) or fans. **Buys 6 mss/year.** Query. Length: 1,000-1,200 words. **Pays up to $150/article for assigned articles.**

REPRINTS Send photocopy of article and information about when and where the article previously appeared. Does not pay for reprints.

COLUMNS Staff written.

💲💲 THE MUSIC & SOUND RETAILER

Testa Communications, 25 Willowdale Ave., Port Washington NY 11050. (516)767-2500. **E-mail:** dferrisi@testa.com. **Website:** www.msretailer.com. **Contact:** Dan Ferrisi, editor. **10% freelance written.** Monthly magazine covering business to business publication for music instrument products. *The Music & Sound Retailer* covers the music instrument industry and is sent to all dealers of these products, including Guitar Center, Sam Ash, and all small independent stores. Estab. 1983. Circ. 11,700. Byline given. Pays on

publication. Offers $100 kill fee. Editorial lead time 1 month. Submit seasonal material 2 months in advance. Accepts queries by e-mail. Accepts simultaneous submissions. Responds in 2 weeks to queries. Responds in 1 month to mss. Sample copy for #10 SASE. Guidelines free.

NONFICTION Needs how-to, new product, opinion, personal experience. Concert and CD reviews are never published; neiter are interviews with musicians. **Buys 25 mss/year.** Query with published clips. Length: 1,000-2,000 words. **Pays $300-400 for assigned and unsolicited articles.** Pays expenses of writers on assignment.

💲💲💲 OPERA NEWS

Metropolitan Opera Guild, Inc., 70 Lincoln Center Plaza, 6th Floor, New York NY 10023. **E-mail:** info@operanews.com. **Website:** www.operanews.com. **Contact:** Kitty March. **75% freelance written.** Monthly magazine for people interested in opera—the opera professional as well as the opera audience. Estab. 1936. Circ. 105,000. Byline given. Pays on publication. No kill fee. Publishes ms an average of 4 months after acceptance. Editorial lead time 4 months. Accepts queries by e-mail. Accepts simultaneous submissions. Sample copy for $5.

NONFICTION Needs historical, interview, informational, think pieces, opera, and CD, DVD and book reviews. Does not accept works of fiction or personal remembrances. Send unsolicited mss, article proposals and queries, along with several published clips. Length: 1,500-2,800 words. **Pays $450-1,200.** Pays expenses of writers on assignment.

COLUMNS Buys 24 mss/year.

💲 OVERTONES

Handbell Musicians of America, P.O. Box 1765, Findlay OH 45839-1765. **E-mail:** jrsmith@handbellmusicians.org. **Website:** http://handbellmusicians.org/music-resources/overtones. **Contact:** J.R. Smith, publications director. **80% freelance written.** Bimonthly magazine covering English handbell ringing and conducting. *Overtones* is a 48-page magazine with extensive educational articles, photos, advertisements, and graphic work. Handbell Musicians of America is dedicated to advancing the musical art of handbell/handchime ringing through education, community, and communication. The purpose of *Overtones* is to provide a printed resource to support that mission. Offers how-to articles, inspirational stories, and interviews with well-known people and unique ensembles. Estab. 1954. Circ. 8,000. Byline given. Pays on publication. No kill fee. Publishes ms an average of 4 months after acceptance. Editorial lead time 4 months. Submit seasonal material 4 months in advance. Accepts queries by mail, e-mail. Accepts simultaneous submissions. Responds in 1 month to queries and to mss. Sample copy available by e-mail. Guidelines available online. Style guideline should follow *The Chicago Manual of Style*.

NONFICTION Needs essays, general interest, historical, how-to, inspirational, interview, religious, technical. Does not want product news or promotional material. **Buys 8-12 mss/year.** Send complete ms via e-mail, CD, DVD, or hard copy. Length: 1,200-2,000 words. **Pays $120.** Pays expenses of writers on assignment.

COLUMNS Handbells in Education (topics covering the use of handbells in school setting, teaching techniques, etc.); Handbells in Worship (topics and ideas for using handbells in a church setting); Tips & Tools (variety of topics from ringing and conducting techniques to score study to maintenance); Community Connections (topics covering issues relating to the operation/administration/techniques for community groups); Music Reviews (recommendations and descriptions of music following particular themes, i.e., youth music, difficult music, seasonal, etc.). Length should be 800-1,200 words. Query. **Pays $80.**

PAPER

⊖⊖ THE PAPER STOCK REPORT

McEntee Media Corp., 9815 Hazelwood Ave., Strongsville OH 44149. (440)238-6603. **Fax:** (440)238-6712. **E-mail:** ken@recycle.cc; psr@recycle.cc. **Website:** www.recycle.cc/psrpage.htm. **Contact:** Ken McEntee, editor/publisher. Bimonthly newsletter covering market trends and news in the paper recycling industry. Audience is interested in new innovative markets, applications for recovered scrap paper, as well as new laws and regulations impacting recycling. Estab. 1990. Circ. 2,000. Byline given. Pays on publication. No kill fee. Publishes ms an average of 1 month after acceptance. Editorial lead time 2 months. Submit seasonal material 2 months in advance. Accepts queries by mail, e-mail, fax, phone. Accepts simultaneous sub-

missions. Responds in 1 month to queries. Sample copy for #10 SAE with 55¢ postage.

NONFICTION Needs book excerpts, essays, expose, general interest, historical, interview, new product, opinion, photo feature, technical, all related to paper recycling. **Buys 0-13 mss/year.** Send complete ms. Length: 250-1,000 words. **Pays $50-250 for assigned articles. Pays $25-250 for unsolicited articles.** Pays expenses of writers on assignment.

⊖⊖ RECYCLED PAPER NEWS

McEntee Media Corp., 9815 Hazelwood Ave., Strongsville OH 44149. (440)238-6603. **Fax:** (440)238-6712. **E-mail:** ken@recycle.cc. **Website:** www.recycle.cc. **Contact:** Ken McEntee, owner. **10% freelance written.** Monthly newsletter covering the recycling and composting industries. Interested in any news impacting the paper recycling industry, as well as other environmental issues in the paper industry, i.e., water/air pollution, chlorine-free paper, forest conservation, etc., with special emphasis on new laws and regulations. Estab. 1990. Pays on publication. No kill fee. Publishes ms an average of 2 months after acceptance. Editorial lead time 1 month. Submit seasonal material 1 month in advance. Accepts queries by mail, e-mail, fax, phone. Accepts simultaneous submissions. Responds in 2 months to queries. Sample copy for 9x12 SAE and 55¢ postage. Guidelines for #10 SASE.

NONFICTION Needs book excerpts, essays, how-to, interview, new product, opinion, personal experience, photo feature. **Buys 0-5 mss/year.** Query with published clips. **Pays $10-500.** Pays expenses of writers on assignment.

COLUMNS Query with published clips. **Pays $10-500.**

PETS

⊖⊖ PET AGE

Journal Multimedia, 220 Davidson Ave., Suite 302, Somerset NJ 08873. (732)246-5734. **Website:** www.petage.com. **Contact:** Glen Polyn, editor-in-chief. **90% freelance written.** Monthly magazine for pet/pet supplies retailers, covering the complete pet industry. Estab. 1971. Circ. 23,022. Byline given. Pays on acceptance. No kill fee. Publishes ms an average of 3 months after acceptance. Accepts simultaneous submissions. Sample copy and writer's guidelines available.

NONFICTION No profiles of industry members and/or retail establishments or consumer-oriented pet articles. **Buys 80 mss/year.** Query with published clips. Length: 1,500-2,200 words. **Pays 15¢/word for assigned articles.** Pays expenses of writers on assignment. Pays documented telephone expenses.

⊛⊛ PET PRODUCT NEWS INTERNATIONAL

I-5 Publishing, LLC, P.O. Box 6050, Mission Viejo CA 92690. (949)855-8822. **Fax:** (949)855-3045. **E-mail:** lwojcik@petproductnews.com. **Website:** www.petproductnews.com. **Contact:** Lindsey Wojcik, managing editor. **70% freelance written.** Monthly magazine. *Pet Product News* covers business/legal and economic issues of importance to pet product retailers, suppliers, and distributors, as well as product information and animal care issues. Looking for straightforward articles on the proper care of dogs, cats, birds, fish, and exotics (reptiles, hamsters, etc.) as information the retailers can pass on to new pet owners. Estab. 1947. Circ. 26,000. Byline given. Pays on publication Offers $50 kill fee. Editorial lead time 3 months. Submit seasonal material 4 months in advance. Accepts queries by mail, fax. Accepts simultaneous submissions. Responds in 2 weeks to queries. Sample copy for $5.50. Guidelines for #10 SASE.

NONFICTION Needs general interest, interview, new product, photo feature, technical. No "cute" animal stories or those directed at the pet owner. **Buys 150 mss/year.** Query. Length: 500-1,500 words. **Pays $175-350.** Pays expenses of writers on assignment.

COLUMNS The Pet Dealer News™ (timely news stories about business issues affecting pet retailers), 800-1,000 words; Industry News (news articles representing coverage of pet product suppliers, manufacturers, distributors, and associations), 800-1,000 words; Pet Health News™ (pet health and articles relevant to pet retailers); Dog & Cat (products and care of), 1,000-1,500 words; Fish & Bird (products and care of), 1,000-1,500 words; Small Mammals (products and care of), 1,000-1,500 words; Pond/Water Garden (products and care of), 1,000-1,500 words. **Buys 120 mss/year.** Query. **Pays $150-300.**

PLUMBING, HEATING, AIR CONDITIONING & REFRIGERATION

♻⊛⊛⊛ HPAC: HEATING PLUMBING AIR CONDITIONING

80 Valleybrook Dr., Toronto Ontario M3B 2S9 Canada. (416)510-5218. **Fax:** (416)510-5140. **E-mail:** smacisaac@hpacmag.com; kturner@hpacmag.com. **Website:** www.hpacmag.com. **Contact:** Sandy MacIsaac, art director; Kerry Turner, editor. **20% freelance written.** Monthly magazine. Estab. 1923. Circ. 19,500. Pays on publication. No kill fee. Publishes an average of 3 months after acceptance. Accepts queries by mail, e-mail. Accepts simultaneous submissions. Responds in 2 months to queries.

NONFICTION Needs how-to, technical. Length: 1,000-1,500 words. **Pays 50¢/word.** Pays expenses of writers on assignment.

REPRINTS Send tearsheet or photocopy with rights for sale noted and information about when and where the material previously appeared.

PRINTING

⊛⊛ THE BIG PICTURE

ST Media Group International, 11262 Cornell Park Dr., Cincinnati OH 45242. (513)421-2050. **E-mail:** adrienne.palmer@stmediagroup.com. **Website:** www.bigpicture.net. **Contact:** Adrienne Palmer, editor-in-chief. **20% freelance written.** Magazine published 9 times/year covering wide-format digital printing. *The Big Picture* covers wide-format printing as well as digital workflow, finishing, display, capture, and other related topics. Readers include digital print providers, sign shops, commercial printers, in-house print operations, and other print providers across the country. Primarily interested in the technology and work processes behind wide-format printing, but also run trend features on segments of the industry (innovations in point-of-purchase displays, floor graphics, fine-art printing, vehicle wrapping, textile printing, etc.). Estab. 1996. Circ. 21,500 controlled. Byline given. Pays on publication. Offers 20% kill fee. Publishes ms an average of 2 months after acceptance. Editorial lead time 2 months. Accepts queries by e-mail. Accepts simultaneous submissions. Responds in 2 weeks to queries. Responds in 1 month to mss. Sample copy available online. Guidelines available.

NONFICTION Needs how-to, interview, new product, technical. Does not want broad consumer-oriented pieces that do not speak to the business and technical aspects of producing print for pay. **Buys 15-20 mss/year.** Query with published clips. Length: 1,500-2,500 words. **Pays $500-700 for assigned articles.** Pays expenses of writers on assignment.

💲💲 IN-PLANT GRAPHICS
NAPCO Media, 1500 Spring Garden St., 12th Floor, Philadelphia PA 19130. (215)238-5321. **Fax:** (215)238-5457. **E-mail:** bobneubauer@napco.com. **Website:** www.inplantgraphics.com. **Contact:** Bob Neubauer, editor. **20% freelance written.** *In-Plant Graphics* features articles designed to help in-house printing departments increase productivity, save money, and stay competitive. *IPG* features advances in graphic arts technology and shows in-plants how to put this technology to use. Audience consists of print shop managers working for (nonprint related) corporations (i.e., hospitals, insurance companies, publishers, nonprofits), universities, and government departments. They often oversee graphic design, prepress, printing, bindery, and mailing departments. Estab. 1951. Circ. 23,100. Byline given. Pays on publication. No kill fee. Publishes ms an average of 3 months after acceptance. Editorial lead time 2 months. Submit seasonal material 3 months in advance. Accepts queries by e-mail. Accepts simultaneous submissions. Guidelines online.

NONFICTION Needs interview, new product, technical. Special issues: See editorial calendar online. No articles on desktop publishing software or design software. No Internet publishing articles. **Buys 5 mss/year.** Query with published clips. Length: 800-1,500 words. **Pays $350-500.** Pays expenses of writers on assignment.

COLUMNS Query with published clips.

💲💲 SCREEN PRINTING
ST Media Group International, 11262 Cornell Park Dr., Cincinnati OH 45242. (513)421-2050, ext. 331. **Fax:** (513)421-5144. **E-mail:** kiersten.wones@stmediagroup.com; ben.rosenfield@stmediagroup.com. **Website:** www.screenweb.com. **Contact:** Kiersten Wones, editorial assistant; Ben Rosenfield, managing editor. **30% freelance written.** Monthly magazine for the screen printing industry, including screen printers

(commercial, industrial, and captive shops), suppliers and manufacturers, ad agencies, and allied profession. Estab. 1953. Circ. 17,500. Byline given. Pays on publication. No kill fee. Publishes ms an average of 3 months after acceptance. Accepts queries by mail, e-mail, fax. Accepts simultaneous submissions. Sample copy available. Guidelines for #10 SASE.

NONFICTION **Buys 10-15 mss/year.** Query. Unsolicited mss not returned. Length: 2,000-3,000 words. **Pays $300-500 for major features.** Pays expenses of writers on assignment.

PROFESSIONAL PHOTOGRAPHY

💲💲 NEWS PHOTOGRAPHER
National Press Photographers Association, Inc., 6677 Whitemarsh Valley Walk, Austin TX 78746-6367. **E-mail:** magazine@nppa.org; tburton@nppa.org. **Website:** www.nppa.org. **Contact:** Tom Burton, editor. Magazine on photojournalism published 10 times/year. *News Photographer* magazine is dedicated to the advancement of still and television news photography. The magazine presents articles, interviews, profiles, history, new products, electronic imaging, and news related to the practice of photojournalism. Estab. 1946. Circ. 11,000. Byline given. Pays on acceptance. Offers 100% kill fee. Publishes ms an average of 4 months after acceptance. Editorial lead time 2 months. Submit seasonal material 2 months in advance. Accepts queries by mail, e-mail, fax, phone. Accepts simultaneous submissions. Responds in 1 month to queries. Sample copy for SAE with 9x12 envelope and 3 first-class stamps. Guidelines free.

NONFICTION Needs historical, how-to, interview, new product, opinion, personal experience, photo feature, technical. **Buys 10 mss/year.** Query. Length: 1,500 words. **Pays $300.** Pays expenses of writers on assignment.

COLUMNS Query.

💲💲 THE PHOTO REVIEW
200 East Maple Avenue, Suite 200, Langhorne PA 19047. (215)891-0214. **Fax:** (215)891-9358. **E-mail:** info@photoreview.org. **Website:** www.photoreview.org. **50% freelance written.** Biannual magazine covering art photography and criticism. "*The Photo Review* publishes critical reviews of photography exhibitions and books, critical essays, and interviews.

We do not publish how-to or technical articles." Estab. 1976. Circ. 2,000. Byline given. Pays on publication. No kill fee. Publishes ms an average of 9-12 months after acceptance. Editorial lead time 3 months. Submit seasonal material 6 months in advance. Accepts queries by mail. Accepts simultaneous submissions. Responds in 2 months to queries. Responds in 3 months to mss. Sample copy for $7. Email for guidelines.

NONFICTION Needs essays, historical, interview, reviews. No how-to articles. **Buys 20 mss/year.** Send complete ms. Length: 2-20 typed pages by email. **Pays $10-250.** Pays expenses of writers on assignment.

REPRINTS Send tearsheet, photocopy, or typed ms with rights for sale noted and information about when and where the material previously appeared. Payment varies.

REAL ESTATE

✪$$ CANADIAN PROPERTY MANAGEMENT

Media Edge, 5255 Yonge St., Suite 1000, Toronto ON M2N 2P4 Canada. (416)512-8186. **E-mail:** barbc@mediaedge.ca. **Website:** www.reminetwork.com/canadian-property-management/home/. **Contact:** Barbara Carss, editor in chief. **10% freelance written.** Magazine published 8 times/year covering Canadian commercial, industrial, institutional (medical and educational), and residential properties. *Canadian Property Management* is a trade journal supplying building owners and property managers with Canadian industry news, case law reviews, technical updates for building operations, and events listings. Building and professional profile articles are regular features. Estab. 1985. Circ. 12,500. Byline given. Pays on publication. No kill fee. Publishes ms an average of 3 months after acceptance. Editorial lead time 2 months. Submit seasonal material 2 months in advance. Accepts queries by mail, e-mail, phone. Accepts simultaneous submissions. Responds in 3 weeks to queries; in 2 months to mss. Sample copy: $5, subject to availability. Guidelines free.

NONFICTION Needs interview, technical. No promotional articles (i.e., marketing a product or service geared to this industry). Query with published clips. Length: 700-1,200 words. **Pays 35¢/word.** Pays expenses of writers on assignment.

$$ THE COOPERATOR

Yale Robbins, Inc., 205 Lexington Ave., 12th Floor, New York NY 10016. (212)683-5700. **Fax:** (212)545-0764. **E-mail:** editorial@cooperator.com. **Website:** www.cooperator.com. **70% freelance written.** Monthly tabloid covering real estate in the New York City metro area. *The Cooperator* covers condominium and cooperative issues in New York and beyond. It is read by condo unit owners and co-op shareholders, real estate professionals, board members and managing agents, and other service professionals. Estab. 1980. Circ. 40,000. Byline given. Pays on publication. No kill fee. Publishes ms an average of 3 months after acceptance. Submit seasonal material 3 months in advance. Accepts queries by mail, e-mail, fax. Accepts simultaneous submissions. Responds in 1 month to queries. Sample copy and writer's guidelines free.

NONFICTION Needs interview, new product, personal experience. No submissions without queries. Query with published clips. Length: 1,500-2,000 words. **Pays $325-425.** Pays expenses of writers on assignment.

COLUMNS Profiles of co-op/condo-related businesses with something unique; Building Finance (investment and financing issues); Buying and Selling (market issues, etc.); Design (architectural and interior/exterior design, lobby renovation, etc.); Building Maintenance (issues related to maintaining interior/exterior, facades, lobbies, elevators, etc.); Legal Issues Related to Co-Ops/Condos; Real Estate Trends, all 1,500 words. **Buys 100 mss/year.** Query with published clips.

$$ FLORIDA REALTOR MAGAZINE

Florida Association of Realtors, 7025 Augusta National Dr., Orlando FL 32822. (407)438-1400. **Fax:** (407)438-1411. **E-mail:** flrealtor@floridarealtors.org. **Website:** www.floridarealtormagazine.com. **Contact:** Doug Damerst, editor-in-chief. **70% freelance written.** Journal published 10 times/year covering the Florida real estate profession. "As the official publication of the Florida Association of Realtors, we provide helpful articles for our 125,000 members. We report new practices that lead to successful real estate careers and stay up on the trends and issues that affect business in Florida's real estate market." Estab. 1925. Circ. 114,592. Byline given. Pays on publication. No kill fee. Publishes ms an average of 2 months after acceptance.

Editorial lead time 3 months. Accepts queries by mail, e-mail, fax. Sample copy available online.

NONFICTION No fiction or poetry. **Buys varying number of mss/year.** Query with published clips. Length: 800-1,500 words. **Pays $500-700.** Pays expenses of writers on assignment.

COLUMNS Some written in-house: Law & Ethics, 900 words; Market It, 600 words; Technology & You, 800 words; ManageIt, 600 words. **Buys varying number of mss/year. Payment varies.**

⊙⊙ OFFICE BUILDINGS MAGAZINE

Yale Robbins, Inc., 205 Lexington Ave., 12th Fl., New York NY 10016. (212)683-5700. **Fax:** (212)497-0017. **E-mail:** mrosupport@mrofficespace.com. **Website:** marketing.yrpubs.com/officebuildings. **15% freelance written.** Annual magazine published in 12 separate editions covering market statistics, trends, and thinking of area professionals on the current and future state of the real estate market. Estab. 1987. Circ. 10,500. Byline sometimes given. Pays 1 month after publication. Offers kill fee. Editorial lead time 2 months. Accepts queries by mail, e-mail. Accepts simultaneous submissions. Sample copy and writer's guidelines free.

NONFICTION **Buys 15-20 mss/year.** Query with published clips. Length: 1,500-2,000 words. **Pays $600-700.** Pays expenses of writers on assignment.

⊙ PROPERTIES MAGAZINE

Properties Magazine, Inc., 3826 W. 158th St., Cleveland OH 44111. (216)251-2655. **Fax:** (216)251-0064. **E-mail:** mwatt@propertiesmag.com. **Website:** www. propertiesmag.com. **Contact:** Mark Watt, managing editor/art director. **25% freelance written.** Monthly magazine covering real estate, residential, commerical construction. *Properties Magazine* is published for executives in the real estate, building, banking, design, architectural, property management, tax, and law community—busy people who need the facts presented in an interesting and informative format. Estab. 1946. Circ. over 10,000. Byline given. Pays on publication. No kill fee. Publishes ms an average of 2 months after acceptance. Editorial lead time 2 months. Submit seasonal material 2 months in advance. Accepts queries by mail, fax. Accepts simultaneous submissions. Responds in 3 weeks to queries. Sample copy for $3.95.

NONFICTION Needs general interest, how-to, humor, new product. Special issues: Environmental issues (September); Security/Fire Protection (Octo-

ber); Tax Issues (November); Computers In Real Estate (December). **Buys 30 mss/year.** Send complete ms. Length: 500-2,000 words. **Pays 50¢/column line.** Pays expenses of writers on assignment.

COLUMNS **Buys 25 mss/year.** Query or send complete ms. **Pays 50¢/column line.**

⊙⊙⊙ REM

Real Estate Magazine, 2255B Queen St. E., Suite #1178, Toronto ON M4E 1G3 Canada. (416)425-3504. **E-mail:** jim@remonline.com. **Website:** www.remonline.com. **Contact:** Jim Adair, managing editor. **35% freelance written.** Monthly Canadian trade journal covering real estate. "*REM* provides Canadian real estate agents and brokers with news and opinions they can't get anywhere else. It is an independent publication and not affiliated with any real estate board, association, or company." Estab. 1989. Circ. 22,000. Byline given. Pays on acceptance. Offers 25% kill fee. Publishes ms an average of 2 months after acceptance. Editorial lead time 3 months. Submit seasonal material 3 months in advance. Accepts queries by mail, e-mail. Accepts simultaneous submissions. Responds in 2 weeks. Sample copy free.

NONFICTION Needs book excerpts, expose, inspirational, interview, new product, personal experience. "No articles geared to consumers about market conditions or how to choose a realtor. Must have Canadian content." **Buys 60 mss/year.** Query. Length: 500-1,500 words. **Pays $200-400.**

⊙⊙ ZONING PRACTICE

American Planning Association, 205 N. Michigan Ave., Suite 1200, Chicago IL 60601. (312)431-9100; (312)786-6392. **Fax:** (312)786-6700. **E-mail:** zoningpractice@planning.org. **Website:** www.planning.org/zoningpractice/. **90% freelance written.** Monthly newsletter covering land-use regulations including zoning. Publication is aimed at practicing urban planners and those involved in land-use decisions, such as zoning administrators and officials, planning commissioners, zoning boards of adjustment, land-use attorneys, developers, and others interested in this field. The material published comes from writers knowledgeable about zoning and subdivision regulations, preferably with practical experience in the field. Anything published needs to be of practical value to our audience in their everyday work. Estab. 1984. Circ. 2,000. Byline given. Pays on publication. Offers 50% kill fee. Publishes ms an average of 3 months after acceptance. Editorial lead time 6 months. Accepts queries by mail, e-mail, fax, phone. Accepts simultaneous submissions. Responds in 2 weeks to queries. Responds in 1 month to mss. Single copy: $10. Guidelines available at www.planning.org/zoningpractice/guidelines.htm.

NONFICTION Needs technical. See description. We do not need general or consumer-interest articles about zoning because this publication is aimed at practitioners. **Buys 12 mss/year.** Query. Length: 3,000-5,000 words. **Pays $300 minimum for assigned articles.** Pays expenses of writers on assignment.

RESOURCES & WASTE REDUCTION

💲💲 COMPOSTING NEWS

McEntee Media Corp., 9815 Hazelwood Ave., Strongsville OH 44149. (440)238-6603. **Fax:** (440)238-6712. **E-mail:** ken@recycle.cc. **Website:** www.compostingnews.com. **Contact:** Ken McEntee, editor. **5% freelance written.** Monthly newsletter about the composting industry. *Composting News* features the latest news and vital issues of concern to the producers, marketers, and end-users of compost, mulch and other organic waste-based products. Estab. 1992. Circ. 1,000. Pays on publication. No kill fee. Publishes ms an average of 1 month after acceptance. Editorial lead time 1 month. Submit seasonal material 1 month in advance. Accepts queries by mail, e-mail, fax, phone. Accepts simultaneous submissions. Responds in 2 months to queries. Sample copy for 9x12 SAE and 55¢ postage. Guidelines for #10 SASE.

NONFICTION Needs book excerpts, essays, general interest, how-to, interview, new product, opinion, personal experience, photo feature. **Buys 0-5 mss/year.** Query with published clips. Length: 100-5,000 words. **Pays $10-500.**

COLUMNS Query with published clips. **Pays $10-500.**

💲💲💲 EROSION CONTROL

Forester Media Inc., P.O. Box 3100, Santa Barbara CA 93130. (805)679-7629. **E-mail:** asantiago@forester.net. **Website:** www.erosioncontrol.com. **Contact:** Arturo Santiago. **60% freelance written.** Magazine published 7 times/year covering all aspects of erosion prevention and sediment control. *Erosion Control* is a practical, hands-on, how-to professional journal. Read-

ers are civil engineers, landscape architects, builders, developers, public works officials, road and highway construction officials and engineers, soils specialists, farmers, landscape contractors, and others involved with any activity that disturbs significant areas of surface vegetation. Estab. 1994. Circ. 23,000. Byline given. Pays 1 month after acceptance. No kill fee. Publishes ms an average of 3 months after acceptance. Editorial lead time 4 months. Submit seasonal material 4 months in advance. Accepts queries by e-mail, phone. Responds in 3 weeks to queries. Sample copy and writer's guidelines free.

NONFICTION Needs photo feature, technical. **Buys 15 mss/year.** Query with published clips. Length: 2,000-4,000 words. **Pays $700-850.** Pays expenses of writers on assignment.

💲💲 WATER WELL JOURNAL

National Ground Water Association, 601 Dempsey Rd., Westerville OH 43081. **Fax:** (614)898-7786. **E-mail:** tplumley@ngwa.org. **Website:** www.waterwelljournal.org. **Contact:** Thad Plumley, director of publications/editor; Mike Price, senior editor. Each month the *Water Well Journal* covers the topics of drilling, rigs and heavy equipment, pumping systems, water quality, business management, water supply, on-site waste water treatment, and diversification opportunities, including geothermal installations, environmental remediation, irrigation, dewatering, and foundation installation. It also offers updates on regulatory issues that impact the ground water industry. Circ. 24,000. Byline given. Pays on publication. Publishes ms an average of 3 months after acceptance. Editorial lead time 6 weeks. Submit seasonal material 3 months in advance. Accepts queries by mail. Accepts simultaneous submissions. Responds in 2 weeks to queries. Responds in 1 month to mss. Guidelines free.

NONFICTION Needs essays, historical, how-to, interview, new product, personal experience, photo feature, technical, business management. No company profiles or extended product releases. **Buys up to 30 mss/year.** Query with published clips. Length: 1,000-3,000 words. **Pays $150-400.** Pays expenses of writers on assignment.

SELLING & MERCHANDISING

$ THE AMERICAN SALESMAN

National Research Bureau, 320 Valley St., Burlington IA 52601. (319)752-5415. **Fax:** (319)752-3421. **E-mail:** contact@salestrainingandtechniques.com. **E-mail:** articles@salestrainingandtechniques.com. **Website:** www.salestrainingandtechniques.com. **80% freelance written.** Monthly magazine covering sales and marketing. *The American Salesman Magazine* is designed for sales professionals. Its primary objective is to provide informative articles that develop the attitudes, skills, and personal and professional qualities of sales representatives, allowing them to use more of their potential to increase productivity and achieve goals. Byline given. Publishes ms an average of 1 month after acceptance. Editorial lead time 1 month. Submit seasonal material 2 months in advance. Accepts queries by e-mail. Accepts simultaneous submissions. Sample copy free. Guidelines by e-mail.

NONFICTION Needs personal experience. **Buys 24 mss/year.** Send complete ms. Length: 500-1,000 words. **Pays 4¢/word.** Pays expenses of writers on assignment.

$$ BALLOONS & PARTIES MAGAZINE

PartiLife Publications, LLC, 65 Sussex St., Hackensack NJ 07601. (201)441-4224. **Fax:** (201)342-8118. **E-mail:** info@balloonsandparties.com. **Website:** www.balloonsandparties.com. **Contact:** Mark Zettler, publisher. **10% freelance written.** International trade journal published bi-monthly for professional party decorators and gift delivery businesses. *BALLOONS & Parties Magazine* is published 6 times/year by PartiLife Publications, LLC, for the balloon, party, and event fields. New product data, letters, mss, and photographs should be sent as "Attention: Editor" and should include sender's full name, address, and telephone number. SASE required on all editorial submissions. All submissions considered for publication unless otherwise noted. Unsolicited materials are submitted at sender's risk and *BALLOONS & Parties*/PartiLife Publications, LLC, assumes no responsibility for unsolicited materials. Estab. 1986. Circ. 7,000. Byline given. Pays on publication. No kill fee. Publishes ms an average of 3 months after acceptance. Submit seasonal material 6 months in advance. Accepts queries by mail, e-mail, fax, phone. Accepts simultaneous submissions. Responds in 6 weeks to queries. Sample copy for SAE with 9x12 envelope.

NONFICTION Needs essays, how-to, interview, new product, personal experience, photo feature, technical. **Buys 12 mss/year.** Send complete ms. Length: 500-1,500 words. **Pays $100-300 for assigned articles. Pays $50-200 for unsolicited articles.** Pays expenses of writers on assignment.

REPRINTS Send typed ms with rights for sale noted and information about when and where the material previously appeared. Length: up to 2,500 words. Pays 10¢/word.

COLUMNS Problem Solver (small business issues); Recipes That Cook (centerpiece ideas with detailed how-to); 400-1,000 words. Send complete ms with photos.

$$ BRAND PACKAGING

BNP Media, 2401 W. Big Beaver Rd., Suite 700, Troy MI 48084. (248)362-3700. **Fax:** (847)362-0317. **E-mail:** kalkowskij@bnpmedia.com. **Website:** www.brandpackaging.com. **Contact:** John Kalkowski, editor-in-chief. **15% freelance written.** Magazine published 10 times/year covering how packaging can be a marketing tool. Publishes strategies and tactics to make products stand out on the shelf. Market is brand managers who are marketers but need to know something about packaging. Estab. 1997. Circ. 33,000. Byline given. Pays on acceptance. Publishes ms an average of 2 months after acceptance. Editorial lead time 3 months. Submit seasonal material 3 months in advance. Accepts queries by mail, fax. Accepts simultaneous submissions. Sample copy free.

NONFICTION Needs how-to, interview, new product. **Buys 10 mss/year.** Send complete ms. Length: 600-2,400 words. **Pays 40-50¢/word.** Pays expenses of writers on assignment.

COLUMNS Emerging Technology (new packaging technology), 600 words. **Buys 10 mss/year.** Query. **Pays $150-300.**

$$ CASUAL LIVING MAGAZINE

Progresive Business Media/Today Group, 7025 Albert Pick Rd., Suite 200, Greensboro NC 27409. (336)605-1122. **Fax:** (336)605-1143. **E-mail:** wgoodson@casualliving.com. **Website:** www.casualliving.com. **Contact:** Waynette Goodson, editorial director. **10% freelance written.** Monthly magazine covering outdoor furniture and accessories, barbecue grills, spas, and more. *Casual Living* is a trade only publication for the casual furnishings and related industries, published monthly. Writes about new products, trends, and casual furniture retailers, plus industry news. Estab. 1958. Circ. 10,000. Pays on publication. Publishes ms an average of 1-2 months after acceptance. Editorial lead time 1-2 months. Submit seasonal material 2 months in advance. Accepts queries by mail, e-mail. Accepts simultaneous submissions. Responds in 2 weeks to queries. Sample copy available online.

NONFICTION Needs how-to, interview. **Buys 20 mss/year.** Query with published clips. Length: 300-1,000 words. **Pays $300-700.** Pays expenses of writers on assignment.

💲💲💲 CONSUMER GOODS TECHNOLOGY

Edgell Communications, 4 Middlebury Blvd., Randolph NJ 07869. (973)607-1354. **Fax:** (973)607-1395. **E-mail:** arajagopal@edgellmail.com. **Website:** www.consumergoods.edgl.com. **Contact:** Alarice Rajagopal, editor. **40% freelance written.** Monthly tabloid benchmarking business technology performance. Estab. 1987. Circ. 25,000. Byline given. Pays on publication. No kill fee. Publishes ms an average of 2 months after acceptance. Editorial lead time 3 months. Accepts queries by e-mail. Accepts simultaneous submissions. Sample copy available online. Guidelines by e-mail.

NONFICTION Needs essays, expose, interview. **Buys 60 mss/year.** Query with published clips. Length: 700-1,900 words. **Pays $600-1,200.** Pays expenses of writers on assignment.

COLUMNS Columns 400-750 words—featured columnists. **Buys 4 mss/year.** Query with published clips. **Pays 75¢-$1/word.**

💲💲💲💲 DIRECT SELLING NEWS

Video Plus, 5800 Democracy Drive, Plano TX 75024. **E-mail:** tday@directsellingnews.com. **Website:** www.directsellingnews.com. **Contact:** Teresa Day, editorial director. **20% freelance written.** Monthly magazine covering direct selling/network marketing industry. Though we are a business publication, we prefer feature-style writing rather than a newsy approach. Circ. 6,000. Byline given. Pays 30 days after publication. Publishes ms an average of 1-2 months after acceptance. Editorial lead time 3 months. Submit seasonal material 3 months in advance. Accepts queries by e-mail. Accepts simultaneous submissions. Responds in 3 weeks to queries. Sample copy available online.

NONFICTION Needs general interest, how-to. Query. Length: 1,500-3,000 words. **Pays 50¢-$1/word.**

💲💲 GIFTWARE NEWS

704 N. Wells St., Chicago IL 60654. (312)849-2220. **Fax:** (312)849-2174. **E-mail:** giftwarenews@talcott.com. **E-mail:** dfields@talcott.com. **Website:** www.giftwarenews.com. **Contact:** Dayna Fields, managing editor. **20% freelance written.** Monthly magazine covering gifts, collectibles, and tabletops for giftware retailers. "*Giftware News* is designed and written for those professionals involved in the retail giftware industry. *Giftware News* serves gift stores, stationary stores, department stores, as well as other retail outlets selling giftware, stationary, party and paper, tabletop, and decorative accessories. *Giftware News* is unique in the industry with an abundance of information, a wealth of product photography, outstanding graphic design, and high-quality printing that all combine with *Giftware News*' digital products to result in a package that is unmatched by any other giftware publication." Estab. 1976. Circ. 21,000. Byline given. Pays on publication. No kill fee. Publishes ms an average of 2 months after acceptance. Submit seasonal material 6 months in advance. Accepts queries by mail, e-mail. Accepts simultaneous submissions. Responds in 2 months to mss. Sample copy: $8.

NONFICTION Needs how-to, new product. **Buys 20 mss/year.** Send complete ms. Length: 1,500-2,000 words. **Pays $400-500 for assigned articles. Pays $200-300 for unsolicited articles.** Pays expenses of writers on assignment.

COLUMNS Stationery, giftbaskets, collectibles, holiday, merchandise, tabletop, wedding market and display—all for the gift retailer. Length: 1,500-2,500 words. **Buys 10 mss/year.** Send complete ms. **Pays $100-250.**

💲💲 NICHE

The Rosen Group, 3000 Chestnut Ave., Suite 112, Baltimore MD 21211. (410)889-3093, ext. 231. **Fax:** (410)243-7089. **E-mail:** hoped@rosengrp.com. **Website:** www.nichemagazine.com. **Contact:** Hope Daniels, editorial director. **50% freelance written.** Quarterly trade magazine for the progressive craft gallery retailer. Each issue includes retail gallery profiles, store design trends, management techniques, financial information, and merchandising strategies for small business owners, as well as articles about craft artists and craft mediums. Estab. 1988. Circ. 15,000. Byline given. Pays on publication. No kill fee. Publishes ms an average of 6-9 months after acceptance. Editorial lead time 9 months. Submit queries for seasonal material 1 year in advance. Accepts queries by e-mail. Accepts simultaneous submissions. Responds in 4-6 weeks to queries; 3 months to mss. Sample copy for $3.

NONFICTION Needs interview. **Buys 15-20 mss/year.** Query with published clips. **Pays $150-300.**

COLUMNS Retail Details (short items at the front of the book, general retail information); Artist Profiles (short biographies of American Craft Artists); Retail Resources (including book/video/seminar reviews and educational opportunities pertaining to retailers). Query with published clips. **Pays $25-100 per item.**

🟢 O&A MARKETING NEWS

KAL Publications, Inc., 559 S. Harbor Blvd., Suite A, Anaheim CA 92805-4525. (714)563-9300. **Fax:** (714)563-9310. **E-mail:** kathy@kalpub.com. **Website:** www.kalpub.com. **3% freelance written.** Bimonthly tabloid. *O&A Marketing News* is editorially directed to people engaged in the distribution, merchandising, installation, and servicing of gasoline, oil, TBA, quick lube, carwash, convenience store, alternative fuel, and automotive aftermarket products in the 13 Western states. Estab. 1966. Circ. 7,500. Byline sometimes given. Pays on publication. No kill fee. Publishes ms an average of 2 months after acceptance. Editorial lead time 1 month. Submit seasonal material 1 month in advance. Accepts queries by mail, e-mail, fax. Accepts simultaneous submissions. Responds in 2 months. Sample copy for SASE with 9x13 envelope and 10 first-class stamps.

NONFICTION Needs interview, photo feature, industry news. Does not want anything that doesn't pertain to the petroleum marketing industry in the 13 Western states. **Buys 35 mss/year.** Send complete ms. Length: 100-500 words. **Pays $1.25/column inch.**

COLUMNS Nevada News (petroleum marketing news in state of Nevada). **Buys 7 mss/year.** Send complete ms. **Pays $1.25/column inch.**

FILLERS Needs gags, short humor. **Buys 7 mss/year.** Length: 1-200 words. **Pays per column inch.**

🟢🟢🟢🟢 OPERATIONS & FULFILLMENT

Primedia, Inc., 761 Main Ave, Second Floor, Norwalk CT 06851. (203)358-4106. **E-mail:** dforte@accessintel.com. **Website:** www.opsandfulfillment.com. **Contact:** Daniela Forte, content manager. **25% freelance written.** Monthly magazine covering catalog/direct mail operations. *Operations & Fulfillment (O&F)* is

a monthly publication that offers practical solutions for catalog online, and direct response operations management. The magazine covers such critical areas as material handling, bar coding, facility planning, transportation, call centers, warehouse management, information systems, online fulfillment and human resources. Estab. 1993. Circ. 17,600. Pays on publication. No kill fee. Publishes ms an average of 2 months after acceptance. Editorial lead time 2 months. Accepts queries by mail, e-mail, phone. Accepts simultaneous submissions. Responds in 1 week to queries. Sample copy and writer's guidelines free.

NONFICTION Needs book excerpts, how-to, interview, new product, technical. **Buys 4-6 mss/year.** Query with published clips. Length: 2,500-3,000 words. **Pays $1,000-1,800.**

🟢🟢 SMART RETAILER

JP Media, P.O. Box 5000, N7528 Aanstad Rd., Iola WI 54945. **Fax:** (715)445-4053. **E-mail:** danb@jonespublishing.com. **Website:** www.smart-retailer.com. **Contact:** Dan Brownell, editor. **50% freelance written.** Magazine published 8 times/year covering independent retail, gift, and home decor. *Smart Retailer* is a trade publication for independent retailers of gifts and home accents. Estab. 1993. Circ. 32,000. Byline given. Pays 3 months after acceptance of final ms. Offers $50 kill fee. Publishes ms an average of 3 months after acceptance. Editorial lead time 4-6 months. Submit seasonal material 6 months in advance. Accepts queries by mail, e-mail. Usually responds in 4-6 weeks (only if accepted). Sample articles are available on website. Guidelines by e-mail.

NONFICTION Needs how-to, interview, new product, finance, legal, marketing, small business, general merchandising, and visual merchandising. No fiction, poetry, fillers, photos, artwork, or profiles of businesses, unless queried and first assigned. **Buys 20 mss/year.** Send complete ms, with résumé and published clips to: Writers Query, *Smart Retailer.* Length: 1,000-1,500 words. **Pays $150-300 for assigned articles. Pays $150-300 for unsolicited articles.** Pays expenses of writers on assignment. Limit agreed upon in advance.

COLUMNS Display & Design (store design and product display), 1,500 words; Retailer Profile (profile of retailer, assigned only), 1,500 words; Vendor Profile (profile of manufacturer, assigned only), 1,200 words; Technology (Internet, computer-related articles as applies to small retailers), 1,500 words; Marketing (marketing ideas and advice as applies to small retailers), 1,500 words; Finance (financial tips and advice as applies to small retailers), 1,500 words; Legal (legal tips and advice as applies to small retailers), 1,500 words; Employees (tips and advice on hiring, firing, and working with employees as applies to small retailers), 1,500 words. **Buys 15 mss/year.** Query with published clips or send complete ms. **Pays $250-350.**

💲💲 TRAVEL GOODS SHOWCASE

Travel Goods Association, 301 North Harrison St., #412, Princeton NJ 08540. (877)842-1938. **Fax:** (877)842-1938. **E-mail:** info@travel-goods.org; cathy@travel-goods.org. **Website:** www.travel-goods. org. **Contact:** Cathy Hays. **5-10% freelance written.** Magazine published quarterly. *Travel Goods Showcase*, the largest trade magazine devoted to travel products, contains articles for retailers, dealers, manufacturers, and suppliers about luggage, business cases, personal leather goods, handbags, and accessories. Special articles report on trends in fashion, promotions, selling and marketing techniques, industry statistics, and other educational and promotional improvements and advancements. Estab. 1975. Circ. 21,000. Byline given. Pays on acceptance. Offers $50 kill fee. Publishes ms an average of 2 months after acceptance. Editorial lead time 3 months. Submit seasonal material 2 months in advance. Accepts queries by mail, e-mail. Accepts simultaneous submissions. Responds in 2 weeks to queries; 1 month to mss. Sample copy and writer's guidelines free.

NONFICTION Needs interview, new product, technical, travel, retailer profiles with photos. No manufacturer profiles. **Buys 3 mss/year.** Query with published clips. Length: 1,200-1,600 words. **Pays $200-400.** Pays expenses of writers on assignment.

💲💲 VENUES TODAY

4952 Warner Ave., Suite 201, Huntington Beach CA 92649. (714)378-5400. **Fax:** (714)378-0040. **E-mail:** linda@venuestoday.com; dave@venuestoday.com. **Website:** www.venuestoday.com. **Contact:** Linda Deckard, publisher and editor in chief. **70% freelance written.** Weekly magazine covering the live entertainment industry and the buildings that host shows and sports. Needs writers who can cover an exciting industry from the business side, not the consumer side. Readers are venue managers, concert promoters, those in the concert and sports business, not the audience for concerts and sports. Need business journalists who can cover the latest news and trends in the market. Estab. 2002. Byline given. Pays on publication. Publishes ms an average of 1 month after acceptance. Editorial lead time 1-2 months. Submit seasonal material 1-2 months in advance. Accepts queries by mail, e-mail, fax. Accepts simultaneous submissions. Responds in 1 week to queries. Sample copy available online. Guidelines free.

NONFICTION Needs interview, photo feature, technical, travel. Does not want customer slant, marketing pieces. Query with published clips. Length: 500-1,500 words. **Pays $100-250.** Pays expenses of writers on assignment.

COLUMNS Venue News (new buildings, trend features, etc.); Bookings (show tours, business side); Marketing (of shows, sports, convention centers); Concessions (food, drink, merchandise). Length: 500-1,200 words. **Buys 250 mss/year. mss/year.** Query with published clips. **Pays $100-250.**

FILLERS Needs gags. **Buys 6 mss/year. Pays $100-300.**

💲💲💲 VMSD

VMSD magazine, ST Media Group International, 11262 Cornell Park Dr., Cincinnati OH 45242. (513)421-2050. **Fax:** (513)421-5144. **E-mail:** jennifer. acevedo@stmediagroup.com; carly.hagedon@stmediagroup.com. **Website:** www.vmsd.com. **Contact:** Jennifer Acevedo, editor-in-chief; Carly Hagedon, managing editor. **10% freelance written.** Monthly magazine covering retailing store design, store planning, visual merchandising, brand marketing. VMSD magazine (Visual Merchandising Store Design) is the leading resource for retail designers and store display professionals, serving the retail industry since its founding by L. Frank Baum in 1897 (then called The Show Window, and later Display World). Articles need to get behind the story, tell not only what retailers did when building a new store, renovating an existing store, mounting a new in-store merchandise campaign, but also why they did what they did: specific goals, objectives, strategic initiatives, problems to solve, target markets to reach, etc. Estab. 1897. Circ. 25,450+. Byline given. Pays on acceptance. Publishes ms an average of 1-2 months after acceptance. Editorial lead time 2-3 months. Submit seasonal material 3-4 months in advance. Accepts queries by e-mail. Accepts simultaneous submissions. Sample copy free. Guidelines available online and by e-mail.

NONFICTION Query with details of project, including a press release if available, high-resolution, professional photos, the date the store opened, and any other information available. Length: 500-1,000 words. **Pays $250-1,000.** Pays expenses of writers on assignment.

COLUMNS Editorial calendar available online. **Buys 5-6 mss/year.** Query. **Pays $500-1,000.**

SPORT TRADE

💲💲 AQUATICS INTERNATIONAL

Hanley Wood, LLC, 6222 Wilshire Blvd., Suite 600, Los Angeles CA 90048. **Fax:** (323)801-4972. **E-mail:** jmcclain@hanleywood.com. **Website:** www.aquaticsintl.com. **Contact:** Joanne McClain, editor-in-chief. Magazine published 10 times/year covering public swimming pools and waterparks. Devoted to the commercial and public swimming pool industries. The magazine provides detailed information on designing, building, maintaining, promoting, managing, programming, and outfitting aquatics facilities. Estab. 1989. Circ. 30,000. Byline given. Pays on publication. No kill fee. Publishes ms an average of 3 months after acceptance. Editorial lead time 3 months. Accepts simultaneous submissions. Responds in 1 month to queries. Sample copy for $10.50.

NONFICTION Needs how-to, interview, technical. **Buys 6 mss/year.** Send query letter with published clips/samples. Length: 1,500-2,500 words. **Pays $525 for assigned articles.**

COLUMNS Pays $250.

💲💲 ARROWTRADE MAGAZINE

Arrow Trade Publishing Corp., 3479 409th Ave. NW, Braham MN 55006. (320)396-3473. **Fax:** (320)396-3206. **E-mail:** info@arrowtrademag.com. **Website:** www.arrowtrademag.com. **Contact:** Tim Dehn, editorial. **80% freelance written.** Bimonthly magazine covering the archery industry. Readers are interested in articles that help them operate their businesses better. They are primarily owners or managers of sporting goods stores and archery pro shops. Estab. 1996. Circ. 13,000. Byline given. Pays on publication. No kill fee. Publishes ms an average of 2 months after acceptance. Editorial lead time 2 months. Accepts queries by mail, e-mail, fax. Accepts simultaneous submissions. Responds in 2 weeks to queries. Responds

in 2 weeks to mss. Sample copy for SAE with 9x12 envelope and 10 First-Class stamps.

NONFICTION Needs interview, new product. "Generic business articles won't work for our highly specialized audience." **Buys 24 mss/year.** Query with published clips. Length: 3,400-4,800 words. **Pays $350-550.** Pays expenses of writers on assignment.

💲💲 BOATING INDUSTRY

EPG Media, 3300 Fernbrook Lane N., Suite 200, Plymouth MN 55447. (763)383-4400. **E-mail:** jonathan.sweet@boatingindustry.com. **Website:** www.boatingindustry.com. **Contact:** Jonathan Sweet, editor-in-chief. **Less than 10% freelance written.** Bimonthly magazine covering recreational marine industry management. "We write for those in the industry—not the consumer. Our subject is the business of boating. All of our articles must be analytical and predictive, telling our readers where the industry is going, rather than where it's been." Estab. 1929. Circ. 23,000. Byline given. Pays on publication. Offers 50% kill fee. Publishes ms an average of 2 months after acceptance. Editorial lead time 2 months. Submit seasonal material 2 months in advance. Accepts queries by mail, e-mail. Accepts simultaneous submissions. Responds in 1 month to queries. Sample copy available online. Guidelines free.

NONFICTION **Buys 30 mss/year.** Query with published clips. Length: 250-2,500 words. **Pays $25-250.** Pays expenses of writers on assignment.

💲💲 BOWLING CENTER MANAGEMENT

Luby Publishing, 122 S. Michigan Ave., Suite 1806, Chicago IL 60603. (312)341-1110. **Fax:** (312)341-1180. **E-mail:** mikem@lubypublishing.com. **Website:** www.bcmmag.com. **Contact:** Michael Mazek, editor. **50% freelance written.** Monthly magazine covering bowling centers, family entertainment. *Bowling Center Management* is the industry's leading business publication and offical trade magazien of the Bowling Proprietor's Association of America. Readers are looking for novel ways to draw more customers. Accordingly, the magazine looks for articles that effectively present such ideas. Estab. 1995. Circ. 12,000. Byline given. Pays on acceptance. Publishes ms an average of 3 months after acceptance. Editorial lead time 3 months. Submit seasonal material 6 months in advance. Accepts queries by e-mail. Accepts simultaneous submissions. Responds in 2-3 weeks to queries. Sample copy for $10.

NONFICTION Needs how-to, interview. **Buys 10-20 mss/year.** Query. Length: 750-1,500 words. **Pays $150-350.** Pays expenses of writers on assignment.

💲💲 *GOLF COURSE MANAGEMENT*

Golf Course Superintendents Association of America (GCSAA), 1421 Research Park Dr., Lawrence KS 66049. (785)832-4456. **Fax:** (785)832-3665. **E-mail:** shollister@gcsaa.org; mhirt@gcsaa.org; tcarson@gcsaa.org. **Website:** www.gcsaa.org. **Contact:** Scott Hollister, editor in chief; Megan Hirt, managing editor; Teresa Carson, science editor. **50% freelance written.** Monthly magazine covering the golf course superintendent. *GCM* helps the golf course superintendent become more efficient in all aspects of their job. Estab. 1924. Circ. 40,000. Byline given. Pays on acceptance. No kill fee. Publishes ms an average of 6 months after acceptance. Editorial lead time 6 months. Submit seasonal material 6 months in advance. Accepts queries by e-mail. Accepts simultaneous submissions. Responds in 3 weeks to queries; in 1 month to mss. Sample copy free. Guidelines available online.

NONFICTION Needs how-to, interview. No articles about playing golf. **Buys 40 mss/year.** Query for either feature, research, or superintendent article. Submit electronically, preferably as e-mail attachment. Send one-page synopsis or query for feature article to Scott Hollister. For research articles, submit to Teresa Carson. If you are a superintendent, contact Megan Hirt. Length: 1,500-2,500 words. **Pays $400-600.** Pays expenses of writers on assignment.

💲💲 INTERNATIONAL BOWLING INDUSTRY

B2B Media, Inc., 12655 Ventura Blvd., Studio City CA 91604. (818)789-2695. **Fax:** (818)789-2812. **E-mail:** info@bowlingindustry.com. **Website:** www.bowlingindustry.com. **40% freelance written.** Online monthly magazine covering ownership and management of bowling centers (alleys) and pro shops. *IBI* publishes articles in all phases of bowling center and bowling pro shop ownership and management, among them finance, promotion, customer service, relevant technology, architecture, and capital improvement. The magazine also covers the operational areas of bowling centers and pro shops such as human resources, food and beverage, corporate and birthday parties, ancillary attractions (go-karts, gaming and the like), and retailing. Articles must have strong how-to emphasis. They must be written specifically in terms of the bowling industry, although content may be applicable more widely. Estab. 1993. Circ. 10,200. Byline given. Pays on acceptance. Offers $50 kill fee. Publishes ms an average of 3 months after acceptance. Submit seasonal material 3 months in advance. Accepts queries by mail, e-mail, fax. Accepts simultaneous submissions. Responds in 2 weeks to queries. Responds in 1 month to mss. Sample copy for #10 SASE. Guidelines free.

NONFICTION Needs how-to, interview, new product, technical. **Buys 40 mss/year.** Send complete ms. Length: 1,100-1,400 words. **Pays $250.** Pays expenses of writers on assignment.

💲💲 NSGA NOW

National Sporting Goods Association, 1601 Feehanville Dr., Suite 300, Mt. Prospect IL 60056-6035. (847)296-6742. **Fax:** (847)391-9827. **E-mail:** info@nsga.org. **E-mail:** kbruce@nsga.org. **Website:** www.nsga.org. **Contact:** Katie Bruce. **5% freelance written. Works with a small number of new/unpublished writers each year.** Bimonthly magazine. *NSGA Now* serves as a bimonthly trade journal for sporting goods retailers who are members of the association. Estab. 1948. Circ. 2,000. Byline given. Pays on publication. Publishes ms an average of 1 month after acceptance. Submit seasonal material 6 months in advance. Accepts queries by e-mail. Accepts simultaneous submissions. Sample copy for sale with 9x12 envelope and 5 first-class stamps.

NONFICTION Needs interview. No articles written without sporting goods retail business people in mind as the audience. In other words, no generic articles sent to several industries. **Buys 12 mss/year.** Query with published clips. **Pays $150-300.** Pays expenses of writers on assignment.

COLUMNS Personnel Management (succinct tips on hiring, motivating, firing, etc.); Sales Management (in-depth tips to improve sales force performance); Retail Management (detailed explanation of merchandising/inventory control); Store Design; Visual Merchandising, all 1,500 words. **Buys 12 columns/year. mss/year.** Query. **Pays $150-300.**

💲💲 POOL & SPA NEWS

Hanley Wood, LLC, 6222 Wilshire Blvd., Suite 600, Los Angeles CA 90048. (323)801-4972. **Fax:** (323)801-4986. **E-mail:** jmcclain@hanleywood.com. **Website:** http://poolspanews.com. **Contact:** Joanne McClain, editor. **15% freelance written.** Semimonthly magazine covering the swimming pool and spa industry for builders, retail stores, and service firms. Estab. 1960. Circ. 16,300. Pays on publication. No kill fee. Publishes ms an average of 2 months after acceptance. Accepts queries by mail, e-mail. Accepts simultaneous submissions. Responds in 1 month to queries. Sample copy for $5 and 9x12 SAE and 11 first-class stamps.

NONFICTION Needs interview, technical. Send résumé with published clips. Length: 500-2,000 words. **Pays $150-550.** Pays expenses of writers on assignment.

REPRINTS Send typed ms with rights for sale noted and information about when and where the material previously appeared. Payment varies.

COLUMNS Payment varies.

💲💲 REFEREE

Referee Enterprises, Inc., 2017 Lathrop Ave., Racine WI 53405. (800)733-6100. **Fax:** (262)632-5460. **E-mail:** submissions@referee.com. **Website:** www.referee.com. **Contact:** Brent Killackey, managing editor. **75% freelance written.** Monthly magazine covering sports officiating. *Referee* is a magazine for and read by sports officials of all kinds with a focus on baseball, basketball, football, softball, and soccer officiating. Estab. 1976. Circ. 40,000. Byline given. Pays on acceptance. Offers kill fee. Kill fee negotiable. Publishes ms an average of 6 months after acceptance. Editorial lead time 6 months. Accepts queries by mail, e-mail. Accepts simultaneous submissions. Responds in 2 weeks to queries; 1 month to mss. Sample copy with #10 SASE. Guidelines online.

NONFICTION Needs book excerpts, essays, historical, how-to, humor, interview, opinion, photo feature, technical. "We don't want to see articles with themes not relating to sport officiating. General sports articles, although of interest to us, will not be published." **Buys 40 mss/year.** Query with published clips. Length: 500-3,500 words. **Pays $50-400.** Pays expenses of writers on assignment.

💲💲 SKI AREA MANAGEMENT

Beardsley Publications, SAM, P.O. Box 644, Woodbury CT 06798. (203)263-0888. **Fax:** (203)266-0452. **E-mail:** donna@saminfo.com; jenn@saminfo.com. **Website:** www.saminfo.com. **Contact:** Donna Jacobs. **85% freelance written.** Bimonthly magazine covering everything involving the management and development of ski resorts. Report on new ideas, developments, marketing, and regulations with regard to ski and snowboard resorts. Estab. 1962. Circ. 4,500. Byline given. Pays on publication. Offers kill fee. Offers kill fee. Editorial lead time 2 months. Submit seasonal material 3 months in advance. Accepts queries by mail, e-mail. Accepts simultaneous submissions. Responds in 2 weeks to queries. Sample copy for 9x12 SAE with $3 postage or online. Guidelines for #10 SASE.

NONFICTION Needs historical, how-to, interview, new product, opinion, personal experience, technical. Does not want anything that does not specifically pertain to resort operations, management, or financing. **Buys 25-40 mss/year.** Query. Length: 500-2,500 words. **Pays $50-400.**

💲💲 SKI PATROL MAGAZINE

National Ski Patrol, 133 S. Van Gordon St., Suite 100, Lakewood CO 80228. (303)988-1111, ext. 2625. **Fax:** (303)988-3005. **E-mail:** editor@nsp.org. **Website:** www.nsp.org. **Contact:** Candace Horgan, editor. **80% freelance written.** Covers the National Ski Patrol, skiing, snowboarding, backcountry travel and recreation, and snow sports safety. *Ski Patrol Magazine* is a triannual publication for the members and affiliates of the National Ski Patrol. Topics are related to patrolling, mountain rescue, and the ski industry. "We cannot consider your ms if it is being reviewed by other publishers or if it has already been published. You must guarantee the originality of your work. If you write about other people's ideas, be sure to credit them where appropriate." Estab. 1984. Circ. 33,000. Byline given. Pays on publication. No kill fee. Publishes ms 3-6 months after acceptance. Editorial lead time 3 months. Submit seasonal material 3 months in advance. Accepts queries by mail, e-mail. Reponds in 1-2 weeks to queries; in 2 months to mss. Sample copy available for SASE with $3 postage. Guidelines available for SASE with 1 first-class stamp.

NONFICTION Needs essays, expose, general interest, historical, how-to, humor, inspirational, interview, nostalgic, opinion, personal experience, photo feature, profile, reviews, technical, travel. Special issues: Fall Issue: Gear Guide. **Buys 10-15 mss/year.** Query with published clips. Length: 700-3,000 words. **Pays $300-400.**

COLUMNS Columns are on NSP education programs. Length: 1,000-1,500 words. **Buys 8-12 mss/year.** Query with published clips. **Pays $100-250.**

STONE, QUARRY & MINING

$$ CANADIAN MINING JOURNAL

BIG Mining Group, 38 Lesmill Rd., Unit 2, Toronto ON M3B 2T5 Canada. (416)510-6742. **E-mail:** editor@canadianminingjournal.com. **Website:** www.canadianminingjournal.com. **Contact:** Marilyn Scales, interim editor. **5% freelance written.** Magazine covering mining and mineral exploration by Canadian companies. *Canadian Mining Journal* provides articles and information of practical use to those who work in the technical, administrative, and supervisory aspects of exploration, mining, and processing in the Canadian mineral exploration and mining industry. Estab. 1882. Circ. 10,000. Byline given. Pays on publication. No kill fee. Publishes ms an average of 3 months after acceptance. Submit seasonal material 3 months in advance. Accepts queries by mail, e-mail, phone. Accepts simultaneous submissions. Responds in 1 week to queries; in 1 month to mss.

NONFICTION Needs new product, personal experience, technical. **Buys 6 mss/year.** Query with published clips. Length: 500-1,400 words. **Pays $100-600.** Pays expenses of writers on assignment.

COLUMNS Guest editorial (opinion on controversial subject related to mining industry), 600 words. **Buys 3 mss/year.** Query with published clips.

$ CONTEMPORARY STONE & TILE DESIGN

Business News Publishing Media, 210 Route 4 East, Suite 203, Paramus NJ 07652. (201)291-9001, ext. 8611. **Fax:** (201)291-9002. **E-mail:** jennifer@stoneworld.com. **Website:** www.stoneworld.com. **Contact:** Jennifer Richinelli, editor. Quarterly magazine covering the full range of stone and tile design and architecture—from classic and historic spaces to current projects. Estab. 1995. Circ. 21,000. Byline given. Pays on publication. No kill fee. Publishes ms an average of 3 months after acceptance. Submit seasonal material 6 months in advance. Accepts simultaneous submissions. Responds in 3 weeks to queries. Sample copy for $10.

NONFICTION Needs interview, photo feature. **Buys 8 mss/year.** Query with published clips. Length: 1,500-3,000 words. **Pays $6/column inch.** Pays expenses of writers on assignment.

COLUMNS Upcoming Events (for the architecture and design community); Stone Classics (featuring historic architecture); question and answer session with a prominent architect or designer. Length: 1,500-2,000 words. **Pays $6/inch.**

$$ MINING PEOPLE MAGAZINE

Al Skinner, Inc., 629 Virginia St. W, P.O. Box 6247, Charleston WV 25362 Kanawha. (304)342-4129. **Fax:** (304)343-3124. **E-mail:** alskinner@ntelos.net; cpm@ntelos.net. **Website:** www.miningpeople.org. **Contact:** Christina Karawan, managing editor; Al Skinner, editor. **50% freelance written.** Most stories are about people or historical—either narrative or biographical on all levels of coal and mining people, past and present—from mining execs down to grass roots miners. Most stories are upbeat—showing warmth of family or success from underground up! Estab. 1976. Circ. 12,300 hard copy, est. 26,000 digital. Byline given. Pays on publication. No kill fee. Publishes ms an average of 3 months after acceptance. Submit seasonal material 2 months in advance. Accepts queries by mail, e-mail, online submission form. Accepts simultaneous submissions. Responds in 3 months to mss. Sample copy for sae with 9x12 envelope and 10 first-class stamps.

NONFICTION Needs book excerpts, historical, humor, interview, personal experience, photo feature. Special issues: Calendar issue for more than 300 annual coal shows, association meetings, etc. (January); Surface Mining/Reclamation Award (July); Christmas in Coal Country (December). No poetry, fiction, or environmental attacks on the mining industry. **Buys 32 mss/year.** Query with published clips. Length: 750-2,500 words. **Pays $150-250.**

REPRINTS Send tearsheet and information about when and where the material previously appeared. Pays 50% of amount paid for an original article.

COLUMNS Length: 300-500 words. Editorials—anything to do with current coal issues (nonpaid); Mine'ing Our Business (bull pen column—gossip—humorous anecdotes); Coal Show Coverage (freelance photojournalist coverage of any coal function across the US). **Buys 10 mss/year.** Query. **Pays $50.**

FILLERS Needs Filler needs: anecdotes. Length: 300 words. **Pays $35.**

💲💲 PIT & QUARRY

Questex Media Group, 1360 E. Ninth St., Suite 1070, Cleveland OH 44114. (216)706-3711; (216)706-3747. **Fax:** (216)706-3710. **E-mail:** info@pitandquarry.com; kyanik@northcoastmedia.net. **Website:** www.pitandquarry.com. **Contact:** Kevin Yanik, managing editor. **10-20% freelance written.** Monthly magazine covering nonmetallic minerals, mining, and crushed stone. Audience has knowledge of construction-related markets, mining, minerals processing, etc. Estab. 1916. Circ. 23,000. Byline given. Pays on acceptance. No kill fee. Publishes ms an average of 2 months after acceptance. Editorial lead time 2 months. Accepts queries by e-mail. Accepts simultaneous submissions. Responds in 1 month to queries. Responds in 4 months to mss.

NONFICTION Needs how-to, interview, new product, technical. No humor or inspirational articles. **Buys 3-4 mss/year.** Query. Length: 2,000-2,500 words. **Pays $250-500 for assigned articles. Does not pay for unsolicited articles.** Pays expenses of writers on assignment.

COLUMNS Brand New; Techwatch; E-business; Software Corner; Equipment Showcase. Length: 250-750 words. **Buys 5-6 mss/year.** Query. **Pays $250-300.**

💲 STONE WORLD

BNP Media, 2401 W. Big Beaver Rd., Suite 700, Troy MI 48084. (201)291-9001. **Fax:** (201)291-9002. **E-mail:** jennifer@stoneworld.com. **Website:** www.stoneworld.com. **Contact:** Jennifer Adams, editor. Monthly magazine on natural building stone for producers and users of granite, marble, limestone, slate, sandstone, onyx, and other natural stone products. Estab. 1984. Circ. 21,000. Byline given. Pays on publication. No kill fee. Publishes ms an average of 4 months after acceptance. Submit seasonal material 6 months in advance. Responds in 2 months to queries. Sample copy for $10.

NONFICTION Needs how-to, fabricate and/or install natural building stone, interview, photo feature, technical, architectural design, artistic stone uses, statistics, factory profile, equipment profile, trade show review. **Buys 10 mss/year.** Send complete ms. Length: 600-3,000 words. **Pays $6/column inch.** Pays expenses of writers on assignment.

REPRINTS Send photocopy with rights for sale noted and information about when and where the material previously appeared. Pays 50% of amount paid for an original article.

COLUMNS News (pertaining to stone or design community); New Literature (brochures, catalogs, books, videos, etc., about stone); New Products (stone products); New Equipment (equipment and machinery for working with stone); Calendar (dates and locations of events in stone and design communities). Query or send complete ms. Length 300-600 words. **Pays $6/inch.**

TRANSPORTATION

💲💲💲 RAILWAY TRACK AND STRUCTURES

Simmons-Boardman Publishing, 55 Broad St., 26th Floor, New York NY 10004. (212)620-7200. **Fax:** (212)633-1165. **E-mail:** Mischa@sbpub-chicago.com; ksenese@sbpub.com. **Website:** www.rtands.com. **Contact:** Mischa Wanek-Libman, editor; Kyra Senese, assistant editor. **1% freelance written.** Monthly magazine covering railroad civil engineering. *RT&S* is a nuts-and-bolts journal to help railroad civil engineers do their jobs better. Estab. 1904. Circ. 9,500. Byline given. Pays on publication. Offers 90% kill fee. Publishes ms an average of 1 month after acceptance. Editorial lead time 2 months. Submit seasonal material 3 months in advance. Accepts queries by mail, fax, phone. Accepts simultaneous submissions. Responds in 1 month to queries and to mss. Sample copy available online.

NONFICTION Needs how-to, new product, technical. Does not want nostalgia or "railroadiana." **Buys 1 mss/year.** Query. Length: 900-2,000 words. **Pays $500-1,000.** Pays expenses of writers on assignment.

💲💲 SCHOOL TRANSPORTATION NEWS

STN Media Co., P.O. Box 789, Redondo Beach CA 90277. (310)792-2226. **Fax:** (310)792-2231. **E-mail:** ryan@stnmedia.com; sean@stnmedia.com. **Website:** www.stnonline.com. **Contact:** Ryan Gray, editor in chief; Sean Gallagherean Gallagher, associate editor. **20% freelance written.** Monthly magazine covering school bus and pupil transportation industries in North America. Contributors to *School Transportation News* must have a basic understanding of K-12 education and automotive fleets and specifically of school buses. Articles cover such topics as manufacturing, operations, maintenance and routing software, GPS, security and legislative affairs. A familiarity with these principles is preferred. Additional industry information is available on website. New writers must perform some research of the industry or exhibit core competencies in the subject matter. Estab. 1991. Circ. 24,000. Byline given. Pays on publication. No kill fee. Editorial lead time 1-2 months. Submit seasonal material 3 months in advance. Accepts queries by e-mail. Accepts simultaneous submissions. Sample copy free. Guidelines free.

NONFICTION Needs book excerpts, general interest, historical, humor, inspirational, interview, new product, personal experience, photo feature, technical. Does not want strictly localized editorial. Wants articles that put into perspective the issues of the day. Query with published clips. Length: 600-1,200 words. **Pays $150-300.** Pays expenses of writers on assignment.

COLUMNS Creative Special Report, Cover Story, Top Story; Book/Video Reviews (new programs/publications/training for pupil transporters), both 600 words. **Buys 40 mss/year.** Query with published clips. **Pays $150.**

TRAVEL

💲💲💲 LEISURE GROUP TRAVEL

Premier Tourism Marketing, 621 Plainfield Rd., Suite 406, Willowbrook IL 60527. (630)794-0696. **Fax:** (630)794-0652. **E-mail:** randy@ptmgroups.com. **E-mail:** editor@ptmgroups.com. **Website:** www.leisuregrouptravel.com. **Contact:** Randy Mink, managing editor. **35% freelance written.** Bimonthly magazine covering group travel. Covers destinations and editorial relevant to the group travel market. Estab. 1994. Circ. 15,012. Byline given. Pays on publication. No kill fee. Editorial lead time 6 months. Submit seasonal material 6 months in advance. Accepts queries by mail, e-mail. Accepts simultaneous submissions. Sample copy available online.

NONFICTION Needs travel. **Buys 75 mss/year.** Query with published clips. Length: 1,200-3,000 words. **Pays $0-1,000.**

💲💲💲 RVBUSINESS

G&G Media Group, 2901 E. Bristol St., Suite B, Elkhart IN 46514. (574)266-7980, ext. 13. **Fax:** (574)266-7984. **E-mail:** bhampson@rvbusiness.com; bhampson@g-gmediagroup.com. **Website:** www.rvbusiness.com. **Contact:** Bruce Hampson, editor. **50% freelance written.** Bimonthly magazine. *RVBusiness* caters to a specific audience of people who manufac-

ture, sell, market, insure, finance, service and supply, components for recreational vehicles. Estab. 1972. Circ. 21,000. Byline given. Pays on acceptance. Offers kill fee. Publishes ms an average of 2 months after acceptance. Editorial lead time 2 months. Accepts simultaneous submissions. Sample copy free.

NONFICTION Needs new product, photo feature, industry news and features. No general articles without specific application to market. **Buys 50 mss/year.** Query with published clips. Length: 125-2,200 words. **Pays $50-1,000.** Pays expenses of writers on assignment.

COLUMNS Top of the News (RV industry news), 75-400 words; Business Profiles, 400-500 words; Features (indepth industry features), 800-2,000 words. **Buys 50 mss/year.** Query. **Pays $50-1,000.**

💲💲 SPECIALTY TRAVEL INDEX

Alpine Hansen, P.O. Box 458, San Anselmo CA 94979. (415)455-1643. **E-mail:** info@specialtytravel.com; aalpine@specialtytravel.com. **Website:** www.specialtytravel.com. **Contact:** Andy Alpine. **90% freelance written.** Semiannual magazine covering adventure and special interest travel. Estab. 1980. Circ. 35,000. Byline given. Pays on receipt and acceptance of all materials. No kill fee. Editorial lead time 3 month. Submit seasonal material 3 months in advance. Accepts queries by mail, e-mail. Accepts simultaneous submissions. Writer's guidelines on request.

NONFICTION Needs how-to, personal experience, photo feature, travel. **Buys 15 mss/year.** Query. Length: 1,250 words. **Pays $300 minimum.** Pays expenses of writers on assignment.

REPRINTS Send tearsheet. Pays 100% of amount paid for an original article.

VETERINARY

💲💲 ANIMAL SHELTERING

The Humane Society of the United States, P.O. Box 15276, North Hollywood CA 91615. (800)565-9226. **E-mail:** asm@humanesociety.org. **Website:** www.animalsheltering.org. **Contact:** Shevaun Brannigan, production/marketing manager; Carrie Allan, editor. **20% freelance written.** Magazine for animal care professionals and volunteers, dealing with animal welfare issues faced by animal shelters, animal control agencies, and rescue groups. Emphasis on news for the field and professional, hands-on work. Readers are shelter and animal control directors, kennel staff, field officers, humane investigators, animal control officers, animal rescuers, foster care volunteers, general volunteers, shelter veterinarians, and anyone concerned with local animal welfare issues. Estab. 1978. Circ. 6,000. Accepts simultaneous submissions. Sample copies are free; contact Shevaun Brannigan at sbrannigan@hsus.org. Guidelines available by e-mail.

NONFICTION Approximately 6-10 submissions published each year from non-staff writers; of those submissions, 50% are from writers new to the publication. **"Payment varies depending on length and complexity of piece. Longer features generally $400-600; short news pieces generally $200. We rarely take unsolicited work, so it's best to contact the editor with story ideas."** Pays expenses of writers on assignment.

REPRINTS "Aquires first publication rights. We also grant permission, with a credit to the magazine and writer, to readers who want to use the materials to educate their supporters, staff and volunteers. Contact asm@humanesociety.org for writers' guidelines."

$$ VETERINARY ECONOMICS

8033 Flint St., Lenexa KS 66214. (800)255-6864. **Fax:** (913)871-3808. **E-mail:** dvmnews@advanstar.com. **Website:** veterinarybusiness.dvm360.com. **20% freelance written.** Monthly magazine covering veterinary practice management. "We address the business concerns and management needs of practicing veterinarians." Estab. 1960. Circ. 54,000. Byline given. Pays on publication. No kill fee. Publishes ms an average of 6 months after acceptance. Editorial lead time 3 months. Submit seasonal material 3 months in advance. Accepts queries by mail, e-mail. Accepts simultaneous submissions. Responds in 3 months to queries. Sample copy free. Guidelines available online.

NONFICTION Needs how-to, interview, personal experience. **Buys 24 mss/year.** Send complete ms. Length: 1,000-2,000 words. **Pays $40-350.** Pays expenses of writers on assignment.

COLUMNS Practice Tips (easy, unique business tips), 250 words or fewer. Send complete ms. **Pays $40.**

PLAYWRITING

For years, *Writer's Market* for has focused solcly on the most traditional publishing formats, including getting published in consumer magazines and trade journals and by book publishers with the assistance of literary agents, as well as writing contests. Those markets aren't going away, but we can add in other venues, including playwriting and screenwriting.

Playwriting is a unique market in that writers have to create scripts that speak to live audiences with live actors. Plus, there are sets to consider, number of roles, and how to engage a captive audience.

PLAYWRITING

///

ACT II PLAYHOUSE

56 E. Butler Ave., Ambler PA 19002. (215)654-0200. **Website:** www.act2.org. Producing Artistic Director: Tony Braithwaite. Estab. 1998. **Produces 4 plays/year. plays/year.** Submit query and synopsis. Include SASE for return of submission. Payment negotiable. Responds in 1 month. Contemporary comedy, drama, musicals. Full length. 6 character limitation; 1 set or unit set. Does not want period pieces. Limited number of scenes per act.

ACTORS THEATRE OF LOUISVILLE

316 W. Main St., Louisville KY 40202-4218. (502)584-1265. **Fax:** (502)561-3300. **E-mail:** awegener@actorstheatre.org. **Website:** www.actorstheatre.org. **Contact:** Amy Wegener, literary director. Estab. 1964. "Professional productions are performed for subscription audience from diverse backgrounds. Agented submissions only for full-length plays, will read 10-page samples of unagented full-length works. Open submissions to National Ten-Minute Play Contest (plays 10 pages or less) are due November 1." **Produces approximately 25 new plays of varying lengths/year. plays/year.** Buys variable rights. Offers variable royalty. Responds in 9-12 months to submissions, mostly in the fall/winter. Full-length and 10-minute plays and plays of ideas, language, humor, experiment and passion.

ACT THEATRE

A Contemporary Theatre, Kreielsheimer Place, 700 Union St., Seattle WA 98101. (206)292-7660. **Fax:** (206)292-7670. **E-mail:** artistic@acttheatre.org. **Website:** www.acttheatre.org. Artistic Director: Kurt Beattie. Estab. 1965. "ACT performs a subscription-based season on 3 stages: 2 main stages (a thrust and an arena) and a smaller, flexible 99-seat space. Although our focus is towards our local Seattle audience, some of our notable productions have gone on to other venues in other cities." **Produces 5-6 mainstage plays/year. plays/year.** *Agented submissions only* or through theatre professional's recommendation. No unsolicited submissions. Query and synopsis only for Northwest playwrights. Pays 5-10% royalty. Responds in 6 months. ACT produces full-length contemporary scripts ranging from solo pieces to large ensemble works, with an emphasis on plays that embrace the contradictions and mysteries of our contemporary world and that resonate with audiences of all backgrounds through strong storytelling and compelling characters.

ALABAMA SHAKESPEARE FESTIVAL

#1 Festival Dr., Montgomery AL 36117. **Website:** www.asf.net. Estab. 1972. The Alabama Shakespeare Festival (ASF), the State's theater, builds community by engaging, entertaining, and inspiring people with transformative theatrical performances and compelling educational and outreach programs. Located in Montgomery, the state capital of Alabama, ASF is a LORT theatre that produces up to ten productions each season in association with Actors' Equity Association, The Stage Directors and Choreographers Society and United Scenic Artists union. Though productions of Shakespeare are at the artistic core of the company, the seasons offer a diverse selection of Broadway musicals, literary classics, children's productions and world premieres of new work developed through the Southern Writer's Project (SWP.) SWP focuses on the diverse, varied heritage of the South and explores who we are today. It offers emerging and established playwrights the opportunity to develop their stories through a collaborative workshop with actors, directors, dramaturgs and an audience. For more information go to http://southernwritersproject.net/.

ALLEYWAY THEATRE

One Curtain Up Alley, Buffalo NY 14202. (716)852-2600. **Fax:** (716)852-2266. **E-mail:** email@alleyway.com. **Website:** www.alleyway.com. **Contact:** Literary Manager. Estab. 1980. **Produces 4-5 full-length, 6-12 one-act plays/year. plays/year.** Seeks first production rights. Submit complete script; include CD for musicals. Alleyway Theatre also sponsors the Maxim Mazumdar New Play Competition. Pays 7% royalty. Responds in 6 months. "Works written uniquely for the theatre. Theatricality, breaking the fourth wall, and unusual settings are of particular interest. We are less interested in plays which are likely to become TV or film scripts."

ALLIANCE THEATRE

1280 Peachtree St. NE, Atlanta GA 30309. (404)733-4650. **Fax:** (404)733-4625. **E-mail:** allianceinfo@alliancetheatre.org. **Website:** www.alliancetheatre.org. **Contact:** Literary Intern. Estab. 1969. Professional production for local audience. Only accepts agent submissions and unsolicited samples from Georgia residents only. Electronic correspondence preferred. **Produces 11 plays/year. plays/year.** Query with synopsis and sample or submit through agent. Enclose SASE. Responds in 9 months. Full-length scripts and scripts for young audiences no longer than 60 minutes.

AMERICAN STAGE

163 3rd St. N., St. Petersburg FL 33701. (727)823-1600. **Website:** www.americanstage.org. Producing Artistic Director: Stephanie Gularte. Development Director: Stephanie Snyder. Estab. 1977. Limited by "Small mainstage venue, 1 touring production conducive to small cast, light technical pieces." Subject matter: classics and original work for children (ages K-12) and families. Recently produced plays: *King Island Christmas for the Mainstage* and *Alexander and the Terrible, Horrible, No Good Very Bad Day* for the School Tour and Mainstage. Query with synopsis, character breakdown and set description. Will consider simultaneous submissions and previously performed work.

ANCHORAGE PRESS PLAYS, INC.

Dramatic Publishing, 311 Washington St., Woodstock IL 60098. (800)448-7469. **Fax:** (800)334-5302. **Website:** www.applays.com. **Contact:** Kevin Wright, submissions coordinator. Estab. 1935. "We are an international agency for plays for young people. First in the field since 1935. We are primarily a publisher of theatrical plays with limited textbooks. "Publishes solicited hardcover and trade paperback originals. "Anchorage Press PLAYS, Inc serves a specialty field of TYA - Theatre for Young Audiences. We publish play scripts and license the performance rights for plays to be presented, by skilled performers, before audiences of children, youth, teens, and young adults or a family audience. Anchorage also has a limited number of plays of faith that are more suitable for a family audience or teen/adult audience in subject complexity. Representing the playwrights of these works, Anchorage serves as the licensing agency for the performance rights. We also publish and distribute a select number of books for the field." **Publishes 4-6 plays/year. plays/year.** "A play manuscript must be computer-printed with dark ink. It should be submitted by mail to (Submissions, Anchorage Press Plays, Linda Habjan, Submissions Editor, 311 Washington St., Woodstock, IL 60098) and accompanied by a SASE. Manuscripts will not be accepted via fax or email. Please send a play script only after it has had staged productions, workshop readings, peer reviews, and rewrites. We cannot accept plays for publication that have not been produced. (Please send information about productions: programs, reviews, etc.) **Send your final version**. We will consider plays with 2 or more characters. See more guidelines online at website." Pays 10-15% royalty. Playwrights also receive 50-75% royalties. Responds in 1-2 years. drama, stage plays, for children and young people.

ARIZONA THEATRE CO.

P.O. Box 1631, Tucson AZ 85702. (520)884-8210. **Fax:** (520)628-9129. **Website:** arizonatheatre.org. **Contact:** Literary Department. Artistic Director: David Ivers. Estab. 1966. "Arizona Theatre Company is the State Theatre of Arizona. Each season reflects the rich variety of world drama—from classics to contemporary plays, from musicals to new works—along with a wide array of outreach programs, educational opportunities, access initiatives, and new play programs." **Produces 6-8 plays/year. plays/year.** Only Arizona writers may submit unsolicited scripts, along with production history (if any), brief bio, and SAE. Out-of-state writers can send a synopsis, 10-page sample dialogue, production history (if any), brief bio, and SAE. Payment negotiated. Responds in 4-6 months. Full length plays of a variety of genres and topics and full length musicals. No one-acts.

ARTISTS REPERTORY THEATRE

Portland OR 97205. **Website:** www.artistsrep.org. Estab. 1982. Plays performed in professional theater with a subscriber-based audience. No unsolicited mss accepted. Pays royalty. No response to unsolicited scripts. Full-length, hard-hitting, emotional, intimate, actor-oriented shows with small casts (rarely exceeds 10-13, usually 2-7). Language and subject matter are not a problem. No one-acts or children's scripts.

　　"We bring Portland the newest and most exhilarating plays being written today and simultaneously showcase the talents of local theater artists."

ART STATION THEATRE

P.O. Box 1998, Stone Mountain GA 30083. (770)469-1105. **Website:** www.artstation.org. Co-founders/directors: David Thomas and Michael Hidalgo. Estab. 1986. ART Station Theatre is a professional theater located in a contemporary arts center in Stone Mountain, GA, which is part of Metro Atlanta. Audience consists of middle-aged to senior, suburban patrons. **Produces 3 plays/year. plays/year.** Query with synopsis and writing samples. Pays 5-7% royalty. Responds in 1 year. Full length comedy, drama and musicals, preferably relating to the human condition in the contemporary South. Cast size no greater than 6.

BLOOMSBURG THEATRE ENSEMBLE

226 Center St., Bloomsburg PA 17815. (570)784-5530. **E-mail:** bte@bte.org. **Website:** www.bte.org. Estab. 1979. Professional productions for a non-urban audience. **Produces 9 plays/year. plays/year.** Buys negotiable rights Submit query and synopsis. Pays 6-9% royalty. Pays $50-70/performance. Responds in 9 months. Because of our non-urban location, we strive to expose our audience to a broad range of theatre—both classical and contemporary. We are drawn to language and ideas and to plays that resonate in our community. We are most in need of articulate comedies and cast sizes under 6.

CELEBRATION THEATRE

1049 Havenhurst Dr., #101-1, West Hollywood CA 90046. (323)957-1884. **Fax:** (323)957-1826. **E-mail:** info@celebrationtheatre.com. **Website:** www.celebrationtheatre.com. **Contact:** Literary Management Team. Co-Artistic Directors: Michael Matthews and Michael A. Shepperd. Estab. 1983. Performed in a small theatre in Los angeles. For all audiences, but with gay and lesbian characters at the center of the plays. **Produces 4 plays/year. plays/year.** Submit query and synopsis. Pays 6-7% royalty. Responds in 5 months. Produce works with gay and lesbian characters at the center of the narrative. There aren't any limitations, but simple productions work best. Don't send coming-out plays/stories.

CHILDSPLAY, INC.

900 S. Mitchell Dr., Tempe AZ 85281. (480)921-5700. **Fax:** (480)921-5777. **E-mail:** info@childsplayaz.org. **Website:** childsplayaz.org. Estab. 1978. Professional touring and in-house productions for youth and family audiences. **Produces 5-6 plays/year. plays/year.** Submit synopsis, character descriptions and 7- to 10-page dialogue sample. Pays royalty of $20-35/performance (touring) or pays $3,000-8,000 commission. Holds a small percentage of royalties on commissioned work for 3-5 years. Responds in 6 months. Seeking theatrical plays on a wide range of contemporary topics. Our biggest market is K-6. We need intelligent theatrical pieces for this age group that meet touring requirements and have the flexibility for in-house staging. The company has a reputation, built up over 30 years, of maintaining a strong aesthetic. We need scripts that respect the audience's intelligence and support their rights to dream and to have their concerns explored. Innovative, theatrical and small is a constant need. Touring shows limited to 5 actors; in-house shows limited to 6-10 actors.

COLONY THEATRE CO.

555 N. Third St., Burbank CA 91502. (818)558-7000. **Fax:** (818)558-7110. **E-mail:** colonytheatre@colony-theatre.org. **Website:** www.colonytheatre.org. **Contact:** Michael David Wadler, literary manager. Professional 276-seat theater with thrust stage. Casts from resident company of professional actors. **Produces 6 plays/year. plays/year.** Negotiated rights. Submit query and synopsis. Pays royalty for each performance. Full length (90-120 minutes) with a cast of 4-12. Especially interested in small casts of 4 or fewer. No musicals or experimental works.

CREEDE REPERTORY THEATRE

P.O. Box 269, Creede CO 81130-0269. (719)658-2541. **E-mail:** litmgr@creederep.com. **Website:** www.creederep.org. **Contact:** Frank Kuhn, Literary Manager. Estab. 1966. Plays performed for a smaller audience. **Produces 6 plays/year. plays/year.** Submit synopsis, 10-page dialogue sample, letter of inquiry, resume; electronic submissions only. Royalties negotiated with each author—paid on a per performance basis. Responds in 6 months. "Special consideration given to plays focusing on the cultures and history of the American West and Southwest."

DALLAS CHILDREN'S THEATER

Rosewood Center for Family Arts, 5938 Skillman, Dallas TX 75231. **E-mail:** artie.olaisen@dct.org. **Website:** www.dct.org. **Contact:** Artie Olaisen, associate artistic director. Estab. 1984. "Professional theater for family and student audiences." **Produces up to 6 youth/family plays/year. Produces 1-2 youth/family musicals/year. plays/year.** Rights negotiable. Query with synopsis, number of actors required, any material regarding previous productions of the work, and a demo tape or lead sheets (for musicals). No materials will be returned without a SASE included. All scripts should be sent to the attention of Artie Olaisen. Pays negotiable royalty. Responds in up to 8 months. "Seeking substantive material appropriate for youth and family audiences. Most consideration given to full-length, nonmusical works, especially classic and contemporary adaptations of literature. Also interested in social, topical, issue-oriented material. Very interested in scripts which enlighten diverse cultural experiences, particularly Hispanic and African-American experiences. Prefers scripts with no more than 15 cast members; 6-12 is ideal."

DIVERSIONARY THEATRE

4545 Park Blvd., Suite 101, San Diego CA 92116. (619)220-6830. **E-mail:** dkirsch@diversionary.org. **Website:** www.diversionary.org. **Contact:** Matt M. Morrow, executive artistic director. Estab. 1986. "Professional non-union full-length productions of gay, lesbian, bisexual and transgender content. Ideal cast size is 2-6." **Produces 5-6 plays/year. plays/year.** Submit application and 10-15 pages of script. Responds in 6 months.

DRAMATIC PUBLISHING, INC.

311 Washington St., Woodstock IL 60098. (800)448-7469. **E-mail:** submissionseditor@dpcplays.com. **Website:** www.dramaticpublishing.com. **Contact:** Linda Habjan, submissions editor. Estab. 1885. Recently published: *Redwall: The Legend of Redwall Abbey*, by Evelyn Swensson, based on the book by Brian Jacques. *Gooney Bird Green and Her True-Life Adventures*, adapted by Kent R. Brown from the book by Lois Lowry; *Anastasia Krupnik*, by Meryl Friedman, based on the book by Lois Lowry; *A Village Fable*, by James Still, adapted from *In the Suicide Mountain*, by John Gardner; *The Little Prince*, adapted by Rick Cummins and John Scoullar. See website for detailed submission guidelines. Accepts submissions by postal mail only. Include your contact information, a cast list with specific character descriptions and set/technical requirements, a synopsis of the play and its production history, and a CD with any written sheet music if it is a musical. Include an SASE for reply. Pays royalties.

EAST WEST PLAYERS

120 N. Judge John Aiso St., Los Angeles CA 90012. (213)625-7000. **E-mail:** literary@eastwestplayers.org. **Website:** www.eastwestplayers.org. Producing Artistic Director: Snehal Desai. Estab. 1965. Professional 240-seat theater performing under LOA-BAT contract, presenting plays which explore the Asian Pacific American experience. **Produces 4 plays/year. plays/year.** Scripts should be submitted in a PDF format and must include the following: 1. A cover sheet, including your name, address, telephone number, website, and e-mail address; 2. A theatrical resume (two pages max) listing major productions, workshops, readings, commissions, publications, awards, education, and training information; 3. A 100-word max synopsis of the play. "Our Literary Committee will read all scripts we deem to be in line with the mission of the theater.

Due to the large volume of submissions, we will only reach out to playwrights whose work we are interested in." Pays royalty against percentage of box office. Responds in 9-12 months. "Whether dramas, comedies, or musicals, all plays must either address the Asian American experience or have a special resonance when cast with Asian American actors."

ELDRIDGE PUBLISHING CO. INC.

P.O. Box 4904, Lancaster PA 17604. (850)385-2463. **E-mail:** info@histage.com. **Website:** www.histage.com; www.95church.com. **Contact:** Meredith Edwards, acquisitions editor. Estab. 1906. Play publisher. Publishes new plays and musicals for junior and senior high school, community theater, and children's theater (adults performing for children), all genres; also religious plays. **Publishes 50 plays and 2-3 musicals a year. plays/year.** Buys all dramatic rights. "Submit complete ms to appropriate online portal; snail mail CD of songs or provide a web link to them." Will consider simultaneous submissions if noted. Pays 50% royalty and 10% copy sales. Responds in 2 months.

THE ENSEMBLE STUDIO THEATRE

545 W. 52nd St., 2nd Floor, New York NY 10019. (212)247-4982. **Fax:** (212)664-0041. **E-mail:** firman@estnyc.org. **Website:** www.ensemblestudiotheatre.org. **Contact:** Linsay Firman, Director of Play Development. Artistic Director: William Carden. Estab. 1972. **Produces 250 projects, readings, workshops and productions/year for off-off Broadway developmental theater in a 100-seat house, 60-seat workshop space. plays/year.** Do not fax mss or resumes. Please check website for current submission guidelines and deadlines. Responds in 10 months. "Full-length plays with strong dramatic actions and situations and solid one-acts, humorous and dramatic, which can stand on their own. Special programs include Going to the River Series, which workshops new plays by African-American women, and the Sloan Project, which commissions new works on the topics of science and technology. Seeks original plays with strong dramatic action, believable characters and dynamic ideas. We are interested in writers who respect the power of language. No verse-dramas or elaborate costume dramas or musicals. Accepts new/unproduced work only."

ENSEMBLE THEATRE OF CINCINNATI

1127 Vine St., Cincinnati OH 45202. (513)421-3555. **Fax:** (513)562-4104. **E-mail:** script@ensemblecincinnati.org. **Website:** www.ensemblecincinnati.org.

Contact: D. Lynn Meyers, producing artistic director. Estab. 1986. Professional year-round theater. **Produces 12 plays/year, including a staged reading series. plays/year.** Query with synopsis, submit complete ms or submit through agent. Pays 5-10% royalty. Responds in 6-9 months. Dedicated to good writing of any style for a small, contemporary cast (prefers a maximum of 8). Small technical needs, big ideas.

SAMUEL FRENCH, INC.

235 Park Ave. S., 5th Floor, New York NY 10003. (866)598-8449. **Fax:** (212)206-1429. **E-mail:** publications@samuelfrench.com. **Website:** www.samuelfrench.com. Estab. 1830. Publishes paperback acting editions of plays. *Not currently accepting unsolicited submissions.* **Publishes 50-60 titles/year. plays/year.** Pays 10% royalty on retail price, plus amateur and stock royalties on productions. Comedies, mysteries, children's plays, high school plays.

WILL GEER THEATRICUM BOTANICUM

P.O. Box 1222, Topanga CA 90290. (310)455-2322. **Fax:** (310)455-3724. **E-mail:** egtree@theatricum.com. **Website:** www.theatricum.com. **Contact:** Ellen Geer, artistic director. Estab. 1973. Professional productions for summer theater. Botanicum Seedlings new plays selected for readings and one play each year developed. **Produces 4 classical and 1 new play if selected/year. plays/year.** Send synopsis, sample dialogue and tape if musical. Pays 6% royalty or $150 per show. Responds in 6 months. Socially relevant plays, musicals; all full-length. Cast size of 4-10 people. "We are a large outdoor theatre—small intimate works could be difficult."

GEVA THEATRE CENTER

75 Woodbury Blvd., Rochester NY 14607. (585)232-1366. **Contact:** Marge Betley, literary manager. Professional and regional theater, modified thrust, 552 seats; second stage has 180 seats. Subscription and single-ticket sales. **Produces 7-11 plays/year. plays/year.** Query with sample pages, synopsis, and resume. Responds in 3 months. Full-length plays, translations, and adaptations.

HORIZON THEATRE CO.

P.O. Box 5376, Atlanta GA 31107. (404)523-1477. **Fax:** (404)584-8815. **Website:** www.horizontheatre.com. **Contact:** Literary Manager. Estab. 1983. Professional productions. **5+ plays/year, and workshops 6 plays as part of New South Playworks Festival plays/year.**

Buys rights to produce in Atlanta area. Accepts unsolicited résumés, samples, treatments, and summaries with SASE. Responds in 1 year. "We produce contemporary plays that seek to bridge cultures and communities, utilizing a realistic base but with heightened visual or language elements. Particularly interested in comedy, satire, plays that are entertaining and topical, but thought provoking. Also particular interest in plays by women, African-Americans, or that concern the contemporary South. No more than 8 in cast."

ILLINOIS THEATRE CENTRE

371 Artists' Walk, P.O. Box 397, Park Forest IL 60466. (708)481-3510. **Fax:** (708)481-3693. **E-mail:** ilthctr@sbcglobal.net. **Website:** www.ilthctr.org. Estab. 1976. Professional Resident Theatre Company in our own space for a subscription-based audience. **Produces 8 plays/year. plays/year.** Buys casting and directing and designer selection rights. Query with synopsis or agented submission. Pays 7-10% royalty. Responds in 2 months. All types of 2-act plays, musicals, dramas. Prefers cast size of 6-10.

INDIANA REPERTORY THEATRE

140 W. Washington St., Indianapolis IN 46204. (317)635-5277. **E-mail:** rroberts@irtlive.com. **Website:** www.irtlive.com. **Contact:** Richard J Roberts, resident dramaturg. Executive Artistic Director: Janet Allen. Estab. 1972. "Modified proscenium stage with 600 seats; thrust stage with 300 seats." Send synopsis with résumé via e-mail to the dramaturg. No unsolicited scripts. Submit year-round (season chosen by January). Responds in 6 months. Full-length plays, translations, adaptations, solo pieces. Also interested in adaptations of classic literature and plays that explore cultural/ethnic issues with a midwestern voice. Special program: Discovery Series (plays for family audiences with a focus on youth). Cast size should be 6-8.

INTERACT THEATRE CO.

The Adrienne, 2030 Sansom St., Philadelphia PA 19103. (215)568-8077. **Fax:** (215)568-8095. **E-mail:** pbonilla@interacttheatre.org. **Website:** www.interacttheatre.org. **Contact:** Peter Bonilla, literary associate.. Estab. 1988. Produces professional productions for adult audience. **Produces 4 plays/year. plays/year.** Query with synopsis and bio. No unsolicited scripts. Pays 2-8% royalty or $25-100/performance. Responds in 6 months. Contemporary dramas and comedies that explore issues of political, social, cultural or historical significance. Virtually all of our productions have political content in the foregound of the drama. Prefer plays that raise interesting questions without giving easy, predictable answers. We are interested in new plays. Limit cast to 8. No romantic comedies, family dramas, agit-prop.

JEWEL BOX THEATRE

3700 N. Walker, Oklahoma City OK 73118-7099. (405)521-7031. **Fax:** (405)525-6562. **Contact:** Charles Tweed, production director. Estab. 1956. Amateur productions. 3,000 season subscribers and general public. **Produces 6 plays/year. plays/year.** Pays $500 contest prize. Annual Playwriting Competition: Send SASE in September-October. Deadline: mid-January.

JEWISH ENSEMBLE THEATRE

6600 W. Maple Rd., West Bloomfield MI 48322. (248)788-2900. **E-mail:** e.orbach@jettheatre.org. **Website:** www.jettheatre.org. **Contact:** Evelyn Orbach, artistic director. Estab. 1989. Professional productions at the Aaron DeRoy Theatre (season), The Detroit Institue of Arts Theatre, and Scottish Rite Cathedral Theatre (schools), as well as tours to schools. **Produces 4-6 plays/year. plays/year.** Obtains rights for our season productions and staged readings for festival. Submit complete script. Pays 6-8% royalty for full production or honorarium for staged reading—$100/full-length play. Responds in 1 year. We do few children's plays except original commissions; we rarely do musicals. Cast limited to a maximum of 8 actors.

KUMU KAHUA

46 Merchant St., Honolulu HI 96813. (808)536-4222. **Fax:** (808)536-4226. **E-mail:** kumukahuatheatre@hawaiiantel.net. **Website:** kumukahua.org. Estab. 1971. Plays performed at new Kumu Kahua Theatre, flexible 120-seat theater, for community audiences. **Produces 5 productions, 3-4 public readings/year. plays/year.** Submit complete script. Pays royalty of $50/performance; usually 20 performances of each production. Responds in 4 months. Plays must have some interest for local Hawai'i audiences.

LOS ANGELES DESIGNERS' THEATRE

P.O. Box 1883, Studio City CA 91614-0883. **Contact:** Richard Niederberg, artistic dir.. Estab. Established 1970. "Professional shows/industry audience." **Produces 8-20 plays/year. plays/year.** Purchases rights by negotiation, first refusal for performance/synchronization rights only. Submit proposal only (i.e., 1 page in #10 SASE) We want highly commercial work without liens, 'understandings,' or promises to anyone. Does not return submissions accompanied by a SASE. Payment varies. Reports in 3 months (minimum) to submission. All types. "No limitations—We seek design challenges. No boring material. Shorter plays with musical underscores are desirable; nudity, street language, and political themes are OK."

MAGIC THEATRE

Fort Mason Center, Bldg. D, 3rd Floor, San Francisco CA 94123. (415)441-8001. **Fax:** (415)771-5505. **E-mail:** info@magictheatre.org. **Website:** www.magictheatre. org. **Contact:** Mark Routhier, director of artistic development.. Artistic Director: Chris Smith. Estab. 1967. Regional theater. **Produces 6 mainstage plays/ year, plus monthly reading series and several festivals each year which contain both staged readings and workshop productions. plays/year.** Bay area residents can send complete ms or query with cover letter, résumé, 1-page synopsis, SASE, dialogue sample (10-20 pages). Those outside the Bay area can query or submit through an agent. Pays royalty or per performance fee. Responds in 6-8 months. Plays that are innovative in theme and/or craft, cutting-edge sociopolitical concerns, intelligent comedy. Full-length only, strong commitment to multicultural work.

MCCARTER THEATRE

91 University Place, Princeton NJ 08540. **E-mail:** literary@mccarter.org. **Website:** www.mccarter.org. **Contact:** Literary Manager. Artistic Director: Emily Mann. Produces professional productions for a 1,077-seat and 360-seat theaters. **Produces 5 plays/year; 1 second stage play/year. plays/year.** Agented submissions only. Pays negotiable royalty. Responds in 4-6 months. Full length plays, musicals, translations.

● MELBOURNE THEATRE COMPANY

129 Ferrars St., Southbank VIC 3006, Australia. (61)(3)9684-4500. **Fax:** (61)(3)9696-2627. **E-mail:** info@mtc.com.au. **Website:** www.mtc.com.au. **Contact:** Aiden Fennessey, associate director. "MTC produces classic plays, modern revivals and the best new plays from Australia and overseas. Victorian work is given emphasis. MTC does not accept unsolicited manuscripts and it is our strict policy to return them unread. MTC does not produce work from previously unproduced Australian playwrights. New Australian plays generally come from three sources: by the commissioning of established writers; by the invitation to submit work to emerging writers with a track record and the potential to write for a mainstream subscription audience; and through a recommendation from an industry body, such as the Australian Script Centre or any of the major playwriting competitions." Responds in 3 months.

MILWAUKEE CHAMBER THEATRE

158 N. Broadway, Milwaukee Chamber Theatre, Milwaukee WI 53202. (414)276-8842. **Fax:** (414)277-4477. **E-mail:** mail@chamber-theatre.com. **Website:** www. chamber-theatre.com. **Contact:** Jaque Troy, Education Director/Literary Manager. Estab. 1975. Plays produced for adult and student audience. **Produces 5 plays/year. plays/year.** Submit query and synopsis. Submissions accompanied by a SASE will be returned. Pays royalty. Responds in 3 months. Produces literary, thought-provoking, biographical plays. Plays require small-unit settings. No plays for a large cast.

NEBRASKA THEATRE CARAVAN

6915 Cass St., Omaha NE 68132. **Fax:** (402)553-6288. **E-mail:** info@omahaplayhouse.com. **Website:** www. omahaplayhouse.com. **Contact:** Alena Furlong, development director. Artistic Director: Carl Beck. Estab. 1976. Nebraska Theatre Caravan is a touring company which produces professional productions in schools, arts centers, and small and large theaters for elementary, middle, high school and family audiences. **Produces 4-5 plays/year. plays/year.** Negotiates production rights unless the work is commissioned by us. Submit query and synopsis. Pays $20-50/performance. Responds in 3 weeks. All genres are acceptable bearing in mind the student audiences. We are truly an ensemble and like to see that in our choice of shows; curriculum ties are very important for elementary and hich school shows; 75 minutes for middle/high school shows. No sexually explicit material.

THE NEW GROUP

410 W. 42nd St., New York NY 10036. (212)244-3380. **Fax:** (212)244-3438. **E-mail:** info@thenewgroup.org. **Website:** www.thenewgroup.org. **Contact:** Ian Morgan, associate artistic director. Artistic Director: Scott Elliott. Estab. 1991. Off-Broadway theater. **Produces 4 plays/year. plays/year.** Submit 10-page sample, cover letter, résumé, synopsis, and SASE. No submissions that have already been produced in NYC. Include SASE for return of script. Pays royalty. Makes outright purchase. Responds in 9 months to submissions.

We produce challenging, character-based scripts with a contemporary sensibility. Does not want to receive musicals, historical scripts or science fiction.

NEW JERSEY REPERTORY COMPANY

179 Broadway, Long Branch NJ 07740. (732)229-3166. **E-mail:** njrep@njrep.org. **Website:** www.njrep.org. **Contact:** Joel Stone, literary manager (literary@njrep.org). Artistic Director: SuzAnne Barabas. Estab. 1997. Professional productions year-round. Previously unproduced plays and musicals only. **Produces 6 plays/year and 20 script-in-hand readings. plays/year.** Rights negotiable. Submit full script via e-mail with synopsis, cast breakdown, playwright bio to literary@njrep.org. For musicals, include mp3 of songs. Hard copies not accepted. Cast of 4 or fewer only, previously unproduced. Response time 12-18 months. For 2018 festival submissions visit http://www.njrep.org/plays/circus.htm. Responds in 12-18 months if interested. Full-length plays with a cast size no more than 4. Unit set.

NEW REPERTORY THEATRE

200 Dexter Ave., Waterton MA 02472. (617)923-7060. **Fax:** (617)923-7625. **E-mail:** artistic@newrep.org. **Website:** www.newrep.org. **Contact:** Rick Lombardo, producing artistic director. Estab. 1984. Professional theater, general audience. **Produces 5 plays/year. plays/year.** Buys production and subsidiary rights. Query with synopsis and dialogue sample. Pays 5-10% royalty. Idea laden, all styles, full-length only. New musicals.

NEW STAGE THEATRE

1100 Carlisle, Jackson MS 39202. (601)948-3533. **Fax:** (601)948-3538. **E-mail:** mail@newstagetheatre.com. **Website:** www.newstagetheatre.com. Estab. 1965. Professional productions, 8 mainstage, 3 in our 'second space.' We play to an audience comprised of Jackson, the state of Mississippi and the Southeast. **Produces 8 plays/year. plays/year.** Exclusive premiere contract upon acceptance of play for mainstage production. Submit query and synopsis. Pays 5-8% royalty. Pays $25-60/performance. Southern themes, contemporary issues, small casts (5-8), single set plays.

NEW THEATRE

4120 Laguna St., Coral Gables FL 33146. (305)443-5373. **Fax:** (305)443-1642. **E-mail:** tvodihn@new-theatre.org. **Website:** www.new-theatre.org. **Contact:** Tara Vodihn, literary manager. Estab. 1986. Profes-

sional productions. **Produces 7 plays/year. plays/year.** Rights subject to negotiation. Submit query and synopsis. Payment negotiable. Responds in 3-6 months. Interested in full-length, non-realistic, moving, intelligent, language-driven plays with a healthy dose of humor. No musicals or large casts.

NEW YORK THEATRE WORKSHOP

83 E. 4th St., New York NY 10003. **Fax:** (212)460-8996. **E-mail:** litern@nytw.org. **Website:** nytw.org. **Contact:** Literary Department. Artistic Director: James C. Nicola. Estab. 1979. "NYTW is renowned for producing intelligent and complex plays that expand the boundaries of theatrical form and in some new and compelling way address issues that are critical to our times. Plays are performed off-Broadway. Audience is New York theater-going audience and theater professionals." **Produces four to five full productions and approximately 50 readings/year. plays/year.** Prefer email submissions. Type "synopsis submission." If mailing: Query with cover letter, synopsis, 10-page dialogue sample, 2 letters of recommendation; SASE if requesting return of materials. Include tape/CD/video where appropriate. Responds in 6-10 months. Full-length plays, translations/adaptations, music theater pieces; proposals for performance projects. Socially relevant issues, innovative form, and language.

NORTHLIGHT THEATRE

9501 Skokie Blvd., Skokie IL 60077. (847)679-9501. **Fax:** (847)679-1879. **E-mail:** kleahey@northlight.org. **Website:** www.northlight.org. **Contact:** Kristin Leahey, Dramaturg. Artistic Director: BJ Jones; Lynn Baber, Artistic Administrator, at lbaber@northlight.org. Estab. 1975. "We are a professional, equity theater, LORT C. We have a subscription base of over 8,000 and have a significant number of single ticket buyers." **Produces 5 plays/year. plays/year.** Buys production rights, plus royalty on future mountings. Query with 10-page dialogue sample, synopsis, resume/bio, and SASE/SASPC for response. Pays royalty. Responds in 3-4 months. Full-length plays, translations, adaptations, musicals. Interested in plays of 'ideas'; plays that are passionate and/or hilarious; accessible plays that challenge, incite, and reflect the beliefs of our society/community. Generally looking for cast size of 6 or fewer, but there are exceptions made for the right play.

OMAHA THEATER CO./ROSE THEATER

2001 Farnam St., Omaha NE 68102. (402)345-9718. **E-mail:** jlarsonotc@msn.com. **Website:** www.rose-theater.org. **Contact:** James Larson, artistic director. "Our target audience is children, preschool through high school, and their parents." **Produces 6-10 plays/year. plays/year.** Submit query and synopsis. Send SASE. Pays royalty. Responds in 9 months. Plays must be geared to children and parents (PG rating). Titles recognized by the general public have a stronger chance of being produced. Cast limit: 25 (8-10 adults). No adult scripts.

☺ ONE ACT PLAY DEPOT

Box 335, Spiritwood Saskatchewan S0J 2M0, Canada. **E-mail:** submissions@oneactplays.net. **Website:** http://oneactplays.net. "Accepts unsolicited submissions only in February of each year." Submit complete script by mail or e-mail. : one-act plays. Does not want musicals or farces. Do not mail originals. Plays should run between 10 and 60 minutes.

O'NEILL MUSIC THEATER CONFERENCE

Eugene O'Neill Theater Center, 305 Great Neck Rd., Waterford CT 06385. (860)443-5378. **Fax:** (860)443-9653. **E-mail:** theaterlives@theoneill.org. **Website:** www.theoneill.org. **Contact:** Jill A. Anderson, general manager.. Estab. 1964. "At The Music Theater Conference, creative artists are in residence with artistic staff and an equity company of actors/singers. Public and private readings, script in hand, piano only." An open submission process begins in the fall of each year and concludes in May. The conference takes place in July and August at the O'Neill Theater Center. Works are accepted based on their readiness to be performed, but when there is still enough significant work to be accomplished that a fully staged production would be premature. For guidelines and application deadlines, send SASE or see guidelines online. Pays stipend, room and board.

PIONEER DRAMA SERVICE, INC.

P.O. Box 4267, Englewood CO 80155-4267. (303)779-4035. **Fax:** (303)779-4315. **E-mail:** editors@pioneerdrama.com. **Website:** www.pioneerdrama.com. **Contact:** Brian Taylor, Acquisitions Editor. Plays are performed for audiences of all ages. Playwrights paid 50% royalty (10% sales) split when there are multiple authors/composers. Publishes plays that are performed by schools, colleges, community theaters, recreation programs, churches, and professional children's theaters for audiences of all ages. For musicals, query with character breakdown, synopsis and set description or submit full ms and CD of music. Include SASE.

Retains all rights. All submissions automatically entered in Shubert Fendrich Memorial Playwriting Contest. SASE for guidelines. Retains all rights. Responds in 6 months. "We seek full length children's musicals, high school musicals, and one-act children's musicals to be performed by children, secondary school students, and/or adults. We want musicals that are easy to perform, simple sets, many female roles, and very few solos. Must be appropriate for educational market. We are not interested in profanity, themes with exclusively adult interest, sex, drinking, smoking, etc."

PITTSBURGH PUBLIC THEATER

621 Penn Ave., Pittsburgh PA 15222. (412)316-8200. **Fax:** (412)316-8216. **Website:** www.ppt.org. **Contact:** Dramaturg. Artistic Director: Ted Pappas. Estab. 1975. O'Reilly Theater, 650 seats, thrust seating. **Produces 7 plays/year. plays/year.** Submit full script through agent, or query with synopsis, cover letter, 10-page dialogue sample, and SASE. Responds in 4 months. Full-length plays, adaptations and musicals.

PLAYSCRIPTS, INC.

450 7th Ave., Suite 809, New York NY 10023. Phone/**Fax:** (866)639-7529. **E-mail:** submissions@playscripts.com. **Website:** www.playscripts.com. Estab. 1998. Audience is professional, community, college, high school, middle school, and children's theaters worldwide. Contracts for exclusive publication and performance licensing rights. See website for complete submission guidelines. "Materials accompanied by SASE will be returned; however, submissions sent through our website at www.playscripts.com/submit are strongly preferred." Pays negotiated book and production royalties. Responds in 3-6 months. "We are open to a wide diversity of writing styles and content. Unsolicited musicals are not accepted."

THE PLAYWRIGHTS' CENTER'S PLAYLABS

2301 Franklin Ave. E., Minneapolis MN 55406. (612)332-7481. **Fax:** (612)332-6037. **E-mail:** info@pwcenter.org. **Website:** www.pwcenter.org. Producing Artistic Director: Polly K. Carl. Estab. 1971. PlayLabs is a 2-week developmental workshop for new plays. The program is held in Minneapolis and is open by script competition. Up to 5 new plays are given reading performances and after the festival, a script sample and contact link are posted on the Center's website. Announcements of playwrights by May 1. Playwrights receive honoraria, travel expenses, room and board. We are interested in playwrights with ambitions for a sustained career in theater, and scripts that could benefit from development involving professional dramaturgs, directors, and actors. US citizens or permanent residents only. Participants must attend entire festival. Submission deadline in October; see website for application and exact deadline. No previously produced materials.

PLAYWRIGHTS HORIZONS

416 W. 42nd St., New York NY 10036. (212)564-1235. **Fax:** (212)594-0296. **E-mail:** lit@phnyc.org. **Website:** www.playwrightshorizons.org. **Contact:** Sarah Lunnie, literary manager. Estab. 1971. Plays performed off-Broadway for a literate, urban, subscription audience. **Produces 6 plays/year. plays/year.** Negotiates for future rights. Submit complete ms with author bio and resume; include CD for musicals. Pays royalty. Makes outright purchase. Responds in 6-8 months. "We are looking for new, full-length plays and musicals by American authors."

PLAYWRIGHTS' PLATFORM

398 Columbus Ave., #604, Boston MA 02116. **Website:** www.playwrightsplatform.org. **Contact:** Regina Eliot-Ramsey, president. Estab. 1972. "Our website contains all information regarding The Platform. The Platform provides dues paying members with the opportunity to read their plays before an audience. Meetings are held at Rosen Auditorium, Brennan Library, Lasell College, Auburndale, MA 02466. Scripts should not be mailed. Readings must be requested through the calendar coordinator. Only dues paying members can submit scripts and are allowed to participate in Platform productions. The Platform produces a short play festival each year in June, held at the Boston Playwrights Theatre, Boston, MA. Only dues paying members can participate. Short one acts, and scenes from full-length plays can be read throughout the calendar year. The festival only produces plays with running times of 20 minutes or less. Members come from the northeast region and are not limited to Massachusetts. There are no restrictions on content." **Produces approximately 50 readings/year plays/year.** Submit script and SASE (or e-mail or hand deliver). Responds in 2 months. "Any types of plays. We will not accept scripts we think are sexist or racist. Massachusetts residents only. There are no restrictions on length or number of characters, but it's more difficult to schedule full-length pieces."

PORTLAND STAGE CO.

P.O. Box 1458, Portland ME 04104. (207)774-1043. **Fax:** (207)774-0576. **E-mail:** literary@portlandstage.org. **Website:** www.portlandstage.org. **Contact:** Todd Brian Backus, literary manager. Artistic Director: Anita Stewart. Estab. 1974. Professional productions at Portland Stage Company. **Produces 7 plays/year. plays/year.** Buys 3- or 4-week run in Maine. Send first 10 pages with synopsis. Pays royalty. Responds in 3-6 months. Developmental Staged Readings: Little Festival of the Unexpected.

PRINCE MUSIC THEATER

1412 Chestnut St., Philadelphia PA 19102. **E-mail:** info@princemusictheater.org. **Website:** www.princemusictheater.org. Estab. 1984. "Professional musical productions. Drawing upon operatic and popular traditions as well as European, African, Asian, and South American forms, new work, and new voices take center stage." **Produces 4 musicals/year. plays/year.** Send synopsis and sample audio tape with no more than 4 songs. Pays royalty. Responds in 6 months. Song-driven music theater, varied musical styles. Nine-member orchestra, 10-14 cast, 36x60 stage.

PRINCETON REP COMPANY

44 Nassau St., Suite 350, Princeton NJ 08542. **E-mail:** prcreprap@aol.com. **Website:** www.princetonrep.org. **Contact:** New Play Submissions. Estab. 1984. Plays are performed in site-specific venues, outdoor amphitheatres, and indoor theatres with approximately 199 seats. Princeton Rep Company works under Actors' Equity contracts, and its directors are members of the SSDC. Rights are negotiated on a play-by-play basis. Query with synopsis, SASE, résumé, and 10 pages of sample dialogue. Submissions accompanied by a SASE will be returned. Payment negotiated on a play-by-play basis. Responds in up to 2 years. Stories that investigate the lives of middle and working class people. Love stories of the rich, famous, and fatuous. If the play demands a cast of thousands, please don't waste your time and postage. No drama or comedy set in a prep school or ivy league college.

THE PUBLIC THEATER

425 Lafayette St., New York NY 10003. (212)539-8500. **Website:** www.publictheater.org. **Contact:** Literary Department. Artistic Director: Oskar Eustis. Estab. 1964. Professional productions. **Produces 6 plays/year. plays/year.** Query with synopsis, 10-page sample, letter of inquiry, cassette with 3-5 songs for musi-

cals/operas. Responds in 3 months. Full-length plays, translations, adapatations, musicals, operas, and solo pieces. All genres, no one-acts.

THE PURPLE ROSE THEATRE CO.

137 Park St., Chelsea MI 48118. (734)433-7782. **Fax:** (734)475-0802. **Website:** www.purplerosetheatre. org. **Contact:** Guy Sanville, artistic director. Artistic Director: Guy Sanville. Estab. 1990. "PRTC is a regional theater with an S.P.T. equity contract which produces plays intended for Midwest/Middle American audience. It is dedicated to creating opportunities for Midwest theatre professionals." **Produces 4 plays/year. plays/year.** Query with synopsis, character breakdown, and 10-page dialogue sample. Pays 5-10% royalty. Responds in 9 months. Modern, topical full length, 75-120 minutes. Prefers scripts that use comedy to deal with serious subjects. 8 cast maximum. No fly space, unit set preferable. Intimate 168 seat 3/4 thrust house.

RESOURCE PUBLICATIONS

160 E. Virginia St., Suite 170, San Jose CA 95112-5176. (408)286-8505. **Fax:** (408)287-8748. **E-mail:** editor@ rpinet.com. **Website:** www.resourcepublications.com. Estab. 1973. Audience includes laity and ordained seeking resources (books/periodicals/software) in Christian ministry, worship, faith formation, education, and counseling (primarily Roman Catholic, but not all). Submit query and synopsis via e-mail. Responds in 3 months. : materials for those in pastoral ministry, faith formation, youth ministry, and parish administration. No fiction, children's books, or music.

SALTWORKS THEATRE CO.

569 N. Neville St., Pittsburgh PA 15213. (412)621-6150. **Fax:** (412)621-6010. **E-mail:** nalrutz@saltworks.org. **Website:** www.saltworks.org. **Contact:** Norma Alrutz, executive director. Estab. 1981. **Produces 8-10 plays/ year. plays/year.** Obtains regional performance rights for educational grants. Submit query and synopsis. Pays $25/performance. Responds in 2 months. Wants plays for children, youth, and families that address social issues like violence prevention, sexual responsibility, peer pressures, tobacco use, bullying, racial issues/diversity, drug and alcohol abuse (grades 1-12). Limited to 5 member cast, 2 men/2 women/1 either.

SEATTLE REPERTORY THEATRE

P.O. Box 900923, Seattle WA 98109. **E-mail:** bradena@ seattlerep.org. **Website:** www.seattlerep.org. **Contact:**

Braden Abraham, associate artistic director. Artistic Director: Jerry Manning. Estab. 1963. **Produces 8 plays/year. plays/year.** Buys percentage of future royalties. Send query, resume, synopsis and 10 sample pages. Pays royalty. Responds in 6 months. "The Seattle Repertory Theatre produces eclectic programming. We welcome a wide variety of writing."

SECOND STAGE THEATRE

305 W. 43rd St., New York NY 10036. (212)246-4422. **Fax:** (212)399-4115. **E-mail:** cburney@2st.com. **Website:** www.2st.com. **Contact:** Christopher Burney, associate artistic director. Estab. 1979. "Second Stage Theatre gives new life to contemporary American plays through 'second stagings'; provides emerging authors with their Off-Broadway debuts; and produces world premieres by America's most respected playwrights. Adult and teen audiences." **Produces 6 plays/year. plays/year.** Query with synopsis and 10-page writing sample or agented submission. Payment varies. Responds in 6 months. "We need socio-political plays, comedies, musicals, dramas—full lengths for full production."

☉ SHAW FESTIVAL THEATRE

P.O. Box 774, Niagara-on-the-Lake ON L0S 1J0, Canada. (905)468-2153. **Fax:** (905)468-7140. **Website:** www. shawfest.com. **Contact:** Jackie Maxwell, artistic director. Estab. 1962. Professional theater company operating 3 theaters (Festival: 869 seats; Court House: 327 seats; Royal George: 328 seats). Shaw Festival presents the work of George Bernard Shaw and his contemporaries written during his lifetime (1856-1950) and in 2000 expanded the mandate to include contemporary works written about the period of his lifetime. **Produces 12 plays/year. plays/year.** We prefer to hold rights for Canada and northeastern US, also potential to tour. Query with SASE or SAE and IRC's, depending on country of origin. Pays 5-10% royalty. We operate an acting ensemble of up to 75 actors; and we have sophisticated production facilities. During the summer season (April-November) the Academy of the Shaw Festival organizes workshops of new plays commissioned for the company.

SOUTH COAST REPERTORY

P.O. Box 2197, Costa Mesa CA 92628-2197. (714)708-5500. **Fax:** (714)545-0391. **Website:** www.scr.org. **Contact:** Kelly Miller, Literary Manager. Artistic Directors: Martin Benson and David Emmes. Estab. 1964. Professional nonprofit theater; a member of LORT and TCG. "We operate in our own facility which houses the 507-seat Segerstrom stage and 336-seat Julianne Argyros stage. We have a combined subscription audience of 18,000. We commit ourselves to exploring the most urgent human and social issues of our time, and to merging literature, design and performance in ways that test the bounds of theatre's artistic possibilities." **Produces 14 plays/year. plays/year.** Acquires negotiable rights. Query with synopsis and 10 sample pages of dialogue, and full list of characters. Pays royalty. Responds in 1-2 months on queries; 6-9 months on full scripts. "We produce full-length contemporary plays, as well as theatre for young audiences, scripts geared toward a 4th grade target audience with a running time of approximately 65 minutes. We prefer plays that address contemporary concerns and are dramaturgically innovative. A play whose cast is larger than 15-20 will need to be extremely compelling, and its cast size must be justifiable."

SOUTHERN APPALACHIAN REPERTORY THEATRE (SART)

P.O. Box 1720, Mars Hill NC 28754. (828)689-1384. **E-mail:** sart@mhc.edu. **Contact:** Bill Gregg, producing artistic director; LoriLynn Mullett, business manager. Estab. 1975. Since 1975, the Southern Appalachian Repertory Theatre has produced over 50 world premieres in the 166-seat Owen Theater on the Mars Hill College campus. SART is a professional summer theatre company whose audiences range from students to senior citizens. SART also conducts an annual playwrights' conference called ScriptFEST in which 4-5 playwrights are invited for a weekend of public readings of their new scripts. The conference is held in the fall of each year. Submissions must be postmarked between August 1 and September 30. If a script read at the conference is selected for production, it will be given a fully-staged production in an upcoming SART summer season. Playwrights receive honorarium and housing. **Produces 5-6 plays/year. plays/year.** "No film or television scripts, translations, or adaptations. Please send 2 hard copies of the script on white paper, standard 3-hole punched, or, better yet, in a binder. Must be full-length plays and musicals, synopsis, and a recording of at least 4 songs (for musicals). No one-acts or children's plays. Include name and contact information only on a separate cover sheet. New plays are defined as those that have not been published and have not received a fully-staged professional produc-

tion. Workshops and other readings do not constitute a fully-staged production. Check website for detailed submission guidelines."

STAGE LEFT THEATRE

3408 N. Sheffield, Chicago IL 60657. (773)883-8830. **E-mail:** scripts@stagelefttheatre.com. **Website:** www.stagelefttheatre.com. **Contact:** Zev Valancy, literary manager. Estab. 1982. "Professional productions for all audiences." **Produces 2-3 mainstage productions and 1 new-play workshop festival per season. "There are also 2 playwright residencies per season, with applications accepted winter/spring. Please see website for details." plays/year.** Submit script through an agent or query with cover letter, 10-page excerpt, 1-page synopsis, SASE, supporting material, and résumé. E-mail submissions preferred. Responds in 3 months. "any length, any genre, any style that fits the Stage Left mission—to produce plays that raise debate on political and social issues. We do have an emphasis on new work."

TEATRO VISIÓN

1700 Alum Rock Ave., Suite 265, San José CA 95116. (408)272-9926. **Fax:** (408)928-5589. **E-mail:** elisamarina@teatrovision.org. **Website:** www.teatrovision.org. **Contact:** Elisa Marina Alvarado, artistic director.. Estab. 1984. Professional productions for a Latino population. **Produces 3 plays/year. plays/year.** Query with synopsis or submit complete ms. Responds in 6 months. We produce plays by Latino playwrights—plays that highlight the Chicano/Latino experience.

THE TEN-MINUTE MUSICALS PROJECT

P.O. Box 461194, West Hollywood CA 90046. **E-mail:** info@tenminutemusicals.org. **Website:** www.tenminutemusicals.org. **Contact:** Michael Koppy, producer. Estab. 1987. "Plays performed in Equity regional theaters in the US and Canada. Deadline August 31; notification by November 30." **Produces 1-10 plays/year. plays/year.** Buys first performance rights. Complete guidelines and information at website. Pays $250 royalty advance upon selection, against equal share of performance royalties when produced. Looking for complete short stage musicals lasting 8-15 minutes. Limit cast to 9. "No parodies—original music only."

THEATER AT LIME KILN

P.O. Box 1244, Lexington VA 24450. **Website:** www.theateratlimekiln.com. Estab. 1984. Outdoor summer theater (May through October) and indoor space

(October through May, 144 seats). **Produces 3 (1 new) plays/year. plays/year.** Buys performance rights. Submit query and synopsis. Include SASE for return of submitted materials. Pays $25-75/performance. Responds in 3 months. Plays that explore the history and heritage of the Appalachian region. Minimum set required.

THEATER BY THE BLIND

306 W. 18th St., New York NY 10011. (212)243-4337. **Fax:** (212)243-4337. **E-mail:** gar@nyc.rr.com. **Website:** www.tbtb.org. **Contact:** Ike Schambelan, artistic director.. Estab. 1979. Off Broadway, Theater Row, general audiences, seniors, students, disabled. If play transfers, we'd like a piece. **Produces 2 plays/year. plays/year.** Submit complete script. Pays $1,000-1,500/production. Responds in 3 months. Genres about blindness.

THEATRE BUILDING CHICAGO

1225 W. Belmont Ave., Chicago IL 60657. (773)929-7367 ext. 229. **Fax:** (773)327-1404. **E-mail:** allan@theatrebuildingchicago.org. **Website:** www.theatre-buildingchicago.org. **Contact:** Allan Chambers, artistic director. "Develops and produces readings of new musicals and Stages festival of new music, some works developed in our writers' workshop. Some scripts produced are unagented submissions. Developmental readings and workshops performed in 3 small off-Loop theaters are seating 148 for a general theater audience, urban/suburban mix." Submit synopsis, sample scene, CD or cassette tape and piano/vocal score of three songs, and author bios along with Stages Festival application, available on our website. Responds in 3 months. "Musicals *only.* We're interested in all forms of musical theater including more innovative styles. Our production capabilities are limited by the lack of space, but we're very creative and authors should submit anyway. The smaller the cast, the better. We are especially interested in scripts using a younger (35 and under) ensemble of actors. We mostly look for authors who are interested in developing their scripts through workshops, readings and production. We rarely work on one-man shows or 'single author' pieces."

THEATRE IV

114 W. Broad St., Richmond VA 23220. (804)783-1688. **Fax:** (804)775-2325. **E-mail:** j.serresseque@theatreivrichmond.org. **Website:** www.theatreiv.org. **Contact:** Janine Serresseque.. Estab. 1975. National tour of plays for young audiences—maximum cast of 5, maximum length of an hour. Mainstage plays for young audiences in 600 or 350 seat venues. **Produces approximately 20 plays/year. plays/year.** Buys standard production rights. Submit query and synopsis. Include SASE for return of submission. Payment varies. Responds in 1 month. Touring and mainstage plays for young audiences. Touring—maximum cast of 5, length of 60 minutes.

THEATRE THREE

P.O. Box 512, 412 Main St., Port Jefferson NY 11777-0512. (631)928-9202. **Fax:** (631)928-9120. **Website:** www.theatrethree.com. **Contact:** Jeffrey Sanzel, artistic director. Estab. 1969. "We produce an Annual Festival of One-Act Plays on our Second Stage. Deadline for submission is September 30. Send SASE for festival guidelines or visit website." We ask for exclusive rights up to and through the festival. Include SASE. No email submissions. Guidelines online. Pays $75 for the run of the festival. Responds in 6 months. One-act plays. Maximum length: 40 minutes. Any style, topic, etc. We require simple, suggested sets and a maximum cast of 6. No adaptations, musicals or children's works.

THEATRE WEST

3333 Cahuenga Blvd. W., Hollywood CA 90068-1365. (323)851-4839. **Fax:** (323)851-5286. **E-mail:** theatrewest@theatrewest.org. **Website:** www.theatrewest.org. **Contact:** Chris DiGiovanni and Doug Haverty, moderators of the Writers Workshop. Estab. 1962. "We operate a 168 seat theater under a letter of agreement with Actors Equity, including a TYA contract for young audiences. Audiences are primarily young urban professionals. Residence in Southern California is vital as it's a weekly workshop." Contracts a percentage of writer's share to other media if produced on MainStage by Theatre West. Submit script, résumé and letter requesting membership. Pays royalty based on gross box office. Responds in 4 months. Full-length plays only, no one-acts. Uses minimalistic scenery, no fly space.

THEATREWORKS

P.O. Box 50458, Palo Alto CA 94303. (650)463-1950. **Fax:** (650)463-1963. **E-mail:** kent@theatreworks.org. **Website:** www.theatreworks.org. **Contact:** Kent Nicholson, new works director. Estab. 1970. Specializes in development of new musicals. Plays are professional productions intended for an adult audience. **Produc-**

es 8 plays/year. **plays/year.** Buys performance rights. Submit synopsis, 10 pages of sample dialogue, and SASE. Include SASE for return of submission. Payment varies per contract. Responds in 6-8 months. TheatreWorks has a high standard for excellence. We prefer well-written, well-constructed plays that celebrate the human spirit through innovative productions and programs inspired by our exceptionally diverse community. There is no limit on the number of characters, and we favor plays with multi-ethnic casting possibilities. We are a LORT C company. Plays are negotiated per playwright. Does not want one-acts, plays with togas. We are particularly interested in plays with musical elements.

UNICORN THEATRE

3828 Main St., Kansas City MO 64111. (816)531-7529. **Fax:** (816)531-0421. **Website:** www.unicorntheatre. org. **Contact:** Herman Wilson, literary assistant.. Producing Artistic Director: Cynthia Levin. "We are a professional Equity Theatre. Typically, we produce plays dealing with contemporary issues." **Produces 6-8 plays/year. plays/year.** Send complete script (to Herman Wilson) with brief synopsis, cover letter, bio, character breakdown. Send #10 SASE for results. Does not return scripts. Responds in 4-8 months. Prefers contemporary (post-1950) scripts. Does not accept musicals, one-acts, or historical plays.

URBAN STAGES

555 8th Avenue #1800, New York NY 10018. (212)421-1380. **Fax:** (212)421-1387. **E-mail:** lschmiedel@ urbanstages.org. **Website:** www.urbanstages.org. **Contact:** Lauren Schmiedel, managing director. Estab. 1986. Professional productions off Broadway—throughout the year. General audience. **Produces 2-4 plays/year. plays/year.** If produced, option for 1 year. Submit complete script year-round, no submission fee. Enter Emerging Playwright Award competition. Prize is $500, plus NYC production. Pays royalty. Responds in 4 months. Full-length; generally 1 set or styled playing dual. Good imaginative, creative writing. Cast limited to 3-6.

WALNUT STREET THEATRE

Ninth and Walnut Streets, Philadelphia PA 19107. (215)574-3550. **Fax:** (215)574-3598. **Contact:** Literary Office. Producing Artistic Director: Bernard Havard. Estab. 1809. Our plays are performed in our own space. WST has 3 theaters—a proscenium (mainstage), 1,052 seats; and 2 studios, 79-99 seats. We have a sub-

scription audience—the largest in the nation. **Produces 10 plays/year. plays/year.** Rights negotiated per project. If you have written a play or musical that you feel is appropriate for the Walnut Street Theatre's Mainstage or Independence Studio on 3, please send the following: 1-2 page synopsis, 5-10 page excerpt from the scrip, a character breakdown, bios for the playwright, composer, lyricist, and any other artistic collaborators, Demo CD with tracks clearly labeled (musicals only). Include SASE for return of materials. Pays negotiable royalty or makes outright purchase. Responds in 5 months. Full-length dramas and comedies, musicals, translations, adaptations, and revues. The studio plays must have a cast of no more than 4 and use simple sets.

WILLOWS THEATRE CO.

636 Ward St., Martinez CA 94553-1651. **Website:** www.willowstheatre.org. Artistic Director: Richard Elliott. Professional productions for a suburban audience. **Produces 6 plays/year. plays/year.** Accepting only commercially viable, small-medium size comedies right now. Guidelines are online at website. Send synopsis, character breakdown, resume, SASE. Do not send full script unless invited to do so. Do not email submission or email the office for information on your submission. Pays standard royalty. Responds in 6 months to scripts. Commercially viable, small-medium size musicals or comedies that are popular, rarely produced, or new. Certain stylized plays or musicals with a contemporary edge to them (e.g., *Les Liasons Dangereuses, La Bete, Candide*). No more than 15 actors. Unit or simple sets with no fly space, no more than 7 pieces. We are not interested in 1-character pieces.

WOMEN'S PROJECT AND PRODUCTIONS

55 West End Ave., New York NY 10023. (212)765-1706. **Fax:** (212)765-2024. **Website:** www.womensproject. org. **Contact:** Megan E. Carter, Associate Artistic Director. Estab. 1978. Professional Off-Broadway productions. Agented submissions only. **Produces 3 plays/year. plays/year.** Please see website for submission guidelines and details. "We are looking for full-length plays written by women."

THREE WAYS FOR WRITERS TO FOLLOW UP

by Robert Lee Brewer

Over the years, I've found many of the most successful writers share one quality in common: They are good at following up. In that vein, here are three practical ways writers can (and probably should) follow up.

FOLLOW UP ON SUBMISSIONS

If there's a typical response time in the submission guidelines, wait for that time to elapse before following up. If there's not, follow up a month after submitting. Be professional and phrase your follow up in a way that doesn't point fingers.

FOLLOW UP ON REJECTIONS

Rejections are opportunities to make a good impression on an editor or agent. When you receive a rejection, thank the person for the response and ask when the next submission period is—or thank the person, while also including a new idea or two. Both strategies have worked on me as an editor.

FOLLOW UP ON PAYMENT

As soon as you receive payment, follow up with the editor to let them know, "Hey! I received my payment. Thanks so much! By the way, I have some new pitches for you, and here they are." If you did a great job, then editors will appreciate knowing they can come back to you for future assignments.

SCREENWRITING

For years, *Writer's Market* for has focused solely on the most traditional publishing formats, including getting published in consumer magazines and trade journals and by book publishers with the assistance of literary agents, as well as writing contests. Those markets aren't going away, but we can add in other venues, including playwriting and screenwriting.

Screenwriting is a unique market in that writers create scripts that are likely to be only the springboard to the collaborative effort involved with films. Whether writing full-length movies or shorter pieces, screenwriters are bound to have revisions to their scripts made by directors, actors, and producers. But that's okay.

What gets the whole process started is an amazing script that could last for two hours or two minutes...or, more likely, somewhere in between.

SCREENWRITING

///

⊘ ALLIANCE FILMWORKS

9595 Wilshire Blvd., Suite 900, Beverly Hills CA 90212. **Website:** www.alliancefilmworks.com. Estab. 2001. Produces 3 movies/year. *Alliance is not accepting unsolicited TV or film submissions, screenplays, pitches, log lines or treatments at this time.* Pays option; makes outright purchase.

○   Produces all genres. Budgets are $1.5 million+.

ALLIED ARTISTS, INC.

2251 N. Rampart Blvd., 1479, Las Vegas NV 89128. (702)991-9011. **E-mail:** query@alliedartistsonline.com. **Website:** www.alliedartistsonline.com. Estab. 1990. Produces material for broadcast and cable television, home video, and film **Buys 3-5 scripts/year. scripts/year. Uses Works with 10-20 writers/year. writers/year.** Buys first or all rights. Submit synopsis, outline. Pays in accordance with writer's guild standards. Responds in 2 months to queries. Responds in 3 months to mss.

TIPS "We are looking for positive, uplifting dramatic stories involving 'real people' situations. Future trend is for more reality-based programming, as well as interactive television programs for viewer participation. Send brief e-mail query only. Do not send scripts or additional material until requested. No phone pitches accepted."

AMERICAN WORLD PICTURES, INC.

16027 Ventura Blvd., Suite 320, Encino CA 91436. (818)380-9100. **Fax:** (818)380-0050. **E-mail:** jason@americanworldpictures.com. **Website:** www.americanworldpictures.com. **Contact:** Jason Corey, acquisitions. **Buys 4 scripts/year. scripts/year. Uses Works with 5 writers/year. writers/year.** Buys all rights. Query. Pays only $15,000 for scripts. Do not contact if price is more than that. Responds in 2 months to queries. Responds in 3 months to mss.

○   Needs feature-length films. Send DVD/VHS to the Acquisitions Department.

TIPS "Use strong characters and strong dialogue."

AUTOMATIC PICTURES

5225 Wilshire Blvd., Ste. 525, Los Angeles CA 90036. (323)935-1800. **Fax:** (323)935-8040. **E-mail:** azentertainment@hotmail.com. **Website:** www.automaticpictures.net. **Contact:** Frank Beddor, producer. Credits include *There's Something About Mary* and *Wicked*.

○   Looking for comedy, horror, or romantic comedy.

BIG EVENT PICTURES

3940 Laurel Canyon Blvd., #1137, Studio City CA 91604. **E-mail:** bigevent1@bigeventpictures.com. **Contact:** Michael Cargile, president. "Produces G, PG, and R-rated feature films for theaters, cable TV, and home video." Query by e-mail. Producers will respond if interested.

TIPS "Interesting query letters intrigue us—and tell us something about the writer. Query letter should include a short log line or pitch encapsulating what this story is about and should be no more than 1 page in length. We look for unique stories with strong characters and would like to see more action and science fiction submissions. We make movies that we would want to see. Producers are known for encouraging new/unproduced screenwriters and giving real consideration to their scripts."

BIZAZZ MEDIA

3760 Grand View Blvd., Los Angeles CA 90066. (310)390-9360. **E-mail:** rupert@bizazzmedia.com. **Website:** www.bizazzmedia.com. **Contact:** Rupert Hitzig. "Bizazz Media is a full service video production company, built around Emmy and Peabody Award winning Producer Rupert Hitzig and a diverse cast of creative professionals with experienced vision. We specialize in the production of documentaries, electronic press kits, marketing videos, corporate videos, industrial videos, and training films. Whether it's for broadcast, non- broadcast presentation, or the Internet, our productions are engaging, informative, and never dull!"

SAM BLATE ASSOCIATES, LLC

10331 Watkins Mill Dr., Montgomery Village MD 20886-3950. (301)840-2248. **Fax:** (301)990-0707. **E-mail:** info@writephotopro.com. **Website:** www.writephotopro.com. **Contact:** Sam Blate, CEO. Produces educational and multimedia for marine, fishing, boating, business, education, institutions and state and federal governments. **Uses Works with 2 local writers/year on a per-project basis—it varies as to business conditions and demand. writers/year.** Buys first rights when possible Query with writing samples and SASE for return. Payment depends on contact with client. Pays some expenses. Responds in 1 month to queries.

TIPS Writers must have a strong track record of technical and aesthetic excellence.

CHEYENNE ENTERPRISES

406 Wilshire Blvd., Santa Monica CA 90401. (310)455-5000. **Fax:** (310)688-8000. **E-mail:** info@rifkin-eberts.com. **Website:** www.rifkin-ebertsproductions.com. Production company of actor Bruce Willis; credits include *Bandits, Hart's War, Timber Falls.*

CONTEMPTIBLE ENTERTAINMENT

c/o USA Films, 9333 Wilshire Blvd., Beverly Hills CA 90210. (310)385-4183. **Fax:** (310)385-6633. Production company of actor/director Neil Labute. Credits include *Your Friends & Neighbors, In the Company of Men, Nurse Betty.*

LEE DANIELS ENTERTAINMENT

315 W. 36th St., Suite 1002, New York NY 10018. (212)334-8110. **Fax:** (212)334-8290. **E-mail:** info@leedanielsentertainment.com. **Website:** www.leedanielsentertainment.com. VP of Development We work in all aspects of entertainment, including film, television, and theater. All nonagency scripts must be accompanied by a signed copy of the submission release form, which can be downloaded from the website. All scripts should be registered or copyrighted for your protection. All scripts should be in standard screenplay format. Include a synopsis, logline, and character breakdown (including lead and supporting roles). Do not send any extraneous materials.

TIPS Lee Daniels produced *Monster's Ball* and *The Woodsman*, and produced/directed *Shadowboxer.* He is the first African-American sole producer of an Academy-Award-winning film.

ESCAPE ARTISTS

10202 W. Washington Blvd., Lean, No. 333, Culver City CA 90232. (310)244-8833. **Fax:** (310)244-2151. Lead developers and producers include Steve Tisch, Todd Black and Jason Blumenthal. Credits include *The Weather Man* (2005), *Alex & Emma* (2003) and *A Knight's Tale (2001).*

TIPS Escape Artists distributes its films domestically via Columbia Pictures and internationally via Summit Entertainment.

FAST CARRIER PICTURES, INC.

820 Majorca Place, Los Angeles CA 90049. (213)300-1896. **E-mail:** fastcarriervp@aol.com. **Website:** www.fastcarrier.com. **Contact:** Rory Aylward. Estab. 2000. Mass market motion picture/TV audience. **Buys 1-2 scripts/year. scripts/year. Uses Works with 1-2 writers/year. writers/year.** No options or cash up front.

Query with synopsis. No teen sex comedies, large science fiction movies, historical epics, serial killer movies, or gross violence and humor at the expense of women, children, or minorities.

O Our bread basket is cable, broadcast, and smaller theatrical films in the following genres: women in jeopardy, low-budget family movies tied to a holiday, low-budget westerns, horror, and romantic comedy.

GINTY FILMS

16255 Ventura Blvd., Suite 625, Encino CA 91436. (310)277-1408. **E-mail:** ginty@robertginty.com. **Website:** www.robertginty.com. **Contact:** Robert Ginty. Estab. 1989. Commercial audience. **Buys 12-15 scripts/year. scripts/year. Uses Works with 10-20 writers/year. writers/year.** Buys first rights, all rights. Query with synopsis. Pays in accordance with WGA standards. Responds in 1 month to queries. Responds in 1 month to mss.

GREY LINE ENTERTAINMENT

115 W. California Blvd., #310, Pasadena CA 91105-3005. (626)943-0950. **E-mail:** submissions@greyline.net. **Website:** www.greyline.net. **Contact:** Sara Miller, submissions coordinator. Grey Line Entertainment is a full-service motion picture production and literary management company. We offer direct management of all services associated with the exploitation of stories. When our clients' motion picture screenplays are ready for the marketplace, we place them directly with studios or with major co-producers who can assist in packaging cast and/or director before approaching financiers (Warner Bros., New Line, Fox, Disney, etc.), or broadcasters (HBO, Showtime, etc.). Query via e-mail only. No attachments. Review online submission guidelines before sending. Responds in 2 weeks to queries.

O Queries for screenplays and treatments should consist of a compelling and business-like letter giving us a brief overview of your story and a 1-sentence pitch. Be sure to include your return address and a phone number. No multiple submissions. Treatments and screenplays submitted without a completed and signed Grey Line submission form will be discarded. Include SASE for reply. We recommend you register your screenplays/treatments with the copyright office or WGA before submitting.

TIPS Your work must be finished and properly edited before seeking our representation (meaning proofread, spell-checked, and rewritten until it's perfect).

BETH GROSSBARD PRODUCTIONS

9696 Culver Blvd., Suite 208, Culver City CA 90232. (310)841-2555. **Fax:** (310)841-5934 or (818)705-7366. **Contact:** Jessica Roach, development executive; Beth Grossbard, executive producer. Estab. 1994. Buys first rights and true-life story rights Query with synopsis, treatment/outline. Responds in 1 month to queries.

TIPS Company develops material for television and the feature film markets. Interested in women's stories/issues, compelling true stories, social issues, contemporary legal issues, literary material, including young adult, children's titles, and small press books. We are also interested in plays, short stories, and original ideas.

INTERNATIONAL HOME ENTERTAINMENT

1440 Veteran Ave., Suite 650, Los Angeles CA 90024. (323)663-6940. **Contact:** Jed Leland, Jr., assistant to the president. Estab. 1976. Buys first rights. Query. Pays in accordance with writer's guild standards. Responds in 2 months to queries.

O Looking for material that is international in scope.

TIPS Our response time is faster on average now (3-6 weeks), but we do not reply without a SASE. No unsolicited mss. We do not respond to unsolicited phone calls or e-mail.

ARNOLD LEIBOVIT ENTERTAINMENT

P.O. Box 33544, Santa Fe NM 87594-3544. **Website:** www.scifistation.com. **Contact:** Barbara Schimpf, V.P., production; Arnold Leibovit, director/producer. Estab. 1988. "Produces material for motion pictures and television." **Uses Works with 1 writer/year. writers/year.** Query with log line and synopsis via e-mail. Do not send full script unless requested. A submission release must be included with all scripts. Pays in accordance with writer's guild standards. Responds in 2 months to queries. Does not want novels, plays, poems, treatments, or submissions on disk.

LEO FILMS

6548 Country Squire Ln., Omaha NE 68152. (323)459-5574. **E-mail:** lustgar@pacbell.net. **Website:** www.leofilms.com. **Contact:** Steve Lustgarten, president. Estab. 1989. Has released over 75 feature films. **Buys 5 scripts/year. scripts/year. Uses Works with 8 writ-**

ers/year. writers/year. Buys all rights. Query by e mail with synopsis. Payment varies—options and sales. Responds in 1 week to queries. Responds in 2 months to mss.

TIPS "Will also consider novels, short stories, and treatments that have true movie potential."

THE MARSHAK/ZACHARY CO.

8840 Wilshire Blvd., 1st Floor, Beverly Hills CA 90211. **Fax:** (310)358-3192. **E-mail:** marshakzachary@aol. com; alan@themzco.com. **Contact:** Alan W. Mills, associate. Estab. 1981. "Audience is film goers of all ages and television viewers." **Buys 3-5 scripts/year. scripts/year. Uses Works with 10 writers/year. writers/year.** Rights purchased vary. Query with synopsis. Payment varies. Responds in 2 weeks to queries. Responds in 3 months to mss.

TIPS "Submit logline (1-line description), a short synopsis of storyline, and a short biographical profile (focus on professional background). SASE required for all mailed inquiries. If submissions are sent via e-mail, subject must include specific information or else run the risk of being deleted as junk mail. All genres accepted, but ideas must be commercially viable, high concept, original, and marketable."

MARULLUS PRODUCTIONS

PO Box 2435, Venice CA 90291. **E-mail:** info@ marullus.com. **Website:** www.marullus.com. Gerhard Schwarz: gerhard@marullus.com; Fernando Ramiros: fernando@marullus.com; Development: development@marullus.com; Company Relations: info@marullus.com. The goal of Marullus Productions Inc. is nothing short of a revolution in independent film, providing both commercially viable and artistically polished films for both the art house and the local cinema around the block. From family films, mainstream feature films to surreal independent dramas and television series.

NITE OWL PRODUCTIONS

126 Hall Rd., Aliquippa PA 15001. (724)775-1993. **Fax:** (801)881-3017. **E-mail:** niteowlprods@aol.com; mark@niteowlproductionsltd.com. **Website:** www. niteowlproductionsltd.com. **Contact:** Bridget Petrella. Estab. 2001. Production credits include *Shopping Cart Commandos* and *American Playhouse: Three Sovereigns for Sarah.* Send a 1-page, single-spaced query letter via e-mail or mail.

○ We will be producing at least 5-10 feature films in the next 2-5 years. We are searching for pol-

ished, well-structured, well-written, and professional-looking screenplays that are ready for production. If your screenplay does not meet these standards, do not send us a query. All screenplays must be in English and be in standard industry format. Provide a working title for your screenplay.

TIPS All submissions must include a dated and signed Submission Release Form or they will be discarded immediately. All full-length feature film screenplays must be 80-130 pages in length. One-hour TV spec scripts must be 55-65 pages in length. Do not send us computer disks. One hardcopy of your screenplay will suffice. Do not cheat on your margins—we will notice. Proofread your screenplay thoroughly before submitting to avoid typos and punctuation and grammar mistakes. Copyright your script with the US Copyright Office and register it with the WGA. All screenplays must be firmly bound and include a cover page with the title of the work and your name, address, and contact information. Your materials will not be returned.

POP/ART FILM FACTORY

23679 Calabasas Rd., Suite 686, Calabasas CA 91302. **E-mail:** popartfilms@earthlink.net. **Website:** popartfilmfactory.com. **Contact:** Daniel Zirilli, CEO/ director. Estab. 1990. Produces material for all audiences/feature films Query with synopsis. Pays on per project basis.

○ "We also have domestic and international distribution, and are always looking for finished films. We're producing 3 feature films/year and 15-20 music-oriented projects."

TIPS "Send a query/pitch letter and let me know if you are willing to write on spec (for the first job only; you will be paid if the project is produced). Be original. Do not play it safe. If you don't receive a response from anyone you have ever sent your ideas to, or you continually get rejected, don't give up if you believe in yourself. Good luck and keep writing!"

THE PUPPETOON STUDIOS

P.O. Box 33544, Santa Fe NM 87594-3544. **Website:** www.scifistation.com. **Contact:** Arnold Leibovit, director/producer. Estab. 1987. "Wants plays geared toward a broad audience." **Uses Works with 1 writer/ year. writers/year.** Query with logline and synopsis via e-mail. Do not send script unless requested. Submission release required with all scripts. Pays in accordance with writer's guild standards. Responds in 2 month to queries. No novels, plays, poems, treatments, or submissions on disk.

SHORELINE ENTERTAINMENT, INC.

1875 Century Park E., Suite 600, Los Angeles CA 90067. (310)551-2060. **Fax:** (310)201-0729. **E-mail:** info@shorelineentertainment.com. **Website:** www.shorelineentertainment.com. Production credits include *Glengarry Glen Ross, The Visit, The Man From Elysian Fields.* Estab. 1993. Mass audience. **Buys 8 scripts/year. scripts/year. Uses Works with 8 writers/year. writers/year.** Buys all rights. Query. Responds in 1 week to queries.

TIPS Looking for character driven films that are commercial as well as independent. Completed screenplays only. Especially looking for big-budget action, thrillers. We accept submissions by mail, e-mail or fax. No unsolicited screenplays, please.

SPENCER PRODUCTIONS, INC.

P.O. Box 2247, Westport CT 06880. **E-mail:** spencerprods@yahoo.com. **Contact:** Bruce Spencer, general manager; Alan Abel, creative director. Produces material for high school students, college students and adults. Occasionally uses freelance writers with considerable talent Query. Payment negotiable. Responds in 1 month to queries.

TIPS "For a comprehensive view of our humor requirements, we suggest viewing our feature film productions, *Is There Sex After Death* (Rated R), starring Buck Henry. It is available at Netflix. Also, *Abel Raises Cain.* Or read *Don't Get Mad . Get Even* and *How to Thrive on Rejection* by Alan Abel (published by W.W. Norton), both available from Amazon.com. Send brief synopsis (one page) and outline (2-4 pages)."

TALCO PRODUCTIONS

279 E. 44th St., New York NY 10017-4354. (212)697-4015. **Fax:** (212)697-4827. **Contact:** Alan Lawrence, president; Marty Holberton, vice president. Estab. 1968. Produces variety of material for TV, radio, business, trade associations, nonprofit organizations, public relations (chiefly political and current events), etc. Audiences range from young children to senior citizens. **20-40% freelance written scripts/year. Uses Buys scripts from published/produced writers only writers/year.** Buys all rights. Submit resume. Makes outright purchase. Pays in accordance with WGA standards. Sometimes pays the expenses of writers on assignment. Responds in 3 weeks to queries.

TIPS We maintain a file of writers and call on those with experience in the same general category as the project in production. *We do not accept unsolicited manuscripts.* We prefer to receive a writer's résumé listing credits. If his/her background merits, we will be in touch when a project seems right. We are doing more public relations-oriented work (print and DVD) and are concentrating on TV productions. Production budgets are tighter.

TOO NUTS PRODUCTIONS, LLC

911 Lakeville St., Suite 201, Petaluma CA 94952. (707)637-0027. **E-mail:** info@toonutsproductions.com. **Website:** toonutsproductions.com. **Contact:** Ralph Scott, executive producer. Estab. 1994. "Produces illustrated kids books, art books, internet animation shorts for internet, music-based kidlit properties, and half-hour tv/video with a twist. Among our projects in development: 'Catscans,' Our Teacher is a Creature, Toad Pizza, The Salivating Salamander, The Suburban Cowboys, The Contest-Ants, The De-Stinktive Skunk, and Sneeks Peaks. Audience for all projects except art books is children, 5-12. Always looking for talented, new kidlit illustrators as well." **Buys 4-10 scripts/year. scripts/year. Uses Works with 4-6 writers/year. writers/year.** Buys both first rights and all rights. Query with synopsis. Submit resume. Submit writing samples. Submit production history. Creative but brief cover letter/e-mail. Works with 20% first time writers. Illustrators query with creative but brief cover letter, samples of work by e-mail or hyperlink to your online portfolio. Pays royalty and makes outright purchase. Responds in less than 3 months to queries; 6 months to mss. "Please do not submit anything with violence, chainsaws, axes, ice picks, and general blood and guts. We're producing for children, not monsters, or those who aspire to become them.".

◐ Really good original—clean—content.

TIPS "Suggestion: Use the words 'Too Nuts' at least twice in your query. (Do the math.) If you don't know how to giggle all the way to the bank, you may want to try someone else. If you've already exorcised your inner child, lizard, monkey, etc., that's a 'no no.' Please visit our website before querying. We receive too many submissions about axe murderers and with clearly adult themes. Even if you're still searching for your inner child through your writing, those subjects are clearly not for our audiences. If you send us anything like this, expect a very 'spirited' response. Find your inner child on your own time!"

⊘ TREASURE ENTERTAINMENT

468 N. Camden Dr., Suite 200, Beverly Hills CA 90210. (310)860-7490. **Fax:** (310)943-1488. **E-mail:** info@ treasureentertainment.net. **Website:** www.treasureentertainment.net. **Contact:** Mark Heidelberger, Treasure Entertainment co-chairman/chief executive officer. Estab. 2000. Management consideration given to writers with produced credits only. Intended audience is theatrical, festival, television, home video/ DVD, Internet. **Buys 1-2 scripts/year. scripts/year. Uses Works with 8-10 writers/year. writers/year.** Query. Pays 1-10% royalty. Makes outright purchase of $1-100,000. Responds in up to 6 months to queries. Responds in up to 6 months to mss.

TIPS "We reserve the right to reject or return any unsolicited material. We also reserve the right not to purchase any material if we don't feel that any submissions are of sufficient merit. Our needs tend to change with the market and will vary from year to year. We are agreeing to look at writer's queries only. Queries should be sent by mail or e-mail only."

VALEO FILMS

P.O. Box 250, Orange Lake FL 32681. (352)591-4714. **E-mail:** screenplays@valeofilms.com. **Website:** www. valeofilms.com. Query by e-mail or mail.

◐ Currently considering projects that contain one or more of the following: character or story driven, identifies moral values, romance/love story, educational/documentary, presents the human condition, strong visual imagery, coming of age/learning, or intellectual drama/mystery.

TIPS "We require that you provide your name, phone number, address, title of your work, and WGA registration or copyright number. We will send an Unsolicited Project Release letter for you to sign and return with a signed copy of your screenplay/treatment. We don't want projects that contain the following characteristics: one character saves the world, SFX based, highly action based, extreme/grotesque violence, high sexual content, or strong explicit language. Although we do have a vast array of production resources available to us, we are a relatively small production company who prefers to limit the number of projects we have in production. Consequently, we tend to be very selective when it comes to choosing new material."

THE THREE C'S OF BLOGGING

by Robert Lee Brewer

Blogging is a great way to build an audience for your writing and communicate with your readership as your audience grows. I've personally found a lot of success blogging, and it's mainly by following the three C's of blogging.

CONTENT

A blog without content isn't really a blog. So pick a general topic to cover that offers you plenty of options to generate new blog posts. Aim for quality content that is relevant to the needs of other people. If you share content that's only relevant to yourself, don't be surprised if you're the only person who reads your blog.

CONSISTENCY

The second C of blogging is consistency. I usually advise new bloggers to aim for one new blog post per week to get started—and to publish that one post at the same time on the same day of the week. This helps set expectations for your audience on when to expect new blog posts, which is key—along with excellent content—in getting return visitors.

COMMUNITY

The third C of blogging is community. I've developed several effective blogs with strong audiences over the years, and I consider community-building the key component of each one. Encourage comments on your blog and respond immediately to comments when they do appear. A blog with a healthy number of comments is a blog with a healthy community.

CONTESTS & AWARDS

The contests and awards listed in this section are arranged by subject. Nonfiction writers can turn immediately to nonfiction awards listed alphabetically by the name of the contest or award. The same is true for fiction writers, poets, playwrights and screenwriters, journalists, children's writers, and translators. You'll also find general book awards, fellowships offered by arts councils and foundations, and multiple category contests.

New contests and awards are announced in various writer's publications nearly every day. However, many lose their funding or fold, and sponsoring magazines go out of business just as often. **Contact names, entry fees,** and **deadlines** have been highlighted and set in bold type for your convenience.

To make sure you have all the information you need about a particular contest, always send a SASE to the contact person in the listing before entering a contest or check their website. The listings in this section are brief, and many contests have lengthy, specific rules and requirements that we could not include in our limited space. Often a specific entry form must accompany your submission.

When you receive a set of guidelines, you'll see some contests are not applicable to all writers. The writer's age, previous publication, geographic location, and length of the work are common matters of eligibility. Read the requirements to ensure you don't enter a contest for which you're not qualified.

Winning a contest or award can launch a successful writing career. Take a professional approach by doing a little extra research. Find out who the previous winner of the award was by investing in a sample copy of the magazine in which the prize-winning article, poem, or short story appeared. Attend the staged reading of an award-winning play. Your extra effort will be to your advantage in competing with writers who simply submit blindly.

CONTESTS & AWARDS

//

PLAYWRITING & SCRIPTWRITING

10 MINUTE PLAY CONTEST & FESTIVAL

Weathervane Playhouse, 1301 Weathervane Lane, Akron OH 44313. (330)836-2626. **E-mail:** mycp@weathervaneplayhouse.com. **Website:** www.weathervaneplayhouse.com. **Contact:** Melanie YC Pepe, Artistic Director. Weathervane Community Playhouse produces high-quality live theater with volunteer artists, designers, and technicians under professional direction, provides education and training in theater arts and appreciation, and engages and entertains its audience and constituents to enrich the quality of life in Northeast Ohio. Weathervane shall be one of the foremost community-based playhouses in the country that serves a region through theater as evidenced by consistent excellence in high caliber, diverse, challenging theater productions that compel our community to attend, participate in, and discuss the ideas and human conditions that are presented on our stages. Maximum running time is 10 minutes. Less is fine. Each year there is a special prop that must be incorporated into that year's plays. See website for details. All entries must be sent electronically, as attachments. Printed plays will not be considered. Guidelines available on website. The mission of the Weathervane Playhouse 8x10 TheatreFest is to promote the art of play writing, present new works, and introduce area audiences to the short play form. The competition will provide Weathervane with recognition for quality and innovative theatre. 2017 Deadline: May 12. Submission period begins November 1. Prizes: Each of 8 finalists receive full productions of their plays during the Festival, held in mid-July. 1st Place: $350; 2nd Place: $250; 3rd Place: $150; 5 runners-up: $50 each. First round judges include individuals with experience in every area of stagecraft, including tech designers, actors, directors, stage managers, and playwrights.

A+ PLAYWRITING CONTEST FOR TEACHERS

Pioneer Drama Service, Inc., P.O. Box 4267, Englewood CO 80155. (303)779-4035. **Fax:** (303)779-4315. **E-mail:** editors@pioneerdrama.com. **E-mail:** submissions@pioneerdrama.com. **Website:** www.pioneerdrama.com. **Contact:** Brian Taylor, acquisitions editor. Playwright must be a current or retired faculty member at an accredited K-12 public or private school in the US or Canada. All plays submitted through this contest must have been produced within the last 2 years at the school where the playwright teaches. Rules and guidelines available online. Encourages the development of quality plays written specifically by teachers and other educators. All qualifying mss accepted for publication will be considered contest finalists. Deadline: Submissions will be accepted on an on-going basis with a June 30 cutoff each year. Prize: $500 royalty advance and a one-time $500 donation to the school theatre program where the play was first produced. Judged by editors.

THE ACADEMY NICHOLL FELLOWSHIPS IN SCREENWRITING

1313 Vine St., Hollywood CA 90028-8107. (310)247-3010. **E-mail:** nicholl@oscars.org. **Website:** www.oscars.org/nicholl. An entrant's total earnings for motion picture and television writing may not exceed $25,000 before the end of the competition. This limit applies to compensation for motion picture and television writing services as well as for the sale of (or sale of an option on) screenplays, teleplays, stage plays, books, treatments, stories, premises and any other source material. Members and employees of the Academy of Motion Picture Arts and Sciences and their immediate families are not eligible, nor are competition judges and their immediate families. Deadline: May 1. The first and quarterfinal rounds are judged by industry professionals who are not members of the Academy. The semifinal round is judged by Academy members drawn from across the spectrum of the motion picture industry. The finalist scripts are judged by the Academy Nicholl Committee.

ACCLAIM FILM AND TV SCRIPT CONTESTS

Acclaim Scripts, 300 Central Ave, Suite 501, St. Petersburg FL 33701. **E-mail:** info@acclaimscripts.com. **Website:** www.acclaimscripts.com. Annual contest for TV and film scripts. Open to all writers worldwide. Work must be original material of the author(s). Must not be sold or optioned at time of submission. Multiple entries may be submitted (include separate entry form for each submission). Two categories for TV: comedy and drama. Contests are ongoing and deadlines change; visit website to check for updated deadlines. Prize: TV: Winner of each category receives $500. Film: 1st Place: $1,000. All winners and finalists may receive consideration by established production companies and agencies.

ACCOLADE COMPETITION

8837 Villa La Jolla Dr., #13131, La Jolla CA 92039. (858)454-9868. **E-mail:** info@accoladecompetition.org. **Website:** www.accoladecompetition.org. The Accolade Global Film Competition is unique in the industry. Attracting both powerhouse companies as well as talented new filmmakers it is an exceptional, truly international awards competition, not a traditional film festival—which allows filmmakers from around the world to enter their films in this prestigious competition. Currently in its 10th year, Accolade Global Film Competition is an avant-garde worldwide competition that strives to give talented directors, producers, actors, creative teams and new media creators the positive exposure they deserve. It discovers and honors the achievements of filmmakers who produce high quality shorts and new media. The Accolade promotes award winners through press releases to over 40,000 filmmakers, industry contacts and additional media/distribution outlets. We are currently creating a filmmaker representative program to assist with the distribution of award winning films. Submissions in other than English must be subtitled or include transcript. Multiple entries are allowed and each entry may be entered in multiple categories. Submit on DVD in NTSC or PAL format. Entries will not be returned. Deadline: March 7. Deadline changes, check website for up-to-date information. Awards include: Annual Humanitarian Award, Fast Focus Short Film Award, $4,800 Post-Production Award, and $1,500 Studio Award. See website for details on these awards. Also recognizes: Best of Show, Awards of Excellence, & Award of Merit. Best of Show honors are granted only if worthy productions are discovered. No more than 15% of entries are granted Awards of Excellence. Notable artistic and technical productions are recognized at the Award Of Merit award level. Judged by in-house staff.

AFC STORYTELLING INTERNATIONAL SCREENWRITING COMPETITION

African Film Commission, 1801 Century Park E., Suite 2400, Los Angeles CA 90067. (310)556-9661. **Fax:** (310)277-1278. **E-mail:** africafilmcommission@gmail.org. **Website:** www.africafilmcommission.org. Conceived to promote understanding of African life through screenplays and documentary projects and to create greater international cooperation in bringing African subject matters and locales to the screen. Scripts must have African content and themes. Three categories have been created for writers to compete: Africa—African Diaspora: Focused on the stories and people of Africa, this category seeks projects with a distinctly African point of view that enlightens, challenges, and informs the reader; Go Green—Sustainability: This subject matter deals with the growing concerns about the state of the self, immediate relationships, the environment, and the planet; International—All Stories: This category has no limits on subject matter or content, but simply seeks to reward the most compelling, well-crafted stories of shared humanity from around the world. Early Bird Deadline: October 2. Regular Deadline: November 20. Final Deadline: December 30. Contest begins September 2. Prizes vary based on awards. Visit website for application and details. Judged by a panel of entertainment industry professionals.

☼ ALBERTA PLAYWRITING COMPETITION

Alberta Playwrights' Network, 2633 Hochwald Ave. SW, Calgary AB T3E 7K2 Canada. (403)269-8564. **Fax:** (403)265-6773. **Website:** www.albertaplaywrights.com. Offered annually for unproduced scripts with full-length and discovery categories. Discovery is open only to previously unproduced playwrights (intended for emerging playwrights). Open only to residents of Alberta. Guidelines and rules available on website. Deadline: March 1. Prize: Grand Prize Category: $3,500 (CAD); Discovery Prize Category: $1,500 (CAD).

ALL ACCESS SCREENWRITING COMPETITION

SellAScript.com, 6506 Green Valley Circle, #313, Culver City CA 90230. (310)577-3181. **Website:** www.sellascript.com. Contest to provide winners with exclusive access to Hollywood. Electronic and mail submissions are both accepted. Script may not be under option at the time of entry nor at the time the material is chosen as a finalist or a winner. Deadline: December 15. Prize: 1st Place: $2,000; 2nd Place: $300; 3rd Place: $100. Each of the 3 winners also receives industry exposure and access, including: screenplay synopsis submitted to 29 participating companies, a free 6-month subscription to the Writer's Rolodex, and more. See website for additional details on prize package. Five finalists are also awarded prizes. Judged by Paul Harvey and Donna Milazzo

ALLIANCE OF WOMEN FILMMAKERS SCRIPT COMPETITION

Alliance of Women Filmmakers, 1317 N. San Fernando Blvd. #340, Burbank CA 91504. (818)749-6162. **E-mail:** info@womenfilmmakersalliance.org. **E-mail:** dmeans25@yahoo.com. **Website:** www.lawomensfest.com. Empowers women filmmakers to make culturally diverse contributions through film to Los Angeles

Communities, as well as educate and inform audiences of social, political, and health issues impacting women globally. Early deadline: September 1. Regular Deadline: September 15. Late deadline: October 1. Prizes are sponsored and vary from year to year.

AMERICAN ZOETROPE SCREENPLAY CONTEST

American Zoetrope, 916 Kearny St., San Francisco CA 94133. **E-mail:** contests@zoetrope.com. **Website:** www.zoetrope.com/contests. Scripts must be between 87 to 130 pages in standard screenplay format. The writer must own all rights to the work. The writer must be at least 18 years old and have never have made more than $5,000 as a screen- or television-writer. The contest's aim is to seek out and encourage compelling film narratives, and to introduce the next generation of great screenwriters to today's leading production companies and agencies. Deadline: August 1; September 2. The grand prize-winner receives $5,000. The winner and top-ten finalists will be considered for representation by icm, uta, paradigm, william morris independent, the gersh agency, caa, exile entertainment, the schiff company, and the firm. Their scripts will be considered for film option and development by leading production companies, including: american zoetrope, samuel goldwyn films, fox searchlight, sony pictures classics, ifc entertainment, paramount classics, icon pictures, working title, dimension films, antidote films, bull's eye entertainment, c/w productions, the film department, first look, frelaine, greenestreet films, matinee pictures, michael london productions, number 9 films, phoenix pictures, pretty pictures, this is that, roserock films, benderspink, room 9 entertainment, industry entertainment, ovie entertainment, nine yards entertainment, and ziskin productions.

THE ANNUAL BLANK THEATRE YOUNG PLAYWRIGHTS FESTIVAL

The Blank Theatre Co., P.O. Box 1094, Los Angeles CA 90078-1094. (323)871-8018. **E-mail:** submissions@youngplaywrights.com. **Website:** www.youngplaywrights.com. Offered annually for unpublished work to encourage young writers to write for the theater by presenting their work as well as through our mentoring programs. Open to all writers 19 or younger on the submission date. Deadline: March 15. Prize: Winning plays will be performed in the Festival in Los Angeles in June. Accomplished professional writers make up a team of mentors who help winning playwrights prepare their work for public performance. Experienced directors and mentors work closely with playwrights during the rehearsal process.

ANNUAL NATIONAL PLAYWRITING COMPETITION

Wichita State University, School of Performing Arts, 1845 Fairmount, Box 153, Wichita KS 67260. (316)978-3646. **Fax:** (316)978-3202. **E-mail:** bret.jones@wichita.edu. **Contact:** Bret Jones, director of theatre. The contest will be open to all undergraduate and graduate students enrolled at any college or university in the United States. Please indicate school affiliation. All submissions must be original, unpublished and unproduced. Both full-length and one-act plays may be submitted. Full-length plays in 1 or more acts should be a minimum of 90 minutes playing time. Two or 3 short plays on related themes by the same author will be judged as 1 entry. The total playing time should be a minimum of 90 minutes. One-act plays should be a minimum of 30 minutes playing time to a maximum of 60 minutes playing time. Musicals should be a minimum of 90 minutes playing time and must include a CD of the accompanying music. Scripts should contain no more than 4-6 characters and setting must be suitable for an 85-seat Black box theatre. Eligible playwrights may submit up to 2 entries per contest year. One typewritten, bound copy should be submitted. Scripts must be typed and arranged in professional play script format. See information provided in *The Dramatist's Sourcebook* or the following website (www.pubinfo.vcu.edu/artweb/playwriting/format.html) for instruction on use of professional format. Two title pages must be included: 1 bound and the other unbound. The unbound title page should display the author's name, address, telephone number, and e-mail address if applicable. The bound title page should only display the name of the script; do not include any personal identifying information on the bound title page. Scripts may be submitted via e-mail. Submit in PDF format. Include all information requested for mail in scripts with electronic submission. Deadline: January 16. Prize: Production or staged reading by the Wichita State University Theatre. Winner will be announced after March 15. No entry may be withdrawn after March 1. Judged by a panel of 3 or more selected from the school faculty. May also include up to 3 experienced, faculty approved WSU School of Performing Arts students.

APPALACHIAN FESTIVAL OF PLAYS & PLAYWRIGHTS

Barter Theatre, Box 867, c/o Barter Theatre, Abingdon VA 24212-0867. (276)619-3316. **Fax:** (276)619-3335. **E-mail:** apfestival@bartertheatre.com. **E-mail:** apfestival@bartertheatre.com. **Website:** www.bartertheatre.com. **Contact:** Nick Piper, Associate Artistic Director/Director, New Play Development. With the annual Appalachian Festival of New Plays & Playwrights, Barter Theatre wishes to celebrate new, previously unpublished/unproduced plays by playwrights from the Appalachian region. If the playwrights are not from Appalachia, the plays themselves must be about the region. Deadline: March 2. Prize: $250, a staged reading performed at Barter's Stage II theater, and some transportation compensation and housing during the time of the festival.

ATLANTIS AWARD

The Poet's Billow, 6135 Avon, Portage MI 49024. **E-mail:** thepoetsbillow@gmail.com. **Website:** thepoetsbillow.org. **Contact:** Robert Evory. Annual award open to any writer to recognize one outstanding poem from its entries. Finalists with strong work will also be published. Submissions must be previously unpublished. Deadline: October 1. Submissions open July 1. Prize: $200 and winning poet will be featured in an interview on The Poet's Billow website. Poem will be published and displayed in The Poet's Billow Literary Art Gallery and nominated for a Pushcart Prize. If the poet qualifies, the poem will also be submitted to The Best New Poets anthology. Judged by the editors, and, occasionally, a guest judge.

BAY AREA PLAYWRIGHTS FESTIVAL

Produced by Playwrights Foundation, 1616 16th Street, Suite 350, San Francisco CA 94103. **E-mail:** literary@playwrightsfoundation.org. **Website:** www.playwrightsfoundation.org. **Contact:** Margot Manburg. Offered annually for unpublished plays by established and emerging theater writers to support and encourage development of a new work. Unproduced full-length plays only. Guidelines available on website. Submissions only accepted as PDFs. Deadline: Mid-July through mid-September. Small stipend and in-depth development process with dramaturg and director, and a professionally staged reading in San Francisco.

BEVERLY HILLS FILM FESTIVAL SCREENPLAY COMPETITION

Beverly Hills Film Festival, 9663 Santa Monica Blvd, Suite 777, Beverly Hills CA 90210. (310)779-1206. **E-mail:** info@beverlyhillsfilmfestival.com. **Website:** www.beverlyhillsfilmfestival.com/. Annual film festival that strives to bring creative new talent to the forefront and make dreams a reality. Selects feature-length and short-length screenplays for competition that will grab the reader and audience passionately and captivate them, whether the characters are likeable or not. Please indicate if the submission is complete, or work in progress. Include a cover page that has the title, writer(s) name, genre, and total number of pages; indicate if the submission is complete, or a work-in-progress; a brief statement from the writer regarding the script; a brieg biography of the writer; and any accompanying artwork. Deadline: August 17 (earlybird), November 17 (regular), January 17, February 15 (extended).

BIG BEAR LAKE SCREENWRITING COMPETITION

P.O. Box 1981, Big Bear Lake CA 92315-1981. (909)866-3433. **E-mail:** BigBearFilmFest@aol.com. **Website:** www.bigbearfilmfestival.com. Deadline: April 1. No confirmed money prizes, but winners receive software and their script submitted to studios.

BIG BREAK INTERNATIONAL SCREENWRITING COMPETITION

Final Draft, Inc., 26707 W. Agoura Rd., Suite 205, Calabasas CA 91302. (818)995-8995. **E-mail:** bigbreak@finaldraft.com. **Website:** www.finaldraft.com/bigbreak. **Contact:** Shelly Mellott, VP events and services. Big Break is an annual, global screenwriting contest designed to launch the careers of aspiring writers with over $80,000 in cash and prizes, as well as A-list executive meetings. Winners and finalists alike have had their screenplays optioned and produced and have secured high-profile representation as well as lucrative writing deals. No rights to submitted materials are acquired or purchased. Contest is open to any writer. Guidelines and rules available online. No paper submissions. Submissions must be unpublished. Enter online. Deadline: April 30 (early bird), July 15 (standard), July 31 (extended). Prizes: 1st Place prizes: $15,000 total cash, plus finalist prizes, airfare to L.A., 3-night hotel stay (unless winner resides in or around L.A.), lunch with executives. 2nd Place prizes:

$4,000 total cash, plus finalist prizes, airfare to L.A., 3-night hotel stay (unless winner resides in or around L.A.), lunch with executives. 3rd Place prizes: $2,000 total cash, plus finalist prizes, airfare to L.A., 3-night hotel stay (unless winner resides in or around L.A.), lunch with executives. 4th and 5th Place prizes: $250 total cash, plus finalist prizes. See 6th through 20th Place Finalist Prizes on website. Judged by industry readers in first 2 rounds. A panel of notable industry professionals conducts the final judging. Information on previous judges can be found on website.

THE BLANK THEATRE COMPANY YOUNG PLAYWRIGHTS FESTIVAL

P.O. Box 38756, Hollywood CA 90038. (323)662-7734. **Fax:** (323)661-3903. **E-mail:** info@theblank.com. **E-mail:** submissions@youngplaywrights.com. **Website:** ypf.theblank.com. Purpose is to give young playwrights an opportunity to learn more about playwriting and to give them a chance to have their work mentored, developed, and presented by professional artists.

BLUECAT SCREENPLAY COMPETITION

P.O. Box 2635, Hollywood CA 90028. **E-mail:** info@bluecatscreenplay.com. **Website:** www.bluecatscreenplay.com/. Founded by Gordy Hoffman, the BlueCat Screenplay Competition's passionate commitment to develop and discover the unknown screenwriter continues to define our work today.

We provide each writer who enters BlueCat one written analysis while supporting screenwriters of all levels and stages of development with the constructive feedback all writers require.

Our Winners and Finalists have been signed by major talent agencies like UTA, CAA and WME, sold their work to studios like Warner Bros., Paramount and Universal, and won major awards at the Sundance, Berlin and Tribeca Film Festivals, all after being discovered by and winning BlueCat. Deadline: February 20. The Feature Screenplay Winner will receive $10,000. Four Feature Finalists will receive $1,000 each. The Pilot Winners will receive $5,000, one Winner for half-hour pilots and one Winner for hour pilots. Four Pilot Finalists for both categories will receive $500 each. The Short Script Winner will receive $5,000. Four Shorts Finalists will receive $500 each. The Fellini Award will be awarded to the Best Feature Screenplay of the 2017 Competition written by a screenwriter residing outside the USA and will receive $1,000. Every script submission will receive a written analysis as a part of their entry fee. See http://www.bluecatscreenplay.com/2018-screenplay-competition-rules-guidelines/ for more information.

BUNTVILLE CREW'S AWARD BLUE

Buntville Crew, 118 N. Railroad Ave., Buckley IL 60918-0445. **E-mail:** buntville@yahoo.fr. **Contact:** Steven Packard, artistic director. "Presented annually for the best unpublished/unproduced play script under 15 pages, written by a student enrolled in any Illinois high school. Submit 1 copy of the script in standard play format, a brief biography, and a SASE (scripts will not be returned). Include name, address, telephone number, age, and name of school." Deadline: May 31. Cash prize and possible productions in Buckley and/or New York City. Judged by panel selected by the theater.

BUNTVILLE CREW'S PRIX HORS PAIR

Buntville Crew, 118 N. Railroad Ave., Buckley IL 60918-0445. **E-mail:** buntville@yahoo.fr. **Website:** www.buntville@yahoo.com. **Contact:** Steven Packard, artistic director. "Annual award for unpublished/unproduced play script under 15 pages. Plays may be in English, French, German, or Spanish (no translations, no adaptations). Submit 1 copy of the script in standard play format, a résumé, and a SASE (scripts will not be returned). Include name, address, and telephone number." Deadline: May 31. $200 and possible production in Buckley and/or New York City. Judged by panel selected by the theater.

CALIFORNIA YOUNG PLAYWRIGHTS CONTEST

Playwrights Project, 3675 Ruffin Rd., Suite 330, San Diego CA 92123-1870. (858)384-2970. **Fax:** (858)384-2974. **E-mail:** write@playwrightsproject.org. **Website:** www.playwrightsproject.org/programs/contest/. **Contact:** Cecelia Kouma, executive director. The California Young Playwrights Contest is open to Californians under age 19. Every year young playwrights submit original scripts to the contest. Every writer who requests feedback receives an individualized script critique. Selected writers win script readings or full professional productions in Plays by Young Writers festival. Distinguished artists from major theatres select festival scripts and write comments to the playwrights. Submissions are required to be unpublished

and not produced professionally. Submissions made by the author. SASE for contest rules and entry form. Scripts must be a minimum of 10 standard typewritten pages. Scripts will *not* be returned. If requested, entrants receive detailed evaluation letter. Guidelines available online. Deadline: June 1. Prize: Scripts will be produced in spring at a professional theatre in San Diego. Writers submitting scripts of 10 or more pages receive a detailed script evaluation letter upon request. Judged by professionals in the theater community, a committee of 5-7; changes somewhat each year.

☼ CANADIAN AUTHORS ASSOCIATION AWARD FOR FICTION

6 West St. N., Suite 203, Orillia ON L3X 5B8 Canada. **Website:** www.canadianauthors.org. **Contact:** Anita Purcell, executive director. Award for full-length, English language literature for adults by a Canadian author. Deadline: January 15. Prize: $1,000. Judging: Each year a trustee for each award appointed by the Canadian Authors Association selects up to 3 judges. Identities of the trustee and judges are confidential.

THE CLAYMORE AWARD

Killer Nashville, P.O. Box 680759, Franklin TN 37068-0759. (615)599-4032. **E-mail:** claymore@killernashville.com. **Website:** www.claymoreaward.com and www.killernashville.com. **Contact:** Clay Stafford, Event Founder. "Although anyone with an unpublished ms is eligible to submit, the award would best benefit authors who have not been previously published, and published authors who are between publishers and would like to get some buzz about their new works. We don't want to exclude anyone, though, so if you're a published author with an unpublished ms not under contract, you'd like to enter, please be our guest." The Claymore Award is Killer Nashville's award for the best opening for an unpublished ms submitted to the judging committee. Deadline: May 31. The Award will be presented at the Killer Nashville Thriller, Mystery, and Crime Literature Conference held annually on the weekend surrounding the fourth Saturday in August. Prize: An engraved dagger award and consideration for publication by the judging publisher. Judged by a committee of experienced readers and writers will review all submissions in a blind judging process. They will recommend and submit 10 mss to the sponsor publisher, whose editors will make the final decision and award the Claymore Award to the winning author. All decisions are final and at the sole discretion of the publisher.

COE COLLEGE PLAYWRITING FESTIVAL

Coe College, 1220 First Ave. NE, Cedar Rapids IA 52402-5092. (319)399-8624. **Fax:** (319)399-8557. **E-mail:** swolvert@coe.edu. **Website:** www.theatre.coe.edu. **Contact:** Susan Wolverton. Offered biennially for a new, full-length, original, unproduced and unpublished play in its final stages of development that would benefit from a week-long workshop at Coe. No musicals, adaptations, translations or collaborations will be considered. Open to any writer. One clean, bound script; a resume; the play's development history; and a statement of development goals for your play (one page). Deadline: November 1 (even years). Submission period begins October 1. Prize: $500, plus 1-week residency as guest artist with airfare, room and board provided. Residency occurs in April (odd years).

CREATIVE WORLD AWARDS (CWA) INTERNATIONAL SCREENWRITING COMPETITION

4712 Admiralty Way #268, Marina del Rey CA 90292. **E-mail:** info@creativeworldawards.com. **Website:** www.creativeworldawards.com. **Contact:** Marlene Neubauer/Heather Waters.. CWA's professionalism, industry innovation, and exclusive company list make this competition a leader in the industry. CWA offers the grand prize winner a production opportunity and has helped many past entrants get optioned and representation. CWA accepts all genres of features, shorts, and television. Check out the website for more details. All screenplays must be in English and in standard spec screenplay format. See website's FAQ page for more detailed information. Deadline: See website. Prize: Over $30,000 in cash and prizes awarded in 10 categories.

DUBUQUE FINE ARTS PLAYERS ANNUAL ONE-ACT PLAY CONTEST

Dubuque Fine Arts Players, PO Box 1160, Dubuque IA 52004-1160. **E-mail:** contact@dbqoneacts.org. **Website:** www.dbqoneacts.org. Annual competition that selects 3 one-act plays each year, awards cash prizes and produces the winning plays in October. Plays for submission must be unpublished and unproduced. Applications may be submitted online or by US mail, as listed on website. Deadline: January 31. Prizes: 1st Place: $600; 2nd Place: $300; 3rd Place: $200. All plays

are read at least twice and as many as 6 times by community readers. Final judging is done by a group of 3 directors and 2 other qualified judges.

EERIE HORROR FILM FESTIVAL SCREENPLAY COMPETITION

P.O. Box 98, Edinboro PA 16412. (814)873-2483. **E-mail:** greg@eeriehorrorfest.com; info@eeriehorrorfest.com. **Website:** www.eeriehorrorfilmfestival.com/. Horror film festival that provides more opportunities and exposure for filmmakers, screenwriters, and video game developers working within the horror, science fiction, and suspense genres, as well as to draw more attention to the Northwestern Pennsylvania region. See website for details as the next festival approaches in October.

THE EMILY CONTEST

West Houston RWA, Houston TX **E-mail:** emily.contest@whrwa.com. **Website:** www.whrwa.com. Annual award to promote publication of previously unpublished writers of romance. Open to any writer who has not published in a given category within the past 3 years. Send up to first 5,600 words and end on a hook. Contest is open to published and unpublished writers. Unpublished authors may enter in any category not contracted in (book-length) by the deadline. Published authors may enter in a category not published (book-length) in the past three years. (Book-length: 40,000+ words.) See website for specific details. The mission of The Emily is to professionally support writers and guide them toward a path to publication. Deadline: October 7. Submission period begins September 1. Prize: $100. Final judging done by an editor and an agent.

ESSENTIAL THEATRE PLAYWRITING AWARD

The Essential Theatre, 1414 Foxhall Ln., #10, Atlanta GA 30316. (404) 212-0815. **E-mail:** pmhardy@aol.com. **Website:** www.essentialtheatre.com. **Contact:** Peter Hardy. Offered annually for unproduced, full-length plays by Georgia resident writers. No limitations as to style or subject matter. Submissions can be e-mailed in PDF or Word Documents, or sent by postal mail. See website for full guidelines. Deadline: April 23. Prize: $600 and full production.

SHUBERT FENDRICH MEMORIAL PLAYWRITING CONTEST

Pioneer Drama Service, Inc., P.O. Box 4267, Englewood CO 80155. (303)779-4035. **Fax:** (303)779-4315.

E-mail: editors@pioneerdrama.com. **E-mail:** submissions@pioneerdrama.com. **Website:** www.pioneerdrama.com. **Contact:** Brian Taylor, acquisitions editor. Annual competition that encourages the development of quality theatrical material for educational, community and children's theatre markets. Previously unpublished submissions only. Only considers mss with a running time between 20-120 minutes. Open to all writers not currently published by Pioneer Drama Service. Guidelines available online. No entry fee. Cover letter, SASE for return of ms, and proof of production or staged reading must accompany all submissions. Deadline: Ongoing contest; a winner is selected by June 1 each year from all submissions received the previous year. Prize: $1,000 royalty advance in addition to publication. Judged by editors.

FESTIVAL OF NEW AMERICAN PLAYS

Firehouse Theatre Project, 1609 W. Broad St., Richmond VA 23220. (804)355-2001. **E-mail:** jase@firehousetheatre.org. **Website:** www.firehousetheatre.org. **Contact:** Jase Smith, artistic director. Annual contest designed to support new and emerging American playwrights. Scripts must be full-length and previously unpublished/unproduced. Submissions should be mailed in standard manuscript form with no fancy binding. Scripts should be secured simply with a binder clip only. All author information must be on a title page separate from the body of the manuscript and no reference to the author is permitted in the body of the script. Scripts must be accompanied by a letter of recommendation from a theater company or individual familiar with your work. Letters of recommendation do not need to be specific to the play submitted; they may be general recommendations of the playwright's work. All letters must be received with the script, not under separate cover. Scripts received without a letter will not be considered. Due to the volume of mail, manuscripts cannot be returned. All American playwrights welcome to submit their work. Deadline: September 1. Prize: 1st Place: $1,000 and a staged reading; 2nd Place: $500 and a staged reading. Judged by a panel of individuals with experience in playwriting and literature.

FILMMAKERS INTERNATIONAL SCREENWRITING AWARDS

Beverly Hills CA 90210 USA. **E-mail:** info@filmmakers.com. **Website:** www.filmmakers.com/screenplay/. Deadlines: Early: Feb. 28; Regular: April 30; Late: May 31; Final: June 30; Extended Final: July 31. Prizes: Grand Prize: $5,000; Elite Prizes: $500 per category.

FLICKERS: SCREENPLAY COMPETITION

FLICKERS: Rhode Island International Film Festival, P.O. Box 162, Newport RI 02840. (401)861-4445. **Fax:** (401)490-6735. **E-mail:** info@film-festival.org. **Website:** www.film-festival.org/enterascreenplay.php. Annual screenplay contest for all genres. Screenplays must have been written in the past 2 years. Full-length scripts, no more than 130 pages. Half-hour shorts or teleplays, no more than 40 pages. Submissions must be in English. Submissions must use 12-point Courier font. Pages should be numbered. 3-hole punch and brads with front and back cover for non-digital files. No promotional material. No shooting scripts. See website for more details. The purpose of the contest is to promote, embolden and cultivate screenwriters in their quest for opportunities within the industry. Deadline: July 15. Prize: The Grand Prize winner will become a central focus during ScriptBiz™ the screenplay pitch forum held during the Festival. The Grand Prize winner will also receive prizes valued at over $10,000. This includes travel, up to four nights accommodations, Final Draft software and screenplay promotions. Judged by a distinguished panel of industry professionals, educators, peers, and film fans. Screenplays will be judged on creativity, innovation, vision, originality and the use of language. The key element is that of communication and how it complements and is transformed by the language of film.

GARDEN STATE FILM FESTIVAL SCREENPLAY COMPETITION

3101 Boardwalk, Tower Two, Suite 1405, Atlantic City NJ 08401. **E-mail:** info@gsff.org. **Website:** www.gsff.org. **Contact:** Diane Raver, executive director. This contest is designed to introduce audiences to the cinematic arts and assist in the revitalization of Asbury Park by filling a cultural void. Entered screenplays must not have been previously optioned, sold, or produced. All screenplays should be registered with the WGA and/or a Library of Congress copyright. Screenplays must be the original work of the writer. If based on another person's life story, a statement attesting to the rights obtained must be attached. No adaptations of other written work will be accepted. Multiple entries are accepted. A separate entry form and fee must accompany each script. Screenplays containing multiple writers are also accepted. Include two cover pages with each screenplay. One that only contains the screenplay's title. A second one that contains all contact information (name, address, phone, and email and Withoutabox tracking number). The writer's name must not appear any where inside the body of the screenplay. All screenplays must abide by proper industry format. All screenplays must be in English, with numbered, plain-write pages. All screenplays MUST be uploaded as a PDF via withoutbox.com. No substitutions of new drafts, or corrected pages, for any screenplay, for any reason, will be accepted after the initial submission. Please enter the draft you are most confident about. No individual feedback or coverage will be made available pertaining to submitted screenplays. **Deadline:** November 1. Submissions are accepted beginning June 1 each year. The winner receives a live staged reading with a professional director and professional actors in a seated venue during the festival.

JOHN GASSNER MEMORIAL PLAYWRITING COMPETITION

New England Theatre Conference, 215 Knob Hill Dr., Hamden CT 06158. **Fax:** (203)288-5938. **E-mail:** mail@netconline.org. **E-mail:** mail@netconline.org. **Website:** www.netconline.org. Annually seeks unpublished full-length plays and scripts. Open to all. Playwrights living outside New England may participate. Submit by Email ONLY **Deadline:** April 15. **Prize:** Staged reading.

THE MARILYN HALL AWARDS FOR YOUTH THEATRE

P.O. Box 148, Beverly Hills CA 90213. **Website:** www.beverlyhillstheatreguild.com. **Contact:** Candace Coster, competition coordinator. The Marilyn Hall Awards consist of 2 monetary prizes for plays suitable for grades 6-8 (middle school) or for plays suitable for grades 9-12 (high school). The 2 prizes will be awarded on the merits of the play scripts, which includes its suitability for the intended audience. The plays should be approximately 45-75 minutes in length. There is no production connected to any of the prizes, though a staged reading is optional at the discretion of the BHTG. Unpublished submissions only. Authors must be U.S. citizens or legal residents and must sign entry form personally. **Deadline:** The last day of February. Submission period begins January 15. **Prize:** 1st Prize: $700; 2nd Prize: $300.

AURAND HARRIS MEMORIAL PLAYWRITING AWARD

The New England Theatre Conference, Inc., 215 Knob Hill Dr., Hamden CT 06518. **Fax:** (203)288-5938. **E-mail:** mail@netconline.org. **E-mail:** mail@netconline.org. **Website:** www.netconline.org. Offered annually for an unpublished full-length play for young audiences. Guidelines available online or for SASE. Open to all. All scripts submitted by email *only*. **Deadline:** May 1.

HOLIDAY SCREENPLAY CONTEST

P.O. Box 450, Boulder CO 80306. (303)629-3072. **E-mail:** Cherubfilm@aol.com. **Website:** www.HolidayScreenplayContest.com. Scripts must be centered around 1 holiday (New Year's Day, President's Day, Valentine's Day, St. Patrick's Day, April Fool's Day, Easter, 4th of July, Halloween, Thanksgiving, Hanukkah, Christmas, Kwanzaa, or any other world holiday you would like to feature). This contest is limited to the first 400 entries. Screenplays must be in English. Screenplays must not have been previously optioned, produced, or purchased prior to submission. Multiple submissions are accepted, but each submission requires a separate online entry and separate fee. Screenplays must be between 90-125 pages. **Deadline:** November 30. **Prize:** Up to $500.

HORROR SCREENPLAY CONTEST

Cherub Productions, P.O. Box 540, Boulder Co 80306. (303)629-3072. **E-mail:** Cherubfilm@aol.com. **Website:** www.horrorscreenplaycontest.com. Annual contest that accepts horror scripts. Contest limited to the first 600 entries. Screenplays must be between 90-125 pages. **Deadline:** July 20. **Prize:** More than $5,000 in cash and prizes.

HRC SHOWCASE THEATRE PLAYWRITING CONTEST

P.O. Box 940, Hudson NY 12534. (518)851-7244. **E-mail:** hrcshowcaseplaycontest@gmail.com. **Website:** www.hrc-showcasetheatre.com. **Contact:** Jesse Waldinger, chair. HRC Showcase Theatre invites submissions of full-length plays to its annual contest from new, aspiring, or established playwrights. Each submitted play should be previously unpublished, run no more than 90 minutes, require no more than 6 actors, and be suitable for presentation as a staged reading by Equity actors. No musicals or children's plays. **Deadline:** February 1. **Prize:** $500. Four runner-ups will receive $100 each.

THE KILLER NASHVILLE SILVER FALCHION AWARD

Killer Nashville, P.O. Box 680759, Franklin TN 37068-0750. (615)599-4032. **E-mail:** awards@killernashville.com. **Website:** www.killernashville.com. **Contact:** Clay Stafford. Any fiction or nonfiction book-length work published for the first time in the previous calendar year, in which a crime drives the storyline, may be nominated by either the publisher or author of the book. Four copies of the work being nominated must be submitted with entry forms to be considered. Deadline: March 1. Entries will be evaluated by judges, who will choose five finalists from the following categories: Best Novel, Best First Novel, Best Paperback, Best e-Book Original, Best Nonfiction, Best Juvenile, Best Young Adult, and Best Anthology. Winners chosen by the Killer Nashville Writers' Conference attendees.

L.A. DESIGNERS' THEATRE-COMMISSIONS

L.A. Designers' Theatre, P.O. Box 1883, Studio City CA 91614-0883. **E-mail:** ladesigners@gmail.com. **Contact:** Richard Niederberg, artistic director. "Quarterly contest to promote new work and push it through a Theatrical Production onto the conveyor belt to Filmed or Digital Origination entertainment. All submissions must be registered with the copyright office and be unpublished. Material will not be returned. Do not submit any proposal that will not fit in a #10 envelope. No rules, guidelines, fees, or entry forms. Just present an idea that can be commissioned into a full work. Proposals for as of yet uncompleted works are encouraged. Unpopular political, religious, social, or other themes are encouraged; 'street' language and nudity are acceptable. Open to any writer." Deadline: March 15, June 15, September 15, December 15. Prize: Production or publication of the work in the Los Angeles market. "We only want 'first refusal' for the Rights and a License that is clear of any legal, stated, unstated, or implied obligation to any other person or entity. You continue to *own* your work."

MCKNIGHT FELLOWSHIP IN PLAYWRITING

The Playwrights' Center, 2301 E Franklin Ave, Minneapolis MN 55406-1099 USA. (612)332-7481. **Fax:** (612)332-6037. **E-mail:** submissions@pwcenter.org. **E-mail:** submissions@pwcenter.org. **Website:** www.pwcenter.org. **Contact:** Julia Brown, Artistic Programs Administrator. The Playwrights' Center today serves more playwrights in more ways than any other organization in the country. Applications are screened for eligibility by the Playwrights' Center and evaluated by an initial select panel of professional theater artists; finalists are then evaluated by a second panel of national theater artists. Selection is based on artistic excellence and professional achievement, and is guided by the Playwrights' Center's mission statement. The McKnight Fellowships in Playwriting recognize playwrights whose work demonstrates exceptional artistic merit and excellence in the field, and whose primary residence is in the state of Minnesota. Deadline: January 5. Prize: 2 fellowships of $25,000 each will be awarded. Additional funds of $2,500 can be used to support a play development workshop and other professional expenses.

MOONDANCE INTERNATIONAL FILM FESTIVAL

970 Ninth St., Boulder CO 80302. (303)818-5771. **E-mail:** director@moondancefilmfestival.com; moondancefestival@gmail.com. **Website:** www.moondancefilmfestival.com; www.moondancefestival.com/blog. Written works submissions: feature screenplays, short screenplays, feature & short musical screenplays, feature & short screenplays for children, 1, 2 or 3-act stageplays, mini-series for TV, television movies of the week, television pilots, libretti, musical film scripts, short stories, radio plays & short stories for children. Submission service: www.withoutabox.com/login/1240. Accepts hard-copies of submissions, as well as digital submissions. Please include your full contact info on the cover page of your entry. Check out our submission guidelines on the website. Regular deadline: May 31; late deadline: June 30, extended deadline: July 15.

NASHVILLE FILM FESTIVAL SCREENWRITING COMPETITION

161 Rains Ave, Nashville TN 37203. (615)742-2500. **E-mail:** info@nashvillefilmfestival.org. **E-mail:** 2019entries@nashfilm.org. **Website:** www.nashvillefilmfestival.org. **Contact:** Robin Robinson. This contest seeks film submissions less than 40 minutes in length, as well as full-length features and documentaries. Deadline: June-January. There are numerous awards: press/industry screenings, $1,000 and option of international representation for one year. Scripts are judged by a carefully curated jury of industry professionals and agents. Past and future juries have included representatives from CAA, Voltage Pictures (The Hurt Locker,

Dallas Buyers Club), APA, and Mosaic (Bad Teacher, Step Brothers, The Other Guys).

NATIONAL LATINO PLAYWRITING AWARD

Arizona Theatre Co., 343 S. Scott Ave., Tucson AZ 85701. (520)884-8210. **Fax:** (520)628-9129. **E-mail:** jbazzell@arizonatheatre.org. **Website:** www.arizonatheatre.org. **Contact:** Jennifer Bazzell, literary manager. Offered annually for unproduced, unpublished plays over 50 pages in length. Plays may be in English, bilingual, or in Spanish (with English translation). The award recognizes exceptional full-length plays by Latino playwrights on any subject. Open to Latino playwrights currently residing in the US, its territories, and/or Mexico. Guidelines online or via e-mail. Deadline: December 31. $1,000

◑ NATIONAL ONE-ACT PLAYWRITING COMPETITION (CANADA)

Ottawa Little Theatre, 400 King Edward Ave., Ottawa ON K1N 7M7 Canada. (613)233-8948. **Fax:** (613)233-8027. **Website:** www.ottawalittletheatre.com. **Contact:** Lynn McGuigan, executive director. Encourages literary and dramatic talent in Canada. Guidelines available online. Deadline: October 15. Prize: 1st Place: $1,000; 2nd Place: $750; 3rd Place: $500; Sybil Cooke Award for a Play Written for Children or Young People: $500. All winning plays will receive a public reading in April, and the winning playwrights will have a one-on-one meeting with a resident dramaturg. Judged by 3 adjudicators, including dramaturgs, directors who develop new work, and playwrights from across Canada.

NEVADA FILM OFFICE SCREENWRITER'S COMPETITION

6655 W. Sahara Ave., Suite C-106, Las Vegas NV 89101. 1-877-NEV-FILM. **E-mail:** lvnfo@nevadafilm.com. **E-mail:** screenwriters@nevadafilm.com. **Website:** www.nevadafilm.com/screenwriting-competition. Competition open to all unsold screenwriters. At least 75% of the locations in the script must be filmable in Nevada. See website for guidelines Deadline: August 31. Prize: Winning script will be eligible for consideration to be pitched to production companies willing to read the winning script. Winner will also receive a complimentary posting of logline, synopsis and full script on the premier screenwriting marketplace InkTip.com, 2 complimentary roundtrip tickets on Southwest Airlines and a complimentary 3 day/ 2 night hotel stay at The D hotel in downtown Las Vegas. Judged by experienced, professional writers and story analysts from a script service company.

NEW WORKS FOR THE STAGE

COE College Theatre Arts Department, 1220 First Ave. NE, Cedar Rapids IA 52402. (319)399-8624. **Fax:** (319)399-8557. **E-mail:** swolvert@coe.edu. **Website:** www.public.coe.edu/departments/theatre. **Contact:** Susan Wolverton. Offered in odd-numbered years to encourage new work, to provide an interdisciplinary forum for the discussion of issues found in new work, and to offer playwright contact with theater professionals who can provide response to new work. Full-length, original, unpublished and unproduced scripts only. No musicals, adaptations, translations, or collaborations. Submit 1-page synopsis, résumé, and SASE if the script is to be returned. Deadline: November 1 even years. Prize: $500, plus travel, room and board for residency at the college.

ONE IN TEN SCREENPLAY CONTEST

Cherub Productions, P.O. Box 540, Boulder CO 80306. **E-mail:** Cherubfilm@aol.com. **Website:** www.OneInTenScreenplayContest.com. Scripts that provide a positive potrayal of gays and lesbians. "A requirement of the competition is that at least one of the primary characters in the screenplay be gay or lesbian (bisexual, transgender, questioning, and the like) and that gay and lesbian characters must be portrayed positively. All writers are encouraged to enter!" Deadline: September 1. Prize: $1,000.

THE PAGE INTERNATIONAL SCREENWRITING AWARDS

7190 W. Sunset Blvd. #610, Hollywood CA 90046. **E-mail:** info@pageawards.com. **Website:** pageawards.com. **Contact:** Zoe Simmons, contest coordinator. Annual competition to discover the most talented new screenwriters from across the country and around the world. Each year, awards are presented to 31 screenwriters in 10 different genre categories: Action/Adventure, Comedy, Drama, Family Film, Historical Film, Science Fiction, Thriller/Horror, Short Film Script, TV Drama Pilot, and TV Comedy Pilot. The contest is open to all writers 18 years of age and older who have not previously earned more than $50,000 writing for film and/or television. (Please visit contest website for entry forms and a complete list of rules and regulations.) Deadlines: January 15 (early), February 15 (regular), March 15 (late), April 15 (last minute). Each year the PAGE Judges present over $50,000 in cash and prizes, including a $25,000 Grand Prize, plus Gold, Silver & Bronze Prizes in all 10 genre categories. Most importantly, the award-winning writers receive extensive publicity and industry exposure for their scripts. As a result of winning the contest, many PAGE Award Winners now have movies and television shows in production, on the air and in theaters. Judging is done entirely by working Hollywood professionals, including industry script analysts, literary agents, managers, producers, and development executives.

SCREENPLAY FESTIVAL

15021 Ventura Blvd., #523, Sherman Oaks CA 91403. (424)248-9221. **Fax:** (866)770-2994. **E-mail:** info@screenplayfestival.com. **Website:** www.screenplay-festival.com. This festival is an opportunity to give all scriptwriters a chance to be noticed and have their work read by the power players. Entries in the feature-length competition must be more than 60 pages; entries in the short screenplay contest must be fewer than 60 pages. The Screenplay Festival was established to solve two major problems. One, it is simply too difficult for talented writers who have no "connections" to gain recognition and get their material read by legitimate agents, producers, directors and investors. Two, agents, producers, directors, and investors complain that they cannot find any great material, but they will generally not accept "unsolicited material." This means that unless the script comes from a source that is known to them, they will not read it. Screenplay Festival was established to help eliminate this "chicken and egg" problem. By accepting all submitted screenplays and judging them based upon their quality—not their source or their standardized formatting or the quality of the brads holding them together—Screenplay Festival looks to give undiscovered screenwriters an opportunity to rise above the crowd. Deadline: September 9. Prize: $500 for feature film categories, $500 for television categories.

SCRIPTAPALOOZA SCREENPLAY & SHORTS COMPETITION

Endorsed by Write Brothers and Robert McKee, (310)594-5384. **E-mail:** info@scriptapalooza.com. **Website:** www.scriptapalooza.com. "From choosing our judges to creating opportunities, our top priority has always been the writer. We surround ourselves with reputable and successful companies, including many producers, literary agents, and managers who read your scripts. Our past winners have won Emmy's, been signed by agents, managers, had their scripts optioned, and even made into movies. Scriptapalooza will promote, pitch and push the semifinalists and higher for a full year." Deadline: January 5, February 1, March 8, April 16, and May 30. Prize: 1st Place: $10,000; over $50,00 in prizes for the entire competition. The top 100 scripts will be considered by over 95 production companies. Judged by over 90 producers.

SCRIPTAPALOOZA TELEVISION WRITING COMPETITION

(310)594-5384. **E-mail:** info@scriptapalooza.com. **Website:** www.scriptapaloozatv.com. Bi-annual competition accepting entries in 4 categories: Reality shows, sitcoms, original pilots, and 1-hour dramas. There are more than 30 producers, agents, and managers reading the winning scripts. Two past winners won Emmys because of Scriptapalooza and 1 past entrant now writes for Comedy Central. Winners announced February 15 and August 30. For contest results, visit website. Length: Standard television format whether 1 hour, 1-half hour, or pilot. Open to any writer 18 or older. Guidelines available on website. Accepts inquiries by e-mail or phone. Deadline: October 15 and April 15 of every year. Prizes: 1st Place: $500; 2nd Place: $200; 3rd Place: $100. Judged by over 25 producers.

SCRIPT PIPELINE SCREENWRITING COMPETITION

2633 Lincoln Blvd. #701, Santa Monica CA 90405. (323)424-4243. **E-mail:** entry@scriptpipeline.com. **Website:** scriptpipeline.com. **Contact:** Matt Misetich, senior executive. Now in its 16th year, the Script Pipeline Screenwriting Competition seeks talented writers to connect with production companies, agencies, and managers. As one of the longest-running screenplay contests, we focus specifically on finding writers representation, supporting diverse voices, championing marketable, unique storytelling, and pushing more original projects into production. The company's distinctive long-term facilitation process helps contest selections gain elite representation and crucial introductions to Hollywood, with $6 million in screenplays and pilots sold by competition finalists and "Recommend" writers since 2010 alone. To circulate exceptional material industry-wide, support our writers long-term, and launch careers. Early deadline:

March 1. Regular deadline: May 1. Late Deadline: May 15. Screenwriting Contest: $25,000 awarded to winner.

SET IN PHILADELPHIA SCREENWRITING COMPETITION

Greater Philadelphia Film Office, 1515 Arch St., 11th Floor, Philadelphia PA 19102. (215)686-2668. **Fax:** (215)686-3659. **Website:** www.film.org. Screenplays must be "shootable" primarily in the Greater Philadelphia area (includes the surrounding counties). All genres and storytelling approaches are acceptable. Feature length screenplays must be between 85-130 pages in length. TV pilot scripts must be 35-70 pages. There are 4 different awards, such as an award for best TV pilot, as well as the best script from a regional writer, and best script from a student. See the website for full details. Prize: $10,000 grand prize, with other prizes offered.

REVA SHINER COMEDY AWARD

Bloomington Playwrights Project, 107 W. 9th St., Bloomington IN 47404. **Website:** www.newplays. org. **Contact:** Susan Jones, literary manager. Annual award for unpublished/unproduced plays. The Bloomington Playwrights Project is a script-developing organization. Winning playwrights are expected to become part of the development process, working with the director in person or via long-distance. Check the website for more details. Deadline: October 31. Prize: $1,000, full production as a part of the Mainstage season. Judged by the literary committee of the BPP.

SHOWTIME'S TONY COX SCREENPLAY COMPETITION

Nantucket Film Festival, 68 Jay St., Suite 319, Brooklyn NY 11201. (646)480-1900. **Fax:** (646)365-3367. **E-mail:** info@nantucketfilmfestival.org. **Website:** www. nantucketfilmfestival.org/. "A once-in-a-lifetime opportunity to participate in the Screenwriters Colony, an annual, month-long retreat where writers are encouraged to find their voice and push the boundaries of their craft under the guidance of established film professionals, an all-expense paid trip to the Festival in June, and a $5,000 cash prize. All competition finalists are invited to a Mentor's Brunch where they can discuss their projects with NFF's annual Screenwriters Tributee." Screenplays must be standard feature film length (90-130 pages) and standard US format only. Regular submission deadline: March 12; WAB extended deadline, March 21.

SHRIEKFEST HORROR/SCI-FI FILM FESTIVAL & SCREENPLAY COMPETITION

P.O. Box 950921, Lake Mary FL 32795. **E-mail:** shriekfest@aol.com. **Website:** www.shriekfest.com. **Contact:** Denise Gossett. Shriekfest, the Los Angeles Horror/SciFi Film Festival continues its tradition as Los Angeles' Premier horror film event, presenting an exciting program of films each fall with beautiful Los Angeles as its backdrop. Now, in it's 18th year, Shriekfest L.A takes place at the legendary Raleigh Studios, which is the largest independent studio operator in the country. Shriekfest Orlando takes place at the famous Wayne Densch Performing Arts Center, which was originally founded in 1923! We offer filmmakers and film fans alike an ideal setting in 2 world-famous cities. Both established and emerging filmmakers gain media exposure, connect with the region's diverse audiences, and participate in an acclaimed event attended by industry professionals as well as horror and scifi fans. Every film accepted into Shriekfest has the opportunity to screen on both coasts for the price of one admission! Over the past Seventeen years, Shriekfest has welcomed numerous indie icons into its family and we are always looking to add to the Shriekfest Family! We are looking for original films and screenplays. We are accepting films/screenplays in five categories: narrative feature, narrative short, narrative super short, music video, feature screenplay, and short screenplay. And these genres: horror, comedy horror, thriller, sci-fi, and fantasy. We will be awarding prizes to the winning filmmaker or screenwriter in each category. Festival Founder and Director Denise Gossett says "We are already planning some exciting things for our 18th year!" Last year's festival was a great success. We had our biggest audience yet and we had more than 55 filmmakers/screenwriters in attendance. Plus, we were able to introduce some amazing indie horror films to Los Angeles and Orlando! "We accept award-winning screenplays. No restrictions as long as it's in the horror/thriller or sci-fi/fantasy genres. We accept shorts and features. No specific lengths." Deadline: February 1, May 1, July 1, July 10. Prize: Trophies, product awards, usually cash. "Our awards are updated all year long as sponsors step onboard." Judged by at least 20-30 judges who are all in different aspects of the entertainment industry, such as producers, directors, writers, actors, and agents.

SKIPPING STONES YOUTH AWARDS

P.O. Box 3939, Eugene OR 97403-0939. (541)342-4956. **Fax:** (541)342-4956. **E-mail:** editor@skippingstones. org. **Website:** www.skippingstones.org. **Contact:** Arun N. Toké. Annual awards to promote creativity as well as multicultural and nature awareness in youth. Cover letter should include name, address, phone, and e-mail. Entries must be unpublished. Length: 1,000 words maximum; 30 lines maximum for poems. Open to any writer between 7 and 17 years old. Guidelines available by SASE, e-mail, or on website. Accepts inquiries by e-mail or phone. Results announced in the October-December issue of *Skipping Stones*. Winners notified by mail. For contest results, visit website. Everyone who enters receives the issue which features the award winners. Deadline: June 25. Prize: Publication in the autumn issue of *Skipping Stones*, honor certificate, subscription to magazine, plus 5 multicultural and/or nature books. Judged by editors and reviewers at *Skipping Stones* magazine.

SOUTHEASTERN THEATRE CONFERENCE HIGH SCHOOL NEW PLAY CONTEST

SETC, 1175 Revolution Mill Dr., Suite 14, Greensboro NC 27405. **E-mail:** setc_hs_new_plays@Yahoo.com. **Website:** www.setc.org. **Contact:** Meredith Levy. Annual contest for one-act plays (no musicals, adaptations, or collaborations) on any subject. The script should be a one-act play that has not been published or professionally produced. Each applicant may submit one play only. E-mail play as a PDF and application form to setc_hs_new_plays@Yahoo.com. Visit website for additional details and required application form. High school student playwrights who currently reside in 1 of the 10 states in the SETC region are eligible. These states include Alabama, Florida, Georgia, Kentucky, Mississippi, North Carolina, South Carolina, Tennessee, Virginia, and West Virginia. Deadline: Submit October 1-December 1. Prize: $250, subsidy to attend the annual SETC convention in March with an adult chaperone, and a staged reading followed by a talkback.

SOUTHEASTERN THEATRE CONFERENCE NEW PLAY PROJECT

Dept. of Theatre & Dance, Austin Peay State Univ., 681 Summer St., Clarksville TN 37044. **Website:** www. setc.org. **Contact:** Chris Hardin, chair. "Annual award for full-length plays or related one acts. No musicals or children's plays. Submissions must be unproduced/ unpublished. Readings and workshops are acceptable. Submit application, and 1 copy of script as an e-mail attachment. Visit website for application. Entries will be accepted between March 1st and June 1st. One submission per playwright only." Eligibility: Playwrights who reside in the SETC region (or who are enrolled in a regionally accredited educational institution in the SETC region) or who reside outside the region but are SETC members are eligible for consideration. SETC Region states include Alabama, Florida, Georgia, Kentucky, Mississippi, North Carolina, South Carolina, Tennessee, Virginia, West Virginia. Mission: The SETC New Play Project is dedicated to the discovery, development and publicizing of worthy new plays and playwrights. Deadline: June 1. $1,000 and a staged reading.

SOUTHERN PLAYWRIGHTS COMPETITION

Jacksonville State University, Department of English, 700 Pelham Rd. N., Jacksonville AL 36265-1602. (256)782-5412. **Fax:** (256)782-5441. **E-mail:** jmaloney@jsu.edu. **E-mail:** jmaloney@jsu.edu. **Website:** www.jsu.edu/depart/english/southpla.htm. **Contact:** Joy Maloney. Competition for playwrights native to or a resident of Alabama, Arkansas, Florida, Georgia, Kentucky, Louisiana, Mississippi, North Carolina, South Carolina, Tennessee, Texas, Virginia, or West Virginia. Plays must deal with the Southern experience. Entries must be original, full-length plays. No musicals or adaptations will be accepted. The playwright may submit only one play. All entries must be typed, securely bound, and clearly identified. Synopsis of script must be included. No electronic entries accepted. Legal clearance of all materials not in the public domain will be the responsibility of the playwright. The Southern Playwrights Competition seeks to identify and encourage the best of Southern playwriting. Deadline: January 15. Prize: $1,000 and production of the play.

TELEVISION OUTREACH PROGRAM (TOP)

Scriptwriters Network (SWN), The Scriptwriters Network Foundation, Inc., P.O. Box 642806, Los Angeles CA 90064 USA. **E-mail:** top@scriptwritersnetwork. org. **E-mail:** top@scriptwritersnetwork.org. **Website:** www.scriptwritersnetwork.org. **Contact:** Melessa Y. Sargent, Director. The Television Outreach Program (TOP) is a Scriptwriters Network program to support undiscovered television writing talent. The program's objective is to help writers improve their craft so that they may achieve their goals of obtaining representation, script development, mentoring and career counseling services, landing writing assignments, and/or selling their work.

TENNESSEE SCREENWRITING ASSOCIATION SCRIPT COMPETITION

2298 Rosa L. Parks Blvd., Nashville TN 37228. (615)316-9448. **E-mail:** info@tennscreen.com. **Website:** www.tennscreen.com. Competition for the best low- or micro-budget scripts. Seeks to promote writers with the potential for investors, crowd-funding proposals, and many other tools. Deadline: February 28. Prize: The grand prize winner will receive notes from professional Hollywood screenwriter Robert Orr, production notes from independent Hollywood producer Guilia Prenna, an estimated budget breakdown for the script, and much more. See website for complete prize package details.

THEATRE CONSPIRACY ANNUAL NEW PLAY CONTEST

Theatre Conspiracy, 10091 McGregor Blvd., Ft. Myers FL 33919. (239)939-2787. **E-mail:** tcnewplaycontest@gmail.com. **Website:** artinlee.org. **Contact:** Bill Taylor, producing artistic director. Offered annually for full-length plays that are unproduced. Work submitted to the contest must be a full length play with 7 actors or less and have simple to moderate technical demands. Plays having up to three previous productions are welcome. No musicals. Deadline: March 30. Prize: $700 and full production. Judged by a panel of qualified theatre teachers, directors, and performers.

☺ THEATRE IN THE RAW BIENNIAL ONE-ACT PLAY WRITING CONTEST

Theatre In the Raw, 3521 Marshall St., Vancouver BC V5N 4S2 Canada. (604)708-5448. **E-mail:** theatreintheraw@telus.net. **Website:** www.theatreintheraw.ca. Biennial contest for an original one-act play, presented in proper stage-play format, that is unpublished and unproduced. The play (with no more than 6 characters) cannot be longer than 25 double-spaced, typed pages equal to 30 minutes. Scripts must have page numbers. Scripts are to be mailed only & will not be accepted by e-mail. Deadline: December 31. Prize: 1st Place: $200, at least 1 dramatic reading or staging of the play at a Theatre In the Raw Cafe/Venue, or as part of a mini-tour program for the One-Act Play Series Nights; 2nd Place: $100; 3rd Place: $75. Winners announced June 30.

TRUSTUS PLAYWRIGHTS' FESTIVAL

Trustus Theatre, 520 Lady St., Columbia SC 29201. (803)254-9732. **Fax:** (803)771-9153. **E-mail:** shammond@trustus.org. **E-mail:** shammond@trustus.org. **Website:** www.trustus.org. **Contact:** Sarah Hammond, literary manager. "Trustus Theatre announces its Annual Playwrights' Festival, a National Contest culminating in the Professional World Premier of an original play." In its 24th year, Trustus is one of America's longest-running play festivals. Since 1988, many of Trustus's winners have been published and produced off-Broadway, in Hollywood or at the Actors Theatre of Louisville. Full-length plays only, with no previous professional productions. Academic productions and workshops are okay. No musicals or no children's shows. One set, minimal production needs preferred. Cast of eight or fewer preferred, ages 15-60. One script per author. No re-submissions. Deadline: March 1. Prize: The winning play will receive a staged-reading at the 2013 Festival and $250. During the following year, the playwright will develop the script for production as he/she wishes and in consultation with members of the Trustus staff and company. In August, the play receive a full production—and the playwright an additional $500.

VERMONT PLAYWRIGHT'S AWARD

The Valley Players, P.O. Box 441, Waitsfield VT 05673. (802)583-6767. **E-mail:** valleyplayer@madriver.com. **Website:** www.valleyplayers.com. **Contact:** Sharon Kellerman. Offered annually for unpublished, non-musical, full-length plays suitable for production by a community theater group to encourage development of playwrights in Vermont, New Hampshire, and Maine. Deadline: February 1. $1,000.

☺ THE HERMAN VOADEN NATIONAL PLAYWRITING COMPETITION

Drama Department, Queen's University, Kingston ON K7L 3N6 Canada. (613)533-6000, ext. 74336. **E-mail:** drama@queensu.ca. **E-mail:** drama@queensu.ca. **Website:** www.queensu.ca/drama. **Contact:** Carol Anne Hanna. Offered every 2 years for unpublished plays to discover and develop new Canadian plays. See website for deadlines and guidelines. Open to Canadian citizens or landed immigrants. Deadline: January 15. Prize: 1st Prize: $3,000; 2nd Prize: $2,000; and 8 honorable mentions. 1st- and 2nd-prize winners are offered a 1-week workshop and public reading by professional director and cast. The 2 authors will be playwrights-in-residence for the rehearsal and reading period.

WATERFRONT FILM FESTIVAL AND INDIE SCREENPLAY COMPETITION

Waterfront Film Festival, P.O. Box 904, South Haven MI 49090. (269)857-8351. **Fax:** (269)857-1072. **E-mail:** info@waterfrontfilm.org. **Website:** www.waterfront-film.org. The festival is non-competitive and open to films of any genre: features, shorts, documentaries, animation, etc. The contest is now accepting entries from writers in any state. Previously, the contest was only for local writers. Scripts must be 80-130 pages in length. Entries are accepted through Withoutabox. Deadline: February 29. Prize includes cash, an industry reception in the winner's honor, lodging, and VIP pass to the festival.

JACKIE WHITE MEMORIAL NATIONAL CHILDREN'S PLAY WRITING CONTEST

1800 Nelwood Dr., Columbia MO 65202-1447. (573)874-5628. **E-mail:** jwmcontest@cectheatre.org **Website:** www.cectheatre.org. **Contact:** Tom Phillips. Annual contest that encourages playwrights to write quality plays for family audiences. Previously unpublished submissions only. Submissions made by author. Play may be performed during the following season. All submissions will be read by at least 3 readers. Author will receive a written evaluation of the script. Guidelines available online. Deadline: June 1. Prize: $500 with production possible. Judging by current and past board members of CEC and by non-board members who direct plays at CEC.

WISCONSIN SCREENWRITERS FORUM CONTEST

P.O. Box 7395, Madison WI 53707. **E-mail:** member-services@wiscreenwritersforum.org. **Website:** www.wiscreenwritersforum.org/contests.html.

WORLDFEST-HOUSTON INDEPENDENT INTERNATIONAL FILM FESTIVAL

51st Annual WorldFest-Houston, 9898 Bissonnet St., Suite 650, Houston TX 77036. (713)965-9955. **Fax:** (713)965-9960. **E-mail:** entry@worldfest.org. **Website:** www.worldfest.org. mixed media art **Contact:** Kelly Mann, entry coordinator. WorldFest discovered Steven Spielberg, George Lucas, Ang Lee, Ridley Scott, the Coen Brothers, Francis Ford Coppola, Randal Kleiser, John Lee Hancock, and David Lynch with their first awards. Screenplays must be submitted as actual printed scripts, 3-hole binders, no on-line reading. Competition for all genres of screenplays, plus 10 other competition categories of films and videos. Deadline: December 31; Final deadline is January 15. Prize: Cash, options, production deals, workshops, master classes, and seminars. Judged by a jury whose members are credentialed, experienced, award-winning writers, producers, and directors. No production assistants.

WRITE NOW

Indiana Repertory Theatre, 140 W. Washington St., Indianapolis IN 46204. 480-921-5770. **E-mail:** info@writenow.co. **Website:** www.writenow.co. The purpose of this biennial workshop is to encourage writers to create strikingly original scripts for young audiences. It provides a forum through which each playwright receives constructive criticism and the support of a development team consisting of a professional director and dramaturg. Finalists will spend approximately one week in workshop with their development team. At the end of the week, each play will be read as a part of the Write Now convening. Guidelines available online. Deadline: August 15.

YEAR END SERIES (YES) FESTIVAL OF NEW PLAYS

Theatre and Dance Program, School of the Arts, Nunn Dr., Northern Kentucky University, Highland Heights KY 41099-1007. 859.572.5648. **Fax:** (859)572-6057. **E-mail:** daniellyc1@nku.edu, or mking@nku.edu. **Website:** http://artscience.nku.edu/departments/theatre.html, https://artscience.nku.edu/content/dam/artscience/theatre/docs/16755YesFestivalFlyer.pdf. **Contact:** Michael King, co-project director; Corrie Danieley, co-project director. Receives submissions until September 30 in even-numbered years for the festivals which occur in April of odd-numbered years. Open to all writers. Flyers with submission guidelines and entry forms available on the website, or via email. Deadline: September 30. Open to submissions on May 1. Prize: $250 and an expense-paid visit (travel and housing) to Northern Kentucky University to see the play produced.

YOUNG PLAYWRIGHTS FESTIVAL NATIONAL PLAYWRITING COMPETITION

Young Playwrights, Inc., P.O. Box 5134, New York NY 10185. (212)594-5440. **Fax:** (212)594-5441. **E-mail:** literary@youngplaywrights.org. **Website:** youngplaywrights.org. **Contact:** Literary Manager. The Young Playwrights Inc. Festival National Playwriting Competition is offered annually to identify talented American playwrights aged 18 or younger. Please include your address, phone number, email address, and date of birth on the title page. Open to US residents only. Deadline: January 2 (postmarked). Prize: Winners receive an invitation to New York City for the annual Young Playwrights, Inc. Writers Conference and a professionally staged reading of their play. Entrants retain all rights to their work.

YOUNG PLAYWRIGHTS INC. WRITE A PLAY! NYC COMPETITION

Young Playwrights, Inc., Young Playwrights Inc. NYC, P.O. Box 5134, New York NY 10185. (212)594-5440. **Fax:** (212)684-4902. **E-mail:** literary@youngplaywrights.org. **Website:** www.youngplaywrights.org. **Contact:** Literary Manager. Offered annually for stage plays of any length (no musicals, screenplays, or adaptations) by NYC elementary, middle, and high school students only. Play must be submitted by students, not teachers. There are no restrictions on length, style, or subject, but collaborations of more than 3 writers will not be accepted. Screenplays and musicals are not eligible, nor are adaptations. Scripts should be typed and stapled, and pages must be numbered. Scripts must have a cover page with title of play, playwright's name, home address (with apartment number and zip code), phone number, school, grade, and date of birth. Submit a copy of your play and keep the original; scripts will not be returned. Deadline: postmarked on or before March 2. Prize varies.

ANNA ZORNIO MEMORIAL CHILDREN'S THEATRE PLAYWRITING COMPETITION

University of New Hampshire, Department of Theatre and Dance, PCAC, 30 Academic Way, Durham NH 03824. (603)862-3038. **Fax:** (603)862-0298. **E-mail:** mike.wood@unh.edu. **Website:** cola.unh.edu/theatre-dance/program/anna-zornio-childrens-theatre-playwriting-award. **Contact:** Michael Wood. Offered every 4 years for unpublished well-written plays or musicals appropriate for young audiences with a maximum length of 60 minutes. May submit more than 1 play, but not more than 3. Honors the late Anna Zornio, an alumna of The University of New Hampshire, for dedication to and inspiration of playwriting for young people, K-12th grade. Deadline: March 1, 2021. Prize: $500.

ARTS COUNCILS & FELLOWSHIPS

$50,000 GIFT OF FREEDOM

A Room of Her Own Foundation, P.O. Box 778, Placitas NM 87043. **E-mail:** awards@aroho.org. **Website:** www.aroomofherownfoundation.org. **Contact:** Tracey Cravens-Gras, associate director. The publicly funded award provides very practical help—both materially and in professional guidance and moral support with mentors and advisory council—to assist women in making their creative contribution to the world. The Gift of Freedom competition will determine superior finalists from each of 3 genres: Creative nonfiction, fiction, and poetry. Open to female residents of the US. Award application cycle dates are yet to be determined. Visit website at www.aroho.org for more information about the next application window. Deadline: November 2. Prize: One genre finalist will be awarded the $50,000 Gift of Freedom grant, distributed over 2 years in support of the completion of a particular creative project. The 2 remaining genre finalists will each receive a $5,000 prize.

✪ ADVANCED ARTIST AWARD

Government of Yukon, P.O. Box 2703, (L-3), Whitehorse YT Y1A 2C6 Canada. (867)667-8789. **Fax:** (867)393-6456. **E-mail:** artsfund@gov.yk.ca. **Website:** www.tc.gov.yk.ca/aaa.html. The Advanced Artist Award (AAA) assists individual Yukon visual, literary and performing artists practicing at a senior level with innovative projects, travel, or educational pursuits that contribute to their personal artistic development and to their community. The intended results and outcomes of the Advanced Artist Award are to encourage artistic creativity, to enable artists to develop their skills, and to improve the ability of artists to promote their works or talents. Guidelines and application available online. Deadlines: April 1 and October 1. Prizes: Level A artists: up to $10,000; Level B artists: up to $5,000. Judged by peer assessment (made up of senior Yukon artists representing the various disciplines seen in applicants for that round).

ALABAMA STATE COUNCIL ON THE ARTS INDIVIDUAL ARTIST FELLOWSHIP

201 Monroe St., Suite 110, Montgomery AL 36130. (334)242-4076, ext. 236. **Fax:** (334)240-3269. **E-mail:** anne.kimzey@arts.alabama.gov. **Website:** www.arts.

state.al.us. **Contact:** Anne Kimzey, Literary Arts Program Manager. Must be a legal resident of Alabama who has lived in the state for 2 years prior to application. Competition receives 30+ submissions annually. Accepts inquiries by e-mail and phone. The following should be submitted: a résumé and a list of published works with reviews, if available; and a minimum of 10 pages of poetry or prose, with a maximum of 20 pages. Please label each page with title, artist's name, and date. If published, indicate where and the date of publication. Please do not submit bound material. Guidelines available in January on website. Recognizes the achievements and potential of Alabama writers. Deadline: March 1. Applications must be submitted online by eGRANT. Judged by independent peer panel. Fellowship recipients notified by mail and announced on website in June.

ALASKA STATE COUNCIL ON THE ARTS CAREER OPPORTUNITY GRANT AWARD

Alaska State Council on the Arts, 161 Klevin St., Suite 102, Anchorage AK 99508-1506. (907)269-6610, (888)278-7424. **Fax:** (907)269-6601. **E-mail:** andrea.noble@alaska.gov. **Website:** www.eed.state.ak.us/aksca. **Contact:** Andrea Noble, visual & literary arts program director. Grants designed to provide financial assistance to professional artists for travel to in-state, national, or international events, programs or seminars and for other activities that will contribute to the strength of the artist's professional standing or skill. These cash awards help professional artists take advantage of impending, concrete opportunities that will significantly advance their work or careers. The awards are for unique, short-term opportunities that do not constitute routine completion of work in progress. Check website for information and details on applying. Deadline: Applications accepted quarterly. Applicants may request grants in variable amounts from $100 to $1,000 rounded to the nearest $100. Career Opportunity Grants will not exceed $1,000.

ARROWHEAD REGIONAL ARTS COUNCIL INDIVIDUAL ARTIST CAREER DEVELOPMENT GRANT

Arrowhead Regional Arts Council, 600 E Superior St., Suite 404, Duluth MN 55802. (218)722-0952 or (800)569-8134. **E-mail:** info@aracouncil.org. **Website:** www.aracouncil.org. Award is to provide financial support to regional artists wishing to take advantage of impending, concrete opportunities that will

advance their work or careers. Applicants must live in the 7-county region of Northeastern Minnesota. Deadline: October and April. Grant awards of up to $3,000. Candidates are reviewed by a panel of ARAC Board Members and Community Artists.

GEORGE BENNETT FELLOWSHIP

Phillips Exeter Academy, 20 Main Street, Exeter NH 03833. **E-mail:** teaching_opportunities@exeter.edu. **Website:** www.exeter.edu/bennettfellowship. Annual award for fellow and family to provide time and freedom from material considerations to a person seriously contemplating or pursuing a career as a writer. Applicants should have a ms in progress which they intend to complete during the fellowship period. Ms should be fiction, nonfiction, novel, short stories, or poetry. Duties: To be in residency at the Academy for the academic year; to make oneself available informally to students interested in writing. Committee favors writers who have not yet published a book with a major publisher. Deadline: November 30. A choice will be made, and all entrants notified in mid-April. Prize: Cash stipend (currently $15,260), room and board. Judged by committee of the English department.

CHLA RESEARCH GRANTS

Children's Literature Association, 1301 W. 22nd Street, Suite 202, Oak Brook IL 60523. (630)571-4520. **Fax:** (708)876-5598. **E-mail:** info@childlitassn.org. **Website:** www.childlitassn.org. **Contact:** ChLA Grants Chair. Offered annually. Three types of grants are available: Faculty Research Grants, Beiter Graduate Student Research Grants, and Diversity Research Grant. The grants are awarded for proposals dealing with criticism or original scholarship with the expectation that the undertaking will lead to publication (or a conference presentation for student awards) and make a significant contribution to the field of children's literature in the area of scholarship or criticism. Funds are not intended for work leading to the completion of a professional degree. Guidelines available online. Deadline: February 1. Prize: $500-1,500. Judged by the ChLA Grants Committee and Diversity Committee, respectively.

DELAWARE DIVISION OF THE ARTS

820 N. French St., Wilmington DE 19801. (302)577-8278. **Fax:** (302)577-6561. **E-mail:** Roxanne.stanulis@state.de.us. **Website:** www.artsdel.org. **Contact:** Roxanne Stanulis. Award to help further careers of emerg-

ing and established professional artists. For Delaware residents only. Guidelines available after May 1 on website. Accepts inquiries by e-mail, phone. Results announced in December. Winners notified by mail. Results available on website. Open to any Delaware writer over 18 years of ages and not in a degree-granting program. Deadline: August 1. Prize: $10,000 for masters; $6,000 for established professionals; $3,000 for emerging professionals. Judged by out-of-state, nationally recognized professionals in each artistic discipline.

DOBIE PAISANO WRITER'S FELLOWSHIP

The Graduate School, The University of Texas at Austin, Attn: Dobie Paisano Program, 110 Inner Campus Drive Stop G0400, Austin TX 78712-0531. (512)232-3609. **Fax:** (512)471-7620. **E-mail:** gbarton@austin.utexas.edu. **Website:** www.utexas.edu/ogs/Paisano. **Contact:** Gwen Barton. Sponsored by the Graduate School at The University of Texas at Austin and the Texas Institute of Letters, the Dobie Paisano Fellowship Program provides solitude, time, and a comfortable place for Texas writers or writers who have written significantly about Texas through fiction, nonfiction, poetry, plays, or other mediums. The Dobie Paisano Ranch is a very rural and rustic setting, and applicants should read the guidelines closely to insure their ability to reside in this secluded environment. At the time of the application, the applicant must meet one of the following requirements: (1) be a native Texan, (2) have resided in Texas at least three years at some time, or (3) have published significant work with a Texas subject. Those who meet requirement 1 or 2 do not have to meet the Texas subject matter restriction. Deadline: January 15. Applications are accepted beginning December 1 and must be post-marked no later than January 15. The Ralph A. Johnston memorial Fellowship is for a period of 4 months with a stipend of $6,250 per month. It is aimed at writers who have already demonstrated some publishing and critical success. The Jesse H. Jones Writing Fellowship is for a period of approximately 6 months with a stipend of $3,000 per month. It is aimed at, but not limited to, writers who are early in their careers.

JOSEPH R. DUNLAP FELLOWSHIP

William Morris Society in the US, Washington D.C., Department of English, University of California-Davis, Davis CA 95616. **E-mail:** us@morrissociety.org. **E-mail:** ecmille1@gmail.com. **Website:** www.morris-

society.org. **Contact:** Prof. Elizabeth Miller, university of California-Davis. Offered annually to promote study of the life and work of William Morris (1834-96), British poet, designer, and socialist. Award may be for research, a creative project, or a translation. Curriculum vitae, 1-page proposal, and 2 letters of recommendation required for application. Applicants must be US citizens or permanent residents. Deadline: December 15 of the year before the award is to be applied. Prize: Up to $1,000; multiple and partial awards possible.

FELLOWSHIPS FOR CREATIVE AND PERFORMING ARTISTS AND WRITERS

American Antiquarian Society, 185 Salisbury St., Worcester MA 01609-1634. (508)755-5221. **Fax:** (508)754-9069. **E-mail:** jmoran@mwa.org; library@americanantiquarian.org. **Website:** www.american-antiquarian.org. **Contact:** James David Moran. Annual fellowship for creative and performing artists, writers, filmmakers, journalists, and other persons whose goals are to produce imaginative, non-formulaic works dealing with pre-20th century American history. Application instructions available online. Website also lists potential fellowship projects. Deadline: October 5. Prize: The stipend will be $1,350 for fellows residing on campus (rent-free) in the society's scholars' housing, located next to the main library building. The stipend will be $1,850 for fellows residing off campus. Fellows will not be paid a travel allowance. Judged by AAS staff and outside reviewers.

GAP (GRANTS FOR ARTIST PROJECTS) PROGRAM

Artist Trust, 1835 12th Ave., Seattle WA 98122. (206)467-8734. **Fax:** (866)218-7878. **E-mail:** miguel@artisttrust.org; info@artisttrust.org. **Website:** www.artisttrust.org. **Contact:** Miguel Guillén, program manager. The GAP grant is awarded annually to 60 Washington state artists of all disciplines. Artist projects may include (but are not limited to): The development, completion or presentation of new work; publication; travel for artistic research or to present or complete work; documentation of work; and advanced workshops for professional development. Full-time students are not eligible. Applications will be posted on website in March. Applicants must be a practicing artist, 18 years of age or older by application deadline date, a generative artist, and a resident of Washington state at the time of application and when the award is granted. Deadline: April. Prize: Up to $1,500 for artist-generated projects.

GUGGENHEIM FELLOWSHIPS

John Simon Guggenheim Memorial Foundation, 90 Park Ave., New York NY 10016. (212)687-4470. E-mail: fellowships@gf.org. Website: www.gf.org. Often characterized as "midcareer" awards, Guggenheim Fellowships are intended for men and women who have already demonstrated exceptional capacity for productive scholarship or exceptional creative ability in the arts. Fellowships are awarded through two annual competitions: one open to citizens and permanent residents of the United States and Canada, and the other open to citizens and permanent residents of Latin America and the Caribbean. Candidates must apply to the Guggenheim Foundation in order to be considered in either of these competitions. The Foundation receives between 3,500 and 4,000 applications each year. Although no one who applies is guaranteed success in the competition, there is no prescreening: all applications are reviewed. Approximately 200 Fellowships are awarded each year. Deadline: September 15.

THE HODDER FELLOWSHIP

Lewis Center for the Arts, 185 Nassau St., Princeton NJ 08544. (609)258-6926. E-mail: ysabelg@princeton.edu. Website: arts.princeton.edu. Contact: Ysabel Gonzalez, fellowships assistant. The Hodder Fellowship will be given to writers of exceptional promise to pursue independent projects at Princeton University during the current academic year. Typically the fellows are poets, playwrights, novelists, creative nonfiction writers and translators who have published one highly acclaimed work and are undertaking a significant new project that might not be possible without the "studious leisure" afforded by the fellowship. Preference is given to applicants outside academia. Candidates for the Ph.D. are not eligible. Submit a resume, sample of previous work (10 pages maximum, not returnable), and a project proposal of 2-3 pages. Guidelines available on website. Princeton University is an equal opportunity employer and complies with applicable EEO and affirmative action regulations. Apply online. Deadline: October 1. Open to applications in July. Prize: $75,000 stipend.

MARILYN HOLLINSHEAD VISITING SCHOLARS FELLOWSHIP

University of Minnesota, 113 Anderson Library, 222 21st Ave. South, Minneapolis MN 55455. Website: http://www.lib.umn.edu/clrc/awards-grants-and-fellowships. Marilyn Hollinshead Visiting Scholars Fund for Travel to the Kerlan Collection is available for research study. Applicants may request up to $1,500. Send a letter with the proposed purpose and plan to use specific research materials (manuscripts and art), dates, and budget (including airfare and per diem). Travel and a written report on the project must be completed and submitted in the previous year. Deadline: June 1.

HENRY HOYNS & POE/FAULKNER FELLOWSHIPS

Creative Writing Program, 219 Bryan Hall, P.O. Box 400121, University of Virginia, Charlottesville VA 22904-4121. (434)924-6074. Fax: (434)924-1478. E-mail: creativewriting@virginia.edu. Website: creativewriting.virginia.edu. Contact: Barbara Moriarty, administrative assistant. Two-year MFA program in poetry and fiction; all students receive fellowships and teaching stipends that total $20,000 in both years of study. Sample poems/prose required with application. Deadline: December 15.

MASS CULTURAL COUNCIL ARTIST FELLOWSHIP PROGRAM

Mass Cultural Council, 10 St. James Ave., 3rd Floor, Boston MA 02116-3803. (617)727-3668. Fax: (617)727-0044. E-mail: mcc@art.state.ma.us. Website: www.massculturalcouncil.org; http://artsake.massculturalcouncil.org. Contact: Dan Blask, program officer. Awards in poetry, fiction/creative nonfiction, and dramatic writing (among other discipline categories) are given in recognition of exceptional original work (check website for award amount). Accepts inquiries by fax, e-mail and phone. Must be 18 years or older and a legal residents of Massachusetts for the last 2 years and at time of award. This excludes students in directly-related degree programs and grant recipients within the last 3 years. Looking to award artistic excellence and creative ability, based on work submitted for review. Judged by independent peer panels composed of artists and arts professionals.

MCKNIGHT ARTIST FELLOWSHIPS FOR WRITERS, LOFT AWARD(S) IN CHILDREN'S LITERATURE/CREATIVE PROSE/POETRY

The Loft Literary Center, 1011 Washington Ave. S., Suite 200, Open Book, Minneapolis MN 55415. (612)215-2575. **Fax:** (612)215-2576. **E-mail:** loft@loft.org. **Website:** www.loft.org. **Contact:** Bao Phi. "The Loft administers the McKnight Artists Fellowships for Writers. Five $25,000 awards are presented annually to accomplished Minnesota writers and spoken word artists. Four awards alternate annually between creative prose (fiction and creative nonfiction) and poetry/spoken word. The fifth award is presented in children's literature and alternates annually for writing for ages 8 and under and writing for children older than 8." The awards provide the writers the opportunity to focus on their craft for the course of the fellowship year. Prize: $25,000.

MINNESOTA STATE ARTS BOARD ARTIST INITIATIVE GRANT

Minnesota State Arts Board, Park Square Court, Suite 200, 400 Sibley St., St. Paul MN 55101-1928. (651)215-1600 or (800)866-2787. **Fax:** (651)215-1602. **E-mail:** kathee.foran@arts.state.mn.us. **Website:** www.arts.state.mn.us. **Contact:** Kathee Foran, program officer. The Artist Initiative Grant Program is designed to support and assist professional Minnesota artists at various stages in their careers by encouraging artistic development, nurturing artistic creativity, and recognizing the contributions of individual artists to the creative environment of the state of Minnesota. Literary categories include prose, poetry, playwriting, and screenwriting. Open to Minnesota residents. Grant amounts of $2,000-10,000

MOONDANCER FELLOWSHIP FOR WRITING ABOUT NATURE AND THE OUTDOORS

The Writers' Colony at Dairy Hollow, 515 Spring St., Eureka Springs AR 72632. (479)253-7444. **E-mail:** director@writerscolony.org. **Website:** www.writerscolony.org. **Contact:** Linda Caldwell, Director. "A two-week residency for writing in any genre about any aspect of nature and the outdoors. Works may be fiction or non-fiction. Supports writing of excellence which aspires to engage the mind, body and soul in the appreciation of nature. Applications accepted until May 31." Deadline: May 31.

JENNY MCKEAN MOORE VISITING WRITER

English Department, George Washington University, Rome Hall, 801 22nd St. NW, Suite 760, Washington DC 20052. (202)994-6180. **Fax:** (202)994-7915. **E-mail:** tvmallon@gwu.edu. **Website:** https://english.columbian.gwu.edu/activities-events. **Contact:** Lisa Page, Acting Director of Creative Writing. The position is filled annually, bringing a visiting writer to The George Washington University. During each semester the Writer teaches 1 creative-writing course at the university as well as a community workshop. Seeks someone specializing in a different genre each year—fiction, poetry, creative nonfiction. Annual stipend between $50,000 and $60,000, plus reduced-rent townhouse on campus (not guaranteed). Application deadline: December 12. Annual stipend varies, depending on endowment performance; most recently, stipend was $60,000, plus reduced-rent townhouse (not guaranteed).

NEBRASKA ARTS COUNCIL INDIVIDUAL ARTISTS FELLOWSHIPS

Nebraska Arts Council, 1004 Farnam St., Plaza Level, Omaha NE 68102. (402)595-2122. **Fax:** (402)595-2334. **E-mail:** nac.info@nebraska.gov. **Website:** www.nebraskaartscouncil.org. Offered every 3 years (literature alternates with other disciplines) to recognize exemplary achievements by originating artists in their fields of endeavor and support the contributions made by Nebraska artists to the quality of life in Nebraska. Funds available are announced in September prior to the deadline. Must be a resident of Nebraska for at least 2 years prior to submission date; 18 years of age; and not enrolled in an undergraduate, graduate, or certificate-granting program in English, creative writing, literature, or related field. Deadline: November 15. Prize: Distinguished achievement awards are $5,000 and merit awards are $1,000-2,000.

NICKELODEON WRITING PROGRAM

Nickelodeon, Viacom, 231 W. Olive Ave., Burbank CA 91502. (818)736-3663. **E-mail:** info.writing@nick.com. **Website:** www.nickwriting.com, www.facebook.com/nickwriting, twitter: @nickwriting. **Contact:** Karen Kirkland, Vice President. Offered annually for unpublished spec scripts. Must be 18 years or older to participate. Deadline: February 28. Prize: The Nickelodeon Writing Program offers aspiring television writers all over the globe, with diverse backgrounds and experiences, the opportunity to hone their skills while writing for our live action and animated shows. Participants will have hands-on interaction with executives writing spec scripts and pitching story ideas.

NORTH CAROLINA ARTS COUNCIL REGIONAL ARTIST PROJECT GRANTS

North Carolina Arts Council, Dept. of Natural and Cultural Resources, MSC #4632, Raleigh NC 27699-4634. (919)807-6512. **Fax:** (919)807-6532. **E-mail:** david.potorti@ncdcr.gov. **Website:** www.ncarts.org. **Contact:** David Potorti, literature and theater director. See website for contact information for the consortia of local arts councils that distribute these grants. Open to any writer living in North Carolina. Deadline: Dates vary in fall/spring. Prize: $500-3,000 awarded to writers to pursue projects that further their artistic development. These grants are awarded through consortia of local arts councils. See our website for details.

NORTH CAROLINA WRITERS' FELLOWSHIPS

North Carolina Arts Council, NC Department of Natural and Cultural Resources, North Carolina Arts Council, Mail Service Center #4632, Raleigh NC 27699-4632. (919)807-6512. **E-mail:** david.potorti@ncdcr.gov. **Website:** www.ncarts.org. **Contact:** David Potorti, literature and theater director. The North Carolina Arts Council offers fellowship grants to support writers of fiction, creative non-fiction, poetry, spoken word, playwrighting, screenwriting and literary translation. Artists must be N.C. residents for at least one year prior to the deadline, and at least 18 years old. They must be a U.S. citizen or holder of permanent resident alien status, remain a N.C. resident during the grant period, and be physically present in the state for the majority of that time. Artists who received the fellowship grant in the past five years or are enrolled in an academic or degree-granting program at the time of application or during the grant period are not eligible. Fellowships are offered to support writers in the development and creation of new work. See website for details. Offered every even-numbered year to support writers of fiction, creative non-fiction, poetry, spoken word, playwriting, screenwriting and literary translation. See website for guidelines and other eligibility requirements. Deadline: November 1 of even-numbered years. Prize: $10,000 grant. Reviewed by a panel of literature professionals (writers and editors).

OREGON LITERARY FELLOWSHIPS

925 S.W. Washington, Portland OR 97205. (503)227-2583. **E-mail:** susan@literary-arts.org. **Website:** www.literary-arts.org. **Contact:** Susan Moore, Director of programs and events. Oregon Literary Fellowships are intended to help Oregon writers initiate, develop, or complete literary projects in poetry, fiction, literary nonfiction, drama, and young readers literature. Writers in the early stages of their career are encouraged to apply. The awards are merit-based. Guidelines available in February for SASE. Accepts inquiries by e-mail, phone. Oregon residents only. Recipients announced in January. Deadline: Last Friday in June. Prize: $3,000 minimum award, for approximately 8 writers and 2 publishers. Judged by out-of-state writers

RHODE ISLAND ARTIST FELLOWSHIPS AND INDIVIDUAL PROJECT GRANTS

Rhode Island State Council on the Arts, State of Rhode Island, One Capitol Hill, 3rd Floor, Providence RI 02908. (401)222-3880. **Fax:** (401)222-3018. **E-mail:** Cristina.DiChiera@arts.ri.gov. **Website:** www.arts.ri.gov. **Contact:** Cristina DiChiera, director of individual artist programs. Annual fellowship competition is based upon panel review of poetry, fiction, and playwriting/screenwriting manuscripts. Project grants provide funds for community-based arts projects. Rhode Island artists who have lived in the state for at least 12 consecutive months may apply without a nonprofit sponsor. Applicants for all RSCA grant and award programs must be at least 18 years old and not currently enrolled in an arts-related degree program. Online application and guidelines can be found at www.arts.ri.gov/grants/guidelines/. You must be a United States citizen or Green Card holder and a current, legal resident of the State of Rhode Island. You must have established legal residence in Rhode Island for a minimum of twelve consecutive months prior to the date of application and you must be a current legal resident of the State of Rhode Island at the time that grant funds are disbursed. Rhode Island State Law (§44-30-5) defines a "resident" as someone "who is domiciled in this state" or "who is not domiciled in this state but maintains a permanent place of abode in this state and is in this state for an aggregate of more than one hundred eighty-three days of the taxable year. If an individual selected for a grant award is no longer a resident of the State of Rhode Island when funds are to be disbursed, the grant award may be withdrawn." Deadline: April 1 and October 1. Fellowship awards: $5,000 and $1,000. Grants range from $500-5,000, with an average of around $1,500. Judged by a rotating panel of artists.

WALLACE E. STEGNER FELLOWSHIPS

Creative Writing Program, Stanford University, Stanford CA 94305-2087. (650)723-0011. **Fax:** (650)723-3679. **E-mail:** stegnerfellowship@stanford.edu. **Website:** http://creativewriting.stanford.edu/about-the-fellowship. Offers 5 fellowships in poetry and 5 in fiction for promising writers who can benefit from 2 years of instruction and participation in the program. Online application preferred. "We do not require a degree for admission. No school of writing is favored over any other. Chronological age is not a consideration." Deadline: December 1. Open to submissions on September 1. Prize: Fellowships of $26,000, plus tuition of over $7,000/year.

TENNESSEE ARTS COMMISSION LITERARY FELLOWSHIP

Tennessee Arts Commission, 401 Charlotte Ave., Nashville TN 37243-0780. **Fax:** (615)741-8559. **E-mail:** lee.baird@state.tn.us. **Website:** tnartscommission.org. **Contact:** Lee Baird, director of literary programs. Awarded annually in recognition of professional Tennessee artists, i.e., individuals who have received financial compensation for their work as professional writers. Applicants must have a publication history other than vanity press. Three fellowships awarded annually to outstanding literary artists who live and work in Tennessee. Categories are in fiction, creative nonfiction, and poetry. Deadline: January 26. Prize: $5,000. Judged by an out-of-state adjudicator.

VERMONT ARTS COUNCIL

136 State St., Montpelier VT 05633-6001. (802)828-3293. **Fax:** (802)828-3363. **E-mail:** zeastes@vermontartscouncil.org. **Website:** www.vermontartscouncil.org. **Contact:** Sonia Rae, (802)828-4325 or by e-mail at srae@vermontartscouncil.org. Annual grants awarded once per year for specific projects. Creation Grants (awards of $3,000) for artists working in any medium including writers, visual artists and performing artists. Three-year Arts Partnership Grants of up to $7,000 and annual Project Grants of up to $3,000 for not-for-profit organizations (including writing pro-

grams and not-for-profit presses). Rolling grants are available in the following categories: Artist Development Grants of up to $1,000 providing professional development funds for individual artists and Technical Assistance Grants of up to $1,500 providing grants for organizational development to non-profit arts organizations. Open to Vermont residents only.

WISCONSIN INSTITUTE FOR CREATIVE WRITING FELLOWSHIP

6195B H.C. White Hall, 600 N. Park St., Madison WI 53706. **E-mail:** rfkuka@wisc.edu. **Website:** creative-writing.wisc.edu/fellowships.html. **Contact:** Sean Bishop, graduate coordinator. Fellowship provides time, space and an intellectual community for writers working on first books. Receives approximately 300 applicants a year for each genre. Judged by English Department faculty and current fellows. Candidates can have up to one published book in the genre for which they are applying. Open to any writer with either an M.F.A. or Ph.D. in creative writing. Please enclose a SASE for notification of results. Results announced on website by May 1. Applicants should submit up to 10 pages of poetry or one story or excerpt of up to 30 pages and a résumé or vita directly to the program during the month of February. See instructions on website for submitting online. An applicant's name must not appear on the writing sample (which must be in ms form) but rather on a separate sheet along with address, social security number, phone number, e-mail address and title(s) of submission(s). Candidates should also supply the names and phone numbers of two references. Accepts inquiries by e-mail and phone. Deadline: Last day of February. Open to submissions on December 15. Prize: $30,000 for a 9-month appointment.

FICTION

🌑 AEON AWARD

Albedo One/Aeon Press, Aeon Award, Albedo One & Yellow Brick Road, 8 Bachelor's Walk, Dublin D1 Ireland. (353)1-8730177. **E-mail:** fraslaw@yahoo.co.uk. **Website:** www.albedo1.com. **Contact:** Frank Ludlow, event coordinator. Prestigious fiction writing competition for short stories in any speculative fiction genre, such as fantasy, science fiction, horror, or anything in-between or unclassifiable. Submit your story (which must be less than 10,000 words in length and previously unpublished) in the body of an e-mail with contact details and "Aeon Award Submission" as the subject. Annual Deadline: November 30. Contest begins January 1. Grand Prize: €1,000; 2nd Prize: €200; and 3rd Prize: €100. The top 3 stories are guaranteed publication in *Albedo One*. Judged by Ian Watson, Juliet E. McKenna, Todd McCaffrey, and Michael Carroll.

🌑 AHWA FLASH & SHORT STORY COMPETITION

AHWA (Australian Horror Writers Association), **E-mail:** ahwacomps@australianhorror.com; ahwa@australianhorror.com. **Website:** www.australianhorror.com. **Contact:** Competitions Officer. Competition/award for short stories and flash fiction. There are 2 categories: short stories (1,001 to 8,000 words) and flash fiction (less than 1,000 words). Writers may submit to one or both categories, but entry is limited to 1 story per author per category. Send submission as an attached rtf or doc. Mail submissions only accepted as a last resort. No previously published entries will be accepted—all tales must be an original work by the author. Stories can be as violent or as bloody as the storyline dictates, but those containing gratuitous sex or violence will not be considered. Please check entries for spelling and grammar mistakes and follow standard submission guidelines (e.g., 12 point font, Ariel, Times New Roman, or Courier New, one and a half spacing between lines, with title and page number on each page). Looking for horror stories, tales that frighten, yarns that unsettle readers in their comfortable homes. All themes in this genre will be accepted, from the well-used (zombies, vampires, ghosts etc) to the highly original, so long as the story is professional and well written. Deadline: May 31. Prize: The authors of the winning Flash Fiction and Short Story entries will each receive paid publication in *Midnight Echo*, the Magazine of the AHWA and an engraved plaque. Judged by previous winners.

SHERWOOD ANDERSON FICTION AWARD

Mid-American Review, Mid-American Review, Dept. of English, Box WM, BGSU, Bowling Green OH 43403. (419)372-2725. **Fax:** (419)372-4642. **E-mail:** mar@bgsu.edu. **Website:** www.bgsu.edu/midamericanreview. **Contact:** Abigail Cloud, editor-in-chief. Offered annually for unpublished mss (6,000 word limit). Contest is open to all writers not associated with a judge or *Mid-American Review*. Guidelines available online or for SASE. Deadline: November 1.

Prize: $1,000, plus publication in the spring issue of *Mid-American Review*. Four Finalists: Notation, possible publication. Judged by editors and a well-known writer, i.e., Aimee Bender or Anthony Doerr. Judged by Charles Yu in 2017.

AUTUMN HOUSE PRESS FULL-LENGTH FICTION PRIZE

Autumn House Press, 5530 Penn Ave., Pittsburgh PA 15206. **E-mail:** info@autumnhouse.org. **Website:** autumnhouse.org. Fiction submissions should be approximately 200-300 pages. All fiction sub-genres (short stories, short-shorts, novellas, or novels), or any combination of sub-genres, are eligible. All finalists will be considered for publication. Deadline: June 30. Prize: Winners will receive book publication, $1,000 advance against royalties, and a $1,500 travel grant to participate in the Autumn House Master Authors Series in Pittsburgh. Judged by Dana Johnson (final judge).

BALCONES FICTION PRIZE

Austin Community College, Department of Creative Writing, 1212 Rio Grande St., Austin TX 78701. (512)584-5045. **E-mail:** joconne@austincc.edu. **Website:** http://www.austincc.edu/crw/html/balconescenter.html. **Contact:** Joe O'Connell. Awarded to the best book of literary fiction published the previous year. Books of prose may be submitted by publisher or author. Send three copies. Deadline: January 31. Prize: $1,500, winner is flown to Austin for a campus reading.

THE BALTIMORE REVIEW CONTESTS

The Baltimore Review, 6514 Maplewood Rd., Baltimore MD 21212. **E-mail:** editor@baltimorereview.org. **Website:** www.baltimorereview.org. **Contact:** Barbara Westwood Diehl, senior editor. Each summer and winter issue includes a contest theme (see submissions guidelines for theme). Prizes are awarded for first, second, and third place among all categories—poetry, short stories, and creative nonfiction. All entries are considered for publication. Open to all writers. Only unpublished work will be considered. Asks only for the right to publish the work for the first time. Deadline: May 31 and November 30. Prize: 1st Place: $500; 2nd Place: $200; 3rd Place: $100. All entries are considered for publication. Provides a small compensation to all contributors. Judged by the editors of *The Baltimore Review* and a guest, final judge.

BARD FICTION PRIZE

Bard College, P.O. Box 5000, Annandale-on-Hudson NY 12504-5000. (845)758-7087. **Fax:** (845)758-7917. **E-mail:** bfp@bard.edu. **Website:** www.bard.edu/bfp. **Contact:** Irene Zedlacher. The Bard Fiction Prize is awarded to a promising, emerging writer who is an American citizen aged 39 years or younger at the time of application. Cover letter should include name, address, phone, e-mail and name of publisher where book was previously published. Entries must be previously published. Open to U.S. citizens aged 39 and below. Guidelines available by SASE, fax, phone, e-mail, or on website. Results announced by October 15. Winners notified by phone. For contest results, e-mail, or visit website. The Bard Fiction Prize is intended to encourage and support young writers of fiction to pursue their creative goals and to provide an opportunity to work in a fertile and intellectual environment. Deadline: June 15. Prize: $30,000 and appointment as writer-in-residence at Bard College for 1 semester. Judged by a committee of 5 judges (authors associated with Bard College).

BELLEVUE LITERARY REVIEW GOLDENBERG PRIZE FOR FICTION

Bellevue Literary Review, NYU Dept of Medicine, 550 First Ave., OBV-A612, New York NY 10016. (212)263-3973. **E-mail:** info@blreview.org; stacy@blreview.org. **Website:** www.blreview.org. **Contact:** Stacy Bodziak, managing editor. The BLR prizes award outstanding writing related to themes of health, healing, illness, the mind and the body. Annual competition/award for short stories. Receives about 200-300 entries per category. Send credit card information or make checks payable to Bellevue Literary Review. Guidelines available in February. Accepts inquiries by e-mail, phone, mail. Submissions open in February. Results announced in December and made available to entrants with SASE, by e-mail, on website. Winners notified by mail, by e-mail. Entries should be unpublished. Anyone may enter contest. Length: No minimum; maximum of 5,000 words. Writers may submit own work. Deadline: July 1. Prize: $1,000 and publication in *The Bellevue Literary Review*. Honorable mention winners receive $250 and publication. BLR editors select semi-finalists to be read by an independent judge who chooses the winner. Previous judges include Nathan Englander, Jane Smiley, Francine Prose, and Andre Dubus III.

BEST LESBIAN EROTICA

BLE 2013, 31-64 21st St., #319, Long Island City NY 11106. **E-mail:** kwarnockble@gmail.com. **Website:** www.kathleenwarnock.com/best-lesbian-erotica. html. **Contact:** Kathleen Warnock, series editor. Call for submissions for *Best Lesbian Erotica*, an annual collection. Categories include: novel excerpts, short stories; poetry will be considered but is not encouraged. Accepts both previously published and unpublished material; will accept submissions that have appeared in other themed anthologies. Open to any writer. All submissions must include an e-mail address for response. No mss will be returned, so please do not include SASE. Include cover page with author's name/pen name if using one, title of submission(s), address, phone, e-mail. All submissions must be typed and double-spaced. Submit double-sided copies. Length: 5,000 words. Submit 2 different pieces of work. Submit 2 hard copies of each submission. "Will only accept e-mail copies if the following conditions apply: You live outside of North America or Europe; the cost of postage would be prohibitive from your home country; the post office system in your country is dreadful (US does not count); the content of your submission may be illegal to send via postal mail in your home country." Deadline: April 1. Prize: $100 for each published story, plus 2 copies of the anthology.

BINGHAMTON UNIVERSITY JOHN GARDNER FICTION BOOK AWARD

Creative Writing Program, Binghamton University, Binghamton University, Department of English, General Literature, and Rhetoric, Library North Room 1149, P.O. Box 6000, Binghamton NY 13902-6000. (607)777-2713. **E-mail:** cwpro@binghamton.edu. **Website:** http://binghamton.edu/english/creative-writing/. **Contact:** Maria Mazziotti Gillan, director. Contest offered annually for a novel or collection of fiction published in previous year in a press run of 500 copies or more. Each book submitted must be accompanied by an application form. Publisher may submit more than 1 book for prize consideration. Send 2 copies of each book. Guidelines available on website. Author or publisher may submit. Deadline: March 1. Prize: $1,000. Judged by a professional writer not on Binghamton University faculty.

JAMES TAIT BLACK MEMORIAL PRIZES

English Literature, University of Edinburgh, School of Literatures, Languages, and Cultures, 50 George

Square, Edinburgh EH8 9LH Scotland. (44-13)1650-3619. **E-mail:** s.strathdee@ed.ac.uk. **Website:** https://www.ed.ac.uk/events/james-tait-black. Open to any writer. Entries must be previously published. Winners notified by phone, via publisher. Contact department of English Literature for list of winners or check website. Accepts inquiries by e-mail or phone. Eligible works must be written in English and first published or co-published in Britain in the year of the award. Works should be submitted by publishers. Deadline: December 1. Prize: Two prizes each of £10,000 are awarded: one for the best work of fiction, one for the best biography or work of that nature, published during the calendar year January 1 to December 31. Judged by professors of English Literature with the assistance of teams of postgraduate readers.

BOULEVARD SHORT FICTION CONTEST FOR EMERGING WRITERS

Boulevard Magazine, 6614 Clayton Rd., PMB #325, Richmond Heights MO 63117. (314)862-2643. **Website:** www.boulevardmagazine.org. **Contact:** Jessica Rogen, editor. Offered annually for unpublished short fiction to a writer who has not yet published a book of fiction, poetry, or creative nonfiction with a nationally distributed press. Holds first North American rights on anything not previously published. Open to any writer with no previous publication by a nationally known press. Guidelines for SASE or on website. Accepts works up to 8,000 words. Simultaneous submissions are allowed, but previously accepted or published work is ineligible. Entries will be judged by the editors of *Boulevard Magazine*. Submit online or via postal mail. Deadline: December 31. Prize: $1,500, and publication in 1 of the next year's issues.

● THE CAINE PRIZE FOR AFRICAN WRITING

51 Southwark St., London SE1 1RU United Kingdom. **E-mail:** info@caineprize.com. **Website:** www.caineprize.com. **Contact:** Lizzy Attree. Entries must have appeared for the first time in the 5 years prior to the closing date for submissions, which is January 31 each year. Publishers should submit 6 copies of the published original with a brief cover note (no pro forma application). "Please indicate nationality or passport held." Submissions should be made by publishers only. Only one story per author will be considered in any one year. Only fiction work is eligible. Indicative length is between 3,000 and 10,000 words. See website

for more details and rules. The Caine Prize is open to writers from anywhere in Africa for work published in English. Its focus is on the short story, reflecting the contemporary development of the African storytelling tradition. Deadline: January 31. Prize: £10,000. Judges change each year.

JOHN W. CAMPBELL MEMORIAL AWARD FOR BEST SCIENCE FICTION NOVEL OF THE YEAR

1445 Jayhawk Blvd, Suite 3001, University of Kansas, Lawrence KS 66045. (785)864-2518. **E-mail:** gunn.sf.center@gmail.com. **Website:** www.sfcenter.ku.edu/campbell.htm. **Contact:** Chris McKitterick. Honors the best science fiction novel of the year. Entries must be previously published. Open to any writer. Accepts inquiries by e-mail. "Ordinarily publishers should submit work, but authors have done so when publishers would not. Send for list of jurors." Results announced in July. For contest results, see website. Deadline: Check website. Prize: Campbell Award trophy. Winners receive an expense-paid trip to the Campbell Conference to receive their award. Their names are also engraved on a permanent trophy. Judged by a jury.

☺ CANADIAN AUTHORS ASSOCIATION AWARD FOR POETRY

6 West St. N, Suite 203, Orillia ON L3V 5B8 Canada. (705)325-3926. **E-mail:** admin@canadianauthors.org. **Website:** www.canadianauthors.org. **Contact:** Anita Purcell, executive director. Offered annually for a full-length English-language book of poems for adults, by a Canadian writer. Deadline: January 31. Prize: $1,000 and a silver medal. Judging: Each year a trustee for each award appointed by the Canadian Authors Association selects up to 3 judges. Identities of the trustee and judges are confidential.

☺ CANADIAN AUTHORS ASSOCIATION EMERGING WRITER AWARD

6 West St. N., Suite 203, Orilla ON L3X 5B8 Canada. **Website:** www.canadianauthors.org. **Contact:** Anita Purcell, executive director. Annual award for a writer under 30 years of age deemed to show exceptional promise in the field of literary creation. Deadline: January 15. Prize: $500. Judging: Each year a trustee for each award appointed by the Canadian Authors Association selects up to 3 judges. Identities of the trustee and judges are confidential.

☼ CANADIAN TALES SHORT STORY COMPETITION

Red Tuque Books, Unit #6, 477 Martin St., Penticton BC V2A 5L2 Canada. (778)476-5750. **Fax:** (778)476-5750. **E-mail:** dave@redtuquebooks.ca. **Website:** www.redtuquebooks.ca. **Contact:** David Korinetz, contest director. Offered annually for unpublished works. Check the guidelines on the website. Purpose of award is to promote Canada and Canadian publishing. Stories require a Canadian element. There are three ways to qualify. They can be written by a Canadian, written about Canadians, or take place somewhere in Canada. Deadline: December 31. Prize: 1st Place: $500; 2nd Place: $150; 3rd Place: $100; and 10 prizes of $25 will be given to honorable mentions. All 13 winners will be published in an anthology. They will each receive a complimentary copy. Judged by Canadian authors/publishers in the appropriate genre. Acquires first print rights. Contest open to anyone.

CASCADE WRITING CONTEST & AWARDS

Oregon Christian Writers, 1075 Willow Lake Road N., Keizer OR 97303. **E-mail:** cascade@oregonchristianwriters.org. **E-mail:** cascade@oregonchristianwriters.org. **Website:** http://oregonchristianwriters.org/. **Contact:** Marilyn Rhoads and Julie McDonald Zander. The Cascade Awards are presented at the annual Oregon Christian Writers Summer Conference (held at the Red Lion on the River in Portland, Oregon, each August) attended by national editors, agents, and professional authors. The contest is open for both published and unpublished works in the following categories: contemporary fiction book, historical fiction book, speculative fiction book, nonfiction book, memoir book, young adult/middle grade fiction book, young adult/middle grade nonfiction book, children's chapter book and picture book (fiction and nonfiction), poetry, devotional, article, column, story, or blog post. Two additional special Cascade Awards are presented each year: the Trailblazer Award to a writer who has distinguished him/herself in the field of Christian writing; and a Writer of Promise Award for a writer who demonstrates unusual promise in the field of Christian writing. For a full list of categories, entry rules, and scoring elements, visit website. Guidelines and rules available on the website. Entry forms will be available on the first day for entry. Annual multi-genre competition to encourage both published and emerging writers in the field of Christian writing. Deadline: March 31. Submissions period begins February 14. Prize: Award certificate and pin presented at the Cascade Awards ceremony during the Oregon Christian Writers Annual Summer Conference. Finalists are listed in the conference notebook and winners are listed online. Cascade Trophies are awarded to the recipients of the Trailblazer and Writer of Promise Awards. Judged by published authors, editors, librarians, and retail book store owners and employees. Final judging by editors, agents, and published authors from the Christian publishing industry.

KAY CATTARULLA AWARD FOR BEST SHORT STORY

Texas Institute of Letters, P.O. Box 609, Round Rock TX 78680. **E-mail:** tilsecretary@yahoo.com. **Website:** www.texasinstituteofletters.org. Offered annually for work published January 1-December 31 of previous year to recognize the best short story. The story submitted must have appeared in print for the first time to be eligible. Writers must have been born in Texas, must have lived in Texas for at least 2 consecutive years, or the subject matter of the work must be associated with Texas. See website for guidelines. See website for details and instructions on entering the competition. Deadline: January 10. Prize: $1,000.

G. S. SHARAT CHANDRA PRIZE FOR SHORT FICTION

BkMk Press, University of Missouri-Kansas City, BkMk Press, University of Missouri-Kansas City, 5100 Rockhill Rd., Kansas City MO 64110-2499. (816)235-2558. **Fax:** (816)235-2611. **E-mail:** bkmk@umkc.edu; newletters@umkc.edu. **Website:** www.umkc.edu/bkmk. **Contact:** Ben Furnish. Offered annually for the best book-length ms collection (unpublished) of short fiction in English by a living author. Translations are not eligible. Initial judging is done by a network of published writers. Final judging is done by a writer of national reputation. Guidelines for SASE, by e-mail, or on website. Short fiction collections should be approximately 125 pages minimum, 300 pages maximum, double spaced. Deadline: January 15. Prize: $1,000, plus book publication by BkMk Press.

☻ PEGGY CHAPMAN-ANDREWS FIRST NOVEL AWARD

P.O. Box 6910, Dorset DT6 9QB United Kingdom. **E-mail:** info@bridportprize.org.uk. **Website:** www.bridportprize.org.uk. **Contact:** Kate Wilson, prize administrator. Award to promote literary excellence and new writers. Enter first chapters of novel, up to 8,000 words (minimum 5,000 words) plus 300 word synopsis. Send SSAE for entry form or enter online. Deadline: May 31. Prize: 1st Place: £1,000 plus mentoring & possible publication; Runner-Up: £500. Judged by Kamila Shamsie with The Literary Consultancy & A.M. Heath Literary Agents.

THE CHARITON REVIEW SHORT FICTION PRIZE

Truman State University Press, 100 East Normal Ave., Kirksville MO 63501-4221. (660)785-7336. **Fax:** (660)785-4480. **E-mail:** chariton@truman.edu; tsup@truman.edu. **Website:** http://tsup.truman.edu. **Contact:** Barbara Smith-Mandell. An annual award for the best unpublished short fiction on any theme up to 5,000 words in English. Mss must be double-spaced on standard paper and bound only with a clip. Electronic submissions are not allowed. Include 2 title pages: 1 with the ms title and the author's contact information (name, address, phone, e-mail), and the other with only the ms title. (The author's name must not appear on or within the ms.) Enclose a SASE for notification when your ms is received. Mss will not be returned. Current Truman State University faculty, staff, or students are not eligible to compete. Deadline: September 30. Prize: $500 and publication in *The Chariton Review* for the winner. Two or three finalists will also be published and receive $200 each. The final judge will be announced after the finalists have been selected in January.

🌀 THE ARTHUR C. CLARKE AWARD

55 Burtt House, Fanshaw Street, London N1 6LE U.K.. **E-mail:** clarkeaward@gmail.com. **Website:** www.clarkeaward.com. **Contact:** Tom Hunter, award director. Annual award presented to the best science fiction novel, published between January 1 and December 31 of the year in question, receiving its first British publication during the calendar year. Deadline: 2nd week in December. Prize: £2,016 (rising by £1 each year), and an engraved bookend. Judged by representatives of the British Science Fiction Association, the Science Fiction Foundation, and Sci-Fi-London Film Festival

THE DANAHY FICTION PRIZE

Tampa Review, University of Tampa, 401 W. Kennedy Blvd., Tampa FL 33606. 813-253-6266. **E-mail:** utpress@ut.edu. **Website:** www.ut.edu/TampaReview. Annual award for the best previously unpublished

short fiction. Prefers mss between 500-5,000 words. Deadline: November 30. Prize: $1,000, plus publication in *Tampa Review*.

DEAD OF WINTER

E-mail: editors@toasted-cheese.com. **Website:** www.toasted-cheese.com. **Contact:** Stephanie Lenz, editor. The contest is a winter-themed horror fiction contest with a new topic/theme each year. Theme and word count parameters announced October 1. Entries must be unpublished. Accepts inquiries by e-mail. Cover letter should include name, address, e-mail, word count, and title. Word count parameters vary each year. Open to any writer. Deadline: December 21. Results announced January 31. Winners notified by e-mail. List of winners on website. Prize: Amazon gift certificates and publication in *Toasted Cheese*. Judged by *Toasted Cheese* editors who blind judge each contest. Each judge uses her own criteria to rate entries.

🌀 DEBUT DAGGER

Crime Writers' Association, Debut Dagger, Dea Parkin, CWA Secretary, The Writing House, 3 Dale View, Chorley Lancashire PR7 3QJ United Kingdom. **E-mail:** secretary@thecwa.co.uk. **Website:** https://thecwa.co.uk/the-debuts/. **Contact:** Dea Parkin. Annual competition for unpublished crime writers. Submit the opening 3,000 words of a crime novel, plus a 500-1,000 word synopsis. Open to any writer who has not had a full-length novel traditionally published. Self-published only is acceptable, including the novel entry. Only accepts entries in Microsoft Word Document. Submissions should not include entrant's name anywhere on the documents. See website for full details on guidelines and submitting. Bring new writers to the attention of publishers. Deadline: February 28. Submission period begins October 1. Prize: £500. All shortlisted entrants will, with their permission, have their entry sent to UK literary agents, and receive brief feedback on their entries. Judged by a panel of top crime editors and agents as well as the CWA's head of Criminal Critiques, and the shortlisted entries are sent to agents.

WILLIAM F. DEECK MALICE DOMESTIC GRANTS FOR UNPUBLISHED WRITERS

Malice Domestic, P.O. Box 8007, Gaithersburg MD 20898-8007. **E-mail:** malicegrants@comcast.net. **Website:** www.malicedomestic.org. **Contact:** Harriette Sackler. Offered annually for unpublished work in the mystery field. Malice awards one grant to unpublished writers in the Malice Domestic genre at its annual convention in May. The competition is designed to help the next generation of Malice authors get their first work published and to foster quality Malice literature. Malice Domestic literature is loosely described as mystery stories of the Agatha Christie type, i.e., traditional mysteries. These works usually feature no excessive gore, gratuitous violence, or explicit sex. Writers who have been published previously in the mystery field, including publication of a mystery novel, short story, or dramatic work, are ineligible to apply. Members of the Malice Domestic Board of Directors and their families are ineligible to apply. Malice encourages applications from minority candidates. Guidelines online. Deadline: November 1. Prize: $2,500, plus a comprehensive registration to the following year's convention and two nights' lodging at the convention hotel.

THE JACK DYER FICTION PRIZE

Crab Orchard Review, Department of English, Mail Code 4503, Faner Hall 2380, Southern Illinois University Carbondale, 1000 Faner Drive, Carbondale IL 62901. (618)453-6833. **Fax:** (618)453-8224. **E-mail:** jtribble@siu.edu. **Website:** www.craborchardreview.siu.edu. **Contact:** Jon C. Tribble, managing editor. Annual award for unpublished short fiction. Entries should consist of 1 story up to 6,000 words maximum in length. *Crab Orchard Review* acquires first North American serial rights to all submitted work. One winner and at least 2 finalists will be chosen. Length: 6,000 words maximum. All submissions must be made through Submittable. Submissions must be unpublished original work, written in English by a U.S. citizen, permanent resident, or person who has DACA/TPS status (current students and employees at Southern Illinois University Carbondale are not eligible). See Submittable guidelines online for complete formatting instructions. The author's name should not appear on any page of the entry. Results announced by end of August. Deadline: May 17. Prize: $2,000, publication and 1-year subscription to *Crab Orchard Review*. Finalists are offered $500 and publication. Judged by editorial staff (pre-screening); winner chosen by genre editor.

MARY KENNEDY EASTHAM FLASH FICTION PRIZE

Category in the Soul-Making Keats Literary Competition, The Webhallow House, 1544 Sweetwood Dr., Broadmoor Village CA 94015-2029. **E-mail:** SoulKeats@gmail.com. **Website:** www.soulmaking-contest.us. **Contact:** Eileen Malone. Keep each story under 500 words. Three stories per entry. One story per page, typed, double-spaced, and unidentified. Deadline: November 30. Prizes: 1st Place: $100; 2nd Place: $50; 3rd Place: $25.

AURA ESTRADA SHORT STORY CONTEST

Boston Review, Short Story Contest, Boston Review, P.O. Box 425786, Cambridge MA 02142. (617)324-1360. **Website:** bostonreview.net. Stories should not exceed 5,000 words and must be previously unpublished. Mailed mss should be double-spaced and submitted with a cover note listing the author's name, address, and phone number. No cover note is necessary for online submissions. Enter using online contest entry manager at website. Aura Estrada (1977-2007), was a promising young Mexican writer and student, and the wife of Francisco Goldman. This prize is meant to honor her memory by supporting other burgeoning writers. Deadline: October 1. Prize: $1,500 and publication in the July/August issue of *Boston Review*. Runners up may also be published.

ETHEL ROHAN NOVEL EXCERPT PRIZE CATEGORY

Soul-Making Keats Literary Competition Category, The Webhallow House, 1544 Sweetwood Dr., Broadmoor Village CA 94015-2029. (650)756-5279. **Fax:** (650)756-5279. **E-mail:** soulkeats@mail.com. **Website:** www.soulmakingcontest.us. **Contact:** Eileen Malone. Open annually to any writer. Send meximum of 25 pages. Include a 1-page synopsis indicating category at top of page. Identify with 3x5 card only. Ongoing Deadline: November 30. Prize: 1st Place: $100; 2nd Place: $50; 3rd Place: $25.

FABLERS MONTHLY CONTEST

818 Los Arboles Lane, Santa Fe NM 87501. **Website:** www.fablers.net. **Contact:** W.B. Scott. Monthly contest for previously unpublished writers to help develop amateur writers. Guidelines posted online. No entry fee. Open to any writer. Deadline: 14th of each month. Prize: $100. Judged by members of website.

☼ THE FAR HORIZONS AWARD FOR SHORT FICTION

The Malahat Review, University of Victoria, P.O. Box 1700, Stn CSC, Victoria BC V8W 2Y2 Canada. (250)721-8524. **Fax:** (250)472-5051. **E-mail:** malahat@uvic.ca. **E-mail:** horizons@uvic.ca. **Website:** www.malahatreview.ca. **Contact:** L'Amour Lisik, Marketing and Circulation Manager. Submissions must be unpublished. No simultaneous submissions. Submit 1 piece of short fiction, 3,500 words maximum; no restrictions on subject matter or aesthetic approach. Include separate page with author's name, address, e-mail, and title; no identifying information on mss pages. E-mail submissions are accepted. Do not include SASE for results; mss will not be returned. Guidelines available on website. Winner and finalists contacted by e-mail. Open to "emerging short fiction writers from Canada, the US, and elsewhere" who have not yet published their fiction in a full-length book (48 pages or more). Deadline: May 1 of odd numbered years. Prize: $1,000 CAD, publication in fall issue of *The Malahat Review*. Announced in fall on website, Facebook page, and in quarterly e-newsletter, *Malahat Lite*.

FAW CHRISTINA STEAD AWARD

Fellowship of Australian Writers, 6-8 Davies St., Brunswick VIC 3095 Australia. **E-mail:** secretary@writers.asn.au; treasurer@writers.asn.au. **Website:** www.writers.asn.au. **Contact:** Awards Co-ordinator. Annual award for a work of fiction published since November 30 the previous year by an Australian writer. Guidelines for SASE or online. Closing date: November 30. Opens on September 1. Prize: $500.

FIRSTWRITER.COM INTERNATIONAL SHORT STORY CONTEST

firstwriter.com, United Kingdom. **Website:** https://www.firstwriter.com/competitions/short_story_contest/. **Contact:** J. Paul Dyson, managing editor. Accepts short stories up to 3,000 words on any subject and in any style. Deadline: April 1. The prize-money for first place is £200 (over $300). Ten special commendations will also be awarded, and all the winners will be published in firstwriter.magazine and receive a voucher that can be used to take out an annual subscription for free. Judged by firstwriter.magazine magazine editors.

FISH PUBLISHING FLASH FICTION COMPETITION

Durrus, Bantry, County Cork Ireland. **E-mail:** info@fishpublishing.com. **Website:** www.fishpublishing.com. **Contact:** Clem Cairns. Annual prize awarding flash fiction. Max length: 300 words. You may enter as many times as you wish. See website for details and rules. "This is an opportunity to attempt what is one of the most difficult and rewarding tasks—to create, in a tiny fragment, a completely resolved and compelling story in 300 words or less." Deadline: February 28. First Prize: $1,200. The 10 published authors will receive 5 copies of the Anthology and will be invited to read at the launch during the West Cork Literary Festival in July. Judged by Nuala O'Connor.

FISH SHORT STORY PRIZE

Durrus, Bantry Co. Cork Ireland. **E-mail:** info@fishpublishing.com. **Website:** www.fishpublishing.com. Annual worldwide competition to recognize the best short stories. Entries must not have been published before. Enter online or by post. See website for full details of competitions, and information on the Fish Editorial and Critique Services, and the Fish Online Writing Courses. Deadline: November 30. Prize: Overall prize fund: $6,000. 1st prize: $3,750. 2nd Prize: 1 week at Anam Cara Writers Retreat in West Cork and $350. 3rd Prize: $350. Closing date 30th November. The best 10 will be published in the Fish Anthology, launched in July at the West Cork Literary Festival. Winners announced March 17.

H.E. FRANCIS SHORT STORY COMPETITION

Ruth Hindman Foundation, University of Alabama in Huntsville, Department of English, Morton Hall Room 222, Huntsville AL 35899. **Website:** www.hefranciscompetition.com. Offered annually for unpublished work, not to exceed 5,000 words. Acquires first-time publication rights. Using the electronic submission system or by mail, submit a story of up to 5,000 words. If submitting by mail, include three copies of the story. Send an SASE or visit the website for complete guidelines. Deadline: January 15. Prize: $2,000, publication as an Amazon Kindle Single, an announcement in Poets and Writers, and publication on the website. Judged by a panel of nationally recognized, award-winning authors, directors of creative writing programs, and editors of literary journals.

THE GHOST STORY SUPERNATURAL FICTION AWARD

The Ghost Story, P.O. Box 601, Union ME 04862. **E-mail:** editor@theghoststory.com. **Website:** www.theghoststory.com. **Contact:** Paul Guernsey. Biannual contest for unpublished fiction. "Ghost stories are welcome, of course—but submissions may involve *any* paranormal or supernatural theme, as well as magic realism. What we're looking for is fine writing, fresh perspectives, and maybe a few surprises in the field of supernatural fiction." Guidelines available online. Length: 1,500-10,000 words. Deadline: April 30 and September 30. Winner receives $1,000 and publication. Honorable Mention wins $250 and publication, and Second Honorable Mention is awarded $100 and publication. Judged by the editors of *The Ghost Story*.

GIVAL PRESS NOVEL AWARD

Gival Press, LLC, P.O. Box 3812, Arlington VA 22203. (703)351-0079. **E-mail:** givalpress@yahoo.com. **Website:** www.givalpress.submittable.com. **Contact:** Robert L. Giron. Offered every other year for a previously original unpublished novel (not a translation). Guidelines by phone, on website, via e-mail, or by mail with SASE. Results announced late fall of same year. Winners notified by phone. Results made available to entrants with SASE, by e-mail, on website. Enter via portal: www.givalpress.submittable.com. Open to any author who writes original unpublished ms/work in English. Length: 30,000-100,000 words. Cover letter should include name, address, phone, e-mail, word count, novel title; include a short bio and short synopsis. Only the title and word count should appear on the actual ms. Writers may submit own work. Purpose is to award the best literary novel. Deadline: May 30. Prize: $3,000, plus publication of book with a standard contract and author's copies. Final judge is announced after winner is chosen. Entries read anonymously.

GIVAL PRESS SHORT STORY AWARD

Gival Press, P.O. Box 3812, Arlington VA 22203. (703)351-0079. **E-mail:** givalpress@yahoo.com. **Website:** www.givalpress.submittable.com. **Contact:** Robert L. Giron, publisher. Annual literary, short story contest. Entries must be unpublished. Open to anyone who writes original short stories, which are not a chapter of a novel, in English. Receives about 100-150 entries per category. Guidelines available online, via e-mail, or by mail. Results announced in the fall of the same year. Winners notified by phone. Results available with SASE, by e-mail, and on website. Enter via portal: www.givalpress.submittable.com. Length: 5,000-15,000 words. Include name, address, phone, e-mail, word count, title on cover letter; include short bio. Only the title and word count should be found on ms. Writers may submit their own fiction. Recognizes the best literary short story. Deadline: August

8. Prize: $1,000 and publication on website. Judged anonymously.

GLIMMER TRAIN'S FAMILY MATTERS CONTEST

Glimmer Train, P.O. Box 80430, Portland OR 97280. (503)221-0836. **Fax:** (503)221-0837. **E-mail:** eds@glimmertrain.org. **Website:** www.glimmertrain.org. **Contact:** Susan Burmeister-Brown. This contest is now held once a year, during the months of November and December. Winners are contacted on March 1. Submit online at www.glimmertrain.org. The word count for this contest generally ranges from 1,000 to 5,000 words, though up 12,000 words is fine. See complete guidelines online. Deadline: December 31. Prize: 1st Place: $2,500, publication in *Glimmer Train Stories*, and 10 copies of that issue; 2nd Place: $500 and consideration for publication; 3rd Place: $300 and consideration for publication. The editors judge.

GLIMMER TRAIN'S FICTION OPEN

Glimmer Train, Inc., Glimmer Train Press, Inc., P.O. Box 80430, Portland OR 97280. (503)221-0836. **Fax:** (503)221-0837. **E-mail:** eds@glimmertrain.org. **Website:** www.glimmertrain.org. **Contact:** Susan Burmeister-Brown. Submissions to this category generally range from 3,000-8,000 words, but up to 20,000 is fine. Held twice a year: March 1 - April 30 and July 1 - August 31. Submit online at www.glimmertrain.org. Winners will be called 2 months after the close of the contest. Deadline: April 30 and August 31. Prize: 1st Place: $3,000, publication in *Glimmer Train Stories*, and 10 copies of that issue; 2nd Place: $1,000 and consideration for publication; 3rd Place: $600 and consideration for publication. Judged by the editors.

GLIMMER TRAIN'S SHORT-STORY AWARD FOR NEW WRITERS

Glimmer Train Press, Inc., P.O. Box 80430, Portland OR 97280. (503)221-0836. **Fax:** (503)221-0837. **E-mail:** eds@glimmertrain.org. **Website:** www.glimmertrain.org. **Contact:** Susan Burmeister-Brown. Offered for any writer whose fiction hasn't appeared in a nationally distributed print publication with a circulation over 5,000. Submissions to this category generally range from 1,000–5,000 words, but up to 12,000 is fine. Held three times a year: January 1–February 28, May 1–June 30, September 1–October 31. Submit online at www.glimmertrain.org. Winners will be called 2 months after the close of the contest. Deadline: February 28, June 30, and October 31. Prize: 1st Place:

$2,500, publication in *Glimmer Train Stories*, and 10 copies of that issue; 2nd Place: $500 and consideration for publication; 3rd Place: $300 and consideration for publication.

GLIMMER TRAIN'S VERY SHORT FICTION CONTEST

Glimmer Train Press, Inc., P.O. Box 80430, Portland OR 97280. (503)221-0836. **Fax:** (503)221-0837. **E-mail:** eds@glimmertrain.org. **Website:** www.glimmertrain.org. **Contact:** Susan Burmeister-Brown. Offered to encourage the art of the very short story. Word count: 3,000 maximum. Held twice a year: March 1–April 30 and July 1–August 31. Submit online at www.glimmertrain.org. Results announced 2 months after the close of the contest. To encourage the art of the very short story. Deadline: April 30 and August 31. Prize: 1st Place: $2,000, publication in *Glimmer Train Stories*, and 10 copies of that issue; 2nd Place: $500 and consideration for publication; 3rd Place: $300 and consideration for publication. Judged by the editors.

● MARJORIE GRABER-MCINNIS SHORT STORY AWARD

ACT Writers Centre, Gorman House Arts Centre, Ainslie Ave., Braddon ACT 2612 Australia. (61)(2)6262-9191. **Fax:** (61)(2)6262-9191. **E-mail:** admin@actwriters.org.au. **Website:** www.actwriters.org.au. Open theme for a short story with 1,500-3,000 words. Guidelines available on website. Open only to unpublished emerging writers residing within the ACT or region. Deadline: September 18. Submissions period begins in early September. Prize: $600 and publication. Five runners-up receive book prizes. All winners may be published in the ACT Writers Centre newsletter and on the ACT Writers Centre website.

● LYNDALL HADOW/DONALD STUART SHORT STORY COMPETITION

Fellowship of Australian Writers (WA), P.O. Box 6180, Swanbourne WA 6910 Australia. (61)(8)9384-4771. **Fax:** (61)(8)9384-4854. **E-mail:** fellowshipaustralianwriterswa@gmail.com. **Website:** www.fawwa.org. Annual contest for unpublished short stories (maximum 3,000 words). Reserves the right to publish entries in a FAWWA publication or on website. Guidelines online or for SASE. Deadline: June 1. Submissions period begins April 1. Prize: 1st Place: $1,00; 2nd Place: $300; 3rd Place: $100.

HAMMETT PRIZE

International Association of Crime Writers, North American Branch, 243 Fifth Avenue, #537, New York NY 10016. **E-mail:** mfrisque@igc.org. **Website:** www.crimewritersna.org.. **Contact:** Mary A. Frisque, executive director, North American Branch. Award for crime novels, story collections, nonfiction by one author. "Our reading committee seeks suggestions from publishers and they also ask the membership for recommendations." Nominations announced in January; winners announced in fall. Winners notified by e-mail or mail and recognized at awards ceremony. For contest results, send SASE or e-mail. For guidelines, send SASE or e-mail. Accepts inquiries by e-mail. Entries must be previously published. To be eligible, the book must have been published in the US or Canada during the calendar year. The author must be a US or Canadian citizen or permanent resident. Award established to honor a work of literary excellence in the field of crime writing by a US or Canadian author. Deadline: December 15. Prize: Trophy. Judged by a committee of members of the organization. The committee chooses 5 nominated books, which are then sent to 3 outside judges for a final selection. Judges are outside the crime writing field.

WILDA HEARNE FLASH FICTION CONTEST

Big Muddy: A Journal of the Mississippi River Valley, WHFF Contest, Southeast Missouri State University Press, One University Plaza, MS 2650, Cape Girardeau MO 63701. (573) 651-2044. **E-mail:** sswartwout@semo.edu. **Website:** www.semopress.com. **Contact:** Susan Swartwout, publisher. Annual competition for flash fiction, held by Southeast Missouri State University Press. Work must not be previously published. Send maximum of 500 words, double-spaced, with no identifying name on the pages, and a separate cover sheet with story title, author's name, address, and phone number. Send SASE for notification of results; all manuscripts will be recycled. Entries should be sent via postal mail. Deadline: October 1. Prize: $500 and publication in *Big Muddy: A Journal of the Mississippi River Valley*. Semi-finalists will be chosen by a team of published writers. The final manuscript will be chosen by Susan Swartwout, publisher of the Southeast Missouri State University Press.

DRUE HEINZ LITERATURE PRIZE

University of Pittsburgh Press, 7500 Thomas Blvd., Pittsburgh PA 15260. **Fax:** (412)383-2466. **E-mail:**

info@upress.pitt.edu. **Website:** www.upress.pitt.edu. Offered annually to writers who have published a book-length collection of fiction or a minimum of 3 short stories or novellas in commercial magazines or literary journals of national distribution. Does not return mss. Deadline: June 30. Open to submissions on May 1. Prize: $15,000. Judged by anonymous nationally known writers such as Robert Penn Warren, Joyce Carol Oates, and Margaret Atwood.

LORIAN HEMINGWAY SHORT STORY COMPETITION

P.O. Box 2011 c/o Cynthia. D. Higgs: Key West Editorial, Key West FL 33045. **E-mail:** shortstorykeywest@hushmail.com. **Website:** www.shortstorycompetition.com. **Contact:** Eva Eliot, editorial assistant. Offered annually for unpublished short stories up to 3,500 words. Guidelines available via e-mail, or online. Accepts inquiries by e-mail, or visit website. Entries must be unpublished. Open to all writers whose work has not appeared in a nationally distributed publication with a circulation of 5,000 or more. Looking for excellence, pure and simple—no genre restrictions, no theme restrictions. We seek a writer's voice that cannot be ignored. All entrants will receive a letter from Lorian Hemingway on the competition's Facebook fan page and a list of winners, via the FB fan page or as requested by e-mail.Results announced the first week of August on the competition's FB fan page, and shortly after on the competition website. Only the first-place winner will be notified by phone prior to announcement. Award to encourage literary excellence and the efforts of writers whose voices have yet to be heard. Deadline: May 15. Prizes: 1st Place: $1,500, plus publication of his or her winning story in *Cutthroat: A Journal of the Arts*; 2nd-3rd Place: $500; honorable mentions will also be awarded. Judged by a panel of writers, editors, and literary scholars selected by author Lorian Hemingway. Lorian Hemingway is the competition's final judge.

TONY HILLERMAN PRIZE

Wordharvest, 1063 Willow Way, Santa Fe NM 87507. (505)471-1565. **E-mail:** wordharvest@wordharvest.com. **Website:** www.wordharvest.com. **Contact:** Anne Hillerman and Jean Schaumberg, co-organizers. Awarded annually, and sponsored by St. Martin's Press, for the best first mystery set in the Southwest. Murder or another serious crime or crimes must be at the heart of the story, with the emphasis on the so-

lution rather than the details of the crime. Multiple entries accepted. Accepts inquiries by e-mail, phone. Entries should be unpublished; self-published work is generally accepted. Length: no less than 220 type written pages, or approximately 60,000 words. Cover letter should include name, address, phone, e-mail, list of publishing credits. Please include SASE for response. Writers may submit their own work. Entries should be mailed to St. Martin's Press: St. Martin's Minotaur/THWC Competition, St. Martin's Minotaur, 175 Fifth Ave., New York, NY 10010. Honors the contributions made by Tony Hillerman to the art and craft of the mystery. Deadline: June 1. Prize: $10,000 advance and publication by St. Martin's Press. Nominees will be selected by judges chosen by the editorial staff of St. Martin's Press, with the assistance of independent judges selected by organizers of the Tony Hillerman Writers Conference (Wordharvest), and the winner will be chosen by St. Martin's editors.

L. RON HUBBARD'S WRITERS OF THE FUTURE CONTEST

Author Services, Inc., 7051 Hollywood Blvd., Los Angeles CA 90028. (323)466-3310. **Fax:** (323)466-6474. **E-mail:** contests@authorservicesinc.com. **Website:** www.writersofthefuture.com. **Contact:** Joni Labaqui, contest director. Foremost competition for new and amateur writers of unpublished science fiction or fantasy short stories or novelettes. Offered to find, reward and publicize new speculative fiction writers so they may more easily attain professional writing careers. Open to writers who have not professionally published a novel or short novel, more than 2 novelettes, or more than 3 short stories. Entry stories must be unpublished. Limit 1 entry per quarter. This is an international contest. Results announced quarterly in e-newsletter. Winners notified by phone. Contest has 4 quarters. There shall be 3 cash prizes in each quarter. In addition, at the end of the year, the 4 first-place, quarterly winners will have their entries rejudged, and a grand prize winner shall be determined. Eligible entries are previously unpublished short stories or novelettes (under 17,000 words) of science fiction or fantasy. Guidelines for SASE or on website. Accepts inquiries by fax, e-mail, phone. Mss: White paper, black ink; double-spaced; typed; each page appropriately numbered with title, no author name. Include cover page with author's name, address, phone number, e-mail address (if available), as well as estimated word count and the title of the work. Online submissions are accepted. Hard copy submissions will not be returned. Deadline: December 31, March 31, June 30, September 30. Prize (awards quarterly): 1st Place: $1,000; 2nd Place: $750; and 3rd Place: $500. Annual grand prize: $5,000. Judged by David Farland (initial judge), then by a panel of 4 professional authors.

INK & INSIGHTS WRITING CONTEST

Critique My Novel, 1802 S Lincoln, Amarillo TX 79102. **E-mail:** contest@inkandinsights.com. **Website:** https://inkandinsights.com. **Contact:** Catherine York, contest administrator. Ink & Insights is a writing contest geared toward strengthening the skills of independent writers by focusing on feedback. Each entry is assigned four judges who specialize in the genre of the manuscript. They read, score, and comment on specific aspects of the segment. The top three mss in the Master and Nonfiction categories move on to the Agent Round and receive a guaranteed read and feedback from a panel of agents. Send the first 10,000 words of your manuscript (unpublished, self-published, or published through a vanity/independent press). Include a cover sheet that contains the following information: novel title, genre, word count of full ms, e-mail address. Do not put name on submission. See website for full details and formatting guidelines. Deadline: May 30 (regular entry), June 30 (late entry). Prize: Prizes vary depending on category. Every novel receives personal feedback from 4 judges. Judges listed on website, including the agents who will be helping choose the top winners this year.

○ INTERNATIONAL 3-DAY NOVEL CONTEST

210-111 West Hastings Street, Vancouver BC V6B 1H4 Canada. **E-mail:** info@3daynovel.com. **Website:** www.3daynovel.com. **Contact:** Brittany Huddart, managing editor. "Can you produce a masterwork of fiction in three short days? The 3-Day Novel Contest is your chance to find out. Each Labour Day weekend, fueled by adrenaline and the desire for literary nirvana, hundreds of writers step up to the challenge. It's a thrill, a grind, a 72-hour kick in the pants and an awesome creative experience. How many crazed plotlines, coffee-stained pages, pangs of doubt and moments of genius will next year's contest bring forth? And what will you think up under pressure?" Entrants write in whatever setting they wish, in whatever genre they wish, anywhere in the world. Entrants may start writing as of midnight on Friday night, and must stop by midnight on Monday night. Then they print entry and mail it in to the contest for judging. Deadline: Friday before Labor Day weekend. Prize: 1st place receives publication; 2nd place receives $500; 3rd place receives $100.

THE IOWA SHORT FICTION AWARD & JOHN SIMMONS SHORT FICTION AWARD

Iowa Writers' Workshop, 507 N. Clinton St., 102 Dey House, Iowa City IA 52242-1000. **Website:** www.uiowapress.org. **Contact:** James McCoy, director. Annual award to give exposure to promising writers who have not yet published a book of prose. Open to any writer. Current University of Iowa students are not eligible. No application forms are necessary. Announcement of winners made early in year following competition. Winners notified by phone. No application forms are necessary. Do not send original ms. Include SASE for return of ms. Entries must be unpublished, but stories previously published in periodicals are eligible for inclusion. The ms must be a collection of short stories of at least 150 word-processed, double-spaced pages. Deadline: September 30. Submission period begins August 1. Prize: Publication by University of Iowa Press. Judged by senior Iowa Writers' Workshop members who screen mss; published fiction author of note makes final selections.

JERRY JAZZ MUSICIAN NEW SHORT FICTION AWARD

Jerry Jazz Musician, 2207 NE Broadway, Portland OR 97232. **E-mail:** jm@jerryjazz.com. **Website:** www.jerryjazzmusician.com. Three times a year, *Jerry Jazz Musician* awards a writer who submits the best original, previously unpublished work of approximately 1,000-5,000 words. The winner will be announced via a mailing of the *Jerry Jazz* newsletter. Publishers, artists, musicians, and interested readers are among those who subscribe to the newsletter. Additionally, the work will be published on the home page of *Jerry Jazz Musician* and featured there for at least 4 weeks. The *Jerry Jazz Musician* reader tends to have interests in music, history, literature, art, film, and theater—particularly that of the counter-culture of mid-20th century America. Guidelines available online. Deadline: September, January, and May. See website for specific dates. Prize: $100. Judged by the editors of *Jerry Jazz Musician*.

JESSE H. JONES AWARD FOR BEST WORK OF FICTION

P.O. Box 609, Round Rock TX 78680. **E-mail:** tilsecretary@yahoo.com. **Website:** http://texasinstituteofletters.org. Offered annually by Texas Institute of Letters for work published January 1-December 31 of year before award is given to recognize the writer of the best book of fiction entered in the competition. Writers must have been born in Texas, have lived in the state for at least 2 consecutive years at some time, or the subject matter of the work should be associated with the state. See website for details and information on submitting. Deadline: January 10. Prize: $6,000.

JAMES JONES FIRST NOVEL FELLOWSHIP

Wilkes University, Creative Writing Department, Wilkes University, 84 West South Street, Wilkes-Barre PA 18766. (570)408-4547. **Fax:** (570)408-3333. **E-mail:** jamesjonesfirstnovel@wilkes.edu. **Website:** www.wilkes.edu/. Offered annually for unpublished novels (must be works-in-progress). This competition is open to all U.S. citizens who have not previously published novels. Submit a 2-page (maximum) outline of the entire novel and the first 50 pages of the novel-in-progress are to be submitted. The ms must be typed and double-spaced; outline may be single-spaced. Entrants submitting via snail mail should include their name, address, telephone number, and e-mail address (if available) on the title page, but nowhere else on the manuscript. For those entrants submitting online, name, address, telephone number, and e-mail address should appear only on your cover letter. Cover letter should be dropped in the cover letter box and outline and ms should be attached as one document. The award is intended to honor the spirit of unblinking honesty, determination, and insight into modern culture exemplified by the late James Jones. Deadline: March 15. Submission period begins October 1. Prize: $10,000; 2 runners-up get $1,000 honorarium.

THE LAWRENCE FOUNDATION AWARD

Prairie Schooner, 123 Andrews Hall, University of Nebraska-Lincoln, Lincoln NE 68588-0334. (402)472-0911. **Fax:** (402)472-9771. **E-mail:** prairieschooner@unl.edu. **Website:** www.prairieschooner.unl.edu. Offered annually for the best short story published in Prairie Schooner in the previous year. Only work published in *Prairie Schooner* in the previous year is considered. Work is nominated by editorial staff. Results announced in the Spring issue. Winners notified by mail in February or March. Prize: $1,000. Judged by editorial staff of *Praire Schooner*.

LAWRENCE FOUNDATION PRIZE

Michigan Quarterly Review, 0576 Rackham Bldg., 915 E. Washington Street, Ann Arbor MI 48109-1070. (734)764-9265. **E-mail:** mqr@umich.edu. **Website:** www.michiganquarterlyreview.com. **Contact:** Vicki Lawrence, managing editor. This annual prize is awarded by the *Michigan Quarterly Review* editorial board to the author of the best short story published in *MQR* that year. The prize is sponsored by University of Michigan alumnus and fiction writer Leonard S. Bernstein, a trustee of the Lawrence Foundation of New York. Approximately 20 short stories are published in *MQR* each year. Guidelines available under submission guidelines on website. Prize: $1,000. Judged by editorial board.

LITERAL LATTÉ FICTION AWARD

Literal Latté, 200 E. 10th St., Suite 240, New York NY 10003. **E-mail:** litlatte@aol.com. **Website:** www.literal-latte.com. **Contact:** Edward Estlin, contributing editor. Award to provide talented writers with 3 essential tools for continued success: money, publication, and recognition. Offered annually for unpublished fiction (maximum 20,000 words). Guidelines online. Open to any writer. Deadline: January 30. Prize: 1st Place: $1,000 and publication in *Literal Latté*; 2nd Place: $300; 3rd Place: $200; also up to 7 honorable mentions. All winners published in *Literal Latté*.

LITERAL LATTE SHORT SHORTS CONTEST

Literal Latté, 200 E. 10th St., Suite 240, New York NY 10003. **E-mail:** litlatte@aol.com. **Website:** www.literal-latte.com. **Contact:** Jenine Gordon Bockman, editor. Keeping free thought free since 1994. Deadline: June 30. Prize: $500. Judged by the editors.

LITERARY FICTION CONTEST

The Writers' Workshop of Asheville, NC, Literary Fiction Contest, 387 Beaucatcher Rd., Asheville NC 28805. **E-mail:** writersw@gmail.com. **Website:** www.twwoa.org. Submit a short story or chapter of a novel of 5,000 words or less. Multiple entries are accepted. All work must be unpublished. Pages should be paper clipped, with your name, address, phone and title of work on a cover sheet. Double-space and use 12-point font. Deadline: August 30. Prize: 1st Place: Your choice of a 2 night stay at the Mountain Muse

B&B in Asheville, 3 free online workshops, or 50 pages line-edited and revised by editorial staff; 2nd Place: 2 free workshops or 35 pages line-edited; 3rd Place: 1 free workshop or 25 pages line-edited; 10 Honorable Mentions. Judged by published writing instructors.

THE MARY MACKEY SHORT STORY PRIZE CATEGORY

Soul-Making Keats Literary Competition, The Webhallow House, 1544 Sweetwood Dr., Broadmoor Village CA 94015-2029. (650)756-5279. **Fax:** (650)756-5279. **E-mail:** soulkeats@mail.com. **Website:** www.soulmakingcontest.us. **Contact:** Eileen Malone. Open annually to any writer. One story/entry, up to 5,000 words. All prose works must be typed, page numbered, and double-spaced. Identify only with 3x5 card. Deadline: November 30. Prize: Cash prizes.

☼ THE MALAHAT REVIEW NOVELLA PRIZE

The Malahat Review, University of Victoria, P.O. Box 1700 STN CSC, Victoria BC V8W 2Y2 Canada. (250)721-8524. **E-mail:** malahat@uvic.ca. **E-mail:** novella@uvic.ca. **Website:** malahatreview.ca. **Contact:** L'Amour Lisik, marketing and circulation manager. Held in alternate (even numbered) years with the Long Poem Prize. Submit novellas between 10,000 and 20,000 words in length. Include separate page with author's name, address, e-mail, and novella title; no identifying information on mss. pages. E-mail submissions are now accepted. Do not include SASE for results; mss will not be returned. Guidelines available on website. 2010 winner was Tony Tulathimutte, 2012 winner was Naben Ruthnum, and the 2014 winner was Dora Dueck. Winner and finalists contacted by e-mail. Offered to promote unpublished novellas. Obtains first world rights. After publication rights revert to the author. Open to any writer. Deadline: February 1 (even years). Prize: $1,500 CAD and one year's subscription. Winner published in summer issue of *The Malahat Review* and announced on website, Facebook page, and in quarterly e-newsletter, *Malahat Lite*. Three recognized literary figures are assigned to judge the contest each year.

☻ THE MAN BOOKER PRIZE

Four Colman Getty PR, 20 St Thomas Street, London SE1 9BF United Kingdom. (44)(207)697 4200. **Website:** www.themanbookerprize.com. **Contact:** Four Colman Getty PR. Books are only accepted through UK publishers. However, publication outside the UK does not disqualify a book once it is published in the UK. Open to any full-length novel (published October 1-September 30). No novellas, collections of short stories, translations, or self-published books. Open to citizens of the Commonwealth or Republic of Ireland. Deadline: July. Prize: £50,000. Judges appointed by the Booker Prize Management Committee.

MARY MCCARTHY PRIZE IN SHORT FICTION

Sarabande Books, 2234 Dundee Rd., Suite 200, Louisville KY 40205. (502)458-4028. **Fax:** (502)458-4065. **E-mail:** info@sarabandebooks.org. **Website:** www.sarabandebooks.org. **Contact:** Sarah Gorham, Editor-in-Chief. Annual competition to honor a collection of short stories, novellas, or a short novel. All mss should be between 150 and 250 pages. All finalists considered for publication. Guidelines available online. Deadline: February 15. Submission period begins January 1. Prize: $2,000 and publication (standard royalty contract).

MEMPHIS MAGAZINE FICTION CONTEST

Memphis Magazine, co-sponsored by booksellers of Laurelwood and Burke's Book Store, Fiction Contest, c/o *Memphis* magazine, P.O. Box 1738, Memphis TN 38101. (901)521-9000, ext. 451. **Fax:** (901)521-0129. **E-mail:** sadler@memphismagazine.com. **Website:** www.memphismagazine.com. **Contact:** Marilyn Sadler. Annual award for authors of short fiction living within 150 miles of Memphis. Each story should be between 2,500 and 3,500 words long. See website for guidelines and rules. Deadline: February 15. Prize: $1,000 grand prize, along with being published in the annual Cultural Issue; two honorable-mention awards of $500 each will be given if the quality of entries warrants.

DAVID NATHAN MEYERSON PRIZE FOR FICTION

Southwest Review, Southern Methodist University, P.O. Box 750374, Dallas TX 75275-0374. (214)768-1037. **Fax:** (214)768-1408. **E-mail:** swr@smu.edu. **Website:** www.smu.edu/southwestreview. **Contact:** Greg Brownderville, editor-in-chief. Annual award given to a writer who has not published a first book of fiction, either a novel or collection of stories. Submissions must be no longer than 8,000 words. Work should be printed without the author's name. Name and address should appear only on the cover letter. Submissions will not be returned. Deadline: May 1 (postmarked). Prize: $1,000 and publication in the *Southwest Review*.

MILKWEED NATIONAL FICTION PRIZE

1011 Washington Ave. S., Suite 300, Minneapolis MN 55415. (612)332-3192. **Fax:** (612)215-2550. **E-mail:** editor@milkweed.org. **Website:** www.milkweed. org. **Contact:** Patrick Thoman, editor and program manager. Annual award for unpublished works. Mss should be one of the following: a novel, a collection of short stories, one or more novellas, or a combination of short stories and one or more novellas. Mss should be of high literary quality and between 150-400 pages in length. Work previously published as a book in the US is not eligible, but individual stories or novellas previously published in magazines or anthologies are eligible. Guidelines available online. Deadline: Rolling submissions. Check website for details of when they're accepting mss. Prize: Publication by Milkweed Editions and a cash advance of $5,000 against royalties, agreed upon in the contractual arrangement negotiated at the time of acceptance. Judged by the editors.

MONTANA PRIZE IN FICTION

Cutbank Literary Magazine, *CutBank*, University of Montana, English Dept., LA 133, Missoula MT 59812. **E-mail:** editor.cutbank@gmail.com. **Website:** www. cutbankonline.org. **Contact:** Allison Linville, editor-in-chief. The Montana Prize in Fiction seeks to highlight work that showcases an authentic voice, a boldness of form, and a rejection of functional fixedness. Accepts online submissions only. Send a single work, no more than 35 pages. Guidelines available online. Deadline: January 15. Submissions period begins November 9. Prize: $500 and featured in the magazine. Judged by a guest judge each year.

THE HOWARD FRANK MOSHER SHORT FICTION PRIZE

Vermont College, 36 College St., Montpelier VT 05602. (802)828-8517. **E-mail:** hungermtn@vcfa.edu. **Website:** www.hungermtn.org. **Contact:** Samantha Kolber, managing editor. The Howard Frank Mosher Short Fiction Prize is an annual contest for short fiction. Enter one original, unpublished story under 10,000 words. Do not put name or address on the story; entries are judged blind. Accepts submissions online or via postal mail. Deadline: March 1. Prize: One first place winner receives $1,000 and publication. Two honorable mentions receive $100 each, and are considered for publication. Judged by Janet Burroway in 2016 and Caitlyn Horrocks in 2017.

NATIONAL READERS' CHOICE AWARDS

Oklahoma Romance Writers of America (OKRWA), **E-mail:** nrca@okrwa.com. **Website:** www.okrwa.com. **Contact:** Kathy L Wheeler. "To provide writers of romance fiction with a competition where their published novels are judged by readers." See the website for categories and descriptions. Additional award for best first book. All entries must have an original copyright date during the current contest year. Entries will be accepted from authors, editors, publishers, agents, readers, whoever wants to fill out the entry form, pay the fee, and supply the books. No limit to the number of entries, but each title may be entered only in one category. Open to any writer published by an RWA approved non-vanity/non-subsidy press. For guidelines, send e-mail or visit website. Deadline: December 1st. Prize: Plaques and finalist certificates awarded at the awards banquet hosted at the Annual National Romance Writers Convention. Judged by readers.

NATIONAL WRITERS ASSOCIATION NOVEL WRITING CONTEST

The National Writers Association, 10940 S. Parker Rd. #508, Parker CO 80134. **E-mail:** natlwritersassn@hotmail.com. **Website:** www.nationalwriters.com. **Contact:** Sandy Whelchel, director. Open to any genre or category. Contest begins December 1. Open to any writer. Entries must be unpublished. Length: 20,000-100,000 words. Contest forms are available on the NWA website or an attachment will be sent upon request via e-mail or with an SASE. Annual contest to help develop creative skills, to recognize and reward outstanding ability, and to increase the opportunity for the marketing and subsequent publication of novel mss. Deadline: April 1. Prize: 1st Place: $500; 2nd Place: $250; 3rd Place: $150. Judged by editors and agents.

NATIONAL WRITERS ASSOCIATION SHORT STORY CONTEST

10940 S. Parker Rd., #508, Parker CO 80134. **E-mail:** natlwritersassn@hotmail.com. **Website:** www.nationalwriters.com. Any genre of short story manuscript may be entered. All entries must be postmarked by July 1. Contest opens April 1. Only unpublished works may be submitted. All manuscripts must be typed, double-spaced, in the English language. Maximum length is 5,000 words. Those unsure of proper manuscript format should request Research Report #35. The entry must be accompanied by an entry form (photocopies are acceptable) and return SASE if you wish the material and rating sheets returned. Submissions will be destroyed, otherwise. Receipt of entry will not be acknowledged without a return postcard. Author's name and address must appear on the first page. Entries remain the property of the author and may be submitted during the contest as long as they are not published before the final notification of winners. Final prizes will be awarded in June. The purpose of the National Writers Assn. Short Story Contest is to encourage the development of creative skills, recognize and reward outstanding ability in the area of short story writing. Prize: 1st Prize: $250; 2nd Prize: $100; 3rd Prize: $50; 4th-10th places will receive a book. 1st-3rd place winners may be asked to grant one-time rights for publication in *Authorship* magazine. Honorable Mentions receive a certificate. Judging will be based on originality, marketability, research, and reader interest. Copies of the judges evaluation sheets will be sent to entrants furnishing an SASE with their entry.

THE NELLIGAN PRIZE FOR SHORT FICTION

Colorado Review/Center for Literary Publishing, Colorado State University, 9105 Campus Delivery, Dept. of English, Colorado State University, Ft. Collins CO 80523-9105. (970)491-5449. **E-mail:** creview@colostate.edu. **Website:** http://nelliganprize.colostate.edu. **Contact:** Stephanie G'Schwind, editor. Annual competition/award for short stories. Receives approximately 900 stories. All entries are read blind by Colorado Review's editorial staff. Ten to fifteen entries are selected to be sent on to a final, outside judge. Stories must be unpublished and between 10 and 50 pages. "The Nelligan Prize for Short Fiction was established in memory of Liza Nelligan, a writer, editor, and friend of many in Colorado State University's English Department, where she received her master's degree in literature in 1992. By giving an award to the author of an outstanding short story each year, we hope to honor Liza Nelligan's life, her passion for writing, and her love of fiction." Deadline: March 14. Prize: $2,000 and publication of story in *Colorado Review*. Judged by a different writer each year. 2017 judge is Richard Bausch.

NEW LETTERS PRIZE FOR FICTION

New Letters, University of Missouri-Kansas City, *New Letters* Awards for Writers, UMKC, University House, 5101 Rockhill Rd., Kansas City MO 64110-2499. (816)235-1168. **Fax:** (816)235-2611. **E-mail:** newletters@umkc.edu. **Website:** www.newletters.org/writers-wanted/writing-contests. **Contact:** Ashley Wann. Offered annually for the best short story to discover and reward new and upcoming writers. Buys first North American serial rights. Open to any writer. Short story should not exceed 8,000 words. Deadline: May 18. 1st Place: $1,500 and publication in a volume of *New Letters*.

✪ SEAN O'FAOLAIN SHORT STORY COMPETITION

The Munster Literature Centre, Frank O'Connor House, 84 Douglas Street, Cork Ireland. +353-0214319255. **E-mail:** munsterlit@eircom.net. **Website:** www.munsterlit.ie. **Contact:** Patrick Cotter, artistic director. Entries should be unpublished. Anyone may enter contest. Length: 3,000 words max. Cover letter should include name, address, phone, e-mail, word count, novel/story title. Purpose is to reward writers of outstanding short stories. Deadline: July 31. Prize: 1st prize €2,000; 2nd prize €500. Four runners-up prizes of €100 (approx $146). All six stories to be published in *Southword Literary Journal*. First-Prize Winner offered week's residency in Anam Cara Artist's Retreat in Ireland.

FRANK O'CONNOR AWARD FOR SHORT FICTION

descant, Texas Christian University's literary journal, TCU Box 298300, Fort Worth TX 76129. **E-mail:** descant@tcu.edu. **Website:** www.descant.tcu.edu. **Contact:** Matthew Pitt, editor. Offered annually for an outstanding story accepted for publication in the current edition of the journal. Publication retains copyright but will transfer it to the author upon request. Deadline: March 31. Open to submissions September 1. Prize: $500.

THE FLANNERY O'CONNOR AWARD FOR SHORT FICTION

The University of Georgia Press, Main Library, 3rd Floor, 320 S. Jackson St., Athens GA 30602. (706)369-6130. **Fax:** (706)369-6131. **Website:** www.ugapress.org. This competition welcomes short story or novella collections. Stories may have been published singly, but should not have appeared in a book-length collection of the author's own work. Length: 40,000-75,000 words. Accepts electronic submissions via website. Accepts multiple submissions, and simultaneous submissions, if identified. Title, author's name, and contact information should appear on a top cover sheet only. Include a table of contents. All submissions and announcement of winners and finalists will be confirmed via e-mail. Deadline: April 1-May 31. 2 winners receive $1,000 and book contracts from the University of Georgia Press.

ON THE PREMISES CONTEST

On The Premises, LLC, 4323 Gingham Court, Alexandria VA 22310. **E-mail:** questions@onthepremises. com. **Website:** www.onthepremises.com. **Contact:** Tarl Kudrick or Bethany Granger, co-publishers. *On the Premises* aims to promote newer and/or relatively unknown writers who can write creative, compelling stories told in effective, uncluttered, and evocative prose. Each contest challenges writers to produce a great story based on a broad premise that the editors supply as part of the contest. Submissions are accepted only through web-based submissions system. Entries should be unpublished. Length: minimum 1,000 words; maximum 5,000. No name or contact info should be in ms. Writers may submit own work. Check website for details on the specific premise that writers should incorporate into their story. Results announced within 2 weeks of contest deadline. Winners notified via e-mail and with publication of *On the Premises*. Results made available to entrants on website and in publication. Deadline: Short story contests held twice a year; smaller mini-contests held four times a year; check website for exact dates. Prize: 1st Prize: $220; 2nd Prize: $160; 3rd Prize: $120; Honorable Mentions receive $60. All prize winners are published in *On the Premises* magazine in HTML and PDF format. Judged by a panel of judges with professional editing and writing experience.

KENNETH PATCHEN AWARD FOR THE INNOVATIVE NOVEL

Eckhard Gerdes Publishing, 1110 Varsity Blvd., Apt. 221, DeKalb IL 60115. **E-mail:** egerdes@experimentalfiction.com. **Website:** www.experimentalfiction. com. **Contact:** Eckhard Gerdes. This award will honor the most innovative novel submitted during the previous calendar year. Kenneth Patchen is celebrated for being among the greatest innovators of American fiction, incorporating strategies of concretism, asemic

writing, digression, and verbal juxtaposition into his writing long before such strategies were popularized during the height of American postmodernist experimentation in the 1970s. See guidelines and application form online at website. Deadline: All submissions must be postmarked between January 1 and July 31. Prize: $1,000 and 20 complimentary copies. Judged by novelist Dominic Ward.

THE PATERSON FICTION PRIZE

The Poetry Center at Passaic Community College, One College Blvd., Paterson NJ 07505. (973)684-6555. **Fax:** (973)523-6085. **E-mail:** mgillan@pccc.edu. **Website:** www.pccc.edu/poetry. **Contact:** Maria Mazziotti Gillan, executive director. Offered annually for a novel or collection of short fiction published the previous calendar year. For more information, visit the website or send SASE. Deadline: February 1. Prize: $1,000.

WILLIAM PEDEN PRIZE IN FICTION

The Missouri Review, 357 McReynolds Hall, Columbia MO 65211. (573)882-4474. **Fax:** (573)884-4671. **E-mail:** mutmrcontestquestion@moreview.com. **Website:** www.missourireview.com. **Contact:** Michael Nye, managing editor. Offered annually for the best story published in the past volume year of the magazine. All stories published in *The Missouri Review* are automatically considered. Guidelines online or for SASE. Prize: $1,000 and a reading/reception.

PEN/FAULKNER AWARDS FOR FICTION

PEN/Faulkner Foundation, 201 E. Capitol St. SE, Washington DC 20003. (202)898-9063. **E-mail:** awards@penfaulkner.org. **Website:** www.penfaulkner.org. **Contact:** Emma Snyder, executive director. Offered annually for best book-length work of fiction by an American citizen published in a calendar year. Deadline: October 31. Prize: $15,000 (one Winner); $5,000 (4 Finalists).

PHOEBE WINTER FICTION CONTEST

Phoebe, MSN 2D6, George Mason University, 4400 University Dr., Fairfax VA 22030. (703)993-2915. **E-mail:** phoebe@gmu.edu. **Website:** http://www.phoebejournal.com/. Offered annually for an unpublished story (25 pages maximum). Guidelines online or for SASE. First serial rights if work is accepted for publication. Purpose is to recognize new and exciting fiction. Deadline: March 19. Prize: $400 and publication in the Spring online issue. Judged by a recognized fiction writer, hired by *Phoebe* (changes each year). For 2016, the fiction judge will be Patricia Park.

EDGAR ALLAN POE AWARD

1140 Broadway, Suite 1507, New York NY 10001. (212)888-8171. **E-mail:** mwa@mysterywriters.org. **Website:** www.mysterywriters.org. Mystery Writers of America is the leading association for professional crime writers in the United States. Members of MWA include most major writers of crime fiction and nonfiction, as well as screenwriters, dramatists, editors, publishers, and other professionals in the field. Categories include: Best Novel, Best First Novel by an American Author, Best Paperback/E-Book Original, Best Fact Crime, Best Critical/Biographical, Best Short Story, Best Juvenile Mystery, Best Young Adult Mystery, Best Television Series Episode Teleplay, and Mary Higgins Clark Award. Purpose of the award: Honor authors of distinguished works in the mystery field. Previously published submissions only. Submissions should be made by the publisher. Work must be published/produced the year of the contest. Deadline: November 30. Prize: Awards ceramic bust of "Edgar" for winner; certificates for all nominees. Judged by active status members of Mystery Writers of America (writers).

THE KATHERINE ANNE PORTER PRIZE FOR FICTION

Nimrod International Journal, The University of Tulsa, 800 S. Tucker Dr., Tulsa OK 74104. (918)631-3080. **Fax:** (918)631-3033. **E-mail:** nimrod@utulsa.edu. **Website:** www.utulsa.edu/nimrod. **Contact:** Eilis O'Neal. Submissions must be unpublished. Work must be in English or translated by original author. Author's name must not appear on ms. Include cover sheet with title, author's name, address, phone number, and e-mail address (author must have a US address by October of contest year to enter). Mark "Contest Entry" on submission envelope and cover sheet if submitting by mail. Include SASE for results only; mss will not be returned. 7,500-word maximum for short stories. Postmark Deadline: April 30. Prizes: 1st Place: $2,000 and publication; 2nd Place: $1,000 and publication. Judged by the *Nimrod* editors, who select the finalists, and a recognized author, who selects the winners.

KATHERINE ANNE PORTER PRIZE IN SHORT FICTION

The University of North Texas Press, 1155 Union Cir., #311336, Denton TX 76203-5017. (940)565-2142. **Fax:** (940)565-4590. **Website:** web3.unt.edu/untpress. **Contact:** Laura Kopchick, editor, University of Texas at Arlington. Contest is offered annually. Prize is awarded to a collection of short fiction. The University of North Texas Press announces the 2012 Katherine Anne Porter Prize in Short Fiction. Entries will be judged by an eminent writer. Entries can be a combination of short-shorts, short stories, and novellas, from 100 to 200 book pages in length (word count between 27,500 and 50,000). Material should be previously unpublished in book form. Once a winner is declared and contracted for publication, UNT Press will hold the rights to the stories in the winning collection. They may no longer be under consideration for serial publication elsewhere and must be withdrawn by the author from consideration. Please include two cover sheets: one with title only, and one with title, your name, address, e-mail, phone, and acknowledgment of any previously published material. Your name should not appear anywhere on the ms except on the one cover page. The winning manuscript will be announced in January 2012. Manuscripts cannot be returned and must be accompanied by a $25 entry fee (payable to UNT Press) and a letter-sized SASE for notification.

PRESS 53 AWARD FOR SHORT FICTION

Press 53, 560 N. Trade St., Suite 103, Winston-Salem NC 27101. (336)770-5353. **E-mail:** kevin@press53.com. **Website:** www.press53.com. **Contact:** Kevin Morgan Watson, Publisher. Awarded to an outstanding, unpublished collection of short stories. Details and guidelines available online. Deadline: December 31. Submission period begins September 1. Finalists and winner announced no later than May 1. Publication in October. Prize: Publication of winning short story collection, $1,500 cash advance and 10 copies of the book. Judged by Press 53 publisher Kevin Morgan Watson.

✪ PRISM INTERNATIONAL ANNUAL SHORT FICTION CONTEST

Creative Writing Program, UBC, Buch. E462 - 1866 Main Mall, Vancouver BC V6T 1Z1 Canada. (604)822-2514. **Fax:** (604)822-3616. **Website:** prismmagazine.ca/contests. **Contact:** Jessica Johns, executive editor, promotions. Maximum word count: 6,000 words. Offered annually for unpublished work to award the best in contemporary fiction. Works of translation are eligible. Guidelines by SASE, by e-mail, or on website. Acquires first North American serial rights upon publication, and rights to publish online for promotional or archival purposes. Open to any writer except students and faculty in the Creative Writing Department at UBC, or people who have taken a creative writing course at UBC with the 2 years prior to the contest deadline. Deadline: January 31. Prize: 1st Place: $1,500; 1st Runner-up: $600; 2nd Runner-up: $400; winner is published.

✪ THOMAS H. RADDALL ATLANTIC FICTION AWARD

Writers' Federation of Nova Scotia, 1113 Marginal Rd., Halifax NS B3H 4P7 Canada. (902)423-8116. **Fax:** (902)422-0881. **E-mail:** director@writers.ns.ca. **Website:** www.writers.ns.ca. **Contact:** Marilyn Smulders, executive director. The Thomas Head Raddall Atlantic Fiction Award is awarded for a novel or a book of short fiction by a full-time resident of Atlantic Canada. Detailed guidelines and eligibility criteria available online. Deadline: First Friday in December. Prize: Valued at $25,000 for winning title.

HAROLD U. RIBALOW PRIZE

Hadassah Magazine, Hadassah WZOA, 40 Wall St., 8th Floor, New York NY 10005. (212)451-6286. **Fax:** (212)451-6257. **E-mail:** magtemp3@hadassah.org. **Website:** www.hadassahmagazine.org. **Contact:** Deb Meisels, coordinator. Offered annually for English-language (no translation) books of fiction (novel or short stories) on a Jewish theme published the previous year. Books should be submitted by the publisher. Administered annually by *Hadassah Magazine*. Deadline: April 15. The official announcement of the winner will be made in the fall.

✪ THE ROGERS WRITERS' TRUST FICTION PRIZE

The Writers' Trust of Canada, 460 Richmond St. W., Suite 600, Toronto ON M5V 1Y1 Canada. (416)504-8222. **Fax:** (416)504-9090. **E-mail:** info@writerstrust.com. **Website:** www.writerstrust.com. **Contact:** Amanda Hopkins. Awarded annually to the best novel or short story collection published within the previous year. Presented at the Writers' Trust Awards event held in Toronto each fall. Open to Canadian citizens and permanent residents only. Deadline: July 18. Prize: $50,000 and $5,000 to 4 finalists.

THE SATURDAY EVENING POST GREAT AMERICAN FICTION CONTEST

The Saturday Evening Post Society, 1100 Waterway Blvd., Indianapolis IN 46202. **E-mail:** fictioncontest@saturdayeveningpost.com. **Website:** www.saturdayeveningpost.com/fiction-contest. "In its nearly 3 centuries of publication, *The Saturday Evening Post* has included fiction by a who's who of American authors, including F. Scott Fitzgerald, William Faulkner, Kurt Vonnegut, Ray Bradbury, Louis L'Amour, Sinclair Lewis, Jack London, and Edgar Allan Poe. The *Post*'s fiction has not just entertained us; it has played a vital role in defining who we are as Americans. In launching this contest, we are seeking America's next great, unpublished voices." Entries must be character- or plot-driven stories in any genre of fiction that falls within the *Post*'s broad range of interest. "We are looking for stories with universal appeal touching on shared experiences and themes that will resonate with readers from diverse backgrounds and experience." Stories must be submitted by the author and previously unpublished (excluding personal websites and blogs), and 1,500-5,000 words in length. No extreme profanity or graphic sex scenes. Submit story via the online at www.saturdayeveningpost.com/fiction-contest. All submissions must be made electronically in Microsoft Word format with the author's name, address, telephone number, and e-mail address on the first page. Do not submit hard copies via the mail; physical mss will not be read. "Due to staff limitations, we will not be able to update entrants on the status of their stories. We will inform winners or runners-up within 30 days of publication. We regret we will not be able to notify non-winning entrants." Deadline: July 1. The winning story will receive $500 and publication in the magazine and online. Five runners-up will be published online and receive $100 each.

SHEEHAN YA BOOK PRIZE

Elephant Rock Books, P.O. Box 119, Ashford CT 06278. **E-mail:** elephantrockbooksya@gmail.com. **Website:** elephantrockbooks.com/ya.html. **Contact:** Jotham Burrello and Amanda Hurley. Elephant Rock is a small independent publisher. Their first YA book, *The Carnival at Bray* by Jessie Ann Foley was a Morris Award Finalist, and Printz Honor Book. Runs contest every other year. Check website for details.

Guidelines are available on the website: http://www. elephantrockbooks.com./about.html#submissions. "Elephant Rock Books' teen imprint is looking for a great story to follow our critically acclaimed novel, *The Carnival at Bray*. We're after quality stories with heart, guts, and a clear voice. We're especially interested in the quirky, the hopeful, and the real. We are not particularly interested in genre fiction and prefer standalone novels, unless you've got the next *Hunger Games*. We seek writers who believe in the transformative power of a great story, so show us what you've got." Deadline: July 1. Prize: $1,000 as an advance. Judges vary year-to-year.

MARY WOLLSTONECRAFT SHELLEY PRIZE FOR IMAGINATIVE FICTION

Rosebud, ROSEBUD MAGAZINE; ROSEBUD, INC., C/O Rosebud Magazine, N3310 Asje Rd., Cambridge WI 53523 USA. (608)423-9780. **E-mail:** jrodclark@ rsbd.net. **Website:** www.rsbd.net. **Contact:** J. Roderick Clark, editor. Publishes eclectic mix of poetry, fiction and nonfiction. Genres with a literary feel okay. The Shelley Award is presented for any kind of unpublished imaginative fiction/short stories, 4,000 words or less. Entries are welcome any time. Acquires first rights. Open to any writer. Deadline: June 15 in even years. Prize: Grand Prize: $1,000. 4 runner-ups receive $100. All winners published in *Rosebud*. Judged by editor Rod Clark in 2016.

STONY BROOK SHORT FICTION PRIZE

Stony Brook Southampton, 239 Montauk Highway, Southampton NY 11968. **Website:** www.stonybrook. edu/fictionprize. "Only undergraduates enrolled full time in United States and Canadian universities and colleges for the current academic year are eligible. This prize has traditionally encouraged submissions from students with an Asian background, but we urge all students to enter." Submissions of no more than 7,500 words. All entries must be accompanied by proof of current undergraduate enrollment, such as a photocopy of a grade transcript, a class schedule or payment receipt showing your full time status. See website for full details. Deadline: March 15. Prize: $1,000.

STORYSOUTH MILLION WRITERS AWARD

E-mail: terry@storysouth.com. **Website:** www.storysouth.com. **Contact:** Terry Kennedy, editor. Annual award to honor and promote the best fiction published in online literary journals and magazines during the previous year. Anyone may nominate one story for the award. To be eligible for nomination, a story must be longer than 1,000 words. See website for details on how to nominate someone. Most literary prizes for short fiction have traditionally ignored web-published fiction. This award aims to show that world-class fiction is being published online and to promote to the larger reading and literary community. Deadline: August 15. Nominations of stories begins on March 15. Prize: Prize amounts subject to donation. Check website for details.

THEODORE STURGEON MEMORIAL AWARD FOR BEST SHORT SF OF THE YEAR

Center for the Study of SF, 1445 Jayhawk Blvd, Room 3001, University of Kansas, Lawrence KS 66045. (785)864-2518. **Fax:** (785)864-1159. **E-mail:** cssf@ ku.edu. **Website:** sfcenter.ku.edu/sturgeon.htm. **Contact:** Kij Johnson, professor and associate director. Entries must be previously published. Guidelines available in December by phone, e-mail or on website. Accepts inquiries by e-mail and fax. Entrants for the Sturgeon Award are by nomination only. Results announced in July. For contest results, send SASE. Award to "honor the best science fiction short story of the year." Prize: Trophy. Winners receive expense-paid trip to the University and have their names engraved on the pernmanent trophy.

THREE CHEERS AND A TIGER

E-mail: editors@toasted-cheese.com. **Website:** tclj. toasted-cheese.com. **Contact:** Stephanie Lenz, editor. Contestants are to write a short story (following a specific theme) within 48 hours. Contests are held first weekend in Spring (mystery) and first weekend in Fall (science fiction/fantasy). Word limit announced at the start of the contest, 5 pm ET. Contest-specific information is announced 48 hours before the contest submission deadline. Results announced in April and October. Winners notified by e-mail. List of winners on website. Entries must be unpublished. Open to any writer. Accepts inquiries by e-mail. Cover letter should include name, address, e-mail, word count and title. Information should be in the body of the e-mail. It will be removed before the judging begins. Prize: Amazon gift certificates and publication. Blind-judged by *Toasted Cheese* editors. Each judge uses his or her own criteria to choose entries.

THE THURBER PRIZE FOR AMERICAN HUMOR

77 Jefferson Ave., Columbus OH 43215. **Website:** www.thurberhouse.org. Entry fee: $65 per title. Published submissions or accepted for publication in U.S. for the first time. Primarily pictorial works such as cartoon collections are not considered. Word length: no requirement. See website for application form and guidelines. Results announced in September. Winners notified in person in New York City. For contest results, visit website. This award recognizes the art of humor writing. Deadline: March 31. Prize: $5,000 for the finalist, non-cash prizes awarded to two runners-up. Judged by well-known members of the national arts community.

STEVEN TURNER AWARD FOR BEST FIRST WORK OF FICTION

6335 W. Northwest Hwy., #618, Dallas TX 75225. **Website:** www.texasinstituteofletters.org. Offered annually for work published January 1-December 31 for the best first book of fiction. Writers must have been born in Texas, have lived in the state for at least 2 consecutive years at some time, or the subject matter of the work should be associated with the state. Guidelines online. Deadline: normally first week in January; see website for specific date. Prize: $1,000.

ANNUAL VENTURA COUNTY WRITERS CLUB SHORT STORY CONTEST

Ventura County Writers Club Short Story Contest, P.O. Box 3373, Thousand Oaks CA 91362. **E-mail:** vcwc.contestchair@gmail.com. **Website:** www.venturacountywriters.com. **Contact:** Contest Chair. Annual short story contest for youth and adult writers. High school division for writers still in school. Adult division for those 18 and older. Club membership not required to enter and entries accepted worldwide as long as fees are paid, story is unpublished and in English. Enter through website. 2,500 word limit. See formatting on website. Winners get cash prizes and are published in club anthology. Deadline: November 15. Adult Prizes: 1st Place: $500; 2nd Place: $250; 3rd Place: $125. High School Prizes: 1st Place: $100; 2nd Place: $75; 3rd Place: $50.

WAASNODE SHORT FICTION PRIZE

Passages North, Department of English, Northern Michigan University, 1401 Presque Isle Ave., Marquette MI 49855. (906)227-1203. **Fax:** (906)227-1096. **E-mail:** passages@nmu.edu. **Website:** www.passag-esnorth.com. **Contact:** Jennifer Howard. Offered every 2 years to publish new voices in literary fiction (maximum 10,000 words). Guidelines for SASE or online. Submissions accepted online. Deadline: April 15. Submission period begins February 15. Prize: $1,000 and publication for winner; 2 honorable mentions are also published; all entrants receive a copy of *Passages North*. Judged by Anne Valente in 2018.

WABASH PRIZE FOR FICTION

Sycamore Review, Department of English, 500 Oval Dr., Purdue University, West Lafayette IN 47907. **E-mail:** sycamore@purdue.edu; sycamorefiction@purdue.edu. **Website:** www.sycamorereview.com/contest/. **Contact:** Kara Krewer, editor-in-chief. Annual contest for unpublished fiction. For each submission, send one story (limit 7,500 words). Ms pages should be numbered and should include the title of the piece. All stories must be previously unpublished. See website for more guidelines. Submit via online submissions manager. Deadline: November 15. Prize: $1,000 and publication.

THE WASHINGTON WRITERS' PUBLISHING HOUSE FICTION PRIZE

Washington Writers' Publishing House, P.O. Box 15271, Washington DC 20003. **E-mail:** wwphpress@gmail.com. **Website:** www.washingtonwriters.org. Fiction writers living within 75 miles of the Capitol are invited to submit a ms of either a novel or a collection of short stories (no more than 350 pages, double-spaced). Author's name should not appear on the manuscript. The title page of each copy should contain the title only. Provide name, address, telephone number, e-mail address, and title on a separate cover sheet accompanying the submission. A separate page for acknowledgments may be included for stories or excerpts previously published in journals and anthologies. Send electronic copies to wwphpress@gmail.com or mail paper copies and/or reading fee (check to WWPH) with SASE to: Washington Writers' Publishing House Fiction Prize, c/o Elisavietta Ritchie, P.O. Box 298, Broomes Island, MD 20615. Deadline: November 15. Submission period begins July 1. Prize: $1,000 and 50 copies of the book.

THOMAS WOLFE PRIZE AND LECTURE

North Carolina Writers' Network, Thomas Wolfe Fiction Prize, Great Smokies Writing Program, Attn: Nancy Williams, CPO #1860, UNC, Asheville NC 28805. **Website:** englishcomplit.unc.edu/wolfe. The

Thomas Wolfe Fiction Prize honors internationally celebrated North Carolina novelist Thomas Wolfe. The prize is administered by Tommy Hays and the Great Smokies Writing Program at the University of North Carolina at Asheville. Competition is open to all writers, regardless of geographical location or prior publication. Submit 2 copies of an unpublished fiction ms (short story or self-contained novel excerpt) not to exceed 12 double-spaced, single-sided pages. Deadline: January 30. Submissions period begins December 1. Prize: $1,000 and potential publication in *The Thomas Wolfe Review*.

TOBIAS WOLFF AWARD FOR FICTION

Bellingham Review, Mail Stop 9053, Western Washington University, Bellingham WA 98225. (360)650-4863. **E-mail:** bellingham.review@wwu.edu. **Website:** www.bhreview.org. **Contact:** Susanne Paola Antonetta, editor-in-chief; Mike Oliphant, managing editor. Offered annually for unpublished work. Guidelines available on website; online submissions only. Categories: novel exceprts and short stories. Entries must be unpublished. Length: 6,000 words or less per story or chapter. Open to any writer. Electronic submissions only. Enter submissions through Submittable, a link to which is available on the website. Winner announced in August and notified by e-mail. Deadline: March 15. Submissions period begins December 1. Prize: $1,000, plus publication and subscription. Judged by Debra Dean.

WORLD FANTASY AWARDS

P.O. Box 43, Mukilteo WA 98275. **E-mail:** sfexecsec@gmail.com. **Website:** www.worldfantasy.org. **Contact:** Peter Dennis Pautz, president. Offered annually for previously published work in several categories, including life achievement, novel, novella, short story, anthology, collection, artist, special award-pro and special award-nonpro. Works are recommended by attendees of current and previous 2 years' conventions and a panel of judges. Entries must be previously published. Published submissions from previous calendar year. Word length: 10,000-40,000 for novella, 10,000 for short story. All fantasy is eligible, from supernatural horror to Tolkien-esque to sword and sorcery to the occult, and beyond. Cover letter should include name, address, phone, e-mail, word count, title, and publications where submission was previously published, submitted to the address above and the panel of judges when they appear on the website. Results announced November 1 at annual convention. For contest results, visit website. Guidelines available in December for SASE or on website. Awards to recognize excellence in fantasy literature worldwide. Deadline: June 1. Prize: Trophy. Judged by panel.

WOW! WOMEN ON WRITING QUARTERLY FLASH FICTION CONTEST

WOW! Women on Writing, P.O. Box 2832, Winnetka CA 91396. **E-mail:** contestinfo@wow-womenonwriting.com. **Website:** www.wow-womenonwriting.com/contest.php. **Contact:** Angela Mackintosh, editor. Contest offered quarterly. Entries must be 250-750 words. "We are open to all themes and genres, although we do encourage writers to take a close look at our literary agent guest judge for the season if you are serious about winning." Deadline: August 31, November 30, February 28, May 31. Prize: 1st place: $400 cash prize, $25 Amazon gift certificate, story published on WOW! Women On Writing, interview on blog; 2nd place: $300 cash prize, $25 Amazon gift certificate, story published on WOW! Women On Writing, interview on blog; 3rd place: $200 cash prize, $25 Amazon gift certificate, story published on WOW! Women On Writing, interview on blog; 7 runners up: $25 Amazon gift certificate, story published on WOW! Women on Writing, interview on blog; 10 honorable mentions: $20 gift certificate from Amazon, story title and name published on WOW!Women On Writing. Judged by a different guest every season, who is either a literary agent, acquiring editor or publisher.

WRITER'S DIGEST SHORT SHORT STORY COMPETITION

Writer's Digest, 10151 Carver Road, Suite 200, Blue Ash OH 45242. (715)445-4612; ext. 13430. **E-mail:** WritersDigestShortShortStoryCompetition@fwmedia.com. **Website:** www.writersdigest.com. **Contact:** Nicole Howard. Looking for fiction that's bold, brilliant, and brief. Send your best in 1,500 words or fewer. All entries must be original, unpublished, and not submitted elsewhere at the time of submission. *Writer's Digest* reserves one-time publication rights to the 1st-25th winning entries. Winners will be notified by Feb. 28. Early bird deadline: November 15. Final deadline: December 15. Prize: 1st Place: $3,000 and a trip to the Writer's Digest Conference; 2nd Place: $1,500; 3rd Place: $500; 4th-10th Place: $100; 11th-25th Place: $50 gift certificate for writersdigestshop.com.

ZOETROPE: ALL-STORY SHORT FICTION COMPETITION

Zoetrope: All-Story, Zoetrope: All-Story, Attn: Fiction Editor, 916 Kearny St., San Francisco CA 94133. (415)788-7500. **E-mail:** contests@all-story.com. **Website:** www.all-story.com/contests.cgi. Acclaimed annual short fiction competition. Considers submissions of short stories no longer than 5,000 words. For details, please visit the website this summer. Deadline: October 1. Submission period begins July 1. Prizes: 1st place: $1,000 and publication on website; 2nd place: $500; 3rd place: $250.

ZONE 3 FICTION AWARD

Zone 3, Austin Peay State University, P.O. Box 4565, Clarksville TN 37044. (931)221-7031. **Fax:** (931)221-7149. **E-mail:** wallacess@apsu.edu. **Website:** www.apsu.edu/zone3/contests. **Contact:** Susan Wallace, Managing Editor. Annual contest for unpublished fiction. Open to any fiction writer. Accepts entries online and via postal mail. Deadline: April 1. Prize: $250 and publication.

NONFICTION

AMERICA & ME ESSAY CONTEST

Farm Bureau Insurance, P.O. Box 30400, Lansing MI 48909. **E-mail:** lfedewa@fbinsmi.com. **Website:** FarmBureauInsurance.com. **Contact:** Lisa Fedewa. Focuses on encouraging students to write about their personal Michigan heroes: someone who lives in the state and who has encouraged them, taught them important lessons, and helped them pursue their dreams. Open to Michigan eighth graders. Contest rules and entry form available on website. Encourages Michigan youth to recognize the heroes in their communities and their state. Deadline: November 18. Prize: $1,000, plaque, and medallion for top 10 winners. Home office volunteers.

ANTHEM ESSAY CONTEST

Ayn Rand Institute, P.O. Box 57044, Irvine CA 92619-7044. (949)222-6550. **Fax:** (949)222-6558. **E-mail:** essays@aynrand.org. **Website:** www.aynrand.org/contests. **Contact:** Anthony Loy. Offered annually to encourage analytical thinking and excellence in writing (600-1,200 word essay), and to expose students to the philosophic ideas of Ayn Rand. "For information contact your English teacher or guidance counselor or visit our website." Open to 8th, 9th and 10th graders.

See website for topics. Deadline: May 1, 2018. Prize: 1st Place: $2,000; 2nd Place (5): $500; 3rd Place (10): $200; Finalist (45): $50; Semifinalist (175): $30.

THE ASCAP DEEMS TAYLOR AWARDS

American Society of Composers, Authors & Publishers, One Lincoln Plaza, New York NY 10023. (212)621-6318. **E-mail:** jlapore@ascap.com. **Website:** www.ascap.com/music-career/support/deems-taylor-guidelines.aspx. **Contact:** Julian Lapore. The ASCAP Deems Taylor Awards program recognizes books, articles, broadcasts, and websites on the subject of music selected for their excellence. Written works must be published in the U.S. in English, during the calendar year of the awards. The subject matter may be biographical or critical, reportorial or historical—almost any form of nonfiction prose about music and/or its creators. However, instructional textbooks, how-to-guides, or works of fiction will not be accepted. Honors the memory of composer/critic/commentator Deems Taylor. Deadline: May 31. Submission period begins February 1. Prize: Several categories of cash prizes are presented to writers of award-winning books and newspaper, journal, or magazine articles (includes program notes, liner notes and on-line publications). Awards are also presented to the authors and journalists as well as to their respective publishers.

ATLAS SHRUGGED ESSAY CONTEST

Ayn Rand Institute, P.O. Box 57044, Irvine CA 92619-7044. (949)222-6550, ext. 269. **Fax:** (949)222-6558. **E-mail:** essays@aynrand.org. **Website:** https://www.aynrand.org/contests. **Contact:** Anthony Loy. Offered annually to encourage analytical thinking and excellence in writing, and to expose students to the philosophic ideas of Ayn Rand. Open to 12th graders, college undergraduates, and graduate students. Essay length: 800-1,600 words. Essays are judged both on style and content. Guidelines and topics available on the website. The winning applicant will be judged on both style and content. Judges will look for writing that is clear, articulate and logically organized. Winning essays must demonstrate an outstanding grasp of the philosophic meaning of *Atlas Shrugged*. Essay submissions are evaluated in a fair and unbiased four-round judging process. Judges are individually selected by the Ayn Rand Institute based on a demonstrated knowledge and understanding of Ayn Rand's works. Deadline: April 28. Prizes: 1st Place: $20,000;

2nd Place (3 awards): $2,000; 3rd Place (5 awards): $1,000; Finalists (25 awards): $100; Semifinalists (50 awards): $50.

BANCROFT PRIZE

Columbia University, c/o Office of the University Librarian, 517 Butter Library, Mail Code 1101, 535 W. 114th St., New York NY 10027. (212)854-7309. **Fax:** (212)854-9099. **Website:** http://library.columbia.edu/about/awards/bancroft.html. **Contact:** Bancroft Prize Committee. The Bancroft Prizes are awarded annually by Columbia University in the City of New York. Two annual prizes are awarded to the authors of distinguished works in either or both of the following categories: American History (including biography) and Diplomacy. Awards are for books published in the previous year. Send 4 copies, 3 for the members of the jury on the award and 1 for the Libraries of Columbia University. Deadline: November 1. Prize: $10,000 for the winning entry in each category.

THE CONGER BEASLEY JR. AWARD FOR NONFICTION

New Letters, University of Missouri-Kansas City, *New Letters* Awards for Writers, UMKC, University House, 5101 Rockhill Rd., Kansas City MO 64110-2499. (816)235-1168. **Fax:** (816)235-2611. **E-mail:** newletters@umkc.edu. **Website:** www.newletters.org. **Contact:** Ashley Wann. Contest is offered annually for unpublished work to discover and reward emerging writers and to give experienced writers a place to try new genres. Acquires first North American serial rights. Open to any writer. Guidelines by SASE or online. Entries should not exceed 8,000 words. Deadline: May 18. 1st Place: $2,500 and publication in a volume of *New Letters*.

☺ THE CANADIAN AUTHORS AWARD FOR CANADIAN HISTORY

6 West St. N, Suite 203, Orillia ON L3V 5B8 Canada. (705)325-3926. **E-mail:** admin@canadianauthors.org. **Website:** www.canadianauthors.org. **Contact:** Anita Purcell, executive director. Offered annually for a work of historical nonfiction on a Canadian topic by a Canadian author. Entry form required. Obtain entry form from contact name or download from website. Deadline: January 15. Prize: $2,000. The CAA Awards Chair appoints a trustee for this award. That trustee selects two judges. The identities of the trustee and judges are confidential throughout the judging process. Decisions of the trustee and judges are

final, and they may choose not to award a prize. A shortlist of the best three entries in each category is announced in June. The winners are announced at the gala awards banquet during the annual CanWrite! conference in June.

☺ CANADIAN LIBRARY ASSOCIATION STUDENT ARTICLE CONTEST

Canadian Library Association, 1150 Morrison Dr., Suite 400, Ottawa ON K2H 8S9 Canada. (613)232-9625, ext. 322. **Fax:** (613)563-9895. **E-mail:** info@cla.ca. **Website:** www.cla.ca. **Contact:** Marketing and Communications Manager. Offered annually to unpublished articles discussing, analyzing, or evaluating timely issues in librarianship or information science. Open to all students registered in or recently graduated from a Canadian library school, a library techniques program, or faculty of education library program. Submissions may be in English or French. Deadline: March 31. Prize: $200 and the winning article will be published in *Feliciter*, the magazine of the Canadian Library Association.

MORTON N. COHEN AWARD

Modern Language Association of America, 85 Broad Street, suite 500, New York NY 10004-2434. (646)576-5141. **Fax:** (646)458-0030. **E-mail:** awards@mla.org. **Website:** www.mla.org. **Contact:** Coordinator of Book Prizes. Awarded in odd-numbered years for a distinguished collection of letters. At least 1 volume of the edition must have been published during the previous 2 years. Editors need not be members of the MLA. Under the terms of the award, the winning collection will be one that provides readers with a clear, accurate, and readable text; necessary background information; and succinct and eloquent introductory material and annotations. The edited collection should be in itself a work of literature. Deadline: May 1. Prize: A cash award and a certificate to be presented at the Modern Language Association's annual convention in January.

CARR P. COLLINS AWARD FOR NONFICTION

The Texas Institute of Letters, P.O. Box 609, Round Rock TX 78680. **E-mail:** tilsecretary@yahoo.com. **Website:** http://texasinstituteofletters.org/. Offered annually for work published January 1-December 31 of the previous year to recognize the best nonfiction book by a writer who was born in Texas, who has lived in the state for at least 2 consecutive years at one point, or a writer whose work has some notable connection with Texas. See website for guidelines and instructions on submitting. Deadline: January 10. Prize: $5,000.

CREATIVE NONFICTION BOOK AWARD

Zone 3, Austin Peay State University, Austin Peay State University, PO Box 4565, Clarksville TN 37044. (931)221-7031. **Fax:** (931)221-7149. **E-mail:** wrighta@apsu.edu; collinsa@apsu.edu. **Website:** www.apsu.edu/zone3/contests. **Contact:** Amy Wright, acquisitions editor; Aubrey Collins, managing editor. This competition is open to all authors writing original works in English. Manuscripts that embrace creative nonfiction's potential by combining lyric exposition, researched reflection, travel dialogues, or creative criticism are encouraged. Memoir, personal narrative, essay collections, and literary nonfiction are also invited. Submit one copy of your ms, 120-300 pages. Accepts entries via postal mail or online. Separate instructions for both, see website for guidelines and details. Submissions Accepted: January 1-April 1. Prize: $1,000 and publication.

☻ CREATIVE NONFICTION CONTEST

PRISM International, Creative Writing Program, UBC, Buch E462—1866 Main Mall, Vancouver BC V6T 1Z1 Canada. **E-mail:** promotions@prismmagazine.ca. **Website:** www.prismmagazine.ca. Maximum word count: 5,000. Offered annually for published and unpublished writers to promote and reward excellence in literary creative nonfiction. *PRISM* buys first North American serial rights upon publication. Also buys limited web rights for pieces selected for the website. Open to anyone except students and faculty of the Creative Writing Program at UBC or people who have taken a creative writing course at UBC in the 2 years prior to contest deadline. All entrants receive a 1-year subscription to *PRISM*. Entries are accepted via Submittable at http://prisminternational.submittable.com/submit or by mail. Deadline: July 15. Prize: $1,500 grand prize, $600 runner-up, and $400 second runner-up.

ANNIE DILLARD AWARD FOR CREATIVE NONFICTION

Bellingham Review, Mail Stop 9053, 516 High St., Western Washington University, Bellingham WA 98225. (360)650-4863. **E-mail:** bellingham.review@wwu.edu. **Website:** www.bhreview.org. **Contact:** Susanne Paola Antonetta, editor-in-chief; Mike Oliph-

ant, managing editor. Offered annually for unpublished essays on any subject and in any style. Guidelines available online. Deadline: March 15. Submission period begins December 1. Prize: $1,000, plus publication and copies. All finalists considered for publication. All entrants receive subscription. Judged by Jenny Boully.

GORDON W. DILLON/RICHARD C. PETERSON MEMORIAL ESSAY PRIZE

American Orchid Society, Inc., American Orchid Society at Fairchild Tropical Botanic Garden, 10901 Old Cutler Rd., Coral Gables FL 33156. (305)740-2010. **Fax:** (305)740-2011. **E-mail:** theaos@aos.org. **E-mail:** rmchatton@aos.org. **Website:** www.aos.org. **Contact:** Ron McHatton. The Gordon W. Dillon\Richard C. Peterson Memorial Essay Prize is an annual writing competition. Open to amateur and professional writers. The theme is announced each May in *Orchids* magazine. All themes deal with an aspect of orchids. Acquires one-time rights. The essay must be an original, unpublished article. Submissions must be no more than 5,000 words in length. Submissions will be judged without knowledge of the identity of the author. Established to honor the memory of two former editors of the *AOS Bulletin* (now *Orchids*). Deadline: November 30. Prize: Cash prize and a certificate. Winning entry usually published in the June issue of *Orchids* magazine.

☻ THE DONNER PRIZE

The Award for Best Book on Public Policy by a Canadian, The Donner Canadian Foundation, 505 Danforth Ave., Suite 201, Toronto ON M4K 1P5 Canada. **E-mail:** sherry@naylorandassociates.com. **Website:** www.donnerbookprize.com. **Contact:** Sherry Naylor. Annual award that rewards excellence and innovation in public policy writing by Canadians. Deadline: November 30. Prize: Winning book receives $50,000; shortlisted titles get $7,500 each.

EDUCATOR'S AWARD

The Delta Kappa Gamma Society International, P.O. Box 1589, Austin TX 78767-1589. (888)762-4685. **Fax:** (512)478-3961. **Website:** www.dkg.org. **Contact:** Carolyn Pittman, chair. Offered annually for quality research and nonfiction published January-December of previous year. This award recognizes educational research and writings of female authors whose work may influence the direction of thought and action necessary to meet the needs of today's complex society. The book must be written by 1 or 2 women who are citizens of any country in which The Delta Kappa Gamma Society International is organized: Canada, Costa Rica, Denmark, Estonia, Finland, Germany, Great Britain, Guatemala, Iceland, Mexico, The Netherlands, Norway, Puerto Rico, Sweden, US, Panama. Guidelines (required) for SASE. The Educators Award Committee is charged with the responsibility of selecting an appropriate book as winner of the annual Educator's Award. Committee members read and evaluate books submitted by publishers that meet the criteria of having been written by women and whose content may influence the direction of thought and action necessary to meet the needs of today's complex society; furthermore, the content must be of more than local interest with relationship, direct or implied, to education everywhere. Deadline: February 1. Prize: $2,500. Judged by Educators Award Committee.

EVANS BIOGRAPHY & HANDCART AWARDS

Mountain West Center for Regional Studies, Room 339, Old Main, 0735 Old Main Hill, Utah State University, Logan UT 84322-0735. (435)797-0299. **Fax:** (435)797-1092. **E-mail:** mwc@usu.edu. **Website:** http://mountainwest.usu.edu/evans.aspx. **Contact:** Patricia Lambert, director. The Evans Biography and Handcart Awards encourage the best in research and writing about the Interior West through the giving of two annual prizes for excellence in biography. The Evans Biography Award is given to the best biography of a person who lived a significant portion of his or her life in the Interior West, or, in the words of the awards' founders, "Mormon Country"—that region historically influenced by Mormon institutions and social practices. The Evans Handcart Award is given to a biography addressing similar subjects as the Evans Biography Award, but often by an emerging author or written as a family history. Send 6 copies of the book and one copy of the author's resume. See website for details. Deadline: January 1 for books published in the previous calendar year. Prize: $10,000 for the Evans Biography Award; and $2,500 for the Evans Handcart Award. Judged by a local jury of five scholars and book experts.

⊙ EVENT CREATIVE NONFICTION CONTEST

EVENT, Poetry and Prose., P.O. Box 2503, New Westminster BC V3L 5B2 Canada. (604)527-5293. **Fax:** (604)527-5095. **E-mail:** event@douglascollege. ca. **Website:** www.eventmagazine.ca. Offered annually for unpublished creative nonfiction. Maximum length: 5,000 words. Acquires first North American serial print rights and limited non-exclusive digital rights for the winning entries. Open to any writer, except Douglas College employees and students. Previously published material, including that which has appeared online or has been accepted for publication elsewhere, cannot be considered. No simultaneous submissions. The writer should not be identified on the entry. Include separate cover sheet with name, address, phone number/email, and title(s). Enter online or send to address above. Multiple entries are allowed; however, each entry must be accompanied by its own entry fee. Pay online or make check or international money order payable to EVENT. Deadline: April 15. Prize: $1,500 in prizes, plus publication in *EVENT*. Judges reserve the right to award 2 or 3 prizes: 3 at $500 or 2 at $750, plus publication payment.

ILA DINA FEITELSON RESEARCH AWARD

International Literacy Association, Awards and Grants, P.O. Box 8139, Newark DE 19714-8139. (302)731-1600, ext. 227. **Fax:** (302)368-2449. **E-mail:** ILAAwards@reading.org. **Website:** www.literacy-worldwide.org/about-us/awards-grants. **Contact:** Wendy Logan, executive programs manager. This is an award for an exemplary work published in English in a refereed journal that reports on an empirical study investigating aspects of literacy acquisition, such as phonemic awareness, the alphabetic principle, bilingualism, or cross-cultural studies of beginning reading. Articles may be submitted for consideration by researchers, authors, et al. Copies of the applications and guidelines can be downloaded in PDF format from the website. Deadline: January 15. Prize: $500 award and recognition at the International Literacy Association's annual conference. Judged by ILA Dina Feitelson Research Award Committee.

THE FOUNTAINHEAD ESSAY CONTEST

The Ayn Rand Institute, P.O. Box 57044, Irvine CA 92619-7044. (949) 222-6550. **Fax:** (949) 222-6558. **E-mail:** essays@aynrand.org. **Website:** https://www. aynrand.org/contests. **Contact:** Anthony Loy. Competition for 11th and 12th grade students. Essays will be judged on whether the student is able to argue for and justify his or her view—not on whether the Institute agrees with the view the student expresses. Judges will look for writing that is clear, articulate and logically organized. Winning essays must demonstrate an outstanding grasp of the philosophic meaning of *The Fountainhead*. Deadline: April 26. Prizes: 1st Place: $10,000; 2nd Place: $2,000 (5 Winners); 3rd Place: $1,000 (10 Winners); Finalists: $100 (45 Winners); Semifinalists: $50 (175 Winners).

THE JOHN GUYON LITERARY NONFICTION PRIZE

Crab Orchard Review, Department of English, Faner Hall 2380 - Mail Code 4503, 1000 Faner Drive, Carbondale IL 62901. (618)453-6833. **Fax:** (618)453-8224. **E-mail:** jtribble@siu.edu. **Website:** www.craborchardreview.siu.edu. **Contact:** Jon C. Tribble, managing editor. Annual award for unpublished creative nonfiction. Not a prize for academic essays. Entries should consist of 1 creative nonfiction piece up to 6,500 words maximum in length. *Crab Orchard Review* acquires first North American serial rights to all submitted work. One winner and at least 2 finalists will be chosen. Length: 6,500 words maximum. All submissions must be made through Submittable. Submissions must be unpublished original work, written in English by a U.S. citizen, permanent resident, or person who has DACA/TPS status (current students and employees at Southern Illinois University Carbondale are not eligible). See Submittable guidelines online for complete formatting instructions. The author's name should not appear on any page of the entry. Results announced by end of August. Deadline: May 31. Submission period begins March 21. Prize: $1,250 and publication. Finalists are each offered online publication.

HENDRICKS AWARD

The New Netherland Institute, Cultural Education Center, Room 10D45, 222 Madison Ave., Albany NY 12230. **Fax:** (518)473-0472. **E-mail:** nyslfnn@nysed.gov. **Website:** www.newnetherlandinstitute.org. Given annually to the best book or book-length ms relating to any aspect of New Netherland and its legacy. Two categories of submissions will be considered in alternate years: (1) recently completed dissertations and unpublished book-length manuscripts, and (2) recently published books. If there is no suitable winner in the designated category in any particular year, submissions from the alternate category will be considered. In addition, submissions from previous years will be reconsidered for the Award. Entries must be

based on research completed or published within three years prior to the deadline for submission. Entries may deal with any aspect of New Netherland and its legacy. Biographies of individuals whose careers illuminate aspects of the history of New Netherland and its legacy are eligible, as are manuscripts dealing with literature and the arts, provided that the methodology is historical. Deadline: March 15. Prize: $5,000 and a framed print of a painting by L.F. Tantillo. Judged by a 5-member panel of scholars.

THE HUNGER MOUNTAIN CREATIVE NONFICTION PRIZE

Vermont College, 36 College St., Montpelier VT 05602. (802)828-8517. **E-mail:** hungermtn@vcfa.edu. **Website:** www.hungermtn.org. **Contact:** Samantha Kolber, Managing Editor. Annual contest for the best writing in creative nonfiction. Submit essays under 10,000 words. Guidelines available on website. Accepts entries online or via mail. Deadline: March 1. Prize: $1,000 and publication. Two honorable mentions receive $100 each. Judged by Joni Tevis in 2017.

ILA TIMOTHY AND CYNTHIA SHANAHAN OUTSTANDING DISSERTATION AWARD

International Literacy Association, Awards and Grants, P.O. Box 8139, Newark DE 19714-8139. (302)731-1600, ext. 227. **Fax:** (302)368-2449. **E-mail:** ILAAwards@reading.org. **Website:** www.literacyworldwide.org/about-us/awards-grants. **Contact:** Wendy Logan, executive programs manager. Dissertations in reading or related fields are eligible for the competition. Studies using any research approach (ethnographic, experimental, historical, survey, etc.) are encouraged. Each study is assessed in the light of this approach, the scholarly qualification of its report, and its significant contributions to knowledge within the reading field. The application process is open to those who have completed dissertations in any aspect of the field of reading or literacy of the calendar year. A routine check is made with the home university of the applicant to protect all applicants, their universities, and the International Reading Association from false claims. Studies may use any research approach (ethnographic, experimental, historical, survey, etc.). Each study will be assessed in light of its approach, its scholarship, and its significant contributions to knowledge within the reading/literacy field. Deadline: January 15.

TILIA KLEBENOV JACOBS RELIGIOUS ESSAY PRIZE CATEGORY

Soul-Making Keats Literary Competition, The Webhallow House, 1544 Sweetwood Dr., Broadmoor Village CA 94015-2029. (650)756-5279. **Fax:** (650)756-5279. **E-mail:** soulkeats@mail.com. **Website:** www.soulmakingcontest.us. **Contact:** Eileen Malone. Call for thoughtful writings of up to 3,000 words. "No preaching, no proselytizing." Open annually to any writer. Previously published material is accepted. Indicate category on cover page and on identifying 3x5 card. Up to 3,000 words, double-spaced. See website for more details. Ongoing Deadline: November 30. Prize: 1st Place: $100; 2nd Place: $50; 3rd Place: $25.

GAIL ANN KENNA CREATIVE NONFICTION PRIZE CATEGORY

Soul-Making Keats Literary Competition, The Webhallow House, 1544 Sweetwood Dr., Broadmoor Village CA 94015-2029. (650)756-5279. **Fax:** (650)756-5279. **E-mail:** soulkeats@mail.com. **Website:** www.soulmakingcontest.us. **Contact:** Eileen Malone. Creative nonfiction is the child of fiction and journalism. Unlike fiction, the characters and events are real, not imagined. Unlike journalism, the writer is part of the story she tells, if not as a participant then as a thoughtful observer. Must be typed, page numbered, and double-spaced. Each entry up to 3,000 words. Identify only with 3x5 card. Open annually to any writer. Deadline: November 30. Prizes: First Place: $100; Second Place: $50; Third Place: $25.

KATHERINE SINGER KOVACS PRIZE

Modern Language Association of America, 85 Broad Street, suite 500, New York NY 10004-2434. (646)576-5141. **Fax:** (646)458-0030. **E-mail:** awards@mla.org. **Website:** www.mla.org. **Contact:** Coordinator of Book Prizes. Offered annually for an outstanding book published in English or Spanish in the field of Latin American and Spanish literatures and cultures. Competing books should be broadly interpretive works that enhance understanding of the interrelations among literature, the other arts, and society. Books must have been published in the previous year. Authors need not be members of the MLA. Must send 6 copies of book. Deadline: May 1. Prize: A cash award and a certificate to be presented at the Modern Language Association's annual convention in January.

THE GILDER LEHRMAN LINCOLN PRIZE

Gettysburg College and Gilder Lehrman Institute of American History, 300 N. Washington St., Campus Box 413, Gettysburg PA 17325. (717)337-8255. **Fax:** (717)337-6597. **E-mail:** lincolnprize@gettysburg.edu. **Website:** www.gettysburg.edu/lincolnprize. **Contact:** Diane Brennan. The Gilder Lehrman Lincoln Prize, sponsored by the Gilder Lehrman Institute and Gettysburg College, is awarded annually for the finest scholarly work in English on Abraham Lincoln, or the American Civil War era. Send 6 copies of the nominated work. Deadline: November 1 at 4:00 p.m. Prize: $50,000.

LITERAL LATTÉ ESSAY AWARD

Literal Latté, 200 E. 10th St., Suite 240, New York NY 10003. **E-mail:** litlatte@aol.com. **Website:** www.literal-latte.com. **Contact:** Jenine Gordon Bockman. Mind-stimulating entertainment. Free since 1994. Acquires first rights. Visit website for guidelines and tastes. Deadline: September 30. Prize: 1st Place: $1,000; 2nd Place: $300; 3rd Place: $200. Judged by the editors.

JAMES RUSSELL LOWELL PRIZE

Modern Language Association of America, 85 Broad Street, suite 500, New York NY 10004-2434. (646)576-5141. **Fax:** (646)458-0030. **E-mail:** awards@mla.org. **Website:** www.mla.org. **Contact:** Coordinator of Book Prizes. For an outstanding literary or linguistic study, a critical edition of an important work, or a critical biography. Open to studies dealing with literary theory, media, cultural history, or interdisciplinary topics. Books must be published in the previous year. Authors must be current members of the MLA. Send 6 copies of the book. Deadline: March 1. Prize: A cash award and a certificate to be presented at the Modern Language Association's annual convention in January.

RICHARD J. MARGOLIS AWARD

c/o Margolis & Bloom, LLP, 667 Boylston St., 5th Floor, Boston MA 02116. (617)294-5951. **Fax:** (617)267-3166. **E-mail:** hsm@margolis.com. **E-mail:** award@margolis.com. **Website:** www.margolisaward.org. **Contact:** Harry S. Margolis. Sponsored by the Blue Mountain Center, this annual award is given to a promising new journalist or essayist whose work combines warmth, humor, wisdom, and concern with social justice. Applicants should be aware that this award is for nonfiction reporting and commentary, not for creative nonfiction, fiction, or poetry. Applications should include at least 2 examples of your work (published or unpublished, 30 pages maximum) and a short biographical note including a description of your current and anticipated work. Also please indicate what you will work on while attending the Blue Mountain residency. Please send to award@margolis.com. Deadline: July 1. Prize: $5,000, plus a one month residency at the Blue Mountain Center.

HOWARD R. MARRARO PRIZE

Modern Language Association of America, 85 Broad Street, suite 500, New York NY 10004-2434. (646)576-5141. **Fax:** (646)458-0030. **E-mail:** awards@mla.org. **Website:** www.mla.org. **Contact:** Coordinator of Book Prizes. Offered in even-numbered years for an outstanding scholarly work on any phase of Italian literature or comparative literature involving Italian. Books must have been published in the previous year. Authors must be members of the MLA. Requires 4 copies of the book. Deadline: May 1. Prize: A cash award and a certificate to be presented at the Modern Language Association's annual convention in January.

KENNETH W. MILDENBERGER PRIZE

Modern Language Association of America, 85 Broad Street, suite 500, New York NY 10004-2434. (646)576-5141. **Fax:** (646)458-0030. **E-mail:** awards@mla.org. **Website:** www.mla.org. **Contact:** Coordinator of Book Prizes. Offered in odd-numbered years for a publication from the previous year in the field of language, culture, literacy, or literature with a strong application to the teaching of languages other than English. Author need not be a member of the MLA. Books must have been published in the previous 2 years. Requires 4 copies of the book. Deadline: May 1. Prize: A cash award, and a certificate, to be presented at the Modern Language Association's annual convention in January, and a year's membership in the MLA.

C. WRIGHT MILLS AWARD

The Society for the Study of Social Problems, 901 McClung Tower, University of Tennessee, Knoxville TN 37996-0490 USA. (865)689-1531. **Fax:** (865)689-1534. **E-mail:** mkoontz3@utk.edu. **Website:** www.sssp1.org. **Contact:** Michele Smith Koontz, Administrative Officer and Meeting Manager. Offered annually for a book published the previous year that most effectively critically addresses an issue of contemporary public importance; brings to the topic a fresh, imaginative perspective; advances social scientific understanding of the topic; displays a theoretically informed view and empirical orientation; evinces quality in style of writing; and explicitly or implicitly contains implications for courses of action. Self-nominations are acceptable. Edited volumes, textbooks, fiction, and self-published works are not eligible. Deadline: December 15. Prize: $1,000 stipend.

MLA PRIZE FOR A BIBLIOGRAPHY, ARCHIVE, OR DIGITAL PROJECT

Modern Language Association of America, 85 Broad Street, Suite 500, New York NY 10004-2434. (646)576-5141. **Fax:** (646)458-0030. **E-mail:** awards@mla.org. **Website:** www.mla.org. **Contact:** Coordinator of Book Prizes. Offered in even-numbered years for an outstanding enumerative or descriptive bibliography, archive, or digital project. Open to any writer or publisher. At least 1 volume must have been published in the previous 2 years. Editors need not be members of the MLA. Criteria for determining excellence include evidence of analytical rigor, meticulous scholarship, intellectual creativity, and subject range and depth. Deadline: May 1. Prize: A cash prize and a certificate to be presented at the Modern Language Association's annual convention in January.

MLA PRIZE FOR A FIRST BOOK

Modern Language Association of America, 85 Broad Street, Suite 500, New York NY 10004-2434. (646)576-5141. **Fax:** (646)458-0030. **E-mail:** awards@mla.org. **Website:** www.mla.org. **Contact:** Coordinator of Book Prizes. Offered annually for the first book-length scholarly publication by a current member of the association. To qualify, a book must be a literary or linguistic study, a critical edition of an important work, or a critical biography. Studies dealing with literary theory, media, cultural history, and interdisciplinary topics are eligible; books that are primarily translations will not be considered. See listing for James Russell Lowe Prize—prize offered for same criteria. Deadline: March 1. Prize: A cash award and a certificate to be presented at the Modern Language Association's annual convention in January.

MLA PRIZE FOR A SCHOLARLY EDITION

Modern Language Association of America, 85 Broad Street, suite 500, New York NY 10004-2434. (646)576-5141. **Fax:** (646)458-0030. **E-mail:** awards@mla.org. **Website:** www.mla.org. Offered in odd-numbered years for an outstanding scholarly edition. Editions may be in single or multiple volumes. At least one volume must have been published in the 2 years prior to the award deadline. Editors need not be members of the MLA. To qualify for the award, an edition should be based on an examination of all available relevant textual sources; the source texts and the edited text's deviations from them should be fully described; the edition should employ editorial principles appropriate to the materials edited, and those principles should be clearly articulated in the volume; the text should be accompanied by appropriate textual and other historical contextual information; the edition should exhibit the highest standards of accuracy in the presentation of its text and apparatus; and the text and apparatus should be presented as accessibly and elegantly as possible. Deadline: May 1. Prize: A cash award and a certificate to be presented at the Modern Language Association's annual convention in January.

MLA PRIZE FOR INDEPENDENT SCHOLARS

Modern Language Association of America, 85 Broad Street, Suite 500, New York NY 10004-2434. (646)576-5141. **Fax:** (646)458-0030. **E-mail:** awards@mla.org. **Website:** www.mla.org. Offered in even-numbered years for a scholarly book in the field of English or other modern languages and literatures. Book must have been published within the 2 years prior to prize deadline. At the time of publication of the book, author must not be enrolled in a program leading to an academic degree or hold a tenured, tenure-accruing, or tenure-track position in postsecondary education. Authors need not be members of the MLA. Requires 6 copies of the book and a completed application. Deadline: May 1. Prize: A cash award, a certificate, and a year's membership in the MLA.

MONTANA PRIZE IN CREATIVE NONFICTION

CutBank Literary Magazine, *CutBank*, University of Montana, English Dept., LA 133, Missoula MT 59812. **E-mail:** editor.cutbank@gmail.com. **Website:** www.cutbankonline.org. **Contact:** Allison Linville, editor-in-chief. The Montana Prize in Creative Nonfiction seeks to highlight work that showcases an authentic voice, a boldness of form, and a rejection of functional fixedness. Accepts online submissions only. Send a single work, no more than 35 pages. Guidelines available online. Deadline: January 15. Submissions period begins November 9. Prize: $500 and featured in the magazine. Judged by a guest judge each year.

LINDA JOY MYERS MEMOIR VIGNETTE PRIZE CATEGORY

Soul-Making Keats Literary Competition, Webhallow House, 1544 Sweetwood Dr., Broadmoor Village CA 94015-2029. (650)756-5279. **Fax:** (650)756-5279. **E-mail:** soulkeats@mail.com. **Website:** www.soul-makingcontest.us. **Contact:** Eileen Malone. Open annually to any writer. One memoir/entry, up to 1,500 words, double spaced. Previously published material is acceptable. Indicate category on first page. Identify only with 3x5 card. Ongoing Deadline: November 30. Prize: 1st Place: $100; 2nd Place: $50; 3rd Place: $25.

NATIONAL BUSINESS BOOK AWARD

BMO Financial Group, 10 Delisle Ave., Suite 214, Toronto ON M4V 3C6 Canada. (416)868-1500. **Website:** www.nbbaward.com. Offered annually for books published January 1-December 31 to recognize excellence in business writing in Canada. Publishers nominate books. TBD. Prize: $30,000 (CAN).

NATIONAL WRITERS ASSOCIATION NONFICTION CONTEST

The National Writers Association, 10940 S. Parker Rd., #508, Parker CO 80134. **E-mail:** natlwritersassn@hotmail.com. **Website:** www.nationalwriters.com. Only unpublished works may be submitted. Judging of entries will not begin until the contest ends. Nonfiction in the following areas will be accepted: articles—submission should include query letter, 1st page of manuscript, separate sheet citing 5 possible markets; essay—the complete essay and 5 possible markets on separate sheet; nonfiction book proposal including query letter, chapter by chapter outline, first chapter, bio, and market analysis. Those unsure of proper manuscript format should request Research Report #35. The purpose of the National Writers Association Nonfiction Contest is to encourage the writing of nonfiction and recognize those who excel in this field. Deadline: December 31. Prize: 1st-5th place awards. Other winners will be notified by March 31st. 1st Prize: $200 and Clearinghouse representation if winner is book proposal; 2nd Prize: $100; 3rd Prize: $50; 4th-10th places will receive a book. Honorable Mentions receive a certificate. Judging will be based on originality, marketability, research, and reader interest. Copies of the judges evaluation sheets will be sent to entrants furnishing an SASE with their entry.

THE FREDERIC W. NESS BOOK AWARD

Association of American Colleges and Universities, 1818 R St. NW, Washington DC 20009. (202)387-3760. **Fax:** (202)265-9532. **E-mail:** info@aacu.org. **Website:** www.aacu.org. **Contact:** Bethany Sutton. Offered annually for work published in the previous year. Each year the Frederic W. Ness Book Award Committee of the Association of American Colleges and Universities recognizes books which contribute to the understanding and improvement of liberal education. Guidelines for SASE or online. "Writers may nominate their own work; however, we send letters of invitation to publishers to nominate qualified books." Deadline: May 1. $2,000 and a presentation at the association's annual meeting—transportation and 1 night hotel for meeting are also provided.

FRANK LAWRENCE AND HARRIET CHAPPELL OWSLEY AWARD

Southern Historical Association, Room 111 A, LeConte Hall, Athens GA 30602-1602. (706)542-8848. **Fax:** (706)542-2455. **E-mail:** sdendy@uga.edu. **Website:** thesha.org. **Contact:** Dr. John B. Boles, Editor. Awarded for a distinguished book in Southern history published in even-numbered years. The decision of the Award Committee will be announced at the annual meeting in odd-numbered years. The award carries a cash payment to be fixed by the Council, a certificate for the author(s), and a certificate for the publisher. Deadline: March 1.

THE PHI BETA KAPPA AWARD IN SCIENCE

The Phi Beta Kappa Society, 1606 New Hampshire Ave. NW, Washington DC 20009. (202)265-3808. **Fax:** (202)986-1601. **E-mail:** awards@pbk.org. **Website:** www.pbk.org/bookawards. **Contact:** Awards Coordinator. Offered annually for outstanding contributions by scientists to the literature of science. To be eligible, biographies of scientists must have a substantial critical emphasis on their scientific research. Entries must have been published in the previous calendar year. Entries must be submitted by the publisher. Entries must be preceded by a letter certifying that the book(s) conforms to all the conditions of eligibility and stating the publication date of each entry. Two copies of the book must be sent with the nomination form. Books will not be entered officially in the competition until all copies and the letter of certification have been received. Open only to original works in English and authors of US residency and publica-tion. The intent of the award is to encourage literate and scholarly interpretations of the physical and biological sciences and mathematics; monographs and compendiums are not eligible. Deadline: January 15. Prize: $10,000.

PRESERVATION FOUNDATION CONTESTS

The Preservation Foundation, Inc, 2313 Pennington Bend, Nashville TN 37214. (615)889-2968. **E-mail:** preserve@storyhouse.org. **Website:** www.storyhouse. org. **Contact:** Richard Loller, publisher. Four contests offered annually for unpublished nonfiction: (1) Biography/Autobiography. (1,000-10,000 words)—a true story of an individual personally known to the author or a true story from the author's life, the whole or an episode. (2) General nonfiction (1,500-10,000 words)—any appropriate nonfiction topic. (3) Travel nonfiction (1,500-10,000 words)—must be the true story of trip by author or someone known personally by author. (4) Animal nonfiction (1,500-10,000 words)—Stories should be true accounts of personal encounters with wild birds, fish, butterflies, snails, lions, bears, turtles, etc. Not pets. Contests are open to any previously "unpublished writer," defined as having earned no more than $750 by creative writing in any previous year. Stories must be submitted by e-mail. No paper mss can be considered. No story may be entered in more than one contest. See website for contest details. Our purpose is to "Preserve the extraordinary stories of 'ordinary' people." Deadline: August 31. Prizes: In each category: First Place $200, Runner-up $100, Finalist $50. Judged by a jury of three judges.

PHILLIP D. REED MEMORIAL AWARD FOR OUTSTANDING WRITING ON THE SOUTHERN ENVIRONMENT

Southern Environmental Law Center, 201 W. Main St., Suite 14, Charlottesville VA 22902-5065. (434)977-4090. **Fax:** (434)977-1483. **E-mail:** cmccue@selcva.org. **Website:** www.SouthernEnvironment.org/phil_reed. **Contact:** Cathryn McCue, writing award coordinator.. Offered annually for nonfiction pieces that most effectively tell stories about the South's environment. Categories include Journalism and Book. Entries must have been published during the previous calendar year and have a minimum of 3,000 words. Guidelines online or for SASE. Deadline: early January. $1,000 for winner in each category. See www.southernenvironment.org/about/phil_reed.

☼ EVELYN RICHARDSON MEMORIAL NONFICTION AWARD

Writers' Federation of Nova Scotia, 1113 Marginal Rd., Halifax NS B3H 4P7 Canada. (902)423-8116. **Fax:** (902)422-0881. **E-mail:** director@writers.ns.ca. **Website:** www.writers.ns.ca. The Evelyn Richardson Memorial Nonfiction Award is awarded for a book of creative nonfiction by a resident of Nova Scotia. Detailed guidelines and eligibility criteria available online. Deadline: First Friday in December. Prize: Valued at $2,000 for the winning title.

ALDO AND JEANNE SCAGLIONE PRIZE FOR COMPARATIVE LITERARY STUDIES

Modern Language Association of America, 85 Broad Street, Suite 500, New York NY 10004-2434. (646)576-5141. **Fax:** (646)458-0030. **E-mail:** awards@mla.org. **Website:** www.mla.org. **Contact:** Coordinator of Book Prizes. Offered annually for outstanding scholarly work in comparative literary studies involving at least 2 literatures. Works of literary history, literary criticism, philology, and literary theory are eligible, as are works dealing with literature and other arts and disciplines, including cinema; books that are primarily translations will not be considered. Books must have been published in the past calendar year. Authors must be current members of the MLA. Requires 4 copies of the book. Deadline: May 1. Prize: A cash award and a certificate to be presented at the Modern Language Association's annual convention in January.

ALDO AND JEANNE SCAGLIONE PRIZE FOR FRENCH AND FRANCOPHONE STUDIES

Modern Language Association of America, 85 Broad Street, Suite 500, New York NY 10004-2434. (646)576-5141. **Fax:** (646)458-0030. **E-mail:** awards@mla.org. **Website:** www.mla.org. Offered annually for an outstanding scholarly work in French or francophone linguistics or literary studies. Works of literary history, literary criticism, philology, and literary theory are eligible for consideration; books that are primarily translations will not be considered. Books must have been published in the previous year. Authors must be current members of the MLA. Requires 4 copies of the book. Deadline: May 1. Prize: A cash award and a certificate to be presented at the Modern Language Association's annual convention in January.

ALDO AND JEANNE SCAGLIONE PRIZE FOR ITALIAN STUDIES

Modern Language Association of America, 85 Broad Street, Suite 500, New York NY 10004-2434. (646)576-5141. **Fax:** (646)458-0030. **E-mail:** awards@mla.org. **Website:** www.mla.org. **Contact:** Coordinator of Book Prizes. Offered in odd-number years for an outstanding scholarly work on any phase of Italian literature or culture, or comparative literature involving Italian. This shall include works that study literary or cultural theory, science, history, art, music, society, politics, cinema, and linguistics, preferably but not necessarily relating other disciplines to literature. Books must have been published in the previous year. Authors must be members of the MLA. Requires 4 copies of the book. Deadline: May 1. Prize: A cash award and a certificate to be presented at the Modern Language Association's annual convention in January.

ALDO AND JEANNE SCAGLIONE PRIZE FOR STUDIES IN GERMANIC LANGUAGES & LITERATURE

Modern Language Association of America, 85 Broad Street, Suite 500, New York NY 10004-2434. (646)576-5141. **Fax:** (646)458-0030. **E-mail:** awards@mla.org. **Website:** www.mla.org. Offered in even-numbered years for an outstanding scholarly work on the linguistics or literatures of any of the Germanic languages (Danish, Dutch, German, Norwegian, Swedish, Yiddish). Works of literary history, literary criticism, philology, and literary theory are eligible for consideration; books that are primarily translations will not be considered. Books must have been published in the previous 2 years. Authors must be members of the MLA. Requires 4 copies of the book. Deadline: May 1. Prize: A cash award, and a certificate to be presented at the Modern Language Association's annual convention in January.

ALDO AND JEANNE SCAGLIONE PUBLICATION AWARD FOR A MANUSCRIPT IN ITALIAN LITERARY STUDIES

Modern Language Association, 85 Broad Street, Suite 500, New York NY 10004-2434. (646)576-5141. **Fax:** (646)458-0030. **E-mail:** awards@mla.org. **Website:** www.mla.org. **Contact:** Coordinator of Book Prizes. Offered annually for an outstanding ms dealing with any aspect of the languages and literatures of Italy, including medieval Latin and comparative studies or intellectual history if the work's main thrust is clearly related to the humanities. Materials from ancient Rome are eligible if related to postclassical developments. Also eligible are translations of classical works of prose and poetry produced in Italy prior to 1900 in any language (e.g., neo-Latin, Greek) or in a dialect of Italian (e.g., Neapolitan, Roman, Sicilian). Eligible are book manuscripts in English or Italian that are ready for submission or already submitted to a press. Mss must be approved or ready for publication before award deadline. Authors must be current members of the MLA, residing in the United States or Canada. Requires 4 copies, plus contact and biographical information. Deadline: June 1. Prize: A cash award and a certificate to be presented at the Modern Language Association's annual convention in January.

WILLIAM SANDERS SCARBOROUGH PRIZE

Modern Language Association of America, 85 Broad Street, Suite 500, New York NY 10004-2434. (646)576-5141. **Fax:** (646)458-0030. **E-mail:** awards@mla.org. **Website:** www.mla.org. **Contact:** Coordinator of book prizes. Offered annually for an outstanding study of black American literature or culture. Books must have been published in the previous year. Authors need not be members of the MLA. Requires 4 copies of the book. Deadline: May 1. Prize: A cash award, and a certificate to be presented at the Modern Language Association's annual convention in January.

SCHOLARLY WRITING AWARD

Saskatchewan Book Awards, Inc., P.O. Box 20025, Regina SK S4P 4J7 Canada. (306)569-1585. **E-mail:** director@bookawards.sk.ca. **Website:** www.bookawards.sk.ca. **Contact:** Courtney Bates-Hardy, Executive Director. Offered annually. This award is presented to a Saskatchewan author for the best contribution to scholarship. The work must recognize or draw on specific theoretical work within a community of scholars, and participate in the creation and transmission of scholarly knowledge. Prize: $2,000 (CAD).

SCIENCE WRITING AWARDS IN PHYSICS AND ASTRONOMY

American Institute of Physics, 1 Physics Ellipse, College Park MD 20740-3843. (301)209-3096. **Fax:** (301)209-0846. **Website:** www.aip.org/aip/writing. Offered for published articles, booklets, or books that improve the general public's appreciation and understanding of physics and astronomy. Four categories: articles or books intended for children, preschool-15 years old; broadcast media for radio or television programming; journalism, written by a professional journalist; books or articles by a scientist. Guidelines by phone, e-mail, or online. Deadline: February 17. $3,000, an engraved Windsor chair, and a certificate awarded in each category.

SCREAMINMAMAS CREATIVE NONFICTION CONTEST

1911 Cleveland St., Hollywood FL 33020. **E-mail:** screaminmamas@gmail.com. **Website:** www.screaminmamas.com/contests. **Contact:** Darlene Pistocchi, editor/managing director. "Looking for stories that revolve around the kids and/or pets. Must be true! Take an incident or scene that is embedded in your brain and share it with us. Story can be dramatic or humorous, happy or sad. Looking for the real deal." Stories should be 600-1,000 words. Open only to moms. Deadline: March 31. Prize: Publication.

THE SHAUGHNESSY COHEN PRIZE FOR POLITICAL WRITING

The Writers' Trust of Canada, 460 Richmond St. W., Suite 600, Toronto ON M5V 1Y1 Canada. (416)504-8222. **Fax:** (416)504-9090. **E-mail:** info@writerstrust.com. **Website:** www.writerstrust.com. **Contact:** Amanda Hopkins. Awarded annually for a nonfiction book of outstanding literary merit that enlarges understanding of contemporary Canadian political and social issues. Presented at the Politics & the Pen event each spring in Ottawa. Open to Canadian citizens and permanent residents only. Prize: $25,000 and $2,500 to 4 finalists.

MINA P. SHAUGHNESSY PRIZE

Modern Language Association of America, 85 Broad Street, Suite 500, New York NY 10004-2434. (646)576-5141. **Fax:** (646)458-0030. **E-mail:** awards@mla.org. **Website:** www.mla.org. **Contact:** Coordinator of Book Prizes. Offered in even-numbered years for a work in the fields of language, culture, literacy, or literature with strong application to the teaching of English. Books must have been published in the previous 2 years. Authors need not be members of the MLA. Requires 4 copies of the book. Deadline: May 1. Prize: A cash prize, a certificate, to be presented at the Modern Language Association's annual convention in January, and a 1-year membership in the MLA.

CHARLES S. SYDNOR AWARD

Southern Historical Association, Rm. 111 A LeConte Hall, Athens GA 30602-1602. (706)542-8848. **Fax:**

(706)542-2455. **E-mail:** sdendy@uga.edu. **Website:** sha.uga.edu/awards/syndor.htm. **Contact:** Southern Historical Association. Offered in even-numbered years for recognition of a distinguished book in Southern history published in odd-numbered years. Publishers usually submit books. Deadline: March 1.

🌀 TONY LOTHIAN PRIZE

Under the auspices of the Biographers' Club, 79 Arlington Ave., London N1 7BA United Kingdom. (44)(20)7 359 7769. **E-mail:** ariane.bankes@gmail.com. **Website:** www.biographersclub.co.uk. **Contact:** Ariane Bankes, prize administrator. Entries should consist of a synopsis and 10 pages of a sample chapter for a proposed biography, plus CV, sources and a note on the market for the book: 20 pages maximum in all, unstapled. Open to any writer who has not previously been published or commissioned or written a biography. Deadline: July 27. Prize: £2,000. Judges have included Michael Holroyd, Victoria Glendinning, Selina Hastings, Frances Spalding, Lyndall Gordon, Anne de Courcy, Nigel Hamilton, Anthony Sampson, and Mary Lovell.

WABASH PRIZE FOR NONFICTION

Sycamore Review, Department of English, 500 Oval Dr., Purdue University, West Lafayette IN 47907. **E-mail:** sycamore@purdue.edu; sycamorenf@purdue.edu. **Website:** www.sycamorereview.com/contest/. **Contact:** Kara Krewer, editor-in-chief. Annual contest for unpublished nonfiction. For each submission, send one nonfiction piece (limit 7,500 words). Ms pages should be numbered and should include the title of the piece. All stories must be previously unpublished. See website for more guidelines. Submit via online submissions manager. Deadline: April 15. Prize: $1,000 and publication.

☯ THE HILARY WESTON WRITERS' TRUST PRIZE FOR NONFICTION

The Writers' Trust of Canada, 460 Richmond St. W., Suite 600, Toronto ON M5V 1Y1 Canada. (416)504-8222. **Fax:** (416)504-9090. **E-mail:** info@writerstrust.com. **Website:** www.writerstrust.com. **Contact:** Amanda Hopkins. Offered annually for a work of nonfiction published in the previous year. Award presented at the Writers' Trust Awards event held in Toronto each fall. Open to Canadian citizens and permanent residents only. Deadline: July 18. Prize: $60,000; $5,000 to 4 finalists.

THE ELIE WIESEL PRIZE IN ETHICS ESSAY CONTEST

The Elie Wiesel Foundation for Humanity, 555 Madison Ave., 20th Floor, New York NY 10022. **Fax:** (212)490-6006. **Website:** www.eliewieselfoundation.org. **Contact:** Leslie Meyers. This annual competition is intended to challenge undergraduate juniors and seniors in colleges and universities throughout the US to analyze ethical questions and concerns facing them in today's complex society. All students are encouraged to write thought-provoking, personal essays. Deadline: December 14. Prize: 1st Prize: $5,000; 2nd Prize: $2,500; 3rd Prize: $1,500; Honorable Mentions (2): $500. Judged by a distinguished panel of readers who evaluate all contest entries. A jury chooses the winners.

WRITING CONFERENCE WRITING CONTESTS

P.O. Box 664, Ottawa KS 66067-0664. (785)242-2947. **Fax:** (785)242-2473. **E-mail:** jbushman@writingconference.com. **E-mail:** support@studentq.com. **Website:** www.writingconference.com. **Contact:** John H. Bushman, contest director. Unpublished submissions only. Submissions made by the author or teacher. Purpose of contest: To further writing by students with awards for narration, exposition and poetry at the elementary, middle school, and high school levels. Deadline: January 8. Prize: Awards plaque and publication of winning entry in The Writers' Slate online, April issue. Judged by a panel of teachers.

YEARBOOK EXCELLENCE CONTEST

100 Adler Journalism Building, Iowa City IA 52242-2004. (319)335-3457. **Fax:** (319)335-3989. **E-mail:** quill-scroll@uiowa.edu. **Website:** www.quilland-scroll.org. **Contact:** Jeff Browne, executive director. High school students who are contributors to or staff members of a student yearbook at any public or private high school are invited to enter the competition. Awards will be made in each of the 18 divisions. There are two enrollment categories: Class A: more than 750 students; Class B: 749 or less. Winners will receive Quill and Scroll's National Award Gold Key and, if seniors, are eligible to apply for one of the Edward J. Nell Memorial or George and Ophelia Gallup scholarships. Open to students whose schools have Quill and Scroll charters. Previously published submissions only. Submissions made by the author or school yearbook adviser. Must be published in the 12-month span

prior to contest deadline. Visit website for list of current and previous winners. Purpose is to recognize and reward student journalists for their work in yearbooks and to provide student winners an opportunity to apply for a scholarship to be used freshman year in college for students planning to major in journalism. Deadline: November 1.

ZONE 3 CREATIVE NONFICTION BOOK AWARD

Zone 3, Austin Peay State University, P.O. Box 4565, Clarksville TN 37044. (931)221-7031. **Fax:** (931)221-7149. **E-mail:** wallacess@apsu.edu. **Website:** www.apsu.edu/zone3/contests. **Contact:** Susan Wallace, Managing Editor. This competition is open to all authors writing original works in English. Looking for manuscripts that embrace creative nonfiction's potential by combining lyric exposition, researched reflection, travel dialogues, or creative criticism. Memoir, personal narrative, essay collections, and literary nonfiction are also invited. Submit one copy of ms of 150-300 pages. Accepts entries online and via postal mail. Deadline: April 1. Prize: $1,000 and publication.

WRITING FOR CHILDREN & YOUNG ADULTS

JANE ADDAMS CHILDREN'S BOOK AWARDS

Jane Addams Peace Association, 777 United Nations Plaza, 6th Floor, New York NY 10017. (212)652-8830. **E-mail:** info@janeaddamspeace.org. **Website:** www.janeaddamspeace.org. **Contact:** Heather Palmer, co-chair. The Jane Addams Children's Book Awards are given annually to the children's books published the preceding year that effectively promote the cause of peace, social justice, world community, and the equality of the sexes and all races as well as meeting conventional standards for excellence. Books eligible for this award may be fiction, poetry, or nonfiction. Books may be any length. Entries should be suitable for ages 2-12. See website for specific details on guidelines and required book themes. Deadline: December 31. Judged by a national committee of WILPF members concerned with children's books and their social values is responsible for making the changes each year.

AMERICAN ASSOCIATION OF UNIVERSITY WOMEN AWARD IN JUVENILE LITERATURE

4610 Mail Service Center, Raleigh NC 27699-4610. (919)807-7290. **E-mail:** michael.hill@ncdcr.gov. **Website:** www.ncdcr.gov. **Contact:** Michael Hill, awards coordinator. Annual award. Book must be published during the year ending June 30. Submissions made by author, author's agent or publisher. SASE for contest rules. Author must have maintained either legal residence or actual physical residence, or a combination of both, in the state of North Carolina for 3 years immediately preceding the close of the contest period. Only published work (books) eligible. Recognizes the year's best work of juvenile literature by a North Carolina resident. Deadline: July 15. Prize: Awards a cup to the winner and winner's name inscribed on a plaque displayed within the North Carolina Office of Archives and History. Judged by three-judge panel.

🐎 HANS CHRISTIAN ANDERSEN AWARD

Nonnenweg 12, Postfach Basel CH-4009 Switzerland. **E-mail:** liz.page@ibby.org. **E-mail:** ibby@ibby.org. **Website:** www.ibby.org. **Contact:** Liz Page, director. The Hans Christian Andersen Award, awarded every two years by the International Board on Books for Young People (IBBY), is the highest international recognition given to an author and an illustrator of children's books. The Author's Award has been given since 1956, the Illustrator's Award since 1966. Her Majesty Queen Margrethe II of Denmark is the Patron of the Hans Christian Andersen Awards. The awards are presented at the biennial congresses of IBBY. Awarded to an author and to an illustrator, living at the time of the nomination, who by the outstanding value of their work are judged to have made a lasting contribution to literature for children and young people. The complete works of the author and of the illustrator will be taken into consideration in awarding the medal, which will be accompanied by a diploma. Candidates are nominated by National Sections of IBBY in good standing. Prize: Awards medals according to literary and artistic criteria. Judged by the Hans Christian Andersen International Jury.

☼ MARILYN BAILLIE PICTURE BOOK AWARD

The Canadian Children's Book Centre, 40 Orchard View Blvd., Suite 217, Toronto ON M4R 1B9 Canada. (416)975-0010, ext. 222. **Fax:** (416)975-8970. **E-mail:**

meghan@bookcentre.ca. **Website:** www.bookcentre.ca. **Contact:** Meghan Howe. The Marilyn Baillie Picture Book Award honors excellence in the illustrated picture book format. To be eligible, the book must be an original work in English, aimed at children ages 3-8, written and illustrated by Canadians. Books published in Canada or abroad are eligible. Eligible genres include fiction, non-fiction and poetry. Books must be published between Jan. 1 and Dec. 31 of the previous calendar year. New editions or re-issues of previously published books are not eligible for submission. Send 5 copies of title along with a completed submission form. Deadline: mid-December annually. Prize: $20,000.

MILDRED L. BATCHELDER AWARD

50 E. Huron St., Chicago IL 60611-2795. **Website:** http://www.ala.org/alsc/awardsgrants/. The Batchelder Award is given to the most outstanding children's book originally published in a language other than English in a country other than the United States, and subsequently translated into English for publication in the US. Visit website for terms and criteria of award. The purpose of the award, a citation to an American publisher, is to encourage international exchange of quality children's books by recognizing US publishers of such books in translation. Deadline: December 31.

JOHN AND PATRICIA BEATTY AWARD

California Library Association, **E-mail:** tbronzan@sonoma.lib.ca.us. **Website:** http://www.cla-net.org/?page=113. **Contact:** Tiffany Bronzan, award chair. The California Library Association's John and Patricia Beatty Award, sponsored by Baker & Taylor, honors the author of a distinguished book for children or young adults that best promotes an awareness of California and its people. Must be a children's or young adult books published in the previous year, set in California, and highlight California's cultural heritage or future. Send title suggestiosn to the committee members. Deadline: January 31. Prize: $500 and an engraved plaque. Judged by a committee of CLA members, who select the winning title from books published in the United States during the preceding year.

✪ THE GEOFFREY BILSON AWARD FOR HISTORICAL FICTION FOR YOUNG PEOPLE

The Canadian Children's Book Centre, 40 Orchard View Blvd., Suite 217, Toronto ON M4R 1B9 Canada. (416)975-0010, ext. 222. **Fax:** (416)975-8970. **Website:** www.bookcentre.ca. **Contact:** Meghan Howe. Awarded annually to reward excellence in the writing of an outstanding work of historical fiction for young readers, by a Canadian author, published between Jan 1 and Dec 31 of the previous calendar year. Open to Canadian citizens and/or permanent residents of Canada.Books must be published between January 1 and December 31 of the previous year. Books must be first foreign or first Canadian editions. Autobiographies are not eligible. Jury members will consider the following: historical setting and accuracy, strong character and plot development, well-told, original story, and stability of book for its intended age group. Send 5 copies of the title along with a completed submission form. Deadline: mid-December annually. Prize: $5,000.

THE IRMA S. AND JAMES H. BLACK AWARD

Bank Street College of Education, 610 W. 112th St., New York NY 10025-1898 (212)875-4458. **Fax:** (212)875-4558. **E-mail:** kfreda@bankstreet.edu. **Website:** http://bankstreet.edu/center-childrens-literature/irma-black-award/. **Contact:** Kristin Freda. Award give to an outstanding book for young children—a book in which text and illustrations are inseparable, each enhancing and enlarging on the other to produce a singular whole. Entries must have been published during the previous calendar year. Publishers submit books. Submit only one copy of each book. Does not accept unpublished mss. Deadline: mid-December. Prize: A scroll with the recipient's name and a gold seal designed by Maurice Sendak. Judged by a committee of older children and children's literature professionals. Final judges are first-, second-, and third-grade classes at a number of cooperating schools.

BOSTON GLOBE-HORN BOOK AWARDS

The Boston Globe, Horn Book, Inc., 300 The Fenway, Palace Road Building, Suite P-311, Boston MA 02115. (617)278-0225. **Fax:** (617)278-6062. **E-mail:** bghb@hbook.com; info@hbook.com. **Website:** www.hbook.com/bghb/. Offered annually for excellence in literature for children and young adults (published June 1-May 31). Categories: picture book, fiction and poetry, nonfiction. Judges may also name up to 2 honor books in each category. Books must be published in the US, but may be written or illustrated by citizens of any country. The Horn Book Magazine publishes speeches given at awards ceremonies. Guidelines for submitting books online. Submit a book directly to each of the judges. See www.hbook.com/bghb-submissions for details on submitting, as well as contest guidelines. Deadline: May 15. Prize: $500 and an engraved silver bowl; honor book recipients receive an engraved silver plate. Judged by a panel of 3 judges selected each year.

✪ ANN CONNOR BRIMER BOOK AWARD

The Ann Connor Brimer Award, P.O. Box 36036, Halifax NS B3J 3S9 Canada. (902)490-2742. **Website:** www.atlanticbookawards.ca/. **Contact:** Laura Carter, Atlantic Book Awards Festival Coordinator. In 1990, the Nova Scotia Library Association established the Ann Connor Brimer Award for writers residing in Atlantic Canada who have made an outstanding contribution to writing for Atlantic Candian young people. Author must be alive and residing in Atlantic Canada at time of nomination. Book intended for youth up to the age of 15. Book in print and readily available. Fiction or nonfiction (except textbooks). Book must have been published within the previous year. Prize: $2,000. Two shortlisted titles: $250 each.

CHILDREN'S AFRICANA BOOK AWARD

Outreach Council of the African Studies Association, c/o Rutgers University -Livingston campus, 54 Joyce Kilmer Ave., Piscataway NJ 08854 USA. (703)549-8208; (301)585-9136. **E-mail:** africaaccess@aol.com. **E-mail:** Harriet@AfricaAccessReview.org. **Website:** www.africaaccessreview.org. **Contact:** Brenda Randolph, chairperson. The Children's Africana Book Awards are presented annually to the authors and illustrators of the best books on Africa for children and young people published or distributed in the U.S. The awards were created by the Outreach Council of the African Studies Association (ASA) to dispel stereotypes and encourage the publication and use of accurate, balanced children's materials about Africa. The awards are presented in 2 categories: Young Children and Older Readers. Entries must have been published in the calendar year previous to the award. Work submitted for awards must be suitable for children ages 4-18; a significant portion of books' content must be about Africa; must by copyrighted in the calendar year prior to award year; must be published or distributed in the US. Books should be suitable for children and young adults, ages 4-18. A significant portion of the book's content should be about Afri-

ca. Deadline: January 31 of the award year. Judged by African Studies and Children's Literature scholars. Nominated titles are read by committee members and reviewed by external African Studies scholars with specialized academic training.

CHILDREN'S BOOK GUILD AWARD FOR NONFICTION

E-mail: theguild@childrensbookguild.org. **Website:** www.childrensbookguild.org. Annual award. "One doesn't enter. One is selected. Our jury annually selects one author for the award." Honors an author or illustrator whose total work has contributed significantly to the quality of nonfiction for children. Prize: Cash and an engraved crystal paperweight. Judged by a jury of Children's Book Guild specialists, authors, and illustrators.

✪ CLA YOUNG ADULT BOOK AWARD

1150 Morrison Dr.,,, Suite 400, Ottawa ON K2H 8S9 Canada. (613)232-9625. **Fax:** (613)563-9895. **E-mail:** cshea@cbvrsb.ca. **Website:** www.cla.ca. **Contact:** Carmelita Cechetto-Shea, chair. This award recognizes an author of an outstanding English language Canadian book which appeals to young adults between the ages of 13 and 18. To be eligible for consideration, the following must apply: it must be a work of fiction (novel, collection of short stories, or graphic novel), the title must be a Canadian publication in either hardcover or paperback, and the author must be a Canadian citizen or landed immigrant. The award is given annually, when merited, at the Canadian Library Association's annual conference. Deadline: December 31. Prize: $1,000.

MARGARET A. EDWARDS AWARD

50 East Huron St., Chicago IL 60611-2795. (312)280-4390 or (800)545-2433. **Fax:** (312)280-5276. **E-mail:** yalsa@ala.org. **Website:** www.ala.org/yalsa/edwards. **Contact:** Nichole O'Connor. Annual award administered by the Young Adult Library Services Association (YALSA) of the American Library Association (ALA) and sponsored by *School Library Journal* magazine. Awarded to an author whose book or books, over a period of time, have been accepted by young adults as an authentic voice that continues to illuminate their experiences and emotions, giving insight into their lives. The book or books should enable them to understand themselves, the world in which they live, and their relationship with others and with society. The book or books must be in print at the time of the nomina-

tion. Submissions must be previously published no less than 5 years prior to the first meeting of the current Margaret A. Edwards Award Committee at Midwinter Meeting. Nomination form is available on the YALSA website. Deadline: December 1. Prize: $2,000. Judged by members of the Young Adult Library Services Association.

DOROTHY CANFIELD FISHER CHILDREN'S BOOK AWARD

Midstate Library Service Center, Dorothy Canfield Fisher Book Award Committee, c/o Vermont Department of Libraries, 109 State St., Montpelier VT 05609. (802)828-6954. **E-mail:** grace.greene@state. vt.us. **Website:** www.dcfaward.org. **Contact:** Mary Linney, chair. Annual award to encourage Vermont children to become enthusiastic and discriminating readers by providing them with books of good quality by living American or Canadian authors published in the current year. E-mail for entry rules. Titles must be original work, published in the U.S., and be appropriate to children in grades 4-8. The book must be copyrighted in the current year. It must be written by an American author living in the U.S. or Canada, or a Canadian author living in Canada or the U.S. Deadline: December of year book was published. Prize: Awards a scroll presented to the winning author at an award ceremony. Judged by children, grades 4-8, who vote for their favorite book.

☺ THE NORMA FLECK AWARD FOR CANADIAN CHILDREN'S NON-FICTION

The Canadian Children's Book Centre, 40 Orchard View Blvd., Suite 217, Toronto ON M4R 1B9 Canada. (416)975-0010 ext. 222. **Fax:** (416)975-8970. **E-mail:** meghan@bookcentre.ca. **Website:** www.bookcentre. ca. **Contact:** Meghan Howe. The Norma Fleck Award was established by the Fleck Family Foundation to recognize and raise the profile of exceptional nonfiction books for children. Offered annually for books published between January 1 and December 31 of the previous calendar year. Open to Canadian citizens and/or permanent residents. Books must be first foreign or first Canadian editions. Nonfiction books in the following categories are eligible: culture and the arts, science, biography, history, geography, reference, sports, activities, and pastimes. Deadline: mid-December annually. Prize: $10,000. The award will go to the author unless 40% or more of the text area is composed of original illustrations, in which case the

award will be divided equally between author and illustrator.

FLICKER TALE CHILDREN'S BOOK AWARD

Morton Mandan Public Library, 609 W. Main St., Mandan ND 58554. **E-mail:** laustin@cdln.info. **Website:** www.ndla.info/flickertale. **Contact:** Linda Austin. Award gives children across the state of North Dakota a chance to vote for their book of choice from a nominated list of 20: 4 in the picture book category; 4 in the intermediate category; 4 in the juvenile category (for more advanced readers); 4 in the upper grade level nonfiction category. Also promotes awareness of quality literature for children. Previously published submissions only. Submissions nominated by librarians and teachers across the state of North Dakota. Deadline: April 1. Prize: A plaque from North Dakota Library Association and banquet dinner. Judged by children in North Dakota.

THEODOR SEUSS GEISEL AWARD

Association for Library Service to Children, Division of the American Library Association, 50 E. Huron, Chicago IL 60611. (800)545-2433. **E-mail:** alscawards@ala.org. **Website:** www.ala.org. The Theodor Seuss Geisel Award is given annually to the author(s) and illustrator(s) of the most distinguished American book for beginning readers published in English in the United States during the preceding year. The award is to recognize the author(s) and illustrator(s) who demonstrate great creativity and imagination in his/her/their literary and artistic achievements to engage children in reading. Terms and criteria for the award are listed on the website. Entry will not be returned. Deadline: December 31. Prize: Medal, given at awards ceremony during the ALA Annual Conference.

GOLDEN KITE AWARDS

Society of Children's Book Writers and Illustrators (SCBWI), SCBWI Golden Kite Awards, 8271 Beverly Blvd., Los Angeles CA 90048-4515. (323)782-1010. **Fax:** (323)782-1892. **E-mail:** bonniebader@sbcwi.org. **Website:** www.scbwi.org. Given annually to recognize excellence in children's literature in 4 categories: fiction, nonfiction, picture book text, and picture book illustration. Books submitted must be published in the previous calendar year. Both individuals and publishers may submit. Submit 4 copies of book. Submit to one category only, except in the case of picture books. Must be a current member of the SCBWI. Deadline: December 1. Prize: One Golden Kite Award Winner and one Honor Book will be chosen per category. Winners and Honorees will receive a commemorative poster also sent to publishers, bookstores, libraries, and schools; a press release; an announcement on the SCBWI website; and on SCBWI Social Networks.

☼ AMELIA FRANCES HOWARD-GIBBON ILLUSTRATOR'S AWARD

1150 Morrison Drie, Suite 400, Ottawa ON K 2H859 Canada. (613)232-9625. **Fax:** (613)563-9895. **Website:** www.bookcentre.ca. **Contact:** Diana Cauthier. Annually awarded to an outstanding illustrator of a children's book published in Canada during the previous calendar year. The award is bestowed upon books that are suitable for children up to and including age 12. To be eligible for the award, an illustrator must be a Canadian citizen or a permanent resident of Canada, and the text of the book must be worthy of the book's illustrations. Deadline: November 30. Prize: A plaque and a check for $1,000 (CAD).

CAROL OTIS HURST CHILDREN'S BOOK PRIZE

Westfield Athenaeum, 6 Elm St., Westfield MA 01085. (413)568-7833. **Fax:** (413)568-0988. **Website:** www. westath.org. **Contact:** Pamela Weingart. The Carol Otis Hurst Children's Book Prize honors outstanding works of fiction and nonfiction, including biography and memoir, written for children and young adults through the age of eighteen that exemplify the highest standards of research, analysis, and authorship in their portrayal of the New England Experience. The prize will be presented annually to an author whose book treats the region's history as broadly conceived to encompass one or more of the following elements: political experience, social development, fine and performing artistic expression, domestic life and arts, transportation and communication, changing technology, military experience at home and abroad, schooling, business and manufacturing, workers and the labor movement, agriculture and its transformation, racial and ethnic diversity, religious life and institutions, immigration and adjustment, sports at all levels, and the evolution of popular entertainment. The public presentation of the prize will be accompanied by a reading and/or talk by the recipient at a mutually agreed upon time during the spring immediately following the publication year. Books must have been copyrighted in their original format during the calendar year, January 1 to December 31, of the year preceding the year in which the prize is awarded. Any individual, publisher, or organization may nominate a book. See website for details and guidelines. Deadline: December 31. Prize: $500.

INTERNATIONAL LITERACY ASSOCIATION CHILDREN'S AND YOUNG ADULT'S BOOK AWARDS

P.O. Box 8139, 800 Barksdale Rd., Newark DE 19714-8139. (302)731-1600, ext. 221. **E-mail:** kbaughman@reading.org. **E-mail:** committees@reading.org. **Website:** www.literacyworldwide.org. **Contact:** Kathy Baughman. The ILA Children's and Young Adults Book Awards are intended for newly published authors who show unusual promise in the children's and young adults' book field. Awards are given for fiction and nonfiction in each of three categories: primary, intermediate, and young adult. Books from all countries and published in English for the first time during the previous calendar year will be considered. See website for eligibility and criteria information. Entry should be the author's first or second book. Deadline: January 15. Prize: $1,000.

☼ THE IODE JEAN THROOP BOOK AWARD

The Lillian H. Smith Children's Library, 239 College St., 4th St., Toronto ON M5T 1R5 Canada. (905)522-9537. **E-mail:** mcscott@torontopubliclibrary.ca; iodeontario@bellnet.ca. **Website:** www.iodeontario. ca. **Contact:** Martha Scott. Each year, the Municipal Chapter of Toronto IODE presents an award intended to encourage the publication of books for children between the ages of 6-12 years. The award-winner must be a Canadian citizen, resident in Toronto or the surrounding area, and the book must be published in Canada. Deadline: December 31. Prize: Award and cash prize of $2,000. Judged by a selected committee.

JEFFERSON CUP AWARD

P.O. Box 56312, Virginia Beach VA 23456. (757)689-0594. **Website:** www.vla.org. **Contact:** Lauri Newell, current chairperson. The Jefferson Cup honors a distinguished biography, historical fiction, or American history book for young people. The Jefferson Cup Committee's goal is to promote reading about America's past; to encourage the quality writing of United States history, biography, and historical fiction for young people; and to recognize authors in these disciplines. Deadline: January 31.

THE EZRA JACK KEATS BOOK AWARD FOR NEW WRITER AND NEW ILLUSTRATOR

University of Southern Mississippi, de Grummond Children's Literature Collection, 118 College Dr., #5148, Hattiesburg MS 39406-0001. **Website:** https://www.degrummond.org/. Annual award to an outstanding new author and new illustrator of children's books that portray universal qualities of childhood in our multicultural world. Many past winners have gone on to distinguished careers, creating books beloved by parents, children, librarians and teachers around the world. Writers and illustrators must have had no more than 3 books previously published. Prize: $3,000 honorarium for each winner. Judged by a distinguished selection committee of early childhood education specialists, librarians, illustrators and experts in children's literature.

EZRA JACK KEATS/KERLAN MEMORIAL FELLOWSHIP

University of Minnesota Libraries, 113 Elmer L. Andersen Library, 222 21st Ave. S, Minneapolis MN 55455. **E-mail:** asc-clrc@umn.edu. **Website:** https://www.lib.umn.edu/clrc/awards-grants-and-fellowships. This fellowship from the Ezra Jack Keats Foundation will provide $1,500 to a talented writer and/or illustrator of children's books who wishes to use the Kerlan Collection for the furtherance of his or her artistic development. Special consideration will be given to someone who would find it difficult to finance a visit to the Kerlan Collection. The Ezra Jack Keats Fellowship recipient will receive transportation costs and a per diem allotment. See website for application deadline and for digital application materials. Winner will be notified in February. Study and written report must be completed within the calendar year. Deadline: January 30.

KENTUCKY BLUEGRASS AWARD

Website: www.kasl.us. The Kentucky Bluegrass Award is a student choice program. The KBA promotes and encourages Kentucky students in kindergarten through grade 12 to read a variety of quality literature. Each year, a KBA committee for each grade category chooses the books for the four Master Lists (K-2, 3-5, 6-8 and 9-12). All Kentucky public and private schools, as well as public libraries, are welcome to participate in the program. To nominate a book, see the website for form and details. Deadline: March 1.

Judged by students who read books and choose their favorite.

CORETTA SCOTT KING BOOK AWARDS

50 E. Huron St., Chicago IL 60611-2795. (800)545-2433. **E-mail:** olos@ala.org. **Website:** www.ala.org/csk. **Contact:** Office for Diversity, Literacy and Outreach Services. The Coretta Scott King Book Awards are given annually to outstanding African American authors and illustrators of books for children and young adults that demonstrate an appreciation of African American culture and universal human values. The award commemorates the life and work of Dr. Martin Luther King, Jr., and honors his wife, Mrs. Coretta Scott King, for her courage and determination to continue the work for peace and world brotherhood. Must be written for a youth audience in one of three categories: preschool-4th grade; 5th-8th grade; or 9th-12th grade. Book must be published in the year preceding the year the award is given, evidenced by the copyright date in the book. See website for full details, criteria, and eligibility concerns. Purpose is to encourage the artistic expression of the African American experience via literature and the graphic arts, including biographical, historical and social history treatments by African American authors and illustrators. Deadline: December 1. Judged by the Coretta Scott King Book Awards Committee.

⊙ THE VICKY METCALF AWARD FOR LITERATURE FOR YOUNG PEOPLE

The Writers' Trust of Canada, 460 Richmond St. W., Suite 600, Toronto ON M5V 1Y1 Canada. (416)504-8222. **E-mail:** info@writerstrust.com. **Website:** www.writerstrust.com. **Contact:** Amanda Hopkins. The Vicky Metcalf Award is presented to a Canadian writer for a body of work in children's literature at The Writers' Trust Awards event held in Toronto each fall. Open to Canadian citizens and permanent residents only. Prize: $25,000.

MILKWEED PRIZE FOR CHILDREN'S LITERATURE

Milkweed Editions, 1011 Washington Ave. S., Suite 300, Minneapolis MN 55415. (612)332-3192. **Fax:** (612)215-2550. **E-mail:** editor@milkweed.org. **Website:** www.milkweed.org. Milkweed Editions will award the Milkweed Prize for Children's Literature to the best mss for young readers that Milkweed accepts for publication during the calendar year by a writer not previously published by Milkweed. All mss for young readers submitted for publication by Milkweed are automatically entered into the competition. Seeking full-length fiction between 90-200 pages. Does not consider picture books or poetry collections for young readers. Recognizes an outstanding literary novel for readers ages 8-13 and encourage writers to turn their attention to readers in this age group. Prize: $10,000 cash prize in addition to a publishing contract negotiated at the time of acceptance. Judged by the editors of Milkweed Editions.

NATIONAL YOUNGARTS FOUNDATION

2100 Biscayne Blvd., Miami FL 33137. (305)377-1140. **Fax:** (305)377-1149. **E-mail:** info@nfaa.org; apply@youngarts.org. **Website:** www.youngarts.org. The National YoungArts Foundation (formerly known as the National Foundation for Advancement in the Arts) was established in 1981 by Lin and Ted Arison to identify and support the next generation of artists and to contribute to the cultural vitality of the nation by investing in the artistic development of talented young artists in the visual, literary, design and performing arts. Each year, there are approximately 11,000 applications submitted to YoungArts from 15-18 year old (or grades 10-12) artists, and from these, approximately 700 winners are selected who are eligible to participate in programs in Miami, New York, Los Angeles, and Washington D.C. (with Chicago and other regions in the works). YoungArts provides these emerging artists with life-changing experiences and validation by renowned mentors, access to significant scholarships, national recognition and other opportunities throughout their careers to help ensure that the nation's most outstanding emerging artists are encouraged to pursue careers in the arts. See website for details about applying. Prize: Cash awards up to $10,000.

JOHN NEWBERY MEDAL

Association for Library Service to Children, Division of the American Library Association, 50 E. Huron, Chicago IL 60611. (800)545-2433, ext. 2153. **Fax:** (312)280-5271. **E-mail:** alscawards@ala.org. **Website:** www.ala.org. The Newbery Medal is awarded annually by the American Library Association for the most distinguished contribution to American literature for children. Previously published submissions only; must be published prior to year award is given. SASE for award rules. Entries not returned. Medal awarded at Caldecott/Newbery banquet during ALA annual conference. Deadline: December 31. Judged by Newbery Award Selection Committee.

NEW VOICES AWARD

95 Madison Ave., Suite 1205, New York NY 10016. **Website:** www.leeandlow.com. Open to students. Annual award. Lee & Low Books is one of the few minority-owned publishing companies in the country and has published more than 100 first-time writers and illustrators. Winning titles include *The Blue Roses*, winner of a Patterson Prize for Books for Young People; *Janna and the Kings*, an IRA Children's Book Award Notable; and *Sixteen Years in Sixteen Seconds*, selected for the Texas Bluebonnet Award Masterlist. Submissions made by author. SASE for contest rules or visit website. Restrictions of media for illustrators: The author must be a writer of color who is a resident of the U.S. and who has not previously published a children's picture book. For additional information, send SASE or visit Lee & Low's website. Encourages writers of color to enter the world of children's books. Deadline: September 30. Prize: $1,000 and standard publication contract (regardless of whether or not writer has an agent) along with an advance against royalties; New Voices Honor Award: $500 prize. Judged by Lee & Low editors.

ORBIS PICTUS AWARD FOR OUTSTANDING NONFICTION FOR CHILDREN

1111 W. Kenyon Rd., Urbana IL 61801-1096. (217)328-3870. **Fax:** (217)328-0977. **E-mail:** elementary@ncte.org. **Website:** www.ncte.org/awards/orbispictus. The NCTE Orbis Pictus Award promotes and recognizes excellence in the writing of nonfiction for children. Orbis Pictus commemorates the work of Johannes Amos Comenius, *Orbis Pictus—The World in Pictures* (1657), considered to be the first book actually planned for children. Submissions should be made by an author, the author's agent, or by a person or group of people. Must be published in the calendar year of the competition. Deadline: November 1. Prize: A plaque given at the NCTE Elementary Section Luncheon at the NCTE Annual Convention in November. Up to 5 honor books awarded. Judged by members of the Orbis Pictus Committee.

THE ORIGINAL ART

128 E. 63rd St., New York NY 10065. (212)838-2560. **Fax:** (212)838-2561. **E-mail:** kim@societyillustrators.org; info@societyillustrators.org. **Website:** www.societyillustrators.org. **Contact:** Kate Feirtag, exhibi-

tion director. The Original Art is an annual exhibit created to showcase illustrations from the year's best children's books published in the US. For editors and art directors, it's an inspiration and a treasure trove of talent to draw upon. Previously published submissions only. Request "call for entries" to receive contest rules and entry forms. Works will be displayed at the Society of Illustrators Museum of American Illustration in New York City October-November annually. Deadline: July 18. Judged by 7 professional artists and editors.

HELEN KEATING OTT AWARD FOR OUTSTANDING CONTRIBUTION TO CHILDREN'S LITERATURE

CSLA, 10157 SW Barbur Blvd. #102C, Portland OR 97219. (503)244-6919. **Fax:** (503)977-3734. **E-mail:** sharper1@kent.edu. **Website:** www.cslainfo.org. **Contact:** S. Meghan Harper, awards chair. Annual award given to a person or organization that has made a significant contribution to promoting high moral and ethical values through children's literature. Recipient is honored in July during the conference. Awards certificate of recognition, the awards banquet, and one-night's stay in the hotel. A nomination for an award may be made by anyone. An application form is available online. Elements of creativity and innovation will be given high priority by the judges.

PATERSON PRIZE FOR BOOKS FOR YOUNG PEOPLE

The Poetry Center at Passaic County Community College, One College Blvd., Paterson NJ 07505. (973)684-6555. **Fax:** (973)523-6085. **E-mail:** mgillan@pccc.edu. **Website:** www.pccc.edu/poetry. **Contact:** Maria Mazziotti Gillan, executive director. Award for a book published in the previous year in each age category (Pre-K-Grade 3, Grades 4-6, Grades 7-12). Deadline: February 1. Prize: $500.

THE KATHERINE PATERSON PRIZE FOR YOUNG ADULT AND CHILDREN'S WRITING

Hunger Mountain, Vermont College of Fine Arts, 36 College St., Montpelier VT 05602. (802)828-8517. **E-mail:** hungermtn@vcfa.edu. **Website:** www.hungermtn.org. **Contact:** Samantha Kolber, Managing Editor. The annual Katherine Paterson Prize for Young Adult and Children's Writing honors the best in young adult and children's literature. Submit young adult or middle grade mss, and writing for younger children, short stories, picture books, poetry, or novel excerpts, under 10,000 words. Guidelines available on website. Deadline: March 8. Prize: $1,000 and publication for the first place winner; $100 each and publication for the three category winners. Judged by a guest judge every year. The 2016 judge is Rita Williams-Garcia, author of Newbery Honor-winning novel, *One Crazy Summer*.

PENNSYLVANIA YOUNG READERS' CHOICE AWARDS PROGRAM

Pennsylvania School Librarians Association, 134 Bisbing Road, Henryville PA 18332. **E-mail:** pyrca.psla@gmail.com. **Website:** www.psla.org. **Contact:** Alice L. Cyphers, co-coordinator. Submissions nominated by a person or group. Must be published within 5 years of the award—for example, books published in 2013 to present are eligible for the 2018-2019 award. Check the Program wiki at pyrca.wikispaces.com for submission information. View information at the Pennsylvania School Librarians' website or the Program wiki. Must be currently living in North America. The purpose of the Pennsylvania Young Reader's Choice Awards Program is to promote the reading of quality books by young people in the Commonwealth of Pennsylvania, to encourage teacher and librarian collaboration and involvement in children's literature, and to honor authors whose works have been recognized by the students of Pennsylvania. Deadline: September 15. Prize: Framed certificate to winning authors. Four awards are given, one for each of the following grade level divisions: K-3, 3-6, 6-8, YA. Judged by children of Pennsylvania (they vote).

PEN/PHYLLIS NAYLOR WORKING WRITER FELLOWSHIP

PEN America, PEN American Center, 588 Broadway, Suite 303, New York NY 10012. **E-mail:** awards@pen.org. **Website:** www.pen.org/awards. **Contact:** Arielle Anema, Literary Awards Coordinator. Offered annually to an author of children's or young-adult fiction. The Fellowship has been developed to help writers whose work is of high literary caliber but who have not yet attracted a broad readership. The Fellowship is designed to assist a writer at a crucial moment in his or her career to complete a book-length work-in-progress. Candidates have published at least one novel for children or young adults which have been received warmly by literary critics, but have not generated sufficient income to support the author. Writers must be nominated by an editor or fellow author. See website for eligibility and nomination guidelines. Deadline: Submissions open during the summer of each year. Visit PEN.org/awards for up-to-date information on deadlines. Prize: $5,000.

PLEASE TOUCH MUSEUM BOOK AWARD

Memorial Hall in Fairmount Park, 4231 Avenue of the Republic, Philadelphia PA 19131. (215)578-5153. **Fax:** (215)578-5171. **E-mail:** hboyd@pleasetouchmuseum.org. **Website:** www.pleasetouchmuseum.org. **Contact:** Heather Boyd. This prestigious award has recognized and encouraged the publication of high quality books. The award was exclusively created to recognize and encourage the writing of publications that help young children enjoy the process of learning through books, while reflecting PTM's philosophy of learning through play. The awards to to books that are imaginative, exceptionally illustrated, and help foster a child's life-long love of reading. To be eligible for consideration, a book must be distinguished in text, illustration, and ability to explore and clarify an idea for young children (ages 7 and under). Deadline: October 1. Books for each cycle must be published within previous calendar year (September-August). Judged by a panel of volunteer educators, artists, booksellers, children's authors, and librarians in conjunction with museum staff.

POCKETS FICTION-WRITING CONTEST

P.O. Box 340004, Nashville TN 37203-0004. (615)340-7333. **Fax:** (615)340-7267. **E-mail:** pockets@upperroom.org. **Website:** www.pockets.upperroom.org. **Contact:** Lynn W. Gilliam, senior editor. Designed for 6- to 12-year-olds, *Pockets* magazine offers wholesome devotional readings that teach about God's love and presence in life. The content includes fiction, scripture stories, puzzles and games, poems, recipes, colorful pictures, activities, and scripture readings. Freelance submissions of stories, poems, recipes, puzzles and games, and activities are welcome. Stories should be 750-1,000 words. Multiple submissions are permitted. Past winners are ineligible. The primary purpose of *Pockets* is to help children grow in their relationship with God and to claim the good news of the gospel of Jesus Christ by applying it to their daily lives. *Pockets* espouses respect for all human beings and for God's creation. It regards a child's faith journey as an integral part of all of life and sees prayer as undergirding that journey. Deadline: August 15.

Submission period begins March 15. Prize: $500 and publication in magazine.

MICHAEL L. PRINTZ AWARD

Young Adult Library Services Association, Division of the American Library Association, 50 E. Huron, Chicago IL 60611. (800)545-2433. **Fax:** (312)280-5276. **E-mail:** yalsa@ala.org. **Website:** www.ala.org/yalsa/printz. **Contact:** Nichole O'Connor, program officer for events and conferences. The Michael L. Printz Award annually honors the best book written for teens, based entirely on its literary merit, each year. In addition, the Printz Committee names up to 4 honor books, which also represent the best writing in young adult literature. The award-winning book can be fiction, nonfiction, poetry or an anthology, and can be a work of joint authorship or editorship. The books must be published between January 1 and December 31 of the preceding year and be designated by its publisher as being either a young adult book or one published for the age range that YALSA defines as young adult, e.g. ages 12 through 18. Deadline: December 1. Judged by an award committee.

PURPLE DRAGONFLY BOOK AWARDS

Story Monsters LLC, 4696 W Tyson St, Chandler AZ 85226-2903. (480)940-8182. **Fax:** (480)940-8787. **E-mail:** linda@storymonsters.com. **Website:** www.dragonflybookawards.com. **Contact:** Cristy Bertini, contest coordinator. The Purple Dragonfly Book Awards are designed with children in mind. Awards are divided into 54 distinct subject categories, ranging from books on the environment and cooking to sports and family issues. The Purple Dragonfly Book Awards are geared toward stories that appeal to children of all ages. We now offer new Marketing/Promotion Categories: Book Trailer, Bookmark, Flyer, Media Kit, and Press Release. The awards are open to books published in any calendar year and in any country that are available for purchase. Books entered must be printed in English. Traditionally published, partnership published and self-published books are permitted, as long as they fit the above criteria. Submit materials to: Cristy Bertini, Attn: Dragonfly Book Awards, 1271 Turkey St., Ware, MA 01082. Deadline: May 1. The grand prize winner will receive a $500 cash prize, a certificate commemorating their accomplishment, 100 Grand Prize seals, a one-hour marketing consulting session with Linda F. Radke, a news release announcing the winners sent to a comprehensive list of media outlets, and a listing on the Dragonfly Book Awards website. All first-place winners of categories will be put into a drawing for a $100 prize. In addition, each first-place winner in each category receives a certificate commemorating their accomplishment, 25 foil award seals, and mention on Dragonfly Book Awards website. All winners receive certificates and are listed in Story Monsters Ink magazine. Judged by industry experts with specific knowledge about the categories over which they preside.

QUILL AND SCROLL WRITING, PHOTO AND MULTIMEDIA CONTEST AND BLOGGING COMPETITION

School of Journalism, Univ. of Iowa, 100 Adler Journalism Bldg., Iowa City IA 52242-2004. (319)335-3457. **Fax:** (319)335-3989. **E-mail:** quill-scroll@uiowa.edu. **E-mail:** quill-scroll@uiowa.edu. **Website:** quilland-scroll.org. **Contact:** Jeffrey Browne, contest director. Entries must have been published in a high school or professional newspaper or website during the previous year, and must be the work of a currently enrolled high school student, when published. Open to students. Annual contest. Previously published submissions only. Submissions made by the author or school media adviser. Deadline: February 5. Prize: Winners will receive *Quill and Scroll*'s National Award Gold Key and, if seniors, are eligible to apply for one of the scholarships offered by *Quill and Scroll*. All winning entries are automatically eligible for the International Writing and Photo Sweepstakes Awards. Engraved plaque awarded to sweepstakes winners.

⚫ THE RED HOUSE CHILDREN'S BOOK AWARD

Red House Children's Book Award, 123 Frederick Road, Cheam, Sutton, Surrey SM1 2HT United Kingdom. **E-mail:** info@rhcba.co.uk. **Website:** www.red-housechildrensbookaward.co.uk. **Contact:** Sinead Kromer, national coordinator. The Red House Children's Book Award is the only national book award that is entirely voted for by children. A shortlist is drawn up from children's nominations and any child can then vote for the winner of the three categories: Books for Younger Children, Books for Younger Readers and Books for Older Readers. The book with the most votes is then crowned the winner of the Red House Children's Book Award. Deadline: December 31.

TOMÁS RIVERA MEXICAN AMERICAN CHILDREN'S BOOK AWARD

Dr. Jesse Gainer, Texas State University, 601 University Drive, San Marcos TX 78666-4613. (512)245-2357. **E-mail:** riverabookaward@txstate.edu. **Website:** www.riverabookaward.org. **Contact:** Dr. Jesse Gainer, award director. Texas State University College of Education developed the Tomas Rivera Mexican American Children's Book Award to honor authors and illustrators who create literature that depicts the Mexican American experience. The award was established in 1995 and was named in honor of Dr. Tomas Rivera, a distinguished alumnus of Texas State University. The book will be written for younger children, ages pre-K to 5th grade (awarded in even years), or older children, ages 6th grade to 12 grade (awarded in odd years). The text and illustrations will be of highest quality. The portrayal/representations of Mexican Americans will be accurate and engaging, avoid stereotypes, and reflect rich characterization. The book may be fiction or non- fiction. See website for more details and directions. Deadline: November 1.

☯ ROCKY MOUNTAIN BOOK AWARD: ALBERTA CHILDREN'S CHOICE BOOK AWARD

Box 42, Lethbridge AB T1J 3Y3 Canada. (403)381-0855. **Website:** www.rmba.info. **Contact:** Michelle Dimnik, contest director. Annual contest. No entry fee. Awards: Gold medal and author tour of selected Alberta schools. Judging by students. Canadian authors and/or illustrators only. Submit entries to Richard Chase. Previously unpublished submissions only. Submissions made by author's agent or nominated by a person or group. Must be published within the 3 years prior to that year's award. Register before January 20th to take part in the Rocky Mountain Book Award. SASE for contest rules and entry forms. Purpose of contest: "Reading motivation for students, promotion of Canadian authors, illustrators and publishers." Gold Medal and sponsored visit to several Alberta Schools or Public Libraries. Judged by students.

SCBWI MAGAZINE MERIT AWARDS

4727 Wilshire Blvd., Suite 301, Los Angeles CA 90010. (323)782-1010. **Fax:** (323)782-1892. **E-mail:** grants@ scbwi.org. **Website:** www.scbwi.org. **Contact:** Stephanie Gordon, award coordinator. The SCBWI is a professional organization of writers and illustrators and others interested in children's literature. Membership

work for young people by an SCBWI member—writer, artist or photographer—is eligible during the year of original publication. In the case of co-authored work, both authors must be SCBWI members. Members must submit their own work. Requirements for entrants: 4 copies each of the published work and proof of publication (may be contents page) showing the name of the magazine and the date of issue. Previously published submissions only. For rules and procedures see website. Must be a SCBWI member. Recognizes outstanding original magazine work for young people published during that year, and having been written or illustrated by members of SCBWI. Deadline: December 15 of the year of publication. Submission period begins January 1. Prize: Awards plaques and honor certificates for each of 4 categories (fiction, nonfiction, illustration and poetry). Judged by a magazine editor and two "full" SCBWI members.

SKIPPING STONES BOOK AWARDS

Skipping Stones, P.O. Box 3939, Eugene OR 97403-0939 USA. **E-mail:** editor@SkippingStones.org. **Website:** www.skippingstones.org. **Contact:** Arun N. Toke', Exec. Editor. Open to published books, publications/magazines, educational videos, and DVDs. Annual awards. Submissions made by the author or publishers and/or producers. Send request for contest rules and entry forms or visit website. Many educational publications announce the winners of our book awards. The winning books and educational videos/DVDs are announced in the July-September issue of *Skipping Stones* and also on the website. In addition to announcements on social media pages, the reviews of winning titles are posted on website. *Skipping Stones* multicultural magazine has been published for over 28 years. Recognizes exceptional, literary and artistic contributions to juvenile/children's literature, as well as teaching resources and educational audio/video resources in the areas of multicultural awareness, nature and ecology, social issues, peace, and nonviolence. Deadline: February 28. Prize: Winners receive gold honor award seals, attractive honor certificates, and publicity via multiple outlets. Judged by a multicultural selection committee of editors, students, parents, teachers, and librarians.

SKIPPING STONES YOUTH HONOR AWARDS

P.O. Box 3939, Eugene OR 97403-0939. (541)342-4956. **E-mail:** editor@SkippingStones.org. **Website:** www.

SkippingStones.org. **Contact:** Arun N. Toké, editor. Now celebrating its 29th year, *Skipping Stones* is a winner of N.A.M.E.EDPRESS, Newsstand Resources, Writer and Parent's Choice Awards. Open to students. Annual awards. Submissions made by the author. The winners are published in the October-December issue of *Skipping Stones*. Everyone who enters the contest receives the Autumn issue featuring Youth Awards. SASE for contest rules or download from website. Entries must include certificate of originality by a parent and/or teacher and a cover letter that included cultural background information on the author. Submissions can either be mailed or e-mailed. Up to ten awards are given in three categories: (1) Compositions (essays, poems, short stories, songs, travelogues, etc.): Entries should be typed (double-spaced) or neatly handwritten. Fiction or nonfiction should be limited to 1,000 words; poems to 30 lines. Non-English writings are also welcome. (2) Artwork (drawings, cartoons, paintings or photo essays with captions): Entries should have the artist's name, age and address on the back of each page. Send the originals with SASE. Black & white photos are especially welcome. Limit: 8 pieces. (3) Youth Organizations: Describe how your club or group works to: (a) preserve the nature and ecology in your area, (b) enhance the quality of life for low-income, minority or disabled or (c) improve racial or cultural harmony in your school or community. Use the same format as for compositions. Recognizes youth, 7 to 17, for their contributions to multicultural awareness, nature and ecology, social issues, peace and nonviolence. Also promotes creativity, self-esteem and writing skills and to recognize important work being done by youth organizations. Deadline: June 25. Judged by *Skipping Stones* staff.

SYDNEY TAYLOR MANUSCRIPT COMPETITION

Association of Jewish Libraries, Sydney Taylor Manuscript Award Competition, 204 Park St., Montclair NJ 07042-2903. **E-mail:** stmacajl@aol.com. **Website:** www.jewishlibraries.org/main/Awards/SydneyTaylorManuscriptAward.aspx. **Contact:** Aileen Grossberg. This competition is for unpublished writers of juvenile fiction. Material should be for readers ages 8-13. The manuscript should have universal appeal and reveal positive aspects of Jewish life that will serve to deepen the understanding of Judaism for all children. Download rules and forms from website. Must be an unpublished fiction writer or a student; also, books must range from 64-200 pages in length. "AJL assumes no responsibility for publication, but hopes this cash incentive will serve to encourage new writers of children's stories with Jewish themes for all children." To encourage new fiction of Jewish interest for readers ages 8-13. Deadline: September 30. Prize: $1,000. Judging by qualified judges from within the Association of Jewish Libraries.

SYDNEY TAYLOR BOOK AWARD

Association of Jewish Libraries, **E-mail:** chair@sydneytaylorbookaward.org. **Website:** www.sydneytaylorbookaward.org. **Contact:** Ellen Tilman, chair. The Sydney Taylor Book Award is presented annually to outstanding books for children and teens that authentically portray the Jewish experience. Deadline: November 30. Cannot guarantee that books received after November 30 will be considered. Prize: Gold medals are presented in 3 categories: younger readers, older readers, and teen readers. Honor books are awarded in silver medals, and notable books are named in each category. Winners are selected by a committee of the Association of Jewish Libraries. Each committee member must receive an individual copy of each book that is to be considered.

❂ TD CANADIAN CHILDREN'S LITERATURE AWARD

The Canadian Children's Book Centre, 40 Orchard View Blvd., Suite 217, Toronto ON M4R 1B9 Canada. (416)975-0010, ext. 222. **Fax:** (416)975-8970. **E-mail:** meghan@bookcentre.ca. **Website:** www.bookcentre.ca. **Contact:** Meghan Howe. The TD Canadian Children's Literature Award is for the most distinguished book of the year. All books, in any genre, written and illustrated by Canadians and for children ages 1-12 are eligible. Only books published in Canada are eligible for submission. Books must be published between January 1 and December 31 of the previous calendar year. Open to Canadian citizens and/or permanent residents of Canada. Deadline: mid-December. Prizes: Two prizes of $30,000, 1 for English, 1 for French. $20,000 will be divided among the Honour Book English titles and Honour Book French titles, to a maximum of 4; $2,500 shall go to each of the publishers of the English and French grand-prize winning books for promotion and publicity.

VEGETARIAN ESSAY CONTEST

The Vegetarian Resource Group, P.O. Box 1463, Baltimore MD 21203. (410)366-VEGE. **Fax:** (410)366-8804.

E-mail: vrg@vrg.org. **Website:** www.vrg.org. Write a 2-3 page essay on any aspect of veganism/vegetarianism. Entrants should base their paper on interviewing, research, and/or personal opinion. You need not be a vegetarian to enter. Three different entry categories: age 14-18; age 9-13; and age 8 and under. Prize: $50.

VFW VOICE OF DEMOCRACY

Veterans of Foreign Wars of the U.S., National Headquarters, 406 W. 34th St., Kansas City MO 64111. (816)968-1117. **E-mail:** kharmer@vfw.org. **Website:** https://www.vfw.org/VOD/. The Voice of Democracy Program is open to students in grades 9-12 (on the Nov. 1 deadline), who are enrolled in a public, private or parochial high school or home study program in the United States and its territories. Contact your local VFW Post to enter (entry must not be mailed to the VFW National Headquarters, only to a local, participating VFW Post). Purpose is to give high school students the opportunity to voice their opinions about their responsibility to our country and to convey those opinions via the broadcast media to all of America. Deadline: November 1. Prize: Winners receive awards ranging from $1,000-30,000.

LAURA INGALLS WILDER MEDAL

50 E. Huron, Chicago IL 60611. (800)545-2433. **E-mail:** alscawards@ala.org. **Website:** www.ala.org/alsc/awardsgrants/bookmedia/wildermedal. Award offered every 2 years. The Wilder Award honors an author or illustrator whose books, published in the US, have made, over a period of years, a substantial and lasting contribution to literature for children. The candidates must be nominated by ALSC members. Medal presented at Newbery/Caldecott banquet during annual conference. Judging by Wilder Award Selection Committee.

RITA WILLIAMS YOUNG ADULT PROSE PRIZE CATEGORY

Soul-Making Keats Literary Competition, The Webhallow House, 1544 Sweetwood Dr., Broadmoor Village CA 94015-2029. (650)756-5279. **Fax:** (650)756-5279. **E-mail:** soulkeats@mail.com. **Website:** www.soulmakingcontest.us. **Contact:** Eileen Malone. For writers in grades 9-12 or equivalent age. Up to 3,000 words in prose form of choice. Complete rules and guidelines available online. Deadline: November 30 (postmarked). Prize: $100 for first place; $50 for second place; $25 for third place. Judged (and sponsored) writers in grades 9-12 or equivalent age. Up to 3,000 words in prose form of choice. Complete rules and guidelines available online. Deadline: November 30 (postmarked). Prize: $100 for first place; $50 for second place; $25 for third place. Judged (and sponsored) by Rita Wiliams, an Emmy-award winning investigative reporter with KTVU-TV in Oakland, California.

PAUL A. WITTY OUTSTANDING LITERATURE AWARD

P.O. Box 8139, Newark DE 19714-8139. (800)336-7323. **Fax:** (302)731-1057. **Website:** www.reading.org. **Contact:** Marcie Craig Post, executive director. This award recognizes excellence in original poetry or prose written by students. Elementary and secondary students whose work is selected will receive an award. Deadline: February 2. Prize: Not less than $25 and a citation of merit.

WORK-IN-PROGRESS GRANT

Society of Children's Book Writers and Illustrators (SCBWI), 8271 Beverly Blvd., Los Angeles CA 90048. (323)782-1010. **E-mail:** grants@scbwi.org; wipgrant@scbwi.org. **Website:** www.scbwi.org. Six grants—one designated specifically for picture book text, chapter book/early readers, middle grade, young adult fiction, nonfiction, and multicultural fiction or nonfiction—to assist SCBWI members in the completion of a specific project. Open to SCBWI members only. Deadline: March 31. Open to submissions on March 1.

● THE YOUNG ADULT FICTION PRIZE

Victorian Premier's Literary Awards, State Government of Victoria, The Wheeler Centre, 176 Little Lonsdale Street, Melbourne VIC 3000 Australia. (61)(3)90947800. **E-mail:** vpla@wheelercentre.com. **Website:** http://www.wheelercentre.com/projects/victorian-premier-s-literary-awards-2016/about-the-awards. **Contact:** Project Officer. Visit website for guidelines and nomination forms. Prize: $25,000.

YOUNG READER'S CHOICE AWARD

Paxson Elementary School, 101 Evans, Missoula MT 59801. **E-mail:** hbray@missoula.lib.mt.us. **Website:** www.pnla.org. **Contact:** Honore Bray, president. The Pacific Northwest Library Association's Young Reader's Choice Award is the oldest children's choice award in the U.S. and Canada. Nominations are taken only from children, teachers, parents and librarians in the Pacific Northwest: Alaska, Alberta, British Columbia, Idaho, Montana and Washington. Nominations will not be accepted from publishers. Nominations may include fiction, nonfiction, graphic novels, anime, and manga. Nominated titles are those published 3 years prior to the award year. Deadline: February 1. Books will be judged on popularity with readers. Age appropriateness will be considered when choosing which of the three divisions a book is placed. Other considerations may include reading enjoyment; reading level; interest level; genre representation; gender representation; racial diversity; diversity of social, political, economic, or religions viewpoints; regional consideration; effectiveness of expression; and imagination. The Pacific Northwest Library Association is committed to intellectual freedom and diversity of ideas. No title will be excluded because of race, nationality, religion, gender, sexual orientation, political or social view of either the author or the material.

GENERAL

● AUSTRALIAN CHRISTIAN BOOK OF THE YEAR AWARD

SparkLit, P.O. Box 198, Forest Hill VIC 3131 Australia. **E-mail:** admin@sparklit.org. **Website:** www.sparklit.org. **Contact:** The Awards Coordinator. SparkLit empowers and encourages Christian writers and publishers. (The Society for Promoting Christian Knowledge Australia and the Australian Christian Literature Society.) The Australian Christian Book of the Year Award is given annually to an original book written by an Australian citizen normally resident in Australia. A short list is released in July. The results are announced and prizes are presented in August. The award recognizes and encourages excellence in Australian Christian writing. Deadline: March 31. Prize: $3,000 (AUD), a framed certificate and extensive promotion.

● J.W. DAFOE BOOK PRIZE

J.W. Dafoe Foundation, 351 University College, University of Manitoba, Winnipeg MB R3T 2M8 Canada. **E-mail:** james.fergusson@umanitoba.ca. **Website:** www.dafoefoundation.ca. **Contact:** Dr. James Fergusson. The Dafoe Book Prize was established to honor John Dafoe, editor of the *Winnipeg Free Press* from 1900 to 1944, and is awarded each year for distinguished writing by Canadians or authors in resident in Canada that contributes to the understanding of Canada, Canadians, and/or Canada's place in the world. Books must be published January-December

THE FOUNTAINHEAD ESSAY CONTEST

Ayn Rand Institute, P.O. Box 57044, Irvine CA 92619-7044. **E-mail:** essays@aynrand.org. **Website:** www.aynrand.org/contests. Offered annually to encourage analytical thinking and excellence in writing, and to expose students to the philosophic ideas of Ayn Rand. "For information contact your English teacher or guidance counselor, or visit our website." Length: 800-1,600 words. Open to 11th and 12th graders. Deadline: April 26, 2017. Prizes: 1st Place: $10,000; 2nd Place (5): $2,000; 3rd Place (10): $1,000; Finalist (45): $100; Semifinalist (175): $50.

THE GLENNA LUSCHEI PRAIRIE SCHOONER AWARDS

Prairie Schooner, 123 Andrews Hall, P.O. Box 880334, Lincoln NE 68588-0334. (402)472-0911. **Fax:** (402)472-1817. **E-mail:** prairieschooner@unl.edu; ps-bookprize@unl.edu. **Website:** http://prairieschooner.unl.edu/. **Contact:** Kwame Dawes. Annual awards for work published in *Prairie Schooner* in the previous year. Offers one large prize and 10 smaller awards. See website for more details. Contact *Prairie Schooner* for further information. Prize: One award of $1,500 and 10 awards of $250 each.

SUE GRANZELLA HUMOR PRIZE

Category in the Soul-Making Keats Literary Competition, The Webhallow House, 1544 Sweetwood Dr., Broadmoor Village CA 94015-2029. (650)756-5279. **Fax:** (650)756-5279. **E-mail:** soulkeats@mail.com. **Website:** www.soulmakingcontest.us. **Contact:** Eileen Malone. Any form, 3,000 words or less. One piece per entry. Previously published material is accepted. Open annually to any writer. Deadline: November 30. Prize: First Place: $100; Second Place: $50; Third Place: $25. Judged by Sue Granzella.

INDEPENDENT PUBLISHER BOOK AWARDS

Jenkins Group/Independent Publisher Online, 1129 Woodmere Ave., Ste. B, Traverse City MI 49686. (231)933-0445. **Fax:** (231)933-0448. **E-mail:** jimb@bookpublishing.com. **Website:** www.independent-publisher.com. **Contact:** Jim Barnes. Honors the year's best independently published English language titles from around the world. The IPPY Awards reward those who exhibit the courage, innovation, and creativity to bring about change in the world of publishing. Independent spirit and expertise comes from publishers of all areas and budgets, and they judge books with that in mind. Entries will be accepted in over 80 categories, visit website to see details. Open to any published author. Accepts books published within the past 2 years. See website for guidelines and details. Deadline: Late February. Price of submission rises in September and December. Prize: Gold, silver and bronze medals for each category; foil seals available to all. Judged by a panel of experts representing the fields of design, writing, bookselling, library, and reviewing.

◑ INSCRIBE CONTESTS

InScribe Christian Writers' Fellowship, PO Box 99509, Edmonton AB T5B 0E1 Canada. **E-mail:** fellowscripteditor@gmail.com. **Website:** www.inscribe.org. **Contact:** Contest Director. Check Website www.inscribe.org for updated details. Contest details are included in *Fellowscript* magazine. Deadline: Contests offered twice per year. See website for details. Prize: 1st Place: $100; 2nd Place: $50; 3rd Place: $30. InScribe reserves the right to publish winning entries in its magazine, *FellowScript*, and/or on its website Judged by a different judge for each category. All judging is blind.

DOROTHEA LANGE–PAUL TAYLOR PRIZE

Center for Documentary Studies, 1317 W. Pettigrew St., Duke University, Durham NC 27705. (919)660-3685. **Fax:** (919)681-7600. **E-mail:** caitlin.johnson@duke.edu; docstudies@duke.edu. **Website:** http://documentarystudies.duke.edu/awards/dorothea-lange-paul-taylor-prize. **Contact:** Caitlin Johnson. Award from the Center for Documentary Studies at Duke University, supporting documentary artists, working alone or in teams, who are involved in extended, on-going fieldwork projects that rely on and exploit the interplay of words and images. More information available at documentarystudies.duke.edu/awards. First announced a year after the Center for Documentary Studies' founding at Duke University, the prize was created to encourage a collaboration between documentary writers and photographers in the tradition of the acclaimed photographer Dorothea Lange and writer and social scientist Paul Taylor. Deadline: May 9. Submissions accepted starting in February. Prize: The winner receives $10,000, features in Center for Documentary Studies' print and digital publications, and inclusion in the Archive of Documentary Arts at Rubenstein Library, Duke University.

MLA PRIZE IN UNITED STATES LATINA & LATINO AND CHICANA & CHICANO LITERARY AND CULTURAL STUDIES

Modern Language Association of America, 85 Broad Street, suite 500, New York NY 10004-2434. (646)576-5141. **Fax:** (646)458-0030. **E-mail:** awards@mla.org. **Website:** www.mla.org. **Contact:** Coordinator of Book Prizes. Offered in odd-numbered years for an outstanding scholarly study in any language of United States Latina and Latino or Chicana and Chicano literature or culture. Books must have been published in the two previous years before the award. Authors must be current members of the MLA. Requires 4 copies of the book. Deadline: May 1. Prize: A cash award, and a certificate to be presented at the Modern Language Association's annual convention in January.

NACUSA YOUNG COMPOSERS' COMPETITION

Box 49256 Barrington Station, Los Angeles CA 90049. **E-mail:** rentows@aol.com. **Website:** nacusa.us. **Contact:** Dr. Wieslaw Rentowski. Applications online. Must be a paid member of NACUSA. The competition is open to all NACUSA members who are American citizens or residents, who have reached their 18th birthday but have not yet reached there 32nd birthday by the submission deadline. Encourages the composition of new American concert hall music. Deadline: December 15. Prize: All prizes come with a possible performance on a NACUSA National concert. First Prize is $400; Second Prize is $300; Third Prize is $200. Judged by a committee of experienced NACUSA composer members.

OHIOANA WALTER RUMSEY MARVIN GRANT

Ohioana Library Association, 274 E. First Ave., Suite 300, Columbus OH 43201. (614)466-3831. **Fax:** (614)728-6974. **E-mail:** ohioana@ohioana.org. **Website:** www.ohioana.org. **Contact:** David Weaver, executive director. Open to unpublished authors born in Ohio or who have lived in Ohio for a minimum of 5 years. Must be 30 years of age or younger. Guidelines for SASE or on website. Winner notified in early summer. Up to 6 pieces of prose may be submitted; maximum 60 pages, minimum 10 pages double-spaced, 12-point type. Entries must be unpublished. Award to encourage young, unpublished writers 30 years of age or younger. Competition for short stories or novels in progress. Deadline: January 31. Prize: $1,000.

PULITZER PRIZES

The Pulitzer Prize Board, Columbia University, 709 Pulitzer Hall, 2950 Broadway, New York NY 10027. (212)854-3841. **E-mail:** pulitzer@.pulitzer.org. **Website:** www.pulitzer.org. **Contact:** Sig Gissler, administrator. Journalism in U.S. newspapers and news websites (published daily or weekly), and in letters, drama, and music by Americans. Deadline: December 31 (music); January 25 (journalism); June 15 and October 15 (letters); December 31 (drama). Prize: $10,000.

DAVID RAFFELOCK AWARD FOR PUBLISHING EXCELLENCE

National Writers Association, 10940 S. Parker Rd., #508, Parker CO 80134. **E-mail:** natlwritersassn@hotmail.com. **Website:** www.nationalwriters.com. **Contact:** Sandy Whelchel. Contest is offered annually for books published the previous year. Published works only. Open to any writer. Guidelines for SASE, by e-mail, or on website. Winners will be notified by mail or phone. List of winners available for SASE or visit website. Purpose is to assist published authors in marketing their works and to reward outstanding published works. Deadline: May 15. Prize: Publicity tour, including airfare, valued at $5,000.

RAMIREZ FAMILY AWARD FOR MOST SIGNIFICANT SCHOLARLY BOOK

The Texas Institute of Letters, P.O. Box 609, Round Rock TX 78680. **E-mail:** tilsecretary@yahoo.com. **Website:** http://texasinstituteofletters.org. Offered annually for submissions published January 1-December 31 of previous year to recognize the writer of the book making the most important contribution to knowledge. Writer must have been born in Texas, have lived in the state at least 2 consecutive years at some time, or the subject matter of the book should be associated with the state. See website for guidelines. Deadline: Visit website for exact date. Prize: $2,500.

BYRON CALDWELL SMITH BOOK AWARD

The University of Kansas, Hall Center for the Humanities, 900 Sunnyside Ave., Lawrence KS 66045. (785)864-4798. **E-mail:** vbailey@ku.edu. **Website:** www.hallcenter.ku.edu. **Contact:** Victor Bailey, director. Offered in odd years. To qualify, applicants must live or be employed in Kansas and have written an outstanding book published within the previous 2 calendar years. Translations are eligible. Guidelines for SASE or online. Deadline: March 1. Prize: $1,500.

FRED WHITEHEAD AWARD FOR DESIGN OF A TRADE BOOK

Texas Institute of Letters, P.O. Box 609, Round Rock TX 78680. **E-mail:** tilsecretary@yahoo.com. **Website:** www.texasinstituteofletters.org. Offered annually for the best design for a trade book. Open to Texas residents or those who have lived in Texas for 2 consecutive years. See website for guidelines. Deadline: early January; see website for exact date. Prize: $750.

☯ THE WRITERS' TRUST ENGEL/FINDLEY AWARD

The Writers' Trust of Canada, 460 Richmond St. W., Suite 600, Toronto ON M5V 1Y1 Canada. (416)504-8222. **Fax:** (416)504-9090. **E-mail:** info@writerstrust.com. **Website:** www.writerstrust.com. **Contact:** Amanda Hopkins. The Writers' Trust Engel/Findley Award is presented annually at The Writers' Trust Awards Event, held in Toronto each fall, to a Canadian writer for a body of work in hope of continued contribution to the richness of Canadian literature. Open to Canadian citizens and permanent residents only. Prize: $25,000.

JOURNALISM

AAAS KAVLI SCIENCE JOURNALISM AWARDS

American Association for the Advancement of Science, AAAS Office of Public Programs, 1200 New York Ave. NW, Washington DC 20005. **E-mail:** sja@aaas.org. **Website:** http://sjawards.aaas.org/. **Contact:** Awards Coordinator. The AAAS Kavli Science Journalism Awards represent the pinnacle of achievement for professional journalists in the science writing field. The awards recognize outstanding reporting worldwide for a general audience and honor individuals (rather than institutions, publishers or employers) for their coverage of the sciences, engineering, and mathematics. Entries are submitted online only at http://sjawards.aaas.org. See website for guidelines and details. Deadline: August 1. Prize: $5,000 and $3,000 awards in each category; award includes travel expenses to AAAS Annual Meeting for awards ceremony. Judged by committees of reporters and editors.

THE AMERICAN LEGION FOURTH ESTATE AWARD

The American Legion, The American Legion, 700 N. Pennsylvania St., Indianapolis IN 46204. (317)630-1253. **E-mail:** pr@legion.org. **Website:** www.legion.org/presscenter/fourthestate. Offered annually for journalistic works published the previous calendar year. Subject matter must deal with a topic or issue of national interest or concern. Entry must include cover letter explaining entry, and any documentation or evidence of the entry's impact on the community, state, or nation. No printed entry form. Guidelines available by SASE or online. Deadline: March 1. Prize: $2,000 stipend to defray expenses of recipient accepting the award at The American Legion National Convention in August/September. Judged by members of the Media & Communications Commission of The American Legion.

AMY WRITING AWARDS

The Amy Foundation, P.O. Box 16091, Lansing MI 48901. (517)323-6233. **Fax:** (517)321-2572. **E-mail:** amyawards@wng.org. **Website:** www.amyfound.org; www.worldmag.com/amyawards. The Amy Foundation Writing Awards program is designed to recognize creative, skillful writing that applies in a sensitive, thought-provoking manner the biblical principles to issues affecting the world today, with an emphasis on discipling. Submitted articles must be published in a secular, non-religious publication (either printed or online) and must be reinforced with at least one passage of scripture. The article must have been published between January 1 and December 31 of the current calendar year. Deadline: January 31. Prize: 1st Prize: $10,000; 2nd Prize: $5,000; 3rd Prize: $4,000; 4th Prize: $3,000; 5th Prize: $2,000; and 10 prizes of $1,000.

INVESTIGATIVE JOURNALISM GRANT

Fund for Investigative Journalism, 529 14th St. NW, 13th Floor, Washington DC 20045. (202)662-7564. **E-mail:** sbergo@fij.org. **Website:** www.fij.org. **Contact:** Sandy Bergo, executive director. Offered 3 times/year for original investigative print, online, radio, and TV stories and books. Guidelines online. See website for details on applying for a grant. Deadlines: Vary. Check website. Grants of $500-10,000. (Typical grant: $5,000.)

ANSON JONES, MD, AWARDS

Texas Medical Association, 401 W. 15th St., Ste. 100, Austin TX 78701-1680. (512)370-1470. **Fax:** (512)370-1693. **E-mail:** ansonjones@texmed.org. **Website:** www.texmed.org. **Contact:** Tammy Wishard, outreach coordinator. Offered annually to Texas news media for excellence in communicating health information to the public. Open only to Texas general-interest media for work published or aired in Texas during the previous calendar year. Guidelines posted online. Deadline: January 10. $500 for winner in each category; $1,000 for Texas Health Journalist of the Year.

LIVINGSTON AWARDS FOR YOUNG JOURNALISTS

University of Michigan, Wallace House, 620 Oxford, Ann Arbor MI 48104. (734)998-7575. **Fax:** (734)998-7979. **E-mail:** livawards@umich.edu. **Website:** www.livawards.org. **Contact:** Charles Eisendrath. Offered annually for journalism published in the previous year to recognize and further develop the abilities of young journalists. Includes print, online, and broadcast. Guidelines available online. Open to journalists who are 34 years or younger as of December 31 of previous year and whose work appears in US-controlled media. Deadline: February 1. Prize: $10,000 each for local reporting, national reporting, and international reporting. Judges include Christiane Amanpour, Ken Auletta, Dean Baquet, Kara Swisher, John Harris, Ellen Goodman, Clarence Page, Anna Quindlen.

FRANK LUTHER MOTT-KAPPA TAU ALPHA RESEARCH AWARD IN JOURNALISM

Kappa Tau Alpha, University of Missouri School of Journalism, 76 Gannett Hall, Columbia MO 65211-1200. (573)882-7685. **E-mail:** umcjourkta@missouri.edu. **Website:** www.kappataualpha.org. **Contact:** Dr. Beverly Horvit, executive director, Kappa Tau Alpha. Offered annually for best researched book in mass communication or journalism. Submit 6 copies; no forms required. Deadline: December 9. Prize: $1,000. Judged by a panel of university professors of journalism and mass communication and national officers of Kappa Tau Alpha.

⊘ NATIONAL MAGAZINE AWARDS

National Magazine Awards Foundation, 2300 Yonge St., Suite 1600, Toronto ON M4P 1E4 Canada. (416)939-6200. **E-mail:** staff@magazine-awards.com. **E-mail:** staff@magazine-awards.com. **Website:** www.magazine-awards.com. **Contact:** Barbara Gould. The National Magazine Awards Foundation is a bilingual, not-for-profit institution whose mission is to recognize and promote excellence in the content and creation of Canadian print and digital publications through an annual program of awards and national

publicity efforts. Deadline: January 20. Cash prizes for winners. Certificates and seals for all finalists and winners. Judged by 200+ peer judges from the Canadian magazine industry.

THE MADELINE DANE ROSS AWARD

Overseas Press Club of America, 40 West 45th Street, New York NY 10036. (212)626-9220. **Fax:** (212)626-9210. **E-mail:** sonya@opcofamerica.org. **Website:** www.opcofamerica.org. **Contact:** Sonya Fry, Executive Director. "Offered annually for best international reporting in the print medium showing a concern for the human condition. Work must be published by US-based publications or broadcast. Printable application available online." Deadline: Late January; date changes each year. $1,000 and certificate

SCIENCE IN SOCIETY AWARDS

National Association of Science Writers, Inc., P.O. Box 7905, Berkeley CA 94707. (510)647-9500. **E-mail:** director@nasw.org. **Website:** www.nasw.org. **Contact:** Tinsley Davis. Offered annually for investigative or interpretive reporting about the sciences and their impact on society. Categories: books, commentary and opinions, science reporting, longform science reporting, and science reporting for a local or regional market. Material may be a single article or broadcast, or a series. Works must have been first published or broadcast in North America between January 1 and December 31 of the previous year. Deadline: February 1. Prize: $2,500, and a certificate of recognition in each category.

⊘ SOVEREIGN AWARD

The Jockey Club of Canada, P.O. Box 66, Station B, Etobicoke ON M9W 5K9 Canada. (416)675-7756. **Fax:** (416)675-6378. **E-mail:** jockeyclub@bellnet.ca. **Website:** www.jockeyclubcanada.com. **Contact:** Stacie Roberts, exec. dir.. The Jockey Club of Canada was founded in 1973 by E.P. Taylor to serve as the international representative of the Canadian Thoroughbred industry and to promote improvements to Thoroughbred racing and breeding, both in Canada and internationally. Submissions for these media awards must be of Canadian Thoroughbred racing or breeding content. They must have appeared in a media outlet recognized by The Jockey Club of Canada. See website for eligibility details and guidelines. Deadline: December 31.

STANLEY WALKER AWARD FOR NEWSPAPER JOURNALISM

The Texas Institute of Letters, P.O. Box 609, Round Rock TX 78680. **E-mail:** tilsecretary@yahoo.com. **Website:** http://texasinstituteofletters.org. Offered annually for work published January 1-December 31 of previous year to recognize the best writing appearing in a daily newspaper. Writer must have been born in Texas, have lived in the state for 2 consecutive years at some time, or the subject matter of the article must be associated with the state. See website for guidelines. Deadline: See website for exact date. $1,000.

TRANSLATION

ALTA NATIONAL TRANSLATION AWARD

American Literary Translators Association, The University of Texas at Dallas, 800 W. Campbell Rd., JO51, Richardson TX 75080-3021. (972)883-2093. **Fax:** (972)883-6303. **E-mail:** maria.suarez@utdallas. edu. **Website:** www.literarytranslators.org. **Contact:** Jeffrey Green. Awarded annualy for the best book-length translation of a work into English. Winner announced each year at ALTA's annual conference. To be eligible, the translation must be by an American citizen or U.S. resident, from any language into English, of a book-length work of fiction, poetry, drama, or creative nonfiction (literary criticism, philosophy, and biographies are not eligible), and published anywhere in the world during the previous year. Honors the translator whose work, by virture of both its quality and significance, has made the most valuable contribution to literary translation in the preceding calendar year. Deadline: March 31. Prize: $5,000; winner announced and featured at annual ALTA conference in the fall; press release distributed to major publications. Judged by a panel of translators.

AMERICAN-SCANDINAVIAN FOUNDATION TRANSLATION PRIZE

The American-Scandinavian Foundation, 58 Park Ave., New York NY 10016. (212)779-3587. **E-mail:** grants@amscan.org; info@amscan.org. **Website:** www.amscan.org. **Contact:** Carl Fritscher, Fellowships & Grants Officer. The annual ASF translation competition is awarded for the most outstanding translations of poetry, fiction, drama, or literary prose written by a Scandinavian author born after 1900. Accepts inquiries by e-mail, or through online applica-

tion. Instructions an application available online. Entries must be unpublished. Length: No more than 50 pages for drama and fiction; no more than 25 pages for poetry. Open to any writer. Results announced in November. Winners notified by e-mail. Results available on the ASF website. Guidelines available online. Deadline: June 15. Prize: The Nadia Christensen Prize includes a $2,500 award, publication of an excerpt in *Scandinavian Review*, and a commemorative bronze medallion; The Leif and Inger Sjöberg Award, given to an individual whose literature translations have not previously been published, includes a $2,000 award, publication of an excerpt in *Scandinavian Review*, and a commemorative bronze medallion.

THE WILLIS BARNSTONE TRANSLATION PRIZE

The Evansville Review, Dept. of Creative Writing, University of Evansville, 1800 Lincoln Ave., Evansville IN 47722. (812)488-1042. **E-mail:** evansvillereview@evansville.edu. **Website:** https://www.evansville.edu/majors/creativewriting/evansvilleReviewBarnstone.cfm. The competition welcomes submissions of unpublished poetry translations from any language and time period (ancient to contemporary). The length limit for each translation is 200 lines. Deadline: December 1. Judged by Willis Barnstone.

DER-HOVANESSIAN PRIZE

New England Poetry Club, 376 School St., Watertown MA 02472. **E-mail:** contests@nepoetryclub. org. **Website:** www.nepoetryclub.org. **Contact:** Audrey Kalajin. For a translation from any language into English. Send a copy of the original. Funded by John Mahtesian. Contest open to members and nonmembers. Poems should be typed and submitted in duplicate with author's name, address, phone, and e-mail address of writer on only 1 copy. Label poems with contest name. Entries should be sent by regular mail only. Entries should be original, unpublished poems in English. No poem should be entered in more than 1 contest, nor have won a previous contest. Deadline: May 31. Prize: $200. Judges are well-known poets and sometimes winners of previous NEPC contests.

SOEURETTE DIEHL FRASER AWARD FOR BEST TRANSLATION OF A BOOK

P.O. Box 609, Round Rock TX 78680. **E-mail:** tilsecretary@yahoo.com. **Website:** http://texasinstituteofletters.org. Offered every 2 years to recognize the best translation of a literary book into English. Translator must have been born in Texas or have lived in the state for at least 2 consecutive years at some time. Check website for guidelines and instructions on submitting. Deadline: January 10. Prize: $1,000.

THE FRENCH-AMERICAN AND THE FLORENCE GOULD FOUNDATIONS TRANSLATION PRIZES

28 W. 44th St., Suite 1420, New York NY 10036. (646)588-6781. **E-mail:** tchareton@frenchamerican. org. **Website:** www.frenchamerican.org. **Contact:** Thibault Chareton. Annual contest to promote French literature in the United States by extending its reach beyond the first language and giving translators and their craft greater visibility among publishers and readers alike. The prize also seeks to increase the visibility of the publishers who bring these important French works of literature, in translation of exceptional quality, to the American market by publicizing the titles and giving more visibility to the books they publish. Entries must have been published for the first time in the United States between January 1 and December 31, of the previous year. Submissions must be completed online and are usually submitted by the publisher. Deadline: January 15. Prize: $10,000 award. Jury committee made up of translators, writers, and scholars in French literature and culture.

☯ JOHN GLASSCO TRANSLATION PRIZE

Literary Translators' Association of Canada, 620-03 Concordia University, 1455 boul. de Maisonneuve Ouest, Montréal QC H3G 1M8 Canada. (514)848-2424, ext. 8702. **E-mail:** info@attlc-ltac.org. **Website:** attlc-ltac.org/john-glassco-translation-prize. **Contact:** Glassco Prize Committee. Offered annually for a translator's first book-length literary translation into French or English, published in Canada during the previous calendar year. The translator must be a Canadian citizen or permanent resident. Eligible genres include fiction, creative nonfiction, poetry, and children's books. Deadline: July 31. Prize: $1,000.

THE HAROLD MORTON LANDON TRANSLATION AWARD

Academy of American Poets, 75 Maiden Lane, Suite 901, New York NY 10038. (212)274-0343. **Fax:** (212)274-9427. **E-mail:** awards@poets.org. **Website:** www.poets.org. **Contact:** Programs Coordinator. This annual award recognizes a poetry collection translated from any language into English and published in the previous calendar year. A noted trans-

lator chooses the winning book. Deadline: February 15. Prize: $1,000.

FENIA AND YAAKOV LEVIANT MEMORIAL PRIZE IN YIDDISH STUDIES

Modern Language Association of America, 85 Broad Street, suite 500, New York NY 10004-2434. (646)576-5141. **Fax:** (646)458-0030. **E-mail:** awards@mla.org. **Website:** www.mla.org. **Contact:** Coordinator of book prizes. Offered in even-numbered years for an outstanding English translation of a Yiddish literary work or the publication of a scholarly work. Cultural studies, critical biographies, or edited works in the field of Yiddish folklore or linguistic studies are eligible to compete. See website for details on which they are accepting. Books must have been published within the past 4 years. Authors need not be members of the MLA. Requires 4 copies of the book. Deadline: May 1. Prize: A cash prize, and a certificate, to be presented at the Modern Language Association's annual convention in January.

☯ MARSH AWARD FOR CHILDREN'S LITERATURE IN TRANSLATION

The English-Speaking Union, Dartmouth House, 37 Charles St., London En W1J 5ED United Kingdom. 020 7529 1590. **E-mail:** emma.coffey@esu.org. **Website:** www.marshchristiantrust.org; www.esu.org. **Contact:** Emma Coffey, education officer. The Marsh Award for Children's Literature in Translation, awarded biennially, was founded to celebrate the best translation of a children's book from a foreign language into English and published in the UK. It aims to spotlight the high quality and diversity of translated fiction for young readers. The Award is administered by the ESU on behalf of the Marsh Christian Trust. Submissions will be accepted from publishers for books produced for readers from 5 to 16 years of age. Guidelines and eligibility criteria available online.

PEN AWARD FOR POETRY IN TRANSLATION

PEN America, 588 Broadway, Suite 303, New York NY 10012. **E-mail:** awards@pen.org. **Website:** www.pen.org/awards. **Contact:** Arielle Anema. This award recognizes book-length translations of poetry from any language into English, published during the current calendar year. All books must have been published in the US. Translators may be of any nationality. US residency/citizenship not required. Submissions must be made publishers or literary agents. Self-published books are not eligible. Books with more than 2 translators are not eligible. Re-translations are ineligible, unless the work can be said to provide a significant revision of the original translation. Deadline: Submissions are accepted during the summer of each year. Visit PEN.org/awards for updated on deadline dates. Prize: $3,000. Judged by a single translator of poetry appointed by the PEN Translation Committee.

PEN TRANSLATION PRIZE

PEN America, 588 Broadway, Suite 303, New York NY 10012. **E-mail:** awards@pen.org. **Contact:** Arielle Anema, Literary Awards Coordinator. *PEN will only accept submissions from publishers or literary agents.* This award is offered for book-length translations from any language into English, published during the current calendar year. No technical, scientific, or bibliographic translations. Self-published books are not eligible. Although all eligible books must have been published in the United States, translators may be of any nationality; US residency or citizenship is not required. PEN will only accept submissions from publishers or literary agents. Deadline: Submissions will be accepted during the summer of each year. Visit PEN.org/awards for up-to-date information on deadlines. Prize: $3,000. Judged by three to five translators and/or writers selected by the PEN Translation Committee.

LOIS ROTH AWARD

Modern Language Association, 85 Broad Street, suite 500, New York NY 10004-2434. (646)576-5141. **Fax:** (646)458-0030. **E-mail:** awards@mla.org. **Website:** www.mla.org. Offered in odd-numbered years for an outstanding translation into English of a book-length literary work. Translators need not be members of the MLA. Translations must have been published in the previous calendar year. Requires 6 copies, plus 12-15 pages of text in the original language. Deadline: April 1. Prize: A cash award and a certificate to be presented at the Modern Language Association's annual convention in January.

ALDO AND JEANNE SCAGLIONE PRIZE FOR A TRANSLATION OF A LITERARY WORK

Modern Language Association, 85 Broad Street, suite 500, New York NY 10004-2434. (646)576-5141. **Fax:** (646)458-0030. **E-mail:** awards@mla.org. **Website:** www.mla.org. **Contact:** Coordinator of Book Prizes. Offered in even-numbered years for an outstand-

ing translation into English of a book-length literary work. Translations must have been published in the previous calendar year. Translators need not be members of the MLA. Requires 6 copies of the book, plus 12-15 pages of text in the original language. Deadline: April 1. Prize: A cash award and a certificate to be presented at the Modern Language Association's annual convention in January.

ALDO AND JEANNE SCAGLIONE PRIZE FOR A TRANSLATION OF A SCHOLARLY STUDY OF LITERATURE

Modern Language Association of America, 85 Broad Street, Suite 500, New York NY 10004-2434. (646)576-5141. **Fax:** (646)458-0030. **E-mail:** awards@mla.org. **Website:** www.mla.org. **Contact:** Coordinator of Book Prizes. Offered in odd-numbered years for an outstanding translation into English of a book-length work of literary history, literary criticism, philology, or literary theory. Translators need not be members of the MLA. Books must have been published in the previous 2 years. Requires 4 copies of the book. Deadline: May 1. Prize: A cash award and a certificate to be presented at the Modern Language Association's annual convention in January.

ALDO AND JEANNE SCAGLIONE PRIZE FOR STUDIES IN SLAVIC LANGUAGES AND LITERATURES

Modern Language Association of America, 85 Broad Street, Suite 500, New York NY 10004-2434. (646)576-5141. **Fax:** (646)458-0030. **E-mail:** awards@mla.org. **Website:** www.mla.org. **Contact:** Coordinator of Book Prizes. Offered in odd-numbered years for an outstanding work on the linguistics or literatures of the Slavic languages. Books must have been published in the previous 2 years. Requires 4 copies of the book. Authors need not be members of the MLA. Deadline: May 1. Prize: A cash award and a certificate to be presented at the Modern Language Association's annual convention in January.

POETRY

49TH PARALLEL AWARD FOR POETRY

Western Washington University, Mail Stop 9053, Bellingham WA 98225. (360)650-4863. **E-mail:** bellingham.review@wwu.edu. **Website:** www.bhreview.org. **Contact:** Susanne Paola Antonetta, editor-in-chief; Mike Oliphant, managing editor. Annual poetry contest, supported by the *Bellingham Review*, given for a poem of any style or length. Upload entries via Submittable online. Up to 3 poems per entry. Deadline: March 15. Submissions period begins December 1. Prize: $1,000. Judged by Oliver de la Paz.

☼ J.M. ABRAHAM POETRY PRIZE

Writers' Federation of Nova Scotia, 1113 Marginal Rd., Halifax NS B3H 4P7 Canada. (902)423-8116. **Fax:** (902)422-0881. **E-mail:** director@writers.ns.ca. **Website:** www.writers.ns.ca. **Contact:** Marilyn Smulders, executive director. The J.M. Abraham Poetry Prize is an annual award designed to honor the best book of poetry by a resident of Atlantic Canada. Formerly known as the Atlantic Poetry Prize. Detailed guidelines and eligibility criteria available online. Deadline: First Friday in December. Prize: Valued at $2,000 for the winning title.

AKRON POETRY PRIZE

The University of Akron Press, 120 E. Mill St., Suite 415, Akron OH 44308. **E-mail:** uapress@uakron.edu. **Website:** www.uakron.edu/uapress/akron-poetry-prize/. **Contact:** Mary Biddinger, editor/award director. Submissions must be unpublished. Considers simultaneous submissions (with notification of acceptance elsewhere). Submit at least 48 pages and no longer than 90 pages. See website for complete guidelines. Manuscripts will be accepted via Submittable. com between April 15 and June 15 each year. Competition receives 500+ entries. 2017 winner was Tyler Mills for *Hawk Parable*. Winner posted on website by September 30. Intimate friends, relatives, current and former students of the final judge (students in an academic, degree-conferring program or its equivalent), and current faculty, staff, students, and alumni of the University of Akron or the Northeast Ohio MFA Program (NEOMFA) are not eligible to enter the Akron Poetry Prize competition. Deadline: June 15. Open to submissions on April 15. Prize: $1,500, plus publication of a book-length ms.

THE AMERICAN POETRY REVIEW/ HONICKMAN FIRST BOOK PRIZE

320 S. Broad St., Hamilton 313, Philadelphia PA 19102. 215 717 6800. **E-mail:** escanlon@aprweb.org. **Website:** www.aprweb.org. **Contact:** Elizabeth Scanlon, editor. The prize is open to poets who have not published a book-length collection of poems with a registered ISBN. Translations are not eligible nor are works written by multiple authors. 2016 guest judge is Gabri-

elle Calvocoressi. Reading period: August 1-October 31. Prize: $3,000, plus publication and reading at the University of the Arts Visiting Writers Series in 2018.

THE ANHINGA PRESS-ROBERT DANA PRIZE FOR POETRY

Anhinga Press, P.O. Box 3665, Tallahassee FL 32315. **E-mail:** info@anhinga.org. **Website:** www.anhinga. org. **Contact:** Kristine Snodgrass, Co-director, Publisher. Offered annually for a book-length collection of poetry by an author writing in English. Guidelines on website. Past winners include Robin Beth Schaer, Hauntie. Mss must be 48-80 pages, excluding front matter. Deadline: Submissions will be accepted from February 15-May 30. Prize: $2,000, a reading tour of selected Florida colleges and universities, and the winning ms will be published. Past judges include Evie Shockley, Eduardo C. Corral, Jan Beatty, Richard Blanco, Denise Duhamel, Donald Hall, Joy Harjo.

THE MURIEL CRAFT BAILEY MEMORIAL AWARD

4956 St. John Dr., Syracuse NY 13215. (315)488-8077. **E-mail:** poetry@comstockreview.org. **Website:** www. comstockreview.org. **Contact:** Peggy Flanders, associate managing editor (poetry@comstockreview.org); Betsy Anderson, managing editor (elanders2@yahoo. com). Annual contest for best previously unpublished poem. Submit unpublished poems, 40 lines or less. Deadline: July 15. Prize: 1st place: $1,000; 2nd place: $250; 3rd place: $100; honorable mentions receive 1-year subscription to *Comstock Review*. Judged by Maggie Smith in 2018.

BARROW STREET PRESS BOOK CONTEST

P.O. Box 1558, Kingston RI 02881. **Website:** www.barrowstreet.org. The Barrow Street Press Book Contest award will be given for the best previously unpublished ms of poetry in English. Submit a 50-80 page unpublished ms of original poetry in English. Please number the pages of your ms and include a table of contents and an acknowledgments page for any previously published poems. Include two title pages. The author's name, address, and telephone number should appear on the first title page only and should not appear anywhere else in the ms. The second title page should contain only the ms title. Deadline: June 30. Prize: $1,000. Judged by Denise Duhamel.

ELINOR BENEDICT POETRY PRIZE

Passages North, Northern Michigan University, 1401 Presque Isle Ave., Marquette MI 49855. **E-mail:** passages@nmu.edu. **Website:** passagesnorth.com/contests/. **Contact:** Jennifer A. Howard, Editor-in-Chief. Prize given biennially for a poem or a group of poems. Check website to see if award is currently being offered this year. Deadline: April 15. Submission period begins February 15. Prize: $1,000 and publication for winner; 2 honorable mentions are also published; all entrants receive a copy of *Passages North*.

BERMUDA TRIANGLE PRIZE

The Poet's Billow, 6135 Avon St., Portage MI 49024. **E-mail:** thepoetsbillow@gmail.com. **Website:** http://thepoetsbillow.org. **Contact:** Robert Evory. Annual award open to any writer to recognize three poems that address a theme set by the editors. Finalists with strong work will also be published. Submissions must be previously unpublished. Please submit online. Deadline: March 15. Submission period begins November 15. Prize: $50 each to three poems. The winning poems will be published and displayed in The Poet's Billow Literary Art Gallery and nominated for a Pushcart Prize. If the poet qualifies, the poem will also be submitted to The Best New Poets anthology. Judged by the editors, and, occasionally, a guest judge.

THE PATRICIA BIBBY FIRST BOOK AWARD

Patricia Bibby Award, Tebot Bach, P.O. Box 7887, Huntington Beach CA 92615-7887. **E-mail:** mifanwy@tebotbach.org; info@tebotbach.org. **Website:** www.tebotbach.org. **Contact:** Mifanwy Kaiser. Annual competition open to all poets writing in English who have not committed to publishing collections of poetry of 36 poems or more in editions of over 400 copies. Offers award and publication of a book-length poetry ms by Tebot Bach. Complete guidelines available by e-mail or on website. Deadline: November 1. Prize: $500 and book publication. Judges for each year's competition announced online.

BINGHAMTON UNIVERSITY MILT KESSLER POETRY BOOK AWARD

Binghamton University Creative Writing Program, Department of English, General Literature, and Rhetoric, Library North Room 1149, Vestal Parkway East, P.O. Box 6000, Binghamton NY 13902-6000. (607)777-2713. **Fax:** (607)777-2408. **E-mail:** cwpro@binghamton.edu. **Website:** www2.binghamton.edu/english/creative-writing/binghamton-center-for-writers. **Contact:** Maria Mazziotti Gillan, creative writing program director. Annual award for a book of poems written in English, 48 pages or more in length, selected by judges as the strongest collection of poems published in that year. Print on demand is acceptable but no self-published or vanity press work will be considered. Each book submitted must be accompanied by an application form available online. Poet or publisher may submit more than 1 book for prize consideration. Send 2 copies of each book. Deadline: February 1. Prize: $1,000.

THE BITTER OLEANDER PRESS LIBRARY OF POETRY AWARD

BOPLOPA, The Bitter Oleander Press, 4983 Tall Oaks Dr., Fayetteville NY 13066-9776. (315)637-3047. **E-mail:** info@bitteroleander.com. **Website:** www.bitteroleander.com. **Contact:** Paul B. Roth. The Bitter Oleander Press Library of Poetry Award (BOPLOPA) is now in its 7th year after replacing the 15-year long run of the Frances Locke Memorial Poetry Award. Guidelines available on website. Entrants may not be friends, previous winners or employees of The Bitter Oleander Press. Deadline: June 15 (postmarked). Open to submissions on May 1. Early or late entries will be disqualified. Prize: $1,000, plus book publication of the winning ms. the following spring.

BLUE LIGHT POETRY PRIZE AND CHAPBOOK CONTEST

1563 - 45th Avenue, San Francisco CA 94122. **E-mail:** bluelightpress@aol.com. **E-mail:** bluelightpress@aol.com. **Website:** www.bluelightpress.com. **Contact:** Diane Frank, Chief Editor. The Blue Light Poetry Prize and Chapbook Contest offers a cash prize and publication by Blue Light Press (see separate listing in Book/Chapbook Publishers). Deadline: June 15. The winner will be published by Blue Light Press, with 20 copies the author's book. We have a group of poets who read manuscripts. Some years, we publish more than one winner.

BLUE MOUNTAIN ARTS

SPS Studios, Inc., Blue Mountain Arts, Inc., P.O. Box 1007, Boulder CO 80306. (303)449-0536. **Fax:** (303)447-0939. **E-mail:** editorial@sps.com. **Website:** www.sps.com. **Contact:** Becky Milanski. Family owned and operated independent greeting card company thriving since its founding in 1971. Specializes in expressing feelings that may be difficult for buyer to express. With its own fine art department creating watercolor paintings and multimedia cards, hand-lettered, Blue Mountain Arts is sold worldwide and is unique with our poetry, artwork, handmade papers that make lifelong buyers. Familiarize yourself with the Blue Mountain Arts writing style, either at a greeting card store or online at our Blue Mountain Arts Amazon store. To put your best writing out there! No deadlines for every day poetry. Write editorial@sps.com for seasonal deadlines. If your poetry is accepted and tests well, you will get $300 and 24 copies of your card. Judged by the Blue Mountain Arts editorial staff.

THE FREDERICK BOCK PRIZE

Poetry, 61 W. Superior St., Chicago IL 60654. (312)787-7070. **Fax:** (312)787-6650. **E-mail:** editors@poetry-magazine.org. **Website:** www.poetryfoundation.org. Several prizes are awarded annually for the best work printed in *Poetry* during the preceding year. Only poems already published in the magazine are eligible for consideration, and no formal application is necessary. The winners are announced in the November issue. Upon acceptance, *Poetry* licenses exclusive worldwide first serial rights, including electronic rights, for publication, as well as non-exclusive rights to reprint, reuse, and archive the work, in any format, in perpetuity. Copyright reverts to author upon first publication. Any writer may submit poems to *Poetry*. Prize: $500.

THE BOSTON REVIEW ANNUAL POETRY CONTEST

Poetry Contest, Boston Review, P.O. Box 425786, Cambridge MA 02142. (617)324-1360. **Fax:** (617)452-3356. **E-mail:** review@bostonreview.net. **Website:** www.bostonreview.net. Offers $1,500 and publication in *Boston Review* (see separate listing in Magazines/Journals). Any poet writing in English is eligible, unless he or she is a current student, former student, or close personal friend of the judge. Submissions must be unpublished. Submit up to 5 poems, no more than 10 pages total, via online contest entry manager. Include cover sheet with poet's name, address, and phone number; no identifying information on the poems themselves. No cover note is necessary for online submissions. No mss will be returned. Guidelines available for SASE or on website. Deadline: June 1. Winner announced in early November on website. Prize: $1,500 and publication.

BOULEVARD POETRY CONTEST FOR EMERGING POETS

PMB 325, 6614 Clayton Rd., Richmond Heights MO 63117. **E-mail:** editors@boulevardmagazine.org. **Website:** www.boulevardmagazine.org. **Contact:** Jessica Rogen, editor. Annual Emerging Poets Contest of-

fers $1,000 and publication in *Boulevard* (see separate listing in Magazines/Journals) for the best group of 3 poems by a poet who has not yet published a book of poetry with a nationally distributed press. All entries will be considered for publication and payment at regular rates. Submissions must be unpublished. Considers simultaneous submissions. Submit 3 poems, typed; may be a sequence or unrelated. On page one of first poem type poet's name, address, phone number, and titles of the 3 poems. Deadline: June 1. Prize: $1,000 and publication.

✪ BP NICHOL CHAPBOOK AWARD

113 Bond St., St. John's NL A1C 1T6 Canada. (416)964-7919. **Fax:** (416)964-6941. **E-mail:** meetthepresses@gmail.com. **Website:** meetthepresses.wordpress.com. **Contact:** Beth Follett. Offered annually to a chapbook (10-48 pages) of poetry in English, published in Canada in the previous year. Open to any Canadian writer. Author or publisher may make submissions. Send 3 copies (non-returnable), plus a short author CV. Deadline: April 30. Prize: $4,000 (Canadian) to author and $500 (Canadian) to publisher.

BARBARA BRADLEY PRIZE

New England Poetry Club, 376 School St., Watertown MA 02472. **E-mail:** contests@nepoetryclub.org. **Website:** www.nepoetryclub.org. **Contact:** Audrey Kalajin. For a lyric poem under 20 lines, written by a woman. Contest open to members and nonmembers. Poems should be typed and submitted in duplicate with author's name, address, phone, and e-mail address of writer on only 1 copy. (Judges receive copies without names.) Copy only. Label poems with contest name. Entries should be sent by regular mail only. Special delivery or signature required mail will be returned by the post office. Entries should be original, unpublished poems in English. No poem should be entered in more than 1 contest, nor have won a previous contest. No entries will be returned. NEPC will not engage in correspondence regarding poems or contest decisions. Deadline: May 31. Prize: $200. Judged by well-known poets and sometimes winners of previous NEPC contests.

BRICK ROAD POETRY BOOK CONTEST

Brick Road Poetry Press, Inc., 513 Broadway, Columbus GA 31901. (706)649-3080. **Fax:** (706)649-3094. **E-mail:** kbadowski@brickroadpoetrypress.com. **Website:** www.brickroadpoetrypress.com. **Contact:** Ron Self and Keith Badowski, co-editors/founders. Annual competition for an original collection of 50-100 pages of poetry. Book-length poetry mss only. Simultaneous submissions accepted. Single sided, single spaced only. Electronic submissions are preferred, see website for details. No cover letter. Deadline: November 1st (Submission period begins August 1st). Prize: $1,000, publication in both print and e-book formats, and 25 copies of the book. May also offer publication contracts to the top finalists. Judged by Keith Badowski & Ron Self, Brick Road poetry editors.

BRIGHT HILL PRESS POETRY CHAPBOOK COMPETITION

Bright Press Hill & Literary Center, 94 Church St., Treadwell NY 13846. (607)829-5055. **E-mail:** brighthillpress@stny.rr.com; wordthur@stny.rr.com. **Website:** www.brighthillpress.org. The annual Bright Hill Press Chapbook Award recognizes an outstanding collection of poetry. Guidelines available for SASE, by e-mail, or on website. Collection of original poetry, 48-64 pages, single spaced, one poem to a page (no name) with table of contents. Ms must be submitted in Times New Roman, 12 pt. type only. No illustrations, no cover suggestions. Bio and acknowledgments of poems that have been previously published should be included in a separate document, or in comments box if submitting online. See website for more details, and information on submitting a hard copy. Deadline: December 31. Prize: A publication contract with Bright Hill Press and $1,000, publication in print format, and 30 copies of the printed book. Judged by a nationally-known poet.

BRITTINGHAM PRIZE IN POETRY

University of Wisconsin Press, 1930 Monroe Street, 3rd Floor, Madison WI 5311-2059. (608)263-1110. **Fax:** (608)263-1132. **E-mail:** rwallace@wisc.edu. **E-mail:** uwiscpress@uwpress.wisc.edu. **Website:** www.wisc.edu/wisconsinpress/poetryguide.html. **Contact:** Ronald Wallace, series editor. The annual Brittingham Prize in Poetry is 1 of 2 prizes awarded by The University of Wisconsin Press (see separate listing for the Felix Pollak Prize in Poetry in this section). Beginning in 2017 the Press will publish two or three additional books annually, drawn from the contest submissions. Submissions must be unpublished as a collection, but individual poems may have been published elsewhere (publication must be acknowledged). Considers simultaneous submissions if notified of selection elsewhere. Submit 60-90 unbound ms pages, typed single-spaced (with double spaces between stanzas). Clean photocopies are acceptable. Include 1 title page with poet's name, address, and telephone number and 1 with title only. No translations. Strongly encourages electronic submissions via web page. SASE required for postal submissions. Will return results only; mss will not be returned. Guidelines available on website. The Brittingham Prize in Poetry is awarded annually to the best book-length manuscript of original poetry submitted in an open competition. The award is administered by the University of Wisconsin–Madison English Department, and the winner is chosen by a nationally recognized poet. The resulting book is published by the University of Wisconsin Press. Deadline: Submit August 15-September 15. Prize: Offers $1,000, plus publication. Judged by a distinguished poet who will remain anonymous until the winners are announced in mid-February.

BURNING BUSH POETRY PRIZE

P.O. Box 1658, Santa Rosa CA 95402. **Website:** www.bbbooks.com. Purpose of contest to reward a poet whose writing inspires others to value human life and natural world instead of values based on short-term economic advantage; speaks for community-centered values, democratic processes, especially those whose voices are seldom heard; demonstrates poetic excellence; and educates readers of the relevance of the past to the present and future. Deadline: June 1.

BOB BUSH MEMORIAL AWARD FOR FIRST BOOK OF POETRY

Texas Institute of Letters, P.O. Box 609, Round Rock TX 78680. **E-mail:** tilsecretary@yahoo.com. **Website:** www.texasinstituteofletters.org. Offered annually for best first book of poetry published in previous year. Writer must have been born in Texas, have lived in the state at least 2 consecutive years at some time, or the subject matter should be associated with the state. Deadline: See website for exact date. Prize: $1,000.

✪ CAA POETRY AWARD

Canadian Authors Association, 74 Mississaga Street E., Orillia ON L3V 1V5 Canada. **Website:** canadianauthors.org/national. Contest for full-length English-language book of poems for adults by a Canadian writer. Deadline: January.

GERALD CABLE BOOK AWARD

Silverfish Review Press, P.O. Box 3541, Eugene OR 97403. (541)344-5060. **E-mail:** sfrpress@earthlink.

net. **Website:** www.silverfishreviewpress.com. **Contact:** Rodger Moody, editor. Awarded annually to a book-length ms of original poetry by an author who has not yet published a full-length collection. There are no restrictions on the kind of poetry or subject matter; translations are not acceptable. Mss should be at least 48 pages in length. Clean photo copies are acceptable. The poet's name should not appear on the ms. Include a separate title page with name, address, and phone number. Poems may have appeared in periodicals, chapbooks, or anthologies, but should not be acknowledged. Simultaneous submissions are accepted. Accepts e-mail submissions. See website for more details and guidelines. Deadline: October 15. Prize: $1,000, publication, and 25 copies of the book. The winner will be announced in March.

CAROLINA WREN PRESS POETRY SERIES CONTEST

120 Morris St., Durham NC 27701. (919)560-2738. **Fax:** (919)560-2759. **E-mail:** carolinawrenpress@earthlink.net. **Website:** www.carolinawrenpress.org. **Contact:** Andrea Selch, Poetry Editor. Carolina Wren Press is a nonprofit organization whose mission is to publish quality writing, especially by writers historically neglected by mainstream publishing, and to develop diverse and vital audiences through publishing, outreach, and educational programs. Submit a copy of a 48-72 page manuscript. Manuscript should be single-spaced and paginated. Please include a table of contents. Title page should not include author information—no name, address, etc. Within the manuscript, do include a page acknowledging individual poems that have been previously published. Open only to poets who have had no more than one full-length book published. Deadline: June 15 of odd-numbered years. Prize: $1,000 and publication.

CAVE CANEM POETRY PRIZE

Cave Canem Foundation, Inc., 20 Jay St., Suite 310-A, Brooklyn NY 11201. (718)858-0000. **Website:** www.cavecanempoets.org. This 1st book award is dedicated to the discovery of exceptional mss by black poets of African descent. Deadline: March 17. 1st place: $1,000, plus publication by University of Pittsburgh Press, 15 copies of the book, and a featured reading.

CHAPBOOK COMPETITION FOR OHIO POETS

Wick Poetry Center, Kent State University, 301 Satterfield Hall, Kent State University, P.O. Box 5190, Kent OH 44242-0001. (330)672-2067. **Fax:** (330)672-3333. **Website:** www2.kent.edu/wick/competitions. **Contact:** David Hassler, director. The Chapbook Competition for Ohio Poets is open to all current residents of Ohio, including students in an Ohio college or university. Does not accept postal submissions. Mss should be 16-30 pages of poetry, with no more than one poem per page. Deadline: October 31. Submissions period begins August 31. Prize: Publication and a reading at Kent State University.

JOHN CIARDI PRIZE FOR POETRY

BkMk Press, University of Missouri-Kansas City, 5101 Rockhill Rd., Kansas City MO 64110. (816)235-2558. **E-mail:** bkmk@umkc.edu. **Website:** www.newletters.org. **Contact:** Ben Furnish. Offered annually for the best book-length collection (unpublished) of poetry in English by a living author. Translations are not eligible. Guidelines for SASE, by e-mail, or on website. Poetry mss should be approximately 50-110 pages, single-spaced. Deadline: January 15. Prize: $1,000, plus book publication by BkMk Press. Judged by a network of published writers. Final judging is done by a writer of national reputation.

CIDER PRESS REVIEW BOOK AWARD

P.O. Box 33384, San Diego CA 92163. **E-mail:** editor@ciderpressreview.com. **Website:** http://ciderpressreview.com/. Annual award from *Cider Press Review*. Submissions must be unpublished as a collection, but individual poems may have been previously published elsewhere. Submit book-length ms of 48-80 pages. Submissions can be made online using the submission form on the website or by mail. If sending by mail, include 2 cover sheets—1 with title, author's name, and complete contact information; and 1 with title only, all bound with a spring clip. Does not require SASE; notification via e-mail and on the website, only. Mss cannot be returned. Online submissions must be in Word for PC or PDF format, and should not include title page with author's name. The editors strongly urge contestants to use online delivery if possible. Review the complete submission guidelines and learn more online at website. Deadline: November 30. Open to submissions on September 1. Prize: $1,500, publication, and 25 author's copies of a book length collection of poetry. Author receives a standard publishing contract. Initial print run is not less than 1,000 copies. CPR acquires first publication rights.

CLEVELAND STATE UNIVERSITY POETRY CENTER BOOK COMPETITIONS

Cleveland State University Poetry Center, Cleveland State University Poetry Center, 2121 Euclid Avenue, Rhodes Tower, Room 1841, Cleveland OH 44115-2214. (216)687-3986. **E-mail:** poetrycenter@csuohio.edu. **Website:** www.csupoetrycenter.com. **Contact:** Caryl Pagel. The Cleveland State University Poetry Center was established in 1962 at the former Fenn College of Engineering to promote poetry through readings and community outreach. In 1971, it expanded its mission to become a national non-profit independent press under the auspices of the Cleveland State University Department of English, and has since published nearly 200 rangy, joyful, profound, astonishing, complicated, surprising, and aesthetically diverse collections of contemporary poetry and prose by established and emerging authors. The Cleveland State University Poetry Center publishes between three and five collections of contemporary poetry and prose a year, with a national distribution and reach. The Poetry Center currently acquires manuscripts through three annual contests (one dedicated to publishing and promoting first books of poetry, one to supporting an established poet's career, and one to publishing collections of literary essays). In addition to publishing, the Poetry Center actively promotes contemporary poetry and prose through an annual reading series, collaborative art events, participation in national writing conferences, and as an educational resource for Cleveland State University's undergraduate, M.A., and N.E.O.M.F.A. students by providing assistantship and internship opportunities as well as involving students in the editorial and production aspects of literary publishing. See website for specific details and rules. Deadline: March 31. Prize: First Book and Open Book Competitions awards publication and a $1,000 prize for an original manuscript of poetry in each category. 2018 Judges: CAConrad (First Book); Samuel Amadon, Leora Fridman, & Jane Lewty (Open Book); Brian Blanchfield (Essay).

CLOCKWISE CHAPBOOK COMPETITION

Tebot Bach, Tebot Bach, Clockwise, P.O. Box 7887, Huntington Beach CA 92615. (714)968-0905. **Fax:** (714)968-4677. **E-mail:** mifanwy@tebotbach.org. **Website:** www.tebotbach.org/clockwise.html. Annual competition for a collection of poetry. Submit 24-32 pages of original poetry in English. Must be previously unpublished poetry for the full collection; individual poems may have been published. Full guidelines, including submission info, available online. Deadline: July 30. Prize: $500 and a book publication in Perfect Bound Editions. Winner announced in September with publication January. Judged by Gail Wronsky.

TOM COLLINS POETRY PRIZE

Fellowship of Australian Writers (WA), P.O. Box 6180, Swanbourne WA 6910 Australia. (61)(8)9384-4771. **Fax:** (61)(8)9384-4854. **E-mail:** fellowshipaustralianwriterswa@gmail.com. **Website:** www.fawwa.org. Annual contest for unpublished poems, maximum 60 lines. Reserves the right to publish entries in a FAWWA publication or on its website. Guidelines online or for SASE. See website for details, guidelines, and entry form. Deadline: No Closed. Prize: 1st Place: $1,000; 2nd Place: $200; 43rd Place: $100 each.

THE COLORADO PRIZE FOR POETRY

Colorado Review,/ Center for Literary Publishing, Department of English, Colorado State University, 9105 Campus Delivery, Ft. Collins CO 80523. (970)491-5449. **E-mail:** creview@colostate.edu. **Website:** coloradoprize.colostate.edu. **Contact:** Stephanie G'Schwind, editor. Submission must be unpublished as a collection, but individual poems may have been published elsewhere. Submit mss of 48-100 pages of poetry on any subject, in any form, double- or single-spaced. Include 2 titles pages: 1 with ms title only, the other with ms title and poet's name, address, and phone number. Enclose SASE for notification of receipt and SASE for results; mss will not be returned. Guidelines available by SASE, e-mail, or online at website. Poets can also submit online via online submission manager through website. Deadline: January 14. Prize: $2,000 and publication of a book-length ms. Judged by John Yau.

CONCRETE WOLF POETRY CHAPBOOK/ LOUIS AWARD CONTEST

P.O. Box 445, Tillamook OR 97141. **E-mail:** concretewolfpress@gmail.com. **Website:** http://concretewolf.com. Prefers collections that have a theme, either obvious (i.e., chapbook about a divorce) or understated (i.e., all the poems mention the color blue). Likes a collection that feels more like a whole than a sampling of work. No preference as to formal or free verse. Slightly favors lyric and narrative poetry to language and concrete, but excellent examples of any style will grab their attention. Considers simultaneous submissions if notified of acceptance elsewhere. See website for details. Deadline: November 30 and March 31. Prize: Publication and author copies of a perfectly-bound collection.

THE CONNECTICUT RIVER REVIEW POETRY CONTEST

P.O. Box 270554, W. Hartford CT 06127. **E-mail:** connpoetry@comcast.net. **Website:** ctpoetry.net. Send up to 3 unpublished poems, any form, 80-line limit. Include 2 copies of each poem: 1 with complete contact informatoin and 1 with no contact information. Include a SASE. Deadline: September 30. Open to submissions on August 1. 1st Place: $400; 2nd Place: $100; 3rd Place: $50.

CPR EDITOR'S PRIZE

P.O. Box 33384, San Diego CA 92163. **E-mail:** editor@ciderpressreview.com. **Website:** http://ciderpressreview.com/bookaward. Annual award from *Cider Press Review*. Submissions must be unpublished as a collection, but individual poems may have been previously published elsewhere. Submit book-length ms of 48-80 pages of original poetry. Submissions can be made online using the submission form on the website or by mail. If sending by mail, include 2 cover sheets—1 with title, author's name, and complete contact information; and 1 with title only, all bound with a spring clip. Check website for change of address coming in the future. Include SASE for results only if no email address included; notification via email and on the website; manuscripts cannot be returned. Online submissions must be in Word for PC or PDF format, and should not include title page with author's name. The editors strongly urge contestants to use online delivery if possible. Review the complete submission guidelines and learn more online at website. Deadline: submit between April 1-June 30. Prize: $1,000, publication, and 25 author's copies of a book length collection of poetry. Author receives a standard publishing contract. Initial print run is not less than 1,000 copies. CPR acquires first publication rights. Judged by *Cider Press Review* editors.

CRAB ORCHARD SERIES IN POETRY FIRST BOOK AWARD

First Book Award, Dept. of English, Mail Code 4503, Southern Illinois University Carbondale, 1000 Faner Drive, Carbondale IL 62901. (618)453-6833. **Fax:** (618)453-8224. **E-mail:** jtribble@siu.edu. **Website:** www.craborchardreview.siu.edu. **Contact:** Jon Trib-

ble, series editor. Annual award that selects a first book of poems for publication from an open competition of manuscripts, in English, by a U.S. citizen, permanent resident, or person who has DACA/TPS status who has neither published, who has neither published, nor committed to publish, a volume of poetry 48 pages or more in length in an edition of over 500 copies (individual poems may have been previously published; for the purposes of the Crab Orchard Series in Poetry, a ms which was in whole or in part submitted as a thesis or dissertation as a requirement for the completion of a degree is considered unpublished and is eligible). Current or former students, colleagues, and close friends of the final judge, and current and former students and employees of Southern Illinois University Carbondale and authors who have published a book with Southern Illinois University Press or have a book under contract with Southern Illinois University Press are not eligible. See website for complete formatting instructions and guidelines. Accepts submissions only through Submittable, online. Mss are recommended to be a minimum of 50 pages to a recommended maximum of 75 pages of original poetry, but no manuscript will be rejected solely because of length. Considers simultaneous submissions, but series editor must be informed immediately upon acceptance. Author's name should appear nowhere in manuscript. Do not include acknowledgments page. Deadline: July 8. Submission period begins May 15. Prize: $4,000 and publication. Judged by a published poet. Check website for current judge.

CRAB ORCHARD SERIES IN POETRY OPEN COMPETITION AWARDS

Department of English, Mail Code 4503, Faner Hall 2380, Southern Illinois University Carbondale, Carbondale IL 62901. (618)453-6833. **Fax:** (618)453-8224. **E-mail:** jtribble@siu.edu. **Website:** www.craborchardreview.siu.edu. **Contact:** Jon Tribble, series editor. Annual competition to award unpublished, original collections of poems written in English by United States citizens, permanent residents, or persons who have DACA/TPS status (individual poems may have been previously published; for the purposes of the Crab Orchard Series in Poetry, a ms which was in whole or in part submitted as a thesis or dissertation as a requirement for the completion of a degree is considered unpublished and is eligible). Two volumes of poems will be selected from the open competition of mss. Current or former students, colleagues, and close friends of the final judge, and current and former students and employees of Southern Illinois University Carbondale and authors who have published a book with Southern Illinois University Press or have a book under contract with Southern Illinois University Press are not eligible. See website for complete formatting instructions and guidelines. Accepts submissions only through Submittable, online. Mss are recommended to be a minimum of 50 pages to a recommended maximum of 80 pages of original poetry, but no manuscript will be rejected solely because of length. Considers simultaneous submissions, but series editor must be informed immediately upon acceptance. Deadline: November 19. Submission period begins October 1. Prize: Both winners will be awarded a publication contract with Southern Illinois University Press, a $2,500 prize, and a $1,500 as an honorarium for a reading at Southern Illinois University Carbondale. Both readings will follow the publication of the poets' collections. Judged by a published poet. Check website for current judge.

THE CRAZYHORSE PRIZE IN POETRY

Crazyhorse, Department of English, College of Charleston, 66 George St., Charleston SC 29424. (843)953-4470. **E-mail:** crazyhorse@cofc.edu. **Website:** http://crazyhorse.cofc.edu. **Contact:** Prize Director. The *Crazyhorse* Prize in Poetry is for a single poem. All entries will be considered for publication. Submissions must be unpublished. Submit online or by mail up to 3 original poems (no more than 10 pages). Include cover page (placed on top of ms) with poet's name, address, e-mail, and telephone number; no identifying information on mss (blind judging). Accepts multiple submissions with separate fee for each. Include SASP for notification of receipt of ms and SASE for results only; mss will not be returned. Guidelines available for SASE or on website. Deadline: January 31. Submissions period begins January 1. Prize: $2,000 and publication in *Crazyhorse*. Judged by genre judges for first round, guest judge for second round. Judges change on a yearly basis.

DANCING POETRY CONTEST

Artists Embassy International, AEI Contest Chair, Judy Cheung, 704 Brigham Ave., Santa Rosa CA 95404-5245. (707)528-0912. **E-mail:** jhcheung@comcast.net. **Website:** www.dancingpoetry.com. Any subject, any form or free verse, suitable for a general audience. **Contact:** Judy Cheung, contest chair. Line Limit:

40 lines maximum each poem. No limit on number of entries. Send 2 typed, clear copies of each entry. Show name, address, telephone number, e-mail and how you heard about the contest on one copy only. Poems must be in English or include English translation. Deadline: April 15. Prizes: Three Grand Prizes will receive $100 each plus the poems will be danced and videotaped at this year's Dancing Poetry Festival; six First Prizes will receive $50 each; twelve Second Prizes will receive $25 each; and thirty Third Prizes will receive $10 each. Judged by members and associates of Artists Embassy International and the Poetic Dance Theater Company.

JAMES DICKEY PRIZE FOR POETRY

Georgia State University, P.O. Box 3999, Atlanta GA 30302-3999. **Website:** fivepoints.gsu.edu. The James Dickey Prize for Poetry is for the best previously unpublished poem. Deadline: December 1. Open to submissions on September 1.

DREAM HORSE PRESS NATIONAL POETRY CHAPBOOK PRIZE

P.O. Box 2080, Aptos CA 95001-2080. **E-mail:** dreamhorsepress@yahoo.com. **Website:** www.dreamhorsepress.com. **Contact:** J.P. Dancing Bear, Editor/Publisher. All entries will be considered for publication. Submissions may be previously published in magazines/journals but not in books or chapbooks. Considers simultaneous submissions with notification. Submit 20-28 pages of poetry in a readable font with table of contents, acknowledgments, bio, e-mail address for results, and entry fee. Poet's name should not appear anywhere on the manuscript. Accepts multiple submissions (with separate fee for each entry). Manuscripts will be recycled after judging. Guidelines available on website. Make checks/money orders made payable to Dream Horse Press. Recent previous winners include M.R.B. Chelko, Cynthia Arrieu-King, and Ariana-Sophia Kartsonis. Deadline: June 30. Prize: $500, publication, and 25 copies of a handsomely printed chapbook. Judged is anonymous.

T.S. ELIOT PRIZE FOR POETRY

Truman State University Press, 100 E. Normal Ave., Kirksville MO 63501. (660)785-7336. **Fax:** (660)785-4480. **E-mail:** tsup@truman.edu. **Website:** tsup.truman.edu. **Contact:** Barbara Smith-Mandell, Editor-in-Chief. The ms may include individual poems previously published in journals or anthologies, but may not include more than 1/3 of the total poems from a published chapbook or self-published book. Submit 60-100 pages. Include 2 title pages: 1 with poet's name, address, e-mail address, phone number, and ms title; the other with ms title only. Include SASE for acknowledgment of ms receipt only; mss will not be returned. Guidelines available for SASE or on website. Deadline: October 31. Prize: $2,000 and publication. Judge announced after close of competition.

✪ FAR HORIZONS AWARD FOR POETRY

The Malahat Review, University of Victoria, P.O. Box 1700, Stn CSC, Victoria BC V8W 2Y2 Canada. (250)721-8524. **Fax:** (250)472-5051. **E-mail:** malahat@uvic.ca. **Website:** www.malahatreview.ca. **Contact:** L'Amour Lisik, Marketing and Circulation Manager. The biennial Far Horizons Award for Poetry offers $1,000 CAD and publication in *The Malahat Review* (see separate listing in Magazines/Journals). Winner and finalists contacted by e-mail. Winner published in fall in *The Malahat Review* and announced on website, Facebook page, and in quarterly e-newsletter, *Malahat lite*. Submissions must be unpublished. No simultaneous submissions. Submit up to 3 poems per entry, each poem not to exceed 60 lines; no restrictions on subject matter or aesthetic approach. Include separate page with poet's name, address, e-mail, and poem title(s); no identifying information on mss pages. E-mail submissions are acceptable: please send to horizons@uvic.ca. Do not include SASE for results; mss will not be returned. Full guidelines available on website. Open to "emerging poets from Canada, the United States, and elsewhere" who have not yet published a full-length book (48 pages or more). Deadline: May 1 (even numbered years). Prize: $1,000.

JANICE FARRELL POETRY PRIZE CATEGORY

Soul-Making Keats Literary Competition, The Webhallow House, 1544 Sweetwood Dr., Broadmoor Village CA 94015. **E-mail:** SoulKeats@mail.com. **Website:** www.soulmakingcontest.us. **Contact:** Eileen Malone. Previously published okay. Poetry may be double- or single-spaced. One-page poems only, and only 1 poem/page. All poems must be titled. Three poems/entry. Identify with 3x5 card only. Open to all writers. Deadline: November 30. Prizes: First: $100, Second: $50, Third: $25. Judged by a local San Francisco Bay Area successfully published poet.

THE JEAN FELDMAN POETRY PRIZE

Washington Writers' Publishing House, 4640 23rd Rd. N., Arlington VA 22207. **E-mail:** wwphpress@gmail.com. **Website:** www.washingtonwriters.org. **Contact:** Holly Karapetkova. Poets living within 75 miles of the Capitol are invited to submit a ms of either a novel or a collection of short stories. Ms should be 50-70 pages, single spaced. Author's name should not appear on the manuscript. The title page of each copy should contain the title only. Provide name, address, telephone number, e-mail address, and title on a separate cover sheet accompanying the submission. A separate page for acknowledgments may be included for stories or excerpts previously published in journals and anthologies. E-mail electronic copies to wwphpress@gmail.com or mail paper copies and/or reading fee (check to WWPH) with SASE to: The Jean Feldman Poetry Prize, WWPH, c/o Holly Karapetkova, 4640 23rd Rd. N., Arlington, VA 22207. Deadline: November 15. Submission period begins July 1. Prize: $1,000 and 50 copies of the book.

FIELD POETRY PRIZE

Oberlin College Press/FIELD, 50 N. Professor St., Oberlin OH 44074-1095. (440)775-8408. **Fax:** (440)775-8124. **E-mail:** oc.press@oberlin.edu. **Website:** www.oberlin.edu/ocpress/prize.htm. **Contact:** Marco Wilkinson, managing editor. Offered annually for an unpublished book-length collection of poetry (mss of 50-80 pages). Contest seeks to encourage the finest in contemporary poetry writing. Open to any writer. Deadline: May 31. Opens to submissions on May 1. Prize: $1,000 and a standard royalty contract.

THE FINISHING LINE PRESS OPEN CHAPBOOK COMPETITION

P.O. Box 1626, Georgetown KY 40324. **E-mail:** finishingbooks@aol.com. **Website:** www.finishinglinepress.com. **Contact:** Christen Kincaid, director. Annual competition for poetry chapbook. $1,000

FIRST BOOK AWARD FOR POETRY

Zone 3, Austin Peay State University, Austin Peay State University, PO Box 4565, Clarksville TN 37044. (931)221-7031. **Fax:** (931)221-7149. **E-mail:** zone3@apsu.edu. **Website:** www.apsu.edu/zone3/. **Contact:** Andrea Spofford, poetry editor; Susan Wallace, managing editor. Annual poetry award for anyone who has not published a full-length collection of poems (48 pages or more). Accepts entries via postal mail or online. Separate instructions for both, see website for guidelines and details. Deadline: May 1. Prize: $1,000 and publication.

🐟 FISH POETRY PRIZE

Fish Poetry Contest, Fish Publishing, Dunbeacon, Durrus, Bantry Co. Cork Ireland. **E-mail:** info@fish-publishing.com. **Website:** www.fishpublishing.com. **Contact:** Clem Cairns. For poems up to 300 words. Age Range: Adult. The best 10 will be published in the Fish Anthology, launched in July at the West Cork Literary Festival. Entries must not have been published before. Enter online or by post. See website for full details of competitions, and information on the Fish Editorial and Critique Services, and the Fish Online Writing Courses. Do not put your name or address or any other details on the poem, use a separate sheet. Receipt of entry will be acknowleged by e-mail. Poems will not be returned. Word count: 300 max for each poem. You may enter as many as you wish, provided there is an entry fee for each one. Full details and rules are online. Entry is deemed to be acceptance of these rules. Publishing rights of the 10 winning poems are held by Fish Publishing for one year after the publication of the Anthology. The aim of the competition is to discover and publish new writers. Deadline: March 31. Prize: $1,000. 2nd Prize: a week at Anam Cara Writers" Retreat in West Cork. Results announced May 15. Judged by Jo Shapcott in 2017.

FOLEY POETRY CONTEST

106 W. 56th St., New York NY 10019. (212)581-4640. **Fax:** (212)399-3596. **Website:** www.americamagazine. org. *America*, the national Catholic weekly by the Jesuits of North America, sponsors the annual Foley Poetry Contest. Offers $1,000 and 2 contributor's copies for the winning poem. Winner will be announced in the mid-June issue of America and on the website. Runners-up will have their poems printed in subsequent issues of *America*. Submissions must be unpublished and may not be entered in other contests. "Submit 1 poem per person, not to exceed 30 lines of verse, in any form. Name, address, telephone number, and e-mail address (if applicable) should be appended to the bottom of the page. Poems will not be returned, and e-mailed submissions are not accepted." Guidelines available in magazine, for SASE, or on website. Competition receives more than 1,000 entries/year. Submissions must be unpublished and may not be entered in other contests. "Submit 1 poem per person, not to exceed 30 lines of verse, in any form. Name, address, telephone number, and e-mail address (if applicable) should be appended to the bottom of the page. Poems will not be returned, and e-mailed submissions are not accepted." Guidelines available in magazine, for SASE, or on website. Deadline: March 31. Open to submissions on January 1.

LITERAL LATTE FOOD VERSE CONTEST

Literal Latte, 200 E. 10th St., Suite 240, New York NY 10003. **E-mail:** litlatte@aol.com. **Website:** www.lit-eral-latte.com. Any topic with Food as an ingredient. **Contact:** Jenine Gordon Bockman, editor. Open to any writer. Poems should have food as an ingredient. Submissions required to be unpublished. Guidelines online at website. Submit poems, up to 10,000 words. Literal Latté acquires first rights. Annual contest to give support and exposure to great writing. Deadline: March 15. Prize: $500. Judged by the editors.

THE FOUR WAY BOOKS LEVIS PRIZE IN POETRY

Four Way Books, Box 535, Village Station, New York NY 10014. (212)334-5430. **Fax:** (212)334-5435. **E-mail:** editors@fourwaybooks.com. **Website:** www.fourwaybooks.com. **Contact:** Ryan Murphy, Assoc. Director. The Four Way Books Levis Prize in Poetry, offered biennially in even-numbered years, offers publication by Four Way Books (see separate listing in Book Publishers), honorarium, and a reading at one or more participating series In New York City. Open to any poet writing in English who has not published a book-length collection of poetry. Entry form and guidelines available on website at www.fourwaybooks.com. Deadline: March 31 (postmark or online submission). Winner announced by e-mail and on website. Prize: Publication and $1,000. Copies of winning books available through Four Way Books online and at bookstores (to the trade through University Press of New England).

GERTRUDE PRESS POETRY CHAPBOOK CONTEST

P.O. Box 28281, Portland OR 97228. **E-mail:** editor@gertrudepress.org; poetry@gertrudepress.org. **Website:** www.gertrudepress.org. Annual chapbook contest for 25-30 pages of poetry. Individual poems may have been previously published; unpublished poems are welcome. Poetry may be of any subject matter, and writers from all backgrounds are encouraged to submit. Include list of acknowledgments and cover letter indicating how poet learned of the contest. Include 1 title page with identifying information and 1 without. Guidelines available in *Gertrude* (see separate listing in Magazines/Journals), for SASE, by e-mail, or on website. Deadline: May 15. Submission period begins September 15. Prize: $200, publication and 25 complimentary copies of the chapbook.

ALLEN GINSBERG POETRY AWARDS

The Poetry Center at Passaic County Community College, One College Blvd., Paterson NJ 07505. (973)684-6555. **Fax:** (973)523-6085. **E-mail:** mgillan@pccc.edu. **Website:** www.pccc.edu/poetry. **Contact:** Maria Mazziotti Gillan, executive director. All winning poems, honorable mentions, and editor's choice poems will be published in *The Paterson Literary Review*. Winners will be asked to participate in a reading that will be held in the Paterson Historic District. Submissions must be unpublished. Submit up to 5 poems (no poem more than 2 pages long). Send 4 copies of each poem entered. Include cover sheet with poet's name, address, phone number, e-mail address and poem titles. Poet's name should not appear on poems. Include SASE for results only; poems will not be returned. Guidelines available for SASE or on website. Deadline: February 1 (postmark). Prize: 1st Prize: $1,000; 2nd Prize: $200; 3rd Prize: $100.

GIVAL PRESS OSCAR WILDE AWARD

Gival Press, LLC, P.O. Box 3812, Arlington VA 22203. (703)351-0079. **E-mail:** givalpress@yahoo.com. **Website:** www.givalpress.com. **Contact:** Robert L. Giron. Award given to the best previously unpublished original poem—written in English of any length, in any style, typed, double-spaced on 1 side only—which best relates gay/lesbian/bisexual/transgendered (GLBTQ) life, by a poet who is 18 years or older. Enter via portal: www.givalpress.submittable.com. Entrants are asked to submit their poems without any kind of identification (with the exception of titles) and with a separate cover page with the following information: name, address (street, city, and state with zip code), telephone number, e-mail address (if available), and a list of poems by title. Checks drawn on American banks should be made out to Gival Press, LLC. May submit via portal: www.givalpress.submittable.com. Deadline: June 27 (postmarked). Prize: $100 and the poem, along with information about the poet, will be published on the Gival Press website. Judged by the previous winner, who reads the poems anonymously.

GIVAL PRESS POETRY AWARD

Gival Press, LLC, P.O. Box 3812, Arlington VA 22203. (703)351-0079. **E-mail:** givalpress@yahoo.com. **Website:** www.givalpress.submittable.com. **Contact:** Robert L. Giron, editor. Offered every other year for a previously unpublished poetry collection as a complete ms, which may include previously published poems; previously published poems must be acknowledged, and poet must hold rights. Guidelines for SASE, by e-mail, or online. Open to any writer, as long as the work is original, not a translation, and is written in English. The copyright remains in the author's name; certain rights fall to the publisher per the contract. Enter via portal: www.givalpress.submittable.com. Must be at least 45 typed pages of poetry, on one side only. Entrants are asked to submit their poems without any kind of identification (with the exception of the titles) and with a separate cover page with the following information: Name, address (street, city, state, and zip code), telephone number, e-mail address (if available), short bio, and a list of the poems by title. Checks drawn on American banks should be made out to Gival Press, LLC. The competition seeks to award well-written, origional poetry in English on any topic, in any style. Deadline: December 15 (postmarked). Prize: $1,000, publication, and 20 copies of the publication. The editor narrows entries to the top 10; previous winner selects top 5 and chooses the winner—all done anonymously.

PATRICIA GOEDICKE PRIZE IN POETRY

CutBank Literary Magazine, *CutBank*, University of Montana, English Dept., LA 133, Missoula MT 59812. **E-mail:** editor.cutbank@gmail.com. **Website:** www.cutbankonline.org. **Contact:** Billy Wallace, editor-in-chief. The Patricia Goedicke Prize in Poetry seeks to highlight work that showcases an authentic voice, a boldness of form, and a rejection of functional fixedness. Accepts online submissions only. Submit up to 5 poems. Guidelines available online. Deadline: January 15. Submissions period begins November 9. Prize: $500 and featured in the magazine. Judged by a guest judge each year.

GOLDEN ROSE AWARD

New England Poetry Club, 654 Green St., No. 2, Cambridge MA 02139. **E-mail:** contests@nepoetryclub.org; info@nepoetryclub.org. **Website:** www.nepoetryclub.org. **Contact:** NEPC contest coordinator. Given annually to the poet, who by their poetry and inspiration to and encouragement of other writers, has made a significant mark on American poetry. Traditionally given to a poet with some ties to New England so that a public reading may take place. Contest open to members and nonmembers. Poems should be typed and submitted in duplicate with author's name, address, phone, and e-mail address of writer on only 1 copy. (Judges receive copies without names.) Copy only. Label poems with contest name. Entries should be sent by regular mail only. Special delivery or signature required mail will be returned by the post office. Entries should be original, unpublished poems in English. No poem should be entered in more than 1 contest, nor have won a previous contest. No entries will be returned. NEPC will not engage in correspondence regarding poems or contest decisions. Deadline: May 31. Judged by well-known poets and sometimes winners of previous NEPC contests.

THE GREEN ROSE PRIZE IN POETRY

New Issues Poetry & Prose, Deptartment of English, Western Michigan University, 1903 W. Michigan Ave., Kalamazoo MI 49008-5463. **E-mail:** new-issues@wmich.edu. **Website:** www.newissuespress.com. Offered annually for unpublished poetry. The university will publish a book of poems by a poet writing in English who has published 1 or more full-length collections of poetry. *New Issues* may publish as many as 2 additional mss from this competition. Guidelines for SASE or online. *New Issues Poetry & Prose* obtains rights for first publication. Book is copyrighted in the author's name. Considers simultaneous submissions, but *New Issues* must be notified of acceptance elsewhere. Submit a ms of at least 40 pages, typed; single-spaced preferred. Clean photocopies acceptable. Do not bind; use manila folder or metal clasp. Include cover page with poet's name, address, phone number, and title of the ms. Also include brief bio, table of contents, and acknowledgments page. Submissions are also welcome through the online submission manager: www.newissuespoetryprose.submittable.com. For hardcopy manuscripts only, you may include SASP for notification of receipt of ms and SASE for results only; mss will be recycled. Guidelines available for SASE, by fax, e-mail, or on website. Winner is announced in January or February on website. The winning manuscript will be published in spring of following year. 2016 winner was Nadine Sabra Meyer (*Chrysanthemum, Chrysanthemum*). Deadline: Submit May 1-September 30. Winner is announced in January or February on website. Prize: $1,000, publication of a book of poems, reading w/ $500 stipend + travel costs.

⊙ THE GRIFFIN POETRY PRIZE

The Griffin Trust for Excellence in Poetry, 363 Parkridge Crescent, Oakville ON L6M 1A8 Canada. (905)618-0420. **E-mail:** info@griffinpoetryprize.com. **Website:** www.griffinpoetryprize.com. **Contact:** Ruth Smith. The Griffin Poetry Prize is one of the world's most generous poetry awards. The awards go to one Canadian and one international poet for a first collection written in, or translated into, English. Submissions must come from publishers. A book of poetry must be a first-edition collection. Books should have been published in the previous calendar year. Deadline: December 31. Prize: Two $65,000 (CAD) prizes. An additional $10,000 (CAD) goes to each shortlisted poet for their participation in the Shortlist Readings. Judges are chosen annually by the Trustees of The Griffin Trust For Excellence in Poetry.

GREG GRUMMER POETRY AWARD

Phoebe, MSN 2C5, George Mason University, 4400 University Dr., Fairfax VA 22030. **E-mail:** phoebe@gmu.edu. **Website:** www.phoebejournal.com. **Contact:** Doug Luman & Janice Majewski, poetry editors. Offered annually for unpublished work. Submit up to 4 poems, no more than 10 pages total. Guidelines online. Requests first serial rights, if work is to be published, and $400 first prize. The purpose of the award is to recognize new and exciting poetry. Deadline: March 19. Prize: $400 and publication in the *Phoebe*. Judged by poet Monica Youn.

THE DONALD HALL PRIZE IN POETRY

AWP, Carty House, Mail Stop 1E3, George Mason University, Fairfax VA 22030-4444. **E-mail:** chronicle@awpwriter.org. **Website:** www.awpwriter.org. The Donald Hall Prize for Poetry offers an award of $5,500, supported by Amazon.com, and publication by the University of Pittsburgh Press. Deadline: March 3. Opens to submissions January 1.

JAMES HEARST POETRY PRIZE

North American Review, University of Northern Iowa, 1222 W. 27th St., Cedar Falls IA 50614-0516. (319)273-3026. **Fax:** (319)273-4326. **E-mail:** nar@uni.edu. **Website:** www.northamericanreview.org. Contest to find the best previously unpublished poem. Deadline: October 31. Prize: 1st place: $1,000; 2nd place: $100; 3rd place: $50. Judged by Major Jackson in 2017.

THE HILARY THAM CAPITAL COLLECTION

The Word Works, Nancy White, c/o SUNY Adiorndack, 640 Bay Rd., Queensbury NY 12804. **E-mail:** editor@wordworksbooks.org. **Website:** www.wordworksbooks.org. **Contact:** Nancy White, editor. The Hilary Tham Capital Collection publishes only poets who volunteer for literary nonprofits. Every nominated poet is invited to submit; authors have until May 1 to send their ms via online submissions at website, or to Nancy White. Details available online. Deadline: May 1. Past judges include Denise Duhamel, Kimiko Hahn, Michael Klein, and Eduardo Corral.

THE BESS HOKIN PRIZE

Poetry, 61 W. Superior St., Chicago IL 60654. (312)787-7070. **Fax:** (312)787-6650. **E-mail:** editors@poetrymagazine.org. **Website:** www.poetrymagazine.org. Offered annually for poems published in *Poetry* during the preceding year (October-September). Upon acceptance, *Poetry* licenses exclusive worldwide first serial rights, including electronic rights, for publication, as well as non-exclusive rights to reprint, reuse, and archive the work, in any format, in perpetuity. Copyright reverts to author upon first publication. "Established in 1947 through the generosity of our late friend and guarantor, Mrs. David Hokin, and is given annually in her memory." Prize: $1,000.

FIRMAN HOUGHTON PRIZE

New England Poetry Club, 53 Regent St., Cambridge MA 02140. **E-mail:** info@nepoetryclug.org. **Website:** www.nepoetryclub.org. **Contact:** Mary Buchinger, co-president NEPC. For a lyric poem in honor of the former president of NEPC. Contest guidelines available on website. Deadline: May 31. Prize: $200. Judged by well-known poets and sometimes winners of previous NEPC contests.

TOM HOWARD/MARGARET REID POETRY CONTEST

Winning Writers, Winning Writers, 351 Pleasant St., PMB 222, Northampton MA 01060-3961. (866)946-9748. **Fax:** (413)280-0539. **E-mail:** adam@winningwriters.com. **Website:** www.winningwriters.com. **Contact:** Adam Cohen. Winning Writers provides expert literary contest information to the public. It is one of the "101 Best Websites for Writers" (*Writer's Digest*). Offers annual awards of Tom Howard Prize, for a poem in any style or genre, and Margaret Reid Prize, for a poem that rhymes or has a traditional style. See website for guidelines and to submit your poem. Nonexclusive right to publish submissions online, in e-mail newsletters, in e-books, and in press releases. Submissions maybe published or unpublished, may have won prizes elsewhere, and may be entered in other contests. Length limit: 250 lines per poem. Deadline: September 30. Submission period begins April 15. Prizes: Two top awards of $1,500 each, with 10 Honorable Mentions of $100 each (any style). All entries that win cash prizes will be published on the Winning Writers website. Judged by Soma Mei Sheng Frazier.

ILLINOIS STATE POETRY SOCIETY ANNUAL CONTEST

Illinois State Poetry Society, 543 E. Squirrel Trail Dr., Tucson AZ 85704. **E-mail:** oasis@alharris.com. **Website:** www.illinoispoets.org. **Contact:** Alan Harris. Annual contest to encourage the crafting of excellent poetry. Guidelines and entry forms available for SASE. Deadline: September 30. Cash prizes of $50, $30, and $10. Three Honorable Mentions. Poet retains all rights. Judged by out-of-state professionals.

INDIANA REVIEW POETRY PRIZE

Indiana Review, Poetry Prize, Indiana Review, Ballantine Hall 529, 1020 E. Kirkwood Ave., Bloomington IN 47405-7103. **E-mail:** inreview@indiana.edu. **Website:** www.indianareview.org. Offered annually for unpublished work. Open to any writer. Guidelines available on website. All entries are considered for publication. Send no more than 3 poems per entry, 8 pages maximum. Each fee entitles entrant to a 1-year subscription. No longer accepts hard-copy submissions. Deadline: March 31. Submission period begins February 1. Prize: $1,000 and publication. Judged by Gabrielle Calvocoressi in 2018. Different judge every year.

IOWA POETRY PRIZE

University of Iowa Press, 119 West Park Rd., 100 Kuhl House, Iowa City IA 52242. (319)335-2000. **Fax:** (319)335-2055. **E-mail:** uipress@uiowa.edu. **Website:** www.uiowapress.org. Offered annually to encourage poets and their work. Submissions must be postmarked during the month of April; put name on title page only. This page will be removed before ms is judged. Open to writers of English (US citizens or not). Mss will not be returned. Previous winners are not eligible. Mss should be 50-150 pages in length.

Poems included in the collection may have appeared in journals or anthologies; poems from a poet's previous collections may be included only in manuscripts of new and selected poems. Deadline: April 30. Prize: Publication under standard royalty agreement.

ALICE JAMES AWARD

Alice James Books, University of Maine at Farmington, 114 Prescott St., Farmington ME 04938. (207)778-7071. **Fax:** (207)778-7766. **E-mail:** ajb@alicejamesbooks.org; info@alice jamesbooks.org. **Website:** www.alicejamesbooks.org. **Contact:** Alyssa Neptune, managing editor. Offered annually for unpublished, full-length poetry collections. Emerging and established poets are welcome. Submit 48-80 pages of poetry. Guidelines for submissions available online. Deadline: November 1. Prize: $2,000, publication, and distribution through Consortium.

RANDALL JARRELL POETRY COMPETITION

North Carolina Writers' Network, Terry L. Kennedy, MFA Writing Program, 3302 MHRA Building, UNC Greensboro, Greensboro NC 27402-6170. **E-mail:** tlkenned@uncg.edu. **Website:** www.ncwriters.org. **Contact:** Terry L. Kennedy, associate director. Offered annually for unpublished work to honor Randall Jarrell and his life at UNC Greensboro, by recognizing the best poetry submitted. The competition is open to any writer who is a legal resident of North Carolina or a member of the North Carolina Writers' Network. Submissions should be one poem only (40-line limit). Poem must be typed (single-spaced) and stapled in the left-hand corner. Author's name should not appear on the poem. Instead, include a separate cover sheet with author's name, address, e-mail address, phone number, and poem title. Poem will not be returned. Include a self-addressed stamped envelope for a list of winner and finalists. The winner and finalists will be announced in May. Deadline: March 1. Prize: $200 and publication at *storySouth* (www.storysouth.com). Judged by Lauren Moseley in 2018.

JUNIPER PRIZE FOR POETRY

University of Massachusetts Press, East Experiment Station, 671 North Pleasant St., Amherst MA 01003. (413)545-2217. **Fax:** (413)545-1226. **E-mail:** info@umpress.umass.edu; kfisk@umpress.umass.edu. **E-mail:** poetry@umpress.umass.edu. **Website:** www.umass.edu/umpress. **Contact:** Karen Fisk, competition coordinator. The University of Massachusetts Press offers the annual Juniper Prize for Poetry, awarded in al-

ternate years for the first and subsequent books. Considers simultaneous submissions, but if accepted for publication elsewhere, please notify immediately. Mss by more than 1 author, entries of more than 1 mss simultaneously or within the same year, and translations are not eligible. Submit paginated ms of 50-70 pages of poetry, with paginated contents page, credits page, and information on previously published books. Include 2 cover sheets: 1 with contract information, 1 without. Mss will not be returned. Guidelilnes available for SASE or on website. Deadline: September 30. Submissions period begins August 1. Winners announced online in April on the press website. Prize: Publication and $1,000 in addition to royalties.

BARBARA MANDIGO KELLY PEACE POETRY AWARDS

Nuclear Age Peace Foundation, PMB 121, 1187 Coast Village Rd., Suite 1, Santa Barbara CA 93108-2794. (805)965-3443. **Fax:** (805)568-0466. **E-mail:** cwarner@napf.org. **Website:** www.wagingpeace.org; www.peacecontests.org. **Contact:** Carol Warner, poetry award coordinator. The Barbara Mandigo Kelly Peace Poetry Contest was created to encourage poets to explore and illuminate positive visions of peace and the human spirit. The annual contest honors the late Barbara Kelly, a Santa Barbara poet and longtime supporter of peace issues. Awards are given in 3 categories: adult (over 18 years), youth between 12 and 18 years, and youth under 12. All submitted poems should be unpublished. Deadline: July 1 (postmarked) or e-mailed (cwarner@napf.org). Prize: Adult: $1,000; Youth (13-18): $200; Youth (12 and under): $200. Honorable Mentions may also be awarded. Judged by a committee of poets selected by the Nuclear Age Peace Foundation. The foundation reserves the right to publish and distribute the award-winning poems, including honorable mentions.

MILTON KESSLER MEMORIAL PRIZE FOR POETRY

Dept. of English, Binghamton University, Library North Room 1149, Vestal Parkway E., P.O. Box 6000, Binghamton NY 13902-6000. **Website:** www.binghamton.edu/english/creative-writing/binghamton-center-for-writers/binghamton-book-awards/kessler-poetry-awards.html. **Contact:** Maria Mazziotti Gillan, director. Annual award for best previously published book (previous year). Deadline: March 1. 1st place: $1,000.

THE JAMES LAUGHLIN AWARD

The Academy of American Poets, 584 Broadway, Suite 604, New York NY 10012. **Website:** www.poets.org. Offered since 1954, the James Laughlin Award is given to recognize and support a second book of poetry forthcoming in the next calendar year. It is named for the poet and publisher James Laughlin, who founded New Directions in 1936. The winner receives a prize of $5,000, an all-expenses-paid weeklong residency at The Betsy Hotel in Miami Beach, FL, and distribution of the winning book to approximately 1,000 Academy of American Poets members. Deadline: May 15.

LEVIS READING PRIZE

Virginia Commonwealth University, Department of English, Levis Reading Prize, VCU Department of English, 900 Park Avenue, Hibbs Hall, Room 306, P.O. Box 842005, Richmond VA 23284-2005. (804)828-1329. **Fax:** (804)828-8684. **E-mail:** bloomquistjmp@mymail.vcu.edu. **Website:** www.english.vcu.edu/mfa/levis. **Contact:** John-Michael Bloomquist. Offered annually for books of poetry published in the previous year to encourage poets early in their careers. The entry must be the writer's first or second published book of poetry. Previously published books in other genres, or previously published chapbooks or self-published material, do not count as books for this purpose. Entries may be submitted by either author or publisher, and must include three copies of the book (48 pages or more), a cover letter, and a brief biography of the author including previous publications. (Entries from vanity presses are not eligible.) The book must have been published in the previous calendar year. Entrants wishing acknowledgment of receipt must include a self-addressed stamped postcard. Deadline: February 1. Prize: $5,000 and an expense-paid trip to Richmond to present a public reading.

THE RUTH LILLY POETRY PRIZE

Poetry, 61 W. Superior St., Chicago IL 60654. (312)787-7070. **Fax:** (312)787-6650. **E-mail:** editors@poetrymagazine.org. **Website:** www.poetrymagazine.org. Awarded annually, the $100,000 Ruth Lilly Poetry Prize honors a living U.S. poet whose lifetime accomplishments warrant extraordinary recognition. Established in 1986 by Ruth Lilly, the Prize is one of the most prestigious awards given to American poets and is one of the largest literary honors for work in the English language. Deadline: No submissions or nominations considered. Prize: $100,000.

LITERAL LATTÉ POETRY AWARD

Literal Latté, 200 E. 10th St., Suite 240, New York NY 10003. **E-mail:** LitLatte@aol.com. **Website:** www.literal-latte.com. **Contact:** Jenine Gordon Bockman, editor. Offered annually to any writer for unpublished poetry (maximum 2,000 words per poem). All styles welcome. Winners published in *Literal Latté*. Acquires first rights. Deadline: Postmark by July 15. Prizes: 1st Place: $1,000; 2nd Place: $300; 3rd Place: $200. Judged by the editors.

LUMINA POETRY CONTEST

Sarah Lawrence College, Sarah Lawrence College Slonim House 1 Mead Way, Bronxville NY 10708. **Website:** www.luminajournal.com. Poetry competition held once every three years by the Sarah Lawrence College's graduate literary journal. Rotates with a fiction and nonfiction contest. Submit online. Include a 100-word bio at the bottom of cover letter. Submit up to 3 poems, 60 lines maximum per poem. Does not accept previously published material or simultaneous submissions. Deadline: October 15. Prize: 1st Place: $500 and publication; 2nd Place: $250 and publication; 3rd Place: $100 and online publication.

THE MACGUFFIN'S NATIONAL POET HUNT CONTEST

The MacGuffin, The MacGuffin, Schoolcraft College, 18600 Haggerty Rd., Livonia MI 48152. (734)462-4400, ext. 5327. **Fax:** (734)462-4679. **E-mail:** macguffin@schoolcraft.edu. **E-mail:** macguffin@schoolcraft.edu. **Website:** www.schoolcraft.edu/a-z-index/the-macguffin. **Contact:** Gordon Krupsky, managing editor. *The MacGuffin* is a national literary magazine from Schoolcraft College in Livonia, Michigan. An entry consists of three poems. Poems must not be previously published, and must be the original work of the contestant. See website for additional details. The mission of *The MacGuffin* is to encourage, support, and enhance the literary arts in the Schoolcraft College community, the region, the state, and the nation. Deadline: June 3. Submissions period begins April 1. Prize: $500. Judged by Li-Young Lee.

NAOMI LONG MADGETT POETRY AWARD

Broadside Lotus Press, Inc., 8300 East Jefferson Ave., #504, Detroit MI 48214. (313)736-5338. **E-mail:** broadsidelotus@gmail.com. **Website:** www.broadsidelotuspress.org. **Contact:** Gloria House. Offered annually to recognize an unpublished book-length poetry ms by an African American. Guidelines available online. Poems in the ms should total *approximately* 60-90 pages, exclusive of a table of contents or other optional introductory material. Poems that have been published individually in periodicals or anthologies are acceptable. Will not consider an entire collection that has been previously published. Deadline: March 1. Submission period begins January 2. Prize: $500 and publication by Lotus Press.

MAIN STREET RAG'S ANNUAL POETRY BOOK AWARD

Main Street Rag Publishing Company, P.O. Box 690100, Charlotte NC 28227-7001. (704)573-2516. **E-mail:** editor@mainstreetrag.com. **Website:** www.mainstreetrag.com. **Contact:** M. Scott Douglass, publisher/managing editor. Submit 48-84 pages of poetry, no more than 1 poem/page (individual poems may be longer than 1 page). Guidelines available on website. The purpose of this contest is to select manuscripts for publication and offer prize money to the manuscript we feel best represents our label. Deadline: January 31. Prize: 1st Place: $1,200 and 50 copies of book; runners-up are also be offered publication. Judged by 1 panel that consists of *MSR* editors, associated editors and college-level instructors, and previous contest winners.

✪ THE MALAHAT REVIEW LONG POEM PRIZE

The Malahat Review, Box 1700 STN CSC, Victoria BC V8W 2Y2 Canada. **E-mail:** malahat@uvic.ca. **Website:** www.malahatreview.ca. **Contact:** L'Amour Lisik, publicity manager. Long Poem Prize offered in alternate years with the Novella Contest. Open to any writer. Offers 2 awards of $1,000 CAD each for a long poem or cycle (10-20 printed pages). Includes publication in *The Malahat Review* and a 1-year subscription. Open to entries from Canadian, American, and overseas authors. Obtains first world rights. Publication rights after revert to the author. Submissions must be unpublished. No simultaneous submissions. Submit a single poem or cycle of poems, 10-20 published pages (a published page equals 32 lines or less, including breaks between stanzas); no restrictions on subject matter or aesthetic approach. Include separate page with poet's name, address, e-mail, and title; no identifying information on mss pages. Do not include SASE for results; mss will not be returned. Guidelines available on website. Deadline: February 1 (odd-numbered years). Prize: Two $1,000 prizes. Winners published in the summer issue of *The Malahat Review*, announced in summer on website, Facebook page, and in quarterly e-newsletter *Malahat lite*. Judged by 3 recognized poets. Preliminary readings by editorial board.

THE MORTON MARR POETRY PRIZE

Southwest Review, Southern Methodist University, P.O. Box 750374, Dallas TX 75275-0374. (214)768-1037. **Fax:** (214)768-1408. **E-mail:** swr@mail.smu.edu. **Website:** www.smu.edu/southwestreview. **Contact:** Prize coordinator. Annual award for poem(s) by a writer who has not yet published a book of poetry. Submit no more than 6 poems in a "traditional" form (e.g., sonnet, sestine, villanelle, rhymed stanzas, blank verse, et al.). Submissions will not be returned. Deadline: September 30. Prizes: $1,000 for 1st place; $500 for 2nd place; plus publication in the *Southwest Review*.

THE LENORE MARSHALL POETRY PRIZE

The Academy of American Poets, 584 Broadway, Suite 604, New York NY 10012. (212)274-0343. **Fax:** (212)274-9427. **E-mail:** awards@poets.org. **Website:** www.poets.org. **Contact:** Programs Coordinator. Established in 1975, this $25,000 award recognizes the most outstanding book of poetry published in the United States in the previous calendar year. The prize includes distribution of the winning book hundreds of Academy of American Poets members. Deadline: May 15. Prize: $25,000.

MARSH HAWK PRESS POETRY PRIZE

Marsh Hawk Press, P.O. Box 206, East Rockaway NY 11518-0206. **E-mail:** marshhawkpress1@aol.com. **Website:** www.MarshHawkPress.org. **Contact:** Prize Director. The Marsh Hawk Press Poetry Prize offers $1,000, plus publication of a book-length ms. Additionally, The Robert Creeley Poetry Prize and The Rochelle Ratner Poetry Award, both cash prizes, go to the runners-up. Submissions must be unpublished as a collection, but individual poems may have been previously published elsewhere. Submit 48-84 pages of original poetry in any style in English, typed single-spaced, and paginated. (Longer mss will be considered if the press is queried before submission.) Contest mss may be submitted by electronic upload. See website for more information. If submitting via Post Office mail, the ms must be bound with a spring clip. Include 2 title pages: 1 with ms title, poet's name, and contact information only; 1 with ms title only (poet's name must not appear anywhere in the ms). Also include table of contents and acknowledgments page. Include SASE for results only; ms will not be returned. Guidelines available on website. Deadline: April 30. Judged by Meena Alexander in 2017.

KATHLEEN MCCLUNG SONNET PRIZE CATEGORY

Soul-Making Keats Literary Competition, The Webhallow House, 1544 Sweetwood Dr., Broadmoor Village CA 94015-2029. (650)756-5279. **Fax:** (650)756-5279. **E-mail:** soulkeats@mail.com. **Website:** www.soulmakingcontest.us. **Contact:** Eileen Malone. Call for Shakespearean and Petrarchan sonnets on the theme of the "beloved." Previously published material is accepted. Indicate category on cover page and on identifying 3x5 card. Open annually to any writer. Ongoing Deadline: November 30. Prize:1st Place: $100; 2nd Place: $50; 3rd Place: $25.

THE KATHRYN A. MORTON PRIZE IN POETRY

Sarabande Books, Inc., 822 E. Market St., Louisville KY 40206. (502)458-4028. **E-mail:** info@sarabandebooks.org. **Website:** www.sarabandebooks.org. **Contact:** Sarah Gorham, editor-in-chief. The Kathryn A. Morton Prize in Poetry is awarded annually to a book-length ms (at least 48 pages). All finalists are considered for publication. Competition receives approximately 1,400 entries. Guidelines available online. Mss can be submitted online or via postal mail. Deadline: February 15. Submissions period begins January 1. Prize: $2,000, publication, and a standard royalty contract.

SHEILA MARGARET MOTTON PRIZE

New England Poetry Club, 2 Farrar St., Cambridge MA 02138. (617)744-6034. **E-mail:** info@nepoetryclub.org. **Website:** www.nepoetryclub.org. **Contact:** Audrey Kalajin. Awarded for a book of poems published in the last 2 years. Send 2 copies of book. Deadline: May 31. Prize: $500. Judged by well-known poets and sometimes winners of previous NEPC contests.

ERIKA MUMFORD PRIZE

New England Poetry Club, 376 School St., Watertown MA 02472. **E-mail:** contests@nepoetryclub.org. **Website:** www.nepoetryclub.org/contests.htm. **Contact:** Audrey Kalajin. Offered annually for a poem in any form about foreign culture or travel. Funded by Erika Mumford's family and friends. Contest open to members and nonmembers. Deadline: May 31. Prize: $250.

Judged by well-known poets and sometimes winners of previous NEPC contests.

⤷ NATIONAL POETRY COMPETITION

The Poetry Society, 22 Betterton St., London WC2H 9BX United Kingdom. 020 7420 9880. **E-mail:** info@poetrysociety.org.uk. **Website:** www.poetrysociety.org.uk. **Contact:** Competition organizer. The Poetry Society was founded in 1909 to promote "a more general recognition and appreciation of poetry". Since then, it has grown into one of Britain's most dynamic arts organizations, representing British poetry both nationally and internationally. Today it has nearly 4000 members worldwide and publishes *The Poetry Review*. With innovative education and commissioning programs and a packed calendar of performances, readings and competitions, The Poetry Society champions poetry for all ages. Open to anyone aged 17 or over. Submissions must be unpublished (poems posted on websites are considered published). Submit original poems in English, on any subject, no more than 40 lines/poem, typed on 1 side only of A4 paper, double- or single-spaced. Each poem must be titled. No identifying information on poems. Do not staple pages. Accepts online submissions; full details available on the National Poetry Competition pages on the Poetry Society website. Entry form (required) available for A5 SAE (1 entry form covers multiple entries, may be photocopied). Include stamped SAE for notification of receipt of postal entries (confirmation of online entries will be e-mailed at time of submission); poems will not be returned. Guidelines available on website. Deadline: October 31. 1st Prize: £5,000; 2nd Prize: £2,000; 3rd Prize: £1,000; plus 7 commendations of £200 each. Winners will be published in *The Poetry Review*, and on the Poetry Society website; the top 3 winners will receive a year's free membership of The Poetry Society.

THE NATIONAL POETRY REVIEW BOOK PRIZE

The National Poetry Review, P.O. Box 2080, Aptos CA 95001-2080. **E-mail:** editor@nationalpoetryreview.com. **Website:** www.nationalpoetryreview.com; www.tnprpress.com. **Contact:** C.J. Sage, editor. Submit 45-80 pages of poetry via e-mail and PayPal (strongly preferred) or via mail. Include cover letter with bio and acknowledgments page. Include e-mail address (no SASE; mss will be recycled). Guidelines available on website. Deadline: June 30 (postmark). Prize: $1,000 plus publication and 15 copies of the book.

NATIONAL WRITERS ASSOCIATION POETRY CONTEST

The National Writers Association, 10940 S. Parker Rd. #508, Parker CO 80134. **E-mail:** natlwritersassn@hotmail.com. **Website:** www.nationalwriters.com. **Contact:** Sandy Whelchel, director. Annual contest to encourage the writing of poetry, an important form of individual expression but with a limited commercial market. Deadline: October 1. Prize: 1st Place: $100; 2nd Place: $50; 3rd Place: $25.

THE PABLO NERUDA PRIZE FOR POETRY

Nimrod International Journal, 800 S. Tucker Dr., Tulsa OK 74104. (918)631-3080. **Fax:** (918)631-3033. **E-mail:** nimrod@utulsa.edu. **Website:** www.utulsa.edu/nimrod. **Contact:** Eilis O'Neal. Annual award to discover new writers of vigor and talent. Open to US residents only. Submissions must be unpublished. Work must be in English or translated by original author. Submit 3-10 pages of poetry (1 long poem or several short poems). Poet's name must not appear on manuscript. Include cover sheet with poem title(s), poet's name, address, phone, and email address (poet must have a US address by October of contest year to enter). Mark "Contest Entry" on submission envelope and cover sheet if submitting by mail. Include SASE for results only; manuscripts will not be returned. Deadline: April 30. Prizes: 1st Place: $2,000 and publication; 2nd Place: $1,000 and publication. Judged by the *Nimrod* editors (finalists). A recognized author selects the winners.

THE NEW ISSUES POETRY PRIZE

New Issues Poetry & Prose, New Issues Poetry & Prose, Department of English, Western Michigan University, 1903 W. Michigan Ave., Kalamazoo MI 49008-5463. **E-mail:** new-issues@wmich.edu. **Website:** www.newissuespress.com. Offered annually for publication of a first book of poems by a poet writing in English who has not previously published a full-length collection of poems in an edition of 500 or more copies. *New Issues Poetry & Prose* obtains rights for first publication. Book is copyrighted in author's name. Guidelines for SASE or online. Additional mss will be considered from those submitted to the competition for publication. Considers simultaneous submissions, but *New Issues* must be notified of acceptance elsewhere. Submit ms of at least 40 pages, typed, single-spaced preferred. Clean photocopies acceptable. Do not bind; use manila folder or metal clasp. Include cover page with poet's name, address, phone number, and title of the ms. Also include brief bio and acknowledgments page. Submissions are also welcome through the online submission manager: www.newissuespoetryprose.submittable.com. For hardcopy submissions only, you may include SASP for notification of receipt of ms and SASE for results only; no mss will be returned. Winning manuscript will be named in May and published in the next spring. Deadline: December 30. Prize: $1,000, publication of a book of poems, reading w/ $500 stipend + travel costs. A national judge selects the prize winner and recommends other manuscripts. The editors decide on the other books considering the judge's recommendation, but are not bound by it. 2018 judge: Cathy Park Hong.

NEW LETTERS PRIZE FOR POETRY

New Letters Awards for Writers, UMKC, University House, 5101 Rockhill Rd., Kansas City MO 64110-2499. (816)235-1168. **E-mail:** newletters@umkc.edu. **Website:** www.newletters.org. **Contact:** Ashley Wann. The annual *New Letters* Poetry Prize awards $1,500 and publication in *New Letters* (see separate listing in Magazines/Journals) to the best group of 3-6 poems. All entries will be considered for publication in *New Letters.* Submissions must be unpublished. Considers simultaneous submissions with notification upon acceptance elsewhere. Accepts multiple entries with separate fee for each. Submit up to 6 poems (need not be related). Include 2 cover sheets: 1 with poet's name, address, e-mail, phone number, prize category (poetry), and poem title(s); the second with category and poem title(s) only. No identifying information on ms pages. Accepts electronic submissions. Include SASE for notification of receipt of ms and entry number, and SASE for results only (send only 1 envelope if submitting multiple entries); mss will not be returned. Guidelines available by SASE or on website. Current students and employees of the University of Missouri-Kansas City, and current volunteer members of the *New Letters* and BkMk Press staffs, are not eligible. Deadline: May 18 (postmarked). $1,500 and publication.

NFSPS POETRY CONVENTION MADNESS CONTEST

2029 103rd Ave. NW, Coon Rapids MN 55433. **E-mail:** pwilliamstein@yahoo.com; schambersmediator@yahoo.com. **Website:** www.mnpoets.com. **Contact:** Peter Stein; Sue Chambers. Enter to win your way to the NFSPS National Poetry Convention in Chaska, MN, June 9th-13th. For more details about the event, visit www.nfspsconvention.com. Must be original work of the contestant. Deadline: January 31. Prizes: 1st Place: Hotel Lodging at Oak Ridge Convention Center for four nights, June 9th-12th. 2nd Place: Meals payed for during the course of the convention. 3rd Place: Registration to the Convention. 1st-3rd Honorable Mentions: Subscription to Poem by Post for one year.

THE NIGHTBOAT POETRY PRIZE

Nightboat Books, P.O. Box 10, Callicoon NY 12723. **E-mail:** info@nightboat.org. **Website:** www.nightboat.org. **Contact:** Stephen Motika. Annual contest for previously unpublished collection of poetry (48-90 pages). Deadline: November 15. 1st place: $1,000, plus publication and 25 copies of published book.

OHIO POETRY DAY CONTESTS

Dept. of English, Heidelberg College, 310 East Market, Tiffin OH 44883. **Website:** ohiopoetryday.blogspot.com. **Contact:** Bill Reyer, Contest Chair. Several poetry categories open to poets from Ohio and out-of-state. Prizes range $5-100. Deadline: May 31.

GUY OWEN AWARD

Southern Poetry Review, Department of Languages, Literature, and Philosophy, Armstrong Atlantic State University, 11935 Abercorn St., Savannah GA 31419-1997. (912)344-3196. **E-mail:** editor@southernpoetryreview.org. **Website:** www.southernpoetryreview.org. **Contact:** Tony Morris, associate editor. The annual Guy Owen Prize offers $1,000 and publication in *Southern Poetry Review* to the winning poem selected by a distinguished poet. All entries will be considered for publication. Submissions must be unpublished. "We consider work published online or posted there as previously published." Considers simultaneous submissions if indicated as such. Submit 3-5 poems (10 pages maximum). Include cover sheet with poet's name and contact information; no identifying information on ms pages. No e-mail or disk submissions. Include SASE for results only; mss will not be returned. Guidelines available in magazine, for SASE, by e-mail, or on website. Deadline: May 31 (postmarked). Open to submissions March 1.

PANGAEA PRIZE

The Poet's Billow, 6135 Avon St, Portage MI 49024. **E-mail:** thepoetsbillow@gmail.com. **Website:** http://thepoetsbillow.org. **Contact:** Robert Evory. Annual award open to any writer to recognize the best series of poems, ranging between two and up to seven poems in a group. Finalists with strong work will also be published. Submissions must be previously unpublished. Please submit online. Deadline: May 1. Prize: $100. The winning poem will be published and displayed in The Poet's Billow Literary Art Gallery and nominated for a Pushcart Prize. If the poet qualifies, the poem will also be submitted to The Best New Poets anthology. Judged by the editors, and, occasionally, a guest judge.

THE PATERSON POETRY PRIZE

The Poetry Center at Passaic County Community College, One College Blvd., Paterson NJ 07505. (973)684-6555. **Fax:** (973)523-6085. **E-mail:** mgillan@pccc.edu. **Website:** www.pccc.edu/poetry. **Contact:** Maria Mazziotti Gillan, executive director. The Paterson Poetry Prize offers an annual award for the strongest book of poems (48 or more pages) published in the previous year. The winner will be asked to participate in an awards ceremony and to give a reading at The Poetry Center. Minimum press run: 500 copies. Publishers may submit more than 1 title for prize consideration; 3 copies of each book must be submitted. Include SASE for results; books will not be returned (all entries will be donated to The Poetry Center Library). Guidelines and application form (required) available for SASE or on website. Deadline: February 1. Prize: $1,000.

PAVEMENT SAW PRESS CHAPBOOK AWARD

321 Empire St., Montpelier OH 43543-1301. **E-mail:** info@pavementsaw.org. **E-mail:** editor@pavementsaw.org. **Website:** www.pavementsaw.org. **Contact:** David Baratier, editor. Pavement Saw Press has been publishing steadily since the fall of 1993. Each year since 1999, they have published at least 4 full-length paperback poetry collections, with some printed in library edition hard covers, 1 chapbook, and a yearly literary journal anthology. They specialize in finding authors who have been widely published in literary journals but have not published a chapbook or full-length book. Submit up to 32 pages of poetry. Include signed cover letter with poet's name, address, phone

number, e-mail, publication credits, a brief biography, and ms title. Also include 2 cover sheets: 1 with poet's contact information and ms title, 1 with the ms title only. Do not put name on mss pages except for first title page. No mss will be returned. Deadline: December 31 (postmark). Prize: Chapbook Award offers $500, publication, and 40 author copies.

JEAN PEDRICK PRIZE

New England Poetry Club, 2 Farrar St., Cambridge MA 02138. **E-mail:** contests@nepoetryclub.org. **Website:** www.nepoetryclub.org. **Contact:** Audrey Kalajin. Prize for a chapbook of poems published in the last two years. Send 2 copies of the chapbook. Deadline: May 31. Prize: $100. Judged by well-known poets and sometimes winners of previous NEPC contests.

PEN/JOYCE OSTERWEIL AWARD FOR POETRY

PEN America, 588 Broadway, Suite 303, New York NY 10012. **E-mail:** awards@pen.org. **Website:** www.pen.org/awards. **Contact:** Arielle Anema, Literary Awards Coordinator. *Candidates may only be nominated by members of PEN.* This award recognizes the high literary character of the published work to date of a new and emerging American poet of any age, and the promise of further literary achievement. Nominated writer may not have published more than 1 book of poetry. Offered in odd-numbered years and alternates with the PEN/Voelcker Award for Poetry. Electronic letters of nomination will be requested during open submissions season. Submissions will be accepted during the summer of even-numbered year. Visit PEN.org/awards for up-to-date information on deadlines. Prize: $5,000. Judged by a panel of 3 judges selected by the PEN Awards Committee.

PENNSYLVANIA POETRY SOCIETY ANNUAL CONTESTS

5 Coachmans Court, Norwalk CT 06850. **Website:** nfsps.com/pa. **Contact:** Colleen Yarusavage. Pennsylvania Poetry Society offers several categories of poetry contests with a range of prizes from $10-100. Deadline: January 15.

PEN/VOELCKER AWARD FOR POETRY

PEN America, 588 Broadway, Suite 303, New York NY 10012. **E-mail:** awards@pen.org. **Website:** www.pen.org/awards. **Contact:** Arielle Anema, Literary Awards Coordinator. The PEN/Voelcker Award for Poetry, established by a bequest from Hunce Voelcker, this award is given to a poet whose distinguished

and growing body of work to date represents a notable and accomplished presence in American literature. The poet honored by the award is one for whom the exceptional promise seen in earlier work has been fulfilled, and who continues to mature with each successive volume of poetry. The award is given in even-numbered years and carries a stipend of $5,000. Please note that submissions will only be accepted from Professional Members of PEN and that it is understood that all nominations made for the PEN/Voelcker Award supplement internal nominations made by the panel of judges. PEN Members are asked to submit a letter of nomination through an online submissions form. Deadline: Nominations from PEN Members will be accepted during the summer of each odd-numbered year. Visit PEN.org/awards for up-to-date information on deadlines. Prize: $5,000. Judged by a panel of 3 poets or other writers chosen by the PEN Literary Awards Committee.

PERUGIA PRESS PRIZE

Perugia Press, P.O. Box 60364, Florence MA 01062. **Website:** www.perugiapress.com. **Contact:** Susan Kan. Submissions must be unpublished as a collection, but individual poems may have been previously published in journals, chapbooks, and anthologies. Considers simultaneous submissions if notified of acceptance elsewhere. Follow online guidelines carefully. Electronic submissions available through website. No translations or self-published books. Multiple submissions accepted if accompanied by separate entry fee for each. Use USPS or electronic submission, not FedEx or UPS. Winner announced by April 1 by e-mail or SASE (if included with entry). The Perugia Press Prize is for a first or second poetry book by a woman. Poet must have no more than 1 previously published book of poems (chapbooks don't count). Deadline: November 15. Open to submissions on August 1. Prize: $1,000 and publication. Judged by panel of Perugia authors, booksellers, scholars, etc.

THE RICHARD PETERSON POETRY PRIZE

Crab Orchard Review, Dept. of English, Mail Code 4503, Faner Hall 2380, Southern Illinois University at Carbondale, 1000 Faner Drive, Carbondale IL 62901. (618)453-6833. **Fax:** (618)453-8224. **E-mail:** jtribble@siu.edu. **Website:** www.craborchardreview.siu.edu. **Contact:** Jon Tribble, managing editor. Annual award for unpublished poetry. Entries should consist of 1 poem up to 5 pages in length. *Crab Orchard Re-*

view acquires first North American serial rights to all submitted work. One winner and at least 2 finalists will be chosen. Entries should consist of 1 poem up to 5 pages in length. All submissions must be made through Submittable. Submissions must be unpublished original work, written in English by a U.S. citizen, permanent resident, or person who has DACA/TPS status (current students and employees at Southern Illinois University Carbondale are not eligible). See Submittable guidelines online for complete formatting instructions. The author's name should not appear on any page of the entry. Results announced by end of August. **Deadline:** May 31. Submission period begins March 21. **Prize:** $1,250 plus publication. Judged by the editors of *Crab Orchard Review*.

THE PLEIADES PRESS EDITORS PRIZE FOR POETRY

Pleiades Press, Pleiades Press, Dept of English, Martin 336, University of Central Missouri, Warrensburg MO 64093. (660)543-8106. **E-mail:** pleiades@ucmo.edu. **Website:** www.ucmo.edu/pleiades/. The annual Pleiades Press Editors Prize for Poetry is open to all American writers, regardless of previous publication. Submission must be unpublished as a collection, but individual poems may have been previously published elsewhere. Submit at least 48 pages of poetry (one copy). Include 2 cover sheets: one with ms title, poet's name, address, and phone number; the second with ms title only. Also include acknowledgments page for previously published poems. Guidelines online. **Deadline:** May 11. **Prize:** $2,000 and the winning collection will be published in paperback and nationally distributed.

THE POETRY CENTER BOOK AWARD

The Poetry Center, San Francisco State University, 1600 Holloway Ave., San Francisco CA 94132. (415)338-2227. **Fax:** (415)338-0966. **E-mail:** poetry@sfsu.edu. **Website:** www.sfsu.edu/~poetry. Offered annually for books of poetry and chapbooks, published in year of the prize. "Prize given for an extraordinary book of American poetry written in English." Please include a cover letter noting author name, book title(s), name of person issuing check, and check number. Will not consider anthologies or translations. **Deadline:** January 31 for books published and copywrited in the previous year. **1st place:** $500 and an invitation to read in the Poetry Center Reading Series.

POETRY SOCIETY OF AMERICA AWARDS

15 Gramercy Park, New York NY 10003. **E-mail:** psa@poetrysociety.org. **Website:** www.poetrysociety.org. Offers 7 categories of poetry prizes between $250-2,500. 5 categories are open to PSA members only. Free entry for members; $15 for non-members. Submit between October 1-December 22.

POETS & PATRONS ANNUAL CHICAGOLAND POETRY CONTEST

Sponsored by Poets & Patrons of Chicago, 416 Gierz St., Downers Grove IL 60515. **E-mail:** eatonb1016@aol.com. **Website:** www.poetsandpatrons.net. **Contact:** Barbara Eaton, director. Annual contest for unpublished poetry. Guidelines available for self-addressed, stamped envelope. The purpose of the contest is to encourage the crafting of poetry. **Deadline:** September 1. **Prize:** 1st Place: $45; 2nd Place: $20; 3rd Place: $10 cash. Poet retains rights. Judged by out-of-state professionals.

POETS OUT LOUD PRIZE

Poets Out Loud, Fordham University at Lincoln Center, 113 W. 60th St., Room 924-I, New York NY 10023. (212)636-6792. **Fax:** (212)636-7153. **E-mail:** pol@fordham.edu. **Website:** www.fordham.edu/pol. Annual competition for an unpublished, full-length poetry ms (50-80 pages). **Deadline:** November 1. **Prize:** $1,000, book publication, and book launch in POL reading series.

FELIX POLLAK PRIZE IN POETRY

University of Wisconsin Press, 1930 Monroe St., 3rd Floor, Madison WI 53711. (608)263-1110. **Fax:** (608)263-1120. **E-mail:** uwiscpress@wisc.edu. **Website:** uwpress.wisc.edu. The Felix Pollak Prize in Poetry is awarded annually to the best book-length ms of original poetry submitted in an open competition. The award is administered by the University of Wisconsin–Madison English department, and the winner is chosen by a nationally recognized poet. The resulting book is published by the University of Wisconsin Press. Submissions must be unpublished as a collection, but individual poems may have been published elsewhere (publication must be acknowledged). Considers simultaneous submissions if notified of selection elsewhere. Submit 50-80 unbound ms pages, typed single-spaced (with double spaces between stanzas). Clean photocopies are acceptable. Include 1 title page with poet's name, address, and telephone number; 1 title page with title only. No translations.

Complete guidelines available online. Deadline: September 15. Prize: $1,000 cash prize, plus publication.

A. POULIN, JR. POETRY PRIZE

BOA Editions, Ltd., P.O. Box 30971, Rochester NY 14603. **E-mail:** contact@boaeditions.org. **Website:** www.boaeditions.org. The A. Poulin, Jr. Poetry Prize is awarded to honor a poet's first book, while also honoring the late founder of BOA Editions, Ltd., a not-for-profit publishing house of poetry, poetry in translation, and short fiction. Published books in other genres do not disqualify contestants from entering this contest. Entrants must be a citizen or legal resident of the US. Poets who are at least 18 years of age, and who have yet to publish a full-length book collection of poetry, are eligible. Translations are not eligible. Individual poems may have been previously published in magazines, journals, anthologies, chapbooks of 32 pages or less, or self-published books of 46 pages or less, but must be submitted in ms form. Submit 48-100 pages of poetry, paginated consecutively, typed or computer generated in 11 point font. Bind physical manuscripts with spring clip (no paperclips) and postmark by November 30. Include cover/title page with poet's name, address, telephone number, and e-mail address. Also include the table of contents, list of acknowledgments, and entry form (available for download on website). Multiple entries accepted with separate entry fee for each. Electronic submissions accepted via Submittable. Deadline: November 30. Open to submissions on August 1. Prize: Awards $1,000 honorarium and book publication in the A. Poulin, Jr. New Poets of America Series.

PRESS 53 AWARD FOR POETRY

Press 53, 560 N. Trade St., Suite 103, Winston-Salem NC 27101. (336)770-5353. **E-mail:** kevin@press53.com. **Website:** www.press53.com. **Contact:** Kevin Morgan Watson, publisher. Awarded to an outstanding, unpublished collection of poetry. Details and guidelines available online. Deadline: July 31. Submission period begins April 1. Winner and finalists announced on by November 1. Publication in April. Prize: Publication of winning poetry collection as a Tom Lombardo Poetry Selection, $1,500 cash advance and 10 copies of the book. Judged by Press 53 poetry series editor Tom Lombardo.

THE PSA NATIONAL CHAPBOOK FELLOWSHIPS

Poetry Society of America, 15 Gramercy Park, New York NY 10003. (212)254-9628. **Fax:** (212)673-2352. **Website:** www.poetrysociety.org. Open to any US citizen or anyone currently living within the US who has not published a full-length poetry collection. Charges $12 entry fee. Winner receives $1,000 and welcomed as guest for a month-long artist's residency at PLAYA and invited to teach a single class at Purchase College for $1,000 under the sponsorshp of the Royal and Shirley Durst Chair in Literature. Deadline: December 22.

RATTLE POETRY PRIZE

RATTLE, 12411 Ventura Blvd., Studio City CA 91604. (818) 505-6777. **E-mail:** tim@rattle.com. **Website:** www.rattle.com. **Contact:** Timothy Green, editor. *Rattle*'s mission is to promote the practice of poetry. To enter, purchase a one-year subscription to *Rattle* at the regular $20 rate. Open to writers, worldwide; poems must be written in English. No previously published works, or works accepted for publication elsewhere. No simultaneous submissions are allowed. Send up to 4 poems per entry. "More than anything, our goal is to promote a community of active poets." Deadline: July 15. Prize: One $10,000 winner and ten $200 finalists will be selected in a blind review by the editors of *Rattle* and printed in the Winter issue; one $1,000 Readers' Choice Award will then be chosen from among the finalists by subscriber and entrant vote. Judged by the editors of *Rattle*.

RHINO FOUNDERS' PRIZE

RHINO, The Poetry Forum, P.O. Box 591, Evanston IL 60204. **E-mail:** editors@rhinopoetry.org. **Website:** rhinopoetry.org. **Contact:** Editors. Send best unpublished poetry (3-5 pages). Visit website for previous winners and more information. Submit online or by mail. Include a cover letter listing your name, address, e-mail, and/or telephone number, titles of poems, how you learned about RHINO, and fee. Mss will not be returned. Deadline: October 31. Open to submissions on September 1. Prize: $500, publication, featured on website, and nominated for a Pushcart Prize. Two runners-ups will receive $50, publication, and will be featured on website. Occasionally nominates runner-up for a Pushcart Prize.

ROANOKE-CHOWAN POETRY AWARD

The North Carolina Literary & Historical Assoc., 4610 Mail Service Center, Raleigh NC 27699-4610. (919)807-7290. **Fax:** (919)733-8807. **E-mail:** michael.hill@ncdcr.gov. **Website:** litandhist.ncdcr.gov. **Contact:** Michael Hill, awards coordinator. Offers annual award for an original volume of poetry published during the 12 months ending June 30 of the year for which the award is given. Open to authors who have maintained legal or physical residence, or a combination of both, in North Carolina for the 3 years preceding the close of the contest period. Submit 3 copies of each entry. Guidelines available for SASE or by fax or e-mail. Winner announced October 15. Deadline: July 15.

LORI RUDNITSKY FIRST BOOK PRIZE

Persea Books, P.O. Box 1388, Columbia MO 65205. **Website:** www.perseabooks.com. "This annual competition sponsors the publication of a poetry collection (at least 40 pages) by an American woman poet who has yet to publish a full-length book of poems." Deadline: October 31. Prize: $1,000, plus publication of book. In addition, the winner receives the option of an all-expenses-paid residency at the Civitella Ranieri Center, a renowned artists retreat housed in a 15th-century castle in Umbertide, Italy.

VERN RUTSALA POETRY PRIZE

P.O. Box 610, Corvallis OR 97339. (541)752-0075. **E-mail:** michael@cloudbankbooks.com. **Website:** http://www.cloudbankbooks.com/Contest.html. **Contact:** Michael Malan. For contest submissions, the writer's name, address, e-mail, and the titles of the poems pieces being submitted should be typed on a cover sheet only, not on the pages of poems. No electronic submissions. Deadline: January 2. Prize: $1,000 plus publication of full-length ms. Judged by Dennis Schmitz.

BENJAMIN SALTMAN POETRY AWARD

Red Hen Press, P.O. Box 40820, Pasadena CA 91114. (818)831-0649. **Fax:** (818)831-6659. **E-mail:** productioncoordinator@redhen.org. **Website:** www.redhen.org. Offered annually for unpublished work to publish a winning book of poetry. Open to any writer. Name on cover sheet only, 48 page minimum. Send SASE for notification. Deadline: August 31. 1st place: $3,000 and publication.

MAY SARTON AWARD

New England Poetry Club, 654 Green St., No. 2, Cambridge MA 02139. (617)744-6034. **E-mail:** contests@nepoetryclub.org. **Website:** www.nepoetryclub.org. **Contact:** NEPC contest coordinator. "Given intermittently to a poet whose work is an inspiration to other poets. Recipients are chosen by the board." "Contest open to members and nonmembers. Poems should be typed and submitted in duplicate with author's name, address, phone, and e-mail address of writer on only 1 copy. (Judges receive copies without names.) Copy only. Label poems with contest name. Entries should be sent by regular mail only. Special delivery or signature required mail will be returned by the post office. Entries should be original, unpublished poems in English. No poem should be entered in more than 1 contest, nor have won a previous contest. No entries will be returned. NEPC will not engage in correspondence regarding poems or contest decisions." To recognize emerging poets of exceptional promise and distinguished achievement. Established to honor the memory of longtime Academy Fellow May Sarton, a poet, novelist, and teacher who during her career encouraged the work of young poets. Deadline: May 31. Prize: $250. Judges are well-known poets and sometimes winners of previous NEPC contests.

SAWTOOTH POETRY PRIZE

Ahsahta Press, Boise State University, 1910 University Dr., MS 1525, Boise ID 83725-1525. (208)426-3134. **Website:** ahsahtapress.boisestate.edu/contest.htm. The Sawtooth Poetry Prize, sponsored by Ahsahta Press (see separate listing in Books/Chapbooks), honors a book of original poetry in English by a single author. Offers a $1,500 for a book of poems. The winning volume will be published in January 2012 by Ahsahta Press. Translations are not eligible for this award. "Students and former students of Boise State University and of this year's judge may not enter; close friends of the judge are also not considered eligible." Considers simultaneous submissions, Submit 48-100 pages of poetry, single-spaced, printed on 1 side of $8\frac{1}{2}x11$ or A4 page only. Include SASP for notification of receipt of ms and SASE (#10 business) for results; mss will not be returned. Guidelines available on website. **Entry fee:** $25/ms. Make checks payable to Ahsahta Press. (See website for payment options outside the U.S.) "Entrants will receive a copy of the winning book when it is printed if they include a 7x10 self-addressed mailer with $3.95 postage. Our books measure 6x8 and will not fit in smaller-sized mailers." **Deadline:** submit January 1-March 1 (postmark). "In addition to announcements in national publications, the winning book and author will be featured on the Ahsahta website, as will lists of finalists and semi-finalists." 2008 winner was Barbara Maloutas with *The Whole Marie* . 2011 judge: Paul Hoover. "Ahsahta Press, a member of the Council of Literary Magazines and Presses, conforms to the CLMP Code of Ethics and participated in its drafting." Winner will be announced in May Poets writing in English are eligible. Previous book publication is not a consideration. No students or former students of Boise State Univ. or of the judge; no close friends of the judge. No email or faxed entries. Eligibility between Jan. 1, 2010 and Mar. 1, 2010. $1,500 for a book of poems upon publication plus 25 copies of the book; announcements in national publications, featured on our website. Rae Armantrout

SCREAMINMAMAS MOTHER'S DAY POETRY CONTEST

1911 Cleveland St., Hollywood FL 33020. **E-mail:** screaminmamas@gmail.com. **Website:** www.scream-inmamas.com/contests. **Contact:** Darlene Pistocchi, editor/managing director. "What does it mean to be a mom? There is so much to being a mom—get deep, get creative! We challenge you to explore different types of poetry: descriptive, reflective, narrative, lyric, sonnet, ballad, limerick.. you can even go epic!" Open only to moms. Deadline: December 31. Prize: Publication.

SLAPERING HOL PRESS CHAPBOOK COMPETITION

The Hudson Valley Writers' Center, 300 Riverside Dr., Sleepy Hollow NY 10591. (914)332-5953. **Fax:** (914)332-4825. **E-mail:** info@writerscenter.org. **Website:** www.writerscenter.org. **Contact:** Margo Stever, editor. The annual competition is open to poets who have not published a book or chapbook, though individual poems may have already appeared. Manuscripts may be either a collection of poems or one long poem and should be a minimum of 16 pages and a maximum of 20 pages (not including the title page or table of contents). Purpose is to provide publishing opportunities for emerging poets. Deadline: June 15. Prize: $1,000, publication of chapbook, 20 copies of

chapbook, and a reading at The Hudson Valley Writers' Center.

SLIPSTREAM ANNUAL POETRY CHAPBOOK CONTEST

Slipstream, Slipstream Poetry Contest, Dept. W-1, P.O. Box 2071, Niagara Falls NY 14301. **E-mail:** editors@slipstreampress.org. **Website:** www.slipstream-press.org. **Contact:** Dan Sicoli, co-editor. *Slipstream Magazine* is a yearly anthology of some of the best poetry you'll find today in the American small press. Send up to 40 pages of poetry: any style, format, or theme (or no theme). Send only copies of your poems, not originals. Manuscripts will no longer be returned. See website for specific details. Offered annually to help promote a poet whose work is often overlooked or ignored. Open to any writer. Deadline: December 1. Prize: $1,000, plus 50 professionally-printed copies of your book.

HELEN C. SMITH MEMORIAL AWARD FOR BEST BOOK OF POETRY

The Texas Institute of Letters, P.O. Box 609, Round Rock TX 78680. **E-mail:** tilsecretary@yahoo.com. **Website:** http://texasinstituteofletters.org/. Offered annually for the best book of poems published January 1-December 31 of previous year. Poet must have been born in Texas, have lived in the state at some time for at least 2 consecutive years, or the subject matter must be associated with the state. See website for submission details and information. Deadline: January 10. Prize: $1,200.

THE RICHARD SNYDER MEMORIAL PUBLICATION PRIZE

Ashland Poetry Press, 401 College Ave., Ashland University, Ashland OH 44805. **E-mail:** app@ash-land.edu. **Website:** www.ashlandpoetrypress.com. **Contact:** Cassandra Brown, managing editor. Submissions must be unpublished in book form. Considers simultaneous submissions. Submit 50-96 pages of poetry. Competition receives 400+ entries/year. Winners will be announced in *Writer's Chronicle* and *Poets & Writers*. Copies of winning books available from Small Press Distribution and directly from the Ashland University Bookstore online. The Ashland Poetry Press publishes 2-4 books of poetry/year. Deadline: April 1. Prize: $1,000 plus book publication. Judged by Elizabeth Spires in 2016.

SOCIETY OF CLASSICAL POETS POETRY COMPETITION

The Society of Classical Poets, 11 Heather Ln., Mount Hope NY 10940. **E-mail:** submissions@classicalpoets.org. **Website:** www.classicalpoets.org. **Contact:** Evan Mantyk, president. Annual competition for a group of poems that address one or more of the following themes: beauty, human rights in China, classical culture, or humor. Poems must incorporate meter and rhyme. All entries are considered for publication. Submit 3-5 poems of up to 50 lines each. Deadline: December 31. Prize: $500. Judged by Evan Mantyk, the society's president.

THE SOW'S EAR CHAPBOOK COMPETITION

The Sow's Ear Review, 1748 Cave Ridge Rd., Mount Jackson VA 22842. (540)955-3955. **E-mail:** sepoetryreview@gmail.com. **Website:** www.sowsearpoetry.org. **Contact:** Sarah Kohrs, managing editor. *The Sow's Ear Poetry Review* sponsors an annual chapbook competition. Open to adults. Open to adults. Send 22-26 pages of poetry plus a title page and a table of contents, all without your name. On a separate sheet list chapbook title, your name, address, phone number, e-mail address if available, and publication credits for submitted poems, if any. No length limit on poems, but no more than one poem on a page. Simultaneous submission is allowed, but if your chapbook is accepted elsewhere, you must withdraw promptly from our competition. Poems previously published are acceptable if you hold publication rights. Send SASE or e-mail address for notification. Entries will not be returned. To submit online, visit our website. Deadline: May 1 (postmark). Prize: Offers $1,000, publication as the spring issue of the magazine, 25 author's copies, and distribution to subscribers.

THE SOW'S EAR POETRY COMPETITION

The Sow's Ear Poetry Review, 1748 Cave Ridge Road, Mount Jackson VA 22842. **E-mail:** SEPoetryReview@gmail.com. **Website:** www.sowsearpoetry.org. **Contact:** Sarah Kohrs, managing editor. Open to adults. Send unpublished poems to the address above. Please do not put your name on poems. Include a separate sheet with poem titles, name, address, phone, and e-mail address if available, or a SASE for notification of results. No length limit on poems. Simultaneous submission acceptable (checks with finalists before sending to final judge). Send poems in September or October. Deadline: November 1. Prize: $1,000, publication, and the option of publication for approximately 20 finalists.

THE EDWARD STANLEY AWARD

Prairie Schooner, 123 Andrews Hall, P.O. Box 880334, Lincoln NE 68588-0334. (402)472-0911. **Fax:** (402)472-9771. **E-mail:** prairieschooner@unl.edu. **Website:** www.prairieschooner.unl.edu. **Contact:** Editor in Chief. Offered annually for poetry published in *Prairie Schooner* in the previous year. Prize: $1,000.

STEVENS POETRY MANUSCRIPT CONTEST

NFSPS Stevens Poetry Manuscript Competition, 4 Bowie Pt, Sherwood AR 72120. **E-mail:** stevens.nfsps@gmail.com. **Website:** www.nfsps.org. **Contact:** Amanda Partridge, chair. National Federation of State Poetry Societies (NFSPS) offers annual award of $1,000, publication of ms, and 50 author's copies for the winning poetry manuscript by a single author. Submit 48-70 pages of poetry by a single author, typewritten, or computer printed. No illustrations. No author identification in the manuscript. No more than one poem per page. May include previously published poems (acknowledgements on separate sheet). Simultaneous and multiple submissions permitted. Deadline: Fall, varies from year to year. For 2018, probably September 15; Submissions open August 15. Prize: $1,000, publication and 50 copies of the book.

THE RUTH STONE POETRY PRIZE

Vermont College, 36 College St., Montpelier VT 05602. (802)828-8517. **E-mail:** hungermtn@vcfa.edu. **Website:** www.hungermtn.org. **Contact:** Samantha Kolber, managing editor. The Ruth Stone Poetry Prize is an annual poetry contest. Enter up to 3 original, unpublished poems. Do not include name or address on submissions; entries are read blind. Accepts submissions online or via postal mail. Deadline: March 1. Prize: One first place winner receives $1,000 and publication on Hunger Mountain online. Two honorable mentions receive $100 and publication on Hunger Mountain online. Judged by Major Jackson in 2017.

THE ELIZABETH MATCHETT STOVER MEMORIAL AWARD

Southwest Review, Southern Methodist University, P.O. Box 750374, Dallas TX 75275-0374. (214)768-1037. **Fax:** (214)768-1408. **E-mail:** swr@mail.smu.edu. **Website:** www.smu.edu/southwestreview. **Contact:** Greg Brownderville, editor-in-chief. Offered annually to the best works of poetry that have appeared in the magazine in the previous year. Please note that mss are submitted for publication, not for the prizes themselves. Guidelines for SASE and online. Prize: $300. Judged by Greg Brownderville and Preston Hutcherson.

STROKESTOWN INTERNATIONAL POETRY COMPETITION

Strokestown International Poetry Festival, Strokestown Poetry Festival Office, Strokestown, County Roscommon Ireland. (+353) 71 9633759. **E-mail:** director@strokestownpoetry.org. **Website:** www.strokestownpoetry.org. **Contact:** Martin Dyar, Director. Poem cannot exceed 70 lines. Ten short-listed poets will be invited to Strokestown for the festival. This annual competition was established to promote excellence in poetry and participation in the reading and writing of it. Acquires first publication rights. Deadline: January. Prize: 1st Place: €1,500; 2nd Place: €500; 3rd Place: €300; 3 shortlisted prizes of €100 each.

THE TAMPA REVIEW PRIZE FOR POETRY

University of Tampa, 401 W. Kennedy Blvd., Tampa FL 33606. 813-253-6266. **E-mail:** utpress@ut.edu. **Website:** www.ut.edu/tampareview. Annual award for the best previously unpublished collection of poetry (at least 48 pages, though preferably 60-100). Deadline: December 31. Prize: $2,000, plus publication.

THE TENTH GATE PRIZE

The Word Works, P. O. Box 42164, Washington D.C. 20015 USA. **E-mail:** editor@wordworksbooks.org. **Website:** www.wordworksbooks.org. **Contact:** Leslie McGrath, Series Editor; Nancy White, Editor. Publication and $1000 cash prize awarded annually by The Word Works to a full-length ms by a poet who has already published at least 2 full-length poetry collections. Submit 48-80 pages. Include acknowledgments and past book publications in the "NOTES" section of the online submissions manager. Submit via online submissions manager: wordworksbooks.org/submissions. Founded in honor of Jane Hirshfield, The Tenth Gate Prize supports the work of mid-career poets. Deadline: July 15. Open to submissions on June 1. Prize: $1,000 and publication. Judged by the editors.

TOR HOUSE PRIZE FOR POETRY

Robinson Jeffers Tor House Foundation, Poetry Prize Coordinator, Tor House Foundation, Box 223240, Carmel CA 93922. (831)624-1813. **Fax:** (831)624-3696. **E-mail:** thf@torhouse.org. **Website:** www.torhouse.org. **Contact:** Eliot Ruchowitz-Roberts, Poetry Prize Coordinator. The annual Prize for Poetry is a living memorial to American poet Robinson Jeffers (1887-1962). Open to well-crafted poetry in all styles, ranging from experimental work to traditional forms, including short narrative poems. Poems must be original and unpublished. Each poem should be typed on 8 1/2" by 11" paper, and no longer than three pages. On a cover sheet only, include: name, mailing address, telephone number and email; titles of poems; bio optional. Multiple and simultaneous submissions welcome. Deadline: March 15. Prize: $1,000 honorarium for award-winning poem; $200 Honorable Mention.

KINGSLEY & KATE TUFTS POETRY AWARDS

Claremont Graduate University, Claremont Graduate University, 160 E. Tenth St., Harper East B7, Claremont CA 91711-6165. (909)621-8974. **E-mail:** tufts@cgu.edu. **Website:** www.cgu.edu/tufts. The $100,000 Kingsley Tufts Poetry Award was created to both honor the poet and provide the resources that allow artists to continue working towards the pinnacle of their craft; the Kingsley Tufts Awards goes to a book published by a mid-career poet. The $10,000 Kate Tufts Award is presented annually for a first book by a poet of genuine promise. "Any poet will tell you that the only thing more rare than meaningful recognition is a meaningful payday. For two outstanding poets each year, the Kingsley and Kate Tufts awards represent both." Deadline: July 1, for books published in the preceding year. Prize: $100,000 for the Kingsley Tufts Poetry Award and $10,000 for the Kate Tufts Discovery Award. Please see website for current judges.

UTMOST CHRISTIAN POETRY CONTEST

Utmost Christian Writers Foundation, 121 Morin Maze NW, Edmonton AB T6K 1V1 Canada. (780)265-4650. **E-mail:** nnharms@telusplanet.net. **Website:** www.utmostchristianwriters.com. **Contact:** Nathan Harms, executive director. Utmost is founded on—and supported by—the dreams, interests and aspirations of individual people. Contest is only open to Christians. Poems may be rhymed or free verse, up to 60 lines, but must not have been published previously or have won any prize in any previous competition of any kind. Submit up to 5 poems. Deadline: February 28. Prizes: 1st Place: $1,000; 2nd Place: $500; 10 prizes of $100 are offered for honorable mention; $300 for best rhyming poem; and $200 for an honorable mention rhyming poem. Judged by a committee of the Directors of Utmost Christian Writers Foundation (who work under the direction of Barbara Mitchell, chief judge).

DANIEL VAROUJAN AWARD

New England Poetry Club, 376 School St., Watertown MA 02472. **E-mail:** contests@nepoetryclub.org. **Website:** www.nepoetryclub.org. **Contact:** Audrey Kalajin. For an unpublished poem (not a translation) worthy of Daniel Varoujan, a poet killed by the Turks in the genocide which destroyed three-fourths of the Armenian population. Previous winners may not enter again. Send entry in duplicate, one without name and address of writer. Deadline: May 31. Prize: $1,000. Judged by well-known poets and sometimes winners of previous NEPC contests.

VASSAR MILLER PRIZE IN POETRY

University of North Texas Press, 1155 Union Circle, #311336, Denton TX 76203. (940)565-2142. **Fax:** (940)565-4590. **Website:** http://untpress.unt.edu. **Contact:** John Poch. Annual prize awarded to a collection of poetry. Submit 50-80 pages. In years when the judge is announced, it is asked that students of the judge not enter to avoid a perceived conflict. All entries should contain identifying material only on the one cover sheet. Entries are read anonymously. Deadline: Mss may be submitted between 9 A.M. on September 1 and 5 P.M. on October 31, through online submissions manager only. Prize: $1,000 and publication by University of North Texas Press. Judged by a different eminent writer selected each year. Some prefer to remain anonymous until the end of the contest.

MARICA AND JAN VILCEK PRIZE FOR POETRY

Bellevue Literary Review, New York University School of Medicine, OBV-A612, 550 First Ave., New York NY 10016. (212)263-3973. **E-mail:** info@BLReview.org. **Website:** www.BLReview.org. **Contact:** Stacy Bodziak. The annual Marica and Jan Vilcek Prize for Poetry recognizes outstanding writing related to themes of health, healing, illness, the mind, and the body. All entries will be considered for publication. No previously published poems (including Internet publication). Submit up to 3 poems (5 pages maximum). Electronic (online) submissions only; combine all poems into 1 document and use first poem as document title. See guidelines for additional submission

details. Guidelines available for SASE or on website. Deadline: July 1. Prize: $1,000 for best poem and publication in *Bellevue Literary Review*. Previous judges include Mark Doty, Cornelius Eady, Naomi Shihab Nye, and Tony Hoagland.

WABASH PRIZE FOR POETRY

Sycamore Review, Department of English, 500 Oval Dr., Purdue University, West Lafayette IN 47907. **E-mail:** sycamore@purdue.edu; sycamorepoetry@purdue.edu. **Website:** www.sycamorereview.com/contest/. **Contact:** Anthony Sutton, editor-in-chief. Annual contest for unpublished poetry. For each submission, send up to 3 poems (no more than 6 total pages). Ms pages should be numbered and should include the title of each poem. See website for more guidelines. Submit online via Submittable. Deadline: December 1. Prize: $1,000 and publication.

THE WASHINGTON PRIZE

The Word Works, Dearlove Hall, SUNY Adirondack, 640 Bay Rd., Queensbury NY 12804. **E-mail:** editor@wordworksbooks.org. **Website:** www.wordworksbooks.org. **Contact:** Rebecca Kutzer-Rice, Washington Prize administrator. In addition to its general poetry book publications, The Word Works runs four imprints: The Washington Prize, The Tenth Gate Prize, International Editions, and the Hilary Tham Capital Collection. Selections announced in late summer. Book publication planned for spring of the following year. Submit a poetry ms of 48-80 pages. Submit online with no identifying information appearing within the manuscript; or, if on paper, include 2 title pages, 1 with and 1 without author information, including an acknowledgments page, a table of contents and a brief bio. Electronic submissions are accepted at www.wordworksbooks.org/submissions. The Washington Prize allows poets from all stages of their careers to compete on a level playing field for publication and national recognition. Deadline: Submit January 15-March 15 (postmark). Prize: $1,500 and publication of a book-length ms of original poetry in English by a living US or Canadian citizen. Judged by two tiers of readers, followed by five final judges working as a panel.

WERGLE FLOMP HUMOR POETRY CONTEST

Winning Writers, 351 Pleasant St., PMB 222, Northampton MA 01060. (866)946-9748. **Fax:** (413)280-0539. **E-mail:** adam@winningwriters.com.

Website: www.winningwriters.com. **Contact:** Adam Cohen. Winning Writers provides expert literary contest information to the public. It is one of the "101 Best Websites for Writers" (*Writer's Digest*). Submit one humor poem online. Length limit: 250 lines. The poem should be in English. Inspired gibberish is also accepted. Submissions may be previously published and may be entered in other contests. Deadline: April 1. Prize: 1st prize of $1,000; 2nd prize of $250; 10 honorable mentions of $100 each. All winners of cash prizes published on website. Judged by Jendi Reiter, assisted by Lauren Singer.

WHITE PINE PRESS POETRY PRIZE

White Pine Press, P.O. Box 236, Buffalo NY 14201. **E-mail:** wpine@whitepine.org. **Website:** www.whitepine.org. **Contact:** Dennis Maloney, editor. Offered annually for previously published or unpublished poets. Manuscript: 60-80 pages of original work; translations are not eligible. Poems may have appeared in magazines or limited-edition chapbooks. Open to any US citizen. Deadline: November 30 (postmarked). Prize: $1,000 and publication. Final judge is a poet of national reputation. All entries are screened by the editorial staff of White Pine Press.

STAN AND TOM WICK POETRY PRIZE

Wick Poetry Center, P.O. Box 5190, Kent OH 44240. (330)672-2067. **E-mail:** wickpoetry@kent.edu. **Website:** www.kent.edu/wick/stan-and-tom-wick-poetry-prize. **Contact:** David Hassler, director. Offered annually to a poet who has not previously published a full-length collection of poetry (a volume of 50 or more pages published in an edition of 500 or more copies). Submissions must consist of 50-70 pages of poetry, typed on one side only, with no more than one poem included on a single page. Also accepts submissions online through Submittable. See website for details and guidelines. Deadline: May 1. Submissions period begins February 1. Prize: $2,500 and publication of full-length book of poetry by Kent State University Press.

MILLER WILLIAMS POETRY PRIZE

University of Arkansas Press, McIlroy House, 105 N. McIlroy Avenue, Fayetteville AR 72701. (479)575-7258. **Fax:** (479)575-6044. **E-mail:** cmoss@uark.edu, mbieker@uark.edu. **Website:** https://www.uapress.com/millerwilliamspoetryseries/. **Contact:** Billy Collins, judge and series editor; Mike Bieker, director. Each year, the University of Arkansas Press accepts submissions for the Miller Williams Poetry Series and from the books selected awards the Miller Williams Poetry Prize in the following summer. Mss should be between 60-90 pages. Individual poems may have been published in chapbooks, journals, and anthologies. Guidelines available online. Submit online. Deadline: September 30. Accepts submissions all year long. Prize: $5,000 and publication. Up to three finalists will also receive publication. Judged by Billy Collins, series editor.

THE J. HOWARD AND BARBARA M.J. WOOD PRIZE

Poetry, 61 W. Superior St., Chicago IL 60654. (312)787-7070. **Fax:** (312)787-6650. **E-mail:** editors@poetrymagazine.org. **Website:** www.poetrymagazine.org. Offered annually for poems published in *Poetry* during the preceding year (October-September). Upon acceptance, *Poetry* licenses exclusive worldwide first serial rights, including electronic rights, for publication, as well as non-exclusive rights to reprint, reuse, and archive the work, in any format, in perpetuity. Copyright reverts to author upon first publication. Prize: $5,000.

WORKING PEOPLE'S POETRY COMPETITION

Blue Collar Review, P.O. Box 11417, Norfolk VA 23517. **E-mail:** red-ink@earthlink.net. **Website:** www.partisanpress.org. Poetry should be typed as you would like to see it published, with your name and address on each page. Include cover letter with entry. Guidelines available on website. Deadline: May 15. Prize: $100, 1-year subscription to *Blue Collar Review* (see separate listing in Magazines/Journals) and 1-year posting of winning poem to website.

JAMES WRIGHT POETRY AWARD

Mid-American Review, Dept. of English, Bowling Green State University, Bowling Green OH 43403. (419)372-2725. **Fax:** (419)372-4642. **E-mail:** clouda@bgsu.edu. **Website:** www.bgsu.edu/midamericanreview. **Contact:** Abigail Cloud, poetry editor. Offered annually for unpublished poetry. Open to all writers not associated with *Mid-American Review* or judge. Guidelines available online or for SASE. Deadline: November 1. Prize: $1,000 and publication in spring issue of *Mid-American Review*. Judged by editors and a well known poet, i.e., Kathy Fagan, Bob Hicok, Michelle Boisseau. Judged by Maggie Smith in 2016.

THE YALE SERIES OF YOUNGER POETS

Yale University Press, P.O. Box 209040, New Haven CT 06520-9040. **Website:** youngerpoets.yupnet.org. The Yale Series of Younger Poets champions the most promising new American poets. The Yale Younger Poets prize is the oldest annual literary award in the United States. Open to U.S. citizens under age 40 at the time of entry who have not published a volume of poetry; poets may have published a limited edition chapbook of 300 copies or less. Poems may have been previously published in newspapers and periodicals and used in the book ms if so identified. No translations. Submit 48-64 pages of poetry, paginated, with each new poem starting on a new page. Accepts hard copy and electronic submissions. Deadline: November 15. Submissions period begins October 1.

THE YEMASSEE POETRY CONTEST

Yemassee, Department of English, University of South Carolina, Columbia SC 29208. **E-mail:** editor@yemasseejournal.com. **Website:** http://yemasseejournal.com. **Contact:** Contest Coordinator. The annual Yemassee Poetry Contest offers a $1000 prize and publication in *Yemassee*. Submissions must be unpublished. Considers simultaneous submissions with notice of acceptance elsewhere. Submit 3-5 poems via Submittable page: https://yemassee.submittable.com/submit. Include cover letter with poet's name, contact information, and poem title(s); no identifying information on ms pages except poem title (which should appear on every page). Deadline: January 15.

ZONE 3 FIRST BOOK AWARD FOR POETRY

Zone 3, Austin Peay State University, Austin Peay State University, PO Box 4565, Clarksville TN 37044. (931)221-7031. **Fax:** (931)221-7149. **E-mail:** spofforda@aspu.edu; wallacess@apsu.edu. **Website:** www.apsu.edu/zone3/. **Contact:** Andrea Spofford, poetry editor; Susan Wallace, managing editor. Offered annually for anyone who has not published a full-length collection of poems (48 pages or more). Submit a ms of 48-80 pages. Deadline: May 1. Prize: $1,000 and publication.

MULTIPLE WRITING AREAS

🐚 ADELAIDE FESTIVAL AWARDS FOR LITERATURE

Arts SA, GPO Box 2308, Adelaide SA 5001 Australia. (61)(8)8463-5444. **Fax:** (61)(8)8463-5420. **E-mail:** artssa@dpc.sa.gov.au. **Website:** www.arts.sa.gov.au. The Adelaide Festival Awards for Literature are presented in even-numbered years during Adelaide Writer's week as part of the Adelaide Festival. Introduced by the South Australia Government, the awards celebrate Australia's writing culture by offering national and State-based literary prizes, as well as fellowships for South Australian writers. Award categories: Premier's Award, Children's Literature, Fiction, John Bray Poetry, Non-Fiction, Young Adult Fiction, Jill Blewett Playwright's and Wakefield Press Unpublished Manuscript. Deadline: June 26. Nominations open on February 27. Prize: $10,000-25,000 for each award.

🐚 AESTHETICA ART PRIZE

Aesthetica Magazine, P.O. Box 371, York YO23 1WL United Kingdom. **E-mail:** info@aestheticamagazine.com; artprize@aestheticamagazine.com. **Website:** www.aestheticamagazine.com. The Aesthetica Art Prize is a celebration of excellence in art from across the world and offers artists the opportunity to showcase their work to wider audiences and further their involvement in the international art world. There are 4 categories: Photograpic & Digital Art, Three Dimensional Design & Sculpture, Painting & Drawing, Video Installation & Performance. See guidelines at Artwork & Photography, Fiction, and Poetry. See guidelines at www.aestheticamagazine.com. The Aesthetica Art Prize is a celebration of excellence in art from across the world and offers artists the opportunity to showcase their work to wider audiences and further their involvement in the international art world. Deadline: August 31. Prizes include: £5,000 main prize courtesy of Hiscox, £1,000 Student Prize courtesy of Hiscox, group exhibition and publication in the Aesthetica Art Prize Anthology. Entry is £15 and permits submission of 2 works in one category.

☯ ALCUIN SOCIETY AWARDS FOR EXCELLENCE IN BOOK DESIGN IN CANADA

The Alcuin Society, P.O. Box 3216, Stn. Terminal, Vancouver BC V6B 3X8 Canada. (604)732-5403. **E-mail:** awards@alcuinsociety.com; info@alcuinsociety.com. **Website:** www.alcuinsociety.com. **Contact:** Leah Gordon. The Alcuin Society Awards for Excellence in Book Design in Canada is the only national competition for book design in Canada. Winners are selected from books designed and published in Canada. Awards are presented annually at appropriate ceremonies held each year. Winning books are exhibited nationally and internationally at the Tokyo, Frankfurt, and Leipzig Book Fairs, and are Canada's entries in the international competition in Leipzig, "Book Design from all over the World" in the following spring. Submit previously published material from the year before the award's call for entries. Submissions made by the publisher, author or designer (Canadian). Deadline: March 1. Prizes: 1st, 2nd, 3rd, and Honourable Mention in each category (at the discretion of the judges). Judged by professionals and those experienced in the field of book design.

MARIE ALEXANDER POETRY SERIES

English Department, 2801 S. University Ave., Little Rock AR 72204. **E-mail:** editor@mariealexanderseries.com. **Website:** mariealexanderseries.com. **Contact:** Nickole Brown. Annual contest for a collection of previously unpublished prose poems or flash fiction by a U.S. writer. Deadline: July 31. Open to submissions on July 1. Prize: $1,000, plus publication.

ALLIGATOR JUNIPER AWARD

Alligator Juniper/Prescott College, 220 Grove Ave., Prescott AZ 86301. (928)350-2012. **Fax:** (928)776-5102. **E-mail:** alligatorjuniper@prescott.edu. **Website:** www.prescott.edu/alligatorjuniper/national-contest/index.html. **Contact:** Skye Anicca, managing editor. Annual contest for unpublished fiction, creative nonfiction, and poetry. Open to all age levels. Each entrant receives a personal letter from staff regarding the status of their submission, as well as minor feedback on the piece. Accepts simultaneous submissions, but inform on cover letter and contact immediately, should work be selected elsewhere. Maximum length: 30 pages or 5 poems. Deadline: October 1. Prize: $1,000 plus publication in all three categories. Finalists in each genre are recognized as such, published, and paid in copies. Judged by the distinguished writers in each genre and Prescott College writing students enrolled in the Literary Journal Practicum course.

AMERICAS AWARD

Consortium of Latin American Studies Program, Stone Center for Latin American Studies, Tulane University, 100 Jones Hall, New Orleans LA 70118-5698. **Website:** http://claspprograms.org/americasaward. **Contact:** Denise Woltering. The Américas Award encourages and commends authors, illustrators, and publishers who produce quality children's and young adult books that portray Latin America, the Caribbean, or Latinos in the United States. Up to 2 awards (for primary and secondary reading levels) are given in recognition of US published works of fiction, poetry, folklore, or selected nonfiction (from picture books to works for young adults). The award winners and commended titles are selected for their (1) distinctive literary quality; (2) cultural contextualization; (3) exceptional integration of text, illustration and design; and (4) potential for classroom use. To nominate a copyright title from the previous year, publishers are invited to submit review copies to the committee members listed on the website. Publishers should send 8 copies of the nominated book. Deadline: January 4. Prize: $500, plaque and a formal presentation at the Library of Congress, Washington DC.

THE AMERICAN GEM LITERARY FESTIVAL

FilmMakers Magazine / Write Brothers, FilmMakers Magazine (filmmakers.com), Beverly Hills CA 90210. **E-mail:** info@filmmakers.com. **Website:** http://filmmakers.com/contests/short_story/. **Contact:** Jennifer Brooks. Worldwide contest to recognize excellent short screenplays and short stories. Ms submissions must be between 3-45 pages (there is an extra fee for anything between 46-65 pages) and up to industry standards. See website for more details. Must not have been previously optioned or sold to market or to a film producer. Preferable that the ms has not yet been adapted to a screenplay. Short stories should be no more than 50 pages, double-spaced, to a maximum of 12,500 words. Must not have been previously published. Deadlines: Early: Feb 29; Regular: April 30; Late: June 30; Final: July 31. Prize: Short Script: 1st Place: $1,000. Other cash and prizes to top 5.

AMERICAN LITERARY REVIEW CONTESTS

American Literary Review, P.O. Box 311307, University of North Texas, Denton TX 76203-1307. (940)565-2755. **E-mail:** americanliteraryreview@gmail.com. **Website:** www.americanliteraryreview.com. Contest to award excellence in short fiction, creative nonfiction, and poetry. Multiple entries are acceptable, but each entry must be accompanied with a reading fee. Do not put any identifying information in the file itself; include the author's name, title(s), address, e-mail address, and phone number in the boxes provided in the online submissions manager. Short fiction: Limit 8,000 words per work. Creative nonfiction: Limit

6,500 words per work. Deadline: October 1. Submission period begins June 1. Prize: $1,000 prize for each category, along with publication in the Spring online issue of the *American Literary Review*.

ANNUAL WRITING CONTEST

Lumina, the literary journal of Sarah Lawrence College, Sarah Lawrence College Slonim House, One Mead Way, Bronxville NY 10708. **E-mail:** lumina@gm.slc.edu. **Website:** www.luminajournal.com/contest. Annual writing contest in poetry, fiction, or creative nonfiction (varies by year). Please visit website in August/September for complete and updated contest rules. Typical reading period: September 1 - November 15. Electronic submissions only. Deadline varies by year. Usually in the early fall. Prize: cash.

ARIZONA LITERARY CONTEST AND BOOK AWARDS

Arizona Authors' Association, 6939 East Chaparral Rd., Paradise Valley AZ 85253-7000. (602)554-8101. **E-mail:** azauthors@gmail.com. **Website:** www.azauthors.com. **Contact:** Lisa Aquilina, president. Arizona Authors' Association sponsors annual literary competition in poetry, short story, essay, unpublished novels, and published books (fiction, nonfiction, and children's literature) and Arizona Book of the Year. Cash prizes awarded ($500 Book of the Year) from Green Pieces Press and 1st, 2nd, and 3rd place in seven categories ($150, $75 and $50, respectively) from Vignetta Syndicate LLC. New category in 2017, New Drama Writing, with a grand prize of $250. All category winners are published in the *Arizona Literary Magazine*. NEW PRIZE in 2018 for Unpublished Novel category. Winner receives a standard, traditional publishing contract through IngramElliott Book Publishers. NEW CATEGORY in 2018 - Published Cookbooks! Must have 2017 or 2018 copyright date at time of submission. Poetry, short story, essay, and new drama writing submissions must be unpublished. Work must have been published in the current or immediate past calendar year. Considers simultaneous submissions. Entry form and guidelines available on website or upon request. Deadline: July 2. Begins accepting submissions January 1. Finalists notified by Labor Day weekend. Prizes: Grand Prize, Arizona Book of the Year Award: $500. All categories except new drama writing: 1st Prize: $150 and publication; 2nd Prize: $75 and publication; 3rd Prize: $50 and publication. New drama writing grand prize $250

and publication. Features in *Arizona Literary Magazine* can be taken instead of money and publication. 1st and 2nd prize winners in poetry, essay, and short story are nominated for the Pushcart Prize. Judged by nationwide published authors, editors, literary agents, and reviewers. Winners announced at an awards dinner and ceremony held the first Saturday in November.

ARTIST TRUST FELLOWSHIP AWARD

1835 12th Ave., Seattle WA 98122. (209)467-8734, ext. 11. **Fax:** (866)218-7878. **E-mail:** info@artisttrust.org. **Website:** www.artisttrust.org. **Contact:** Miguel Guillen, program manager. Fellowships award $7,500 to practicing professional artists of exceptional talent and demonstrated ability. The Fellowship is a merit-based, not a project-based award. Recipients present a Meet the Artist Event to a community in Washington state that has little or no access to the artist and their work. Awards 14 fellowships of $7,500 and 2 residencies with $1,000 stipends at the Millay Colony. Artist Trust Fellowships are awarded in two-year cycles. Applicants must be 18 years of age or older, Washington State residents at the time of application and payment, and generative artists. Deadline: January 17. Applications available December 3. Prize: $7,500.

ARTS & LETTERS PRIZES

Arts & Letters Journal of Contemporary Culture, Campus Box 89, GC&SU, Milledgeville GA 31061. (478)445-1289. **E-mail:** al.journal@gcsu.edu. **Website:** al.gcsu.edu. **Contact:** The Editors. Offered annually for unpublished work. Deadline: March 31. Prize: $1,000 prize for each of the four major genres. Fiction, poetry, and creative nonfiction winners are published in Fall or Spring issue. The prize-winning one-act play is produced at the Georgia College campus (usually in March). Judged by the editors (initial screening); see website for final judges and further details about submitting work.

THE ATHENAEUM LITERARY AWARD

The Athenaeum of Philadelphia, 219 S. 6th St., Philadelphia PA 19106-3794. (215)925-2688. **Fax:** (215)925-3755. **E-mail:** jilly@PhilaAthenaeum.org. **Website:** http://www.philaathenaeum.org/literary.html. **Contact:** Jill LeMin Lee, Librarian. The Athenaeum Literary Award was established to recognize and encourage literary achievement among authors who are bona fide residents of Philadelphia or Pennsylvania living within a radius of 30 miles of City Hall at the time their book was written or published. Any volume of general literature is eligible; technical, scientific, and juvenile books are not included. Nominated works are reviewed on the basis of their significance and importance to the general public as well as for literary excellence. Only published works are eligible. Deadline: All nominations must be submitted prior to December 1st of the year of publication.

AUTUMN HOUSE POETRY, FICTION, AND NONFICTION PRIZES

5530 Penn Ave., Pittsburgh PA 15206. (412)362-2665. **E-mail:** info@autumnhouse.org. **Website:** autumnhouse.org. **Contact:** Christine Stroud, editor-in-chief. Offers annual prize and publication of book-length ms with national promotion. Submission must be unpublished as a collection, but individual poems, stories, and essays may have been previously published elsewhere. Considers simultaneous submissions. "Autumn House is a nonprofit corporation with the mission of publishing and promoting poetry and other fine literature. We have published books by Chana Bloch, Ellery Akers, Gerald Stern, Ruth L. Schwartz, Ed Ochester, Andrea Hollander, George Bilgere, Ada Limon, and many others." Submit 50-80 pages of poetry or 200-300 pages of prose (include 2 cover sheets requested). Guidelines available for SASE, by e-mail, or on website. Competition receives 1,500 entries/year. Winners announced through mailings, website, and ads in *Poets & Writers*, *American Poetry Review*, and *Writer's Chronicle* (extensive publicity for winner). Copies of winning books available from Amazon.com, Barnes & Noble, and other retailers. Deadline: June 30. Prize: The winner (in each of three categories) will receive book publication, $1,000 advance against royalties, and a $1,500 travel/publicity grant to promote his or her book. Judged by Kimiko Hahn (poetry), Dana Johnson (fiction), and Daisy Hernandez (nonfiction).

AWP AWARD SERIES

Association of Writers & Writing Programs, George Mason University, 4400 University Drive, MSN 1E3, Fairfax VA 22030. **E-mail:** supriya@awpwriter.org. **Website:** www.awpwriter.org. **Contact:** Supriya Bhatnagar, director of publications. AWP sponsors the Award Series, an annual competition for the publication of excellent new book-length works. The competition is open to all authors writing in English regardless of nationality or residence, and is available to published and unpublished authors alike. Guidelines on website. Entries must be unpublished. Open to any writer. Entries are not accepted via postal mail. Offered annually to foster new literary talent. Deadline: Postmarked between January 1 and February 28. Prize: AWP Prize for the Novel: $2,500 and publication by New Issues Press; Donald Hall Prize for Poetry: $5,500 and publication by the University of Pittsburgh Press; Grace Paley Prize in Short Fiction: $5,500 and publication by the University of Massachusetts Press; and AWP Prize for Creative Nonfiction: $2,500 and publication by the University of Georgia Press.

AWP INTRO JOURNALS PROJECT

The Association of Writers & Writing Programs, Dept. of English, Bluffton University, 1 University Dr., Bluffton OH 45817-2104. **E-mail:** awp@awpwriter.org. **Website:** www.awpwriter.org. **Contact:** Susan Streeter Carpenter. This is a prize for students in AWP member-university creative writing programs only. Authors are nominated by the head of the Creative Writing Department. Each school may nominate no more than 1 work of nonfiction, 1 work of short fiction, and 3 poems. Open to students in AWP member-university creative writing programs only. Deadline: December 1. Prize: $100, plus publication in participating journal. Judged by AWP.

THE BASKERVILLE PUBLISHERS POETRY AWARD & THE BETSY COLQUITT POETRY AWARD

descant, Texas Christian University's literary journal, TCU, Box 297270, Fort Worth TX 76129. **Fax:** (817)257-6239. **Website:** www.descant.tcu.edu. **Contact:** Matthew Pitt, Editor. Annual award for an outstanding poem published in the latest issue of *descant*. Deadline: September-April. Prize: $250 for Baskerville Award; $500 for Betsy Colquitt Award. Publication retains copyright, but will transfer it to the author upon request.

THE BLACK RIVER CHAPBOOK COMPETITION

Black Lawrence Press, 279 Claremont Ave, Mount Vernon NY 10552. **E-mail:** editors@blacklawrencepress.com. **Website:** www.blacklawrence.com. **Contact:** Kit Frick, senior editor. Twice each year Black Lawrence Press will run the Black River Chapbook Competition for an unpublished chapbook of poems or short fiction between 16-36 pages in length. Submit through Submittable. Spring deadline: May 31. Fall deadline: October 31. Prize: $500, publication, and

10 copies. Judged by a revolving panel of judges, in addition to the Chapbook Editor and other members of the BLP editorial staff.

THE BOARDMAN TASKER PRIZE FOR MOUNTAIN LITERATURE

The Boardman Tasker Charitable Trust, 8 Bank View Rd., Darley Abbey Derby DE22 1EJ UK. 01332 342246. **E-mail:** steve@people-matter.co.uk. **Website:** www.boardmantasker.com. **Contact:** Steve Dean. Offered annually to reward a work with a mountain theme, whether fiction, nonfiction, drama, or poetry, written in the English language (initially or in translation). Subject must be concerned with a mountain environment. Previous winners have been books on expeditions, climbing experiences, a biography of a mountaineer, novels. Guidelines available in January by e-mail or on website. Entries must be previously published. Open to any writer. Writers may obtain information, but entry is by publishers only (includes self-publishing). Awarded for a work published or distributed for the first time in the United Kingdom during the previous year. Not an anthology. The award is to honor Peter Boardman and Joe Tasker, who disappeared on Everest in 1982. Deadline: August 1. Prize: £3,000 Judged by a panel of 3 judges elected by trustees.

BOOK OF THE YEAR AWARD

Saskatchewan Book Awards, Inc., P.O. Box 20025, Regina SK S4P 4J7 Canada. (306)569-1585. **E-mail:** director@bookawards.sk.ca. **Website:** www.bookawards.sk.ca. Offered annually. This award is presented to a Saskatchewan author for the best book, judged on the quality of writing. Books from the following categories will be considered: children's; drama; fiction (short fiction by a single author, novellas, novels); nonfiction (all categories of nonfiction writing except cookbooks, directories, how-to books, or bibliographies of minimal critical content); poetry. Visit website for more details. Deadline: November 1. Prize: $3,000 (CAD).

BOROONDARA LITERARY AWARDS

City of Boroondara, 340 Camberwell Rd., Camberwell VIC 3124 Australia. **E-mail:** bla@boroondara.vic.gov.au. **Website:** www.boroondara.vic.gov.au/literary-awards. Contest for unpublished work in 2 categories: Young Writers who live, go to school or work in the City of Boroondara: 5th-6th grade (Junior), 7th-9th grade (Middle), and 10th-12th grade

(Senior), prose and poetry on any theme; and Open Short Story from residents of Australia (1,500-3,000 words). Deadline: 5pm on August 28. Prizes: Young Writers, Junior: 1st Place: $150; 2nd Place: $100; 3rd Place: $50. Young Writers, Middle and Senior: 1st Place: $600; 2nd Place: $400; 3rd Place: $200. Open Short Story: 1st Place: $1,500; 2nd Place: $1000; 3rd Place $500.

THE BRIAR CLIFF REVIEW FICTION, POETRY, AND CREATIVE NONFICTION COMPETITION

The Briar Cliff Review, Briar Cliff University, 3303 Rebecca St., Sioux City IA 51104-0100. **E-mail:** tricia.currans-sheehan@briarcliff.edu (editor); jeanne.emmons@briarcliff.edu (poetry). **Website:** www.bcreview.org. **Contact:** Tricia Currans-Sheehan, editor. *The Briar Cliff Review* sponsors an annual contest offering $1,000 and publication to each 1st Prize winner in fiction, poetry, and creative nonfiction. Previous year's winner and former students of editors ineligible. Winning pieces accepted for publication on the basis of first-time rights. Considers simultaneous submissions, "but notify us immediately upon acceptance elsewhere. We guarantee a considerate reading." No mss returned. Word limit for short story and creative nonfiction is 5,000. For poetry, three poems, no more than five pages total. Submit via Submittable or post. To reward good writers and showcase quality writing. Deadline: November 1. Prize: $1,000 and publication to each prize winner in fiction, poetry, and creative nonfiction. Judged by *Briar Cliff Review* editors.

THE BRIDPORT PRIZE

P.O. Box 6910, Dorset DT6 9QB United Kingdom. **E-mail:** info@bridportprize.org.uk; kate@bridportprize.org.uk. **Website:** www.bridportprize.org.uk. **Contact:** Kate Wilson, Bridport Prize administrator. Award to promote literary excellence, discover new talent. Categories: Short stories, poetry, flash fiction, first novel. Entries must be unpublished. Length: 5,000 maximum for short stories; 42 lines for poetry, 250 words for flash fiction and 8,000 words max for opening chapters of a novel. Deadline: May 31. Prize: £5,000; £1,000; £500; various runners-up prizes and publication of approximately 13 best stories and 13 best poems in anthology; plus 6 best flash fiction stories. 1st Prize of £1,000 for the best short, short story of under 250 words. £1,000 plus up to a year's mentoring for winner of Peggy Chapman-Andrews Award for a first novel. Judged by 1 judge for short stories (in 2018, Monica Ali), 1 judge for poetry (in 2018, Daljit Nagra) and 1 judge for flash fiction (in 2018 Monica Ali). The Novel award is judged by a group comprising representatives from The Literary Consultancy, A.M. Heath Literary Agents, and (in 2018) judge Kamila Shamsie.

🌑 BRITISH CZECH AND SLOVAK ASSOCIATION WRITING COMPETITION

24 Ferndale, Tunbridge Wells Kent TN2 3NS England. **E-mail:** prize@bcsa.co.uk. **Website:** www.bcsa.co.uk/specials.html. Annual contest for original writing (entries should be 1,500-2,000 words) in English on the links between Britain and the Czech/Slovak Republics, or describing society in transition in the Republics since 1989. Entries can be fact or fiction. Topics can include history, politics, the sciences, economics, the arts, or literature. Deadline: June 30. Winners announced in November. Prize: 1st Place: £300; 2nd Place: £100.

❂ BURNABY WRITERS' SOCIETY CONTEST

E-mail: info@bws.ca. **Website:** www.bws.ca; www.burnabywritersnews.blogspot.com. **Contact:** Contest Committee. Offered annually for unpublished work. Open to all residents of British Columbia. Categories vary from year to year. Send SASE for current rules. For complete guidelines see website or burnabywritersnews.blogspot.com. Purpose is to encourage talented writers in all genres. Deadline: May 31. Prizes: 1st Place: $200; 2nd Place: $100; 3rd Place: $50; and public reading.

CALIFORNIA BOOK AWARDS

Commonwealth Club of California, 110 The Embarcadero, San Francisco CA 94105. (415)597-6700. **Fax:** (415)597-6729. **E-mail:** bookawards@commonwealthclub.org. **Website:** www.commonwealthclub.org/. **Contact:** Renee Miguel. Offered annually to recognize California's best writers and illuminate the wealth and diversity of California-based literature. Award is for published submissions appearing in print during the previous calendar year. Can be nominated by publisher or author. Open to California residents (or residents at time of publication). Submit at least 6 copies of each book entered with an official entry form. Open to books, published during the year prior to the contest, whose author must have been a legal resident of California at the time the manuscript was submitted for publication. Entry form and guidelines available for SASE or on website. Deadline: December 22. Prize: Medals and cash prizes to be awarded at publicized event. Judged by 12-15 California professionals with a diverse range of views, backgrounds, and literary experience.

❂ CANADIAN AUTHORS ASSOCIATION AWARDS PROGRAM

6 West St. N, Suite 203, Orillia ON L3V 5B8 Canada. (705)325-3926. **E-mail:** admin@canadianauthors.org. **Website:** www.canadianauthors.org. **Contact:** Anita Purcell. Offered annually for fiction, poetry, and Canadian history. Entrants must be Canadians by birth, naturalized Canadians, or landed immigrants. Entry form required for all awards. Obtain entry form from contact name or download from website. Deadline: January 15. Prize: Cash and a silver medal.

CBC LITERARY PRIZES/PRIX DE LA CRÉATION RADIO-CANADA

CBC/Radio-Canada, Canada Council for the Arts, *enRoute* magazine, Banff Centre for Arts and Creativity, P.O. Box 6000, Montreal QC H3C 3A8 Canada. (877)888-6788. **E-mail:** canadawrites@cbc.ca. **Website:** www.cbcbooks.ca. **Contact:** Daphné Santos-Vieira, coordinator. The CBC Literary Prizes competitions are the only literary competitions that celebrate original, unpublished works in Canada's two official languages. There are 3 categories: short story, nonfiction and poetry. Submissions to the short story and nonfiction categories must be 1,200-1,800 words; poetry submissions must be up to 600 words (no minimum word count). Poetry submissions can take the form of a long narrative poem, a sequence of connected poems, or a group of unconnected poems. Canadian citizens, living in Canada or abroad, and permanent residents of Canada are eligible to enter. Deadline: September 1 for short story; February 28 for nonfiction; April 1 for poetry. See website for when each competition is accepting entries. Prize: For each category, in both English and French: 1st Prize: $6,000; 4 finalists each receive $1,000. In addition, winning entries are published in Air Canada's *enRoute* magazine and broadcast on CBC radio. Winning authors also get a 10-day residency at the Banff Centre for Arts and Creativity. First publication rights are granted by winners to *enRoute* magazine and broadcast rights are given to CBC radio. Submissions are judged blind by a jury of qualified writers and editors from around the country. Each category has 3 jurors.

CHAUTAUQUA LITERARY JOURNAL ANNUAL EDITORS PRIZES

Chautauqua Literary Journal, P.O. Box 2039, York Beach ME 03910 (for contest entries only). **E-mail:** clj@uncw.edu. **Website:** www.ciweb.org/literary-arts/literary-journal. **Contact:** Jill and Philip Gerard, co-editors. Annual award for work that best captures the spirit of Chautauqua Institution and the theme. Offered for unpublished work in the categories of poetry and prose (short stories, flash, and/or creative nonfiction). First place winner automatically nominated for the Pushcart Prize. All submissions must be submitted through Submittable. Guidelines available online at http://ciwebdev.squarespace.com/submission-guidelines/. Deadline: Reading periods are August 15-November 15 and February 15-April 15. Prize: 1st Place: $500; 2nd Place: $250; 3rd Place: $100.

CHRISTIAN BOOK AWARD® PROGRAM

Evangelical Christian Publishers Association, 5801 S. McClintock Dr, Suite 104, Tempe AZ 85283. (480)966-3998. **Fax:** (480)966-1944. **E-mail:** info@ecpa.org. **Website:** www.ecpa.org. **Contact:** Stan Jantz, ED. The Evangelical Christian Publishers Association (ECPA) recognizes quality and encourages excellence by presenting the ECPA Christian Book Awards® (formerly known as Gold Medallion) each year. Categories include Christian Living, Biography & Memoir, Faith & Culture, Children, Young People's Literature, Devotion & Gift, Bibles, Bible Reference Works, Bible Study, Ministry Resources and New Author. All entries must be evangelical in nature and submitted through an ECPA member publisher. Books must have been published in the calendar year prior to the award. Publishing companies submitting entries must be ECPA members in good standing. See website for details. The Christian Book Awards® recognize the highest quality in Christian books and is among the oldest and most prestigious awards program in Christian publishing. Submission period runs September 1-30. Judged by experts, authors and retailers with years of experience in their field.

☼ THE CITY OF VANCOUVER BOOK AWARD

Cultural Services Dept., Woodward's Heritage Building, 111 W. Hastings St., Suite 501, Vancouver BC V6B 1H4 Canada. (604)871-6634. **Fax:** (604)871-6005. **E-mail:** marnie.rice@vancouver.ca; culture@vancouver.ca. **Website:** https://vancouver.ca/people-programs/city-of-vancouver-book-award.aspx. The annual City of Vancouver Book Award recognizes authors of excellence of any genre who contribute to the appreciation and understanding of Vancouver's history, unique character, or the achievements of its residents. The book must exhibit excellence in one or more of the following areas: content, illustration, design, format. The book must not be copyrighted prior to the previous year. Submit four copies of book. See website for details and guidelines. Deadline: May 18. Prize: $3,000. Judged by an independent jury.

CLOUDBANK JOURNAL CONTEST

P.O. Box 610, Corvallis OR 97339. (541)752-0075. **E-mail:** michael@cloudbankbooks.com. **Website:** www.cloudbankbooks.com. **Contact:** Michael Malan. *Cloudbank* is a 96-page print journal published annually. Included are poems, flash fiction and book reviews. Regular submissions and contest submissions are accepted. An annual book contest, entitled the Vern Rutsala Book Prize, results in a published book of poetry and/or flash fiction. For *Cloudbank* contest submissions, the writer's name, address, e-mail, and the titles of the poems/flash fiction pieces being submitted should be typed on a cover sheet only, not on the pages of poems or flash fiction. Submit no more than 5 poems or flash fiction pieces (500 words or less) for the contest or for regular submissions. For the book contest, submit an unpublished manuscript of 60 to 90 pages. Deadline: *Cloudbank* contest due date is the last day in February. The Vern Rutslala Book contest due date is the last day in October. Prize: $200 and publication, plus an extra copy of the issue in which the winning poem appears. Two contributors' copies will be sent to writers whose work appears in the magazine. The book contest winner receives $1,000 and publication of the manuscript. The *Cloudbank* contest is judged by Michael Malan and editorial staff. The Vern Rutsala Book contest is judged by an outside author.

COLORADO BOOK AWARDS

Colorado Humanities & Center for the Book, 7935 E. Prentice Ave., Suite 450, Greenwood Village CO 80111. (303)894-7951. **Fax:** (303)864-9361. **E-mail:** bess@coloradohumanities.org. **Website:** www.coloradohumanities.org. **Contact:** Bess Maher. An annual program that celebrates the accomplishments of Colorado's outstanding authors, editors, illustrators, and photographers. Awards are presented in at least ten categories including anthology/collection, biography, children's, creative nonfiction, fiction, history, nonfiction, pictorial, poetry, and young adult. To be eligible for a Colorado Book Award, a primary contributor to the book must be a Colorado writer, editor, illustrator, or photographer. Current Colorado residents are eligible, as are individuals engaged in ongoing literary work in the state and authors whose personal history, identity, or literary work reflect a strong Colorado influence. Authors not currently Colorado residents who feel their work is inspired by or connected to Colorado should submit a letter with his/her entry describing the connection. Deadline: January 9.

THE CRUCIBLE POETRY AND FICTION COMPETITION

Crucible, Barton College, College Station, Wilson NC 27893. (800)345-4973 x6450. **E-mail:** crucible@barton.edu. **Website:** www.barton.edu. **Contact:** Terrence L. Grimes, editor. Open annually to all writers. Entries must be completely original, never published, and in ms form. Does not accept simultaneous submissions. Fiction is limited to 8,000 words; poetry is limited to 5 poems. Guidelines online or by email or for SASE. All submissions should be electronic. Deadline: May 1. Prize: 1st Place: $150; 2nd Place: $100 (for both poetry and fiction). Winners are also published in *Crucible*. Judged by in-house editorial board.

THE CUTBANK CHAPBOOK CONTEST

CutBank Literary Magazine, *CutBank*, University of Montana, English Dept., LA 133, Missoula MT 59812. **E-mail:** editor.cutbank@gmail.com. **Website:** www.cutbankonline.org. **Contact:** Kate Barrett, editor-in-chief. This competition is open to original English language mss in the genres of poetry, fiction, and creative nonfiction. While previously published stand-alone pieces or excerpts may be included in a ms, the ms as a whole must be an unpublished work. Looking for startling, compelling, and beautiful original work. "We're looking for a fresh, powerful manuscript. Maybe it will overtake us quietly; gracefully defy genres; satisfyingly subvert our expectations; punch us in the mouth page in and page out. We're interested in both prose and poetry—and particularly work that straddles the lines between genres." Accepts online submissions only. Submit up to 25-40 pages of poetry or prose. Guidelines available online. Deadline: March 31. Submissions period begins January1. Prize: $1,000

and 25 contributor copies. Judged by a guest judge each year.

CWW ANNUAL WISCONSIN WRITERS AWARDS

Council for Wisconsin Writers, 4964 Gilkeson Rd, Waunakee WI 53597. **E-mail:** karlahuston@gmail.com. **Website:** www.wiswriters.org. **Contact:** Geoff Gilpin, president and annual awards co-chair; Karla Huston, secretary and annual awards co-chair; Sylvia Cavanaugh, annual awards co-chair; Edward Schultz, annual awards co-chair, Erik Richardson, annual awards co-chair. Offered annually for work published by Wisconsin writers during the previous calendar year. Nine awards: Major Achievement (presented in alternate years); short fiction; short nonfiction; nonfiction book; poetry book; fiction book; children's literature; Lorine Niedecker Poetry Award; Christopher Latham Sholes Award for Outstanding Service to Wisconsin Writers (presented in alternate years); Essay Award for Young Writers. Open to Wisconsin residents. Entries may be submitted via postal mail only. See website for guidelines and entry forms. Deadline: January 31. Submissions open on November 1. Prizes: First place prizes: $500. Honorable mentions: $50. List of judges available on website.

DANA AWARDS IN THE NOVEL, SHORT FICTION, AND POETRY

200 Fosseway Dr., Greensboro NC 27445. (336)644-8028. **E-mail:** danaawards@gmail.com. **Website:** www.danaawards.com. **Contact:** Mary Elizabeth Parker, chair. Three awards offered annually for unpublished work written in English. Works previously published online are not eligible. The Dana Awards are re-vamping. The Novel Award is now increased to $2,000, based on a new partnership with Blue Mary Books: Blue Mary has agreed to consider for possible publication not only the Novel Award winning manuscript, but the top 9 other Novel finalists, as well as the 30 top Novel semifinalists. The Short Fiction and Poetry Awards offer the traditional $1,000 awards each and do not offer a publishing option (currently, Blue Mary publishes only novels). See website for further updates. Categories: Novel: For the first 40 pages of a novel completed or in progress; Fiction: Short fiction (no memoirs) up to 10,000 words; Poetry: For best group of 5 poems based on excellence of all 5 (no light verse, no single poem over 100 lines). Purpose is monetary award for work that has not been previously

published or received monetary award, but will accept work published simply for friends and family. Deadline: October 31 (postmarked). Prizes: $2,000 for the Novel Award; $1,000 each for the Short Fiction and Poetry awards awards.

DIAGRAM CHAPBOOK CONTEST

Department of English, University of Arizona, P.O. Box 210067, Tucson AZ 85721-0067. **E-mail:** nmp@thediagram.com; editor@thediagram.com. **Website:** www.thediagram.com/contest.html. **Contact:** Ander Monson, editor. Contest for prose, poetry, or hybrid manuscript between 18-44 pages. Deadline: April 28. Check website for more details. Prize: $1,000 and publication. Finalist essay also published. Judged by editor Ander Monson.

DIAGRAM/NEW MICHIGAN PRESS CHAPBOOK CONTEST

New Michigan Press, P.O. Box 210067, English, ML 424, University of Arizona, Tucson AZ 85721. **E-mail:** nmp@thediagram.com. **Website:** www.thediagram.com. **Contact:** Ander Monson, editor. The annual *DIAGRAM*/New Michigan Press Chapbook Contest offers $1,000, plus publication and author's copies, with discount on additional copies. Submit 18-44 pages of poetry, fiction, mixed-genre, or genre-bending work. Do not send originals of anything. Include SASE. Guidelines available on website. Deadline: April 28. Prize: $1,000, plus publication. Finalist chapbooks also considered for publication. Judged by editor Ander Monson.

EATON LITERARY AGENCY'S ANNUAL AWARDS PROGRAM

Eaton Literary Agency, P.O. Box 49795, Sarasota FL 34230-6795. (941)366-6589. **Fax:** (941)365-4679. **E-mail:** eatonlit@aol.com. **Website:** www.eatonliterary.com. **Contact:** Richard Lawrence, President. Offered biannually for unpublished mss. Entries must be unpublished. Open to any writer. Guidelines available for SASE, by fax, e-mail, or on website. Accepts inquiries by fax, phone, and e-mail. Results announced in April and September. Winners notified by mail. For contest results, send SASE, fax, e-mail, or visit website. Deadline: March 31 (short story); August 31 (book-length). Prize: $2,500 (book-length); $500 (short story). Judged by an independent agency in conjunction with some members of Eaton's staff.

THE VIRGINIA FAULKNER AWARD FOR EXCELLENCE IN WRITING

Prairie Schooner, 123 Andrews Hall, University of Nebraska-Lincoln, Lincoln NE 68588-0334. (402)472-0911. **Fax:** (402)472-1817. **E-mail:** PrairieSchooner@unl.edu. **Website:** www.prairieschooner.unl.edu. **Contact:** Kwame Dawes. Offered annually for work published in *Prairie Schooner* in the previous year. Categories: short stories, essays, novel excerpts, and translations. Accepts inquiries by fax and e-mail. Reads unsolicited mss between May 1 and September 1. Winning entry must have been published in *Prairie Schooner* in the year preceding the award. Results announced in the Spring issue. Winners notified by mail in February or March. Prize: $1,000. Judged by editorial board.

THE WILLIAM FAULKNER-WILLIAM WISDOM CREATIVE WRITING COMPETITION

Faulkner - Wisdom Competition, Pirate's Alley Faulkner Society, Inc., The Pirate's Alley Faulkner Society, Inc., 624 Pirate's Alley, New Orleans LA 70116-3233. (504)586-1609. **E-mail:** faulkhouse@aol.com. **Website:** www.wordsandmusic.org. general craft **Contact:** Rosemary James, award director. See guidelines posted at www.wordsandmusic.org. Deadline: May 15. Prizes: $750-7,500 depending on category. Judged by established authors, literary agents, and acquiring editors.

FINELINE COMPETITION FOR PROSE POEMS, SHORT SHORTS, AND ANYTHING IN BETWEEN

Mid-American Review, Dept. of English, Bowling Green State University, Bowling Green OH 43403. (419)372-2725. **E-mail:** mar@bgsu.edu. **Website:** www.bgsu.edu/midamericanreview. **Contact:** Abigail Cloud, editor-in-chief. Offered annually for previously unpublished submissions. Contest open to all writers not associated with current judge or *Mid-American Review*. Deadline: June 1. Prize: $1,000, plus publication in fall issue of *Mid-American Review*; 10 finalists receive notation plus possible publication. Judge will be a contemporary writer of note.

FIRST NOVEL CONTEST

Harrington & Harrington Press, 3400 Yosemite, San Diego CA 92109. **E-mail:** press@harringtonandharrington.com. **Website:** www.harringtonandharrington.com. **Contact:** Laurie Champion, contest/

award director. Annual contest for any writer who has not previously published a novel. Entries may be self-published. Accepts full-length works in literary fiction, creative nonfiction, memoir, genre fiction, and short story collections. No poetry. Guidelines available online. Harrington & Harrington Press aims to support writers, and the First Novel Contest will provide many ways to promote authors through networks and connections with writers, artists, and those involved in the technical production of art. Deadline: August 15. Prize: $500 advance royalty and publication by Harrington & Harrington Press. Judged by the Harrington & Harrington staff for the preliminary round. A respected author with numerous publications will act as the final judge.

🌑 FISH SHORT MEMOIR PRIZE

Fish Publishing, Durrus, Bantry Co. Cork Ireland. **E-mail:** info@fishpublishing.com. **Website:** www.fishpublishing.com. Annual worldwide contest to recognize the best memoirs submitted to Fish Publishing. Submissions must not have been previously published. Enter online or via postal mail. See website for full details. Word limit: 4,000. Deadline: January 31. Prize: 1st Prize: $1,000. The 10 best memoirs will be published in the Fish Anthology, launched in July at the West Cork Literary Festival.

THE FLORIDA REVIEW EDITOR'S PRIZE

Dept. of English, P.O. Box 161346, University of Central Florida, P.O. Box 161346, Orlando FL 32816. **E-mail:** flreview@mail.ucf.edu. **Website:** http://floridareview.cah.ucf.edu/. Annual awards for the best unpublished fiction, poetry, and creative nonfiction. Deadline: March 17. Prize: $1,000 (in each genre) and publication in *The Florida Review*. Judged by the editors in each genre. Judging is blind, so names should not appear on mss.

FOREWORD'S INDIES BOOK OF THE YEAR AWARDS

Foreword Magazine, 425 Boardman Ave, Traverse City MI 49684. (231)933-3699. **Website:** www.forewordreviews.com. **Contact:** Michele Lonoconus. Awards offered annually. In order to be eligible, books must have a current year copyright and be independently published which includes university presses, privately held presses, and self-published authors. International submissions are welcome. New editions of previously published books are eligible if significant content has been changed and the book has a new ISBN. Reissued editions in new formats are not eligible. *Foreword's*INDIES Book of the Year Awards were established to bring increased attention from librarians, booksellers, and avid readers, to the literary achievements of independent publishers and their authors. Deadline: January 15th. Prize: $1,500 cash will be awarded to a Best Fiction and Best Nonfiction choice. Our awards process is unique and well respected because we assemble a jury of volunteer booksellers and librarians to make the final judgment on the books and who select winners based on their experience with readers. Their decisions also take into consideration editorial excellence, professional production, originality of the narrative, author credentials relative to the subject matter, and the value the title adds to its genre.

♻ FREEFALL SHORT PROSE AND POETRY CONTEST

Freefall Literary Society of Calgary, 922 9th Ave. SE, Calgary AB T2G 0S4 Canada. **E-mail:** editors@freefallmagazine.ca. **Website:** www.freefallmagazine.ca. **Contact:** Ryan Stromquist, managing editor. Offered annually for unpublished work in the categories of poetry (5 poems/entry) and prose (3,000 words or less). Recognizes writers and offers publication credits in a literary magazine format. Contest rules and entry form online. Acquires first Canadian serial rights; ownership reverts to author after one-time publication. Deadline: December 31. Prize: 1st Place: $500 (CAD); 2nd Place: $250 (CAD); 3rd Place: $75; Honorable Mention: $25. All prizes include publication in the spring edition of *FreeFall Magazine*. Winners will also be invited to read at the launch of that issue, if such a launch takes place. Honorable mentions in each category will be published and may be asked to read. Travel expenses not included. Judged by current guest editor for issue (who are also published authors in Canada).

♻ GOVERNOR GENERAL'S LITERARY AWARDS

Canada Council for the Arts, 150 Elgin St., P.O. Box 1047, Ottawa ON K1P 5V8 Canada. (800)263-5588, ext. 5573. **Website:** ggbooks.ca. The Canada Council for the Arts provides a wide range of grants and services to professional Canadian artists and art organizations in dance, media arts, music, theatre, writing, publishing, and the visual arts. Books must be first edition literary trade books written, translated, or illustrated by Canadian citizens or permanent residents of Canada and published in Canada or abroad in the previous year. In the case of translation, the original work must also be a Canadian-authored title. For complete eligibility criteria, deadlines, and submission procedures, please visit the website at www.canadacouncil.ca. The Governor General's Literary Awards are given annually for the best English-language and French-language work in each of 7 categories, including fiction, non-fiction, poetry, drama, young people's literature (text), young people's literature (illustrated books), and translation. Deadline: Depends on the book's publication date. See website for details. Prize: Each GG winner receives $25,000. Non-winning finalists receive $1,000. Publishers of the winning titles receive a $3,000 grant for promotional purposes. Evaluated by fellow authors, translators, and illustrators. For each category, a jury makes the final selection.

GREAT LAKES COLLEGES ASSOCIATION NEW WRITERS AWARD

The Great Lakes Colleges Association, 535 W. William St., Suite 301, Ann Arbor MI 48103. (734)661-2350. **Fax:** (734)661-2349. **E-mail:** wegner@glca.org. **Website:** glca.org/program-menu/new-writers-award. **Contact:** Gregory R. Wegner, Director of Program Development: wegner@glca.org.. The Great Lakes Colleges Association (GLCA) is a consortium of 13 independent liberal arts colleges in Ohio, Michigan, Indiana, and Pennsylvania. Nominations should be made by the publisher and should emphasize literary excellence. A publisher can nominate only one author per year for any given category. A publisher can nominate one author in each of the three categories (poetry, fiction, creative nonfiction) in a single year if desired. The Award's purpose is to celebrate literary achievement in a writer's first-published volume of fiction, poetry, or nonfiction. Deadline: June 25, 2018. Prize: Honorarium of at least $500 from each member college that invites a winning to give a reading on its campus. Each award winner receives invitations from several of the 13 colleges of the GLCA to visit campus. At these campus events an author will give readings, meet students and faculty, and occasionally visit college classes. In addition to the $500 honorarium for each campus visit, travel costs to colleges are paid by GLCA and its member colleges. Judged by professors of literature and writers in residence at GLCA colleges.

HACKNEY LITERARY AWARDS

4650 Old Looney Mill Rd, Birmingham AL 35243. **E-mail:** info@hackneyliteraryawards.org. **Website:** www.hackneyliteraryawards.org. **Contact:** Myra Crawford, PhD, executive director. Offered annually for unpublished novels, short stories (maximum 5,000 words), and poetry (50 line limit). Guidelines on website. Deadline: September 30 (novels), November 30 (short stories and poetry). Prize: $5,000 in annual prizes for poetry and short fiction ($2,500 national and $2,500 state level). 1st Place: $600; 2nd Place: $400; 3rd Place: $250; plus $5,000 for an unpublished novel. Competition winners will be announced on the website each March.

ERIC HOFFER AWARD

Hopewell Publications, LLC, P.O. Box 11, Titusville NJ 08560-0011. **Fax:** (609)964-1718. **E-mail:** info@hopepubs.com. **Website:** www.hofferaward.com. **Contact:** Dawn Shows, EHA Coordinator. Annual contest for previously published books. Recognizes excellence in independent publishing in many unique categories: Art (titles capture the experience, execution, or demonstration of the arts); Poetry (all styles); Chapbook (40 pages or less, artistic assembly); General Fiction (nongenre-specific fiction); Commercial Fiction (genre-specific fiction); Children (titles for young children); Young Adult (titles aimed at the juvenile and teen markets); Culture (titles demonstrating the human or world experience); Memoir (titles relating to personal experience); Business (titles with application to today's business environment and emerging trends); Reference (titles from traditional and emerging reference areas); Home (titles with practical applications to home or home-related issues, including family); Health (titles promoting physical, mental, and emotional well-being); Self-help (titles involving new and emerging topics in self-help); Spiritual (titles involving the mind and spirit, including relgion); Legacy Fiction and Nonfiction (titles over 2 years of age that hold particular relevance to any subject matter or form); E-book Fiction; E-book Nonfiction. Open to any writer of published work within the last 2 years, including categories for older books. This contest recognizes excellence in independent publishing in many unique categories. Also awards the Montaigne Medal for most though-provoking book, the Da Vinci Eye for best cover, and the First Horizon Award for best new authors. Results published in the US Review of

Books. Deadline: January 21. Grand Prize: $2,500; honors (winner, runner up, honorable mentions) in each category, including the Montaigne Medal (most thought-provoking), da Vinci Art (cover art), First Horizon (first book), and Best in Press (small, academic, micro, self-published).

TOM HOWARD/JOHN H. REID FICTION & ESSAY CONTEST

Winning Writers, 351 Pleasant St., PMB 222, Northampton MA 01060-3961. (866)946-9748. **Fax:** (413)280-0539. **E-mail:** adam@winningwriters.com. **Website:** www.winningwriters.com. **Contact:** Adam Cohen, president. Since 2001, Winning Writers has provided expert literary contest information to the public. Sponsors four contests. One of the "101 Best Websites for Writers" (*Writer's Digest*). Open to all writers. Submit any type of short story or essay. Both published and unpublished works are welcome. If you win a prize, requests nonexclusive rights to publish your submission online, in e-mail newsletters, in e-books, and in press releases. See website for guidelines and to submit your entry. Prefers inquiries by e-mail. Length: 6,000 words max per entry. Writers may submit own work. Winners notified by e-mail. Results made available to entrants on website. Deadline: April 30. Prizes: Two 1st prizes of $2,000 will be awarded, plus 10 honorable mentions of $100 each. Top 12 entries published online. Judged by Dennis Norris II, assisted by Lauren Singer.

THE JULIA WARD HOWE/BOSTON AUTHORS AWARD

The Boston Authors Club, The Boston Authors Club, 36 Sunhill Lane, Newton Center MA 02459. **E-mail:** bostonauthors@aol.com;. **Website:** www.boston-authorsclub.org. **Contact:** Alan Lawson. This annual award honors Julia Ward Howe and her literary friends who founded the Boston Authors Club in 1900. It also honors the membership over 110 years, consisting of novelists, biographers, historians, governors, senators, philosophers, poets, playwrights, and other luminaries. There are 2 categories: trade books and books for young readers (beginning with chapter books through young adult books). Authors must live or have lived (college counts) within a hundred 100-mile radius of Boston within the last 5 years. Subsidized books, cook books and picture books are not eligible. Deadline: January 15. Prize: $1,000. Judged by the members.

INSIGHT WRITING CONTEST

Insight Magazine, 55 W. Oak Ridge Dr., Hagerstown MD 21740-7390. **Fax:** (301)393-4055. **E-mail:** insight@rhpa.org. **Website:** www.insightmagazine.org. **Contact:** Omar Miranda, editor. Annual contest for writers in the categories of student short story, general short story, and student poetry. Unpublished submissions only. General category is open to all writers; student categories must be age 22 and younger. Deadline: July 31. Prizes: Student Short and General Short Story: 1st Prize: $250; 2nd Prize: $200; 3rd Prize: $150. Student Poetry: 1st Prize: $100; 2nd Prize: $75; 3rd Prize: $50.

THE IOWA REVIEW AWARD IN POETRY, FICTION, AND NONFICTION

308 EPB, University of Iowa, Iowa City IA 52242. **E-mail:** iowa-review@uiowa.edu. **Website:** www.iowareview.org. *The Iowa Review* Award in Poetry, Fiction, and Nonfiction presents $1,500 to each winner in each genre and $750 to runners-up. Winners and runners-up published in *The Iowa Review*. Submissions must be unpublished. Considers simultaneous submissions (with notification of acceptance elsewhere). Submit up to 25 pages of prose, (double-spaced) or 10 pages of poetry (1 poem or several, but no more than 1 poem per page). Submit online. Include cover page with writer's name, address, e-mail and/or phone number, and title of each work submitted. Personal identification must not appear on ms pages. Guidelines available on website. Deadline: January 31. Submission period begins January 1. Judged by Joyelle McSweeney, Amy Gray, and Charles D'Ambrosio in 2017.

JAPAN-U.S. FRIENDSHIP COMMISSION PRIZE FOR THE TRANSLATION OF JAPANESE LITERATURE

Japanese Literary Translation Prize, Donald Keene Center of Japanese Culture, Columbia University, 507 Kent Hall

1140 Amsterdam Ave., New York NY 10027 USA. **Website:** http://www.keenecenter.org/. **Contact:** Yoshiko Niiya, Program Coordinator. The Donald Keene Center of Japanese Culture at Columbia University annually awards Japan-U.S. Friendship Commission Prizes for the Translation of Japanese Literature. A prize is given for the best translation of a modern work or a classical work, or the prize is divided between equally distinguished translations. Translators must be citizens or permanent residents of the United States. Deadline: June 1. Prize: $6,000.

THE STEPHEN LEACOCK MEMORIAL MEDAL FOR HUMOUR

149 Peter St. N., Orillia ON L3V 4Z4 Canada. (705)326-9286. E-mail: bettewalkerca@gmail.com. Website: www.leacock.ca. Contact: Bette Walker, award committee, Stephen Leacock Associates. The Leacock Associates awards the prestigious Leacock Medal for the best book of literary humor written by a Canadian and published in the current year. The winning author also receives a cash prize of $15,000 thanks to the generous support of the TD Financial Group. 2 runners-up are each awarded a cash prize of $1,500. Deadline: December 31. Prize: $15,000.

LEAGUE OF UTAH WRITERS CONTEST

The League of Utah Writers, The League of Utah Writers, P.O. Box 64, Lewiston UT 84320. (435)755-7609. E-mail: luwcontest@gmail.com; luwriters@gmail.com. Website: www.luwriters.org. Open to any writer, the LUW Contest provides authors an opportunity to get their work read and critiqued. Multiple categories are offered; see website for details. Entries must be the original and unpublished work of the author. Winners are announced at the Annual Writers Round-Up in September. Those not present will be notified by e-mail. Deadline: June 15. Submissions period begins March 15. Prize: Cash prizes are awarded. Judged by professional authors and editors from outside the League.

LES FIGUES PRESS NOS BOOK CONTEST

P.O. Box 7736, Los Angeles CA 90007. (323)734-4732. E-mail: info@lesfigues.com. Website: www.lesfigues.com. Contact: Teresa Carmody, director. Les Figues Press creates aesthetic conversations between writers/artists and readers, especially those interested in innovative/experimental/avant-garde work. The Press intends in the most premeditated fashion to champion the trinity of Beauty, Belief, and Bawdry. Submit a 64-250 page unpublished manuscript through electronic submissions manager. Eligible submissions include: poetry, novellas, innovative novels, anti-novels, short story collections, lyric essays, hybrids, and all forms *not otherwise specified*. Guidelines available online. Deadline: September 15. Prize: $1,000, plus publication by Les Figues Press. Each entry receives LFP book.

LET'S WRITE LITERARY CONTEST

The Gulf Coast Writers Association, P.O. Box 4808, Biloxi MS 39535. E-mail: writerpllevin@gmail.com. Website: www.gcwriters.org/contest.html. Contact: Philip Levin. The Gulf Coast Writers Association sponsors this nationally recognized contest, which accepts unpublished poems, prose, and short stories from authors all around the US. This is an annual event which has been held for 29 years. Deadline: April 10. Prize: 1st Prize: $80; 2nd Prize: $60; 3rd Prize: $40.

THE HUGH J. LUKE AWARD

Prairie Schooner, 123 Andrews Hall, University of Nebraska-Lincoln, Lincoln NE 68588-0334. (402)472-0911. Fax: (402)472-1817. E-mail: prairieschooner@unl.edu. Website: www.prairieschooner.unl.edu. Contact: Kwame Dawes. Offered annually for work published in *Prairie Schooner* in the previous year. Results announced in the Spring issue. Winners notified by mail in February or March. Prize: $250. Judged by editorial staff of *Prairie Schooner*.

THE MCGINNIS-RITCHIE MEMORIAL AWARD

Southwest Review, Southern Methodist University, P.O. Box 750374, Dallas TX 75275-0374. (214)768-1037. Fax: (214)768-1408. E-mail: swr@mail.smu.edu. Website: www.smu.edu/southwestreview. Contact: Greg Brownderville, editor-in-chief. The McGinnis-Ritchie Memorial Award is given annually to the best works of fiction and nonfiction that appeared in the magazine in the previous year. Mss are submitted for publication, not for the prizes themselves. Guidelines for SASE or online. Prize: $500. Judged by Greg Brownderville and Preston Hutcherson.

A MIDSUMMER TALE

E-mail: editors@toasted-cheese.com. Website: www.toasted-cheese.com. Contact: Theryn Fleming, editor. A Midsummer Tale is open to non-genre fiction and creative nonfiction. There is a different theme each year. Entries must be unpublished. Accepts inquiries by e-mail. Cover letter should include name, address, e-mail, word count, and title. Length: 1,000-5,000 words. Open to any writer. Guidelines available in April on website. Deadline: June 21. Results announced on July 31. Winners notified by e-mail. List of winners on website. Prize: Amazon gift certificates and publication in Toasted Cheese. Entries are blind-judged by at least one Toasted Cheese editor

MINNESOTA BOOK AWARDS

The Friends of the Saint Paul Public Library, 1080 Montreal Ave., Suite 2, St. Paul MN 55116. (651)222-3242. **Fax:** (651)222-1988. **E-mail:** mnbookawards@thefriends.org. **Website:** www.mnbookawards.org. A year-round program celebrating and honoring Minnesota's best books, culminating in an annual awards ceremony. Recognizes and honors achievement by members of Minnesota's book and book arts community. All books must be the work of a Minnesota author or primary artistic creator (current Minnesota resident who maintains a year-round residence in Minnesota). All books must be published within the calendar year prior to the Awards presentation. Deadline: Books should be entered by 5 p.m. on the third Friday in November.

MISSISSIPPI REVIEW PRIZE

Mississippi Review, 118 College Dr., #5144, Hattiesburg MS 39406-0001. (601)266-4321. **Fax:** (601)266-5757. **E-mail:** msreview@usm.edu. **Website:** www.mississippireview.com. Annual contest starting August 1 and running until January 1. Winners and finalists will make up next spring's print issue of the national literary magazine *Mississippi Review*. Each entrant will receive a copy of the prize issue. Contest is open to all writers in English except current or former students or employees of The University of Southern Mississippi. Fiction entries should be 1,000-8,000 words, poetry entries should be 3-5 poems totaling 10 pages or less. There is no limit on the number of entries you may submit. Online submissions must be submitted through Submittable site: mississippireview.submittable.com/submit. No mss will be returned. Previously published work is ineligible. Winners will be announced in March and publication is scheduled for June of following year. Entries should have "MR Prize," author name, address, phone, e-mail and title of work on page 1. Deadline: January 1. Prize: $1,000 in fiction and poetry. Judged by Andrew Malan Milward in fiction, and Angela Ball in poetry.

MOUNTAINS & PLAINS INDEPENDENT BOOKSELLERS ASSOCIATION READING THE WEST BOOK AWARDS

Mountains & Plains Independent Booksellers Association, 3278 Big Spruce Way, Park City UT 84098 USA. **E-mail:** Submission is via an online form, posted on the website (www.mountainsplains.org) in the fall of each year. **Website:** http://www.mountainsplains.

org/reading-the-west-book-awards/. **Contact:** Laura P Burnett. Mountains & Plains Independent Booksellers Association is a professional trade organization with the primary mission of supporting independent bookseller members in a 12-state region in the West. Also welcomes as members colleagues in the book industry including authors, publishers, sales representatives, and others. The purpose of these annual awards is to honor outstanding books published in the previous calendar year which are set in the region (Arizona, Colorado, Kansas, Montana, Nebraska, Nevada, New Mexico, Oklahoma, South Dakota, Texas, Utah, and Wyoming) or that evoke the spirit of the region. The author's place of residence is immaterial for these awards. Deadline: Nomination period September 1 to December 31 for books published in the previous calendar year. Prize: All nominated titles are listed on the website (www.mountainsplains.org). Shortlist and winning titles are recognized via a press release, e-announcement, and on the website. Winners are recognized at a Reading the West luncheon at the Fall Discovery Show and in promotional materials. Judged by 2 panels of judges, 1 for adult titles and 1 for children's titles. Other categories/panels may be convened at the Association's discretion.

NATIONAL BOOK AWARDS

The National Book Foundation, 90 Broad St., Suite 604, New York NY 10004. (212)685-0261. **E-mail:** nationalbook@nationalbook.org; agall@nationalbook.org. **Website:** www.nationalbook.org. **Contact:** Amy Gall. The National Book Foundation and the National Book Awards celebrate the best of American literature, expand its audience, and enhance the cultural value of great writing in America. The contest offers prizes in 4 categories: fiction, nonfiction, poetry, and young people's literature. Books should be published between December 1 and November 30 of the past year. Submissions must be previously published and must be entered by the publisher. General guidelines available on website. Interested publishes should phone or e-mail the Foundation. Deadline: Submit entry form, payment, and a copy of the book by July 1. Prize: $10,000 in each category. Finalists will each receive a prize of $1,000. Judged by a category specific panel of 5 judges for each category.

NATIONAL OUTDOOR BOOK AWARDS

921 S. 8th Ave., Stop 8128, Pocatello ID 83209. (208)282-3912. **E-mail:** wattron@isu.edu. **Website:**

www.noba-web.org. **Contact:** Ron Watters. Nine categories: History/biography, outdoor literature, instructional texts, outdoor adventure guides, nature guides, children's books, design/artistic merit, natural history literature, and nature and the environment. Additionally, a special award, the Outdoor Classic Award, is given annually to books which, over a period of time, have proven to be exceptionally valuable works in the outdoor field. Application forms and eligibility requirements are available online. Applications for the Awards program become available in early June. Deadline: August 23. Prize: Winning books are promoted nationally and are entitled to display the National Outdoor Book Award (NOBA) medallion.

THE NEUTRINO SHORT-SHORT CONTEST

Passages North, Dept. of English, Northern Michigan University, 1401 Presque Isle Ave., Marquette MI 49855. (906)227-1203. **Fax:** (906)227-1096. **E-mail:** passages@nmu.edu. **Website:** www.passagesnorth. com. **Contact:** Jennifer Howard. Offered every 2 years to publish new voices in literary fiction, nonfiction, hybrid-essays and prose poems (maximum 1,000 words). Guidelines available for SASE or online. Deadline: April 15. Submission period begins February 15. Prize: $1,000, and publication for the winner; 2 honorable mentions also published; all entrants receive a copy of *Passages North*. Judged by T Fleischmann in 2018.

NEW ENGLAND BOOK AWARDS

1955 Massachusetts Ave., #2, Cambridge MA 02140. (617)547-3642. **Fax:** (617)547-3759. **E-mail:** nan@neba.org. **Website:** www.newenglandbooks.org/programs/awards-scholarships/new-england-book-awards/. **Contact:** Nan Sorensen, administrative coordinator. All books must be either written by a New England based author or be set in New England. Eligible books must be published between September 1, 2017 and August 31, 2018 in either hardcover or paperback. Submissions made by New England booksellers; publishers. Submit written nominations only; actual books should not be sent. $25 fee per title for non-member submissions. Award is given to a specific title, fiction, non-fiction, children's. The titles must be either about New England, set in New England or by an author residing in the New England. The titles must be hardcover, paperback original or reissue that was published between September 1 and August 31. Entries must be still in print and available. Deadline:

June 8. Prize: Winners will receive $250 for literacy to a charity of their choice. Judged by NEIBA membership.

NEW LETTERS LITERARY AWARDS

New Letters, University of Missouri-Kansas City, 5101 Rockhill Rd., Kansas City MO 64110-2499. (816)235-1168. **Fax:** (816)235-2611. **Website:** www.newletters.org/writers-wanted/writing-contests. **Contact:** Ashley Wann. Award has 3 categories (fiction, poetry, and creative nonfiction) with 1 winner in each. Offered annually for previously unpublished work. For guidelines, send an SASE to *New Letters*, or visit http://www.newletters.org/writers-wanted/writing-contests. Deadline: May 18. 1st place: $1,500, plus publication in poetry and fiction category; 1st place: $2,500, plus publication in essay category. Judged by regional writers of prominence and experience. Final judging by someone of national repute. Previous judges include Maxine Kumin, Albert Goldbarth, Charles Simic, and Janet Burroway.

NEW MILLENNIUM AWARDS FOR FICTION, POETRY, AND NONFICTION

New Millennium Writings, 4021 Garden Dr., Knoxville TN 37918. (865)254-4880. **Website:** www.newmillenniumwritings.org. **Contact:** Alexis Williams, Editor and Publisher. No restrictions as to style, content or number of submissions. Previously published pieces acceptable if online or under 5,000 print circulation. Simultaneous and multiple submissions welcome. Each fiction or nonfiction piece is a separate entry and should total no more than 6,000 words, except for the Short-Short Fiction Award, which should total no more than 1,000 words. (Nonfiction includes essays, profiles, memoirs, interviews, creative nonfiction, travel, humor, etc.) Each poetry entry may include up to 3 poems, not to exceed 5 pages total. All 20 poetry finalists will be published. Include name, phone, address, e-mail, and category on cover page only. Apply online via submissions manager. Send SASE or IRC for list of winners or await your book. Deadline: Postmarked on or before January 31 for the Winter Awards and July 31 for the Summer Awards. Prize: $1,000 for Best Poem; $1,000 for Best Fiction; $1,000 for Best Nonfiction; $1,000 for Best Short-Short Fiction.

NEW SOUTH WRITING CONTEST

English Department, Georgia State University, P.O. Box 3970, Atlanta GA 30302-3970. **E-mail:** newsoutheditors@gmail.com. **Website:** newsouthjournal. com/contest. **Contact:** Anna Sandy, editor-in-chief. Offered annually to publish the most promising work of up-and-coming writers of poetry (up to 3 poems) and fiction (9,000 word limit). Rights revert to writer upon publication. Guidelines online. Deadline: March 21. Prize: 1st Place: $1,000 in each category; 2nd Place: $250; and publication to winners. Judged by Safiya Sinclair in poetry and Alissa Nutting in prose.

NORTHERN CALIFORNIA BOOK AWARDS

Northern California Book Reviewers Association, c/o Poetry Flash, 1450 Fourth St. #4, Berkeley CA 94710. (510)525-5476. **E-mail:** ncbr@poetryflash.org; editor@poetryflash.org. **Website:** www.poetryflash.org. **Contact:** Joyce Jenkins, executive director. Annual Northern California Book Award for outstanding book in literature, open to books published in the current calendar year by Northern California authors. NCBR presents annual awards to Bay Area (northern California) authors annually in fiction, nonfiction, poetry and children's literature. Previously published books only. Must be published the calendar year prior to spring awards ceremony. Submissions nominated by publishers; author or agent could also nominate published work. Send 3 copies of the book to attention: NCBR. Encourages writers and stimulates interest in books and reading. Deadline: December 28. Prize: $100 honorarium and award certificate. Judging by voting members of the Northern California Book Reviewers.

◑ NOVA WRITES COMPETITION FOR UNPUBLISHED MANUSCRIPTS

Writers' Federation of Nova Scotia, 1113 Marginal Rd., Halifax NS B3H 4P7. (902)423-8116. **Fax:** (902)422-0881. **E-mail:** programs@writers.ns.ca. **Website:** www.writers.ns.ca. **Contact:** Robin Spittal, communications and development officer. Annual program designed to honor work by unpublished writers in all 4 Atlantic Provinces. Entry is open to writers unpublished in the category of writing they wish to enter. Prizes are presented in the fall of each year. Categories include: short form creative nonfiction, long form creative nonfiction, novel, poetry, short story, and writing for children/young adult novel. Judges return written comments when competition is concluded. Page lengths and rules vary based on categories. See website for details. Anyone resident in the Atlantic Provinces since September 1st immediately prior to the deadline date is eligible to enter. Only one entry per category is allowed. Each entry requires its own entry form and registration fee. Deadline: December 13. Prizes vary based on categories. See website for details.

OHIOANA BOOK AWARDS

Ohioana Library Association, 274 E. First Ave., Suite 300, Columbus OH 43201-3673. (614)466-3831. **Fax:** (614)728-6974. **E-mail:** ohioana@ohioana.org. **Website:** www.ohioana.org. **Contact:** David Weaver, executive director. Writers must have been born in Ohio or lived in Ohio for at least 5 years, but books about Ohio or an Ohioan need not be written by an Ohioan. Finalists announced in May and winners in July. Winners notified by mail in early summer. Offered annually to bring national attention to Ohio authors and their books, published in the last year. (Books can only be considered once.) Categories: Fiction, nonfiction, juvenile, poetry, and books about Ohio or an Ohioan. Deadline: December 31. Prize: $1,000 cash prize, certificate, and glass sculpture. Judged by a jury selected by librarians, book reviewers, writers and other knowledgeable people.

OKLAHOMA BOOK AWARDS

200 NE 18th St., Oklahoma City OK 73105. (405)521-2502. **Fax:** (405)525-7804. **E-mail:** connie.armstrong@libraries.ok.gov. **Website:** www.odl.state. ok.us/ocb. **Contact:** Connie Armstrong, executive director. This award honors Oklahoma writers and books about Oklahoma. Awards are presented to best books in fiction, nonfiction, children's, design and illustration, and poetry books about Oklahoma or books written by an author who was born, is living or has lived in Oklahoma. SASE for award rules and entry forms. Winner will be announced at banquet in Oklahoma City. The Arrell Gibson Lifetime Achievement Award is also presented each year for a body of work. Previously published submissions only. Submissions made by the author, author's agent, or entered by a person or group of people, including the publisher. Must be published during the calendar year preceding the award. Deadline: January 10. Prize: Awards a medal. Judging by a panel of 5 people for each category, generally a librarian, a working writer in the genre, booksellers, editors, etc.

✪ OPEN SEASON AWARDS

The Malahat Review, University of Victoria, P.O. Box 1700, Stn CSC, Victoria BC V8V 2Y2 Canada. (250)721-8524. **Fax:** (250)472-5051. **E-mail:** malahat@uvic.ca. **Website:** www.malahatreview.ca. **Contact:** L'Amour Lisik, publicity manager. The Open Season Awards accepts entries of poetry, fiction, and creative nonfiction. Winners published in spring issue of *Malahat Review* announced in winter on website, facebook page, and in quarterly e-newsletter, *Malahat lite*. Submissions must be unpublished. No simultaneous submissions. Submit up to 3 poems of 100 lines or less; 1 piece of fiction 2,500 words maximum; or 1 piece of creative nonfiction, 2,500 words maximum. No restrictions on subject matter or aesthetic approach. Include separate page with writer's name, address, e-mail, and title(s); no identifying information on mss pages. E-mail submissions now accepted: season@uvic.ca. Do not include SASE for results; mss will not be returned. Guidelines available on website. Winners and finalists will be contacted by e-mail. Deadline: November 1. Prize: $6,000 over three categories (poetry, fiction, creative nonfiction) and publication in *The Malahat Review* in each category.

OREGON BOOK AWARDS

925 SW Washington St., Portland OR 97205. (503)227-2583. **Fax:** (503)241-4256. **E-mail:** la@literary-arts.org. **Website:** www.literary-arts.org. **Contact:** Susan Denning, director of programs and events. The annual Oregon Book Awards celebrate Oregon authors in the areas of poetry, fiction, nonfiction, drama and young readers' literature published between August 1 and July 31 of the previous calendar year. Awards are available for every category. See website for details. Entry fee determined by initial print run; see website for details. Entries must be previously published. Oregon residents only. Accepts inquiries by phone and e-mail. Finalists announced in January. Winners announced at an awards ceremony in November. List of winners available in April. Deadline: August 26. Prize: Grant of $2,500. (Grant money could vary.) Judged by writers who are selected from outside Oregon for their expertise in a genre. Past judges include Mark Doty, Colson Whitehead and Kim Barnes.

JUDITH SIEGEL PEARSON AWARD

Judith Siegel Pearson Award, c/o Department of English, Wayne State University, Attn: Royanne Smith, 5057 Woodward Ave., Ste. 9408, Detroit MI 48202. **E-mail:** fm8146@wayne.edu. **Website:** https://wsu-writingawards.submittable.com/submit. **Contact:** Donovan Hohn. Offers an annual award for the best creative or scholarly work on a subject concerning women. The type of work accepted rotates each year: nonfiction in 2018; fiction in 2019; drama in 2020, poetry in 2021. Open to all interested writers and scholars. Only submit the appropriate genre in each year. Submit electronically on the web site listed here. Deadline: February 22. Prize: $500. Judged by members of the writing faculty of the Wayne State University English Department.

PEN CENTER USA LITERARY AWARDS

PEN Center USA, P.O. Box 6037, Beverly Hills CA 90212. (323)424-4939. **E-mail:** awards@penusa.org. **Website:** www.penusa.org. Offered for work published or produced in the previous calendar year. Open to writers living west of the Mississippi River. Award categories: fiction, poetry, research nonfiction, creative nonfiction, translation, young adult, graphic literature, drama, screenplay, teleplay, journalism. Guidelines and submission form available on website. No anthologies or self-pubished work. Deadline: See website for details. Prize: $1,000.

PENGUIN RANDOM HOUSE CREATIVE WRITING AWARDS

One Scholarship Way, P.O. Box 297, St. Peter MN 56082. (212)782-9348. **Fax:** (212) 782-5157. **E-mail:** creativewriting@penguinrandomhouse.com. **Website:** www.penguinrandomhouse.com/creativewriting. **Contact:** Melanie Fallon Hauska, director. Offered annually for unpublished work to NYC public high school seniors. 72 awards given in literary and nonliterary categories. Four categories: poetry, fiction/drama, personal essay, and graphic novel. Applicants must be seniors (under age 21) at a New York high school. No college essays or class assignments will be accepted. Word length: 2,500 words or less. Applicants must be seniors (under age 21) at a New York high school. Results announced mid-May. Winners notified by mail and phone. For contest results, send SASE, fax, e-mail or visit website. Deadline: February 3 for all categories. Graphic Novel extended deadline: March 1st. Prize: Awards range from $500-10,000. The program usually awards just under $100,000 in scholarships.

THE PINCH LITERARY AWARDS

Literary Awards, The Pinch, Department of English, The University of Memphis, Memphis TN 38152-6176. (901)678-4591. **Website:** www.pinchjournal.com. Offered annually for unpublished short stories of 5,000 words maximum or up to three poems. Guidelines on website. Cost: $20, which is put toward one issue of *The Pinch*. Deadline: March 15. Prize: 1st place Fiction: $1,500 and publication; 1st place Poetry: $1,000 and publication. Offered annually for unpublished short stories and prose of up to 5,000 words and 1-3 poems. Deadline: March 15. Open to submissions on December 15. Prizes: $1,000 for 1st place in each category.

PLOUGHSHARES EMERGING WRITER'S CONTEST

Ploughshares, 120 Boylston St., Boston MA 02116. **Website:** www.pshares.org/submit/emerging-writers-contest.cfm. Writers who have not published a book or chapbook are eligible. Submit three to five poems or up to 5,000 words of prose with a $24 entry fee, which includes a subscription to Ploughshares, by April 2. Visit the website for complete guidelines. "Three prizes of $1,000 each and publication in Ploughshares will be given annually for a poem or group of poems, a short story, and an essay." April 2.

PNWA LITERARY CONTEST

Pacifc Northwest Writers Association, PMB 2717, 1420 NW Gilman Blvd., Suite 2, Issaquah WA 98027. (452)673-2665. **Fax:** (452)961-0768. **E-mail:** pnwa@pnwa.org. **Website:** www.pnwa.org. Annual literary contest with 12 different categories. See website for details and specific guidelines. Each entry receives 2 critiques. Winners announced at the PNWA Summer Conference, held annually in mid-July. Deadline: February 20. Prize: 1st Place: $600; 2nd Place: $300; 3rd Place: $100. Judged by an agent or editor attending the conference.

PRAIRIE SCHOONER BOOK PRIZE

Prairie Schooner and the University of Nebraska Press, Prairie Schooner Prize Series, 123 Andrews Hall, Lincoln NE 68588-0334. (402)472-0911. **E-mail:** PSBookPrize@unl.edu. **Website:** prairieschooner.unl.edu. **Contact:** Kwame Dawes, editor. Annual competition/award for poetry and short story collections. The Prairie Schooner Book Prize Series welcomes manuscripts from all living writers, including non-US citizens, writing in English. Both unpublished and published writers are welcome to submit manuscripts. Writers may enter both contests. Simultaneous submissions are accepted, but we ask that you notify us immediately if your manuscript is accepted for publication somewhere else. No past or present paid employee of Prairie Schooner or the University of Nebraska Press or current faculty or student at the University of Nebraska will be eligible for the prizes. Deadline: March 15. Prize: $3,000 and publication through the University of Nebraska Press.

THE PRESIDIO LA BAHIA AWARD

Sons of the Republic of Texas, 1717 Eighth St., Bay City TX 77414-5033. (979)245-6644. **Fax:** (979)244-3819. **E-mail:** srttexas@srttexas.org. **Website:** www.srttexas.org. **Contact:** Scott Dunbar, chairman. "Material may be submitted concerning the influence on Texas culture of our Spanish Colonial heritage in laws, customs, language, religion, architecture, art, and other related fields." Offered annually to promote suitable preservation of relics, appropriate dissemination of data, and research into Texas heritage, with particular attention to the Spanish Colonial period. Deadline: September 30. Prizes: $2,000 available annually for winning participants; 1st Place: Minimum of $1,200; 2nd and 3rd prizes at the discretion of the judges. Judged by members of the Sons of the Republic of Texas on the Presidio La Bahia Award Committee.

PRIME NUMBER MAGAZINE AWARDS

Press 53, 560 N. Trade St., Suite 103, Winston-Salem NC 27101. (336)770-5353. **Fax:** N/A. **E-mail:** kevin@press53.com. **Website:** www.press53.com. **Contact:** Kevin Morgan Watson, Publisher. Awards $1,000 in poetry and short fiction. Details and guidelines available online. Deadline: April 15. Submission period begins January 1. Finalists and winners announced by August 1. Winners published in Prime Number Magazine in October. Prize: $1,000 cash. All winners receive publication in Prime Number Magazine online. Judged by industry professionals to be named when the contest begins.

✪ PRISM INTERNATIONAL ANNUAL SHORT FICTION, POETRY, AND CREATIVE NONFICTION CONTESTS

PRISM International, Creative Writing Program, UBC, Buch. E462, 1866 Main Mall, Vancouver BC V6T 1Z1 Canada. **E-mail:** promotions@prismmagazine.ca. **Website:** www.prismmagazine.ca. **Contact:** Claire Matthews. Offered annually for unpublished work to award the best in contemporary fiction, poetry, drama, translation, and nonfiction. Works of translation are eligible. Guidelines are available on website. Acquires first North American serial rights upon publication, and limited web rights for pieces selected for website. Open to any writer except students and faculty in the Creative Writing Department at UBC, or people who have taken a creative writing course at UBC within 2 years of the contest deadline. Entry includes subscription. Deadlines: Creative Nonfiction: July 15; Fiction: January 15; Poetry: October 15. Prize: All grand prizes are $1,500, $600 for first runner up, and $400 for second runner up. Winners are published.

PUSHCART PRIZE

Pushcart Press, P.O. Box 380, Wainscott NY 11975. (631)324-9300. **Website:** www.pushcartprize.com. **Contact:** Bill Henderson. Published every year since 1976, The Pushcart Prize - Best of the Small Presses series "is the most honored literary project in America. Hundreds of presses and thousands of writers of short stories, poetry and essays have been represented in the pages of our annual collections." Little magazine and small book press editors (print or online) may make up to six nominations from their year's publicatoins by the deadline. The nominations may be any combination of poetry, short fiction, essays or literary whatnot. Editors may nominate self-contained portions of books — for instance, a chapter from a novel. Deadline: December 1.

☻ THE RBC BRONWEN WALLACE AWARD FOR EMERGING WRITERS

The Writers' Trust of Canada, 460 Richmond St. W., Suite 600, Toronto ON M5C 1P1 Canada. (416)504-8222. **Fax:** (416)504-9090. **E-mail:** info@writerstrust.com. **Website:** www.writerstrust.com. **Contact:** Amanda Hopkins. Presented annually to a Canadian writer under the age of 35 who is not yet published in book form. The award, which alternates each year between poetry and short fiction, was established in memory of Bronwen Wallace. Deadline: March 5. Prize: $10,000. Two finalists receive $2,500 each.

SUMMERFIELD G. ROBERTS AWARD

Sons of the Republic of Texas, 1717 Eighth St., Bay City TX 77414-5033. (979)245-6644. **Fax:** (979)244-3819. **E-mail:** aa-srt@son-rep-texas.net. **Website:** www.srttexas.org. **Contact:** Edward A. Heath, Chairman. The manuscripts must be written or published

during the calendar year for which the award is given. No entry may be submitted more than one time. There is no word limit on the material submitted for the award. The manuscripts may be fiction, nonfiction, poems, essays, plays, short stories, novels, or biographies. The competition is open to all writers everywhere; they need not reside in Texas nor must the publishers be in Texas. Judges each year are winners of the award in the last three years. The purpose of this award is to encourage literary effort and research about historical events and personalities during the days of the Republic of Texas,1836-1846, and to stimulate interest in this period. Deadline: January 15. Prize: $2,500.

ERNEST SANDEEN PRIZE IN POETRY AND THE RICHARD SULLIVAN PRIZE IN SHORT FICTION

University of Notre Dame, Dept. of English, 356 O'Shaughnessy Hall, Notre Dame IN 46556-5639. (574)631-7526. **Fax:** (574)631-4795. **E-mail:** creativewriting@nd.edu. **Website:** http://english.nd.edu/creative-writing/publications/sandeen-sullivan-prizes. **Contact:** Director of Creative Writing. The Sandeen & Sullivan Prizes in Poetry and Short Fiction is awarded to the author who has published at least one volume of short fiction or one volume of poetry. Awarded biannually, but judged quadrennially. Though the Sandeen Prize is open to any author, with the exception of graduates of the University of Notre Dame, who has published at least one volume of short stories (Sullivan) or one collection of poetry (Sandeen), judges pay special attention to second volumes. Please include a vita and/or a biographical statement which includes your publishing history. Will also see a selection of reviews of the earlier collection. Please submit two copies of mss and inform if the mss is available on computer disk. Include an SASE for acknowledgment of receipt of your submission. If you would like your manuscript returned, please send an SASE. Manuscripts will not otherwise be returned. Submissions Period: May 1 - September 1. Prize: $1,000, a $500 award and a $500 advance against royalties from the Notre Dame Press.

SANTA FE WRITERS PROJECT LITERARY AWARDS PROGRAM

Santa Fe Writers Project, 369 Montezuma Ave., #350, Santa Fe NM 87501. **E-mail:** info@sfwp.com. **Website:** www.sfwp.com. **Contact:** Andrew Gifford. Annual contest seeking fiction and nonfiction of any genre. The Literary Awards Program was founded by a group of authors to offer recognition for excellence in writing in a time of declining support for writers and the craft of literature. Past judges have included Richard Currey, Jayne Anne Phillips, Chris Offutt, Emily St. John Mandel, and David Morrell. Deadline: July 20th. Prize: $3,300 and publication. Judged by Benjamin Percy and Mat Johnson in 2017.

SASKATCHEWAN BOOK AWARDS

315-1102 8th Ave., Regina SK S4R 1C9 Canada. (306)569-1585. **E-mail:** director@bookawards.sk.ca. **Website:** www.bookawards.sk.ca. **Contact:** Courtney Bates-Hardy, executive director. Saskatchewan Book Awards celebrates, promotes, and rewards Saskatchewan authors and publishers worthy of recognition through 14 awards, granted on an annual or semiannual basis. Awards: Fiction, Nonfiction, Poetry, Scholarly, First Book, Prix du Livre Français, Regina, Saskatoon, Indigenous Peoples' Writing, Indigenous Peoples' Publishing, Publishing in Education, Publishing, Children's Literature/Young Adult Literature, Book of the Year. November 1. Prize: $2,000 (CAD) for all awards except Book of the Year, which is $3,000 (CAD). Juries are made up of writing and publishing professionals from outside of Saskatchewan.

MARGARET & JOHN SAVAGE FIRST BOOK AWARD

Halifax Public Libraries, 60 Alderney Dr., Dartmouth NS B2Y 4P8 Canada. (902)490-5991. **Fax:** (902)490-5889. **E-mail:** mackenh@halifaxpubliclibraries.ca. **Website:** www.halifax.ca/bookawards. **Contact:** Heather MacKenzie. "Recognizes the best first book of fiction or nonfiction written by a first-time published author residing in Atlantic Canada. Books may be of any genre, but must contain a minimum of 40% text, be at least 49 pages long, and be available for sale. No anthologies. Publishers: Send 4 copies of each title and submission form for each entry." Children's Books not accepted. Deadline: December 2.

THE MONA SCHREIBER PRIZE FOR HUMOROUS FICTION & NONFICTION

3940 Laurel Canyon Blvd., #566, Studio City CA 91604. **E-mail:** brad.schreiber@att.net. **Website:** www.bradschreiber.com. **Contact:** Brad Schreiber. Established in 2000, to honor Mona Schreiber, a writer and teacher. Entry fees are the same as in 2000 and money from entries helps pay for prizes. No SASEs.

Non-US entries should enclose US currency or checks written in US dollars. Include e-mail address. No previously published work. The purpose of the contest is to award the most creative humor writing, in any form, under than 750 words, in either fiction or nonfiction, including but not limited to stories, articles, essays, speeches, shopping lists, diary entries, and anything else writers dream up. Complete rules and previous winning entries on website. Deadline: December 1. Prize: 1st Place: $500; 2nd Place: $250; 3rd Place: $100. Judged by Brad Schreiber, journalist, consultant, instructor, author of among other books, the humor writing how-to *What Are You Laughing At?*

SHORT GRAIN CONTEST

P.O. Box 3986, Regina SK S4P 3R9 Canada. (306)791-7749. **E-mail:** grainmag@skwriter.com. **Website:** www.grainmagazine.ca/short-grain-contest. **Contact:** Jordan Morris, business administrator (inquiries only). The annual Short Grain Contest includes a category for poetry of any style up to 100 lines and fiction of any style up to 2,500 words, offering 3 prizes. Each entry must be original, unpublished, not submitted elsewhere for publication or broadcast, nor accepted elsewhere for publication or broadcast, nor entered simultaneously in any other contest or competition for which it is also eligible to win a prize. Entries must be typed on 8½x11 paper. It must be legible. No simultaneous submissions. A separate covering page must be attached to the text of your entry, and must provide the following information: Author's name, complete mailing address, telephone number, e-mail address, entry title, category name, and line count. Online submissions are accepted, see website for details. An absolutely accurate word or line count is required. No identifying information on the text pages. Entries will not be returned. Names of the winners and titles of the winning entries will be posted on the *Grain Magazine* website in August; only the winners will be notified. Deadline: April 1. Prize: $1,000, plus publication in *Grain Magazine*; 2nd Place: $750; 3rd Place: $500.

SKIPPING STONES HONOR (BOOK) AWARDS

P.O. Box 3939, Eugene OR 97403 USA. (541)342-4956. **Fax:** (541)342-4956. **E-mail:** editor@skippingstones.org. **Website:** www.skippingstones.org. **Contact:** Arun N. Toké. *Skipping Stones* is a well respected, multicultural literary magazine now in its 29th year. For multicultural and nature books and teaching resources. Entries must be previously published. Open to published books and teaching resources that appeared in print during a 2-year period prior to the deadline date. Guidelines for SASE or e-mail and on website. Accepts inquiries by e-mail or phone. The Annual Honors list includes approximately 25 books and teaching resources in three categories. Annual award to promote multicultural and/or nature awareness through creative writings for children and teens and their educators. Seeks authentic, exceptional, child/youth friendly books that promote intercultural, international, intergenerational harmony, or understanding through creative ways. Deadline: February 29. Prize: Honor certificates; gold seals; reviews; press release/publicity. Judged by a multicultural committee of teachers, librarians, parents, students and editors.

THE BERNICE SLOTE AWARD

Prairie Schooner, 123 Andrews Hall, PO Box 880334, Lincoln NE 68588-0334. (402)472-0911. **Fax:** (402)472-1817. **E-mail:** PrairieSchooner@unl.edu. **Website:** www.prairieschooner.unl.edu. **Contact:** Kwame Dawes. Categories: short stories, essays and poetry. For guidelines, send SASE or visit website. Only work published in the journal during the previous year will be considered. Work is nominated by the editorial staff. Offered annually for the best work by a beginning writer published in *Prairie Schooner* in the previous year. Celebrates the best and finest writing that they have published for the year. Prize: $500. Judged by editorial staff of *Prairie Schooner*.

JEFFREY E. SMITH EDITORS' PRIZE IN FICTION, ESSAY AND POETRY

The Missouri Review, 357 McReynolds Hall, UMC, Columbia MO 65211. (573)882-4474. **Fax:** (573)884-4671. **E-mail:** contest_question@moreview.com. **Website:** www.missourireview.com. **Contact:** Editor. Offered annually for unpublished work in 3 categories: fiction, essay, and poetry. Guidelines online or for SASE. Deadline: October 15. Prize: $5,000 and publication for each category winner.

KAY SNOW WRITING CONTEST

Willamette Writers, Willamette Writers, 2108 Buck St., West Linn OR 97068. (503)305-6729. **Fax:** (503)344-6174. **E-mail:** reg@willamettewriters.com. **Website:** www.willamettewriters.org. Willamette Writers is the largest writers' organization in Oregon and one of the largest writers' organizations in the

United States. It is a non-profit, tax-exempt Oregon corporation led by volunteers. Elected officials and directors administer an active program of monthly meetings, special seminars, workshops, and an annual writing conference. Continuing with established programs and starting new ones is only made possible by strong volunteer support. See website for specific details and rules. There are six different categories writers can enter: Adult Fiction, Adult Nonfiction, Poetry, Juvenile Short Story, Screenwriting, and Student Writer. The purpose of this annual writing contest, named in honor of Willamette Writer's founder, Kay Snow, is to help writers reach professional goals in writing in a broad array of categories and to encourage student writers. Deadline: April 23. Submission deadline begins January 15. Prize: One first prize of $300, one second place prize of $150, and a third place prize of $50 per winning entry in each of the six categories. Student first prize is $50, $20 for second place, $10 for third.

SOCIETY OF MIDLAND AUTHORS AWARD

Society of Midland Authors, Society of Midland Authors, P.O. Box 10419, Chicago IL 60610-0419. **E-mail:** marlenetbrill@comcast.net. **Website:** www.midlandauthors.com. **Contact:** Marlene Targ Brill, awards chair. Since 1957, the Society has presented annual awards for the best books written by Midwestern authors. The Society began in 1915. The contest is open to any title published within the year prior to the contest year. Open to adult and children's authors/poets who reside in, were born in, or have strong ties to a Midland state, which includes Illinois, Indiana, Iowa, Kansas, Michigan, Minnesota, Missouri, Nebraska, North Dakota, South Dakota, Ohio, and Wisconsin. The Society of Midland Authors (SMA) Award is presented to one title in each of 6 categories: adult nonfiction, adult fiction, adult biography and memoir, children's nonfiction, children's fiction, and poetry. There may be honor book winners as well. Books and entry forms must be mailed to the 3 judges in each category; for a list of judges and the entry and payment forms, visit the SMA website. Do not mail books to the society's P.O. box. The fee can be sent to the SMA P.O. box or paid via Paypal. Deadline: The first Saturday in January for books from the previous year. Prize: $500 and a plaque that is awarded at the SMA banquet in May in Chicago. Honorary winners receive a plaque. Check the SMA website for each year's judges.

SOUL-MAKING KEATS LITERARY COMPETITION

The Webhallow House, 1544 Sweetwood Dr., Broadmoor Village CA 94015-2029. (650)756-5279. **Fax:** (650)756-5279. **E-mail:** soulkeats@mail.com. **Website:** www.soulmakingcontest.us. **Contact:** Eileen Malone, contest founder/director. Annual open contest offers cash prizes in each of 12 literary categories. Competition receives 600 entries/year. Names of winners and judges are posted on website. Winners announced in January by SASE and on website. Winners are invited to read at the Koret Auditorium, San Francisco. Event is televised. Submissions in some categories may be previously published. No names or other identifying information on mss; include 3x5 card with poet's name, address, phone, fax, e-mail, title(s) of work, and category entered. Include SASE for results only; mss will not be returned. Guidelines available on website. Ongoing Deadline: November 30. Prizes: 1st Prize: $100; 2nd Prize: $50; 3rd Prize: $25.

STORY MONSTER APPROVED BOOK AWARDS

Story Monsters LLC, 4696 W. Tyson St., Chandler AZ 85226. (480)940-8182. **Fax:** (480)940-8787. **E-mail:** linda@storymonsters.com. **E-mail:** cristy@story-monsters.com. **Website:** www.dragonflybookawards.com. **Contact:** Cristy Bertini. Recognizes and honors accomplished authors in the field of children's literature who inspire, inform, teach, or entertain. A Story Monsters seal of approval on your book tells teachers, librarians, and parents they are giving children the very best. Offered on an annual basis, we have expanded our program to include 23 distinct categories which cover a variety of genres and target ages. Guidelines available online. Send submissions to Cristy Bertini, Attn.: Dragonfly Book Awards, 1271 Turkey St., Ware, MA 01082. Deadline: December 1. The Book of the Year winner will receive an advertorial, which includes a feature interview and a full-page ad in Story Monsters Ink® magazine (a $1,600 value), a certificate commemorating their accomplishment, and 50 Story Monsters Approved! seals. All books earning a Story Monsters Approved! Gold Medal Honor receive a gold medal, a certificate, and 25 award seals. All books earning a Story Monsters Approved! designation receive a certificate and 15 award seals. All winners are listed in a news release sent to a comprehensive list of media outlets, on the Dragonfly Book Awards website, and in Story Monsters Ink® magazine. Our judging panel includes industry experts in specific fields as well as experts in education and publishing.

⚙ SUBTERRAIN MAGAZINE'S LUSH TRIUMPHANT LITERARY AWARDS COMPETITION

P.O. Box 3008 MPO, Vancouver BC V6B 3X5 Canada. (604)876-8710. **Fax:** (604)879-2667. **E-mail:** subter@portal.ca. **Website:** www.subterrain.ca. Entrants may submit as many entries in as many categories as they like. Fiction: Max of 3,000 words. Poetry: A suite of 5 related poems (max of 15 pages). Creative Nonfiction (based on fact, adorned with fiction): Max of 4,000 words. All entries must be previously unpublished material and not currently under consideration in any other contest or competition. Deadline: May 15. Prize: Winners in each category will receive $1,000 cash (plus payment for publication) and publication in the Winter issue. First runner-up in each category will be published in the Spring issue of *subTerrain*.

THE TEXAS INSTITUTE OF LETTERS LITERARY AWARDS

E-mail: Betwx@aol.com. **Website:** www.texasinstituteofletters.org. The Texas Institute of Letters gives annual awards for books by Texas authors and writers who have produced books about Texas, including Best Books of Poetry, Fiction, and Nonfiction. Awards are also given for best Short Story, Magazine or Newspaper Article, Essay, and best Books for Children and Young Adults. Work submitted must have been published in the year stipulated, and entries may be made by authors or by their publishers. Complete guidelines and award information is available on the Texas Institute of Letters website.

TOMMY AWARD FOR EXCELLENCE IN WRITING

International Book Management Corporation, 3468 Babcock Blvd., Pittsburgh PA 15237-2402. (412)837-2423. **E-mail:** info@internationalbookmanagement.com; editor@writersnewsweekly.com. **Website:** writersnewsweekly.com. **Contact:** Christopher Stokum and Sarah Schiavoni. The Tommy Award For Writing Excellent recognizes and rewards excellence in full length literary works in adult fiction and nonfiction. Books must be published in the U.S. between June 1 and May 31 of the following year. Textbooks, e-books, children's books, young adult books, poetry and audio-books will not be considered, nor will manuscripts. Judges will selected one winner and may designate up to two Honorable Mention books in each of the following categories: fiction, nonfiction, shosrt story collection. Books can be submitted by the publisher or the author. A copy of each book submitted should be mailed directly to: International Book Management Corporation, 3468 Babcock Blvd., Pittsburgh, PA 15237. Please send submissions as soon as possible after publication. No books will be accepted after May 21, 2011. There will be no extensions to this deadline. Winners and honorable mentions will be announced on August 15th. The awards are presented in October. Winners receive a certificate and trophy. An author interview and book review of the winning submission will appear on WritersNewsWeekly. Entries will not be returned. International Book Management Corp. reserves the right to donate or dispose of entries. No entry fee. More more information contact International Management at: info@internationalbookmanagement.com. "The Tommy Award honors and encourages outstanding novelists and short story authors by separating them from the bulk of contemporary fiction writers for recognition. Authors may submit previously published novels or unpublished short stories for consideration." May 21. The winning novelist will receive a trophy and a certificate. WritersNewsWeekly will feature a review of his/her book and indicate where the book can be purchased. The winning short story author will also receive a trophy and a certificate, and his/her winning story will be featured on WritersNewsWeekly. Novelists retain all rights to their submitted material. Short Story authors agree to a one-time online publication upon submitting their work but retain all rights. Judged by the combined staff of WritersNewsWeekly and International Book Management Corportation.

TORONTO BOOK AWARDS

City of Toronto c/o Toronto Arts & Culture, Cultural Partnerships, City Hall, 9E, 100 Queen St. W., Toronto ON M5H 2N2 Canada. **E-mail:** shan@toronto.ca. **Website:** www.toronto.ca/book_awards. The Toronto Book Awards honor authors of books of literary or artistic merit that are evocative of Toronto. There are no separate categories; all books are judged together. Any fiction or nonfiction book published in English for adults and/or children that are evocative of Toronto are eligible. To be eligible, books must be published between January 1 and December 31 of previous year.

Deadline: April 30. Prize: Each finalist receives $1,000 and the winning author receives$10,000 ($15,000 total in prize money available).

THE JULIA WARD HOWE AWARD

The Boston Authors Club, 33 Brayton Road, Brighton MA 02135. (617)783-1357. **E-mail:** alan.lawson@bc.edu. **Website:** www.bostonauthorsclub.org. **Contact:** Alan Lawson, president. Julia Ward Howe Prize offered annually in the spring for books published the previous year. Two awards are given: one for adult books of fiction, nonfiction, or poetry, and one for children's books, middle grade and young adult novels, nonfiction, or poetry. No picture books or subsidized publishers. There must be two copies of each book submitted. Authors must live within 100 miles of Boston the year their book is published. Deadline: January 15. Prize: $1,000 in each category. Several books will also be cited with no cash awards as Finalists or Highly Recommended.

THE ROBERT WATSON LITERARY PRIZE IN FICTION AND POETRY

The Robert Watson Literary Prizes, *The Greensboro Review*, MFA Writing Program, 3302 MHRA Building, Greensboro NC 27402-6170. (336)334-5459. **E-mail:** jlclark@uncg.edu. **Website:** www.greensbororeview.org. **Contact:** Jim Clark, editor. Offered annually for fiction (up to 25 double-spaced pages) and poetry (up to 10 pages). Entries must be unpublished. Open to any writer. Guidelines available online. Submit online: https://greensbororeview.submittable.com/submit. Deadline: September 15. Prize: $1,000 each for best short story and poem. Judged by editors of *The Greensboro Review*.

WESTERN AUSTRALIAN PREMIER'S BOOK AWARDS

State Library of Western Australia, Perth Cultural Centre, 25 Francis St., Perth WA 6000 Australia. (61)(8)9427-3151. **E-mail:** premiersbookawards@slwa.wa.gov.au. **Website:** pba.slwa.wa.gov.au. **Contact:** Karen de San Miguel. Annual competition for Australian citizens or permanent residents of Australia, or writers whose work has Australia as its primary focus. Categories: children's books, digital narrative, fiction, nonfiction, poetry, scripts, writing for young adults, West Australian history, and Western Australian emerging writers. Submit 5 original copies of the work to be considered for the awards. All works must have been published between January 1 and December 31 of the prior year. See website for details and rules of entry. Deadline: January 31. Prize: Awards $25,000 for Premier's Prize; awards $15,000 each for the Children's Books, Digital Narrative, Fiction, and Nonfiction categories; awards $10,000 each for the Poetry, Scripts, Western Australian History, Western Australian Emerging Writers, and Writing for Young Adults; awards $5,000 for People's Choice Award.

WESTERN HERITAGE AWARDS

National Cowboy & Western Heritage Museum, 1700 NE 63rd St., Oklahoma City OK 73111-7997. (405)478-2250. **Fax:** (405)478-4714. **Website:** www.national-cowboymuseum.org. **Contact:** Jessica Limestall. The National Cowboy & Western Heritage Museum Western Heritage Awards were established to honor and encourage the legacy of those whose works in literature, music, film, and television reflect the significant stories of the American West. Accepted categories for literary entries: western novel, nonfiction book, art book, photography book, juvenile book, magazine article, or poetry book. Previously published submissions only, must be published the calendar year before the awards are presented. Requirements for entrants: The material must pertain to the development or preservation of the West, either from a historical or contemporary viewpoint. Literary entries must have been published between December 1 and November 30 of calendar year. Five copies of each published work must be furnished for judging with each entry, along with the completed entry form. Works recognized during special awards ceremonies held annually at the museum. There is an autograph party preceding the awards. Awards ceremonies are sometimes broadcast. The WHA are presented annually to encourage the accurate and artistic telling of great stories of the West through 16 categories of western literature, television, film and music; including fiction, nonfiction, children's books and poetry. See website for details and category definitions. Deadline: November 30. Prize: Awards a Wrangler bronze sculpture designed by famed western artist, John Free. Judged by a panel of judges selected each year with distinction in various fields of western art and heritage.

WESTERN WRITERS OF AMERICA

271CR 219, Encampment WY 82325. (307)329-8942. **E-mail:** wwa.moulton@gmail.com. **Website:** www. westernwriters.org. **Contact:** Candy Moulton, executive director. Eighteen Spur Award categories in vari-

ous aspects of the American West. Send entry form with your published work. Accepts multiple submissions, each with its own entry form, available on our website. The nonprofit Western Writers of America has promoted and honored the best in Western literature with the annual Spur Awards, selected by panels of judges. Awards, for material published last year, are given for works whose inspirations, image and literary excellence best represent the reality and spirit of the American West. Deadline: January 4.

WESTMORELAND POETRY & SHORT STORY CONTEST

Westmoreland Arts & Heritage Festival, 252 Twin Lakes Road, Latrobe PA 15650-9415. (724)834-7474. **Fax:** (724)850-7474. **E-mail:** info@artsandheritage.com. **Website:** www.artsandheritage.com. **Contact:** Diane Shrader. Offered annually for unpublished work. Two categories: Poem and Short Story. Short story entries no longer than 4,000 words. Family-oriented festival and contest. Deadline: February 17. Prizes: Award: $200; 1st Place: $125; 2nd Place: $100; 3rd Place: $75.

WILLA LITERARY AWARD

Women Writing the West, 8547 East Arapaho Rd., #J-541, Greenwood Village CO 80112-1436. **E-mail:** jcpeone@gmail.com. **Website:** www.womenwritingthewest.org. **Contact:** Carmen Peone. The WILLA Literary Award honors the year's best in published literature featuring women's or girls' stories set in the West. Women Writing the West (WWW), a nonprofit association of writers and other professionals writing and promoting the Women's West, underwrites and presents the nationally recognized award annually (for work published between January 1 and December 31). The award is named in honor of Pulitzer Prize winner Willa Cather, one of the country's foremost novelists. The award is given in 8 categories: historical fiction, contemporary fiction, original softcover fiction, creative nonfiction, scholarly nonfiction, poetry, children's fiction and nonfiction and young adult fiction/nonfiction. Entry forms available on the website. Deadline: November 1–February 1. Prize: $150 and a trophy. Finalist receives a plaque. Both receive digital and sticker award emblems for book covers. Notice of Winning and Finalist titles mailed to more than 4,000 booksellers, libraries, and others. Award announcement is in early August, and awards are presented to the winners and finalists at the annual WWW Fall

Conference. Also, the eight winners will participate in a drawing for 2 two week all expenses paid residencies donated by Playa at Summer Lake in Oregon. Judged by professional librarians not affiliated with WWW.

TENNESSEE WILLIAMS/NEW ORLEANS LITERARY FESTIVAL CONTESTS

Tennessee Williams/New Orleans Literary Festival, 938 Lafayette St., Suite 514, New Orleans LA 70113. (504)581-1144. **E-mail:** info@tennesseewilliams.net. **Website:** www.tennesseewilliams.net/contests. **Contact:** Paul J. Willis. Annual contests for: Unpublished One Act, Unpublished Short Fiction, Unpublished Flash Fiction, and Unpublished Poem. Plays should run no more than one hour in length. Unlimited entries per person. Production criteria include scripts requiring minimal technical support for a 100-seat theater. Cast of characters must be small. See website for additional guidelines and entry form. Fiction must not exceed 7,000 words. Poetry submissions should be 2-4 poems not exceeding 400 lines total. "Our competitions provide writers a large audience during one of the largest literary festivals in the nation." Deadline: October 1 (One Act, Fiction); October 15 (Poetry, Very Short Fiction). Prize: One Act: $1,500, staged read at the next festival, VIP All-Access Festival pass, and publication in Bayou. Poetry: $1,000, public reading at next festival, VIP all-access pass, publication in Louisiana Cultural Vistas Magazine. Fiction: $1,500, public reading at next festival, publication in Louisiana Literature, VIP all-access pass. Very Short Fiction: $500, publication in the New Orleans Review, VIP all-access past. Judged by special guest judges, who change every year.

⟳ THE WORD AWARDS

The Word Guild, The Word Guild, Suite # 226, 245 King George Rd, Brantford ON N3R 7N7 Canada. 800-969-9010 x 1. **E-mail:** info@thewordguild.com. **E-mail:** info@thewordguild.com. **Website:** www.thewordguild.com. **Contact:** Karen deBlieck. The Word Guild is an organization of Canadian writers and editors who are Christian, and who are committed to encouraging one another and to fostering standards of excellence in the art, craft, practice and ministry of writing. Memberships available for various experience levels. Yearly conference Write Canada (please see website for information) and features keynote speakers, continuing classes and workshops. Editors and agents on site. The Word Awards is for work published in the past year, in almost 30 categories including books, articles, essays, fiction, nonfiction, novels, short stories, songs, and poetry. Please see website for more information. Deadline: January 15. Prize $50 CAD for article and short pieces; $100 CAD for book entries. Finalists book entries are eligible for the $5,000 Grace Irwin prize. Judged by industry leaders and professionals.

WORLD'S BEST SHORT-SHORT STORY CONTEST, NARRATIVE NONFICTION CONTEST & SOUTHEAST REVIEW POETRY CONTEST

The Southeast Review, Florida State University, English Department, Tallahassee FL 32306. **E-mail:** southeastreview@gmail.com. **Website:** www.southeastreview.org. **Contact:** Erin Hoover, editor. Annual award for unpublished short-short stories (500 words or less), poetry, and narrative nonfiction (6,000 words or less). Visit website for details. Deadline: March 15. Prize: $500 per category. Winners and finalists will be published in *The Southeast Review*.

WRITER'S DIGEST ANNUAL WRITING COMPETITION

Writer's Digest, a publication of F+W Media, Inc., 10151 Carver Rd., Suite 300, Cincinnati OH 45242. (715)445-4612, ext. 13430. **E-mail:** writing-competition@fwmedia.com. **Website:** www.writersdigest.com. Writing contest with 9 categories: Inspirational Writing (spiritual/religious, maximum 2,500 words); Memoir/Personal Essay (maximum 2,000 words); Magazine Feature Article (maximum 2,000 words);Children's/Young Adult Fiction (maximum 2,000 words) Short Story (genre, maximum 4,000 words); Short Story (mainstream/literary, maximum 4,000 words); Rhyming Poetry (maximum 32 lines); Nonrhyming Poetry (maximum 32 lines); Stage Play/TV/Movie Script (first 15 pages and 1-page synopsis). Entries must be original, in English, unpublished/unproduced (except for Magazine Feature Articles), and not accepted by another publisher/producer at the time of submission. Writer's Digest retains one-time publication rights to the winning entries in each category. Deadline: May (early bird); June. Grand Prize: $5,000 and a trip to the Writer's Digest Conference to meet with editors and agents; 1st Place: $1,000 and $100 of Writer's Digest Books; 2nd Place: $500 and $100 of Writer's Digest Books; 3rd Place: $250 and $100 of Writer's Digest Books; 4th Place: $100 and

$50 of Writer's Digest Books; 5th Place:$50 and $50 of Writer's Digest Books; Sixth through Tenth place winners in each category:$25; and more.

WRITER'S DIGEST SELF-PUBLISHED BOOK AWARDS

Writer's Digest, 10151 Carver Road, Suite 300, Blue Ash OH 45242. (715)445-4612, ext. 13430. **E-mail:** writersdigestselfpublishingcompetition@fwmedia. com. **Website:** www.writersdigest.com. **Contact:** Nicole Howard. Contest open to all English-language, self-published books for which the authors have paid the full cost of publication, or the cost of printing has been paid for by a grant or as part of a prize. Categories include: Mainstream/Literary Fiction, Genre Fiction, Nonfiction, Inspirational (spiritual/new age), Life Stories (biographies/autobiographies/family histories/memoirs), Children's Books, Reference Books (directories/encyclopedias/guide books), Poetry, and Middle-Grade/Young Adult Books. Judges reserve the right to re-categorize entries. Judges reserve the right to withhold prizes in any category. All winners will be notified in October. Entrants must send a printed and bound book. Entries will be evaluated on content, writing quality, and overall quality of production and appearance. No handwritten books are accepted. Books must have been published within the past 5 years from the competition deadline. Books which have previously won awards from *Writer's Digest* are not eligible. Early bird deadline: April 2. Prizes: Grand Prize: $8,000, a trip to the Writer's Digest Conference, promotion in *Writer's Digest*, 10 copies of the book will be sent to major review houses, and a guaranteed review in *Midwest Book Review*; 1st Place (9 winners): $1,000 and promotion in *Writer's Digest*; Honorable Mentions: $50 worth of Writer's Digest Books and promotion on writersdigest.com. All entrants will receive a brief commentary from one of the judges.

WRITER'S DIGEST SELF-PUBLISHED E-BOOK AWARDS

Writer's Digest, 10151 Carver Road, Suite 300, Blue Ash OH 45242. (715)445-4612, ext. 13430. **E-mail:** writersdigestselfpublishingcompetition@fwmedia. com. **Website:** www.writersdigest.com. **Contact:** Nicole Howard. Contest open to all English-language, self-published e-books for which the authors have paid the full cost of publication, or the cost of publication has been paid for by a grant or as part of a

prize. Categories include: Mainstream/Literary Fiction, Genre Fiction, Nonfiction (includes reference books), Inspirational (spiritual/new age), Life Stories (biographies/autobiographies/family histories/memoirs), Children's Books, Poetry, and Middle-Grade/Young Adult Books. Judges reserve the right to re-categorize entries. Judges reserve the right to withhold prizes in any category. All winners will be notified by December 31. Entrants must enter online. Entrants may provide a file of the book or submit entry by the Amazon gifting process. Acceptable file types include: .epub, .mobi, .ipa. Word processing documents will not be accepted. Entries will be evaluated on content, writing quality, and overall quality of production and appearance. Books must have been published within the past 5 years from the competition deadline. Books which have previously won awards from *Writer's Digest* are not eligible. Early bird deadline: August 1; Deadline: September 4. Prizes: Grand Prize: $5,000, promotion in *Writer's Digest*, $200 worth of Writer's Digest Books, and more; 1st Place (9 winners): $1,000 and promotion in *Writer's Digest*; Honorable Mentions: $50 worth of Writer's Digest Books and promotion on writersdigest.com. All entrants will receive a brief commentary from one of the judges.

☯ WRITERS' GUILD OF ALBERTA AWARDS

Writers' Guild of Alberta, Percy Page Centre, 11759 Groat Rd., Edmonton AB T5M 3K6 Canada. (780)422-8174. **Fax:** (780)422-2663. **E-mail:** mail@ writersguild.ca. **Website:** writersguild.ca. **Contact:** Executive Director. Offers the following awards: Wilfrid Eggleston Award for Nonfiction; Georges Bugnet Award for Fiction; Howard O'Hagan Award for Short Story; Stephan G. Stephansson Award for Poetry; R. Ross Annett Award for Children's Literature; Gwen Pharis Ringwood Award for Drama; Jon Whyte Memorial Essay Award; James H. Gray Award for Short Nonfiction. Eligible entries will have been published anywhere in the world between January 1 and December 31 of the current year. The authors must have been residents of Alberta for at least 12 of the 18 months prior to December 31. Unpublished mss, except in the drama and essay categories, are not eligible. Anthologies are not eligible. Works may be submitted by authors, publishers, or any interested parties. Deadline: December 31. Prize: Winning authors receive $1,500; short piece prize winners receive $700.

WRITERS' LEAGUE OF TEXAS BOOK AWARDS

Writers' League of Texas, 611 S. Congress Ave., Suite 200A-3, Austin TX 78704. (512)499-8914. **Fax:** (512)499-0441. **E-mail:** sara@writersleague.org. **Website:** www.writersleague.org. **Contact:** Sara Kocek. Open to Texas authors of books published the previous year. To enter this contest, you must be a Texas author. "Texas author" is defined as anyone who (whether currently a resident or not) has lived in Texas for a period of 3 or more years. This contest is open to indie or self-published authors as well as traditionally-published authors. Deadline: February 28. Open to submissions October 7. Prize: $1,000 and a commemorative award.

LAMAR YORK PRIZE FOR FICTION AND NONFICTION CONTEST

The Chattahoochee Review, Georgia Perimeter College, 2101 Womack Rd., Dunwoody GA 30338-4497. (770)274-5479. **E-mail:** gpccr@gpc.edu. **Website:** thechattahoocheereview.gpc.edu. **Contact:** Anna Schachner, Editor. Offered annually for unpublished creative nonfiction and nonscholarly essays and fiction up to 5,000 words. *The Chattahoochee Review* buys first rights only for winning essay/ms for the purpose of publication in the summer issue. Entries should be submitted via Submittable. See website for details and guidelines. Deadline: January 31. Submission period begins October 1. Prize: 2 prizes of $1,000 each, plus publication. Judged by the editorial staff of *The Chattahoochee Review*.

THE YOUTH HONOR AWARDS

Skipping Stones Youth Honor Awards, Skipping Stones Magazine, Skipping Stones Magazine, P.O. Box 3939, Eugene OR 97403 USA. (541)342-4956. **E-mail:** info@skippingstones.org. **E-mail:** editor@skippingstones.org. **Website:** www.skippingstones.org. **Contact:** Arun N. Toke, Editor and Publisher. *Skipping Stones* is an international, literary, and multicultural, children's magazine that encourages cooperation, creativity, and celebration of cultural and linguistic diversity. It explores stewardship of the ecological and social webs that nurture us. It offers a forum for communication among children from different lands and backgrounds. *Skipping Stones* expands horizons in a playful, creative way. This is a non-commercial, non-profit magazine with no advertisements. In its 28th year. Original writing and art from youth, ages 7 to 17, should be typed or neatly handwritten. The entries should be appropriate for ages 7 to 17. Prose under 1,000 words; poems under 30 lines. Word limit: 1,000. Poetry: 30 lines. Non-English and bilingual writings are welcome. To promote multicultural, international and nature awareness. Deadline: June 25. Prize: An Honor Award Certificate, a subscription to Skipping Stones and five nature and/or multicultural books. They are also invited to join the Student Review Board. Everyone who enters the contest receives the autumn issue featuring the ten winners and other noteworthy entries. Editors and interns at the *Skipping Stones* magazine

PRAIRIE SCHOONER GLENNA LUSCHEI AWARDS

201 Andrews Hall, P.O. Box 880334, Lincoln NE 68588-0334. (402)472-0911. **Fax:** (402)472-9771. **E-mail:** jengelhardt2@unl.edu. **Contact:** Hilda Raz, editor-in-chief. Awards to honor work published the previous year in Prairie Schooner, including poetry, essays and fiction. Prize: $250 in each category. Judged by editorial staff of Prairie Schooner. No entry fee. For guidelines, send SASE or visit website. "Only work published in Prairie Schooner in the previous year is considered." Work nominated by the editorial staff. Results announced in the Spring issue. Winners notified by mail in February or March.

◑ QUEBEC WRITERS' FEDERATION BOOK AWARDS

1200 Atwater, Westmount QC H3Z 1X4 Canada. (514)933-0878. **Website:** www.Qwf.org. Award "to honor excellence in writing in English in Quebec." Prize: $2,000 (Canadian) in each category. Categories: fiction, poetry, nonfiction, first book, translation, and children's and young adult. Each prize judged by panel of 3 jurors, different each year. $20 entry fee. Guidelines for submissions sent to Canadian publishers and posted on website in March. Accepts inquiries by e-mail. Deadline: May 31, August 15. Entries must be previously published. Length: must be more than 48 pages. "Writer must have resided in Quebec for 3 of the previous 5 years." Books may be published anywhere. Winners announced in November at Annual Awards Gala and posted on website.

SPUR AWARDS

1080 Mesa Vista Hall MSC06 3770, 1 University of New Mexico, Alberquerque NM 87131. (615)791-1444. **E-mail:** wwa@unm.edu. **Website:** www.westernwriters.org. Purpose of award is "to reward quality in the fields of western fiction and nonfiction." Prize: Trophy. Categories: short stories, novels, poetry, songs, scripts and nonfiction. No entry fee. **Deadline: January 10.** Entries must be published during the contest year. Open to any writer. Guidelines available in Sept./Oct. for SASE, on website or by phone. Inquiries accepted by e-mail or phone. Results announced annually in Summer. Winners notified by mail. For contest results, send SASE.

JOHN STEINBECK FICTION AWARD

Reed Magazine. San Jose State University, Dept. of English, One Washington Square, San Jose CA 95192. **E-mail:** reed@email.sjsu.edu. **Website:** www.reed-mag.org/drupal/. **Contact:** Nick Taylor, editor. "Award for an unpublished short story of up to 6,000 words." Annual. Competition/award for short stories. Prize: $1,000 prize and publication in Reed Magazine. Receives several hundred entries per category. Entries are judged by a prominent fiction writer; 2007 judge was Tobias Wolff. Entry fee: $15 (includes issue of Reed). **Submission period is June 1 - November 1.** Anyone may enter contest. "Do not submit any pornographic material, science fiction, fantasy, or children's literature. The work must be your own, (no translations)." Results announced in April.

PROFESSIONAL ORGANIZATIONS

///

AGENTS' ORGANIZATIONS

ASSOCIATION OF AUTHORS' AGENTS (AAA), 5-8 Lower John St., Golden Square, London W1F 9HA. E-mail: anthonygoff@david-higham.co.uk. Website: www.agentsassoc.co.uk.

ASSOCIATION OF AUTHORS' REPRESENTATIVES (AAR). E-mail: info@aar-online.org. Website: www.aar-online.org.

ASSOCIATION OF TALENT AGENTS (ATA), 9255 Sunset Blvd., Suite 930, Los Angeles CA 90069. (310)274-0628. E-mail: shellie@agentassociation.com. Website: www.agentassociation.com.

WRITERS' ORGANIZATIONS

ACADEMY OF AMERICAN POETS 584 Broadway, Suite 604, New York NY 10012. E-mail: academy@poets.org. Website: www.poets.org.

AMERICAN CRIME WRITERS LEAGUE (ACWL), 17367 Hilltop Ridge Dr., Eureka MO 63205. Website: www.acwl.org.

AMERICAN INDEPENDENT WRITERS (AIW), 1001 Connecticut Ave. NW, Suite 701, Washington DC 20036. E-mail: info@aiwriters.org. Website: americanindependentwriters.org.

AMERICAN MEDICAL WRITERS ASSOCIATION (AMWA), 30 West Gude Dr., Suite 525, Rockville MD 20850-4347. E-mail: amwa@amwa.org. Website: www.amwa.org.

AMERICAN SCREENWRITERS ASSOCIATION (ASA), 269 S. Beverly Dr., Suite 2600, Beverly Hills CA 90212. (866)265-9091. E-mail: asa@goasa.com. Website: www.asascreenwriters.com.

AMERICAN TRANSLATORS ASSOCIATION (ATA), 225 Reinekers Ln., Suite 590, Alexandria VA 22314. (703)683-6100. E-mail: ata@atanet.org. Website: www.atanet.org.

EDUCATION WRITERS ASSOCIATION (EWA), 2122 P St., NW Suite 201, Washington DC 20037. E-mail: ewa@ewa.org. Website: ewa.org.

HORROR WRITERS ASSOCIATION (HWA), 244 5th Ave., Suite 2767, New York NY 10001. E-mail: hwa@horror.org. Website: www.horror.org.

THE INTERNATIONAL WOMEN'S WRITING GUILD (IWWG), P.O. Box 810, Gracie Station, New York NY 10028. Website: www.iwwg.com.

MYSTERY WRITERS OF AMERICA (MWA), 1140 Broadway, Suite 1507, New York NY 10001. (212)888-8171. E-mail: mwa@mysterywriters.org. Website: www.mysterywriters.org.

NATIONAL ASSOCIATION OF SCIENCE WRITERS (NASW), P.O. Box 7905, Berkeley, CA 94707. (510)647-9500. E-mail: lfriedmann@nasw.org. Website: www.nasw.org.

NATIONAL ASSOCIATION OF WOMEN WRITERS (NAWW), 24165 IH-10 W., Suite 217-637, San Antonio TX 78257. Phone/Fax: (866)821-5829. Website: www.naww.org.

ORGANIZATION OF BLACK SCREENWRITERS (OBS). 1999 W. Adams Blvd., Mezzanine, Los Angeles CA 90018. Website: www.obswriter.com.

OUTDOOR WRITERS ASSOCIATION OF AMERICA (OWAA), 121 Hickory St., Suite 1, Missoula MT 59801. E-mail: krhoades@owaa.org. Website: www.owaa.org.

POETRY SOCIETY OF AMERICA (PSA), 15 Gramercy Park, New York NY 10003. Website: www.poetrysociety.org.

POETS & WRITERS, 90 Broad St., Suite 2100, New York NY 10004. (212)226-3586. Fax: (212)226-3963. Website: www.pw.org.

ROMANCE WRITERS OF AMERICA (RWA), 114615 Benfer Rd., Houston TX 77069. (832)717-5200. Fax: (832)717-5201. E-mail: info@rwanational.org. Website: www.rwanational.org.

SCIENCE FICTION AND FANTASY WRITERS OF AMERICA (SFWA), P.O. Box 877, Chestertown MD 21620. E-mail: execdir@sfwa.org. Website: www.sfwa.org.

SOCIETY OF AMERICAN BUSINESS EDITORS & WRITERS (SABEW), University of Missouri, School of Journalism, 30 Neff Annex, Columbia MO 65211. (602) 496-7862. E-mail: sabew@sabew.org. Website: www.sabew.org.

SOCIETY OF AMERICAN TRAVEL WRITERS (SATW), 7044 S. 13 St., Oak Creek WI 53154. E-mail: satw@satw.org. Website: www.satw.org.

SOCIETY OF CHILDREN'S BOOK WRITERS & ILLUSTRATORS (SCBWI), 8271 Beverly Blvd., Los Angeles CA 90048. E-mail: scbwi@scbwi.org. Website: www.scbwi.org.

WESTERN WRITERS OF AMERICA (WWA). E-mail: spiritfire@kc.rr.com. Website: www.westernwriters.org.

INDUSTRY ORGANIZATIONS

AMERICAN BOOKSELLERS ASSOCIATION (ABA), 200 White Plains Rd., Suite 600, Tarrytown NY 10591. (914)591-2665. E-mail:

info@bookweb.org. Website: www.bookweb.
org.

AMERICAN SOCIETY OF JOURNALISTS & AU-THORS (ASJA), 1501 Broadway, Suite 302, New York NY 10036. (212)997-0947. E-mail: director@asja.org. Website: www.asja.org.

ASSOCIATION FOR WOMEN IN COMMUNI-CATIONS (AWC), 3337 Duke St., Alexandria VA 22314. (703)370-7436. E-mail: info@womcom.org. Website: www.womcom.org.

ASSOCIATION OF AMERICAN PUBLISHERS (AAP), 71 5th Ave., 2nd Floor, New York NY 10003. Website: www.publishers.org.

THE ASSOCIATION OF WRITERS & WRITING PROGRAMS (AWP), Mail Stop 1E3, George Mason University, Fairfax VA 22030. Website: www.awpwriter.org.

THE AUTHORS GUILD, INC., 31 E. 32nd St., 7th Floor, New York NY 10016. E-mail: staff@authorsguild.org. Website: authorsguild.org.

CANADIAN AUTHORS ASSOCIATION (CAA), P.O. Box 581, Stn. Main Orilla ON L3V 6K5 Canada. Website: www.canauthors.org.

CHRISTIAN BOOKSELLERS ASSOCIATION (CBA), P.O. Box 62000, Colorado Springs CO 80962. Website: www.cbaonline.org.

THE DRAMATISTS GUILD OF AMERICA, 1501 Broadway, Suite 701, New York NY 10036. Website: www.dramatistsguild.com.

NATIONAL LEAGUE OF AMERICAN PEN WOMEN (NLAPW), 1300 17th St. NW, Washington DC 20036-1973. Website: www.americanpenwomen.org.

NATIONAL WRITERS ASSOCIATION (NWA), 10940 S. Parker Rd., #508, Parker CO 80134. Website: www.nationalwriters.com

NATIONAL WRITERS UNION (NWU), 256 West 38th St., Suite 703, New York, NY 10018. E-mail: nwu@nwu.org. Website: www.nwu.org.

PEN AMERICAN CENTER, 588 Broadway, Suite 303, New York NY 10012-3225. E-mail: pen@pen.org. Website: www.pen.org.

THE PLAYWRIGHTS GUILD OF CANADA (PGC), 215 Spadina Ave., Suite #210, Toronto ON M5T 2C7 Canada. E-mail: info@playwrightsguild.ca. Website: www.playwrightsguild.com.

VOLUNTEER LAWYERS FOR THE ARTS (VLA), One E. 53rd St., 6th Floor, New York NY 10022. (212)319-2787. Website: www.vlany.org.

WOMEN IN FILM (WIF), 6100 Wilshire Blvd., Suite 710, Los Angeles CA 90048. E-mail: info@wif.org. Website: www.wif.org.

WOMEN'S NATIONAL BOOK ASSOCIATION (WNBA), P.O. Box 237, FDR Station, New York NY 10150. E-mail: publicity@bookbuzz.com. Website: www.wnba-books.org.

WRITERS GUILD OF ALBERTA (WGA), 11759 Groat Rd., Edmonton AB T5M 3K6 Canada. E-mail: mail@writersguild.ab.ca. Website: writersguild.ab.ca.

WRITERS GUILD OF AMERICA-EAST (WGA), 555 W. 57th St., Suite 1230, New York NY 10019. E-mail: info@wgaeast.org. Website: www.wgaeast.org.

WRITERS GUILD OF AMERICA-WEST (WGA), 7000 W. Third St., Los Angeles CA 90048. Website: www.wga.org.

WRITERS UNION OF CANADA (TWUC), 90 Richmond St. E., Suite 200, Toronto ON M5C 1P1 Canada. E-mail: info@writersunion.ca. Website: www.writersunion.ca.

GLOSSARY

#10 ENVELOPE. A standard, business-size envelope.

ADVANCE. A sum of money a publisher pays a writer prior to the publication of a book. It is usually paid in installments, such as one-half on signing contract; one-half on delivery of complete and satisfactory manuscript.

AGENT. A liaison between a writer and editor or publisher. An agent shops a manuscript around, receiving a commission when the manuscript is accepted. Agents usually take a 10-15% fee from the advance and royalties.

ARC. Advance reader copy.

ASSIGNMENT. Editor asks a writer to produce a specific article for an agreed-upon fee.

AUCTION. Publishers sometimes bid for the acquisition of a book manuscript that has excellent sales prospects. The bids are for the amount of the author's advance, advertising and promotional expenses, royalty percentage, etc. Auctions are conducted by agents.

AVANT-GARDE. Writing that is innovative in form, style, or subject.

BACKLIST. A publisher's list of its books that were not published during the current season, but that are still in print.

BIMONTHLY. Every two months.

BIO. A sentence or brief paragraph about the writer; can include education and work experience.

BIWEEKLY. Every two weeks.

BLOG. Short for weblog. Used by writers to build platform by posting regular commentary, observations, poems, tips, etc.

BLURB. The copy on paperback book covers or hard cover book dust jackets, either promoting the book and the author or featuring testimonials from book reviewers or well-known people in the book's field. Also called flap copy or jacket copy.

BOILERPLATE. A standardized contract.

BOUND GALLEYS. Prepublication edition of book, usually photocopies of final galley proofs; also known as "bound proofs."

BYLINE. Name of the author appearing with the published piece.

CATEGORY FICTION. A term used to include all types of fiction.

CHAPBOOK. A small booklet usually paperback of poetry, ballads, or tales.

CIRCULATION. The number of subscribers to a magazine.

CLIPS. Samples, usually from newspapers or magazines, of a writer's published work.

COFFEE-TABLE BOOK. A heavily illustrated oversize book.

COMMERCIAL NOVELS. Novels designed to appeal to a broad audience. These are often broken down into categories such as western, mystery and romance. See also genre.

CONTRIBUTOR'S COPIES. Copies of the issues of magazines sent to the author in which the author's work appears.

CO-PUBLISHING. Arrangement where author and publisher share publications costs and profits of a book. Also known as cooperative publishing.

COPYEDITING. Editing a manuscript for grammar, punctuation, printing style, and factual accuracy.

COPYRIGHT. A means to protect an author's work.

COVER LETTER. A brief letter that accompanies the manuscript being sent to an agent or editor.

CREATIVE NONFICTION. Nonfictional writing that uses an innovative approach to the subject and creative language.

CRITIQUING SERVICE. An editing service in which writers pay a fee for comments on the salability or other qualities of their manuscript. Fees vary, as do the quality of the critiques.

CV. Curriculum vita. A brief listing of qualifications and career accomplishments.

ELECTRONIC RIGHTS. Secondary or subsidiary rights dealing with electronic/multimedia formats (i.e., the Internet, CD-ROMs, electronic magazines).

ELECTRONIC SUBMISSION. A submission made by modem or on computer disk.

EROTICA. Fiction that is sexually oriented.

EVALUATION FEES. Fees an agent may charge to evaluate material. The extent and quality of this evaluation varies, but comments usually concern salability of the manuscript.

FAIR USE. A provision of the copyright law that says short passages from copyrighted material may be used without infringing on the owner's rights.

FEATURE. An article giving the reader information of human interest rather than news.

FILLER. A short item used by an editor to "fill" out a newspaper column or magazine page. It could be a joke, an anecdote, etc.

FILM RIGHTS. Rights sold or optioned by the agent/author to a person in the film industry, enabling the book to be made into a movie.

FOREIGN RIGHTS. Translation or reprint rights to be sold abroad.

FRONTLIST. A publisher's list of books that are new to the current season.

GALLEYS. First typeset version of manuscript that has not yet been divided into pages.

GENRE. Refers either to a general classification of writing, such as the novel or the poem, or to the categories within those classifications, such as the problem novel or the sonnet.

GHOSTWRITER. Writer who puts into literary form an article, speech, story, or book based on another person's ideas or knowledge.

GRAPHIC NOVEL. A story in graphic form, long comic strip, or heavily illustrated story; of 40 pages or more.

HI-LO. A type of fiction that offers a high level of interest for readers at a low reading level.

HIGH CONCEPT. A story idea easily expressed in a quick, one-line description.

HONORARIUM. Token payment.

HOOK. Aspect of the work that sets it apart from others and draws in the reader/viewer.

HOW-TO. Books and magazine articles offering a combination of information and advice in describing how something can be accomplished.

IMPRINT. Name applied to a publisher's specific line of books.

JOINT CONTRACT. A legal agreement between a publisher and two or more authors, establishing provisions for the division of royalties the book generates.

KILL FEE. Fee for a complete article that was assigned and then cancelled.

LEAD TIME. The time between the acquisition of a manuscript by an editor and its actual publication.

LITERARY FICTION. The general category of serious, non-formulaic, intelligent fiction.

MAINSTREAM FICTION. Fiction that transcends popular novel categories such as mystery, romance and science fiction.

MARKETING FEE. Fee charged by some agents to cover marketing expenses. It may be used to cover postage, telephone calls, faxes, photocopying or any other expense incurred in marketing a manuscript.

MASS MARKET. Non-specialized books of wide appeal directed toward a large audience.

MEMOIR. A narrative recounting a writer's (or fictional narrator's) personal or family history; specifics may be altered, though essentially considered nonfiction.

MIDDLE GRADE OR MID-GRADE. The general classification of books written for readers approximately ages 9-11. Also called middle readers.

MIDLIST. Those titles on a publisher's list that are not expected to be big sellers, but are expected to have limited/modest sales.

MODEL RELEASE. A paper signed by the subject of a photograph giving the photographer permission to use the photograph.

MULTIPLE CONTRACT. Book contract with an agreement for a future book(s).

MULTIPLE SUBMISSIONS. Sending more than one book or article idea to a publisher at the same time.

NARRATIVE NONFICTION. A narrative presentation of actual events.

NET ROYALTY. A royalty payment based on the amount of money a book publisher receives on the sale of a book after booksellers' discounts, special sales discounts and returns.

NOVELLA. A short novel, or a long short story; approximately 7,000 to 15,000 words.

ON SPEC. An editor expresses an interest in a proposed article idea and agrees to consider the finished piece for publication "on speculation." The editor is under no obligation to buy the finished manuscript.

ONE-TIME RIGHTS. Rights allowing a manuscript to be published one time. The work can be sold again by the writer without violating the contract.

OPTION CLAUSE. A contract clause giving a publisher the right to publish an author's next book.

PAYMENT ON ACCEPTANCE. The editor sends you a check for your article, story or poem as soon as he decides to publish it.

PAYMENT ON PUBLICATION. The editor doesn't send you a check for your material until it is published.

PEN NAME. The use of a name other than your legal name on articles, stories or books. Also called a pseudonym.

PHOTO FEATURE. Feature in which the emphasis is on the photographs rather than on accompanying written material.

PICTURE BOOK. A type of book aimed at preschoolers to 8-year-olds that tells a story using a combination of text and artwork, or artwork only.

PLATFORM. A writer's speaking experience, interview skills, website and other abilities which help form a following of potential buyers for that author's book.

POD. Print on demand.

PROOFREADING. Close reading and correction of a manuscript's typographical errors.

PROPOSAL. A summary of a proposed book submitted to a publisher, particularly used for nonfiction manuscripts. A proposal often contains an individualized cover letter, one-page overview of the book, marketing information, competitive books, author information, chapter-by-chapter outline, and two to three sample chapters.

QUERY. A letter that sells an idea to an editor or agent. Usually a query is brief (no more than one page) and uses attention-getting prose.

REMAINDERS. Copies of a book that are slow to sell and can be purchased from the publisher at a reduced price.

REPORTING TIME. The time it takes for an

editor to report to the author on his/her query or manuscript.

REPRINT RIGHTS. The rights to republish a book after its initial printing.

ROYALTIES, STANDARD HARDCOVER BOOK. 10 percent of the retail price on the first 5,000 copies sold; 12 percent on the next 5,000; 15 percent thereafter.

ROYALTIES, STANDARD MASS PAPERBACK BOOK. 4-8 percent of the retail price on the first 150,000 copies sold.

ROYALTIES, STANDARD TRADE PAPERBACK BOOK. No less than 6 percent of list price on the first 20,000 copies; 7½ percent thereafter.

SASE. Self-addressed, stamped envelope; should be included with all correspondence.

SELF-PUBLISHING. In this arrangement the author pays for manufacturing, production and marketing of his book and keeps all income derived from the book sales.

SEMIMONTHLY. Twice per month.

SEMIWEEKLY. Twice per week.

SERIAL. Published periodically, such as a newspaper or magazine.

SERIAL FICTION. Fiction published in a magazine in installments, often broken off at a suspenseful spot.

SERIAL RIGHTS. The right for a newspaper or magazine to publish sections of a manuscript.

SHORT-SHORT. A complete short story of 1,500 words.

SIDEBAR. A feature presented as a companion to a straight news report (or main magazine article) giving sidelights on human-interest aspects or sometimes elucidating just one aspect of the story.

SIMULTANEOUS SUBMISSIONS. Sending the same article, story or poem to several publishers at the same time. Some publishers refuse to consider such submissions.

SLANT. The approach or style of a story or article that will appeal to readers of a specific magazine.

SLICE-OF-LIFE VIGNETTE. A short fiction piece intended to realistically depict an interesting moment of everyday living.

SLUSH PILE. The stack of unsolicited or misdirected manuscripts received by an editor or book publisher.

SOCIAL NETWORKS. Websites that connect users: sometimes generally, other times around specific interests. Four popular ones at the moment are Facebook, Twitter, Instagram and LinkedIn.

SUBAGENT. An agent handling certain subsidiary rights, usually working in conjuction with the agent who handled the book rights. The percentage paid the book agent is increased to pay the subagent.

SUBSIDIARY RIGHTS. All rights other than book publishing rights included in a book publishing contract, such as paperback rights, book club rights and movie rights. Part of an agent's job is to negotiate those rights and advise you on which to sell and which to keep.

SUBSIDY PUBLISHER. A book publisher who charges the author for the cost to typeset and print his book, the jacket, etc., as opposed to a royalty publisher who pays the author.

SYNOPSIS. A brief summary of a story, novel or play. As part of a book proposal, it is a comprehensive summary condensed in a page or page and a half, single-spaced.

TABLOID. Newspaper format publication on about half the size of the regular newspaper page.

TEARSHEET. Page from a magazine or newspaper containing your printed story, article, poem or ad.

TOC. Table of Contents.

TRADE BOOK. Either a hardcover or softcover book; subject matter frequently concerns a special interest for a general audience; sold mainly in bookstores.

TRADE PAPERBACK. A soft-bound volume published and designed for the general public; available mainly in bookstores.

TRANSLATION RIGHTS. Sold to a foreign agent or foreign publisher.

UNSOLICITED MANUSCRIPT. A story, article, poem or book that an editor did not specifically ask to see.

YA. Young adult books.

BOOK PUBLISHERS SUBJECT INDEX

HOBBIES

GENERAL INDEX